THE HANDBOOK OF
BIRD FAMILIES

JONATHAN ELPHICK

Published by the Natural History Museum, London

For my children Tom, Alys and Becky, and my grandsons Jacob and Callum, with all my love and the heartfelt hope that they can still enjoy the beauty of birds and other wildlife in years to come.

First published by the Natural History Museum, Cromwell Road, London SW7 5BD
© The Trustees of the Natural History Museum, London 2019.

All rights reserved. No part of this publication may be transmitted in any form or by any means without prior permission from the British Publisher.

The Author has asserted his right to be identified as the Author of this work under the Copyright, Designs and Patents Act 1988.

ISBN 978 0 565 09378 5

A catalogue record for this book is available from the British Library.

10 9 8 7 6 5 4 3 2 1

Internal design by Mercer Design London
Reproduction by Saxon Digital Services
Printed by Toppan Leefung Printing Limited

Front cover: Australasian Gannet, *Morus serrator* © David Tipling
Back cover from top left to bottom right: Bald Eagle, *Haliaeetus leucocephalus*, Marabou, *Leptoptilos crumenifer*, Hawk-owl, *Surnia ulula*, Zebra Dove, *Geopelia striata*, Regent Bowerbird, *Sericulus chrysocephalus*, Wandering Albatrosses, *Diomedea exulans*, Emperor Penguins, *Aptenodytes forsteri*, Magnificent Hummingbird, *Eugenes fulgens*, Common Ostrich, *Struthio camelus*, Purple Martin, *Progne subis*, Dalmatian Pelican, *Pelecanus crispus*, Dusky Thrush, *Turdus naumanni* © David Tipling

CONTENTS

INTRODUCTION 4

THE BIRD FAMILIES 6
Related families are grouped into orders as follows:
Struthioniformes 6 Rheiformes 8 Tinamiformes 9 Apterygiformes 10
Casuariiformes 11 Anseriformes 13 Galliformes 19
Phoenicopteriformes 27 Podicipediformes 29 Columbiformes 31
Mesitornithiformes 36 Eurypygiformes 37 Phaethontiformes 39
Caprimulgiformes 40 Opisthocomiformes 56 Cuculiformes 57
Gruiformes 61 Otidiformes 69 Musophagiformes 71 Gaviiformes 73
Sphenisciformes 74 Procellariiformes 77 Pelacaniformes 88
Charadriiformes 105 Accipitriformes 131 Strigiformes 141
Coliiformes 148 Leptosomiformes 149 Trogoniformes 150
Bucerotiformes 153 Piciformes 160 Coraciiformes 173
Cariamiformes 183 Falconiformes 184 Psittaciformes 188
Passeriformes 198

Glossary 394

Appendix 396

Further information 397

Index 398

Picture credits 416

Acknowledgements 416

INTRODUCTION

THE FIRST BIRD I CAN REMEMBER having really noticed was a Common Pochard drake on a small lake. This was at the age of about six in North Wales, where I had the good fortune to be born and raised. The most recent, 66 years later, included the privilege of being able to watch a mighty Harpy Eagle at its nest deep in the Darien National Park on one of my trips to Panama, and just a few weeks ago, thrilling encounters in Extremadura, southwest Spain, with a huge melee of vultures jostling for food at a 'vulture restaurant', as well as a host of other birds, from stately Common Cranes, Great and Little Bustards and sandgrouse to Thekla Larks and Azure-winged Magpies. As I write this, I can see in black and white contrast Little Egrets mingling with the Rooks in the wood opposite where both roost and breed, and Greenshank and Black-tailed Godwits flying over my house, situated next to the bird-rich Exe Estuary in beautiful Devon. In between, birds have delighted, inspired and fascinated me on a daily basis in many parts of the world. Although I consider myself an all-round naturalist, at least in my interest if not my detailed knowledge, birds have always held my main attention. This is true for many zoologists, for birds have figured hugely in scientific research. They are so noticeable, due to being largely active by day and living virtually everywhere. We admire their mastery of flight or their colourful plumage, and regard the songs and calls of many species as the most attractive or beautiful of all natural sounds. As well as providing ornithologists such excellent subjects for research, they give delight to birders and all who love nature, and inspire writers, poets, artists and photographers. Today, their importance as a crucial part of all ecosystems, and as indicators of the damage we are wreaking on their – and our – environment, is established beyond question, but is, regrettably, all too often unheeded by politicians and other decision makers. If, as well as providing information, this book helps the reader to feel passionate about the birds with which we share the world, and to do something to help them, then I will be doubly pleased. Since our earliest prehistoric encounters with these remarkable creatures, they have been deeply enmeshed in our collective consciousness, embedded in so many myths, proverbs and parts of speech. A world devoid of birds would be an immensely poorer place.

No single work, even one of many volumes, can be comprehensive; ornithology is such a vast subject today, with so many advances in the last few decades alone. In this book my aim is to provide a succinct and accessible account of every one of the 36 orders and 234 families of birds alive today.

A few words about scientific classification are apposite here, for those unfamiliar with how it works. Whether applied to birds or to any other living organisms, it uses the same hierarchical arrangement of ranks. In all cases the scientific names are either in Latin or the Latinised form of words derived from Greek or other languages, often describing some distinctive feature or the place where the bird lives, or celebrating the name of a person. This means that unlike common names, which vary from one language to another, the scientific names are truly international. The basic unit of classification is the species.

This is given a binomial name consisting of two parts, as originally proposed in the eighteenth century by the Swedish naturalist Linnaeus. It is always printed in italics. The first part, always given an initial capital, is the generic name. This is the name of the genus – the group of similar, closely related species to which the species belongs (in some cases a genus may contain only a single particularly distinctive species). The second part, always in lower case type, is the specific name; although this may be the same for many species (for instance, alba, white, minor, smaller, or americana, from America) the combination of generic and specific names is unique. Similar genera of birds are gathered together into families, whose names end in –idae, similar families into orders, with names ending in –iformes. All the orders combined form the Class Aves, the birds. In addition to this basic scheme, species may be divided into subspecies, more informally called races, which are given a third name, or trinomial. There are other, intermediate, rankings too, such as superfamilies and subclasses. The two used most in this book are subfamilies (ending in -inae) and within some subfamilies, tribes (ending in –ini).

ABOVE I spent many hours watching this male Satin Bowerbird, *Ptilinorhynchus violaceus*, gathering material for constructing his bower to entice a female to mate with him, at Bina Burra Lodge in Lamington National Park, Queensland, Australia.

Just as the birds have evolved since they first appeared more than 150 million years ago, and continue to evolve today, our classification system itself is subject to a process of evolution. In contrast to some other groups of animals, birds have not left a rich fossil record. Nevertheless, new fossils are being discovered, and through many other studies more data is being continually added. In addition, similar features that initially suggested relationships may turn out to be the result of convergent evolution, in which two unrelated groups have evolved similarities due to adopting similar lifestyles. Most profound in its effect on how birds are classified have been the revolutionary techniques of DNA analysis in the past couple of decades. This has led to often surprising reassessments of relationships, including the realisation that some species in a family may not belong there but are better placed in a different family. It also has an impact on whether a subspecies should be promoted to species rank or a species demoted to subspecies level, although there is a degree of subjectivity involved in such decisions between the classifiers known as 'lumpers' and those dubbed 'splitters'.

Because taxonomists – the scientists who classify organisms – do not always agree about the interpretation of the data, there is no single definitive list of the world's bird species or how they should be arranged into families, and families into orders. Although a consensus is emerging in many cases, in others there is still considerable disagreement about the wisdom of following some proposals. As a result, my policy in this book is to adopt a conservative approach, and (apart from a few exceptions) to follow the arrangement set out in the fourth edition of The Howard and Moore Complete Checklist of the Birds of the World, edited by E.C.Dickinson and J.V. Remsen Jr., Volume 1. Non-passerines, 2013, and Volume 2, Passerines, 2014, published by Aves Press, Eastbourne, UK. As for the common names of species, I have generally followed those used in Howard and Moore, fourth edition, but in a few cases I have used alternatives that I regarded as preferable. In this book, the common names always have initial capitals.

The accounts dealing with the orders and families summarise their salient features and in most cases, also include brief mention of their relationships to other birds. The family accounts, which vary in length according to the size and diversity of the family, detail the appearance, behaviour and lifestyle of its members (or member in the case of families containing just a single species), and where appropriate, include a summary of distinct subgroups within it. Each family text has a box containing key facts under standardised headings. The species whose names are listed under 'Conservation' are many of those identified by BirdLife International as experiencing various levels of threat. Space restrictions do not permit a complete listing, but this can be found in the Data Zone of BirdLife's website (see Further Information, p. 397 for details). In some cases, species are recognised by BirdLife but not Howard and Moore, fourth edition, where they have merely subspecies status. For a list of the definitions of the various threat categories see the Appendix, on p. 396. As far as possible, I have explained any necessary technical terms in the text as they arise, but there is also a glossary at the end of the book, on pp. 394–396.

BELOW I photographed these Greater Crested Terns, *Thalasseus bergii*, with their flamboyantly spiky headgear, at Byron Bay, New South Wales, Australia.

The 30 or so living orders into which the 10,000 or so species of modern birds can be classified consist of two main divisions: the superorder Palaeognathae ('ancient jaws'), thought to be among the most primitive of today's birds, and the superorder Neognathae ('new jaws'). Just five orders of palaeognaths survive. The first are the tinamous (order Tinamiformes), which can fly but do so reluctantly and poorly. The other four are mainly huge and entirely flightless birds, the living representatives of the group collectively known as the ratites. This informal grouping includes the few surviving species – the two species of ostrich (order Struthioniformes), the three species of rhea (order Rheiformes), the three species of cassowary and the single species of emu (order Casuariiformes), and the five species of kiwi (order Apterygiformes) – as well as a larger number of extinct ones. Among the latter are extinct members of the preceding orders, and those placed in two other orders with no surviving relatives, the elephant birds (Aepyornithiformes) of Madagascar and the moas (Dinornithidae) of New Zealand. Most ratites are prehistoric, but the moas and elephant birds survived until historic times. The name 'ratite' denotes their supposed common ancestry and also refers to one of their features: the flat breastbone, lacking the keel that serves for attachment of the big flight muscles on most birds ('ratite' comes from the Latin word *ratis*, meaning 'raft'). Ratites share various other features, including a penis in males, found in only a few other groups of birds.

ORDER STRUTHIONIFORMES

This order contains just a single family of ostriches, with only two species in existence today.

OSTRICHES Struthionidae

GENERA: 1   **SPECIES**: 2

LENGTH: males 2.1–2.75 m (7–9 ft); females 1.75–1.9 m (5.75–6.25 ft)

WEIGHT: males 100–156 kg (220–344 lb); females 90–110 kg (198–242 lb)

RANGE AND HABITAT: Africa, in southern Sahara and Sahel, East Africa, from Somalia to Tanzania, and South Africa; small feral population in South Australia derived from escaped farmed birds; open, arid and semi-arid areas; savannah

SOCIAL BEHAVIOUR: live mainly in small family groups outside the breeding season, but some groups amalgamate to form larger, looser associations of up to 100 individuals, and single birds also occur; when breeding, males gather harems of several females (including a dominant major hen) or birds live as monogamous pairs; the male defends a breeding territory

NEST: a shallow scrape in the soil or sand, made by the male

EGGS: 10–40; glossy, creamy white

INCUBATION: 42–46 days

FLEDGING PERIOD: 4–5 months

SEXUAL MATURITY: 3–4 years

FOOD: grasses, seeds, leaves, fruits, flowers; also some small animals, such as locusts or other insects and lizards

VOICE: booming roar of male during courtship display and territorial defence; both sexes utter a variety of hissing, snorting, whistling and other sounds

MIGRATION: nomadic movements determined by availability of food and water

CONSERVATION STATUS: the range of the Common Ostrich is considerably reduced; the Arabian subspecies *syriacus* was hunted to extinction by 1966. The north-east African species *molybdophanes*, called the Somali ostrich, is at risk of extinction in the Horn of Africa and is currently classified as Vulnerable

The Common Ostrich, *Struthio camelus*, and its close relative the Somali Ostrich, *S. molybdophanes*, are easily the world's largest and heaviest living birds: the biggest males tower above humans, at up to 2.5 m (8 ft) or more in height, and especially large ones may weigh over 120 kg (19 stone). The huge, rounded body is densely clothed in fluffy plumage (the feathers are soft and smooth because they lack the tiny hooks linking the barbules found in most other birds). These birds have a striking pattern of black with white wings and tail in males, which they use to full advantage in threat and courtship displays, and brown with pale fringes and dull cream in females, reducing their visibility to predators when breeding. The young are similarly camouflaged. The huge wings are used not only in displays, but also as fans to cool the body, and as balancing organs when running at high speed. The bare skin on the upper neck and on the legs is pink or blue in males (the colour depends on the subspecies), becoming much brighter during the breeding season.

The long legs and small feet of ostriches are modified for terrestrial life. They are powered by big muscles, and the foot is adapted for fast running in a rather similar way to that of horses, with the toes reduced more than any other birds, to just two: one large and one small. Ostriches can run faster than any other bird and are able to outrun most predators, especially as they have great

ABOVE The Common Ostrich, *Struthio camelus*, is always on the alert for the approach of predators, especially lions, as here in Masai Mara, Kenya.

ABOVE Although there may be twice as many eggs laid by several hens, a female Common Ostrich can cover only about 20 of them when incubating.

stamina. They can maintain speeds of 50 km/h (31 mph) for over 30 minutes and can sprint briefly at up to 70 km/h (43 mph), taking great strides of 3.5 m (11.5 ft). The feet can also serve as formidable weapons against predators such as jackals, and even lions. The big claw is up to 10 cm (4 in) long and can inflict slashing wounds, or even disembowel a pursuer, as the ostrich kicks out forwards.

ABOVE With its large eyes at a height of about 2.0–2.2 m (6.5–7.2 ft) above ground, the long-necked Common Ostrich is able to detect danger at long range.

Their very long necks, topped by a proportionately small head, give them a clear view all round, even above tall grasses, enabling the great birds to scan for predators with their large, keen eyes. These are the largest of any vertebrates and are among the few birds' eyes to be fringed by eyelashes, in this case large, luxuriant ones. They protect the eyes against injury as the birds feed and perhaps also against dust and sand.

A group of ostriches will roam great distances, walking slowly and tirelessly for hours on end, searching for food by lowering their heads and moving them from side to side. They eat mainly plants, including seeds, leaves, flowers and roots from a very wide range of species of herbaceous plants, shrubs, trees and grasses. They supplement this with occasional animal food. They have a powerful digestive system (including 14 m-/46 ft-long intestines) that allow them to break up often tough plant material in the gizzard with the aid of sand or stones, which may make up half its contents.

During the breeding season, males strut about and threaten or chase off rivals with raised and flicked wings and loud, deep booming calls. They attract females by squatting and waving their spread wings alternately. If they are receptive, females lower their heads and quiver their wings. A successful male mates with several females, only one of which, the 'major hen' will remain with him. After she has chosen one of several nest scrapes he has made, she lays her eggs; then up to six or more 'minor hens' each lay their clutch, until there are up to 40 eggs in the nest. The major hen and the male then take it in turns to incubate the eggs. Although the eggs are huge, the biggest of any living bird's, each measuring on average 16 cm (6.25 in) long and weighing up to 2 kg (4.4 lb) or more, they are the smallest of any bird's relative to the huge size of the female. This enables the birds to incubate so many of them, although for particularly big clutches the major hen will roll any she cannot cover to the outside, where they will fail to hatch (she only does so with those of the minor hens).

Although not threatened overall, ostriches have declined considerably in many areas, mainly as a result of loss of habitat to agriculture. Today, they are native in the wild only to Africa, although until recently they occurred in Asia (in Arabia): the extinct Middle Eastern subspecies *syriacus* had probably disappeared by about 1966. The Common Ostrich is also farmed in many parts of the world for its meat (valued as it is low in fat), feathers (used in fashion and decoration) and skin (for making fine leather products). The distinctive northeastern species *S. molybdophanes* is threatened by habitat loss, hunting, egg collection and many decades of warfare in parts of its range. Found in Somalia, southeast Ethiopia and northern and eastern Kenya. Other closely related species of ostrich are known widely as fossils from southern Europe and Asia, from Greece to Central Asia and India, as well as across most of Africa.

ORDER RHEIFORMES

This order of very big flightless birds contains only a single family of two species, the Greater Rhea, *Rhea americana*, and the Lesser Rhea, *Rhea pennata*. Populations of the latter in the Andes, although traditionally regarded as a subspecies, *R.p.tarapacensis*, may merit treatment as a separate species.

RHEAS Rheidae

GENERA: 1   **SPECIES:** 2

LENGTH: 0.93–1.40 m (3–4.6 ft)

WEIGHT: 10–50 kg (22–110 lb)

RANGE AND HABITAT: South America; greatest diversity in Patagonia (both species); grassland and open scrub; Greater Rheas are lowland dwellers, while Lesser Rheas, especially the Puna Rhea, are upland birds, the latter to altitudes of 4,500 m (14,800 ft)

SOCIAL BEHAVIOUR: gregarious for much of the year, in mixed groups of adults of both sexes and juveniles; in breeding season, females form exclusive small groups, while males become territorial

NEST: a shallow scrape in the soil about 1 m (3 ft) across, lined with pieces of dried grass or other vegetation

EGGS: 10–70 eggs, golden or olive coloured (soon becoming discoloured)

INCUBATION: 35–40 days

FLEDGING PERIOD: chicks independent at about 6 months

FOOD: a wide range of plant foods, from seeds and fruits to roots and leaves, from a very wide range of plant species; also invertebrates and small vertebrates

VOICE: females silent; males give booming calls

MIGRATION: sedentary

CONSERVATION STATUS: both species have declined, especially in less remote areas; the Greater Rhea, *R. americana*, and the Puna Rhea, *R. (p.) tarapacensis*, are both regarded as Near Threatened

ABOVE This is a Lesser Rhea, *Pterocnemia pennata*, in Chile, South America.

Their rather ostrich-like appearance, with fluffy, mainly grey-brown plumage, led to the two species of rhea being dubbed 'the South American ostriches'; Charles Darwin referred to them thus in his first great work, *The Voyage of the Beagle*, published in 1839. In fact, though, the similarities between the birds are the result of convergent evolution to a similar lifestyle, and the rheas are more closely related to the tinamous with which they share the subcontinent. They are smaller than the Ostrich, with males of the Greater Rhea reaching only a maximum of 1.4 m (5 ft), half the height of a large male Ostrich, and have retained three toes on each foot. Also unlike the Ostrich, rheas have a fully feathered head and neck and feathered thighs (the feathering even extending down onto the upper part of the tarsus in the Lesser Rhea). Lesser Rheas in particular are the most rotund looking of the ratites and have been likened to 'a powder-puff on legs'. Males are larger and heavier than females, and males of the Greater Rhea generally have darker plumage than the females, with black on the lower neck and forebody. There are some plumage and size differences between the various races of both species, but also considerable individual variation.

Like Ostriches, rheas eat a very wide range of plants, including those such as thistles that are rejected by most other birds and mammals because of their unpalatability. They also eat a few insects and small vertebrates such as lizards.

The breeding system in rheas is complex, with males adopting one of four distinct strategies: (1) many mate with females and then incubate the eggs alone; (2) some mate and do not incubate; (3) some do not mate but incubate; (4) and some take no part at all in breeding. Males that mate attract wandering groups of females to their nest scrape by displaying and uttering booming cries. Several males will mate with the females in a group. When the females lay their eggs, the male gathers the eggs together, using his bill, and rolls any that are outside the scrape into it. There may be as many as 70 eggs in a single scrape, although 18–25 is more usual. The incubating male becomes more and more belligerent, driving off any other rheas that approach.

A dominant male may be joined by a subordinate male, who mates less often with the females and incubates the first complete clutch while the dominant male goes off and makes another nest, attracts females and then incubates the eggs. The dominant male

benefits by using a helper in this way as more of his young are raised successfully (and thus more of his genes are perpetuated) than for males without subordinates. In any one year only about 5% of males and 30% of females breed successfully.

Males accompanied by chicks are very belligerent towards any intruders, including not only other rheas but anything perceived as a threat, from potential predators of their young, such as foxes or birds of prey, to humans: they have even been known to attack light aircraft. They are disliked by gauchos as they will attack them when on horseback, causing the horse to throw the rider or bolt; for this reason, the men are usually preceded by dogs.

ORDER TINAMIFORMES

This group of unusual New World birds forms a sister group to the ratites. Unlike the latter, tinamous can fly (and possess a keel, albeit a reduced one, on their breastbone, for attachment of the flight muscles) but do so poorly and usually reluctantly.

TINAMOUS Tinamidae

GENERA: 9   **SPECIES**: 47

LENGTH: 15–53 cm (6–21 in)

WEIGHT: 43–2,300 g (1.5 oz–5 lb)

RANGE & HABITAT: Mexico, and Central and South America; greatest diversity in tropical South America, especially in the Amazon basin; forests, savannah and grassland

SOCIAL BEHAVIOUR: some species are largely solitary, some live in pairs year round, and others live in groups; territorial, with some species defending territory all year

NEST: on ground, either a simple scrape in soil or leaf litter, often between tree roots, or a nest of grass and sticks

EGGS: 1–16 (over 12 probably by more than one female); glossy green, blue, yellow, purplish, violet or almost black

INCUBATION: 16–20 days

FLEDGING PERIOD: about 20 days for few species where it is known; maybe as short as 10 days in some

FOOD: mainly seeds; also some fruits and invertebrates; occasionally small vertebrates such as frogs, lizards and mice

VOICE: loud, liquid whistles in forest species; higher pitched or rattling calls in open-country species; harsher trills of alarm

MIGRATION: do not migrate

CONSERVATION STATUS: seven species are listed as Vulnerable, including the Hooded Tinamou, *Nothocercus nigrocapillus*, Grey Tinamou, *Tinamus tao*, the Choco Tinamou, *Crypturellus kerriae*, and Dwarf Tinamou, *Taoniscus nanus*; and seven species including the Great Tinamou, *Tinamus major*, and the Solitary Tinamou, *T. solitarius*, are Near Threatened

Tinamous are among the most persistently terrestrial of all flying birds. They are very reluctant to take wing, and when they do it is usually when suddenly surprised at close quarters. Their flight is generally weak and clumsy, and they often collide with trees or other obstacles, when they may be injured or even killed. They have thick, strong legs that appear well adapted for running, but they become exhausted rapidly if chased by predators or humans and often stumble. They usually prefer to escape danger by relying on their superb camouflage.

Tinamous are generally very wary: this is hardly surprising, as they are extensively hunted for their oddly translucent but tender and very tasty meat. Coupled with their camouflage, this makes the forest-dwelling species in particular usually very hard to see. Often the only signs of their presence are their calls. In forest species their advertising calls may be uttered by night as well as by day, and include a series of mellow or mournful flute-like whistles, among the most characteristic sounds of Neotropical forests.

LEFT The Great Tinamou, *Tinamus major*, is a very wary bird, due to hunting pressure. Usually, the only sign of its presence is its song of seven tremulous whistles.

Looking superficially like partridges or guineafowl but with longer bills, these plump-bodied, small-headed, very short-tailed birds range in size from the Dwarf Tinamou, *Taoniscus nanus*, no larger than a week-old poultry chick, to species such as the Great Tinamou, *Tinamus major*, and Grey Tinamou, *Tinamus tao*, which are as big as a fair-sized cockerel.

Their plumage is highly cryptic, often streaked, barred or spotted in subtle shades of grey and brown. Females average slightly bigger and heavier than males, usually have somewhat brighter, paler or more strongly patterned plumage and may have differently coloured legs.

Feeding on the ground, tinamous do not use their feet to scratch for food, as do partridges or other game birds, but use their bills to dig in soil or leaf litter and to break up termite mounds.

The usual sexual roles are normally reversed in tinamous, with females playing a more active role in courtship and being more aggressive in territorial defence, and males building the nest and caring for the eggs and young. The eggs are among the most beautiful of all birds' eggs, with their brilliant, clear colours and high gloss, like fine porcelain. Tinamou chicks are well developed on hatching and run about soon after; they can often fly after a fashion when still only half grown. The young of the Spotted

Nothura, *Nothura maculosa*, are known to be physiologically capable of breeding less than 2 months after hatching, although any attempt to mate is unlikely to be fruitful at such an early age, before they have developed the technique of successful copulation.

ORDER APTERYGIFORMES

This order contains only a single small and unusual family, that of the kiwis, which evolved in isolation on the islands of New Zealand.

KIWIS Apterygidae

GENERA: 1   **SPECIES**: 5

LENGTH: 30–60 cm (12–24 in)

WEIGHT: 1.2–2.3 kg (2.6–5 lb)

RANGE AND HABITAT: New Zealand; mainly in forest and scrub of various types, some in tussock grassland and pasture or other more open habitats

SOCIAL BEHAVIOUR: live in pairs and unlike other ratites, partners are monogamous

NEST: usually in a hollow under dense vegetation; unlined or sparsely lined with leafmould and leaves

EGGS: 1–2, white

INCUBATION: 65–85 days

FLEDGING PERIOD: young may be independent at only 2 or 3 weeks old but may be protected by parents for up to 1–3 years.

FOOD: earthworms, spiders, beetles, insect larvae and other invertebrates, as well as seeds, fruits and other plant food

VOICE: loud whistling cries at night, harsher in females; also various growls, hisses, snorts and other sounds in alarm or aggression

MIGRATION: pairs rarely move from their territory

CONSERVATION STATUS: four subspecies, the Northern Brown Kiwi, *Apteryx mantelli*, the Southern Brown Kiwi, *A. australis*, the Okarito, *A. rowi*, and the Great Spotted Kiwi, *A. haastii*, are Vulnerable; and one, the Little Spotted Kiwi, *A. owenii*, has been downlisted to Near Threatened as a result of conservation successes

Looking more like bizarre mammals than birds, the kiwis are by far the smallest of the ratites, the largest species being only about the size of a domestic hen. They are among the most unusual of all birds and have the most reduced wings (tiny stumps hidden beneath their shaggy brown or grey plumage, which looks more like fur than feathers). The legs are very stout and the bill long and subtly downcurved.

There are three larger species. The Great Spotted Kiwi, *Apteryx haastii*, about 50–60 cm (20–24 in) long, found only on South Island, in forested mountains from sea level up to 1,500 m (4,900 ft) but mainly in the subalpine zone between 700 m (2,300 ft) and 1,100 m (3,600 ft). The Northern Brown Kiwi, *A. mantellii*, 50–65 cm (20–26 in) long, was once widespread throughout the North Island and the north of the South Island, but today is found only as fragmented populations, mostly in the north of North Island but also including some small offshore islands. It prefers dense, subtropical or temperate forests, but also occurs in shrublands, scrub, regenerating forest, plantations of introduced pines and pasture. The similarly sized Southern Brown

ABOVE Kiwis, such as this Northern Brown Kiwi, *Apteryx mantelli*, are nocturnal, usually remaining active until dawn, when they return to their burrows.

Kiwi, *A. australis*, is restricted today to two areas of South Island: in localised parts of Fiordland and a tiny isolated population near Haast on the west coast of South Island. Almost 75% of the total population of the Southern Brown Kiwi is of the subspecies *lawryi*, confined to Stewart Island, off the south coast of South Island. Southern Brown Kiwis occur in a wide range of habitats, including forest, scrub and tussock grassland in Fiordland and among coastal sand dunes on Stewart Island. The Okarito Brown Kiwi, *Apteryx rowi*, is about 55 cm (22 in) long. It is restricted to the Okarito forest on the west-central coast of South Island, (plus some successfully introduced to two offshore islands) in the Cook Strait between South Island and North Island, with a total population estimated at just 400–450 individuals. The smallest species at about 35–45 cm (14–18 in) long, the Little Spotted Kiwi, *A. owenii*, occurred in forests throughout both islands before European settlers arrived, but today is restricted to five offshore islands on which it has been introduced, and one mainland site where it was reintroduced. It occurs in various habitats, from forest to grassland.

All species of kiwi are nocturnal, and pairs spend the day resting in one or other of many burrows or dens that they maintain in their territory and that they defend fiercely against other pairs. They emerge after dark to feed, again resembling mammals in using their sense of smell to locate prey. The nostrils are not situated near the base of the bill as with most birds, but near its tip. They have an unusually acute olfactory sense compared with many other birds, and sniff out buried invertebrate prey such as worms or beetle larvae by making test probes into soft soil or leaf litter, then seizing the item in the bill tip and swallowing it by a series of jerks. Nesting occurs in one of the burrows or dens. In complete contrast to the eggs of other ratites (several laid by each female and though large representing only a very small proportion of the bird's weight), the one or two eggs laid by a female kiwi are, relative to her weight, astonishingly big. Each egg takes a long time to produce. Unlike most other birds, which can lay an egg at intervals of between one day (as in most songbirds, as well as the domestic chicken) and one week, the kiwi can take up to a month to produce a second egg if laying more than one. A kiwi egg weighs up to a quarter of the female's entire weight (four times the typical egg weight for a bird of this size) and fills much of her body. It has a huge yolk, which sustains the chick not only for the very long 2–3-month incubation period but also for over a week after it has hatched: the remaining yolk is available in a sac attached to the chick's stomach.

All but one of the kiwi species are threatened and suffer ongoing declines. Although the birds were of great symbolic importance to the Maori people, providing both food and feathers for making ceremonial cloaks, serious declines began when European settlers arrived in the mid-nineteenth century, converting large areas for agriculture and introducing various plants and animals. A particular threat to the kiwis (and other native birds) were mammalian predators – dogs (which had also been introduced earlier by the Maori), cats, rats, brush-tailed possums, ferrets and stoats. Intensive conservation programmes have had considerable success in translocating kiwis to islands from which predators have been removed, but stoats in particular still pose a major problem, constituting the single most significant threat: 94% of young kiwis are killed by or before they reach 100 days old, in many areas about half of this total by stoats. Predatory mammals had such a devastating effect on kiwis and other New Zealand birds because they evolved on islands where there were no native mammalian predators: the only native mammals were a few species of bats. Furthermore, they were not free from predation from the air: in prehistoric times, there was a wide range of avian predators, which may have contributed to the kiwis' adoption of a nocturnal lifestyle.

ORDER CASUARIIFORMES

This order of big flightless birds has one family of three living species of cassowary, *Casuarius*, found in New Guinea and as two isolated populations in northeastern Queensland, Australia, and a single extant species of emu, *Dromaius*, restricted to Australia.

CASSOWARIES AND EMU Casuariidae

GENERA: 1   **SPECIES:** 4

LENGTH: cassowaries 1–1.7 m (3.3–5.6 ft); emus 1.5–1.9 m (5–6.2 ft)

WEIGHT: cassowaries 18–58 kg (40–128 lb); emu 30–55 kg (66–120 lb)

RANGE AND HABITAT: cassowaries, New Guinea and a few nearby islands, northeast Queensland, Australia, with greatest diversity in New Guinea (all three species compared to only one, the Southern Cassowary, in Australia), in rainforest, swamp forest and humid savannah woodland, mainly in lowlands, except for the Dwarf Cassowary in montane forest; the Emu widespread across much of Australia in various drier habitats, including open woodland, grassland, scrub, heath, and semi-arid plains of the interior

SOCIAL BEHAVIOUR: cassowaries seen singly, in pairs or family groups; emu usually singly or in pairs or family groups; gregarious when nomadic and especially at good sources of food or water

NEST: shallow scrape on forest floor, lined with leaves and grasses

EGGS: cassowaries, 3–5 pale to dark green; emu, 5–15, dark green

INCUBATION: cassowaries, about 50 days; emu, about 56 days

FLEDGING PERIOD: cassowary chicks usually independent by 9 months, emu chicks after 7–8 months

FOOD: cassowaries, mainly fruit, also fungi, invertebrates (especially snails) and sometimes small vertebrates; emu omnivorous, eating leaves, roots, fruits, seeds and various invertebrates and small vertebrates

VOICE: cassowaries, grunts, hisses, roars, snorts; emu, grunting and booming

MIGRATION: cassowaries are mainly sedentary, with some evidence of nomadic movements, and altitudinal migrations by Dwarf Cassowary; emu are sedentary if conditions are right, but make long seasonal nomadic movements in search of food or water

CONSERVATION STATUS: although all three species of cassowary were until recently classified as Vulnerable, new estimates of population sizes and ability to cope with threats have led to their being downgraded to Least Concern though the situation will be monitored; the emu has increased greatly since European colonisation of Australia

In contrast to ostriches, rheas and Emu, the cassowaries are birds of dense forest. A cassowary's body is clothed in glossy black plumage in the adults, and rich brown in the immature birds. This looks more like hair than feathers and appears denser, sleeker and less shaggy, than the plumage of other living ratites. Like the Emu, the cassowaries have unusual, double-shafted feathers. However, the most prominent features are the brightly coloured bare skin on the head and (in two of the three species) the hanging neck

ABOVE Largest of the three cassowary species, the Southern Cassowary, *Casuarius casuarius*, is second only to ostriches in weight, and in New Guinea, the largest land animal.

flaps (called wattles), and the big blade-shaped casque that tops the head, a remarkable structure of uncertain function.

The casque may serve to help the bird force its way through dense undergrowth or to dig for fruits, fungi or small animals in the soil or leaf litter on the forest floor. Another possible function is as a badge of status or breeding condition, as it is larger in adults and highest in females. It consists of a delicate framework of bone or calcified cartilage, fused with the skull and covered with a hardened keratinised skin. The fragile internal network closely reflects the shape of the whole structure, in contrast to the anatomy of the casques of hornbills (Family Bucerotidae, see p. 153), in which the bone does not resemble the shape of the largely hollow casque when it is exposed by removal of the keratinised skin.

The brightly coloured bare parts – in various combinations of red, blue, purple, yellow and white, depending on species – are indicators of sex (brighter in females), and age (absent in younger birds), as well as changing according to 'mood' and acting as social signals in the gloom of the rainforest interior. By contrast, the chicks are camouflaged, with striped plumage breaking up their outline in the dappled shade of the forest.

The cassowaries' food is largely fruit of up to 75 or so different species of forest trees and shrubs. The survival of the birds depends on mature forests with diverse food-plant species, guaranteeing their access to a year-round supply of fruit. In turn, the cassowaries ensure the survival of the trees as they eat the fruit whole and excrete the seeds, dispersing species with fruit that is too big for any other rainforest animals to eat.

Cassowaries are generally solitary, and when individuals do meet (except when courting and adults and their young) often fight fiercely. They may defend themselves by spreading their very reduced wings, which bear enlarged, spike-like quills. As well as serving as a deterrent to an attacker, they may provide some shielding to the body beneath. Far more dangerous, though, is when they use the innermost of their three toes as a terrifying weapon. This toe bears a 10 cm (2.5 in) long, dagger-like claw, which the bird can use in a downward slash as it leaps up and strikes out with its feet to rip open an adversary, whether a rival of its own species or a threatening human. Despite this, and the fact that a good number of people in New Guinea, especially children, have been killed, it is often kept in captivity by the native peoples of that island for its feathers (used to decorate headdresses), quills (for nose ornaments), dangerous claws (used as spear points) and meat.

In reality, though, cassowaries are far more threatened by humans than the other way round – especially in Australia, where the only species occurring there, the Southern (or Two-wattled) Cassowary, *Casuarius casuarius*, is at risk from being killed by ever-increasing road traffic and attacks by dogs (especially on young birds) as well as from habitat damage by grazing cattle. In New Guinea, extensive logging, exploitation of mineral resources and an intensification of hunting pressure pose further threats to the three species living there – the Southern Cassowary, the Northern (or Single-wattled) Cassowary, *C. unappendiculatus*, and the Dwarf Cassowary, *C. bennetti*. Despite this, the latest research into the status of these remarkable birds indicates that, for the present at least, they are holding their own overall.

The single living species of Emu (*Dromaius novaehollandiae*) is a big, bulky bird (second in size only to the Ostrich) with a long neck and legs, and a long, round-backed body. The plumage hangs loosely, giving it a particularly shaggy appearance, and there is a distinct central 'parting'. As in its relatives the cassowaries, each feather in the Emu is double, with a greatly enlarged secondary aftershaft (the feather that branches off the base of the main feather and is small in most birds), which is as long as the main feather. For much of the year, the plumage is pale brown with darker mottling, having faded in the hot Australian sun, but after the annual moult the new feathers are much darker. The top of the head and the neck are black, but for much of the time the bare skin of the neck shows through its sparse feathering at the front; in the breeding season the black feathers are much denser in females, and they also have bright blue bare skin on the head behind the eye.

The wings are very stunted, at less than 20 cm (8 in) long, and are hidden beneath the plumage; however, they are important in keeping the birds cool on hot summer days, when they raise them to allow heat to evaporate from the network of surface veins on the underside. Emus also take advantage of the shade cast by trees when resting, but unlike kangaroos will feed in the open during the heat of the summer days, as long as they can obtain enough water. Many populations, especially in the arid interior where the high-quality plant food they need is often only available in certain widely scattered places, have to spend a good deal of time on the move. Some clock up over 500 km (300 miles) in a year.

The female attracts males by making loud, booming calls known as 'drumming'. The sound carries far, amplified by resonating within an air sac in the neck, which connects to the windpipe. A pair of Emus will spend several months together defending a large territory of about 30 km² (12 sq. miles). After she has laid the eggs, some females may defend the male as he incubates the eggs. Others though, leave the territory to mate with another male. For almost 2 months, the male

ABOVE Emus, *Dromaius novaehollandiae*, are often alone or in pairs, although small groups like this one form at good feeding sites and water sources.

remains on or next to the eggs, and does not eat, drink or defecate. The male is a solicitous father, driving off or attacking any intruders that approach the striped chicks, from his partner to dogs and humans.

Emus occur over much of Australia, being absent only from dense rainforest and urban areas. They survived heavy persecution during the early days of European colonisation as the settlers killed them for their meat and oil (for use in lamps) and ate their eggs. The development of agriculture in Australia has proved a mixed blessing for these great birds. Although many have been killed by farmers because the emus relish their crops, the species has benefited from the provision of water supplies for livestock in arid areas in the centre of the continent, where they were previously unable to survive. They are farmed in other parts of the world as well as in Australia for their skin, oil, meat and feathers. The Emu is also celebrated as one of the continent's national emblems. Two other species of emu, the King Island Emu, *Dromaius minor*, and Kangaroo Island Emu, *D. baudinianus*, became extinct in the early nineteenth century, while the Tasmanian race of the emu, *D. novaehollandiae diemenensis*, lasted until about 1850.

ORDER ANSERIFORMES

The reason for uniting the two distinct groups in this order – the large assemblage of swans, geese and ducks (Family Anatidae) and the Magpie Goose (with just one modern species in the Family Anseranatidae) on the one hand and the very different-looking screamers (Family Anhimidae) on the other – is that they share a range of characters, including a reduced or absent aftershaft on the feathers, a feathered oil gland and various details of the syrinx ('voice box'), skull and sternum.

The Anseriformes are related to the game birds and other families in the Order Galliformes, and are united within the major subdivision Galloanserae; this has long been reflected in the 'fowl' part of the name in 'wildfowl' (North American waterfowl).

SCREAMERS Anhimidae

GENERA: 2   **SPECIES:** 3

LENGTH: 70–95 cm (23–28 in)

WEIGHT: 3–4.5 kg (6.6–10 lb)

RANGE AND HABITAT: South America; the Northern Screamer, *Chauna chavaria*, is found only in Venezuela and northern Colombia; the other two species are far more widespread; wetlands in tropical or subtropical lowlands

SOCIAL BEHAVIOUR: probably pair for life; usually in pairs or family groups in the breeding season but may gather in small groups for winter

NEST: large structure of sticks and other vegetation, built by both sexes just above the surface of the water

EGGS: 2–7, white with pale spots

INCUBATION: 40–45 days

FLEDGING PERIOD: 8–10 weeks

FOOD: mainly leaves, stems, flowers and roots of aquatic plants; also some seeds, insects and other invertebrates

VOICE: various loud calls, ranging from guttural drumming to harsh trumpeting, audible at up to 3 km (1.8 miles) away

MIGRATION: sedentary, apart from post-breeding dispersal of young and non-breeding adults

CONSERVATION STATUS: Northern Screamer is Near Threatened

These unusual birds are exclusively South American, and although they are generally classified with swans, geese and ducks in the Order Anseriformes, they are a basal group that probably constitutes a link between the game birds and the wildfowl proper. Screamers have smallish, chicken-like heads and large, bulky bodies; on the ground they resemble large game birds or geese, but when they take off they look more like big birds of prey – apart from their long legs. They are strong fliers, and often soar to great heights on their long, broad wings. Despite their size and weight, they perch on the topmost branches of trees and shrubs. Their toes

ABOVE Although mainly a bird of wetlands, the Southern Screamer, *Chauna torquata*, is also found in drier habitats, than the other two screamer species.

ABOVE The screamers maintain long-term pair bonds, probably sometimes for life. This pair of Horned Screamers, *Anhima cornuta*, are in the Peruvian Amazon.

are only slightly webbed at the base, and adults do not often swim, although they often wade, and their widely splayed toes allow them to walk across floating vegetation.

Instead of being arranged in distinct tracts as with most modern birds, the plumage is evenly distributed. The Northern Screamer, *Chauna chavaria*, and the Southern Screamer, *C. torquata*, have grey plumage, darker above than below. The former species has a white patch on the throat and face that contrasts with the black neck, and the latter has a thin white neck ring above a black collar. Both have a scruffy grey crest at the rear of the head. The Horned Screamer, *Anhima cornuta*, is mainly black with a white belly, a barred black-and-white neck

and a head with a broad black band. The head is downy, and there is a patch of bare skin from the base of the bill to around the eyes, red in the Southern and Northern species, blackish in the Horned Screamer. The latter takes its name from the long 'horn' of gleaming white cartilage that curves forward from the middle of its forehead, where it is attached to a little bony nub on the skull. The legs of the Horned Screamer are greenish grey, but the other two species have bright reddish legs.

Screamers are exceptional among living birds in lacking the uncinate processes on the ribs (extensions from the middle of each rib that overlap with the next rib in front to strengthen and rigidify the ribcage). Another odd feature is the air sacs beneath their skin, which crackle when they are handled; of all birds, their bones are the most honeycombed with air spaces, including even the toe bones. There is a long, sharp, curved spur at the bend of each wing, which is used in territorial disputes.

Screamers have very loud voices, true to their name, although it is a misnomer in that they do not really scream, but utter gargled trumpeting, honking, yelping or other sounds. Among the loudest of any birds' calls, they can carry for 3 km (1.8 miles). Pairs often call to one another or in unison incessantly, especially during the breeding season. Members of a big flock produce an amazingly loud and cacophonous chorus, for instance when they assemble at their treetop roost as night falls. Their propensity for making so much noise when alarmed has led to screamers being kept in captivity by local people to serve as watchdogs, but also earns them the wrath of hunters as their calls alert every other creature to the presence of danger.

MAGPIE GOOSE Anseranatidae

GENERA: 1   **SPECIES:** 1

LENGTH: 75–90 cm (30–35 in)

WEIGHT: 2–2.8 kg (4.4–6 lb)

RANGE AND HABITAT: restricted to Australia, almost entirely in the north, and southern New Guinea; margins of shallow wetlands with fringing vegetation, flooded grassland and swamps

SOCIAL BEHAVIOUR: gregarious outside the breeding season, often occurring in flocks of up to many hundreds or occasionally even thousands of birds; nest in small colonies; polygamous, with each male usually pairing with a couple of females

NEST: large floating mound of reeds and spike-rushes, built mainly in swamps

EGGS: usually 5–20 (depending on whether one, two or up to four females lay in the same nest), whitish or buff

INCUBATION: 23–25 days

FLEDGING PERIOD: about 11 weeks

FOOD: grazes on leaves of grasses and sedges, eats seeds, and uses hook on bill to dig for bulbs of rushes and rhizomes of sedges

VOICE: loud honking calls

MIGRATION: not a true migrant, but wanders extensively in dry periods in search of food

CONSERVATION STATUS: not threatened

ABOVE The big, ungainly Magpie Goose, *Anseranas semipalmata*, of Australia and New Guinea is often nomadic, wandering widely in search of food and water.

The Magpie Goose (*Anseranas semipalmata*) is an odd bird that is placed in a family of its own. It may be among the oldest and most primitive of all the wildfowl, forming a link between the screamers and the ducks, geese and swans. Anseranatids have a widespread and diverse fossil record going back into the Tertiary, with a range that included North America and Europe. The modern species seems to be the sole survivor of this ancient lineage. Found only in Australia and New Guinea, it is a gangly, goose-like bird with a large peaked bulge on the top of the head, which is more pronounced in males. Most of the body is white, contrasting with the black of the long neck, head, large rounded wings, longish tail and neat 'thigh' feathers. This bird has bare pink skin at the base of the disproportionately large, hook-tipped bill, and has long, sturdy pink legs; its toes have only rudimentary webs at their base. Unlike other wildfowl, it does not moult all its wing feathers at once, and so does not have a flightless 'eclipse' period.

Until the end of the nineteenth century, the species range extended to many parts of South Eastern Australia, but hunting, drainage and agricultural development virtually eliminated it from there and threatens its future in the north and north east of the continent, where indigenous populations are confined today – although there are current attempts at reintroduction to the south east.

DUCKS, GEESE AND SWANS Anatidae

GENERA: 53   **SPECIES:** 157

LENGTH: 30–180 cm (1–6 ft)

WEIGHT: 215 g–15 kg (0.5–33 lb)

RANGE AND HABITAT: worldwide except Antarctica; all sorts of aquatic and wetland habitats, both freshwater and marine

SOCIAL BEHAVIOUR: swans and geese pair for life, ducks usually only seasonally; nest as separate pairs, often in small to medium colonies; outside breeding season generally in flocks, often large

NEST: most build nest of vegetation lined with down on land; some nest in tree holes or holes in ground

EGGS: average clutch size in most species is 4–13 (but sometimes 'egg dumping' by other females results in up to 35 or more in a nest); typically white or pastel coloured

INCUBATION: 22–40 days

FLEDGING PERIOD: 4–10 weeks

Food: wide range of plant matter, especially seeds, leaves, roots and tubers; some feed exclusively on small animals such as insects and their larvae, molluscs and crustaceans, or on fish

VOICE: wide range of calls, including trumpeting of swans and honking, cackling and yelping of geese and the huge variety of duck sounds, from whistling, grating, rattling, yodelling and cooing sounds uttered by males during courtship to the more familiar quacks, louder and more frequent in females

MIGRATION: many northern species in particular make long migrations

CONSERVATION STATUS: two species (and perhaps 19 more known only as sub-fossils) are Extinct: species became extinct in historic times, including the Reunion Shelduck, *Alopochen kervazoi*, the Labrador Duck, *Camptorhynchus labradorius*, and the Auckland Islands Merganser, *Mergus australis*; six species – the Laysan Duck, *Anas laysanensis*, the Madagascar Pochard, *Aythya innotata*, Baer's Pochard, *Aythya baeri*, the Brazilian Merganser, *Mergus octosetaceus*, the Pink-headed Duck, *Rhodonessa caryophyllacea*, and the Crested Shelduck, *Tadorna cristata* – are Critically Endangered; eight species, including the Madagascar Teal, *Anas bernieri*, the Brown Teal, *A. chlorotis*, the Hawaiian Duck, *A. wyvilliana*, the Blue Duck, *Hymenolaimus malacorhynchos*, the Scaly-sided Merganser, *Mergus squamatus*, and the White-headed Duck, *Oxyura leucocephala*, are Endangered; 18 species, including the Lesser White-fronted Goose, *Anser erythropus*, the Swan Goose, *A. cygnoides*, the Hawaiian Goose, *Branta sandvicensis*, the Red-breasted Goose, *Branta ruficollis*, and Steller's Eider, *Polysticta stelleri*, are Vulnerable; there are 10 species that are Near Threatened

The worldwide representatives of this well-known family of waterbirds are collectively known as wildfowl in Britain and waterfowl in North America. Placed first in the sequence following the Magpie Goose is the small subfamily of whistling ducks, containing eight species in the genus *Dendrocygna*, and one in *Thalassornis*. The rest are almost all in two familiar subgroups: the 23 species of swans and geese (subfamily Anserinae) and a much larger one containing most of the ducks (subfamily Anatinae), with 99 species.

The subfamily Anserinae are sometimes divided into two main tribes, the Cygnini, the swans, and the Anserini, the geese. There are six species of swans in the genus *Cygnus*: the Mute Swan, *C. olor*, of Europe to Central Asia; three far northern breeding swans, the Whooper Swan, *C. cygnus*, of Eurasia, the Tundra Swan, *C. columbianus*, in both Eurasia and North America, and the Trumpeter Swan, *C. buccinator*, restricted to North America; the Black Swan, *C. atratrus*, native to Australia and introduced to New Zealand; and the Black-necked Swan, *C. melanocoryphus*, in southern South America and the Falkland Islands. A second southern South American species, the Coscoroba Swan, is given a genus of its own, *Coscoroba*, and is likely to be more closely related to another, Australian, oddity in the subfamily, the Cape Barren Goose, *Cereopsis novaehollandiae*, rather than to the 'true' swans. There are two main geese genera: *Anser* (known as the 'grey geese'), whose 10 species include the Greylag Goose of Eurasia, *A. anser*, from which most of the world's domestic geese have been bred, and *Branta* (the 'black geese'), with 5 species including the Canada Goose, *Branta canadensis*, a native of northern North America that is also familiar in the British Isles and New Zealand, where introductions were successful, and, by contrast, the rare Hawaiian Goose, *B. sandvicensis*, rescued from extinction by captive breeding and reintroduction.

Turning to the ducks, several species somewhat confusingly contain the word 'goose' in their name: the five species of sheldgeese, *Chloephaga*, of South America, two African species, the Egyptian Goose, *Alopochen aegyptiaca* and the Blue-winged Goose, *Cyanochen cyanoptera*, and the Orinoco Goose, *Neochen jubata* of South America. All these, together with their relatives the seven species of shelducks, *Tadorna*, have traditionally, as here, been separated in a subfamily of their own, the Tadorninae, although recent analysis suggests that they may be better placed within a tribe Tadornini within the Anatinae. They are generally thought to represent a transitional group between the true geese and the ducks. Various other species of uncertain affinities have been lumped with them, including the steamer ducks, *Tachyeres*, the Torrent Duck, *Merganetta armata*, both from South America, the Spur-winged Goose, *Plecopterus gambensis* of Africa, the Comb Duck, *Sarkidiornis melanotos* with a wide range in Africa, southern Asia and South America, and the Blue Duck, *Hymenolaimus malacorhynchos* of New Zealand. Another oddity, the Freckled Duck, *Stictonetta naevosa*, of Australia, is distinctive enough to have been given a subfamily (Stictonettinae) of its own.

The subfamily Anatinae includes several well recognised groupings as well as a number of species whose relationships with the rest are less certain. Examples of the latter are the Muscovy Duck, *Cairina moschata*, a native of Central and South America that in its domesticated form is widespread across the world; the little Mandarin Duck, *Aix galericulata* of the Far East of Asia and the Wood Duck, *A. sponsa* of North America, both of which have strikingly beautiful and flamboyantly plumages males and have been introduced to Europe; the Maned Duck, *Chenonetta jubata* of Australia; and the three species of pygmy geese, *Nettapus* from Africa, southern Asia and Australia. All these and several others have often been united in a tribe Cairinini, popularly known as perching-ducks, from their habit of nesting in tree-holes and perching and walking on branches, but this may not indicate that they are so closely related. Other species of uncertain relationships include a very distinctive Australian endemic, the Pink-eared Duck, *Malacorhynchus membranaceus*: it has recently been suggested that it might be more closely related to the geese and swans, and even placed in the Anserinae.

The largest genus of the Anatinae, *Anas*, with 25 species, is sometimes included with other genera in a tribe, Anatini. It includes the most familiar of the ducks to most people in Europe, Asia and North America, the Mallard, *Anas platyrhynchos*. The three species of wigeon (the Eurasian Wigeon, *Mareca penelope*, the American Wigeon, *M. americana*, of North America, and the Chiloe Wigeon, *M. sibilatrix*, of southern South America), have short, stubby bills rather like those of geese, and, like the latter, obtain much of their food by grazing vegetation on land. A number of ducks are called teal, including the Green-winged Teal, *Anas crecca* of Eurasia and North America, the Blue-winged Teal, *Spatula discors* of North America, the Baikal Teal, *Sibirionetta formosa*, of north-east Asia, and the Hottentot Teal, *Spatula hottentota* of Africa. Other members include the Northern Pintail, *A. acuta*, of Eurasia and North America, and the four species of *Spatula* in North America and Asia; southern Africa; South America; and Australasia.

The tribe Aythyini are the pochards, diving ducks that are mainly birds of freshwaters. They include three species in the genus *Netta*, one in Eurasia, one in South America, and the other in Africa, and 12 species of *Aythya*. The latter include two familiar North American species, the Canvasback, *A. valisineria* and Redhead, *A. americana*, and the Common Pochard, *A. ferina* of Eurasia. Other members of this group are the Ring-necked Duck, *A. collaris*, of North America,

LEFT When it dives, this drake Red-breasted Merganser, *Mergus serrator*, will use its long slender bill with sharply serrated inner edges to grasp a slippery fish firmly.

the very similar Tufted Duck, *A. fuligula* of Eurasia and the more marine Greater Scaup, *A. marila*, of North America and Eurasia.

The tribe Mergini comprise a group of 18 mainly marine species often known as the sea ducks. The eiders are in two genera, with a single species in one genus, Steller's Eider, *Polysticta stelleri*, and three very closely related species in *Somateria*. All four are birds of coastal waters and nearby freshwaters in various parts of northern Eurasia and North America. The Labrador Duck, *Camptorhynchus labradorius*, extinct since the late nineteenth century, is thought to have shown some similarities to the eiders. Two unique species are the little Harlequin Duck, *Histrionicus histrionicus* and the Long-tailed Duck, *Clangula hyemalis*. Both breed in the north of North America and Eurasia; the Harlequin Duck by fast-flowing upland streams and the Long-tailed Duck mainly by tundra pools and on bogs, and both winter at sea along the coasts, the latter much farther from shore.

A trio of close relatives are the three species of scoters, *Melanitta*, again with a breeding range across the tundra and open boreal forests of northern North America and Eurasia, and a habit of wintering mainly at sea. Yet another group of three close relatives are the goldeneyes, *Bucephala*. Unlike the other members of the Mergini, two of the goldeneyes, the Common Goldeneye, *B. clangula*, and the exclusively North American Bufflehead, *B. albeola*, breed in tree hollows (or artificial nestboxes) in forests bordering rivers, lakes or pools, while the third, Barrow's Goldeneye, *B. islandica*, may conceal its nest among vegetation or in a hole at ground level, as its range includes open, treeless country, as in Iceland and Greenland.

The sawbills are a group of very distinctive fish-eating specialists. Like the goldeneyes, they are hole nesters, either in trees or on the ground. The Smew, *Mergellus albellus*, is exclusively Eurasian, while the Hooded Merganser, *Lophodytes cucullatus*, is endemic to North America. The four other extant species are all in the genus *Mergus*. Two are common and widespread across Eurasia and North America; these are the Red-breasted Merganser, *Mergus serrator* and the larger Goosander (called the Common Merganser in North America), *Mergus merganser*. The other two, the Brazilian Merganser, *Mergus octosetaceus*, and a localised Far Eastern species, the Scaly-sided Merganser, *M. squamatus* are both rare and threatened. A fifth species, the Auckland Islands Merganser, *M. australis*, from the Auckland Islands of New Zealand, became extinct in 1902.

The tribe Oxyurini are the stifftails, so called because of their rather long, stiffened tail feathers, which they often hold cocked vertically. There are six species of *Oxyura*, three restricted to the New World, although one of these, the Ruddy Duck, *O. jamaicensis*, was introduced to England, where it spread widely across Britain and Ireland and into parts of Europe. Because of fears that they would interbreed with Mediterranean populations of the far scarcer White-headed Duck, *O. leucocephala*, and replace them with hybrids, a controversial culling programme was instigated to eradicate them in their introduced range. Another one of the six *Oxyura* species, the Lake Duck, *O. vittata* of southern South America, is notable as the possessor of the longest avian penis.

Also included are three species in monotypic genera: The Black-headed Duck, *Heteronetta atricapilla*, of South America, the Masked Duck, *Nomonyx dominicus*, in the Caribbean, Mexico, Central America and South America and the Musk Duck, *Biziura lobata*. The last of these may prove not to belong in this group.

Members of the family vary hugely in size, from the tiny African Pygmy Goose, *Nettapus auritus*, and Hottentot Teal, *Spatula hottentota*, only 30–36 cm (12–14 in) long and weighing 215–285 g (8–10 oz), to the huge *Cygnus* swans, at up to 1.8 m (6 ft) and 15 kg (33 lb) or more.

Features shared by all species include feet that are webbed between the front three toes (the hind one being elevated) and the classic flattened 'duck bill', which differs considerably in size, shape and structure between various species. There is great variety in the size, shape and arrangement of the projections (lamellae) along the cutting edges of the bill, and the hardened 'nail' at the tip may be blunt, expanded or slightly hooked. The bills of some wildfowl bear knobs or caruncles, typically restricted to – or larger in – the males: examples are seen in the Mute Swan, Black-necked Swan, Common Shelduck, and Rosy-billed Pochard, *Netta peposaca*. The male Comb Duck, *Sarkidiornis melanotos*, has a particularly bizarre bill-knob, which grows to disproportionate size in the breeding season. Other odd-billed species are the Musk Duck, *Biziura lobata*, in which the male has a highly distensible throat pouch, especially large during the breeding season, the very large bill of the shovelers, with a particularly complex structure for filter-feeding, and the Pink-eared Duck, *Malacorhynchus membranaceus*, whose bizarre-looking bill, with its side flaps, is also highly adapted for sieving food.

ABOVE This drake Eurasian Wigeon, *Mareca penelope*, is uttering its loud whistling call, Caerlaverock, Scotland.

Many wildfowl species have a long, slim neck; the wings are pointed and used for fast-flapping flight rather than gliding, and most species are powerful fliers (notable exceptions are three of the four species of steamer ducks, *Tachyeres*, of southern South America, which are flightless). The tail is usually short. This is one of the few bird families in which males have a penis. The plumage consists of a dense coat of strong, highly waterproof feathers overlying a thick insulating layer of down. All species undergo a more or less simultaneous moult of their flight feathers after breeding and are flightless for several weeks during this 'eclipse' period. During this vulnerable time, the brightly patterned males of many species of ducks adopt a dull, cryptic eclipse plumage similar to that of the females.

Plumage varies from all white, black, or black and white in the swans, through various combinations of greys, browns, white and black in most geese, to the colourful patterns of most male ducks. A distinctive feature of many of the ducks is the speculum, a contrastingly coloured panel of feathers on the secondary wing-feathers. This found in both sexes and also in immature birds. In many species it is an iridescent, metallic blue, green or bronze, and is often bordered by black and white bars. The bill of some species is boldly coloured, especially in males during the breeding season; examples include the bright pinkish bills of the Common Shelduck,

ABOVE A drake Pochard, *Aythya ferina*, takes off from a lake in Norfolk, England.

ABOVE Barrow's Goldeneye, *Bucephala islandica*, is one of three related species that feed mainly by diving for molluscs and other invertebrates.

ABOVE A pair of Mute Swans, *Cygnus olor*, with their day-old cygnets at Cley, Norfolk, England.

Tadorna tadorna, and various other species, or the brilliant blue ones of the stifftails, *Oxyura*.

Although most species are closely tied to water, especially during the breeding season, wildfowl occupy many different habitats, from cold arctic seas and lakes to tropical swamps, and even hot deserts and almost barren lava fields. Although many spend most of their lives on or under the water, some (such as many swans and geese) feed a lot on land; like other wildfowl, when not breeding they prefer to roost on water, where they are safer from predators. By contrast, the most accomplished aquatic members of the family include the little Harlequin Duck, *Histrionicus histrionicus*, of northwest and northeast North America, Greenland, Iceland and north-east Asia; the Torrent Duck, *Merganetta armata*, of Andean South America, and the Blue Duck, *Hymenolaimus malacorhynchos*, of alpine New Zealand. All three are adapted for life in fast-flowing water, with rushing torrents and waterfalls. Dabbling ducks, such as the Mallard, teal and relatives, *Anas*, are adapted to finding their food in relatively shallow water, while the diving ducks – such as the pochards, scoters, goldeneye, Long-tailed Duck, sawbills and stifftails – often feed at much greater depths. The Long-tailed Duck is a particularly deep diver, recorded at depths of over 150 m (480 ft).

There is considerable variety in diet and feeding methods in this family. For instance, the dabbling ducks are filter-feeders that sift tiny animals and seeds using the fine, comblike lamellae on their bills, those of the shovelers and the Pink-eared Duck being especially well developed for this purpose; geese and swans graze on plants, including crops in fields; diving ducks wrench molluscs from the rocks on the seabed with their short, powerful bills; while fish-eating specialists such as the sawbills grasp their slippery, wriggling prey in long, fine, hooked bills equipped with modified lamellae like the teeth of a saw.

Swans and geese generally mate for life, protect their young and maintain strong family bonds year-round; male swans (and whistling ducks) even share incubation duties. By contrast, most ducks pair for only one season, and the drakes usually play no part in rearing the family. Some species, such as the Mute Swan, *Cygnus olor*, of Eurasia and the Torrent Duck, are highly territorial; others, including many ducks, are loosely colonial; and some, such as geese, nest in tighter-knit colonies. Nests are usually built by the female alone, except in most swans and whistling ducks, in which the male helps, and the South American Coscoroba Swan, *Coscoroba coscoroba*, and Australian Cape Barren Goose, *Cereopsis novaehollandiae*, in which the male does all the work. In most species, nests are shallow scrapes on the ground near water, sparsely lined with grass or other vegetation, but shelducks, *Tadorna*, nest in old mammal burrows, tree hollows or even haystacks. Others, such as the Common Goldeneye, *Bucephala clangula*, and Mandarin and Wood Ducks, *Aix galericulata* and *A. sponsa*, nest in holes high in tree trunks (or nest boxes), from which the young must leap to the ground after fledging. Most wildfowl nests are lined with a snug layer of soft down, which the female plucks from her own breast. The ducklings can run about, dive and feed themselves within hours of hatching.

Outside the breeding season, many species, such as the Snow Goose, *Anser caerulescens*, of North America, gather in huge flocks. The sight of such vast assemblages flying high overhead on migration, or landing to feed, is one of the greatest of all wildlife spectacles. In many ducks, the wintering flocks often consist entirely or predominantly of one sex. Then, when males and females meet, the drakes impress the attendant ducks with elaborate, stereotyped courtship rituals.

Species breeding in the north make long migrations to and from their wintering grounds. Most tropical and subtropical species remain in the same general area if possible, but may be forced to move in search of food or breeding sites by drought. During their flightless period, many species migrate to special moulting grounds where they can find abundant food as well as protection from predators through strength of numbers.

Along with game birds (particularly the domestic fowl), wildfowl have been intimately associated with humans for longer than any other group of birds. They have long played an important part in mythology and folk tales of many cultures, from the deception by the Greek god Zeus in taking on the form of a swan when seducing Leda, to the swan's representation as the 'swan-maiden', a symbol of purity, in numerous Celtic and Nordic legends. Another reflection of this intimate bond is the way in which references to these birds are part of everyday speech, as in expressions such as 'swanning around' or 'like water off a duck's back'. In turn, these are often related to ancient myths, as in the 'goose that laid the golden egg'.

As well as being embedded in our minds, swans, geese and ducks have long been satisfying our stomachs. For millennia they have been hunted for their tasty flesh wherever they occur, and hunting continues today on a large scale, for both subsistence and sport. Duck hunting is still big business in countries such as the USA.

In addition, several species have been domesticated for at least 2,000 years. Among the ducks the most important is the widespread Mallard, *Anas platyrhynchos*, the world's most abundant wild duck and the one most often kept in captivity everywhere, with selective breeding producing many varieties; there are also domesticated forms of the Muscovy Duck, *Cairina moschata*, a native of South America. The ancestor of domestic geese in Europe was the Greylag Goose, *Anser anser*, while in China the species involved was the Swan Goose, *Anser cygnoides*. Many species, especially of ducks, are kept in waterfowl collections, often with the flight feathers of their wings trimmed annually or pinioned (by removing the outer part of the wing completely while the bird is only a few days old, which normally renders it flightless for the rest of its life) so that they cannot escape.

Although many species, such as the Canada Goose, Mallard and Long-tailed Duck, are abundant, all wildfowl are adversely affected by human activities – especially as the result of pollution and the draining of wetlands – and some are declining or are already rare and endangered.

ABOVE A Greylag Geese, *Anser anser*, comes in to land at Caerlaverock, Scotland.

ORDER GALLIFORMES

This is a widespread group of mainly medium to large terrestrial birds, divided into five families. Two of these families (the New World quail and the pheasants, grouse and relatives) are often known collectively as the game birds. This reflects the fact that many of them are indeed major quarry for hunters, although of course the same applies to various other birds, especially the other galliform families and birds in the Order Anseriformes – the wildfowl (North American: waterfowl), and some of the waders and pigeons, for instance.

Although a typical game bird such as a pheasant or quail looks very different from a duck or goose, the Galliformes share many internal features with the Anseriformes. The members of both orders share the ability to lay large clutches of eggs relative to the birds' size, and their young are remarkably precocious; most are strongly polygamous, and often different species and even genera interbreed. In addition, their relationship has been strongly supported by DNA studies and other molecular analysis, and the two orders are now generally regarded as forming a major subdivision, called the Galloanserae, distinct from all the rest of modern birds, the latter being united in a huge group called the Neoaves.

MEGAPODES Megapodiidae

GENERA: 7   **SPECIES:** 22

LENGTH: 35–65 cm (14–26 in)

WEIGHT: 0.3–3 kg (0.66–6.6 lb)

RANGE AND HABITAT: Nicobar Islands, Philippines, East Indonesia, New Guinea, North Australia, some Pacific islands; greatest diversity in New Guinea and adjacent islands (nine species); rainforest, other tropical woodland, scrub; Malleefowl in semi-arid low-eucalypt shrubland (mallee)

SOCIAL BEHAVIOUR: probably live mainly singly or in pairs; some roost in groups; chiefly monogamous apart from brush-turkeys

NEST: a burrow warmed by sun or decaying tree roots, in hot volcanic soil, or buried deep inside a huge mound of rotting vegetation and soil

EGGS: 12–30, white, brownish or pink, abandoned by parents, who also play no part in rearing chicks

INCUBATION: 50–96 days

FLEDGING PERIOD: hatch almost fully feathered; can fly within a few hours

FOOD: many species are omnivorous, although Malleefowl are largely vegetarian and some scrubfowl eat mainly invertebrates; for most, fruits and seeds are important; chicks feed mainly on invertebrates

VOICE: loud whistles, cackling and grunting calls; some mae booming sounds, amplified by inflating neck sac

MIGRATION: little known, though some scrubfowl can move from island to island

CONSERVATION STATUS: four species, Bruijn's Brush-turkey, *Aepypodius bruijnii*, the Maleo, *Macrocephalon maleo*, the Micronesian Megapode, *Megapodius laperouse*, and the Tongan Megapode, *Megapodius pritchardii*, are Endangered; six species, including the Moluccan Megapode, *Eulipoa wallacei*, and the Malleefowl, *Leipoa ocellata*, are Vulnerable; one species, the Tanimbar Megapode, *Megapodius tenimberensis*, is Near Threatened

The most primitive members of the galliform order, the megapodes are stout-bodied birds whose plumage in most species is brown, grey or black, although there are a few with white areas; some species have brightly coloured bare skin on the head and neck. These birds can be subdivided

ABOVE The Orange-footed Scrub Fowl, *Megapodius reinwardt,* lives in various habitats in Indonesia, New Guinea and northern Australia.

into five groups: 14 species of megapodes and 1 species of scrubfowl in the genus *Megapodius* and one megapode in *Eulipoa;* the *Talegalla* brush-turkeys (three species); the *Aepypodius* brush-turkeys (two species); and two distinctive species: the Malleefowl, *Leipoa ocellata,* and the Maleo, *Macrocephalon maleo.* All are ground dwellers that rarely use their big, rounded wings for flight except in an emergency to escape a predator.

The genus *Megapodius* occurs very widely, on many south Asian islands, including the Nicobar Islands, Indonesia and the Philippines, New Guinea, the Solomon Islands and (one species, the Orange-footed Scrubfowl, *M. reinwardt*), Australia. The Moluccan Megapode, *Eulipoa wallacei,* is endemic to the Moluccan islands off the west coast of New Guinea. The *Talegalla* brush-turkeys are birds of New Guinea and adjacent islands, as are two of the *Aepypodius* brush-turkeys; the other one, *A. lathami,* often known simply as *the* Brush Turkey, is endemic to Queensland and New South Wales in Australia. The Malleefowl is another Australian endemic, in this case restricted to southern Australia, whereas the Maleo occurs only on Sulawesi and Buton Island, Indonesia.

Megapodes have big, powerful legs and feet with strong claws (the family name is from the Greek for 'big feet'). These are useful not only in scratching for food in typical galliform style but are also well adapted for their unique method of producing young, which is more akin to that used by many reptiles such as crocodiles and marine turtles. To incubate their eggs, they adopt one of three strategies, depending on species. Some lay the eggs in shallow holes that they dig in beach sand, and then cover them over and leave them to be heated by the sun. Others excavate more permanent burrows (up to 3 m/10 ft deep and 2 m/6 ft long) in soil that is heated by volcanic activity or as a result of rotting tree roots. The third strategy, found in all three Australian species, is for the pair to pile up huge mounds of soil and vegetation in which to bury the eggs. These mounds produce the necessary warmth as they rot, as a result of the respiration of

micro-organisms, especially fungi. These mounds, when used year after year, can reach prodigious sizes. One built by a pair of Orange Scrubfowl measured 18 m (almost 60 ft) long, 5 m (16 ft) wide and 3 m (10 ft) high, while another was 8 m (26 ft) high and 51 m (167 ft) in circumference. Such huge constructions are likely to weigh well over 50 tonnes.

Every aspect of reproduction in megapodes is remarkable. The eggs, abandoned by the female once she has laid them, are incubated in conditions of low oxygen/high carbon dioxide concentrations and high humidity that would be likely to prevent eggs of other birds from surviving. The eggs are adapted to facilitate gas exchange and water removal by being especially thin-shelled and furnished with large pores that can change shape.

The male Malleefowl works on his mound, which is heated by sunshine as well as decomposition, for much of each year, regularly adjusting the thickness of the covering soil to maintain the correct temperature (averaging 33°C/91.4°F) for incubation. He is able to assess this accurately by probing into the surface of the mound with his bill. Each female lays up to 34 eggs, (typically 15–24) per season, one at a time, at intervals of several to many days. As the embryo starts to develop immediately, the young emerge continuously over a period of many weeks. Megapode chicks are the most well developed at hatching of all birds. Each chick explodes out of the egg by forcing the shell apart with its strong legs, back and head, and then digs its way up to the light and fresh air. Buried typically 30–120 cm (1–4 ft) deep in the mound, it must lose no time in fighting its way to the surface.

Once it reaches the surface of the mound, the chick must fend entirely for itself. The parents do not even show they recognise it on the infrequent occasions when their paths cross and do nothing to help it. The relatively few offspring that survive have to cope with finding food, water and shelter, avoiding overheating and cooling, and escaping predators totally alone.

Predation is a major problem affecting many megapode species. Concentrated in colonies of burrows or in such huge mounds, their eggs have provided an important food source for humans for

ABOVE A male Malleefowl visits the immense mound of rottting vegetation and soil he and his mate have accumulated. Its heat will incubate the eggs the female lays in a chamber dug in the top.

thousands of years. Some harvests are sustainable, but others have contributed to the extinction of over 30 species in the past or serious declines in others, which continue today. Humans are also indirectly responsible for other grave threats of predation, by their long history of introducing mammals such as foxes, cats and pigs, which dig out the eggs or kill the birds. In addition, habitat destruction is a serious threat, from fires as well as logging and other developments.

CHACHALACAS, CURASSOWS AND GUANS Cracidae

GENERA: 11 **SPECIES:** 54

LENGTH: 42–92 cm (16.5–36 in)

WEIGHT: 390 g to 4.3 kg (14 oz to 9.5 lb)

RANGE AND HABITAT: extreme southern USA (Plain Chachalaca, *Ortalis vetula*, in Rio Grande, Texas), Mexico, Central America, South America; greatest diversity in Colombia (22 species); guans and curassows in dense tropical forests, chachalacas in more open woods and thickets, including near human settlements

SOCIAL BEHAVIOUR: chachalacas are highly gregarious, often in groups; others are usually in pairs or small family parties; mostly monogamous, pairs defending breeding territory

NEST: sparse platform of sticks or leaves and other vegetation, in tree or shrub

EGGS: 1–2 in curassows, 3–4 in chachalacas and guans; white or cream

INCUBATION: 24–36 days

FLEDGING PERIOD: as little as a few days, but remain with parents for several weeks or even a few months

FOOD: mainly fruit, seeds, buds, flowers, shoots, twigs and leaves, supplemented by some invertebrate food, especially in young; rarely frogs or other small vertebrates

VOICE: wide range of whistling, piping and harsher notes, often very loud

MIGRATION: local seasonal movements only

CONSERVATION STATUS: one species, the Alagoas Curassow, *Mitu mitu*, is Extinct in the Wild; six species including the Blue-billed Curassow, *Crax alberti*, the Horned Curassow, *Pauxi unicornis*, the White-winged Guan, *Penelope albipennis*, and the Trinidad Piping Guan, *Pipile pipile*, are Critically Endangered; six species, including the Wattled Curassow, *Crax globulosa*, the Horned Guan, *Oreophasis derbianus*, the Helmeted Curassow, *Pauxi pauxi*, and the Black-fronted Piping Guan, *Pipile jacutinga*, are Endangered; seven species, including the Rufous-headed Chachalaca, *Ortalis erythroptera*, and Highland Guan, *Penelopina nigra*, are Vulnerable; and five species are Near Threatened

Collectively known as cracids, the two subfamilies of birds making up the Family Cracidae are restricted to wooded parts of the warmer regions of the New World. All share the same basic shape, having a bulky body with a thinnish neck, smallish head, long, broad tail and short rounded wings. Unlike most other galliformes, they are primarily tree-dwelling, although most descend to the ground to feed. They can fly well but usually do so for only short distances, often climbing up and then gliding down from the treetops instead.

The subfamily Penelopinae contains the chachalacas and guans. The 15 species of chachalaca, all in the genus *Ortalis*, have bodies the size of scrawny hens. They are the smallest cracids, and also have the dullest plumage, in various shades of brown and grey, relieved only by a chestnut or white tip to the tail, and chestnut primary wing feathers and head in some species. There is also a small patch of red bare skin on the throat and pinkish, reddish or grey bare skin around each eye. The name chachalaca is onomatopoeic, from the birds' loud calls, which form a distinctive chorus at dawn and dusk when a party of these gregarious birds are preparing to leave or return to their roosting tree. These raucous performances can continue for up to 2 hours or more.

Guans, of which there are 24 species in 6 genera, are bigger and more boldly patterned or coloured than chachalacas. They have brown to black plumage, often with whitish edges to some of the feathers, striped, spotted or scalloped patterns, or a greenish, purplish or bluish gloss to the back and wings. Many species have long feathers on the crown that can be raised to form a crest, brightly coloured red, orange (or in the piping guans, *Pipile*, blue) throat wattles and duller bluish bare skin around the eye. The Horned Guan, *Oreophasis derbianus*, has a bizarre and unique red horn sticking up from the centre of its head. This very distinctive species is not closely related to other guans, and may form a link between the rest of the guans and the curassows. It appears to be the sole survivor of a distinctive and ancient lineage. In both chachalacas and guans, the sexes are generally very similar, except in the Highland Guan, *Penelopina nigra*, in which the male is black with a large red wattle and the female has dark-barred brown plumage. Several species have shorter, weaker legs and spend much more time in the trees.

The 15 species of curassow in the subfamily Cracinae are the biggest and sturdiest members of the family, and spend much of their time on the ground. They show more difference between the sexes than the chachalacas and typical guans. Males have dark plumage, ranging from deep blue to black, shot through with a purple or violet gloss; females often have variable plumage within a species, some

ABOVE The smallest, plainest-plumaged members of the family are the chachalacas. These two are Grey-headed Chachalacas, *Ortalis cinereiceps*, in Costa Rica.

LEFT Largest of the guans, the Crested Guan, *Penelope purpurascens*, has a big, bushy crest, blue facial skin and a red dewlap, used in courtship and other displays.

RIGHT Like almost half of all cracid species, the Great Curassow, *Crax rubra*, is threatened, by habitat destruction, disturbance and hunting; this male is at La Selva Reserve, Costa Rica.

individuals being all dark, others reddish-brown and other barred – or in some cases a mixture. Many curassows have prominent curly crests, and some have blue or red bill, whereas others have bright blue, red, yellow or chestnut knobs and wattles on their heads. Two species of helmeted curassow, *Pauxi*, have big bluish-grey casques sticking up from the bill, which they use in courtship displays.

All cracids are predominantly vegetarian, eating mainly fruit but also leaves, flowers, buds and seeds; some also snap up invertebrates, such as insects, spiders or molluscs, if they get the chance. Chachalacas and curassows use their strong feet to scratch for food on the ground, whereas guans feed more in the trees.

Cracids are noisy birds with a great repertoire of songs and calls, ranging from squawks, growls, grunts and yelps to whistling, piping or mooing sounds. Some of these, such as the choruses of chachalacas

or the crowing of some of the guans, can carry for more than 1 km (0.6 miles). Many species have a long and looping trachea, which helps them produce loud trumpeting and booming calls.

Courtship displays include mutual preening and chasing. All guans except for the Horned Guan have stiffened, curving outer flight feathers that produce a strange drumming sound, usually heard in special pre-dawn display flights, whereas curassows perform elaborate dancing displays on the forest floor.

Nests are usually built mainly or entirely by the male, and are surprisingly small and fragile in relation to the birds' size. The chicks develop rapidly and those of some species can fly within a matter of days.

Many species suffer from serious hunting pressure, their relative tameness and reluctance to fly making them easy targets; added to this is the relentless pressure of logging and other forms of habitat destruction.

GUINEAFOWL Numididae

GENERA: 4   **SPECIES:** 6

LENGTH: 40–72 cm (16–28 in)

WEIGHT: about 0.7–1.6 kg (1.5–3.5 lb)

RANGE AND HABITAT: Africa, south of the Sahara, with greatest diversity in the west and the centre; Helmeted Guineafowl, *Numida meleagris*, domesticated almost worldwide, with feral populations in various places, including Madagascar, Florida and the Caribbean; wide range, including dense primary rainforest in White-breasted Guineafowl, *Agelastes meleagrides*, Black Guineafowl, *A. niger*, and Plumed Guineafowl, *Guttera plumifera*, forest edge, open woodland, savannah and thorn scrub in Helmeted Guineafowl and Crested Guineafowl, *Guttera pucherani*, and semi-desert in Vulturine Guineafowl, *Acryllium vulturinum*.

SOCIAL BEHAVIOUR: very sociable outside the breeding season

NEST: a simple hollow or scrape on the ground, sometimes sparsely lined with grass, leaves and feathers

EGGS: 4–20, white, yellowish, pinkish or pale brown

INCUBATION: 23–28 days

FLEDGING PERIOD: 2–3 weeks

FOOD: mainly insects; also spiders, scorpions, small molluscs, millipedes and other invertebrates, seeds, fallen fruit, bulbs, tubers, roots, leaves and grain

VOICE: loud trilling, squealing or rattling alarm calls

MIGRATION: highly sedentary

CONSERVATION STATUS: the White-breasted Guineafowl, *Agelastes meleagrides*, with a restricted range in forests of West Africa, is classified as Vulnerable; the Moroccan race of the Helmeted Guineafowl, *Numida meleagris sabyi*, is probably now extinct in the wild

This small family of highly terrestrial game birds is one of the few bird families that are entirely restricted to Africa, where the different species occur in various forested and open habitats.

Guineafowl have very bulky bodies, emphasising their small head. The bill is short, stout and strong, with an arched upper mandible. The plumage is basically entirely black, dark grey or

brown except in one of the two West African *Agelastes* species, the White-breasted Guineafowl *A. meleagrides*, which has a boldly contrasting pure white lower neck, upper back and breast. The two *Guttera* species, the Plumed Guineafowl, *G. plumifera* and the Crested Guineafowl, *G. pucherani*, have chestnut-and-white and brown-and-white wing markings, respectively, while the dark

LEFT The Vulturine Guineafowl, *Acryllium vulturinum*, found mainly in arid thorn-scrub and grassland, is the most strikingly plumaged member of the family.

RIGHT A pair of Helmeted Guineafowl, *Numida meleagris*, step out briskly in Samburu National Reserve, Kenya.

plumage of both these species, as well as the Helmeted Guineafowl, *Numida meleagris*, and the Vulturine Guineafowl, *Acryllium vulturinum*, is densely peppered with small white spots, visible only at close range. The Vulturine Guineafowl also has beautiful rich blue underparts, and striking, long, slender, black-and-white feathers (hackles) cascading from its long, extremely slender neck.

The head and neck of all species are almost featherless, with the bare skin bright blue, red, pink, yellow, grey or white, according to species, and bearing wattles, convolutions or bristles. The head of both the Crested Guineafowl and the Plumed Guineafowl has a prominent crest, while that of the Helmeted Guineafowl has an erect bony casque. Sexes appear alike except that males are slightly larger than females.

Except when breeding, guineafowl live in flocks for much of the year, with a complex social hierarchy. These groups vary from fewer than 10 birds in the two *Agelastes* species to huge ones of more than 2,000 in Helmeted Guineafowl, which travel in single file as they make their way to waterholes or other drinking sites, with dominant males acting as scouts and alerting the flock to the presence of predators. The Vulturine Guineafowl is an exception: adapted to arid habitats, this bird is rarely seen drinking.

Even when threatened by predators such as leopards, jackals or baboons, guineafowl often escape by running rather than flying, but do take wing regularly each night to roost in trees. Despite their reluctance to fly, they cover considerable distances each day on foot, spending much of each day foraging. All species are ground feeders, scratching for both invertebrates and plant food with their strong legs and feet, and digging up tubers. Flocks often forage line abreast (that is, advancing in a row, side by side), so that they cover the maximum area possible.

As well as being the most widespread species in its native range, the Helmeted Guineafowl is a familiar bird across much of the world, as it has been domesticated repeatedly since ancient times.

NEW WORLD QUAILS Odontophoridae

GENERA: 10   **SPECIES:** 33

LENGTH: 17–37 cm (6.5–14.5 in)

WEIGHT: 115–460 g (4–16 oz)

RANGE AND HABITAT: North America, Central America, Caribbean, South America; the greatest diversity is in southern Mexico and Guatemala; forests, forest edge, savannah and agricultural land; two aberrant African members of the Family Phasianidae may be better included in this family, as ancient Old World relict representatives.

SOCIAL BEHAVIOUR: highly gregarious outside the breeding season

NEST: in most species, a shallow scrape on the ground lined with vegetation and usually concealed among dense vegetation; some wood-quails construct a domed or canopied nest accessed by a long tunnel

EGGS: typically 10–15 in North American species, and 3–6 in tree-quails and wood-quails of Central and South America; white, cream or buff, sometimes spotted or blotched with brown, usually as a result of staining

INCUBATION: 16–30 days

FLEDGING PERIOD: often less than 2 weeks; first flights often at only a few days old

FOOD: mainly seeds, bulbs, buds, also some fruit, supplemented with insects in some species

VOICE: varied, with many species having a large range of calls, including whistling sounds, as with the double-note call of the Northern Bobwhite, *Colinus virginianus*, for which the bird was named, as well as shrieks, grunting and hooting sounds; the wood-quails and wood-partridges are very noisy, especially at dawn and dusk, when their loud, guttural rolling cries ring out through Neotropical forests, amplified further in some species when pairs duet or groups perform raucous choruses

MIGRATION: almost all species are highly sedentary, apart from altitudinal migration in one or two species

CONSERVATION STATUS: the Gorgeted Wood-quail, *Odontophorus strophium*, with a very restricted range in Colombia, is Endangered, and five species are Vulnerable: the Bearded Wood-partridge, *Dendrortyx barbatus*, the Ocellated Quail, *Cyrtonyx ocellatus*, and three wood-quails (the Black-fronted Wood-quail, *Odontophorus atrifrons*, the Dark-backed Wood-quail, *O. melanonotus*, and the Tacarcuna Wood-quail, *O. dialeucos*); five species are Near Threatened, including the Northern Bobwhite, *Colinus virginianus*

In their plump-bodied shape, general plumage colours and patterns, and lifestyle, these game birds resemble the Old World quails from which they were named. However, DNA–DNA hybridisation studies suggest they are not so closely related to the Old World quails or the rest of the Family Phasianidae to justify inclusion in that large family, so they are generally placed in a separate family of their own. Just five of the 32 species occur in the USA (all but one, the Northern Bobwhite, *Colinus virginianus*, in the west). The fact that the least specialised species and greatest number of genera are found in southern Mexico and Guatemala suggests that the family evolved here and then radiated north and south. Recent research suggests that two African game birds, the Stone Partridge, *Ptilopachus petrosus* and Nahan's Francolin, *Francolinus nahani*, currently classified within the Family Phasianidae, are likely to be members of this family instead, representing a relict Old World branch.

Most species have intricate streaked or barred plumage patterns in browns and greys, often with black and white spots, but some have strikingly patterned heads, and some also have long crests. The sexes are similar in most species, but in some the males are distinctly brighter and more strongly patterned. In contrast to the generally promiscuous behaviour of most game birds, New World quail seem to be mostly monogamous, living as separate pairs, and usually as family groups after breeding. Outside the breeding season, however, many of the temperate zone species may form large flocks of up to several hundreds or even 1,000 individuals.

A feature these game birds share with the other members of their order, wherever they occur and throughout history, is their popularity

ABOVE Gambel's Quail, *Callipepla gambelii*, is a desert dweller of southwest USA and northwest Mexico. This is a male, with bold plumage and a large crest.

with hunters. In North America, several species are the basis of a lucrative sport hunting industry, with the Northern Bobwhite being by far the major quarry species. Until recently, about 20 million individuals of the latter species were being killed each year by hunters. Although well-regulated hunting can benefit the birds when habitat is conserved, poor management can lead instead to declines.

TURKEYS, GROUSE, PARTRIDGES AND OLD WORLD QUAIL, PHEASANTS Phasianidae

GENERA: 49   **SPECIES:** 180

LENGTH: 12 cm–2.3 m (4.75 in–7.5 ft)

WEIGHT: 43 g–6 kg (1.5 oz–13 lb)

RANGE AND HABITAT: almost worldwide except for southern South America and Antarctica; greatest diversity in Africa and southern Asia; wide range, from open habitats (including grassland, croplands, scrub and semi-desert) to open woodlands and dense forests, and from sea level to high mountains

SOCIAL BEHAVIOUR: ranges from living a solitary existence or as pairs year-round in some forest-dwelling partridges, to dwelling in larger family groups, or coveys, which may amalgamate to form large groups after breeding; this is typical of more open-country partridges and quails; turkeys and many pheasants and grouse are polygamous, while most of the partridges and quail are monogamous

NEST: typically a shallow scrape hidden among vegetation, sometimes lined with leaves, grass or twigs

EGGS: 2–15, whitish to pale brownish, with brown markings in grouse, turkeys and some of the pheasants and partridges

INCUBATION: 50–96 days

FLEDGING PERIOD: young leave the nest within 1–2 days of hatching and can fly within about 5 days in some especially precocial quail species, to about 2–3 weeks

FOOD: most partridges and pheasants feed mainly on seeds, flowers, leaves, buds, bulbs, roots and tubers, as well as variable amounts of insects and other invertebrate foods; grouse are almost entirely vegetarian, concentrating on tough food such as conifer needles in winter, and buds, leaves, flowers, fruit and seeds for the rest of the year; turkeys eat insects almost exclusively when young, but gradually shift to a mixed diet including seeds, acorns and other plant matter

VOICE: varied, with calls including harsh cackling, hissing or grunting calls; some species have more melodious whistles; displaying males make some extraordinary sounds, including clucking, hooting, bubbling, crowing, clicking, cooing, gobbling, popping and purring notes; sounds are amplified by air sacs in North American plains grouse; many species also make loud, rattling, hissing, whirring or drumming sounds by rapid beating or striking together of their wings, or tail movements

MIGRATION: most species are more or less sedentary, but some grouse move south or downslope in winter, and three quail species make long migrations, especially the Common Quail, *Coturnix coturnix*, breeding in Eurasia and wintering as far south as north-central Africa and India

CONSERVATION STATUS: two species (the Himalayan Quail, *Ophrysia superciliosa*, and the Djibouti Francolin, *Francolinus ochropectus*) are Critically Endangered; nine species are Endangered; 33 species are Vulnerable

This is by far the largest family in the order Galliformes, with 180 species accounting for 62% of the whole order. Research is ongoing into the precise relationships between the various families and subfamilies of Galliformes, and several schemes have been suggested for the classification of this big family, with turkeys and grouse each traditionally regarded as deserving separate family status. Nevertheless, often, as here, they are included as subfamilies together with the partridges and pheasants, also each constituting a subfamily, within a single big family, the Phasianidae.

There are just two species of turkeys in the subfamily Meleagridinae: the Wild Turkey, *Meleagris gallopavo*, ranging from southern USA to Central Mexico, and the other, the smaller Ocellated Turkey, *M. ocellata*, found in southeast Mexico, Belize and Guatemala. As well as having been introduced to various regions outside their natural range, from Europe to Australia, they were domesticated by Native Americans up to 2,000 years ago, after which the Spanish conquistadors introduced the birds to Europe during the early sixteenth century. These are among the largest members of the family, males of the Wild Turkey reaching 1.2 m (4 ft) long, and weighing up to 10 kg (22 lb). The broad, rounded wings are very large, but the ratio of body weight to wing area in males is still one of the highest of any bird. As a result, turkeys are generally reluctant to fly unless absolutely necessary. Females, however, are only half the weight of males, and do usually take to the air to escape danger.

Both species have dark, barred plumage with iridescent, coppery, blue and green highlights, especially bright in the males. Their naked heads and necks are strikingly ornamented, also especially in the males, with lines of berry-like bright orange caruncles on bright blue skin in the Ocellated species. The male Wild Turkey has the skin more convoluted into wattles and can rapidly change the colour of these appendages from red and white to blue. He also has a tuft of bristle-like feathers projecting from his chest that probably helps him position himself correctly on the female when mating, as she is otherwise hidden from his view by his protruding breast when he has climbed aboard her back to copulate. Both species have a bizarre erectile fleshy appendage called a 'snood' dangling down over or to one side of the bill.

The subfamily Tetraoninae contains 18 species of grouse in 10 genera. They are medium to large birds, measuring 30–90 cm (1–3 ft) long and weighing 280 g to 6 kg (0.6–13 lb). The male plumage is mainly black or brown with white markings, with prominent fleshy red or yellow combs on the head; the females are brown, with camouflaging barring and flecking. Both sexes of ptarmigan are mainly or entirely white in winter, again for camouflage to protect against eagles, foxes and other predators.

Grouse are thought to have evolved in northern latitudes, where they became adapted to life in cold climates with a monotonous winter diet of low-nutrient but abundant plant food. The northernmost are a group of three Arctic-alpine species in the genus *Lagopus*. The hardiest is the Rock Ptarmigan, *L. muta*, which occurs from Iceland right across Eurasia, Greenland and the whole of far northern North America, while the range of the Willow Grouse, *L. lagopus*, which includes the famous Red Grouse (race *scoticus*) of Britain and Ireland, is even greater in area, extending farther south. The third species, the White-tailed Ptarmigan, *L. leucura*,

ABOVE A male Wild Turkey, *Meleagris gallopavo*, performs a 'strutting' courtship display, with fanned tail and back feathers making him appear even larger.

ABOVE A displaying male Greater Prairie-Chicken, *Tympanuchus cupido*, erects long neck feathers and inflates yellow-orange neck sacs to make a deep booming sound.

occurs only in western North America. Another ecological grouping is that containing species adapted to woodlands, from young conifers and forest edges to mature deciduous and coniferous forests: in Eurasia these are the two species of capercaillie, *Tetrao* (the largest of all grouse), two species of black grouse, *Lyrurus*, and two of hazel grouse, *Tetrastes*; in North America there is the Ruffed Grouse, *Bonasa umbellus*, and the Blue Grouse, *Dendragapus obscurus*, mainly a mountain specialist; finally, there are two genera of prairie grassland grouse in North America, comprising two species of sage grouse, *Centrocercus*, and the two prairie-chicken species and single species of sharp-tailed grouse, *Tympanuchus*. The other two genera each contain a single species: the Spruce Grouse, *Canachites canadensis* of North America and the Siberian Grouse, *Falcipennis falcipennis*.

Nine species are polygamous, with several or many males displaying dramatically at communal leks: these include both the open-country North American plains species such as the Sage Grouse, *Centrocercus urophasianus*, and its four relatives, and Old World forest-edge and forest grouse, such as the Eurasian Black Grouse, *Lyrurus tetrix*, the Western Capercaillie, *Tetrao urogallus*, and the Black-billed Capercaillie, *T. parvirostris*.

The largest subfamily (Perdicinae) is that of the partridges and relatives, with 110 species in 22 genera. Native to the Old World, they range from the diminutive quails, with the King Quail, *Coturnix chinensis*, only about 12–15 cm (4.75–6 in) long and weighing 20–57 g (0.7–2 oz), to the big snowcocks, *Tetraogallus*, of which the Himalayan Snowcock, *T. himalayensis*, is the largest, with males measuring up to 72 cm (28 in) and weighing up to 3.6 kg (8 lb). As well as grey partridges, *Perdix*, and the Red-legged Partridge, *Alectoris rufa*, and relatives, this large group includes the hill-partridges, *Arborophila*, of Asia, the francolins, *Francolinus*, of Africa and Asia, and the quails, *Coturnix*, found from Europe and Africa to Asia and Australia.

Recent genetic research has strongly suggested that two African species, the Stone Partridge, *Ptilopachus petrosus*, and Nahan's Francolin, *Francolinus nahani*, might actually be only distant relatives of the Old World Family Phasianidae in which they were generally included, and that it might be better to position them within the Odontophoridae. Equally unexpected was that the evidence also seems to indicate a close relationship between the two: the researchers have suggested that Nahan's Francolin, in a different genus, may in fact belong in *Ptilopachus*. Reflecting their closeness by including them both in *Ptilopachus* is supported not only by the genetic data but also by previously unrecognised behavioural and vocal similarities between the two species. They constitute a relict group from which the American members of the family diverged about 37.4 million years ago, and thus the origin of the New World quail may actually be in the Old World.

The 16 genera and 50 species of pheasants in the subfamily Phasianinae include some of the most spectacular and beautiful members of the galliform order. They range in size from 36 cm to 2.3 m (14 in to 7.5 ft) long, but in the longest species, the male's huge tail (or in the case of the two Asian peafowl, *Pavo*, the upper tail coverts overlying the short true tail) constitutes over half the length. Weights are from 410 g to 6 kg (1–13 lb).

Most of the more sexually dimorphic species of pheasants are polygamous, with males performing elaborate displays. Those with particularly spectacular performances include the five *Tragopan* species (mountain dwellers of the Himalayas and eastern Asia), Bulwer's Pheasant, *Lophura bulweri* (Borneo), the two argus pheasants, *Rheinardia* and *Argusianus*, (Vietnam, Malaysia, Sumatra and Borneo) and, best known of all, the Indian peafowl, *Pavo cristatus* (the Indian subcontinent).

In many species, the male leaves the female after mating, but in the Common Pheasant, *Phasianus colchicus*, and the four junglefowl species, *Gallus*, of southern Asia, males bond with a harem of females until the eggs have been laid. The junglefowls are of interest, too, since they include the ancestor of the domestic chicken. All chickens have until recently been thought to have been derived from a single species that is widespread in southern Asia, from northeast India east to Java. This is the Red Junglefowl, *G. gallus*, and its scientific name is accordingly also that of the domesticated form. Recent research, however, suggests that another, more localised junglefowl species, the Grey Junglefowl, *G. sonneratii*, that is endemic to parts of northwest India and

ABOVE A male Grey Partridge, *Perdix perdix*, in Norfolk, England, utters his 'rusty-gate' advertising call to attract females and challenge rivals.

much of peninsular India, may also have been involved in the process. Evidence in favour of such a hybrid origin is that the Grey Junglefowl carries a gene that produces the yellow skin found in some chickens. While the Common Pheasant and the Indian Peafowl have been widely introduced outside their native Asian ranges to Europe, North America and other areas, the domestic chicken has a truly global distribution. It is the most numerous of all birds, with a global population estimated at a minimum of 12 billion and perhaps as many as 20 billion individuals alive at any one time – almost two to three chickens for every human on the planet. More than 50 billion are raised annually. This compares with the most abundant wild species, the little Red-billed Quelea of Africa (see p. 292), which probably has a total peak post-breeding population of about 1.5 billion individuals.

ORDER PHOENICOPTERIFORMES

This order contains only one family: that of the highly distinctive flamingos (Phoenicopteridae), with their very long necks and legs and greatly specialised bill. Traditionally, resemblances to herons, storks and relatives led to their being considered closest relations to birds in the Order Ciconiiformes, especially to ibises and spoonbills (Family Threskiornithidae); however, some researchers postulated a link with the swans, geese and ducks (Order Anseriformes) and others to the waders (Order Charadriiformes), especially the stilts and avocets (Family Recurvirostridae). Like grebes (Order Podicipediformes), which are usually now considered their closest relatives, the flamingos are a very ancient group, with fossil evidence stretching back at least as far as 34 million years ago. Later fossils provide evidence that the birds were widespread throughout much of Europe, North America and Australia, as well as in places where they are far more restricted today.

Unmistakable and resembling a mixture of outlandishness and beauty, these are extraordinary and unique birds whose relationships with other birds were largely enigmatic. Their huge, bizarrely shaped bill, which is almost as big as the head, gives them an odd, ungainly appearance at close range, especially when they are feeding with the head upside down. However, seen en masse, moving in tight packs with balletic grace, or flying strongly in close formation with long necks and legs outstretched, they provide some of the most spectacular, lovely and unforgettable of all sights in nature.

Although in most respects the five species are very similar, they can be divided into two main subgroups. The first consists of the two *Phoenicopterus* species: the Greater Flamingo, *P. ruber* (whose two subspecies, the Eurasian Flamingo, *P. r. roseus*, and the American Flamingo, *P. r. ruber*, are sometimes considered as separate species), and the Chilean Flamingo, *P. chilensis*, with a more primitive bill structure and more generalised diet. The second subgroup contains the Lesser Flamingo, *Phoeniconaias minor*, of Africa, Pakistan and India and the two *Phoenicoparrus* species – the Andean Flamingo, *P. andinus*, and James's Flamingo (or Puna Flamingo), *P. jamesi*. These three all have more specialised bills and a narrower diet than the other two; in addition, a peculiarity of *Phoenicoparrus* is that both species lack the small hind toe of the other genera.

Flamingos have an oval body, a very long, thin, sinuous neck, a small head and extremely long legs. Their legs and neck are longer in relation to the body than in any other birds. Males are larger and longer-legged than females – up to 20% in the Greater Flamingo – but otherwise the sexes look very similar. The head, neck and body plumage is mainly pink, although this varies between species and subspecies from delicate pastel pink to deep rose pink, whereas the wings have a contrasting pattern of intense crimson with black flight feathers. The bill and bare facial skin at its base varies from various shades of pink to near-white or apricot, with a black tip of varying size, and the legs and feet of most species are pink (although the Chilean Flamingo has yellowish-grey legs with red 'knees' and feet, and the feet and legs of the Andean Flamingo are all yellow).

FLAMINGOS Phoenicopteridae

GENERA: 3 **SPECIES**: 5

LENGTH: 80–145 cm (31–57 in)

WEIGHT: 1.9–3 kg (4.2–6.6 lb)

RANGE AND HABITAT: tropical and subtropical regions, mainly in the Caribbean, South America, the Mediterranean, Africa and southern Asia, from sea level to very high altitudes; mainly restricted to highly alkaline or saline lakes and lagoons

SOCIAL BEHAVIOUR: highly sociable at all times, often in large flocks, which in some species can be vast; may be monogamous for more than one season, but Greater Flamingos, *Phoenicopterus ruber*, have been found to have a very high 'divorce' rate; nest colonially

NEST: sited on mud or other substrate at edge of lake or on island, a conical mound of mud baked hard by sun, with a shallow depression at the top in which the female lays her single egg

EGGS: 1, white

INCUBATION: 27–31 days

FLEDGING PERIOD: 65–90 days

FOOD: algae and diatoms; small aquatic invertebrates, especia lly crustaceans, insect larvae and molluscs

VOICE: noisy, with flocks typically producing a low gabbling murmur when feeding and louder, nasal, honking contact calls in flight; also a range of grunting, growling and other sounds during group displays or aggressive encounters when breeding

MIGRATION: mainly sedentary, although movement patterns are complex; some populations living on lakes that freeze in winter (such as Greater Flamingos in Russia and Kazakhstan) regularly migrate to ice-free waters, while all species may make erratic movements depending on factors such as food supply, water levels and seasonal weather; in some cases these can involve many birds travelling thousands of kilometres

CONSERVATION STATUS: one species, the Andean Flamingo, *Phoenicoparrus andinus*, is Vulnerable; three species, the Chilean Flamingo, *Phoenicopterus chilensis*, James's Flamingo, *Phoenicoparrus jamesi*, and the Lesser Flamingo, *Phoeniconaias minor*, are Near Threatened

ABOVE A Lesser Flamingo, *Phoeniconaias minor*, on top of its mud nest. Breeding time is irregular and many adults do not breed every year.

Their very long legs enable flamingos to wade into deeper water than other wading birds, and the webbing between their three front toes gives them extra support when walking on mud, as well as being used to swim in water too deep for them to stand. Here, they can also upend, their greatly elongated necks allowing them to extend their downward reach still further. The neck has only 17 vertebrae – not that many compared to the 25 of swans – but they are considerably elongated. This can give the neck a curiously stepped appearance when the bird bends it.

When feeding, the extraordinary bill is held upside down and submerged. As the bird sweeps it through the water, the big fleshy tongue acts like a piston in a pump to suck in mouthfuls of water and sometimes mud. As the liquid is forced through the bill and expelled, it passes through many fine comblike lamellae, which filter out the algae and other tiny food items on which the birds depend in an analogous way to the filter feeding of the baleen whales. Backward-pointing spines on the tongue and palate direct the food particles towards the throat.

The larger Greater and Chilean Flamingos have a shallow-keeled bill, an adaptation for feeding mainly in the mud at the bottom of the lake, from where they select generally larger food items – small shrimps, molluscs and flies – than those preferred by their relatives. The smaller Lesser, Andean and James's species have a deep-keeled bill with a more complex system of lamellae, including microscopic extruders to keep out all but the finer particles; they feed mainly on microscopic blue-green algae and diatoms near the surface. In this way, the differences in bill structure enable pairs of species (Greater and Lesser in Eurasia and Africa, and Chilean and Andean or James's) to coexist on the same lakes by concentrating on different foods.

Courtship displays are very inconspicuous and low-key, but flamingos perform dramatic group displays that may involve hundreds or thousands of birds. Beginning several months before breeding, these provide hormonal stimulation to help all the birds in a colony become ready to mate at more or less the same time, so that they can gain maximum benefit from the narrow window of opportunity when conditions in their unstable environments are most suitable for egg laying and rearing young. These displays involve elaborate sequences of ritualised movements that are exaggerated versions of their stretching and preening actions, such as head flagging, wing saluting, twist preening and wing–leg stretching, as well as marching close together in the same direction, then suddenly turning.

Flamingo chicks look rather like goslings or cygnets, clad in greyish white down on hatching and with a straight bill. For their first few days, the chicks remain on the nest or snuggled into their parents' back feathers, but then they form large crèches, often numbering hundreds or thousands, under the watchful eyes of a few non-breeding adults. The youngsters are fed for several weeks by both their parents on a milk-like secretion from the adults' upper digestive tract. By the time they fledge at about 10–12 weeks of age, the bill has acquired the swollen, bent shape of the adult's, and is equipped for filter feeding. The birds do not acquire adult plumage for several years, however, being a mixture of grey with brown and pink markings, and their bill, feet and legs are greyish or blackish.

The pinks and reds of maturity are the result of feeding on algae that have synthesized substances called carotenoids or on small shrimps and other invertebrates that have eaten the algae. The flamingos then use enzymes in the liver to break down these carotenoids into the bright pigment canthaxanthin. Until this process was understood, the many zoos and waterfowl collections keeping flocks of these popular birds found that their plumage soon faded and the birds did not breed successfully, but later they dealt with the problem by feeding them first on such foods as dried shrimps, carrots or peppers, and more recently with greater success on synthetic canthaxanthin. Most species attain sexual maturity at 3–4 years, but Greater Flamingos generally do not do so until 5–6 years old.

These exquisitely coloured birds live in some of the bleakest and most inhospitable environments for wildlife. The shallow, highly alkaline or saline lakes they favour contain concentrations of soda or salt that can cause agony to a human who ventures into the water. In Africa, adult Greater and Lesser Flamingos can tolerate levels of fluorides, sulphates, chlorides and other salts that would be deadly to most animals; they are also able to endure temperatures exceeding 68°C (155°F) at noon, and to drink water as hot as 65°C (150°F) near hot springs. By contrast, the three South American species live on lakes at heights of up to 4,500 m (14,760 ft), or in the case of the Andean Flamingo 4,950 m (16,240 ft), and may experience night-time temperatures as low as –30°C (–22°F); they depend on hot springs to keep their roosting areas free of ice when the rest of the lake is frozen.

Breeding success in flamingos is notoriously variable from one year to the next. The eggs and chicks can be taken in large numbers by predators such as big gulls or, in East Africa, Marabou Storks, *Leptoptilos crumenifer*. In addition, after being crippled by great anklets of soda that build up around their legs, thousands may die as a result of starvation or becoming an easy target for the predators. By contrast, adult flamingos suffer very little predation and are generally very long-lived compared with many other birds. Birds in many populations average about 20–30 years and some wild birds live for over 50 years, and birds in captivity 60 years. Breeding can be abandoned completely, however, when disturbance from predators or humans reaches a level that causes the birds to desert en masse. Other serious threats include egg collecting, water pollution and other effects of habitat exploitation on a group of birds with relatively few breeding sites. Even the most numerous species, the Lesser Flamingo, with a total population of 2–3 million, is concentrated in just three major sites in Africa. If proposed soda-ash mining and hydroelectric power schemes go ahead at the main site, Lake Natron in Tanzania, these could have a devastating impact.

ABOVE Two Greater Flamingos, *Phoenicopterus ruber roseus*, touch bills at one of the bird's few European breeding sites, in the Camargue, southern France.

ORDER PODICIPEDIFORMES

This order contains just the single family of grebes (Podicipedidae). These waterbirds bear a superficial resemblance to divers (known as loons in North America) in the Order Gaviiformes and were formerly thought to be related to them. Nowadays, however, divers are generally considered to be more closely related to penguins (Order Sphenisciformes) and albatrosses and other tubenoses (Order Procellariiformes), and are accordingly placed between those two groups in this book (see p. 73). Surprisingly, recent DNA research suggests that grebes' closest living relatives are likely to be the flamingos (Order Phoenicopteriformes), so they are situated next to them in this account. Both groups are among the most ancient of all modern birds; the earliest grebe fossils are about 80 million years old, and specimens in the largest present-day genus *Podiceps* have been dated back to at least 25 million years.

GREBES Podicipedidae

GENERA: 6   **SPECIES:** 22

LENGTH: 20–78 cm (8–31 in)

WEIGHT: 115 g–1.8 kg (4 oz–4 lb)

RANGE AND HABITAT: all continents except Antarctica, with greatest diversity in South America; freshwater lakes, ponds, rivers, canals, marshes and brackish lagoons or bays; many species winter along sheltered coasts

SOCIAL BEHAVIOUR: usually seen singly or in pairs during the breeding season, but some species form large or even huge feeding assemblies after breeding at moulting sites or rich feeding sites; monogamous, with pairs sometimes remaining together over winter; territorial, although some species are colonial nesters

NEST: a damp, decaying mass of aquatic vegetation floating on the water and attached to emergent plants such as reeds, to which the pair must continually add material to prevent it submerging completely

EGGS: 2–8 (rarely as few as 1 or as many as 10); white, cream, pale buff or (especially in New World species) pale blue or greenish at first but soon becoming stained brown when covered by the birds with vegetation during periods of absence from incubation

INCUBATION: 20–31 days

FLEDGING PERIOD: 44–79 days

FOOD: fish, aquatic insects, crustaceans, molluscs and other invertebrates, occasionally tadpoles; smaller species feed mainly on insects and larvae, larger ones on small fish

VOICE: largely silent outside the breeding season, but they utter various barking, whistling, wailing or trilling sounds during courtship

MIGRATION: some species are sedentary, remaining on a single large lake, for instance, but many in temperate climates abandon freshwaters prone to freezing to winter in coastal waters or larger or more southerly ice-free freshwaters

CONSERVATION STATUS: three species, the Atitlan Grebe, *Podilymbus gigas*, Alaotra Grebe, *Tachybaptus rufolavatus*, and Colombian Grebe, *Podiceps andinus*, are Extinct; two species, the Junin Flightless Grebe, *Podiceps taczanowskii*, endemic to Lake Junin in the Peruvian Andes, and the Hooded Grebe, *Podiceps gallardoi*, are Critically Endangered; one species, the Titicaca Grebe, *Rollandia microptera*, is Endangered; two species, the New Zealand Grebe, *Poliocephalus rufopectus*, and the Madagascar Grebe *Tachybaptus pelzelnii*, are Vulnerable

ABOVE A Little Grebe, *Tachybaptus ruficollis*, carries one of its chicks on its back, keeping it warm and safe from predators.

Few birds are as comprehensively aquatic as the grebes. Except when on the nest, they normally spend almost their entire lives on or under the water. They are superbly adapted for diving, and obtain almost all their prey underwater, where they pursue fish and other aquatic prey with great speed and agility, propelling themselves by kicking backwards with both feet together. They do not use their wings for propulsion, normally holding them closed tightly to their sides – although they may open them when executing a tight turn or swimming through dense submerged vegetation.

Adaptations for an aquatic life include impressively waterproof and very dense plumage (a typical grebe has over 20,000 feathers), a streamlined body with an extremely short tail (reducing drag) and highly modified legs and feet. The legs are positioned far to the rear, enabling efficient propulsion, but making progress an awkward shuffle if the bird finds itself on land. The three front toes are expanded into broad lobes, as well as being very slightly webbed at the base (and the tiny raised hind toe also bears a miniature lobe). The bones of the tarsi (lower part of the leg) are flattened from side to side, minimising water resistance. Also, during the backward power stroke the lobes are spread, while as they move forward on the recovery stroke they are collapsed to reduce resistance further. Laboratory studies suggest that the feet do not simply move back and forth as with ducks or other web-footed swimmers, but with a rotary motion (like the stroke of a kayak paddle), which makes them more efficient. The very short tail reduces drag, but cannot serve as a rudder as with many other aquatic birds,

LEFT Resplendent in their breeding plumage, a pair of Great Crested Grebes, *Podiceps cristatus*, prepare to display by a reedbed in Norfolk, England.

RIGHT The Pied-billed Grebe, *Podilymbus podiceps*, has a vast range, from central Canada to southern Argentina. This one is in the Everglades, Florida.

so the highly manoeuvrable legs and feet, with their flexible tibiotarsal and tarsometatarsal joints, are used instead for steering.

As well as feeding underwater, grebes also submerge to escape enemies. As they are heavier than most aquatic birds, owing to their dense bones with few hollows and air sacs, they float very low in the water and can dive more rapidly. They are also able to position themselves more precisely and can remain almost completely submerged with just the top of the head and bill visible above the surface. This enables them to avoid detection by predators, especially when among reeds or other dense aquatic plant cover. Another characteristic action of grebes is seen when they preen their underparts, rolling right over on one side in the water to expose their belly feathers.

Grebes do not often fly, except when migrating or making other movements from one water body to another. Their wings are small and narrow. Two species, the Titicaca (or Short-winged) Grebe, *Rollandia microptera*, of south-east Peru and western Bolivia and the Junin Flightless Grebe (or Junin Grebe), *Podiceps taczanowskii*, of Lake Junin, Peru, are completely flightless, as was the extinct Atitlan Grebe, *Podylimbus gigas* of Lake Atitlan, Guatemala.

The Least Grebe, *Tachybaptus dominicus*, and the three other surviving *Tachybaptus* species are only about the size of a thrush, while the rest of the family range from pigeon-sized birds to the size of a large duck but slimmer. Grebes all have a relatively long neck, which is particularly long and slim in some larger species such as the Western Grebe, *Aechmophorus occidentalis*, and its close relative Clark's Grebe, *A. clarkii*.

The bill varies from short and stout in species such as the Pied-billed Grebe, *Podilymbus podiceps*, and the extinct Atitlan Grebe through medium-length and dagger-like in species such as the Great Crested Grebe, *Podiceps cristatus*, and the Red-necked Grebe, *P. grisegena*, to long and slender like a stiletto in the two *Aechmophorus* species (the name of this genus translates as 'spear-carrier'). Some grebes use the sharply pointed bill to spear their prey rather than the more usual method of grasping it in the mandibles; fish killed by Western Grebes, for instance, have been found marked with holes through the body. Smaller species that include a good deal of invertebrates in their diet quite often pick them off the water surface, and a few even snatch flying insects while swimming.

In all species of grebe, the sexes look alike. Non-breeding plumage is generally a rather drab combination of brown, grey or blackish and white. With the approach of the breeding season, however, many species acquire striking patches of contrasting

colours on the head or elsewhere (often chestnut or red), whereas in others a blackish head and hindneck contrasts with a gleaming white foreneck and breast. In addition, some grow bright, usually erectile, head plumes in the shape of a ruff (also known as a tippet), crest or ear-tufts. In many species, these are bright gold or chestnut, usually emphasised by adjacent areas of black.

Many species have spectacular courtship displays involving complex sequences of ritualised movements; those of the Great Crested Grebe were the subject of pioneering studies of bird behaviour in the early twentieth century by the British biologists Edmund Selous and later (and most famously) Julian Huxley. These involve elaborate 'dances' with the pair of birds facing one another and shaking their heads to show off the magnificent tippets, and presenting waterweed held in the bill. Western and Clark's Grebes perform extraordinary 'rushing' ceremonies, with both birds rising up and paddling furiously across the water close together line abreast (that is, advancing in a row, side by side).

Grebes (especially those whose diet consists mainly of fish) are unusual in regularly ingesting their own small breast, belly and flank feathers, and also feeding them to their young as soon as they hatch, even before they take their first meal. The partially digested feathers form a spongy, felt-like mass that protects the delicate, thin-walled intestine from being damaged by sharp fish bones. The feathers seem to do this in two ways: by forming a plug at the entrance to the duodenum; and by becoming wrapped around the bones before they are regurgitated as pellets. Also, some species have been found to have small pebbles in their stomach; the birds are likely to have swallowed these to help grind up their food in the muscular part of the stomach (the gizzard).

All species face various threats from humans, especially drainage and pollution of their shallow wetland habitats, introduction of alien fish species, changes in water level resulting from human activities such as hydroelectric schemes, disturbance, hunting and egg collecting. Indeed three species – the Atitlan Grebe, the Alaotra Grebe, *Tachybaptus rufolavatus*, of Lake Alaotra, Madagascar, and the Colombian Grebe, *Podiceps andinus* – are already extinct, and three others – the Junin Grebe, Titicaca Grebe, endemic to the Andean lakes for which they are named, and Hooded Grebe, *P. gallardoi*, which has a scattered range in southern South America – are at risk of joining them. In all, just over a quarter of the surviving species are given official threatened status.

ORDER COLUMBIFORMES

This order contains the large, worldwide family (Columbidae) of pigeons and doves; there is no biological distinction between the two names, although the word 'dove' tends to be used for the smaller species. The order also contains two unique, flightless, extinct species from Indian Ocean islands – the Dodo, *Raphus cucullatus*, of Mauritius and the Rodrigues Solitaire, *Pezophaps solitaria*, of nearby Rodrigues. They are placed in a family (Raphidae) of their own. Both were wiped out between about 1680 and 1800 as a result of relentless hunting by sailors and colonists and also the mammals that those people introduced (the depredations of eggs and young and habitat alteration caused by pigs were especially damaging to the Dodo, and cats were major predators of the Solitaire). A third extinct species that for a long while was thought to be a close relative of the Dodo and named the 'Reunion Solitaire' from the island where it lived, turned out to be a species of ibis, and hence completely unrelated to the other two. Apart from the Raphidae, and a probable connection with the sandgrouse (see introduction to the next order, Pterocliformes, p. 34), pigeons appear to have no close living relatives.

PIGEONS Columbidae

GENERA: 42   **SPECIES**: 308

LENGTH: 14–79 cm (5.5–31 in)

WEIGHT: 24 g–2.4 kg (0.8 oz–5.3 lb)

RANGE AND HABITAT: worldwide, except for Antarctica, and apart from a very few species, the far north; almost all land habitats, from dense humid tropical forests and grassland to dry deserts; most in wooded habitats

SOCIAL BEHAVIOUR: most species are seen in pairs or small flocks, but some form huge groups outside the breeding season, especially when feeding or migrating ; most are monogamous, at least for a single season and sometimes for life; most are solitary nesters, but a few nest in dense colonies

NEST: most species build a sparse, fragile looking though often tightly woven platform or shallow cup consisting mainly of sticks and twigs in a tree or shrub; some nest in tree-holes, crevices in cliffs or cavities in buildings, others on the ground

EGGS: 1 or (more often) 2, white

INCUBATION: 13–18 days in most species, up to 30 days in the largest

FLEDGING PERIOD: about 12 days in seed-eating species, up to 22 days in fruit eaters

FOOD: some species are seed eaters, some also eat plant parts (especially green leaves), others are almost exclusively fruit eaters; many supplement their plant diet with snails, worms, insects or other small invertebrates

VOICE: soft, rhythmic cooing in many species; others make very different sounds, including chattering, quacking, drumming or froglike notes

MIGRATION: many species are sedentary, some nomadic and others migratory

CONSERVATION STATUS: At least 7 species, including the Bonin Pigeon, *Columba versicolor*, Passenger Pigeon, *Ectopistes migratorius*, Mauritius Blue Pigeon, *Alectroenas nitidissima*, and Red-moustached Fruit Dove, *Ptilinopus mercierii*, are Extinct; one species, the Socorro Dove, *Zenaida graysoni*, is Extinct in the Wild; 9 species, including the Silvery Pigeon, *Columba argentina*, Sulu Bleeding-heart, *Gallicolumba menagei*, Mindoro Bleeding-heart, *G. platenae*, Negros Bleeding-heart, *G. keayi*, and Grenada Dove, *Leptotila wellsi*, are Critically Endangered; 15 species, including the Timor Imperial Pigeon, *Ducula cineracea*, Pink Pigeon, *Nesoenas mayeri*, Tooth-billed Pigeon, *Didunculus strigirostris*, and Timor Green Pigeon, *Treron psittaceus*, are Endangered; 37 species, including the Sri Lanka Pigeon, *Columba torrington*, Mindanao Bleeding-heart, *Gallicolumba crinigera*, and Victoria Crowned Pigeon, *Goura victoria*, are Vulnerable; and 40 species are Near Threatened

ABOVE Australia is home to many pigeon species, including this Squatter Pigeon, *Geophaps scripta*, from the east of the continent.

ABOVE The little Zebra Dove, *Geopelia striata*, has a wide range in Southeast Asia; it has been widely trapped for the cagebird trade.

One of the world's most familiar birds belongs to this very large worldwide family – the Feral Pigeon, which (together with almost all the domesticated forms of pigeon, including the great variety of fancy pigeons and racing, or 'homing,' pigeons) is entirely descended from the wild Rock Dove (or Rock Pigeon), *Columba livia*. The original stock stemmed almost completely from semi-domesticated, semi-wild birds kept from ancient times in dovecotes and other buildings, mainly for food. Over the centuries these successful, adaptable and fast-breeding birds colonised most of the inhabited areas of the world. As a result, the species is so widespread and well known that often it is referred to simply as 'the pigeon'.

The pigeon family also includes many little-known or rare and endangered species, especially in the tropics, such as the bleeding-hearts, *Gallicolumba*, of the Philippine jungles and the Tooth-billed Pigeon, *Didunculus strigirostris*, of Samoa. The greatest variety of species is in the Indomalayan and Australasian regions. Most species are highly or partially arboreal, although some, such as the Rock Dove, are cliff-nesters and some are ground dwellers, including species that inhabit treeless habitats. Some pigeons are able to live in very hot places, such as baking deserts. One such, the Australian Spinifex Pigeon, *Geophaps plumifera*, has been found to have various adaptations that enable it to cope with extremely high temperatures. As well as having a lower metabolic rate they can lose heat rapidly by water evaporation through the skin, but whenever possible they avoid becoming overheated by feeding in shady places during the late morning, resting in crevices among boulders during the hottest period later in the day.

There is a great size range, from the sparrow-sized ground-doves, *Columbina*, of open habitats in the New World, only about 30 g (1 oz) in weight, to the crowned pigeons, *Goura*, of the New Guinea rainforests, which are as big as a plump chicken, and weigh up to 2.4 kg (5.3 lb). Most species are 25–45 cm (10–18 in) long.

Pigeons are generally stocky and compact-bodied birds, though some of the smaller species commonly called doves have a rather more slender, elongated body. They have a small head relative to the body, and a short neck. The bill is short and quite slender, with an area of soft, swollen skin at its base called the cere, which lies above a flap, the operculum, overhanging the nostrils.

The wings vary in length but are generally broad with rounded tips, although those of strongly migratory species are somewhat narrower and more tapered. The tail varies considerably in size and length between different groups, but is longest in species that need to make rapid changes in direction, such as the cuckoo-doves, *Macropygia*, which live in dense forests in Asia and Australasia, where they fly fast on rounded wings and use their tail to help manoeuvre between tree trunks.

Flight muscles are large and powerful, constituting about 30–45% of the total body mass. These features give pigeons strong, fast flight, with rapid, almost vertical, take-off and the ability to fly for long distances (racing pigeons can fly at an average speed of about 70 km/h (44 mph) nonstop for hundreds of kilometres). Pigeons are also highly manoeuvrable in flight, an ability that often stands them in good stead when escaping from aerial predators. Most species have relatively short legs, although those of some of the ground-dwelling species are longer, suiting them to spend more time walking or running.

Most pigeons are primarily either seed eaters or fruit eaters. The seed eaters eat mainly seeds on the ground, while the fruit eaters feed largely in trees. Seed eaters have a thick-walled gizzard for preliminary grinding up of their tough food and longer intestines for digesting it, while fruit eaters are more agile in trees, able to cling to small branches and even hang upside down to reach fruit. Many species (especially Indopacific *Gallicolumba* ground-doves and various New World quail-doves) supplement their seed diet with various invertebrates, such as small snails, worms and insects, while one, the Atoll Fruit Dove, *Ptilinopus coralensis*, which lives on treeless atolls in the Pacific Ocean archipelago of Tuamoto, specialises in eating mainly insects and lizards.

<small>**ABOVE** With up to 10 million or so plump birds after each breeding season, the Wood Pigeon, *Columba palumbus*, has the greatest biomass of any UK bird.</small>

In contrast to other birds, except for some estrildid finches (see p. 296), all pigeons except for the Tooth-billed Pigeon, *Didunculus strigirostris*, of Samoa have a special method of drinking, in which they keep the bill immersed and suck up the water with a pumping action. This contrasts with the usual method of dipping the bill in the water, scooping it up into the buccal cavity and then raising the head so that the water runs down the oesophagus by gravity.

The plumage is soft and dense, and easily pulled out, especially on the rump and tail. This may help reduce the chance of the bird being caught and killed by a predator, such as a bird of prey or a fox or cat, as when its attacker seizes it from behind it can be left with nothing more than a foot, beak or mouth full of feathers.

Despite the presence of a uropygial (preen) gland in some species, pigeons, unlike most other birds which use the waxy oil it produces for feather maintenance, instead rely on the powder-down (produced by the wearing away of tips of special feathers) for this purpose. Evidence of this is graphically demonstrated when a pigeon collides with a glass window, as it often leaves behind a ghostly imprint of its wings, body and tail formed from the powder. (Owls, too, use powder down for preening and leave such impressions.)

The seed-eating pigeons have relatively dull plumage in various shades of grey or brown, often with black lines or spots and black-and-white wing bars (although in many species this is brightened somewhat by iridescent purple, green or bronze markings on the neck, face, breast, back or wings, and also often a pinkish tinge to the underparts).

Most of the fruit-eating species are far more colourful. This is particularly true of the fruit doves, *Ptilinopus*, with mainly brilliant green plumage, in many species contrasting with a silvery grey head and breast, and often also with yellow, red, pink, purple, black or white markings on the crown, breast, rump or undertail coverts. Even so, the bright green provides excellent camouflage against the foliage, where they spend most of their lives.

Some species have striking crests. The Crested Pigeon, *Ocyphaps lophotes*, and Spinifex Pigeon of more open country in Australia both have a long, slender, pointed crest, while the Topknot Pigeon, *Lopholaimus antarcticus*, of eastern Australian forests is unique within the family in having two separate crests, larger in males than females: a shorter, more curved, grey one extending from the forehead, and a longer, straighter one composed of rust-red feathers with black edges. They are erected during courtship displays. The most spectacular crests are sported by the three species of New Guinea crowned pigeons: they are large and fan-shaped with lacy feathers. The Nicobar Pigeon, *Caloenas nicobarica*, from woodlands in Southeast Asian islands, New Guinea and the Solomons, has unique, long, pointed feathers hanging from the neck, like the hackles of a cockerel. Many species have brightly coloured areas of bare skin on the cere at the base of the bill, or in rings or patches around each eye.

The sexes of most species have almost identical plumage, and in those where there is a difference, it is usually confined to the colours of head, neck and breast. Courtship displays performed on the ground or on a perch involve the birds, especially the males, in bowing, strutting about with a puffed-out breast, wing-twitching and raising and spreading the tail. Aerial displays include slow, shallow wingbeats, rising at an angle, wing-clapping and gliding downwards.

Although pigeons lay small clutches of just one or two eggs that are very small in relation to the female's body size, they make up for this in that incubation and fledging periods are very short and breeding seasons often very long. Some species can rear up to eight broods in a year. Nestlings (called 'squabs') grow extremely quickly, due largely to their diet of nutrient-rich 'milk' produced in the crop of both parents, although the young fledge at well below adult weight in all open-nest species. The ungainly looking nestlings are covered in sparse, whitish, cream, or pale yellow, grey or brown down. Often, in a brood of two, one will be a male and the other a female.

<small>**ABOVE** The Wonga Pigeon, *Leucosarcia melanoleuca*, is a large pigeon of rainforest and other wooded habitats endemic to eastern Australia.</small>

Five subfamilies are generally recognised. The first is the Columbinae, the 'typical pigeons', a large group of seed eaters. It includes the major genus *Columba*, with 50 extant species (32 spread right across the Old World, one endemic to Australia, and 17 in the New World), as well as the 16 Old World species of turtle doves, *Streptopelia*, nine species of Old World and Australasian cuckoo-doves, *Macropygia*, seven species of *Zenaida* in the New World, including the familiar Mourning Dove, *Z. macroura*, nine species of New World ground doves, *Columbina*, 16 species of quail-doves, *Geotrygon*, from Central and South America and the Caribbean, and 18 species of Indopacific ground-doves, *Gallicolumba*. The second subfamily, Otidiphabinae, contains just a single species, the large, crested Pheasant Pigeon, *Otidiphaps nobilis*, of the New Guinea region, named for its large, laterally compressed tail like that of some pheasants. The subfamily Gourinae, also confined to New Guinea, contains the three very large species of crowned pigeon *Goura*. The odd-looking Tooth-billed Pigeon, *Didunculus strigirostris*, of western Samoa, the sole member of the subfamily Didunculinae, was given its common name because of the three toothlike projections and two notches in either side of the lower mandible of its stout, bulbous, red-and-yellow bill. The shape of the bill superficially recalls that of the Dodo, and the generic name *Didunculus* is from the Latin words meaning 'little dodo'. Richard Owen, the great nineteenth-century anatomist and opponent of Darwin, referred to this bird as the 'Dodlet', figuring a skeleton of *Didunculus* as a comparison to the Dodo in his major work on the latter bird. However, researchers today think that the Dodo is more likely to be closely related to another odd-looking species, the Nicobar Pigeon, found from Southeast Asia to the Solomon Islands. The fifth subfamily, the Treroninae, includes 23 species of green pigeons, *Treron*, from Africa and Asia, 50 species of fruit doves, *Ptilinopus*, from Southeast Asia, Australasia and the Pacific, and 34 species of imperial pigeons, *Ducula*, from south Asia, Australasia and the Pacific.

Recent molecular research suggests that some of the traditional families delineated above may include several less closely related groups that may deserve separate subfamilies of their own. In addition, some major genera appear to be paraphyletic; for instance this appears to be true for the large genus *Columba*, in which the Old World species are apparently more closely related to the smaller (exclusively Old World) turtle doves, *Streptopelia*,

RIGHT The New Zealand Pigeon, *Hemiphaga novaeseelandiae*, is the only member of the pigeon family that is native to New Zealand.

than to the New World species, which should then be moved to a different genus, *Patagioenas*.

The pigeon order contains the fourth highest number of recently extinct species of all bird orders; only the perching birds (Order Passeriformes), the rails and relatives (Order Gruiformes) and the parrots (Order Psittaciformes) have more. Today, almost a third of all extant species of pigeon are threatened to some degree; most of these are restricted to small islands (as were about 80% of extinct species). Most threats are the result of human actions, from habitat destruction and the introduction of alien predators (as with the Pink Pigeon, *Nesoenas mayeri*, of Mauritius) to overhunting for food and sport. The most notorious example of the latter is the rapid decline to extinction of the North American Passenger Pigeon, *Ectopistes migratorius*. This handsome blue-grey and pinkish pigeon once bred in vast numbers in deciduous woodlands across the northern USA and southern Canada, from the Atlantic coast west as far as the Great Plains, migrating to winter in woodlands in the southeastern USA. Migratory flocks were so immense that they darkened the sky, and were reported in the 1860s to stretch for as much as 1.6 km (1 mile) wide and 480 km (300 miles) long, and contain many millions of birds. It went from being one of the most abundant of all birds to extinction in just over 40 years. Relentless slaughter, combined with habitat loss, ensured that by 1914 just a single individual remained in captivity in Cincinnati Zoo; 'Martha' died in September of that year.

ORDER PTEROCLIDIFORMES

This order contains just the single small family of sandgrouse. These birds look rather like a cross between a pigeon (in the order Columbiformes, p. 31) and a game bird (Order Galliformes, p. 19), the latter comparison accounting for the 'grouse' part of their common name. Although sandgrouse are now generally regarded as deserving an order of their own, they were originally classified by the eighteenth century 'father of taxonomy' Linnaeus with the tree grouse, and some ornithologists argued for a close relationship with the grouse (subfamily Tetraoninae of the Family Phasianidae) or other game birds in the Order Galliformes, until the early years of the twentieth century. However, superficial similarities with

game birds are due to convergent evolution not relationship. On the other hand, there has long been an alternative view that sandgrouse are closest to the pigeons, and they have at times been included as a family within the pigeon order. Such a relationship is supported by recent molecular data. Such evidence has also been used to suggest a relationship with the small and enigmatic order of mesites (Order Mesitiformes), endemic to Madagascar. Another possibility is that sandgrouse might be more related to one or other of the wader families of the order Charadriiformes, such as the thick-knees (Family Burhinidae), plovers (Family Charadriidae) or coursers (Family Glareolidae, subfamily Cursoriinae).

SANDGROUSE Pteroclididae

GENERA: 2   **SPECIES:** 16

LENGTH: in most species, 24–35 cm (9.5–14 in), but males of the two *Syrrhaptes* species and some *Pterocles* species have a pair of elongated central tail feathers that in *Syrrhaptes* and Pin-tailed Sandgrouse, *P. alchata*, increase their total length to about 40 cm (16 in)

WEIGHT: 150–550 g (5.3–19.5 oz)

RANGE AND HABITAT: parts of southern Europe, Africa, Madagascar and central and southern Asia; open country, mainly in arid or semi-arid areas

SOCIAL BEHAVIOUR: generally intensely social outside breeding season, and some species nest in small, loose colonies, others as separate pairs; monogamous but not strongly territorial

NEST: a simple scrape on ground in open, often within the footprint of a grazing mammal, or against a grass tuft, bush or boulder; sometimes sparsely lined with dry grass or other plant matter or small stones

EGGS: 3 (rarely 2), cream, greyish, pink or greenish, heavily marked with brown and grey

INCUBATION: 21–30 days

FLEDGING PERIOD: about 4 weeks

FOOD: almost entirely small seeds

VOICE: most vocal when flying to and from waterholes, when pairs or flocks give loud, far-carrying churring, chuckling, or melodious whistling calls

MIGRATION: some species are sedentary or are partial nomads, while some populations of others make regular migrations

CONSERVATION STATUS: none threatened

ABOVE This Painted Sandgrouse, *Pterocles indicus*, at Ranthambore National Park, India, is a male, with brighter plumage than the female.

Of the two genera in this small Old World family, the first, *Syrrhaptes*, contains just two of the 16 species, distinguished only by the lack of a rear toe, and the partial fusion and feathering of the three forward ones (the generic name comes from the Greek words meaning 'sewn together'). Both are found only in central Asia, where the feathered feet may help them keep warm on the cold ground at night and in winter.

The major genus, *Pterocles*, includes two species in North Africa, both breeding marginally in south-west Europe, and one in the Canaries; six species restricted to Africa, one endemic to Madagascar; one endemic to the Indian subcontinent; and four in both Africa and southwest Asia.

All species have a plump, compact body and a small head on a short neck. The bill is small with fine feathers at the base covering the nostrils, helping to prevent the entry of wind-blown sand. The wings are broad-based with pointed tips, and are equipped with powerful muscles for strong, rapid flight after a sudden, almost vertical, take-off. The legs are short and strong, suited for walking and fast running, and the toes are short and broad so that they spread the bird's weight to make it easier to walk on sand.

Living in arid environments and being restricted to a very dry diet consisting almost entirely of seeds of various mainly leguminous plants, sandgrouse need to drink regularly, usually every day. Given the general scarcity of water in deserts and semi-deserts, they are often forced to fly long distances of up to 50 km

(30 miles) or more to drink at lakes, waterholes and other water sources, assembling beforehand and flying there in noisy flocks that may contain dozens, hundreds or even thousands of birds. Contrary to what was once believed to be the case, sandgrouse do not drink as pigeons do, by sucking up water with the bill immersed, but need to take a beakful then raise their heads to swallow it, like most other birds. One remarkable feature that is borne out by observation, though, is that male sandgrouse have highly absorbent belly feathers that enable them to carry water back to their chicks daily until they fledge. Before entering the water to soak them, a male will first remove the waterproofing preen oil from the feathers by rubbing his belly in dry sand or soil. He then wades in and lifts wings and tail to expose his belly to the water and pumps his body up and down until the feathers are saturated. On his return, he stands over the chicks as they sip the water from a vertical groove in the centre of his belly plumage.

Plumage is cryptic, camouflaging the birds well against a background of sand, rocks and sparse vegetation, but has some colourful markings. The upperparts are mainly buff, chestnut, orange and yellow, and may be barred, spotted or mottled, and some species are yellowish, chestnut or blue-grey on the head and breast. Many have single or double, thin, crescent-shaped black and white or pale yellowish breast bands, and several have black or chestnut patches on the belly, while in others the belly is barred and in two species it is pure white. Females are slightly duller than males.

ORDER MESITORNITHIFORMES

This enigmatic family of birds was formerly lumped together with a very varied assemblage of families in the Order Gruiformes, but recent research suggests that they deserve to occupy an order of their own.

MESITES Mesitornithidae

GENERA: 2 **SPECIES:** 3

LENGTH: 30–32 cm (12–13 in)

WEIGHT: 103–172 g (3.6–6 oz)

RANGE AND HABITAT: Madagascar; both *Mesitornis* species inhabit forests (the White-breasted Mesite in the north and west of the island and the Brown Mesite in the east); the Sub-desert Mesite, *Monias benschi*, lives in dry marginal spiny woodland and scrublands in the southwest

SOCIAL BEHAVIOUR: generally forage in small family groups; breeding may be monogamous, with female incubating eggs, but in the Subdesert Mesite at least there is evidence of polygamy, with both sexes having more than one sexual partner during a single breeding season (rare in birds)

NEST: platform of twigs, leaves and bark strips, usually sited low down in a shrub

EGGS: 1–3, whitish with brown spots

INCUBATION: 21–27 days in Subdesert Mesite

FLEDGING PERIOD: unknown; downy young leave nest soon after hatching but remain with parents for up to a year

FOOD: mainly small insects and seeds; also small fruits and various invertebrates

VOICE: all three species are highly vocal, especially in early morning; calls include clicks and hisses, and songs consist of rapidly delivered harsh chuckling notes or whistled phrases, either simply repeated or ending with a brief trill; White-breasted Mesite pairs often duet

MIGRATION: sedentary, apart from altitudinal movements of the Brown Mesite outside the breeding season

CONSERVATION STATUS: all three species are Vulnerable

ABOVE This White-breasted Mesite, *Mesitornis variegatus*, was photographed in the western deciduous forest of Ankarafantsika Nature Reserve, Madagascar.

This small family of ground-dwelling birds is endemic to the island of Madagascar. In size and general appearance they are superficially reminiscent of thrushes, while they share some behavioural traits with rails. These odd birds have most often been classified with rails, cranes and relatives in the order Gruiformes. Despite this, various analyses of recent molecular data suggests that they might be most closely related to pigeons (Order Columbiformes), or perhaps to sandgrouse (Order Cuculiformes). They may be a relict group, the three survivors of an ancient, once more widespread family.

Mesites have a slim body, a small head, a broad, longish tail and strong legs and feet. The bill of the forest-dwelling White-breasted Mesite, *Mesitornis variegatus*, and Brown Mesite, *M. unicolor*, is short and straight, whereas the Subdesert Mesite, *Monias benschi*, has a much longer, distinctly decurved bill. Although their short wings are functional, mesites have only a rudimentary collarbone, and fly only weakly and briefly, mainly when going up to roost in a tree or shrub or to escape danger, by flying to a low perch and 'freezing'. Although they may nest a couple of metres high in a shrub, they scramble up instead of flying to it. They feed mainly by walking around with head bobbing and flicking fallen leaves or other vegetation aside to flush out insects and other invertebrates. All three species are generally shy and secretive, and various aspects of their lives are still relatively little known. They are all considered globally threatened, with fragmented populations thought to be declining rapidly as a result of forest destruction by slash-and-burn agriculture and logging, as well as hunting and predation by dogs.

The plumage is basically brownish or greyish above and paler below. The Brown Mesite is the plainest, whereas the White-breasted Mesite and Subdesert Mesite both have a strongly striped head pattern and bold dark chevrons on their underparts. The sexes look the same in the first two species, but female Subdesert Mesites have duller underparts with dense red-brown markings.

ABOVE Startled by the photographer, this male Sub-desert Mesite, *Monias benschi*, in the Ifaty spiny forest, southwest Madagascar, adopts a defence posture.

ORDER EURYPYGIFORMES

Another recently proposed order, this contains just two single-species families from different parts of the world – the Neotropical Sunbittern Family Eurypygidae, and the Family Rhynochetidae, endemic to the island of New Caledonia, in the Southwest Pacific Ocean.

SUNBITTERN Eurypygidae

GENERA: 1 **SPECIES**: 1

LENGTH: 43–48 cm (17–19 in)

WEIGHT: about 180–220 g (6–8 oz)

RANGE AND HABITAT: Central and South America, from Guatemala to Brazil; open lowland forest and woodlands alongside rivers, streams, lakes or floodwaters

SOCIAL BEHAVIOUR: mainly solitary; sometimes seen in pairs, especially in the breeding season; probably territorial

Nest: bulky cup of sticks, leaves, stems and grass, bound together with mud, sited on a narrow branch of a tree or shrub, at heights of up to 7 m (23 ft)

EGGS: 1–2, pinkish-buff, with dark spots

INCUBATION: about 30 days

FLEDGING PERIOD: about 22–30 days, but may depend on parents for food for up to 2 months after fledging, or longer

FOOD: small fish, molluscs, crustaceans, insects and other freshwater invertebrates

VOICE: soft, melancholy, drawn-out whistles; peeping calls, and a series of sharp notes followed by a trill during courtship; also non-vocal bill-rattling

MIGRATION: sedentary

CONSERVATION STATUS: not threatened

This exclusively Neotropical family contains just a single, unusual and elegant species, the Sunbittern, *Eurypyga helias*. It acquired the first part of its evocative common name and specific name (*helias* is the Greek word for 'of the sun') from the striking patches of golden buff, chestnut and black on the uppersides of its very large, rounded wings: these were, rather fancifully, thought to resemble the rising sun. The dramatic patterns, which look like huge, staring eyes, are suddenly revealed when the bird opens its wings to fly or suddenly spreads them in a threat display to startle and intimidate predators. Spreading the wings as it tilts forward also makes it look much larger than it really is, and the effect is heightened by fanning the tail. The generic name (and name of the family) is derived from two Greek words meaning 'broad rump', and refers to the wide circle formed by the tail when it is fanned. The rest of the bird's plumage is intricately striped, barred and mottled in browns, greys, black and white. This is as beautiful as the uppersides of the wings but in contrast to them has evolved to provide effective camouflage against the background of waterside vegetation, where the Sunbittern seeks cover when disturbed.

The second part of the common name refers to its superficial resemblance to the unrelated bitterns, although unlike those birds, it does not adopt an upright posture as they often do. Moreover, not only is the Sunbittern not related to the bitterns or other members of the heron family, but like the mesites opposite, and the equally odd species on the next page, the Kagu, *Rhynochetos jubatus*, has now been shown to be unrelated to the rails, cranes and other birds in the large order Gruiformes. Their true relationship to other birds is far from certain, but recent research suggests they might be closest to the tropicbirds of the order Phaethontiformes or to the order Caprimulgiformes, composing the nightjars, and relatives, together with the swifts and hummingbirds.

The Sunbittern hunts rather like a true bittern, stalking along a riverbank stealthily or pausing motionless, then suddenly stabbing or seizing a fish or other small animal with its long, daggerlike black and orange bill. The head is small, with big red eyes, and the body is long and slender, although it looks bigger because of the big wings and longish, broad tail.

ABOVE This Sunbittern, *Eurypyga helias*, on a riverbank in the Peruvian Amazon is performing its threat display in response to danger.

KAGU Rhynochetidae

GENERA: 1   **SPECIES**: 1

LENGTH: 55 cm (22 in)

WEIGHT: 700–1,100 g (25–39 oz)

RANGE AND HABITAT: New Caledonia; mainly in humid forests, including high-altitude cloud forest, but also drier forests at low altitude in the centre of the island; sometimes in closed-canopy scrub in the wet season

SOCIAL BEHAVIOUR: usually solitary except during breeding season; monogamous and territorial

NEST: simple structure made of leaves, sited on the ground

EGGS: 1, cream or buff, blotched dark brown

INCUBATION: 33–37 days

FLEDGING PERIOD: chick leaves nest about 3 days after hatching, but continues to be fed by both parents and brooded at night for about 6 weeks thereafter

FOOD: invertebrates, mainly snails, worms, millipedes and insects, and small lizards

VOICE: variety of soft hissing and rattling calls; far-carrying song, rather like a cross between the barking of a young dog and the crow of a cockerel, usually heard as a duet by paired birds just before dawn and in early morning; can last for up to an hour

MIGRATION: sedentary

CONSERVATION STATUS: this species is Endangered

ABOVE A pair of Kagus, *Rhynochetos jubatus*, erect their flamboyant crests and expose their chequered wing markings in a courtship display.

This strange bird, the sole member of its family today, resembles a cross between a rail and a small heron, but with a very large, shaggy, erectile crest. Indeed the Kagu, *Rhynochetos jubatus*, was once thought to be related to the herons, owing to its appearance and possession of powder down, together with other plumage features and bill structure. Later it was lumped with cranes, rails and other members of the Order Gruiformes. Recent molecular evidence does not support this view, however, and the Kagu is likely to be an ancient species with no obvious relatives apart from the next species in this book, the Sunbittern, *Eurypyga helias*, which also appears to be misplaced in the Gruiformes. The relationship of these two odd birds is strongly supported by both molecular data and similarities in morphology, and as a result they now appear here in an order of their own, Eurypygiformes.

Standing at about knee-height to a human, the Kagu has a large, rounded head, with a strong, slightly decurved, pointed bill, a short neck and a plump body. The tail is short and the legs long. The Kaku is flightless, but can glide downslope on its broad rounded wings, which it also uses for balance when running away from predators.

When foraging, Kagus spend much time standing still (often on one leg), sometimes on a rock or fallen tree, or walking slowly through the dark forest interior, where the large, dark red eyes presumably help the birds to see well as they forage among the leaf litter or soil for invertebrates such as snails, worms and millipedes, or small lizards. They listen for prey, too, and once it is located, thrust out their head to seize it in their bill. Sometimes, they use the bill to toss leaves aside or dig in the soil.

Plumage is uniformly very pale ash-grey, apart from dark bands on the wings, which are revealed as a striking, bold chequered pattern when they are spread during displays, during courtship or defence of territory or young. The bill and legs are bright orange-red. The almost white plumage is celebrated in the native Kanak islanders' name, *kagou*, meaning 'ghost of the forest'. The chicks are camouflaged in fawn and brown.

Endemic to the Pacific island of New Caledonia, the Kagu has become extirpated from much of its former range mainly because of a combination of habitat destruction, human persecution and introduced mammals. The forests in many parts of the island have been destroyed or degraded chiefly by agriculture, logging, nickel mining and fires, and by introduced deer in some areas. Hunting and capture for the cage bird trade or for the local habit of keeping the birds as pets made further inroads. Introduced dogs still pose a major threat, killing both adult and young birds. Currently there are estimated to be only 250 to 1,000 mature individuals in the wild. Although the Kagu now has such a small population and a fragmented range, it is still widespread and even increasing in places, and conservationists are combating further declines with legislation, education and captive breeding.

ORDER PHAETHONTIFORMES

The tropicbird Family Phaethontidae was formerly included as an atypical family of the Order Pelecaniformes, as a result of shared anatomical characters, but recent molecular research indicates that they do not belong there. Nevertheless, their true relationships are decidedly uncertain, so they have been given an order of their own, that may possibly be nearest to the Sunbittern and Kagu in the Order Eurypygiformes.

TROPICBIRDS Phaethontidae

GENERA: 1   **SPECIES:** 3

LENGTH: 70–110 cm (28–43 in), including tail streamers of 30–56 cm (12–22 in)

WEIGHT: 220–835 g (7.8–29 oz)

RANGE AND HABITAT: tropical and subtropical oceans; eastern Pacific, central and south-central Atlantic, Indian Ocean; mostly live far out to sea, coming to land only for breeding, on remote oceanic islands where they prefer inaccessible crevices on cliffs

SOCIAL BEHAVIOUR: usually solitary or in small groups; breeds in loose colonies; experienced pairs at least are monogamous

NEST: a scrape on the bare ground (often in the shade of a shrub, grass tussock or overhanging rock), or in a hole in a cliff or tree

EGGS: 1, ranges from unmarked pale pastel colours to grey, purplish, red or brown with a sprinkling of blotches or spots in various colours

INCUBATION: 40–47 days

FLEDGING PERIOD: about 70–90 days

FOOD: mainly fish (especially flying fish) and squid; occasionally other cephalopods or crustaceans

VOICE: usually silent at sea, but utter shrill, whistling, screaming, shrieking or grating calls when at breeding colonies, especially during courtship

MIGRATION: range very widely across oceans but do not usually make true migrations

CONSERVATION STATUS: none threatened

ABOVE A Red-billed Tropicbird, *Phaethon aethereus*, flies over the Pacific Ocean off South Plaza Island, in the Galapagos archipelago.

The three tropicbird species are among the most striking and beautiful of all seabirds. Their graceful, buoyant and agile flight is a delight to watch. It is strong and direct with rapid beats of the long, narrow, sharply pointed wings, sometimes interspersed with brief glides or soaring. The tropicbird tail is wedge shaped or diamond shaped, and is tipped by the family's most striking and distinctive feature – the extremely long, narrow central pair of feathers, or streamers. These may exceed the entire length of the rest of the bird. They are flexible, and play an important part in the birds' courtship displays, which involve pairs or sometimes trios breaking away from a flock to perform dramatic aerobatics. They include closely synchronised manoeuvres, such as zig-zagging,

one bird flying just above another, and then lowering its wings at the same moment as the lower bird raises its own, so that their wingtips almost touch. Their appearance may be the primary role of these flamboyant accoutrements, but as with terns, swallows and other birds that have elongated tail streamers, they may also help stabilise their owners during such dashing manoeuvres. The true element of tropicbirds is the air – as is instantly apparent when they are seen at their nesting sites. The legs are extremely short and set far back at the rear of the body, and the webbed feet small and weak, so they are very clumsy on land, shuffling along with their bellies scraping the ground, and are barely able to stand.

With a deep-chested body about the same size as that of a domestic pigeon, tropicbirds have a large head and a stout, slightly decurved, sharply pointed bill with finely serrated cutting edges. Their plumage contrasts dramatically with the blue of tropical skies, as it is mainly dazzling white, apart from a black eyestripe common to all three species and black markings on the upperparts that vary between them and help identify the adults. The Red-billed Tropicbird, *Phaethon aethereus*, has a black wedge on the wingtips and extensive black barring on the back and the inner part of the upperwings. Of all three, the Red-tailed Tropicbird, *P. rubricauda*, has the least black on its upperparts, restricted to the tips of the scapulars and the shafts of the outer primaries. As its name implies, it has red tail streamers rather than the white ones of the other two species. The white on the body is flushed with pale pink when newly moulted, but this usually wears away. The White-tailed Tropicbird, *P. lepturus*, considerably smaller and only about half the weight of the others, has a black diagonal bar on each wing as well as a black wedge on each wingtip. The race *fulvus* of this bird, which breeds on Christmas Island in the Indian Ocean, has a rich apricot tinge to its head, body and tail streamers. The bill of the first two species is bright red, while that of the White-tailed Tropicbird is yellowish or orange. The legs and feet of the Red-billed and White-tailed

Tropicbirds are yellowish, while those of the Red-tailed species are blue-grey; the webs of all species are mainly black. The sexes are alike. Juveniles of all species are strongly barred blackish above.

Tropicbirds are unusual among open ocean seabirds in their great capacity for sustained, mainly flapping, flight; most seabirds that are aerial for much of their lives, such as shearwaters, albatrosses and frigatebirds, use air currents to sail on the wind. Although tropicbirds spend most of their time airborne, they sometimes swim, riding high on the water with their long tail arched behind them. Severe storms can blow these lovely, delicate-looking but very tough birds far from their normal range and, albeit very rarely, even well inland.

They are highly skilled plunge divers, patrolling at up to 25 m (80 ft) above the waves, and often hovering like terns to detect or get an exact fix on prey before hurtling down with wings half closed. They often concentrate on catching flying fish, which they take at or just below the surface, or sometimes when the fish are in the air.

The feet of tropicbirds are too small to provide enough warmth to the egg as in most other Pelecaniformes, and the parents incubate like most birds, with their body covering it.

ABOVE This White-tailed Tropicbird, *Phaethon lepturus*, and its single chick are at their ground nest in the Seychelles.

ORDER CAPRIMULGIFORMES

In traditional schemes of classification, this order comprised five families of largely nocturnal or crepuscular, cryptically plumaged birds. All have short legs, and most have small, weak feet and claws. Uniquely in the order, the nightjars and nighthawks of the Family Caprimulgidae have a pectinated (comblike) claw on the middle toe, which they use in preening. Most caprimulgiforms have a large head and all have big eyes suited for night vision. The bill is very small but with an extraordinarily wide gape, an adaptation in most members for catching insect prey in flight. In many, it is fringed with highly modidied, stiff whisker-like feathers, called rictal bristles. These may help funnel the prey into the mouth and/or protect the birds' eyes from damaging contact with the hard or spiny exoskeletons of their prey; additionally, they might serve as tactile organs like a cat's whiskers, helping their owner to sense prey or in those that nest in dark holes, to locate eggs and nestlings.

Unlike the birds in the other four traditional caprimulgiform families, which nest on bare ground or in a cavity of some sort, the frogmouths of the Family Podargidae build small platform-like or cushion-shaped nests.

The Oilbird, *Steatornis caripensis*, of Panama and South America, sole member of its Family Steatornithidae, is a very distinctive, large, highly specialised nocturnal fruit-eating bird that roosts and nests in the pitch dark interior of caves, navigating by echolocation; in contrast to the rest of the order, whose members are generally not gregarious, it roosts, breeds and feeds in large colonies.

The relationships of the birds in this order with other birds have long been uncertain and controversial. At various times,

the five traditional caprimulgiform families have been linked to hummingbirds, trogons, todies, motmots, bee-eaters, rollers, jacamars, puffbirds and even swallows. However, they have usually been classified between the owls (Order Strigiformes) and the swifts and hummingbirds (Order Apodiformes). They do bear various resemblances to the owls (including such features as soft plumage, cryptic coloration, and nocturnal habits with excellent night-time vision) and have long been regarded as being their closest relatives. The pioneering DNA studies of Sibley and Ahlquist even led them to unite the two groups in a single order, Caprimulgiformes. On the other hand, there is more recent molecular evidence suggesting strongly that the similarities are instead the result of convergent evolution of unrelated groups to a similar lifestyle. They do, however, show similarities with the swifts (both groups being highly aerial insectivores that have a very short bill with a broad gape, and small, weak legs and feet).

The relationships of many of the families with the others in the order remains uncertain, but it appears likely that nightjars, nighthawks and eared-nightjars, together with potoos, are closely related, while the oilbird and frogmouths are more distant, and owlet-nightjars are perhaps closest to swifts, treeswifts and hummingbirds (the last four families have been linked in a superfamily Trochiloidea). Recent evidence suggests that the order should be enlarged to include the diurnal swifts (Family Apodidae), treeswifts (Family Hemiprocnidae) and hummingbirds (Family Trochilidae). Although the evidence from morphology is sometimes contradictory, this apparently rather radical proposal is supported by molecular research, and it is the arrangement that we follow here.

OILBIRD Steatornithidae

GENERA: 1   **SPECIES:** 1

LENGTH: 40–49 cm (16–19 in)

WEIGHT: 350–485 g (12–17 oz)

RANGE AND HABITAT: Breeds Colombia, Venezuela (the latter with largest numbers), Trinidad, northern Brazil, Ecuador, Peru and Bolivia and recorded from Panama and Costa Rica; tropical and subtropical forest, with caves for roosting and nesting

SOCIAL BEHAVIOUR: extremely gregarious at all times; monogamous

NEST: shallow bowl of fruit pulp, pits and the birds' excrement, glued together with saliva, sited on cave ledge, usually near the ceiling

EGGS: 1–4, white (but soon stained brown)

INCUBATION: 32–35 days

FLEDGING PERIOD: about 88–125 days

FOOD: entirely ripe fruit from more than 80 tree species, mainly of palms throughout the year, and seasonally on other, aromatic, fruit, mainly in the laurel family (Lauraceae) and gumbo-limbo or incense-tree family (Burseraceae)

VOICE: harsh shrieks, screams and snarling sounds when the colony is disturbed in their cave; also echolocation clicks, and outside in the open, less harsh, shorter clucking calls

MIGRATION: many colonies disperse after breeding

CONSERVATION STATUS: not threatened

The Oilbird *Steatornis caripensis*, restricted as a breeder to parts of northwestern South America and Trinidad, is so specialised and atypical in its anatomy, ecology and behaviour that it is placed in a family of its own. This remarkable bird may be nearest to the potoos (Family Nyctibiidae), although none of the caprimulgiform families appear to be especially closely related. It might have once been far more widespread, judging by fossil remains of early relatives found in Wyoming and France. Both its common and generic names (*Steatornis* is from the Greek for 'fat (or tallow) bird') refer to the clear, odourless oil obtained from the thick layers of fat laid down beneath the skin of the plump nestlings. These were traditionally harvested by Venezuelan Indians, who extracted the oil, which they used for cooking and, locally, as lamp oil, by boiling the young birds they killed to render the fat.

The Oilbird is a crow-sized bird with rich chestnut brown plumage peppered with white diamonds and spots edged with black. The flight feathers of the wing and the tail feathers are banded with blackish bars edged with a broad patch of speckled black. The wings are long in proportion to the rather slender body, spanning over a metre (3.2 ft), and the long, graduated tail is held in an inverted 'V', probably helping the birds hover and manoeuvre slowly when feeding or approaching the nest site. The brown eyes are large, providing good night vision for this strictly nocturnal bird. The Oilbird's bill has the broad base and wide gape typical of the caprimulgiforms, but it is also laterally compressed and distinctly hooked, adding to the long wings and long graduated tail to give it a rather raptor-like appearance. The short legs, set far forward on the body with three toes pointing forwards and the hind toe held at right angles, account for the bird's awkward front-heavy posture when perching or shuffling along the nesting ledge. Oilbirds are unable to stand on one leg to preen the plumage of the head with a foot: instead they have to prop themselves up with one or both wings first.

Oilbirds breed and roost packed closely together in colonies that can contain many thousands of birds. They avoid most natural predators (but not human ones) by doing so mainly deep within huge cave systems, on narrow ledges high up on the walls – although eggs or chicks that fall out of the nest may be eaten by crabs or rats. They also feed together, streaming out of their caves in large numbers at dusk. They are the world's only nocturnal fruit-eating birds, and apart from some swiftlets (see p. 406) in Southeast Asia, the only birds known to use echolocation for navigation in the complete darkness deep within the nesting caves, preventing them from striking one another or the cave walls. The sonar clicks they produce are of much lower frequency than those of insect-eating bats (which enable their owners to pinpoint fast-flying, weaving moths when feeding), and at about 700 cycles per second are audible to humans. If a colony is disturbed, the birds produce an almost continual, ear-splitting cacophony of eerie, snarling screaming calls.

The prominent white markings show up well in dim light, and may serve to help the birds avoid colliding with one another and causing injury (their wing bones are relatively thin) as they forage silently close together in flocks of up to 20 or more, hovering high up in the forest canopy in front of the clumps of ripe palm and other fruits. Thanks to the wide gape of the bill, Oilbirds can swallow each fruit whole, regurgitating the single large seed later. When feeding nestlings, they carry considerable weights of fruit back to them. This may involve trips of up to 93 miles (150 km), perhaps more, and the long wings with their deeply slotted primary flight feathers help them to fly efficiently with the extra weight.

ABOVE These Oilbirds, *Steatornis caripensis*, are at their nesting site within a large cave in Ecuador.

FROGMOUTHS Podargidae

GENERA: 3   **SPECIES:** 13

LENGTH: 19–60 cm (7.5–23.5 in); Australasian species (*Podargus*) are larger

WEIGHT: 46–680 g (1.6–24 oz)

RANGE AND HABITAT: parts of southern and southeast Asia, and throughout New Guinea and Australia; mostly in tropical forests, also other woodlands, plantations, bamboo groves and scrub; in Australia, in evergreen forests, eucalypt and other dry woodlands and scrub, also urban areas with trees

SOCIAL BEHAVIOUR: usually solitary or in mated pairs, which remain year-round in their breeding territory

NEST: Asian species (*Batrachostomus*) build dense little cushion-pad nests largely of their own down, plucked from their breasts and matted together, with a camouflaging outer layer of moss, lichen, leaves and spiders' webs; Australasian species (*Podargus*) build larger nests consisting mainly of twigs; both types usually sited on branches of a tree or shrub, sometimes on an epiphyte or atop the old nest of another bird

EGGS: mostly 1 or 2, sometimes 3, 4 or even 5 in the Tawny Frogmouth, white

INCUBATION: 28–32 days (in the Tawny Frogmouth, *P. strigoides*, the only species for which details are known)

FLEDGING PERIOD: 25–35 days (in the Tawny Frogmouth, the only species for which details are known)

FOOD: insects, mainly large ones, including beetles, grasshoppers, cockroaches and moths; large frogmouths, especially the three *Podargus* species, also eat frogs, lizards, small mammals and birds

VOICE: mellow or booming hooting calls and song, including duets by mated pairs

MIGRATION: all are sedentary

CONSERVATION STATUS: five species, including the Short-tailed Frogmouth, *Batrachostomus poliolophus*, and Large Frogmouth, *B. auritus*, are Near Threatened

Frogmouths have a very large head relative to the body, and a very short but strong and wide bill with an immense gape that accounts for their common name. This is far stouter than the bill of other caprimulgiforms, and ends in a short hook, enabling these birds to catch relatively large, tough, highly active prey such as large beetles, cicadas and other insects, as well as other invertebrates such as scorpions and centipedes, and in the largest *Podargus* species even small lizards, birds and mammals. Their broad, rounded wings and a long tail give the completely nocturnal frogmouths great manoeuvrability in their woodland habitat as they swoop down to seize prey from the ground or from tree branches, trunks or foliage. Like their relatives the owlet-nightjars, frogmouths are especially well-endowed with facial bristles. As well as those surrounding the bill that are found in other members of the order, *Batrachostomus* species may have well-developed bunches of bristles sprouting from the forehead and semi-bristles extending over the ear-coverts. Suggestions for possible functions include shedding rainwater and serving like a cat's whiskers as touch sensors.

The thirteen species are classified in three genera. The three mainly larger species of *Podargus* are birds of Australia and New Guinea. The largest – and biggest of all frogmouths – is the Papuan Frogmouth, *P. papuensis*, found mainly in New Guinea but also in north-east Australia. The Marbled Frogmouth, *P. ocellatus*, has a similar distribution (though also occurring in other small islands and in a small area of eastern Australia), while the Tawny Frogmouth, *P. strigoides*, is exclusively Australian, found throughout the mainland and in Tasmania.

There are nine *Batrachostomus* species, all living in southern Asia. Most are smaller than *Podargus* frogmouths, although one, the aptly named Large Frogmouth, *B. auritus* of Thailand, Malaysia, Sumatra and Borneo, overlaps in size with the smallest of the *Podargus* trio, the Tawny Frogmouth.

The third genus, *Rigidipenna*, contains just one species, the Solomon Islands Frogmouth (or Cinnamon Frogmouth). This was first scientifically described from a single specimen collected in

ABOVE With plumage like tree-bark, a Tawny Frogmouth, *Podargus strigoides*, roosts inconspicuously during the day in Queensland.

1890 from one of the many islands of the Solomon Islands group in the Pacific, east of Papua New Guinea. It was not until more than a century later, in 2007, that researchers recognised that it was sufficiently distinctive to deserve a genus of its own. It was originally misclassified as a subspecies of the Marbled Frogmouth, but then, after three more specimens had been obtained and sent to the Natural History Museum at Tring, England, it was realised in 1901 that it was a new species, and given the name *Podargus inexpectatus*. After an expedition by the Florida Museum of Natural History collected a new specimen in 1998, analysis of its DNA and morphology showed it to warrant placement in a new genus. Distinctive features include having only eight tail feathers rather than the 10 or 12 of other frogmouths, and much coarser feathers, reducing the flying ability of this isolated island species. Although new species of birds are still being identified (typically at the rate of a few per year worldwide), discovery of a new genus is far more of a rare event (fewer than one genus per year).

All frogmouths have intricately patterned plumage in various combinations of brown, buff, rufous, grey or whitish, often mottled, streaked or barred that camouflage them superbly against tree bark, lichen and foliage during the daytime when they roost on a perch, typically a branch high up in a tree, when they appear like a snag. In some species, the sexes differ, with females generally browner or brighter and with less cryptic countershading, probably because males tend to take the daytime shift when incubating, when the best possible camouflage is more important. In some species, there are considerable differences in plumage colour between different races, and sometimes within a race; this may involve a rufous form and a greyer form or a mottled one or a black-and-white one, and sometimes there are also intermediates.

POTOOS Nyctibiidae

GENERA: 1 **SPECIES:** 7

LENGTH: 21–55 cm (8–21.5 in)

WEIGHT: 46—620 g (1.6–21.9 oz)

RANGE AND HABITAT: tropics of Central and South America and the Caribbean; all but one species in lowland forest; the Andean Potoo, *Nyctibius maculosus*, in Andean cloud forest at altitudes up to 2,800 m (9,200 ft)

SOCIAL BEHAVIOUR: usually solitary; monogamous, probably for many years, and territorial

NEST: none; egg laid in a crevice on top of a bare branch

EGGS: 1, white

INCUBATION: typically probably 28 days or longer

FLEDGING PERIOD: about 56 days

FOOD: large insects, including moths, beetles, grasshoppers, winged ants and termites; the Great Potoo may sometimes take bats

VOICE: song of clear, mournful whistles, croaks or grunts, uttered at night

MIGRATION: sedentary

CONSERVATION STATUS: none threatened

No other birds are better camouflaged from predators than the potoos: it is possible to walk past a tree, stump or log on which a potoo is perched bolt upright at its daytime roost many times and never see it unless one is told it is there. This is due not only to its plumage, beautifully patterned in browns and greys to mimic tree bark and lichen, but also to its ability to 'freeze' for very long periods when it detects approaching danger – it points its head and bill skywards, so that it looks just like a snag or other extension from the branch or other perch on which it rests, barely moving all day. Potoos rely so much on their camouflage for defence that they have been captured by people approaching and reaching out with their hands. Another remarkable adaptation is that there are two or three small notches in each of its upper eyelids, so that although these are closed, avoiding the risk of the eyes being spotted, it can peep through the slits at the intruder.

The seven species, all classified in the single genus *Nyctibius* inhabit a variety of tropical forest habitats in Central and South America, with two species in the Caribbean. They range in size from the thrush-sized Rufous Potoo, *N. bracteatus*, of lowland Amazonia to the crow-sized Great Potoo, *N. grandis*, widespread from extreme southern Mexico to northern Paraguay and

ABOVE Resembling a broken section of a tree stump, a Common Potoo, *Nyctibius griseus*, remains immobile near Iquitos, Peru.

southeast Brazil. They all have a disproportionately big head. The long wings and tail relative to the small, slender, lightweight body permit them to be very agile and buoyant in the air, able to catch flying insects in twilight or at night even in dense forest without touching the foliage or making a sound. Unlike nightjars, which hawk over wide areas for their aerial insect prey, potoos usually hunt from one or more favoured perches, sallying out to snatch their prey and then returning to the perch. The eyes are huge and because they bulge outwards and upwards give the bird a very wide field of view so that it doesn't need to turn its head, which would reveal its position when it is 'freezing'. Although the head is large, a potoo's brain is remarkably small, only the size of a peanut in the smaller species. The bill is short and slender but has the very wide gape typical of the caprimugiform order;

its upper mandible is strongly hooked and bears a toothlike projection unique among the order, which may help its owner grasp or break the wings of large insect prey. Potoos lack the rictal bristles at the edges of the mouth, found in nightjars and some other caprimulgiforms, but do have thin bristles emerging from the loral region between the base of the bill and the eyes.

The loud wailing calls that emanate from these strange-looking crepuscular and nocturnal birds can alarm the unwary traveller, and (as with owls in many cultures), it is hardly surprising that they were thought by natives of the Caribbean and tropical America to be omens of disaster.

NIGHTJARS Caprimulgidae

GENERA: 20   **SPECIES:** 92

LENGTH: 15–40 cm (6–16 in); species with long tail streamers up to about 1 m (3.2 ft)

WEIGHT: 28–155 g (1–5.5 oz)

RANGE AND HABITAT: worldwide apart from the far north, Antarctica, largest deserts and some islands, including New Zealand and Tasmania; the great majority are residents in the tropics and subtropics, although some species are summer visitors to temperate regions; most species prefer semi-open habitats with trees, shrubs and ground cover, but the family as a whole ranges from deserts and high mountains to dense rainforests

SOCIAL BEHAVIOUR: mostly solitary (although some migratory species roost semi-communally locally in their winter range); most are monogamous (although the two *Macrodipteryx* species from Africa and the two species of *Uropsalis* from South America are polygynous, with males displaying at leks) and territorial (a few are sometimes semi-colonial or even colonial)

NEST: none built, the female laying her egg(s) among dead leaves or on bare soil, sand, gravel or rocks (or in three species, one habitually, in a tree)

EGGS: 1–2 (occasionally 3 or 4), ground colour whitish (sometimes pinkish or brownish in some species), with an intricate pattern of darker markings

INCUBATION: typically 16–22 days

FLEDGING PERIOD: 16–28 days

FOOD: winged insects caught in the air, sometimes insects taken from vegetation or branches or even from the ground; there have been a few incidences of other prey such as small vertebrates

VOICE: contact calls include various croaking, twittering, chattering or whistling sounds; in many species, male song is a series of whistling notes; in others it is made up of purring, bubbling, trilling or twittering as well as mechanical clapping or booming sounds caused by the bird clapping its wings together in flight

MIGRATION: some northern temperate zone species are long-distance migrants to warmer areas in the southern hemisphere winter; many other members of the family make shorter migrations; some tropical and subtropical species make local migrations, a few make altitudinal ones or are nomadic, and a few are sedentary

CONSERVATION STATUS: two species, the Jamaican Pauraque, *Siphonorhis americana*, and the Silver Nightjar, *Eurostopodus exul*, are Critically Endangered (Possibly Extinct); three species, the Puerto Rican Nightjar, *Antrostomus noctitherus*, the Itombwe Nightjar, *Caprimulgus prigoginei*, and the White-winged Nightjar, *Eleothreptus candicans*, are Endangered; three species, Heinrich's Nightjar, *Eurostopodus diabolicus*, Bonaparte's Nightjar, *C. concretus*, and the Nechisar Nightjar, *C. solala*, are Vulnerable; five species are Near Threatened

ABOVE This male Swallow-tailed Nightjar, *Uropsalis segmentata*, at his roost in Ecuador will shed his long streamers after the breeding season.

Constituting the largest family by far in the caprimulgiform order, the members of the Caprimulgidae are small to medium-sized aerial insect eaters. They are all large-headed with a neck that appears very short. The bill is tiny but the gape very wide, as evidenced when they open it to reveal an enormous mouth, during crepuscular or night-time feeding flights to trap insects in mid-air, or in hot weather when they need to cool down, by gaping and fluttering the throat area. In most species, the bill is fringed by very long, stiff rictal bristles. They have a specialised lower jaw with a spreading mechanism that allows it to open horizontally as well as vertically.

Although, like swifts (Family Apodidae, see p. 48) they have short legs and very small, weak feet, nightjars and nighthawks are able to walk fairly well. All species have partly webbed toes, and the middle toe has a long claw that is pectinated (comblike) and used to preen the feathers. It may be important in removing parasites from the feathers or in cleaning or straightening the rictal bristles, if insect parts are trapped in them. Although almost all species nest on the ground and many roost there too, many perch on tree branches, often aligned along the length of the branch, in contrast to the crosswise posture of most birds.

Most species have long, narrow wings with fairly pointed tips, although some, such as the poorwills of the New World, have somewhat shorter, broader, rather rounder wings. Although a few have a rather short tail, those of most species are long and highly mobile, combining with the large wing area relative to body weight to give these superb flyers great control and manoeuvrability. Males of seven nightjar species have elongated wing or tail feathers that give them a bizarre appearance, especially in flight. Two African species, the Standard-winged Nightjar, *Caprimulgus longipennis*, and Pennant-winged Nightjar, *C. vexillarius*, have extremely elongated second innermost primary wing feathers. Those of the former are bare for about two-thirds of their total length of 45–54 cm (18–21 in), the last third of each feather having a broad web, so that they resemble wires ending in flags. When on the ground, the bird holds them at right angles to its body, but when it performs a slow, undulating courtship display flight along with other males at a lek to impress watching females, the 'standards' are borne aloft as the male circles round, quivering his wings so that the standards tremble in time with them. The male Pennant-winged Nightjar's accoutrements may grow even longer: a pair of largely whitish pennants that trail behind for 48–78 cm (19–31 in). He has both a flight display, when he resembles a giant swallowtail butterfly, and a perched performance. After the breeding season, the elongated feathers are lost. In five South American species, it is the tail feathers that are dramatically elongated in different ways, as suggested by their names: Ladder-tailed Nightjar, *Hydropsalis climacocerca*, Scissor-tailed Nightjar, *H. torquata*, Swallow-tailed Nightjar, *Uropsalis segmentata*, Lyre-tailed Nightjar, *U. lyra*, and Long-trained Nightjar, *Macropsalis forcipata*.

Nightjar plumage is highly cryptic. In most species the upperparts and breast feature an intricate mixture of browns, greys, rufous, cinnamon and buff, with dark brown or blackish streaks, spots or fine wavy barring (vermiculations). The underparts, normally visible only in flight, are off-white or pale buff with brown bars. Like the plumage, the eggs are subtly camouflaged, with their complex patterns of spots, blotches and scrawls in various colours – blackish, greyish, brownish, reddish or lilac. Apart from being distinguished by the large white spots on their wings, tail and throat, males of most species are very similar to females, and in some species, females, too, have similar white markings. These are important in courtship or aggressive

ABOVE A male European Nightjar, *Caprimulgus europaeus*, distinguished by his white wing and tail spots makes a display flight.

flight displays and defence or distraction displays at the nest site, and show up well in dim light.

Many species hunt in much the same way as flycatchers, by launching themselves from a perch such as a tree branch to snap up an insect in mid-air and then return to the perch. Others hawk for insects in sustained flight like swifts or swallows, actively targeting their prey and often twisting and turning in pursuit, rather than trawling with the bill open. Some species use both perch-and-sally hunting and hawking at different times and for different prey. The biggest of the North American nightjars, Chuck-will's-widow, *Antrostomus carolinensis*, occasionally scoops up small birds such as hummingbirds, swallows, wood-warblers and American sparrows in its capacious mouth.

Although most species are largely silent for much of the year, all are more vocal during the early stages of the breeding season. The European Nightjar, *C. europaeus,* is well known for the remarkable churring song, sounding rather like a distant two-stroke motorbike, which the male utters for hours on end with only brief pauses, from dusk onwards. It has a ventriloquial quality and rises and falls in pitch; these qualities may be linked to the bird's breathing rhythm. A few African and Asian species have similar songs. By contrast, males of most species advertise their presence by very different whistling, knocking, high-pitched twittering or bubbling sounds. The whistlers include the Eastern and Mexican Whip-poor-wills, *Antrostomus vociferus* and *A. arizonae*, and Chuck-will's-widow, *A. carolinensis*, whose English names are an approximation of their songs; the name of the Common Pauraque, *Nyctidromus albicollis*, is another example of such onomatopoeia, in this case in

Spanish, from a common Mexican name for the bird. The Common Nighthawk, *Chordeiles minor*, has a distinctive nasal 'peent' song. Flight calls, too, are varied, and some species also make clapping, booming or other sounds with their wings. Another, very different, use of sound is when a nightjar faces some immediate threat, such as an attack by a predator or being handled by a human. At such times, the bird will open its huge gape to reveal its interior (conspicuously pink or red in many species) and emit a loud, harsh, hissing sound that rises in volume and pitch.

There are two subfamilies. The Eurostopodinae are the eared nightjars, with eight species in two genera. There are two species of *Eurostopodus* in New Guinea, two in Australia and one (possibly extinct) in New Caledonia, and three species of *Lyncornis* in Southern Asia. The bigger subfamily by far is the Caprimulginae (84 species in 17 genera). This is the group with the widest distribution, in much of Europe, Africa, Asia and the New World; moreover, a single race, schlegelii, of one species, the Large-tailed Nightjar, *Caprimulgus macrurus*, extends the subfamily's range to New Guinea and Australia.

The Eurostopodinae include some of the larger members of the family: the Great Eared Nightjar, *Lyncornis macrotis*, is the bulkiest of all nightjars, with some individuals exceeding 150 g (5.3 oz), and can be as much as 40 cm (15.75 in) long. The name 'eared nightjars' for this subfamily is derived from the elongated earlike feathers extending from the rear crown of the two Asian species, the Malaysian Eared Nightjar, *L. temminckii*, and the Great Eared Nightjar. Eared nightjars lack the rictal bristles that fringe the gape of most other members of this family.

A distinctive exclusively New World subgroup of the subfamily Caprimulginae are the nighthawks, with 10 species in four genera. They probably originated in South America and spread northward, with two species breeding in North America. They are generally distinguished by having particularly long, pointed wings and a rather short, square-ended tail; an exception is a South American species, the Nacunda Nighthawk, *Chordeiles nacunda*, which has much broader, rounded wings. Unlike most other members of the subfamily Caprimulginae, they do not have white tail markings, and few have white spots on the outer wings. There are also differences in the structure of the palate, and (like the eared nightjars) most species lack prominent rictal bristles. Nighthawks fly fast and erratically as they hawk for insects, and often do so for long periods. Unlike other nightjars, most nighthawk species start hunting in the late afternoon. Each species favours a particular height and has a characteristic flight pattern. They may roost on or near the ground like the rest of the family, but sometimes do so quite high up in trees. The Common Nighthawk, a widespread and common breeding bird in North America, has adapted to many habitats altered by humans, including towns and cities, and often roosts and breeds on gravel rooftops. The mainly Neotropical Lesser Nighthawk, *C. acutipennis*, is restricted to southwestern USA.

The rest of the Caprimulginae have well-developed, long rictal bristles and are widespread across temperate and tropical regions of the world. The sole member of the genus *Nyctidromus* is the Common Pauraque, *N. albicollis*, whose extensive range, from northern Argentina north through South and Central America

into Mexico just extends to southern Texas, is often detected by its golden-red eyeshine as it waits on the warm surface of roads to fly out and catch moths and other insects. There are two other species of pauraque, both in the genus *Siphonorhis*, and both Caribbean; the Jamaican Pauraque, *S. americana*, may be extinct. Five New World species are known as poorwills. The Common Poorwill, *Phalaenoptilus nuttallii*, is a widespread bird of western Canada, the USA and northern Mexico; it has the distinction of being the only bird to hibernate. The four other poorwills, in the genus *Nyctiphrynus*, are variously found in Mexico, Central America and South America.

Apart from the pauraques and poorwills, the small and distinctive Brown Nightjar, *Veles binotatus*, found in a few rainforests of west and central Africa, the Sickle-winged Nightjar, *Eleothreptus anomalus* of South Africa, and the five genera of long-tailed or long-winged species mentioned above, the rest of the subfamily were all traditionally regarded as members of the very large genus *Caprimulgus*. However, the genetic differences between some appeared too great to justify inclusion in the same genus, and some were thus moved to new genera, or to some of the other genera mentioned above. Africa has the greatest number of breeding species, followed by Asia and South America. *Caprimulgus* is still the most speciose and widespread genus, with 36 species, followed by the exclusively New World Antrostomus, with 11 species.

The name of the genus *Caprimulgus* (and of the Family Caprimulgidae, and Order Caprimulgiformes) comes from the Latin word meaning 'goatsucker', which was one of several old English names for these formerly little-known and enigmatic birds, often applied to the one of the best-known members of the family, the European Nightjar, *C. europaeus*. It derives from an ancient superstition, persisting for centuries since the days of Aristotle, that when nightjars flew near or landed next to goats (or other grazing mammals), they were trying to suck the mammals' milk. There is no evidence whatsoever for this, and when these mysterious nocturnal birds are seen among the herds, they are most likely feeding on moths, beetles or other flying insects attracted by the animals' dung or the lights of their herders.

ABOVE The only thing that gave away the position of this Common Pauraque, *Nyctidromus albicollis*, among leaves in Panama was its eye.

OWLET-NIGHTJARS Aegothelidae

GENERA: 1   **SPECIES:** 11

LENGTH: 18–30 cm (7–12 in)

WEIGHT: 29–85 g (1–3 oz)

RANGE AND HABITAT: Australasia; mostly in lowland primary tropical forests; the Australian Owlet-nightjar is also found in open woodlands, *Eucalyptus* and *Acacia* scrub, and especially in sclerophyll forests, tropical woodland and taller, mallee scrub; rarely in rainforests

SOCIAL BEHAVIOUR: usually seen alone, although in the Australian Owlet-nightjar, *Aegotheles cristatus*, at least, pairs roost close together and usually mate for life, living in well-spaced territories

NEST: detailed information only for the Australian Owlet-nightjar; usually nests in a tree hole, but sometimes uses a fallen log, riverbank burrow, a fence-post or other site; lays eggs on a mound of bark fragments or fresh leaves

EGGS: 2–5, usually 3 or 4, white

INCUBATION: 25–27 days

FLEDGING PERIOD: 21–32 days

FOOD: mainly insects, in flight and from foliage, branches or the ground; also some other invertebrates (spiders and millipedes taken by the Australian Owlet-nightjar)

VOICE: rattling, trilling or churring songs; whistling notes in the Mountain Owlet-nightjar, *A. albertisi*, and loud screaming and cackling sounds in the Moluccan Owlet-nightjar, *Euaegotheles crinifrons*

MIGRATION: all species are completely sedentary

CONSERVATION STATUS: one species, the New Caledonian Owlet-nightjar, *A. savesi*, is Critically Endangered

ABOVE Little is known about the Barred Owlet-nightjar of New Guinea, *Aegotheles bennettii*. This one is in its tree roost, in Varirata National Park.

The common name of this small family of nocturnal insect eaters suggests that they may be related to small owls as well as nightjars. They do look more owl-like than other members of the Order Caprimulgiformes, and there are various anatomical features that might seem to suggest a possible ancestral link with the owls. Also, they adopt an upright, owl-like posture when perched, and nest in tree holes or rotted tree stumps rather than on the ground. Nevertheless, despite earlier suggestions of an ancestral link with owls from the DNA hybridization studies of Sibley and Ahlquist, the recent molecular data do not bear out any such relationship. Some recent research indicates that they may not be as closely related to the rest of the Caprimulgiformes as they have appeared to be and may be closer to the swifts and hummingbirds; they might even share a common ancestor.

Owlet-nightjars are today exclusively Australasian, with the overall range of the family extending from the islands of the Moluccas, in eastern Indonesia, to New Guinea, the Solomon Islands and Australia, including Tasmania. In New Zealand, bones of a large, long-extinct species are known from both North and South Islands and this may have survived until as recently as the twelfth century AD. Fossilized remains that may possibly be those of an owlet-nightjar were discovered in 1982 in France, dating back to Upper Eocene to Upper Oligocene times, about 40 million to 30 million years ago.

The nine present-day species, all in the genus *Aegotheles*, range in size from that of a small thrush to a small pigeon. They have a large head with very big, rounded, prominent eyes. The bill is very short and decurved, with a very wide gape. The legs and feet are larger and stronger than those of most other Caprimulgiformes, and the claw of the middle toe lacks the comb-like pectination.

All species have facial bristles around the base of the bill and much longer ones on the forehead that extend above the top of the head; these are especially luxurious and whiskery in the aptly named Feline Owlet-nightjar, *Aegotheles insignis*, from the mountains of New Guinea. The wings are more or less rounded, and the tail long. The cryptic plumage is generally brown to rufous or grey, with fine pale or dark barring; the two biggest species have bold white lines or spots. There are differences between subspecies and several species have different colour morphs, some individuals being grey or brown and others rufous.

Strictly nocturnal, owlet-nightjars roost in a concealed site by day: usually in a tree hole, but in some cases among a vine tangle or dense foliage, in a hollow in a termite mound, in a fence post, in a log in the ground, in a crevice in a cliff or earth bank, an abandoned nest of a babbler or in a derelict building.

Owlet-nightjars use various methods for catching their insect prey. The only well-known species, the Australian Owlet-nightjar, hunts mainly from a low perch, from which it may chase moths and other flying insects and snap them up in mid-air; it also gleans various insects from foliage while hovering, and picks insects or other invertebrates, such as spiders, millipedes and earthworms, from the ground, either while hovering, or on foot.

SWIFTS Apodidae

GENERA: 20   **SPECIES:** 99

LENGTH: 9–25 cm (3.5–10 in)

WEIGHT: 5.5–185 g (0.2–6.5 oz)

RANGE AND HABITAT: worldwide, except for far north and south; greatest diversity in tropics and subtropics; very wide ranging, as their hunting 'ground' is the sky and many species travel long distances in search of food, mainly over open habitats but also forests for a few species; need suitable well-concealed nest sites with a clear flight path to the nest

SOCIAL BEHAVIOUR: most species are highly gregarious all year, foraging and roosting in groups; some breed as isolated single pairs, while others form small or large nesting colonies; most of those that have been studied are generally monogamous

NEST: most species build bracket-shaped nests of feathers, plant matter, such as leaves, straw and small twigs, or other material, mainly collected in the air; they use their saliva to glue them together and attach them to the substrate, often the vertical wall of a cliff, tree or rock cavity or other site

EGGS: 1–7, white

INCUBATION: 16–30 days

FLEDGING PERIOD: 28–70 days

FOOD: small insects caught on the wing, also small spiders drifting through the air on silk lines

VOICE: foraging and roosting groups are often noisy, as are pairs and flocks during the breeding season, most species uttering shrill, piercing screams, trills or chattering sounds

MIGRATION: most tropical, subtropical and island species are sedentary; most in temperate regions migrate, in some cases crossing the equator; many species also may move far to avoid bad weather

CONSERVATION STATUS: one species, the Mariana Swiftlet, *Aerodramus bartschi*, is Endangered; three species, the Seychelles Swiftlet, *A. elaphrus*, Schouteden's Swift, *Schoutedenapus schoutedeni*, and the Dark-rumped Swift, *Apus acuticauda*, are Vulnerable; six species, including the Chimney Swift, *Chaetura pelagica*, the Philippine Spinetail, *Mearnsia picina*, and the Waterfall Swift, *Hydrochous gigas*, are Near Threatened

These include the most aerial of all land birds, spending almost all their waking hours on the wing. No other birds are so profoundly adapted for such a lifestyle. The extreme is seen in the best-known species, the Common Swift, *Apus apus*, of Eurasia and North Africa. This remarkable bird not only feeds and drinks exclusively in the air, but also gathers nest material and sometimes mates aerially. Groups of Common Swifts even sleep in the air, by circling up to heights of 1,000–2,000 m (3,300–6,600 ft) or even more, then staying aloft by flying or gliding slowly into the wind, which provides enough lift to maintain their altitude. To cope at high altitudes, they have an extremely high haemoglobin concentration in their blood. Typically, a Common Swift does not come down to roost or nest for an average of 2 years after fledging, and in some cases not for 3 or even 4 years. When roosting terrestrially, as with other swifts, this species does so in the nest or clinging to a vertical surface such as a wall, the inside of a tree hollow or on a tree trunk, or among foliage.

Most species are distinctively and highly aerodynamically shaped, with a smoothly rounded head that merges almost necklessly into the cigar-shaped body. The large eyes are generally deeply recessed into the face, with a ridge of dark, bristly feathers in front that they can move by means of muscles to create a miniature sunshade, helping them to avoid being confused by glare when homing in on prey. The bill is small, very short and weak but broad based, giving the bird a very wide gape, suited for catching flying insects.

Like their relatives the hummingbirds, swifts have tiny feet that are useless for perching or walking. If a swift is grounded, its combination of very long wings and very short feet make it very difficult for it to flap its wings to take off, although – particularly if there is a wind to contribute lift – it is not impossible as is sometimes erroneously thought to be the case. However, swifts' feet are surprisingly strong for their size, and the toes end in well-developed and very sharp claws, both adaptations for clinging securely to vertical or sharply angled surfaces when breeding or roosting.

Again, as with hummingbirds, the wings of swifts are highly specialised, in this case not enabling such tricks as hovering or flying backwards but fast and aerobatic forward flight instead, using a combination of fast beats of their usually stiffly held wings and gliding. The larger species tend to make long glides, while the smallest often have a rather fluttering flight style more like that of some swallows and martins. Swifts are also skilled at taking advantage of winds to augment their flight speed.

A swift's distinctive sickle-shaped wings have a very short arm, formed from the humerus, and the ulna/radius, to which is attached a narrow span of short secondary feathers; the much longer carpus ('hand') bones bear the elongated primaries. Gliding as well as flapping enables the birds to conserve energy, particularly useful when travelling great distances, especially when feeding and migrating. Such wings do not need very large breast muscles to power them. Most of the time, swifts travel at relatively moderate speeds, which as well as saving energy presumably helps facilitate spotting, chasing and catching their diminutive prey. Recent research in Sweden on Common Swifts, using sophisticated methods to make very accurate measurements of their flight speeds, showed that they usually fly at speeds of 36–43 km/h (22–26 mph), whether en route to roost, migrating or flying in a wind tunnel. However, at certain times swifts clearly live up to their collective common name. When engaged in 'screaming party' display flights (when they bunch together to fly fast and often low, uttering screaming calls) birds in the study attained speeds as great as 75 km/h (47 mph). Moreover, one individual clocked a top speed of 116.6 km/h (69.3 mph). This is the highest speed reliably recorded for any bird in self-powered level flight. Remarkably, these swifts reached top speeds of twice the normal speed when making steep climbs. Another swift, the White-throated Needletail, *Hirundapus caudacutus*, is often said to be the fastest of all birds in self-powered level flight at an estimated speed of 169 km/h (105 mph), but this claim is difficult to verify as the methods used to measure it have never been verified. Swifts may be able to switch from a slower,

ABOVE Great Dusky Swifts, *Cypseloides senex*, cling to their roost sites behind a huge wall of water at Igauzu Falls, South America.

energy-saving flight style to very fast flight by sweeping back their wings, rather like variable-sweep-wing fighter planes. Also, each wing appears to operate aerodynamically independently to some degree, which may increase agility.

Swifts fly astonishing distances in a lifetime. Common Swifts not only make a long two-way annual migration between the southern half of Africa and their breeding grounds in Eurasia, but also cover huge distances (as much as 800 km/500 miles a day) when feeding, especially when they have young in the nest and bad weather forces them to search for better feeding conditions.

All members of the family feed on what has been dubbed 'aerial plankton', which includes a variety of different kinds of (mainly small) insects and small or young spiders borne aloft on detached silken strands. They do not simply fly around with their bill open, 'vacuuming' up flying prey, but are selective, targeting and chasing a particular range of prey. At the same time, they are opportunistic, taking advantage of swarms of insects or the emergence of young insects. When feeding, a swift collects insects in an expandable pouch of skin (the sublingual pouch) beneath the tongue at the back of the throat and binds them with its copious saliva into a glutinous mass called a bolus. When this is large enough, the swift will swallow its neatly packaged food, or if it has young in the nest, take it back to regurgitate it into their throats.

The precise range of prey differs between the various species of swifts, as well as varying according to weather and time of year (including whether they have young in the nest to feed). On the whole, the larger the swift species, the bigger the insects they prefer and the fewer they catch in a given time, as researchers can tell by examining and taking apart the boluses. For instance, each bolus of a Common Swift, for instance, contains an average of 300–500 prey

items, while that of the much larger Alpine Swift, *Tachymarptis melba*, typically holds only 156–220.

Most swifts feed mainly at heights of about 50–100 m (165–330 ft) above ground, although weather conditions may drive them lower, and when insects are occasionally concentrated at higher altitudes by turbulence, they may follow them to as high as 1,000 m (3,300 ft) or so. Swifts are generally less manoeuvrable than swallows and martins, and generally they appear to stay in open areas of sky when hunting, avoiding trees and other obstructions. However, some species do feed close to forest canopies, and a few have even been seen taking insects from the foliage.

Like swallows and martins, swifts drink regularly by flying down close to a large or small body of water, and dipping in the lower mandible of the bill to scoop up a mouthful of water. They sometimes take insects as well from the water surface, and can also drink by swallowing raindrops.

There are three subfamilies of swifts. The Cypseloidinae comprise a small group of just two genera of exclusively New World species. They include the Black Swift, *Cypseloides niger*, of western North America, Central America and the Caribbean, which is the only member of the subfamily to occur in the USA and Canada, and the Great Dusky Swift, *C. senex*, a powerful South American bird that is one of three swift species habitually roosting and nesting on sheer cliff faces behind waterfalls, flying through the spray to enter and exit.

The second, major, subfamily, the Apodinae, is divided into three tribes. All but three species in the tribe Collocalini are known as swiftlets. Generally they are divided into two genera, *Collocalia* and *Aerodramus*, although the taxonomy of the swiftlet group is highly contentious; often included with them in a separate genus is a large Southeast Asian waterfall-dwelling species, the Waterfall Swift, *Hydrochous gigas*, and two African species, in the little-known genus *Schoutedenapus*. The 25–30 or so swiftlets include the smallest of all swifts, the Pygmy Swiftlet, *Collocalia troglodytes*, of the Philippines. Its specific name *troglodytes* reflects the roosting and nesting sites used by almost all swiftlets, in caves – although the abundant and widespread Glossy Swiftlet, *Collocalia esculenta*, breeds outside on overhanging rocks, holes in rocks, hollow trees or among tree roots as well as in shallow caves or the mouths of large caves, and this and some other species have also adapted to nesting on buildings or tunnels. Along with the unique, unrelated Oilbird, *Steatornis caripensis*, a relative of the nightjars (see pp. 44–46), swiftlets are the only birds known to use echolocation, which helps them avoid obstacles in the pitch darkness of their breeding caves and navigate back to them on dark nights. In contrast to the ultrasound echolocation clicks of bats, those of the swiftlets are audible to most humans.

The tribe Chaeturini comprises the spinetails, needletails and relatives. There are 11 species of spinetail in five genera, and four species of needletail in a single genus, *Hirundapus*. In contrast to other swifts, which have tails that are notched, forked, square-ended or slightly round-tipped, these have the shafts of their tails (which are often very short) extending beyond the vane to form a row of stiff 'spines' and 'needles'. Like the stiff tail feathers of woodpeckers or treecreepers, they help support the swifts when

ABOVE These Glossy Swiftlets, *Collocalia esculenta*, are nesting inside a dwelling on the island of Cebu in the Philippines.

they land on vertical surfaces. This group includes some very small species but also the largest of all the swifts, two of the four needletails: these are the Brown-backed Needletail, *Hirundapus giganteus*, widespread from India to Southeast Asia, and the Purple Needletail, *H. celebensis*, of Sulawesi and the Philippines, both of which are 25 cm (10 in) long. The remaining 11 species in the Chaeturini all belong to the genus *Chaetura*. They include two North American species, Vaux's Swift, *C. vauxi*, and the well-known Chimney Swift, *C. pelagica*. The southern Canadian and US breeding populations of both migrate south for winter, the former to Mexico and Central America, where several local races also breed, and the latter much farther, to west-central South America.

The third tribe is the Apodini, or typical swifts, comprising 27 species in six genera. It contains small species, such as several species in the major genus *Apus*, including the Little Swift, *A. affinis*, of Africa and Asia, medium-sized ones such as the Common Swift, *A. apus*, and the African Swift, *A. barbatus*, and large ones, such as the two species of *Tachymarptis*, the Alpine Swift, *T. melba* of southern Europe, Africa, Madagascar and parts of southern Asia, and the Mottled Swift, *T. aequatorialis*, of Africa. Other members of this tribe include three mountain-dwelling swifts, *Aeronautes*. The North American White-throated Swift, *A. saxatilis*, has been recorded foraging at up to 4,270 m (14,000 ft) in Yosemite National Park, California. Almost all the New World palm swifts *Tachornis* and the African and Asian palm swifts *Cypsiurus* have long, deeply forked tails, as do the swallow-tailed swifts, *Panyptila*.

Swift plumage is usually dull, dark brownish or blackish, paler or mainly white below, or with white patches or a white rump. Many species have a distinct bluish, purplish or greenish gloss to the dark areas. Brighter areas of plumage are found in two Neotropical species, the Chestnut-collared Swift, *Streptoprocne rutila*, and the Tepui Swift, *S. phelpsi*, which both have a bright chestnut throat and collar, while the Purple Needletail lives up

to its common name by having a particularly bright gloss on its upper body.

Many swifts build self-supporting, bracket-shaped nests, often attached to a vertical surface. They use their own saliva to glue together nest materials. These are typically straw, seeds, feathers, moss and other aerial debris, but some species, such as the Chimney Swift, use twigs that they break off from trees in flight. Swifts also use their sticky saliva to fix the nest firmly to such sites as a crevice in a rock face, a hollow or hole in a tree, beneath the eaves of a building or on other artificial site. In much of Europe, Common Swifts nowadays breed almost exclusively in holes and hollows in buildings and other structures, or in nest boxes. Hollow 'swift bricks' are sometimes included in new buildings that are otherwise devoid of suitable nesting holes for the birds. Chimney Swifts, too, have almost entirely forsaken natural nest sites such as tree holes and hollows for the artificial structures from which the species acquired its common name, whereas its close relative Vaux's Swift still prefers traditional tree hollow sites to chimneys.

Swift salivary glands grow especially large (up to 10 or more times bigger than normal) during the nest-building period to produce the large amounts of saliva required for this purpose. Swiftlets build their nests largely of saliva, mixed with a few of their own feathers, or entirely of saliva. The nests of several species, especially the Edible-nest Swiftlet, *Aerodramus fuciphagus*, and the Black-nest Swiftlet, *A. maximus,* are highly valued in Chinese cuisine as the principal ingredient of bird's nest soup, and form the basis of a multi-million dollar industry. These small birds probably generate more profit than any other wild bird. In 2011, a bowl of authentic bird's nest soup might cost the diner as much as US$100, with a wholesale price of the processed nests from US$2,000 up to US$15,000 per kilogram. It is believed to bring great health benefits to those who can afford to eat it, including an increase in libido and a strengthening of the immune system. The nests originally came mainly from vast limestone caves in Sarawak on the island of Borneo. Sited high up on the towering cave walls, they are still traditionally harvested by skilled local men using a system of bamboo poles lashed together and wedged against the cave roof. Nests are also collected from other countries, including Malaysia, Vietnam and Thailand, and a recent development has been a huge increase in the provision of very large artificial nest sites, often converted from shops, blocks of apartments and other buildings into swiftlet 'farms'.

Some other swift species also build unusual nests. The two species of swallow-tailed swift, *Panyptila*, make very long tube-shaped nests on vertical surfaces that may be completely attached or free-hanging. They make these striking nests of a felt-like mixture of plant down and saliva. The palm swifts (three New World *Tachornis* species, two Old World *Cypsiurus* species, one in Africa and one in southern Asia) are so called because they attach their small cup-shaped nests, made of plant down and feathers mixed with sticky saliva, to the outward-facing surfaces of palm fronds. The *Cypsiurus* palm swifts are not always tied to palms, having adapted in places to nesting on artificial structures, such as thatched roofs of houses. The African Palm Swift, *C. parvus*, (and perhaps the Fork-tailed Palm Swift, *Tachornis squamata*, too) glue the eggs to the nest using their saliva.

The *Cypseloides* species of the New World, such as the Black Swift of North and Central America and the Caribbean, are unusual in not employing saliva for nest building, using mud instead to bind together the moss, twigs and even pebbles they use in their construction. The Old World needletails, too, probably build nests without saliva, and along with two tropical American *Streptoprocne* species, the White-collared Swift, *S. zonaris*, and White-naped Swift, *S. semicollaris*, often build no nest at all, using a simple scrape in the cave, tree hole or other hidden nest site as a repository for their eggs.

Particularly reptilian looking, the naked swift nestlings are often very fat when food supplies are good. However, those of temperate zone species such as the Common Swift may receive little food if the weather is bad. Despite this, they can survive surprisingly long periods of semi-starvation, up to several weeks on end. Their weight may fall by half, but they can cope by becoming torpid (as can adult White-throated Swifts and perhaps the adults of some other species too).

The third, very small, subfamily is that of the treeswifts (Hemiprocninae) (just four species in a single genus, *Hemiprocne*) is largely restricted to southern Asia, with just the largest species, the Moustached Treeswift, *H. mystacea*, extending the family's range to the Moluccas, New Guinea and the Solomon Islands. The three others are the Crested Treeswift, *H. coronata*, which occurs from India and Sri Lanka east to south-central China, southwest Thailand and Indochina, and the very similar Grey-rumped Treeswift, *H. longipennis* (once regarded by some ornithologists as conspecific with the former species), whose range is farther south, from southern Myanmar to Borneo, Java and nearby islands, and Sulawesi. The much smaller Whiskered Treeswift, *H. comata*, is found in Malaysia, Sumatra, Borneo and the Philippines.

The treeswifts are often placed in a family of their own, the Hemiprocnidae. Even so, they are clearly most closely related to typical swifts (Family Apodidae), and thus are here included within them as a subfamily. They share a morphology and lifestyle in some ways similar to those of swallows (Family Hirundinidae), (by a process of convergent evolution – in which unrelated groups have evolved similar adaptations to a particular lifestyle) and in others to those of swifts. With their long, sickle-shaped wings on a short arm and long hand, the tiny bill with a very broad gape and proportionately large eyes fronted by short bristles, treeswifts resemble typical swifts in shape, but like some of the swallows all four species have very long and deeply forked tails; depending on species, the forking extends for 45–70% of the length of the tail – far greater than in any swift, and giving it a very distinctive silhouette that helps identify these birds as treeswifts at long range. When perched, the long outer tail streamers are often pressed tightly together, forming a long spike extending beyond the crossed wingtips. In flight, the fork is opened for manoeuvring when gliding and soaring, producing a silhouette reminiscent of some long-tailed swallows. Treeswifts are very fast fliers, and glide or soar with ease.

Even so, compared with typical swifts (subfamily Apodinae) treeswifts are less aerial. Their legs are short but their feet are less stout and have a non-reversible hind toe, which enables them to

ABOVE A Moustached Treeswift, *Hemiprocne mystacea*, scans for flying insect prey from a perch in New Guinea.

grasp a perch strongly, unlike swifts. They often perch upright on a tree branch or overhead wire, like swallows. Whiskered Treeswifts usually use these as lookout posts as they scan for insects flying past or on nearby foliage, then sally out briefly to catch their prey. The three other species most often hunt for flying insects swallow-style in long flights with much circling and gliding above the tree canopy in a forest or over more open terrain.

These are very handsome birds, with softer plumage than the typical swifts that is much more colourful and boldly patterned. In all but the Whiskered Treeswift, the head and body are largely grey (blue-grey in the Moustached Treeswift), while all have very dark glossy green or blue on the head and wings. The Crested and Grey-rumped Treeswifts have a prominent, dark greenish-blue, narrow fan-shaped crest extending vertically from the forecrown, while the other two species have only small, insignificant crests. The sexes of Crested, Grey-rumped and Whiskered Treeswifts differ in that males have contrasting chestnut ear-coverts, while there is little difference in appearance between male and female Moustached Treeswifts. Both sexes of Whiskered and Moustached species have a striking head pattern, with a bold white stripe above and below each eye; they also have white tertial patches on the wings.

HUMMINGBIRDS Trochilidae

GENERA: 105   **SPECIES:** 338

LENGTH: 5–22 cm (2–8.7 in)

WEIGHT: 1.6–21 g (0.05–0.7oz)

WORLD RANGE: the New World, from southern Alaska and Canada south through North, Central and South America to as far south as Tierra del Fuego; including the Caribbean; the greatest diversity is in parts of tropical South America, especially the Andean regions near the equator

HABITAT: a wide range of habitats as long as they provide sufficient flowering plants of the right kind for nectar feeding, from sea-level mangroves and tropical forests of various kinds to arid regions, high-altitude cloud forests and exposed high mountains (up to over 4,000 m/13,000 ft in the Andes)

SOCIAL BEHAVIOUR: usually solitary; except for hermits, both sexes defend nectar sources of flowering trees and shrubs against competitors; polygynous, males territorial, each mating with several females each season; male hermits display communally at leks to attract females (only a few typical hummingbirds are lek breeders)

NEST: almost all species in the subfamily Trochilinae build a small open cup nest, usually of vegetable down and animal hairs, camouflaged with moss, lichens or other material, and bound together and fixed to the support, typically a twig or small branch, with spiders' webs; sylphs *Aglaiocercus* build domed nests, and a few trochiline species nesting on rock faces, caves or buildings glue their thick-walled, pendant nests to the walls; hermits (subfamily Phaethornithinae) construct hanging, cone-shaped nests attached to the undersides of palm fronds or other vegetation

EGGS: 2 (rarely 1), white

INCUBATION: 14–23 days

FLEDGING PERIOD: 23–40 days

FOOD: a major part of the diet is nectar; many species also supplement this with small insects and spiders, and in those most studied, the nestlings are often fed almost exclusively on invertebrates

VOICE: calls are typically high-pitched chirps, squeaks, whistles and chattering or buzzy notes; these kind of sounds also make up territorial songs, but some species have much more melodious warbling songs; some make non-vocal sounds using specialised wing or tail feathers

MIGRATION: most species are sedentary; many northern hemisphere species are true migrants, some travelling great distances; a few species in the far south of South America migrate northwards; some Andean species make altitudinal migrations

CONSERVATION STATUS: two species, Brace's Emerald, *Chlorostilbon bracei*, and the Caribbean Emerald, *C. elegans*, are Extinct; one species, the Turquoise-throated Puffleg, *Eriocnemis godini*, is Critically Endangered (possibly Extinct); six species, the Gorgeted Puffleg, *E. isabellae*, Colourful Puffleg, *E. mirabilis*, Black-breasted Puffleg, *E. nigrivestis*, Sapphire-bellied Hummingbird, *Lepidopyga lilliae*, Short-crested Coquette, *Lophornis brachylophus*, and Juan Fernandez Firecrown, *Sephanoides fernandensis*, are Critically Endangered; 17 species, including the Hook-billed Hermit, *Glaucis dohrnii*, Honduran Emerald, *Amazilia luciae*, Venezuelan Sylph, *Aglaiocercus berlepschi*, Santa Marta Sabrewing, *Campylopterus phainopeplus*, Purple-backed Sunbeam, *Aglaeactis aliciae*, Royal Sunangel, *Heliangelus regalis*, and Marvellous Spatuletail, *Loddigesia mirabilis*, are Endangered; eight species, including the Blossomcrown, *Anthocephala floriceps*, Black Inca, *Coeligena prunellei*, Glow-throated Hummingbird, *Selasphorus ardens*, and Mexican Woodnymph, *Thalanuria ridgwayi*, are Vulnerable; and 16 species are Near Threatened

Almost all of the members of this large family of nectar-feeding birds (one of the largest of all in the New World) are very small and (especially the males) brilliantly plumaged. Hummingbirds are renowned for their beauty and for their astonishing and unique prowess in the air. They are able to hover in one position for long periods, to fly upside down and even backwards as well as forwards. They are the only birds able to hover in completely still air (other hoverers fly into the wind to remain stationary) and the only birds able to fly backwards (as opposed to brief fluttering movements in that direction by other birds). They can achieve such feats not only because of the structure of the wing, shared with the swifts, but also because of their unique flight action, involving rotary figure-of-eight movements made possible by the uniquely flexible shoulder joint. The family's vernacular name refers to the humming sound produced by the rapidly whirring wings. Their ability to hover for sustained periods and adjust their position in front of flowers with great precision is an adaptation to nectar feeding.

The family includes the world's smallest birds, the Bee Hummingbird, *Mellisuga helenae*, of Cuba and the slightly larger Reddish Hermit, *Phaethornis ruber*, of Guyana and Brazil. Both weigh less than 2 g (0.07 oz), making them not only the lightest birds but also the smallest of all warm-blooded animals. They are no larger than big species of bumblebees, and smaller than some insects with which they share the air. Most species measure just 6–12 cm (2.4–4.7 in) from bill-tip to tail-tip and many have a body length of only 5 cm (2 in) or less; weights

ABOVE This female Magnificent Hummingbird, *Eugenes fulgens*, lacks the iridescent purple crown and green throat patch of the male.

typically range from 2.5 g (0.09 oz) to 10 g (0.35 oz). In some cases, where the overall length is greater, it includes a long bill or tail, or both. The largest species is the Giant Hummingbird, *Patagonia gigas*, and even this is a giant only in relative terms, with a length of 20–22 cm (8–8.75 in), including a long bill and long forked tail, and a weight of 18.5–22 g (0.65–0.78 oz).

Hummingbirds have an extraordinarily high metabolic rate, higher than that of any other animals apart from insects. Their demand for oxygen is the highest found in any vertebrates, and typically they take 300 breaths per minute at rest (about 10 times the rate measured in a pigeon), and as many as 500 when hovering, when the flight muscles make huge oxygen demands. For comparison, a human breathes about 14–18 times a minute. A hummingbird's heart represents 2–5% of its body mass about twice the proportion in most birds, and five times that in a human. The heart rate of some hummingbirds has been measured beating at a rate of 500–600 times while the bird is at rest, and at over 1,000 beats per minute during territorial chases between rivals. Although some of the larger species have wingbeat frequencies of just 20 to 30 per second, many small species beat their wings at the rate of up to 80 times per second, and in some this can rise briefly to as much as 100 beats per second during aerial courtship or aggressive displays. Due to the extremely high energy demands resulting from flight, hummingbirds typically spend only about 20% of their waking time in the air. During the remaining 70–80% they are resting, digesting food, preening, singing or sunbathing while perched.

To maintain their high-energy lives, hummingbirds must eat up to 12 times their body weight each day. They live on a knife-edge, potentially rarely more than hours from starvation. This necessitates taking regular small nectar meals throughout the day, often every 10–15 minutes or so, and typically by visiting hundreds of flowers. This enables them to store sufficient energy to survive for the night without feeding – unless it is cold, when their small size means they risk losing heat quickly. To cope with this, during cooler nights and at high altitudes, many species can conserve energy by greatly reducing their metabolic rate, and become torpid.

Despite their high-octane lifestyles, hummingbirds have surprisingly long lifespans for such small birds. The average lifespan in the wild appears to be about 5–8 years, and some individuals have been recorded reaching 11 or 12. Captive birds attain an average age of 10 years, with the record being 17 years.

Hummingbirds are traditionally divided into two subfamilies. By far the smaller of the two is the subfamily Phaethornithinae, comprising the 34 species of hermits, in six genera. Most have 'hermit' as part of their name (given them because they are more retiring and spend much time among dense vegetation), but two (in the genus *Threnetes*) are known as barbthroats (from the spiky feathers on their throat) and two (in the genus *Eutoxeres*) with strongly downcurved bills are called sicklebills. The far larger subfamily Trochilinae contains the 297 species of typical hummingbirds, in 98 genera. A recent, more comprehensive examination of molecular data suggests there might be further subdivision of the Trochilinae. In this scheme, one subfamily, the Florisuginae, containing just four species in two genera, the two species of topaz, *Topaz*, and two jacobins, *Florisuga*, is considered

ABOVE A Snowy-bellied Hummingbird, *Amazilia edward*. This is a species in which the sexes look very similar.

the basal group of the family, which split off first from the rest of the family. The 7 species of mango, *Anthracocorax*, 4 violetears, *Colibri*, 2 lancebills, *Doryfera*, and relatives are given a new subfamily, the Polytminae, containing a total of 12 genera and 27 species. The unusually sized and dull-plumaged Giant Hummingbird is given a subfamily of its own, Patagoninae. The 9 sunangels, *Heliangelus*, 10 coquettes, *Lophornis*, 9 metaltails, *Metallura*, 14 pufflegs, *Haplophaedia*, Marvellous Spatuletail, *Lodigesis mirabilis*, 11 incas and starfontlets, *Coeligena*, Sword-billed Hummingbird, *Ensifera ensifera*, and relatives are placed in a subfamily Lesbiinae, containing a total of 18 genera and 61 species. All the rest – 42 genera and 59 species – are in the smaller but still largest subfamily Trochilinae, which includes the 18 species of emerald, *Chlorostilbon* (two of which are extinct), 11 species of sabrewing, *Campylopyterus*, five species of woodnymph, *Thalurania*, 29 variously named species in the large genus *Amazilia*, the Bee Hummingbird, *Mellisuga helenae*, and several species breeding in the USA and Canada, including the Ruby-throated Hummingbird, *Archilochus colubris*, Black-chinned Hummingbird, *A. alexandri*, Anna's Hummingbird, *Calypte anna*, Rufous Hummingbird, *Selasphorus rufus*, and Allen's Hummingbird, *S. sasin*.

Living in dim light and being non-territorial, the hermits and relatives have relatively dull plumage in shades of brown, rufous or grey, and with bronze or green iridescence usually only on the upperparts. By contrast, in the rest of the family, males typically have bright plumage with iridescent green, blue, purple, red or bronze feathers that are transformed from their plain, dark appearance in shade to a gem-like brilliance in sunlight. There are often contrasting colours on the throat (gorgets) or crown, and in many species elongated feathers form crests, cheek plumes or throat plumes. These are used in display to females and rival males. Females are generally far duller than males – usually iridescent green above and dull whitish below.

The male finery of most hummingbirds accounts for the wonderfully flamboyant names given to so many of them by the Victorian ornithologists who first described them: examples plucked at random from a huge list are Lazuline Sabrewing, Sparkling Violet-ear, Spangled Coquette, Glittering-bellied Emerald, Fiery Topaz, Purple-crowned Woodnymph, Sapphire-spangled Emerald, Bronze-tailed Plumeleteer, Green-breasted Mountain-gem, Shining Sunbeam, Rainbow Starfrontlet, Amethyst-throated Sunangel, Sapphire-vented Puffleg, Hyacinth Visorbearer, Purple-crowned Fairy, Horned Sungem and Amethyst Woodstar.

The bill is slender and pointed, and generally long. In some cases it is very long indeed: the extreme example is that of the Sword-billed Hummingbird, *Ensifera ensifera*, in which it is longer than the head and body combined (the only bird species for which this is so), and is an adaptation for feeding at flowers with particularly long corollas, whose nectar other birds cannot reach. It is so long that the bird has to hold it at a steep angle towards the vertical when perching or during flight to maintain its balance. The bills of most hermits are not only long but gently decurved, whereas those of the two species of sicklebill, *Eutoxeres*, are strongly decurved. In most cases, the length and shape of the bill is intimately related to the shape and length of the tubular flowers on which it feeds. These have coevolved with the hummingbirds to their mutual advantage, relying on the birds for pollination. Short bills are found in a few species, such as the Purple-backed Thornbill, *Ramphomicron microrhynchum*, which 'cheats' flowers by 'stealing' nectar from the nectary at the base of the flower by taking advantage of the holes made by unrelated birds called flowerpiercers, *Diglossa*. Other short-billed species, such as the two species of fairy, *Heliothryx*, do the piercing themselves. The hummingbird tongue is long and highly extensible, with its tip bifurcated to form two curled troughs, along which the nectar passes as a result of capillary action when the bird thrusts its bill into the flower.

Like their relatives the swifts (Family Apodidae, p. 48), hummingbirds have tiny legs and feet, which allow perching but not movement along the ground. In some species that can feed by hanging onto flowers rather than hovering, they are stronger. The wings are relatively long and pointed. Hummingbird tails are generally large relative to the body, but vary greatly in shape and length. In many species the tail is square-ended or notched, but some genera, such as the woodnymphs, *Thalurania*, and brilliants, *Heliodoxa*, have a forked tail, and the tail of hermits is long and graduated, with the longest feathers being the central ones. The males of various genera and species have a very elongated tail: examples are the topazes, *Topaz*, streamertails, *Trochilus*, trainbearers, *Lesbia*, sylphs, *Aglaiocercus*, and the Peruvian Sheartail, *Thaumastura cora*. Most remarkable is the tail of the aptly named (and sadly Endangered) Marvellous Spatuletail, *Loddigesia mirabilis*, in which the extremely long outermost pair of feathers are reduced to wirelike shafts crossing one another and each terminating in a racquet-shaped expansion. During courtship displays, the male can move these extraordinary appendages independently.

Hummingbirds follow one of two main strategies for obtaining food. Many species, especially smaller hummingbirds with short bills, aggressively defend flowering bushes or trees within a single feeding territory. This necessitates obtaining all their nectar needs within an area small enough for them to defend against incursion by rivals, both hummingbirds and other nectar-feeding birds. Others, especially hermits and some other long-billed hummingbirds, practise 'traplining'. Instead of defending food supplies within a territory, they visit many scattered flowers repeatedly on a regular circuit. Sometimes, in tropical environments with many species, the situation is more complex, with some of them acting like food parasites, dashing in and stealing nectar from flowers in a clump belonging to a territory holder: these invaders may be very small and fast-moving, such as coquettes, *Lophornis*, and less likely to be noticed by the rightful owner, or large and unafraid of being challenged. Other species are opportunists that feed both at flower clumps and by traplining, depending on the availability of food supplies and the degree of competition from other nectar feeders.

As they sip nectar from flowers, hummingbirds frequently supplement their staple diet of nectar with pollen, which supplies some amino acids. However, they fulfil most of their protein requirements by eating small insects and spiders. These they obtain while hovering either by gleaning them from vegetation (including flowers), tree bark and spiders' webs, or by hawking or hovering to catch aerial insects. The long bill of the male Toothbilled Hummingbird, *Androdon aequatorialis*, has a hooked tip and several tiny toothlike serrations near the tip of the upper mandible, used to help extract spiders from narrow cavities or rolled-up leaves. Of those species studied, nestlings appear to be fed mainly on insects, and migratory species eat many insects to build up fat reserves before embarking on long flights.

All species of hummingbirds are polygynous. Trapliners usually have a lek mating system, where several or many males sing and advertise territory ownership by displaying at perches near one another. Males of other species attract mates by performing from perches scattered about their territory. The female is solely responsible for nest building, incubation and rearing of the young. Most hummingbirds build tiny cup-shaped nests, ranging in size from smaller than half a walnut shell in the Bee Hummingbird to only 2.5 cm (1 in) or a little more in diameter in most species. These are typically constructed from plant material such as moss and plant fibres, lined with soft, insulating material such as plant down, small feathers and animal hair. The exterior is usually adorned with the addition of lichens, bark fragments, dead leaves or other material that serves as effective camouflage. The whole structure is bound together with spiders' webs. Generally the nest is attached to a branch or twig, often where there is a fork between two twigs, but a variety of other sites are used by some species. They may fasten their nest to the surface of a large leaf or palm frond, beneath dense overhanging vegetation, onto a liana or other epiphytic plant, or even onto an exposed tree root near ground level. The nests of high-mountain dwelling species, such as hillstars, are typically much bulkier, with plentiful insulation, and sited in sites such as the walls of caves, gullies, or a rock face beneath an overhang that provide shelter from the wind. The nests of some montane hummingbirds, such as the metaltails, are partially roofed, while the sylphs build bulky domed nests with a side entrance. The Giant

ABOVE This tiny male Rufous-crested Coquette, *Lophornis delattrei*, is adept at 'stealing' nectar from a larger hummingbird's patch of flowers.

Hummingbird often sites its tiny nest atop a cactus. Hermits build very distinctive, pendant, cone-shaped nests which they typically attach to the underside of a long, hanging leaf or palm frond.

The two elliptical eggs are tiny, about the size of a pea or a small jellybean and include the smallest of all birds' eggs. Those of the Bee Hummingbird measure, on average, just 11 x 8 mm (0.4 x 0.3 in), and even the Giant Hummingbird's eggs are only 20 x 12 mm (0.8 x 0.5 in). Despite this, they are very large in relation to the size of the female's body.

Hummingbirds are today found only in the New World. The family has a vast overall range, from southern Alaska and Canada to Tierra del Fuego, although only a few species occur at the highest latitudes. Extreme examples include the Rufous Hummingbird, *Selasphorus rufus*, extending as far north as about 60°N in Alaska and the Green-backed Firecrown, *Sephanoides sephaniodes*, which breeds as far south as Tierra del Fuego, at a latitude of about 54°S. A few species live on islands in both the Atlantic and Pacific, from as far east as Barbados to as far west as the Juan Fernandez archipelago, some 650 km (400 miles) from the coast of Chile. The great majority, however, are birds of the tropics, with the greatest species richness in Colombia (131 species) and Ecuador (100). By contrast, just 23 species have ever been recorded from the USA and Canada, of which 17 species have nested there, most of them only occasionally and in the southern USA.

Hummingbirds occupy a remarkably wide range of habitats, from sea level to over 4,000 m (13,000 ft), where various species thrive in the bleak treeless plateaus of the Andean paramo or survive in sheltered canyons near glaciers and snowfields. Relatively few species occur in lowland rainforest; the greatest diversity is found in the cloud forests on the slopes of the Andes. Hummingbirds are also found in arid scrub, coastal mangroves and conifer forests, among various other habitats where they can find nectar-producing flowers.

A few species have a very wide breeding range – for example, the Ruby-throated Hummingbird, *Archilochus colubris*, is widely distributed across the eastern half of the USA and southern Canada, where it extends as far west as central Alberta (and winters from central Mexico to Panama), and the Black-throated Mango, *Anthracothorax nigricollis*, is found in Panama and South America to as far south as northeast Argentina. The great majority, though, have more restricted ranges and many are highly localised. To take just a single example, the Critically Endangered Colourful Puffleg, *Eriocnemis mirabilis*, is known from only four locations in Colombia.

Most species are largely or entirely sedentary, although some temperate zone breeders, such as the Ruby-throated Hummingbird, the Calliope Hummingbird, *Stellula calliope*, and the Rufous Hummingbird from North America, and the Green-backed Firecrown from southern South America, are long-distance migrants. Others make regular seasonal movements from mountains to lower altitudes.

ABOVE A Long-tailed Hermit, *Phaethornis supercilosus*, at Canopy Tower, Panama, demonstrates its manoeuvrability.

ABOVE A female Green-breasted Mango, *Anthracothorax prevostii*. Unlike many of its family, this species is expanding its range with deforestation.

ORDER OPISTHOCOMIFORMES

This order includes just a single monotypic family containing the very distinctive Hoatzin, *Opisthocomus hoazin*. The relationships of this remarkable bird to other birds has long been a topic of controversy, and uncertainty about its relationships with other birds remains: originally thought to be closest to the game birds such as curassows and guans (Order Galliformes), it has more recently been considered (from morphological similarities) somewhat closer to the cuckoos (Order Cuculiformes), or alternatively to the turacos, (Order Musophagiformes), pigeons (Order Columbiformes), sandgrouse (Order Pteroclidiformes), and grebes (Order Podicipediformes), or with even groups, such as the cranes (Order Gruiformes) and relatives or the shorebirds and relatives (Order Charadriiformes). The hoatzin order is likely to be very ancient, perhaps constituting one of the earliest of all modern bird groups, with no really close living relatives.

HOATZIN Opisthocomidae

GENERA: 1   **SPECIES**: 1

LENGTH: 61–70 cm (24–27.5 in)

WEIGHT: 0.7–0.9 kg (1.5–2 lb)

RANGE AND HABITAT: much of northern South America, east of the Andes; trees along rivers, streams and lakes of fresh, brackish and salt water in lowland tropics, often where there are giant arum plants; along coasts, often among mangroves

SOCIAL BEHAVIOUR: very social year-round, with groups of up to 40 birds; usually monogamous, each pair living in groups with up to six helpers, mainly their own young from previous season, which defend small breeding and feeding territory next to water

NEST: a flat, unlined platform of sticks and twigs, sometimes so loosely assembled that the eggs are visible from below, sometimes with an overhead canopy, sited in a dense bush or tree up to 5 m (16 ft) above water

EGGS: 2–4, white, heavily spotted with reddish brown and lavender

INCUBATION: 30–31 days

FLEDGING PERIOD: 55–65 days

FOOD: almost exclusively green leaves and buds of various tree and other plant species, supplemented by a few flowers and fruits

VOICE: noisy birds, adults uttering various grunting, growling, screeching, clucking, croaking and hissing sounds; chicks beg for food with rasping peeps

MIGRATION: sedentary

CONSERVATION STATUS: not threatened

ABOVE The Hoatzin, *Opisthocomus hoazin*, is a clumsy, strangely proportioned bird of waterside trees and shrubs in northern South America.

Unmistakable in appearance, the Hoatzin is one of the most unusual of all the world's birds. Ungainly and rather prehistoric-looking, it is a common denizen of the permanently flooded forests of the Orinoco, Amazon and various rivers of the Guianan region of South America. Here, loose flocks clamber about in trees and shrubs bordering slow-moving rivers, streams or lakes. Social units usually consist of just a few birds, but sometimes up to eight; these groups may coalesce into larger assemblages of up to 100 or more.

The Hoatzin is about the size of a big chicken, with a large bulky body, contrasting with the very small head on a long neck. The head is crowned by a prominent, scruffy, erect, bristly, reddish-brown crest and there is a large patch of naked blue skin around each eye, which is red with long eyelashes. The upperparts are olive-brown, with white streaks on the neck and back, and creamy white shoulders, forewings and wing bars. The underparts are rich orange-buff, with the belly rufous, like the outermost nine primary wing feathers and the underwing coverts. The bill is short and heavy, with its upper mandible articulated with the skull so that it is in independently movable, as in parrots and a few other families of birds. Although the wings are very large and broad, Hoatzins are weak flyers, due to their reduced flight muscles. Although they take to the air for short distances to cross water, alternating clumsy flight with much gliding, they use their wings, along with the long, broad, round-tipped tail, mainly as balancing organs as they move clumsily around in the trees.

Hoatzin chicks have an extra adaptation to help them climb. The first and second digits at the bend of the wing bear large, movable claws with which the young birds can grasp branches. This feature recalls the claws found on the wings of the prehistoric *Archaeopteryx*, a fact that led to misleading suggestions that the Hoatzin was a 'living fossil'. Should danger threaten, the chicks drop from their perch into the water, where they can swim and dive. Once it is safe, they can use their claws to climb back up through overhanging vegetation to rejoin the flock.

The Hoatzin is one of very few birds feeding almost entirely on green plant leaves and buds, which form about 80% of the diet. Over 50 species of tree, shrub and other plant have been recorded in their diet. Unlike other herbivorous birds, such as grouse, which digest tough pine needles and other plant food in their hindgut, Hoatzins store the leaves in their capacious crop and ferment the leaves in the foregut with the help of micro-organisms acting on the mush produced by the grinding of powerful muscles, just like ruminant mammals such as cows or sheep. So large is the crop that it comprises about one-third of the body, and during the slow process of digestion, the bird perches with the breastbone resting on a branch to support its considerable weight (about a quarter of its total weight). Its unusual method of digestion probably accounts for the Hoatzin's reputation as foul smelling (various local names translate as 'stinking bird').

Highly gregarious and noisy, a group of Hoatzins often draws attention by a cacophony of grunting and other calls, especially when they feed on moonlit nights. They also feed mainly at dusk and in the early morning. Nest helpers in each social group aid not only territory defence and incubation of the eggs, but also assist the breeding pair with brooding, feeding and protection of the chicks.

ORDER CUCULIFORMES

This order contains a single family. Until recently, it also included the turacos, the Family Musophagidae (p. 71), on grounds of similarities in their morphology, notably the zygodactyl (yoke-toed) arrangement of the feet which the two families share. Current evidence suggests that the two families are only distantly related, and that the turacos, a very distinctive group that is endemic to sub-Sahara Africa, may also be related to various other orders. The cuckoo family (Cuculidae) is large, very widely distributed, and a few of its species at least are familiar and well-studied birds.

With a long and complex evolutionary history, the cuckoo family poses problems for taxonomists trying to unravel the relationships of the different groups within the family. The approach taken in this book differs considerably from that adopted until recently, to reflect new research.

CUCKOOS Cuculidae

GENERA: 35   **SPECIES:** 138

LENGTH: 15–76 cm (6–30 in)

WEIGHT: 17–620 g (0.6–22 oz)

RANGE AND HABITAT: on all continents except Antarctica; most species in tropics and subtropics, but some migratory species extend to temperate latitudes; most live in forests, woods and scrublands, often near water; some in more open habitats, including deserts and moorland

SOCIAL BEHAVIOUR: most are solitary or live in pairs, though some occur in flocks; apart from those that are interspecific brood parasites, most are monogamous; a few are polyandrous; the three species of ani, *Crotophaga*, live and breed in groups, defending a big territory and a communal nest where two or more females lay eggs; while in the Guira Cuckoo, *Guira guira*, some pairs nest separately within the communal territory while others share a nest, and intraspecific parasitism occurs

NEST: apart from brood parasites, which build no nest, most cuckoos build a shallow nest of sticks and twigs in a tree or shrub, or on the ground among dense vegetation; coucals, *Centropus*, construct big spherical or dome-shaped nests of grass and green leaves with a side entrance, in shrubs, trees or among ground cover, and roadrunners *Geococcyx* make large, untidy bundles of sticks, twigs and bones lined with leaves, snake skin, fragments of mesquite seed-pods and animal dung, 1–3 m (3–10 ft) up in a shrub, low tree or clump of cactus

EGGS: most brood parasites lay eggs that vary in ground colour and any markings as they mimic those of the host; non-parasitic species mostly lay 1–5 white or blue eggs

INCUBATION: 11–16 days

FLEDGING PERIOD: 16–24 days

FOOD: for many species, mainly insects, especially large adult insects and caterpillars, including hairy toxic ones avoided by other birds; some species also eat small vertebrates, including lizards, snakes, birds and rodents; some koels, couas and the Channel-billed Cuckoo, *Scythrops novaehollandiae*, eat mainly fruit

VOICE: wide range of calls and songs, from the well-known repeated 'cuckoo' of the male Common Cuckoo (the female's main call is a very different bubbling sound) to the often equally repetitive and generally simple whistling, fluting, chuckling or hiccuping sounds; many species, though diurnal, call at night

MIGRATION: most tropical and subtropical species are sedentary, although several move in response to rainfall; most temperate zone species are migrants

CONSERVATION STATUS: one species, the Snail-eating Coua, *Coua delalandiae*, is Extinct; two species, the Sumatran Ground Cuckoo, *Carpococcyx viridis*, and Black-headed Coucal, *Centropus steerii*, are Critically Endangered; two species, the Bay-breasted Cuckoo, *Coccyzus rufigularis*, and Banded Ground Cuckoo, *Neomorphus radiolosus*, are Endangered; six species, including the Red-faced Malkoha, *Phaenicophaeus pyrrhocephalus*, Green-billed Coucal, *Centropus chlororhynchos*, and Rufous-vented Ground Cuckoo, *Neomorphus geoffroyi*, are Vulnerable; 8 species are Near Threatened

Popular awareness of cuckoos, at least in the Old World, is confined mainly to a single species, the Common Cuckoo, *Cuculus canorus*, named for the male's distinctive onomatopoeic song. It provides the universal image as the bird that tricks other species into rearing its young. This is celebrated in the English word 'cuckold', to describe both the husband deceived by an unfaithful wife and the act of duplicity itself. Many people might assume that all cuckoos have similar breeding habits, but in fact brood parasitism, as this behaviour is known, is found in just 40% of the family, in 51 of the 104 extant cuckoo species of the Old World and Australasia, and in only three of the 33 New World species. Overall, the cuckoos exhibit a wide range of breeding strategies, among the most diverse

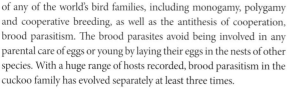

ABOVE A Common Cuckoo, *Cuculus canorus*, proclaims its presence to females and rival males in spring by its persistent onomatopoeic song.

ABOVE The Black-bellied Cuckoo, *Piaya melanogaster*, is a long-tailed, non-parasitic species from the Amazon.

of any of the world's bird families, including monogamy, polygamy and cooperative breeding, as well as the antithesis of cooperation, brood parasitism. The brood parasites avoid being involved in any parental care of eggs or young by laying their eggs in the nests of other species. With a huge range of hosts recorded, brood parasitism in the cuckoo family has evolved separately at least three times.

Widespread on every continent save Antarctica, the cuckoos are a fairly diverse group in appearance as well as lifestyle. Most species are sedentary inhabitants of scrubland and woodlands in the tropics and subtropics, often in the vicinity of rivers or streams, although some live in hot deserts and others in mountains, moorlands or mangroves. Migratory species extend the family's range to temperate latitudes, with the Common Cuckoo of Eurasia being found as far north as northern Scandinavia and northern China.

There are three subfamilies of cuckoos, each of which is divided into two tribes. The first subfamily, Crotophaginae, with 14 species in seven genera, is endemic to the New World. It comprises the tribes Crotophagini and Neomorphini. The Crotophagini contains two genera: Crotophaga, with three species of ani, found mainly in the Neotropics but with two of them extending as far north as southern Florida and Texas; and Guira, with a single, distinctive South American species, the Guira Cuckoo, *G. guira*. These four birds are cooperative breeders, with several females laying a total of up to 20 eggs in the same nest, and both male and female breeders as well as the offspring of previous seasons caring for the young. On the other hand, adults may compete with one another when they toss eggs out of the nest or bury them in its base, or kill nestlings, as fellow nestlings have also been seen to do. The tribe Neomorphini, also endemic to the Americas, contains five genera and ten species of long-tailed, ground-dwelling cuckoos. They include the roadrunners, *Geococcyx*, with two species, the Greater Roadrunner, *G. californianus*, found from south-west USA to south-central Mexico, subject of the famous American cartoon series, and its smaller relative, the Lesser Roadrunner, *G. velox*, of western Mexico, Yucatan and Central America. The genus *Neomorphus* contains four large species of ground cuckoos of humid forests in tropical America. Solitary, shy and very secretive, they are generally scarce birds that are threatened by forest clearance. Two

other genera, *Tapera* and *Dromococcyx*, contain the only three New World species that are brood parasites, a fact that was not discovered until the early years of the twentieth century. They are the Striped Cuckoo, *Tapera naevia*, found in scrubland or open country with scattered trees, from Mexico to northern South America; its hosts are small passerines with domed nests, such as various species of wrens, spinetails and New World sparrows. The hosts of the other two species, the Pheasant Cuckoo, *Dromococcyx phasianellus*, with a similar range to *Tapera* but in tropical forest, and the Pavonine Cuckoo, *D. pavoninus*, restricted to northern South America, include tyrant flycatchers and antbirds that build open or bag-shaped nests as well as closed ones.

The second subfamily, with 38 species in three genera, is the Centropodinae, subdivided into the tribe Couini and the tribe Centropodini. There are two genera in the Couini. The genus Coua, which is endemic to Madagascar, contains nine large mainly ground-dwelling species in forests and scrub in various parts of the island. They have soft plumage, brown and rufous in most species, with one all-blue. The largest species, the boldly pied Snail-eating Coua, *C. delalandei*, became extinct during the early nineteenth century as a result of the complete deforestation of Ile de Sainte-Marie, off the northeast coast of the main island. As its name suggests, it specialized in eating snails. There are three species of large ground cuckoos in the genus *Carpococcyx*, one on Borneo, one on Sumatra, and the biggest, the Coral-billed Ground Cuckoo, *C. renauldi*, in Thailand, Vietnam, Cambodia and Laos. One of the largest of all cuckoos at 60 cm (2 ft) long from the tip of its big bright red bill to the tip of its long violet-glossed black tail, it preys on small mammals, birds and reptiles as well as insects. The tribe Centropodini contains just a single genus, *Centropus*. This is the most speciose genus in the entire cuckoo family, containing 26 sombre black or black-and-brown plumaged species known as coucals. Of these, seven live in Africa, one in Madagascar, 11 in southern Asia (mainly on islands), and seven in New Guinea and other nearby islands, with two races of one of these, the Pheasant Coucal, *C. phasianinus*, occurring in Australia. With a very long, rather pheasant-like, barred tail, this is the longest of all cuckoos, with some individuals as much as 80 cm (31 in) long.

The third subfamily, Cuculinae, is by far the largest, with 26 genera and 86 species. It is subdivided into two tribes, the Phaenicophaeini and the Cucculini. The Phaenicophaeini contains 35 species in 12 genera, and is the only tribe to include representatives from both the Old World and Australasian regions and the New World. The Old World group of 25 species, all non-parasitic in breeding habits, include 12 Asian and a single African species of malkohas. Six of the Asian species are in the genus *Phaenicophaeus*, with the others divided between seven other monotypic genera. These are large and striking cuckoos, with big, brightly coloured red, yellow or multicoloured bills and bare skin around the eyes and mostly with glossy dark green, purple or blue upperparts and grey or reddish-brown underparts. Other Old World members of the Phaenicophaeini include the four slightly crested species in the genus *Clamator*. These are brood parasites and are unusual in choosing the nests of larger birds in which to lay their eggs. The hosts of the two African and single Asian species include bulbuls and shrikes, while the Great Spotted Cuckoo, *C. glandarius* (whose range includes Iberia, southern France, western Italy, Turkey and parts of the Middle East as well as Africa), specialises in parasitising crows and Black-billed Magpies, as well as starlings in Africa. The New World members of this tribe comprise 18 species of slender cuckoos with similar chestnut, brown and grey plumage, and distinctive, boldly patterned undertails bearing large white and black spots. Thirteen are classified in the genus *Coccyzus*, and these include two well known North American species, the Black-billed Cuckoo, *C. erythropthalmus*, and the Yellow-billed Cuckoo, *C. americanus*; both are long-distance migrants, breeding as far north as southern Canada and wintering in South America. There are two species of *Piaya*, including the Squirrel Cuckoo, *P. cayana*, with 15 races in its very wide geographical range, from Mexico to northern Argentina, and three Central and South American species in the genus *Coccyua*.

ABOVE The Brush Cuckoo, *Cacomantis variolosus*, is one of several Asian species dubbed the 'brain-fever bird' due its incessant singing day and night.

These two are usually nest builders that raise their own young, but when food is unusually plentiful, females not only follow this 'normal' route but also parasitise the nests of their own kind or of other species.

The tribe Cuculini is made up of the Old World and Australasian brood parasites. The largest genus, *Cuculus*, includes, as well as the Common Cuckoo, nine other similar species across the world from West Africa to Australia. They parasitise a wide range of small birds such as warblers, pipits, flycatchers, honeyeaters and robins. Other members of the Cuculini include six African and Asian species in the genus *Chrysococcyx*, such as the Asian and African emerald cuckoos, *C. maculatus* and *C. cupreus*, and the eight *Chalcites* species of bronze cuckoos, with representatives in Southeast Asia, New Guinea and nearby islands and Australia, with a race of one species, the Shining Bronze Cuckoo, *Chalcites lucidus*, in New Zealand. Small birds parasitized by these two genera include sunbirds, weavers and sparrows. The tribe Cuculini also contains four Asian and Australasian species called koels, divided between three genera. The Common Koel, *Eudynamys scolopaceus*, is an abundant, familiar bird of the Indian subcontinent, Southeast Asia and Australasia. In parts of its huge range it parasitizes starlings and mynahs, but it generally chooses crows, which are as large as itself. Another, very distinctive member of the Cuculini is one of the giants among cuckoos, the Channel-billed Cuckoo, *Scythrops novaehollandiae*, of eastern Indonesia and Australia. It parasitizes crows, butcherbirds and currawongs.

There is a great variation in how closely cuckoo eggs mimic those of the hosts, ranging from eggs that do not resemble them at all (as in the plain white eggs of South African Jacobin Cuckoos, *Clamator jacobinus*, so different from the spotted eggs of their bulbul hosts), via the perfect matching of colour and pattern of spots but size and shape difference, as seen in Common Cuckoos, to the blue eggs of some cuckoos that are so similar to those of their babbler hosts in size, shape and colour that ornithologists can distinguish them only by weighing them. It is likely that this variation reflects an 'arms race' that has evolved over millennia between cuckoo and host. During the earliest stages of this arms race, when the host has little experience of parasitism, they do not reject the alien looking eggs; but as some individuals start to reject them, and thereby raise more young, natural selection favours this trait and it becomes more common. This in turn means that the cuckoos that lay eggs more closely resembling those of the host will produce more young, and this is selected for in the cuckoo population. So as the hosts evolve better egg rejection, the cuckoos evolve better egg mimicry.

Members of the cuckoo family range considerably in size, with tree dwellers tending to be smaller and with a more slender body than ground dwellers. Smallest are the mainly south Asian and Australasian *Chrysococcyx* species, with the Little Bronze Cuckoo, *Chalcites minutillus*, being the smallest member of the entire family, at 15–16 cm (6 in) and about 17 g (0.6 oz); in the New World the smallest are two Neotropical species, the Dwarf Cuckoo, *Coccycua pumila*, at 21 cm (8 in) and about 36 g (1.25 oz), and the Little Cuckoo, *Coccycua minuta*, at 25 cm (10 in) and about 40 g (1.4 oz). The largest cuckoos are from Indonesia, New Guinea and Australia, including some of the coucals, notably the Greater Black Coucal, *Centropus menbeki*, at up to 67 cm (26 in) and 553 g (19.5 oz), the Channel-billed Cuckoo, *Scythrops novaehollandiae*, which is shorter but the heaviest of all cuckoos at up to 623 g (22 oz), and the Pheasant Coucal, *Centropus phasianinus*, of Timor, New Guinea and Australia, which is lighter but up to 80 cm (31.5 in) long. Most species are between about 30 cm and 50 cm (12 and 20 in).

One of the major common features of all cuckoos is that the feet have what is known as the zygodactyl arrangement of toes, with the inner and outer toes facing backwards and the other two toes pointing forwards. This helps many species move with facility along branches or even climb slender, swaying reed stems and helps the female of brood parasitic species such as the Common Cuckoo to maintain a good grip on the rim of the small nest of her host as she quickly removes the host's egg and lays her own. Arboreal species have short legs, but the legs of most of the terrestrial cuckoos are longer, and their toes more flexible, suiting them for fast running. This reaches its apogee in the ground-cuckoos, especially the roadrunners, which can run at speeds of up to 30 km/h (18.5 mph); they often do this while chasing insect or lizard prey along roadsides or dried-up riverbeds.

Wing and tail shape, too, varies according to habitat and lifestyle. Tree dwellers have pointed or slightly rounded wings, whereas ground-cuckoos tend to be short-winged, with very long tails, which they use for balance when running. Flight is usually by flapping alternating with glides. Some of the ground-cuckoos fly only infrequently, while most others do so more often, with a flapping and gliding action, and long-distance migrants such as the Common Cuckoo and the Shining Bronze Cuckoo, *Chalcites lucidus*, can fly fast and direct on relatively longer, pointed wings.

The bill is generally short, strong and slightly decurved, due to an arched upper mandible. In members of the Cuculinae it is slender, but in others, such as the coucals and especially the malkohas and the Neotropical ground-cuckoos, *Neomorphus*, it is much thicker. Roadrunners have a slender, spikier bill, while the lizard-cuckoos, *Saurothera*, of the Caribbean region have a longer bill with a hooked tip, anis have a deep, laterally compressed bill, with a high arching ridge near the base of the upper mandible in the Greater Ani, *Crotophaga major*, and the Channel-billed Cuckoo has a massive bill to match its great body size.

The plumage is generally soft, delicate and loose, and tends to become soaked in the rain; cuckoos often spend time sunbathing to dry it off. Roadrunners have areas of blackish skin on the back that they expose by fluffing out their feathers to warm themselves up quickly after the cold desert night (they can also go into slight torpor to cope with the cold. Many species, especially the brood parasites, which need to be as unobtrusive as possible when approaching a host nest, have relatively dull plumage of browns, rufous hues and greys. But some are much brighter, notably the males of many of the *Chrysococcyx* species, with iridescent upperparts of bronzy green, brilliant emerald, or in one species, the Violet Cuckoo, *C. xanthorhynchus*, intense reddish or bluish violet (though females are generally duller). The Coral-billed Ground Cuckoo, *Carpococcyx renauldi*, has a black head, neck and throat, contrasting with pale bluish wings, a glossy violet tail, finely vermiculated white underparts and a bright coral-red bill and legs. Various species, such as some of the koels and the coucals, the Black Cuckoo, *Cuculus clamosus*, and the Drongo Cuckoo, *Surniculus lugubris*, are entirely black (in some cases males only), while others are pied, and there are some species with variable colour morphs. Many of the parasitic cuckoos, especially *Cuculus* species, have a resemblance to *Accipiter* hawks, with barred underparts; this similarity may have evolved as an adaptation to make it more likely that incubating hosts will react with alarm by flying off the nest, allowing the female cuckoo to sneak in and deposit its egg. In most species, males and females have very similar plumage, but some of the Old World parasitic species are sexually dimorphic. Females of various species, including the Common Cuckoo and most other *Cuculus* species from Africa and Asia, have a distinctive rufous colour variant (morph). Many species have eyes with brightly coloured irides (such as red, yellow or blue) and often there are coloured eye-rings; those of Cuculus species are yellow. Couas have a blue area of bare skin around each eye; the same areas in malkohas are bright red. Similar adornments are found in many other species; for instance, the Coral-billed Ground Cuckoo has a violet patch surrounding a scarlet eye-ring, and the Bornean Ground Cuckoo, *Carpococcyx radiceus*, has a pale green area, the same colour as the bill.

Most cuckoos feed mainly on insects. Many specialise in eating hairy, toxic caterpillars, benefiting from a food supply that is avoided by almost all other birds. The lizard-cuckoos are well named, taking large numbers of small lizards, as well as snakes and large insects. Roadrunners are opportunists, running down all manner of creatures from grasshoppers, beetles, scorpions, centipedes and spiders to lizards, snakes (including rattlesnakes), other birds and small rodents, as well as eating some fruit and seeds. Pairs sometimes cooperate in overpowering a snake. A few species of koels and couas, as well as the Channel-billed Cuckoo, feed mainly on fruit, especially when raised by fruit-eating hosts such as figbirds (see p. 256), but also eat animal prey.

ABOVE A Greater Roadrunner, *Geococcyx californianus*, lives up to its reputation as a snake-killer, at the Salton Sea in California.

ORDER GRUIFORMES

The birds in this diverse order vary greatly in size and build, from the smallest rails, scarcely larger than sparrows, to the stately cranes, standing taller on their long legs than any other birds apart from ratites such as the Ostrich; the tallest crane species are as high as a human adult, at up to 1.8 m (6 ft). Until recently, the Gruiformes were essentially a 'ragbag' grouping, an unwieldy assemblage of bird familes, some of which were included because there was no other order to which they could be assigned. Relatively few features unified all members of this large group, apart from some skeletal and palatal similarities, but a smaller subgroup of families, comprising those of the rails and relatives, finfoots, trumpeters, limpkin and cranes, did show stronger similarities that were supported by evidence from DNA studies. It is this core group that now forms the greatly reduced order. The families no longer considered as Gruiformes are the mesites (Family Mesitornithidae, now given an order of their own, Mesitornithiformes, p. 36); the Kagu (Family Rhynochetidae) and Sunbittern (Family Eurypygidae), now united in the Order Eurypygiformes (p. 37); the buttonquails (Family Turnicidae), now included in the Order Charadriiformes (p. 105); the bustards (Family Otididae), now placed in an order of their own, Otidiformes (p. 69); and the seriemas (Family Cariamidae), also in their own order, Cariamiformes (p. 183), remarkably now regarded as very distant from their former home in the Gruiformes as a result of evidence indicating their new place in a radical major grouping linking them with the falcons, parrots and passerines.

RAILS Rallidae

GENERA: 33   **SPECIES:** 141

LENGTH: 12–63 cm (5–25 in)

WEIGHT: 20 g–3.2 kg (0.7 oz–7 lb)

RANGE AND HABITAT: on every continent except for Antarctica and the far north of the northern hemisphere, including many remote oceanic islands or (for two coot species) high-altitude lakes in the Andes; mainly wet or at least damp habitats, from lakes, rivers, freshwater, brackish and saltwater marshes, mangroves, bogs, reed beds, scrublands, meadows and flooded fields to moist forests and woodlands

SOCIAL BEHAVIOUR: depending on species, ranges from being mainly solitary or occurring in pairs to highly gregarious, especially in the case of the coots and relatives; most species are apparently monogamous and territorial, fewer than 4% are probably polygamous; young from earlier broods and sometimes adult helpers may aid in chick rearing in a few species

NEST: made of sticks or other vegetation, sometimes roofed, low among vegetation such as among grasses or reeds, in a few species in shrubs or trees; coots build bulky aquatic nests in shallow water on a foundation of sticks or stones

EGGS: 1–19, whitish to dark brownish, very variable individually, often with darker spots

INCUBATION: 20–30 days

FLEDGING PERIOD: 28–56 days

FOOD: most species are omnivorous and opportunistic, taking a wide range of animal and plant food, including insects, molluscs, worms and other invertebrates, small fish and amphibians, some birds and eggs, carrion, seeds and other parts of many plants, including crops; sometimes also carrion and discarded food

VOICE: most species are very vocal, with many calling or singing mainly at night; the range of sounds is very wide, including soft whistles or cooing sounds, mechanical clicks, rasps, squeaks and loud squeals and grunts, often very unlike typical bird sounds; some species duet

MIGRATION: tropical and subtropical species and the many flightless species of oceanic islands are generally sedentary or make relatively short seasonal or dispersal movements; most temperate zone species migrate to winter in warmer regions

CONSERVATION STATUS: At least 24 species have become Extinct since about 1600, mostly during the nineteenth century, and one, the Guam Rail, *Gallirallus owstoni*, is Extinct in the Wild; four species, the New Caledonian Rail, *Gallirallus lafresnayanus*, Zapata Rail, *Cyanolimnas cerverai*, Samoan Moorhen, *Pareudiastes pacificus*, and Makira Moorhen, *P. silvestris*, are Critically Endangered; 9 species, including the Okinawa Rail, *Hypotaenidia okinawae*, Bogota Rail, *Rallus semiplumbeus*, and South Island Takahe, *Porphyrio hochstetteri*, are Endangered; 18 species, including the Weka, *Gallirallus australis*, Invisible Rail, *Habroptila wallacii*, and Galapagos Rail, *Laterallus spilonota*, are Vulnerable; 14 species are Near Threatened

Members of this large family of birds live in a wide variety of mainly damp habitats, from freshwater marshes, reed beds, coastal salt marshes or lush meadows or other vegetation to large bodies of open water. Most are very secretive, spending much of their lives hidden in dense vegetation; as a result, often birdwatchers and ornithologists detect their presence only by their loud vocalisations. To the uninitiated, these can sound alarming: for example, the Western Water Rail, *Rallus aquaticus*, often proclaims its presence by 'sharming', an old name for the medley of squeals like the sounds of a distressed piglet that issue forth from deep within a marsh.

All species have rather short, rounded wings and a short tail and strong, sturdy legs with large feet and long toes. These allow them to walk across swampy or floating vegetation or clamber among reeds and other water plants, and in a few cases even to forage, shelter or nest in small trees or shrubs.

The family has been traditionally divided into three subfamilies on the basis of their general shape and habits, although these are not taxonomic divisions and there is little to justify them. Also, there was considerably inconsistency as to which subfamily a genus belonged to, and names such as 'crake' and 'rail' were often assigned arbitrarily. Body shape and particularly bill length, size and shape vary considerably across the family. A more recent division recognised by many researchers divided the family into just two broad 'natural groups': the crakes, rails, wood-rails, bush-hens and forest-rails and relatives, which are mainly terrestrial, and the swamphens, gallinules and coots, which tend to be more aquatic.

In the first group, a large number of species have rail as part of their common name (the word 'rail' is also used for the family as a whole). These birds have a longish bill and a body that is narrowed from side to side, allowing them to slip easily between vertical stems in dense vegetation such as reeds.

The second subgroup includes the plump-bodied coots, *Fulica*, as well as moorhens, gallinules and swamphens. The swamphens, the biggest of all rails, have a huge, deep bill. Although all species in the family can swim and most can sink underwater or dive to escape predators, and the moorhens and gallinules, *Gallinula*, spend a fair amount of time swimming, the coots are by far the most aquatic, rarely found far from water, and have become specialised at diving for food. Unlike the rest of the family, they have lobed feet that help them swim and dive efficiently, and they spend much of their lives on open waters, including huge lakes.

Plumage patterns in most species are combinations of browns, buffs, greys and rusty hues that camouflage the bird very well among dense vegetation. However, there are exceptions. These include the flufftails, with bright reddish-chestnut heads and breasts, contrasting with the rest of the plumage which is mainly black or dark brown with white bars or spots; many of the rails in the genus *Rallina* also have similar colours and patterns; in all but one of the flufftails the bright plumage is restricted to the males. There are also a few species which are entirely black, or sooty grey or brown, such as the Black Crake, *Amaurornis flavirostra*, a widespread African species, or the aptly named Invisible Rail, *Habroptila wallacii*, endemic to the Indonesian island of Halmahera. Coots are very dark grey and sooty black. Gallinules, whose Old World species are called moorhens, are slate grey or purplish blue, sometimes with areas of green, whereas the swamphens (such as the very widespread Purple Swamphen, *Porphyrio porphyrio*, and the very rare and endangered Southern Takahe, *P. hochstetteri*, of New

ABOVE The Grey-necked Wood Rail, *Aramides cajanea*, is a large rail found in a wide range of wetland habitats from southern Mexico to northern Argentina.

ABOVE A South Island Takahe, *Porphyrio hochstetteri*, feeds its chick at a translocation site on Tiri Matangi Island, North Island, New Zealand.

ABOVE A Common Coot, *Fulica atra*, carries material to build its floating nest at Titchwell RSPB Reserve in Norfolk, England in March.

Zealand) are brilliant, glossy blue, purple and green. An extinct close relative of the Purple Swamphen, the Lord Howe Swamphen (or White Swamphen), *P. albus*, from Lord Howe Island in the Tasman Sea, was white.

In many species, the bill, legs and feet of adults are brightly coloured – usually red, orange, green or yellow – and the eyes are bright red. Coots and some gallinules in particular have conspicuous, large, smooth, horny 'frontal shields' extending back onto the forehead from the upper bill and continuous with the bill's outer covering. These are white or very pale pinkish in most coot species, red and yellow in most moorhens. The largest coot species, the Horned Coot, *Fulica cornuta*, of remote high Andean lakes, has a strange appendage extending forwards from the base of its bill, which consists of three joined wattles, each ending in a frill of bristlelike feathers, called filoplumes. The function of all these coot adornments is unknown.

Although most rails prefer to run or swim from danger and appear to fly only weakly, a good many are long-distance migrants or make prodigious dispersal movements. This has enabled them to colonise many remote oceanic islands, where many evolved into new species. Originally free of predators, many of these islands were relative havens and many island species accordingly became flightless. Unfortunately, this made them particularly vulnerable as humans arrived and killed them directly or accidentally or deliberately introduced alien mammals that were even more effective at predation. As a result, most of the extinct species of rails are island ones. The Rallidae is among the most threatened of all bird families, with almost 40% of species either threatened or already extinct. The number of species (at least nine and perhaps as many as 20, depending on taxonomy and whether or not subfossils are included) that are known to have become extinct since about 1600 is very high compared with most other bird families. But it is probable that many more unknown species have been lost; one estimate by an expert on the family's history suggests that anything from a very conservative 442 to almost 1,600 species may once have occurred on the many islands of the Pacific Ocean, and the total could be even greater.

FLUFFTAILS Sarothruridae

GENERA: 1   **SPECIES:** 9

LENGTH: 13.5–17 cm (5–6.5 in)

WEIGHT: 30–60 g (1–2 oz)

RANGE AND HABITAT: sub-Saharan Africa and Madagascar; flooded grasslands, swamps, some species in forests or scrub

SOCIAL BEHAVIOUR: monogamous and territorial; young may remain in the territory until the next breeding season

Nest: well-hidden pad, bowl or domed structure of grass and other plant material

EGGS: 2–5, white, sparsely spotted in a few species

INCUBATION: 14–18 days

FLEDGING PERIOD: about 5–6 weeks

FOOD: invertebrates, including insects, spiders and snails, also small frogs, seeds and other plant matter

VOICE: very varied, including high-pitched hoots, squeaks, rattles, growls, grunts, and bubbling, wailing, or hissing sounds

MIGRATION: although most seem to be sedentary or make only local movements, evidence suggests some make seasonal migrations

CONSERVATION STATUS: one species, the White-winged Flufftail, *S. ayresi*, is Critically Endangered; one species, the Slender-billed Flufftail, *S. watersi*, is Endangered

This small family contains nine species of rail-like birds known as flufftails, all in a single genus, *Sarothrura*. Seven species are endemic to Africa and two to Madagascar.

The family name refers to the fluffy appearance of the tail feathers in most species, which are fragmented at their tips. These diminutive, sparrow-sized, birds have a short, conical bill, compact body, short tail, strong feet and short, rounded wings. Unlike the great majority of rails, the sexes differ markedly in appearance. Males are boldly patterned, with the head and neck chestnut (in some species extending to the mantle and breast and also on the tail) and the body black with white or buff streaks or spots. Females of most species are much duller, brown or blackish with pale bars and spots; in two species they have a similar plumage pattern to the male, but duller. Another difference between the flufftails and rails is that compared with the strongly marked eggs of most of the rails, those of the flufftails are plain or only sparsely spotted.

It appears from recent genetic research that their closest relatives are not the rails, which they resemble so much in general features, and with which they have long been classified, but the finfoots (Family Heliornithidae, p. 64). Some molecular data suggest that the Grey-throated Rail, *Canirallus oculeus*, a denizen of West and Central African rainforests, should also be included in the flufftail family.

FINFOOTS Heliornithidae

GENERA: 3   **SPECIES**: 3

LENGTH: 26–59 cm (10–23 in)

WEIGHT: ranges from 120–150 g (4–5 oz) in the Sungrebe, *Heliornis fulica*, to 340–880 g (12–31 oz) in the African Finfoot, *Podica senegalensis*

RANGE AND HABITAT: one species in tropical central and South America, one in sub-Saharan Africa and one in Southeast Asia; slow-moving rivers and lakes, especially bordered by forests with plenty of overhanging vegetation; the Masked Finfoot, *Heliopais personatus*, also in swamps, flooded forests and mangroves

SOCIAL BEHAVIOUR: usually seen singly but sometimes in pairs or small family groups; appear to defend sizeable territories up to several hundred metres long, probably for most of the year

NEST: a shallow bowl of sticks, twigs and reeds, lined with dead leaves and sited above water, often among dense tangles of dead vegetation carried along by floodwaters and caught up on fallen trees or on low, branches overhanging water

EGGS: 2–3, 5–7 in the Masked Finfoot, cream or reddish-brown

INCUBATION: reputedly very short incubation period of 10–11 days in the Sungrebe and at least 12 days in the African Finfoot

FLEDGING PERIOD: unknown

FOOD: typical diet is little known but includes insects, crustaceans and molluscs; also some fish, frogs and seeds

VOICE: largely silent, but may utter a variety of growling, barking, booming or bubbling sounds during territorial defence or a soft clucking sound during courtship

MIGRATION: generally sedentary

CONSERVATION STATUS: one species, the Masked Finfoot, is Endangered

ABOVE This male African Finfoot, *Podica senegalensis*, was photographed on a river in Lope National Park, Gabon, West Africa.

This very small family comprises three species of highly aquatic birds that are largely restricted to the tropics and subtropics. Each is very far removed geographically from the others: the Sungrebe, *Heliornis fulica*, is in the New World, from southern Mexico to northeast Argentina; both the other species are in the Old World – the African Finfoot, *Podica senegalensis*, in much of sub-Saharan Africa apart from the southeast and northeast, and the Masked Finfoot, *Heliopais personatus*, in southern Asia, from Bangladesh and northeast India to Indochina and Sumatra. They differ enough from one another that they are classified in three separate genera.

Wherever they live, all finfoots need dense cover next to the water; where they inhabit large lakes or rivers, these wary, elusive birds usually stay close to the shore where they can hide easily among the vegetation. They rarely dive, securing most of their staple diet of insects and other invertebrates from the surface.

With their long, slim neck, daggerlike bill and lobed toes, the birds in this family superficially resemble grebes (as celebrated in an alternative family name of sungrebes) but are unrelated. The closest relatives of these odd birds appear to be the flufftails (Family Sarothruridae, see p. 63). As in cormorants and anhingas, the tail has a graduated shape and its feathers are stiffened in the two finfoot species, though not in the Sungrebe. Adult and young

African Finfoots have a well-developed claw at the bend of each wing that may help them clamber about in vegetation, in a similar way to the young of the unrelated Hoatzin, *Opisthocomus hoazin*, of Amazonia (see p. 56). At night, they climb up into overhanging branches to roost, from where they can drop into the water if threatened.

All three species are basically mainly brownish above and paler below, with striking head markings, but otherwise plumage details, and also colours of bare parts in the breeding season, differ markedly between species. The Sungrebe is plain olive-brown above, with a black-and-white-striped head and neck. The bill is horn coloured below, dark above in males, and red above in females, and the feet are strikingly banded yellow and black. The African Finfoot has a white-spotted back (much darker or entirely blackish in western birds), a long white stripe across the head continuing down the neck, dark barring on the breast and flanks and an orange-red bill and legs. The Masked Finfoot has a black face and throat bordered by a white stripe and a yellow bill and green legs. Size, too, varies between species: the smallest is the Sungrebe, at about 26–33 cm (10–13 in) long; the Masked Finfoot is a good deal bigger, at about 43–55 cm (17–22 in); in the African Finfoot there is marked variation in size between the four distinct subspecies, from 35 cm (14 in) to 59 cm (23 in), and between males and females.

Owing to these birds' highly secretive habits, many aspects of their biology are still relatively little known. One remarkable feature observed in the Sungrebe is that males carry their young in flight as well as on the water. They are able to transport tiny, naked, just-hatched chicks safely within a pair of special cavities formed by skin folds beneath each wing, found in no other birds.

TRUMPETERS Psophiidae

GENERA: 1   **SPECIES**: 3

LENGTH: 45–52 cm (18–20 in)

WEIGHT: 1–1.5 kg (2.2–3.3 lb)

RANGE AND HABITAT: northern half of South America; dense tropical rainforest

SOCIAL BEHAVIOUR: highly sociable, living in groups of 3–12 or so birds that cooperate to defend territory and care for the young

NEST: in a hole (often excavated by another species) in a tree, from which the dominant female or male removes all debris except for a shallow layer on which the eggs are laid, and from where the young leap down to the ground soon after hatching

EGGS: 2–5, white

INCUBATION: 23–29 days

FLEDGING PERIOD: about 42 days

FOOD: mainly large fruit; also some insects and other invertebrates; occasionally small snakes and lizards

VOICE: very loud, resonant trumpeting or low hooting or booming sounds, which may accelerate into gurgling or bubbling noises; also cackling, grating or clucking alarm and other calls

MIGRATION: sedentary

CONSERVATION STATUS: four races, regarded as separate species by some authorities, are threatened: the Black-winged Trumpeter, *P. viridis obscura*, is Critically Endangered, the Olive-winged Trumpeter, *P. v. dextralis*, is Endangered; and the Green-winged Trumpeter, *P. v. viridis*, is Vulnerable; also another race, the Ochre-winged Trumpeter, *P. leucoptera ochroptera*, and the Grey-winged Trumpeter, *P. crepitans* are Near Threatened

ABOVE Like the other two trumpeter species, this Grey-winged Trumpeter, *Psophia crepitans*, feeds mainly on fruit pulp.

This family comprises just three similar species, all living in the lowland tropical forests of the northern half of South America, mainly in the Amazon and Orinoco river basins. They live up to their common name, all proclaiming their presence with very loud, resonant, far-carrying trumpeting threat calls. These are amplified

ABOVE A patch of iridescent neck feathers gleams in the sunlight on this Grey-winged Trumpeter in the Peruvian Amazon.

as a result of their long, coiled windpipe, a feature shared by some of the members of another family in the Order Gruiformes: the cranes (Family Gruidae, see p. 67).

Trumpeters look rather like the unrelated chickens or guans (see p. 65) in shape, with a small head in relation to the large body, but they have longer legs. They hold their short, rounded wings folded loosely, which, combined with the neck held in an S-shape, gives them a rather hunchbacked appearance; the long, drooping secondary feathers almost completely hide the short tail. The head and neck feathers in particular are very short, so that they resemble soft, velvety fur. They have big, dark eyes, giving good vision in the gloom of the forest interior, where they forage for fallen fruit, including that dropped by monkeys or other fruit-eating creatures. They can swallow large fruit with their short, stout, slightly curved bill. Trumpeters are poor fliers (usually using their wings only to flutter laboriously up to roost as much as 9 m/30 ft high in trees) but tireless walkers, and they can run very fast to escape danger.

To find enough food, family groups wander through their large territory all year round, and may combine to fight with other groups when they meet. In groups of Pale-winged Trumpeters, *Psophia leucoptera*, hierarchy is reinforced by subordinate members giving a crouching, spread-wing display accompanied by high-pitched chicklike twittering calls, to which dominant birds respond by flicking their wings. The unusual breeding system of this species, with a single dominant female mating with several males (including a dominant male), is known as cooperative polyandry.

All species are mainly black, with a purple, bronze or green iridescence – especially on the lower neck and wing coverts – and patches of dark green, grey, buff or white on the inner wing coverts that vary with age and play a part in the social displays.

LIMPKIN Aramidae

GENERA: 1   **SPECIES**: 1

LENGTH: 56–71 cm (22–28 in)

WEIGHT: 0.9–1.3 kg (2–2.9 lb)

RANGE AND HABITAT: southern USA (Florida), Caribbean, Mexico, Central America, South America; swampy woodland, freshwater marshes, lake edges and mangroves

SOCIAL BEHAVIOUR: usually solitary, occasionally seen in small groups; some pairs are monogamous, but in others the female changes mate with a second clutch; males defend their territory year-round

NEST: big, bulky shallow structure varying with location, from floating, piled-up platform of aquatic vegetation on water, and dead reeds or grasses woven among living reeds, to nest of vines, palm fronds or sticks in shrubs or trees

EGGS: 4–8, buff or whitish, blotched with brown

INCUBATION: 26–28 days

FLEDGING PERIOD: about 42 days

FOOD: mainly large freshwater snails and mussels (clams), and some frogs, lizards and insects

VOICE: males very noisy, especially in the breeding season, uttering loud rattling, clucking, wailing and screaming sounds (often simultaneously)

MIGRATION: in most places essentially sedentary, apart from movements in response to drought or flooding reducing the food supply

CONSERVATION STATUS: not threatened

ABOVE The long, sturdy bill of the Limpkin, *Aramus gaurauna*, is beautifully adapted for opening snail shells.

The bird that is the sole member of this New World family, the Limpkin, *Aramus guarauna*, looks rather like a dully plumaged crane or ibis – it has a long, slightly decurved bill, long slim neck and long legs – and also bears some resemblance to a large rail. Its plumage is dark brown, spangled with white to a varying extent, depending on subspecies. The odd common name is often said to refer to the bird's odd, high-stepping walk, although this does not really look like limping.

Although many people are unlikely to know a Limpkin when they see one, those living near these relatively common birds are bound to have heard them. Loops in the male's windpipe help him amplify his voice, to produce a cacophony of penetrating shrieks, mournful wails, and other weird sounds. These are often uttered for much of the day and night by males trying to attract mates, and the performance is particularly dramatic when several males call together. Far more people will have been unaware that the loud dramatic calls are among the animal sounds used on various old Hollywood movies to create the atmosphere of the African or Asian jungle, where no Limpkin lives. Limpkin calls were also used more recently for the voice of the mythical hippogriff in the film of *Harry Potter and the Prisoner of Azkaban*.

The Limpkin is a highly specialised feeder. It concentrates mainly on large freshwater apple snails, *Pomacea*, removing the soft body from the shell with great adroitness. Wading in the shallows on its long legs or walking about on floating vegetation, it probes for its prey with its long, strong bill. Once it makes contact

with an apple snail, it seizes the mollusc in the downcurved tip of its bill and carries it to the shore or a perch, then holds it down firmly in one foot with the operculum (the horny cover over the opening of the shell) facing upwards. The bird then inserts the lower mandible of its bill, which is curved to the right, into the narrow gap between the shell and the operculum, while bracing the upper mandible against the shell. Using its bill like scissors to snip the muscle attached to the inside of the shell, it pulls out the soft body of the snail, and swallows it. The whole process may take only 10–20 seconds. The Limpkin deals with clams, which are bivalves, in a similar fashion, in this case hacking at the weakest point between the two valves to reach the muscle. In areas where snails or clams are plentiful, a Limpkin can dispose of one every 2 or 3 minutes, and leaves behind a large pile of empty shells.

CRANES Gruidae

GENERA: 4   **SPECIES:** 15

LENGTH: 90–180 cm (36–72 in)

WEIGHT: 2.7–12 kg (6–26 lb)

RANGE AND HABITAT: all continents except South America and Antarctica; most species in Asia (eight breeding) and Africa (five breeding, one wintering); marshes and other shallow wetlands during the breeding season; steppes, other grasslands and cultivated land during the non-breeding season

SOCIAL BEHAVIOUR: intensely social, at least wintering and migrating in flocks, sometimes large; many species nest in loose colonies, but some larger species do so as isolated pairs; monogamous, usually for life

NEST: a bulky platform or mound of sedges or other vegetation on the ground among grass or other vegetation or in shallow water; the Grey Crowned Crane, *Balearica regulorum*, very occasionally nests in trees

EGGS: 1–4, white or heavily marked

INCUBATION: 28–36 days

FLEDGING PERIOD: 2–4 months

FOOD: a wide range of small animals, including insects, snails, crustaceans, worms and other invertebrates, fish, frogs, reptiles and young or small birds; also a variety of plant material, including roots, bulbs and tubers, shoots and seeds

VOICE: varied, from soft guttural notes to loud shrill trumpeting or piping sounds that are among the most far-carrying of all bird utterances; important during dancing displays and for flocks keeping in contact during flight

MIGRATION: six species are sedentary or make short movements only; the rest are long-distance migrants, wintering in warmer regions

CONSERVATION STATUS: one species, the Siberian Crane, *Leucogeranus leucogeranus*, is Critically Endangered; three species, the Grey Crowned Crane, *Balearica regulorum*, Whooping Crane, *G. americana*, and Red-crowned Crane, *G. japonensis*, are Endangered; seven species are Vulnerable, including the Black Crowned Crane, *B. pavonina*, the Sarus Crane, *Antigone antigone*, the Hooded Crane, *G. monacha*, and the Blue Crane, *Grus paradiseus*

The large, elegant and stately birds in this small family have a long neck, and long legs that enable them to wade in shallow water. They include the tallest of all flying birds, standing as tall as most adult humans. The Sarus Crane, *Antigone antigone*, is the biggest of all, reaching up to 1.76 m (5.8 ft) high. Even the smallest species, the Demoiselle Crane, *Grus virgo*, stands 0.85–1.0 m (2.8–3.3 ft) tall.

There are two very distinctive species in the genus *Balearica*: the Grey Crowned Crane, *B. regulorum*, resident in eastern and southern Africa; and the Black Crowned Crane, *B. pavonina*, whose range lies to the north, occupying a broad band across the continent, from Senegambia to Ethiopia.

The most speciose of the four genera is *Grus*, containing 8 of the 15 species. Just a single species of crane, the Common Crane, *G. grus*, breeds in northern Europe, with most of its population in Asia. It winters in southern Europe, northern Africa and southern Asia. Asia, by contrast, is home to seven crane species. The Demoiselle Crane, *G. virgo*, breeds from south-east European Russia and eastern Turkey to inner Mongolia, and winters in north-east Africa and southern Asia. The Blue Crane, *G. paradiseus*, is a sedentary species found only in part of South Africa and as a small, isolated population in Namibia. The Wattled Crane, *G. carunculatus*, lives in eastern and southern Africa. The White-naped Crane, *G. vipio*, breeds from northern Mongolia to the far east of Russia and China, wintering in Korea, southern Japan and east-central China; the Hooded Crane, *G. monacha*, breeds in southern Siberia and north China and winters in Japan, South Korea and east and central China; the Black-necked Crane, *G. nigricollis*, breeds on the Tibetan plateau and winters from Bhutan and northeast India to south-central China; the Red-crowned Crane (often called the Japanese or Manchurian Crane), *G. japonensis*, breeds in northern Japan and north-east China. The only wild population of the Whooping Crane, *G. americana*, breeds at Wood Buffalo Park, central Canada, and winters in southeast Texas; there are reintroduced birds in Wisconsin, Louisiana and Florida. The Siberian Crane, *G. leucogeranus*, is in a genus of its own and breeds in Siberia and winters in Iran, northwest India and China. There are four species in the genus *Antigone*. The Sarus Crane, *A. antigone*, comprises one race resident in the north of the Indian subcontinent, a migratory race breeding in Cambodia and Laos that winters in Vietnam, and a resident race in northeast Australia. A more widespread northern and eastern Australian species is the Brolga, *A. rubicunda*, with a separate population in southern New Guinea. There are two crane species in North America: the rare Whooping Crane mentioned above, and the more widely distributed Sandhill Crane, *A. canadensis*. This has a huge breeding range with populations in northeast Siberia, Alaska, Canada, and north and west-Central USA; these birds migrate to winter in the southern US and northern Mexico. There are also resident subspecies in Mississippi, Georgia, Florida and Isla de la Juventud, Cuba.

Cranes seem to be most closely related to the trumpeters (Family Psophidae) and Limpkin (Family Aramidae). The most primitive members of the family are the two crowned cranes, classified in a separate subfamily, the Balearicinae, from that of the rest, which are classified in the subfamily Gruinae. Their fossil record dates them as among the earliest of all extant bird groups, back to the Eocene epoch: between 56 and 34 million years ago, as many as 11 species of crowned

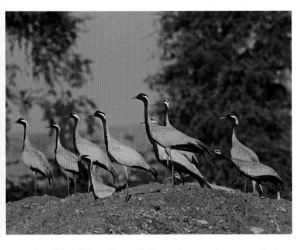

ABOVE A few of the 9,000 or so Demoiselle Cranes, *Grus virgo*, that winter at Khichan, Rajasthan, India, where local people feed and protect them.

ABOVE Red crowned Cranes, *Grus japonensis*, perform a dramatic dance on the snow at Akan International Crane Centre, Hokkaido, Japan.

cranes lived in North America and Europe, when those regions were warmer. With the advent of the ice ages, they presumably retreated to ice-free Africa. Typical cranes, by contrast, are more cold hardy, able to live in temperate climates. They evolved more recently, during the Miocene epoch, between 24 and 5 million years ago.

All cranes have long, broad wings – those of the Sarus Crane span up to 2.8 m (10 ft) – adapted for gliding and soaring flight. The elongated inner secondary feathers at the trailing edge of each wing droop over the wingtips when the bird is on the ground and hide the short, rounded tail, forming a distinctive 'bustle' or 'false 'tail'. Like herons, cranes usually extend their long legs behind them when in the air (although in cold conditions they fold them and tuck their feet beneath their breast feathers); however, unlike herons and like storks, they hold the neck fully extended forward. The bill is long but not as stout as those of storks. It varies in length – that of the crowned cranes, Demoiselle Crane and Blue Crane, for instance, is shorter, adapted for plucking grass like geese as well as feeding on seeds or insects while most *Grus* species have a longer,

more powerful bill that they use mainly for digging in soil or mud for tubers, roots and small animals.

With a long prehensile hind toe, the crowned cranes are the only members of the family able to perch in trees when roosting. Demoiselle and Blue Cranes have short-toed feet similar to those of bustards, suited to fast running in their grassland habitats. Other cranes have longer legs and broader feet, adapted for walking in marshy and muddy terrain and wading.

Males and female cranes look alike, though males are, on average, slightly larger and heavier. Several species have plumage of uniform or almost uniform colour: these include the all-white Siberian Crane and almost all-white Whooping Crane, and the Sandhill Crane, with entirely grey plumage. In other species, the plumage is in various combinations of grey and white, in some species contrasting with black on the head and neck and a black 'bustle'. In all but the Blue Crane and Demoiselle Crane (which can elongate the long plumes on the sides of the head) there are bright red areas of bare skin on the head. These can be expanded and intensified in colour by muscle action to communicate fear, threat or other behavioural states. The crowned cranes have flamboyant golden crowns of long, stiff bristlelike feathers.

All species have complex courtship behaviour. They are famous for their 'dancing' displays, in which the pair may bow, toss sticks or vegetation into the air, spread their wings, leap into the air, run about and circle one another. These may continue for hours on end (up to four in Blue Cranes, for example). The displays are accompanied by loud calls as the birds point head and neck skywards. Young, unpaired adults dance the most. However, it does not only serve to establish the pair bond, for even chicks less than 2 days old have been seen dancing.

Pairs also duet, males typically uttering longer, deeper sounds, and females shorter, higher-pitched ones. The 'unison call' not only helps maintain the pair bond but also serves as a warning to neighbouring pairs not to encroach on the pair's territory. All but the crowned cranes have a long windpipe that is coiled within the breastbone, and greatly amplifies their stirring, strident calls.

ABOVE This flock of wintering Sandhill Cranes, *Antigone canadensis,* is at Bosque del Apache National Wildlife Refuge, New Mexico.

Northern species make impressive migrations, saving energy on their long journeys to distant wintering grounds by soaring and gliding with the aid of thermals. After departing from their breeding grounds, family groups gather at traditional staging areas in flocks that may number thousands of birds. Some Common Cranes reach their winter quarters in northern India by crossing the Himalayas, reaching greater heights than the summit of Mt Everest: flocks have been seen at altitudes of almost 10,000 m (33,000 ft).

Cranes have been admired, revered – and hunted – by humans for millennia. They appear in cave paintings and in the art of ancient Egyptians, Greeks and Romans, and of China and Japan. Native peoples from all over the world where cranes live – including the Great Plains Indians of the US, and inhabitants of Siberia, China, Japan and Australia – have developed ceremonial dances of their own based on the birds' dramatic nuptial performances. Wherever they occur, cranes have been invested by people with various supposed attributes: as symbols of good fortune, happiness, marital fidelity, peace and longevity.

Cranes are, indeed, among the world's most long-lived birds: a few individuals in captivity have survived into their eighties. However, 11 of the 15 species face a barrage of threats, all resulting from human activity. The major threats comes from drainage, overgrazing by livestock and other habitat destruction and degradation, disturbance and hunting. Captive breeding and release has had some success in increasing numbers of some species, such as the Whooping Crane, but the future looks especially bleak for the most threatened of all – the Siberian Crane – unless education programmes can prevent the hunting and habitat alteration that imperil it, especially on migration.

ABOVE A Common Crane, *Grus grus*, calls at dawn in spring, at Lake Hornborga, Sweden, a vital staging site on the species' northward migrations to breed.

ORDER OTIDIFORMES

Recent molecular analysis indicates that the bustards, which were traditionally included in the Order Gruiformes, do not belong there. With no clear relationships to other birds, they are now given an order of their own.

BUSTARDS Otididae

GENERA: 11   **SPECIES:** 26

LENGTH: 40–120 cm (16–48 in)

WEIGHT: 0.45–18 kg (1–40 lb)

RANGE AND HABITAT: Europe, Africa, Asia, Australia; greatest diversity in Africa; grasslands of many types, from downland and steppes to open thornscrub, acacia savannah and semi-desert with scrub; also on agricultural land, especially edges of traditionally managed farmland

SOCIAL BEHAVIOUR: most species are social to a greater or lesser degree, in loose flocks of up to 50 birds for at least part of the year; some smaller species live for most of the year in small family groups, while some of the largest ones are more solitary, with single-sex flocks outside the breeding season; some species are monogamous and territorial, but many are polygamous, with males assembling at traditional lek sites to display to attending females. In all species, except for those in the African genus *Eupodotis*, the female selects the nest site, incubates the eggs and rears the chicks alone and there is no real pair bond

NEST: Bare scrape on ground

EGGS: 1–6, 1 or 2 in larger species; olive, buff or reddish

INCUBATION: 20–25 days

FLEDGING PERIOD: 30–40 days

FOOD: wide range of food from ground or low foliage, from scorpions and snails to small mammals and reptiles, but mainly eat insects and plant matter, including leaves, shoots and buds

VOICE: mainly silent apart from breeding season, when displaying males utter a range of generally unmusical sounds; wheezing, snoring, popping, yelping or quacking sounds in smaller species and booming, barking, croaking, grunting or drumming noises in larger ones

MIGRATION: generally sedentary, apart from relatively short nomadic movements, though northern populations of a few species migrate from central Europe and Asia to southern Asia for winter

CONSERVATION STATUS: two species, the Bengal Florican, *Houbaropsis bengalensis*, are Critically Endangered; two species, the Great Indian Bustard, *Ardeotis nigriceps*, and Ludwig's Bustard, *Neotis ludwigii*, and the Lesser Florican, *Sypheotides indicus*, are Endangered; four species are Vulnerable including the Great Bustard, *Otis tardai*, and the Asian Houbara, *Chlamydotis macqueenii*; seven species are Near Threatened

ABOVE A male Little Bustard, *Tetrax tetrax*, erects the feathers around his fleshy neck 'collar' and utters a 'snort' call in a territorial display on a Spanish steppe in May.

Bustards are a family of Old World medium-sized to large ground-dwelling birds. They have a stout but often tapering body, a rather flattened head, a long neck (slender in many smaller species but much thicker in larger ones), and a powerful, short, bill. Their longish, strong, sturdy legs, with just three toes on each foot, thick soles and flattened claws, are well adapted for walking great distances in search of often sparsely distributed food without tiring. Living in dry country, with little need for waterproofing their plumage, bustards lack a preen gland. They are thought to have evolved in Africa, and indeed today 21 of the total 26 species have all or part of their range within this continent, with 17 species endemic to the region.

Bustards range from medium-sized superficially gamebird-like birds to some of the world's heaviest flying birds, which stand about 1 m (3.3 ft) tall. The smallest include the Lesser Florican, *Sypheotides indicus*, of India, which weighs only about 0.45 kg (1 lb) and the Little Bustard, *Tetrax tetrax*, of southern Europe, northwest Africa and Asia, which although more compact weighs up to twice as much, at 0.6–0.9 kg (1.3–2 kg), and is roughly the size of a Willow Grouse or a female Pheasant. The biggest are large, stately species such as the Great Bustard, *Otis tarda*, of Eurasia and the Houbara Bustard, *Chlamydotis undulata*, of North Africa, the Middle East and western Asia. The two latter species are among the world's heaviest flying birds, with males regularly attaining 16 kg (35 lb) or more, and exceptional individuals claimed by hunters to weigh over 20 kg (44 lb). The bigger species look like shorter, stouter-necked versions of their relatives the cranes (Family Gruidae,

p. 67) as they stride across open country on their sturdy long legs, or even a smaller version of a rhea (Family Rheidae, p. 8) or other ratite. Unlike cranes, which are found mainly in swampy or marshy habitats, bustards are primarily birds of dry land.

Despite their weight, even the largest bustard species are strong fliers, probably capable of reaching speeds of up to about 60 km per hour (37 mph). They need to run across the ground before becoming airborne, although smaller species can rise almost vertically. The second part of the name 'bustard' may not, as might be expected (and as the Roman scholar Pling the Elder stated), come from the Latin word *tardus*, meaning 'slow', but from an old Spanish word *tarda*, which has a connection to the English word 'tread'. This could refer to their deliberate, measured gait when foraging.

In all species, the plumage of the upperparts in particular provides camouflage when the bird hides or 'freezes' pressed to the ground to try and avoid danger and for incubating females, which are duller than the males' brighter plumage in some species. The upperparts are generally brownish or greyish with darker mottling, streaking or barring and the underparts are whitish in the larger species and all black or black and white in some of the smaller ones. In many species, the head and neck have distinctive patterns, combining two or more colours, typically including bluish grey, buff, chestnut, black or white. The larger bustards have loose crown and neck feathers that they erect during displays, as well as an inflatable neck sac. In flight, the wings of the large species show extensive white patches.

Courtship displays at communal leks are particularly dramatic. The male Great Bustard, for instance, inflates his neck sac to produce a great feathery balloon and billows out his secondary

ABOVE This young male Great Bustard, *Otis tarda*, appears to be turning himself inside out during his courtship display in Extremadura, Spain, in April.

wing feathers and tail feathers into huge fans that conceal the brown plumage of the body so that they are transformed into a giant white powder-puff shape, visible to females at long range. Several small species (such as Little Bustards in Eurasia and North Africa, the African Black-bellied Bustard, *Lissotis melanogaster*, and the Lesser Florican of the Indian subcontinent) are usually concealed from females by long grass, so they display in flight or by leaping vertically up to 4 m (13 ft) in the air while vibrating their wings and uttering nasal calls; the Red-crested Bustard, *Lophotis ruficrista*, of southern Africa flies up vertically to reach as high as 30 m (100 ft) above ground, then flips over on its back and plummets down to pull out at the last moment and glide down to land.

Bustards are very wary birds: even if a human, dog or other threatening creature is as far as 1 km (0.6 miles) away, often they will spot the threat and take avoiding action. They prefer to run and then hide in dense vegetation or other cover, or flatten themselves on the ground, hoping to rely on their cryptic plumage to escape detection, but they may take flight if necessary.

Their cautiousness is with good reason, as this family has a high proportion of threatened species, with over a quarter of all species facing varying degrees of threat and a further six classified as Near Threatened. These birds eat huge quantities of insects such as locusts, various beetles and termites, that are harmful to agriculture, but ironically this has not protected them from the damage wrought by intensive agriculture and other habitat destruction. They have also always been highly prized by hunters, particularly in the Middle East, Africa, Pakistan and India, where they are hunted not only with the traditional falcons, but also using modern technology, from the latest firearms or global positioning systems to air-conditioned, four-wheel-drive vehicles.

ORDER MUSOPHAGIFORMES

At various times, ornithologists have suggested that this small family of endemic African birds was related to a wide range of other birds, from gamebirds and pigeons to parrots, mousebirds, trogons and woodpeckers. More recently, they were thought to be most closely related to cuckoos, and were included with that big family of birds in the Order Cuculiformes (p. 57). Recent genetic analysis suggests they are not close relatives of cuckoos, but may possibly be linked to the gamebirds (Order Galliformes, p. 19) or even to various waterbird orders, including pelicans, gannets and storks. Because of the uncertainty about their relationship they are now given an order of their own.

TURACOS Musophagidae

GENERA: 6   **SPECIES**: 23

LENGTH: 38–46 cm (15–18 in), except for the Great Blue Turaco, *Corythaeola cristata*, 70–75 cm (27.5–29.5 in)

WEIGHT: 170–548 g (6–19 oz), Great Blue Turaco 0.82–1.23 kg (1.8–2.7 lb)

RANGE AND HABITAT: Africa, south and east of the Sahara; wide range of woodlands for family as a whole include dense, humid forests at various altitudes (typical for most turacos), some also in wooded suburban gardens and plantations; go-away birds mainly in *Acacia* and thornbush savanna, plantain-eaters in wide range of scrubby open grasslands

SOCIAL BEHAVIOUR: mainly in family parties or other small groups; all turacos breed as solitary pairs that defend territory vigorously; most are probably monogamous, though some go-away birds with helpers to defend territory and feed young

NEST: flat, usually rather flimsy nest of sticks and twigs, generally well hidden in dense foliage of tree or shrub, but in go-away birds usually in acacias with little attempt if any at concealment

EGGS: usually 2 in turacos, 2–3 in others, white, cream, or very pale greyish, bluish or greenish

INCUBATION: 16–31 days

FLEDGING PERIOD: 25–38 days

FOOD: mostly fruit, also buds, shoots, flowers and leaves; a few caterpillars, termites, snails or other invertebrates eaten by some species, especially in the breeding season

VOICE: most turacos utter loud, gruff, barking sounds, often preceded by a higher-pitched hoot, pairs sing in duet, one at a higher pitch; go-away birds give loud, nasal calls that sound like their common name, repeated with a rising pitch; plantain-eaters make a series of cackling or laughing calls ending in a gradually fading chatter

MIGRATION: mainly sedentary, but most make local movements in search of fruiting trees

CONSERVATION STATUS: one species, Bannerman's Turaco, *Tauraco bannermani*, is Endangered; one species, Ruspoli's Turaco, *T. ruspolii*, is Vulnerable; and one species, Fischer's Turaco, *T. fischeri*, is Near Threatened

The turacos are mainly brightly plumaged arboreal birds living in forests, woodlands and savannahs of sub-Saharan Africa; they are among the few bird families endemic to continental Africa. The scientific name of the family, Musophagidae, is from the Greek words meaning 'plantain-eater' and by extension this was often used in the past as the common name. Even today, the two species in the genus *Crinifer* contain these two words as part of their common name. However, this is a misnomer, as in their natural habitat turacos never or only very rarely eat either wild plantains or the cultivated forms of those plants, bananas. Turacos (formerly also spelled Tauraco or Touraco) were alternatively often called 'louries' (or 'loeries') from a South African name for the birds.

All turacos have an elongated but sturdy body, with a thick neck and short, strong, stout bill with a decurved upper mandible. They have short, rounded wings and a long tail. Nearly all species have a prominent, large erectile crest and most have a striking pattern of markings on the head. All species have unusual feathers on their head and breast, which are hairlike due to the

ABOVE Go-away birds, like this White Bellied Go-away Bird, *Corythaixoides leucogaster*, are so named from their nasal calls.

The second subfamily comprises three species of go-away birds, *Corythaixoides*, and the two plantain-eaters, *Crinifer*. The Grey Go-away Bird, *Corythaixoides concolor*, is uniform grey, while the White-bellied Go-away Bird, *C. leucogaster*, is mainly grey apart from the white where its name indicates; both these have a tall, squared-off crest. The Bare-faced Go-away Bird, *C. personatus*, has most of its dark brown face almost bare of feathers, a rather floppy pointed pale greenish-brown crest, grey upperparts and whitish and pale olive chest and the rest of the underparts pinkish brown. Both species of plantain-eaters are mainly grey and brownish-grey, contrasting with a bright yellow bill, which is shared by females of the White-bellied Go-away Bird.

By far the largest subfamily is the Musophaginae, with 14 species in the major genus *Turaco*, one species of *Ruwenzorornis*, the Ruwenzori Turaco, *R. johnstoni*, and two species of *Musophaga*. All have bright red flight feathers, usually visible only when the bird is in flight or performing courtship displays involving wing spreading. Most have mainly bright green plumage, darker on the wings, in various different subspecies with purple, blue, yellow or buff gloss on the wings and tail; others have bright violet or blue or grey-blue wings and tail throughout their range, and two are almost entirely bright violaceous blue. Crests are green, with a narrow white, black-and-white or orange-and-black border in many species, but are entirely orange, red, purple, black or white in others, while head markings vary from white lines, spots or commas to black patches. Eye-rings are usually red, while the two *Musophaga* species have a large yellow shield of bare skin on the bill, extending back into a broad eye-ring in the Violet Turaco, *Musophaga violacea*.

very small number of barbules normally found in abundance on the side branches (barbs) of most birds' feathers. Also atypical is the anatomy of the feet, in which the outer toe is usually held at right angles to the main axis of the foot but can be moved further backwards or straight forwards. This versatility enables turacos to climb, leap and bound at high speed and with great agility when necessary along the branches of trees and shrubs and among dense vegetation, making up for their weak, laboured flight. Indeed, they seldom come to the ground except sometimes to drink or bathe.

Another, unique, feature of the family is the chemistry of the green and red pigments responsible for the very bright colours of the beautiful, glossy plumage of most species. These are copper compounds, red turacin and green turacoverdin, and are not found in any other birds, or indeed in the entire animal kingdom.

The subfamily Corythaeolinae contains just the Great Blue Turaco, *Corythaeola cristata*, which as its common name implies, is the largest member of the family. Indeed, it is far bigger than all the other species, at a length of 70–75 cm (27.5–29.5 in). The rest are all medium sized, at 40–54 cm (16–21 in). It is mainly quite pale greenish to greyish blue with a patch of greenish-yellow on the lower breast and one on the tail, a chestnut belly and black undertail and terminal tail band. It has a very large blue black crest and a bright yellow and red bill.

ABOVE The intensely glossy plumage of Ross's Turaco, *Musophaga rossae*, contains a very high proportion of melanin pigment.

ORDER GAVIIFORMES

This order contains just a single family (Gaviidae) of highly aquatic birds that occur on both freshwaters (mainly when breeding) and coastal waters of the seas (especially in winter). They propel themselves in the water using their webbed feet. They were formerly regarded as relatives of the grebes (Order Podicipediformes, p. 29), but this relationship has been disputed and grebes are now generally regarded as being closest to flamingos. Divers, by contrast, are members of an ancient group that includes the penguins. There is some evidence from the anatomy of their wing bones that their ancestors may have used their wings, like penguins, for propulsion under water, rather than their feet, and may have evolved foot propulsion later, as well as the ability to fly in the air.

DIVERS OR LOONS Gaviidae

GENERA: 1   **SPECIES**: 5

LENGTH: 53–91 cm (21–36 in)

WEIGHT: 1.4–5.4 kg (3–12 lb)

RANGE AND HABITAT: Northern Europe, Asia and North America; the greatest diversity is in North America; breed mainly on fresh water and winter mainly on inshore waters of sea

SOCIAL BEHAVIOUR: all five species are monogamous and highly territorial and may pair for life

NEST: large mound of aquatic vegetation on shore, usually less than 1 m (3 ft) from the water's edge

EGGS: usually 2, glossy olive brown with dark spots

INCUBATION: 24–30 days

FLEDGING PERIOD: 38–77 days

FOOD: mainly fish; also some crustaceans, molluscs and amphibians

VOICE: in breeding season, loud eerie wailing, yodelling and cooing; also croaking, barking and cackling calls; generally silent in winter

MIGRATION: most winter farther south

CONSERVATION STATUS: one species, the White-billed Diver (Yellow-billed Loon), *Gavia adamsii*, is Near Threatened

ABOVE A Great Northern Diver (Common Loon), *Gavia immer*, in winter plumage at Whitlingham Country Park, Norwich, England.

This very small family of fish-eating birds is restricted to the northern hemisphere. Among adaptations for a life spent almost entirely on or under the water are their streamlined, cigar-shaped body, legs set very far back on the body and feet with broad webs between their three front toes. This makes for very efficient swimming and diving, but renders the birds very clumsy on land, where they must shuffle along on flat surfaces (although they can run upslope) and cannot stand upright for more than a few seconds; the name 'loon' used for these birds in North America (and formerly in Scotland) probably derives from the Old Norse word *lomr*, meaning 'lame'. (Another possible alternative is that it relates to the birds' eerie wailing cries.)

Another distinctive feature of the anatomy of the divers is that the tibia and tarsus of each leg is flattened laterally to offer least resistance to the water. As with several other groups of specialised diving birds, the bones are heavy to enable the diver to counteract its natural buoyancy and sink effortlessly beneath the surface. When swimming or diving, divers propel themselves by their feet, using their short, pointed wings underwater only for steering – in contrast to birds such as auks and penguins. During their frequent dives for fish or other prey, they descend on average to between 2 m (6.5 ft) and 10 m (33 ft) and stay under for about a minute. Not infrequently though they go deeper, and have been recorded reaching depths of about 75 m (250 ft) and staying submerged for as long as 8 minutes.

The breeding plumage is subtly but beautifully patterned, with dove-grey head and neck in the Red-throated Diver (known as the Red-throated Loon in North America), *Gavia stellata*, Black-throated Diver (Arctic Loon), *G. arctica*, and Pacific Diver (Pacific Loon), *G. pacifica*, contrasting with a dark red or black throat and narrow black-and-white stripes; the last two species also have a chequerboard black-and-white pattern on the back. This is also a feature of the two larger species, the Great Northern Diver (Common Loon), *Gavia immer*, and the White-billed Diver (Yellow-billed Loon), *Gavia adamsii*, which have all-black heads and striped patches on the neck. In winter, the plumage is much duller, greyish above and paler beneath. The sexes are alike.

Although their wings are relatively small and their bodies bulky, divers are good flyers, and can cover long distances, especially when migrating. The smallest species, the Red-throated Diver, flies several times each day from the small freshwater lakes or pools where it prefers to breed to the coast to find fish for itself and its offspring. This enables it to exploit much smaller water bodies compared with other species, which normally obtain all their food from the larger lakes (or rivers in the case of some White-billed Divers) where they breed. In winter, all species mainly move to

LEFT A pair of Red-throated Divers (Red-throated Loons), *Gavia stellata*, perform a dramatic threat display on a pool in Finland to drive off rivals from their territory.

sheltered coastal waters, but some will winter on fresh waters, as long as these remain unfrozen.

In the breeding season, divers are very vocal, and their loud, wild wailing, yodelling and laughing calls are a feature not only of northern lakes but also of Hollywood films as a stereotypical sound evoking wilderness. Divers are highly territorial, and pairs or individuals perform dramatic ritualised aggressive displays when defending their domain against intruders. These include raising the neck to display the throat markings, circling, bill-dipping and 'splash-diving'; usually such warnings suffice, but if not a fight may ensue that can result in the death of one or both protagonists by drowning or spearing with the formidable bill.

All species favour undisturbed habitat for breeding, and human disturbance poses a major problem, often resulting in breeding failure. Other important causes of egg and chick losses are flooding of the nests, which lie very near the water's edge, and predation by mammals such as foxes, stoats and other mustelids, birds such as gulls and skuas, and fish such as pike. In addition, divers often do not attempt to breed in some years (typically doing so in three out of every four years). As adults, they face threats ranging from oil spills to drowning in fishing nets, and are likely to suffer in the future from global warming.

ORDER SPHENISCIFORMES

This order contains just a single, highly distinctive family (Spheniscidae) of exclusively marine birds, highly adapted to swimming and diving in the oceans, propelled by their 'flippers' (modified wings). Their closest relatives appear to be the divers (North American: loons) of the Order Gaviiformes and the albatrosses, shearwaters and petrels and relatives ('tubenoses') of the Order Procellariiformes (see p. 77), but they may also share a relationship with the storks in the Family Ciconiidae (see p. 88). Like these two orders, penguins are an ancient group of birds, with many of the oldest fossil penguins being recent discoveries. It is likely that they diverged from their relatives at least 62 million years ago, during the early Tertiary period. The common ancestors of the three orders of seabirds mentioned above appear to date back as far as the late Cretaceous period, about 74 million years ago, when they are thought to have diverged from the shorebird lineage (Order Charadriiformes), which includes the waders (North American: shorebirds), gulls, auks and relatives.

PENGUINS Spheniscidae

GENERA: 6   **SPECIES:** 16

LENGTH: 40–115 cm (16–45 in)

WEIGHT: 1–46 kg (2.2–101 lb)

RANGE AND HABITAT: Antarctic, Atlantic and Pacific oceans, with the greatest diversity in the sub-Antarctic region; mostly at sea (some species spend months on end without leaving the water), but breeding and moulting on land (mainland coasts and islands) or even ice (Emperor Penguin, *Aptenodytes forsteri*)

SOCIAL BEHAVIOUR: most species are very social, especially when breeding, maintaining only very small territory around the nest; monogamous

NEST: rudimentary assemblage of stones, vegetation and moulted feathers, on ground in the open, among vegetation, beneath rocks or among tree roots, or in a burrow or cave; the Emperor Penguin nests on bare ice and, like the King Penguin, *Aptenodytes patagonicus*, builds no nest, keeping the egg and chick warm resting on the feet, wrapped in a special fold of skin above the vent

EGGS: two in most species; one in the King and Emperor Penguins; white

INCUBATION: 33–65 days

FLEDGING PERIOD: 2–13 months

FOOD: small fish, squid, krill and other crustaceans

VOICE: at breeding colonies, cacophony of braying, trumpeting, cackling or other sounds, individually recognisable to the birds among the din; usually silent at other times

MIGRATION: dispersal from breeding colonies to spend the winter at sea

CONSERVATION STATUS: five species, the Erect-crested Penguin, *Eudyptes sclateri*, Northern Rockhopper Penguin, *E. moseleyi*, Yellow-eyed Penguin, *Megadyptes antipodes*, African Penguin, *Spheniscus demersus*, and Galapagos Penguin, *S. mendiculus*, are Endangered; five species, including the Macaroni Penguin, *E. chrysolophus*, and Fiordland Penguin, *E. pachyrhynchus*, are Vulnerable; two species, and the Magellanic Penguin, *S. magellanicus*, and Emperor Penguin, *Aptenodytes forsteri*, are Near Threatened other birds, which have alternating tracts of feathers and bare patches, this forms a uniform layer over the whole body, wings and tail.

The most striking adaptation of the penguin is that the shortened wings have become flippers, able to deliver powerful flicks that drive the birds fast through the water when they are submerged (when swimming on the surface their progress is much slower, as they cannot flap their wings fully and they experience more turbulence). This evolutionary transformation involved the wing bones becoming flattened and fitting together like the pieces of a jigsaw, producing a very strong, rigid bladelike structure. A result of this is that the penguin cannot fold its wings like other birds.

Other adaptations to swimming and diving in cold water include the thick layer of fat beneath the skin, which provides excellent insulation, reinforced by a layer of warmed air immediately above. Warming is facilitated by complex network of blood vessels in the flippers (the vascular rete, or net) that acts as a heat exchanger, with the cooled blood passing from the flipper back into the body being warmed by the outward-flowing blood, so that there is minimal heat loss from the body.

Another adaptation is the behavioural one of 'porpoising', in which most penguins gain extra speed at the surface by bouncing through the waves like cetaceans. The short legs and sturdy webbed feet, situated at the rear of the body, are used in the water as a rudder, aided by the short, stiff tail. In contrast to some other highly adapted diving birds with legs at the rear, such as divers or grebes, penguins stand upright on land and most can walk and climb relatively well when ashore or on ice. Species breeding on ice move faster by tobogganing on their belly.

ABOVE A pair of Rockhopper Penguins, *Eudyptes chrysocome*, on the Falkland Islands, in the South Atlantic.

Although penguins are among the most familiar of all birds and are among the most popular zoo animals, they are not often encountered by most people in the wild. Many are surprised to learn that they are not restricted to the Antarctic, with one species, the Galapagos Penguin, *Spheniscus mendiculus*, occurring on the islands for which it is named, as far north as the equator. All others dwell in the southern hemisphere, with most species in the sub-Antarctic and Antarctic regions. No penguins occur in the Arctic.

Penguins are perfectly adapted to life in – and especially under – the sea, with their whole structure and biology modified for their lifestyle, more than in any other birds. Although they vary considerably in size, from the Little Penguin, *Eudyptula minor*, standing 40 cm (16 in) high and weighing 1 kg (2.2 lb), to the Emperor Penguin, *Aptenodytes forsteri*, which can attain almost 1.2 m (4 ft) and 46 kg (101 lb), they share the same stout but streamlined body shape, with a rounded head and tapering towards the short tail at the rear. This facilitates their swift progress through the water, made even more efficient by the smooth surface of their dense, well-oiled waterproof plumage, which is unique in consisting of small, very tough, stiff spear-shaped feathers. Unlike that of most

ABOVE A parent Emperor Penguin, *Aptenodytes forsteri*, with its chick, on the ice in the Weddell Sea, Antarctica.

Gentoo Penguins, *Pygoscelis papua*, are probably the fastest swimmers of all birds, able to 'fly' underwater at up to 36 km/h (22 mph); Emperor Penguins hold the world deep diving record for birds, one having been recorded near the bed of the Ross Sea at up to 500 m (1,650 ft). They are capable of remaining underwater for up to 18 minutes.

The plumage in penguins is black or bluish-grey above and white below. The sexes look the same, but males are slightly bigger than females. Differing patterns on the head enable different species to recognise one another, even when in the water. The Emperor Penguin and King Penguin, *Aptenodytes patagonicus*, have prominent orange markings on the sides of the neck and on the bill as well as a golden flush to the chest, whereas seven species have bright yellow to gold crests above their eyes. The colours of bill and legs are pinkish, reddish or black.

In most species, the bill (which is lined within by backward-facing spines to grip prey) is laterally compressed, and is shorter and stouter in species that feed largely on plankton. In the mainly fish- and squid-eating King Penguin and Emperor Penguin it is longer and more slender. Apart from these two largest penguins, species living around Antarctica, such as the Adélie and Chinstrap Penguins, *Pygoscelis adeliae* and *P. antarctica*, prey largely on crustaceans, especially the shrimplike krill. Most species eat more fish and squid, but diet within a species often varies with locality and seasonal availability. Penguins may travel huge distances to feed: up to 800 km (500 miles) or more in King Penguins, for instance.

Almost all species breed in dense colonies, sometimes containing several hundreds of thousands of pairs. All penguins are monogamous, at least for one season, and some may reunite from one year to the next.

ABOVE King Penguins, *Aptenodytes patagonicus*, in a huge, tightly packed nesting colony, or 'rookery', at Royal Bay, South Georgia.

ABOVE King Penguins, *Aptenodytes patagonicus*, huddle together during a storm at Right Whale Bay, South Georgia.

ORDER PROCELLARIIFORMES

The birds in this order are all normally totally marine, except when individuals are occasionally driven inland by storms. Outside the breeding season, they stay mostly well out to sea, travelling huge distances in search of food and on migration to and from their breeding colonies, typically on remote islands. Here they cope with the roughest weather, and indeed in most cases rely on strong winds for their energy-saving flight. They include both the smallest seabirds, the sparrow to thrush-sized storm-petrels, and the biggest, the albatrosses and giant petrels.

The most distinctive feature uniting all four families in this order is their large tubular external nostrils on the culmen (the ridge on top of the bill), from which they earn the group name 'tubenoses'. These are related to the birds' exceptionally well-developed sense of smell, which they use to locate nest sites, mates and young when returning to the breeding colony and probably also to locate food. The bill is hooked, and made up of a number of horny plates. The wings are generally long (except in the diving-petrels), and the feet webbed. Except in the albatrosses and giant petrels, whose short legs are positioned more centrally, allowing them to stand and waddle about with relative ease on land, the legs are set far back on the body, permitting only an awkward shuffling motion when visiting their breeding colonies. Other morphological features the four families have in common include the enlarged salt-extracting nasal gland above the eyes, which removes salt from the seawater the birds drinks.

The clutch consists of a single egg, large in relation to the female. Incubation, and especially rearing of the young bird, is very prolonged. Chicks are fed, often at intervals of many hours or days, on a rich, highly calorific diet, consisting of a soup-like or paste-like mixture of partially digested food and its parents' stomach oil. They put on a great deal of weight, and before they eventually leave the nest are often heavier than an adult.

Evidence from both molecular and morphological data support the long-held view that the closest relatives of the Procellariformes appear to be the penguins (Order Sphenisciformes). A recent proposal, which is based on both morphological and genetic differences, has been for the separation of the southern storm-petrels as a separate family, Oceanitidae, from the northern storm-petrels, in the Family Hydrobatidae (see also p. 83), and it is this scheme that we follow here.

Molecular studies suggest that these two groups have undergone a very long period of evolution in separate hemispheres and might be better regarded as separate families. The Hydrobatidae breed mainly in the northern hemisphere and the Oceanitidae almost entirely in the southern hemisphere, but they overlap in the tropics. Some species in each group make very long migrations between breeding colonies and wintering areas in the opposite hemisphere; examples are Wilson's Storm-petrel, a member of the Oceanitidae, which travels each year between breeding grounds on sub-Antarctic islands and Antarctica to the Indian, Atlantic and Pacific oceans, reaching as far north as the sea off Newfoundland. In a reverse of this pattern, the European Storm-petrel, *Hydrobates pelagicus*, from the Hydrobatidae, breeds in northwest Europe and winters as far south as the waters around South Africa.

Another recent suggestion, also followed here, is to subsume the diving petrels, within the shearwater and petrel family, Procellariidae (see also p. 84).

SOUTHERN STORM-PETRELS Oceanitidae

GENERA: 5   **SPECIES: 8**

LENGTH: 15–26 cm (6–10 in)

WEIGHT: 14–86 g (0.5–3 oz)

RANGE AND HABITAT: breed mainly on small islands in all oceans in the Southern Hemisphere and one species, the white-faced storm-petrel, *Pelagodroma marina*, with colonies on islands in the North Atlantic; for most of the year, they live in open oceans, with some migrating far into the Northern Hemisphere

SOCIAL BEHAVIOUR: gregarious throughout the year, especially at concentrations of food at sea; breed in colonies, sometimes very large; monogamous, probably pairing for life

NEST: mostly in a chamber at the end of a short burrow dug out by both sexes, or in crevices among rocks

EGGS: 1, white, sometimes with very fine spots at larger end

INCUBATION: 35–59 days

FLEDGING PERIOD: 46–97 days

FOOD: mainly planktonic crustaceans (especially krill and amphipods), as well as small squid and fish; also molluscs and other marine invertebrates, offal and other refuse (especially oily and fatty waste) from ships, and whale or dolphin faeces

VOICE: generally silent at sea, apart from chattering or peeping sounds when competing for food; at breeding colonies, extremely noisy, uttering a bizarre or eerie cacophony of grating, cooing, purring, squeaking, twittering, moaning, peeping or whistling sounds

MIGRATION: some species are more or less sedentary, making only local movements to and from the breeding colonies, but others are long-distance migrants, in some cases reaching far into the Northern Hemisphere

CONSERVATION STATUS: one species, the recently (2003) rediscovered New Zealand Storm-petrel, *Fregetta maoriana*, is Critically Endangered; one species, the Polynesian Storm-petrel, *Nesofregetta fuliginosa*, is Endangered

ABOVE A Wilson's Storm-petrel, *Oceanites oceanicus*, appears to walk across the water as it plucks food from the surface off the island of Madeira in August.

This family of little seabirds was originally lumped together with the northern storm-petrels as one of two subfamilies in a single storm-petrel family, Hydrobatidae. Recently, however, it has been established from DNA studies (which in turn corroborate historic evidence based on differences in the wing and skeletons and muscles) that the two groups are not so closely related, and so should be classified as separate families. Surprisingly, the diminutive southern storm-petrels may be most closely related to the huge albatrosses of the Family Diomedeidae (see p. 79), although their precise relationships within the Order Procellariiformes is the subject of ongoing research. The southern storm-petrels are far more diverse taxonomically than the northern ones, with five genera, three of which contain only a single species each.

Compared to the northern storm-petrels, the southern storm-petrels have proportionately shorter wings, a shorter, generally square-ended tail and longer legs, which often project beyond the tail in flight. Most species have dark brown or blackish plumage with white on the rump and often on the underwings and underparts, and with pale diagonal upperwing bars. They also have more variable plumage than southern storm-petrels, often with several different plumage forms in a single species. There is no difference in plumage between the sexes.

Despite their very small size (ranging from the size of sparrows to small thrushes, they include the world's smallest seabirds) and delicate appearance, storm-petrels of both families are immensely hardy birds, spending most of their lives flying low above the open ocean, far from shore. They can cope with extreme conditions,

except very occasionally when forced inland by severe storms, and come to land only to breed, chiefly on small isolated offshore islands. Superb fliers, they only occasionally land on the water, though their webbed feet equip them well for swimming. Their flight style varies between species, from erratic and fluttering – in some cases rather batlike – to stronger and faster, more like a swallow, with sudden changes in direction in some species. Southern storm-petrels alternate fluttering flight with slow glides, in which they often hold their wings in a shallow 'V'.

Storm-petrels of both families feed on the wing, chiefly by fluttering or hovering just above the surface of the sea, with their legs dangling, and dip their heads down to pluck food from the water, often following the face of a wave. Some species patter with their feet held along or just beneath the surface, so they appear to be walking on the water. (This may be the origin of the name 'petrel', from a supposed link to the biblical disciple Peter, who tried to walk on the water.) One of the best known members of this family, Wilson's Storm-petrel, *Oceanites oceanicus*, not only patters but often faces into the wind, effectively soaring on the spot with its wings spread wide and feet submerged to serve as anchors, as it looks around for food.

Their keen sense of smell helps storm-petrels of both families detect food from a distance. When they have located it, they usually reach down and peck their prey from the ocean surface or just below it, with only the bill or head contacting the water. Since the bill is relatively small and with a narrow gape, they are restricted to smaller prey, from planktonic invertebrates or small squid to little fish.

All species visit their breeding colonies only after nightfall, to reduce the chances of attack by gulls, skuas, birds of prey or other predators. Their long legs (as with the northern storm-petrels, proportionately longer than those of other members of the Procellariiformes) are very weak and cannot support their weight for any distance, so they shuffle along and rest every few steps on their bellies. Colonies vary in size: some may contain only a few dozen pairs while others may hold tens of thousands. Although they are highly vulnerable to habitat destruction and especially the depredations of introduced rats, cats or other predators to their remote breeding islands, some species are still very successful; Wilson's Storm-petrel is one of the world's most numerous birds, with a total population estimated at between 12 million and 30 million individuals.

As their name suggests, the southern storm-petrels breed almost entirely in the southern hemisphere, compared to the northern storm-petrels that breed mainly in the northern hemisphere, but the families' distribution overlaps in the tropics. Some species in each family make very long migrations between breeding colonies and wintering areas in the opposite hemisphere: examples include Wilson's Storm-petrel, which travels each year between its breeding grounds on sub-Antarctic islands and Antarctica to winter in the Indian, Atlantic and Pacific oceans, reaching as far north as the sea off Newfoundland. In a reverse of this pattern, the European Storm-petrel, *Hydrobates pelagicus*, best known member of the northern storm-petrel family, breeds in northwest Europe and winters as far south as the waters around South Africa.

ALBATROSSES Diomedeidae

GENERA: 4 **SPECIES**: 13

LENGTH: 71–140 cm (28–55 in)

WEIGHT: 1.8–11.9 kg (4–26.2 lb)

RANGE AND HABITAT: nine southern hemisphere species range mainly across the Southern Ocean, while three breed and feed in the North Pacific and one (the Waved Albatross) in the east-central Pacific; most stay far out in open ocean for most of their lives, coming ashore only to breed on islands, mostly remote

SOCIAL BEHAVIOUR: most are solitary at sea but some may gather at good sources of food; mostly colonial breeders, some in large colonies; monogamous, pairing for life; most are not usually mature until 7–15 years old

NEST: all southern species build a raised nest of mud, grass and moss on the ground; the three North Pacific species make far more rudimentary nests; the Waved Albatross is unique in making no nest but laying its egg on the bare ground

EGGS: 1, white, often with a sprinkling of pale red-brown markings

INCUBATION: usually 60–79 days

FLEDGING PERIOD: 120–280 days

FOOD: squid, fish, krill and other invertebrates; some offal and carrion

VOICE: groans, croaks and shrieks when feeding; courtship displays are accompanied by loud braying, trumpeting, grunting or whistling notes, as well as bill-clattering

MIGRATION: most species make long journeys from their breeding grounds in search of food and after breeding often travel huge distances

CONSERVATION STATUS: one species, the Waved Albatross, *Phoebastria irrorata*, and two subspecies of Wandering Albatross, *Diomedea exulans dabbenena* (which breeds on Tristan da Cunha and Gough Island) and *D. e. amsterdamensis* (which breeds on Amsterdam Island), are Critically Endangered; three species, the Sooty Albatross, *Phoebetria fusca*, the Yellow-nosed Albatross, *T. chlororhynchos*, and the Grey-headed Albatross, *T. chrysostoma*, the northern subspecies of Royal Albatross, *D. epomophora sanfordi* (which breeds on Otago Peninsula, New Zealand, Chatham Islands) and the subspecies of Wandering Albatross, *D. e. antipodensis*, breeding on Antipodes and Campbell Islands, are Endangered; one species the Short-tailed Albatross, *Phoebastria albatrus*, and five subspecies are Vulnerable; (four species and two subspecies) are Near Threatened

These magnificent birds are the biggest of all seabirds, and include in the pair of species making up the genus *Diomedea* the largest of all flying birds, at least in terms of wingspan (hence their collective name of 'great albatrosses'). Their wings are narrow as well as very long, up to 3.63 m (almost 12 ft) in *Diomedea*, with the bones of the 'forearm' exceptionally long in relation to those of the 'hand'. These are ideally suited to soaring above the waves. They have a large but compact body, a longish, stout neck, short legs and a short tail. The bill is massive, sharp-edged and distinctly hooked, well adapted for seizing elusive and slippery squid, octopuses and fish.

Albatrosses are among the most accomplished of all flying creatures, able to use the updraughts rising from the windward slopes of the waves to slope-soar like a glider. At times they may also take advantage of the differential speeds of the wind near the wave surface and high above it to perform another type of soaring known as 'dynamic soaring'. Both are extremely energy-efficient forms of locomotion, enabling these birds to travel vast distances in search of food and when dispersing and migrating. The great albatrosses in particular, with the huge length of their wings providing maximum lift, can fly with scarcely a wingbeat for many days on end. They have a locking system based on a sheet of tendon that allows them to hold their wings spread constantly with virtually no muscular effort. Most albatrosses rely on the steadily blowing winds that surround the Antarctic continent and those further north in the southern oceans, north to a latitude of about 35°S, (including the 'furious fifties' and 'roaring forties' well known to mariners). Many albatrosses follow ships, not only to feed on food scraps or fishery discards, but also in periods of relative calm to gain extra lift from the air displacement off the vessels' sides and superstructure. Without a strong wind, swimming albatrosses must patter laboriously across the surface with their feet to take off, and during rare periods of total calm, they may have to sit it out until they can become airborne.

Some species of albatross are capable of circumnavigating the globe, and some of the great albatrosses in particular may cover staggering distances in remarkably short times, as demonstrated by satellite tracking. One radio-collared Wandering Albatross was found to have covered 33,000 km (20,500 miles) in just 10 weeks. Parents of this species often travel up to 10,000 km (6,000 miles) to find food for their chick. Few other birds can move unaided so far so quickly, in some cases as much as 1,000 km (600 miles) in a day.

ABOVE A Black-browed Albatross, *Thalassarche melanophris*, soars with consummate skill over the south Atlantic Ocean.

ABOVE A pair of Grey-headed Albatrosses, *Thalassarche chrysostoma*, manouevre in air currents at a cliff-top nesting site.

The family comprises four genera. The two species of 'great albatrosses' make up the genus *Diomedea*. Of these, the Wandering Albatross, *D. exulans*, is the more widespread breeder, breeding on many islands in the south Atlantic, Indian and Pacific oceans. There are five distinguishable populations, here regarded as constituting five distinctive subspecies but afforded full species rank by some taxonomists. The form inhabiting Amsterdam Island is by far the rarest, and indeed has the smallest population of any albatross – at the time of writing constituting a total population of fewer than 200 individuals. The Royal Albatross, *D. epomophora*; with two distinctive subspecies (or species, according to some), breeds on islands in the New Zealand region.

The great albatrosses share the vastness of the Southern Ocean with five smaller (but still impressively sized) species in the largest genus, *Thalassarche*, collectively known as 'mollymawks'. (Again, as with the great albatrosses, alternative taxonomies recognise some distinctive island populations as forming full species, up

to nine or even 11.) Mollymawks range in size from the Yellow-nosed Albatross, *T. chlororhynchos*, with a wingspan of less than 2 m (6.6 ft), via a group of three medium-sized species, the Black-browed Albatross, *T. melanophris*, the Grey-headed Albatross, *T. chrysostoma*, and Buller's Albatross, *T. bulleri*, to the largest, the Shy Albatross, *T. cauta*. The Yellow-nosed Albatross has two widely separated populations, one breeding on Gough and Tristan da Cunha islands in the south Atlantic, and the other on various south Indian Ocean islands. The Grey-headed and Black-browed species both have a circumpolar breeding range. The Shy and Buller's albatrosses, by contrast, have far more restricted breeding ranges – in both cases on islands around New Zealand, with a population of the former species also on Tasmania. The Black-browed Albatross is one of the most widespread and the most numerous of all albatrosses, although it is a mark of the threats facing the family as a whole that even this species has suffered huge declines.

All but one of the four *Phoebastria* species (sometimes called 'gooneys') are, in contrast to the rest of the family, denizens of the northern hemisphere, breeding far away from their relatives on islands in the central and north Pacific Ocean. The Black-footed Albatross, *P. nigripes*, and the Laysan Albatross, *P. immutabilis*, breed mainly on islands of western Hawaii with outlying colonies far away on islands of Japan and, for the Laysan Albatross, also off the west coast of Mexico. The Laysan Albatross is the next most abundant species after the Black-browed Albatross (both with several hundred thousand breeding pairs) but the Short-tailed Albatross, *P. albatrus*, is now one of the rarest. It breeds only on an outermost island of Japan, Tori-shima, and the island of Minami-kojima (Senkaku), claimed jointly by Japan, China and Taiwan. It was thought to be extinct after the depredations of plume-hunters during the nineteenth and early twentieth centuries. Following its rediscovery in 1951, rigorous protection has seen the numbers steadily increase from 25 birds (including perhaps as few as six breeding pairs) in 1954 to a total of about 4,200 individuals, including about 650 breeding pairs. But its very small breeding range and threats including deaths due to fisheries, oil and other pollution and an active volcano. Uniquely, the fourth member of this genus, the Waved Albatross, *P. irrorata*, is tropical, breeding almost entirely on Hood Island in the Galapagos apart from a very small colony on La Plata Island, off the coast of mainland Ecuador. Thought to be the most primitive member of the family, with less wind assistance around the equator, it relies far more on powered flight than the others. It also has by far the smallest range, where it is the sole albatross species and is declining at a worrying rate.

The fourth genus, *Phoebetria*, comprises a pair of sooty albatrosses. The Sooty Albatross, *P. fusca*, breeds on islands in the south Atlantic and Indian oceans, whereas the Light-mantled Albatross, *P. palpebrata*, is more widespread, with a circumpolar range; it is also the only albatross that regularly ventures into the pack-ice zone fringing the Antarctic continent. Both species are the most sleek and streamlined members of the family, with especially long, tapering wings and a long, wedge-shaped tail. They prefer to nest in solitary pairs on cliff ledges rather than on the ground, and they catch much of their food by diving.

ABOVE A Light-mantled Albatross, *Phoebetria palpebrata*, comes in to land at a breeding colony on South Georgia.

The plumage of most adult albatrosses is black or brown above, in some species also with a white (or grey) head, neck and body; the tail is typically white with a broad dark terminal band – all white in the great albatrosses. The plumage generally becomes whiter with age, with particularly complex variations by sex as well as age in the great albatrosses. The Waved Albatross has a pale brown body, and the Black-footed Albatross and *Phoebetria* albatrosses have all-dark plumage (the Light-mantled Albatross, as its name suggests, has a contrasting ashy-grey area around the hind-neck, mantle and upper back).

Wandering Albatrosses appear to catch their main prey, squid and fish, at or near the sea surface, mainly by swimming and lunging at the prey. They may also make the occasional very shallow dive to a depth of no more than 1 m (3.3 ft) or so from the surface, or from flight just above it. Some of the smaller albatrosses, such as the mollymawks, dive far more frequently, typically to about 2–3 m (6.5–10 ft), while the two sooty species habitually catch much of their food by diving, to considerably greater depths than the rest of the family, reaching 12 m (40 ft) or more. As well as live prey, albatrosses take advantage of dead or dying prey, including that discarded by fishing vessels or stolen from their compatriots or from other seabirds; the great albatrosses, in particular, appear to obtain a good deal of food by scavenging.

Albatrosses often choose sloping sites for breeding, so that they can easily take off by facing into the wind and jumping into the air. Although their long narrow wings make them superb gliders, their high wing loading (total weight to wing area ratio), combines with turbulence created off the trailing edge of the wings to increase their stalling speed. The result is that they are very unstable when taking off and landing, and often tumble head over heels in a most undignified manner.

Courtship is a dramatic affair, involving elaborate rituals in which a pair of birds point the bill skywards with wings spread out in heraldic poses, bow, or perform stylised preening motions, turning the head to jab their great bills into their shoulder feathers. These are all accompanied by loud braying or other calls and clapping the mandibles of the bill together to produce a sound like a football supporter's wooden rattle. The various different movements have

ABOVE A breeding colony of Black-browed Albatrosses, *Thalassarche melanophris*, at Steeple Jason Island in the Falkland archipelago.

ABOVE A male Wandering Albatross, *Diomedea exulans*, reaches the climax of his 'ecstatic' display at Albatross Island, Bay of Isles, South Georgia.

been given evocative names such as 'bill circling', 'bill clappering', 'sky pointing', 'sway walking' and 'flank touching'. Many of them are common to all species of albatross, and they often involve the pair facing one another. The calls accompanying some postures are more specific; Waved Albatrosses, for instance, utter rapid 'ha-ha-ha-ha' notes with their bills wide open as they abruptly extend their necks vertically.

The egg is very large in relation to the size of the bird (6–10% of the female's total body weight) and in the two great albatrosses is incubated for longer than in any other birds (apart from the kiwis, with a similar range of incubation period): in most individuals for 78–79 days, but in some for as 'few' as 74 days or as many as 85 days. It takes so long for the great albatrosses to rear a family that they are only able to breed every 2 years at best. Added to this is the fact that they are not fully mature until at least 9 years old, usually 10 or 11, and sometimes not until they are 15.

However, albatrosses can live a very long time, with among the longest potential lifespans of any birds. The oldest recorded albatross – and the oldest known seabird – was a female Royal Albatross. First named Blue-white, she was ringed in 1937, when already adult (and probably at least 9 years old, the age when great albatrosses usually first breed), on arrival at a breeding colony on Taiaroa Head, New Zealand. In November 1988, when she was 60 years old, and renamed Grandma, she still managed to lay an egg, before disappearing in 1990.

Of all the bird families, this one contains the highest proportion of threatened species. Indeed, all species of albatrosses face a range of threats resulting from human activity, from destruction or degradation of their nesting habitat to the introduction of animals such as pigs, goats, cattle, cats, dogs and rats; in the case of

Wandering Albatrosses on Gough Island, the culprit is the House Mouse, which eats the helpless young chicks alive. The major threat for decades until very recently came from the practice of longlining, in which fishing vessels (often operating illegally) pay out lines of 100 km (62 miles) or more, to which are attached baited hooks every few metres – up to 3,000 or so in total. The seabirds clamouring over this easy food source included many thousand of albatrosses, which were drowned as they snagged their bill on the hooks and were dragged under the water surface. At its height, this appalling 'by-catch' may have resulted in the deaths of almost 50,000 albatrosses each year. Various simple devices and methods for ensuring albatross and hook do not meet have been developed and are being employed on a large scale, and the death rate has fallen greatly, so there are grounds for cautious optimism.

ABOVE The Waved (or Galapagos) Albatross, *Phoebastria irrorata*, is the only albatross species that is restricted to the tropics.

NORTHERN STORM-PETRELS Hydrobatidae

GENERA: 1   **SPECIES**: 15

LENGTH: 13–27 cm (5–10.6 in)

WEIGHT: 14–112 g (0.5–4 oz)

RANGE AND HABITAT: worldwide, in all oceans except the Arctic; greatest abundance in the cold waters around Antarctica and areas of marine upwelling such as the Humboldt Current, off Peru; open ocean, ranging far from land, which they visit only to breed; on remote coasts or islands

SOCIAL BEHAVIOUR: generally solitary or in small groups (especially at concentrations of food) at sea; breed in colonies, sometimes very large; monogamous, probably pairing for life

NEST: in a chamber at the end of a short burrow dug out by both sexes, or among rocks or grass tussocks or other vegetation; sometimes lined with feathers, vegetation or pebbles

EGGS: 1, white, sometimes with very fine spots at the larger end in some species

INCUBATION: 38–70 days

FLEDGING PERIOD: 52–119 days

FOOD: mainly planktonic crustaceans (especially krill and amphipods), as well as small squid and fish; also molluscs and other marine invertebrates, offal and other refuse (especially oily and fatty waste) from ships, and whale or dolphin faeces

VOICE: generally silent at sea, apart from chattering or peeping sounds when competing for food; at breeding colonies, extremely noisy, uttering a bizarre or eerie cacophony of grating, cooing, purring, squeaking, twittering, moaning, peeping or whistling sounds

MIGRATION: some species are more or less sedentary, making only local movements to and from the breeding colonies; others make long migrations, often between the northern and southern hemispheres

CONSERVATION STATUS: one species, the Guadalupe Storm-petrel, *Hydrobates macrodactylus*, is Critically Endangered (Possibly Extinct); one species, the Ashy Storm-petrel, *Hydrobates homochroa* is Endangered; three species, Monteiro's Storm-petrel, *H. monteiroi*, Matsudaira's Storm-petrel, *H. matsudairae*, and Leach's Storm-petrel, *H. leucorhous*, are Vulnerable; and two species, Swinhoe's Storm-petrel, *H. monorhis*, and Tristram's Storm-petrel, *H. tristrami*, are Near Threatened

This family of diminutive seabirds was originally lumped together with the southern storm-petrels (see p. 77) as one of two subfamilies in a single storm-petrel Family Hydrobatidae. Recent molecular research, however, backs up studies from as long ago as the late nineteenth century of the wing and leg skeletons and musculature of the two groups and shows that they are not so closely related and should be separated into two distinct familes. The relationships of both these families to the rest of the order Procellariiformes are not certain, though it seems that the northern storm-petrels may be most closely related to the petrels and shearwaters of the Family Procellariidae. The general features of storm-petrels of both families can be found in the account of the southern storm-petrel family.

The northern storm-petrel family is more speciose, with almost twice as many species, 15, as there are of southern storm-petrels, with eight species. But although they were traditionally assigned to three different genera, they are now considered to all belong to the same genus, *Hydrobates*. This contrasts with the situation in the southern storm-petrel family, where there is greater taxonomic diversity, with five genera that have long been recognised, three of which contain only a single species each.

Compared to the southern storm-petrels, the members of this family have longer wings, wedge-shaped or forked tails, and shorter legs. They feed less often than the southern storm-petrels by hovering or pattering across the ocean surface, usually fluttering low over the water and frequently making use of dynamic soaring, gaining energy by gliding along the front of waves.

The plumage of most species is very similar, being dark blackish or brownish all over apart from pale upperwing bars and in some species a white rump, although two species differ markedly: the Fork-tailed Storm-petrel, *H. furcatus*, is almost uniformly pale grey, and Hornby's Storm-petrel, *H. hornbyi*, is grey above with a dark cap and white below with a grey collar.

ABOVE A European Storm-petrel, *Hydrobates pelagicus*, at its nest site on Mousa Broch, an Iron Age tower on the island of Mousa, Shetland.

More species in this family are endangered than in the southern storm-petrel family. One, the Guadalupe Storm-petrel, *H. macrodactylus*, endemic to the Pacific island of Guadalupe, off the west coast of Mexico's Baja California peninsula, may already be extinct: it has not been recorded since 1912 and may have succumbed to predation by introduced cats and nesting habitat destruction by goats.

PETRELS AND SHEARWATERS Procellariidae

GENERA: 16   **SPECIES**: 84

LENGTH: 23–99 cm (9–39 in)

WEIGHT: 90 g–5 kg (3 oz–11 lb)

RANGE AND HABITAT: worldwide, in all oceans; greatest diversity in the southern hemisphere; spend most of their lives at sea, often far out in open ocean; most breed on remote islands or coasts

SOCIAL BEHAVIOUR: most species forage in small to large groups, especially at rich food sources, and breed in colonies; monogamous and probably mate for life

NEST: most nest in crevices or burrows they dig themselves or take over from another animal, some among boulders or on the ground beneath bushes or other cover; those in the fulmar-petrel group nest on cliff ledges, on the ground, or in crevices

EGGS: 1, white

INCUBATION: 43–60 days

FLEDGING PERIOD: 41–132 days

FOOD: most are adaptable feeders on a wide range of marine prey, from fish and their eggs to squid, jellyfish and krill and other crustaceans, as well as carrion and offal, much of it discarded from fishing vessels; the two giant petrels feed on land as well as at sea, on carrion and bird and mammal prey

VOICE: great variety of mainly harsh sounds, including croaks, wails, cackles, screams, throaty coos, grunts, whistles, trills and squeaks delivered in a bizarre cacophony from courting birds and pairs at breeding colonies in nest burrows or other sites and in the air; some species make croaks, grunts and other sounds when feeding, especially during disputes over food

MIGRATION: most migrate after breeding, and some move huge distances across the oceans between the southern and northern hemispheres, in giant loops or figures of eight

CONSERVATION STATUS: one race of the Black-capped Petrel, *Pterodroma hasitata caribbaea*, is Critically Endangered (Possibly Extinct); eight species, the Mascarene Petrel, *Pseudobulweria aterrima*, Beck's Petrel, *Pseudobulweria becki*, the Fiji Petrel, *Pseudobulweria macgillivrayi*, the Magenta Petrel, *Pterodroma magentae*, and the Galapagos Petrel, *Pterodroma phaeopygia*, Townsend's Shearwater, *Puffinus auricularis*, Bryan's Shearwater, *Puffinus bryani*, and the Balearic Shearwater, *Puffinus mauretanicus*, are Critically Endangered; ten species, including the Phoenix Petrel, *Pterodroma alba*, the Bermuda Petrel, *Pterodroma cahow*, Madeira Petrel, *Pterodroma madeira*, and Hutton's Shearwater, *Puffinus huttoni*, and three subspecies are Endangered; 19 species, including the Chatham Petrel, *Pterodroma axillaris*, the Hawaiian Petrel, *Pterodroma sandwichensis*, Cook's Petrel, *Pterodroma cookii*, Juan Fernandez Petrel, *Pterodroma externa*, and the Pink-footed Shearwater, *Ardenna creatopus*, are Vulnerable; and nine species are Near Threatened

This is the largest family of the tubenose order Procellariiformes, with representatives occurring worldwide in all oceans. It also has one of the widest overall distributions of any bird family, from the high Arctic, where the Northern Fulmar, *Fulmarus glacialis*, breeds on the northernmost islands and headlands and has been observed at the North Pole, to Antarctica, where the Snow Petrel, *Pagodroma nivea*, nests up to at least 300 km (186 miles) inland and has occurred at the South Pole.

Like albatrosses, the petrels and shearwaters are superb fliers, able to cope with the roughest weather far out in the open oceans. The different groups have a range of distinct flight styles and diets.

Fulmar-petrels are a small group of seven stout-bodied cold-water species that include the two closely related species in the genus *Fulmarus* known simply as fulmars (the Northern Fulmar and its Southern counterpart, *F. glacialoides*). The fulmar-petrel group are thought to have evolved in the southern hemisphere: the Northern Fulmar is the only northern representative of the group.

Apart from the other pair of very closely related (sibling) species, the giant petrels *Macronectes*, the fulmar-petrels are widespread and numerous, with populations in the millions. The Northern Fulmar has made a spectacularly successful expansion, colonising huge areas in the relatively short period of 100 years or so from its original far northern breeding grounds. The reasons for this are unclear, but may be to do with the birds' exploitation of the huge food resource provided by offal from the fishing industry, or perhaps to genetic changes, or to a combination of these and other factors.

Fulmars are superb fliers, rather like miniature albatrosses, gliding on stiffly held wings, interspersed with few wingbeats, for many hours on end. They can cope skilfully with high winds but also spend much of the year at their breeding colonies, incessantly

wheeling round their narrow nesting ledges on sheer cliffs and making precise adjustments of their wings as they hang in the updraught to position themselves precisely for a landing, or soaring off over the sea again.

The two species of giant petrels are heavier than medium-sized albatrosses such as the Black-browed Albatross, *Thalassarche melanophris*, and can have wings as long as those of some of the smaller albatrosses, with a span of up to 2.1 m (almost 7 ft). They are mostly dark grey with paler patches on the neck and face, but the Southern species has an almost all-white morph (colour form). Unlike other members of the family, they often feed on land as well as in the water, where they are far more agile than any other members of the tubenose order. They are formidable predators as well as inveterate scavengers of penguin, seal and cetacean carcasses and offal from ships. They use their massive, sharp and strongly hooked bill to seize and batter or drown vulnerable prey, such as penguin chicks, seal pups and adult seabirds such as other petrels and even immature albatrosses, and thrust the head and bill deep into carcasses like vultures do.

The three other fulmar-petrel species are all distinct enough from one another to be placed in separate genera. The Antarctic Petrel, *Thalassoica antarctica*, is a grey-brown-and-white species that is the only bird that breeds solely on the Antarctic continent. The chequered brownish-black-and-white Cape Petrel, *Daption capense*, by contrast, breeds not only at coastal sites on the Antarctic continent and peninsula but also on islands of the Antarctic and sub-Antarctic eastwards as far as New Zealand. It is often seen in huge flocks, especially around trawlers in winter. The Snow Petrel, which breeds on various adjacent islands as well as on the Antarctic continent, is one of the world's most beautiful seabirds, with its

ABOVE A Southern Giant Petrel, *Macronectes giganteus*, prepares to feed atop a seal carcass on South Georgia.

entirely snow-white plumage, contrasting with its tiny black bill and eyes, and graceful fluttering flight with slow, elastic wingbeats and short glides, and has been dubbed 'the Angel of the Antarctic'. In contrast to the image this conjures, its diet includes whale blubber, seal placentae, animal excreta and dead birds and marine mammals as well as krill, fish and squid.

The prions are classified in two genera: *Pachyptila* comprises six extremely similar grey-and-white species with a black M-shaped marking across the wings; *Halobaena* comprises a single species, the Blue Petrel, *H. caerulea*, which is distinguished from the other prions by the black hood on its head. All are restricted to the southern hemisphere. They feed mainly on krill and other planktonic crustaceans, and have a specialised broad bill equipped with comblike lamellae in the upper mandible, which filter out their diminutive prey. They supplement this basic diet with squid and fish. Some feed mainly by hydroplaning, skimming with their feet rapidly across the water surface, wings spread and bill – or

sometimes the whole head – held underwater. The smaller species feed mainly by snatching prey while swimming, dipping down as they fly or patter low over the surface, or occasionally in shallow dives. Prions are very active in the air, with a very fast erratic flight, including sudden twists and turns; one species, the Fulmar Prion, *Pachyptila crassirostris*, even performs loop-the-loops.

The gadfly-petrels are also very fast, with rapid wingbeats alternating with long glides, and they often fly up high above the sea. They constitute the largest group in the family, widespread across many ocean areas and comprising 32 species, with all-dark or dark-and-white plumage. All but one, the Kerguelen Petrel, *Aphrodroma brevirostris*, belong to the genus *Pterodroma*. Sturdy and stout-bodied, these birds have a short, stubby bill adapted for seizing squid, small fish and crustaceans in flight as they dip down to the water surface. They feed mainly by night, rarely alight on the water, unlike other members of this family, and do not dive. Many species in this genus are threatened.

The petrels comprise three small genera: *Pseudobulweria*, *Procellaria* and *Bulweria*. *Pseudobulweria* contains four species, three of which are rare and Critically Endangered. Perhaps only a few dozen pairs of Mascarene Petrels, *P. aterrima*, breed on the island of Réunion in the Indian Ocean, and the Fiji Petrel, *P. macgillivrayi*, is one of the rarest of all petrels, unrecorded for 129 years until it was rediscovered in 1984 and with a tiny population now assumed to be reduced to fewer than 50 mature individuals. Beck's Petrel, *P. becki*, was known only from two museum specimens collected in 1928 and 1929 until its survival was confirmed in 2007 by sightings at sea off New Ireland in the Bismark Archipelago northwest of New Guinea. Currently, the total world population is estimated at just 50–249 mature individuals. For the two latter species, the breeding sites are unknown.

There are five species of big, heavy-bodied *Procellaria* petrel, all but one entirely restricted to the southern oceans. There are two species of *Bulweria* petrel; one is far more widespread in tropical and temperate waters of the Atlantic, Indian and Pacific oceans, and one is restricted to tropical areas of the northwest Indian Ocean.

The shearwaters are a distinctive group, found in oceans worldwide, with seven species in the genus *Ardenna*, four in the genus *Calonectris*, 13 in the genus *Puffinus*. They may be blackish or dark brown above and white below, or all dark, and have a long, cigar-shaped body and a long, slim bill. These birds include a few particularly well-studied species – notably the Manx Shearwater, *P. puffinus*, renowned for its prowess in navigation. Several individuals from a colony on the island of Skokholm, Wales, in the UK, found their way back to their breeding burrows after being flown by researchers to various distant places, including Boston, from where one found its way back across almost 5,000 km (3,100 miles) of the Atlantic Ocean in just 13 days. As their name suggests, shearwaters almost touch the surface of the sea as they bank down after ascending in a high arc to soar on the updraughts from waves like miniature albatrosses.

Many species of shearwater nest in very large colonies. Some, such as those of the Sooty Shearwater, *Ardenna grisea*, on the Snares Islands, New Zealand, contain several million pairs. Most visit

ABOVE A Cape Petrel, *Daption capense*, flies just above the surface of the Southern Ocean off Chile.

abundant, the family also includes many that are scarce or seriously endangered, and some may be teetering on the brink of extinction.

A homogenous family of just four species of stout-bodied seabirds with a short, thick neck and short wings, the diving-petrels are probably close relatives of the shearwaters. Whatever their precise taxonomic position, they are a distinctive group of birds that have evolved adaptations to a different, far less aerial, lifestyle, and, as their name suggests, are specialised divers. They have a shorter, broad-based bill than other tubenoses, suited to a diet consisting mainly of krill and other planktonic crustaceans. The tubular nostrils open upwards rather than forwards, presumably as an adaptation that helps to prevent water from being forced in when diving.

The four species are all very similar, very dark grey or brown above (with some white fringes to the feathers, especially in the Magellanic Diving-petrel, *Pelecanoides magellani*) and white below, making them difficult for even experienced observers to identify at sea.

ABOVE This Antarctic Prion, *Pachyptila desolata*, was photographed in the Drake Passage, between Cape Horn and the South Shetland Islands.

their breeding colonies only under cover of darkness, when avian predators such as large gulls are not a threat. This has not deterred their exploitation by humans, not only for their eggs, as with many seabirds, but also for their tasty, strongly flavoured meat, especially that of the plump nestlings. For this reason, several species are known locally as 'muttonbirds'. Such exploitation occurred mainly in the past but some still continues to this day – for instance, in the case of the Great Shearwater, *A. gravis*, several thousand adults and about 50,000 chicks are taken annually by Tristan da Cunha islanders from a large colony on nearby Nightingale Island in the south Atlantic Ocean.

The chief threats today are from introduced predators such as rats, cats and mongooses at the breeding colonies, and being caught and drowned by longline fisheries. Although some species are very

ABOVE The Sooty Shearwater, *Ardenna grisea,* is a long distance migrant between the southern and northern hemispheres.

ABOVE Most widespread of the four species of diving petrel is the Common Diving Petrel, *Pelecanoides urinatrix;* this one is in New Zealand.

Through a process of convergent evolution, they have developed similar adaptations to the unrelated auks (Family Alcidae, see p. 123) of the northern hemisphere, including short, powerful wings with which they propel themselves fast when underwater, and (like the plankton-eating auk species) a well developed gular (throat) pouch for storing food to bring back to their young in the nest burrows – this is in contrast to the rest of the tubenoses, which transport semi-digested food in their stomachs. In the air, they fly fast and straight with whirring wingbeats, again like auks and in dramatic contrast to the soaring or fluttering flight of other members of the tubenose order. Diving-petrels have a unique ability to fly through tall waves, emerging on the other side without slowing down or deviating from their direct course.

The Common Diving-petrel, *P. urinatrix,* and the Magellanic Diving-petrel do most of their foraging close to coasts, around their breeding colonies in bays, channels or fjords. The other two species, the South Georgia Diving-petrel, *P. georgicus,* and the Peruvian Diving-petrel, *P. garnotii,* feed further offshore and occasionally far out to sea.

Many colonies suffer badly from predation by introduced predators such as cats and rats, as well as natural predators, including skuas, gulls and owls. Although the birds try to avoid being attacked by these predators by visiting the colonies only on moonless nights, and choosing sloping sites for their burrows from which they can take off and land quickly, they are vulnerable because of their inability to do more than scramble along clumsily on their rear-positioned legs. Even so, these birds manage to survive in colonies that may each number several million pairs. The exception is the Peruvian Diving-petrel, which is now scarce and with a very small breeding range as a result of the damage done to the nesting sites in the past by the commercial extraction of their guano and hunting by the guano workers, as well as fishermen.

ABOVE The White-chinned Petrel, *Procellaria aequinoctialis,* is one of many members of this family threatened with extinction, in this case mainly as a result of accidental bycatch by longline fishing boats.

ORDER PELECANIFORMES

Previously, the six families regarded as belonging to this order were the tropicbirds (Family Phaethontidae), gannets and boobies (Family Sulidae), cormorants (Family Phalacrocoracidae), darters (Family Anhingidae), pelicans (Family Pelecanidae) and frigatebirds (Family Fregatidae). Recent molecular research suggests that neither this order as previously recognised nor the traditionally recognised order Ciconiiformes (which contained the herons, Family Ardeidae; the ibises and spoonbills, Family Threskiornithidae), storks, Family Ciconiidae; the Hamerkop, Family Scopidae; and the Shoebill, Family Balaenicipitidae; are monophyletic (that is, having a single evolutionary ancestry). Instead, each of these orders turns out to be polyphyletic, consisting of some families that are indeed close relatives of one another, some that are more closely related to members of the other order, and one that appears to be related to neither. For instance, the molecular data strongly suggest that the pelicans do not belong at all in the order Pelecaniformes as traditionally defined, but are most closely related to the herons, the Shoebill, *Balaeniceps rex*, the Hamerkop, *Scopus umbretta*, and the ibises and spoonbills, all formerly included in the Ciconiiformes (or in another former arrangement, with the shoebill and hamerkop included in the Pelecaniformes).

One suggestion put forward to deal with this is to retain the storks in a single-family Ciconiiformes, and separate four clearly related families, the gannets and boobies, cormorants, darters and frigatebirds into a new order, Suliformes. This leaves six of the remaining six families – the storks, herons, ibises and spoonbills, Hamerkop, Shoebill and pelicans – in the Pelecaniformes. Another arrangement, which we follow here, unites the two orders in a greatly enlarged single order Pelecaniformes, and dispenses with the name Ciconiiformes.

Despite some morphological similarities, the tropicbirds differ from all the other families in other ways (for instance they have very prominent external nostrils and chicks that hatch with a full covering of down); recent molecular evidence suggests that they do not belong here at all but should be given an order, Phaethontiformes, of their own, close to a putative and very varied assortment of birds called the Metaves, and so they are separated in this book (see p. 39).

The enlarged order Pelecaniformes can be divided into two major groups in terms of habitat and lifestyle. The first consists of six families of birds that are adapted to life mainly in freshwater habitats – the storks, ibises and spoonbills, herons, Shoebill, Hamerkop and pelicans. Apart from the pelicans, these are long-legged birds capable of wading in shallow waters. All have long bills, with that of the Shoebill being uniquely huge and clog-shaped, while the pelicans are renowned for the immense length and size of the bill with its capacious gular (throat) pouch. The second group of four families comprise two – the gannets and boobies, and the frigatebirds – that are exclusively marine, the mainly marine cormorants, and the mainly freshwater darters. Like the pelicans, all these have a well-developed (though smaller) gular pouch and feet webbed between all four toes which power them through the water. They all lack the brood patch(es) of naked skin on the underparts used by most birds to incubate their eggs by heat transfer from blood capillaries, and use the broad webs of their feet instead for this purpose, as they too become richly supplied with warm blood. Pelicans, cormorants and anhingas rest the eggs on top of their feet, but gannets and boobies hold their eggs beneath them, and their shells are especially thick and strong to bear the parents' weight without cracking.

STORKS Ciconiidae

GENERA: 6   **SPECIES:** 19

LENGTH: 75–152 cm (29–60 in)

WEIGHT: 1.3–8.9 kg (2.9–19.6 lb)

RANGE AND HABITAT: widespread worldwide; absent from North America, except for the extreme south, the Sahara and most of Arabia, and much of central Asia, Australia and northern Eurasia; most species live mainly in freshwater wetlands, including marshes, swamps, wet grasslands and savannahs, rice paddies, and the banks of lakes and rivers; several species inhabit coastal mudflats, lagoons and mangroves; some also forage in drier habitats

SOCIAL BEHAVIOUR: most species are very social, in many cases feeding, roosting and nesting closely or loosely together, sometimes in large numbers

NEST: very large piles of sticks, often with other material, such as clods of earth and leafy twigs added; in most species usually sited in a tree, but in some cases on a cliff or (as with most White Storks in Europe) on the roof of a building or atop another artificial structure such as a water tower; Abdim's Stork, *Ciconia abdimii*, sometimes nests on the roofs of African native huts, and the Maguari Stork, *C. maguari*, of South America often nests on the ground in dense reed beds

EGGS: 1–7, white

INCUBATION: 25–38 days

FLEDGING PERIOD: 50–almost 100 days

FOOD: all but one of the seven *Ciconia* species are generalists, taking a wide range of prey, from fish, amphibians, reptiles and small mammals to insects such as swarming locusts (Abdim's Stork specialises on insects); the four *Mycteria* species, two species of *Ephippiorhynchus*, the Lesser Adjutant, *Leptoptilos javanicus*, and the Jabiru, *Jabiru mycteria*, eat mainly fish, whereas the two openbills, *Anastomus*, use their strange bill to open the shells of freshwater molluscs, especially apple snails, *Pila*; the Greater Adjutant, *Leptoptilos dubius*, and Marabou, *L. crumenifer*, eat large amounts of carrion

VOICE: generally silent except at nesting sites, when (despite lacking a syrinx) some utter vocal sounds such as croaking, honking, hissing, whistling, whining or mooing, as well as noisy bill-clattering

MIGRATION: European White Stork, Oriental White Stork and Black Stork migrate south after breeding in Europe and Asia to winter in southern Africa; Abdim's Stork is a trans-equatorial migrant in Africa, breeding in the north and wintering in the south, following the rains; most tropical breeders are sedentary or make only local post-breeding movements

CONSERVATION STATUS: four species – Storm's Stork, *Ciconia stormi*, the Oriental White Stork, *C. boyciana*, the Milky Stork, *Mycteria cinerea*, and the Greater Adjutant, *Leptoptilos dubius* – are Endangered; two species – the Lesser Adjutant, *L. javanicus*, and the Woolly-necked Stork, *C. episcopus*, are Vulnerable; two species are Near Threatened

Tall and imposing birds, storks bear a superficial resemblance to their relatives the herons. They generally have a relatively heavier build and have a rather ungainly appearance, especially as the bill is even more prominent than in the herons – it is generally long and heavy and ends in a sharp point. Its precise shape varies between different groups, related to the diet and method of feeding.

In the seven species that make up the genus *Ciconia* (such as the European White Stork, *C. ciconia,* the Black Stork, *C. nigra,* of Eurasia, the Woolly-necked Stork, *C. episcopus,* of Africa and Asia, and the Maguari Stork, *C. maguari,* of South America, the bill is straight, conical and of medium size, fitting these adaptable species for opportunistic feeding on a wide range of prey in various habitats.

The four wood storks of the genus *Mycteria* (two Asian species, one African and one American) have a long bill with a circular cross section and a slight downward curve at the tip, which is richly supplied with sensory receptors, enabling these birds to catch fish in muddy waters where they cannot see their prey.

The two small *Anastomus* species, one in Africa (*A. lamelligerus*) and one in Asia (*A. oscitans*), are aptly called openbills – they share a unique bill structure, in which there is a permanent opening between the two mandibles. This is an adaptation to their highly restricted diet of aquatic snails, especially large apple snails. The upper mandible is virtually straight with 20–30 small pads along the edges towards the tip that probably serve to grip the shell and hold it still against the river or lake bed or the ground while the bird extracts the snail's body by inserting the razor-sharp tip of its lower mandible under the hard horny shield (operculum), of the mollusc which normally prevents access. In the case of the Asian Openbill at least this is facilitated by saliva flowing down the bill; this saliva contains a narcotic secretion that relaxes the snail's adductor muscle holding the body tight against the shell.

The two large species of *Ephippiorhynchus* – the Black-necked Stork, *E. asiaticus,* of the Indian subcontinent, New Guinea and northern Australia, and the Saddle-billed Stork, *E. senegalensis,* of Africa – along with the Jabiru, *Jabiru mycteria,* of Central and South America have a very long, massive, dagger-like, slightly upturned bill (particularly deep in the Jabiru) with which they stab at and seize fish in shallow water.

The biggest bills of all are found in two of the three *Leptoptilos* storks, the Greater Adjutant, *L. dubius,* of southern Asia and the Marabou, *L. crumenifer,* of Africa (the latter's bill can reach 34.6 cm/13.6 in long). They use their massive bills not for cutting meat but mainly for seizing pieces of carrion at carcasses of large animals killed by predators, or at abattoirs and garbage dumps, including those in villages and towns. Their formidable appearance also helps them to intimidate adult birds or small mammals trying to defend helpless young. Marabous, for instance, are adept at killing birds as large as flamingos (usually the young but also adults on occasion) and even young crocodiles. Both species also readily eat insects or fish if available.

Storks generally have bold plumage colours or patterns, and the sexes look alike. Most species are patterned in varying proportions of black and white, although one, the African Openbill, *Anastomus lamelligerus,* is all black with a purple-and-green gloss, and the Wood Stork of southeast USA to South America, the Milky Stork,

ABOVE A Wood Stork, *Mycteria americana,* at a nesting colony in the trees, Florida.

ABOVE As well as being an expert scavenger, the Marabou, *Leptoptilos crumenifer,* can stab nestling and even adult flamingos with its huge bill.

M. cinerea, of Southeast Asia, and the Jabiru, *Jabiru mycteria*, of Central and South America are almost all white. Two, the Yellow-billed Stork, *Mycteria ibis*, of Africa and the Painted Stork, *M. leucocephala*, of southern Asia, have pink upperparts and tertial feathers of the wings, respectively. About half of all species have areas of bare skin on the head, which is yellowish or pinkish in most but blue or grey in some. These become more vividly coloured during the breeding season. As well as having the bare grey, scaly-looking skin on its head extending to its neck, the Wood Stork also has two bony plates on the crown of its head, whereas the Lesser Adjutant has a single one. Bills may be greyish, dirty whitish, black, yellow or red, or in the Saddle-bill Stork a combination of the last three. Legs are red or pinkish in most species, black in a few, black with red 'knees' and feet in the Saddle-bill Stork, and grey in the three *Leptopilos* storks. The Greater Adjutant and Marabou each have a pair of large, bulbous, inflatable air sacs – one less obvious one extending down the upper back and the other hanging down from the throat – used in display and as a cooling device.

Like cranes, storks fly with their neck held out straight, rather than drawn back into the body in an S-shape like herons; as with both cranes and herons, their long legs extend well behind their short tail. All storks have long, broad wings that are well suited to a mainly soaring and gliding flight. Those of the Marabou are among the longest of any birds, with a wingspan of up to 3 m (9.8 ft) or possibly rarely even 3.2 m (10.5 ft). Migratory species such as White Storks are skilled at using energy-saving soaring in thermals (warm air currents) while migrating overland in large flocks between their temperate breeding sites and African winter quarters. During the first half of the nineteenth century, before bird migration was well understood (and at a time when some naturalists still disputed that it occurred at all), this species provided valuable early evidence of the truth of migration. Some individuals injured by arrows in or en route from their African winter quarters survived the journey with the arrow still stuck in the body, and were easily noticed when they returned to their traditional nest sites in spring. A couple of dozen such *pfeilstorches* (from the German for 'arrow storks') are known, the first and most famous being the bird that returned in 1822 to near the village of Klütz in north-east Germany. This was stuffed and is still preserved, complete with the arrow through its neck, in the zoological collection of the University of Rostock.

To this day, the return of White Storks to their European nest sites, often in the midst of towns or villages on the roofs of houses, churches or other large buildings, is still an event eagerly awaited by local people as a sign not only of the return of spring and evidence of the survival of nature but also because of the ancient beliefs that their presence brings prosperity and fertility (among which was the famous legend of the birds actually bringing human babies). As a result, the birds have long been protected, as have their huge and highly conspicuous nests: like other non-colonial breeders in the family, White Storks often reuse their nests for several years at least, so that they may reach colossal proportions, sometimes as many as 3 m (10 ft) deep. Their courtship and other rituals are equally obvious, as a pair raise and then lower their heads to the accompaniment of a bout of noisy bill-clattering.

ABOVE A White Stork, *Ciconia ciconia*, at its huge stick nest beneath the huge bell of a cathedral at Alfaro, northern Spain.

ABOVE A pair of White Storks perform their 'up-down' greeting display on the roof of Alfaro Cathedral, including loud bill-clattering.

However, despite the high regard felt by many people for 'their' White Storks, this species has experienced declines of over 80% across western Europe over the past century. Many other stork populations have suffered similar reductions over the past century, as a result of human impacts such as wetland drainage, pollution and hunting and other persecution. Today, several species, such as the Greater Adjutant, are rare throughout almost all their range, while others, though quite numerous overall, are found only locally compared with their former far wider ranges.

PELICANS Pelecanidae

GENERA: 1　　　**SPECIES**: 8

LENGTH: 1.1–1.8 m (3.6–5.9 ft)

WEIGHT: 2.5–15 kg (5.5–33 lb)

RANGE AND HABITAT: south-east Europe, Africa, Asia, from Turkey east to central Siberia and eastern China; eastern India, Sri Lanka; the Philippines; Indonesia; New Guinea; Australia; North America, the Caribbean, Central America, South America; most species on shallow lakes and estuaries; Brown Pelican, *Pelecanus occidentalis*, and Peruvian Pelican, *P. thagus*, the two truly marine species, in coastal waters

SOCIAL BEHAVIOUR: generally very gregarious, feeding and roosting in groups and breeding in colonies, often intermixed with other waterbirds such as herons, cormorants and (Brown Pelican) boobies; pair bond in most species loose and not lasting more than a single year

NEST: differs according to species, from a shallow scrape on the ground, which may be lined with sticks, reeds or leaves, to large nests of sticks up to 30 m (100 ft) above ground in tree-nesting species

EGGS: 1–6, white

INCUBATION: 30–36 days

FLEDGING PERIOD: 70–85 days

FOOD: almost entirely fish; occasionally amphibians, young waterbirds and small mammals

VOICE: usually silent, but (mainly chicks) utter hisses, squawks and grunts at nesting colonies

MIGRATION: some northern European and Asian populations of Great White Pelican, *Pelecanus onocrotalus*, and Dalmatian Pelican, *P. crispus*, and northern populations of American White Pelican, *P. erythrorhynchos*, migrate south after breeding to subtropical regions; others make dispersive movements, to newly flooded areas inland or (Brown Pelican) northward up coasts

CONSERVATION STATUS: three species, the Dalmatian Pelican, the Spot-billed Pelican, *P. philippensis*, and the Peruvian Pelican, *P. thagus*, are Near Threatened

With an appearance familiar to most people, if only from cartoons and zoos, these unmistakable birds are among the largest and heaviest of all flying birds, up to 1.8 m (5.9 ft) long, with a wingspan of up to 3.4 m (11 ft) and a weight of up to 13 kg (29 lb) or occasionally more. The instantly noticeable feature that sets them apart from all other birds is the immense bill, in which the lower mandible is joined to the huge, capacious gular (throat) pouch to form a unique natural 'net' for catching fish. The Australian Pelican, *Pelecanus conspicillatus*, has the longest bill of all birds, up to 50 cm (20 in) long in males.

This remarkable bill is not used to store fish as some people have thought, but as a highly efficient scoop. The bird opens its bill wide and positions the mandibles so that they are above and below the prey, then, as the pouch expands, the fish, along with a large volume of water, is trapped. When the pelican lifts its bill out of the water, it must first allow the water, which may weigh more than the bird itself, to drain off from both sides of the bill before it can raise its head to swallow the prey; also, it would be unable to fly if it did not do this. The draining process may take almost a minute, so this is a risky time when other birds are around waiting to steal its catch; these include gulls, which may even land on the pelican's head as it emerges from the water. However, pelicans are themselves not averse to stealing food from other waterbirds if they get the chance.

ABOVE A Dalmatian Pelican, *Pelecanus crispus*, bows the flexible lower mandible of its huge bill, fully distending the skin pouch attached to it.

ABOVE The Australian Pelican, *Pelecanus conspicillatus*, is the only member of its family to occur in Australia, where it is a widespread breeder.

The six species of largely freshwater white pelicans forage chiefly while swimming powerfully with their large webbed feet, sometimes upending or submerging to reach prey at lower depths. Often, they feed cooperatively, advancing in rows or chevrons to surround a shoal of fish and drive them into the shallows, where they can scoop large numbers up more readily. By contrast, the two strictly marine species, the Brown Pelican, *P. occidentalis*, of North America, the Caribbean, Central America and South America, and the Peruvian Pelican, *P. thagus*, of Peru and Chile are plunge divers, albeit with a distinctly ungainly style, from heights of up to 20 m (65 ft).

Pelicans have very long, broad wings with a larger number of secondary flight feathers (30–35) compared with most other birds. They often fly with a few deep wingbeats alternating with a long glide, and are well suited to making use of the lift from air currents near the water surface, as they fly just above it. They also take advantage of thermal air currents over land, and can soar in spirals up to 1,000 m (3,300 ft) or more.

Flocks adopt a straggling diagonal line or V-formation when travelling any distance. Using soaring and gliding with few wing flaps, they can cover as many as 500 km (310 miles) in a day, and are capable of travelling non-stop for up to 24 hours. Such impressive

ABOVE The Brown Pelican, *Pelecanus occidentalis*, like the Peruvian Pelican, *P. thagus*, is strictly marine and feeds by diving from the air.

ABOVE The American White Pelican, *Pelecanus erythrorhynchos*, breeds inland in North America, this one is at the Salton Sea, California.

feats of endurance are enabled by a layer of 'slow' fibres buried deep within the breast muscles. These enhance muscle endurance, in contrast to 'fast twitch' fibres, which are used for sudden actions. Pelicans bend their neck and retract the head between the shoulders when in the air, so the huge bill rests on the chest, where it is closer to the overall centre of gravity, increasing stability. They often also adopt this posture when sleeping or resting on land.

As its name indicates, the Brown Pelican has dark brown and grey plumage, with yellow, white and chestnut markings on the head and neck. Its bill is grey and orange, and the pouch dark grey, although the colours are brighter in the breeding season, often with a scarlet base to the pouch. Its close relative the Peruvian Pelican has similar plumage but with even brighter breeding colours is almost twice as heavy and longer. The other six species are largely white,

with dusky or black flight feathers. The white of the Pink-backed Pelican, *P. rufescens*, of Africa is tinged with grey and the back, flanks and underwings have a pinkish hue, whereas that of the Spot-billed Pelican, *P. philippensis*, of southern Asia usually has a dusky grey or brown tone above. The bill and pouch are mainly yellow or orange in most species and, like the ring of bare skin around each eye, become much brighter during the breeding season, whereas that of the Australian Pelican is two shades of pink, dark blue and scarlet at that time. Most species develop a short crest on the nape, and some, most notably the American Pelican, sport a large knob on the upper mandible for much of the year.

Sadly, the numbers of many species of these splendid and unusual birds are greatly reduced, and huge colonies containing millions of pairs are a thing of the past.

HAMERKOP Scopidae

GENERA: 1   **SPECIES:** 1

LENGTH: 50–56 cm (19.5–22 in)

WEIGHT: 415–430 g (14.5–15 oz)

RANGE AND HABITAT: sub-Saharan Africa, southwest Arabia, Madagascar; variety of wetlands, from lakesides, fish ponds, riverbanks and canal banks and irrigated land to estuaries and rocky coasts; needs trees for nesting and roosting

SOCIAL BEHAVIOUR: usually alone or in pairs, but sometimes in groups of up to 10 or so birds, and occasionally up to 50 may gather at roosts in reed beds or other vegetation; monogamous and weakly territorial

NEST: huge domed structure of sticks and vegetation bound with mud, with central chamber, sited in fork of a tree or sometimes on a cliff or wall, or rarely on the ground

EGGS: 3–7, white, soon stained brown with mud

INCUBATION: 28–32 days

FLEDGING PERIOD: 44–50 days

FOOD: mainly amphibians, especially *Xenopus* frogs and tadpoles, also small fish; sometimes crustaceans such as freshwater shrimps, insects, worms and even small mammals

VOICE: mainly silent, apart from shrill, piping flight call, loud, nasal cackles from flocks, and croaking sounds during courtship flights

MIGRATION: sedentary, apart from dispersal in the wet season from drier areas to benefit from temporary feeding opportunities created by rainfall elsewhere

CONSERVATION STATUS: not threatened

The common name of the Hamerkop, *Scopus umbretta*, nowadays generally used for this odd-looking bird, is its Afrikaans name and means 'hammer-head' (which is one of its alternative English names). These names refer to its very distinctive profile, rather

resembling a hammer, with the long heavy bill and large, stiff, rearward-pointing crest. The plumage is rich brown all over, with a slight purple iridescence on the back. The neck and blackish legs are shorter than those of most habitually wading birds,

ABOVE The Hamerkop, *Scopus umbretta*, has such a distinctive profile that even in silhouette it can be identified easily, as here at Masai Mara, Kenya.

and it is restricted to feeding in shallow water. The middle toe is pectinate (comb-shaped), like that of a heron. The Hamerkop has large, wide, rounded wings and a short tail, and resembles an owl in flight, with its head partly retracted towards its shoulders, coiled like a heron's. It also glides and soars, when it stretches its neck out like that of a stork or ibis.

The black bill superficially resembles a smaller, and far narrower version of the Shoebill's. But on the Hamerkop's bill the terminal half of the lower mandible is very thin and the whole bill appears thin as well as flattened when viewed from the front.

The species is renowned not only for its strange and unique appearance, but also for its huge nests, built by both sexes in 3–6 weeks. These are elaborate structures of sticks, grass and other vegetation, strengthened with mud, and dwarf their builders, averaging some 1.5 m (5 ft) in height and with an equal or greater circumference. Containing up to 8,000 or more sticks, they may sometimes reach over 100 times the bird's weight, and are strong enough to support a human adult. They are among the biggest of all birds' nests and also one of the most complex, with a platform of sticks being erected first, followed by the building of walls made of big sticks interwoven with grass and cemented with mud, and then a domed roof to cover the whole structure. The roof is often decorated with a strange assortment of scavenged materials, including paper, clothing, plastic and other rubbish and pieces of skin and bone. Entry is via a small hole in the base, which the pair reinforce with mud, with which they also plaster an inner nesting chamber big enough for parents and young. This inner sanctum is reached via a tunnel up to 60 cm (2 ft) long.

Nest building appears to be a compulsive activity for much of a pair's lives, with an average of three to five nests being built annually, and older ones being constantly added to or repaired. Often, an abandoned nest will be used by an assortment of other birds, from ducks and geese to pigeons and even kestrels, and often other animals, including snakes, monitor lizards, mongooses, genets, or honeybees. Frequently, small birds such as sparrows or weaverbirds move in as lodgers to nests in use by a pair of Hamerkops, and append their own nests, like tenements hanging from its great bulk. Sometimes, more formidable invaders such as Verreaux's Eagle Owls, *Bubo lacteus*, and Barn Owls, *Tyto alba*, usurp the rightful owners.

SHOEBILL Balaenicipitidae

GENERA: 1   **SPECIES:** 1

LENGTH: 110–140 cm (43–55 in); males larger than females

WEIGHT: 4.4–6.7 kg (9.7–14.8 lb)

RANGE AND HABITAT: Central and East Africa, especially in vast papyrus swamps of north-east Africa; swamps, usually with floating papyrus sedges; some in reed beds and marshes at lake edges

SOCIAL BEHAVIOUR: usually solitary, even pairs feeding separately, and breed in widely separated, territorial pairs; monogamous

NEST: large mound of aquatic vegetation, concealed on floating vegetation or on an isolated island or termite nest in dense swamp

EGGS: 2–3, pale blue or white

INCUBATION: about 30 days

FLEDGING PERIOD: 95–105 days

FOOD: mainly large fish, also aquatic snakes, frogs and turtles, lizards, young crocodiles, young birds and small mammals

VOICE: guttural croak in flight, soft mooing or whinnying sounds and bill-clattering at nest

MIGRATION: sedentary

CONSERVATION STATUS: Vulnerable

ABOVE The remarkable Shoebill, *Balaeniceps rex*, is threatened by habitat destruction, hunting and capture for the cagebird trade.

One of the most bizarre-looking of all animals, this unique waterbird of densely vegetated African swamps has long puzzled taxonomists trying to adduce its relationships to other birds. It shares various skeletal and other features with storks and also has some similarities to herons (it has a tract of powder down, flies with its neck hunched into its shoulders and shows some biochemical likenesses), and was for long placed in the Order Ciconiiformes. Now, however, it is more often (as here) considered to be an odd member of the Pelecaniformes, and thought to be closest to the pelicans (Family Pelecanidae). Many researchers think that the line between the Ciconiiformes and Pelecaniformes is blurred, as highlighted by the Shoebill and Hamerkop, and some even consider the pelican lineage should be subsumed within the Ciconiiformes. Features shared by the Shoebill and the equally distinctive and remarkable pelicans include various details of its skull and a little shaggy tuft of feathers forming a topknot on the nape, and DNA studies further support a close relationship.

The Shoebill is impossible to confuse with any other bird, thanks to its most noticeable feature – its huge, clog-shaped bill (an alternative common name was Whale-headed Stork, and its scientific name, *Balaeniceps rex*, translates as 'King Whalehead'). This is up to about 20 cm (8 in) long, about 10 cm (4 in) wide, and about 10 cm (4 in) deep, with the maximum depth at the base. Like the bills of pelicans, it has a strong ridge, or keel, running down the centre of the upper mandible, which ends in a very sharp, hooked 'nail'. This presumably helps the bird grasp its slippery and wriggling prey. The bird often rests its bill on its chest when it stands almost motionless for hours on end, its only movement its head turning around now and then to look for prey. It holds it in this way, pointing downwards, mainly so that it can see past it with both eyes, as it depends on binocular vision to spot prey beneath the water. Sometimes, it searches a wider area, moving very slowly and stealthily.

As soon as it spots suitable food, it lunges powerfully at great speed into the water, launching its whole body forwards and downwards at the target, and toppling onto its head. This is when the huge bill's reinforced structure comes into its own, as it takes most of the impact. Even large fish or other prey can easily be engulfed in its capacious interior. The Shoebill then pushes down against the ground or water with its wings and sometimes also its bill, and tosses it head backwards, to right itself and stand upright. It may decapitate its catch by moving the mandibles, with their sharp cutting edges, from side to side (a procedure that also helps it eject the clumps of plant matter often taken in with the prey) before swallowing it. Occasionally, a shoebill may perform this dramatic 'collapsing' trick directly from the air without pausing to land. As it does so, it flicks its very noticeable opaque nictitating membranes ('third eyelids') across the eyes to protect them.

The Shoebill is a big bird, standing 1.2 m (almost 4 ft) or more tall, with a rather short, thick neck and a large head to support the giant bill. Its plumage is blue-grey, with a dull green iridescence on the back; the sexes look alike but juveniles are darker.

The large, broad wings of the Shoebill are well adapted for soaring, which this bird frequently does, often after a big leap and some deep wingbeats to get its bulk airborne until it reaches a thermal air current. It flies with its neck retracted into its shoulders to bring the heavy bill nearer to the overall centre of gravity for stability. The wings serve a secondary function in helping the bird to maintain its balance as it clambers about over the floating islands of dense aquatic vegetation, and also to right itself after its violent lunges onto its prey. The giant bill also has subsidiary uses, in carrying water to the nest to wet eggs or chicks to cool them on very hot days, and as a deterrent when waved vertically at rivals flying over the bird's territory.

HERONS Ardeidae

GENERA: 18   **SPECIES:** 63

LENGTH: 27 cm–1.5 m (11 in–4.9 ft)

WEIGHT: 100 g–4.5 kg (3.5 oz–9.9 lb)

RANGE AND HABITAT: worldwide apart from Antarctica, far northern Eurasia and North America and extensive desert regions; wetlands of all kinds, from lakes, rivers, marshes and reed beds to mangroves, estuaries and coasts; some, such as the Cattle Egret, feed in drier habitats such as grasslands and farmland fields

SOCIAL BEHAVIOUR: some species are usually solitary or occur in pairs most of the time, whereas others often roost and feed together, but many are flexible when feeding, depending on fluctuations in the availability of food; most species are colonial breeders, often in mixed colonies with other heron species and other waterbirds, but some are solitary; most are monogamous

NEST: a platform of sticks, reeds or other vegetation, sited in a tree, shrub, near the base of a dense reed bed or other aquatic vegetation

EGGS: 1–10, white or pale blue, or in large bitterns, *Botaurus*, olive-brown; in almost all species unmarked

INCUBATION: 14–30 days

FLEDGING PERIOD: 25–91 days

FOOD: mainly fish, amphibians and crustaceans; also small reptiles, birds and their eggs or young, mammals, insects, molluscs and other invertebrates

VOICE: a variety of squawking, grunting, cooing and groaning sounds, mostly at breeding sites (although some species, such as some of the egrets, *Egretta*, and the Grey Heron, *Ardea cinerea*, are regularly vocal); the large bitterns produce a loud booming 'song' via a modified, inflatable oesophagus; also various bill-snapping and bill-clattering sounds

MIGRATION: many species and populations are sedentary, but some make regular migrations south from temperate breeding quarters

CONSERVATION STATUS: One species, the New Zealand Bittern, *Ixobrychus novaezelandiae*, is Extinct, one species, the White-bellied Heron, *Ardea insignis*, is Critically Endangered; five species, the Australasian Bittern, *Botaurus poiciloptilus*, White-eared Night Heron, *Gorsachius magnificus*, Japanese Night Heron, *G. goisagi*, Madagascan Pond Heron, *Ardeola idae* and Humblot's Heron, *Ardea humbloti*, are Endangered; three species, the Agami Heron, *Agamia agami*, Chinese Egret, *Egretta eulophotes*, and Slaty Egret, *E. vinaceigula*, are Vulnerable; three species are Near Threatened

ABOVE A scarce sight, a Eurasian Bittern, *Botaurus stellaris*, emerges from its home in a dense reedbed.

Most members of this diverse family are medium to large birds with a long, sharply pointed, dagger-like bill, a long neck characteristically held kinked in an 'S' shape, and long legs for wading in water. Most species are found largely in more open wetlands of various types, including those with fresh, brackish and salt water, but a few are adapted to life in dry habitats far from water, or to rivers and lakes in densely forested regions. All possess paired tracts of powder down (used for preening) among the rest of their plumage, mainly on the breast and rump.

The family is traditionally divided into four subfamilies (although none of these appear to be monophyletic, they are included here as they form a useful guide to the varied forms). The Tigrisomatinae contains a single, New Guinea species of Forest Bittern, *Zonerodius heliosylus*, two genera of tiger-herons (the African *Tigriornis*, with one species, and the Neotropical *Tigrisoma*, with three species), and another monotypic Neotropical genus, containing the Agami Heron, *Agamia agami*. The Cochleariinae contains just a single, unusual, Neotropical species, the Boat-billed Heron, *Cochlearius cochlearius*. The Botaurinae comprises the Neotropical Zigzag Heron, *Zebrilus undulatus*, the widespread bitterns, with four large species of *Botaurus* and eight small extant species and one extinct species of *Ixobrychus*. The Ardeinae comprises the widespread typical herons (12 *Ardea* species, including the Great Egret, *A. alba*), two Neotropical species, the Capped Heron, *Pilherodius pileatus*, and the Whistling Heron, *Syrigma sibilatrix*, the 12 species of egrets, *Egretta*, the night herons (*Gorsachius*, with three Asian and one African species, the widespread *Nycticorax*, with two species, and the single New World species of *Nyctanassa*), and the widespread pond herons (six *Ardeola* species, the Cattle Egret, *Bubulcus ibis*, with a vast range across much of the world and two *Butorides* species, the Green Heron, *B. virescens* in much of the New World, and the even more widespread Striated Heron, found from South America to Africa, Indian Ocean islands, the Far East and Australia and Pacific islands).

There is a great size range in the family as a whole, from the smallest bitterns, such as the widespread Least Bittern *Ixobrychus minutus*, little more than 25 cm (10 in) long and with wings spanning only 40 cm (16 in), to the huge Goliath Heron, *Ardea goliath*, of Africa, which can attain 1.5 m (4.9 ft) in length and a wingspan of 2.3 m (7.5 ft). The build, bill length and leg length also vary: from small bitterns, pond herons and night herons, with a compact body and shorter, proportionately thicker neck, shorter bill and legs; through the larger, more slender egrets with longer, more slender neck, bill and legs; to the stouter, bigger bitterns and the largest *Ardea* herons, with the longest neck and generally long but rather sturdier bill and longest legs. Two species with an unusually shaped bill are the Agami Heron, with a bill that is relatively very long and slender, and the Boat-billed Heron, with its massive, deep, broad bill.

In this family the wings are long and broad, and the tail is very short. Most of the time, herons use flapping flight, often with slow wingbeats, especially in the larger species, in which the wings may be arched. However, they can maintain powered flight for long periods and distances. Some species, notably the night herons and bitterns, have rather faster wingbeats. All species except the unusual, monotypic Whistling Heron of South American wet grasslands, fly with the neck completely retracted, hunched in an 'S'-shaped coil into the body. As with the storks, ibises and spoonbills, these birds hold their legs extended behind the tail.

The legs have partly unfeathered tibia (the upper visible part of the leg above the 'knee') and the feet have long toes to spread the bird's weight when walking on mud or across aquatic vegetation (notably in the bitterns, clambering about with great agility in reed beds or marshes). Many herons also roost or nest in trees, and can climb about and perch with ease. The middle claw is pectinate (comblike), and the bird uses it when preening to remove the powder down it has spread on its plumage when this is saturated with fish slime and other food remains.

Plumage colour includes various combinations of white, grey, grey-blue, dark green, brown, rufous buff and black, often with complex patterns. In a few species, it is pure white: in one colour morph of the North American Great Blue Heron *Ardea herodias*, the

ABOVE Some herons are migrants, like this Purple Heron, *Ardea purpurea*, flying in April through the Great Caucasus Mountains to winter in Africa.

ABOVE These Grey Herons, *Ardea cinerea*, are at a nesting colony (or heronry) in trees in Regents Park, central London.

Great Egret, *A. alba*, of Eurasia, three species of *Egretta* egrets, the white morph of four more, and the Madagascan Pond Heron *Ardeola idae*. In a few others, it is all dark, as in the slate-grey Galapagos race *sundevalli* of Striated Heron, *Butorides striata*, of the Galapagos Islands, the dark slate-blue Little Blue Heron, *Egretta caerulea*, ranging from the southern USA to central South America, and dark morphs of several other *Egretta* egrets, such as the Western Reef Egret, *E. gularis*, of Africa to Sri Lanka and the Pacific Reef Egret, *E. sacra*, found from Southeast Asia to Australasia and Polynesia. In most species the sexes look alike, but four of the small bittern species in the genus *Ixobrychus* are exceptions to this rule, with males being far brighter and more boldly patterned than females.

Some species, particularly the large herons, the *Egretta* egrets and the night herons, develop striking display plumes before the breeding season. Apart from the unique sickle-shaped neck plumes of the Agami Heron, they are of three types. The first type comprise very long, narrow black or white lanceolate plumes, such as those extending back from the nape of various species of *Ardea*, including the common Eurasian species *A. cinerea* and the North American Great Blue Heron, most of the *Egretta* egrets, and the *Nycticorax* night herons. The second type, of long, delicate, hairlike filoplumes, with free barbs, are characteristic of the pond herons, such as the Squacco Heron, *Ardeola ralloides*, which also has handsome black-and-white lanceolate plumes, and are even more prominent in the Reddish Egret, *E. rufescens*. The third type, known as aigrettes, are looser than the usual filoplumes and occur on both scapulars ('shoulders') and breast; these delicate, wispy plumes are characteristic of the egrets and the three *Butorides* herons.

The possession of luxuriant aigrettes was almost the complete downfall of various members of this family – especially the Great Egret, the Snowy Egret, *Egretta thula*, and the Little Egret, *E. garzetta* – when they were killed in huge numbers for the plume trade in North America and Europe during the nineteenth and early twentieth centuries.

The iris of the eye, the bill, the legs and the bare facial skin of many species become far brighter during the courtship period, and sometimes may change colour within minutes or even seconds during aggressive encounters. The non-breeding colours of these bare parts are typically brown, yellowish, greenish or black. In some species the bill is bicoloured, with a paler base or lower mandible and a dark tip or upper mandible, and the legs of some egrets are black with contrasting yellow feet, as if they had dipped them in yellow paint. The bare part colours change to orange, red or blue in the breeding season.

All herons catch their prey by seizing it or spearing it with the bill. They are able to strike with lightning speed, thanks to a hinged 'trigger' mechanism involving the elongated sixth neck vertebrae, which produces the marked kink in the neck. This enables them to straighten the neck almost instantaneously.

Different groups or species use different foraging techniques. The most common is to stand motionless by the water's edge or in the shallows and wait until fish or other prey comes within reach of the bill. Often, herons will seek prey more actively, by walking along slowly, both in the water and on land. Some species such the Little Egret, Reddish Egret and Cattle Egret, move much faster and may make short dashes or leaps after very active prey.

Sometimes, a heron will open and close its wings, presumably to scare prey that is hidden or motionless, or hold its wings spread over its head, perhaps to entice prey into the shade this produces, or maybe to reduce glare from the water surface so that it can see more clearly. One species, the Black Heron, *Egretta ardesiaca*, of Africa, uses this strategy habitually, having perfected it to a fine art: it stretches its wings so far forward and downward that their tips meet and touch the water surface, forming an almost complete sunshade. Often, at the same time, it stirs the bottom mud with its feet to flush out fish or other prey. Other herons, too, stir or probe the substrate or sink their feet into it – particularly

ABOVE Grey Herons are opportunistic feeders; this one in London has just caught a European Water Vole, *Arvicola amphibius*.

those species of egrets with bright yellow feet, which may be extra effective in alarming prey. Most remarkable is the method of foraging evolved by the very widespread Green Heron, *Butorides virescens*, and the almost cosmopolitan Striated Heron, *B. striata*. Reminiscent of an angler using a dry fly, these small herons select a lure – a piece of bread or other food morsel, a stick or a feather – and place it onto the water surface, where it attracts the fish.

Some species feed mainly on insects on land. Least aquatic of all the herons, the Cattle Egret, *Bulbucus ibis*, is a very adaptable and successful species that has achieved a vast expansion in range over the past 100 or so years. It was named for its regular habit of foraging close to cattle, sheep or other large grazing livestock as well as wild mammals such as antelopes or elephants, and also behind tractors and farming machinery, to take advantage of the rich bounty of insects and other small animals they disturb. As well as eating other animals – from lizards and frogs to fish, small birds and rodents – in addition to their staple diet of insects, these opportunistic foragers take waste food at rubbish dumps and insects fleeing from grassland fires.

Some herons, such as the Cattle Egret, many of the large herons and the *Egretta* egrets, are conspicuous and easy to see; others, such as the bitterns, both large and small, are notoriously difficult to spot as they spend much of their lives hidden among reeds or other dense aquatic vegetation, where their cryptic plumage provides superb camouflage. In addition, when threatened, they 'freeze' with bill pointing skywards, and may even sway slightly to heighten their resemblance to the background of reeds.

IBISES AND SPOONBILLS Threskiornithidae

GENERA: 13   **SPECIES**: 34

LENGTH: 46–110 cm (17–40 in)

WEIGHT: 420 g–2.1 kg (0.9–4.5 lb)

RANGE AND HABITAT: wide range in temperate to tropical regions worldwide; most in the tropics and subtropics; most species in wetlands of various sorts, from freshwater marshes, flooded grasslands, rice paddies, and on lake- and riverbanks to coastal mudflats, lagoons, estuaries and mangroves; also in much drier habitats, including arid savannahs, montane grasslands, dense forests and farmland

SOCIAL BEHAVIOUR: range from highly gregarious to largely solitary or in pairs; social species often join other ibis species and other waterbirds such as herons, storks, anhingas or cormorants when feeding, roosting and breeding; monogamous, in some cases for more than a year; most are colonial nesters

NEST: usually a platform of sticks, twigs, reeds or other vegetation, often lined with softer material, sited in a tree or shrub, among aquatic or other low vegetation, or sometimes on the ground, especially on small islands with little risk of predation

EGGS: 1–7, white, pale green or pale blue

INCUBATION: 20–31 days

FLEDGING PERIOD: 28–56 days

FOOD: mainly insects, crustaceans, snails and worms; also fish and their eggs or young, small amphibians, reptiles, birds and mammals; some species also include some plant food (such as aquatic plant shoots and rhizomes, or berries) in their diet

VOICE: generally silent except at breeding sites, where they utter a range of grunting, wheezing and whistling sounds; also non-vocal sounds produced by clattering or snapping the bill

MIGRATION: species breeding in temperate zones migrate south or north to subtropical or tropical regions for winter; some subtropical breeders move to the tropics; tropical breeders are mainly sedentary

CONSERVATION STATUS: one species is Extinct, the Reunion Ibis, *Threskiornis solitarius*, four species, the White-shouldered Ibis, *Pseudibis davisoni*, the Giant Ibis, *P. gigantea*, the Northern Bald Ibis, *Geronticus eremita*, and the São Tomé Ibis, *Bostrychia bocagei*, are Critically Endangered; three species, the Crested Ibis, *Nipponia nippon*, the Black-faced Spoonbill, *Platalea minor*, and the Madagascar Sacred Ibis, *Threskiornis bernieri*, are Endangered; one species the Southern Bald Ibis, *Geronticus calvus*, is Vulnerable; two species are Near Threatened

ABOVE Southernmost of the ten species of ibis in South America is the Black-faced Ibis, *Theristicus melanopis*, this pair are in Tierra del Fuego.

This family of wading birds comprises two distinctive subfamilies. Both are similar to herons in build, but the ibises (subfamily Threskiornithinae) have a long, slender, decurved bill, whereas the spoonbills (subfamily Plataleinae) have a remarkable long, broad, spatula-shaped bill flattened from top to bottom and narrowing then expanding into a broad tip. Despite this dramatic difference in bill shape, the two subfamilies are closely related and share a number of features – most noticeably a pair of grooves extending from the nostrils to the tip of the bill – and several instances of successful hybridisation between an ibis and a spoonbill are known.

These are medium to large birds with an elongated, stocky body, a proportionately small head, longish neck and short tail. The length of the sturdy legs varies. The tail is short and wedge-shaped or slightly rounded. The wings are relatively long and broad and are generally used for flapping flight alternating with short glides, faster in ibises. Both groups fly with neck and legs outstretched (although in some ibises, the legs are short enough not to extend as far as the tailtip, let alone beyond it).

Most ibises have largely or entirely blackish, greyish, brown or white plumage. The sexes look alike. Many ibises have strongly iridescent feathers that produce a handsome green, coppery or purplish gloss. Two of the three species in the South American genus *Theristicus* have warm buff on head, neck and upper body, whereas another South American species, the Scarlet Ibis, *Eudocimus ruber*, is one of the most strikingly plumaged of all larger non-passerine birds – its dazzling red colour is the result of pigments ingested by eating bright red crabs. Along with macaws and toucans, it is often used as a symbol of the tropical and exotic in media of many sorts, from inclusion in the odd assortments of species in sixteenth century Old Master paintings of menagerie birds, to modern travel posters and films.

All species have areas of bare skin on the head, throat or nape. These are particularly noticeable in species such as the Sacred Ibis, *Threskiornis aethiopicus*, in which the dark grey scaly and folded skin extends all over the head and neck, and two very rare species, the Northern Bald Ibis, *Geronticus eremita*, and the Crested Ibis, *Nipponia nippon,* which have bright red skin contrasting with dark head plumage extending on the nape into a long shaggy crest. In some cases, the bare parts serve as important

ABOVE It is easy to see how the spoonbills acquired their common name. This is a Eurasian Spoonbill, *Platalea leucorodia*, at Cley, Norfolk, England.

badges of breeding condition as they show a striking change in colour preceding pair formation.

The 28 species of ibis are more diverse in their habitat range, some being found in drier or wooded terrain in contrast to the open wetlands that are the preferred habitat of most of the subfamily and all the 6 species of spoonbills. These include the two *Geronticus* species, the Critically Endangered Northern Bald Ibis (see p. 97) and the Vulnerable Southern Bald Ibis, *G. calvus* of parts of southern Africa, whose remnant populations live in open grasslands, pastures and arid habitats. By contrast, they also include the adaptable and numerous, mainly African, Sacred Ibis and its close relative the Australian Ibis, *Threskiornis moluccus*: these species are equally at home in swamps, floodplains and other freshwater wetlands, on sheltered coasts, in dry grasslands (especially after fires when insect prey is flushed out), on farmland, and in urban environments, such as abattoirs, rubbish dumps and even the centres of large cities such as Sydney, where they can be seen plodding around on traffic islands and fossicking in rubbish bins. Sacred Ibises that have escaped from zoos or waterfowl collections have already started to colonise parts of Europe in similar environments. The Sacred Ibis earned its common name through being regarded as a divine bird in ancient Egypt, where it was identified with the god Thoth.

A few species, such as the very localised Olive Ibis, *Bostrychia olivacea*, with a scattered range right across equatorial Africa, the Madagascan Crested Ibis, *Lophotibis cristata*, and the Green Ibis, *Mesembrinibis cayennensis*, of Central and South America are forest dwellers, whereas a few others, like the Black-faced Ibis, *Theristicus melanopis*, and Puna Ibis, *Plegadis ridgwayi*, of the Andes, live at high altitudes.

There are six species of spoonbill in the single genus *Platalea*. All but one has all-white or almost entirely white plumage. The exception is the Roseate Spoonbill, *P. ajaja*, which although not as dramatically flamboyant as the Scarlet Ibis, is nonetheless an extremely striking and colourful bird – the white neck and upper body contrasts with the bright rose-pink wings and underparts for which it is named, with a broad, darker reddish-pink band running back from the bend of the wing. In the southern USA, the loveliness of this plumage was the bird's undoing, for it was nearly wiped out there during the nineteenth century and early 1900s when people hunted it for its wings, used to make decorative fans.

Both ibises and spoonbills locate their prey mainly by touch rather than vision, and the tip of their bill is richly endowed with sensory cells for this purpose. Ibises feed mainly by probing with their long bill into mud, soil or other soft substrates; sometimes they even insert the bill into cracks in dry ground. Spoonbills generally feed by sweeping their unusually shaped bill from side to side through shallow water, snapping up small fish or invertebrates they encounter, including those stirred up from the mud at the bottom. The broad tip contains a particularly rich concentration of touch receptors and its broadness also increases the chance of contact. In both subfamilies, the external nostrils are reduced to slits, so that the bird can still breathe while its long bill is immersed in the water or mud.

FRIGATEBIRDS Fregatidae

GENERA: 1   **SPECIES**: 5

LENGTH: 71–114 cm (28–45 in)

WEIGHT: 0.75–1.6 kg (26–57 oz); females 25–30% heavier than males

RANGE AND HABITAT: tropical and subtropical areas of the Atlantic, Pacific and Indian Oceans; forage mainly over coastal waters and around oceanic islands during breeding season, but otherwise range widely at sea; nest mainly on wooded or shrubby islands (Ascension Frigatebird on bare ground)

SOCIAL BEHAVIOUR: highly gregarious when roosting and breeding; generally forage alone or in pairs over open ocean, but at rich feeding sources may form large concentrations; pair bond weak

NEST: rough, loosely woven structure of sticks and twigs, usually with additions of grass, leaves, seaweed, feathers or other material; sited in trees where available, otherwise on bare ground

EGGS: 1, white

INCUBATION: 40–55 days

FLEDGING PERIOD: 135–210 days

FOOD: mainly fish (especially flying fish) and squid; also offal, often from ships, eggs or chicks of other seabirds, baby turtles, crabs

VOICE: usually silent away from breeding colonies, where they make rattling, twittering or whinnying calls (differing between the sexes) as well as bill-rattling, and the males also drum with their bill on their greatly inflated throat pouch

MIGRATION: do not make true migrations; young birds especially disperse widely after leaving the breeding colony

CONSERVATION STATUS: the Christmas Island Frigatebird, *F. andrewsi*, is Critically Endangered; the Ascension Frigatebird, *F, aquila*, is Vulnerable

ABOVE Most threatened of all frigatebirds is the Critically Endangered Christmas Island Frigatebird, *Fregata andrewsi*.

This small family of large seabirds is named for its habit of robbing other seabirds of their prey, by reference to the fast sailing ships originally used by pirates; another older seaman's name with a similar origin is 'man-o'-war birds'. In reality, though, these birds usually obtain only small amounts of food in this way.

Two species, the Great Frigatebird, *Fregata minor*, and the Lesser Frigatebird, *F. ariel*, are widespread in tropical and subtropical waters across the Indian, Pacific and part of the south Atlantic Ocean, breeding on various small, remote islands. The Magnificent Frigatebird, *F. magnificens*, is found off both Pacific and Atlantic coasts of the Americas, from California to Ecuador and from Florida to southern Brazil, with a relict population on and around the Cape Verde islands off West Africa. The other two species are far less numerous and have more restricted distributions, especially the Ascension Frigatebird, *F. aquila*, which now breeds only on Boatswainbird Islet, next to Ascension Island in the St Helena archipelago in the south Atlantic; the Critically Endangered Christmas Island Frigatebird, *F. andrewsi*, breeds only on Christmas Island, in the Indian Ocean between Australia and Indonesia, dispersing on both sides of the equator after breeding.

All species have very long wings and tail, giving them a very distinctive silhouette when in the air, where they usually spend every day except when at the nest site. Although females are on average about 25% bigger and heavier than males, both are remarkably lightweight for their size, owing to the lightness of the skeleton. The combined weight of all a frigatebird's bones is less than 5% of its total weight: the lowest ratio of any bird. Many of the bones, including the long wing bones, are essentially thin-walled, relatively flexible hollow tubes full of air.

Their wings are huge, with a span of 1.75 m (5.75 ft) even in the smallest male Lesser Frigatebird, and up to almost 2.5 m (8.2 ft) in a large female Magnificent Frigatebird. Their low weight and huge wing area combine to give them the lowest wing loading of any birds. They can take off from a perch on a roosting or nesting tree merely by opening their wings, and soar and glide endlessly on air currents for many hours on end at speeds of up to 50 km/h (31 mph) or so, and single birds or small groups can travel huge distances when foraging. A frigatebird may expend more energy perched on a branch than when sailing through the air. These champion flyers are capable of astonishing feats of aerobatics, aided not only by their wing and tail plan and aerodynamic body shape, but also by fusion of the bones of the pectoral (shoulder) girdle (the coracoid and the furcula, or wishbone) a feature not found in any other birds.

Although the deeply forked long tail is often held closed, it is opened wide like a huge pair of scissors during manoeuvres to serve as a rudder. Frigatebirds can hang virtually motionless, buoyed up on rising currents, for long periods, and perform amazingly abrupt turns and side-slips. They use these skills to outmanoeuvre other seabirds when stealing their food or when diving down to snap up prey with the formidable, long, sharply hooked bill, ranging from schools of flying fish as they emerge from the waves to the eggs or chicks of other seabirds on nesting beaches.

In contrast to the wings, tail and bill, the legs and feet are tiny and weak and, unlike those of most other Pelecaniformes, only slightly webbed at the base. Although the sharp claws enable the big birds to grip branches tightly when perching at their breeding and roosting sites, the feet are useless for walking or swimming. They very rarely land on the water anyway, having only a tiny uropygial (preen) gland producing minimal oil for waterproofing the plumage, which rapidly becomes sodden if immersed; also, with their huge wings, it is impossible for them to take off from the water by flapping.

ABOVE A male Magnificent Frigatebird, *Fregata magnificens*, displays to females at North Seymour Islet, in the Galapagos.

Plumage differs little between the five species, but there is considerable variation within each species and – unusually for Pelecaniformes – the sexes differ. Adult males are mainly or almost entirely black, but some feathers, especially the long, lance-shaped scapulars have an iridescent green, purple or blue gloss. Male Christmas Island Frigatebirds have a white belly patch, whereas male Lesser Frigatebirds have a small white axillary patch (on the underside of each wing where it meets the body). Female Ascension Frigatebirds have a brown collar and breastband, while females of all other species have a large white area on the breast

and belly and, in Christmas Island and Lesser Frigatebirds, white axillary patches. There is also a complex series of juvenile and subadult plumages that add to the problem of identifying these birds at sea. After moulting from their thick coat of white down, the first black plumage of the juvenile has extensive contrasting white, rusty brown or speckled areas on the head and underparts, and a paler brown bar on the upperwing, which they lose gradually over a period of several years.

At the breeding colonies, the males perform one of the most impressive – and bizarre – of all seabird courtship displays. Groups of up to 30 males assemble in the trees or bushes (or where there are no trees or bushes, as on Boatswainbird Islet, on the ground) and await the arrival of the females. Each male inflates his bright red gular pouch, which for the rest of the year is hidden from view among the throat feathers, into a huge balloon. As the females fly overhead, their suitors spread their wings and vibrate them, and throw back their head so it rests on their back, pointing the long bill skywards as they call or clatter their mandibles.

As with the tropicbirds, frigatebirds' feet are too small to provide enough warmth to the egg, unlike those of the other major families of Pelecaniformes, and the parents incubate like most birds, with their body covering it. Although the young fledge when between 4.5 and 7 months old, parental care is far from over. It can involve the adults in caring for their offspring for another 4 months at least, and in some cases for 14 months or occasionally for a further 15 or 18 months in Christmas and Great Frigatebirds, respectively.

GANNETS AND BOOBIES Sulidae

GENERA: 3   **SPECIES:** 10

LENGTH: 70–95 cm (28–38 in)

WEIGHT: 0.8–3.6 kg (2–8 lb)

RANGE AND HABITAT: gannets in North Atlantic, South Africa and Australasia; boobies throughout tropical and subtropical oceans, with Peruvian Booby extending to cool Humboldt Current region of Pacific off western South America; breed mainly on islands and offshore stacks, with some on sheer mainland cliffs; forage in inshore waters (except for Abbott's Booby, *Papasula abbotti*, and, to a lesser extent, the Red-footed Booby, *Sula sula*, which feed in open ocean)

SOCIAL BEHAVIOUR: gregarious, generally foraging and breeding together; gannets and Abbott's Booby remain with the same mate (and at the same nest site) for many seasons, whereas others may change either or both in succeeding years

NEST: sited on the ground in gannets and most boobies; a rudimentary affair consisting of a slight depression surrounded by a rim of excreta (guano); Abbott's Booby and the Red-footed Booby build rather flimsy stick nests, cemented with their droppings, in trees

EGGS: 1–3, whitish, pale blue, green or pink

INCUBATION: 42–55 days in all species except Abbott's Booby, in which it is about 57 days

FLEDGING PERIOD: 70–84 days

FOOD: fish, squid and offal, including fish discarded from fishing boats

VOICE: usually silent at sea, though may call when feeding, otherwise gannets very noisy at colonies, giving loud, harsh grunts, moans or rasping cries; male boobies utter hoarse whistling sounds, females quacking or grunting sounds

MIGRATION: some gannets winter south into subtropical waters; most boobies disperse out to sea or along coastal waters after breeding

CONSERVATION STATUS: two species, Abbott's Booby, *Papasula abbotti*, and the Cape Gannet, *Morus capensis*, are Endangered

These two groups of large, exclusively marine birds are similar enough to be united in a single family, the Sulidae, and are collectively known as sulids. The three gannets, all classified in the genus *Morus*, are birds of cooler, temperate waters, with the Northern Gannet, *M. bassanus*, in the North Atlantic, the Cape Gannet, *M. capensis*, off southern Africa and the Australasian

Gannet, *M. serrator*, off Australasia. The boobies (all but one in the genus *Sula*) live mainly in tropical and subtropical seas, although the Peruvian Booby, *S. variegata*, fishes in the particularly food-rich cool Humboldt Current off western South America. The other six species include two very localised species, Abbott's Booby *Papasula abbotti*, which breeds only on the small Australian territory of

ABOVE Northern Gannets, *Morus bassanus*, dive for mackerel off the island of Noss, Shetland, in June.

ABOVE A pair of Australasian Gannet, *Morus serrator*, perform a bill-fencing greeting ceremony, Cape Kidnappers, North Island, New Zealand.

Christmas Island in the Indian Ocean about 360 km (220 miles) south of Java, and the Nazca Booby, *Sula granti*, which breeds on the Galapagos Islands and three other tiny Pacific islands. The latter was until recently regarded as a subspecies of the widespread Masked Booby, *S. dactylatra*. Also widely distributed are the Red-footed Booby, *S. sula*, and the Brown Booby, *S. leucogaster*.

All sulid species have a tapering, torpedo-shaped body with a sturdy, longish neck, a long, conical sharp-tipped bill and a long wedge shaped tail (shorter in gannets), which provides excellent streamlining during both their powerful, fast, sustained flight on long, narrow, angled wings, and when diving for their food. Level flight involves flapping alternating with brief glides.

Adding to their imposing size and appearance, sulids provide a dramatic sight when fishing, being the most impressive of all plunge divers. The sight of a large flock of hundreds of gannets diving for prey is one of the most thrilling in all of nature, as the great gleaming white birds rain down from on high like living arrows and manage to just miss one another as they cross one another's paths before folding their wings and striking the waves

ABOVE A posse of Blue-footed Boobies, *Sula nebouxii*, plunge into the water of the Gulf of California, just off the coast of Mexico, targeting a large shoal of fish.

with a resounding thwack, which sends up a plume of water. The momentum of the dive takes the gannets only a metre or two below the surface, but they may swim down farther with powerful strokes of the wings and broadly webbed feet to home in on a school of fish before emerging. As well as the gannets, Peruvian Boobies, *Sula variegata*, often hunt in such large groups, but other sulids generally do so in smaller groups or even alone.

Adaptations for plunge diving include inflatable air sacs between skin and muscles that cushion the body against the impact, the lack of external openings to the nostrils to prevent an inrush of water into the lungs, and well-developed binocular vision. Gannets and most boobies concentrate mainly on schooling fish such as mackerel, whereas Abbott's Booby and the Red-footed Booby feed largely on squid and flying fish. The bill has serrated cutting edges, and the bird can move its upper mandible upwards, so that it can accommodate large prey. All species except for Abbott's Booby forage in inshore waters, although the gannets in particular often travel several hundred kilometres from their breeding colonies to find sufficient food.

Except for some all-brown races of the very widespread Red-footed Booby, all sulids have some white on the underparts. The gannets and three species of boobies (Masked, Nazca and Red-footed) have an all-white or mainly white body, head, neck and inner wings and black flight feathers and tail, whereas the Peruvian Booby has a similar pattern but with brown and white in place of black; in Abbott's Booby (which is placed in a different genus from the other boobies and is more closely related to the gannets) the black is flecked with white. The Blue-footed Booby, *Sula nebouxii*, has greyish-brown streaks on the head and neck and similarly coloured back and wings. The Brown Booby has a dark brown head and upper breast, with white only on the belly. The boobies have brightly coloured bills, facial skin and legs and feet – the latter in particular being important in courtship rituals, when the birds walk with exaggerated foot-lifting actions. Gannets have patches of golden yellow on the head and neck.

All sulids breed colonially, although the arrangement varies from small groups with dispersed pairs nesting high up in tall rainforest trees in the rare Abbott's Booby to huge noisy colonies of gannets packed together so closely they almost touch on the flat tops of small rocky offshore islands. Along with Guanay Cormorants, *Phalacrocorax bougainvillii*, and Peruvian Pelicans, *Pelecanus thagus*, Peruvian Boobies nest in huge (but fluctuating) colonies. The guano produced by these three species accumulates to depths of several metres and was the basis of a major industry, being extracted for worldwide use as fertilizer.

Such great concentrations of birds inevitably spelled trouble when humans arrived, and huge numbers of most species were hunted or their eggs were taken. The guano industry also had adverse effects as a result of disturbance during the breeding season. Today most gannetries are well protected, although some booby species are still exploited. Abbott's Booby has a population currently in the low thousands of breeding pairs – its decline is due largely to past habitat destruction as a result of logging of the nesting trees between 1965 and 1987 to clear the ground for phosphate mining, which destroyed about a third of the breeding habitat. This species is now seriously at risk from a variety of other threats, including damage to nesting trees by cyclones, marine pollution and overfishing, Another problem has been the accidentally introduced Yellow Crazy Ants, *Anoplolepis gracilipes*, which build huge, high-density supercolonies that alter the habitat adversely by their predation of beneficial red crabs and their 'farming' of scale insects, which damages the trees.

CORMORANTS Phalacrocoracidae

GENERA: 2   **SPECIES:** 31

LENGTH: 45–100 cm (18–39 in)

WEIGHT: 0.9–4.09 kg (2–11 lb)

RANGE AND HABITAT: worldwide, including the Arctic and Antarctic, although fewer at high latitudes; along sea coasts and in near-shore waters, most species are restricted to colder waters, with a few in the tropics; some species on freshwater lakes, reservoirs, rivers and marshes inland; a few (such as the Double-crested Cormorant, *Phalacrocorax auritus*, in North America, the Neotropic Cormorant, *P. brasilianus*, in Central America, the Caribbean and South America and the Great Cormorant, *P. carbo*, in Eurasia) occupy both marine and freshwater habitats

SOCIAL BEHAVIOUR: some species may feed solitarily, but most are often gregarious when foraging, roosting and breeding; many nest in large colonies

NEST: in marine species, often a pile of seaweed, often admixed with other materials such as grass, bones and feathers, and cemented with the birds' own droppings or mud; inland breeders (such as the three mentioned under Range and habitat above, or exclusively inland ones, such as the Pygmy Cormorant, *Microcarbo pygmeus*) usually build nests largely of sticks; marine species or populations usually site their nests on rocky, gravelly or sandy ground or ledges on cliffs, islands or sea stacks; inland breeders typically nest in trees, shrubs or dense reed beds

EGGS: 2–7, pale green or blue

INCUBATION: 23–35 days

FLEDGING PERIOD: 35–80 days

FOOD: most species live almost entirely on fish, but many cold-ocean species also eat a wide variety of crustaceans, squid and other marine invertebrates

VOICE: generally silent away from breeding colonies, where the birds (especially males) are noisy, making loud, guttural croaking, barking, gargling and groaning calls

MIGRATION: some temperate-zone species make short migrations, many inland breeders moving to ice-free coasts in hard winters, while many marine species disperse along coastlines; most others are sedentary

CONSERVATION STATUS: one species, the Spectacled Cormorant, *Phalacrocorax perspicillatus*, is Extinct; one species, the Chatham Shag, *P. onslowi*, is Critically Endangered; three species, the Bank Cormorant, *P. neglectus*, the Cape Cormorant, *P. capensis* and the Pitt Shag, *P. featherstoni*, are Endangered; seven species, including the Socotra Cormorant, *P. nigrogularis*, the Rough-faced Shag, *P. carunculatus* and the Flightless Cormorant, *P. harrisi*, are Vulnerable; three species are Near Threatened

ABOVE A Pygmy Cormorant, *Microcarbo pygmeus*, at Varna, Bulgaria, adopts the wing-drying posture typical of cormorants.

ABOVE An Imperial Shag, *Phalacrocorax atriceps*, carries nest material to a nest site on an island in the Beagle Channel, Ushuaia, Argentina.

Often easily recognisable as members of their family at long range from their habit of standing with their wings spread, the mainly large, fish-eating seabirds in this family are variously known as 'cormorants' or 'shags'. As with 'pigeon' and 'dove' in the Family Columbidae (see p. 31) these names are more or less arbitrary, although the smaller, crested species do tend to be called shags.

These birds range in size from the Mallard-sized Pygmy Cormorant, *Microcarbo pygmeus*, to the Great Cormorant *P. carbo*, which is as big as a goose. Although smaller than the latter, the Flightless Cormorant, *P. harrisi*, of the Galapagos, is the heaviest member of the family.

In contrast to the entirely marine members of the order Pelecaniformes, such as the gannets and boobies (Family Sulidae), cormorants also include some freshwater representatives. Four species live exclusively on and around fresh or brackish waters; a further six occur in freshwaters, estuaries and inshore coastal waters; and the remaining 26 are exclusively marine, or almost so.

Wherever they live, all the birds in this family have a strong but slender, sharply hooked bill, a bare gular (throat) pouch, a long neck, a sturdy body and a rather long, wedge-shaped tail with stiffened feathers. Most have broad, medium-length wings, although those of the Flightless Cormorant are tiny and atrophied. On sea or lake shores or on perches such as breakwaters or tree branches, they usually adopt an upright posture, but with their feet situated well to the rear of the body, they walk clumsily with a shuffling gait.

The plumage of cormorants is generally black, in about half of all species relieved by a white breast, white on the head, neck, wing coverts or flanks, or completely white underparts. The black often has an iridescent green, blue, purple or bronze sheen. Many species sport crests (single or, in a few species, double) and long hairlike feathers called filoplumes on the head and neck, as well as brightly coloured red, blue or yellow naked skin on the face or gape of the bill and as rings around the eyes. These adornments are present only in the breeding season or are more prominent then. In all cormorant species, the sexes look alike.

A few species differ in appearance from the typical plumage pattern outlined above. Most distinctive is the Red-legged Cormorant, *P. gaimardi*, of southern South America. It has a smoky grey head and body, with a large white neck patch in the breeding season, speckled silvery wing coverts and black wingtips.

This is set off by a red-and-yellow bill and bright red legs and feet. Another distinctive species is the Spotted Shag, *P. punctatus*, of New Zealand, in which the white of the underparts (which can be very pale grey when seen close up) extends as a narrow band up the side of the neck and onto the face as an eyestripe; its upperparts are brown rather than black. A few species have distinct dark and pale plumage variants (morphs). An example is the New Zealand race *brevirostris* of the Little Pied Cormorant, *Microcarbo melanoleucos*, found on coasts and interior of New Zealand. The dark morph of this subspecies is entirely black apart from variable white flecks on the chin and throat. In the white-throated morph the white is restricted to the head and neck, contrasting with the black of the rest of the plumage. The pied morph has the white extending onto the entire underparts, while an intermediate morph has its white underparts variably speckled with black.

Cormorants are expert divers, catching their prey underwater. They have much denser bones than most birds, and together with their lack of body fat, this helps them reduce buoyancy so that they can easily slip beneath the water and chase prey with less effort. For this reason, too, cormorants swim low in the water, and often do so almost completely submerged. They can chase and catch fast-moving fish or other prey with powerful strokes of their broadly webbed feet, and steer with their webs and tail; they hold their wings tightly pressed to the body for streamlining. With their large volume of blood relative to body weight, they can store enough oxygen to remain underwater for a few minutes if necessary – up to about 4 minutes in some species. Most species fish at relatively modest depths of less than 7 m (25 ft), but some marine species are known to go down to 30 m (100 ft).

Cormorants usually fly with continuous flapping, although on occasion many species regularly soar up to considerable heights. More characteristically, they often fly very low over the water, and this probably helps them use the 'ground effect', their slow wingbeats producing vortices that rebound from the water surface to provide extra lift.

The distinctive spread-wing resting posture is generally thought to be for drying the wings after swimming or diving, since the plumage does become easily wetted. Additionally, the looseness of the feathers helps cormorants shed water and probably also aids insulation by trapping air; various species are perfectly at home in very cold waters.

DARTERS Anhingidae

GENERA: 1   **SPECIES:** 4

LENGTH: 81–97 cm (32–38 in)

WEIGHT: 1–1.8 kg (2.2–4 lb)

RANGE AND HABITAT: southern USA, Cuba, Mexico, Central America, South America, Africa, India and Southeast Asia, New Guinea, Australia; still or slow-moving freshwaters (lakes, reservoirs, ponds and rivers) and freshwater swamps; less often in estuaries, tidal inlets and coastal lagoons or mangroves; needs trees, forest edges or islets with dense vegetation for nesting

SOCIAL BEHAVIOUR: usually solitary, but may be seen in pairs or small, loose groups; monogamous, perhaps for more than one season; usually nest as single pairs or in loose assemblages of a few pairs, but sometimes form large colonies of several hundred pairs

Nest: a platform of sticks and leaves or reeds, usually sited in trees, often overhanging water

EGGS: 2–6, pale green or bluish-white, with an outer chalky layer that wears off during incubation, sometimes with dark brown spots

INCUBATION: 25–30 days

FLEDGING PERIOD: 40–50 days

FOOD: mainly fish; also some amphibians, aquatic reptiles and aquatic invertebrates (such as crustaceans, leeches and aquatic insects and larvae)

VOICE: usually silent outside the breeding season, when they utter guttural, croaking, chattering or grunting calls or explosive notes

MIGRATION: most populations are sedentary, but northernmost breeders in the USA migrate south to the Gulf Coast or Mexico for the winter

CONSERVATION STATUS: one species, the Oriental Darter, *A. melanogaster*, is Near Threatened

ABOVE A male Anhinga, *Anhinga anhinga*, in the Florida Everglades erects the feathers of his hindneck during a courtship display.

ABOVE Anhingas, like this Anhinga, *Anhinga anhinga*, have body plumage that becomes even wetter than that of cormorants when they submerge, so they need to perch with open wings to dry it after each dive. This posture also maximises the heat these poorly insulated birds can absorb from sunlight.

Sometimes called snakebirds or darters, these large but extremely attenuated waterbirds look rather like a cross between a heron and an emaciated cormorant, with their very small head with its long, slender, very sharp pointed bill, merging into a long, thin snakelike neck. The wings are long and broad and the tail long and fan-shaped, and anhingas often use thermals to soar with minimal energy expenditure. These birds look most snakelike when swimming along with their body submerged and just the sinuous neck and head above water.

There is one species, the Anhinga, *Anhinga anhinga*, in the New World, from southeast USA to Argentina, and three in the Old World: the African Darter, *A. rufa*, in Iran, sub-Saharan Africa and Madagascar, the Oriental Darter, from Pakistan, India and Sri Lanka to south-east Asia, the Philippines and parts of Indonesia, and the Australasian Darter, *A. novaehollandiae*, in New Guinea and Australia. All have dark plumage, but there are differences in appearance between the sexes. Male Anhingas are black with white shoulder and wing-covert markings; females are similar but brown rather than black. Male Darters are brighter, with areas of chestnut or brown and white on the throat and neck; females are mainly brown, with whitish underparts. In both species, the bill is yellowish; male Anhingas have bright greenish-blue eye-rings.

In contrast to the mainly exclusively marine cormorants, anhingas are found mainly on freshwater wetlands of various types, though some occur on brackish estuaries and lagoons with mangroves.

Anhingas hunt their prey underwater, where they are accomplished divers, propelling themselves with their broadly webbed feet. The feeding technique of anhingas is unusual in that the prey is invariably speared on the long, thin, very sharply pointed bill rather than being grasped by it as with most other aquatic feeders. The neck has a unique joint between the eighth and ninth vertebrae that enables them to strike the prey with lightning speed.

ORDER CHARADRIIFORMES

This large, diverse order contains over 300 species in 17 families. Despite their variety, these families do have anatomical features in common, such as details of the leg tendons, bones making up the palate and the structure of the syrinx ('voice box'). There are four major subgroups: the waders (known in North America as shorebirds), classified in 14 families; the gulls, terns and skimmers (Family Laridae); the skuas (Family Stercorariidae); and the auks (Family Alcidae). The buttonquails (Family Turnicidae, which were formerly included within the Order Gruiformes, seem more likely to belong to the Charadriiformes, and are included here.

THICK-KNEES Burhinidae

GENERA: 2 **SPECIES:** 9

LENGTH: 35–57 cm (14–22 in)

WEIGHT: 0.3–1.1 kg (0.7–2.4 lb)

RANGE AND HABITAT: Europe, Africa, Asia, Australasia, South America; most in dry open country with sparse vegetation, including semi-deserts, grasslands and cultivated areas; the Water Dikkop, *Burhinus vermiculatus*, of Africa and the Great Stone-curlew, *Esacus recurvirostris*, of southern Asia occurs almost entirely by lakes, rivers and streams, whereas the Beach Stone-curlew, *E. magnirostris*, lives mainly on beaches, or among mangroves from Southeast Asia to Australia

SOCIAL BEHAVIOUR: during the breeding season usually in pairs (though after that most species form flocks that are usually quite small but may number several hundreds)

NEST: a shallow scrape in soil, sand or shingle, sometimes unlined but often lined with small stones, shells, wood, animal droppings and other items

EGGS: 2 (rarely 3), except in the Beach Stone-curlew, which has a single egg clutch; whitish or buff with brown markings

INCUBATION: 24–27 days

FLEDGING PERIOD: 42–50 days

FOOD: insects and other invertebrates (including crabs and molluscs in coastal species), frogs, lizards and other small vertebrates

VOICE: loud, bisyllabic wailing or whistling cries; usually quieter by day, but very noisy at dusk and through the night, often in chorus

MIGRATION: most species are strictly sedentary, but some northern Senegal Thick-knee, *Burhinus senegalensis*, make southward movements in relation to rainfall, and Bush Stone-curlews, *B. grallarius*, in Australia may wander widely after breeding; the northern European and Asian populations of the Eurasian Stone-curlew, *B. oedicnemus*, are true migrants, moving south to winter in the Mediterranean region, North Africa and the Arabian peninsula

CONSERVATION STATUS: two species, the Great Stone-curlew, and the Beach Stone-curlew, are Near Threatened

ABOVE A Eurasian Stone-curlew, *Burhinus oedicnemus*, returns to incubate its eggs at nest, in a field of crops in Breckland, Suffolk, England.

This is a small family of ground-dwelling birds of open country. They are thought to be an ancient group that from molecular analysis appear to be most closely related to the sheathbills and Magellanic Plover (see p. 106). The vernacular name 'thick-knees' refers to the prominent leg joints of these birds. Most species in this small family are also known as stone-curlews (although unrelated to the curlews in the Family Scolopacidae, they have similar calls, and they often inhabit stony terrain). Two African species are called dikkops, from the Afrikaans word meaning 'thick-head', named for their domed crown.

All but two species live in the Old World – especially Africa, where there are four species. Two of them, the Senegal Thick-knee, *Burhinus senegalensis*, and the Water Dikkop, *B. vermiculatus*, are endemic to that continent, and one, the Spotted Dikkop, *B. capensis*, is virtually so, with an outlying population in southern Arabia. The fourth, found breeding in parts of North Africa, is the most widespread Old World species, and the best known member of the family: this is the Eurasian Stone-curlew *B. oedicnemus*, whose range also extends from the Canary Islands and Europe into Central and southern Asia. The Great Stone-curlew, *Esacus recurvirostris*, occurs from southeast Iran across the Indian subcontinent to Indochina and southern China, there are two species in Australia, one of which, the Bush Stone-curlew, *Burhinus grallarius*, is also found in New Guinea and the other, the Beach Stone-curlew, *Esacus magnirostris*, is also found from the Andaman Islands through Malaysia, the Philippines and Indonesia to New Guinea. Two species inhabit the New World: they are the Double-striped Thick-knee, *Burhinus bistriatus*, with a range encompassing southern Mexico to Costa Rica, Hispaniola and part of northern South America, and the Peruvian Thick-knee, *B. superciliaris*, from extreme southern Ecuador and Peru.

All thick-knees have a large, broad head with very big, prominent yellow eyes that give them staring or glaring 'expression', which is heightened by the pale eyebrow stripes above. These large eyes are well adapted for seeing in dim light, for thick-knees are mainly active at dusk and through the night. The bill is strong and thick – in *Burhinus* species no longer than the length of the head but in the two *Esacus* species much longer and more massive, and with the lower mandible curving upwards. The body is long and slim, the legs long and sturdy, well suited to walking and running, and the wings long and narrow.

The plumage of all species is cryptic – essentially pale brown above, and whitish from the lower breast to the undertail. In the

Burhinus species, the head, neck, upperparts and breast are streaked and spotted with darker brown, with a pattern of pale head-stripes, whereas the two *Esacus* species have plainer, greyer upperparts and a bolder, black-and-white head pattern. Many also have white markings on the wings. The legs are yellow, in different species ranging from dull greenish or greyish yellow to bright yellow.

Thick-knees search for food, which includes some small vertebrates as well as large insects and other invertebrates, by walking about slowly; once they have spotted suitable prey, they may make a brief dash before seizing it in the strong bill. These birds often adopt an odd position on the ground, with the tibia vertical and the entire tarsi stretched out horizontally. They spend much of the day resting motionless, assisted by their highly cryptic plumage. If disturbed, they may 'freeze' in a hunched position, or may even stretch the head, neck and body right out flat on the ground, relying on their camouflage to avoid detection; this strategy is used even by young chicks, with their striped down. Thick-knees prefer to run from any imminent danger, although they are strong flyers.

SHEATHBILLS AND MAGELLANIC PLOVER Chionidae

GENERA: 2   **SPECIES:** 3

LENGTH: sheathbills 34–41 cm (13.5–16 in); the Magellanic Plover, 19.5–21.5 cm (7.5–8.5 in)

WEIGHT: sheathbills 450–780 g (15.9–27.5 oz); the Magellanic Plover 70–100 g (2.5–3.5 oz)

RANGE AND HABITAT: sheathbills in the Antarctic Peninsula, sub-Antarctic islands and Indian Ocean islands; the Magellanic Plover in extreme southern Chile and Argentina; sheathbills live on sea coasts and islands, especially around penguin, albatross and cormorant colonies; the Magellanic Plover breeds on the exposed shores of shallow pools or lakes in highlands or steppes

SOCIAL BEHAVIOUR: sheathbills are loosely colonial, gathering to feed at breeding colonies of seabirds; pairs are monogamous and highly faithful to mate, territory and nest-site; the Magellanic Plover in separate pairs during the breeding season; pairs defend not only a nesting territory but also a separate feeding territory; in winter feeds in small flocks

NEST: sheathbills, untidy, often foul-smelling pile of tussock grass, seaweed, moss, bones and feathers, with cup on top for eggs, concealed under overhang of rock, crevice or small cave, sometimes in a petrel burrow; Magellanic Plovers make a scrape, which they line with gravel, on exposed shore very close to water

EGGS: sheathbills 1–4, whitish, heavily blotched with dark grey, brown or black; the Magellanic Plover 2, pale ground colour with very dense black or dark brown speckling

INCUBATION: 28–32 days in sheathbills; unknown in the Magellanic Plover

FLEDGING PERIOD: sheathbills 50–60 days; the Magellanic Plover, 28–30 days

FOOD: sheathbills have a very wide diet of fish, squid, krill stolen from penguins or other seabirds, eggs and small chicks of these birds, carrion, bird and seal faeces, invertebrates, seaweeds, seal blood and placentae, and human refuse; the Magellanic Plover feeds on tiny invertebrates during the breeding season, mainly chironomid midge larvae in winter

VOICE: sheathbills utter loud, harsh high-pitched calls, especially when defending or advertising ownership of territory; the Magellanic Plover produces soft, dovelike cooing whistles

MIGRATION: the Snowy Sheathbill migrates after breeding to winter mainly on the Falkland Islands, Tierra del Fuego and southern Patagonia; the Black-faced Sheathbill is sedentary; the Magellanic Plover is mostly migratory, moving to coasts; some birds are sedentary or dispersive

CONSERVATION STATUS: one species, the Magellanic Plover, *Pluvianellus socialis*, is Near Threatened

Until recently this family included only the two species of sheathbills, *Chionis*, which had the distinction of being the only bird family endemic to the Antarctic and sub-Antarctic regions. Sheathbills may form an evolutionary link between the waders (shorebirds in the USA) and the gulls. Recent research strongly suggests that another very different-looking bird, the Magellanic Plover, *Pluvianellus socialis*, originally classified with the plovers (Family Charadriidae, p. 111) should also be included within this family, in a subfamily of its own (Pluvianellinae) distinct from the sheathbill subfamily, Chioninae. This arrangement is followed here.

The sheathbills are rather ungainly-looking, pigeon-sized birds that look rather like a cross between a plump, short-tailed pigeon and a chicken, with a small head and a short, stout, conical bill. The nostrils are partly covered by a saddle-shaped horny sheath that accounts for the common name for these birds. They have a short neck, stout body and strong legs and feet. Their feet are unwebbed, and although they wade in shallows, they do not swim, preferring to forage on land or ice. Sheathbills have strong, direct flight, but except on migration, on journeys to and from roosting sites,

or when escaping danger such as a predatory skua, they do not generally fly; instead they walk or run fast and purposefully, with a pigeon-like bobbing of the head. The wings have well-developed carpal spurs, which the birds use when fighting over territory. They are usually very tame, allowing close approach by humans.

The Snowy (or Pale-faced or American) Sheathbill, *Chionis alba*, inhabits rocky coasts on the islands of South Georgia, South Orkney and South Shetland and the Antarctic Peninsula, migrating to winter on the Falkland Islands and the coasts of Argentina and Uruguay. The slightly smaller Black-faced (or Lesser) Sheathbill, *C. minor*, lives as a year-round resident on rocky coasts and inland meadows of Prince Edward, Marion, Crozet, Kerguelen and Heard Islands.

Both sheathbill species have very similar snow-white plumage, are well insulated from their bitterly cold surroundings by an extra-thick underlayer of down and differ only in the colours of their bare parts. On the Snowy Sheathbill, the bill is yellowish with a black ridge and tip and the sheath is greenish, as is the caruncle-covered area at the bill's base; the legs are grey. The Black-faced Sheathbill has a black bill and caruncles, and legs that vary between races from pinkish to

ABOVE A Snowy Sheathbill, *Chionis alba*, scavenges scraps of meat clinging to the skull of a King Penguin, *Aptenodytes patagonicus*, on South Georgia Island.

purplish black. The fleshy eye-rings are pinkish in both species.

Sheathbills have a scavenging lifestyle, using their powerful bill to break into birds' eggs, batter small penguin chicks, scoop up the krill brought back to the colony by penguins for their chicks, tear the flesh off seal, whale and bird carcasses, scrape algae off rocks or

glean anything edible, from invertebrates to faeces, offal and human refuse. They are intimately tied to seabird colonies, especially those of penguins, and the time of breeding is determined by that of the seabirds on which they depend for much of their food.

The Magellanic Plover is an unusual wader that breeds by upland lakes in Patagonia and Tierra del Fuego and migrates to the Atlantic coast of Argentina for the winter. It is unobtrusive, with plain grey or grey-brown upperparts and breast and white underparts. Its short bill is black with a pinkish base, and its eyes and legs are bright pinkish-red. The legs are very short and thick, and it has a pigeon-like waddling gait. As well as looking unlike the true plovers, it feeds in a very different way from them, digging into the sand to obtain buried fly larvae or other invertebrates, or uses its bill to turn over stones (and seaweeds on the shore in winter) like a turnstone (*Arenaria*) to flush out prey. Other unplover-like features include the well-developed crop in which it carries food back to regurgitate to its young (it is unique among all waders in this behaviour). Its distinctive morphology, plumage and behaviour, together with molecular studies, led to it being placed in a separate subfamily of the Chionidae (as here) – or by some researchers in a family (Pluvianellidae) of its own.

EGYPTIAN PLOVER Pluvianidae

GENERA: 1   **SPECIES:** 1

LENGTH: 19–22 cm (7.5–8.5 in)

WEIGHT: 73–92 g (2.6–3.2 oz)

RANGE AND HABITAT: Sub-Saharan Africa south to northern Uganda; formerly along River Nile into Egypt but now extinct there; lives in lowlands along large rivers, with sand or gravel bars, including next to human settlements, also by ditches, reedbeds and vegetated lakes

SOCIAL BEHAVIOUR: solitary breeder, monogamous; often in small groups

NEST: a deep scrape dug by both sexes in an exposed sandbank in the riverbed; no lining

EGGS: 2–3, ochre, with small grey and red-brown spots

INCUBATION: 28–31 days

FLEDGING PERIOD: about 30–35 days

FOOD: molluscs, worms, insects and larvae

VOICE: noisy, with loud 'cherk' and 'chee-chee-chee' calls, especially in flight; clucks of alarm near nest

MIGRATION: movements are mainly associated with changes in water level; most are local but some are longer, up to about 800 km (500 miles)

CONSERVATION STATUS: not threatened

The common name of this beautiful little bird is a double misnomer. It no longer occurs in Egypt, although it was abundant during the nineteenth century along the banks of the River Nile south of Cairo, until becoming extinct early in the twentieth century; and it is not a plover.

An aberrant species of uncertain affinities, the Eygptian Plover, *Pluvianus aegyptius*, was traditionally placed with the coursers and pratincoles in the Family Glareolidae (see p. 122). Recent molecular research suggests that it does not belong there and that it is a very ancient and distinctive bird that probably deserves to be placed in a family (Pluvianidae) of its own. One of the African endemics, distributed in a broad belt across Africa south of the Sahara, this strikingly patterned little blue-grey, orange, black and white bird lives not in the arid habitats occupied by the coursers, but along the banks of large rivers and lakes. In many places it has become acclimatised to the presence of humans, and is very tame. It is popularly supposed to enter crocodiles' mouths to feed on the scraps of food left between their teeth, earning the species its popular name of Crocodile Bird. No reliable evidence has come to light to back up the story, which appears in the writings of the Ancient Greek historian Heredotus and has been repeated ever since.

An unusual aspect of the Egyptian Plover's breeding behaviour is the way in which the adults enable their eggs and subsequently the chicks to survive in the extreme heat of the exposed river islands where they dig their nest scrapes. When both members of the pair are away from the nest, the incubating bird tosses sand over the eggs (using its bill and not its feet) before it departs. Later in the morning, when the heat starts to become so intense that the eggs would be at risk of overheating and killing the developing chicks inside, the parent goes to the river and immerses its belly, using a rocking motion to soak the feathers, then returns to the nest and settles so that the water wets the sand covering the eggs, thus cooling them. During the hottest part of the day, the parent may have to soak its feathers every few minutes. After hatching, the adults cover the chicks with sand if they have to leave them, and also wet them if they are in danger of overheating.

OYSTERCATCHERS AND IBISBILL Haematopodidae

GENERA: 1   **SPECIES:** 13

LENGTH: oystercatchers, 41–51 cm (16–20 in); Ibisbill, 39–41 cm (15–16 in)

WEIGHT: oystercatchers, 0.53–0.78 kg (1.2–1.7 lb); Ibisbill, 0.27–0.32 kg (0.6–0.7 lb)

RANGE AND HABITAT: oystercatchers, North, Central and South America, the Caribbean, Europe, Africa, Asia, Australasia; coasts of all types, with sand, mud, rocks or shingle, estuaries, salt marshes; three species also breed inland (but winter mainly on coasts); Ibisbill, central and south-central Asia; mountain valleys, along shingle-bed and boulder-bed rivers at 500–4,400 m (1,600–14,400 ft), descending lower in winter

SOCIAL BEHAVIOUR: oystercatchers, in pairs during the breeding season, monogamous, defending territory, outside breeding season usually in flocks; Ibisbill, usually in pairs or small groups, monogamous, highly territorial

NEST: oystercatchers, a scrape on the ground, in some species lined with rock chips and shell fragments; Ibisbill, a scrape, sometimes lined with small pebbles, sited on a shingle bank, island or peninsula

EGGS: oystercatchers, 1–4, usually 2–3, grey-buff or grey-blue (darker and greenish in the Magellanic Oystercatcher, *H. leucopodus*) with darker markings; Ibisbill 2–4, grey to greenish grey, speckled dark brown

INCUBATION: oystercatchers, 24–39 days; Ibisbill, unknown

FLEDGING PERIOD: oystercatchers, 33–49 days; Ibisbill, 45–50 days

FOOD: oystercatchers, on rocky shores, mainly bivalve molluscs, especially mussels and limpets, also chitons, crabs, amphipods and echinoderms; on soft shores mostly bivalves such as clams, and polychaete worms; inland mainly insects and earthworms; Ibisbill, insects and their larvae, crustaceans, small fish

VOICE: oystercatchers, loud, penetrating, piping calls; Ibisbill, mainly sedentary, apart from moving down to lower altitudes in winter

MIGRATION: oystercatchers, most species are sedentary, apart from inland breeders moving to coasts in winter; only Eurasian Oystercatchers, *H. ostralegus*, are truly migratory, some populations travelling south in winter

CONSERVATION STATUS: oystercatchers, one species, the Canary Islands Oystercatcher, *H. meadewaldoi*, is Extinct; one species, the Chatham Island race of the Variable Oystercatcher, *H. unicolor chathamensis*, is Endangered; one species, the Eurasian Oystercatcher, is Near Threatened; the Ibisbill is not threatened

This family is divided into two subfamiles, the subfamily Haematopodinae containing 12 species of oystercatchers and the subfamily Ibidorhynchidae, containing just one species, the Ibisbill, *Ibidorhyncha struthersii*. the oystercatchers are plump, boldly pied or all-black, stout-billed waders ('shorebirds' in the USA) with a very wide distribution, being found on all continents except Antarctica. There are 10 surviving species and one recently extinct one, all placed in a single genus, *Haematopus*.

Six very similar species are pied, black from head to chest and on the upperparts, with the rest of the body white, and with a white wing bar, prominent in flight. Of these, the American Oystercatcher, *H. palliatus*, the most widespread species, occurs in both North and South America, the Caribbean and the Galapagos Islands; the Magellanic Oystercatcher, *H. leucopodus*, is restricted to the far south of South America; the Eurasian Oystercatcher, *H. ostralegus*, is a very widespread member of the family, breeding right across Europe and Asia and wintering from North Africa to southern Asia; the Pied Oystercatcher, *H. longirostris*, lives in Australia, Tasmania, New Guinea and the Kai and Aru islands; the South Island Pied Oystercatcher, *H. finschi*, is restricted to New Zealand , breeding on South Island. Another pied species is the Chatham Oystercatcher, *H. chathamensis*; this is endemic to the Chatham Islands, which belong to New Zealand, lying about 800 km (500 miles) east of South Island.

Four very similar species with all-black plumage are the American Black Oystercatcher, *H. bachmani*, found on the west coast of North America; the Blackish Oystercatcher, *H. ater*, of South America; the African Black Oystercatcher, *H. moquini*, and the Sooty Oystercatcher, *H. fuliginosus*, of Australia. A fifth black species, the Canary Islands Oystercatcher, *H. meadewaldoi*, is now considered extinct, probably as a result of overharvesting of its mollusc food and disturbance by people, and predation by rats and cats.

The eleventh species, found in New Zealand, is polymorphic, occurring as an-all black form, a pied form, and a form with intermediate plumage. Its common name (but not its specific one) is apt: this is the Variable Oystercatcher, *H. unicolor*. One of its races, *chathamensis*, endemic to the Chatham Islands, is often now regarded as a separate species, the Chatham Oystercatcher, *H. chathamensis*. All oystercatchers have a bright orange-red bill and legs of various shades of pinkish or pinkish-red. Eyes and eye-rings are red in most species and races, yellow in a few.

Although most species are coastal, many Magellanic Oystercatchers breed inland on grasslands and by pools, including in the uplands of the species' range in the far south of South America. In addition, over the last hundred or so years two seashore species – the Eurasian Oystercatcher and the South Island Pied Oystercatcher in New Zealand – have extended their ranges up into rivers, especially where shingle banks provide good nesting sites. In both cases this has been accompanied by major increases in the overall populations.

The long, stout, bladelike bill is well adapted for breaking into the hard shells of molluscs. Despite their common name, these birds rarely include oysters in their diet, but eat various other bivalve molluscs. Both Eurasian and Variable Oystercatchers deal with them in two main ways: to get at the mollusc's soft body within they either use the bill to stab between the slightly open valve edges, as the bivalve feeds, severing the adductor muscle that closes the shell, or hammer at the shell to smash it open. In Eurasian Oystercatchers, at least, the method of shell opening is culturally transmitted from adults to young, but as the novices mature, they may alter their technique. Females are on average longer-billed than males, and this difference probably relates to their taking different prey or feeding in different types of habitat, and thus avoiding competition.

Oystercatchers are at their most noticeable when performing their complex piping territorial defence displays, when many birds may run along side by side calling loudly. They also perform display flights to advertise territory ownership, flying around with shallow wingbeats and calling loudly.

The Ibisbill, *Ibidorhyncha struthersii*, is a unique wader ('shorebird' in the USA), the sole member of its genus. The latest molecular research indicates that its closest relatives appear to be the oystercatchers (Family Haematopodidae), although it has been classified with the stilts and avocets in the next family. Indeed the oystercatchers and the Ibisbill together form a sister group to the stilts and avocets. This habitat specialist dwells only in river valleys in the mountains of central and south-central Asia, albeit over a huge range. Here it finds nesting sites and food among extensive shingle and boulder beds. As its common name indicates, the bill resembles that of an ibis, being very long and strongly decurved. The Ibisbill uses it to search for its invertebrate food by pecking at the prey on the water surface, probing for hidden prey under boulders and among pebbles, or dislodging it by putting its head on one side and raking the bill sideways across the pebbles.

Relative to the rounded head, thick neck and long, stout body, the sturdy, greyish-purple legs are relatively short, giving the bird a top-heavy appearance like that of oystercatchers (*Haematopus*). The head, neck and breast are strikingly patterned in blue-grey, contrasting with the bright crimson bill, a black face with a narrow white border and a narrow, white-bordered breast band. The back and wings are mainly brownish grey and the underparts aft of the breast band white. Despite this boldly marked plumage, the Ibisbill is very hard to spot, as the frontal pattern is disruptive, breaking up the bird's outline so it merges into the background of pebbles, rocks and water.

ABOVE Despite their common name, oystercatchers such as this Eurasian Oystercatcher, *Haematopus ostralegus*, feed extensively on mussels.

ABOVE The Ibisbill, *Ibidorhyncha struthersii*, is a specialist feeder restricted to slow-moving high-altitude rivers in Asia.

STILTS AND AVOCETS Recurvirostridae

GENERA: 3   **SPECIES:** 7

LENGTH: 35–51 cm (14–20 in)

WEIGHT: 1.65–4.60 kg (3.6–10.1 lb)

RANGE AND HABITAT: worldwide except for far north and Antarctic regions; greatest diversity in Australasia; mostly in large lowland shallow freshwater, brackish and saline wetlands, usually bordered by sandy shores, dunes or other suitable open areas for nesting

SOCIAL BEHAVIOUR: often in small groups throughout the year, and most breed in colonies of 5–100 pairs (but the rare Black Stilt, *Himantopus novaezelandiae*, is nowadays a solitary breeder, defending its territory all year); monogamous (often only for one breeding season, although Black Stilts pair for life)

NEST: a shallow scrape in sand, sometimes with a sparse lining of grass or other vegetation

EGGS: 3–4, brownish or yellowish with darker markings (except for those of the Banded Stilt, which are pure white)

INCUBATION: 19–26 days

FLEDGING PERIOD: 28–55 days

FOOD: small crustaceans, molluscs, aquatic insects and worms and small fish

VOICE: loud calls, especially when defending eggs or young and in flight; stilts utter harsh, high-pitched yelping and piping notes, whereas avocet calls have nasal or shrill calls, often disyllabic

MIGRATION: mostly sedentary, but in Australia Banded Stilts, *Cladorhynchus leucocephalus*, and Red-necked Avocets, *Recurvirostra novaehollandiae*, are nomadic, travelling after seasonal rainfall to breed by temporary lakes; three more northerly breeding species (the Black-winged Stilt, *Himantopus himantopus*, the Pied Avocet, *R. avosetta*, and the American Avocet, *R. americana*) migrate south for winter

CONSERVATION STATUS: one species, the Black Stilt, is Critically Endangered

This is a small family of distinctive, elegant waders ('shorebirds' in the USA), which all share striking, mainly black-and-white, plumage, a long, very fine bill (straight in stilts and upcurved at the tip in avocets) and very long legs. The legs are especially long in stilts, as their common name suggests: in the most widespread member of the entire family, the Black-winged Stilt, *Himantopus himantopus*, they are longer in proportion to the body than those of any other birds except flamingos. Stilts (subfamily Himantopodinae) and avocets (subfamily Recurvirostrinae) are among the most conspicuous birds of shallow wetlands across much of the world, not only because all but one has a gleaming white body, but also because they have loud calls and are pugnacious in defence of their eggs or young.

In addition to the Black-winged Stilt (which is found over a vast range from Europe and Africa to Asia, Australasia, New Zealand, Hawaii, the Americas and the Caribbean) there are two other far more local stilt species. The rare Black Stilt, *H. novaezelandiae*, is restricted today to a small area in New Zealand, whereas the Banded Stilt, *Cladorhynchus leucocephalus*, is a distinctive species of Australia, which shares features of both stilts and avocets, such as the straight (or very slightly upcurved) bill of the former and the basal webbing uniting the front three toes, found in the avocets. Recent molecular research suggests it may be better moved to the avocet subfamily.

The four species of avocet, all in the single genus *Recurvirostra*, are also collectively spread across the world. The Pied Avocet, *R. avosetta*, breeds across parts of Europe and Asia and in Africa, mainly in the east and south, whereas the American Avocet, *R. americana*, also has a very extensive range in North America, the Caribbean, Mexico and Guatemala. The Red-necked Avocet, *R. novaehollandiae*, is spread widely across Australia. Although the other avocet species – and all stilts except some Black-winged Stilts – live at lower altitudes, the Andean Avocet, *R. andina*, lives year-round by saline lakes and pools, mainly above 5,000 m (16,500 ft).

ABOVE This juvenile Pied Avocet, *Recurvirostra avosetta*, demonstrates the distinctive feeding action of these graceful birds.

ABOVE The Black-winged Stilt, *Himantopus himantopus*, has the longest legs of its family, with those of males being the longest of all.

All members of the family have a black bill; stilts have bright reddish or orange-pink legs, whereas avocets have blue-grey legs. The plumage of the Black-winged Stilt is pied, with black upperparts and white underparts; the extent of black markings on head and neck varies between the five subspecies. The Banded Stilt is distinguished by a chestnut breast band, and the Black Stilt is coloured as its name suggests. Avocets are also pied, with the American Avocet having an apricot-coloured head and neck, whereas those areas are a richer, deeper chestnut red in the Red-necked Avocet.

With their long legs, both stilts and avocets can wade up to their knee joints into shallow water more deeply than most other birds, and both can swim. They forage by pecking at visible prey on or just below the water surface or on the ground, and by touch: a characteristic method, used especially by avocets, is to sweep the slightly opened bill sideways at a low angle through the water to contact and ingest prey.

Stilts and avocets breed in loose colonies. In these, nests are typically spaced 5–30 m (16–98 ft) apart. An exception is seen in Banded Stilts – sporadic, opportunistic breeders that travel considerable distances to congregate at ephemeral saline lakes as these fill following heavy rainfall. Here they pack their nests together (at some sites as many as 18 nests in a square metre) in colonies that can be huge, up to almost 180,000 in one case.

Another contrast is provided by New Zealand's Black Stilt, which today is one of the world's rarest waders and has largely abandoned colonial breeding. Fewer than 100 adults (including some captive-bred birds) survive, all breeding solely in the Upper Waitiki Valley on South Island. There were only 19 productive breeding pairs recorded in February 2016. The huge decline in this bird's fortunes is due mainly to predation by introduced mammals such as cats, stoats, ferrets, hedgehogs and rats. With such low population levels, an additional major threat comes from hybridisation with the more common Black-winged Stilt.

PLOVERS AND LAPWINGS Charadriidae

GENERA: 11   **SPECIES:** 67

LENGTH: 12–38 cm (5–15 in)

WEIGHT: 20–440 g (0.7–15.5 oz)

RANGE AND HABITAT: worldwide, from the High Arctic to the tropics and sub-Antarctic, and on many islands, absent only from the Antarctic continent; wide range of both wet and dry open habitats, including all sorts of wetlands, sea coasts, steppes and other grasslands, cultivated land, tundra and semi-deserts; a few in high mountains

SOCIAL BEHAVIOUR: seen singly, in pairs or in flocks (largest on migration); most species are seasonally monogamous (the Northern Lapwing, *Vanellus vanellus*, is sometimes polygamous and the Eurasian Dotterel, *Eudromias morinellus*, is polyandrous, with sex-role reversal); some territorial and solitary breeders, others loosely colonial

NEST: most species build a simple scrape in sand or soil, sometimes lined with vegetation or small pebbles or shell fragments; marsh-nesting lapwings assemble a mound of plant material

EGGS: 2–5, whitish, beige or greenish, with dark markings

INCUBATION: 21–30 days

FLEDGING PERIOD: 22–days

FOOD: mostly invertebrates, including insects, spiders, crustaceans, snails and worms; some small fish, amphibians and lizards, and berries or seeds

VOICE: a variety of whistling, piping, trilling or rattling calls; those of lapwings are harsher and more strident, those of plovers more melodious, often sounding plaintive

MIGRATION: many species are sedentary, or make only local altitudinal or dispersal movements; some, notably the tundra plovers, *Pluvialis*, are long-distance migrants

CONSERVATION STATUS: three species, the Sociable Lapwing, *Vanellus gregarius*, the Javan Wattled Lapwing, *V. macropterus*, and the southern race *obscurus* of the Red-breasted Plover, *Charadrius obscurus*, are Critically Endangered; one species, the Shore Dotterel, *Thinornis novaeseelandiae*, is Endangered; four species, the St Helena Plover, *C. sanctaehelenae*, the Madagascan Plover, *C. thoracicus*, the Hooded Dotterel, *T. cucullatus* and the Wrybill, *Anarhynchus frontalis*, are Vulnerable; 10 species, including the Northern Lapwing, *V. vanellus* and the Snowy Plover, *C. nivosus*, are Near Threatened

ABOVE The Masked Lapwing, *Vanellus miles*, is a common sight in parks, playing fields and other urban habitats in Australia.

This is the second largest group of waders ('shorebirds' in the USA) after the sandpipers and snipes (Scolopacidae). In appearance they are a more homogeneous group than the latter. All have a plump, neatly tapering body ranging in length in different species from that of a Canary almost to that of a Eurasian Coot or American Coot. They have a short, thick neck and a rounded head, with big eyes that contain a high ratio of retinal rod to cone cells, giving good vision in dim light; many species feed at twilight or at night. Almost all species have a relatively short bill in which the upper mandible is slightly swollen near the tip; two South American species, the Tawny-throated Dotterel, *Oreopholus ruficollis*, and the Diademed Plover, *Phegornis mitchellii*, have a longer, thin bill (slightly decurved in the latter), whereas a New Zealand endemic, the Wrybill, *Anarhynchus frontalis*, has a bill unlike that of any other bird, curving sideways, invariably to the right. Leg length varies considerably, from the short legs of many of the *Charadrius* species to the long ones of some of the lapwings, *Vanellus*. The front toes are relatively short and the hind toe is tiny or vestigial, suited to fast running on flat surfaces. There are three subfamilies: the tundra plovers (Pluvialinae) and the ringed plovers (Charadiinae), and the lapwings (Vanellinae). Despite their morphological similarity, analysis of recent molecular data suggests that the subfamily containing the four tundra plover species, *Pluvialis*, are not as closely related to the other two subfamilies as each of those is to one another, and that they constitute a more ancient group.

The tundra plovers breed mainly on the Arctic and sub-Arctic tundra and moorland of North America and Eurasia. These birds form the smallest subfamily, with just four similar species in the genus *Pluvialis*, between 23 cm (9 in) and 31 cm (12 in) long. The difference between breeding and non-breeding plumage is greatest in this group, all of them having patterns of black and white from the face to the breast and belly, the black being lost in winter. In three of them, the Eurasian, Pacific and American Golden Plovers, *P. apricaria*, *P. fulva*, and *P. dominica*, the upperparts are spangled gold, black and white, brightest in the breeding plumage. The fourth species, the equally appropriately named Grey Plover (known from its breeding plumage as the Black-bellied Plover in North America), *P. squatarola*, has spangled silvery grey upperparts.

The ringed plover subfamily contains 36 species. These birds are mainly small – 27 species are between 16.5 and 21 cm (6.5 and 8 in) long; the others measure 22–29 cm (8.5–11.5 in). All but seven are in the genus *Charadrius*, which includes the very widespread, mainly coastal Common Ringed Plover, *C. hiaticula*, which breeds in northeast Canada, Greenland and Eurasia, the Semi-palmated Plover, *C. semipalmatus*, which breeds in Alaska and right across Canada, and the bigger Killdeer, *C. vociferus*, a largely inland species that is often seen on playing fields and golf courses and even breeds in cities on gravel-topped roofs. Plumage is typically brown above and white below. Many species have black, white and sometimes chestnut markings on the head, and often also one or two black or chestnut breast bands; the markings are bolder in the breeding plumage. The subfamily Charadriinae includes eight species called dotterels, scattered among six different genera. The best known of these, the Eurasian Dotterel, *Eudromias morinellus*, is remarkable in exhibiting a pronounced sex role reversal. Females are rather larger, heavier and more brightly plumaged than males, and take the lead in courtship and territorial defence. Depending on local sex ratios, a female may practise serial polyandry, leaving her mate to incubate the eggs and rear the chicks while she mates with another male, and sometimes after that with another; alternatively, a female may have two or even three mates at the same time, or may take a single mate for the season.

The 24 species of lapwing in the genus *Vanellus* are found worldwide except for North America and Antarctica. They include common and conspicuous species of farmland and other open habitats, such as: the most studied species, the Northern Lapwing, *V. vanellus*, widespread across Eurasia; several African species; the Red-wattled Lapwing, *V. indicus*, of southern Asia, which can be seen searching for food around muddy pools or on lawns even in the heart of crowded cities; the Masked Lapwing, *V. miles*, of Australasia; and the Southern Lapwing, *V. chilensis*, of South America.

Lapwings are larger than the other plovers, mostly 25–35 cm (10–14 in) long, and with a proportionately smaller head. The largest, at 32–38 cm (12.5–15 in), is the Southern Lapwing. They have broad wings with broad tips, unlike almost all other waders – including the other plovers – which have narrower, tapering wings. It is the wing shape and the slow, floppy flight that earned them their common name. The most extreme shape is seen in the Northern Lapwing, whose wingtips are almost semicircular.

ABOVE A Eurasian Golden Plover, *Pluvialis apricaria*, gives an alarm call as an observer approaches its nest on a bog on Shetland, Scotland.

ABOVE The Common Ringed Plover, *Charadrius hiaticula*, is a very widespread species across northern Eurasia and North America.

Most lapwings have brown upperparts and white or pale underparts, often with contrasting black-and-white head markings or breast bands. Sixteen species have head adornments in the form of a crest, bright red or yellow fleshy facial wattles, or sharp bony spurs on the wings that are used in fighting over territory; although no species has all three of these accoutrements, some have two.

Almost all species in the family have a very distinctive feeding method. They stand still and watch for prey (typically small crustaceans and marine worms on coasts, and insect larvae, earthworms and spiders inland). As soon as they detect an animal emerging from the substrate or already moving on it, they run forward rapidly and, bending the head, snap it up; then they pause before moving on to another watch-point and repeating the process. They often make tapping or trembling movements with their legs on the surface, to stimulate buried prey to emerge. The exception is the Wrybill, which uses its laterally bent bill to probe and sweep about beneath stones for mayfly larvae and other invertebrates hiding there.

Most of the lapwings are sedentary or make only relatively short seasonal or altitudinal movements, or move in response to rainfall or fires affecting their food supply. However, most Northern Lapwings winter to the south of their breeding range, as far as North Africa, the Middle East, northern India and southern China, and the rare Sociable Lapwing, *V. gregarius*, which breeds in Central Asia also migrates south. Truly migrant species include the ringed plovers, mainly those breeding in the northern hemisphere, but also some southern hemisphere species, such as the Double-banded Plover, *C. bicinctus*, which crosses the Tasman sea between New Zealand and Australia. Some ringed plovers travel great distances, but the champion migrants in the family are members of the tundra plover subfamily, which are among the fastest flying of all birds in level flight, at up to 96 km/h (60 mph). This enables them to perform impressively rapid migrations. The Pacific Golden Plover, *Pluvialis fulva*, for instance, is known to make a non-stop journey of about 4,800 km (3,000 miles) across the Pacific in autumn between its breeding grounds on the Alaskan tundra and Hawaii. Using tiny geolocator data-loggers attached to the birds' legs, researchers have found that some can do this in as little as 3 days (including a record of 70 hours) on their northward flight in spring, and about 4 days on the return trip in autumn. Some were found to maintain a minimum flight speed of 56 km/h (35 mph) and an average of 63 km/h (40 mph), and record maximum ground speeds of 167–185 km/h (104–115 mph) have been recorded for three birds, presumably involving the benefit of a strong wind behind them.

PLAINS-WANDERER Pedionomidae

GENERA: 1   **SPECIES**: 1

LENGTH: 15–19 cm (6–7.5 in)

WEIGHT: 40–95 g (1.4–3.4 oz)

RANGE AND HABITAT: fragmented range across eastern Australia; extensive, open, treeless tracts of native grassland and saltbush; occasionally in fields of low crops and stubble fields

SOCIAL BEHAVIOUR: usually solitary outside the breeding season; females probably breed with several males in turn (serial polyandry) and males play a major or sole part in incubation and are totally responsible for the care of the young while females pair with the next male

NEST: a hollow scratched in ground, lined with grasses, sometimes with grasses pulled over the top to conceal the contents

EGGS: 2–5, yellowish buff, marked with grey and olive

INCUBATION: about 23 days

FLEDGING PERIOD: chicks leave the nest almost immediately after hatching, but they are not fully independent until 2 months old

FOOD: small seeds and insects

VOICE: usually silent except in the breeding season, when birds (possibly females only) make repeated low, resonant cooing or mooing sounds; the males also communicate with the chicks by low clucking calls and longer piping notes

MIGRATION: sedentary unless forced out of an area by changes in habitat or rainfall

CONSERVATION STATUS: Critically Endangered

ABOVE A rare sight, a female Plains-wanderer, *Pedionomus torquatus*, emerges from cover in its Australian grassland home.

Although formerly considered as a member of the Order Gruiformes, and most closely related to the buttonquails (Family Turnicidae, see p. 120), this odd little Australian endemic is now known to be a member of the Order Charadriiformes, probably closest to the seedsnipes (Family Thinocoridae, see p. 114), and the remnant of an ancient lineage. Apart from the DNA evidence, differences from the buttonquails include its possession of a hind toe, more upright posture, and pear-shaped rather than oval eggs.

Only the size of an Old World quail, the Plains-wanderer, *Pedionomus torquatus*, is cryptically plumaged, brown above and whitish below, with black or dark brown crescent markings. It often stands on tiptoe to scan for predators over the top of the vegetation, and rarely flies, preferring to run from danger. Sometimes, it lies flat on the ground in an effort to evade detection. The female is distinctly brighter, with her black-and-white collar above a chestnut breast patch, and she is also larger.

As with various other families in the Charadriiformes, she is the more dominant sex; she takes the initiative in courtship, and often takes a second mate, leaving the first one to rear the chicks alone.

Despite its common name, the Plains-wanderer is essentially sedentary, making nomadic movements only when forced by food shortages resulting from habitat changes, prolonged drought or especially heavy rainfall (which reduces the supply of seeds from native plants as non-native ones outcompete them). It depends almost entirely on native plants for its sustenance, eating just the seeds. The intensification of agriculture, including overgrazing, has greatly reduced the area of natural lowland grassland, and as a result this unusual and enigmatic bird has declined immensely. Other threats include pesticides, introduced foxes, wildfires and increased drought due to climate change. Today, the species has become extinct from many former haunts, especially in its former stronghold in South Australia and Victoria.

SEEDSNIPES Thinocoridae

GENERA: 2   **SPECIES:** 4

LENGTH: 16–30 cm (6.25–12 in)

WEIGHT: 50–400 g (1.75–14 oz)

RANGE AND HABITAT: western and southern South America, in the Andes and Patagonia; open country, often at high altitudes; mainly in grassland and semi-desert; one species in highland bogs

SOCIAL BEHAVIOUR: mostly in pairs or small flocks, including family groups; sometimes in larger flocks at good food sources; apparently monogamous and territorial and without sexual role reversal

NEST: a scrape on the ground, often lined with vegetation or mammal dung, sited against a stone, grass tussock or dense, dwarf shrub; many among mammal dung

EGGS: 4, cream, buff, pinkish, very pale green or olive, with dark brown markings

INCUBATION: about 26 days in the Least Seedsnipe, *Thinocorus rumicivorus*

FLEDGING PERIOD: 49–55 days in the Least Seedsnipe

FOOD: mainly plant leaves and buds, also occasionally seeds and berries

VOICE: the song is a fast sequence of cooing and other notes; they also give sharp, short grating, grunting, rasping or peeping alarm calls

MIGRATION: some are sedentary, but others make local movements, including seasonal altitudinal changes; some Least Seedsnipes in Peru may be nomadic

CONSERVATION STATUS: none threatened

LEFT The Grey-breasted Seedsnipe, *Thinocorus orbignyianus*, is a characteristic species of puna grassland of the Andes, often near bogs.

These elusive birds inhabit wild open country, including that in some of the most inhospitable parts of South America, so it is not surprising that much still remains to be learned about them. They are rather like very small grouse in general appearance, with a small chicken-like bill, plump body and short, strong legs and feet; however, they differ from those birds in having long, pointed wings and being strong flyers. They have a fast, snipe-like escape flight when disturbed by a predator or human intruder, dashing off on a zig-zagging course, calling loudly, and may soon drop down to hide in dense cover. Males of the two small *Thinocorus* species perform a lark-like display flight, flying up high into the air and then descending on stiffly held wings, singing their repetitive songs as they glide down to earth.

These birds are hard to see, superbly camouflaged against the vegetation, earth or rocks by the cryptically patterned plumage of their upperparts – an intricate scalloped mixture of browns, black, grey and golden buff. In the two larger species, in the genus *Attagis*, which are a bit smaller than a town pigeon, the sexes have similar plumage. The Rufous-bellied Seedsnipe, *A. gayi*, has reddish underparts; the other three seedsnipes have white bellies. In the two *Thinocorus* species, the males have a grey head and breast, whereas those parts of the females are brown with black markings.

In contrast to those of other waders ('shorebirds' in the USA), the external nostrils of seedsnipes are covered with a thin flap of skin (the operculum), which presumably protects them from being clogged with wind-blown dust.

PAINTED-SNIPES Rostratulidae

GENERA: 2   **SPECIES:** 3

LENGTH: 19–28 cm (7.5–11 in)

WEIGHT: 65–200 g (2.3–7 oz)

RANGE AND HABITAT: the Greater Painted-snipe, *Rostratula benghalensis*, lives in Africa, Madagascar, Southern Asia, Japan, China, the Philippines and Indonesia; the Australian Painted-snipe, *R. australis*, in parts of Australia, mainly in the east; the South American Painted-snipe, *Nycticryphes semicollaris*, is a bird of southern South America, from Paraguay and southeastern Brazil to central Argentina; swamps, marshes, reed beds, rice fields, lake and pool shores, banks of rivers and streams, mangroves

SOCIAL BEHAVIOUR: solitary, in pairs and sometimes in loose groups when feeding or breeding; the Greater Painted-snipe and Australian Painted-snipe are usually polyandrous (monogamous in some areas where it occurs at low density, including South Africa), the South American Painted-snipe apparently monogamous; females, which are the dominant sex and incubate the eggs and care for the young, are territorial

NEST: cup of plant stems and leaves on ground, concealed among dense vegetation

EGGS: 2–4, cream or buff, heavily spotted black and brown

INCUBATION: 15–21 days

FLEDGING PERIOD: period unknown; young leave the nest soon after hatching and remain with the father for a few days

FOOD: insects, snails, worms, crustaceans, seeds

VOICE: mainly silent outside the breeding season, but then females display to males with mellow hooting or booming sounds (Greater Painted-snipe and Australian Painted-snipe) or brief, plaintive whistles (South American Painted-snipe)

MIGRATION: many populations are sedentary, although those breeding in northern China and Japan migrate to winter in Southeast Asia, and those in Africa and Australia are nomadic; the South American Painted-snipe may also move in response to rainfall

CONSERVATION STATUS: one species, the Australian Painted-snipe, *R. australis*, is Endangered

This family contains just three species of small, rather snipe-like waders ('shorebirds' in the USA) with a long, slightly drooping bill; two are found over a huge range in the Old World and Australia and the other one in the New World, with a more restricted but still very extensive range in South America. Although they have at times been thought to be linked to true snipes, *Gallinago*, and woodcocks, *Scolopax*, the latest molecular data indicates that they are best placed near the jacanas (Family Jacanidae, see below), seedsnipes (Family Thinocoridae, see opposite page) and Plains Wanderer (Family Pedionomidae, p. 113).

The vernacular family name of these relatively little known birds refers to the bright plumage of the female of the two Old World species. In contrast to the situation in most sexually dimorphic birds, in which the male is usually the more brightly or boldly plumaged sex, in this species, females are distinctly bigger and heavier, and much brighter plumaged and more boldly marked than males. They have dark bronze green upperparts, a large patch of rich chestnut colour from the head below the eye to the breast and a broad white patch around the eye. Males are mottled grey-brown and golden buff above, providing excellent camouflage when sitting on the nest. The females defend their territories and mates against rival females, take the lead in courtship, and play no part in nest building, incubation or chick rearing. They are usually polyandrous, with each female mating with more than one male sequentially. They usually have two mates, but may take three or even four in the course of a single season.

The South American Painted-snipe, *Nycticryphes semicollaris*, is distinguished from its relatives by its smaller size, more decurved bill, and small webs between the toes; also the sexes differ little if at all in plumage, although females average very slightly larger. Its head, neck and the front of the body are very dark reddish brown, while the rest of the underparts are white, as with the Greater Painted-snipe. It also shares the latter birds' white stripe extending from the breast around the shoulders onto the back, where it becomes golden.

ABOVE Two male Greater Painted-snipe, *Rostratula benghalensis*, at Keoladeo National Park, Bharatpur, Rajasthan, India in November.

All three species have a short neck, a plump body, and long legs with long, slender toes – well adapted for foraging in the shallow water and soft oozy mud of swamps and other wetlands. They also have big eyes, aiding vision as they feed, mainly at dusk and dawn and on moonlit nights. They spend much of the daytime roosting among dense aquatic vegetation, from where they are difficult to flush out, preferring to 'freeze'; not surprisingly, birdwatchers usually find them notoriously difficult to see. They are normally silent, but the females utter advertising calls during the breeding season, which are particularly far-carrying in the two *Rostratula* species.

JACANAS Jacanidae

GENERA: 6 **SPECIES**: 8

LENGTH: 15–30 cm (6–12 in); the Pheasant-tailed Jacana 39–58 cm (15–23 in), including 23–35 cm (9–14 in) tail in breeding plumage in both sexes

WEIGHT: 40–260 g (1.4–9 oz)

RANGE AND HABITAT: sub-Saharan Africa, India, Southeast Asia, New Guinea, North and East Australia, Mexico (and rarely, Texas), Central and South America; marshes, lakes, ponds and slow-flowing rivers covered with floating vegetation

SOCIAL BEHAVIOUR: outside breeding season, often gregarious; in all species but the Lesser Jacana, *Microparra capensis* (which breeds as monogamous pairs), the females are dominant and polyandrous

NEST: circular pad of leaves of aquatic plants, usually sited on floating vegetation or a raised platform of plant material, sometimes partly submerged; several platforms may be built, from which the female chooses one

EGGS: 3–4, brownish, very glossy, very heavily marked with black or dark brown spots and lines, except in the Pheasant-tailed Jacana, *Hydrophasianus chirurgus*, whose eggs are unmarked

INCUBATION: 21–28 days

FLEDGING PERIOD: 50–60 days for species where it is known

FOOD: aquatic insects and other invertebrates, occasionally seeds of aquatic plants

VOICE: noisy, with various piping, squawking, squeaking, chattering, rattling and whistling notes; many are loud and harsh, but adults call young with soft and quieter sounds

MIGRATION: mainly sedentary, but the Pheasant-tailed Jacanas in the north of their range move south for winter

CONSERVATION STATUS: One species, The Madagascar Jacana, *Actophilornis albinucha*, is Near Threatened

Found in tropical and subtropical wetlands of various kinds throughout the world, jacanas have long legs and remarkably long toes. The latter are an adaptation for walking on floating vegetation, including lily leaves – a habit that has earned these birds their old alternative common name of 'lily-trotters'. These are the only birds to really exploit this unique niche, and do so thoroughly, not only foraging but also defending territories, pairing, mating and raising families on the living raft that is their home for most of their lives. Except for males incubating eggs or rearing young, they spend up to 90% of their time foraging, using their bill to pick insects or other invertebrates from the water surface or to flip over water-lily leaves and glean prey hiding on their undersurfaces. They also take prey from the root systems of floating plants and flutter up into the air to catch flying insects.

Most jacanas range in size from roughly that of a thrush to that of a domestic pigeon but with a longer neck, but one species, the Lesser Jacana, *Microparra capensis*, of Africa is much smaller, with a body not much larger than a sparrow's. The tail is short in all species, except for the Pheasant-tailed Jacana, *Hydrophasianus chirurgus*, in the breeding season, when both sexes sport very long tail feathers (lost after breeding).

All species have colourful plumage but are often very hard to spot; in some species the bold patterns are disruptive, breaking up their outline against the background of vegetation. Most are mainly bronzy brown with variable amounts of glossy black, in two species with contrasting yellow flight feathers, and five species have a complex pattern of bright orange or yellow on a black and white head and neck. In addition, all species except for the Pheasant-tailed Jacana have conspicuous yellow, red or blue bare fleshy protrusions on the head or bill. These may take the form of a frontal shield extending from the upper bill onto the forehead, a fleshy comb on the head or a larger combination of comb and wattles in the Wattled Jacana, *Jacana jacana*; most dramatic is

ABOVE A Northern Jacana, *Jacana spinosa*, 'walks on the water' across a lake at Tikal, Guatemala.

the large comb of the Comb-crested Jacana, *Irediparra gallinacea*. When the bird is excited during courtship displays or other social interactions, the comb becomes engorged with blood and erected, and changes colour from yellow to bright red.

In all species except for the monogamous Lesser Jacana, the females are considerably larger and more dominant than males, and play no real part in nest building, incubation or chick rearing, sometimes mating with as many as four different males. However (in contrast to the situation with other polyandrous families in this order), there is little difference in plumage between the sexes. Males are solicitous fathers; if they need to move young chicks from the nest to avoid danger, they walk away with the offspring tucked up under their wings, their long legs dangling.

SANDPIPERS AND SNIPES Scolopacidae

GENERA: 16   **SPECIES**: 94

LENGTH: 13–66 cm (5–26 in)

WEIGHT: 18 g–1 kg (0.6 oz–2.2 lb)

RANGE AND HABITAT: on all continents except Antarctica; most species breed in the northern hemisphere; most breed in wetlands, moorland and grasslands, both coastal and inland; a few, notably woodcocks, breed in woodland; most winter on coasts, estuaries and wetlands

SOCIAL BEHAVIOUR: some species are mainly solitary, some generally live in pairs or small groups, and others form large flocks outside the breeding season; many species are monogamous and territorial, but some are polyandrous, with reversed sex roles

NEST: typically a shallow scrape in the ground, which may be lined with pebbles, shell fragments or vegetation

EGGS: 2–4 (typically 4), usually buff or greenish with darker markings

INCUBATION: 18–30 days

FLEDGING PERIOD: 16–50 days

FOOD: mainly molluscs, crustaceans, aquatic worms, flies; some seeds or other plant matter

VOICE: wide range of whistling, fluting, yodelling, purring and trilling sounds, and rattling, yelping or other shriller ones

MIGRATION: some species are sedentary; others make only local movements; many are long-distance migrants travelling many thousands of kilometres

CONSERVATION STATUS: three species, the Tahiti Sandpiper, *Prosobonia leucoptera*, the Christmas Island Sandpiper, *P. cancellata* and the Moorea Sandpiper, *P. ellisi*, are Extinct; one species, the Eskimo Curlew, *Numenius borealis*, is Critically Endangered (Possibly Extinct); two species, the Spoon-billed Sandpiper, *Calidris pygmea*, and Slender-billed Curlew, *N. tenuirostris*, are Critically Endangered; five species, the Tuamotu Sandpiper, *P. parvirostris*, Moluccan Woodcock, *Scolopax rochussenii*, the Far Eastern Curlew, *N. madagascariensis* and the Great Knot, *C. tenuirostris* and Nordmann's Greenshank, *Tringa guttifer*, are Endangered; five species, including the Madagascar Snipe, *Gallinago macrodactyla*, the Amami Woodcock, *S. mira*, and Bristle-thighed Curlew, *Numenius tahitiensis*, are Vulnerable; and 10 species are Near Threatened

ABOVE In their coastal winter quarters, Eurasian Curlews, *Numenius arquata*, catch large numbers of burrowing crabs.

This is the largest and most diverse family of waders ('shorebirds' in the USA), with a wide range of size, bill shape and leg length. In many parts of the world, they often constitute the majority of these birds to be seen on coasts in winter. Vast numbers are often involved, as revealed by the counts of migrants at stopover sites: almost half a million individuals of just one North American species, the Semipalmated Sandpiper, *Calidris pusilla*, have been counted in autumn at the Bay of Fundy on the border between the eastern USA and Canada as they fatten up ready for their long journeys to winter in South America. At the major wintering site for waders breeding in northern Europe, Siberia and Greenland – the Banc d'Arguin, off the coast of Mauritania, west Africa – up to 3 million birds, many of them belonging to this family, have been recorded. Huge flocks of these birds perform astonishingly well-coordinated aerial manoeuvres like those of schooling fish across estuaries and bays between feeding and roosting. With their dark uppersides and pale undersides alternately in view, they appear to shimmer or twinkle; at a distance they resemble clouds of smoke blowing in the wind.

The family is divided into five subfamilies. The first subfamily, Numeniinae, contains the largest members of the family, the long-billed curlews, with eight species in the genus *Numenius*. These range in length from 28 to 32 cm (11 to 12.5 in) in the Little Curlew, *N. minutus*, to the Far Eastern Curlew, *N. madagascariensis*, in which the larger females may reach 66 cm (26 in). All have a downcurved bill that varies in length between species and within species between the sexes; that of the female Far Eastern Curlew is the longest of any wader, at up to 18.4 cm (7.25 in). The legs are relatively short, especially in the smaller species. The Eurasian Curlew, *N. arquata*, is the largest European wader. Also included in the Numeniinae is the short-billed, much smaller Upland Sandpiper, *Bartramia longicauda*.

The next subfamily, Limosinae, comprises the four species of godwit, in the genus *Limosa*: two, the Black-tailed Godwit, *L. limosa*, of Eurasia and the larger and mainly inland breeding Marbled Godwit, *L. fedoa*, of North America have especially long legs. All have a very long, straight or almost straight, bill.

The third subfamily, Calidridinae, contains 24 species in the genus *Calidris*, as well as two distinctive turnstone species, *Arenaria* and a third genus, *Prosobonia*, with only one living representative (the Endangered Tuamotu Sandpiper, *P. parvirostris*) and three extinct species.

The two species of turnstone have evolved a special way of foraging. Moving among slippery seaweed-covered rocks with a sure balance from their short legs, they use their strong, short bill that is flattened from top to bottom to heave aside stones or seaweed fronds to find invertebrates beneath. The more widespread Ruddy Turnstone, *Arenaria interpres*, which breeds right around the Arctic, has a chestnut, black and white tortoiseshell plumage pattern, duller in females and in males in their winter plumage; the Black Turnstone, *A. melanocephala*, of Pacific shores of North America is largely black with a white belly.

The 24 calidrid sandpipers known to birders in North America as 'peeps', often make up the largest number of waders to be seen on estuaries and sheltered coasts on migration and in winter.

The most flamboyant male breeding plumage of any wader – indeed one of the most remarkable of all bird plumages – is that of an atypical member of this subfamily: the Ruff, *Philomachus pugnax*. Winter-plumage males and females of this unusual member of the calidrine subfamily are rather nondescript, mainly barred and mottled grey or rufous birds. In spring, however, the males, which are much bigger than the females, acquire a spectacular ruff of long feathers that cloak the neck and breast and smaller ear-tufts. The colour and pattern of these adornments vary individually, bright chestnut, buff, deep purple, black or white, either unpatterned or marked with contrasting bars or spots, and they serve both as a badge of attraction for females and a mark of status when the birds gather at traditional lek sites.

ABOVE One of the small sandpipers known in North America as 'peeps,' this is a Western Sandpiper, *Calidris mauri*, in its brighter breeding plumage.

Most members of the family use various methods of obtaining food. These include picking at the surface of mud or water and chasing more active prey. They often feed by probing into mud, soil or other soft substrates. The bill is particularly sensitive, its tip packed with touch sensors called Herbst's corpuscles. Some of the long-billed waders, such as snipe, godwits and curlews, can also move the tip of the bill independently of the rest, in a process called rhynchokinesis. This enables them to tweezer buried prey while the bill is inserted into the ground. The curlews' curved bills are adapted for probing into deep burrows to remove prey such as crabs, enabling them to reach more of the space behind the entrance.

The fourth subfamily, Scolopacinae, is that of the woodcocks, snipes and dowitchers. There are eight eight very similar species of woodcocks in the single genus *Scolopax*. All are plump-bodied, with rather short legs and a very long, straight, thick-based bill. They have very broad, rounded wings and relatively slow flight, in contrast to other members of the family, although they are adept at escaping shots from hunters as they jink and weave through the trees. There are two widespread species, one, the Eurasian Woodcock, *S. rusticola,* in Europe and Asia, and the smallest of the six, the American Woodcock, *S. minor,* in the eastern half of the USA and southern Canada. Three of the remaining four species live in rainforest or hill forest on islands in Indonesia, one of these also in New Guinea, while the fourth lives on the Japanese Ryuku Islands, including Okinawa. Unusually for waders, they live in moist woodlands and forests, although they often feed in more open habitats. The plumage of woodcocks is a particularly intricate pattern of barred and mottled browns, greys, cream and black above and often barred underparts (although those of two of the island species and the American Woodcock are unmarked rich orange-buff). Their resemblance to dead leaves is so effective that even researchers studying them for years find it very rare to spot a resting

ABOVE A flock of Common Snipe, *Gallinago gallinago*, roost at daybreak on an icy pool in Kent, England in winter.

or incubating bird. Compared with other members of the family, woodcocks have especially large eyes, suited for nocturnal feeding and other activities, including courtship, which typically begins at dusk, when males of the two widespread species perform 'roding' flights, with exaggeratedly slow wingbeats to attract females waiting on the forest floor below. As he does so, the male of the Eurasian species announces his presence by making several quiet froglike croaks or grunts followed by a loud sneezing sound; although the male American Woodcock gives a buzzy courtship call on the ground, the chirping and twittering sounds he makes as he rises, circles and descends during his display flight are not vocal but mechanical, resulting from air rushing past his narrowed primary wing feathers. The eyes are set very high up on the side of the head towards the rear, giving their owner all-round vision, of great value in checking for predators as it inserts its long bill deep into leaf litter or soil.

Related to the woodcocks are the snipes and relatives (subfamily Gallinaginae). There are 22 species of snipe in three genera. There are 18 species in the main genus *Gallinago*; the other three are the two *Coenocorypha* species from islands off New Zealand and the little Jack Snipe, *Lymnocryptes minimus.* The other members of the subfamily are the three species of dowitchers, all in the genus *Limnodromus.* They look like small godwits, with their chestnut breeding plumage. Snipe and dowitchers are less plump-bodied than woodcocks, and some have a proportionately even longer bill. Snipe live mainly in marshy or boggy habitats, both inland and on the coast. Like woodcocks, they have a twisting escape flight, but unlike the latter they rapidly 'tower' up into the sky to evade predators. Snipe have striped head patterns rather than the barred crown of woodcocks, and similarly cryptic plumage. Except for the largest species, the Great Snipe, *Gallinago media*, which breeds in northern and eastern Europe and western Siberia, those for which details are known have aerial display flights during which they make a curious, penetrating bleating or humming sound called 'drumming'; this results from the air rushing past the stiffened outer tail feathers, which they hold out at right angles as they dive. The drumming of the New Zealand Snipe, *Coenocorypha aucklandica*, was the basis for the Maori myth of a giant bird, variously known as the Hakawai, Hokioi or similar names. It was said to be one of the gods of the winds, and hearing it was thought to be a bad omen, presaging war.

The final subfamily, Tringinae, consists of two distinct subgroups – the tringine sandpipers and the phalaropes. As well as the largest genus, *Tringa*, the Tringinae contains two species of *Actitis* sandpipers, the Common Sandpiper, *A. hypoleucos,* in Eurasia and the Spotted Sandpiper, *A. macularius*, its equivalent in North America; both breed mainly on fresh waters. The 12 species of shanks and other tringine sandpipers, *Tringa*, include common and widespread coastal and estuary birds such as the Common Redshank, *T. totanus*, of Eurasia, the Greater and Lesser Yellowlegs, *T. melanoleuca* and *T. flavipes*, all with the brightly coloured legs celebrated by their names.

In their non-breeding plumage, most members of the Tringinae are rather dull, mainly streaked brown or grey above and pale buff or white below, with darker streaks. Some have much brighter breeding plumage, usually with chestnut and black fringes to the feathers

ABOVE The Common Sandpiper, *Actitis hypoleucos*, breeds by freshwaters in Eurasia and migrates to winter in Africa, southern Asia and Australia.

of the upperparts, and sometimes with large areas of chestnut or orange on the head and breast and in some, such as the Red Knot, *Calidris canutus*, and the Curlew Sandpiper, *C. ferruginea*, more extensively on the underparts. Males are typically rather brighter. The Spotted Redshank, *Tringa erythropus*, has a particularly stunning breeding plumage, entirely jet-black apart from a white eye-ring, a constellation of fine white spots on the upperparts and small patches of white below, which contrast with the deep crimson bill and legs.

The three species of phalaropes are highly specialised, elegant little 18–24 cm (7–9.5 in) long waders that spend much of their lives far out in the oceans. Although other members of the family, such as the sandpipers and shanks, do swim regularly when foraging, they do not do so for prolonged periods. The phalaropes have lobed and partially webbed feet that help them to swim buoyantly. Both the Grey Phalarope (Red Phalarope in the USA), *Phalaropus fulicarius*, and the smaller Red-necked Phalarope, *P. lobatus*, breed in arctic North America and Asia (and in the case of the latter, also in northern Europe). The largest of the three, Wilson's Phalarope, *P. tricolor*, breeds by inland wetlands in North America, mainly in the prairie region, and also unlike the other two species, winters almost entirely inland too, in South America.

The phalaropes – especially the two ocean-going species – have evolved a special method of obtaining their tiny invertebrate prey; they spin around rapidly in tight circles, stirring up zooplankton from the water column, so that they can then deftly pick them off the surface with their bill. The prey is trapped within a water droplet, which then passes up the bill to the mouth by capillary action. Wilson's Phalarope by contrast, feeds mainly by pecking prey from the surface of water or mud without spinning round (although it sometimes does so), by probing into mud, scything its bill through the shallows, or upending to reach slightly deeper prey.

This family includes some prodigious migrants. The dainty-looking phalaropes journey across the globe from the Arctic and northern North America as far as Australasia and the sub-Antarctic islands. Red Knots migrating from the Arctic, where they breed nearer the North Pole than any other waders, to South Africa must make a round trip of up to 32,000 km (20,000 miles). This may involve non-stop flights, often across open sea, of up to 3,000 km (1,900 miles) or more, and they may be on the move for 7 months of each year. Wandering and Grey-tailed Tattlers, *Heteroscelus brevipes* and *H. incanus*, also travel immense distances between breeding grounds in Siberia, Alaska and northwest Canada and winter quarters that may be as far away as Australia and New Zealand. Most impressive of all, making greater non-stop migrations over water than any other land bird, are Bar-tailed Godwits breeding in eastern Siberia and western Alaska. They fly ceaselessly across the Pacific for more than 10,400 km (6,460 miles), aided by favourable winds. They must more or less double their weight before leaving so that they have enough fat reserves, as they cannot feed en route. One record-holding satellite-tracked individual flew 11,500 km (7,145 miles) from its breeding territory in Alaska to its wintering site in New Zealand without stopping to eat or drink. It took just 9 days to accomplish this prodigious feat, and was found to have lost over half its body weight.

All waders, like most wetland birds, face the problem of drainage and other habitat destruction, but a few species in this family are on the brink of extinction – notably the little Spoon-billed Sandpiper, *Calidris pygmea*, with its extraordinary spatulate bill, and the Slender-billed Curlew, *Numenius tenuirostris*. The latter species was confirmed breeding only in one small area of bog-forest transition zone north of Omsk, Siberia between 1909 and 1925, with flocks on migration in central and eastern Europe and at wintering sites in southern Europe and North Africa declining dramatically during the twentieth century; the last confirmed record is from Hungary in 2001. The Eskimo Curlew, *N. borealis*, which once nested in great numbers in the far north of North America and migrated to Argentina, is already almost certainly extinct.

ABOVE A female Red-necked Phalarope, *Phalaropus lobatus*, on a breeding loch on the island of Fetlar, Shetland.

BUTTONQUAILS Turnicidae

GENERA: 2   **SPECIES:** 16

LENGTH: 10–23 cm (4–9 in)

WEIGHT: 20–130 g (0.7–4.6 oz)

RANGE AND HABITAT: a few individuals of the Common Buttonquail, *Turnix sylvaticus*, may still occur in Spain, southern Portugal or northwest Africa; otherwise widespread in sub-Saharan Africa, southern Asia from Pakistan to Burma and in Thailand, Indochina, the Philippines and Indonesia; open grassland, including semi-desert and steppe, scrub, cultivated fields, savannah and forest clearings, among forest undergrowth and leaf litter

SOCIAL BEHAVIOUR: may be seen singly, in pairs or small family groups; territorial, with defence by the female; females may be monogamous during a single season, but in some species mate with several males in turn; the males incubate the eggs and care for the young

NEST: varies between species, from a simple hollow in vegetation, lined and sometimes roofed with grass stems to a domed structure with a side entrance (and sometimes a runway leading to it)

EGGS: 3–7, white or buff, with dark markings

INCUBATION: 12–15 days

FLEDGING PERIOD: about 14 days

FOOD: small seeds and small insects

VOICE: female gives low-pitched booming or drumming calls in the breeding season; otherwise mostly silent

MIGRATION: most species are highly sedentary; some move in response to rainfall; the northern race of the Yellow-legged Buttonquail, *Turnix tanki blanfordii*, is truly migratory, breeding in the Russian Far East, Korea, north-east China, Burma, Thailand and Indochina and wintering from northeast India to Southeast Asia

CONSERVATION STATUS: one race (*novaecaledoniae*) of the Painted Buttonquail, *T. varius*, often regarded as a separate species, is Critically Endangered (perhaps Extinct); one species, the Buff-breasted Buttonquail, *Turnix olivii*, and one race (*hottentotus*) of the Black-rumped Buttonquail, *T. nanus*, are Endangered; one species, the Sumba Buttonquail, *T. everetti*, is Vulnerable; one species, the Black-breasted Buttonquail, *T. melanogaster*, is Near Threatened

ABOVE Buttonquail are among the most secretive of all birds; this is an Asian species, the Yellow-legged Buttonquail, *Turnix tanki*.

The small, plump-bodied members of this Old World family look similar to Old World quails (p. 24): indeed, they appear so similar to quails in the genus *Coturnix* that even when captured, their true identity can be determined only by examining their feet – quails have four toes whereas buttonquails have only three, lacking the hind toe (hallux). The two families also have a similar skulking lifestyle. They are, however, unrelated – an example of convergent evolution (the true quails are not only placed in a different family, Phasianidae, but in a completely different order, the gamebird order Galliformes). Indeed, the buttonquails' relationships to other birds have long been shrouded in mystery. Although there are morphological similarities that suggest they might be related to mesites (order Mesitornithiformes), rails (Gruiformes), bustards (Otidiformes), pigeons (Columbiformes) or sandgrouse (Pteroclidiformes), more recent molecular studies suggest they should be included within the Charadriiformes, as they are in this book; they appear to occupy a basal position as one of its most ancient members, perhaps with closer relationships to the crab-plover (Family Dromadidae), coursers and pratincoles (Family Glareolidae), Skuas (Family Stercorariidae), Auks (Family Alcidae) and gulls and terns (Family Laridae), rather than to the main grouping of waders (North American: shorebirds) such as the plovers (Family Charadriidae) and sandpipers (Scolopacidae).

Buttonquails exhibit a very marked sexual role reversal: the females are more brightly plumaged and bigger in species in which the sexes differ in size. It is they who defend the territory, driving off rival females. In some species (such as the Common Buttonquail, *Turnix sylvaticus*) females may be monogamous – at least under certain conditions – perhaps related to food supply (if this is limited then it may be an advantage for the female to remain with a single mate and share the task of rearing the family). However, often females are polyandrous, mating with several males sequentially and leaving each one to rear the young. In regions where there are no marked seasons, these birds can breed at any time of year. These birds produce large numbers of offspring that reach maturity very early; young hatched early in the season can themselves be breeding at only four months. This means that populations can increase very rapidly. Such fecundity is presumably an adaptation to life in challenging habitats and high mortality rates.

Extraordinarily shy and secretive, buttonquails are very difficult to see, with their cryptic plumage and habit of 'freezing' among cover. All species have a short neck and small head, with a short strong bill, short, rounded wings and a short tail. They have strong legs and feet, and their lack of a hind toe is an adaptation for fast running, as these birds fly only as a last resort. The absence of the hind toe was celebrated in the old name of 'hemipodes' (half-foot). In addition to lacking the hind toe, they also differ from true quails in their lack of a crop. A unique feature of the females is their enlarged trachea and the inflatable bulb in their oesophagus, enabling them to produce loud booming, mooing or moaning calls to advertise their presence to potential mates or rival females. Plumage is buff or brown with cryptic black, brown and cream spots, chevrons or barring on the upperparts (and breast in two species) and areas of chestnut below, as well as a black throat in the females of two species.

CRAB PLOVER Dromadidae

GENERA: 1   **SPECIES**: 1

LENGTH: 38–41 cm (15–16 in)

WEIGHT: 230–325 g (8–11.5 oz)

RANGE AND HABITAT: breeds on coasts of the Red Sea, Persian Gulf and northwest Indian Ocean, wintering mainly on east African and west Indian coasts and Indian Ocean islands, also some farther east; only on coasts, on mud- and sandflats, sandy beaches, estuaries, lagoons and coral reefs

SOCIAL BEHAVIOUR: highly social at all times, feeding in flocks of about 20 or more birds and gathering at high tide in big roosts that may number over 1,000 birds; breeds in colonies that may include many hundreds of pairs

NEST: in unlined chamber at end of a burrow in sand on islets or among dunes

EGGS: 1 (rarely 2), white

INCUBATION: unknown

FLEDGING PERIOD: unknown

FOOD: mainly crabs, especially small burrowing species, supplemented by other marine invertebrates such as molluscs, marine worms and shrimps, and also mudskippers

VOICE: noisy, with a variety of raucous barking calls and sharp whistles and constant chattering from flocks

MIGRATION: after breeding, most migrate south to winter along coasts, mainly of east Africa, Madagascar and the Seychelles; some east to western India, Sri Lanka and the Andaman Islands; a few to South Africa and southwest Thailand

CONSERVATION STATUS: not threatened

The sole member of this family, the Crab Plover, *Dromas ardeola*, is a relatively little-known bird of uncertain relationships. It may be related to thick-knees (Burhinidae), but DNA studies suggest it may have a closer affinity with pratincoles and coursers (Glareolidae).

The Crab Plover's plumage is mainly pure white with black markings. Its pattern is reminiscent of the Pied Avocet, *Recurvirostra avosetta* (but without a black cap and hindneck), and like that bird it has a black bill and blue-grey legs. However, the bill shape is very different; rather than the delicate needle-like upcurved one of the avocet, the Crab Plover has a very thick, powerful bill, laterally compressed and with a slight but distinct angle (gonys) in the ventral surface of the bill towards its end, at the junction between the two halves of the lower mandible; this is visible when the bird is viewed in profile (a feature more marked in many gulls).

True to its common name, this unique wader's diet consists mainly of crabs, especially small fiddler crabs. As these emerge after sunset to feed and search for mates, the Crab Plover feeds mainly at dusk and by night. The bird uses its formidable daggerlike bill to stab the prey; then if it is a small crab, it will swallow it whole. It will hold a bigger crab in its bill and shake it to remove the legs and claws, and then take it apart with blows of the bill.

Unlike any other shorebird, the Crab Plover nests in a burrow, which it digs out of the sand. Up to 2 m (6.6 ft) long and sloping downward, the burrow ends in an unlined nest chamber. In large colonies, the burrows are usually close to one another, in a honeycomb-like arrangement. With no need for the camouflage against predators provided by the heavy blotching and speckling of the eggs of other waders, the Crab Plover's eggs are pure white (like those of hole-nesting birds such as woodpeckers).

ABOVE Young Crab Plovers, *Dromas ardeola*, unlike those of any other wader, are at least partly dependent on parents for food for several months.

COURSERS AND PRATINCOLES Glareolidae

GENERA: 4   **SPECIES**: 17

LENGTH: 17–29 cm (6.5–11.5 in)

WEIGHT: 37–172 g (1.3–6 oz)

RANGE AND HABITAT: southern Europe, Africa, central, eastern and southern Asia, New Guinea, Australia; most species in the tropics; coursers mainly in drier habitats, including desert, semi-desert scrub and dry grassland, some in open woodland; pratincoles are associated with water, mainly rivers (especially with sand and shingle bars or banks) and lakes in open country, occasionally along estuaries and coasts

SOCIAL BEHAVIOUR: coursers usually occur singly, in pairs or small groups; pratincoles are much more sociable, more or less gregarious at all times and often seen in very large flocks outside the breeding season; all are monogamous; coursers are mainly solitary breeders, whereas pratincoles nest in colonies, often large

NEST: a scrape in sand or gravel, unlined or sparsely lined with grass or other vegetation

EGGS: coursers usually lay 1–2 eggs, pratincoles 3–4; cream, buff, yellowish or greyish brown, with dense darker markings

INCUBATION: 17–21 days in pratincoles; 18–27 days in coursers

FLEDGING PERIOD: 21–35 days

FOOD: chiefly insects, particularly larger ones, such as grasshoppers and beetles; coursers are ground-feeders, but pratincoles catch most insects in the air

VOICE: pratincoles are noisy birds, especially on the wing, uttering sharp, high-pitched ternlike calls, shrill whistles and (in the smaller species) more musical liquid calls or trilling calls and songs; coursers are less vocal, and their calls are mainly harsh and grating, often heard by night

MIGRATION: coursers are mostly sedentary, although most northerly breeding populations of Cream-coloured Coursers, *Cursorius cursor*, move south across the Sahara for winter; some pratincoles are migratory (the longest movements are made by the Black-winged Pratincole, *Glareola nordmanni*, between Central Asia and southern Africa, and the Oriental Pratincole, *Glareola maldivarum*, between Australia and Indonesia

CONSERVATION STATUS: Jerdon's Courser, *Rhinoptilus bitorquatus*, is Critically Endangered; the Madagascar Pratincole, *Glareola ocularis*, is Vulnerable; the Black-winged Pratincole, *G. nordmanni*, is Near Threatened

ABOVE A Cream-coloured Courser, *Cursorius cursor*, walks briskly across the arid surface of the Sahara Desert in Morocco.

This small family is divided into two subfamilies. Distinctive features include the short, arched bill, found in no other waders (North American: shorebirds). Molecular studies indicate that this family, which includes the rather tern-like species known as pratincoles, may be more closely related to the terns, gulls, skuas and auks (Family Laridae) than to the various families of waders. The Egyptian Plover, *Pluvianus aegyptius*, was formerly included with the coursers in this family, but is now regarded as a unique species with no close relatives and placed in a family of its own (see p. 107).

The coursers (Cursoriinae) are superficially plover-like, with an upright stance, and are well adapted for fast running on flat terrain, with long legs and short toes. Ground-feeders, they take invertebrates from the surface or (particularly those with longer bills) by digging in sand or soil. They have largely cream, buff or yellowish brown plumage; many species have black markings on the head and breast. All are superbly camouflaged against sand or soil, and are often extremely difficult to spot unless they move. They prefer to run rather than fly to escape danger, but when they do take to the air, they reveal striking wing or tail patterns. They are divided between two genera, with five species in *Cursorius* and four in *Rhinoptilus*, the latter differing in plumage from the plainer *Cursorius* species by having the crown and upperparts handsomely spangled in black, brown and buff. The *Rhinoptilus* coursers appear to be less closely related to the other coursers and may deserve to be placed in a subfamily of their own. Eight of the 10 courser species live in Africa, and all but one of them, the Cream-coloured Courser, *C. cursor*, which also lives in the Middle East and southwest Asia, are endemic to that continent. The remaining two species are birds of southern Asia. One, the Indian Courser, *C. coromandelicus*, is widespread, occurring across much of Pakistan, India, Nepal and Sri Lanka. The other, Jerdon's Courser, *Rhinoptilus bitorquatus*, is by contrast one of the world's rarest birds, found only in a few places in the Eastern Ghats of southeast India. After 1900, when what was thought to be the last individual was seen, it was considered extinct – until 1986, after a year-long survey by the Bombay Natural History Society, it was rediscovered.

The pratincoles (Glareolinae) are more streamlined than the coursers and stand and walk with the body held more or less horizontally and low to the ground, owing to the short legs. With their long pointed wings and deeply forked tail they look rather like a cross between a plover and a tern or swallow (an old name for pratincoles was 'swallow-plover'). The bill has a much wider gape than that of the coursers, an adaptation for catching flying insects. Unlike coursers – and all other waders – pratincoles obtain most of their food on the wing, although they do chase insects across the ground at times.

ABOVE This pair of Collared Pratincoles, *Glareola pratincola*, are at their nest site on the ground, in Oman.

There are just two genera of pratincoles – *Stiltia*, containing only the Australian Pratincole *S. isabella*, which has much longer legs than the others – and *Glareola*, with seven species: the Collared Pratincole, *G. pratincola*, in southern Europe, western Asia and parts of Africa; two exclusively African species; one endemic to Madagascar; and three in Asia. The Black-winged Pratincole, *G. nordmanni*, which breeds in small numbers in southeast Europe as well as its main range in Central Asia, is unusual in that it nests mainly on saline and alkaline steppes and grassland, and not always near water.

The plumage of pratincoles is darker than that of the coursers, typically brown or grey above and white from belly to rump; three species have a striking throat pattern of ochre yellow bordered with black; four are plainer, mainly brown, dark grey or pale grey; and the Grey Pratincole, *G. cinerea*, of West Africa is pale grey above and white below with a black, white and apricot pattern on the head reminiscent of some of the coursers. All have a bright red base to the blackish bill.

AUKS Alcidae

GENERA: 11   **SPECIES:** 25

LENGTH: 12–43 cm (4.75–17 in)

WEIGHT: 140 g–1.1 kg (5 oz–2.4 lb)

RANGE AND HABITAT: right across the oceans of the northern hemisphere, with 87% of species in the north Pacific; breeding along coasts and on offshore islands; mostly in inshore waters at other times

SOCIAL BEHAVIOUR: all species are gregarious, almost all breeding in colonies, some of them vast, and feeding together; all are monogamous, often pairing for life

NEST: some species nest on bare cliff ledges or in caves or crevices on cliffs, among or beneath boulders or on scree, others in burrows they excavate themselves or take over from other animals such as rabbits or shearwaters, in holes or scrapes in sandy soil, between exposed tree roots or beneath logs, or among dense vegetation; most make no nest but puffins, the Rhinoceros Auklet, *Cerorhinca monocerata*, and the Ancient Murrelet, *Synthliboramphus antiquus*, may line nest chamber sparsely with grasses, twigs and feathers, while the Marbled Murrelet, *Brachyramphus marmoratus*, lays on moss or lichen platforms on conifer branches

EGGS: one in most species apart from *Cepphus* guillemots and *Synthliboramphus* murrelets, which usually lay two eggs; wide variation in shape and colour, from ovoid to pear-shaped and whitish with pale markings to bright green, blue, greyish, buff or white with dark scribbles

and blotches in murres or cryptic dark-spotted olive or yellowish ones in Kittlitz's Murrelet, *B. brevirostris*, and the Marbled Murrelet

INCUBATION: 27–46 days, shortest in the Little Auk, *Alle alle*, *Cepphus* guillemots and *Brachyramphus* murrelets and longest in puffins

FLEDGING PERIOD: the age of leaving the colony is very variable, from a few days to 50 days; actual fledging takes longer

FOOD: fish and marine invertebrates, including squid, adult crustaceans and various planktonic creatures

VOICE: many species are very noisy at breeding sites, with hoarse and harsh groaning and growling sounds in larger species and mewing, whistling, piping, cheeping or trilling notes in smaller species

MIGRATION: some, such as *Cepphus* guillemots and *Brachyramphus* murrelets are essentially sedentary, but most species are at last partly migratory, and some make long and complex movements

CONSERVATION STATUS: one species, the Great Auk, *Pinguinus impennis*, is Extinct; two species, the Marbled Murrelet, *Brachyramphus marmoratus*, and the Guadalupe Murrelet, *Synthliboramphus hypoleucus*, are Endangered; four species, the Atlantic Puffin, *Fratercula arctica*, Craveri's Murrelet, *S. craveri*, Scripps's Murrelet, *S. scrippsi*, the Japanese Murrelet, *S. wumizusume*, are Vulnerable; four species, including the Long-billed Murrelet, *B. perdix* and the Razorbill, *Alca torda*, are Near Threatened

This is a wholly marine family of diving seabirds, whose members normally come to land only to breed. They have the smallest geographic range of any family of seabirds, being restricted to the cooler waters of the northern hemisphere. Despite a superficial similarity, they are unrelated to penguins (Order Sphenisciformes, p. 74). Of the total of 24 extant species, just two, the Atlantic Puffin, *Fratercula arctica*, and the Razorbill, *Alca torda*, are endemic to the Atlantic; four are found in both the Atlantic and the Pacific, although one of these, the Little Auk (known in North America as the Dovekie), *Alle alle*, has huge colonies in the far north Atlantic but only a few colonies maintaining a toehold in the Pacific, in the

Bering Straits region. By contrast, 18 species live only in the North Pacific. This suggests that the origin of the family is there.

Auks can be divided into two subfamilies, the Aethinae and the Alcinae. The Aethinae comprises the three species of puffins, *Fratercula* – the Atlantic Puffin, *F. arctica*, the Horned Puffin, *F. corniculata*, and the Tufted Puffin, *F. cirrhata* – and six smaller species called auklets, divided between three genera. The genus *Cerorhinca* contains just a single distinctive species, the Rhinoceros Auklet, *C. monocerata*. This is smaller than the puffins but larger than the other auklets in the genera *Aethia*, with four species, and another genus containing a single species,

ABOVE Guillemots (Common Murres), *Uria aalge*, flying back to their nest ledges on Hornoya Island, Varangerfjord, Norway, in early spring.

ABOVE A Guillemot (Common Murre), *Uria aalge*, lands at its breeding colony on Inner Farne Island, Northumberland, in front of a pair of Razorbills, *Alca torda*.

Cassin's Auklet, *Ptychoramphus aleuticus*. The subfamily Alcinae contains six extant genera (and one other genus, *Pinguinus*, containing the extinct Great Auk). Two of them contain small species known as murrelets (pronounced 'merrlets'), with three species in the genus *Brachyramphus* and five species in the genus *Synthliboramphus*. The genus *Cepphus* contains three species called guillemots, while the genus *Alca* has only one representative, the Razorbill, *A. torda*. The Little Auk, *Alle alle*, is the sole member of its genus, and the genus *Uria* contains two species known as guillemots in Britain and as murres (pronounced 'merrs') in North America.

Auks range in size from the Least Auklet, *Aethia pusilla*, little bigger than a sparrow, to Brünnich's Guillemot (known in North America as the Thick-billed Murre), *Uria lomvia*, which is about the size of a crow. All species have a compact, stocky body and a short neck. The tail is very short and the wings are relatively small and short, suited for powering them through the water when diving for fish or other prey, though large enough to enable them to fly fast and direct with rapidly whirring beats. The legs, ending in large feet webbed between the three toes, are positioned near the rear of the body. They are used for swimming on the surface, and also as efficient rudders and brakes, but not for propulsion when underwater (in contrast to foot-propelled diving birds such as divers, grebes and cormorants, whose legs are set even farther back). They also serve as air brakes when landing. When the birds come ashore to breed, their posture and ease of movement depends on the exact position of the legs. Most awkwardly placed in this respect are the two *Uria* guillemots (murres) and the Razorbill, which stand most erect and shuffle along awkwardly on their tarsi

ABOVE A pair of Crested Auklets, *Aethia cristatella*, at their breeding site on St Paul Island, in the Pribilof archipelago, Alaska, USA.

this was also true of the Razorbill's close relative, the extinct Great Auk, *Pinguinus impennis* (see the end of this family account). By contrast, the *Cepphus* guillemots, the Little Auk and most of the small murrelets and auklets, as well as the puffins, have their feet placed somewhat farther forward and can walk on their toes like most birds, and even run when necessary. Some of them, such as the Atlantic and Tufted Puffins also use their feet for digging out their nest burrows, aided by the bill.

Bill and mouth structure is varied, depending mainly on diet. Species such as the Guillemot, *Cepphus* guillemots and *Brachyramphus* murrelets that feed mainly on fish, have rather long, narrow, pointed bills. Another fish-eater, the Razorbill, has a bill that is narrow but deep, somewhat resembling an old fashioned cut-throat razor. The fish-eaters have hard tongues that work with few toothlike denticles on the palate to grip their slippery prey. Auks that eat mainly plankton, as do the auklets and Little Auk, have a shorter, wider bill, a softer, muscular tongue and many tiny denticles. More generalist feeders, such as Brünnich's Guillemot (Thick-billed Murre), and the Rhinoceros Auklet, are intermediate between these extremes.

Plumage is in various permutations of black and white and, in some species, dark grey; several species are almost entirely dark, several have grey or brown mottling on their white underparts, some have dark-barred flanks and the *Cepphus* guillemots are mainly white in winter. The bright red, orange-red or yellow colours of some species are restricted to the bill, mouth, legs and feet, and are generally brighter in the breeding season. As well as bright red legs, the three *Cepphus* guillemots have brilliant red mouths that contrast with the black bill and plumage. Most brightly adorned of all are the three puffins, *Fratercula*, with their huge multicoloured triangular bill sheathed in distinct red and yellow plates (and a blue basal one in the Atlantic Puffin, *F. arctica*). After playing an important part in courtship, these are shed after the breeding season so that the bill becomes smaller as well as duller. Some species, such as the Tufted Puffin, *F. cirrhata*, and the Crested Auklet, *Aethia cristatella*, grow long head plumes for the breeding season.

The Least Auklet is the most abundant North American seabird, and one of the most numerous of all seabirds worldwide, with a total population estimated at about 24 million mature individuals. Most auks normally breed colonially, often in huge colonies, and although Razorbills may breed in discrete pairs, the three *Brachyramphus* murrelets are the only major exception. Kittlitz's Murrelet, *B. brevirostris*, breeds around coasts and islands in the Bering and Chukchi seas and the Gulf of Alaska, while the Marbled Murrelet, *B. marmoratus*, has a more restricted breeding range on either side of the Bering Sea and the Long-billed Murrelet, *B. perdix*, breeds around the Sea of Okhotsk and in the North Pacific from Kamchatka south to Hokkaido, northern Japan. This trio of diminutive auks is remarkable in nesting inland, up to 75 km (46 miles) from the coast, and in the case of the Marbled Murrelet, high up in a tree.

A much larger relative of the Razorbill, the flightless Great Auk once bred on islands around the north Atlantic. This remarkable bird was far larger than any of the living members of the family, standing about 75–85 cm (30–33 in) tall and weighing at least 5 kg (11 lb) and perhaps up to 8 kg (17.6 lb). It has the unfortunate distinction of being the only member of the auk family – and the only European bird – to have been wiped out by humans in historical times. Unable to fly, it was easy to catch on land at its breeding colonies, and, due entirely to hunting for its feathers, meat, fat and oil, and egg and specimen collecting, was extinct by the mid-1800s. Its Welsh name *pengwyn* ('white head'), from the white patch near the top of its head, was misappropriated by European explorers to the southern hemisphere, who encountered the birds we now know as penguins. These are, however, completely unrelated to the auks, which have evolved similarities in appearance, some of their adaptations and lifestyle by convergent evolution.

SKUAS Stercorariidae

GENERA: 1　　　**SPECIES**: 7

LENGTH: 48–64 cm (19–25 in)

WEIGHT: 230 g–2.2 kg (8 oz–4.9 lb)

RANGE AND HABITAT: in all oceans worldwide, though mostly at high latitudes; most species breed on coastal moorland or tundra, or on grassy islands; after breeding they usually range far out over oceans; jaegers sometimes fly long distances over land on migration

SOCIAL BEHAVIOUR: mainly solitary outside the breeding season, apart from gathering at good food sources; nests may be widely spaced (as in arctic tundra or close together, as on many small islands); generally monogamous and territorial

NEST: simple scrape on the ground

EGGS: usually 2, occasionally 1, olive, sparsely blotched with brown

INCUBATION: 24–27 days in jaegers, 28–32 in larger skuas

FLEDGING PERIOD: 24–32 days in jaegers, 45–55 days in larger skuas

FOOD: fish (often robbed from other seabirds), squid, crustaceans, birds and their eggs and young, lemmings, rabbits and other small mammals, or insects during the breeding season; carrion, offal and other discarded food

VOICE: generally silent at sea, but on breeding grounds they utter various mewing, yelping, quacking or screaming sounds

MIGRATION: Chilean Skuas, *Stercorarius chilensis*, and Brown Skuas, *S. antarcticus*, disperse after breeding; some Brown Skuas are more sedentary, and the other five species are long-distance migrants, all but the Great Skua, *S. skua*, crossing the equator

CONSERVATION STATUS: none threatened

ABOVE A dark-morph Arctic Skua, *Stercorarius parasiticus*, stands guard near its nest site on Handa Island, Scotland, UK.

ABOVE A Brown Skua, *Stercorarius antarcticus*, steals an egg from a colony of Gentoo Penguins, *Pygoscelis papua*, at Sea Lion Island, on the Falklands.

This small family of exclusively marine birds has traditionally been regarded as close relatives of the gulls. They are generally gull-like in appearance, with long, angled and pointed wings, a hooked bill and feet with webs between the three front toes; their plumage, wholly or partially brown or brownish, resembles that of many juvenile gulls, although they generally appear darker than these, and have a distinctive white 'flash' near the wingtips. Also, they have a more strongly hooked tip to their bill than most gulls, too, and their claws are longer and sharper. Since their ancestors split from the gulls about 10 million years ago, they have evolved a more predatory and piratical lifestyle. An unexpected result of recent sampling of molecular data has suggested that the skuas are more closely related to the auks (Family Alcidae, p. 123) than to the gulls.

Three smaller species are known in North America as jaegers, from the German word for 'hunter'. Smallest of all, the Long-tailed Skua (known in North America as the Long-tailed Jaeger), *S. longicaudus*, develops in the breeding season a very long pair of wirelike central tail feathers (12–24 cm/4.75–9.5 in), which may account for over half its total length.

The two other species are the rather larger Arctic Skua (known in North America as the Parasitic Jaeger), *S. parasiticus*, and the bigger still, stouter-chested Pomarine Skua, *Stercorarius pomarinus* (known in North America as the Pomarine Jaeger). These three have dimorphic plumage, with individuals of each species being either a dark phase (morph) bird, with entirely dark brown or grey-brown plumage, or a pale (light) morph one, with dark upperparts, a dark cap and whitish below. Arctic Skuas may have an ill-defined, smudgy dark breast band, whereas Pomarine Skuas have a more prominent barred one. The proportion of light to dark morph birds increases towards the north of these species' range. The light phase is very rare in Long-tailed Skuas.

The other four species are the large, bulky and powerful northern hemisphere Great Skua, *S. skua*, and three similar species that breed only in the southern hemisphere: the South Polar Skua

S. maccormicki, the Brown (or Southern) Skua, *S. antarcticus*, and the Chilean Skua, *S. chilensis*. Apart from the Chilean Skua, which has a dark and a light phase, they generally have all-brown plumage, with pale flecks on the upperparts. The South Polar Skua, *S. maccormicki*, lives in the most extreme conditions, breeding as it does on the Antarctic continent and peninsula; this species has been recorded nearer to the South Pole than any other wild vertebrate. Some nest inland, on bare rock, gravel or patches of lichen or moss, often near nesting colonies of penguins or petrels. Most of their loose colonies, though, are found on coasts or grassy offshore islands.

In gulls, as with most other birds, males are on average larger than females, but in skuas, as with birds of prey, the opposite is true. All species in the family are skilled at pirating food from other birds as well as killing prey ranging from insects and lemmings in the smaller species to penguins, geese and hares in the larger ones. They have faster, more agile and aerobatic flight than gulls and are very persistent at harrying other seabirds (from small terns to big gannets) to steal their food. Once a suitable victim has been spotted, the skua will chase it mercilessly, sometimes tweaking a wingtip with the bill to destabilise it, until it disgorges its catch and the skua swoops down deftly to take it in mid-air.

GULLS, TERNS AND SKIMMERS Laridae

GENERA: 24   **SPECIES**: 99

LENGTH: gulls 25–79 cm (10–31 in); terns 22–56 cm (8.5–22 in); skimmers 34–46 cm (13–18 in)

WEIGHT: gulls 88 g–2.3 kg (3 oz–5 lb); terns 39 g–0.78 kg (1.4 oz–1.7 lb); skimmers 110–375 g (3.8–13 oz)

RANGE AND HABITAT: gulls worldwide, mainly in temperate zones, especially in the northern hemisphere; terns worldwide, with most species in the tropics and subtropics; skimmers across the tropics and subtropics from North, Central and South America to Africa and Asia and just extending in places into temperate zones; gulls in many habitats, both on coasts and inland, including sandy and rocky shores, sea cliffs, sand dunes, coastal and inland marshes, moorland, islands in lakes and rivers and on roofs in cities; one species, the Grey Gull, *Leucophaeus modestus*, breeds in deserts; many feed on coasts and in inshore waters, only a few (such as kittiwakes, *Rissa*, and Sabine's Gull, *Xema sabini*) far out at sea, while inland feeding sites range from ploughed fields to rubbish dumps; terns are mainly coastal breeders that feed inshore, though some breed inland on islands in lakes or rivers or on marshes, and a few wander open oceans after breeding, or, in the case of Sooty Terns, *Onychoprion fuscatus*, sometimes also during the breeding season; skimmers mainly along large rivers, also lakes and marshes with areas of open water; the Black Skimmer, *Rynchops niger*, almost entirely coastal in North America

SOCIAL BEHAVIOUR: all are largely sociable, breeding in colonies, sometimes huge, and often feeding together (although skimmers often feed singly or in pairs); mainly monogamous, with pair bonds that may be lifelong in large gulls but are usually seasonal in others

NEST: gulls usually build a cup of seaweed or vegetation on a cliff ledge (or building), on the ground, or among aquatic plants, although Bonaparte's Gull, *Chroicocephalus philadelphia*, is unusual in nesting in coniferous trees; most terns make little or no nest, laying in a scrape on the ground that may have sparse lining, among rocks or vegetation, or

on cliff ledges, although marsh-nesting species make floating nests of vegetation, noddies build nests of seaweed and twigs in shrubs and trees, and the White Tern, *Gygis alba*, usually lays its single egg directly onto a branch, although it will sometimes lay it on the ground; skimmers lay in unlined scrapes in sand or shell beach

EGGS: usually 2–3 in gulls, olive, greenish or brownish, heavily mottled; 1–3 in terns, cream to brownish or greenish, with dark blotches; 2–6 in skimmers, pale grey, sandy, buff or olive with dark blotches

INCUBATION: 21–28 days in gulls and terns (except for some tropical terns, incubating for 30–41 days); 21–26 days in skimmers

FLEDGING PERIOD: 4–8 weeks in gulls and terns; 3–4 weeks in skimmers

FOOD: gulls eat a wide range of food, from fish, marine invertebrates and insects to birds, small mammals, food pirated from other birds, carrion, human refuse, seeds and fruits; terns feed mainly on fish, also squid and crustaceans, with marsh terns taking insects, amphibians and snails; skimmers feed almost entirely on small fish, also sometimes shrimps

VOICE: gulls utter a wide range of mainly loud, harsh yelping, mewing, whining or laughing sounds; terns give mainly shrill or hoarse calls; skimmers make barking or chattering noises

MIGRATION: many gulls are sedentary or make short seasonal movements only in response to weather, although a few species are long-distance migrants; most terns make long migrations; most populations of skimmers migrate or disperse widely after breeding

CONSERVATION STATUS: one species, the Chinese Crested Tern, *Thalasseus bernsteini*, is Critically Endangered; four species, the Black-billed Gull, *Chroicocephalus bulleri*, Black-fronted Tern, *Chlidonias albostriatus*, Black-bellied Tern, *Sterna acuticauda* and the Peruvian Tern, *Sternula lorata*, are Endangered; nine species, including the Lava Gull, *Leucophaeus fuliginosus*, the Red-legged Kittiwake, *Rissa brevirostris*, the Fairy Tern, *Sternula nereis*, and the Indian Skimmer, *Rynchops albicollis*, are Vulnerable; 10 species are Near Threatened

This major group of mainly marine, web-footed birds has often been considered to constitute three separate families. These are generally now regarded as subfamilies (Larinae, gulls; Sternidae, terns and Rynchopinae, skimmers) within an enlarged Family Laridae, which formerly included only the gulls. The three subgroups are still well defined and easily assigned to their subfamily by appearance in the field alone. However, the latest molecular data suggest that the terns known as noddies, *Anous* and *Procelsterna*, and the White Tern, *Gygis alba*, constitute two more ancient, basal groups that evolved

before the typical terns, gulls and skimmers. These are the subfamily of noddies, Anoinae (containing the two genera *Anous* and *Procelsterna*) and the Gyginae (containing the simple genus *Gygis*).

The gulls (subfamily Larinae) comprise 51 species in seven genera. Most of these were traditionally included in the genus *Larus*, with 43 species worldwide. However, evidence suggests this genus is polyphyletic and that its members should be divided among as many as 11 genera as in this book. Although popularly known as 'seagulls', many species do not normally range beyond

ABOVE Like most of the world's gulls, the Herring Gull, *Larus argentatus*, is mainly a bird of coastal waters, but it has also spread inland.

continental shelf waters, and some regularly or even mainly occur inland. Many are common and widespread. Although most eat fish and invertebrates, many have become omnivorous, and this dietary adaptability has helped them flourish. These inquisitive and resourceful birds are generally very successful at adapting to coexist alongside humans, from following the plough on farmland to snap up the invertebrates it disturbs, attending fishing vessels to feed on discarded fish and offal, to snatching food from the hands of seaside tourists or gorging themselves on the piles of waste food at garbage dumps.

Mainly crow-sized or larger, gulls have a streamlined but sturdy body and long, narrow wings for skilful gliding and soaring on air currents around cliffs where many nest or across the sea when foraging. Thanks to their broadly webbed feet, they are good swimmers and they also walk well, with a slight waddle. The tail is short and slightly rounded in almost all species; exceptions are the forked tail of the Swallow-tailed Gull, *Creagrus furcatus*, of the Galapagos Islands and Sabine's Gull, *Xema sabini*, of arctic North America and Eurasia, and the wedge-shaped tail of another Arctic specialist, Ross's Gull, *Rhodostethia rosea*. The bill is strong, stout and distinctly hooked in the larger species, in which there is a marked bulge in the lower mandible near the tip. The smaller, hooded species have a more slender, pointed bill. The feet are usually short and the legs of medium length, longer than the short legs of their relatives the terns. There is no difference in plumage between the sexes, but males are slightly larger and bigger-billed than females.

Most gulls are basically pale to dark grey or black above and white below, but some have different plumage colours and patterns. Almost all have black wingtips, usually bearing small white spots, known to birdwatchers as 'mirrors'. Two major divisions are between the bigger, white-headed species, such as the Herring Gull, *L. argentatus*, of Eurasia and North America, and the smaller, slighter 'hooded' or 'masked' species that mostly have a dark brown or black hood on the head in the breeding season: examples of the latter are a common Eurasian species, the Black-headed Gull,

Chroicocephalus ridibundus, and the Laughing Gull, *Leucophaeus atricilla* of North America, the Caribbean and Central America. Juvenile plumage of all these gulls is usually mottled brown, and then moults produce a series of two or more intermediate immature plumages. The smaller hooded gulls take only two years to gain their adult plumage but the larger white-headed gulls may not attain it until their fifth year.

The bill is mainly yellow in the white-headed gulls, and generally with a red spot at the gonydeal angle, which serves as a stimulus for the chick to peck at to persuade its parent to regurgitate food. Most of the smaller gulls have a red or black bill. The feet, too, are often brightly coloured – yellow or pink in the white-headed group and usually red in the hooded gulls – and the eye-rings and irides are also often bright red or yellow.

Although most gulls do not venture far out to sea, a few do. The two species of kittiwake, *Rissa*, are true ocean-goers, at home in the strongest gales, when they travel fast in a series of arcs. The more common kittiwake species, the Black-legged Kittiwake, *R. tridactyla*, breeds all round the north of the northern hemisphere on Atlantic and Pacific coasts, and the rarer and highly localised Red-legged Kittiwake, *R. brevirostris*, nests only on islands in the Bering Sea. Despite its large and extensive populations, the Black-legged Kittiwake has recently joined its rarer Red-legged relative in being classified as Vulnerable, due to major declines. Three other highly marine species are arctic breeders. All are small, elegant gulls with distinctive plumage and buoyant, tern-like flight. Sabine's Gull, which breeds around much of the Arctic tundra, has a slate grey head in the breeding season and a striking wing pattern with three triangles of grey, black and white. Ross's Gull is the smallest of the three, with a unique black collar encircling its white head and with its white underparts delicately suffused with pale rosy pink in summer, due to pigments from its invertebrate prey. It breeds in marshy tundra in the High Arctic of North America and Siberia. The considerably larger Ivory

ABOVE A Black-headed Gull, *Chroicocephalus ridibundus*, chases an Atlantic Puffin, *Fratercula arctica*, to steal its sandeel catch, off the Farne Islands, Northumberland.

Gull, *Pagophila eburnea*, has almost all-white plumage and is, like Sabine's Gull, an almost circumpolar breeder, although not on the tundra; it nests mainly on inaccessible cliffs and broken ice fields. It winters out on the vast expanses of pack ice, sometimes travelling north even nearer to the pole. In this inhospitable environment it feeds not only on fish and invertebrates but also on carrion, and is able to swallow large chunks of frozen food. It follows Polar Bears and human hunters to feed on scraps from their kills and also on faeces, as well as seal placentae.

Other unusual gulls are the Grey Gull, *Leucophaeus modestus*, and the Swallow-tailed Gull. The Grey Gull, grey all over apart from its whitish head and trailing edge to the wings, lives in the driest of the world's deserts. Here in the barren, waterless, montane landscape of the Atacama Desert, 35–100 km (22–62 miles) inland, it must fly to the coast every day to feed. The Swallow-tailed Gull of the Galapagos, with a dark grey hood, grey upperparts and breast, white underparts and deeply forked tail, is largely nocturnal, feeding mainly on squid that come to the surface at night.

Although no gulls migrate as far as some of the terns, populations of two of the North American black-hooded gulls, the Laughing Gull and Franklin's Gull, *Leucophaeus pipixcan*, are transequatorial migrants, as is Sabine's Gull.

Terns (subfamily Sterninae) comprise 44 species in 12 genera. The smallest species, the North American Least Tern, *Sternula antillarum*, and its Old World and Australasian counterpart, the Little Tern, *S. albifrons*, are rather smaller than even the smallest gulls, at 22–24 cm (8.5–9.5 in) and 22–28 cm (8.5–11 in) respectively; the largest, the widespread Caspian Tern, *Hydroprogne caspia*, is almost the size of a Herring Gull, at 48–56 cm (19–22 in), but not so bulky.

All terns are more slightly built than gulls, with a far more streamlined, tapering body, relatively longer, narrower, more pointed wings, shorter legs and a longer, spiky bill. Many species have a forked tail, which aids in aerial manoeuvrability. Some have particularly elegant, long outer tail feathers or streamers. This feature and their graceful buoyant flight earned them the old name of sea-swallows. Although they have webbed feet, they do not generally swim, in contrast to gulls.

Despite their more delicate appearance than gulls, terns are hardy creatures. Temperate and Arctic breeding species travel immense distances on migration, spending most of their lives in the air. They include the champion migrant of all birds, the Arctic Tern, *S. paradisaea*, with many individuals travelling from one polar region to the other and back again each year.

Another remarkable species is the Sooty Tern, *Onychoprion fuscatus*, distributed across all the world's tropical oceans. It is the most aerial of all birds – once fledglings have left the breeding colony they remain aloft continuously until they reach maturity and return to land to nest – occasionally at 4 or 5 years old, but usually 6 to 8 years later, and in some individuals, up to 10 years hence. Their plumage is poor at repelling water so they do not swim and rarely even land on the water. Instead, they seize fish or squid in flight from the surface or by dipping the head underwater, just below it, and sleep on the wing in a series of short naps. Far from land, terns hunt particularly over shoals of predatory fish, such as tuna, that drive prey to the surface.

ABOVE This graceful Arctic Tern, *Sterna paradisaea*, hovers before diving for fish on a loch on the island of Fetlar, Shetland, Scotland, in June.

Terns are more specialised in their diet than gulls, feeding mainly on small fish and often also some invertebrates. Some of the four marsh terns, *Chlidonias*, which commonly live far inland on freshwaters, are largely insectivorous. So, too, are a few other species, such as the Gull-billed Tern, *Geochelidon nilotica*.

Terns also have distinctive foraging methods. Most species catch their prey by plunge diving. This involves quartering back and forth at heights of about 3–15 m (10–50 ft) above a stretch of water in the sea, river or lake as they search for signs of prey. Once they have spotted it, they hover to fix its exact location and then plummet down to plunge below the surface to seize the fish.

Marsh terns, by contrast, usually catch insects and other invertebrates and sometimes small fish, frogs and tadpoles, by swooping down to the surface or dropping vertically, snatching the prey without their body entering the water. They often hawk in the air for dragonflies and swarming insects such as mayflies or flying ants. The Gull-billed Tern is unusual in that it regularly hunts over land rather than water.

The 13 species in the largest genera *Sterna*, along with those in several other genera, are often collectively known as 'sea terns', although some occur on freshwaters inland as well as along coasts. Their plumage is typically pale to dark grey above and white or very pale grey below, with a jet-black cap in breeding plumage that forms a spiky crest at the rear in some species, such as the Royal Tern, *Thalasseus maximus*, of the Americas and Africa, the Elegant Tern, *T. elegans*, with a restricted breeding range on the southern Pacific coast of North America, and the Sandwich Tern, *T. sandvicensis*, of Europe and the Americas. Many of the sea terns have a more or less deeply forked tail. After their post-breeding moult, the birds lose most of the all-black cap, which is restricted to the hind part of the crown. The bill is red in many species, yellow in some and orange in a few, and sometimes has a black tip. The feet are similarly coloured or black.

ABOVE This close-up reveals the extraordinary bill of a Black Skimmer, *Rynchops niger*, at a breeding colony in Florida.

The genus *Chlidonias* contains the four marsh terns. These have only a slightly forked tail. They are darker than the sea terns, especially the Black Tern, *C. niger* and White-winged Black Tern, *C. leucopterus*, having a black head and body and paler wings, dark grey in the Black Tern and very pale silvery grey in the latter species; the Whiskered Tern, *C. hybrida*, and the Black-fronted Tern, *C. albostriatus*, are all grey apart from a black cap, white cheeks and a white vent.

The oceanic species commonly known as noddies are divided between two genera. There are three species of *Anous* noddies, all with mainly dark chocolate brown plumage, rather paler on the breast and with a grey or whitish crown. There are two species of *Procelsterna* noddies: one, the Blue Noddy, *P. cerulea*, is entirely pale grey apart from blackish wingtips and tail; and the other, the Grey Noddy, *P. albivitta*, is much paler grey with a white head and body. All but one of the noddies are found mainly in tropical waters, extending in places to the subtropics, breeding on small oceanic islands. The exception is the Grey Noddy, which occurs in temperate as well as subtropical waters, as far south as those off northern New Zealand and central Chile.

The remaining species in the tern subfamily are each distinctive enough to be given a genus of their own. They include one of the most lovely of all seabirds, the ethereal and immaculate looking little White Tern, *Gygis alba*. Dazzling white and with an unusual slightly upcurved black bill, it breeds on islands in the tropical Atlantic, Indian and Pacific Oceans. It is also remarkable for laying its single egg directly onto a bare tree branch, usually in a slight hollow at a fork or on the midrib of a banana leaf or palm frond.

Another unusual species is the striking Inca Tern, *Larosterna inca*, of the Pacific coastal waters, found from northern Peru to central Chile. Its plumage is entirely dark slate grey, apart from the contrasting white trailing edge to the wings, blackish flight feathers and a white stripe on the head which extends from the base of the bill to the side of the neck, where it expands into a satiny curl.

The three species of skimmer (subfamily Rynchopinae) are by far the most specialised of the three subfamilies of Laridae, and among the most unusual of all birds in their bill anatomy and method of feeding. All are very similar in appearance, structure and habits, and are placed in a single genus, *Rynchops*. Indeed, they are so closely related that they have been considered as constituting a single species. The Black Skimmer, *R. niger*, is found in the New World, where there are three races, one (*niger*) along both Atlantic and Pacific coasts of the USA and the Caribbean and Pacific shores of Mexico, one (*cinerascens*) in northern South America, including along the coast and far up rivers, including the Amazon and Orinoco, and one (*intercedens*) in eastern South America, south of the Amazon, as far south as northern Argentina. The African Skimmer, *R. flavirostris*, is distributed on coasts and rivers of much of sub-Saharan Africa except for the south. The scarcest of the three species, with a population that may number only 6,000–10,000 mature individuals at most, is the Indian Skimmer, *R. albicollis*, which occurs patchily from East Pakistan across north and east-central India. It has suffered major declines as a result of habitat damage, pollution and destruction of breeding colonies resulting from flooding or drought, often linked to dam projects.

All species have a curious low-slung appearance when ashore, because of their slim attenuated body with long slim wings and very short legs, and their great bills make them look ungainly and front-heavy. They feed in flight by skimming low over shallow water, with the tip of the much longer lower mandible of the bill ploughing through the water just below the surface. The upper mandible is raised at an angle while the lower one, which is laterally flattened like a knife blade, is depressed. As soon as the sharp edge of the lower mandible strikes a fish, the bird jerks its head back under its body and snaps its jaws shut on the prey. Skimmers are truly programmed by evolution to skim. Even newly fledged chicks instinctively try to skim; if they are not by the water they will attempt to do so on the sand of a beach or dune.

The boldly pied plumage pattern of skimmers is very similar in all species. All have black upperparts and black upperwings with a white trailing edge, and white underparts; there is a neat black crown contrasting with the white of the forehead and rest of the head. In the Black and African Skimmers the white extends down from the head to the foreneck, with the black of the crown extending down the hindneck and joining with the black of the upperparts in breeding plumage; the Indian Skimmer is distinguished in the breeding season at least by its all-white neck (in winter the other two share this feature). The huge bill is bright red with a yellow tip in the African and Indian species, and half red, half black in the Black Skimmer. The legs, which are moderately webbed, are also red.

ORDER ACCIPITRIFORMES

This large order comprises all the diurnal birds of prey, or raptors in the large Order Accipitriformes. There is some woolliness about the definition of these terms, with some popular and historical accounts referring to owls as nocturnal raptors. Today, ornithologists do not include owls in the category of raptors, although these birds do hunt and kill similar prey (and a few species do so in daylight), as they are classified in a completely different order, Strigiformes (see p. 141). It should be said that although most birds of prey do live up their name by hunting and killing prey, the vultures subsist almost entirely on carrion and a good many other groups include carrion as part of their diet.

Currently, four families are generally recognised within the order Accipitriformes. Although all vultures share similarities of appearance and lifestyle, the New World vultures are not necessarily closely related to those of the Old World, and so they are given a family of their own, the Cathartidae. (Some authorities go further and even place them in a separate order Cathartiformes.) The Old World vultures are included in the largest and most varied by far of the four families, that of the Accipitridae, which also includes kites, harriers, eagles of various kinds, sparrowhawks and goshawks, buzzards (known in the New World as Buteo hawks) and other subgroups. Two highly distinctive species, the Secretary Bird, *Sagittarius serpentarius*, and the Osprey, *Pandion haliaetus*, which were often traditionally included within the family, are now deemed to each deserve families of their own, Sagittaridae and Pandionidae respectively.

Until recently, another large and familiar family, that of the falcons and caracaras, Falconidae, has for a long time been included within the order (indeed, the order was often generally known as Falconiformes in preference to Accipitriformes). Despite its members having many features in common with the Accipitriformes, recent genetic evidence supported a single dissenting review of morphological features from 40 years ago that showed that the two groups were not in fact related. Even more surprising, the analysis again supported that earlier review and showed that the closest relatives of the Falconidae are in fact the parrots (Order Psittaciformes, p. 188) and the seriemas (Order Cariamiformes, p. 183) and, more distantly, that they are related to the vast order of Passeriformes (the perching birds, containing the songbirds and relatives, p. 198).

As for the relationships between the Accipitriformes and other birds, recent analyses suggest that their closest relatives are the owls, mousebirds (Order Coliiformes, p. 148), trogons (Order Trogoniformes, p. 150) and the rollers, kingfishers and relatives (Order Coraciiformes, p. 173).

NEW WORLD VULTURES Cathartidae

GENERA: 5   **SPECIES:** 7

LENGTH: 56–135 cm (22–53 in)

WEIGHT: 850 g–15 kg (1.9–33 lb)

RANGE AND HABITAT: the Americas, from southern Canada to the southern tip of South America, including the Caribbean and Central America; three species in North America and six in South America; wide range, from lowlands to high mountains such as the Andes; includes seashores, agricultural land, grasslands, deserts and semi-deserts, and tropical forests; two species (the Turkey Vulture and the Black Vulture) have become adapted to life close to humans

SOCIAL BEHAVIOUR: feeding and roosting behaviour varies between species from largely solitary, as in condors, to gregarious, as in the Black Vulture; all species are solitary and monogamous when breeding; most species breed annually but condors do so at best only every 2 years

NEST: none, all species laying their egg on a bare cliff ledge, cave or other cavity, including large tree cavities in some species

EGGS: 1–2, white; in the Turkey Vulture blotched with brown and lilac at the larger end

INCUBATION: 38–60 days

FLEDGING PERIOD: 70–180 days

FOOD: carrion; some species also eat fruit, other plant matter, the eggs of birds or reptiles, or animal dung; some species, especially Black Vultures, are known to occasionally kill helpless sick, injured or young animals

VOICE: despite the lack of a syrinx, they do make hissing or rattling sounds, especially at the breeding site

MIGRATION: most species are essentially sedentary, although they may range considerable distances in search of carrion; northern populations of Turkey Vulture are long-distance migrants, from as far north as southern Canada, to winter in northern South America

CONSERVATION STATUS: one species, the California Condor, *Gymnogyps californianus*, is Critically Endangered; another species, the Andean Condor, *Vultur gryphus*, is Near Threatened

Also known as the cathartid vultures, the seven living species in this small family have a similar scavenging lifestyle to the vultures of the Old World. Old World vultures, which live in Europe, Africa and Asia, are included together with hawks, eagles and relatives in the major raptor Family Accipitridae. The members of the Old World and New World vulture groups also have a generally similar appearance, and for a long time they were considered to be closely related. However, more recently, the similarities between them are thought to have resulted from convergent evolution instead. The fossil record of the cathartid vultures includes species that lived in Europe up to about 20 million years ago, during the Miocene period, but today the family is restricted to the Americas. By far the oldest cathartid fossils are not from America, but from France, and it is possible that the family evolved in the Old World rather than the New World.

A while ago, there was a good deal of support for the view that the New World vultures may be most closely related to the storks

ABOVE The naked, wrinkled grey skin on the head and neck of this Black Vulture, *Coragyps atratus*, is only partly visible until it extends its neck.

(Family Ciconiidae, p. 88). This may seem surprising, given the great differences in such features as bill shape, leg length and absence of nest building in cathartids, but there are also various similarities. For instance, like storks, the New World vultures share various anatomical details, including the lack of a syrinx ('voice box') and a reduced or non-functioning hind toe, as well as the pattern of feather development in chicks and behavioural traits – notably the habit of defecating on their legs in hot weather to cool themselves by evaporation of the liquid droppings. Some storks (such as the formidable Marabou and Greater Adjutant storks, *Leptoptilos*) also feed mainly on carrion. Despite this, the idea of such a relationship has been overturned by the DNA evidence.

Cathartid vultures are large-bodied, with a strong chest and powerful leg muscles for holding down carcasses when they are feeding, but weak feet with blunt talons, unsuited for seizing or carrying prey. The head and upper neck are more or less bare, helping to avoid soiling when thrust deep into a carcass, as well as being used in display and maybe also for cooling in hot climates. The bill is strongly hooked, and unlike that of Old World vultures or almost all other birds – in which there is a wall (septum) between the two nostrils – it has completely perforate external nostrils so that it is possible to see right through them from one side of the bill to the other.

The genus *Cathartes* comprises three species. The Turkey Vulture, *C. aura*, is the most common of the three, and by far the most widespread, with a vast range from southern Canada to southern South America (although it is a summer visitor only to much of North America). This is the only species in Canada and the one most often encountered in the USA, where it is often known colloquially (and incorrectly in taxonomic terms) as the 'buzzard' (or 'turkey buzzard'). The two others (the Greater and Lesser Yellow-headed Vultures, *C. melambrotus* and *C. burrovianus*) are restricted to tropical and subtropical Central and South America. The Greater Yellow-headed Vulture is a bird of moist lowland forests. By contrast, the more common Lesser-headed species is a bird of open country, especially savannah. The Black Vulture, *Coragyps atratus*, is a very widespread bird, found in the southern USA, Mexico, Central America and much

of South America, to as far south as central Chile and Uruguay. With a wide range from southern Mexico to northern Argentina, the King Vulture, *Sarcoramphus papa*, is essentially restricted to undisturbed tropical and subtropical lowland forests and nearby savannahs and grasslands.

The two condor species are huge birds. With a wingspan of up to 3.1 m (10.2 ft), and a weight of up to 15 kg (33 lb), the Andean Condor, *Vultur gryphus*, is among the very largest of all flying birds, almost equalled by the biggest Old World Vulture, the Cinereous Vulture, *Aegypius monachus*, with the same maximum wingspan and a slightly smaller maximum weight of 14 kg (31 lb). Although some of the great albatrosses, *Diomedea* (see p. 79), have slightly longer wings, they are far lighter, whereas Mute Swans, *Cygnus olor*, and Great Bustards, *Otis tarda*, though rivalling them in weight, have a rather smaller wingspan. Andean Condors have a huge range down the western side of South America, although they are sparsely distributed and have declined considerably in modern times. They live mainly in remote mountainous terrain, up the highest Andean peaks, searching far and wide for carcasses of Guanacos, *Lama guanicoe*, and other medium to large mammals, including domestic livestock, mainly on alpine grassland but also on plains at lower altitudes. In Peru and Chile, they visit coasts to feast on the carcasses of seals, seabirds and stranded whales. With a wingspan almost as great as the Andean Condor, the California Condor, *Gymnogyps californianus*, once ranged from British Colombia to Baja California in northern Mexico. Its range today is far more restricted. Consisting entirely of reintroduced birds, it includes only parts of California and Arizona, as well as a much smaller reintroduction area in Baja California in Mexico. The habitat includes rocky scrubland, coniferous forest and oak savannah.

Prehistoric relatives of the condors known as teratorns were even larger than their modern-day counterparts; one species, *Argentavis magnificens*, whose fossils date from the Miocene of Argentina about

ABOVE Like the rest of the family, the Turkey Vulture, *Cathartes aura*, is superbly adapted for soaring and gliding.

ABOVE Lacking a good sense of smell, the King Vulture, *Sarcoramphus papa*, depends mainly on Turkey Vultures, *Cathartes aura*, to find carrion.

2 to 5 million years ago, soared on wings spanning up to 6.07 m 19.9 ft), making it by far one of the largest known flying birds.

Both condors have largely black plumage, relieved by white patches r bands on the wings, more pronounced in males; these are on he upperwings in Andean Condors and on the underwings in the Californian species. The Andean Condor has a prominent, contrasting white neck ruff, whereas that of the California Condor is black.

As well as preventing soiling of feathers as the bill is plunged deep into a carcass, the skin on the head of cathartid vultures also serves as a means of signalling social status and information about readiness to mate. In all but the Black Vulture, in which this skin is grey, it is brightly coloured – red and purplish in the Turkey Vulture, contrasting with the sombre dull blackish brown plumage, and bright yellow, as well as orange or bluish in the two yellow-headed species, again relieving the monotony of their black plumage. The King Vulture is one of the most strikingly ornamented of all birds of prey. Its bare skin is a riot of purple, blue, red, orange and yellow, elaborated into fleshy folds around the bill base and behind he eyes, and contrasting with its pale grey neck ruff and the bold black-and-white pattern of the rest of its plumage. The colour of he skin changes with mood; in condors, for example, from yellow to bright orange-red in the California Condor and from dull red to bright yellow in the male Andean Condor; the skin can also be inflated. In the Andean Condor, it is extended into deep folds and here is a large comblike wattle on the top of the head.

All species feed mainly on carrion. Some rarely if ever kill any animals, although Black Vultures and to a lesser extent Turkey Vultures sometimes attack small or defenceless creatures, including

nestling birds, hatchling turtles, small lizards and insects, or injured, sick and dying animals. In many areas, several species coexist together, and they have evolved specialisations for taking different parts of a carcass, as well as a dominance hierarchy, in a similar way to the guilds of Old World vultures. Where they still occur, the condors are the only species able to tear through the tough hides of large mammals such as deer or cattle, and while they are doing so and taking their fill of the meat inside, they dominate the smaller vultures. In tropical forests, the King Vulture is the dominant species, as it is able to break through the skins of smaller mammals such as sloths or monkeys. After them, it is the turn of the Black Vultures, which specialise in feeding on muscles and body organs thanks to their very wide gape, which enables them to gulp down large quantities of meat rapidly. Black Vultures are especially aggressive, jostling one another or even King Vultures for access to meat. Finally, it is left to the Turkey Vultures or the two yellow-headed vultures to clean up the carcass, removing any scraps of meat ignored by the larger species, such as those adhering to the bones.

An interesting adaptation possessed by the Turkey and yellow-headed vultures is a highly developed sense of smell. When flying over forests they invariably are the first to find a carcass, although unless it is of a smaller animal, they have to wait for the larger species (which, flying high above, soon spot any sign of another vulture locating prey) to open the carcass.

The California Condor is the rarest of all New World vultures, and one of the rarest of all raptors. It faces a range of threats, chief of which is lead poisoning resulting from ingestion of lead shot or bullets from carcasses of game animals (the condors' powerful digestive juices break down the lead readily, and they are especially prone to poisoning due to their longevity and the great areas over which they forage, so that the lead builds up in their bodies to dangerous levels). Other threats are shooting and, in the past, collision with power lines. As a result, the total wild population declined to just 21 individuals by 1983. In 1987, the species was deemed extinct in the wild after all 22 individuals were taken into captivity in the USA, to join a breeding stock of 26 others at San Diego Wild Animal Park and the Los Angeles Zoo. One of the most

LEFT This California Condor, *Gymnogyps californianus*, photographed in the wild in Arizona, is one of the rarest of all the world's raptors.

intensive of all bird conservation initiatives, this has also been one of the most expensive conservation projects for any animal species undertaken in the USA. The captive breeding, rearing of chicks and carefully controlled release has generally proved successful, although the birds still suffer from human impacts. 2015 was a milestone year, in which more young condors successfully fledged than the number of individuals that died in the wild. By the end of 2016, there was a total of 446 birds – 276 of them in the wild and 170 in captivity. Also, although condors may live to a considerable age (potentially up to 50 years), they have a very low reproductive rate, taking 2 years to produce at most only a single chick, which then requires extensive parental care and will not breed until 6–8 years old.

SECRETARY-BIRD Sagittariidae

GENERA: 1   **SPECIES:** 1

LENGTH: 1.25–1.5 m (4–4.9 ft)

WEIGHT: 2.3–4.3 kg (5–9.5 lb)

RANGE AND HABITAT: Africa, in a broad belt from Senegal to Somalia and south in east and southern Africa; savannah grassland with scattered trees for nesting and roosting; also in cereal-growing farmland and subdesert

SOCIAL BEHAVIOUR: sometimes solitary, but usually in pairs or family groups; larger numbers may gather where prey is plentiful, especially at grass fires; breeding pairs typically occupy territory of 25–45 sq km (9.6–17.4 sq miles), and both parents incubate eggs and care for young

NEST: big platform, up to 2.5 m (8 ft) across, of sticks, with a thick lining of grass, mammal dung and wool, usually on top of a low tree

EGGS: 1–3, white, with very sparse dark markings

INCUBATION: 42–46 days

FLEDGING PERIOD: 64–106 days, usually 75–90 days

FOOD: mainly insects such as grasshoppers and beetles, also a wide range of other prey, from frogs to birds and small mammals

VOICE: usually silent, but utters drawn-out growling sounds or deep croaks during courtship displays on the ground or in the air

MIGRATION: mostly nomadic, travelling about, mainly on foot, in response to changes in grazing regimes of grassland, rainfall and fires

CONSERVATION STATUS: Vulnerable

The Secretary-bird, *Sagittarius serpentarius*, is a unique, extraordinary-looking African bird, the sole member of its genus. In the past it has been included as a subfamily within the Family Accipitridae, although it is now generally regarded as being so distinctive that it warrants placement in a family (Sagittariidae) of its own, as in this book (although not so distinct as to merit erecting a separate order, Sagittariiformes, for it, as some researchers have proposed).

Standing up to 1.5 m (almost 5 ft) tall, this is an imposing bird with a long mobile crest, very long central feathers in its tail and extremely long legs (uniquely among living raptors), and looks rather like an emaciated, long-tailed eagle on stilts. Another analogy is that it resembles a cross between a raptor and a crane or stork. In the past, its odd appearance even led to its being classified in the Order Gruiformes, along with the cranes. It has blue-grey upperparts contrasting with black flight feathers and, and whitish underparts, with black feathers on its abdomen and covering its upper legs like culottes; its lower legs are pink. The crest and tail feathers are tipped with black and it has a bare area of orange-red skin around each eye. Females are a little smaller with a slightly shorter crest and tail.

The generic name *Sagittarius*, dating from the late eighteenth century, is from the Latin word for 'archer', and was said to have derived from the way in which the bird marched about in different directions like a crossbowman advancing on the enemy, while the specific name *serpentarius* (Latin for snake) refers to its prey. The origin of its curious common name is debatable, but it has been long thought to be derived from the supposed resemblance of the bird's long crest to the bunches of quill pens that eighteenth and nineteenth century secretaries tucked behind their ears. The national emblem of Sudan, the Secretary-bird is also included on the national coat-of-arms of South Africa and appear on postage stamps of over 30 countries.

Largely terrestrial, the Secretary-bird strides about in grasslands, savannahs and other open habitats, with its head jerking back and forth like that of a pigeon, searching for prey on foot. As well as large insects, usually its main prey, it kills a wide range of other animals, such as mammals up to the size of hares and including rodents, mongooses and hedgehogs, chickens and wild birds, their eggs and young, lizards, small tortoises, crabs and snakes, some of which are venomous ones like cobras and puff-adders. It deals with prey either by striking it with its bill or, in the case of larger prey, including snakes, by rapid forward kicks of its long legs ending with large, short, blunt-clawed toes or by stamping on them until they are stunned or dead. The thick scales on their legs doubtless protect them from snakebites. They also use the stamping technique to flush out prey from hiding places. They are able to swallow most prey whole, thanks to the very wide gape of their small bill. During the course of a day, a Secretary-bird may cover as much as 20–30 km (12.4–18.6 miles) in its search for food.

Although they prefer walking to running, and running to flying they do take to the wing when visiting their nests, and especially during courtship displays, when pairs soar high into the air and dive at one another, as well as performing an undulating 'sky-dance' – behaviour they share with many members of the Family Accipitridae. Secretary-birds may nest in almost any month, as long as they can find enough food to provide for the family. Although they may three eggs (and even, rarely, four), pairs hardly ever raise more than two chicks, but they may breed again less than a month later.

Although they are traditionally regarded as beneficial for their destruction of snakes and rodents, Secretary-birds face increasing threats today, from loss of grassland to collision with power lines and fences, and are declining rapidly across much of their range.

OSPREY Pandionidae

GENERA: 1   **SPECIES:** 1

LENGTH: 50–66 cm (20–26 in)

WEIGHT: 1–2 kg (2.2–4.4 lb)

RANGE AND HABITAT: almost cosmopolitan in its breeding and wintering ranges; breeds almost entirely in Eurasia, North America and Australasia, and winters mainly in Central America and much of South America, sub-Saharan Africa and southern Asia; lakes, reservoirs, large rivers, estuaries, coastal lagoons and shorelines

SOCIAL BEHAVIOUR: generally breeds as solitary pairs, but sometimes males (or occasionally females) are polygamous, and in some areas pairs group into loose colonies, of up to 300 pairs

NEST: very large structure of branches and twigs, 1.2–1.5 m (4–5 ft) across, sometimes incorporating flotsam such as seaweed, driftwood and even bones, often lined with moss, grass, reeds and heather, wedged high in an isolated tree (often dead), or on a rock ledge, and on the ground on islands free of nest predators; also on artificial structures such as power line poles or pylons, large buoys, ruined buildings or platforms specially provided by conservationists; often used and added to for many years, eventually reaching a depth of up to 2 m (6.5 ft)

EGGS: 1–4, usually 2–3, white, cream, yellow-buff, or brown, usually heavily marked with chestnut, dark brown and pale grey spots and blotches

INCUBATION: 34–43 days

FLEDGING PERIOD: 44–59 days

FOOD: almost entirely live fish; very occasionally other prey; rarely eats carrion

VOICE: noisy when intruders, human or avian, approach nest and during displays between pairs, giving a range of different calls, from short harsh staccato sounds to longer yelps, screams and whistles, often rising and falling or wavering in pitch; mainly silent otherwise

MIGRATION: except for pairs breeding in the tropics and subtropics, they are migratory, often making long journeys between breeding sites and wintering areas, generally to latitudes around the equator

CONSERVATION STATUS: not threatened

ABOVE Shaking off droplets of water after its dive, an Osprey, *Pandion haliaetus*, flies off with a trout, in Speyside, Scotland.

Like the Secretary-bird, the Osprey, *Pandion haliaetus*, is such a distinctive species that although formerly included in within the Family Accipitridae (see next page), it is now separated from all the other diurnal raptors in its own family, Pandionidae. It is the most highly adapted of all the specialist fish-hunting birds of prey; indeed it rarely eats any other prey. Unlike the Secretary-bird, which is restricted to Africa, the Osprey is one of the world's most widespread birds. They breed on every continent except Antarctica, by shallow waters both inland and coastal, and on many islands too. Furthermore, the prodigious migratory journeys undertaken by most populations mean that they are seen in many areas across the world where they do not breed, briefly as passage migrants and for longer as winter visitors.

Ospreys catch fish, occasionally from a perch but usually in flight, by a spectacular plunge from heights ranging from 5–75 m (16–245 ft), but usually from 10–30 m (33–99 ft), above the water.

If there is enough of a breeze, they often hover, sometimes in stages, to pinpoint their prey. They dive headlong, but enter the water feet-first with a resounding splash, partially or completely submerging except for the open wings, to sink their talons deep into the body of the prey. They can seize and carry away large fish up to 2 kg (4.4 lb) in weight, although they generally catch much smaller ones. They usually carry the fish head-first, slung like a torpedo beneath their body, often with one foot behind the other for an extra secure grip.

Adaptations to their specialised lifestyle include dense, very oily, waterproof plumage, nasal valves that close off the nostrils to prevent water entering, long legs for reaching into the water, big, strong feet with a reversible outer toe and tiny sharp spines (spicules) on their soles that combine with the very sharp curved talons to gaff the slippery, wriggling prey.

From a distance, an Osprey in flight, with its white underparts seen from below, and its habit of gliding and soaring on long, upwardly kinked wings, can be mistaken for a large gull. The Osprey has a proportionally smaller head, longer and less pointed wings and flaps less often. When it does flap, its flight is powerful, with stiff, shallow wingbeats; seen from below, the blackish carpal (wrist) patches at the bend of each wing are prominent. Its dark brown upperparts contrast with the underparts, which are all-white apart from a variable brown-streaked breast-band. This is generally less developed in males and often absent in the North American race *carolinensis*. The white head is bisected by a blackish brown band that runs through the eyes, and the brown-streaked nape feathers are raised into a short crest.

KITES, HAWKS, EAGLES AND RELATIVES Accipitridae

GENERA: 69   **SPECIES**: 240

LENGTH: 20–150 cm (8–59 in)

WEIGHT: 75 g–12.5 kg (2.6 oz–28 lb)

RANGE AND HABITAT: worldwide, except Antarctica; very wide range, including woodlands of all types, from northern coniferous forests to tropical rainforests, grasslands, farmland, deserts, mountains and in some species, towns and cities

SOCIAL BEHAVIOUR: most species live as pairs in the breeding season but are solitary for the rest of the year; some gather together at good feeding sites, at roosts outside the breeding season, or on migration; a few such as the insect-eating and snail-eating kites in the genera *Rostrhamus*, *Gampsonyx*, *Ictinia* and *Elanoides*, and the griffon vultures, *Gyps*, are gregarious both when foraging and breeding; most are monogamous and many pair for life; the harriers, *Circus*, are polygamous, and Harris's Hawk, *Parabuteo unicinctus*, is often polyandrous; the latter may also breed cooperatively, with related nest helpers, and groups hunt together as well as share the tasks of nest building, incubation, feeding of young and defence against predators

NEST: all species build their own nests from sticks and plant stems, often lining them with fresh foliage; nest sites range from high up in trees or on cliffs to low in vegetation such as reed beds or on the ground among cover

EGGS: 1–7, white, buff or pale greenish, often with brownish or purplish markings

INCUBATION: 28–60 days

FLEDGING PERIOD: 24–148 days

FOOD: most species kill and eat live prey, including insects and other invertebrates, fish, amphibians, reptiles, birds and mammals; many also eat carrion, and vultures specialise in feeding on it; a few species have very restricted diets – examples are the Snail Kite, which subsists almost entirely on apple snails in the genus *Pomacea*, honey buzzards, *Pernis*, which feed largely on wasp and bee larvae, the Bat Hawk, which feeds on bats, the Bearded Vulture, surviving mainly on bones, and the Palm-nut Vulture, which eats the fruits of *Elaeis* and *Raphia* oil palms

VOICE: the calls, which are often high-pitched, include yelping, whistling, barking, chattering and croaking sounds; most species are generally quiet when not courting or breeding, but some forest dwellers are much noisier; vultures hiss when squabbling over a carcass

MIGRATION: varies from sedentary through dispersive or nomadic to migratory, with some species making very long migrations between North American or northern European breeding grounds and tropical and subtropical wintering quarters in Central and South America and Africa

CONSERVATION STATUS: 11 species, the Philippine Eagle, *Pithecophaga jefferyi*, White-rumped Vulture, *Gyps bengalensis*, Slender-billed Vulture, *G. tenuirostris*, Indian Vulture, *G. indicus*, White-backed Vulture, *G. africanus*, Rüppell's Vulture, *G. rueppelli*, White-headed Vulture, *Trigonoceps occipitalis*, Red-headed Vulture, *Sarcogyps calvus*, Hooded Vulture, *Necrosyrtes monachus*, Madagascar Fish-eagle, *Haliaeetus vociferoides*, and Ridgway's Hawk, *Buteo ridgwayi*, are Critically Endangered; 17 species, including the Egyptian Vulture, *Neophron percnopterus*, Cape Vulture, *Gyps coprotheres*, Reunion Harrier, *Circus maillardi*, and Crowned Solitary Eagle, *Buteogallus coronatus*, are Endangered; 23 species, including the Steller's Sea Eagle, *Haliaeetus pelagicus*, are Vulnerable; 33 species, including the Harpy Eagle, *Harpia harpyja*, Bearded Vulture, *Gypaetus barbatus* and Red Kite, *Milvus milvus*, are Near Threatened

This major family of predatory birds is by far the largest group of diurnal birds of prey, with representatives spread across every continent apart from the Antarctic continent, and in all kinds of habitat, from deserts and high mountains to tropical rainforests and sea coasts.

There is a huge range of size within the family. The smallest, such as the Pearl Kite, *Gampsonyx swainsonii*, and the Tiny Hawk, *Accipiter superciliosus*, are only the size of a large thrush, and may weigh as little as 62 g (2.2 oz) for males of the hawk and 94 g (3.3 oz) for the kite, with a wingspan of about 38–48 cm (15–19 in) and 54–55 cm (21–22 in) respectively. At the other end of the scale are the biggest vultures, such as the Himalayan Vulture, *Gyps himalayensis*, the Cinereous Vulture, *Aegypius monachus*, or the Bearded Vulture (Lammergeier), *Gypaetus barbatus*, and eagles, such as the huge Steller's Sea-eagle, *Haliaeetus pelagicus*, the Harpy Eagle, *Harpia harpyja*, and the Philippine Eagle, *Pithecophaga jefferyi*. These imposing birds weigh up to 150–200 times as much as the two smallest species – up to 9 kg (20 lb) in the eagles and up to 12 kg (26 lb) and 14 kg (31 lb) respectively in the Himalayan Griffon and Cinereous Vulture – and have wingspans up to 2 m (6.5 ft) in the eagles and about 3 m (10 ft) in the vultures.

Most species have a relatively sturdy body. Generally, in contrast to the situation in most other birds, females are distinctly larger and heavier on average than males, a phenomenon known as reversed sexual size dimorphism. This may relate to the greater demand on females during incubation and chick rearing, or to the sexes taking different prey, as in the *Accipiter* hawks. The more predatory and aggressive the species, and the more it feeds on birds, the greater the size disparity: for instance, a female Eurasian Sparrowhawk, *A. nisus*, can be twice as heavy as her mate.

Although the wings are not sharply pointed as with many of the falcons (p. 184), their shape varies considerably between the different groups. Vultures and sea eagles and fish eagles, for instance, have evolved huge, long and broad plank-like wings while booted eagles also have long, but narrower, wings; in both cases the

ABOVE A falconer's Goshawk, *Accipiter gentilis*, feeds on a Pheasant, *Phasianus colchicus*, it has just caught in Scotland.

ABOVE One of the world's 10 fish and sea eagles, the Bald Eagle, *Haliaeetus leucocephalus*, has increased greatly in numbers in North America over the last 70 years.

wingtip feathers can be widely 'fingered'. This wing-plan is suited to much soaring and gliding with few wingbeats. By contrast, the sparrowhawks and relatives (or accipiters) have much shorter, more rounded wings, which, together with the long tail, give them great agility when weaving among the trees of densely wooded habitats.

The tail, too, varies a good deal, from short and broad to long and narrow, with a square or rounded tip. Some species have a wedge-shaped tail, as in the Bearded Vulture (or Lammergeier), *Gypaetus barbatus*, or some of the sea eagles, *Haliaeetus*, whereas in some of the kites, the tail is strongly forked, helping these gracefully aerobatic birds to make precise manoeuvres and preventing stalling when foraging at slow speeds.

The bill, which is powered by strong jaw muscles, is invariably hooked – the extent differing between species – but its overall shape and size vary greatly. Extremes are the thin, delicate meat-hook-like structure of the Snail Kite, *Rostrhamus sociabilis*, and the huge, deep bill of species such as Steller's Sea-eagle, the Harpy and Philippine eagles, and some of the vultures.

Many species have a pronounced flange of bone (the supraorbital ridge) projecting out over the eye socket so that it has the effect of deepening the socket. This feature is especially well developed in the 'true' or booted eagles, such as the Golden Eagle, *Aquila chrysaetos*, and Wedge-tailed Eagle, *A. audax,* giving these birds their characteristically 'fierce' look. This may have the dual function of protecting the eyes from being injured by struggling prey, and acting like a sun visor to shield the eyes from glare in bright light. The legs and feet are generally strong, being used to seize and carry prey, and in most the claws are strongly hooked and very sharp, able to subdue struggling prey and even to pierce vital organs.

The plumage colour of most species is in various combinations of brown, chestnut, buff and grey, with paler underparts, often with barring or streaking, and many have barred underwings and barred or banded tail. A number of species, from harriers to eagles, have a white patch on the rump. Many Neotropical forest dwellers are mainly black or white. Quite a few species are polymorphic, with light and dark (melanistic) or rufous (erythristic) morphs or forms, and in some cases a confusing range of different plumage patterns, as with the honey buzzards, *Pernis*. A few species have spiky crown feathers or crests.

The food eaten by different groups and species is very diverse, including mammals as small as shrews and as big as young deer, birds of a similar size range, reptiles, amphibians and fish, as well as insects; many species include carrion in their diet if they come across it – not just the vultures that specialise in feeding on carcasses. Some other specialists eat a diet consisting mainly or almost entirely of bats, crabs, snails or fruit, for examples.

Hunting styles vary greatly, not only between species but also within a single species, depending on environmental conditions or the type of prey being hunted. Many species practise the 'sit-and-wait' technique from a perch, which may be hidden or exposed, then swooping down onto prey or chasing it. Some use a refinement of this approach, reminiscent of that used by big cats or other mammalian predators, concealing themselves on a branch over known trails, such as those used by prey travelling to a river or other watering place. Others look for prey (or carrion, as with the vultures) by soaring high above the land. Many raptors, including eagles and harriers, search more actively, quartering a particular area and then dropping down on prey to take it by surprise, or chasing it if necessary. All members of the family have very acute vision, enabling them to spot and track prey at long range. None, including the vultures, are known to have a very well-developed sense of smell (unlike some of the New World vultures).

The Accipitridae can be divided into three subfamilies, within which there are five tribes. Terms such as 'buzzard', 'hawk' and 'eagle' bear little taxonomic relevance, and are used to describe a wide range of unrelated birds. Although generally the name 'eagle' is used for large, powerful species, some hawks are bigger than the smallest eagles, and the birds known in the Old World as buzzards are called hawks in the New World. The birds known as kites are distributed between all three of the subfamilies, though in general they share features of behaviour and lifestyle.

The first subfamily, Elaninae, contains six species of small, slim kites with pointed wings divided between three genera. Four are in the very widespread genus *Elanus*: these all have a similar plumage of grey upperparts with black areas on the wings and white underparts. The Black-winged Kite, *E. caeruleus*, occurs over a huge range, including southwestern Europe, Africa, southern Asia and New Guinea. Australia has two species, the widespread Black-shouldered Kite, *E. axillaris*, and the Letter-winged Kite, *E. scriptus* of central Australia. The fourth species, the White-tailed Kite, *E. leucurus*, has a huge range in the New World, from western and southern USA to central Argentina and Chile. The Scissor-tailed Kite, *Chelictinia riocourii*, endemic to Africa, has a similar plumage pattern to the *Elanus* species, but has a long, deeply forked tail like a tern or a swallow. The Pearl Kite, *Gampsonyx swainsonii*, is a Neotropical species ranging from Nicaragua to northern Argentina. This is the smallest of all the kites and one of the smallest members of the entire Family Accipitridae, just 20–25 cm (8–10 in) long, and differs from the rest of this subfamily in its plumage, with blackish upperparts contrasting with white underparts and orange on its head and in its northern race also on the flanks. All these kites feed on insects or small vertebrates, in most cases taking them from the ground.

The second subfamily, Gypaetinae, containing 23 species in 13 genera, is subdivided into two tribes. The first, Pernini, containing 9 genera, comprise 18 species of kites, honey-buzzards and cuckoo-hawks, or bazas. The kites include the Swallow-tailed Kite, *Elanoides forficatus*, from southern USA, Central America and much of South America. This is one of the most elegant and beautiful of all diurnal raptors, with its blue-black back, wings and tail glossed with violet, purple, bronze and green iridescence and pure white head and underparts. It spends much of its time in the air, where it deftly seizes large flying insects and often eats them in flight. By contrast, another Neotropical kite, the Hook-billed Kite, *Chondrohierax uncinatus*, one of three kites to specialize in eating snails, finds much of its food in the forest understorey, leaping from branch to branch and even swinging upside down to reach its prey. The six species of honey-buzzards (four in the genus *Pernis*, one in Europe and northern Asia and three in different parts of eastern and southern Asia, and at least one of the two species in the genus Henicopernis, from New Guinea) are also highly specialised, in this case feeding mainly on the larvae, pupae and combs of wasps and bees. They excavate the insects' nests with their straight, quite blunt claws, sometimes making such a large hole to reach its food that the bird disappears from sight. The group name is however a classic misnomer, as they do not feed on honey and are not buzzards! The five species of African, Asian and Australasian bazas in the genus *Aviceda* acquired their alternative common name of cuckoo-hawks from the resemblance of the plumage pattern of some of them to cuckoos of the genus *Cuculus*. Feeding mainly on insects and reptiles, they are medium sized, relatively plump bodied and their heads are adorned with an erectile crest.

The second tribe of the Gypaetinae, the Gypaetini, is a small group of just five distinctive species in four genera found mainly in Africa and Asia. The two species of harrier hawks, *Polyboroides*, one in Africa and the other in Madagascar, are gangling, long-winged grey and black birds with a narrow head and long, double-jointed legs, which they thrust deep into tree holes and other crevices to pull out nesting birds and their young. The other members of the group, each in a genus of its own, are three atypical vultures. The Palm-nut Vulture, *Gypohierax angolensis*, of Africa is the only member of the Accipitridae that is largely vegetarian. This striking, black-and-white bird is the smallest of the Old World vultures, about the size of a Herring Gull, but with short, very broad wings. It feeds mainly on the fruits of the oil palm and raffia palm, although it also catches a wide variety of animal prey, from crabs and fish to small mammals, as well as eating carrion. At the other end of the size scale, the huge Bearded Vulture, *Gypaetus barbatus*, is another highly specialised feeder, in this case on animal bones and the marrow concealed within them, which form 70–90% of its diet. With its dense plumage, including a fully feathered head and neck, often stained a rich glowing orange-red by the iron in the water in which it bathes, this dweller of remote mountainous regions of southern Europe, Africa and Asia breaks the bones left by vultures and mammalian scavengers from large animal carcasses by flying up with them held in its talons and dropping them from a height, often repeatedly, onto flat expanses of rock (many of them, known as ossuaries, are regularly used sites), when they dislocate, or shatter

and liberate the nutritious marrow. They concentrate especially on large leg bones, and can lift bones of 4 kg (8 3/4 lb) or more. The bill has a very wide gape, enabling them to swallow surprisingly large fragments, up to 25 cm (10 in) or more in length. They can dissolve the bone because they have extremely strong stomach acid. The third vulture species is the Egyptian Vulture, *Neophron percnopterus*. This relatively small, black-and-white vulture, with bare yellow skin on its face and a slender bill, is found in southern Europe, Africa and southwest Asia. It is one of the few birds known to use a tool – in this case a stone, which the bird picks up and throws at the egg of an Ostrich, *Struthio camelus*, to break it.

The third subfamily, Accipitrinae, is by far the biggest of the subfamilies, with 211 species in 53 genera, and is subdivided into three tribes. The first tribe, Circaetini, of 14 species in five genera, includes five species in the genus *Spilornis* and a single species of *Dryotriorchis* known as serpent eagles and six species of *Circaetus* snake eagles; as their common names suggest, they feed mainly on snakes. A very distinctive member of this tribe is the boldly patterned black, grey and chestnut plumaged Bateleur, *Terathopius ecaudatus*. It has an extremely short tail, and spends most of its time in the air, gliding low over the African savannahs on its specialised bow-shaped wings with upturned tips, searching for its prey – small mammals, birds and reptiles. It is easily identified in flight by its side-to-side rocking motion, like a tightrope walker, a feature reflected in its common name – 'bateleur' is the French word for that particular acrobat. The other species in this tribe, the Critically Endangered Philippine Eagle, *Pithecophaga jefferyi*, is a huge, immensely powerful and imposing predator, with a massive deep strongly hooked bill and a bushy erectile crest. It shares features with the Central and South American Harpy Eagle, *Harpya harpyja* and Crested Eagle, *Morphnus guianensis* and the smaller Papuan Eagle, *Harpyopsis novaeguineae*, and was formerly thought to be closely related to them but it now classified within the third and largest subfamily Accipitrinae (see later). It snatches arboreal mammals from trunks or branches, in this case mainly colugos (originally misnamed 'flying lemurs') and palm civets. Despite its old name of 'Monkey-eating Eagle' it does not feed that often on monkeys.

The second tribe of the Accipitrinae is the Gypini, comprising all the Old World vultures apart from the three atypical species already described. Its 13 species are classified in six genera, and range from the small, scruffy-looking, thin-billed Hooded Vulture, *Necrosyrtes monachus*, to two huge, massive-billed species, the Lappet-faced Vulture, *Torgos tracheliotos*, and Cinereous Vulture, *Aegypius monachus*, the first two in Africa and the third in southern Europe and Asia. Old World vultures have evolved a very similar lifestyle to their New World counterparts in the Family Cathartidae, with bare skin on the head and neck to avoid soiling when thrusting their head deep inside a carcass. As with the New World vultures, too, they obey distinct pecking orders in which the smaller, weaker-billed species wait their turn while their bigger relatives open the carcass and take their fill. The main genus is *Gyps*, comprising eight large species in Europe, Africa and Asia, many of which are known as 'griffon vultures'. They include three species of the Indian subcontinent (the White-rumped Vulture, *Gyps bengalensis*, the

Slender-billed Vulture, *G. tenuirostris*, and the Long-billed Vulture, *G. indicus*) that were once among the world's commonest raptors, numbered in the millions; these birds provide a salutary warning of how quickly birdlife can suffer reversals of fortune as a result of human impact. Over a disturbingly short period of just 15 years they were reduced in numbers by a staggering 96.8–99.9% and have been put on the Critically Endangered list. The chief cause of this decline was poisoning by the drug diclofenac, used in cattle as a veterinary drug; ingestion by the birds leads to their deaths from kidney failure. The same drug has more recently been widely used in Africa and approved for use in parts of Europe, including Spain, where 90% of European vultures are found. This adds to existing threats facing all species, from deliberate poisoning and shortages of carcasses to hunting for food and traditional medicine in Africa.

The third tribe of the Accipitrinae, the Accipitrini, is by far the biggest, with 184 species in 42 genera. In a genus of its own, the Bat Hawk, *Macheirhamphus alcinus*, as its name implies, is a specialist predator. Found in Africa, Madagascar and southern Asia, it feeds mainly on bats, supplemented by birds. Aided by very large eyes, it catches at its prey at dusk and dawn and on moonlit nights, and

ABOVE The Crowned Eagle, *Stephanoaetus coronatus*, although not the biggest of Africa's raptors, is the most powerful, able to seize and kill monkeys and small antelopes.

is able to swallow them whole in flight, thanks to the very wide gape of its bill. Three very large eagles are found in tropical and subtropical rainforests: two are found Central America and South America. The biggest of all and one of the world's biggest raptors, is the huge and supremely powerful Harpy Eagle, *Harpia harpyja*. With legs that are as thick as a baby's, and fearsomely huge talons, it watches hidden in deep foliage and then flies silently between the tree trunks and branches before powering into its chosen target – a sloth sunning itself high in a *Cecropia* tree or an equally unaware monkey feeding on leaves – and ripping it from its perch. Its close relative is the smaller and lighter Crested Eagle, *Morphnus guianensis*. The other one of these formidable predators is the Papuan Eagle, *Harpyopsis novaeguineae*.

The 35 species in ten genera of 'true' eagles are often called booted eagles, because, unlike those of the most of the rest of the family, they have feathered tarsi (lower legs). The core of this group – containing the eagles best known to most people – are the 11 species in the genus *Aquila*. Most of these, such as the well-known Golden Eagle, *A. chrysaetos*, found across Eurasia and North America and the even larger Wedge-tailed Eagle, *A. audax*, of Australia, eat much carrion as well as hunting a range of live bird and mammal prey. The black-plumaged Verreaux's Eagle, *A. verreauxii*, of Africa specialises in catching small mammals called hyraxes. Another specialist is the Black Eagle, *Ictinaetus malayensis*, of southern Asian forests. This has evolved a unique hunting technique: it glides very slowly just above the treetops on its long wings, twisted at the tips, and snatches entire nests of birds, containing eggs, nestlings and even the parents. Other booted eagles include an assortment of 20 species, some of which are known as hawk eagles, divided between seven genera. *Spizaetus* contains four species, all of which occur in Central and South America, while the eight species of *Nisaetus* live in southern Asia. The genus *Hieraaetus* contains five species in Europe, Africa, Asia, New Guinea and Australia. The biggest known eagle was the extinct Haast's Eagle, *Harpagornis moorei*, of New Zealand, which may have flourished until as recently as about 1400, and fed on the flightless birds called moa, including giant species. This giant eagle is thought to have weighed up to 15 kg (33 lb), making it about 40% heavier than the biggest of today's eagles. Surprisingly, it appears that its closest living relatives are two of the smallest Hieraaetus eagles, the Little Eagle, *H. morphnoides*, of Australia and Booted Eagle, *H. pennatus*, of Eurasia. Two especially large and powerful species are found in Africa, the Martial Eagle, *Polemaetus bellicosus*, Africa's largest eagle, and the Crowned Eagle, *Stephanoaetus coronatus*, which although smaller is also capable of killing prey as large as small or young antelopes. has Another specialist feeder with black plumage is the Long-crested Eagle, *Lophaetus occipitalis*, of Africa, which preys almost entirely on Vlei Rats.

Another distinctive genus is that of the 14 species of harriers, *Circus*. Collectively they occur over a huge range. Four species are found in Europe and Asia, with one of them, the Hen Harrier, *C. cyaneus*, also breeding in North Africa, and right across North America into Central America, wintering farther south in the Caribbean and northern South America. Two are African, and two are endemic to Indian Ocean islands, one to Réunion and the other to Madagascar and the Comoros. Two are found only in Asia, and two in Australia, one also in eastern Indonesia and the other also in New Zealand and various Pacific islands. Finally, there are two South American species. All are graceful, slender-bodied open-country raptors with long wings, which they hold in a characteristic V-shape as they float over grasslands and marshes, dropping down like a stone to seize a rodent or small bird. They have a prominent, well-defined facial ruff of stiffened feathers, giving them a rather owl-like appearance; this helps to funnel the squeaking, rustling and other sounds of their usually hidden prey to their ears.

By far the biggest genus in the whole family is *Accipiter*, comprising 46 species. Together with two species of *Erythrotriorchis* and one each in the genera *Megatriorchis* and *Urotriorchis*, these are the sparrowhawks and goshawks, often referred to as 'accipiters'. (Two other African genera are also called goshawks, but they are now thought not to be very close relatives). These are mainly woodland and forest dwellers with short broad wings and a long tail; they hunt for birds and other vertebrate prey. They include well-known and common species such as the Eurasian Sparrowhawk, *A. nisus*, the Northern Goshawk, *A. gentilis*, which lives right across North America and northern Eurasia, and the North American Cooper's and Sharp-shinned Hawks, *A. cooperii* and *A. striatus*, as well as rare and little-studied species such as Gundlach's Hawk, *A. gundlachi*, of Cuba and the Imitator Sparrowhawk, *A. imitator*, of the Solomon Islands.

The next group comprises the 10 species (in two genera) of sea eagles and fish eagles. There are eight species of sea eagles, *Haliaeetus*, in Europe, Africa, Madagascar, Asia, Australia, New Guinea, the Solomon Islands and North America. These mainly very large eagles eat a good deal of carrion as well as fish and waterbirds. They include the Bald Eagle, *H. leucocephalus*, of North America, famous as the national emblem of the USA, as well as one of the largest of all birds of prey, Steller's Sea Eagle, *H. pelagicus*, particularly dramatic looking with its bold black-and-white plumage and huge, deep yellow bill. There are two species of fish eagles *Ichthyophaga*, both in Asia.

ABOVE A juvenile Red-tailed Hawk, *Buteo jamaicensis*, soars overhead in New Mexico; this is one of the commonest 'buteos'.

Other members of the tribe Accipitini include eight kites: two species of *Haliastur*, the Whistling Kite, *H. sphenurus*, of Australia, New Guinea and New Caledonia, and the Brahminy Kite, *H. indus*, one of the commonest and best known of raptors from India and the rest of southern Asia to New Guinea and Australia. Two other kites, in the genus *Milvus*, are also familiar birds: the Red Kite, *M. milvus*, occurring widely in Europe, which despite declines, has, following virtual extinction in the UK by the early twentieth century, become very well known there, thanks to successful reintroduction programmes; and the Black Kite, *M. migrans*, which may be the world's most numerous raptor with an estimated maximum population of 2,500,000 individuals. It occurs over a vast range in Europe, Africa, Asia and Australia. The four other kites are the Mississippi Kite, *Ictinia mississippiensis*, in the southern USA and the Plumbeous Kite, *I. plumbea*, from Mexico to northern Argentina, and two specialist mainly Neotropical snail-eating kites, the Snail Kite, *Rostrhamus sociabilis*, which also has a small population in the Florida Everglades, and the Slender-billed Kite, *Helicolestes hamatus*.

The Crane Hawk, *Geranospiza caerulescens*, of Mexico, Central America and South America, now generally thought to be unrelated to the two Old World species of Harrier Hawk, *Polyboroides*, and included in the Tribe Gypaetini of the subfamily Gypaetinae (see above) has independently evolved the same structure and feeding niche, using its long, double-jointed legs to plunder nesting birds and their young hidden in holes .

A mixed bag of hawks (sometimes referred to as 'sub-buteonine' hawks), include the Harris's Hawk (or Bay-winged Hawk), *Parabuteo unicinctus*, with mainly blackish-and-rufous plumage, it is often kept in captivity and seen at falconry displays. This species is unusual in hunting in small groups, and the North American race *harrisi* from southwestern USA also breeds cooperatively. One of the most strikingly plumaged raptors, the White Hawk, *Pseudastur albicollis*, has a pure white head and underparts, with one race almost entirely white. The three largest and most powerful sub-buteonine species are the Black-chested Buzzard Eagle, *Geranoaetus melanoleucus*, and the two black and grey species of solitary eagles in the genus *Buteogallus*. Another, smaller *Buteogallus* is the Rufous Crab Hawk, *B. aequinoctialis*, a highly specialised feeder whose diet consists entirely of crabs.

Finally, the 26 species of buzzard (known as hawks in North America), are all classified in the genus *Buteo* and hence often called 'buteos'. Mostly broad-winged and short-tailed, they hunt a wide variety of prey using different methods, from watching from a perch and swooping down to soaring high over the ground or hovering to spot prey below. Representatives are found in every continent except Australia and Antarctica, and they include common and widespread species such as the Common Buzzard, *Buteo buteo*, of Eurasia and in the Americas, the Red-tailed Hawk, Broad-winged Hawk and Swainson's Hawk, *B. jamaicensis*, *B. platypterus* and *B. swainsoni*. The Rough-legged Buzzard, *B. lagopus* (Rough-legged Hawk), is found around the northern hemisphere, across northern Eurasia and North America, as far north as northwest Siberia and northern Alaska and Canada.

ORDER STRIGIFORMES

This order contains just two closely related families of owls, the small group of barn owls and relatives (Family Tytonidae) and the large one of 'typical' owls (Family Strigidae). The relationship of the owl order to other birds is uncertain. They have been thought for a long time to be related to the nightjars and allies of the Order Caprimulgiformes (p. 40), another group of highly nocturnal birds, on the basis of similarities in some morphological characters. The genetic evidence, however, suggests that a close relationship with that order is not likely, and that they may be close to the diurnal raptors in the Order Accipitriformes (p. 131), though not to those in the Falconiformes, now completely separated from the other diurnal raptors (p. 184). Another possible relationship suggested by molecular data, is (surprisingly) that they may be related to an odd group of non-predatory birds endemic to Africa, the mousebirds (Order Coliiformes, p. 148), with both owls and mousebirds also being related to the Cuckoo Roller (Order Leptosomiformes, p. 149), trogons (Order Trogoniformes, p. 150), as well as woodpeckers (Order Piciformes, p. 160), rollers (Order Coraciiformes, p. 173) and hornbills (Order Bucerotiformes, p. 153).

Owls are among the most recognisable of all bird families to everyone from early childhood. The most obvious and important distinguishing features are the flattened face with big, forward-facing eyes, set in the facial disc, formed of concentric rings of feathers around each eye, framed by a narrow ring of stiff feathers. The function of the facial disc is to funnel the slightest sound from prey into the ears: it may magnify sounds up to 10 times in species where it is particularly well developed, such as the Great Grey Owl, *Strix nebulosa*, which can detect rodent prey under deep snow. (A less well-defined version is found in a few other birds, notably the diurnal raptors called harriers).

The birds in both the owl families share a number of other features: a large, rounded head on a compact, stout though lightweight body, large, forward-facing eyes and acute vision and very sensitive hearing; a strongly hooked, sharp-tipped raptorial bill, and strong legs and feet with long, extremely sharp talons. Most species have quite long but broad and rounded wings and a short tail. The plumage is dense and very soft. The upper surface of the flight feathers is downy, and the leading and trailing edges of many flight feathers are soft fringes, and in most species there are comblike serrations on the leading edges of the outer primaries. These plumage features muffle the sound so that as the owl swoops down towards it, the prey is unaware of the owl's approach until it is too late. No owl is brightly coloured; almost all are beautifully camouflaged. Most owls are active only or mainly at twilight and through the night, although a few are diurnal.

Although their hooked bill and powerful feet with prominent, razor-sharp, curved talons might make one think that owls are simply nocturnal equivalents of the diurnal raptors, owls have many different features from the raptors. These include the lack of a crop for storing food; the facial disc, in which the bill points downwards and is obscured by feathers for much of its length; large, deep, tubular eyes with markedly spherical lenses that can be moved only a little if at all in their sockets, so that the bird must turn its head to look sideways or behind it, aided by the flexible neck found in most birds (some owls can rotate their heads through 270° or more); and feet with a reversible outer toe to give a wide spread and a secure grip to engulf and subdue struggling prey.

BARN OWLS AND RELATIVES Tytonidae

GENERA: 2   **SPECIES**: 19

LENGTH: 23–57 cm (9–22.5 in)

WEIGHT: 187 g–1.26 kg (6.6 oz–2.78 lb)

RANGE AND HABITAT: all continents except Antarctica; none in the higher latitudes of northern Europe, Asia or North America, or in New Zealand; most species in the tropics; most species in tropical forests and forest edge, with some in plantations and more open habitats, especially for hunting; grass-owls in grassland, savannah and marshes; some species have adapted to cultivated land, notably the Barn Owl, *Tyto alba*, in Europe, in farmland with scattered trees or old buildings for nesting.

SOCIAL BEHAVIOUR: usually solitary or in pairs, usually monogamous and territorial (although loose colonies recorded in the Barn Owl)

NEST: the two grass-owls site their nest, a flattened pad of grass, in a grass tuft (often beneath a bush) at the end of one of the network of tunnels the birds make by forcing their way through dense grass; most other species usually nest in tree cavities, although some may use a rock crevice or cave, especially where there is a shortage of absence of tree sites and the Barn Owl often uses barns or other buildings and nest boxes; the eggs are usually laid on the bare surface of the cavity, among debris, including pellets (regurgitated prey remains)

EGGS: Barn Owl 2–4, others 2–6 white

INCUBATION: 29–42 days

FLEDGING PERIOD: 42–90 days in the relatively few species for which details are known

FOOD: mostly rodents and other small mammals; other prey taken seasonally, locally or occasionally includes birds, reptiles, frogs and insects

VOICE: most calls are harsh, many screeching or hissing; a wider range at nest including snoring, wheezing, rasping, cackling and twittering sounds

MIGRATION: most are sedentary; some are nomadic or dispersive

CONSERVATION STATUS: one species, the Congo Bay Owl, *Phodilus prigoginei*, is Endangered; four species, the Bismarck Masked Owl (or Golden Owl), *T. aurantia*, the Minahassa Masked Owl, *T. inexpectata*, the Manus Masked Owl, *T. manusi*, and the Madagascan Red Owl, *T. soumagnei*, are Vulnerable

ABOVE The Greater Sooty Owl, *Tyto tenebricosa*, of New Guinea and Australia preys mainly on mammals such as giant rats, possums and bats.

The barn owls and their relatives the bay owls and grass owls are separated from the rest of the owls (the 'typical' owls in the Family Strigidae) in a small family of their own, because they differ in various respects. Their different characteristics include a heart-shaped facial disc (more angular and incomplete in *Phodilus*); long legs, feathered throughout in *Phodilus*, and variably in the other genus, *Tyto*; middle toes of equal length, with the talon on the middle toe pectinated (serrated like a comb); and the wishbone fused to the breastbone.

The genus *Tyto* contains all but one of the 19 species. Despite the usual family name, only three have 'barn owl' as part of their common name. These include the best-known species, the Common Barn Owl, *T. alba*. The other two are the Andaman Barn owl, *T. deroepstorffi*, restricted to the Andaman Islands, and the far more widespread Australian Barn Owl (or Pearly Owl), *T. delicatula*, found from eastern Indonesia and New Guinea to Australia and on various Pacific islands. With investigations of its breeding habits and other aspects of its biology extending back over 200 years, the Barn Owl is the most extensively studied of all owl species. It is also one of the most widespread of all birds, which has evolved 24 distinct subspecies across its vast range across the world. By contrast, the Congo Bay Owl, *T. prigoginei*, has a very restricted range, in the Albertine Rift Mountains of eastern Zaire and northwest Tanzania, and was not known to ornithologists until 1951. The Greater Sooty Owl, *T. tenebricosa*, lives in eastern Australia, while the Lesser Sooty Owl, *T. multipunctata*, is found in northeast Queensland, Australia and New Guinea. Eight species of masked owl live variously in New Guinea, Australia and Indonesia. The Ashy-faced Owl, *T. glaucops*, is endemic to Hispaniola and the Tortuga Islands. Finally there are the Madagascan Red Owl, *T. soumagnei*, the African Grass Owl, *T. capensis*, which lives in sub-Saharan Africa, and the Eastern Grass Owl, *T. longimembris*, in southern Asia (from India to southeast Asia and China), and in New Guinea and Australia. Some ornithologists still lump these two geographically separated grass owl species together as a single species, the Grass Owl, *T. capensis*.

The genus *Phodilus* comprises just a single species. The Oriental Bay Owl, *P. badius*, is small and slight, and in addition to the complete leg-feathering characteristic of the genus, has a more square-shaped facial disc. In front view, its head appears more concave than convex, and uniquely in the family, has a pair of short, rounded ear-tufts projecting from the sides of the head. Although scarce or rare in most places, it has an extensive range, from the Himalayas east to southwest China and south to Java, as well as two isolated races in south-west India and Sri Lanka.

The very soft plumage of most species is golden-brown and ash-grey or blackish on the upperparts and paler golden-buff or white, but the Greater Sooty Owl lives up to its common name by being the larger and darker of the sooty owl pair, with almost entirely blackish plumage peppered with small silvery spots. The Lesser Sooty Owl is like a paler shadow of its relative. The many races of the Barn Owl vary considerably in appearance, with the underparts ghostly white in some, pale to rich buff in others; some have much darker upperparts than most. The Madagascan Red Owl has its dark-spotted plumage suffused with orange-red. Generally, females are larger and darker than males, although they become paler with age.

The barn owls are capable of hunting in total darkness, using their phenomenally acute sense of hearing and ability to pinpoint the position of prey, thanks to their asymmetrical ears.

The Barn Owl has an unusual reproductive strategy that is unlike that of most other owls (although grass owls in this family may share it) and, indeed, most diurnal raptors. It is more like that of a small passerine such as one of the tits (Family Paridae, p. 335), producing a large number of young within a short breeding season. More typical of raptor breeding habits, during years when there is a dearth of prey, the youngest chicks are often eaten by their older, larger and stronger siblings.

ABOVE A Barn Owl, *Tyto alba*, turns its head, showing the heart-shaped facial disk characteristic of its genus.

TYPICAL OWLS Strigidae

GENERA: 28   **SPECIES:** 194

LENGTH: 13–75 cm (5–29.5 in)

WEIGHT: 41 g–4.2 kg (1.5 oz–9.25 lb)

RANGE AND HABITAT: worldwide except Antarctica; about 80% of species are tropical; almost all land habitats, with almost all species in woodlands of many kinds, from tropical rainforest and cloud forest to temperate woodlands and northern coniferous forests, as well as savannah and scrub; a few inhabit treeless grasslands, moorland, deserts and tundra

SOCIAL BEHAVIOUR: generally seen singly or in pairs, although a few species, notably the *Asio* owls (at least some of the long-eared owls and the Short-eared Owl, *A. flammeus*, and the Marsh Owl, *A. capensis*) and the related Striped Owl, *Pseudoscops clamator*, roost in groups of up to 100 or so; most species are monogamous, often with long-term pair-bonds

NEST: most use natural or woodpecker-excavated tree holes, artificial nest boxes or larger natural tree hollows, rock ledges, or caves; some larger species take over the nests of crows, raptors and other birds or squirrel dreys; some nest on the ground (or, uniquely, in the Burrowing Owl, *Athene cunicularia*, beneath it); none make any nest, at most laying eggs on a raking of wood chips or other litter, or trampled vegetation in ground nesters

EGGS: 2-7, up to 9 or more in some species when food is abundant

INCUBATION: 20–37 days

FLEDGING PERIOD: 24–80 days

FOOD: mainly small mammals, especially rodents (although some of the largest species take much larger mammals), also birds, reptiles, frogs, fish and crabs (the last three mainly by fish owls), insects and earthworms (especially by small owls)

VOICE: variety of calls, including hooting, whistling, piping, trilling, barking and shrieking sounds, especially during courtship and territorial disputes

MIGRATION: most are sedentary, a few are nomadic or migratory

CONSERVATION STATUS: one species, the Laughing Owl, *Sceloglaux albifacies*, is Extinct; one species, the Pernàmbuco Pygmy Owl, *Glaucidium mooreorum*, is Critically Endangered; 14 species, including Blakiston's Eagle Owl, *Bubo blakistoni*, Seychelles Scops Owl, *Otus insularis*, Flores Scops Owl, *O. alfredi*, Forest Owlet, *Heteroglaux blewitti*, Least Boobook, *Ninox sumbaensis*, and Long-whiskered Owlet, *Xenoglaux loweryi*, are Endangered; 19 species, including the Philippine Eagle Owl, *B. philippensis*, Snowy Owl, *Bubo scandiacus*, Fearful Owl, *Nesasio solomonensis*, and Christmas Island Boobook, *Ninox natalis*, are Vulnerable; and 20 species, including the Spotted Owl, *Strix occidentalis*, Shelley's Eagle Owl, *B. shelleyi*, and Cloud-Forest Screech Owl, *Megascops marshalli*, are Near Threatened

ABOVE The ground-dwelling Burrowing Owl, *Athene cunicularia*, is one of the few owls that is regularly active by day, though it hunts mainly at night.

This is the major owl family, containing over 90% of species in the Order Strigiformes. Although they share the basic structure described above, with a rounded facial disc rather than the heart-shaped ones of the barn owl family, there is a very great size range,

from tiny species like the Elf Owl, *Micrathene whitneyi*, the Long-whiskered Owlet, *Xenoglaux loweryi*, and the Least Pygmy Owl, *Glaucidium minutissimum*, measuring only 13–15 cm (5–6 in) from beak tip to tail tip, and just 41–51 g (1.4–1.8 oz) in weight, to extremely large ones, such as the Snowy Owl, *Bubo scandiacus*, Blakiston's Eagle Owl, *B. blakistoni*, and the Eurasian Eagle Owl, *B. bubo*, at 55–76 cm (22–30 in) long, with wings that span 1.6–1.9 m (5.25–6.25 ft) and weights of 0.7–4.2 kg (1.5–9.25 lb).

Most owls have short legs and a short tail, and their wings are generally broad and rounded, fitting them for manoeuvring in flight between tree trunks and branches in woodland, though they are longer and narrower in species such as the Eurasian Scops Owl, *Otus scops*, that are long-distance migrants and species such as the Long-eared Owl, *Asio otus*, and the Short-eared Owl, *A. flammeus*, that hunt in open country (and also are nomadic).

Plumage is generally a highly cryptic mix of browns, buffs, greys and black, usually darker above and paler, often streaked or barred below. The sexes typically have very similar plumage, although there is a marked difference in a few species, notably the Snowy Owl, in which mature males are almost pure white, and females have the white marked with dark speckles and barring. Similarly, juvenile birds typically differ little from the adults, although as well as dark-marked juvenile Snowy Owls, young of the striking Neotropical species aptly named the Spectacled Owl, *Pulsatrix perspicillata*, look like negative photos of the adults, with a white head and black 'goggles' rather than the black head and white 'spectacles' of their parents.

In contrast to the barn owl family, in which only one species has short ear-tufts, over 40% of typical owls include 'eared' species. Their feathery extensions of the forecrown plumage are not external

ABOVE A Hawk Owl, *Surnia ulula*, flies off with a vole it has just caught, in a snowy woodland clearing in Finland.

ears at all (the huge ear openings are hidden in the plumage on the side of the head). Many of the scops-owl group, for instance, have short ear-tufts, while in other species, such as the eagle-owls, the tufts may be long and far more noticeable. They may enhance camouflage at daytime roosts as they break up the outline of the head, although it is possible that the owls may also use them for species recognition and behavioural signalling.

Typical owls are found worldwide, being absent only from Antarctica and some remote oceanic islands. The greatest diversity of species is in the tropics and subtropics. The vast majority of owls are birds of wooded habitats. Only 10 species live regularly in treeless terrain. The huge Snowy Owl is an Arctic specialist. Hume's Owl, *Strix butleri*, also dwells in a restricted habitat, in this case rocky gorges and canyons in semi-desert and desert, at scattered locations across the Middle East. The Elf Owl of southwestern USA and Mexico is also a desert specialist, often nesting in saguaro cacti. Two species of *Athene* live in grasslands, scrub and deserts. The Burrowing Owl, *A. cunicularia*, a New World species, is restricted to such habitats, whereas some populations of the Little Owl, *A. noctua*, of the Old World live in open woodland and farmland. Two *Asio* species, the very widespread Short-eared Owl and the Marsh Owl, endemic to Africa, are very much open-country species; the former has the more catholic requirements, occurring in grassland, marshland, moorland and tundra, with some populations in savannah or even montane woodland; the Marsh Owl prefers moist grassland and marshes.

Most typical owls are normally strictly or largely nocturnal. They spend the day resting or sleeping in a concealed spot such as on a branch against the trunk of a tree or among dense foliage, or within a hole or other cavity in a tree or cliff. Their cryptic plumage camouflages them so that they are less likely to be spotted by predators (mainly powerful diurnal raptors) or by other birds (such as songbirds) that may mob them and reveal their position. Some

owls will hunt by day or in twilight as well as at night, especially when they have young to feed, or during periods when prey is sparse or more difficult to catch, as in harsh winter weather; Snowy Owls and Hawk Owls, *Surnia ulula*, living in the north of their range have to hunt in daylight in the Arctic summer, as it does not get dark then. A few species, though, regularly hunt prey by day. These include the Short-eared and Marsh Owls, and various species of *Glaucidium*, such as the Eurasian Pygmy Owl, *G. passerinum*, the Asian Barred Owlet, *G. cuculoides*, the African Barred Owlet, *G. capense*, and the Northern Pygmy Owl, *G. gnoma*, of western North America.

ABOVE Second largest of the world's largest owls is the mainly fish-eating Blakiston's Eagle Owl, *Bubo blakistoni*, seen here in Hokkaido, Japan.

Typical owls generally use one or both of two hunting methods; by far the most common is 'perch-and-pounce', which is the preferred method of most woodland owls; the other technique is active searching in flight, and this is characteristic of open-country hunters. Other methods may be used by certain species or for some prey. Burrowing Owls and Little Owls, for instance, may run after insect prey, Little Owls, Tawny Owls, *Strix aluco*, and Eurasian Scops-owls haul worms out of their burrows with their bill, Burrowing Owls and some scops owls and hawk-owls hawk in the air for flying insects, while fish-owls and fishing owls may wade in the water to catch fish or other aquatic creatures.

An owl usually kills its prey by striking it with its widely spread toes, gripping the victim with great power and squeezing it with its razor-sharp talons; if necessary, it will finish it off with a swift bite to the back of the skull. The owl often swallows whole small prey such as mice or voles and small birds; larger species deal with larger prey by tearing pieces of flesh from the body. The owl later regurgitates the undigestible parts of the food such as bones, fur, feathers or beetle wing cases in the form of compact pellets.

Owls detect prey using their acute senses of vision and hearing. Two myths are that owls can see well in complete darkness and are near-blind in daylight. Neither is true. Their sight is good enough to see objects in very low light, such as starlight, but only slightly better than the average human's; their large pupils (those of many owls being larger than those of humans) create a brighter image and they are highly sensitive to motion (it helps an owl if its prey moves: this may help the owl hear it, but also enables it to get a visual fix on the prey in low light). Owls supplement their vision with a highly developed spatial memory to avoid striking branches when flying in woodland, much as a human car driver relies on familiarity with a regularly travelled road to drive faster at night than they would if relying on sight alone. For this reason, it is vital for woodland-hunting owls such as the Tawny Owl to maintain a feeding territory where they can build up knowledge of the obstacles over the years. The daytime vision of owls is better than that of many nocturnal mammals such as rats and cats, and similar to that of most other birds.

Hearing is particularly well developed, and owls can hear better across a wide range of frequencies than most other birds and humans. Many species have ears that are asymmetrically positioned on the head, enabling them to determine the precise source of a sound, such as the squeaking or rustling sounds of a rodent. Great Grey Owls, *Strix nebulosa*, have been found to be able to pinpoint the position of mice concealed under 45 cm (18 in) of snow.

In such largely nocturnal birds voice is a very important method of communication, and owls communicate with a rich repertoire of sounds. These can be vital for both birds and ornithologists in distinguishing very similar-looking species, such as the Eastern and Western Screech Owls, *Megascops asio* and *M. kennicottii*. Although most people would associate hooting with owls, and many species do make hooting sounds of various kinds, there are many others that do not sound like the conventional owl heard in many films to add atmosphere. The various piping and high-pitched trilling sounds of some smaller species, for instance, are often thought to emanate from insects or frogs.

In many species, mated pairs duet, especially early in the breeding season. A good example is provided by the Tawny Owl, in which the female responds with a loud 'kewick' call to the male's long, quavering hoot (two very different sounds that since their transliteration in Shakespeare's *Love's Labour's Lost* over 400 years ago have been referred to as 'tu-whit, tu-whoo'). By contrast, the male and female parts of the Eurasian Scops Owl's duet are so alike and closely synchronised that the short, deep, fluty whistling calls, repeated monotonously for up to 40 minutes on end sound as if they are made by a single bird.

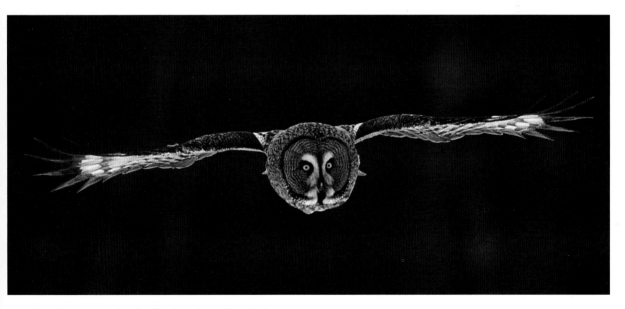

ABOVE A huge but lightweight Great Grey Owl, *Strix nebulosa*, floats silently over meadow in Finland as it hunts voles in winter.

Few other families of birds are so thoroughly non-nest-builders. Most owls lay their eggs in cavities of various kinds, from woodpecker holes for small woodland owls to larger tree hollows, caves or crevices in cliffs, old corvid or raptor nests and even on the ground. Lining is at most a sparse layer of wood chips or other debris. The Burrowing Owl uses underground burrows. Sometimes these small owls dig out their own, but usually use those excavated by mammals such as the North American ground squirrels called prairie dogs, skunks, American Badgers, gopher tortoises or armadillos. They often line the egg chamber with animal dung, and also scatter it around the entrance, probably to help maintain an equable microclimate for incubation and chick rearing and also to attract insect food, rather than to disguise the scent of the young from predators as was once suggested.

Eggs are usually laid at intervals of 1 to 3 days, and unlike the case with many other birds, hatching is staggered, resulting in broods with chicks of different sizes. Older, stronger chicks are more likely to survive when food is scarce, rather than all dying. Species such as the Short-eared Owl, Ural Owl, *Strix uralensis*, and Great Horned Owl, *Bubo virginianus*, that feed mainly on prey such as voles or hares whose populations have cycles of abundance and scarcity adjust the number of eggs they lay according to the available food supply; in good years, they may lay large clutches and may have two broods, but in lean ones lay few eggs or may not breed at all. Sometimes older chicks kill and eat younger ones. Many owls, especially the females, are extremely aggressive at or near their nests when breeding, and attack intruders as large as dogs or bears, as well as humans, who run the risk of being struck on the head and gashed; on occasion, their habit of targeting the eyes has resulted in unfortunate individuals being blinded.

Of the 28 genera in this large family, 14 are monotypic, and six contain just two, three or four species. The monotypic genera include, as well as the Snowy Owl, at the other end of the size scale, the Elf Owl of the deserts of southwestern USA and Mexico and, almost as tiny, the Long-whiskered Owlet, *Xenoglaux loweryi*, known only from three localities in elfin forests (a rare dwarf type of cloud forest) clothing the eastern Andean slopes of northern Peru, where it remained unknown to science until 1976.

There are three subfamilies. The first is the Ieraglaucinae, containing just 33 living species in two genera and one recently extinct species. The largest genus *Ninox* is thought to be the basal group of the Family Strigidae. Its 33 species, called boobooks, are distributed almost entirely across southern Asia and Australasia, with one species, the Northern Boobook, *N. japonica*, breeding in the far east of Russia, Korea, China and Japan, though migrating to winter in Southeast Asia. These birds used to be known as southern hawk-owls, from their superficially hawk-like appearance. This is due to their lack of the distinct facial disc of most other owls, their longer, more pointed wings and relatively long tail, features they shared with the Hawk-owl, *Surnia ulula*, of northern Eurasia and North America, formerly known as the Northern Hawk-owl: this is classified in the next subfamily, and by contrast is the sole member of its genus. The single other living member of the Ieraglaucinae is the Papuan Boobook, *Uroglaux albifacies*. Until the early twentieth century, another species, the Laughing Owl or Whekau, *Sceloglaux*

ABOVE Diminutive Northern Saw-whet Owls, *Aegolius acadicus*, have a distinctive territorial song of whistling notes repeated about 100 times a minute.

albifacies, survived in New Zealand. It was still relatively abundant and widespread there in the first half of the nineteenth century, but had become much scarcer by the 1840s, and the last specimen was collected in 1914. Despite unconfirmed reports until the 1960s, it is now considered extinct, possibly due to predation by introduced mammals or habitat destruction.

The second subfamily is the Surniinae, with 38 species in seven genera. The Hawk-owl has a vast range across the boreal forests of northern Eurasia and North America. It can often be seen perching in summer in broad daylight at the top of a tall conifer in full view, when it looks like a cross between a typical owl and a hawk. This impression is heightened when it takes off, with its bluntly pointed wings and long tail, and flight action of a few flaps followed by a glide. The Surniinae also contains three other very distinctive monotypic genera and three larger ones. The three species in the monotypic genera are the Elf Owl and Long-whiskered Owlet, described above, and the Forest Owlet, which was considered extinct after what was thought to be the last specimen (one of only seven ever known to science) was collected in 1884, until it was rediscovered in 1997; a very small and declining population survives at a few sites in central India. Threats to its survival include forest destruction and hunting. The largest genus in the Surniinae is *Glaucidium*, comprising 26 similar species of pygmy owls and owlets. All are small, mainly crepuscular or diurnal species that prey on insects, small reptiles and small birds. Of the 17 species known as pygmy owls, just one, the Eurasian Pygmy-owl, *G. passerinum*, occurs in the Old World (and is the only European species), with the rest in the New World. Of the latter, only one, the Northern Pygmy Owl, *G. gnoma*, is widespread in North America, with one more, the Ferruginous Pygmy Owl, *G. brasilianum*, breeding only in the USA in Arizona; all the others are birds of Mexico and/or Central and South America, apart from one, the Cuban Pygmy Owl, *G. siju*.

The nine *Glaucidium* species called owlets include five species in Asia, from the Himalayas to southern China and south to Java, and four in Africa, mainly in the tropics. The genus *Athene* comrpises three species of small owls with a flat-topped head and relatively long legs, suiting them for living mainly in open country. Two are birds of the Old World: the widespread Little Owl, *A. noctua*, found in Europe, northern Africa and Asia, and the exclusively Asian Spotted Owlet, *A. brama*. The other is the Burrowing Owl, *A. cunicularia*, with especially long legs and an upright stance, as it perches outside its nesting burrow in open grassland. It occurs over a huge range from southern Canada through the USA, Caribbean and Central America to much of South America. The final genus in this subfamily is *Aegolius*, containing four species of small woodland owls with large rounded heads, compact bodies and short tails. There are four species, all but one of them restricted to the New World. The exception is the Tengmalm's (or Boreal) Owl, *A. funereus*, which is found right across northern North America, Europe and northern Asia. Two of the the other three are known as saw-whet owls, one in North America and one in southern Mexico and parts of Central America, while the fourth is the Buff-fronted Owl, *A. harrisii* from northern South America.

The third subfamily, Striginae, is by far the largest of the three, containing 121 species in 18 genera. There are four large genera, with the remainder containing just one to four species each. The biggest genus is that of the scops owls, *Otus* of the Old World, with 40 mostly very similar species. All are small owls with (mainly short) ear-tufts. For most of them, insects form a major part of the diet, which typically also includes other invertebrates and small vertebrates. They include such well-known species as the Eurasian Scops Owl, *O. scops*. The seven species of 'eared' owls in the genus *Asio* include the well-known Long-eared Owl, *A. otus*, found across North America, Europe, North Africa and Asia, and three similar looking species – one in the Neotropics, one in East Africa, and one endemic to Madagascar. The Short-eared Owl, *A. flammea*, is one of the most widespread of all owls, while its close relative the Marsh Owl, *A. capensis*, is restricted to Africa. Three close relatives are the Jamaican Owl, *Pseudoscops grammicus*, the Flammulated Owl, *Psiloscops flammeolus*, which lives in the mountains of western North America and Mexico, and the Fearful Owl, *Nesasio solomonensis*, found only in the Solomon Islands. The 21 exclusively New World species of screech owls in the large genus *Megascops* were until recently lumped with the Old World scops owls in the genus *Otus* but genetic research has led to their being reclassified. Almost all are birds of Mexico, Central America and South America, but two families North American owls: the Eastern and Western Screech Owls, *M. asio* and *M. kennicottii*. These two were classified as the same species until 1983 – an indication of how extremely similar-looking many of these small owls are. The major genus of a group often known as the wood-owls is *Strix*, which contains 14 species of medium-sized to large owls. They include the widespread Tawny Owl, *S. aluco*, of Eurasia, in addition to the African Wood Owl, *S. woodfordi*, the Brown Wood Owl, *S. leptogrammica*, of India, China and Southeast Asia, and the very large (though lightweight) Great Grey Owl, *S. nebulosa*, found in forests right around the high latitudes of North America, Europe

and Asia. Exclusively New World species include the well-known Spotted Owl, *S. occidentalis*, and the Barred Owl, *S. varia*, of North America; the former, restricted to old-growth forests in western Canada, USA and Mexico, is threatened by logging; the latter is widespread across the continent. An unusual member of the genus is Hume's Owl, *S. butleri*, a scarce and localised resident of parts of the Middle East. Uniquely among a subgroup of owls that are particularly closely tied to wooded habitats, it lives in deserts, nesting in holes in cliffs. An odd and little-known member of the wood-owl tribe is the bizarre-looking Crested Owl, *Lophostrix cristata*, the sole member of its genus: the 'crest' of this Neotropical species is actually a continuation of the white eyebrows into very long ear-tufts. The other monotypic genus in this tribe is a West and Central African bird, the Maned Owl, *Jubula lettii*, with a mane of spiky brown-and-white feathers extending from the eyebrows to the nape. Also in the Neotropics, the three species of *Pulsatrix* have striking plumage, a combination of blackish-brown, white and golden buff; they include the widespread Spectacled Owl, *P. perspicillata*, found from southern Mexico to north-west Argentina.

The fourth of the larger genera is that of the eagle owls *Bubo*. These are very large and powerful predators, and include the biggest of all owls. In plumage and behaviour the Snowy Owl, *B. scandiacus*, is so distinctive that it was traditionally placed in a genus (*Nyctea*) of its own, although due to similarities in anatomy and genetics it is now included in *Bubo* with the eagle-owls. It is a High Arctic specialist that breeds farther north than any other owl species. Despite its great size, it feeds mainly on lemmings and other voles, although it will also supplement this staple diet with birds up to the size of ptarmigans and medium-sized geese, and mammals as big as hares. Some of the other big eagle-owls, by contrast, regularly include large prey in their very diverse diet. The Great Horned Owl, *Bubo virginianus*, found from Alaska to central Argentina, feeds mainly on mammals such as rabbits, hares, voles and mice (and the occasional farmyard cat), also taking small to medium-sized birds, reptiles, amphibians, fish and insects, but can overpower large geese, herons, other owls and diurnal raptors. The mighty Eurasian Eagle Owl, *B. bubo*, has similar tastes, and has even been known to tackle prey as large as Roe Deer fawns, Chamois and young foxes, as well as killing (and often eating) – or driving off – other predatory birds, including owls, Ravens, *Corvus corax*, and powerful diurnal raptors such as Peregrine, *Falco peregrinus*, Gyr Falcon, *F. rusticolus*, and Goshawk, *Accipiter gentilis*. Another huge species, Blakiston's Eagle Owl, *Bubo blakistoni*, was formerly regarded as a species of *Ketupa*, with the common name Blakiston's Fish Owl, a reference to its specialization for eating fish. On the other hand, the three other species of Asian fish owls, which have at times been included in *Bubo*, are better left in a genus of their own, *Ketupa*. The same applies to another trio of piscivorous owls, endemic to Africa, in the genus *Scotopelia*. They are distinguished from the Asian fish-eaters by their common name of fishing-owls. The diet of these six species, and of Blakiston's Eagle Owl, consists mainly of fish, but they do take other prey on occasion, ranging from frogs and crabs to mammals and birds (which can be as large as grouse in the case of Blakiston's Eagle Owl).

ORDER COLIIFORMES

This single-family order is one of just three bird orders endemic today to the African continent (the others being those of the ostrich (p. 6) and the turacos (p. 71)). Fossil evidence of the ancestors has come from Europe and North America. Their true relationships with other birds have long been uncertain. Some recent molecular studies combined with an analysis of morphology suggest that mousebirds are near the base of

a group of birds that includes five orders: the Cuckoo-roller (Leptosomiformes, p. 149), trogons (Trogoniformes, p. 150), rollers, kingfishers, bee-eaters and relatives (Coraciformes), hornbills (Bucerotiformes) and barbets, toucans and woodpeckers (Piciformes). Other studies have linked it with owls (Order Strigiformes), parrots (Order Psittaciformes) and perching birds (Order Passeriformes).

MOUSEBIRDS Coliidae

GENERA: 2   **SPECIES**: 6

LENGTH: 14–79 cm (5.5–31 in)

LENGTH: 29–38 cm (11.5–15 in), including a very long tail of 18–28 cm (7–11 in)

WEIGHT: 28–82 g (1–3 oz)

RANGE AND HABITAT: sub-Saharan Africa; varied wooded and shrubby habitats, from open thornbush and *Acacia* savannah to open woodland, and also gardens, but not in dense forest

SOCIAL BEHAVIOUR: extremely sociable, usually seen year-round in family groups, or larger flocks at good feeding sites; monogamous, but generally cooperative breeders, with young of both sexes acting as nest helpers

NEST: an untidy bowl of twigs a few metres up in a dense or thorny bush

EGGS: usually 2 or 3, whitish in *Colius* species, and whitish with brownish-red markings in *Urocolius*

INCUBATION: 10–13 days

FLEDGING PERIOD: 16–18 days

FOOD: a wide range of plant food, mainly fruits, but also including leaves, flowers, buds, nectar and bark

VOICE: very vocal, with a wide variety of calls, mostly of harsh chattering, clicking, buzzing or twittering notes; the two *Urocolius* species utter long, clear melodious whistles

MIGRATION: basically sedentary, but sometimes nomadic, and *Urocolius* species may make seasonal movements to avoid driest months

CONSERVATION STATUS: none threatened

ABOVE A Speckled Mousebird, *Colius striatus*, hangs acrobatically from a vine, helped by its exceptionally flexible feet.

ABOVE A Blue-naped Mousebird, *Urocolius macrourus*, peers out from foliage in Samburu National Reserve, Kenya.

The common name 'mousebirds' refers to these generally abundant African birds' superficial resemblance to mice, with their drab brown, buff or grey coloration, very long tail and habit of running or clambering under or through dense scrub and other cover, including in gardens. In Africa, they are sometimes called colies;

this and the scientific name of the major genus (*Colius*) and the family and order may be derived from the Greek word *koleos*, for 'sheath', possibly referring to these birds' long tails.

The tail, which accounts for about two-thirds of the total length, is graduated and stiff-feathered, and can look spiky.

The neck is short and the head small, with a strong, stubby, moderately decurved bill, rather like that of many finches. The head bears a prominent crest, which is often raised in a fan shape. The shortish legs have four very flexible toes; all four can turn to point forwards or one or two swing back. In addition, the toes are equipped with strong, sharp, hooked claws for a sure grip when moving around in cover and when perching. These birds usually perch, as when resting or roosting, in a most distinctive posture, hanging from a narrow branch with their feet held level with the upper breast. Mousebirds have short, rounded wings, and whirring flight; they often climb to the top of a bush before making an explosive take-off.

The plumage is soft and hairlike, and is less waterproof than that of most birds, so they can quickly become soaked in heavy rain. To compensate, mousebirds are great sunbathers, drying themselves and maintaining their body temperature with the help of blackish skin that absorbs solar radiation most efficiently. Conversely, when their food supply is scarce, they are able to become torpid.

There are four *Colius* species. The Speckled Mousebird, *C. striatus*, is the most widespread and perhaps most abundant of all the family, contrasting with two species that have restricted ranges. These are the White-headed Mousebird, *C. leucocephalus*, in central East Africa and the Red-backed Mousebird, *C. castanotus*, in western Angola and southern Democratic Republic of Congo. The fourth *Colius* species is the White-backed Mousebird, *C. colius*, of southern Africa. The two, widespread, *Urocolius* species are the Blue-naped Mousebird, *U. macrourus*, and the Red-faced Mousebird, *U. indicus*. All mousebird species look similar, but each has a distinctive patch of colour somewhere on the head or body, as reflected in their common names. The sexes look similar.

Intensely social, especially outside the breeding season, mousebirds may also nest near one another, and family rearing often involves the pair being aided by nest helpers, usually young from an earlier brood. Pairs and extended family groups roost packed tightly together. They also feed together, and when moving from one bush to the next, they usually fly in single file. Large flocks may build up where there are concentrations of fruit and other plant food; these are alleged to cause considerable damage to fruit and vegetable crops, and the birds are often shot or poisoned by farmers. Despite this, all species are generally common.

ORDER LEPTOSOMIFORMES

The sole member of the Leptosomidae, this endemic arboreal bird of Madagascar and the nearby Comoro islands, was thought to belong to the cuckoo family (Cuculidae) when it was first described scientifically in 1783, and was given the name *Cuculus discolor*. Later study of its morphology indicated that it was not a cuckoo at all, but a relative of the rollers (Coraciidae). However, it proved to have enough distinctive features from that family to warrant being given a family of its own. It now appears to be a 'living fossil' with no close living relatives, and accordingly deserves an order of its own, the Leptosomiformes.

CUCKOO-ROLLER Leptosomidae

GENERA: 1   **SPECIES:** 1

LENGTH: 38–50 cm (15–19.5 in)

WEIGHT: 192–270 g (6.8–9.5 oz)

RANGE AND HABITAT: Madagascar and the Comoro Islands; wide range, including rainforest, deciduous forest, spiny bush-forest and parkland to more open habitats with trees for nesting

SOCIAL BEHAVIOUR: usually seen in pairs, sometimes solitary or in groups of up to 10 birds; probably monogamous and territorial

NEST: within a natural tree hollow, without any material added to the nest chamber

EGGS: 4–5, whitish, slightly tinted beige-green

INCUBATION: at least 20 days

FLEDGING PERIOD: about 30 days

FOOD: often includes many chameleons, also other small reptiles and various large insects, such as grasshoppers, stick insects, beetles and caterpillars, especially noxious hairy ones

VOICE: whistling sounds, varying from loud contact or territorial calls to softer ones from birds approaching the nest

MIGRATION: probably largely sedentary

CONSERVATION STATUS: not threatened

ABOVE A male of the oddly proportioned Cuckoo-roller, *Leptosomus discolor*, waits patiently for signs of insect or lizard prey.

Sometimes known by its French name, Courol, the Cuckoo-roller, *Leptosomus discolor*, is widespread in wooded habitats of many kinds in Madagascar and the major islands of the Comoros archipelago, though patchily distributed in some areas. The repeated, bisyllabic whistling cries of this species are among the most characteristic of all bird sounds in wooded areas. Loud yet plaintive, they are usually heard from a bird in flight, gliding above the tree canopy, but sometimes also from perched individuals. Since it tends to remain perched motionless for long periods and is then hard to see among foliage, its distinctive voice is often the main clue to its presence. Generally tame, it is fortunate in not usually being harmed by people; indeed, seeing one is often regarded as a good omen.

The crow-sized Cuckoo-roller has a stout body and a proportionally massive head, contrasting rather oddly with its small and rather delicate legs. The steeply rounded forehead has upwardly curving feathers and the crown extends into a short, loose crest. The bill is sturdy and broad-based, with a slightly hooked and serrated tip, and the eyes large and set far back on the head. Unlike most other members of the Coraciiformes, which have a syndactyl arrangement of the toes (with third and fourth toe fused at the base), the Cuckoo-roller has unfused toes. The toes also seem to have a zygodactyl arrangement, like those of the ground rollers, so that they perch with two toes pointing forwards and two backwards. The wings are very broad and rounded and the tail fairly long.

In contrast to the rollers and ground rollers (Brachypteraciidae), the sexes have very different plumage. Males of all three subspecies have a pale grey breast and head, the latter with a black cap joined by stripes through and above each eye; the lower underparts are white. The upperparts and tail are deep metallic green with a purple or violet gloss when viewed from some angles. The bill is black and the legs red. Females are completely different, barred rich rufous and blackish on head and upperparts and pale buff below with dark spots, a plumage that superficially resembles that of some female cuckoos (and may thus partly account for the species' common name). The three races differ in size and details of coloration.

ORDER TROGONIFORMES

One of the main distinguishing features of these birds is that the arrangement of toes on their feet is different from that of any other birds: the first and second toes face backwards and the third and fourth forwards – an arrangement known as heterodactyl. This is a very distinctive, ancient and highly uniform group of birds that are placed in an order of their own because of uncertainty about their relationships to other birds. They appear to have some morphological similarities to the mousebirds (Order Coliiformes) though genetic analysis suggests they may be closer to hornbills (Order Bucerotiformes), woodpeckers and relatives (Order Piciformes) and rollers, kingfishers and relatives (Order Coraciiformes).

TROGONS Trogonidae

GENERA: 7   **SPECIES:** 44

LENGTH: 23–40 cm (9–16 in); Resplendent Quetzal, *Pharomachrus mocinno*, males 36–40 cm (14–16 in) plus tail streamers up to 65 cm (25.5 in) extra

WEIGHT: 34–210 g (1.2–3.9 oz)

RANGE AND HABITAT: extreme southern USA, Mexico, Central America, the Caribbean, South America, sub-Saharan Africa, India, Sri Lanka and Southeast Asia; various wooded habitats, from lowland rainforests to arid woodlands and high-altitude mountain forests; some in savannah and other sparsely wooded regions, plantations and even bamboo thickets, but most in denser tropical forests

SOCIAL BEHAVIOUR: usually solitary or in pairs, although males of some species may gather in noisy groups of up to 10 or so birds; monogamous and strongly territorial

NEST: an unlined nest chamber at the end of a tunnel dug into rotting wood (or a termite's nest, or, in the Violaceous Trogon, *Trogon violaceus*, a wasp's nest) with the bill; in some cases, the nest may be placed in a much shallower, more open hollow, so the sitting bird is visible

EGGS: 2–4, usually white or cream (but sometimes very pale grey, green or buff), pale blue in quetzals; all unmarked

INCUBATION: 16–19 days

FLEDGING PERIOD: 16–30 days

FOOD: the three African species eat only insects and other arthropods and, in some cases, small vertebrates such as lizards; the Asian trogons eat mainly animal food but also some fruit; the New World species eat variable proportions of fruits and animals, with quetzals being almost entirely fruit eaters

VOICE: songs uttered by both sexes consist of simple series of loud whistles, coos or hoots, varying between species from mellow to harsh; calls include quite soft churring sounds, and chattering, clucking or squawking notes

MIGRATION: most species are sedentary but some, including the Resplendent Quetzal, make altitudinal migrations

CONSERVATION STATUS: one species, the Javan Trogon, *Apalharpactes reinwardtii*, is Vulnerable; 9 species, including the Red-naped Trogon, *Harpactes kasumba*, the Baird's trogon, *Trogon bairdii*, the Hispaniolan Trogon, *Priotelus roseigaster* and the Resplendent Quetzal are Near Threatened

ABOVE Although not so bright as the male, this female Violaceous Trogon, *Trogon violaceus*, is nevertheless a strikingly plumaged bird.

With their brilliantly coloured plumage, trogons are generally regarded as among the most beautiful of all tropical birds. Males of many species are especially stunning, their brilliant plumage featuring a green, blue or violet head and chest that contrast with bright red, orange or yellow underparts. Females have similar colours, albeit rather duller, beneath, but a drabber, usually brown or grey, head.

In the American and African species (but not most of the Asian ones), the effect is enhanced by iridescence, producing colour changes as one views them from different angles, as with some other birds, notably hummingbirds. However, their unobtrusive behaviour means that these virtually entirely arboreal birds can easily escape detection. They are not shy like some hard-to-find birds, but rely on their ability to spend much of the day perched, motionless, in the subcanopy or at mid-levels of tall forest for long periods on branches, which helps them avoid being noticed by predators. If they sense danger, they turn so that their green, dark grey or brown upperparts face the observer, and blend into the background of branches and foliage, with the brilliant areas of red or yellow on the underparts not visible. They do, however, have penetrating and distinctive songs and calls. The flesh, nest and excrement of trogons has a distinctive odour, foul to humans at least, which may help to deter mammalian predators. This may result from these birds eating many noxious caterpillars.

Most trogons are thrush-sized, though the quetzals are bigger, about the size of a small pigeon. All species have a compact, stocky body and a short neck. Although lightness is a feature of all flying birds' skeletons, those of trogons are particularly thin, especially the

bones of the skull. Trogon skin is also unusual in being remarkably fragile, contributing to the ease with which the feathers can fall out, which is probably an adaptation to foil predators that may seize the bird only to be left with a mouthful of feathers. The legs and feet are so underdeveloped that they are of little use for movement, as exemplified by the fact that a trogon cannot turn around on a perch unless it uses its wings. Walking is generally restricted to a brief shuffle along a branch. The yoke-toed arrangement of the feet is an adaptation to perching on branches. The ratio of leg muscle to body weight is a mere 3%, the lowest recorded for any bird, which is only half that for most other birds sampled. The wings are short and broad, the tail is relatively long and quite broad, and the wing muscles are large and powerful. These enable trogons to make efficient, swift, and manoeuvrable though brief flights in their forest habitats.

Trogons feed mainly by sallying out from a perch to snatch caterpillars, beetles, moths and other large insects (as well as spiders and occasionally small vertebrates) in flight from branches and foliage. They are also skilled at catching flying insects. Unlike most fruit-eating birds, all trogons except the exclusively animal-eating African trogons use a similar in-flight method to pluck fruit from trees and shrubs, briefly hovering or stalling in front of it. The bill of all species is short and strong with a wide gape, especially in the quetzals, which include many large fruits in their diet.

ABOVE The Slaty-tailed Trogon, *Trogon massena*, is widespread from southern Mexico to Panama, and also occurs in western Colombia.

Although the family is often thought to have its origin in Africa, the greatest diversity today is in the Neotropics, followed by southern Asia. The three African trogons are all placed in a single genus, *Apaloderma*. Best known is Narina's Trogon, *A. narina*. As well as being the most widespread African species, it is unusual among the family in its more catholic choice of habitats, able to live in quite open savannah, plantations and even suburban gardens, as well as various types of forest.

Ten of the 12 species of Asian trogons are in the genus *Harpactes*. The other two are given a separate genus, *Apalharpactes*: both the Javan Trogon, *A. reinwardtii* and the Sumatran Trogon, *A. mackloti*, have a different song, and a very different plumage from that of all other Asian species, including green upperparts and a metallic sheen, on the blue tail.

The 29 species of American trogons are divided among four genera. The main genus, *Trogon*, with 21 species, includes the well-known Collared Trogon, *T. collaris*, with a wide range from central Mexico to northwestern Brazil, and the Elegant

Trogon, *T. elegans*. The genus *Priotelus* contains just two atypical Caribbean species, the Cuban Trogon, *P. temnurus*, and the Hispaniolan Trogon, *P. roseigaster*. The quetzals are divided between two genera, with one species in *Euptilotis* – the Eared Quetzal, *E. neoxenus* – and the other five in *Pharomachrus*, including the Golden-headed Quetzal, *P. auriceps*, found from extreme southeastern Panama and along the Andean slopes from Colombia south to eastern Peru and northern Bolivia and, most spectacular of all trogons, the Resplendent Quetzal, *P. mocinno*, of southern Mexico and Central America. The northern limits of the range of two species just reaches the USA. The Elegant Trogon breeds in small numbers in woodland along streams and rivers in mountain canyons of extreme southern Arizona. The other species, the Eared Quetzal, does not breed but is a rare visitor only to the same state.

Plumage colours and patterns differ between the three geographical groups. Male African trogons have iridescent green upperparts, head and breast, and a bright red belly. Apart from the Javan and Sumatran Trogons (see opposite) male Asian trogons are rich orange-brown above and pinkish red below, with a black head in many species. The New World species have upperparts and breast iridescent blue-green, golden green or violet-blue and the belly bright red, orange or yellow; quetzals are more uniform in colour, being mainly brilliant, shimmering, metallic green, with red underparts.

All trogons apart from the quetzals have densely barred or vermiculated wing panels. The undertail, too, bears distinctive patterns of broad or narrow dark barring; both wing-panel and tail patterns differ between species and also between age groups, and form an important clue to identification, presumably for the birds as well as their human watchers.

The common and scientific names of the family come from the Greek word meaning 'gnawing' and probably refer either to the piecemeal biting of fruits by those species that do not eat them whole, or to the way these birds excavate their nest holes. With their short and not especially powerful bills, they are restricted to doing this in rotting wood or termite (or wasp) nests.

The name 'quetzal' used for the six New World species in the genus *Pharomacrus* is derived from a native American (*Nahuatl*) word for 'tail feather'. It is the 'tail' sported by the male of the most spectacular of the six, the aptly named Resplendent Quetzal, that is celebrated in this context. The streamers consist of four greatly elongated, filamentous tail coverts that extend up to 65 cm (26 in) beyond the tip of the actual tail, and cover it above. Aztec and Maya peoples harvested the showy green feathers from living birds as well as dead ones, while in more recent times many individuals of this species and other trogons have been killed for their plumage, adding to the main threat of habitat destruction.

It used to be believed that when male Resplendent Quetzals took their turn at incubation (a task shared by both sexes – also in most other trogons for which details are known), they positioned themselves in the nest hole with their head pointing away from the entrance, allowing the long tail streamers to cascade out of the hole, but in fact they face the outside world, with the flexible streamers curled around and protruding next to the head and shoulders.

ABOVE An aptly named male Resplendent Quetzal, *Pharomachrus mocinno*, brings food to his nestlings in the Central Highlands of Costa Rica.

ORDER BUCEROTIFORMES

Although the ground hornbills have at times been regarded as meriting a separate family status in a Family Bucorvidae, or at least as a subfamily Bucorvinae, here they are united as a distinctive genus with the rest of hornbills in a single Family Bucerotidae. The closest relatives of these remarkable and very distinctive birds are the hoopoes (Upupidae) and wood-hoopoes (Phoeniculidae). All three families were formerly classified within the order Coraciiformes (see p. 173) but recent morphological and molecular research indicates they should be included in an order of their own, the Bucerotiformes, as here.

HORNBILLS Bucerotidae

GENERA: 15   **SPECIES:** 53

LENGTH: 30–120 cm (1–4 ft)

WEIGHT: 85 g–6.2 kg (3 oz–13.6 lb)

RANGE AND HABITAT: sub-Saharan Africa, extreme southwest Arabian peninsula (one species), southern Asia, and New Guinea east to the Solomon Islands (one species); many species inhabit forests, most of them only evergreen tropical forests; others live in more open woodland, and about a quarter of all species are savannah dwellers, all but one in south Asia; some have also adapted in places to plantations, while a few can survive in semi-arid scrublands

SOCIAL BEHAVIOUR: usually in pairs or family groups, with some species assembling in bigger flocks of up to 20 or more birds to feed or sometimes roost together; almost all species are monogamous, for more than one season, and usually stay together year-round; many are territorial; some species are cooperative breeders

NEST: generally in natural tree holes or hollows, sometimes in old nests of barbets or woodpeckers, and where trees are scarce, in rock faces, earth banks or nest boxes or other artificial structures; the nest hole is sealed from outside and then from within by the female, helped by the male outside, with a mixture of mud, her own droppings, wood chips and sticky food remains, which harden when dry, leaving just a slit for the male to pass food to his mate; the nest chamber is lined either with dry materials such as bark flakes and dry leaves, or in some species a moist lining of fresh green grass or leaves

EGGS: 1–8, white

INCUBATION: 23–42 days

FLEDGING PERIOD: 39–96 days

FOOD: mainly fruit and insects in varying proportions for different species; also most eat various other small animals, such as scorpions, millipedes, earthworms, small lizards and snakes, birds and their eggs and young, and small mammals

VOICE: most are noisy, making a wide variety of calls, including softer clucking, grunting and whistling notes and loud and far-carrying roaring, hooting, booming, braying, cackling and squealing sounds

MIGRATION: most species are sedentary, but many make local movements during dry seasons or in response to shortages of particular fruits in forest species; in some cases the birds can travel much farther and possibly in a regular and predictable pattern

CONSERVATION STATUS: three species, the Rufous-headed Hornbill, *Rhyticeros waldeni*, the Helmeted Hornbill, *Rhinoplax vigil*, and the Sulu Hornbill, *Anthracoceros montani*, are Critically Endangered; three species, the Narcondam Hornbill, *Rhyticeros narcondami*, are Endangered; nine species, the Sumba Hornbill, *R. everetti*, the Rufous-necked Hornbill, *Aceros nipalensis*, the Plain-pouched Hornbill, *R. subruficollis*, the Palawan Hornbill, *Anthracoceros marchei*, the Knobbed Hornbill, *Rhyticeros cassidix*, the Brown-cheeked Hornbill, *Bycanistes cylindricus*, the Yellow-casqued Hornbill, *Ceratogymna elata* and the Sulwesi Hornbill, *Penelopides exarhatus*, are Vulnerable; nine species are Near Threatened

ABOVE Like other hornbills, this Eastern Yellow-billed Hornbill, *Tockus flavirostris*, flies with a series of flaps followed by glides.

Among the most striking and distinctive of all Old World birds, hornbills are named for their outsized bill, superficially similar in shape to that of the unrelated New World toucans. The similarity is the result of convergent evolution that enables both groups of birds to reach tree fruit. A major difference is that the hornbill's long, deep, decurved bill is topped by a unique outgrowth known as the casque. Depending on species, this can be simply a small ridge or a flamboyantly large, elaborate structure, which may be cylindrical, folded or upturned, and in some cases exceeds the size of the bill itself.

Mainly tropical, with some species occurring in the subtropics, hornbills are almost all birds of continental Africa south of the Sahara and southern Asia. Just one species is found in the Arabian peninsula – the African Grey Hornbill, *Tockus nasutus*, a widespread species in Africa, whose range extends to extreme southwest Saudi Arabia and western Yemen, where it is also common. There is a single species in New Guinea, the Papuan Hornbill, *Rhyticeros plicatus*, which also lives in the Indonesian islands of the South Moluccas to the west, and the Solomon Islands and other smaller islands to the east.

Most hornbills are birds of forests and woodlands of various kinds, but about a quarter are savannah dwellers, in some cases in very arid habitats. There are 25 species in Africa, of which 13 live in open deciduous woodland or savannah, in some species including arid thorn-scrub or even semi-desert and the remaining nine in evergreen forest. The division by habitat among Asian species is very different, with just one savannah dweller, the Indian Grey Hornbill, *Ocyceros birostris*, and the other 27 in forests, most of them in evergreen rainforest. The Papuan Hornbill, too, is a forest bird.

There is a huge size range in the family as a whole, from the females of the smallest *Tockus* species, weighing as little as 85 g (3 oz), to males of the Great Hornbill, which can be 120 times as heavy, attaining up to 3.4 kg (7.5 lb). These birds have evolved skeletal features found in no other birds that enable the head to support such an immense, heavy bill. The first two neck vertebrae are fused, and the skull articulates on the neck with the aid of an additional, second protuberance on the skull and corresponding socket on the fused vertebrae to the single ones of other birds. Also, hornbills have powerful neck muscles. The body is relatively small and slender compared with the bill and the large, broad wings and (in most cases) the long tail. The legs are short and sturdy and the feet have the three forward-facing toes partly fused at the base. The soles of the feet are broad, which is an adaptation for perching. Most hornbills move about on land or the larger branches of trees with a succession of long hops, with both feet held together, though some of the small, more ground-dwelling *Tockus* species of Africa can walk or run. The eyelashes are long, and are thought to serve as a sunshade, though they are not as well developed as the flattened ones of the ground-hornbills.

Like the common name, the scientific name for the family refers to the shape of the bill, being derived from the Greek word meaning 'cow-horn'. Although often large, the casque is light in weight, being hollow in almost all species and developed from the outer keratin covering of the upper mandible. It is strengthened internally by a network of thin, bony struts. There is usually a small opening at the head end leading to the mouth, and one function of the casque is thought to be to serve as a resonating chamber, amplifying the birds' often very loud calls. Such a prominent feature is also likely to be important as a badge of status during rivalry between individuals of the same sex or for recognition of potential mates.

The body, neck and head plumage is rather coarse, hairlike and loose, and in many species the head feathers can be erected to form a modest crest, or in a few, an impressive tall crown or fan. The plumage of many species exhibits various striking, bold patterns of black and white or black and buff. Many of the *Tockus* species of Africa have a chequered black-and-white pattern on the upperparts, a black and white crown and mainly pure white underparts. Some hornbills have mainly or partly brown and rufous plumage. Differences in plumage between the sexes are minor, but males are often much bigger and heavier, and develop a larger bill and casque. The bill, the casque and the bare skin on the face, throat and around the eyes are in many species patterned in bright red, blue, yellow or buff. These colours, together with the size of the bill and the development of the casque, indicate the age and sex of each individual. In species with a large casque, its development to full size may take up to 6 years.

ABOVE One of the smaller African species, the Red-billed Hornbill, *Tockus erythrorhynchus*, is widespread and locally common.

In Africa, two very similar species, the ground hornbills of the genus *Bucorvus*, are distinctive enough to merit being placed, as here, in a subfamily, Bucorvinae, with the rest of the family constituting the subfamily Bucerotinae; indeed they are sometimes treated as a separate family, Bucorvidae. These are the bulkiest of all hornbills.

They differ from the rest of the family in various ways, including the number of neck vertebrae (15 instead of 14), walking instead of hopping, and details of breeding behaviour (see below). Also, they are unique among all birds in lacking a carotid artery. They are now thought to be the earliest surviving offshoot of the hornbill group.

The Northern Ground Hornbill, *Bucorvus abyssinicus*, is found in a broad belt in the arid Sahel region along the southern edge of the Sahara, from Senegal and Gambia east to northwest Kenya, Uganda and Ethiopia. The Southern Ground Hornbill, *B. leadbeateri*, occurs from southern Kenya to Angola, West Zaire, northern Namibia and eastern Cape Province.

Both are very big birds, standing up to 1 m (3.3 ft) tall. This is taller than a male Wild Turkey, but only about half its weight – ground hornbills typically weigh about 4 kg (8.8 lb), while Wild Turkey males are about 8–10 kg (17.6–22 lb) – though especially large males of the Southern Ground Hornbill can weigh up to 6.2 kg (13.6 lb). They have a large head on a thick neck, and are equipped with a formidable weapon in the massive, sharply pointed bill, resembling the blade of a pickaxe. The upper mandible bears a tall, short casque in the Northern species but only a hump-shaped ridge in its Southern relative. Both species have large areas of bare brightly coloured skin surrounding the eyes and on the inflatable throat sac. The eyes are encircled by big, stiff flattened eyelashes, each up to 1.8 cm (0.7 in) long and overhanging the upper part

ABOVE A Southern Ground Hornbill, *Bucorvus leadbeateri*, passes food to another member of its cooperative breeding group.

ABOVE A close-up of the head of a captive male Rhinoceros Hornbill, *Buceros rhinoceros*, shows the beauty of its cosmetic colours.

of each eye. The birds seem to use these as sunshades, deliberately angling their head so that the lashes reduce glare from the bright light on the open savannah. The lashes may also protect the eyeballs from damage by struggling prey. Ground hornbills have longer, thicker legs than the hornbills, and feet with rather short toes – adaptations for a terrestrial lifestyle.

Both species have almost entirely black plumage, apart from the white primary flight feathers. Male Northern Ground Hornbills have blue facial skin and a red and blue throat sac, but these areas are completely blue in females. In Southern Ground Hornbills these areas are entirely red in the male, while the female has a partly blue throat sac. The birds can use this sac to make loud, deep booming or grunting calls, often heralding the dawn.

Far more carnivorous than their hornbill relatives, ground hornbills may kill and eat quite sizeable vertebrate prey as well as their staple diet of large insects and other invertebrates. Animals they have been seen to overpower include squirrels, mongooses, hares, tortoises and large snakes, including dangerous ones such as cobras. Northern Ground Hornbills forage in pairs, sometimes with their single offspring, while members of the Southern species also hunt in larger groups of up to eight or so. The birds often cooperate when tackling larger or more dangerous prey. The birds use the massive bill like a pickaxe to strike the victim and kill it, and then to dismember it. They also take advantage of carrion – and the insects attracted to the carcasses.

As their name suggests, ground hornbills spend most of the time on the ground, where they stride along with a stately gait in pairs or small groups, digging for hidden prey, walking and running after other creatures, and occasionally climbing trees to catch them. At a golf course in Kenya, ground hornbills occasionally used to make off with golf balls, presumably mistaking them for food. Despite their bulk, ground hornbills are accomplished fliers when necessary, capable of reaching speeds of up to 29 km/h (18 mph) on their broad, rounded wings. Southern Ground Hornbills fly up to their roosts in trees.

Unlike bucerotid hornbills, female ground hornbills do not seal themselves up inside the nest hole, nor do they exhibit any sign of nest sanitation. They differ, too, from their relatives in another feature of reproduction, which has evolved to make it more likely that the number of offspring doesn't exceed the available food supply. Although they normally lay two eggs, and both hatch, only one chick survives to fledge. The eggs are laid at intervals of 3 to 5 days and as the female starts to incubate as soon as the first egg is laid, the chick that hatches from it is larger and stronger than the second one. It is far more successful at in competing for the food brought to the nest by the adults, and the young chick virtually always dies of starvation within 4 days in the Northern Ground Hornbill and a week in its Southern relative (in which helpers also feed the young as well as both parents). Birds that survive to adulthood may live a long time; at least 40 years for a pair of Northern Ground Hornbills in captivity.

Ground hornbills are traditionally regarded as sacred by many Africans, and killing one was thought to bring bad luck. But they are often killed for the supposed magical powers of their body parts, or when they break glass windows of buildings, mistaking the reflection for a rival male. They also experience major threats from clearance for agriculture, fires, and poisoning when they eat carcass baits set out to kill other animals.

Over half of all African species (14) are in the genus *Tockus*. These are small compared with most other hornbills, ranging in size from the Red-billed Dwarf Hornbill, *T. camurus*, just 30 cm long including its big bill and long tail, to about 58 cm (23 in) in the largest species. They are mainly savannah and open woodland birds, although the two dwarf species are strictly tied to forests. As well as *Bucorvus* and *Tockus*, there are three other genera endemic to Africa. Although it was regarded as being closely related to the *Tockus* species, the monotypic Long-tailed Hornbill, *Tropicranus albocristatus*, is a very distinctive species now classified along with the two other African genera within the large assemblage of 10 Asian genera. True to its name the Long-tailed Hornbill has an extremely long, markedly graduated tail, considerably longer than its body. It favours dense tangled vegetation in primary forest and has a unique feeding method for a hornbill, catching insects in mid-air like an oversized flycatcher, steering by movements of its tail. It also has a howling call unlike the sounds made by other hornbills. The six medium-sized to large species of *Bycanistes* are primarily birds of evergreen forests. Two other African hornbills, in the genus *Ceratogymna*, are larger forest dwellers.

Asian species are divided between nine genera. The three small *Ocyceros* species superficially resemble the African *Tockus* hornbills, and include the single Asian savannah-dwelling species, the Indian Grey Hornbill, the commonest and most widespread Indian species. There are five species of *Anthracoceros*, medium-sized hornbills in which the female's casque is, unusually, almost as large as that of the male.

The largest and most imposing of the Asian hornbills are the three *Buceros* species: males of the biggest and most widespread, the Great Hornbill, *B. bicornis*, grow to a length of just over a metre (3.3 ft) and, with their huge, broad wings are particularly impressive in flight. Even bigger, at up to 1.2 m (almost 4 ft) long, though not as heavy, is the Helmeted Hornbill, *Rhinoplax vigil*, of Southeast Asia, in a genus of its own. It has a large area of coloured bare skin on the neck, red in males and pale turquoise in females. Although relatively short, and straight, its bill is very stout, and topped by a short but tall casque that ends abruptly halfway along the bill in a solid block of 'ivory'. This makes the bill far heavier than that of other hornbills, so that the skull, bill and casque together constitute 10% or more of the total body weight. The very long tail of this species may help the Helmeted Hornbill counterbalance the extremely heavy casque. One use to which the formidable bill is put is in aerial casque-butting contests between rival males. The skull includes additional strengthening behind the ivory, aligned so that it helps withstand strikes to the front of the casque. The casque may also help provide extra momentum when the birds are chiselling off bark to get at insect food beneath, like huge woodpeckers. Another interesting feature of the Helmeted Hornbill and the three *Buceros* species is that they all apply a natural 'cosmetic' in the form of their preen oil to colour the bill and casque – red in the Helmeted Hornbill and yellow, orange and red respectively in the others. They apply this by wiping the bill and casque against a special tuft on the preen gland.

The single *Anorrhinus* species and the two species of *Ptilolaemus* are medium sized and distinguished by their all-brown or brown and rufous plumage and bushy head feathers. There are also two small species of *Penelopides*, collectively known as taristic hornbills, from the distinctive cackling calls they make. Recent research suggests that they should be split into at least four and perhaps six species. Two genera of mainly large species are *Aceros* and *Rhyticeros*. There is just a single very large species of *Aceros*, the Rufous-necked hornbill, *A. nipalensis*, in which the sexes differ strikingly in plumage, the male being bright rufous, contrasting with its black wings and tail base, and the almost all-black female. There are nine species of *Rhyticeros*. These two genera are often collectively known as the pouched hornbills, from the brightly coloured, inflatable sac or wattle of bare skin on the throat.

The final Asian species, the White-crowned Hornbill, *Berenicornis comatus*, is usually placed in a genus of its own, although has often

ABOVE Like many hornbills, this Taristic Hornbill, *Penelopides manillae*, in the Philippines is threatened by loss of its forest habitat.

been included in *Aceros* and is thought to be related to the Long-tailed Hornbill, *Tropicranus albocristatus*. It has very striking plumage, with a tall spiky crest, and is unusual in that male and female plumage differ quite markedly. Males are pure white with a black back, black wings with white tips, and black thighs, while females are all black apart from the white crest, wingtips and tail.

Hornbills are omnivores, eating both fruit and a wide range of small animals. The proportions vary between species, and also depending on the availability of particular foods seasonally. Also, each species has its preferred foraging techniques and in forest-dwelling hornbills, its preferred foraging height. In this way the birds avoid competing with one another for limited resources. Up to eight species may coexist in a particular area, each one occupying a distinct niche.

The small savannah-dwelling *Tockus* hornbills feed mainly on a wide range of insects and other invertebrates. Most take the majority of their food from the ground. Most of the forest-dwelling hornbills rely on fruit as the staple items in their diet but opportunistically supplement this with various small invertebrate and vertebrate animals; the animal part of the diet is often increased during the breeding season, probably to meet extra calcium requirements following depletion during egg laying, and for bone development when fed to the young. The powerful bill is used as a pair of forceps to pick up food items. Its length serves to keep dangerous prey such as scorpions or small vertebrates at a distance, and to reach otherwise inaccessible fruit. Hornbills may also use the bill to dig out food from soil or other places, while some smaller species also hawk for flying insects. The birds' binocular vision enables them to see the tip of the bill, which helps in precision food handling. Hornbills have much shorter tongues than toucans, so with a toss of the head they throw the food item back into the throat, with great precision.

The loud calls of hornbills, including clucking, cackling, whistling, barking, hooting and roaring sounds, enable them to communicate over considerable distances and in densely wooded habitats. Another method of long-range communication is by rapping with the bill against a dead branch or log, especially to convey aggression. Also, as the bigger species fly from tree to tree with deep beats of their huge wings, the air rushes through the gaps resulting from the reduced underwing coverts, which leave the bases of their flight feathers exposed, to make a remarkably loud whooshing sound. Humans – and surely also the birds themselves – can distinguish many species from the particular sound of its wingbeats.

One of the most remarkable aspects of hornbill biology, unique among birds, is the habit of females of sealing themselves into the nest hole. Most choose a hole with as narrow an entrance as possible, to reduce the amount of sealing needed to a minimum. When she is nearing the time for egg laying, she enters the nest hole, and starts to seal it by plastering it with a mixture of her own droppings, mud and sticky food remains until only a narrow slit remains through which her mate will pass her food during incubation and for a variable time, depending on species, after the young hatch. The sealing process may take only a few hours, and at most a few days. A popular myth is that the male forces her in and seals up the hole himself, but this is not true; the most he does in some species is to supply some sealing material. Once the female is sealed within the nest chamber she usually waits for a few days or sometimes as long as 3 weeks before laying, presumably to ensure that she is safe from predators and can rely on her partner to feed her while she spends the 3 to 6 weeks it takes to incubate the eggs, incarcerated within the cramped nest chamber. Often the space is so limited that she must hold her tail vertically above her back. In some species, including small *Tockus* hornbills and the three *Buceros* hornbills, the female typically emerges when the chicks are one-third to a half grown, so that the total period of her incarceration from when she sealed herself in ranges from about 6 to 16 weeks depending on the size of the species; after she has broken her way out by chipping away the seal with her bill, the young reseal the entrance from within. In other species she waits until the young are ready to leave.

Some hornbills have survived in captivity for 30 years or more; the record is held by a female Great Hornbill named Josephine that was kept in London Zoo. Acquired as a young bird, she lived there for 49 years, and died in 1998 at the age of 53. For many years she also held the record of being the oldest animal at the zoo. And hornbill researchers estimate that members of this species are likely to have a potential lifespan of 35–40 years in the wild. However, almost 20% of species, mainly island species with very small ranges, are threatened to varying degrees, chiefly by deforestation, but also in some cases as a result of hunting.

HOOPOE Upupidae

GENERA: 1   **SPECIES**: 1

LENGTH: 26–32 cm (10–12.5 in)

WEIGHT: 47–89 g (1.6–3 oz)

RANGE AND HABITAT: much of Europe apart from the north, Madeira, Canary Islands, Africa, Madagascar, southern and eastern Asia; open or lightly wooded country, in light woodland, orchards, olive groves, vineyards, gardens, sandy heathland; also in semi-desert scrub in the Canary Islands, dry savannah and dense forest edge in Africa and Madagascar, in steppe grassland in central Asia and coastal dune scrub in southern Asia

SOCIAL BEHAVIOUR: usually singly or in pairs, but may occur in small loose flocks after breeding, when feeding and on migration; monogamous and territorial

NEST: a nest chamber unlined or sparsely lined with vegetation, feathers, wool or rubbish, within a natural tree hole, or especially in treeless areas, a hollow among boulders or in a sandbank, termite mound, or an old building, as well as in nest boxes

EGGS: 4–8, pale milky blue when laid, soon changing to pale dull greenish grey and stained by increasingly dirty nest interior

INCUBATION: 16–18 days

FLEDGING PERIOD: 25–30 days

FOOD: chiefly large insects, including many soil-dwelling larvae and pupae such as those of cockchafers and other beetles, as well as other insects, such as crickets, mole-crickets, moths, bugs and cicadas; also other invertebrates such as spiders, centipedes and snails; small lizards and other vertebrates; small amounts of fruits, seeds, rhizomes and other plant food

VOICE: mellow, often trisyllabic 'hoop hoop hoop' advertising call of the male (the Madagascar race has a different, purring song); also various other unmelodious rasping, rattling, cawing or chirping calls

MIGRATION: tropical and southern subspecies are generally sedentary or partially migratory; northern ones are regular long-distance migrants to Africa and southern Asia

CONSERVATION STATUS: not threatened

The only living member of its family, the Hoopoe, *Upupa epops*, is one of the most distinctive of all birds with its unique combination of chestnut and cinammon-buff head and body, a bold black-and-white wing pattern, a long, slightly decurved bill and a striking, big, black-tipped crest. Restricted to the Old World, it has a very wide range in Europe, Africa and central to southern Asia. Eight subspecies, which differ mainly in size, depth of coloration, and other plumage details, especially the width and number of the black bands; also, migratory races have longer wings, and the Madagascar race a very different song. Up to four of the eight subspecies have been regarded as full species by some researchers. The Hoopoe has often been linked to hornbills (Family Bucerotidae, p. 153), and this relationship has been essentially borne out by the latest molecular and morphological data; its closest relatives appear to be the wood-hoopoes (Family Phoeniculidae); for these reasons, both the Hoopoe and wood-hoopoes are now included together with the hornbills in the Order Bucerotiformes.

The Hoopoe is about the size of a large thrush. The slender bill is black with a pinkish base, and strongly compressed laterally. Its large, black-tipped crest is erectile, shaped like a mohican hairstyle (known as a mohawk in North America) when fully raised and expanded, as it frequently is when the bird is excited or alarmed, and briefly whenever it lands after a short flight. The black wings are very broad and rounded, with up to five broad parallel white bars forming a banded pattern along each inner wing and, in some races, a single white band at right angles to the others along the base of the primaries. There is a small white patch on the rump, and the broad, square-ended black tail is crossed by a broad white inverted chevron at about its mid-point. The Hoopoe's flight is as distinctive as its wing pattern, with a brief burst of erratic beats of the wings followed by their partial closure. This produces a floating, undulating action, the effect reminiscent of a giant butterfly.

The Hoopoe spends a good deal of its time on the ground, walking and running well; when feeding it moves with a series of short, shuffling steps as it probes with its bill for insects or other invertebrates in soil, leaf litter, grass or other vegetation, or among animal dung. The thick neck houses strong muscles working the bill, and the skull and jaws are modified in such a way that they enable the bill to be opened while inserted in the ground to tweezer out prey.

The very distinctive, far-carrying advertising call of the male is one of the quintessential sounds of the spring and early summer in Mediterranean countries and other parts of its huge range. A

ABOVE A Hoopoe, *Upupa epops*, spreads out its wings and ruffles its feathers to absorb as much heat as possible.

sequence of short, mellow, resonant hooting notes, usually three in each phrase, with only a second or so between phrases, it is repeated steadily for long periods throughout the day.

Protected in many parts of its range, the Hoopoe eats large amounts of insects that are pests of agriculture or forestry. It was considered sacred in Ancient Egypt and in Crete during Minoan times, and features in the mythology of Ancient Greece; it is the state bird of the Punjab province of India and in recent times was chosen as the national bird of Israel in 2008. Unfortunately, it is still hunted in parts of southern Europe and Asia, adding to more general declines due to intensive agriculture.

WOOD-HOOPOES Phoeniculidae

GENERA: 2   **SPECIES:** 8

LENGTH: 21–38 cm (8–15 in)

WEIGHT: 18–99 g (0.6–3.5 oz)

RANGE AND HABITAT: sub-Saharan Africa; forest, open *Acacia* woodlands, thornbush, wooded savannah, palm groves and gardens

SOCIAL BEHAVIOUR: *Rhinopomastus* species are usually solitary, in pairs or briefly as family groups, but *Phoeniculus* wood-hoopoes are far more sociable, occurring year-round in groups; monogamous and territorial, probably all *Phoeniculus* species (except perhaps the Forest Wood-hoopoe, *P. castaneiceps*) are cooperative breeders

NEST: an unlined nest cavity inside a tree hole, either a natural one or one excavated by woodpeckers or barbets, or in a larger hollow in a tree

EGGS: 2–5, blue, turquoise, olive green or grey, typically with little chalky white pits; those of the White-headed Wood-hoopoe, *P. bollei*, are also covered with dark brown spots and blotches

INCUBATION: about 17 or 18 days

FLEDGING PERIOD: 28–30 days

FOOD: mainly insects and their young and eggs, and other invertebrates; also some berries and seeds; larger species also occasionally take small lizards; the Violet Wood-hoopoe, *P. damarensis*, steals eggs from the nests of small birds such as weavers

VOICE: very vocal; most species have loud, harsh chattering or cackling calls that are important in group displays, as well as other calls including quacking, whistling, twittering and growlings; those of the less social species, the Forest Wood-hoopoe and the three *Rhinopomastus* species, have softer and less noticeable calls

MIGRATION: largely sedentary

CONSERVATION STATUS: none threatened

One of the very few bird families endemic to Africa, the wood-hoopoes take their name from their superficial resemblance to the Hoopoe, *Upupa epops* (above), which is their closest relative.

The eight species are divided between two genera, *Phoeniculus* and *Rhinopomastus*. Surprisingly, although they look broadly similar, they show marked genetic differences, apparently diverging about

10 million years ago; there is a good case for elevating them to subfamilies or even to separate the two groups farther, in families of their own.

All but one of the five species of typical wood-hoopoes, *Phoeniculus*, are noisy, group-living birds, with some practising cooperative breeding, in contrast to the *Rhinopomastus* species, which are quieter, more unobtrusive and breed as solitary pairs. The exception to this rule is the Forest Wood-hoopoe, *P. castaneiceps*, which seems to share characteristics of both genera, and may be a primitive member of the family. Of the five, the Green Wood-hoopoe, *P. purpureus*, is by far the most widespread member of the family and common in many parts of its range. The three species of *Rhinopomastus* comprise two species of scimitarbills and the Black Wood-hoopoe, *R. aterrimus*.

Like the Hoopoe, wood-hoopoes are very distinctive birds. The bill is the most prominent feature, long and slightly to markedly decurved according to genera and species: in the five species of *Phoeniculus* and also one of the *Rhinopomastus* wood-hoopoes, the Black Wood-hoopoe, the curvature is slight or moderate, and the bill varies in size from medium-length and slight in the smallest wood-hoopoe, the Forest Wood-hoopoe to long and massive in the three biggest ones, the Green Wood-hoopoe, Black-billed Wood-hoopoe, *P. somaliensis*, and Violet Wood-hoopoe, *P. damarensis*. Both the two scimitarbills have a strongly decurved bill.

All eight species have a relatively long and slender body and a long and strongly graduated tail, and all normally spend almost all their lives on trees, where they are skilled climbers up trunks and branches like woodpeckers. The legs and feet are strong and the toes, three facing forwards and one backwards, are equipped with long, sharp claws for this arboreal lifestyle.

In all species, the predominant plumage colour is black, with variable amounts of white barring on the wings and tail of some species. In many species, the black is strongly iridescent, with a

ABOVE The scimitarbills, *Rhinopomastus*, like this Common Scimitarbill, *R. cyanomelas*, are placed in a separate subfamily, and may even deserve a family of their own.

ABOVE Among the noisiest of African birds is the Green Wood-hoopoe, *Phoeniculus purpureus*, like this one cackling in Kenya.

green, purple, violet or blue gloss. Atypical plumage patterns are found in the small Forest Wood-hoopoe, which has a bright chestnut head and chest, and in the White-headed Wood-hoopoe, *Phoeniculus bollei*. Some males of the polymorphic race of the Forest Wood-hoopoe also have a white head, and it may be in both species an adaptation for helping the birds detect prey in the deep shade of their dense primary forest habitat, the white reflecting what little light there is. The bill and legs are bright red in most of the *Phoeniculus* species and black in *Rhinopomastus*, except for the Abyssinian Scimitarbill, *R. minor*, in which the bill is bright orange.

Wood-hoopoes all feed mainly on invertebrates, including many spiders, millipedes, centipedes and a wide range of insects, especially beetles, cockroaches, earwigs, ants, termites, grasshoppers and moths and their larvae or pupae. They travel about from tree to tree in search of food, probing with their long bill into crevices and holes and sometimes stripping off loose bark to get at prey hiding beneath. Wood-hoopoes occasionally descend to the ground to feed, which scimitarbills do only rarely.

Apart from the Forest Wood Hoopoe, *Phoeniculus* wood-hoopoes are very vocal birds, communicating with a variety of different calls, often loud and far-carrying, especially in chorus from flocks performing territorial displays known as 'rallies', when the birds rock back and forth with wings partly open and raise and lower their long tail. Often the species in South Africa are known colloquially in Afrikaans as *kakelaars*, meaning 'cacklers'. Males also make mammal-like growls, for instance when they spot a rival entering their territory.

ORDER PICIFORMES

This order comprises four families of arboreal birds: the jacamars, in the Family Galbulidae, the puffbirds (Family Bucconidae), both of which are endemic to the Neotropics, the honeyguides (Family Indicatoridae), from Africa and Asia, the very widespread woodpeckers (Family Picidae) and the toucans and barbets (Family Ramphastidae), with five subfamilies in the tropics and subtropics of Central and South America, Africa and Asia. All Piciformes (along with some other tree-dwelling birds such as owls and parrots) have similarities between the muscle arrangements of their legs and feet, and their feet have the zygodactyl, or yoke-toed, arrangement of toes, that is with toes two and three facing forwards and toes one and four facing backwards in the shape of an X. Woodpeckers can alter this arrangement when climbing, to give a better grip. Other features common to the order are that these birds lack down feathers at any age, they nest in holes or cavities of various sorts (apart from the honeyguides, which are brood parasites like many cuckoo species, laying their eggs in other birds' nests), and have altricial young (born helpless and dependent on their parents until they leave the nest).

The jacamars appear most closely related to the puffbirds and the honeyguides to the woodpeckers. Relationships among the toucans and barbets are less certain, but the toucans appear to be closest to the other Neotropical members of the Ramphastidae, the two species of Prong-billed Barbets and the 15 species of New World barbets, and so these three groups are here regarded as forming three tribes (Ramphastini, Semnornithini and Capitonini respectively) in the subfamily Ramphastinae, leaving the rest of the barbets in three other subfamilies, Megalaiminae and Caloramphinae (Asian barbets) and Lybiinae (African barbets).

JACAMARS Galbulidae

GENERA: 5 **SPECIES:** 18

LENGTH: 14–34 cm (5.5–13.5 in)

WEIGHT: 17–76 g (0.6–2.7 oz)

RANGE AND HABITAT: Central and South America; range of one very widespread species extends northwards to southeastern Mexico; most inhabit lowland tropical forest, especially along edges and in clearings, though some in more open woodland and savannah, shrubby land and even marshes with scattered trees or bushes

SOCIAL BEHAVIOUR: usually singly or in pairs, though sometimes join mixed-species flocks; most monogamous, nesting in separate pairs but some may be polygamous and some, especially the Three-toed Jacamar, *Jacamaralcyon tridactyla*, sometimes breed cooperatively

NEST: in a hole excavated by the birds, usually either in an earth bank or in a termite nest in a tree (if neither is available, may make a hole in soil between the roots of a large fallen tree); nest chamber unlined but becomes littered with chitinous parts of insects regurgitated by incubating adults and excrement from nestlings

EGGS: usually 2–4, white

INCUBATION: 18–26 days

FLEDGING PERIOD: 20–26 days

FOOD: in all but one species, almost entirely aerial insects caught in flight, such as butterflies, wasps and beetles; the Great Jacamar, *Jacamerops aureus*, gleans some insects from foliage while it is in flight, as well as in mid-air, and also takes some spiders and even small lizards

VOICE: most species have high-pitched calls, mainly whistles, squeals and trills, that are prolonged into complex songs; the Great Jacamar makes catlike mewing calls and has a song consisting of a clipped note followed by a long mournful whistle

MIGRATION: sedentary

CONSERVATION STATUS: two species, the Three-toed Jacamar and the Coppery-chested Jacamar, *Galbula pastazae*, are Vulnerable

This is a small exclusively Neotropical family of mainly forest-dwelling insectivorous birds with brilliant iridescent plumage that alternate periods of perching quietly and unobtrusively in the forest

ABOVE A male Rufous-tailed Jacamar, *Galbula ruficauda*, grasps insect prey in its stiletto-shaped bill at La Selva, Costa Rica.

canopy with sudden agile and aerobatic dashes to seize their prey in mid-air. As they scan their surroundings for prey, they have a characteristic habit of perching upright with the bill held upward at an angle, like a bee-eater or hummingbird. Exclusively arboreal except when feeding or when breeding in earth banks or termite mounds, they are generally restricted to more or less wooded habitats. Of the 18 species in the family, 13 occur in the Amazon Basin, and 15 in Brazil. Just two species, the Yellow-billed Jacamar, *Galbula albirostris*, and the Great Jacamar, *Jacamerops aureus*, are birds of forest interiors as well as forest edges and open second growth; most of the rest are birds of forest clearings and edges. They show some resemblance to the Old World bee-eaters (Meropidae) in appearance and certain habits, such as their predilection for targeting insects such as bees, wasps and some butterflies that are avoided by most other birds because of their unpalatability or toxicity and beating these on a branch to remove the stings or venom.

In all but three species, the bill is long, almost straight (in most it is actually slightly decurved but usually looks straight in the field) and slender, tapering to a needle point: it resembles a letter-opener in shape (or a slender pair of scissors when open). The Great Jacamar, by contrast, has a relatively shorter, stouter, more powerful bill, which is decurved, suited for gleaning insects and also spiders and small lizards from the foliage as well as catching insects in the air like other jacamars, while the two species of *Galbalcyrhynchus* have a bill that is deeper, heavier and more daggerlike, resembling that of many kingfishers and perhaps an adaptation for taking larger or harder insect prey. The bill may become broken at the tip when used for digging out nesting burrows. The legs are short and feet small and weak, with the toes arranged in the zygodactylous pattern, the second and third digits pointing forward and the first and fourth facing rearward, except in the Three-toed Jacamar, *Jacamaralycon tridactyla*, which has lost its first toe. The wings of all species are short and rounded, and 12 species have a long, strongly graduated tail that may enhance their agility in the air. On the other hand, the two

Galbalcyrhynchus species have a very short, square-ended tail, and the four species of *Brachygalba* have a proportionally shorter, narrower tail.

The plumage of seven species (six in the genus *Galbula* and the Great Jacamar) is basically rich rufous or cinnamon below, contrasting with darker upperparts and breast, which have a strong iridescent sheen, mainly green, blue or bronze. The sexes differ only slightly, females being a little duller and with a buff or rufous throat patch, which is white in the males of some species. A further seven species are duller, with even less sexual dimorphism. Of these, the two *Galbalcyrhynchus* species are mainly chestnut, and three of the four *Brachygalba* jacamars and the Three-toed Jacamar are dull brownish, bronzy or greenish-black above with varying amounts of white (the other *Brachygalba* species is very like the six *Galbula* species described above). The Paradise Jacamar, *Galbula dea*, is mainly metallic blue-black with a strikingly contrasting white half collar.

PUFFBIRDS Bucconidae

GENERA: 10   **SPECIES:** 35

LENGTH: 13–29 cm (5–11.5 in)

WEIGHT: 17–101 g (0.6–3.6 oz)

RANGE AND HABITAT: southern Mexico, Central America, South America; tropical rainforest and forest edge, dry open woodlands, scrub, savannah

SOCIAL BEHAVIOUR: most species are solitary or sometimes in family parties or other small groups; nunbirds, *Monasa*, occur in larger flocks; most species are monogamous and territorial, nesting as isolated pairs, though nunbirds breed cooperatively, as may the Swallow-winged Puffbird, *Chelidoptera tenebrosa*, which often nests in loose, non-territorial colonies

NEST: little is known for many species; otherwise most species nest in a cavity excavated by the pair in a termite nest in a tree; *Nystalus* species and the Swallow-winged Puffbird nest at the end of a burrow dug in an earth bank or the ground, while nunlets *Monasa* and *Malacoptila* species may use either type of nest site

EGGS: 2–3, occasionally 4, white

INCUBATION: unknown for all except the Swallow-winged Puffbird, 15 days

FLEDGING PERIOD: about 20–30 days

FOOD: a wide range of large insects, such as beetles, grasshoppers, cicadas and butterflies, and other invertebrates, including small crabs, spiders, scorpions and millipedes; occasionally small lizards, snakes, frogs or toads; sometimes also berries or other fruit

VOICE: often silent, but may utter high-pitched trills and whistles or hissing sounds, especially at dawn and dusk; nunbirds are more vocal, with loud, melodious contact calls between flock members

MIGRATION: sedentary

CONSERVATION STATUS: one race (minor) of the Crescent-chested Puffbird, *Malacoptila striata*, is Endangered; one species, the Sooty-capped Puffbird, *Bucco noanamae*, and the other race (striata) of the Crescent-chested Puffbird, are Near Threatened

ABOVE The Semi-collared Puffbird, *Malacoptila semicincta*, has a relatively restricted range in northern South America.

The members of this small family of Neotropical birds are superficially rather like kingfishers in body shape, although none is brightly coloured. The odd common name is derived from the birds' habit of frequently fluffing out their lax plumage and retracting the large rounded head into the shoulders, giving them an almost spherical appearance reminiscent of an old-fashioned powderpuff.

Ranging from sparrow-sized birds to species the size of a small pigeon, puffbirds are stout-bodied, short-necked and large-headed; they have big, often bright red or yellow eyes and well-developed rictal bristles. Some species have extra bristles on the face and elongated throat feathers that may play a part in display. Most have powerful, heavy bills with a hooked tip. An unusual feature of some puffbirds is that the tip of the upper mandible is forked, and the tip of the lower mandible fits into the narrow gap between the two forks. This is thought to serve as a 'vice' for holding insect prey while the bird deals with it. The legs are short and the feet small and a zygodactyl arrangement of the toes (two facing forward, two backwards). Most species have short, rounded wings and a short tail.

The family can be divided into six main groups. The 'typical' puffbirds comprise 15 species divided between four genera, *Notharchus*, *Bucco*, *Nystalus* and *Hypnelus*, the latter with just a single species. Medium-sized, they have heavy hooked bills, capable of despatching the occasional lizard or small snake. *Nystalus* puffbirds take far more of their prey from the ground compared with their relatives. Plumage varies from mainly black and white in *Notharchus* and complex patterns of brown, buff, rufous, black and white in *Bucco* and *Hypnelus*, often including a black collar and underparts that are barred and spotted black, to mainly brown, rufous and buff above with black bars, streaks or spots on white or buff underparts in *Nystalus*.

The seven species in the genus *Malacoptila* are similar to the typical puffbirds but have more strongly streaked plumage. Collectively known as softwings, they have particularly lax and fluffy plumage, enabling silent flight for approaching prey unawares. The smallest member of the family at just 13–15 cm (5–6 in) long, the Lanceolated Monklet, *Micromonacha lanceolata*, is dull brown above and with white underparts strongly streaked with black; despite its small size, it catches large insects which it dismembers with its heavy bill. It is unusual in also eating fruit. The genus *Nonnula* comprises six small species called nunlets, with a slender, slightly decurved and sharply pointed bill, and plainer, unpatterned plumage, brown above and cinnamon below. Despite the similar common name, the five species of nunbirds differ markedly from nunlets. They are among the largest members of the family, with a far more massive bill, and some of the most active, chasing insects in fast flight or hovering to glean them from vegetation. There are two genera: *Hapaloptila*, with a single species, the White-faced Nunbird *H. castanea*, with similar plumage to the nunlets except for the white face; and the four species of *Monasa*, which live up to the group's common name with their sombre, black or dark grey plumage (with patches of white in three species). This contrasts with the brilliantly coloured bill, red in three species and yellow in the other. Finally, the monotypic Swallow-winged Puffbird, *Chelidoptera tenebrosa*, is very distinctive, looking rather like a martin (Family Hirundinidae, p. 350) or an Australian wood-swallow (Family Artamidae, p. 259) with its pointed wings and short tail and more aerial lifestyle than other puffbirds. It has mainly black plumage with white on the underwings, a rufous or orange-buff lower belly and a white rump. Although it shares the other puffbirds' habit of spending much time watching for prey from a perch, it is adapted to more sustained flight as it flutters, glides and wheels about, with a flight action reminiscent of a bat or a butterfly, chasing flying insects and catching them in its shorter bill with a wide gape.

With their plump, fluffy body, big head and sluggish habits, puffbirds have long been considered lazy or stupid by local people and early ornithologists alike. In reality, they are efficient, well-camouflaged sit-and-wait predators, which save energy by perching absolutely still apart from the occasional head movement, and then leaping into action to dart out and snatch a passing insect or other small animal from the air, a branch or the ground.

HONEYGUIDES Indicatoridae

GENERA: 4   **SPECIES:** 16

LENGTH: 10–20 cm (4–8 in)

WEIGHT: 9–62 g (0.3–2.2 oz)

RANGE AND HABITAT: 15 species in sub-Saharan Africa, two in southern Asia; mostly in tropical forests and woodlands; some species range into montane or temperate woodland, orchards, plantations, trees lining suburban streets, parks and gardens, wooded grassland or semi-deserts with bushes or trees

SOCIAL BEHAVIOUR: usually solitary except when breeding, but may gather in groups of up to 50 or more birds (often of different species) at sources of beeswax; mostly territorial, males are promiscuous, as are at least some females

NEST: none; all species are brood parasites (hosts include barbets, small woodpeckers, warblers, flycatchers and white-eyes), choosing species nesting in tree holes or building deep cup nests

EGGS: clutch size is little known, in the Greater Honeyguide, *Indicator indicator*, and the Lesser Honeyguide, *I. minor*, about 20 eggs; white (apart from some eastern Green-backed Honeyguides, *Prodotiscus zambesiae*, that lay blue eggs to match usual white-eye hosts' eggs)

INCUBATION: 12–18 days

FLEDGING PERIOD: 20–22 days in *Prodotiscus* species; 30–40 days in those species of other genera for which information is known

FOOD: most species feed mainly on the wax of honeybees; all species also eat a variety of insects and their eggs or larvae, including bees, 'waxworms' (caterpillars of wax moths that feed on the wax in bees' nests), beetles, termites, ants and also wax scale-insects; the latter form most of the diet of the three *Prodotiscus* honeyguides

VOICE: varied calls include chattering, piping, whistling, squeaking, buzzing or trilling notes; songs consist of trills or more melodic sounds

MIGRATION: mostly sedentary; some Yellow-rumped Honeyguides, *Indicator xanthonotus*, make altitudinal migrations

CONSERVATION STATUS: four species, the Dwarf Honeyguide, *Indicator pumilio*, the Malaysian Honeyguide, *I. archipelagicus*, the Yellow-rumped Honeyguide, and the Yellow-footed Honeyguide, *Melignomon eisentrauti*, are Near Threatened

All but two species of this small family of soberly plumaged, sparrow-sized to thrush-sized birds of tropical woodlands are restricted to sub-Saharan Africa, with the remaining two species in southern Asia. Although they all have relatively drab plumage, these relatives of woodpeckers and barbets are remarkable in their feeding behaviour. They are among the very few birds that can

ABOVE A Greater Honeyguide, *Indicator indicator*, perches next to the honeycomb it is plundering in Natal, South Africa.

digest pure wax, mainly in the form of beeswax, and in the case of at least one and perhaps one other African species, they lead humans to bee nests that they have already spotted, then access the contents after their follower has broken into them. Although the story is perpetuated in many books, and even set-up footage in TV documentaries, there is no evidence for the supposed similar 'guiding' association with ratels (honey-badgers).

There are four genera, each of which has representatives in Africa. The most diverse genus is *Indicator*, with two Asian species and eight in Africa. As its name suggests, it includes the species – the Greater Honeyguide, *I. indicator* – that is well known for its habit of guiding people to the bees' nests. Another of the African *Indicator* species, the Scaly-throated Honeyguide, *I. variegatus*, may also be an 'indicator-bird', but researchers disagree about whether or not this is true.

There is just a single species in the genus *Melichneutes*, also restricted to Africa. This is the Lyre-tailed Honeyguide, *M. robustus*, of West Africa, whose tail shape contrasts with that of other honeyguides, which have a longish, graduated tail. It uses its 'lyre' in a spectacular aerial display: as it dives steeply, it spreads the outer tail feathers so that the air rushing over them makes a loud tooting sound (audible for up to 1 km/0.6 mile). The genus *Melignomon* contains two species, both African, which are intermediate in appearance and behaviour between the typical honeyguides and the last group.

This comprises three small African species in the genus *Prodotiscus*, which differ from the rest of the honeyguides in their fine, pointed bill, softer plumage and only 10 rather than 12 tail feathers. Also, they lack the thickened skin of other species that confers a degree of protection from the stings of the bees (although the combined attack from a large swarm has been known to kill a honeyguide), and none of them appear to feed on beeswax (see also below, regarding diet). They are sometimes known as honeybirds.

Most honeyguides have a stout, blunt-tipped bill. The legs are relatively short, but vary in length from species to species, with zygodactyl feet ending in strong, curved claws. The wings are rather long, narrow and pointed and the flight swift and often gently undulating. The plumage is generally olive, greyish or brownish above, and paler below, with rather faint streaking or barring in some species, and the outer tail feathers have white or off-white patches; some also have small yellow or white wing, head or rump patches. One, the Yellow-rumped Honeyguide, *Indicator xanthonotus*, a montane species living in the Himalayas, has a bright orange-yellow rump and face, while the Greater Honeyguide shows more difference between the sexes than other species, the male being distinguished by his black and white head pattern and pink bill.

A major part of the diet of most honeyguides is beeswax from the combs in the nests of honeybees of the genus *Apis*. The three *Prodotiscus* species also feed mainly on wax, though they obtain it not from bees but from scale insects (Coccidae); these are also important in the diet of the two *Melignomon* species. In addition, all honeyguides eat various insects and spiders, and also some fruits. The insects include other bees, wasps, ants, termites and caterpillars, especially those of the wax-eating moths *Galleria* that infest the honeycombs. There is a strict dominance hierarchy between different species at a bees' nest, rather like that seen in vultures at a carcass; superimposed on this is the hierarchy within species, where immature birds are generally dominant, followed by adult females, with adult males feeding last.

Honeyguides are capable of opening up bees' nests for themselves, and often select nests that have been recently abandoned by the insects and easy to access. Greater Honeyguides do not always obtain wax by guiding, and the behaviour seems to have arisen relatively recently rather than being deeply entrenched genetically. A guiding bird starts by attracting humans' attention with a chattering call. If they follow, it stops frequently to call and check that they are still following. Traditionally, the African follower leaves some of the honeycomb for the honeyguide. Remarkably, that research has proved the birds are able to understand the special calls made by

ABOVE Like all other honeyguides apart from the Greater Honeyguide, this Lesser Honeyguide, *Indicator minor*, does not guide humans to bees' nests.

the human African honey-hunters to attract them and maintain their attention. This two-way communication has evolved by natural selection, in contrast to the training involved in cooperation between humans and other hunting animals such as falcons or dogs.

Honeyguides also have interesting breeding behaviour. Like some cuckoos and other birds, they are brood parasites, laying their eggs in the nests of various host species, especially woodpeckers and barbets. The eggs are white in most species, as are those of most of the hole-nesting hosts. The young are cared for and fed by the hosts, on the diet of insects and fruit that they would normally bring to their own nestlings. As many as 40 or so hosts have been recorded for the Greater Honeyguide. Both male and female adults apparently monitor the activities and nests of their

hosts. Egg laying has been most studied in the Greater Honeyguide and its African relative the Lesser Honeyguide, *Indicator minor*; females were found to lay a total of about 20 eggs per season. These were separated temporally into four or five batches each of five or four eggs, with the female usually laying a single egg in a host nest at more or less at 2-day intervals. When it hatches, the young honeyguide makes use of a sharp, curved, projection from the downward-pointing tip of its bill – unique among all birds – to kill the host nestlings. Although its eyes are not yet open, it locates the young by touch, and then grasps each one firmly, aided by the bill projection, and shakes it to death. Once it has finished its grisly task and removed all competition, it can then eat all the food brought to the nest by the hosts.

WOODPECKERS Picidae

GENERA: 33   **SPECIES:** 217

LENGTH: 7.5–60 cm (3–23.5 in)

WEIGHT: 7–570 g (0.25–20 oz)

RANGE AND HABITAT: across much of the world except for the polar regions, large deserts, oceanic islands and Australasia; mostly in forests and woodlands of many kinds, including boreal or montane coniferous forest, temperate broadleaf and mixed woodland and tropical rainforest; many species also occur in parks, gardens, orchards and other plantations, and other agricultural habitats with trees; a few live in savannahs and even grasslands or deserts with scattered trees, shrubs or cacti

SOCIAL BEHAVIOUR: mainly solitary, or in the breeding season in pairs or family groups; a few species live year-round in complex social groups that defend a joint territory; most are monogamous and territorial; a few are colonial breeders, some in cooperative groups that may include young from previous years

NEST: most woodpeckers and piculets nest in holes in trees that they excavate themselves; a few woodpecker species excavate holes in ant nests, termite mounds in earth banks or in the ground; wrynecks use natural tree holes, take over holes made by other birds or use nest boxes; no material is used to line the nest chamber except wood chips and finer wood particles

EGGS: 2–10, rarely up to 12 in wrynecks, white

INCUBATION: 9–14 days in most species, up to 19 days in a few larger ones

FLEDGING PERIOD: for most species, 20–28 days; up to 31 days in a few large species and less in some piculets, even as brief as 11 days in the Speckled Piculet, *Picumnus innominatus*

FOOD: for most species, insects form the main part of the diet, with many specialising in wood-boring insects and their larvae and many others on ants or termites; some eat many seeds for much of the year, while others harvest sap by drilling 'wells' into trees; many supplement an insect diet with seeds and fruits; some species kill nestlings of other hole-nesting birds such as tits and feed them to their young

VOICE: calls are varied, including sharp, short sounds, piercing cries, churring, chattering, rattling, whinnying, laughing or crowing notes; main territorial and mate-seeking advertising is done non-vocally, by drumming rapidly with the bill on a dead branch or other resonant surface

MIGRATION: most species are sedentary; some make altitudinal or other movements, mainly in response to food shortages, including irregular dramatic mass irruptions; a few north temperate species are strongly migratory

CONSERVATION STATUS: one species, the Imperial Woodpecker, *Campephilus imperialis*, is Critically Endangered (Possibly Extinct); two species, the Ivory-billed Woodpecker, *C. principalis*, and Okinawan Woodpecker, *Dendrocopos noguchii*, are Critically Endangered; three species, the Speckle-chested Piculet, *Picumnus steindachneri*, Varzea Piculet, *P. varzeae*, and Kaempfer's Woodpecker, *Celeus obrieni*, are Endangered; six species, the Fernandina's Flicker, *Colaptes fernandinae*, the Helmeted Woodpecker, *Dryocopus galeatus*, Andaman Woodpecker, *Dryocopus hodgei*, the Sulawesi Pygmy Woodpecker, *Picoides ramsayi*, the Great Slaty Woodpecker, *Mulleripicus pulverulentus* and the White-bellied Piculet, *Picumnus spilogaster*, are Vulnerable; 20 species are Near Threatened

Among the most distinctive of all bird families, woodpeckers – at least those in the subfamily of typical or 'true' woodpeckers – are the most familiar of all tree-climbing and wood-chiselling birds. The true woodpeckers occur right across the world, though they are absent from Madagascar, Australasia, Antarctica and oceanic islands. In addition to this large subfamily, Picinae, containing all but four of the family's 33 genera and 186 species (86% of the total) there are two smaller subfamilies: the wrynecks, Jynginae, with just two species in a single genus, *Jynx* and the diminutive piculets, Picumninae, with 29 species in three genera.

The wrynecks, with one species, the Northern Wryneck, *Jynx torquilla*, breeding right across Europe and northern and central

Asia and wintering in Africa and southern Asia, and the other, the Rufous-breasted Wryneck, *J. ruficollis*, confined to sub-Saharan Africa, are the most different, and probably branched off from the rest of the family very early in its evolution. Only a little larger than a sparrow, these birds have a cryptic, bark-like plumage pattern of intricately mottled, blotched and spotted browns, buffs, greys and black. Like piculets they lack the stiffened tail feathers of the rest of the family, that serve as a prop when climbing, and like the piculets and ground-dwelling species of woodpecker, they have the ancestral unmodified zygodactyl foot plan, Wrynecks do not often cling to trees, instead perching sideways on branches and hopping along them like a songbird, and spending much of their time on the ground, which is where they find most of their food. Their short bill is not strong enough for them to chisel out their own nest holes, and they rely instead on natural tree holes or those abandoned by other woodpeckers. They sometimes steal nest holes from other birds, including tits, flycatchers, sparrows and even starlings and other woodpeckers, and may also take eggs and nestlings to eat or feed to their own young (as do some other woodpecker species such as Great Spotted Woodpecker, *Dendrocopos major*, of Eurasia and the Red-headed Woodpecker, *Melanerpes erythrocephalus*, of North America). Feeding mainly on ground-dwelling ants, like many woodpeckers, wrynecks share the long tongue characteristic of the family, although not the barbs or bristles found in the others. A wryneck's tongue is in fact the longest tongue of any bird in the world in relation to its body size. The common name 'wryneck' and the specific name *torquilla* (Latin for 'little twister') derives from its habit (seen in both adults and young), when threatened by a predator, of stretching out the extraordinarily mobile neck and writhing the head while erecting the crown feathers and hissing, in imitation of a menacing snake. If picked up either by a persistent pursuing predator or, for instance, by a bird ringer (known in North America as a bird bander), it will often feign death. Such behaviour led to the bird being associated in ancient Greek and Rome with fertility rites involving a rotating wheel-like charm called a Iynx, on which the bird itself could be spread with its wings open: with its spelling transmuted to 'jynx' this is celebrated in the generic name *Jynx*, and the word has also come to signify 'bad luck' or a curse.

The piculets are tropical, almost all in the New World and in the genus *Picumnus*. All but one of the 25 American species of *Picumnus* have relatively restricted ranges in various parts of South America; the Olivaceous Piculet, *P. olivaceus*, is found in Central America as well as northeastern South America. In a separate genus, the Antillean Piculet, *Nesoctites micromegas*, is endemic to the Caribbean islands of Hispaniola and Gonave. There are just four Old World species. One is the sole non-American member of the genus *Picumnus*, the Speckled Piculet, *P. innominatus*, with a very extensive range in central and southern Asia, from Afghanistan east to China and south to Sumatra and northern Borneo. Two others, in the genus *Sasia*, are Asian, with more restricted ranges, while the sole African species is a member of the monotypic genus *Verreauxia*: the African Piculet, *V. africana*, of West and west-central Africa. All piculets are small, the great majority only 9–11 cm (3.5–4 in) long, and the smallest, the Bar-breasted Piculet, *Picumnus aurifrons*, just 7.5 cm (3 in). The Antillean Piculet is the odd one out, being the giant of the group, at up to 16 cm (over 6 in).

The 186 species of true woodpeckers have a considerable range in size, from diminutive species such as the Scarlet-backed Woodpecker, *Veniliornis callonotus*, only 13 cm (5 in) long, or the Philippine and Japanese pygmy woodpeckers, *Dendrocopos maculatus* and *D. kizuki*, both about 14 cm (5.5 in) and weighing just 18–33 g (0.6–11.6 oz), to the giants of the family. The biggest are the possibly extinct Ivory-billed Woodpecker, *Campephilus principalis,* up to 53 cm (21 in) and 570 g (20 oz), whose two races may possibly still occur in tiny numbers in southeast USA and Cuba, and the Imperial Woodpecker, *C. imperialis*, biggest of them all, at up to 60 cm (24 in) and a weight of perhaps as much as 650 g (23 oz) that is, or was, endemic to

ABOVE One of just three Old World piculets, this is a Rufous Piculet, *Sasia abnormis*, at Sepilok Forest Reserve, Borneo, Malaysia.

the pine/oak montane forests of northwest Mexico. The biggest of all Old World species is the Great Slaty Woodpecker, *Mulleripicus pulverulentus*, of southern and southeast Asia. This measures about 50 cm (20 in) long and may weigh up to 563 g (20 oz).

Nesting in tree holes, the great majority of species are birds of wooded habitats. These include a wide range of types, from vast, dark northern conifer forests and broadleaved or mixed temperate forests to open woodlands, savannahs, scrublands, bamboo forests and mangroves. A few species even thrive in grasslands and deserts, where they nest in holes they dig in the ground, in earth banks or in cacti. Occasionally, woodpeckers bore their nest holes in human-made structures such as earth huts, wooden buildings, fence-posts and telephone poles, while a few species do so in termite mounds on the ground or termite or ant nests in trees. Insects form the staple diet of most species but many also eat – and often cache – seeds or fruit.

Most species of woodpecker are sexually dimorphic to a degree. The main plumage features distinguishing the sexes – and also juveniles from adults – are the head pattern, often incorporating black-and-white stripes, and boldly contrasting, often bright red or yellow, crown, crest or undertail markings.

The large subfamily Picinae can be divided into several distinctive subgroups, or tribes. The first two tribes are both very small groups. The Nesoctitini contains just a single species, the Antillean Piculet, *Nesoctites micromegas*, endemic to the Caribbean islands of Hispaniola and Gonave. It is included within the main woodpecker subfamily Picinae rather than with the other piculets, to which it is less closely related. The tribe Hemicircini comprises two very small southern Asian species in a single genus, *Hemicircus*.

The Picini is a large tribe of 13 genera and 78 species, with representatives shared almost equally between the Old World (43 species) and New Worlds (35 species). The first member is an oddity, the sole member of its genus – the Ground Woodpecker, *Geocolaptes olivaceus*. This is a medium-sized specialised ant-eater with a grey head and brownish upperparts and mottled pinkish-

ABOVE This male Black Woodpecker, *Dryocopus martius*, distinguished by his more extensive scarlet crown, is at his nest hole in Finland.

red underparts. It lives in barren open rocky terrain in the uplands of South Africa and Lesotho, to as high as 2,100 m (6,900 ft), and nests and roosts in a tunnel it excavates in earth banks or among rocks. Next, and also endemic to Africa, is the large genus *Campethera*, with 11 species of small to medium sized, mainly greenish brown or yellowish green with much barring or spotting. Many of them live in open woodland and savannah, but some are found in denser forests. The following eight genera are almost all restricted to Asia. They include four species of colourful medium sized species forming the genus *Dinopium*. Known as flame-backed woodpeckers from the deep red and gold on their uppparts, they also sport a black-and-white striped head topped with a striking red crest. This plumage pattern and common name are echoed by a larger species in the next tribe, Campephilini. The 12 species in the

ABOVE The Green Woodpecker, *Picus viridis*, is often seen on lawns or grass fields, digging for ants, its main prey, with its powerful bill.

genus *Picus* are mainly medium-sized green and yellow birds, some with a conspicuous yellow crest, all but two restricted to Asia. The exceptions are the Green Woodpecker, *P. viridis*, familiar from its habit of feeding on ants in short grass, including garden lawns, which lives in Europe and southwest Asia, and the less well-known Grey-headed Woodpecker, *P. canus*, which is more patchily distributed in Europe, absent from Britain, Iberia and much of the Mediterranean and with most of its range in Asia, extending as far east as Japan. The three species in the genus *Mulleripicus* are all-black, grey-and-white or all grey with red on the head in males; the biggest of them, the Great Slaty Woodpecker, *M. pulverulentus*, is one of the world's largest woodpeckers. The seven species of *Dryocopus* have a very wide geographic range: there are four species in the New World, including the crow-sized Pileated Woodpecker, *D. pileatus*, found in Canada and parts of the USA, two in Asia, and just one in Eurasia, the Black Woodpecker, *D. martius*. This is the biggest member of the genus, with a range extending from western Europe to Japan. *Dryocopus* woodpeckers all have a red crest or crown and mostly are black with white on the underparts or as stripes on the head, neck or upper back, but the Black Woodpecker and the Andaman Woodpecker, *D. hodgei*, are all-black. One of the two largest genera in the Picini is Celeus, with 12 Neotropical species of small to medium-sized woodpeckers with mainly dark-barred reddish-brown plumage, with black-and-white or cream in some species, including the striking almost entirely cream Cream-coloured Woodpecker, *C. flavus*, of northern South America. The other largeish genus, also found only in the New World, and almost all in the Neotropics, is *Colaptes*, containing the 12 species of flickers and relatives. These are mainly medium-sized open-country dwellers that feed on the ground and nest in burrows they excavate in earth banks, termite mounds or large cacti or in holes in rocks, buildings or trees. Most have strongly barred sandy-brown upperparts and paler or whitish underparts that are barred or spotted with black. There are two species of flickers in North America, the Northern Flicker, *C. auratus*, with a huge range in open woodlands and farmland, from Alaska and Canada to Nicaragua and Cuba, and the Gilded Flicker, *C. chrysoides*, found in the US only in the southwest, and also in Mexico. The Andean Flicker, *C. rupicola*, manages to thrive at altitides of 2,000–5,000 m (6,560–16,400 ft).

The tribe Campephilini comprises four genera and 16 species. All but one genus are found in the Old World, with five species, divided between three genera, in southern Asia. The 11 New World species, all in the genus *Campephilus*, are large to very large mainly black-plumaged species and a big, prominent red crest (generally smaller and in some cases black rather than red in females). Seven of them are found in South America, with one species just extending into Central America, in Panama. Another occurs along the whole of the Central American isthmus and in Mexico, while the last two are the huge and probably extinct Imperial Woodpecker of Mexico, and the Ivory-billed Woodpecker of southeast USA and Cuba, mentioned above. The southern Asian representatives of this tribe include the striking Greater Flame-backed Woodpecker, *Chrysocolaptes lucidus*, which lives up to its name by having a deep crimson back, at least in some of its variably plumaged 14 races (which some authorities split into as many as seven species).

LEFT This photo of a female Great Spotted Woodpecker, *Dendrocopos major*, shows how long the fourth toe is when moved to a lateral position to maintain a secure grip.

RIGHT The Yellow-tufted Woodpecker, *Melanerpes cruentatus*, is widespread in southeast Brazil, eastern Paraguay and northeast Argentina.

Finally, another very large tribe, with 10 genera and 89 species, is the Melanerpini, with 60% of the total (53 species) in the New World and 40% (36 species) in the Old World. The genus *Sphyrapicus* contains four small North American species called sapsuckers, from their predilection for feeding on the sap of many species of trees, both conifers and broadleaves. They obtain this by drilling the trunks with many small holes (called 'sap wells') that fill up with the sugary and protein-rich sap. They are not alone in this habit: tree sap is also an important part of their diet for other North American members of this tribe, in the genus *Melanerpes*, as well as for a few Eurasian woodpeckers. *Melanerpes* is the largest genus in this tribe, with 23 species that are mostly very similar in appearance, with a red crown in males, reduced to the nape or absent in females, strongly barred black-and-white upperparts and pale buff underparts. The barred species are mostly found in Mexico, Central America, the Caribbean and South America, but there are three in the USA: the Gila Woodpecker, *M. uropygialis*, of southwestern deserts and the Red-bellied Woodpecker, *M. carolinus*, of eastern woodlands and also parks and gardens with trees. Two other North American species with simpler, bolder plumage patterns are the Red-headed Woodpecker, *M. erythrocephalus* and its black-and-white counterpart Lewis's Woodpecker, *M. lewis*. Another is the Acorn Woodpecker, *M. formicivorus*, a small, boldly marked, black, white and red species that stores acorns, a major food, by ramming them into funnel-shaped holes it drills in tree trunks, or sometimes in telephone poles other human-made wooden structures. Accumulated by small social groups, these form 'granaries' or 'larders' that may contain as many as 50,000 holes, whose contents are defended by all group members against rivals. Thirteen small species divided between four genera, *Dendropicos*, *Chloropicus*, *Mesopicos* and *Ipophilus*, are endemic to Africa: they typically have dull green backs and paler or strongly streaked or barred underparts and red on the head. The genus *Dendrocopos* is a large group of 22 species of small to medium sized pied woodpeckers found mainly in Asia, with several species also occurring in Europe. Two well-known Eurasian species are the Great Spotted and Lesser Spotted Woodpeckers, *D. major* and *D. minor*.

They have vast ranges, from Britain and Portugal to the Far East, and also extend marginally into northwest Africa.

The 12 species of small pied woodpeckers in the genus *Picoides* are almost entirely endemic to the New World; the single exception is the small Eurasian Three-toed Woodpecker, *P. tridactylus*, found from northern Europe right across northern Asia and also in high mountains to the south. Its close relative, the American Three-toed Woodpecker, *P. dorsalis*, until recently considered conspecific, also has a huge range extending right across the north of the North American continent and on high southern mountains, as far south in the USA as New Mexico. Other, more familiar North American members of the genus are the little Downy Woodpecker, *P. pubescens*, and the very similar, slightly bigger Hairy Woodpecker, *P. villosus*, which often visit bird feeders; the Downy Woodpecker even breeds in Central Park, in the heart of New York. The 14 species of *Veniliornis* are exclusively Neotropical. Small, with olive green upperparts and barred underparts, they include species at home in the Amazon, as well as others that live in the Andes.

True woodpeckers chisel into wood both to extract insect food hidden within and to excavate nest holes. Although they often seek out soft, decaying or dead wood, they also drill into hard, healthy, live wood. To carry out their arduous tasks, they have a strong, straight, usually rather long bill, powered by a very efficient system of muscles and tendons. In those species that do a lot of excavating, it is strengthened with longitudinal ridges and furnished with a tip shaped like that of a chisel. The powerful pecking action continually wears away the horny covering so that the tip maintains this shape.

Both the bill and the woodpecker's skull are specialised for withstanding the shock of repeated percussion. The front of the skull protrudes so that the impact of each blow does not drive the upper jaw upwards. Also, the hinge between the front of the skull and the upper mandible is folded inwards in such a way that when the bird is hammering, the bone experiences a tension rather than being compressed. This tension is counteracted by a special muscle lying beneath the cranium that acts as a shock absorber and protects the brain. To prevent the entry of damaging wood-dust and wood-chips, the nostrils are covered by small, tough feathers, and in some specialised woodpeckers are reduced to slits, protected by a ridge.

Among the most remarkable of all avian structures, the woodpecker's tongue is highly specialised, especially in those species that probe deeply for their food, whether into holes they drill in trees or into the nests of ants or termites. They need to have great control over the tongue, including the precise movements of its tip as they flick it in and out a long way beyond the bill tip. This is enabled by very long, specialised muscles sheathing the greatly elongated hyoid bones, which act to stiffen the flexible tongue when the muscles contract. The hyoids are so long that they wind right around the back of the woodpecker's skull, and over the top to meet in its frontal region; in particularly long-tongued species, they usually they enter the bill at the nostril cavity, but in some, they extend around the right eye instead. For trapping insect prey, glands provide sticky mucous secretions, and the tip of the tongue is furnished with several to many backward-pointing barbs. Several woodpeckers drink tree sap at particular seasons, but the sapsuckers that specialise for much of the time on this source of food have a shorter tongue with a brushlike tip for lapping up this nutritious liquid.

Woodpeckers have short legs that help them maintain their centre of gravity when tree climbing, and strong feet with powerful, strongly curved, sharp claws that help them grip onto the bark. The arrangement of the toes is modified in almost all species from the zygodactyl pattern into one known as ectropodactyl: when climbing or pecking they usually move the longer, rear-facing fourth toe up until it is sticking out to one side, to reduce the pulling force due to gravity, which is increased when pecking. The small hind toe is usually not of much use and several woodpeckers, including some of the flamebacks, *Dinopium*, as well as the three-toed *Picoides* species have lost it completely. Large species in the genera *Campephilus* and *Drycopus* have an elongated hind toe, directed forwards. Woodpeckers proceed up (though not down) tree trunks and branches (also along the ground) by a series of bipedal hops, so that for a fraction of a second their legs are not in contact with the bark and they are completely in the air. Except in wrynecks and piculets, the tail acts as a brace for maintaining balance, especially when the bird is hammering with its bill. It has strong, tough feathers, the central ones in particular stiffened, with rigid shafts. In many species the tail curls upwards at the tip, providing more of a surface area to press down onto the trunk. Woodpeckers have broad, rather rounded wings and most have a distinctly undulating flight action.

No woodpeckers have a well-developed song. Instead many species rely on the loud and far-carrying rattling sounds – called drumming – that they make by repeatedly striking the bill extremely rapidly on a hard surface, usually a hollow dead trunk or branch, but sometimes a human-made structure, ranging from wooden or metal posts, poles or buildings (including church towers).

Woodpeckers are of great importance for other wildlife through providing holes that when abandoned serve as nest sites for many other birds and various small mammals. They also perform a valuable service to people by eating many wood-boring insects and their larvae, which can cause considerable damage to commercial forestry.

TOUCANS AND BARBETS Ramphastidae

GENERA: 20   **SPECIES:** 120

LENGTH: toucans 30–65 cm (12–25.5 in); barbets 9–35 cm (3.5–14 in)

WEIGHT: toucans 95–860 g (3.3–30 oz); barbets 6–295 g (0.2–10.4 oz)

RANGE AND HABITAT: toucans only in Mexico, Trinidad, Central America and South America; barbets in sub-Saharan Africa (greatest diversity there), southern Asia, Central and South America; most toucans are restricted to forests, with many in lowland tropical forest, some only or mainly in montane forest, some also in gallery forest in savannahs, plantations, gardens; barbets in various habitats with dead trees for excavating nesting and roosting holes, from dense tropical rainforest to open woodland, scrub and even deserts with trees, as well as farmland and gardens

SOCIAL BEHAVIOUR: most seen singly or in pairs, but a few barbet species and some toucans are more social outside the breeding season, foraging in small groups or joining mixed-species flocks; mostly monogamous and strongly territorial; some African barbets and some toucans (*Pteroglossus* araçaris) breed cooperatively; some African barbets and one Asian barbet nest in colonies in a single tree, those of the former often made up of closely related species

NEST: most barbets and toucans nest in tree holes; barbets often excavate their own holes, but toucans rarely do, using natural holes or enlarging those made by woodpeckers or barbets; a few barbets and toucans excavate or take over holes in earth banks, while a few barbets use nest boxes, fence-posts or termite mounds

EGGS: 1–7 in barbets; 1–6 in toucans, white

INCUBATION: 12–19 days

FLEDGING PERIOD: 40–60 days in toucans; 17–46 days in barbets

FOOD: toucans eat mainly fruit, but also insects, spiders, scorpions and other invertebrates, frogs, toads, small lizards and snakes, small birds and their eggs and nestlings, or small mammals; barbets also mostly eat fruit (some species also taking buds, flowers and nectar) supplemented in some species by insects and other invertebrates and small vertebrates

VOICE: toucans utter a wide range of mainly unmusical sounds, including grunts, croaks, retching sounds, barks, rattles or yelps; non-vocal sounds include those made by bill-clattering or striking the bill against a branch, also loud rustling sounds made by the two modified outer primary wing feathers; barbets make sounds ranging from harsh squawks, nasal honks, chattering, rattling and grating sounds, to trills, popping noises and softer more melodic whistling or piping sounds; many species perform song duets; some also make non-vocal bill-snapping sounds

MIGRATION: generally sedentary; some species make seasonal altitudinal migrations and many respond to dearths or gluts of fruit supplies

CONSERVATION STATUS: one species, the Yellow-browed Toucanet, *Aulacorhynchus huallagae*, is Endangered; six species, the Channel-billed Toucan, *Ramphastos vitellinus*, Five-coloured Barbet, *Capito quinticolor*, Scarlet-banded Barbet, *C. wallacei*, Black-girdled Barbet, *C. dayi*, White-mantled Barbet, *Capito hypoleucus* and Zambian Barbet, *Lybius chaplini*, are Vulnerable; 12 species are Near Threatened

This family of mainly tropical birds comprises four subfamilies. The taxonomic treatment followed in this book begins with the subfamily Megalaiminae. This contains all but one of the 28 species of Asian barbets, in the single genus *Psilopogon*. The remaining species, the brown barbet, *Caloramphus fuliginosus*, is distinctive enough to merit placement in a subfamily of its own, the Caloramphinae. Next comes the subfamily Ramphastinae, uniting the five genera and 34 species of toucans, in the tribe Ramphastini, and the two tribes of American barbets, the Semnornithini, containing just two unusual species in a single genus *Semnornis*, and the Capitonini, comprising the remaining 15 species in two genera, *Capito* and *Eubucco*. Finally, the 41 species of African barbets in the subfamily Lybiinae are split between two tribes, the *Trachyphonini*, with a single genus Trachyphonus containing four species, and the Lybiini, with the remaining 37 species in nine genera.

The general account that follows deals with the toucans and barbets as two groups, rather than in the more complex taxonomic treatment outlined above, as they differ in appearance and lifestyle.

TOUCANS

The toucans are instantly distinguishable from all the barbets by virtue of their remarkable, massive, long, colourful, banana-shaped bill (the only other birds with which they might be confused in a zoo aviary or photograph by the uninitiated are hornbills, but these are found only in Africa and Asia, and their superficially similar bills, also evolved for reaching food items, mainly have a distinctive large casque on top. The toucan bill is laterally compressed and has a serrated cutting edge that helps the bird seize and manipulate food items, both fruit and insects or other animals. The tongue is long, up to 15 cm (6 in) long in the larger species, and unusually frayed at the sides, greatly increasing its surface area, which may help to increase its sensitivity as an organ of touch and taste when manipulating food. It also has a brushlike tip.

ABOVE The strong serrations on the cutting edges of the bill characteristic of the araçaris are clearly visible on this Collared Araçari, *Pteroglossus torquatus*.

ABOVE The Emerald Toucanet, *Aulacorrhynchus prasinus*, is the smallest member of the toucan family.

In some of the largest toucans in the genus *Ramphastos*, the bill may even be half the length of the body. Although the size of these impressive appendages compared with the relatively small, compact body makes them look top-heavy and in danger of falling over, the bill is actually lightweight, having a honeycomb-like interior, criscrossed by an intricate system of very thin bony struts that provide strength; in between these, the spaces are filled with a spongy tissue of keratin fibres. The length of the bill enables toucans to reach tree fruit at the otherwise inaccessible tips of small branches that are too thin to bear their weight. Furthermore, the birds can insert the bill deep into tree holes to find insects and other food, including the eggs and chicks of hole-nesting birds, and also to plunder the hanging nests of birds such as oropendolas. The bright colours and formidable size of the bill may even intimidate other birds, allowing toucans to ransack their nests unmolested or dominate other birds at fruiting trees. Another, recently discovered, function of their huge bill is in thermoregulation. Toco Toucans, *Ramphastos toco*, have been shown to use them like a radiator to dissipate heat by modifying the blood flow to the bill. Relative to the size of the bird's body, the bill is one of the largest such heat dispersers known in animals, rivalling the ears of elephants in effectiveness. Toucans may also use these versatile structures to assert dominance during jousting contests between rivals, sometimes grasping their opponent's bill and pushing until it is forced off its perch. Not all interactions using the bill are boisterous, though: mated pairs gently proffer food, held in the bill tip, to one another, and also indulge in mutual preening. Sometimes, a group of toucans will throw a piece of fruit from one to the other, each bird catching it deftly in the bill tip before passing it on to the next.

Toucans have a short, thick neck and rounded tail that often measures about half the length of the body but may equal its whole length in some of the smaller species of toucans known as araçaris (pronounced 'arassarees'). A distinctive feature, unique to toucans, is that their three rearmost tail vertebrae are fused, and attached to the others by a fluid-bearing ball-and-socket joint. This allows the birds to snap the tail forwards over the back so that it touches the head. They adopt this posture when roosting, when they resemble a ball of feathers. This may well protect them from discovery by

ABOVE The head feathers of the Curl-crested Araçari, *Pteroglossus beauhamaesii*, look as if they have been permed or lacquered.

ABOVE A Keel-Billed Toucan, *Ramphastos sulfuratus*, plucks a fruit from a twig, at Tikal, Guatemala.

predators. Smaller toucans often roost in tree cavities, either alone or in pairs, or in groups after the breeding season, while the large *Ramphastos* species usually sleep on branches.

The wings are small, suited only for relatively short flights within wooded habitats. When crossing a clearing or a river, a group of toucans often climb to the tops of trees then take off one after the other, forming a straggling line as they travel in single file. Larger species have a distinctive flap-glide action, and an undulating flight path; their flight is rather weak, and they may even fail to cross a wide river, soon losing height as they set out. Small toucans, however, especially some of the araçaris, have a more direct, fast flight with a whirring wing action. The legs are short and the feet strong, enabling the bird to move about with great agility, cling to vertical trunks or even hang from branches.

Toucans are among the most strikingly plumaged of all tropical birds, with patterns of bright green, red, blue, yellow and other colours – as well as black and white, especially in the large *Ramphastos* species (see below for details of the various subgroups). They also have strikingly coloured areas of bare skin around the eyes. Although a few species have a more or less unicoloured bill, that of most toucans has complex patterns in various permutations of yellow, orange, red, green, blue, black, white or cream. A distinctive feature is the narrow vertical band at the base of the bill, often in a contrasting colour.

The five genera of toucans form distinctive subgroups. The first genus, *Ramphastos*, with seven species, includes the largest toucans. Most are species of lowland forests or the lower slopes of mountains, though the Toco Toucan, *R. toco*, is unusual in being the only non-forest dweller among the whole family, inhabiting forest edges and areas of woodland, wooded savannah, plantations and orchards. This is the best-known of all toucans, familiar from its appearance as a logo in many places, including classic Guinness advertisements. The plumage of all species is mainly black on the crown, upperparts, hind body and tail, and white, orange or yellow from the throat to the breast, ending in a red band. These toucans also have a red undertail and a red, orange, yellow or white rump. All species have a much shorter tail than the other toucans. The bill of most species is largely black, usually with a narrow or broad yellow or greenish ridge along the top, but in some species it has a more complex pattern. The Keel-billed Toucan, *R. sulfuratus*, found from southern Mexico to Panama and extreme northern South America, has perhaps the most beautiful of all toucan bills, a lovely mixture of yellow, green, orange and blue intergrading into one another, contrasting with a red tip, an appearance celebrated in its alternative name of Rainbow-billed Toucan.

The genus *Aulacorhynchus* comprises the seven species of green toucanets, which live mainly in moist or wet montane forest. As the diminutive name 'toucanet' suggests, they are relatively small: indeed they include the smallest of all toucans, the Emerald Toucanet, *A. prasinus*, which is just 30–37 cm (12–14.5 in) long. This is the only very widespread species, with a huge range from Mexico to Bolivia. The other five have relatively far less extensive ranges within the northern half of South America. All six have almost entirely bright green plumage, with small areas of red, chestnut, violet, blue or yellow on the head, breast, rump, vent or tail. The bill is either black and yellow, black and maroon, or black and ivory. The four species of mountain toucans *Andigena* are much larger than the *Aulacorhynchus* toucanets, and occur in forests clothing the slopes of the Andes, from Colombia and Venezuela to Bolivia. All have dense, soft, loose plumage that is particularly effective at trapping an insulating layer of air, fitting them for life in their relatively cool, high-altitude habitats. They have a black cap and greenish-brown upperparts contrasting with blue-grey underparts, a yellow rump and red patches on the thighs, undertail and tailtip. The bill is mainly marked with bands of red, black and yellow or green.

A fourth group of six small species are the *Selenidera* toucanets. Four species are birds of lowland or hill forests of Amazonia, with one species in the Atlantic forest of southeast Brazil and one in Central America. They are unusual not only among the family but within the whole order Piciformes in their striking sexual dimorphism. Males have a black head and foreparts, while those areas in females are rufous or grey. The upperparts are green, duller and more olive than the green of *Aulacorhynchus* toucanets, and most species have tufted yellow, orange or tawny ear coverts, similarly coloured flank patches and a yellow collar.

The final genus, *Pteroglossus*, consists of 10 species of small to medium-sized toucans, called araçaris, the Portuguese name derived from a Tupi Indian word for these very colourful birds. Most are birds of lowland forests, and the genus ranges from Mexico to Paraguay. The head is chestnut or black and the wings green, but their most striking plumage features are the bands of yellow, red and/or black below. Their bills are also strikingly marked, mainly in yellow, orange, red or ivory with a black lower mandible, and the serrations are very apparent, being highlighted in black and ivory. One species, the Curl-crested Araçari, *P. beauharnaesii*, is distinguished by its odd, curly, shiny black feathers, resembling pieces of enamel or hard plastic, on the crown and black-spotted whitish cheeks. Another distinctive species, the Saffron Toucanet, *P. bailloni*, was formally accorded a genus of its own, *Baillonius*. Found mainly in the lowland Atlantic forests of Brazil, it has distinctively fluffy feathers with a very different, simple plumage pattern of olive-green upperparts and yellowish underparts, unmarked apart from a red rump, and a far less colourful bill.

ABOVE A Red-fronted Barbet, *Tricholaema diademata*, peers out of its nest hole with a berry for one of its nestlings, near Lake Baringo, Kenya.

BARBETS

Barbets are mainly tropical in distribution, with their greatest diversity in Africa, which contains just over half of all species. Some range into subtropical and even marginally into temperate regions. Most barbets live in woodlands and forests, although some are birds of the edges of these habitats and more open areas, including scrubland and gardens.

All are smaller than toucans, mostly a good deal smaller, at 15–23 cm (6–9 in) long; a very few are bigger, the largest reaching 35 cm (14 in), bigger than some small toucans, while most of the African tinkerbirds *Pogoniulus* are really tiny, at just 9 cm (3.5 in) long, and weighing as little as 6 g (0.2 oz). As with toucans, many species are renowned for the beauty of their colourful plumage, although a good number of African species are far duller. In most barbets the sexes look alike, though some show marked sexual dimorphism.

All species are compact, stout-bodied, almost neckless birds with a large head and a powerful, short, often conical, sharp-tipped bill. As well as being highly effective for dealing with fruit and insect food, it is used for excavating the birds' nest holes, typically in the dead wood of trees, in posts or in earth banks, but in some species in the nests of termites or ants. Most species have tough bristles around the gape of the bill and covering the nostrils. The common name of the family, derived from the Latin word for 'bearded' refers to this characteristic. In most African and American species the bristles are short and insignificant, but they are far more prominent in almost all Asian barbets: in some they are so long that they reach the tip of the bill or even extend slightly beyond it.

African barbets (subfamily Lybiinae) are found in forests, woodlands and arid open woodland and scrub throughout sub-Saharan Africa, except in the extreme south-western desert. There are

ABOVE The diet of the Red-and-Yellow Barbet, *Trachyphonus erythocephalus*, includes fruit, insects, small birds and edible household refuse.

ABOVE The Golden-fronted Barbet, *Psilopogon franklinii*, lives in montane forest at up to 2,700 m (8,800 ft), from the Himalayan foothills south to the Malaysian peninsula.

ABOVE These Toucan-barbets, *Semnornis ramphastinus*, are having a tug of war with their hefty bills over insect prey in Ecuador.

two groups: the majority of species (36, in eight genera) are arboreal, while the rest (just four species of *Trachyphonus* and a single one of *Tracholaemus*, the Yellow-billed Barbet, *T. purpuratus*) are ground feeders, with relatively long legs and tail. Most species have boldly patterned plumage, with various combinations of black, white, red or orange, and yellow, often featuring strikingly spotted or striped black-and-white upperparts, but others are much more cryptically coloured in various shades of brown. A few species have white or mainly white body and black upperparts, while two are black and red. Two genera, *Tricholaema* and *Lybius*, have a heavy bill with a large notch and one or two teeth that help their owners grip food items.

All but one of the 28 species of Asian barbets, in the subfamily Megalaiminae, are in a single genus, *Psilopogon*. The exception is the very distinctive, little-known Brown Barbet, *Calorhamphus fuliginosus*, found in the Thai-Malaysian peninsula, Sumatra and Borneo, which is given a subfamily (Caloramphinae) of its own. As its common name suggests, this is a dull plumaged bird, in contrast to the most of the other Asian barbets, which are bright green, with contrasting brilliant red, yellow and blue markings. These are overwhelmingly forest birds, with just one species, the widespread Coppersmith Barbet, *P. haemacephalus*, found in much of south and southeast Asia along forest edges and in scrub, plantations and gardens, even in cities. The Megalaiminae includes the largest of all barbets, the Great Barbet, *P. virens*, which is bigger and heavier than some small toucans.

American barbets (almost all in the subfamily Capitoninae) are all birds of humid forests, in various parts of Central and South America. Of the three genera, the most diverse is *Capito*, with 11 species. One species is olive green and yellow with a red crown, and the rest have combinations of black, white, red or orange and yellow, often with bold black streaks or spots below. The four species of *Eubucco* are gaudily attired in green, red, blue and yellow, with a bright yellow bill. The third genus, *Semnornis*, contains two particularly plump and unusual species with restricted ranges, the Prong-billed Barbet, *S. frantzii*, in Costa Rica and western Panama and the Toucan-barbet, *S. ramphastinus*, on the Andean slopes of part of western Colombia and Ecuador. They are distinguished from all other members of the barbet and toucan family by their unusual bill structure: the tip of the upper mandible has a tooth-like projection just behind where the lower mandible juts up past the upper mandible. This 'tooth' fits into a deep cleft in the tip of the lower mandible. It appears to be a very secure arrangement for gripping food items or scissoring chunks out of fruits. This pair of unusual species are placed in a subfamily (Semnornithinae) of their own.

Although the largest species can appear sluggish and cumbersome, many barbets are agile, especially when feeding, restlessly moving about through the foliage and hanging from small branches. They proceed by hopping on their rather short, strong legs. Their strong feet have the zygodactyl arrangement of toes and, like woodpeckers, they are able to cling onto and climb about on the trunks and branches of trees. They often use the tail as a support when doing so, although its feathers are not stiffened as in woodpeckers and other specialised tree climbers. Barbets eat mainly fruit, although most supplement this with insects and other invertebrates, especially during the breeding season, and some species also include lizards, nestlings of other birds and other small vertebrates in their diet. The nestlings are fed on a mixture of fruit and animal food or exclusively on the latter.

The songs of many barbets, though most intense in the breeding season, are often heard throughout the year and in many species consist of monotonously repeated, unmusical sounds that are very loud for the size of the bird. Duetting between members of a pair or chorus singing by cooperative breeding groups is a very important method of communication in African barbets of the genus *Trachyphonus* and *Lybius*. They are complex and melodic, with male and female singing different parts that are so perfectly synchronised that they sound as if they come from a single bird. These performances seem to be important in coordinating territorial defence, and for maintaining the dominant pair's hierarchy as well as ensuring its synchronisation of breeding.

ORDER CORACIIFORMES

Most members of this order are confined to the Old World, although there are many members of the kingfisher family in New Guinea and other nearby islands, two species of roller and three of bee-eaters in Australasia, and two families (the todies and motmots), plus a small number of kingfishers, endemic to the New World tropics.

Here, we include seven families in this order: those of the rollers (Coraciidae), ground rollers (Brachypteraciidae), the monotypic Cuckoo-roller (Leptosomidae), kingfishers (Alcedinidae), todies (Todidae), motmots (Momotidae), and Bee-eaters (Meropidae). The monotypic Hoopoe (Upupidae) and wood-hoopoes (Phoeniculidae) were traditionally included in this order, along with the hornbills (Bucerotidae), but are now judged to deserve an order of their own (Bucerotiformes), as in this book.

Clearly, not all the seven coraciiform families listed above are each other's relatives, but no consensus seems to have been reached in subdividing them. Recent molecular analysis suggests that only six of these nine families should remain in the order. The rollers (Family Coraciidae) and ground rollers (Family Brachypteraciidae) are each other's closest relatives, and, these in turn are both related to the bee-eaters (Family Meropidae). The kingfishers (Family Alcedinidae), todies (Family Todidae) and motmots (Family Momotidae) form another group of close relatives. The Cuckoo Roller, *Leptosoma discolor*, is not closely related to any of the others, being a 'living fossil', a relict of a family known from fossils in Europe and North America, with its restricted range on Madagascar and the Comoro Islands. It has therefore been given an order of is own (Leptosomatiformes).

Features all these families have in common include the structure of the palate and leg muscles, and the anatomy of the feet. Most have four toes, with the forward-facing three in a syndactyl arrangement (with the inner and middle toes fused for the first half of their length and the middle joined to the outer one for half their length), although in some kingfishers there are only three toes altogether. Most nest in holes or other cavities in trees, in banks of soil or sand or in the ground.

BEE-EATERS Meropidae

GENERA: 3   **SPECIES:** 27

LENGTH: 17–35 cm (6.5–14 in) including the elongated central tail feathers of many species

WEIGHT: 13–93 g (0.5–3.3 oz)

RANGE AND HABITAT: Old World and Australasia, in warm climates; most species in open country of various types, including savannah, grassland with scattered trees, thickets and desert margins; several species in forest clearings and forest edge; some usually near water; Red-bearded and Blue-bearded Bee-eaters, *Nyctyornis*, mainly in forest interior

SOCIAL BEHAVIOUR: except for bearded bee-eaters and some of the other forest-dwelling species, which live mainly as isolated pairs, they are highly sociable, often foraging together and usually roosting and nesting in colonies; mostly monogamous; colonial species are cooperative breeders

NEST: a nest chamber at the end of a tunnel in an earth bank or cliff, sand dune, or in some species in flat ground, lined with pellets of regurgitated insect remains

EGGS: 2–4 in tropical species, up to 7 in Eurasian ones, white

INCUBATION: 18–23 days

FLEDGING PERIOD: 27–32 days

FOOD: flying insects, especially wasps and bees, also dragonflies, butterflies, ants, termites, beetles, cicadas, crickets and grasshoppers

VOICE: frequent soft, rolling contact calls; the two *Nyctyornis* bearded bee-eaters have harsher calls

MIGRATION: tropical forest species are mainly sedentary, open-country species are partially or completely migratory

CONSERVATION STATUS: one species, the Blue-moustached Bee-eater, *Merops mentalis*, is Near Threatened

ABOVE One of the strongholds of the European Bee-eater, *Merops apiaster*, is Spain, where these two were photographed.

These graceful, intensely colourful and highly aerial birds delight birdwatchers across most of the warmer parts of the Old World – in southern Europe, Africa and southern Asia – as well as in Australia and New Guinea. There are only three genera. The two species of *Nyctyornis* are the largest in the family, up to the size of a large thrush, with a particularly sturdy bill that has an arched, ridged and grooved culmen, and nostrils that are protected by feathers. The Red-bearded Bee-eater, *N. amictus*, is found from southern Myanmar and Thailand to the Malay peninsula, Sumatra and Borneo, while the even larger Blue-bearded Bee-eater, *N. athertoni*, has a far greater range, from western India to Indochina and Hainan, China. There is just a single species in the second genus, *Meropogon*: the Purple-bearded Bee-eater, *M. forsteni*, endemic to the island of Sulawesi. Both this and the two *Nyctyornis* species are forest dwellers, and both have long throat feathers and shorter ones on the neck sides that the bird can erect to form a ruff.

The rest of the family, 24 species in total, are all members of the genus *Merops*. Most are about the size of a European starling *Sturnus vulgaris* or a thrush *Turdus*, while a few are smaller. They are overwhelmingly African in distribution: 20 species breed there, of which 15 are endemic to the African continent, two almost so (the Olive Bee-eater, *M. superciliosus*, whose range extends to Madagascar, and the White-throated Bee-eater, *M. albicollis*, also breeding in Yemen), and the other two (the Blue-cheeked Bee-eater, *M. persicus*, and the European Bee-eater, *M. apiaster*) have the main part of their extensive range in west and central Asia, and in the case of the last named species, also in southern and central Europe. The Green Bee-eater, *M. orientalis*, occurs in a wide belt across Africa from the southern Sahara south to South Sudan, and also from Egypt and the Arabian Peninsula across southern Asia east to Thailand. Just two *Merops* species are exclusive to Asia, while one breeds there and east to New Guinea, and just one, the Rainbow Bee-eater, *M. ornatus*, mainly in Australia (also in south-eastern New Guinea).

All bee-eaters have a streamlined shape, with a slender body and a fairly large head (though not as big relative to the body as that of a kingfisher or roller) on a short neck. All feed on flying insects caught in the air. They have a distinctively shaped bill – long, sharply pointed and decurved, and relatively slender, though more robust in the two *Nyctyornis* species, the Black-headed Bee-eater, *Merops breweri*, and the Northern and Southern Carmine Bee-eaters, *M. nubicus* and *M. nubicoides*. This serves as a pair of forceps for seizing the prey in its tip, which is also where small insects are crushed and then swallowed without landing. Bee-eaters carry larger prey one at a time to a branch or other hard perch to deal with before eating them or feeding them to young; they rub the bodies of larger bees and wasps on the perch to remove the sting, and beat other large insects, such as butterflies and dragonflies, against the hard surface to detach the wings.

The carmine bee-eaters are frequently seen hitching a ride on large grassland birds or mammals, benefiting not only from saving energy but from the insects disturbed from the vegetation by their 'mount'. Animals used in this way include the Kori Bustard, the Ostrich and various other birds and mammals such as zebras, camels, antelopes, cattle and donkeys, and the bird will also follow vehicles for the same reason. These beautiful bee-eaters are also especially attracted to bush fires, where they take easy pickings from the concentrations of grasshoppers and other insects fleeing from the flames.

The wings vary considerably in shape between species, according to habitat and lifestyle. Those living in open country have wings that are almost triangular in shape, with a pointed tip. These species are wonderful to watch in flight, buoyant and graceful as they glide and wheel about overhead. They make fast, tight twists and turns when chasing aerial insect prey, which may include dragonflies, beetles, flying ants or termites and locusts as well as the bees (and wasps) that make up the bulk of the diet for many species, and give the family its common name. Their strong flight helps several species migrate long distances. The wings are proportionally shorter and more rounded in forest-dwelling bee-eaters, including the two *Nyctyornis* species from south Asia, and in various small species living among dense vegetation such as reed beds, tall grasses or bushes. These all tend to be solitary breeders, with each pair defending a territory, and also sedentary.

ABOVE One of two bee-eater species endemic to Southeast Asia, this is a Blue-throated Bee-eater, *Merops viridis*, in Luzon, Philippines.

In most species, the central two tail feathers are elongated into short, sharply pointed streamers that appear as a projecting spike. The Swallow-tailed Bee-eater, *M. hirundineus*, of Africa differs from the rest of the family in having a forked tail, as suggested by its common and specific names. These projections do not appear to have an aerodynamic function; rather, they may help the birds recognise other members of their own species or provide a measure of fitness when assessing a mate.

The legs are very short, with relatively weak feet that have all three forward-facing toes unable to spread on the perch, the outer two being joined at their base, and small, curved, sharp claws. Although they highly adapted for life in the air, bee-eaters do spend a fair amount of time perched, watching for signs of prey, resting or roosting, and sometimes land on the ground, where they are fond of sunbathing. The shortness of their legs means that they must move about with a shuffling gait, but they can run fast when in their nest burrows.

The dazzling plumage of most species includes striking patterns in various combinations of bright green, blue, red, chestnut or yellow; most have thick black eye-stripes. Several species differ from this typical appearance. As their common names indicate, the two *Nyctyornis* species – the Red-bearded Bee-eater, *N. amictus*, and Blue-bearded Bee-eater, *N. athertoni* – are largely green, with differently coloured long, shaggy 'beards'. In addition to a red 'beard' the crown of the former species is an intense, glossy lilac colour in males (restricted to a small patch in females), while both sexes of the latter species have a bright azure blue 'beard' and forehead. Other species are patterned in purplish blue, deep wine red, black or brilliant azure, while the pair of carmine bee-eaters and the Rosy Bee-eater, *M. malimbicus*, are among the most spectacular of all African birds, with the body of the former and the underparts of the latter glowing carmine-pink, a colour rarely found in birds. In most species the sexes look alike or similar, with males generally brighter and longer tailed.

Most open-country species are very social throughout the year and are generally very vocal. Pairs and group members of *Merops* bee-eaters repeatedly keep in contact with liquid rolling or purring calls that are very pleasing to the human ear and carry fair distances. Often the first sign of an approaching flock is their collective sound, as it can be heard long before the birds themselves are seen, for instance from migrants high overhead. These mellifluous sounds contrast strikingly with the calls of the two *Nyctyornis* species, which are harsh and croaking.

In West Africa, Rosy Bee-eaters nest in huge colonies, tunnelling into sandbars exposed as the water level falls in major rivers. By contrast, another African endemic, the Little Bee-eater, *M. pusillus*, is a solitary nester that often bores into the sloping roof of a deep Aardvark burrow. In the European Bee-eater, the process of digging out the nest takes a pair from 10 to 20 days, and in harder earth, their bill is noticeably worn away at the tip by about 2 mm (0.08 in), although it will regrow. Sometimes, a pair can manage to excavate almost 40 cm (16 in) of tunnel in a single day.

ABOVE This breeding colony of Southern Carmine Bee-eaters, *Merops nubicoides*, is in a steep sandy riverbank in Zambia, Africa.

The nest tunnel is usually between 1 and 3 m (3.3 and 10 ft) long. A blackish carpet of regurgitated hard insect parts builds up and forms a lining that can almost bury the clutch of shiny, porcelain-like, almost round white eggs. The colonial breeders have complex family lives, with up to eight adults (the nesting pair and related adults) bringing food to the nestlings.

ROLLERS Coraciidae

GENERA: 2   **SPECIES:** 12

LENGTH: 25–40 cm (10–16 in)

WEIGHT: 82–214 g (3–7.5 oz)

RANGE AND HABITAT: southern Europe, Africa, western and southern Asia, Australasia; open woodland, forest edge, savannah and a few species within or at edges of lowland rainforest

SOCIAL BEHAVIOUR: solitary or in pairs for much of the time, but on migration they may form large flocks; monogamous, highly territorial; the Blue-bellied Roller, *Coracias cyanogaster*, may breed cooperatively

NEST: in a hole or other cavity in a tree; some species may also use crevices in cliffs or the walls of buildings

EGGS: 2–6, white

INCUBATION: 18–20 days

FLEDGING PERIOD: 25–30 days

FOOD: mainly insects, especially big ones such as large beetles, cockroaches and grasshoppers, scorpions and other invertebrates; also some small vertebrates, including lizards, small snakes, rodents and small or young birds

VOICE: harsh cawing, chacking and rattling notes in *Coracias* rollers; more limited range in *Eurystomus* species, including squawks and guttural sounds

MIGRATION: most species are sedentary, but the European Roller, *C. garrulus*, migrates from southern Europe and Asia to winter in much of Africa south of the Sahara; populations of the Dollarbird, *Eurystomus orientalis*, breed in northern China and eastern Australia and winter in Southeast Asia and Indonesia; and the Broad-billed Roller, *E. glaucurus*, migrates within Africa

CONSERVATION STATUS: one species, the Purple Roller, *Eurystomus azureus*, is Near Threatened

These are birds of warm climates, restricted to the Old World and Australasia, with most species in Africa, fewer in Asia and just one in Australasia (though not Tasmania and New Zealand). Their common name refers to the dramatic aerobatic rolling and diving displays that some species perform during courtship, for pair bonding, and especially to defend their territory.

There are just two genera. Birds in the first, *Coracias*, are sometimes called 'true rollers' and they include eight of the 12 species in the family. They are rather crow-like in shape, with a strong bill and similar harsh, raucous calls: the name of this genus,

and of the Family Coraciidae and Order Coraciiformes, comes from the Latin word meaning 'raven-like'. Although not particularly close to ravens (members of the huge order of perching birds, Passeriformes), rollers and the other families in the Coraciiformes do appear to be related to that order. Five species are endemic to Africa, (the Rufous-crowned Roller, *C. naevius*, Racquet-tailed Roller, *C. spatulatus*, Lilac-breasted Roller, *C. caudatus*, Abyssinian Roller, *C. abyssinicus*, and Blue-bellied Roller, *C. cyanogaster*), while one, the European Roller, *C. garrulus*, breeds from Iberia and North Africa across southern and east-central Europe and the

ABOVE This Lilac-breasted Roller, *Coracias caudatus*, tosses a locust in the air before swallowing it whole.

slight hook. The wings are rather broad but also quite long, and rollers are strong fliers. The tail of most species is square-ended or slightly notched, but four African species of *Coracias* have long projecting tail streamers; in one, the Racquet-tailed Roller, these have an enlarged spoon-shaped tip.

The four broadbilled rollers of the genus *Eurystomus* are similar in shape but have a much shorter bill that is very broad at the base and longer wings suiting them for their more aerobatic flight. Two species inhabit Africa. One, the Blue-throated Roller, *E. gularis*, is restricted to West and west-central Africa and the other, the Broad-billed Roller, *E. glaucurus*, is far more widespread in Africa and occurs too in Madagascar. The best-known species, the Dollarbird (so-called because of the coin-sized whitish or pale blue markings on its wings), *E. orientalis*, is widespread in southern Asia and Australasia. The Purple Roller, *E. azureus*, is restricted to the north Moluccas.

Rollers have beautiful brilliantly coloured plumage, in various combinations of blues, turquoise, pink, lilac, rich brown and cinnamon, with areas of black and white in some species. The two Asian/Australasian *Eurystomus* species are far more uniform in appearance, almost entirely dark purplish or greenish blue in the Dollarbird and glossy purplish blue in the Purple Roller. The bill is blackish in the *Coracias* species, bright yellow in African *Eurystomus* rollers and brilliant red in the other two members of that genus. The sexes look alike.

Coracias species hunt for their food – large insects and lizards or other small vertebrates – mainly by using the 'watch-and-wait' technique. They have a number of favoured perches, in a treetop, on a fence, or on an overhead wire, on which they perch, often for long periods, and scan their surroundings for prey, rather like outsized shrikes. And like those unrelated birds, too, once they have spotted suitable prey, they drop or fly down to seize it. *Eurystomus* rollers also hunt in this way at times, but they concentrate more on flying insects, catching them deftly in the air, assisted by the wide gape of their broad bill.

Middle East to central Asia, and winters in Africa. The remaining two are the widespread Indian Roller, *C. benghalensis*, which – despite its common name – occurs from eastern Iraq across to the Indian subcontinent and Sri Lanka, and then east as far as south-central China, and the Purple-winged (or Sulawesi) Roller, *C. temminckii*, endemic to the large Indonesian island of Sulawesi and some of its offshore islands.

These are sturdily built birds, mostly about the size of a town pigeon. They have a large head on a short sturdy neck, and a strong bill. The legs are short and the feet, which have the two inner front toes connected, are rather weak and used mainly for perching: the birds spend a lot of time perched in trees, on wires, rocks or other vantage points, and usually only make clumsy hops on the ground. The shortish bill is strong and powerful and ends with a

GROUND ROLLERS Brachypteraciidae

GENERA: 4   **SPECIES:** 5

LENGTH: 24–47 cm (9.5–18.5 in)

WEIGHT: 75–215 g (2.6–7.6 oz)

RANGE AND HABITAT: Madagascar; four species in tropical and subtropical rainforest; the Long-tailed Ground Roller, *Uratelornis chimaera*, in sub-arid thorn scrub and deciduous woodland

SOCIAL BEHAVIOUR: solitary for most of the year, in pairs or family groups during the breeding season and after the young fledge; appear to be monogamous and territorial

NEST: all but one species excavate a burrow in the ground with a nest chamber at its end, a shallow scrape covered with pellets of earth and dry leaves; the exception is the Short-legged Ground Roller, *Brachypteracias leptosomus*, which nests in tree cavities

EGGS: 1–4 (usually 2), white

INCUBATION: at least 18 days and 22–26 days in the Scaly Ground Roller, *Geobiastes squamiger*, and the Short-legged Ground Roller, respectively

FLEDGING PERIOD: about 18 days in the Scaly Ground Roller; maybe as many as 30 days in the Short-legged Ground Roller

FOOD: mainly insects; also other invertebrates and small vertebrates

VOICE: generally silent except during the breeding season, when pairs utter far-carrying territorial calls; these consist of low, guttural sounds in the four rainforest species and soft hooting or chuckling sounds in the Long-tailed Ground Roller; various other calls include soft whooping, clucking or croaking contact calls and harsh hisses when alarmed

MIGRATION: sedentary

CONSERVATION STATUS: three species, the Short-legged Ground Roller, *Brachypteracias leptosomus*, Scaly Ground Roller, *Geobiastes squamiger*, and Long-tailed Ground Roller, *Uratelornis chimaera*, are Vulnerable; one species, the Rufous-headed Ground Roller, *Atelornis crossleyi*, is Near Threatened

This very small family of just five species of largely terrestrial birds is endemic to Madagascar. All species are extremely wary, skulking and difficult to see and there is much still to learn about their biology. The tree nest of the Short-legged Ground Roller, *Brachypteracias leptosomus*, in a genus of its own, was not known to ornithologists until 1996 and came as a surprise, as the other four species all nest in burrows in the ground.

Ground rollers spend much of the daytime roosting or resting in dense cover, becoming active as dusk approaches and also in the

ABOVE Despite its colourful plumage, the Pitta-like Ground Roller, *Atelornis pittoides*, is very secretive and usually hard to see.

ABOVE The Long-tailed Ground Roller, *Uratelornis chimaera*, has a very restricted range in the spiny forest of southwest Madagascar.

early morning. Then they can be seen to be sturdily built, with a large head, big eyes and a short, stout bill. The relatively long tongue has a brushlike tip, presumably helping the bird to grasp its invertebrate prey. The tail is graduated and in all but one species about as long as the body: the exception is the aptly named Long-tailed Ground Roller, *Uratelornis chimaera*, the sole member of its genus, in which the tail is over two-thirds the bird's total length. The wings are generally short and quite rounded, and all species generally fly but little, preferring to freeze or run away if alarmed. Ground rollers have strong legs, which are long in all species except for the Short-legged Ground Roller, which spends more time perching and also has rather longer wings. The toes have a zygodactyl arrangement, with the first and fourth toes pointing outwards while those of the second and third toes face inwards.

Compared with the brightly plumaged rollers (Family Coraciidae, see p. 175), ground rollers are, with one exception, duller in appearance. The exception is, as its common and specific names suggest, the Pitta-like Ground Roller, *Atelornis pittoides*, which although not as brilliantly coloured as a pitta (see p. 200), has a complex pattern of cobalt blue, black and white on the head and breast, rich rufous and buff on the neck and flanks, a white underbody, and mainly bronzy green upperparts. The Rufous-headed Ground Roller *A. crossleyi* has a mainly deep rufous head and underparts, becoming lighter on the belly, contrasting with a white-streaked black crescent on the throat and mainly dark green upperparts and tail. The Short-legged Ground Roller and Scaly Ground Roller *Geobiastes squamiger* have mainly green and bronze upper body and tail, with the head and underparts white with bold blackish or brown bars (in the former) or crescents (in the latter). The Long-tailed Ground Roller is intricately streaked and mottled brown, rufous, fawn and black above, and on the tail, with a striking black and chestnut eye patch and breastband and white underparts. Females are somewhat smaller in the Short-legged and Long-tailed species, and with a shorter tail in the latter.

The Long-tailed Ground Roller is the only member of the family to live in the west of Madagascar, where it occupies a small area in the south-west of the island. All the others are found in the eastern half of Madagascar, although they are far more widespread than the Long-tailed species, occurring from near the northern tip to the far south.

The prey of these birds consists mainly of insects, both adult and larval, including butterflies, caterpillars, grasshoppers, wasps and praying mantises, but they also eat a wide range of other invertebrates, such as spiders, millipedes, woodlice, snails, slugs and earthworms, and some small vertebrates such as chameleons, geckos, small snakes and frogs.

Ground rollers forage alone or in pairs, usually standing alert for any sign of prey, often for long periods, before rummaging in leaf litter for insects or chasing them across the ground. They also clamber about on logs or through thick undergrowth and sometimes leap up to seize an insect from a branch or foliage. The Short-legged Ground Roller is the exception in foraging mainly in trees and tall shrubs. It perches on a branch to scan for prey, and usually makes a short flight to snatch it from a branch or foliage or seize it in the air.

TODIES Todidae

GENERA: 1   **SPECIES:** 5

LENGTH: 10–11.5 cm (4–4.5 in)

WEIGHT: 5–7.5 g (0.17–0.26 oz)

RANGE AND HABITAT: Greater Antilles islands of Cuba (and some small offshore islands), Hispaniola and Gonave Island, Jamaica and Puerto Rico; varied wooded habitats with dense undergrowth, from rainforest and deciduous dry forest to pine forest, plantations, semi-desert scrub and mangroves, from sea level to highlands (up to 3,200 m/10,500 ft for the Narrow-billed Tody, *Todus angustirostris*)

SOCIAL BEHAVIOUR: mostly singly or in pairs; monogamous and territorial

NEST: in a chamber at the end of a short burrow excavated by both the male and female, usually in a low earth bank

EGGS: 1–4, white

INCUBATION: about 21–22 days

FLEDGING PERIOD: 19–20 days for the Puerto Rican Tody, *T. mexicanus*

FOOD: a great variety of insects and their eggs and larvae; also other small invertebrates, such as earthworms, millipedes and spiders

VOICE: all but one species frequently give nasal, buzzing calls; the main call of the Cuban Tody, *T. multicolor*, is a soft, rolling trill; todies also make non-vocal sounds – wing rattling (similar to guttural vocal throat-rattling) and bill-snapping

MIGRATION: sedentary, although the Narrow-billed Tody may make altitudinal movements

CONSERVATION STATUS: none threatened

ABOVE A pair of Broad-billed Todies, *Todus subulatus*, take a rest from digging out their nest in an earth bank in the Dominican Republic.

Endemic to the Greater Antillean islands of the Caribbean, the five species of tody all look extremely similar. Classified in the single genus *Todus*, these are tiny insectivorous forest birds with brilliant green head and upperparts, a bright crimson throat patch that they puff out when calling, a narrow white 'moustache' and white, grey, yellow and pink underparts. The extent and position of the different underpart colours and the presence or absence of a blue patch below the ear coverts distinguishes each species. The Cuban Tody, *T. multicolor*, lives only in Cuba and the Isle of Pines, the Jamaican Tody, *T. todus*, is restricted to Jamaica, and the Puerto Rican Tody, *T. mexicanus*, is found on Puerto Rico. Hispaniola (divided between Haiti and the Dominican Republic) is home to two species: the Broad-billed Tody, *T. subulatus*, lives at low altitudes, and its range also includes neighbouring Gonave island, while the Narrow-billed Tody, *T. angustirostris*, is the scarcest of the five, restricted to higher altitudes, in moss forests at 1,000–3,200 m (3,300–10,500 ft).

With a big head, long, slender, pointed bill, an even more compact, almost spherical body, short broad wings and a very short tail, todies look rather like miniature kingfishers. Their rapid darting flights (sometimes making a whirring sound), often restless bobbing action and brief hovering as well as their brilliant semi-iridescent plumage also recall hummingbirds. They are, however, thought to be most closely related to the motmots (Family Momotidae, see p. 179). The bill is flattened from top to bottom, and edged with serrations that are microscopic in adults but visible to the naked eye in nestlings. Motmots, too, have serrations on their bill, but these are more substantial than those of todies, and motmots also differ strikingly in that all but one species has a long tail, with each of the elongated outer pair of feathers ending in a racquet shape. The exception is the Tody Motmot, *Hylomanes momotula*, whose common name may be an accurate reflection of an evolutionary position as the closest living relative of the todies. Todies' legs are very small and, as with most other members of the Order Coraciiformes, the third and fourth toes are partly united at their bases (syndactylous).

Todies spend much time perching beneath the canopy, with their bill pointing upwards at an angle, scanning the foliage above for any sign of a meal, usually one of many kinds of insect, or sometimes a millipede, spider or other invertebrate, or perhaps a little lizard. When they spot suitable prey, they make brief, very fast, upward flights to sweep it off the underside of foliage with a sideways movement of the bill. At times, they will also approach from above to take the prey from the upper surface of a leaf, and sometimes from a branch or tree trunk. These engaging and highly energetic little birds often call almost constantly, for instance when feeding, during courtship or territorial chases, or entering the nest burrow, with very distinctive buzzing 'beep' calls. During chases, todies also make loud rattling or explosive 'cracking' sounds with their wings, similar to the display sounds made by the unrelated passerine family of manakins (Family Pipridae, see p. 205).

A pair of todies usually dig out a new nesting chamber each year. Male and female alternate bouts of digging, thrusting their long strong bill into the bank to chisel out the soil, and scraping out the debris with their tiny feet. Unusual sites have included crab burrows in Cuba. Tody nest burrows themselves are attractive to other creatures, and the rightful owners may be turfed out of their homes by lizards, tree frogs, scorpions, cave crickets and stinging ants. On Puerto Rico, they are vulnerable to formidable whip scorpions that are longer than the birds themselves.

MOTMOTS Momotidae

GENERA: 6   **SPECIES**: 13

LENGTH: 16–48 cm (6–19 in), including elongated tail feathers in all but the Tody Motmot, *Hylomanes momotula*

WEIGHT: Tody Motmot 25–30 g (0.9–1 oz); Rufous Motmot, *Baryphthengus martii*, 146–208 g (5–7.3 oz); other species 44–151 g (1.5–5.3 oz)

RANGE AND HABITAT: Mexico, Central America, Trinidad, the northern half of South America; Rufous and Rufous-capped Motmots, *B. ruficapillus*, inhabit a wide variety of tropical wooded habitats, from rainforests to dry deciduous forest, as well as semi-open country with tall trees; the Blue-crowned Motmot, *Momotus momota*, is also in plantations and gardens, visiting bird feeders; the other three species are restricted to primary and old-growth secondary rainforest

SOCIAL BEHAVIOUR: usually seen alone or in pairs; monogamous and territorial; mostly solitary nesters, although some Turquoise-browed Motmots, *Eumomota superciliosa*, may nest alone or colonially, depending on the availability of nest sites

NEST: a nest chamber at the end of a burrow up to 5 m (16.4 ft) long in larger species, usually excavated in an earth bank

EGGS: 3–5, white

INCUBATION: 18–20 days in the Turquoise-browed Motmot; 21–22 days in the Blue-throated Motmot, *Aspatha gularis*

FLEDGING PERIOD: about 24–32 days

FOOD: mainly fairly large insects, including beetles, dragonflies and butterflies; also some other invertebrates such as scorpions and small crabs, and vertebrates such as small frogs and lizards and occasionally fish; larger species also eat much fruit

VOICE: generally silent, but call loudly at dawn and dusk, some larger species with deep, bisyllabic hoots and bubbling sounds, and others with hoarse honking or nasal twanging notes

MIGRATION: generally strictly sedentary

CONSERVATION STATUS: one species, the Keel-billed Motmot, *Electron carinatum*, is Vulnerable

ABOVE The Amazonian Motmot, *Momotus momota*, has an extensive range from Mexico to northern Argentina.

Among the most colourful and exquisitely plumaged of all tropical birds, this small family is confined to the Neotropical forests of southern Mexico, Central America and the northern half of South America. Unusually, there are more species (eight of the total of ten) in the far smaller northerly area of its distribution, in Mexico and Central America. Four species are endemic to those regions: the Blue-throated Motmot, *Aspatha gularis*, the Turquoise-browed Motmot, *Eumomota superciliosa*, the Keel-billed Motmot, *Electron carinatum*, and the Russet-crowned Motmot, *Momotus mexicanus* – and another, the Tody Motmot, *Hylomanes momotula*, is almost so, just extending its range across the border from Panama into north-west Colombia. A further three occur more widely in South America as well as farther north: the Amazonian Motmot, *Momotus momota*, the Broad-billed Motmot, *Electron platyrhynchum*, and the Rufous Motmot, *Baryphthengus martii*. Just two are endemic to South America, the Rufous-capped Motmot, *Baryphthengus ruficapillus*, in Brazil, Paraguay and northeast Argentina and the Highland Motmot, *Momotus aequatorialis*, confined to the northern Andes.

With the exception of the aberrant Tody Motmot, which is little larger than a sparrow, motmots range in size from starling-sized or thrush-sized species to the biggest species, the Rufous Motmot, which is about as big as a magpie. All 10 species have a large head, and a longish, sturdy, slightly decurved bill, which – in all species apart from the Tody Motmot – has serrated cutting edges on both mandibles. These vary from very fine in species that feed mainly on smaller, flying insects to extremely coarse in those that concentrate on taking larger prey, more often from the ground. The bill is guarded by strong rictal bristles.

Motmots have short legs with small, weak feet. The outer two of the three forward-pointing toes are partially united. The wings are quite short and rounded, suited to occasional short-range flights among trees. The most distinctive feature of all but the Tody Motmot is the long tail. In seven species the two central feathers each have the shaft bare (for varying lengths, according to species) and end in an expanded 'racquet', which is blue tipped with black in most species. This arrangement is absent in the nominate race of the Turquoise-browed Motmot and in three races of the Broad-billed Motmot. The Blue-throated Motmot has a long, graduated tail and the Rufous-capped Motmot a long tapering tail. When the feathers are newly grown, the racquets are not apparent, but result from the weakly attached barbs of the lower part of the central feathers wearing away to produce the bare shafts. The Tody Motmot has a much shorter tail with no racquets.

The plumage, similar in both sexes, is in various combinations of soft greens, blues and rufous, with a bold head pattern that generally features a black mask and, in most species, iridescent turquoise, blue or violet patches. Most species have one or two black spots or teardrop-shaped patches on the chest, in some species edged with blue or turquoise. Formed by clusters of elongated feathers, they vary in appearance within species, changing with preening.

The odd family name is from the Aztec name for the birds, imitative of the distinctive deep, powerful disyallabic hooting calls of the Blue-crowned species. Their calls are often the first clue to the presence of these birds, which spend much time perching quietly upright on a branch in a shady spot in the subcanopy. Here, they may remain almost motionless for long periods, apart from their very characteristic habit of swinging the tail from side to side, slowly and deliberately, or faster if they spot prey – or approaching humans.

Motmots make brief, rapid flights from their perch to snatch prey from foliage, twigs or branches, as well as from the ground. Smaller species also catch flying insects. They feed mainly on large insects, such as beetles, and other invertebrates, supplemented with some fruit, but the larger species also eat small lizards and snakes and even small birds or nestlings. Compared with most other diurnal Neotropical forest birds, motmots usually go to roost later, often remaining active well into dusk.

LEFT The Broad-billed Motmot, *Electron platyrhynchum*, has suffered declines in parts of its range due to deforestation.

The male and female take turns in digging out a long, narrow nesting tunnel, ending in an oval egg chamber, usually in an earth bank. The entrance can be distinguished from that of other birds or mammals as it is usually broader than it is high, though it is often concealed by leaves and other debris, and sometimes due to the birds choosing a site behind a tree root or trunk. Studies of Blue-throated and Turquoise-browed Motmots have revealed that the hard beetle wing cases and other hard parts of insects and other prey regurgitated as pellets by the incubating pair accumulate to form a nest lining.

KINGFISHERS Alcedinidae

GENERA: 18   **SPECIES:** 91

LENGTH: 10–46 cm (4–18 in)

WEIGHT: 9–465 g (0.3–16.4 oz)

RANGE AND HABITAT: worldwide, except in the far north of North America and Europe, much of northern Asia, large deserts and Antarctica; various species on oceanic islands; many species live beside rivers, streams or lakes of many kinds, often bordered by trees, but others (especially in the tropics) live in open areas of forests and woodlands far from water and seek prey on dry land, and some even inhabit fairly arid country, such as *Acacia* savanna and semi-desert or desert edge scrubland; a few hunt along seashores or among mangroves and some live in parks and gardens

SOCIAL BEHAVIOUR: usually solitary or in pairs, but some, such as kookaburras, form family groups that stay together for a year or more; most are monogamous and strongly territorial, but there is occasional polygamy and some are cooperative breeders in colonies

NEST: sited in a chamber at the end of a tunnel in an earth or sand bank, sometimes in a heap of soil or soil accumulated between tree roots, or in a tree hole or a termite nest; rarely any lining apart from the excreta and regurgitated pellets (containing bones, fish scales and other discarded parts of prey) of the young

EGGS: 2–10, white

INCUBATION: 13–28 days

FLEDGING PERIOD: 21–44 days

FOOD: for many species, mainly fish and aquatic invertebrates; some also eat land insects, earthworms, small reptiles, amphibians, mammals and birds; some do not eat fish

VOICE: most species are very vocal, different species having various sharp staccato calls, loud whistling, piping, screaming or rattling calls; kookaburras have loud, complex laughing calls

MIGRATION: a few species are true migrants, and many make seasonal movements, especially to escape freezing weather

CONSERVATION STATUS: two species, the Tuamotu Kingfisher, *Todiramphus gambieri*, and the Marquesan Kingfisher, *T. godeffroyi*, are Critically Endangered; one species, the Moustached Kingfisher, *Actenoides bougainvillea*, is Endangered; six species, the Blue-capped Kingfisher, *Actenoides hombroni*, the Bismarck Kingfisher, *Ceyx websteri*, the Sombre Kingfisher, *Todiramphus funebris*, the Rufous-lored Kingfisher, *T. winchelli*, the Kafiau Paradise Kingfisher, *Tanysiptera ellioti*, and the Philippine Dwarf Kingfisher, *Ceyx melanurus*, are Vulnerable; 19 species, including the Sulawesi Dwarf Kingfisher, *Ceyx fallax*, the Numfor Paradise Kingfisher, *Tanysiptera carolinae*, and the Brown-winged Kingfisher, *Pelargopsis amauroptera*, are Near Threatened

This large family of mainly colourful birds is found across most of the world apart from the upper latitudes, major deserts, high mountains and the Antarctic region. During the group's evolution, many species have managed to colonise both offshore and oceanic islands, including many in the Pacific Ocean.

As well as their impressively wide geographic range, there is a great size range in the family, from species such as the tiny African

Dwarf Kingfisher, *Ispidina lecontei*, which may weigh as little as 9 g (0.3 oz), to the sturdy Australasian Laughing Kookaburra, *Dacelo novaeguineae*, about 50 times as heavy. Most species, however, weigh between 30 and 100 g (1 and 3.5 oz).

Kingfishers are large headed with a compact, dumpy body, short wings and, in most species, a short tail. In most species, the powerful bill is long, straight, and dagger-shaped, used for seizing and holding fish or other prey, and also in nest building. The wings are short and rounded. The legs of most species are very short, although ground-feeding kingfishers have longer tarsi for efficient hopping. The small feet usually have four toes, three pointing forwards and one backwards. The front toes are partially fused, the inner one to the middle one for the first third of its length, and the middle to the outer toe for over half its length. Several species in the genera *Ceyx* and *Alcedo* have only three toes, lacking the inner one. Many species are brilliantly coloured, often blue, green or turquoise above, frequently with a metallic gloss, and in many with rufous or white underparts, but some are black and white and a few mainly or entirely blue or chestnut. The head feathers are typically loose and fluffy and some species sport crests of various lengths, which are usually mottled or barred. The sexes usually look alike or very similar, though a few species show fairly marked sexual dimorphism.

The family is divided into three subfamilies. The largest by far is the Halcyoninae, with 59 species in 11 genera. It includes the eight species of paradise kingfisher, *Tanysiptera*, distributed on various islands of the Moluccan archipelago, New Guinea and nearby islands, with one, the Buff-breasted Paradise Kingfisher, *T. sylvia*, including a race that breeds in northern Queensland, Australia, and migrates to winter in New Guinea. All are stunningly plumaged, with brilliant blue upperparts and white or orange (or in one species blue) underparts, and a long blue, white or blue-and-white tail extended even farther by a pair of very long central feathers; in all but one species, these each end in a small racquet. In all eight species, the striking plumage contrasts with the bright sealing-wax-red bill.

The most famous member of this subfamily is one of the five species of kookaburra, *Dacelo*: the Laughing Kookaburra, which despite its specific name (*D. novaeguineae*) is not found in New Guinea. It is a widespread and well-known bird in eastern Australia, and following introductions in the nineteenth and early twentieth centuries, it is also found in Tasmania, south-west Australia and Kawau Island, one of the islands in the Hauraki Gulf in North Island, New Zealand. With some females just exceeding 0.5 kg (1.1 lb) in weight, this is the heaviest and one of the largest of all kingfishers. It

ABOVE The Common Kingfisher, *Alcedo atthis*, prefers clear, slow-flowing rivers with plenty of perches from which it can dive for fish.

has a massive, powerful, hook-tipped bill that it can use to make short work of surprisingly large snakes (up to 1 m/3.3 ft long), including venomous species, stunning them by dropping them from a height and bashing them on a branch, against a rock or on the ground before swallowing them whole, head first. Familiar from the loud chuckling or gurgling cries celebrated in its common name, it is a successful and adaptable bird, found from the wildest forests and woodlands to suburban gardens and urban parks. As well as snakes, its wide diet may also include hand-outs at bird feeders, discarded sandwiches and other human waste, as well as a variety of large insects, mice, lizards, young or injured birds and other small vertebrates. Australia is also home to a less well-known kookaburra species, the Blue-winged Kookaburra, *D. leachii*, which is restricted to the north and north-east of the continent, and also lives in New Guinea. Both are mainly whitish with blackish streaks on the crown, and a dark grey back and wings; the Blue-winged species has mainly blue wings, while its bigger relative has only a little blue in the wing coverts. The other three kookaburra species are restricted to New Guinea and adjacent islands. Two are brighter than the Australian species: the Rufous-bellied Kookaburra, *D. gaudichaud*, with a black head, white collar, bright blue wings and rich rufous underparts and an all-white bill, and the Spangled Kookaburra, *D. tyro*, with a black head and nape spotted with golden-buff. The third, described in more detail below, is mainly brown and orange, with a blue rump (and blue tail in the male), and a massive pale conical bill.

The 11 species of *Halcyon* comprise four in Asia, including the striking and widespread Ruddy Kingfisher, *H. coromanda*, and the White-throated Kingfisher, *H. smyrnensis*, and seven species in Africa. The largest genus is *Todiramphus*, with 21 species, including one of the most widespread of all kingfishers, the Collared Kingfisher, *T. chloris*, which has diversified into 50 subspecies covering an overall range extending from Somalia and Arabia across India, Southeast Asia and Australia to many islands in the Pacific. Some of these are often thought to deserve full species rank.

The subfamily Alcedininae is the next largest, with 22 species in four genera. The genus *Ceyx* comprises nine species of small kingfisher, found in Africa, Madagascar, Southeast Asia and the New Guinea region. Most are brilliant blue with rufous underparts. The genus *Ispidina* with just two species includes the smallest of all kingfishers, the African Dwarf Kingfisher, *I. lecontei*, which weighs a mere 9–12 g (0.3–0.4 oz). The seven species of *Alcedo* are also brilliantly plumaged small blue-and-rufous species, but have a wider distribution. They include one of the most studied and greatly admired species, the Common Kingfisher, *A. atthis*, with a huge range encompassing Europe (where it is the only species) and much of Asia and east to the Moluccas, New Guinea and the Solomon islands. The fourth genus of the Alcedinidae is *Corythornis*, with four small species, two from Africa, and two from Madagascar (one also occurring on the Comoros Islands).

The third subfamily, Cerylinae, is the smallest, with just nine species in three genera. The four species of *Chloroceryle* are all restricted to the New World, mainly in the tropics, and are similarly plumaged, green above and mainly rufous or rufous and white below, but of different sizes: they range from the very small American Pygmy Kingfisher, *C. aenea*, and the Green Kingfisher, *C. americana*, twice

ABOVE With a raucous cackling call to match its common name, this is the Laughing Kookaburra, *Dacelo novaeguineae*.

ABOVE The Grey-headed Kingfisher, *Halcyon leucocephala*, Samburu Kenya.

as heavy as the former species, via the Green-and-rufous Kingfisher, *C. inda*, twice as heavy again, to the big Amazon Kingfisher, *C. amazona*, again double the weight of the preceding species. All four have almost identical ranges, and the regularly increasing size and length of bill may be related to the size of fish and invertebrates hunted by each species, which would minimise mutual competition for resources. The northern margin of the Green Kingfisher's range includes part of southern Texas and extreme southeastern Arizona.

As its name suggests, the genus *Megaceryle* comprises four large fish-eating species; all have a prominent, shaggy crest. The biggest of the four is the Giant Kingfisher, *M. maxima,* of Africa, which at 42–46 cm (16.5–18 in) averages slightly longer than the Laughing Kookaburra, though is not as heavy. It has blackish upperparts peppered with white spots and grey-spotted and rufous underparts. The Crested Kingfisher, *M. lugubris,* of Afghanistan to Japan is almost as big and sports the biggest and shaggiest crest, which like the upperparts has a striking pepper-and-salt pattern. Two species inhabit the New World. The Ringed Kingfisher, *M. torquata*, the third largest member of the genus, is very widespread from Mexico to Argentina, and just penetrates the USA, breeding in extreme southern Texas. The only common kingfisher of the USA and Canada is the smallest of the four, the Belted Kingfisher, *M. alcyon*. Both these species have a blue-grey head, crest, upperparts and breastband and are rufous or rufous and white below.

Surprising to many people is the fact that many kingfishers do not catch fish and some do not even live near rivers or other water. Many hunt for insects or small vertebrates in woodlands of all kinds. Some kingfishers live in more open, drier country. They include the little Striped Kingfisher, *Halcyon chelicuti*, which looks like a miniature kookaburra. It inhabits dry woodlands and thornbush in Africa, where it feeds mainly on grasshoppers. Several species, such as the Red-backed Kingfisher, *Todiramphus pyrrhopygius*, of Australia, another grasshopper eater, even live in desert scrubland. Two remarkable and unusual species in the subfamily Halcyoninae that may be related to kookaburras and are endemic to the forests of New Guinea are the Hook-billed Kingfisher, *Melidora macrorrhina*, and the Shovel-billed Kingfisher, *Dacelo rex*. The former has a

hefty, strongly hooked bill, which it uses for rummaging about in the leaf litter and probably also for digging in the soil of the forest floor for large insects such as stick insects, and frogs. It is also unusual among kingfishers in feeding mainly at dusk and by night. The Shovel-billed Kingfisher has an immense conical bill with which it ploughs up a patch of soil by thrusting it into the ground at an angle and then pushing it forwards, to reveal and catch earthworms, insects, snails, lizards and snakes.

The many fish-catching kingfishers have a number of specialisations for hunting aquatic prey, which also includes insects and other invertebrates (such as crabs, molluscs, water beetles and dragonflies and their larvae) in many cases. Sometimes fish and other prey can be snatched from the surface, but often the kingfisher must dive beneath the surface. Such species are able to compensate for the effects of light reflection and refraction at the surface, even when the water is moving. The Common Kingfisher is so adept at plunge diving that it has been observed to dive through shallow ice to reach fish trapped beneath.

Some fish-eating kingfishers are skilled at hovering, employing this technique especially when there is no perch from which to scan for underwater prey. The Pied Kingfisher, *Ceryle rudis*, of Africa and Asia, is one species that has perfected this technique. It obtains a large percentage of its food by hovering for long periods, and its skill and stamina in this respect gives it an advantage over other species as it does not need to return to a perch and can exploit feeding grounds and a wider range of fish species far from the shore of lakes or rivers. Another skilled hoverer is the Beach Kingfisher, *Todiramphus saurophagus*, found from the north Moluccas to New Guinea and the Solomon Islands. Although it hunts mainly from a perch in a tree, or on a post or rock, over the shore for crabs at low tide and for lizards behind the shore when the tide is in, it also will also hover and plunge dive for fish in rock pools and in the sea, sometimes as much as 100 m (330 ft) from shore.

Kingfishers are often heard before they are seen. Their loud calls are used especially for territorial defence and courtship. Often solitary individuals or pairs of many species jealously guard their hunting rights along a stretch of river and are aggressive in seeing

ABOVE The Green Kingfisher, *Chloroceryle americana*, is one of only six species of the large kingfisher family to occur in the New World.

off interlopers. Extended family groups of kookaburras and other more social species gang up to repel rivals; kookaburras use their laughing cries to warn them off.

All kingfisher species nest at the end of a tunnel excavated by both members of the pair. Depending on the depth of the earth bank, tree trunk or other site, the nest tunnel may be fairly short, but in most species it is of considerable length. The record is held by a pair of Giant Kingfishers, *Megaceryle maxima*, whose tunnel measured 8.5 m (28 ft). Several species excavate the tunnel by flying at the chosen bank of soil or tree, striking the substrate with the bill to hack out earth or wood, and then using the feet to dig out the soil or sawdust. Some species use termite nests instead, while Ruddy Kingfishers, *Halcyon coromanda*, may dig out their holes in the mud walls of village huts. One pair of Stork-billed Kingfishers, *Pelargopsis capensis*, even spent several weeks trying to dig out a tunnel in a brick wall. Sometimes, kingfishers are fatally injured during initial attempts at excavation, when they fly at a particularly hard substrate and bounce off.

ORDER CARIAMIFORMES

This very small order, containing just two species in a single family, has been created to reflect the distinctiveness of these unusual birds. Until recently, they were usually considered to belong to the Order Gruiformes (p. 61), and their closest relatives within that formerly much larger order have variously thought to be the cranes (Family Gruidae), Trumpeters (Family Psophiidae) or, most often, the bustards (Family Otididae) – which are now also given an order (Otidiformes) of their own.

But despite the resemblances in appearance and lifestyle to the bustards, seriemas are now known not to be related to them or to any of the Gruiformes. The molecular evidence indicates that they are best classified in a large grouping (the superorder Passerimorphae) together with the falcons and relatives of the Order Falconiformes (p. 184), parrots Psittaciformes (p. 188) and the huge of passerines (Order Passeriformes, p. 198).

SERIEMAS Cariamidae

GENERA: 2   **SPECIES:** 2

LENGTH: 70–90 cm (28–36 in)

WEIGHT: about 1.2–1.5 kg (2.6–3.3 lb)

RANGE AND HABITAT: central South America; grassland, savannah, scrub and open woodland

SOCIAL BEHAVIOUR: usually alone or in pairs, sometimes in small family groups, including well-grown young; strongly territorial and apparently monogamous, with both parents incubating eggs and caring for the young

Nest: large stick nest low down (up to 3 m/10 ft above ground) in a tree or shrub

EGGS: 2–3, white to buff, with brown markings

INCUBATION: 24–30 days

FLEDGING PERIOD: about 30 days in the Red-legged Seriema, *Cariama cristata*

FOOD: omnivorous, eating mainly insects but also snakes, lizards, small birds, young birds, rodents and other small mammals, as well as small amounts of plant matter, including crops such as beans and maize

VOICE: loud, very far-carrying yelping or cackling sounds; pairs often duet

MIGRATION: sedentary

CONSERVATION STATUS: neither species is threatened

ABOVE A Red-legged Seriema, *Cariama cristata*, utters its very loud yelping song as it strides across the cerrado savannah of Piaui State, Brazil.

Both species of seriema are tall, long-legged birds of open country that are found only in South America. With their strong, distinctly hooked bill, long, powerful legs and long, graduated tail, seriemas look rather like small versions of the Secretary-bird, *Sagittarius serpentarius*. They are unrelated to that African raptor but have evolved similar adaptations to killing prey, including snakes and lizards, in similar habitats, on the ground in open grassland and scrub. The length of the legs and of the neck enables them to scan for danger over the top of long grasses or shrubs.

Seriemas differ from their African ecological counterpart in one major respect, though: whereas the Secretary-bird spends a good deal of time soaring above its habitat on its long, broad wings, the seriemas rarely fly, although their short wings are perfectly functional. Instead, they generally escape danger or disturbance by running, when they can reach speeds of over 50 km/h (30 mph). Their usual gait, however, is a slow, stately walk. They do occasionally fly short distances – for example, if a dangerous predator gets too close, or to reach their roosts in trees.

The hooked bill and powerful legs and feet armed with strong claws are effective weapons when dealing with potentially dangerous snakes, lizards or rodents; also the length of the legs and their strong scales presumably protect them from the venomous snake species that they sometimes tackle, as they are not immune to their poison. In addition, the inner toe bears a particularly long, sickle-shaped claw; this is normally held raised above the ground and partially retracted but is brought down to hold or kill struggling prey. Seriemas usually use the bill to seize and kill smaller animals such as insects, devouring them quickly. They may also hold prey in the bill if it is too big to swallow whole, while using the big sickle claw of one foot to dismember their catch. Seriemas have also been observed throwing reptiles against the ground or other hard surface to stun or kill them or break their bones.

Seriemas are very wary birds, reacting quickly to the least sound or sight of danger. For this reason, they are valued by rural people in South America as highly efficient 'watchdogs'; they are often trapped when young, tamed and kept along with poultry, to warn their owners of approaching foxes or other predators.

The Red-legged Seriema, *Cariama cristata*, which occurs from Brazil to Uruguay and northern Argentina, is a bird of grasslands, savannah and open scrublands. It has brownish plumage, paler below, with streaks on the head, neck and breast, and a white-tipped tail. Most distinctive is a long, bristly crest sticking up from the front of the crown; although shorter, the throat feathers can also be erected. Like the legs, the bill is bright red.

The slightly larger Black-legged Seriema, *Chunga burmeisteri*, lives in rather less open country – dry, open woodlands, forest edges and thick scrub. It has a more restricted range, in western Paraguay and northern Argentina. It has a black bill and legs and a very small crest, and its plumage is greyish, paler below and with a black-tipped tail.

The seriemas thought by some ornithologists to be the closest living relatives of a group of long extinct South American birds, the formidable, carnivorous phorusrhacids. These were up to 3 m (10 ft) tall with immense hooked bills, and lived between 62 million and 2 million years ago. One species, *Titanus walleri*, lived in southern USA, with fossil evidence from Florida, dated at 3 to 2.9 million years ago.

ORDER FALCONIFORMES

The falcons and caracaras were traditionally included together with the very large group of hawks, eagles and other diurnal birds of prey in the Order Accipitriformes, but recent molecular research (as well as a much earlier morphological analysis) indicates they are likely to be unrelated and that their likeness results from having evolved adaptations to a similar lifestyle. The recent evidence points to the likelihood that the Falconiformes belong to the other members of a huge group of landbirds, the Passerimorphae, that includes the two species of seriemas (Order Cariamiformes, p. 183), which are likely to be their closest relations, as well as the large order of parrots (Psittaciformes, p. 188) and the immense order of passerines, or perching birds (Passeriformes, p. 198) that make up over half the world's bird families and two-thirds of bird species. All members of the Falconiformes are classified in a single family, Falconidae.

FALCONS AND CARACARAS Falconidae

GENERA: 11   **SPECIES:** 64

LENGTH: 14–65 cm (5.5–25 in)

WEIGHT: 28 g–2.1 kg (1 oz–4.6 lb)

RANGE AND HABITAT: worldwide, except for Antarctica; wide range of more or less open habitats, from treeless Arctic tundra, desert, and moorland to savannah; the Red-throated Caracara, *Ibycter americanus*, and the forest-falcons, *Micrastur*, live in the interior of dense rainforest, and the Black Caracara, *Daptrius ater*, Laughing Falcon, *Herpetotheres cachinnans*, and falconets prefer open woodland and forest edges or clearings; individuals of 15 or so species, notably the Peregrine Falcon, *Falco peregrinus*, and Common Kestrel, *F. tinnunculus*, have become adapted to life in urban areas; the Lesser Kestrel, *Falco naumanni*, regularly breeds on old buildings and roosts in winter with Red-footed Falcons, *F. vespertinus*, in trees in African villages

SOCIAL BEHAVIOUR: generally solitary or in pairs, and mostly monogamous, some pairing for life; a few species, notably the Lesser Kestrel, Red-footed Falcon and Amur Falcons, *A. amurensis*, are highly gregarious, breeding and roosting together; Eleonora's Falcon, *F. eleonorae*, breeds in smaller colonies on sea cliffs, and also often feed in groups where prey is abundant; Red-throated Caracaras nest cooperatively, with the family group sharing incubation, care of young and nest defence

NEST: caracaras build untidy stick nests and debris in trees, on cliff ledges or in cover on ground, but all other members of the family make no nest, laying their eggs on a bare cliff ledge or crevice, in a tree hole or other hollow sometimes on a building, pylon or in an open-front nest-box, and occasionally on the ground; many use the old nests of other birds, for instance Red-footed and Amur Falcons use nests abandoned by Rooks, *Corvus frugilegus*, whereas falconets nest in the huge nests of communally breeding birds such as Monk Parakeets, *Myiopsitta monachus*, or weavers, or in old woodpecker holes

EGGS: 1–7, in most species buff with dark reddish speckles and blotches; white in falconets

INCUBATION: 28–35 days

FLEDGING PERIOD: 28–55 days

FOOD: mostly small mammals, birds, reptiles and large insects caught on the ground or (for forest species) trees; many of the true falcons (*Falco*) catch birds in the air by chasing them or diving on them, whereas some catch flying insects such as dragonflies and locusts; most caracaras eat a good deal of carrion, as well as birds, small animals and dung, and some eat fruit, grains or other plant matter; Red-throated Caracaras specialise in eating wasp and bee larvae

VOICE: mainly harsh chattering, cackling, yelping and whining calls; especially noisy around nest sites; forest falcons and the Laughing Falcon are generally more vocal, including duets between pair members

MIGRATION: some species are sedentary, especially in the tropics and on islands; some are nomadic, moving in times of prey scarcity; others make regular migrations

CONSERVATION STATUS: one species, the Guadalupe Caracara, *Caracara lutosa*, is extinct ; two species, the Mauritius Kestrel, *Falco punctatus*, and the Saker Falcon, *F. cherrug*, are Endangered; five species, the Plumbeous Forest-falcon, *Micrastur plumbeus*, Seychelles Kestrel, *F. araea*, Grey Falcon, *F. hypoleucos*, Sooty Falcon, *F. concolor*, and Taita Falcon, *F. fasciinucha*, are Vulnerable; eight species, including the Striated Caracara, *Phalcoboenus australis*, and White-fronted Falconet, *Microhierax latifrons*, New Zealand Falcon, *F. novaeseelandiae*, and Red-footed Falcon, *F. vespertinus*, are Near Threatened

The best-known wild examples of this family to most people include various species of kestrel (such as the Common Kestrel, *Falco tinnunculus*, of Eurasia and Africa and the American Kestrel, *F. sparverius*) hovering by a busy roadside, and the powerful, dashing Peregrine Falcon, *F. peregrinus*, with its ability to dive on prey from great heights at record-breaking speed; with one of the widest of all distributions of any bird in the world, this magnificent raptor breeds both in the wildest habitats and in the centres of great cities, such as London, Bristol, Manchester, Berlin, Florence, Warsaw, Hong Kong, New York, Boston, Chicago, San Francisco, Toronto and Vancouver, where it enthrals those who look up to see it in action. Many people also come into contact with Peregrines and various other falcon species such as the big Gyr Falcon, *F. rusticolus*, and the Saker, *F. cherrug*, kept by falconers, when they attend public flying displays, where they can more easily marvel at the birds' prowess in the air. Although the above-mentioned species have a high public profile, most of the species in the genus *Falco* are impressive in flight.

Despite the differences between all the different subgroups, and the wide adaptive radiation into different ecological niches, numerous common features support their classification as a single family, distinct from hawks, eagles and other birds of prey. These include a unique moulting sequence for the primary flight feathers, the same feather lice, the structure of the syrinx ('voice box'), a shortened neck (except in caracaras), similarities in the chemical composition and blotched rufous colouring of the eggshells (except for the white eggs of the pygmy falcons) and – apart from the atypical caracara subgroup – the fact that they build no nest. Fossil evidence suggests that the falcon family contains the most recent and specialised of the diurnal raptors.

The second largest family of diurnal birds of prey, after the unrelated Accipitridae (p. 136), the Falconidae is divided into two subfamilies. The subfamily Herpetotherinae is by far the smaller of the two. Its members are restricted to tropical and subtropical Central and South America, most of them in dense humid forests. They are the six species of forest falcons, *Micrastur*, and the unique Laughing Falcon, *Herpetotheres cachinnans*. The forest falcons are very secretive birds of tropical forests that superficially resemble the unrelated sparrowhawks, *Accipiter*, with their short, rounded wings and long tail – an example of convergent evolution in that both groups need to manoeuvre between trees and branches when hunting, but forest falcons are not specialist bird catchers and lack the accipiters' long, narrow toes. Forest falcons spend long periods perched motionless watching for prey, and swoop down to seize prey such as lizards, birds and insects. In contrast to most other falcons, which probably locate and track prey mainly by using their very keen vision, hearing is likely to be important in forest falcons, as they have a ruff of stiffened feathers around each ear like a small version of the facial ruff of harriers (see p. 140). The Laughing Falcon spends long periods perched upright high in a tree, head bowed to scan below for snakes (including venomous ones), which form the bulk of its diet. Its common and specific names refer to some of its loud calls; this is one of the most vocal of all raptors, its calls, often given as a duet by a mated pair, a feature of Neotropical forests, especially at dawn or dusk.

The subfamily Falconinae is divided into two tribes. The tribe Polyborini comprises the 12 species of caracara (one of which is extinct), in six genera. These are the most atypical members of the family. Along with the vultures (both Old and New World), caracaras are generally the least predatory of the raptors, feeding extensively on carrion, food at waste disposal sites, insects and other invertebrates, fruit and other plant matter, although they do take more live prey than vultures, especially small, young or incapacitated animals. Slow flyers, they have long, broad wings, a long tail and long legs, and they do a lot of their foraging on the ground; some species take almost anything edible. The largest and most widespread species are the Crested Caracara, *Caracara cheriway*, whose range extends from extreme southern USA to South America, north of the River Amazon, and the Southern Caracara, *C. plancus*, found south of the Amazon to Tierra del Fuego and the Falkland Islands. It is a determined kleptoparasite, chasing other raptors, including caracaras and vultures, and forcing them to disgorge their prey. It is often seen feeding on animals killed on roads. With its deep, strongly hooked bill it takes more live prey – such as young birds (and eggs), small turtles, crabs, earthworms and insects – than do most other caracaras. The third species in the genus *Caracara*, the Guadalupe Caracara, *C. lutosa*, was endemic to the Mexican island off Baja California whose name it bears, but was driven from abundance in the 1870s to extinction by the early 1900s as a result of hunting and a poisoning campaign by settlers. The five species of *Phalcoboenus* caracaras includes the Mountain Caracara, *P. megalopterus*, of the Andes and the Striated Caracara, *P. australis*, found on remote shores and islands off extreme south of South America, but with most on the British Overseas Territory of the Falkland Islands, where it is known by its nickname of 'Johnny Rook'. Its numbers have been greatly reduced as a result of persecution in the past by sheep farmers. Unlike the other caracaras, the Red-throated Caracara, *Ibycter americanus*, is a specialist feeder, subsisting mainly on the larvae of wasps and bees. Formerly regarded as the only South American falconet, the Spot-winged Falconet, *Spiziapteryx circumcinctus*, is now thought to be an unusual diminutive member of the caracara tribe.

The second tribe of the Falconinae, the Falconini, is the largest of all the subgroups of the family and the most speciose, with 44 species in four genera. It contains the best known members of the family, and some with very extensive ranges; indeed, the Peregrine Falcon, *Falco peregrinus*, is one of the world's most widespread birds, and the world's most cosmopolitan diurnal raptor, found on every continent except Antarctica. The Falconini also includes both the largest members of the entire family and its smallest members – indeed, the smallest of all diurnal birds of prey. The five species of southern Asian falconets, *Microhierax*, are all tiny; the smallest of these is the Black-thighed Falconet, *M. fringillarius*, which is only the size of a House Sparrow, *Passer domesticus*, although longer winged, at just 14–17 cm (5.5–6.5 in) long, with a wingspan of 27–32 cm (10.5–12.5 in) and weighing 28–55 g (1–2 oz). The African Pygmy Falcon, *Polihierax semitorquatus*, is only a little bigger, but the other species in the genus *Polihierax*, the White-rumped Pygmy Falcon, *P. insignis*, is a little bigger again. As with most other diurnal birds of prey, and unlike most other birds, females are on average larger than males, a situation called reversed sexual size dimorphism.

The other 44 members of the tribe Falconini, all in the single genus *Falco*, are often known as the 'true' falcons. Apart from a few forest or woodland dwellers, they have long, pointed wings and large breast muscles suiting them for fast, aerobatic, powered flight, although they are also accomplished soarers when necessary. They can be divided into several distinct groups. Many of the first group, the 13 species of kestrels, use hovering as one method of locating prey, such as voles hiding in long grass or other cover. There is just one species in the New World, the American Kestrel, albeit with many races occupying a huge range, from Alaska and northern Canada to Tierra del Fuego. The rest include species that are widespread in Europe, Africa and Asia, one in Australia, and three restricted to three Indian Ocean island groups, Madagascar, Mauritius and the Seychelles. Most are open-country birds – exceptions being the Mauritius Kestrel, *F. punctatus*, the little Seychelles Kestrel, *F. araea* (the smallest of all the true falcons) and the Banded Kestrel of Madagascar, *F. zoniventris*, which have shorter, more rounded wings and a proportionately longer tail, like accipitrine hawks (see p. 136); the last named even has plumage that resembles that of many sparrowhawks, *Accipiter*, having underparts that are barred rather than streaked as in most other kestrels.

The hobbies are a group of four similar species. The Eurasian Hobby, *F. subbuteo*, breeds from western Europe to China, and winters in Africa or southern Asia (apart from a resident race in Burma, Indonesia and southern China); two resident species are the African Hobby, *F. cuvieri*, and Oriental Hobby, *F. severus*, and the fourth is the Australian Hobby *F. longipennis*, which breeds mainly in Australia, with some wintering in New Guinea. All have a very streamlined profile with long, sickle-shaped wings. They are exceptionally manoeuvrable in their fast flight. As well as eating large insects such as dragonflies, usually in flight by deft transfer from talons to bill, they are speedy and agile enough to catch birds such as swifts and hirundines (swallows and martins). Other species resembling hobbies in many respects and probably allied to them include another species pair, Eleonora's Falcon, *F. eleonorae*, and the Sooty Falcon, *F. concolor*. Both are very elegant, especially long-winged birds that specialise in catching

ABOVE A pale morph Eleonora's Falcon, *Falco eleonorae*, scans for prey in Cyprus, in autumn, when it catches many migrant songbirds to feed its chicks.

insects and migrating birds on the wing. They are remarkable in timing their breeding season so that the young hatch in the autumn to coincide with the peak passage of small autumn migrant birds between Eurasia and Africa, which they feed to their chicks. Two other species considered likely to be close relatives of the hobbies are the Aplomado Falcon, *F. femoralis*, of southern USA, Central and South America and the Bat Falcon, *F. rufigularis* of Central and South America. As its common name suggests, the Bat Falcon does indeed catch bats, and generally hunts around dusk and dawn; adaptations for pursuing such agile prey in dim light are its fast flight and big eyes. Another pair of close relatives, the mainly insect-eating Red-footed Falcon, *F. vespertinus*, and Amur Falcon, *F. amurensis*, may form a link between the kestrels and the hobbies. The Merlin, *F. columbarius*, is a small falcon (the male especially so, being little bigger than a thrush) with a very wide range across North America and Eurasia. It is renowned for its determined fast pursuit of small songbird prey such as pipits and larks, following their every twist and turn, often low over the ground, but also by climbing high into the air.

The last two groups of true falcons are large and powerful predators specialised for killing mainly birds in flight. They do this by striking them with a blow from a foot or raking them with a talon in mid-air, or seizing them in their feet and killing them on the ground by severing the spinal cord with a powerful bite from the bill. The bill is specially adapted with a notch (known as the 'tomial tooth' although it is not a real tooth at all) in the edge of the upper mandible for this purpose. This enables these predators to deal rapidly with struggling prey that is large relative to the falcon's size compared with hawks, which generally subdue the prey with talons alone.

The penultimate group comprises four species sometimes collectively called 'hierofalcons', 'great falcons' or 'desert falcons'. Three of these, the Lanner Falcon, *F. biarmicus*, the Laggar Falcon, *F. jugger*, and the Saker Falcon, *F. cherrug*, are found in the Old World, the Lanner in Europe, the Middle East and Africa, the Laggar in Asia, from Pakistan and India to Myanmar, and the

ABOVE The Chimango Caracara, *Milvago chimango*, is the commonest raptor over much of its range; this one is in Tierra del Fuego, Argentina.

Saker in Europe and Asia. The imposing Gyr Falcon, *F. rusticolus*, the largest member of the subfamily Falconinae, lives around the entire Arctic region right across Alaska and Canada and from Scandinavia to far eastern Siberia. Most hunt birds, typically by closing in on them in level flight, although during the breeding season the Saker concentrates mainly on mammals.

The final group includes a pair of fast, very powerful species – the Peregrine Falcon, *F. peregrinus*, and its close relative the smaller, desert-dwelling Barbary Falcon, *F. pelegrinoides*. The Peregrine is one of the world's supreme predators, renowned for its especially dramatic hunting method – soaring high into the air to spot pigeons, wildfowl or other prey and then diving down at an acute angle in an awe-inspiring 'stoop' to strike the victim in mid-air. Reaching as much as 290 km/h (180 mph) or more, they are the world's fastest living creatures. The Prairie Falcon, *F. mexicanus*, with a range extending from southern Canada south to Arizona, Texas and Mexico, was traditionally included in the hierofalcon group, but is now generally thought to be more closely related to the Peregrine Falcon. The Taita Falcon, *F. fasciinucha*, a rare species of eastern and southern Africa, though sometimes grouped near the hobbies, is more likely to be related to the Peregrine too.

Plumage in the Falconidae varies between the different groups. Many species of caracaras are black or dark brown with varying amounts of white or pale buff or cream, whereas the Black Caracara,

ABOVE The American Kestrel, *Falco sparverius*, is the smallest of a group of falcons that often search for prey by hovering in the wind.

Daptrius ater, is entirely black apart from a white base to the tail, the Chimango Caracara, *Milvago chimango*, is all brown with darker streaks, and the Striated Caracara, *Phalcoboenus australis*, is dark brown and rufous, with pale streaks on the dark underparts; most have brightly coloured yellow, orange or red bare facial skin. The plumage of forest falcons is generally grey or blackish above with pure white or barred underparts; all have a dark tail barred with white. The Laughing Falcon is strikingly patterned, with the blackish brown of its upperparts contrasting with the creamy white to rich buff of its underparts and large head, the latter with a broad blackish mask through the eyes.

Pygmy falcons and falconets have boldly patterned plumage in various permutations of grey, black, white and, in some cases, rufous too. Plumage in most true falcons is blackish, brown, chestnut or grey above and paler below, often patterned with darker streaking, barring, spotting or mottling. Some species, such as the American Kestrel, the Orange-breasted Falcon, *F. deirolucus*, and the sooty grey and rich chestnut males of the Red-footed and Amur Falcons, are more striking.

Males and females are similar in many species, but in some (particularly the American Kestrel, the Orange-breasted Falcon, the Red-footed Falcon, *Falco vespertinus*, the Amur Falcon and the Merlin) the males are brighter or more boldly patterned. Females of both pygmy falcons and one species of falconet have areas of bright chestnut, lacking in males. Several species are polymorphic (although not as many as in the Accipitridae); examples are the Barred and Collared Forest-falcons, *Micrastur ruficollis* and *M. semitorquatus*, with a bewildering range of plumage variations between races and individuals, including partly rufous forms, the Gyr Falcon, *Falco rusticolus*, with colour forms ranging from almost pure white through grey to an almost uniform very dark grey, and Eleonora's Falcon *F. eleonorae*, with a scarcer all dark form as well as the usual one with streaked buff underparts.

ABOVE The Peregrine Falcon, *Falco peregrinus*, is an immensely powerful raptor that usually catches its bird prey in mid-air after an astoundingly fast dive.

Falcons include some of the most impressive migrants among the raptors. As befits its common and specific names, the Peregrine is a great wanderer, with some northern breeders in Alaska or northern Canada clocking up a round trip of almost 16,000 km (9,900 miles) to and from winter quarters in southern South America; Amur Falcons breeding in far eastern Asia travel almost twice as far to winter in southern Africa, the longest of any raptor migration. Eleonora's and Sooty Falcons nest on cliffs in the Mediterranean and North Africa and winter in Madagascar. They are unique in timing their breeding so that they have young in the nest in autumn, when they can feed them plentiful supplies of birds migrating to Africa; at this time of year, there are many inexperienced young migrants that are easier to catch.

ORDER PSITTACIFORMES

The birds in this major order were until recently often classified within a single family, Psittacidae, with eight subfamilies comprising the cockatoos, lories, lorikeets, parakeets, macaws, and amazons as well as birds whose common names include the word 'parrot'. The cockatoos are a very distinctive group, and as a result have often been given a separate family of their own. Recent research incorporating molecular studies suggested that a revision was necessary. The scheme set out here recognises the distinctiveness of the cockatoos by giving them family status, as the Cacatuidae, and does the same for the extraordinary Kakapo, *Strigops habroptila*, uniting it in a Family Strigopidae with two other New Zealand parrots, the Kea, *Nestor notabilis* and Kaka, *N. meridionalis*. These are divided between two subfamilies, Strigopinae for the Kakapo and Nestorinae for the other two species. This small group is regarded as the basal group of the whole family, which might have appeared as long as 65 million years ago. The remaining species are divided between two large families, the Psittacidae, containing most of the African parrots and all the New World species, and the Psittaculidae, comprising most of the Old World and Australasian parrots. In the latter family, one of the more radical differences from the traditional scheme is the the the uniting of various Asian and Australasian species, including the fig parrots, *Psittaculirostris* and *Cyclopsitta* of New Guinea and *Bolbopsittacus* of the Philippines, the hanging parrots *Loriculus*, the Budgerigar, *Melopsittacus undulatus* of Australia and various lories and lorikeets with the lovebirds, *Agapornis*, from Africa, in an enlarged subfamily Loriinae. Even more radical is the decision to move the parrots from their conventional placement immediately following the pigeons, as in this book, to a position next to the great group of passerines (Order Passeriformes, p. 198) and their proposed grouping in a superorder Passerimorphae, to include the seriemas (Family Cariamidae, p. 183) and falcons (Family Falconidae, p. 184) as well as the passerines. The four families that make up this large order have various features in common, so these will be dealt with here, rather than being repeated in the account for each family.

Parrots are found in most tropical and subtropical regions worldwide, with some species extending their range into temperate regions, just a few in the northern hemisphere but more in the southern hemisphere. They are particularly abundant in the New World tropics and Australasia, with fewer species in sub-Saharan Africa, Madagascar, Indian Ocean islands, southern Asia, New Zealand and Pacific islands. The greatest diversity occurs in and around New Guinea, in the Wallacean and Australo-Papuan region, extending from the Indonesian island of Sulawesi to the Solomon Islands.

Most parrots are tree dwellers, with representatives from all types of wooded habitat, including dense lowland tropical rainforests, high-altitude cloud forests, open woodland and savannahs. Some species have become adapted to life in plantations and other agricultural land. A few live in more open country, such as scrubland, in some cases in arid areas, or even in treeless grassland, as long as there are cliffs or banks of earth or soft rock where they can nest in holes.

Almost everyone can identify a bird as a parrot, thanks to the distinctive short, broad-based, deep, hook-tipped bill on a large head. The bill of most cockatoos and macaws is especially big. The shorter, upwardly curved lower mandible has a sharp cutting edge, which moves against the flat portion of the strongly decurved upper mandible, which has a sharp tip. Parrot skulls are remarkable pieces of natural engineering. The upper mandible is not fused to the skull, but articulates with the skull via a hinge joint, with additional articulations towards the back of the skull to allow it independent movement and maximise the biting pressure. To help power the bite, the mandible is especially deep to accommodate the big jaw muscles, and the quadrate bones in the points of the jaw have a special 'rocker' articulation to allow a wide range of movement. Coupled with the well-developed, highly mobile tongue, this gives the parrot great power and control in the handling and processing of food items. When eating a seed or a nut, the tongue positions and holds it so that the mandibles can crack it. Nuts are cracked by being held in the basal part of the bill, where the greatest pressure can be exerted. Large macaws are particularly impressive in this respect: the biggest species, the Hyacinth Macaw, *Anodorhynchus hyacinthinus*, can shear Brazil nuts. A parrot can deal with a large number of seeds quickly and efficiently. It holds each seed between the front edge of the lower mandible and the 'step' in the upper mandible. The cutting edge of the lower mandible penetrates the husk and removes it. The parrot then rotates the seed with the tip of its tongue so that the detached husk is gripped in corrugations on the inside of the upper mandible, and then discarded. The parrot then splits the seed and swallows it. The whole process happens with lightning speed. Parrots are mainly seed eaters: even when they feed on fruit, they usually extract the seeds and discard the flesh, and they crack nuts to get at the kernels. However, a considerable number of species feed mainly on nectar and pollen, which they gather from flowers using their long, narrow, brush-tipped tongue. Some parrots include insects in their diet. Various cockatoo species, for instance, eat wood-boring insects and their larvae.

Other distinctive features of parrots include a short neck, a stocky body, and short, strong legs with a yoke-toed (zygodactyl) foot pattern, two toes facing forward and two backward. This gives the bird optimum stability when clambering about in trees or on other perches, or hanging upside down, and the shortness of the legs keeps the centre of gravity low. Parrots also increase their agility when climbing by using the bill as a grappling hook to grasp onto the perch to steady themselves or help them ascend or descend. Their feet are used not only for perching and climbing, but also for powerful grasping of objects, especially food items, which are then often held up to the bill. No other birds have such dexterity.

There is a great range in size and weight between the different groups of this large family of birds. The smallest are the tiny pygmy parrots – the smallest of all, the Buff-faced Pygmy Parrot, *Micropsitta pusio*, is only 10 cm (4 in) long and weighs just 10 g (0.35 oz). At the other extreme are the huge macaws and the far bulkier-bodied Kakapo, *Strigops habroptila*. The longest parrot is the Hyacinth Macaw, measuring up to 1 m (3.3 ft), and the heaviest is the Kakapo, with males weighing up to 3 kg (6.6 lb), about twice the weight of a Hyacinth Macaw. Wing and tail shape vary considerably, from the short, broad, blunt-tipped wings and short, square-ended tail of amazons, *Amazona*, and some cockatoos to the long, pointed wings and very long tail of macaws and some parakeets. The small parrots in the genus *Prioniturus*, from the Philippines and some Indonesian islands, have unique, racquet-shaped tail-tips.

In general, parrots are among the most brightly coloured of all birds, although most cockatoos are mainly black, white or salmon pink, and a few other species have largely black, grey, brown or dull greenish plumage. The most common colour is bright green, which camouflages the birds well against their usual background of foliage. Many species also have red, orange, yellow or blue markings, and some are brilliantly multicoloured. Often, there are bright colours on the rump, tail, forewing and underwing; generally hidden, they are suddenly revealed to dramatic effect when the birds display or take flight. In many species, the bill, eyes, eye-rings or bare facial skin are also brightly coloured. Crests are highly developed in the cockatoos; the birds erect or lower them to communicate mood and intentions. In some, they are relatively short and simple, as with the jaunty spike of the Cockatiel, *Nymphicus hollandicus*, or the wispy, forwardly curving tufts of the Gang-gang Cockatoo, *Callocephalon fimbriatum*. Others have more elaborate adornments, such as the fans of the white cockatoos. In larger species these are shaped like an Indian chief's war-bonnet, and in three of them, the long white feathers are tipped with bright yellow, while the Salmon-crested Cockatoo, *Cacatua moluccensis*, has a rather shaggy, pink-tipped crest, and Major Mitchell's Cockatoo, *C. leadbeateri*, sports the most elaborate version, with concentric bands of red

and yellow. The Palm Cockatoo, *Probosciger aterrimus*, has a striking cascade of spiky, black plumes.

In many parrots there is only a slight difference in appearance between the sexes, but some show marked sexual dimorphism. Indeed, the greatest plumage difference between males and females of any bird species is seen in the Eclectus Parrot, *Eclectus roratus*, of New Guinea and extreme north-east Australia: males are green with red flanks and underwing coverts, and blue primary feathers, while females are mainly red and blue.

Because of the variability of their food supplies, most parrots must move about a good deal. Many are nomadic, and search for seeds, nectar or other plant food a long way from roosts or nest sites. Nomadism is often in response to alternating wet and dry seasons, or to sporadic drought. Regular seasonal migration is known only for two species that breed in Tasmania, the Orange-bellied Parrot, *Neophema chrysogaster*, and the Swift Parrot, *Lathamus discolor*. Both cross the Tasman Sea (at its narrowest about 240 km/150 miles) to winter in Australia, the Orange-bellied Parrot in the coastal strip from southeast South Australia to south-central Victoria, and the Swift Parrot more widely and extending rather further inland, in south-eastern and eastern Australia.

Almost all parrots nest as single pairs in holes and other cavities in trees, sometimes in cavities in cliffs, or in termite nests. Breeding species with unusual nesting arrangements include the Monk Parakeet, *Myiopsitta monachus*, a common parrot in much of the southern half of South America, which has also been introduced to (or escaped from captivity in) many other parts of the world, from North America and Europe to Japan. Uniquely among parrots, it builds huge, enclosed communal nests of sticks in trees. These may hold up to 200 or more pairs and their families, each in a separate chamber. The massive structures, which can be the size of a small car, are used not only for nesting but also for roosting outside the breeding season. Sometimes Monk Parakeet nests are taken over and modified from the old nest of another bird; for example, in Argentina the great pile of sticks accumulated by the furnariid aptly known as the Firewood Gatherer, *Annumbius annumbi*. The nests often attract avian tenants of various kinds, including Great Horned Owls, *Bubo virginianus*, American Kestrels, *Falco sparverius*, and other birds of prey, and ducks such as whistling ducks, *Dendrocygna*. Another unusual nester is the Burrowing Parakeet, *Cyanoliseus patagonus*, of Argentina and Chile, which, as its common name indicates, nests at the end of burrows it excavates in soft earth, sandstone or limestone cliffs, often near a river or the sea.

Sadly, the parrot order is one of the most threatened of all groups of birds. Over a third of all species are officially classified as threatened to some degree. For centuries, their beauty, intelligence and the ability of some species to mimic human speech have all made parrots greatly in demand as cage birds, and there is still a thriving illegal trade as well as responsible captive breeding. Some are regarded by fruit-growers and other farmers as pests and many suffer from habitat loss, while island species in particular are vulnerable to introduced mammalian predators.

KEA AND ALLIES Strigopidae

GENERA: 2   **SPECIES**: 4

LENGTH: Kakapo, 58–64 cm (23–25 in); Kea, *c.* 48 cm (19 in); New Zealand Kaka, *c.* 45 cm (18 in)

WEIGHT: Kakapo, 0.95–4 kg (2–8.8 lb); Kea, 0.8–1 kg (1.8–2.2 lb); New Zealand Kaka, 0.4–0.6 kg (0.9–1.3 lb)

RANGE AND HABITAT: all three species are endemic to New Zealand; the Kakapo is restricted to native forests (mainly of Southern Beech, *Nothofagus*) bordering subalpine scrub or open ground along riversides on a few, predator-free islands off South Island; the Kea occurs only in the mountains of South Island; and the New Zealand Kaka is found only in remnant areas of native forest on both North and South Islands and some offshore islands

SOCIAL BEHAVIOUR: unlike other parrots, the Kakapo is polygynous with no pair bonds and the Kea may be monogamous or polygamous, with only the Kaka being monogamous; the Kakapo is mainly solitary, but males gather within earshot of one another at display sites where they attract females with their loud booming calls; Kea spend much of their time in flocks; New Zealand Kaka are usually seen in pairs, but often form flocks after the breeding season

NEST: Kakapo, in cavities in rotten trees, other holes or among dense vegetation, adding a bed of feathers and wood dust; Kea, in a burrow or hollow log, lined with leaves, twigs and lichen; New Zealand Kaka, usually in a tree hollow, often higher than the other two species, and lined with wood dust

EGGS: white in all three species, clutch in Kakapo, 1–2, rarely 3; Kea, 2–4; New Zealand Kaka, 1–8, usually 3–5

INCUBATION: Kakapo, about 4 weeks; Kea, 3–4 weeks; New Zealand Kaka, about 3 weeks

FLEDGING PERIOD: Kakapo 10–13 weeks; Kea, 13 weeks; New Zealand Kaka, about 10 weeks

FOOD: the Kakapo eats leaves, stems, roots, nectar, fruit, nuts and seeds; the Kea and the New Zealand Kaka have a wide diet of fruit, nuts, seeds and invertebrates, and occasionally meat from carcases; the New Zealand Kaka eats honeydew produced by scale insects in the breeding season

VOICE: Kakapo, include loud, far-carrying booming by males to attract females in breeding season and high-pitched *ching* calls that indicate their exact position to a female, and shrieks between rival males; Kea, mainly far-carrying, ringing *keeee-aa* calls; New Zealand Kaka, various harsh grating calls and liquid whistles

MIGRATION: none are migratory, and the flightless Kakapo is sedentary, but Keas move from scrub and grassland in autumn (when juveniles form wandering flocks) to find berries and then lower down below the timberline in winter, and New Zealand Kakas are sometimes nomadic, and may move in winter to more open country

CONSERVATION STATUS: the Norfolk Island Kaka, *Nestor productus*, is Extinct; the Kakapo, *Strigops habroptilus*, is Critically Endangered; the Kea, *N. notabilis*, and the New Zealand Kaka, *N. meridionalis*, are Endangered

LEFT Surviving only in tiny numbers on three islands off New Zealand's South Island, the Kakapo, *Strigops habroptilus*, is one of the world's rarest birds. After declining by over 80 percent during the last 100 years, its numbers are now slowly increasing, thanks to intensive conservation, but the total population is still only 150 or so birds, including just over 100 mature adults.

All three of the remarkable – and sadly endangered – living species in this small family are endemic to New Zealand; a fourth, the Norfolk Island Kaka, *Nestor productus*, lived on the Pacific Ocean island after which it is named (and adjacent Philip Island), but hunting and trapping by settlers rendered it extinct in the wild by the early nineteenth century; the last captive specimen died in London in 1851. There are two subfamilies: the Strigopinae, containing just the Kakapo, *Strigops habroptilus*, and the Nestorinae, comprising the two extant species of *Nestor*, the Kea, *N. notabilis*, and the New Zealand Kaka, *N. meridionalis*.

They are all stocky, thick-necked birds, the Kea and New Zealand Kaka about the size of a large pigeon and the Kakapo considerably larger, more rotund and appearing almost neckless. The plumage is mainly brown or green, with dark edges to the feathers giving a scaly appearance. The Kakapo has green upperparts with brown wings and tail mottled with black, and yellowish below, barred green and buff; the Kea is bronzy green above and brown on the head and underparts, with green and dark blue flight feathers, dull reddish back and rump, and a reddish-orange patch under the wing; the New Zealand Kaka is mainly brownish grey, with a whitish crown, pinkish face and dull rust red on the mantle and rear half of the underparts. The Norfolk Island Kaka was brighter than its surviving relative, with more extensive bright red and orange.

The Kakapo is in many ways the most atypical member of the whole parrot order, and one of the most remarkable of all birds. It is the world's heaviest parrot, and the only flightless one: despite having large rounded wings, it cannot glide, let alone use them for powered flight. It uses them instead for balance when running fast on its big, strong and stout legs or clambering among shrubs or along sloping tree branches or to break its fall as it tumbles from them or down a slope. Another oddity is that it has a distinctive sweet aroma, and is likely to have a well developed sense of smell. The Kakapo is one of the very few parrots that are nocturnal, hiding in vegetation during the day, where its mottled earth and leaf coloured plumage renders it virtually invisible to humans unless they are using tracker dogs or the bird is fitted with a radio telemetry device. Unlike other parrots, which are among the most sociable of all birds, Kakapos are solitary except during courtship, and then the males are highly competitive. They are also unique within the parrot order in having a lek mating system in which several males gather at a traditional site to advertise their presence to females. This they do by making very loud booming notes throughout the night, keeping up this performance every night for two or three months, mainly between January and March

These strange sounds, like that made by blowing over the top of a bottle, are among the loudest made by any bird, carrying for up to 5 km (3 miles). This is achieved by the bird taking in gulps of air, possibly into his oesophagus, and then expelling it to produce what is essentially a spectacularly loud belch, his whole body swelling so that he resembles a large ball. To add to the impact, he flaps his wings as he calls.

This remarkable bird is the most seriously threatened with extinction. Before the first Maori settlers arrived in New Zealand at least 700 years ago, it was abundant throughout both North, South and Stewart Islands. But its numbers and range contracted as the Maori and then to a far greater degree the European settlers altered and destroyed habitat. Even more damaging was their introduction of dogs, cats, rats, stoats and other predators to which the Kakapo had no natural defences (having evolved on predator-free islands). It is also at risk because of its slow rate of reproduction – it breeds only every two to five years, coinciding with periodic fruiting and seeding of its main food plants – added to the threats it faces, added to which it has very low egg fertility and chicks are susceptible to disease. By 1927, it could not be found on North Island, and the last ones on the mainland of South Island were recorded in 1987, and on Stewart Island in 1997. Today, it is likely to be extinct in its native range, and all surviving birds have been moved to small offshore islands from which predators have been removed.

COCKATOOS Cacatuidae

GENERA: 7   **SPECIES:** 21

LENGTH: 29–64 cm (11–25 in)

WEIGHT: 80 g–1 kg (2.8 oz–2.2 lb)

RANGE AND HABITAT: Philippines, Eastern Indonesia, New Guinea and nearby islands, Australia; inhabit a wide range of habitats, including tropical rainforest, other forests, scrub and semi-desert; some tolerate human presence and are found even in major cities

SOCIAL BEHAVIOUR: monogamous, with long-lasting pair bonds; all except the *Calyptorhynchus* black cockatoos share incubation and brooding of unfeathered young, with young often remaining with parents for a long time; generally very sociable, often forming large flocks that feed, fly and roost together

NEST: in holes or other cavities in trees formed by decay, breaking of branches or by animals such as woodpeckers or termites, not excavated by the cockatoos themselves; nest hollow lined with wood chips or (as in Galahs) leafy branches or (Palm Cockatoo) a platform of sticks

EGGS: 1–8, white

INCUBATION: 19–29 days

FLEDGING PERIOD: 5–13 weeks

FOOD: some take a wide range of food, including seeds, grain, fruit, nuts and other plant matter, as well as insects (especially when breeding and to feed to young) while others are specialists (such as the Glossy Black Cockatoo feeding on seeds from cones of just one genus of she-oak trees)

VOICE: mainly a variety of loud, harsh screeching calls, but some species also have chuckling, growling or whistling calls

MIGRATION: a few species make regular migrations but most are relatively sedentary or make nomadic movements

CONSERVATION STATUS: two species, the Yellow Crested Cockatoo, *Cacatua sulphurea*, and the Philippine Cockatoo, *C. haematuropygia*, are Critically Endangered; three species, the Long-billed Black Cockatoo, *Zanda baudinii*, the Short-billed Black Cockatoo, *Zanda latirostris*, and the White Cockatoo, *Cacatua alba*, are Endangered; two species, the Blue-eyed Cockatoo, *Cacatua ophthalmica*, and the Salmon-crested Cockatoo, *C. moluccensis*, are Vulnerable: and one species, the Tanimbar Corella, *C. goffiniana*, is Near Threatened.

The 21 species of cockatoo of the Family Cacatuidae are found in the Philippines, Indonesia and Australasia; by far the most species (11) are endemic to Australia. There are three more species whose range includes Australia and New Guinea; four species are restricted to Indonesia, and one each to the islands of the Philippines, the Solomons, and New Britain.

Compared to most other parrots, cockatoos have less colourful plumage – generally white, black or grey with only small areas of bright colour on the head, crest or tail – although the Galah and Major Mitchell's Cockatoo have pink bodies. Crests are highly developed; they are highly movable, and the birds often erect or lower them to communicate mood and intentions. In some, they are relatively short and simple, as with the jaunty spike of the Cockatiel, *Nymphicus hollandicus*, or the wispy, forwardly curving tufts of the Gang-gang Cockatoo, *Callocephalon fimbriatum*, which are contrastingly bright red (as well as the face) in males. Others have more elaborate adornments, such as the fans of the white cockatoos. In larger species these are shaped like an Indian chief's war-bonnet, and in three of them, the long white feathers are tipped with bright yellow, while the Salmon-crested Cockatoo, *Cacatua moluccensis*, has a rather shaggy, pink-tipped crest, and Major Mitchell's Cockatoo, *C. leadbeateri*, sports the most elaborate version, with concentric bands of red and yellow.

Most cockatoos are medium sized to large birds, with a deep, strongly hooked bill. The six black species include the biggest of all, and the largest Australian parrot, the monotypic Palm Cockatoo, *Probosciger aterrimus*, of New Guinea and extreme north-east Australia – at 55–60 cm (22–30 in), it is about the size of a Common Raven, *Corvus corax*, and also possesses a massive, very strongly hooked bill. Adding to its impact, its head is adorned with a huge, striking cascade of spiky black plumes. This impressive bird is remarkable for its use of a tool – during courtship or territorial displays at the nest site both males and females hold a stick or a stone or large nut in the bill and use it to strike a hollow branch and produce a loud drumming sound. Other cockatoos have dramatic displays too, including swinging down while perched on a branch to hang vertically, accompanied by loud calls. The other five species of black cockatoos, which are not much smaller than the Palm Cockatoo, are divided between two genera, *Calyptorhynchus* and *Zanda*. They live in various parts of Australia, two, the Glossy Black

ABOVE Its elegant crest raised, a Sulphur-crested Cockatoo, *Cacatua galerita*, feeds on figs in Queensland, Australia.

Cockatoo, *C. lathami*, and Yellow-tailed Black Cockatoo, *C. funerea*, in the east; two far more restricted and scarcer species (both classified as Endangered), the Long-billed and Short-billed Black Cockatoos, *Z. baudinii* and *Z. latirostris*, in the extreme southwest; and one, the Red-tailed Black Cockatoo, *C. banksii*, most widespread, found mainly in the west, north and northeast. Pairs or flocks are splendid in flight circling high overhead, when their long, narrow wings and long tails are distinctive.

A further dark-plumaged species, the smaller mainly grey Gang-gang Cockatoo, *Callocephalon fimbriatum*, is restricted to the extreme south-east of that continent. The smallest member of the family, the monotypic Cockatiel occurs across much of Australia (and is a common cagebird worldwide), while another monotypic species is the even more widespread and abundant Galah, *Eolophus roseicapillus*. The rest of the family are the 12 species of mainly white-plumaged cockatoos in the genus *Cacatua*. The best known by far of these is the Sulphur-crested Cockatoo, *Cacatua galerita*. Although it has a more restricted range in Australia than the preceding two species it is also familiar as a cagebird. It also occurs in the wild in the eastern Moluccas and most of New Guinea, and has been introduced to New Zealand, where small numbers still survive. Four other *Cacatua* species occur in Australia, of which three medium-sized species are called corellas. The Little Corella, *C. sanguinea*, (which also lives in parts of New Guinea), is the most widespread, the other two having restricted ranges, one in Western Australia and one with a much smaller range in the southwest. Major Mitchell's Cockatoo has a patchy range, mainly across the Australian interior. The remaining seven species of white cockatoos are all island endemics and include three rare and declining species, the Critically Endangered Philippine Cockatoo, *C. haematuropygia*, and the Yellow Crested Cockatoo, *C. sulphurea*, of various Indonesian islands, and the Endangered White Cockatoo, *C. alba*, of the northern Moluccas, and all but one of the others face varying degrees of threat, largely from habitat destruction and the cagebird trade. Overall, a third of the family is at variable risk of extinction.

AFRICAN AND NEW WORLD PARROTS Psittacidae

GENERA: 36   **SPECIES**: 167

LENGTH: 12 cm–100 cm (4.7–39 in)

WEIGHT: 20 g–1.7 kg (0.7 oz–3.7 lb)

RANGE AND HABITAT: some in tropical Africa (two genera), most in the New World tropics and subtropics; the majority live in forests of various types, but some in open country, including savannah, scrub and semi-desert

SOCIAL BEHAVIOUR: almost all are extremely social, many forming small or large flocks at feeding sites and roosts and when flying between them; most breed as isolated pairs or in small colonies, though some form larger colonies; monogamous, with many species pairing for life

NEST: most species breed in holes or other hollows in trees, some in old termite nests, or in cavities in cliffs, under rocks or in burrows in soil; most build no nest apart from scraping the interior of the nest cavity to accumulate a platform of wood dust for the eggs to lie on; some line the base with leaves or other vegetation, a few weave a nest of grass, bark or twigs within the cavity; one (Monk Parakeet) builds huge communal nests of sticks in treetops or on poles, pylons or other human structures, or on cliff ledges

EGGS: 1–11, white

INCUBATION: 18–30 days

FLEDGING PERIOD: 28–110 days

FOOD: mainly seeds and nuts, with fruits eaten mainly for the seeds they contain rather than their flesh; some also may eat other plant matter, such as flowers, leaves and bark; macaws and some other species also ingest clay exposed in river banks, which probably renders harmless toxins contained in some of their food

VOICE: very vocal, typically uttering loud, harsh screeching, squawking and chattering sounds; some species famed for mimicking human speech

MIGRATION: many make seasonal movements (including altitudinal migrations), or are nomadic, driven by geographical or temporal variations in food supply, and some make long daily journeys between good feeding areas and roosting or nesting sites

CONSERVATION STATUS: two species, the Carolina Parakeet, *Conuropsis carolinensis*, and Cuban Macaw, *Ara tricolor*, have become Extinct in recent historic times, and other Extinct species are known from subfossils or fossils; one species, Spix's Macaw, *Cyanopsitta spixii*, is Critically Endangered (Perhaps Extinct in the Wild); four species, the Indigo-winged Parrot, *Hapalopsittaca fuertesi*, Puerto Rican Amazon, *Amazona vittata*, Glaucous Macaw, *Anodorhynchus glaucus*, and Blue-throated Macaw, *Ara glaucogularis*, are Critically Endangered; 20 species, including the Grey Parrot, *Psittacus erithacus*, Sun Parakeet, *Aratinga solstitialis*, Lilac-crowned Amazon, *Amazona finschi*, Imperial Amazon, *A. imperialis*, Yellow-headed Amazon, *A. oratrix*, Lear's Macaw, *Anodorhynchus leari*, Great Green Macaw, *Ara ambiguus*, Red-fronted Macaw, *A. rubrogenys*, are Endangered; 32 species, including the Yellow-faced Parrotlet, *Forpus xanthops*, Red-fronted Parrotlet, *Touit costaricensis*, Vulturine Parrot, *Pyrilia vulturina*, Red-spectacled Amazon, *Amazona pretrei*, St Vincent Amazon, *A. guildingii*, St Lucia Amazon, *A. versicolor*, Hyacinth Macaw, *Ara hyacinthus*, and Military Macaw, *A. militaris*, are Vulnerable; and 16 species are Near Threatened

This is a very big bird family, almost as large as the next family (Psittaculidae), which in the classification followed in this book, is the largest in the parrot Order Psittaciformes. These two families, together with the previous two, Strigopidae and Cacatuidae, have previously been lumped together in a single huge family, when they formed one of the largest of all bird families, with as many as 390 species in some schemes. Recently, as here, the birds in the Strigopidae and Cacatuidae have each been recognised as deserving separate family status, though some systematists prefer to still unite the members of the two larger families, Psittacidae and Psittacidulidae as subfamilies within in a single enlarged Psittacidae.

There are two subfamilies in the Psittacidae, the Psittacinae and Arinae. The Psittacinae comprises just two genera and 10 species of African parrots. The monotypic genus *Psittacus* is that of one of the most familiar of all parrots, the Grey Parrot (or African Grey Parrot), *P. erithacus*, found in rainforest and woodland across a broad belt in Africa from Sierra Leone to western Uganda. Its pale silvery grey plumage has a distinctive and beautiful scalloped pattern due to the feathers' white edges contrasts with a patch of bare white skin extending from the base of the bill to behind the eye and a bright red tail (the smaller West African race *timneh*, sometimes regarded as a separate species, has a maroon tail and darker grey plumage). The Grey Parrot has long been popular as a cagebird, from the fifteenth century onwards, as trade with Africa gradually made the birds available as pets to amuse the rich and powerful (including Henry VIII of England). Grey Parrots are among the most long lived of parrots, with 40–50 years recorded in captivity and up to almost 23 years in the wild. This is one of the world's most intelligent birds, as demonstrated by Alex, studied for 30 years by US biologist Irene Pepperberg. Alex was able to use words in a way she showed via experiments indicated he understood their meaning and even coined new words. Sadly, today the Grey Parrot is the second most commonly trapped of all the world's parrots. As with many other species of parrot caught for the cagebird trade, large numbers of trapped birds die before export. The other genus in the Psittacinae is *Poiocephalus*, with nine species of mainly green or brown and green parrots, mostly with relatively restricted ranges in various parts of Africa.

The subfamily Arinae, containing all the New World parrots, comprises 157 species in 34 genera. It is divided into four tribes. The small tribe Amoropsittacini has 15 species in four genera. The genus *Touit* is one of two genera whose common name of 'parrotlet' reflects their small size. The odd scientific name is an approximation of the sound of some of the eight species' flight calls. These are sturdy little bright green birds with red feathers in the tail and wings. The three other genera in this tribe are mainly birds of mountain forests, occuring from altitudes of about 1,000 m (3,300 ft) to 4,000 m (13,100 ft) or more – the Andean Parakeet, *Bolborhynchus orbygnesius*, has been recorded at about 6,000 m (19,700 ft); the little Tepui Parrotlet, *Nannopsittaca panychlora*, commutes daily, sometimes in big flocks, between its roosts in the famous isolated table-top mountains (tepuis) of Venezuela and Guyana to the lowlands where it feeds.

The 10 genera and 61 species in the tribe Androglossini include the monotypic Monk Parakeet, *Myiopsitta monachus*, a thrush-sized bird famed for building huge communal nests. Other members of this tribe include the eight *Brotogeris* species, smallish, sturdy lowland

ABOVE The Festive Amazon, *Amazona festiva*, is an inhabitant of lowland South American rainforest in the Amazon and Orinoco basins.

dwelling parakeets that fly around in noisy flocks high above the forest in search of food. The genus *Pyrilia* includes the Vulturine Parrot, *P. vulturina*, of northern Brazil. Like the unrelated Pesquet's Parrot, *Psittrichas fulgidas*, of New Guinea (see p. 194), which is sometimes also confusingly referred to by the same common name, it has a black and yellow area of bare skin covered with bristles on its head. As with Pesquet's Parrot, this may be an adaptation to avoid the feathers being matted by the fruit that it eats. The best known and largest genus in the Androglossini is that of the amazon parrots, *Amazona*. These medium to large parrots are highly prized as cage birds, which (in combination with loss of habitat) has had a serious impact on the survival of many species. The various species are distinguished by the details of red, yellow, blue or white colours on their faces and wings. They are sturdy with short, square tails, rounded wings and distinctive flight, with fast, shallow beats of their stiff wings.

The tribe Forpini contains just a single genus, *Forpus*, of parrotlets, with six species. These tiny, rotund parrots are even smaller than the *Touit* and *Nannopsittaca* parrotlets, most being just 12–13 cm (4.7–5 in) long.

The tribe Arini is the largest of the four tribes, with 74 species in 19 genera. They include the family's largest and most easily recognisable members, the macaws, with 16 living species divided between four genera. Apart from the great size of many of them, these striking, long-bodied and long-tailed birds are renowned for their beautiful bright colour patterns. The two most familiar, through their popularity as cagebirds and ubiquitous use as symbols of the tropics in advertising, are among the eight extant species in the main genus, *Ara*: the Scarlet Macaw, *A. macao*, found from Mexico to the Amazon, and the Blue-and-yellow Macaw, *A. ararauna*, whose range extends from Panama to southern Brazil. Largest and most spectacular of all (and at about 1 m (3.2 ft) from bill tip to tail tip) the longest of all parrots) is the Hyacinth Macaw, *Anodorhynchus hyacinthinus*; smallest is an Amazonian species, the Red-shouldered Macaw, *Diopsittaca nobilis*, which is only 30 cm (12 in) long.

One species is already extinct – the Cuban Macaw, *Ara tricolor*, last seen in 1885 – and a further eight macaw species are classified as threatened with extinction: the rarest is the all-blue Spix's Macaw, *Cyanopsitta spixii*, of the dry caatinga woodland of eastern Brazil, which is likely now to be extinct in the wild, only surviving in captivity, due to trapping for the illegal cagebird trade and habitat loss.

Other members of the Arini include many parakeets, divided among several genera. These long-tailed, fast flying parrots include 23 in the largest genus *Pyrrhura* and an extinct monotypic species, the beautiful orange-red and yellow headed Carolina Parakeet, *Conuropsis carolinensis*, the sole native North American representative of the order until its demise in the wild by 1910 (the last captive individual died in Cincinatti Zoo in 1918). Although still common at the beginning of the nineteenth century, Audubon commented on their decline in 1832, resulting from increasing colonisation of the bird's range in the southeastern US by human settlers, who killed huge numbers for food, to prevent destruction of crops, for feathers to adorn women's hats and for the cagebird trade, as well as destroying habitat. The six species of the genus *Aratinga*, often known, especially in the cagebird trade, as conures, include some of the most exquisitely plumaged parakeets, for example the aptly named Sun Parakeet, *A. solstitialis*, of Guyana, Surinam and Brazil and the Jandaya Parakeet, *A. jandaya*, of Brazil, which have mainly brilliant golden orange and yellow plumage. A much larger and duller, mainly olive green species, the Burrowing Parakeet, *Cyanoliseus patagonicus*, lives in open country in Argentina and Chile, with an unusual habit of colonial nesting in burrows in earth banks. Another unusual monotypic member of the tribe Arini is

ABOVE Sun Parakeets, *Aratinga solstitialis*, are native to northern Brazil and adjacent Guyana, where they have suffered huge declines due to trapping for the cagebird trade.

the Red-fan Parrot, *Deroptyus accipitrinus*, which as its specific name indicates, is sometimes known as the Hawk-headed Parrot. The bright red and blue banded feathers of its hind crown and nape are usually laid back like a cowl around its neck but can be fanned out.

OLD WORLD AND AUSTRALASIAN PARROTS Psittaculidae

GENERA: 45   **SPECIES:** 184

LENGTH: 8–50 cm (3–20 in)

WEIGHT: 10–550 g (0.35–19 oz)

RANGE AND HABITAT: nine species in Africa (lovebird genus Agapornis), the rest spread across southern Asia and Australasia, also on many islands, including Madagascar and other Indian Ocean islands, Philippines, Indonesia, New Guinea, New Zealand and some Pacific islands; most in forests of various types, but some in in open country, including savannah, scrub and semi-desert

SOCIAL BEHAVIOUR: almost all are extremely social, many forming small or large flocks at feeding sites and roosts and when flying between them; most breed as isolated pairs or in small colonies, though some form larger colonies; monogamous, with many species pairing for life

NEST: most species breed in holes or other hollows in trees, some in old termite nests, or in cavities in cliffs, under rocks or in burrows in soil; most build no nest apart from scraping the interior of the nest cavity to accumulate a platform of wood dust for the eggs to lie on; some line the base with leaves or other vegetation, a few weave a nest of grass, bark or twigs within the cavity

EGGS: 2–9, white

INCUBATION: 18–26 days

FLEDGING PERIOD: 30–84 days

FOOD: mainly seeds and nuts, with fruits eaten mainly for the seeds they contain rather than their flesh; some also may eat other plant matter, such as flowers, leaves and bark; lories have narrower bills and highly specialised tongues with brushlike tips for lapping up nectar and pollen from flowers

VOICE: very vocal, typically uttering loud, harsh screeching, squawking and chattering sounds but also quieter chattering or warbling songs in some species; the Budgerigar, *Melopsittacus undulatus*, is well known for mimicking the human voice in captivity

MIGRATION: many species make seasonal movements or are nomadic in response to variations in food supply, or may commute long distances daily between good feeding areas and roosting or nesting sites; a few make regular migrations

CONSERVATION STATUS: six species, the Black-fronted Parakeet, *Cyanoramphus zealandicus*, Raiatea Parakeet, *C. ulietanus*, Seychelles Parakeet, *Psittacula wardi*, Rodrigues Parakeet, *P. exsul*, Mascarene Parrot, *Mascarinus mascarin*, and Paradise Parrot, *Psephotellus pulcherimmus* have become Extinct in recent historic times, with two more known only from fossils or subfossils; seven species, the Blue-fronted Lorikeet, *Charmosyna toxopei*, New Caledonian Lorikeet, *C. diadema*, Red-throated Lorikeet, *C. amabilis*, Ultramarine Lorikeet, *Vini ultramarina*, Blue-winged Racquet-tail, *Prioniturus verticalis*, Orange-bellied Parrot, *Neophema chrysogaster*, and Swift Parrot, *Lathamus discolor*, are Critically Endangered; eight species, including Wallace's Hanging Parrot, *Loriculus flosculus*, Green Racquet-tail, *P. luconensis*, Night Parrot, *Pezoporus occidentalis*, and Echo Parakeet, *Psittacula eques*, are Endangered; 17 species, including the Seychelles Black Parrot, *Coracopsis barklyi*, Black-winged Lory, *Eos cyanogenia*, Chattering Lory, *Lorius garrulus*, Pesquet's Parrot, *Psittrichas fulgida*, and Black-cheeked Lovebird, *Agapornis nigrigenis*, are Vulnerable; and 30 species are Near Threatened

In the classification followed in this book, the Family Psittaculidae is the largest of all families in the order Psittaciformes, with 184 species in 45 genera – slightly bigger than the other big family, the Psittacidae. There are three subfamilies: a very small one, the Psittrichasinae, a larger one, the Psittaculinae, and the largest, the Loriinae.

The Psittrichasinae comprises just four living species divided between two genera. The genus *Psittrichas* contains just a single unusual and increasingly scarce species, Pesquet's Parrot, *P. fulgidas*, patchily distributed in the mountain forests of New Guinea. This striking crow-sized bird is black, with pale fringes creating a scalloped pattern on its breast and a contrasting bright red belly, rump and big wing patches. Its long, strongly hooked bill, with bare skin at the base, on a long, thin neck, account for its alternative common name of Vulturine Parrot, though its food is not carrion but soft fruit, especially sticky figs and mangoes; the bare facial skin is probably an adaptation, as with vultures, to prevent its plumage being soiled. (There is another, similarly bare faced but unrelated South American species in the Family Psittacidae called the Vulturine Parrot: see p. 192.) The other genus in the tribe Psittirchasinae, *Coracopsis*, contains three large all-black parrots. Two are endemic to the Indian Ocean islands of Madagascar and the Comoros (the Greater and Lesser Vasa Parrots, *C. vasa* and *C. nigra*), and one, the Seychelles Black Parrot, *C. barklyi*) on Praslin Island in the Seychelles (which is sometimes regarded as conspecific with the Lesser Vasa Parrot). Their plumage is unusually sombre for a parrot, being dull brownish black and grey. Even more atypical is the reproductive behaviour of the Greater Vasa, in which females are larger than males and during the breeding season develop a bright orange patch of bare skin on the head after feathers fall out; they are promiscuous and attract males by singing an individually distinctive song, then copulate with several males over a period of days. Males mate with females over a wide range, and several males provide food for a female during incubation and for her chicks. The females' intense promiscuity has resulted in the evolution of intense sperm competition between the males. They have exceptionally large testes and a penis-like cloacal organ that becomes locked in a copulatory tie (reminiscent of that seen in mating dogs, though with the protagonists side-by-side in the parrot) within the female's cloaca for up to an hour and a half.

The Psittaculinae is subdivided into two tribes. The Tribe Micropsittini contains just a single genus of six species, *Micropsitta*, with the apt common name of pygmy parrots, for these are the world's smallest parrots, at 8–9 cm (3–3.5 in) long even smaller than a Eurasian Wren, *Troglodytes troglodytes*, or in North America a Winter Wren, *T. hiemalis*. Endemic to New Guinea and nearby islands, they are adept at climbing on tree trunks, aided (as are woodpeckers) by short, stiff, spiny tail feathers. There they feed mainly on fungus and lichens, a diet found in few other birds, let alone parrots. They roost and nest in holes made in the nests of tree-dwelling termites.

The tribe Psittaculini, with 42 species in nine genera, includes several well-known Australian species. The male Australian King Parrot, *Alisterus scapularis*, is adorned with brilliant scarlet and green plumage, while in the female the red is confined to her belly and undertail. Despite this gaudy plumage, the birds can be difficult to see as they tend to feed unobtrusively in the forest canopy. Another distinctive and much admired Australian species is the monotypic Eclectus Parrot, *Eclectus roratus*, in which the sexual dimorphism is even more exaggerated than that of the Australian King Parrot – so much so that the male and female were once thought to be different species. Uniquely among parrots, it is the male that is the less brightly plumaged of the pair, being all green save for blue and red patches on the wings and a narrow yellow tail tip; the female is brilliant red apart from a blue lower breast and belly. This reverse sexual dichromatism is associated with the females having to compete for nest holes with one another, and are (unlike almost all other parrots) promiscuous, copulating with several males; up to five males have been seen feeding a single female at the nest. This is partly reminiscent of the situation with another unusual parrot, the Greater Vasa Parrot, described above. The 10 species of racquet-tails, *Prioniturus*, are found on various islands of the Philippines (six species) and islands in eastern Indonesia (three species) or in both groups (one species). The largest genus in the tribe Psittaculini is *Psittacula*, with 13 extant species distributed widely across southern Asia. Best known is the Rose-ringed Parakeet, *P. krameri*, both as an extremely common bird in its native lands (it is probably the world's most numerous parrot species), where it occurs over a huge area in southern Asia, and unlike the other Psittacula species, also in Africa. In countries such as India where it occurs in vast numbers, it can cause major losses of grain crops. It is also increasingly well known in various other parts of the world to which it has been introduced, usually as a result of escapes of cagebirds or birds brought back home by sailors. In the UK, it is thriving and still increasing in numbers and range, and may pose problems by competing for nest sites with native hole-nesting birds. Large screeching flocks are now a common sight in major cities, such as London, Amsterdam and Los Angeles. This very successful bird is often called the Ring-necked Parakeet, but this is a poor name, as two other parrots in the genus also have similar coloured neck rings, brighter and redder or more intense pink. By contrast, two Psittacula species endemic to the Indian Ocean islands of the Seychelles (*P. wardi*) and Rodrigues (*P. exsul*) are extinct. The Rodrigues Parakeet suffered from a combination of hunting and habitat loss and was last recorded in 1875, with the last survivors probably wiped out by the worst cyclone the island has experienced in the nineteenth century; the last known individual of the Seychelles species was seen in 1893, the fate of this species sealed by clearing of forest for coconut plantations and being shot and trapped, especially because of its feeding on maize crops.

The big subfamily Loriinae comprises 131 species divided between 32 genera, and is divided into four tribes. The Tribe Psitacellini contains just a single genus, with four distinctively plumaged New Guinea species called tiger-parrots, referring to the bold black stripes on the upperparts, running from the nape to the upper back, and in females also on the underparts.

The tribe Platycercini comprises 39 species in 13 genera. The three living species of *Psephotellus*, a genus of brightly multi-coloured, long-tailed parrots endemic to Australia, include the Mulga Parrot, *P. varius*, found in scrubland and lightly wooded grassland, especially where the acacia shrub called mulga occurs, from the extreme west to as far east as western New South Wales. A fourth species, the Paradise Parrot, *P. pulcherimmus*, is now extinct. It was last recorded for certain in 1928, its demise resulting from a range of threats, including variation in the fire regime, predation by introduced and native animals, egg collecting and trapping disease, clearance of eucalypt woodland, other habitat damage and the reduction in its food supply due to overgrazing and drought.

The genus *Platycercus* contains some of Australia's most popular parrots, the six species of rosellas, attired in various combinations of bright red, blue, orange, yellow and green, with a distinctive scaled pattern on the upperparts, resulting from black feathers having coloured edges. The best known species is the Crimson Rosella, *Platycercus elegans*, with intense red and blue plumage. Along with another very abundant and equally gorgeously plumaged visitor, the Rainbow Lorikeet, large flocks, often numbering many hundreds, visit parks, nature reserves and open-air cafes in search of food. The birds become so confiding that they will land on the hands, arms, shoulders and heads of people proffering the seeds and fruit that these establishments sell to attract both birds and their human admirers. Such encounters are the closest most people have with wild birds. As a complete contrast, the pair of species making up the genus *Eunymphicus*, the Long-horned and Short-horned Parakeets, *E. cornutus* and *E. uvaeensis*, are rarely encountered, being restricted to remote parts of the islands of New Caledonia and Ouvea. Worryingly, both are threatened and classified as Vulnerable: the Long-horned species has declined as a result of logging and destruction of their forest home by introduced deer, as well as the effects of wet weather on breeding success, while the Short-horned species is at more imminent risk of extinction since it is restricted to part of a very small island and suffers from various threats, including habitat fragmentation, capture for the cagebird trade, predation and competition for nest holes with bees. Both species are unique among parrots in having a crest of narrow feathers on the head. The genus *Cyanoramphus* include six species of parakeets endemic to New Zealand and/or its offshore islands, as well as one from the island of New Caledonia and two extinct species from the Pacific islands of Tahiti and Raiatea. There are three very unusual endemic and enigmatic terrestrial Australian species in the genus *Pezoporus*: the Eastern and Western ground-parrots, *P. wallicus* and *P. flaviventris*, and the Night Parrot, *P. occidentalis*. With few confirmed sightings since 1935, the mottled green, brown and yellow Night Parrot was thought to have become extinct until its recent rediscovery. It is remarkable in being active at night (the only other nocturnal parrot is the Kakapo, *Strigops habroptilus* (see p. 190). Together with its very sparse distribution across a huge range in remote arid and semi-arid regions, this contributes to it being one of the most elusive and mysterious of all the world's birds. It is currently regarded as Endangered, with a guesstimated population that may number only 50–250 birds. Together with the Night Parrot, the two species of ground parrots (often regarded as a single species) are the only truly terrestrial parrots in the world, apart from two New Zealand species, the Antipodes Parakeet, *Cyanoramphus unicolor*, and the Kakapo. Both are threatened by habitat destruction, including by fire, as well as by dogs and other predators. The Eastern species is

very sparsely distributed in coastal grasslands of south-east Australia and Tasmania, while its Western relative, with a far smaller current range in the extreme southwest, is very rare.

The tribe Loriini is the largest in the Loriinae, with 65 species in 15 genera. Most live on islands, including the very large island of New Guinea but with the majority on small island archipelagos, from Indonesia to the western Pacific. Its best known member – indeed, one of the most familiar and most loved of all birds as the most abundant of all cagebirds, is the Budgerigar, *Melopsittacus undulatus*, in a genus of its own. Known as the 'Warbling Grass Parakeet', they were first scientifically described in 1805, and became popular in the West after they were seen by the famous nineteenth century English ornithologist, artist and publisher John Gould on his visit to Australia (when his Aboriginal assistants told him they called the bird 'betcherrygah'. Subsequently, Gould succeeded, despite the length of the sea voyage, in bringing back a live pair to England in 1840, when they caused a sensation. Today they are the third most popular pets in the world, after dogs and cats. In striking contrast to the image of the solitary cagebird, wild Budgerigars roam in flocks across arid and semi-arid grassland, scrub and open woodland over much of inland Australia. Their numbers and the size of the flocks vary with their food supply (seeds of grasses and other plants), which in turn depends on rainfall. Another difference between the wild and captive birds is that the former are always green-bodied, the various different colours and patterns of cagebirds, from blue and violet to white, and from clear-winged to spangled and crested, having been created by selective breeding. This attractive little bird is one of those parrots renowned

ABOVE A Rainbow Lorikeet, *Trichoglossus haematodus*, in Queensland, Australia, uses its brush-tipped tongue to lap up nectar.

as talkers, exemplified by one of several exceptional individuals, an American bird called Puck, who had memorised over 1,728 words or phrases, earning him a place in the *Guinness Book of World Records*. Of these only 50 or so had been taught him by his owner; the rest he picked up by listening to people's conversations or the radio. Another well known member of the Loriini is the Rainbow Lorikeet, *Trichoglossus haematodus*. The 10 other species in its genus are spread across various islands of eastern Indonesia, with one on Mindanao in the Philippines and one on Pohnpei, one of the Caroline Islands. Along with the Crimson Rosella, described above, it is hugely popular as a tourist attraction, when the beauty of its multicoloured plumage, from which it deserves its common name, adds to its tameness when offered food.

The Loriini also includes the two genera of fig-parrots, *Psittaculirostris*, with three species and *Cyclopsitta*, with four species. All are endemic to New Guinea and adjacent islands. As their common group name indicates, these small mainly green parrots feed mainly on figs, supplemented by other fruits, nectar and insects.

The final tribe, Agapornithini, comprises 23 species in three genera. The single species in the genus *Bolbopsittacus*, *B. lunulatus*, is known by its Spanish name, Guaiabero. Endemic to the Philippines, it is a little known, small almost all-green species that, like the species in the previous family of fig-parrots, feeds on figs and other fruit, including guavas (from which its common name

ABOVE A devoted pair of Rosy-faced Lovebirds, *Agapornis roseicollis*, from Angola, demonstrate the affection celebrated in their common and generic names.

derives). The 13 species in the genus *Loriculus* are the hanging parrots, their name referring to their extraordinary habit of resting by day and roosting at night hanging upside-down by their strong legs from a branch. The last members of the Agapornithini are the nine species of lovebirds, *Agapornis*, which are endemic to Africa. Small (13–16 cm/5–6 in long) and stocky, with short rounded tails, they are mainly green, with contrasting head colours in all but one species: various shades of red, pink or orange in five of them, pale grey in another, and blackish brown and blackish brown and buff in the other two. Four species also have a prominent white eye-ring. Their common name and the genus name (made up of the equivalent Greek words) refers to the habit of mated pairs of spending long periods perched close together, often touching, and preening one another, a habit that along with their pretty plumage has made them yet another parrot group that are very popular as cagebirds. As with Budgerigars, many colour varieties have been produced by selective breeding. Agile, noisy little parrots, Lovebirds are colonial nesters, siting their grass in crevices in rocks under the eaves of buildings or by invading the multi-chambered nests of colonial weaverbirds. Females have the odd habit of carrying strips of grass, bark or other material in flight to the nest by tucking them between their body feathers.

ABOVE The Rose-ringed Parakeet, *Psittacula krameri*, lends an exotic air to the places where the accidental introduction of this Asian species has led to its spreading in the wild.

ORDER PASSERIFORMES

The passerines (from the Latin word *passer* for sparrow) are sometimes known as perching birds as they have feet specialised to grasp branches and other perches by wrapping their long and strong hind toe (hallux) right around the perch. (This is however a misleading name, as many non-passerine birds, can perch too, but most have a different arrangement of their feet, such as parrots with two toes pointing forward and two back.) Features unique to the order include the shape of their sperm, the arrangement of bones in their palate, a distinctive arrangement of wing muscles and oil glands that differ from those of other birds. They generally have a relatively big brain and are good at learning, especially in relation to song repertoires.

The passerines are alternatively referred to as songbirds, a term that is strictly restricted to just one of their three constituent suborders the Oscines, in which song is most highly developed, although many members of the other main sub-order, and non-passerines too, produce sounds that effectively serve as songs. Some families, such as those of the crows (Corvidae), show great plasticity in behaviour and can learn new tasks quickly. Such assets are likely to be a major factor in the success and diversity of the whole order.

Most passerines are small birds, although the overall size range is great. It extends from tiny species, such as the kinglets, New Zealand wrens and pygmy-tyrants, with one of the latter, the Short-tailed Pygmy-tyrant, *Myiornis ecaudatus*, the smallest of all, at a mere 6.5 cm (2.5 in) long and 4.2 g (0.15 oz) in weight, to birds the size of umbrellabirds (*Cephalopterus*) or ravens, with the largest passerine, the Common Raven, *Corvus corax*, with large individuals of some races up to 69 cm (27 in) long and weighing 2 kg (4.4 lb). The order contains many birds that are familiar to people from watching them at bird feeders or providing breeding sites in the form of nest boxes, from tits, thrushes and finches in the UK and USA to honeyeaters and fairy-wrens in Australia.

About half of all bird families and over half of all the world's species of birds – some 6,000 species – are passerines. The order is one of the most species-rich of all land vertebrate orders, with almost 2.5 times as many species as the largest order of mammals, the rodents (Order Rodentia). There are a few really big families: three contain over 300 species each – the tanagers (Thraupidae), with 371, the tyrant-flycatchers (Tyrannidae), with 306, and the chats and flycatchers (Muscicapidae), with 303. A further three families have species totals in the 200s: the antbirds (Thamnophilidae), with 232, the horneros and relatives (Furnariidae), with 228, and the finches and relatives (Fringillidae), with 221, and there are 15 families that contain over 100 species each, including the honeyeaters (Meliphagidae), thrushes (Turdidae) and the New World wood warblers (Parulidae). Six families have between 77 and 93 species, while a further 12 families have species totals in the 50s and 60s. The rest consist of families ranging from just a few species (or in some cases only one) to the 40s. The history of this remarkable order has been one of often rapid adaptive radiations to different habitats and lifestyles, over timespans that, geologically speaking are very short (in some cases of the order of a few million years).

The order is divided into three suborders: a tiny relict group of just two tiny species, the Acanthisitti, which form the remnants of a basal group that evolved much earlier than the others; the Tyranni, or Suboscines; and the Passeri, or Oscines (the largest of the three suborders, popularly known as 'songbirds').

There is general agreement that the order as a whole is monophyletic, and that none of the species included within it belong to any other order. What is not at all clear is the relationship of this order to other orders, and many of the relationships of species within the order. Regarding the first of these uncertainties, the traditional view has long been that the passerines' closest relatives – often dubbed 'near passerines' – include the cuckoos (Order Cuculiformes), kingfishers, and relatives (Order Coraciiformes), hornbills and relatives (Bucerotiformes) and woodpeckers and relatives (Order Piciiformes). A recent molecular analysis, by contrast, suggests that the parrots (Order Psittaciformes) are closest to the Passeriformes, with falcons (Order Falconiformes) and seriemas (Order Cariamiformes) as the closest relatives of the parrots and passerines, and this is the scheme followed in this book.

As to relationships within the order, passerine taxonomy at family level is currently under more or less constant revision, particularly using new molecular techniques. The classification presented here is intended to represent a sensible compromise between topicality and uncertainty, but future arrangements are likely to end up looking very different to such a standard reference. The state of upheaval extends to the basal groups, with considerable disagreement regarding the relative merits of various proposals for classifying them. It is likely that some of the larger families, such as those of the Old World warblers (Sylviidae), Old World chats and flycatchers (Muscicapidae) have proved to be paraphyletic and thus, some of their members have been moved to other families or to new ones.

The origin of the order, both in space and time, is also clouded in uncertainty. There is quite strong evidence that they are a relatively ancient group that originated in the Southern Hemisphere, perhaps in Australia, where some of the oldest fossils known to date have been recently discovered.

SUBORDER ACANTHISITTI

There has long been uncertainty about the taxonomic position of the very small family, Acanthisittidae, of rockwrens and bushwrens, endemic to New Zealand. The current consensus is that they are a unique and ancient group, separate from all other passerines, that should be placed on its own in a separate suborder of the Passeriformes. Recent DNA studies suggest it should appear, as here, at the base of the Passerine radiation.

ROCKWRENS AND BUSHWRENS Acanthisittidae

GENERA: 3   **SPECIES:** 4

LENGTH: 7–10 cm (2.75–4 in)

WEIGHT: 5.5–22 g (0.2–0.8 oz)

WORLD RANGE AND HABITAT: New Zealand; Rifleman, *Acanthisitta chloris*, in forest, especially of southern beech (*Nothofagus*), with fewer at lower altitudes in temperate rainforest; Alpine Rockwren, *Xenicus gilviventris*, in open rocky alpine/subalpine terrain with stunted vegetation

SOCIAL BEHAVIOUR: monogamous and territorial; some Rifleman pairs breed cooperatively, with unmated adult males and juveniles helping in feeding and caring for young

NEST: spherical or ovoid, built by both sexes from sticks, grass and other plant matter, lined with feathers and with a side entrance, sited in a cavity (in a tree-trunk, branch, fence or other structure in the Rifleman and among rocks, tree-roots, moss or soft mud or clay in the Alpine Rock Wren)

EGGS: 2–5, white to cream

INCUBATION: 18–22 days

FLEDGING PERIOD: 21–27 days

FOOD: mainly insects, also other invertebrates such as spiders and small snails; occasionally nectar, seeds and berries

VOICE: sharp, very high-pitched calls

MIGRATION: essentially sedentary

CONSERVATION STATUS: Two species, the Bushwren, *Xenicus longipes*, and Lyall's Rockwren (Stephens Island Wren), *Traversia lyalli*, are recently Extinct; one species, the Alpine Rockwren (New Zealand Rockwren), is Endangered

The two living species, the Rifleman, *Acanthisitta chloris*, and the Alpine Rockwren (or New Zealand Rockwren), *Xenicus gilviventris*, are both tiny birds with relatively long legs, short, rounded wings and a very short tail, giving them a slight resemblance to the unrelated wrens (Family Troglodytidae, p. 376), although without the wrens' cocked tails. They are rather more like miniature versions of pittas (Family Pittidae, p. 200) but with finer bill although without the wrens' cocked tails. Unusually for passerines, females are larger than males.

The Rifleman is widespread in much of the North and South islands of New Zealand, and locally common, although some populations are fragmented; the Alpine Rockwren was once also found on North Island, before the arrival of European settlers, but is today found only on South Island. Its range includes much of the western part of the island, but is now fragmented, and in many places it is declining; a third species, the Bushwren, *Xenicus longipes*, is extinct, the last certain sightings in 1972. It was a very poor flier.

The fourth species, Lyall's Rockwren (or Stephens Island Wren), *Traversia lyalli*, was one of just a very few passerines known to have been completely flightless, the others both being long extinct species known only from subfossil remains: two of these were also species of New Zealand wrens, the Long-billed Wren, *Dendroscansor decurvirostris*, and the Stout-legged Wren, *Pachyplichas yaldwyni*. (The other was a bunting from Tenerife, one of the Canary Islands: the Long-legged Bunting, *Emberiza alcoveri*.) The Lyall's Rockwren was exterminated in 1894 (soon after its discovery) by a lighthouse keeper's cat on tiny island for which it was named; fossil deposits indicate it was widespread on both North Island and South Island in prehistoric times. It was the smallest of all known flightless birds.

ABOVE This is a male Rifleman, *Acanthisitta chloris*, the female is far duller, with streaked brown upperparts.

SUBORDER TYRANNI

Containing almost 1,300 species, this suborder is the smaller of the two major suborders of passerines. (Its scientific name, Tyranni, has been used sometimes, although not in this book, to refer to one of the subdivisions of this suborder, which we call the Tyrannides.) The Tyranni, or suboscines, have a more primitive syrinx (the avian voicebox) than the oscines, and generally are not capable of producing the complex songs of many of the birds in the latter group.

By far the greatest diversity among the suboscines today is seen in the New World, where the vast majority of species (about 96%) live, especially in the tropics of Central and South America. Here they form a dominant part of the entire passerine avifauna: the tyrant-flycatchers alone make up one of the biggest of all the world's bird families, with 79 genera and 306 species. By contrast, the Old World suboscines contain just 13 genera and 48 species.

The suborder is often divided into two main groups. The first of these is the Infraorder Eurylaimes, comprising the few Old World representatives of the suboscines and a single New World one. It contains five families, those of the pittas (Pittidae), typical broadbills (Eurylaimidae), asities (Philepittidae), African and green broadbills (Calyptomenidae), and the Sapayoa from the Neotropics (Sapayoidae).

The second is the exclusively New world Infraorder Tyrannides, which has two major subdivisions: the Parvorder Tyrannida and the Parvorder Furnariida. The Tyrannida contains the following ten families: manakins (Pipridae), cotingas (Cotingidae), Sharpbill (Oxyruncidae), the royal flycatcher and relatives (Onychorhynchidae), tityras (Tityridae), spadebills (Platyrhynchidae), piprites (Pipritidae), Rush Tyrant (Tachuridae), flatbills (Pipromorphidae), and tyrant-flycatchers (Tyrannidae). The Furnariida contains nine families: the antbirds (Thamnophilidae), crescentchests (Melanopareiidae), gnateaters (Conopophagidae), antpittas (Grallariidae), tapaculos (Rhinocryptidae), ant-thrushes (Formicariidae), leaftossers (Sclerruidae), woodcreepers (Dendrocolaptidae), horneros and relatives (Furnariidae).

ABOVE The Noisy Pitta, *Pitta versicolor*, is the most common and widespread of the three pitta species breeding in Australia.

PITTAS Pittidae

GENERA: 1   **SPECIES:** 29

LENGTH: 15–29 cm (6–11.5 in)

WEIGHT: 42–205 g (1.5–7.25 oz)

WORLD RANGE AND HABITAT: tropical sub-Saharan Africa, south and southeast Asia, Australasia; most species live in moist lowland tropical forest; others in upland or mountain forest; some in bamboo thickets or scrub; the Mangrove Pitta, *Pitta megarhyncha*, mainly in mangroves; the Giant Pitta, *Pitta caerulea*, sometimes in marshes

SOCIAL BEHAVIOUR: normally solitary outside the breeding season, and strongly territorial year-round; monogamous

NEST: loosely built, domed and with a side entrance, made of sticks, dead leaves, moss and grass, built by both sexes on the ground, between tree roots or in fork of tree branch

EGGS: 2–6, whitish with darker markings

INCUBATION: 14–18 days

FLEDGING PERIOD: 15–17 days

FOOD: mainly invertebrates, especially earthworms, also snails, ants, termites, beetles, spiders and centipedes; less often, small lizards, snakes and frogs and plant matter

VOICE: loud calls, mainly by males, especially at dusk, dawn or on moonlit nights; range from fluty or whistling sounds to yelping or whirring ones; the Noisy Pitta, *P. versicolor*, has a call that sounds like '*walk-to-work*'

MIGRATION: most species are sedentary, but four (the African Pitta, *P. angolensis*, the Indian Pitta, *P. brachyura*, the Fairy Pitta, *P. nympha*, and the Blue-winged Pitta, *P. moluccensis*) are medium- to long-distance migrants, and some populations of four others make more local movements

CONSERVATION STATUS: two species, Gurney's Pitta, *Pitta gurneyi*, and the Superb Pitta, *P. superba*, are Endangered; seven species, the Fairy Pitta, *P. nympha*, Graceful Pitta, *P. venusta*, Superb Pitta, *P. superba*, and Whiskered Pitta, *P. kochi*, Azure-breasted Pitta, *P. steerii*, Giant Pitta, *P. caerulea*, Blue-headed Pitta, *P. baudii*, and Black-faced Pitta, *P. anerythra* are Vulnerable; four species are Near Threatened

With their combination of brilliantly coloured plumage and very elusive habits, pittas are among the most highly sought-after of all birds by birdwatchers. Plump-bodied, big-headed, with a strong, slightly decurved bill, and almost tailless, pittas are ground dwellers that hop about on the forest floor on their rather long, sturdy legs. Their superficial likeness to thrushes (to which they are not related) in body shape and feeding behaviour, and their gorgeous plumage, led to pittas once also being known as jewel-thrushes. Here, we include all 29 species in a single genus, *Pitta*; some researchers prefer to place some in two additional genera, *Erythropitta* and *Hydromis*.

This small family exhibits a great range of plumage colours and patterns. Many species have green or mostly green upperparts, whereas others have mainly blue or brown. About half have bold head patterns, with broad black 'bandit's-mask' eyestripes and paler buff or yellow supercilia. A red belly, often with a blue breast-band above it, adorns many species. In most species the patches of colour are unmarked, but several species have dark barring on the underparts. In all but nine species, in which females are duller, the sexes look alike, or almost so.

Brilliant plumage is relatively unusual in ground-dwelling birds, but in the gloom of the dense forests where most pittas live, their intensely bright, almost iridescent colour patches on the coverts may serve as highly effective 'flags' or 'badges' to others of their own kind when flashed in display; also, as birds can see into the ultraviolet spectrum, their may be other plumage signals that are apparent to each other. For humans, though, and presumably most predators, it is normally surprisingly hard to see a pitta as it spends long periods standing motionless (often on one leg) during much of the day, feeding mostly in the cooler early morning or evening. When disturbed, it is likely to hop away into cover rather than fly, though the few migratory species are capable of making long flights. They normally leave the ground layer only at night, when they roost on tree branches.

Pittas feed like thrushes by sweeping aside dead leaves to expose insects and other invertebrates. They also dig into soft leaf litter and soil for prey such as earthworms, and are likely to locate it using their unusually well developed sense of smell. Several species have been found to use a stone, branch or root as an 'anvil' for breaking into the shells of snails, a method far better known in the Eurasian Song Thrush, *Turdus philomelos*.

A few species (such as the Blue-winged Pitta, *Pitta moluccensis*, of Southeast Asia, which can live in gardens and plantations) are more tolerant of habitat alteration, but most suffer from human disturbance. With their beautiful plumage, pittas have always been popular as cage birds, and trapping for this purpose and even more so for food, is a secondary threat.

TYPICAL BROADBILLS Eurylaimidae

GENERA: 7   **SPECIES:** 8

LENGTH: 13.5–28.5 cm (5–11 in)

WEIGHT: 29–140 g (1–4.9 oz)

WORLD RANGE AND HABITAT: all but a single African species in Asia; greatest diversity (nine species) in Southeast Asia; mostly forests, some in open woodland, bamboo thickets or scrub

SOCIAL BEHAVIOUR: monogamous with cooperative breeding in a few species; often gregarious outside breeding season

NEST: elaborate, tightly woven bag or ball shaped nest with a drooping 'tail' at the base, built by both sexes or female alone, of grasses, vines and other vegetation suspended from vine or tip of tree branch, camouflaged with leaves, moss, lichens, insect and spider cocoons and excreta held together with spiders' webs

EGGS: 1–8 (but usually only 2–3 young reared in each breeding attempt); white, cream or pinkish with darker markings

INCUBATION: unknown

FLEDGING PERIOD: unknown

FOOD: for most species, the staple diet is insects, spiders and other invertebrates; some species also eat fruit, which may form the main food of Grauer's Broadbill, *Pseudocalyptomena graueri*

VOICE: great range of calls, including whistling, mewing, trilling, squeaking, screaming, rattling and wheezing sounds

MIGRATION: mostly sedentary, although some make limited altitudinal or nomadic movements

CONSERVATION STATUS: two species, the Wattled Broadbill, *Sarcophanops steerii* and Grauer's Broadbill, *Pseudocalyptomena graueri*, are Vulnerable; one, the Black-and-Yellow Broadbill, *Eurylaimus ochromalus*, is Near Threatened

ABOVE The Black-and-red Broadbill, *Cymbirhynchus macrorhynchus*, of Southeast Asia uses its big bill to catch small crabs as well as insects.

It was not until the mid-nineteenth century that ornithologists considered the broadbills to be members of the Passeriformes; they had often been thought to be related to such birds as rollers and kingfishers in the Order Coraciiformes, or even to nightjars (Caprimulgiformes).

These sparrow-sized to dove-sized birds of forests and woodlands are sturdy bodied, with a big head and large eyes. They are all restricted to southern Asia, apart from one unusual species, the little Grauer's Broadbill, *Pseudocalyptomena graueri*, which is a scarce relict species inhabiting forests in two separate small areas of the Albertine Rift mountains of eastern Zaire and western Uganda. All but this species, which has a small, narrower black bill, have a very broad, slightly hooked distinctively coloured bill that is flattened from top to bottom and has a very wide gape. The two largest species, the Black-and-red Broadbill, *Cymbirhynchus macrorhynchos*, and the Dusky Broadbill, *Corydon sumatranus*, have especially big and wide bills; indeed that of the Dusky Broadbill is the broadest in relation to its overall size of any passerine.

Apart from Grauer's Broadbill, which is almost uniformly green and the mainly sombre blackish-brown Dusky Broadbill, typical broadbills have strikingly patterned plumage in various combinations of black, yellow, orange, red, maroon, pink, blue or white, as well as much green in the Long-tailed Broadbill, *Psarisomus dalhousiae*. The sexes are generally similar, although females of some species are a little duller. In addition to the bright plumage colours, the bills of all but Grauer's Broadbill are contrastingly coloured, silver, blue, blue-and-yellow or, in the Dusky Broadbill, pinkish red; the eyes of the two *Eurylamus* species too have bright colours in the iris, yellow in the Black-and-yellow Broadbill, *E. ochromalus*, and yellow in the Banded Broadbill, *E. javanicus*. The Silver-breasted Broadbill, *Serilophus lunatus*, has dark blue to green eyes surrounded by an orange ring of bare skin, while the Wattled Broadbill, *Sarcophanops steerii*, has eyes with a blue iris further enhanced by a blue wattle of skin encircling them.

Little is known of the biology of most species apart from anecdotal accounts. On the whole, broadbills are gregarious birds, and most species are often seen in small flocks. This is especially true of the Dusky Broadbill, which occurs in groups of up to 10 or more year-round. They eat a wide range of insects, especially big grasshoppers, crickets, mantids, bugs and beetles, and ants and other hymenopterans; the larger species are capable of dealing with small lizards and tree-frogs. Mostly, they feed on flying insects by waiting quietly on a perch, sometimes for long periods, head tucked in, until they spot the prey. Then they sally out, with whirring wingbeats of their short wings, in the manner of a flycatcher to intercept it and snap it up in the capacious gape of the broad bill before returning to deal with it, often to a different perch. They also glean insects from foliage or branches, either snatching them in flight or by hopping after them. Their short legs, with two of the forward facing toes partly fused and a weak hind toe, are not suited to walking or running. With its small bill unspecialised for dedicated insect eating, Grauer's Broadbill lives mainly on berries and other small fruits.

ASITIES Philepittidae

GENERA: 2   **SPECIES:** 4

LENGTH: 12.5–16.5 cm (5–6.5 in) in the two *Philepitta* asities; 9–10.5 cm (3.5–4 in) in the sunbird asities

WEIGHT: about 30–38 g (1–1.3 oz) in the two *Philepitta* asities; about 6–8 g (0.25–0.3 oz)

WORLD RANGE AND HABITAT: Madagascar; Schlegel's Asity lives in seasonally dry rainforest in western Madagascar; the three other species inhabit rainforest in the east of the island

SOCIAL BEHAVIOUR: often solitary, although they gather in large numbers at good food sources, and may join mixed-species flocks; the Velvet Asity at least is polygamous

NEST: untidy, pear-shaped or spherical structure suspended from a branch and constructed of grass, leaves, bamboo fibre, moss or other vegetation, tapering towards the base, and with an overhanging 'porch' above the entrance hole; the Velvet Asity and Common Sunbird Asity at least are unique among all birds in making the hole by poking their bill through the wall of the finished nest rather than weaving it into the nest as they build it

EGGS: unknown for Schlegel's Asity; 2 or 3 eggs recorded for other species; pale green in one nest of Common Sunbird Asity, unknown colour for others

INCUBATION: unknown

FLEDGING PERIOD: unknown

FOOD: mainly fruit in the two *Philepitta* asities; nectar in the two *Neodrepanis* sunbird-asities; also some insects

VOICE: weak, squeaky calls; whistling songs heard from the two asities

MIGRATION: none; may make some altitudinal or food-seeking movements

CONSERVATION STATUS: the Yellow-bellied Sunbird Asity, *Neodrepanis hypoxantha*, is Vulnerable; Schlegel's Asity, *Philepitta schlegeli*, is Near Threatened

ABOVE This male Common Sunbird Asity, *Neodrepanis coruscans*, will lose the blue bare skin around his eyes with the post-breeding moult.

Small, round-bodied, brightly plumaged birds with an extremely short tail and forked, brush-tipped tongues for nectar feeding, the asities form a tiny family restricted entirely to the island of Madagascar.

The genus *Philepitta* contains two shorter-billed birds: the Velvet Asity, *P. castanea*, and Schlegel's Asity, *P. schlegeli*. During the breeding season, the male of the first of these species, which is the biggest member of the family, acquires an almost entirely intensely velvety black breeding plumage. He acquires this by wearing away of the bright yellow fringes of the otherwise black feathers (apart from a small concealed 'shoulder' patch). He also develops a large wattle of iridescent bright green naked skin above each eye. This is extended into little 'horns' at the front that meet over the bill when he expands them during breeding displays to attract females or challenge rival males. Once breeding is over, the male moults back to his yellow-scaled non-breeding plumage, and the head wattles shrink until they are almost invisible. Schlegel's Asity is rather smaller. The male is mainly olive above and bright yellow below, and in breeding plumage has a bright blue and pale green wattle encircling most of each eye.

The other genus, *Neodrepanis*, also comprises two species, distinguished by the name sunbird asities: the Common Sunbird Asity, *N. coruscans*, and the Yellow-bellied Sunbird Asity, *N. hypoxantha*. The sunbird asities were originally thought to be relatives of starlings (Family Sturnidae, p. 381) and birds-of-paradise

(Paradisaeidae, p. 277) and later of sunbirds (Nectariniidae), all of which are oscine passerines (songbirds). With their green or bright blue and yellow plumage and long curved bills, they do bear a strong superficial resemblance to the sunbirds, but after examination of their simpler syrinx (voicebox) it became clear that they were suboscines, and then by DNA and morphological evidence, close relatives of the typical broadbills (Eurylaimidae, p. 201). Both species are tiny birds with a very long, slender, strongly decurved bill. The males of both species have deep, iridescent blue plumage on the back and on the head, which has a large green and blue bare skin wattle around the eye, and bright yellow underparts. In all four asity species, the males are much the brighter sex. Females are dark olive-green above and dull yellowish below.

The brilliant colour of the male wattles does not come from pigments, but is a result of light scattering from collagen fibres, a feature that may be unique not only among birds, but among all animals.

The *Philepitta* asities feed mainly on fruits (especially small berries that provide a lot of energy), supplemented by nectar, which they lap up with the forked, brush-tipped tongues. The sunbird asities are more highly adapted for drinking nectar, having an extra refinement in that their long tongues are also tubular. As well as nectar, they eat insects and spiders, as do the *Philepitta* species.

Little is known about the breeding biology of the two sunbird asities and Schlegel's Asity, though there is some evidence that some of them at least may be monogamous. It appears that the Velvet Asity is polygynous, with males performing to females on branches at special display sites (leks), and each male mating with several females. A range of displays include the male perching erect, stretching out his neck and inflating his wattle; flapping his wings to reveal the hidden bright yellow spot; and opening his bill to show off the bright yellow gape, on occasion then suddenly falling forward to hang from the perch; at the peak of display fervour, he may even swing completely round it. The males of at least some asity species make mechanical noises resulting from air vibrating the enlarged outer primary feather of each wingtip. This may be used in display flights; the buzzing sound produced by the Yellow-bellied Sunbird Asity is particularly loud.

Although the Yellow-bellied Sunbird Asity was listed as Endangered as recently as 1994, it has since been found to be somewhat more numerous. Accordingly, its status has been downgraded to Vulnerable, although it is still thought to be declining. Indeed, all four species of asity, along with many other Malagasy birds, are at risk from further fragmentation, degradation or destruction of the country's already savagely depleted forests, as a result of logging, slash-and-burn agriculture and mining.

AFRICAN AND GREEN BROADBILLS Calyptomenidae

GENERA: 2 **SPECIES:** 6

LENGTH: 11.5–27 cm (4.5–10.5 in)

WEIGHT: 18–171 g (0.6–6 oz)

RANGE AND HABITAT: the three *Smithornis* species live in tropical Africa, the African Broadbill, *S. capensis*, with the widest distribution in a range of wooded habitats, as well as scrub and more open agricultural land and around villages, and the other two species with more restricted ranges and tied to dense forest; the three *Calyptomena* species are found in Southeast Asia in humid forests, with one, the Green Broadbill, *C. viridis*, widespread across the south, and the other two restricted to the island of Borneo

SOCIAL BEHAVIOUR: often seen in small groups; breeding possibly polygynous, with males displaying at leks

NEST: a bag-like structure of grass, leaves, rootlets, vines, moss, lichen and other material with a side entrance and an untidy 'tail', suspended from a branch

EGGS: 1–3, white in *Smithornis*, cream in *Calyptomena*

INCUBATION: known only from captive individuals of the Green Broadbill, *C. viridis*: 17–18 days

FLEDGING PERIOD: known only from captive individuals of the Green Broadbill, *C. viridis*: 22-23 days

FOOD: insects and spiders in *Smithornis*, mainly fruit but also some insects in *Calyptomena*

VOICE: quiet whistling or mewing notes in *Smithornis* (as well as much louder non-vocal sounds), and a wide range of wheezing, chattering, cooing, harsh grating and other sounds in *Calyptomena*

MIGRATION: mainly sedentary, apart from local movements in response to weather or (in *Calyptomena*) relative abundance of fruit

CONSERVATION STATUS: two species, the Green Broadbill and Hose's Broadbill, *C. hosii*, are Near Threatened

The six species in this small family were until recently lumped with the typical broadbills in the Family Eurylaimidae, with the three Asian green broadbills in the genus *Calyptomenus* given a subfamily (Calyptomeninae) of their own. Recent DNA studies indicate that their closest relatives are the three African species in the genus *Smithornis* and that together they merit placement in a family (Calyptomenidae) of their own separate from the typical broadbills. For a long time, until the early years of the twentieth century, most ornithologists considered the broadbills to be endemic to Asia, and regarded *Smithornis* as a member of the very large and diverse assortment of the Family Muscicapidae of Old World flycatchers and relatives.

The three *Smithornis* species all have a black or grey crown, dark-streaked brown upperparts, orange or buff breast sides and dark streaked white underparts. The sexes are have a similar plumage pattern but the females are duller. The African Broadbill, *S. capensis*, is widespread across tropical southern, central and eastern Africa; the Rufous-sided Broadbill, *S. rufolateralis*, has a more discontinuous range in Central and West Africa; and the Grey-headed Broadbill, *S. sharpei*, is restricted to the Congo Basin and the small island of Bioko, and requires undisturbed rainforest. In contrast to the green broadbills, *Smithornis* species feed on insects. They sit patiently upright and motionless on a perch, often for long periods, before dashing out like a flycatcher

ABOVE Stiffened feathers almost cover the wide, hooked bill of this handsome male Green Broadbill, *Calyptomena viridis*.

The green broadbills are plump bodied, with short but wide bills and very short tails. There is a gradation in size between the three species, from the smallest, the Green Broadbill, *Calyptomena viridis*, at 14–17 cm (5.5–6.5 in) long, via Hose's Broadbill, *C. hosii*, 19–21 cm (7.5–8 in) to Whitehead's Broadbill, *C. whiteheadi*, 24–27 cm (9.5–10.5 in). All have a very distinctive tuft of feathers on the forehead that is particularly pronounced in males, virtually hiding the bill and iridescent green plumage, especially bright in the males. Apart from the Green Broadbill, in which the female is almost uniformly green, they have contrasting black markings, more prominent in the males. Male Hose's Broadbills also have bright blue underparts; the blue is paler and confined to the rear in females. Despite their bright plumage, these beautiful birds can be hard to see, as the green blends in with the sun-dappled foliage of the middle and upper storeys of the humid tropical forests that are their home. The Green Broadbill has the largest range, encompassing southern Myanmar, southwest Thailand, the Malaysian Peninsula, Sumatra, and much of Borneo as well as smaller islands. The two other species are endemic to the island of Borneo. The Green and Hose's Broadbills have declined considerably as a result of logging.

In contrast to almost all of the typical broadbills, these birds are primarily fruit-eaters, although they eat some insects too, especially to feed to their young. They eat a wide range of fruit, from small berries to large fruit, in Whitehead's Broadbill including some as big as plums. They swallow most fruit whole, thanks to their broad bills.

to catch flying insects in mid-air, and also glean insects from the branches or foliage of trees. A distinctive feature of these little birds is that during their tight circular display flights, they make loud, far-carrying, trilling and buzzing sounds. These were long thought to be vocal, but in fact they are mechanical, produced as air rushes over the stiffened outer primary feather of each wing. They share this ability with their relatives the asities of Madagascar (Family Philepittidae, p. 202).

SAPAYOA Sapayoaidae

GENERA: 1   **SPECIES:** 1

LENGTH: 13.5–15.5 cm (5–6 in)

WEIGHT: about 21 g (0.75 oz)

WORLD RANGE AND HABITAT: eastern Panama and western Colombia south to northwest Ecuador; humid lowland forest, understorey to mid-level, often near streams and ravines

SOCIAL BEHAVIOUR: solitary for much of time but regularly joins in feeding with roaming mixed-species flocks

NEST: few known: pear-shaped, made of bark and fibres, suspended from tree branch

EGGS: unknown

INCUBATION: unknown

FLEDGING PERIOD: unknown

FOOD: mostly small invertebrates, also some fruit; sallies out from perch to snap up insect in mid-air or glean it (or fruit) from foliage

VOICE: soft, nasal trill and louder '*chip, ch-ch-ch*' contact call

MIGRATION: sedentary

CONSERVATION STATUS: not threatened

The Sapayo, *Sapayoa aenigma*, is a dull-plumaged little bird of the rainforests of Panama and northwest South America that is distinctive enough to be placed in a family of its own, as here. As its specific name, *aenigma*, suggests, it has for a long time posed a taxonomic riddle, with uncertain relationships to other passerines and no obvious relatives. Its drab olive plumage and habit of perching motionless for long periods make it unobtrusive and easily overlooked, but it appears to be more common than once thought to be over much of its range in northwestern South America and Panama.

Although traditionally placed, with reservations, in the tropical American manakin family, Pipridae, or with the tyrant-flycatchers, Tyrannidae, it clearly differs from these in various ways. However, recently, DNA research showed that it is actually more closely related to the Old World suboscines. The most likely scenario is that the Sapayoa is the last surviving member of a group of birds that evolved in Australia or New Guinea and spread to the New World via Antarctica before plate tectonics split the supercontinent of Gondwanaland and separated the southern continents from South America. It has sometimes been linked to the broadbill family, whereas other taxonomists tentatively put it nearer to the asity family, and it may also be more distantly related to the pittas.

MANAKINS Pipridae

GENERA: 17 **SPECIES**: 48

LENGTH: 7–16.5 cm (2.75–6.5 in)

WEIGHT: 6–35 g (0.2–1.25 oz)

WORLD RANGE AND HABITAT: Central and South America, from southern Mexico to southern Brazil, Paraguay and northern Argentina; most species in lowland humid tropical forest, a few in dry forests, thickets and scrub, or at higher altitudes in the Andes

SOCIAL BEHAVIOUR: often solitary when feeding, although females are more social; may gather at fruiting trees, join mixed-species flocks and bathe communally in forest streams in the late afternoon, often several species together; polygamous, with a small number of males at each lek performing most matings

NEST: usually tiny, flimsy, hammock-like nests of vegetable fibres, fungal threads and other fine material, slung between two twigs or fern fronds

EGGS: 2, whitish, cream, buff or grey, with brown markings

INCUBATION: 16–21 days recorded in a few species

FLEDGING PERIOD: 13–15 days recorded in a few species

FOOD: mainly small fruits, snatched from a tree or shrub in flight; also some insects and spiders

VOICE: mostly silent, although at leks males make a variety of calls, including piping, chirping, hiccupping and froglike sounds, including precisely synchronised duets between a dominant and subdominant male; also a whole range of non-vocal sounds, produced by the wings (in many species as they are clapped together or against the body or tail)

MIGRATION: most species are highly sedentary; a few make seasonal altitudinal movements

CONSERVATION STATUS: one species, the Araripe Manakin, *Antilophia bokermanni*, is Critically Endangered; four species, Wied's Tyrant-manakin, *Neopelma aurifrons*, the Opal-crowned Manakin, *Lepidothrix iris*, the Golden-crowned Manakin, *L. vilasboasi*, and the Yellow-headed Manakin, *Chloropipo flavicapilla*, are Vulnerable; one species, the Blue-rumped Manakin, *L. isidorei*, is Near Threatened

ABOVE This Bearded Manakin, *Manacus manacus*, of the distinctive race *candei* (often regarded as a separate species) is displaying at a lek in Costa Rica.

Small tropical forest birds of Central and South America, manakins are stout-bodied and short-tailed. The bill is short but with a very wide gape, evolved for swallowing fruits that are large relative to the bird's size (the fruit may be only the size of a grape, but this is equivalent to a turkey swallowing a coconut-sized fruit). These birds are exceptional in having great variation in the structure of their syrinx ('voice box'), with every genus and many species being distinguishable on this basis, in contrast to almost all other families of songbirds.

Males of most species are boldly plumaged, with contrasting areas of brilliant colour. Many are largely black, with patches of red, orange, yellow, blue or white, while a few have a white, blue or yellow body and black wings. The females of these gaudy males, by contrast, are mostly well camouflaged olive-green – as are the immature males in many species; in others a distinct subadult plumage is acquired and worn for 2–4 years until the birds attain sexual maturity and moult into adult plumage. In some species both male and female are mainly olive-green or brown.

All species are essentially fruit-eating specialists that appear to have evolved from insect-eating stock; they make swift sallies to snatch small fruit in the bill from the tree or shrub in flight and then return to the perch to swallow it whole. They also supplement their staple diet with insects and spiders taken in the same way from foliage or hawk for flying insects such as swarms of termites. Sometimes they will pluck more accessible fruit without leaving the perch.

Manakins are renowned for the great range of spectacular courtship displays performed by males of many species. These are accompanied by special calls and distinctive mechanical sounds produced by modified wing feathers. These include clicking, whirring, popping, softer 'pooping' sounds and snapping wing noises that sound like miniature firecrackers; the latter are remarkably loud in species such as the Bearded Manakin, *Manacus manacus*.

Although females travel over a wide range in search of good fruit sources, males spend much of their time at the communal display site, or lek (often foraging for fruit for less than 10% of each day). The Helmeted Manakin, *Antilophia galatea*, is the only species known to form pairs, and even then the male's contribution seems to be limited to defending the territory: all the others are polygynous, with females visiting the lek and choosing to mate each year with just a few dominant males.

The males' courtship displays are particularly elaborate in the genera *Pipra* and *Chiroxiphia*: indeed, they are the most complex such rituals performed by any passerines. *Pipra* manakins perch on a branch about 3–10 m (10–33 ft) above ground and then perform a whole series of stereotyped movements. These include rapid backward slides that give the impression that the little bird is gliding along the perch, sudden about-faces, twists, back-and-forth pivoting, and swift flights to another perch and back. They are performed by two or more males, often with highly coordinated actions. The displays of the Wire-tailed Manakin, *P. filicauda*, culminate in the male tickling the chin of his intended mate with the very long wire-thin filaments that project from the tail.

The displays of *Chiroxiphia* manakins are even more remarkable. Here, coordination reaches its zenith, with two unrelated males opening the proceedings with a duet of whistling notes to attract a female. When one arrives at the lek, the males fly down to land on a special perch from which the dominant male has stripped

ABOVE With a distinctive syrinx and courtship display, the White-crowned Manakin, *Dixiphia pipra*, is sometimes given a separate genus, *Dixiphia*.

ABOVE The snapping sounds made by this male Red-capped Manakin, *Ceratopipra mentalis*, helps females locate his lek in the gloom of the forest.

the leaves. Here they woo her with a display of vertical leaps, alternating precisely with one another so that as one rises the other lands on the perch. They accompany this display with a curious nasal twanging call. If the female then flies to their perch, they switch to the high spot of their act. Facing her, the nearest male jumps up, calls, hovers, and flies back behind the other male, who slides forward, then repeats these actions. Faster and faster they rotate in this strange revolving wheel dance, the calls building up to a frantic crescendo; then suddenly the dominant male dismisses his subordinate with a sharp 'zeek' call. Alone with the female, he clinches the affair with a series of butterfly-like display flights and wing-cracking before mating with her. The subordinate male benefits in the long run, as he inherits the dominant male's display site – although he may have a long wait, for manakins are long-lived compared with most other passerines. A study of Long-tailed Manakins, *Chiroxiphia linearis*, found that some subordinates may have to wait as long as 10 years to gain their reward.

ABOVE A male Wire-tailed Manakin, *Pipra filicauda*, prepares to display at a lek near Iquitos, in the Peruvian Amazon.

COTINGAS Cotingidae

GENERA: 25   **SPECIES:** 65

LENGTH: 12–51 cm (5–20 in)

WEIGHT: about 6–500 g (0.2–17.6 oz)

WORLD RANGE AND HABITAT: Central and South America, Trinidad; most in tropical and subtropical forest; a few species in temperate mountain woodlands

SOCIAL BEHAVIOUR: most live alone or in pairs or family groups; breeding systems vary from monogamy and cooperative breeding to polygamy (with or without leks)

NEST: varies widely from group to group, from very small to large, and includes neat cups, untidy, loosely woven platforms, and the unusual bracket-shaped nests of mud and vegetation cemented to a rock face or ledge built by the two cock-of-the-rock (*Rupicola*) species

EGGS: 1–4 in most species, but only 1 or 2 in cocks-of-the-rock and fruiteaters; usually buff, khaki or olive, with darker markings

INCUBATION: 15–28 or more days

FLEDGING PERIOD: 28–33 days in most species, but only 17 or so in plantcutters, *Phytotoma*, and up to 48 in cocks-of-the-rock

FOOD: either mainly or almost entirely fruit, or fruit and insects (and some small vertebrates in a few species); young are fed more on insects; the three species of plantcutter are unusual in feeding on leaves, shoots, buds and flowers

VOICE: hugely varied, mainly by males, including insect-like calls of fruiteaters, loud grunts, booms or hoots of umbrellabirds, the mooing of the capuchinbird, the very loud whistles of the pihas, the even louder clanging of bellbirds and the squeals, squawks and clucks of cocks-of-the-rock; by contrast, some cotingas have never been heard to make any calls

MIGRATION: mostly sedentary, but a few (notably bellbirds) make seasonal altitudinal migrations

CONSERVATION STATUS: one species, the Chestnut-capped Piha, *Lipaugus weberi*, is Critically Endangered; four species, the Banded Cotinga, *Cotinga maculata*, Peruvian Plantcutter, *Phytotoma raimondii*, Yellow-billed Cotinga, *Carpodectes antoniae*, and Bare-necked Umbrellabird, *Cephalopterus glabricollis*, are Endangered; 11 species, including the Turquoise Cotinga, *Cotinga ridgwayi*, Three-wattled Bellbird, *Procnias tricarunculatus* and Long-wattled Umbrellabird, *Cephalopterus penduliger*, are Vulnerable; seven species are Near Threatened

ABOVE This male Three-wattled Bellbird, *Procnias tricarunculatus*, is calling and displaying from a perch in a Costa Rican cloud forest.

ABOVE The Long-wattled Umbrellabird, *Cephalopterus penduliger*, is a rare and local species due to habitat destruction and hunting.

Cotingas are extremely varied in size, form and plumage, with the widest length, wingspan and weight range of all passerine families. At one extreme is the sparrow-sized Fiery-throated Fruiteater, *Pipreola chlorolepidota*; at the other is the crow-sized Red-ruffed Fruitcrow, *Pyroderus scutatus*, and the three species of umbrellabirds, *Cephalopterus*, of which the Amazonian Umbrellabird, *C. ornatus*, is the largest of all Neotropical passerines – almost the size of a Northern Raven, *Corvus corax*. Bill shape and size differ in relation to diet, which consists mainly of fruit, especially the protein- and fat-rich fruits of palms, laurels, incense trees, nutmeg and mistletoes. The smaller species (such as the fruiteaters, *Pipreola*, and berryeaters, *Carpornis*) generally have a short, slightly hooked bill for dealing with small fruits; larger species that specialise in swallowing big fruits whole (such as the bellbirds, *Procnias*) have a bill with a very wide gape; the biggest species (the fruitcrows, *Haematoderus*, *Querula* and *Pyroderus*, and umbrellabirds, *Cephalopterus*) eat large insects (and in the case of the umbrellabirds, small lizards, snakes and frogs) as well as large fruits, and have a long, powerful bill.

About half of all cotinga species are brightly plumaged, at least the males in those species in which the sexes differ markedly. The males of the seven *Cotinga* species are mainly stunningly intense blue, with deep purple or rich plum-coloured patches (for instance, the aptly named Lovely Cotinga, *Cotinga amabilis*, has large purple patches on the throat and belly) in contrast to the sober brown and mottled females. The blue colours of these species are structurally produced by light interference, whereas the other colours of cotingas are the result of carotenoid pigments. Males of the three *Xipholena* species are glossy crimson-purple or purplish-black with white wings (and in one, a white tail too), whereas the females have a grey body. The fruiteaters have a bold colour scheme of bright green upperparts, vivid yellow underparts that are mottled, barred or streaked with green in most species, and a brilliant red bill, eye-rings and legs, with a black hood in most males of most.

Several species are among the few all-white landbirds. Males of the three *Carpodectes* cotingas have all-white plumage; females are grey-bodied. The males of the four bellbirds, *Procnias*, are partly or wholly white-feathered too, and three of them have extensible skin wattles dangling from the bill. The White Bellbird, *P. albus*, and Bare-throated Bellbird, *P. nudicollis*, are entirely white, contrasting in the first of these with the extraordinary, long, single, snakelike wattle,

which is grey and adorned with tiny white starlike feathers, and in the second with a bright turquoise patch of bare skin on the throat and round the eye. The Three-wattled Bellbird, *P. tricarunculatus*, has a white head and foreparts and chestnut hindbody and wings, with three dark grey wattles, whereas the Bearded Bellbird, *P. averano*, has a dark brown hood, white body and tail and black wings, and a 'beard' of many very thin black wattles. The females of all species are similar: green above and streaked green and yellow below.

The three umbrellabird species have all-black plumage, which includes a bizarre umbrella-like crest on the head – bigger in the males. The males are also distinguished from the females by the long, hanging wattles, black and densely feathered in the Amazonian and Long-wattled species, *Cephalopterus ornatus* and *C. penduliger*, and the bare, red skin terminating in a brushlike tuft of hairlike feather barbs in the Bare-necked Umbrellabird (*C. glabricollis*). The Capuchinbird, *Perissocephalus tricolor*, is a very odd-looking species, with a rich brown body, darker brown wings, and a virtually bare blue-grey face sunk into a cowl of feathers. Red-and-black plumage is a feature of the three fruitcrows, and also of males of the two species of red cotingas, *Phoenicircus*. The two species of cocks-of-the-rock, *Rupicola*, are amazing-looking birds, the males being adorned with glowing orange plumage (or blood-red in one race of the Andean species) and a big fanlike crest.

Tree dwellers, cotingas perch for long periods. They are mainly solitary, or found in pairs or small family groups, although they will join mixed-species foraging flocks. Just as with their appearance, cotingas are very variable in their breeding systems. Some, such as the plantcutters and fruiteaters are monogamous, and share incubation and rearing of the young, whereas many are polygynous: in some of these, the females assume all parental duties. The Purple-throated Fruitcrow, *Querula purpurata*, is a cooperative breeder, with one or more helpers at the nest. Some of the polygynous species perform courtship displays at communal mating grounds (leks): these include some of the pihas, *Lipaugus*, the bellbirds, umbrellabirds and cocks-of-the-rock.

Many species have a very restricted range, and they are particularly vulnerable to the destruction of their forest homes. Just one example is that of the Swallow-tailed Cotinga, *Phibalura flavirostris*. A striking and beautiful black, olive green and yellow bird with a

LEFT Among the most beautiful of all Neotropical birds are the seven Cotinga species, like this male Spangled Cotinga, *Cotinga cayana*.

RIGHT This Orange-breasted Fruiteater, *Pipreola jucunda*, is in a cloud forest in Ecuador, on the western slope of the Andes.

BELOW RIGHT A male Andean Cock-of-the-Rock, *Rupicola peruvianus*, displays at a lek high up in the cloud forest at Manu, Peru.

yellow bill and legs, this cotinga has a long, deeply forked tail that accounts for its common name. Of its two subspecies, the nominate, *phibalura*, with almost all its population in southeast Brazil, is Near Threatened, and is generally rare and declining, while the Bolivian race, *boliviana*, which is sometimes regarded as a separate species, is Endangered. Its single, very small population was unrecorded for 98 years until its rediscovery in the year 2000 at the edge of a fragment of forest in the upper Amazon basin of Bolivia. Here it is at grave risk from destruction and degradation of its forest habitat for crop growing and cattle ranching. Its low breeding success is exacerbated by predation and the effects of extreme weather.

SHARPBILL Oxyruncidae

GENERA: 1 **SPECIES:** 1

LENGTH: 16.5–17 cm (6.5–6.7 in)

WEIGHT: about 40 g (1.4 oz)

RANGE AND HABITAT: fragmented range, from Costa Rica to southeast Brazil; humid tropical foothill or montane forest at altitudes of about 500–1,800 m (1,600–5,900 ft)

SOCIAL BEHAVIOUR: usually seen singly or in pairs, and often forages with mixed flocks of other species, especially tanagers; may have a polygynous breeding system with males displaying to females at a dispersed lek

NEST: small cup of leaf stalks, liverworts, moss and spiders' webs, glued with saliva; situated high in the tree canopy

EGGS: possibly 2

INCUBATION: 14–24 days

FLEDGING PERIOD: unknown

FOOD: mainly berries and larger fruits, also insects, spiders and other invertebrates

VOICE: song of male a very shrill, clear whistle lasting up to three seconds and descending in pitch; has been compared to the sound of a falling bomb; various calls include chattering and high-pitched tremulous sounds

MIGRATION: probably largely sedentary, but some descend to lower altitudes after breeding

CONSERVATION STATUS: not threatened

This enigmatic little bird *Oxyruncus cristatus* has puzzled taxonomists for a long time. Its close relationships have long been unclear, and so for a long period since it was first scientifically described in the early eighteenth century it was given a family of its own. In recent years, however, DNA research led to it being variously included in the cotinga family (Cotingidae), tyrant-flycatcher family (Tyrannidae) or tityra family (Tityridae). Despite this, there are good arguments for retaining its family status pending further good evidence for its precise relationships. Currently, it appears that its closest relatives may turn out to be a small group of three genera of tyrant-flycatchers in three genera, *Onychorhynchus*, *Myiobius* and *Terenotriccus*. The relationship may prove close enough to justify placing all these birds together with the Sharpbill in an enlarged Family Oxyruncidae.

True to both its common and scientific names (*Oxyruncus* being from the Greek words for sharp bill), it has a very sharply pointed, conical bill. Stocky bodied with a relatively small head, it has bright olive green above, with a long, contrastingly coloured crest of silky feathers running from its crown to its nape, more prominent in males; this varies from orange to red, perhaps reflecting a difference between some of the four subspecies but maybe due also to individual variation. The crest is partially concealed and generally hard to see unless the bird is in the hand. The ground colour of the underparts, which are marked with dark grey spots, varies from white to pale yellow, depending on the subspecies. The eyes are striking, having a brightly coloured iris, red in males and orange in females.

This is generally a very inconspicuous bird, spending long periods perching quietly. Even when it is feeding, it is hard to see as it stays up in the canopy, where its green plumage provides camouflage. Its presence is usually confirmed by the male's distinctive whistling song which carries a considerable distance.

It is an agile feeder, running or hopping along branches and hanging upside down like a tit. It probes with its wide-based, sharp bill into the leaf clusters of epiphytic plants and into clumps of moss. It also uses it as a wedge, inserted into fruit to extract the seeds or into rolled dead leaves to find insects or spiders.

ROYAL FLYCATCHERS AND ALLIES Onychorhynchidae

GENERA: 2 **SPECIES**: 4

LENGTH: 12.5–17.5 cm (5–7 in)

WEIGHT: 12–21 g (0.4–0.7 oz)

RANGE AND HABITAT: southern Mexico to south-central Brazil; tropical humid and deciduous forest and woodland

SOCIAL BEHAVIOUR: usually seen alone or in pairs; monogamous, with pairs defending a territory

NEST: Royal Flycatcher, *Onychorhynchus coronatus*, a very long, untidy hanging structure of rootlets, moss, dead leaves and plant fibres hanging from a branch or vine, often over a stream, with a small chamber for the eggs and young in the middle, accessed by a side entrance, below which is a long 'tail'; *Myiobius* species, a hanging, bell-shaped nest of plant fibres with an entrance hole at the bottom, and often a roof of twigs, typically suspended from a branch overhanging water

EGGS: 2, reddish brown in Royal Flycatcher and white with brown speckling in Sulphur-rumped Flycatcher, *Myiobius barbatus*

INCUBATION: about 22–23 days

FLEDGING PERIOD: about 22 days (known only for Sulphur-rumped Flycatcher)

FOOD: insects, including butterflies and moths, dragonflies, crickets, beetles and bees

VOICE: Royal Flycatcher, mellow whistling calls and song a series of higher, sharper whistles; *Myiobius* species, sharp or softer 'psik' calls; dawn song of Sulphur-rumped Flycatcher is a series of musical whistling notes, rising and falling in pitch

MIGRATION: sedentary

CONSERVATION STATUS: two races (may deserve full species status) of the Royal Flycatcher, the Pacific Royal Flycatcher, race *occidentalis* and the Atlantic Royal Flycatcher, race *swainsoni*, are Vulnerable

RIGHT The usual view of a Royal Flycatcher, *Onychorhynchus coronatus*, is of a small bird with an oddly shaped head, due to its crest being lowered and almost hidden.

This small family has recently been created to include two genera of birds that were previously classified in the very large tyrant-flycatcher family (Tyrannidae, p. 215). There is still uncertainty about their relationships with other birds formerly included in the Tyrannidae, and these two genera are now often included as a subfamily (Onychorhynchinae) of the tityra family, Tityridae, together with the single species in a third genus, *Terenotriccus*, the Ruddy-tailed Flycatcher, *T. erythrurus*, traditionally regarded, as here, as a tyrant-flycatcher. Whatever approach is adopted, the DNA evidence indicates that they do form a closely related

group whose closest relative seems to be the Sharpbill, *Oxyruncus cristatus* (p. 208).

Although many species of tyrant-flycatchers have a short, bushy crest, the Royal Flycatcher, *Onychorhynchus coronatus*, is unique in having a long, brilliantly coloured transverse crest that is (to the disappointment of birdwatchers) normally inconspicuously unfurled, giving the bird an odd, hammer-headed appearance. However, the few lucky observers who witness an individual defending its territory, or performing a courtship or post-copulatory display, may be treated to the stunning sight of the crest being raised and fanned like a peacock's tail. Other occasions when the crest can be seen fanned in all its glory are when a bird is handled for ringing or to take measurements. During such displays, the bird slowly opens and closes its bill to reveal the bright orange lining of its mouth, and it twists its head rhythmically from side to side. The crest is bright red in the males and orange in the female and with contrasting iridescent violet blue and black tips. From three to five subspecies have been recognised, and recently four subspecies have often been regarded as deserving full species status. Royal Flycatchers are brown above and buff below, with a rufous tail, and have a long, heavy flattened bill surrounded by very long rictal bristles (modified feathers like cat's whiskers) that presumably have the function of protecting the eyes as the bird flies out from a perch to snap up large insects with their hard-bodies, barbed legs and flapping wings. Another singular feature of these remarkable birds is their exceptionally long hanging nest, at up to 1.8 m (6 ft) longer than that of any of its tyrant flycatcher relatives.

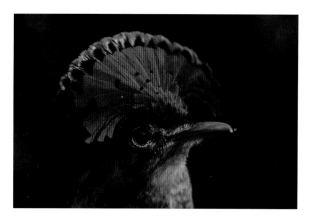

ABOVE Lucky observers may see the Royal Flycatcher, *Onychorhynchus coronatus*, with its crest fully raised, revealing its splendour in a brilliantly coloured fan.

The *Myiobius* flycatchers, by contrast, build a much squatter, bell-shaped nest, but as with the Royal Flycatcher, it is suspended from a branch. Other features shared between the two genera are large eyes, extremely long rictal bristles, and a concealed patch of (yellow) feathers on the crown (though these are far smaller and not fanned as in *Myiobius*) as well as several details of anatomy. The three species (or four according to some taxonomists) are distinctly smaller than the Royal Flycatcher, and all very similar, with an olive brown head, back and wings and apricot buff underparts, with a bright yellow rump contrasting with the black tail. They have a very distinctive habit of fanning their tails and drooping their wings to show off the yellow rump. Their insect catching technique is also unusual: they move about restlessly, opening their wings and fanning the tail to fully reveal the sulphur yellow rump, then suddenly dash at a leaf to knock an insect off and chase it in flight until they have caught it.

TITYRAS AND RELATIVES Tityridae

GENERA: 7   **SPECIES:** 35

LENGTH: 9.5–24 cm (3.75–9.5 in)

WEIGHT: 10–88 g (0.35–3 oz)

WORLD RANGE AND HABITAT: Central and South America; one species in Jamaica and a few species extending into North America in Mexico and (one species) the extreme southern USA; forests, forest edges, open woodlands, plantations

SOCIAL BEHAVIOUR: most forage in pairs or family groups, but some are more solitary

NEST: variable, from tiny hummingbird-like nests of purpletufts to large, untidy balls of dry grasses with a side entrance in the becards; usually in tree branches but some in tree holes

EGGS: 2 or 3, whitish, cream or brown with darker markings

INCUBATION: about 18–20 days (in the few species for which information is available)

FLEDGING PERIOD: little known; about 20–30 days in some species

FOOD: fruit is the main food of most species, with some insects; others are mainly insectivorous

VOICE: varies from the melodious whistles of *Laniocera* mourners to the grunts, croaks and rattles of tityras, *Tityra*

MIGRATION: sedentary; some may make altitudinal or other local movements

CONSERVATION STATUS: two species, the Slaty Becard, *Pachyramphus spodiurus*, and the Buff-throated Purpletuft, *Iodopleura pipra*, are Endangered; one species, the Elegant Mourner, *Laniisoma elegans*, is Near Threatened

ABOVE The Masked Tityra, *Tityra semifasciata*, is a conspicuous, boldly patterned bird that spends a lot of time perched on a bare branch in the forest canopy.

Different genera within this new family were formerly classified with the tyrant-flycatchers, cotingas, or (in the case of *Schiffornis*) in the manakin family. Recently, this assemblage of birds was found to be more closely related to the manakins and is now given separate family status, as here.

The four species of tityras in the genus *Tityra* are boldly plumaged thrush-sized birds – black and white in males and brown and grey in females. Two species have bright red bare facial skin around each eye and a powerful, black-tipped red bill. They are sturdy birds that are often aggressive to other species as they hop heavily around trees in search of fruit or large insects.

An assortment of smallish to medium-sized secretive birds called mourners include seven species of *Schiffornis*, two species of *Laniocera*, and one of *Laniisoma* – the Elegant Mourner, *L. elegans*. The *Schiffornis* species have olive and warm brown or cinnamon plumage and large dark eyes, and they forage solitarily or in pairs in dense undergrowth. Their presence is usually discovered by their melodious whistling calls. Males of the two *Laniocera* mourners, one mainly grey and the other a rich rufous brown gather at loose leks in shady spots, where they utter their whistling songs endlessly throughout the day. The Elegant Mourner is smaller, with bright olive-green upperparts and dark-scaled golden underparts, set off by a black crown in the male. Even more unobtrusive than the other species, it is generally rare.

The purpletufts, *Iodopleura*, comprise three species of very small plump-bodied, blackish, brown and white birds that have disproportionately long swallow-like wings adapted for manoeuvrable flight as they hawk for flying insects from the treetops, catching them in their short but wide-based bills. The common name of the genus refers to the small tufts of violet feathers on the upper flanks of the males.

The 17 species of becards, *Pachyramphus*, are mainly sparrow-sized birds with a disproportionately large head bearing a very slight crest, and a short, broad bill. Most species are sexually dimorphic: males have black, grey and white plumage, with a black crown, sometimes with yellow or olive, or all black; the females are typically chestnut, paler below, in some cases with yellow or grey as well. In two species, the sexes are very similar: chestnut or chestnut and grey. The range of the Central American and Mexican Rose-throated Becard, *P. aglaiae*, just reaches the USA in extreme southern Texas.

The White-naped Xenopsaris, *Xenopsaris albinucha*, a smart little black-and-white bird that twists and turns when it chases insects in flight. It is in many respects similar to the becards and may be better classified with them.

SPADEBILLS AND ALLIES Platyrinchidae

GENERA: 3   **SPECIES:** 9

LENGTH: 7.5–12.5 cm (3–5 in)

WEIGHT: about 6–17 g (0.2–0.6 oz)

RANGE AND HABITAT: tropical America, from southern Mexico to northeast Argentina; among dense vegetation in humid forests, with some in montane forest and a few also in secondary woodland

SOCIAL BEHAVIOUR: generally solitary; no information for Kinglet Calyptura, *Calyptura cristatus*

NEST: spadebills, a tiny but sturdy cup of fine fibres, sited low down in the fork of a tree or shrub; no information for Cinnamon Tyrant or Kinglet Calyptura

EGGS: 2, yellowish-white with a rufous wreath in the best-known species, the White-throated Spadebill, *Platyrinchus myastaceus*; reliable information unavailable for other species

INCUBATION: about 12–21 days in two spadebill species; otherwise unknown

FLEDGING PERIOD: about 14–19 days in two spadebill species; otherwise unknown

FOOD: insects and spiders

VOICE: songs of spadebills are squeaky, bubbling or buzzing and insect-like trills rising or falling in pitch; brief, sharp squeaking, twittering or insect-like calls and mechanical wing-whirring in flight displays

MIGRATION: resident in spadebills; unknown but probably resident in the other species

CONSERVATION STATUS: the Kinglet Calyptura, *Calyptura cristata*, is Critically Endangered; the Russet-winged Spadebill, *Platyrinchus leucoryphus*, is Vulnerable

ABOVE The tiny, chubby bodied White-throated Spadebill, *Platyrinchus mystaceus*, is unobtrusive as it remains quietly for long periods in the forest understorey.

The seven species of spadebills are very small, plump-bodied, short-tailed birds of the forest understorey. As their name suggests, they have disproportionately broad bills. These are surrounded by long, whisker-like rictal bristles that most likely protect their eyes from being damaged by the hard or spiny bodies, legs and wings of their insect prey as they snatch them in mid-air or from the underside of a leaf. They have mainly brown upperparts and yellowish buff underparts, and a partly concealed coloured crown patch. These are unobtrusive little birds, as they perch quietly in dense foliage or other undergrowth or motionless on a more exposed branch. Generally, they forage alone and do not usually join mixed feeding flocks of tanagers or other species.

The Cinnamon Tyrant, *Neopipo cinnamomea*, was until recently classified in the manakin Family Pipridae (p. 205), when its common name was Cinnamon Manakin or Cinnamon Tyrant-manakin. It has a grey upper back and head with a concealed yellow crown-patch, rufous back and plain cinnamon underparts; it lacks the rictal bristles that are a feature of the spadebills. It does resemble a manakin in its general appearance, with its big, rounded head and large eyes, but DNA studies indicate that this tiny bird's nearest relatives are in fact the spadebills and the Kinglet Calyptura. One scheme is to group these together in a subfamily (Platyrinchinae), but here these three groups are united in the small Family Platyrinchidae. This is closest to the three families that follow, and these four are together most closely related to the tyrant-flycatchers (Tyrannidae, p. 215).

The final member of this small family is one of the world's rarest and most enigmatic birds. The Kinglet Calyptura, *Calyptura cristata*, was for a long time considered to be the smallest member of the cotinga family (Cotingidae, p. 206), entirely on the basis of the arrangement of scales on its legs, but DNA studies showed that it belonged elsewhere. Recently, taxonomists have established by further molecular studies that it belongs with the spadebills and the Cinnamon Tyrant, as described above. This minuscule bird is strikingly plumaged, bright olive green above with a bold orange crown stripe bordered on either side by a broad black stripe, and bright yellow below. During the nineteenth century, specimens were collected as prepared skins (but not as skeletons or whole birds preserved in alcohol), the last one in about 1890; about 55 are in museums, but these are very poorly documented. Since then, since there were no sightings for over 100 years, the species was considered likely to be extinct. Then, in 1996, there was a miraculous rediscovery, when birders found a pair in tall mainly secondary forest to the northeast of Rio de Janeiro. Other reports have been too vague for acceptance. Its extremely small size makes it hard to find in dense cover. As for locating it by sound, one of the few descriptions of its calls referred to its uttering a sparrow-like chirp, while another describes its calls as 'brief, sharp and disagreeable'!

Although reliable nineteenth century records were only from a few localities in Rio de Janeiro state, it may have been quite common there. Since then, though, almost all forest below 1,000 m (3,200 ft) has been felled for growing coffee or mining gold and diamonds.

PIPRITES Pipritidae

GENERA: 1   **SPECIES**: 3

LENGTH: 12–14 cm (5–5.5 in)

WEIGHT: 15–21 g (0.5–0.75 oz)

RANGE AND HABITAT: one species, the Grey-headed Piprites, *Piprites griseiceps*, is restricted to the Caribbean slope of Central America, from extreme eastern Guatemala to extreme northwest Panama, while the other two species are South American, the Wing-barred Piprites, *P. chloris*, having by far the greatest range, across a large area of northern South America and with a smaller, disjunct population in Brazil, Paraguay and extreme northeast Argentina, and the Black-capped Piprites, *P. pileata*, in a small area of southeast Brazil and a tiny area of northeast Argentina; humid forest and mature secondary woodland, with the Black-capped Piprites restricted mainly to montane forest

SOCIAL BEHAVIOUR: usually seen singly or in pairs, and sometimes joins mixed flocks of other birds when feeding; probably monogamous

NEST: few details; cup-shaped, one of Wing-barred Piprites in tree cavity

EGGS: unknown

INCUBATION: unknown

FLEDGING PERIOD: unknown

FOOD: mainly insects in the Wing-barred Piprites; the other two species eat mainly small fruits as well as insects

VOICE: varied songs and calls of whistling, chortling or staccato notes

MIGRATION: probably mainly resident, but some Black-capped Piprites in Brazil may make regular altitudinal movements

CONSERVATION STATUS: the Black-capped Piprites, *P. pileata*, is Vulnerable

ABOVE The Black-capped Piprites, *Piprites pileata*, is a rare and threatened inhabitant of montane Atlantic forest in southeast Brazil.

The birds in this tiny family have at various times meandered from one family to another, as new research suggested different relationships. After having been traditionally included in the manakin family (Pipridae, p. 205), some researchers thought it might belong instead in the great family of tyrant-flycatchers (Tyrannidae, p. 215) or with the tityras and relatives in the Tityridae (p. 210). Currently, it is generally regarded as forming a distinctive subfamily within the Tyrannidae or, as here, deserving a family of its own, with its closest relatives the spadebills and relatives (Platyrichidae) and the Many-coloured Rush-tyrant, *Tachuris rubrigastra*.

With mainly green upperparts and yellow or pale grey underparts, and prominent eyes with a contrasting yellow eye-ring, the Grey-headed Piprites, *P. griseiceps*, and Wing-barred Piprites, *P. chloris*, look rather like a cross between a large female manakin or some tyrant-flycatchers. As well as being the scarcest and most threatened of the three species, the Black-capped Piprites, *P. pileata*, is far more distinctive, with its striking plumage pattern of jet black crown and nape contrasting with rich chestnut upperparts and cinnamon-buff and yellow underparts. All three species are also rather similar to some of the becards, *Pachyramphus*, of the Family Tityridae. Unlike most manakins, which are often encountered in undergrowth, they forage mainly at mid-levels of the forest and in the canopy. The Wing-barred Piprites, on the other hand, appears to eat little fruit, feeding mainly on insects, which it catches largely by gleaning while on branches rather than by flying out from a perch.

RUSH TYRANT Tachurididae

GENERA: 1   **SPECIES:** 1

LENGTH: 11–11.5 cm (4.3–4.5 in)

WEIGHT: 6.5–8 g (0.2–0.3 oz)

RANGE AND HABITAT: coastal central and southern Peru, Chile, with few in extreme southern Brazil and Paraguay, central and southern Argentina; restricted to reedbeds, from sea level to altitudes of about 4,000 m (13,000 ft)

SOCIAL BEHAVIOUR: may be encountered alone, in pairs, or in small family groups

NEST: tiny, deep, cone shaped structure of dried pieces of reed leaves, attached to a single stem, and with a smooth coating of a gum-like substance, attached to a single reed stem, usually over water

EGGS: 3

INCUBATION: no information

FLEDGING PERIOD: no information

FOOD: insects

VOICE: a sweet, gurgling and buzzing song, nasal sounds, and rapid, dry insect-like trills

MIGRATION: birds from southern breeding populations move north in winter

CONSERVATION STATUS: not threatened

ABOVE This colourful little bird is a Many-coloured Rush Tyrant, *Tachuris rubigastra*, in a reedbed in Patagonia, Argentina.

A beautiful little bird, and one that is very aptly named: unlike many of its tyrant-flycatcher relatives which are relatively drab, it is truly many-coloured. It sports a striking pattern of black crown and glossy blue-black sides to its head, the two separated by a long golden stripe running from the base of its black bill and extending above each eye on each side to almost join at the rear. In the middle of the crown there is an often almost hidden crimson stripe. Its back is bright olive green, the wings are mainly black, with a broad angled white bar and its tail is black with white outer feathers.

Below, apart from its white throat it is bright yellow, with an apricot tinge to its breast, a broad black bar extending down the sides of the breast, and a bright red undertail. Despite its Spanish name of *siete colores* (seven colours), it actually has a total of eight colours.

Restless, agile, and acrobatic, it is constantly on the move. Its rather long legs suit it well to perching briefly on vertical reed stems in the reedbeds of marshes and lake margins where it lives. It often lowers the tips of its wings and flicks them in and out and holds its tail partly cocked and flicks that too. It raises the crimson central feathers of its crown when alarmed or excited. It usually catches insects by picking them off the reeds or other marsh vegetation or from the water surface, generally remaining low down, though it will sometimes fly out to seize midges or other prey.

The Many-coloured Rush Tyrant makes its deep, cone-shaped nest from wet reed fragments, which dry and harden to give a strong cardboard-like structure. The covering of a gumlike substance gives it a neat appearance, resembling a conical ice-cream cone.

FLATBILLS Pipromorphidae

GENERA: 17   **SPECIES:** 101

LENGTH: 6.5–18 cm (2.5–7 in)

WEIGHT: 4–25 g (0.1–0.9 oz)

RANGE AND HABITAT: southern Mexico to northern Argentina; mainly in tropical forests and woodlands, with a few in other habitats, such as arid scrub

SOCIAL BEHAVIOUR: may be seen singly, in pairs or in family groups, and many join mixed-species groups; those for which information is available appear to be monogamous

NEST: materials include rootlets, leaves, dry grass, moss and plant fibres; in some genera a globular structure with a covered side entrance, but most build a purse-shaped or pear-shaped structure with an entrance tube at the side, suspended from a thin branch or vine

EGGS: 2–3 in the few species for which information is available

INCUBATION: unknown for most species

FLEDGING PERIOD: unknown for most species

FOOD: insects and other invertebrates and some fruit

VOICE: a variety of whistling, trilling, twittering, chattering, chirping songs and calls

MIGRATION: most species are thought to be resident, though some are known to make altitudinal movements

CONSERVATION STATUS: one species, the Alagoas Tyrannulet, *Phylloscartes ceciliae*, is Critically Endangered; four species, Johnson's Tody Tyrant, *Poecilotriccus lululae*, the Bahia Tyrannulet, *Phylloscartes beckeri*, Minas Gerais Tyrannulet, *P. roquettei*, and Antioquia Bristle Tyrant, *Pogonotriccus lanyoni*, are Endangered; five species, the Rufous Twistwing, *Cnipodectes superrufus*, Restinga Tyrannulet, *Phylloscartes kronei*, Kaempfer's Tody Tyrant, *Hemitriccus kaempferi*, Fork-tailed Tody Tyrant, *H. furcatus*, and Cinnamon-breasted Tody Tyrant, *H. cinnamomeipectus*; 10 species are Near Threatened

Like the preceding six families, this is an example of a family that has traditionally been included within the very large family of tyrant-flycatchers (Tyrannidae, p. 215). Although many researchers today prefer to retain all but the tityras and relatives (Tityridae, p. 210) as six distinctive subfamilies within the Tyrannidae, pending further research, in this book we give family status to all of these groups, including this one. The flatbills are by far the largest of the six, with almost twice as many species (101) and two more genera (17) than all the rest of those groups together. In terms of species, it is almost exactly one-third the size of the tyrant-flycatcher family as constituted here.

This is a varied assemblage, but can be divided into three subfamilies, all sharing the flattened bills that give the family its name. The first, the subfamily Pipromorphinae, consists of 40 species in eight genera. The three species of pygmy tyrants in the genus *Pseudotriccus* are, as their name suggests, very small, and all three are restricted to different parts of the Andes, where they live in dense rainforest and cloudforest, foraging for insects low down in the undergrowth. Two are brown and buff, while the Rufous-headed Pygmy Tyrant, *P. ruficeps*, found from Colombia to northwest Bolivia, lives up its name, with a bright orange-rufous head, as well as similarly coloured wings. The two species of ant-pipits, *Corythopis*, by contrast, are lowland rainforest birds, are long-legged, long-tailed and mainly terrestrial birds. They are dark olive-brown above, and their white underparts are marked with a black necklace that extends down the breast as black streaks. They walk around, nodding the head and pumping the tail up and down, flying up to snatch insects from the undersurface of the leaves. Birdwatchers are often made aware of their presence by their habit of loudly snapping their bills. The subfamily Pipromorphinae also includes four genera of small mainly green and yellow birds with quite long and slender bills. Some of them have a distinctive habit of raising one wing over the back, either repeating the action with the same wing or flicking both up alternately, often during courtship or other displays. The two species of twistwings in the genus *Cnipodectes* are the largest members of the family, at up to

18 cm (7 in) long. Mainly dull brown, they acquired their commo[n] name from the oddly stiffened and twisted outer primary win[g] feathers. Their function is not known for sure, but they probab[ly] used in displays.

The second subfamily is the Rhynchocyclinae. It contains nin[e] green and yellow species in two genera. The five *Tolmomyia[s]* species are all very similar; with large heads and broad, flat bill[s] they are inconspicuous inhabitants of a wide range of woode[d] habitats. As well as being the common name for the famil[y] the name flatbill is also used for the four species in the genu[s] *Rhynchocyclus*, and with good reason, as they have even wider fl[at] bills than the *Tolmomyias* species.

The third subfamily, the Triccinae, comprises 52 species in seve[n] genera. These are all very small – especially the four grey-green an[d] species of pygmy tyrants, *Myiornis*, which are among the world[s] tiniest bird species. The Black-capped and Short-tailed Pygm[y] Tyrants, *M. atricapillus* and *M. ecaudatus*, are the most diminutiv[e] of these, both only 6.5 cm (2.5 in) long, which is smaller than man[y] hummingbirds. Slightly bigger are the four species of *Lophotricc[us]* pygmy tyrants, with prominent erectile crests. Two genera ar[e] known as tody tyrants, due to their superficial resemblance t[o] the non-passerine family of birds called todies. These are plump[-] bodied, short-tailed little birds. The 22 species of *Hemitriccus* ar[e] dull olive green or brown with paler underparts. Many of the 1[?] species in the genus *Poecilotriccus* are, by contrast, boldly patterne[d] in various combinations of russet, black, olive, yellow and whit[e] Three species are sexually dimorphic, two of them slightly (wit[h] the females somewhat duller) and one markedly so: the mal[e] Black-and-white Tody Tyrant, *P. capitalis*, has a glossy black hea[d] and upperparts and white underparts, while the female is mainl[y] olive above and white below with a chestnut cap.

The two olive and yellow species in the genus *Oncostoma* ar[e] called bentbills, from their heavy, downwardly bent bills, whil[e] the seven species of *Todirostrum* tody flycatchers are very strikin[g] mostly with a black head, olive back and bright yellow underpart[s] They have longer bills than most of their relatives, and perch mor[e] horizontally, frequently holding their short black tails cocked at [a] jaunty angle.

ABOVE This Yellow-olive Flycatcher, *Tolmomyias sulphurescens*, is the most widespread of a group of five very similar species; it is found from Mexico to northern Argentina.

ABOVE The Common Tody Flycatcher, *Todirostrum cinereum*, is a very active littl[e] bird that darts about in the foliage searching for insect food, mainly gleaned from under leaves.

TYRANT-FLYCATCHERS Tyrannidae

GENERA: 79   **SPECIES:** 306

LENGTH: 6.5–29 cm (2.5–11.5 in) or to 30–40 cm (12–16 in), including a very long tail, in a few species

WEIGHT: 4–88 g (0.1–3 oz)

WORLD RANGE AND HABITAT: the Americas, from the far north of Canada and Alaska south to Tierra del Fuego in southernmost South America; also in the Caribbean and other islands such as the Galapagos and the Falklands; a huge range, from tropical rainforests and mangrove swamps to temperate broadleaved and conifer woodlands, high mountains, grasslands, scrub, deserts

SOCIAL BEHAVIOUR: some species are mainly solitary; some spend most time in pairs; others are gregarious; most are monogamous and territorial

NEST: varies widely, from open cups of vegetation to purse-shaped structures, hanging nests, spherical ones or other shapes; may be sited in trees or shrubs, in natural or artificial holes in trees, rocks or elsewhere, or on or beneath the ground. Some species take over the abandoned nests of other birds, while the Piratic Flycatcher, *Legatus leucophaius*, evicts the owners

EGGS: 2–6, sometimes brown-mottled whitish

INCUBATION: 12–23 days

FLEDGING PERIOD: 12–28 days

FOOD: mainly insects, although almost all species also eat fruit and in some it forms an important part of the diet; a few eat some small vertebrates

VOICE: calls in all but a few species consist of rather unmusical whistles, chirps and trills; songs are mainly simple elaborations of similar sounds, but they are vital in helping the birds (and birdwatchers!) distinguish one of their own kind from a very similar-looking species

MIGRATION: many species are migratory, some making long annual journeys between North America or southern South America and the tropics; other North American breeders make even longer migrations, from as far north as Newfoundland to as far south as southern Argentina

CONSERVATION STATUS: five species, the Cuban Tyrannulet, *Tyrannus cubensis*, Ash-breasted Tit Tyrant, *Anairetes alpinus*, Rufous Flycatcher, *Myiarchus semirufus*, Santa Marta Bush Tyrant, *Myiotheretes pernix*, Urich's Tyrannulet, *Philomyias urichi*, are Endangered; 15 species, including the Red-billed Tyrannulet, *Zimmerius cinereicapilla*, Sharp-tailed Tyrant, *Culicivora caudacuta*, Black-and-white Monjita, *Xolmis dominicanus*, Ochraceous Attila, *Attila torridus*, Cock-tailed Tyrant, *Alectrurus tricolor*, and Strange-tailed Tyrant, *A. risora*, are Vulnerable; 13 species are Near Threatened

ABOVE The Scissor-tailed Flycatcher, *Tyrannus forficatus*, is the only long-tailed tyrant-flycatcher species to breed in the USA.

LEFT The Streaked Flycatcher, *Myiodynastes maculatus*, occurs over a huge range, from southern Mexico to northern Argentina.

Even after the removal of various groups into separate families (the Oxyruncidae, p. 208; Onychorhynchidae, p. 209; Tityridae, p. 210; Pipritidae, p. 212; Tachurididae, p. 213; Platyrinchidae, p. 211; and Pipromorphidae) according to the classificatory system followed in this book, this is still the most diverse family of birds in the New World. Indeed it is one of the largest of all the world's bird families, and with 306 species only one of four containing more than 300 species – only the tanager Family Thraupidae (p. 329), with 371 species, and the non-passerine hummingbird Family Trochilidae (p. 52), with 335 species, are larger. The huge biodiversity of tyrant-flycatchers we see today represents a dramatic, explosive evolutionary radiation in which different groups became adapted to exploit almost the entire range of habitats and food niches within the Americas. Indeed, the only habitat they do not inhabit is the high-Arctic tundra and polar regions.

The family includes various familiar and common birds of North America, such as the pewees, *Contopus*, elaenias, *Elaenia*, and the *Empidonax* flycatchers, as well as the hugely greater number of species in the Neotropics, which include many that are localised and scarce or endangered.

Tyrant-flycatchers are extremely diverse in appearance and habits. They range from tiny birds like the Brown-capped Tyrannulet, *Ornithion brunneicapillus*, just 8 cm (3 ¼ in) long to the bulky thrush-sized Great Shrike-Tyrant, *Agriornis lividus*, 4.5 times longer and over 20 times heavier. The bill is generally fairly short, strong and flat and broad, but bills vary among species according to diet and lifestyle. Tail length is also variable: most have medium-length tails, but some have very short ones, as with the pygmy-tyrants, and a few, such as the Scissor-tailed Flycatcher, *Tyrannus forficatus*, have a very long, forked tail, up to three times as long as the body. Others have much smaller brightly coloured crown patches that they can fan and flaunt at rivals.

In the great majority of species, the sexes are similar. Most are drably plumaged in various combinations of grey, brown, olive-green and white or whitish. Many of these duller and less distinctively marked birds, such as the numerous species of *Empidonax* flycatchers, are a challenge for birdwatchers to tell apart. A few tyrant-flycatchers are black and white, almost all black or all white. Many have yellow

ABOVE The White-ringed Flycatcher, *Conopias albovittatus*, often perches prominently on a wire or high in the tree canopy.

underparts; a whole suite of several genera of larger species (such as the Social Flycatcher *Myiozetetes similis*, and relatives, the two kiskadees, *Pitangus*, and the big Boat-billed Flycatcher, *Megarynchus pitangua*) have brown or chestnut upperparts, bright lemon yellow underparts and a black-and-white striped head with a yellow, orange or red crown patch. Some have even brighter colours – for example, the stunning red-and-black Vermilion Flycatcher, *Pyrocephalus rubinus*.

Although some of these birds include a large amount of fruit in their diet and almost all eat some (especially in winter), most tyrant-flycatchers feed mainly on insects. Some (including most of the North American species) do so by making short flights out from a perch to seize a flying insect in mid-air. This is the same method used by various other bird families, including the Old World flycatchers, although the two groups are unrelated (this being a good example of convergent evolution).

Different groups have evolved other styles of obtaining their food. Some spend far more time in the air, hawking for insects, their long wings and tail giving them increased manoeuvrability. Others fly from a perch down onto the ground to find their prey, or are ground dwellers that chase prey on foot, running fast on strong legs. Some, such as the Pied Water-Tyrant, *Fluvicola pica*, feed on aquatic insects, in this case chasing them across floating vegetation. Various species catch insects by fluttering into the air or hovering like miniature kestrels above land or water.

Many species (including most in the Neotropics) are foliage gleaners that search for non-flying insects or fruit among trees and other vegetation on foot or by making short flights. These tend to be warbler-like in build, with a slim body, longish legs, a longish tail for balancing while reaching for prey, and a slender, sharp-tipped bill for tweezering insects from foliage or other hiding places.

Some larger species (such as the Great Kiskadee, *Pitangus sulphuratus*, and the Giant Kingbird, *Tyrannus cubensis*) tackle small vertebrates such as fish, lizards, snakes, frogs or rodents, which they dispatch with their big, powerful, distinctly hook-tipped bill.

Many members of the family that hunt by flying out to catch prey have a cluster of tough rictal bristles around the base of the bill, and sometimes around the face and eyes too; these help protect the eyes from injury as the birds fly fast into foliage to strike prey or deal with the sharply toothed legs and claws, flapping wings and toxic hairs of lively, tough-bodied insects.

The Tyrannidae is divided into five subfamilies. The small subfamily Hirundineinae (with its name a reference to the completely unrelated oscine Family Hirundinidae, of swallows and martins, p. 350) contains just six species in four genera. There are three single-species genera, including *Hirundinea*: the Cliff Flycatcher, *H. ferruginea*, with a patchy distribution in South America, is a dark brown and cinnamon bird that is unique in the family in its resemblance to a swallow, especially when it glides and banks as it hunts insects in flight.

Another far larger subfamily, Elaeniinae, is subdivided into two tribes. The smaller of the two is the Euscarthmini, with 25 species in six genera. Five of the six genera contain little, mainly long-tailed birds with the diminutive common name of tyrannulets; the two species in the sixth genus, *Stigmatura*, have the longest tails of all, which they constantly move energetically while they forage; this earns them their common name of wagtail-tyrants, celebrating their superficial similarity to the unrelated oscine birds called wagtails (Family Motacillidae, p. 302). The other tribe in the Elaeniinae is the Elaeniini, whose 74 species are spread between 16 genera. Most species are small or very small, but the elaenias, in two genera, are larger; the genus *Elaenia* contains some larger species up to 19 cm (7.5 in) long. This is the largest genus in the tribe, with 19 similar species that have olive-brown upperparts, greyish breasts and pale yellow bellies. The seven species in the other elaenia genus, *Myiopagis*, are rather smaller, with greener upperparts and yellower underparts. Other members of this tribe include 29 very small species of tyrannulets, divided between seven genera; the five doraditos, *Pseudocolopteryx*, handsome little birds with olive or brown upperparts and bright yellow underparts that live in reedbeds and other dense marshland vegetation; and the six little tit-tyrants, *Anairetes*, all but one (endemic to the island of Juan Fernandez, 670 km (415 miles) off the coast of Chile) found in the Andes and Patagonia. All but one rare species of *Anairetes* have boldly streaked plumage and all have striking crests. There are two other duller plumaged crested species called tit-tyrants, also found in the Andes, but placed in a different genus, *Uromyias*.

The subfamily Muscigrallinae contains only a single species, the Short-tailed Field Tyrant, *Muscigralla brevicauda*. This is a plump

ABOVE A stunning male Vermilion Flycatcher, *Pyrocephalus rubinus*, pauses with insect prey in its bill in winter quarters in Peru.

little mainly grey-and-cream bird with a very short tail, extremely long sturdy legs, very short, rounded wings and an upright posture. It is a habitat specialist – it is restricted to arid coastal lowlands in southern Ecuador and northern Chile, especially on sandy ground (including farmland) that is barren or with sparse vegetation. Among the most terrestrial of all members of the family, it runs or hops rapidly in bursts, chasing its insect prey. It has provided taxonomists with a challenge, at various times being regarded first as a member of the cotinga family (Cotingidae, p. 206), then as an antbird (Thamnophilidae, p. 218) and then placed with the ground tyrants, *Muscisaxicola*, in the fifth subfamily of tyrant flycatchers (Fluvicolinae, below). Since then, its distinctive features have led to it being given a subfamily of its own: these include the tibia (the part of the leg above the 'knee' joint) being bare instead of feathered, making it look like a diminutive wader. Only one other (unrelated) passerine, the equally terrestrial Golden Pipit, *Tmetothylacus tenellus*, of Africa (p. 304), shares this anatomical distinction.

The fourth subfamily, with 34 species in 11 genera, is the Tyranninae, which contains several of the species that occur in North America. It is divided into two tribes. The Tyrannini includes six genera that share a striking black-and-white and yellow plumage pattern as described above. The range of one, the Great Kiskadee, just extends into the extreme south of the USA, as does the duller, streaky Sulphur-bellied Flycatcher, *Myiodynastes luteiventris*. Other members of this tribe include the 13 species of kingbirds in the genus *Tyrannus*. These are sturdy, mostly thrush-sized birds that are usually very conspicuous as they perch high on an exposed tree branch, sallying out now and then to snap up a beetle, grasshopper or other insect from mid-air, or from foliage or the ground. Eight species breed in the USA, but four are restricted to parts of the far south; the two common species are the Western Kingbird, *T. verticalis*, and the even more widespread Eastern Kingbird, *T. tyrannus*. Six species look similar, with grey heads, white throats, dark grey or olive backs, darker wings and mainly yellow underparts; the others are black, grey and white, mostly with a black head. Two of these, the Scissor-tailed Flycatcher, *T. forficatus*, and Fork-tailed Flycatcher, *T. savana*, have extraordinarily elongated outer tail feathers, twice as long as the body or longer (longest in males). The Fork-tailed Flycatcher is a tropical species that only occurs in the USA as a wanderer to Texas and the Atlantic coast, whereas the Scissor-tailed Flycatcher is a common breeder in much of south-central USA. It is an especially beautiful bird, its ash grey upperparts contrasting with a pale salmon pink belly and in flight with bright pink underwing coverts.

The tribe Myiarchini comprises 31 species in four genera. The largest genus by far is *Myiarchus*, with 22 species. They are generally smaller than the *Tyrannus* species, ranging from 15–22 cm (6–8.5 in) long, and almost all look very similar, with darker grey or brown upperparts, a pale grey throat and upper breast and the rest of the underparts pale yellow. Four species breed in North America, although only two are widely distributed there – the Great Crested Flycatcher, *M. crinitus*, common across most of eastern and central USA, and the Ash-throated Flycatcher, *M. cinerascens*, in much of the west.

The final subfamily is the Fluvicolinae. This is further divided into three tribes. The Fluvicolini contains 28 species in 10 genera.

These are birds of tropical South America, apart from five whose range extends into Central America, and one species with a vast range, from southwest USA to southern Argentina. This is the Vermilion Flycatcher, *Pyrocephalus rubinus*. The male is the most brilliantly coloured member of the entire tyrant-flycatcher family, with his intensely red and sooty black plumage. The three species of water-tyrants in the genus *Fluvicola* are striking little black-and-white birds tied to marshes, lakes and ponds, rivers and streams. Two members of the Fluvicolini with distinctively shaped, very long tails are the Streamer-tailed Tyrant, *Gubernetes yetapa*, and the Strange-tailed Tyrant, *Alectrurus risora*, which has broad, twisted outer tail feathers that extend from the bare shafts at their base like a pair of blades. These are reminiscent of the tail streamers of the African paradise whydahs and widowbirds (p. 299).

There are 11 genera and 49 species in the entirely South American tribe Xolmiini. They include a genus, *Knipolegus*, of forest and woodland species in which males are all-black and females brown. Their close relative, the Spectacled Tyrant, *Hymenops perspicillatus*, has similar plumages, but the male has contrasting white primary wing feathers and a very striking white eye ring of bare skin surrounding its white eyes that account for its common and specific names. There are eight species in the genus *Xolmis*, all but one with the common name of monjita. This means 'little nun' in Spanish, and refers to their plumage in various simple patterns of black, white and grey. They live in open country with scattered bushes or low trees, typically feeding by dropping to the ground from a perch. The 13 species of ground tyrants, *Muscisaxicola*, are slim-bodied, slender billed, mainly brown or greyish plumaged birds. Highly terrestrial, with many species in the Andes, they alternate standing erect and motionless with bursts of fast running on their long legs.

The five species of shrike-tyrants, *Agriornis*, are also open-country birds, mostly found in the Andes and Patagonia. Large and sturdy with strong legs, they are named for their powerful, hook-tipped bills (like those of the unrelated shrikes, p. 270) with which they catch and dismember large insects and occasionally small vertebrates. All have brown plumage with dark-streaked white throats.

Finally, the tribe Contopini contains 40 species in 10 genera. Three genera have well-known representatives in North America. All three species of phoebes, *Sayornis*, breed there, the Eastern Phoebe, *S. phoebe*, in east and central USA and in Canada as far north as northwest Canada, and Say's Phoebe, *S. saya*, in the west, extending farther north into Alaska. All but the southern populations of both species migrate to winter as far south as southern Mexico. The Black Phoebe, *S. nigricans*, is resident over its vast range, which extends from western USA to northwest Argentina. The 14 species of pewees, *Contopus*, include four North American species. Like the phoebes, these are medium sized flycatchers, but they look more similar to one another, with dull brown-and-grey plumage. The common species are the Eastern Wood Pewee, *C. virens*, and Western Wood Pewee, *C. sordidulus*, both extending north into Canada, and the western species as far north as Alaska. The 15 species of *Empidonax*, smaller than the pewees and almost all extremely similar to one another, contain the greatest number of North American species of any of the genera of tyrant flycatchers – 11 species breed there.

ANTBIRDS Thamnophilidae

GENERA: 59   **SPECIES**: 232

LENGTH: 7.5–34 cm (3–13 in)

WEIGHT: 6–155 g (0.2–5.5 oz)

RANGE AND HABITAT: Mexico, Central America and South America; greatest diversity in Amazonia; most species in humid lowland and foothill forest; some in arid or semi-arid woodland or thorn-scrub; a few in marshes

SOCIAL BEHAVIOUR: most species live in monogamous pairs for life, defending a year-round territory; some are more solitary; many join mixed-species feeding flocks, including those at army-ant swarms; seven genera feed exclusively by following such swarms

NEST: most build a shallow open cup in the fork of a branch; some make hanging purse-shaped structures or domed nests; sites vary from the ground to among tree roots or vines or in trees or shrubs, often low down or at moderate heights but up to canopy level

EGGS: 2 (rarely 1 or 3), white to buff or pale pinkish eggs with darker markings

INCUBATION: 14–20 days in the few species in which breeding data are known

FLEDGING PERIOD: 8–15 days in the few species in which breeding data are known

FOOD: insects and other invertebrates, including spiders; larger species may take small frogs or reptiles; some include fruit in the diet

VOICE: many species are very vocal; calls are varied, often harsh, from trills and rattles to barking, buzzing, whistling or piping; simple, often loud songs

MIGRATION: mostly sedentary, with some making local movements in search of army-ant swarms or other food sources

CONSERVATION STATUS: four species, the Marsh Antwren, *Formicivora paludicola*, Rio Branco Antbird, *Cercomacra carbonaria*, Orange-bellied Antwren, *Terenura sicki*, and the Alagoas Antwren, *Myrmotherula snowi*, are Critically Endangered; 9 species, including the Recurve-billed Bushbird, *Clytoctantes alixii*, the Black-hooded Antwren, *Formicivora erythronotos*, the Scalloped Antbird, *Myrmoderus ruficauda*, the Fringe-backed Fire-eye, *Pyriglena atra*, and the Yellow-rumped Antwren, *Euchrepomis sharpei*, are Endangered; 19 species, including the White-bearded Antshrike, *Biatas nigropectus*, the Bananal Antbird, *Cercomacra ferdinandi*, the Plumbeous Antvireo, *Dysithamnus plumbeus*, the Pectoral Antwren, *Herpsilochmus pectoralis*, and the Spiny-faced Antshrike, *Xenornis setifrons*, are Vulnerable; 19 species are Near Threatened

ABOVE One of three antbird species that attend ant swarms together, the big Ocellated Antbird, *Phaenostictus mcleannani*, is generally dominant.

ABOVE The Spotted Antbird, *Hylophylax naevioides*, unlike the other two members of the trio, sometimes forages away from ant-swarms.

The members of this large family of Neotropical birds do not eat ants; the name refers to their habit of following huge swarms of army ants, to take advantage of the abundant supply of insects, spiders and other invertebrates – and sometimes small lizards or other vertebrates too – that are attempting to flee from the formidable jaws of the advancing ant columns. Although many antbird species will join in mixed flocks of antbirds and other birds, such as tanagers, woodcreepers and cuckoos, to take advantage of this mobile feast, fewer than 30 species of 'professional' ant-followers regularly feed in this way. They include a hard core of about 20 species of 'obligate' ant-followers, which are never seen feeding away from ant swarms. The only other birds known to show such extreme specialisation are a few species of woodcreepers (Dendrocolaptinae, p. 227). Often a strict hierarchy operates, with some species keeping just ahead of the ant column, some in the centre of the mixed flock of antbirds, others farther back, and some on the flanks. There is often a vertical stratification too, with

some species restricted to lower branches and undergrowth, and others at varying levels above. Another way in which resources are partitioned is that some species search for food among living leaves, others look among dead ones hanging from a tree, others among vine tangles, and yet others specialise in turning over leaf litter, and different species take different types of prey.

Small to medium sized, many with relatively large heads, most antbirds hold themselves horizontally. They have short, broad, rounded wings for limited flights among dense vegetation. Their bills are short to medium in length, and variably but distinctly hooked at the tip. Most have relatively strong and often longish legs and big feet, with toes adapted for gripping perches firmly – this is particularly true of those like the ant-following species that cling onto vertical branches. Powerful leg muscles allow them to jump from one perch to another and make swift, deft movements when chasing fast-moving invertebrate prey. Their feathers are typically soft and fluffy. Although none are brilliantly coloured, males are generally much more boldly coloured than females, with dark grey, black or bright chestnut plumage and striking patterns, including black or white spots or (especially in male antshrikes) barring, and they look very different from the mainly brown females. Many species look very similar to one another. Some have brighter white or yellowish underparts, and many have contrasting bright crown, face, throat or rump patches, or bright blue, green, red or yellow bare skin around the eyes. The eyes themselves may be yellow, white or red. Both sexes of all species have concealed white patches on the back or around the 'shoulder' area that they suddenly expose during courtship or threat displays. Some species have a prominent erectile crest, which is especially pronounced in antshrikes. The crest of the bright grey and chestnut White-plumed Antbird, *Pithys albifrons*, is forked and is continuous with its white beard, contrasting with the bird's jet-black head. Unusually, both sexes share this flamboyant plumage.

The various compound common names that many of these birds have acquired relate to a supposed resemblance to familiar Eurasian and North American families that the Western naturalists who named them saw – for example, the small, fine-billed, foliage gleaning antwrens and antvireos, and the larger antshrikes, with their much heavier, hooked bill. Other species are just called antbirds.

In the past, the members of this big family have been lumped with the ant-thrushes, Formicariidae (p. 224), the antpittas, Grallariidae (p. 222) and gnateaters, Conopophagidae (p. 221) in a single, considerably enlarged Family Formicariidae. More recently, DNA studies have revealed that the antbirds are not so closely related to the ant-thrushes and antpittas as was once thought, and that they are probably closest to the gnateaters and to another very small family, the crescentchests, Melanoparaeiidae (p. 220), which were formerly included within the tapaculo Family Rhinocryptidae (p. 223).

Almost 90% of genera and 80% of species in the former enlarged family remain in the Thamnophilidae. It is divided into three subfamilies. The smallest is the Euchrepomidinae, containing just four species in a single genus, *Euchrepomis*. This is one of nine genera in the family whose members are called antwrens; all are small, agile and highly active birds, many of which seek food by hanging head-down from the tips, edges or undersides of large leaves. Males of this genus have bright yellow or rufous patches of colour on the shoulders and rump. The second and by far the largest subfamily is the Thamnophilinae, which is subdivided into five tribes. The tribe Microrhopini, with eight genera and 16 species, includes a strikingly plumaged antwren, the Dot-winged Antwren, *Microrhopias quixensis*, named for the rows of white dots that stand out against the glossy black plumage of the male. He often fans and cocks his long tail, showing off the white tips to its feathers. This species has a very wide distribution from southern Mexico to central Brazil. Also in this tribe are three scarce and local species of bushbirds in two genera in which males are entirely black and females mainly rufous or black with a rufous breast. As well as this distinctive plumage, they have remarkable, deep and laterally compressed bills with the lower mandible strongly upcurved, which they use to peel bark from trees, vines or rotten logs to get at insects hiding beneath, as well as taking them from among dense clusters of dead leaves. The tribe Formicivorini includes three genera of antwrens. The ten species of *Formicivora* antwrens are small birds, at 11–14 cm (4–5.5 in) long, and boldly plumaged in various

ABOVE The Bicoloured Antbird, *Gymnopithys bicolor*, is often the most numerous of the three species commonly seen together.

combinations of chestnut, black and white. The most speciose group of antwrens are those in the genus *Myrmotherula*, with 24 species. Ten of these have boldly streaked plumage, especially in the males, while the rest are attired in plainer browns and greys. These are tiny birds, the smallest members of the antbird family, mostly just 9–10 cm (3.5–4 in) long – the smallest of all, the Pygmy Antwren, *M. brachyura*, and Moustached Antwren, *M. ignota*, measuring a mere 7.5–8 cm (3 in) and weighing only 6–8 g (0.2–0.3 oz).

By contrast, the 79 species in 17 genera of the tribe Thamnophilini, include the largest members of the family among the 44 species in twelve genera known as antshrikes. Largest of all by far is the appropriately named Giant Antshrike, *Batara cinerea*, which with its long tail, as long as its body, has a total length of 28–36 cm (11–14 in), and weighs 100–155 g (3.5–5.5 oz). Males have a black cap ending in a slight crest, white barred black upperparts and tail and white underparts, while females have the black replaced by reddish-brown. With disjunct populations in the Bolivian Andes and in Brazil, Paraguay and Argentina, it is often hard to see among dense undergrowth, but its very loud song of a series of musical ringing notes is audible for well over 1 km (0.6 mile). Six of the antshrike genera, including *Batara*, contain only one species, and all but one of the remaining six contain two or three; by contrast there are 30 species in the genus *Thamnophilus*. These include the Barred Antshrike, *T. doliatus*, with 12 subspecies over its huge range, from southern Mexico to northern Argentina. The common name is well deserved, as males are completely barred black-and-white above and below, while females have a rufous crown and upperparts and buff underparts, with black-and-white barring only on the head and nape. Most antshrikes search for food by travelling through dense foliage in series of rather ungainly hops, but can move with lightning speed when they spot a beetle or other insect prey. At the smaller end of the size range, the Thamnophilini includes 20 species of antwrens in three genera, which are larger than the little *Myrmotherula* antwrens, and also the similarly sized antvireos, all eight species of which are in the same genus, *Dysithamnus*. The antvireos resemble the antshrikes in some ways, being sturdier, less active and with heavier, more distinctly hooked bills than the antwrens, and they are closely related to four small Amazonian antshrike species in the genus *Thamnomanes*. The latter differ though in that while the antvireos are foliage gleaners, they fly out to catch their prey.

The tribe Pithyini, with 51 species in 10 genera, includes all the obligate ant followers, in five genera. There is a well established hierarchy of species queuing for prey fleeing an ant swarm. The largest species, the Ocellated Antbird, *Phaenostictus mcleannani*, a rich brown and black bird with a blue patch of bare skin around each eye, is generally dominant over other antbirds. The obligate antbirds have a complex social structure, with many individuals, pairs or family groups following an ant swarm and a distinct pecking order within the species; this is especially true of the Ocellated Antbirds, which form clans in which the dominant pair tolerate their offspring and their mates for several years, bunching together to drive off rival clans. Up to 20 individuals of the White-plumed Antbird and as many as 26 Rufous-throated Antbirds, *Gymnopythis rufigula* have been observed at large swarms.

The final tribe of the subfamily Thamnophilinae is the Pyriglenini, with 41 species and 15 genera, each containing between one and eight species. They include regular ant followers, such as the Bare-crowned Antbird, *Gymnocichla nudiceps*, from Central America and northern Colombia, unique in the family in that its bare bright blue skin extends onto the crown, in males only. Other members of this tribe that are regular 'professional' ant-swarm feeders include the three species of fire-eyes, *Pyriglena*, long-tailed antbirds named for their fiery red eyes that stand out against their all-black plumage.

The third subfamily, Myrmornithinae, contains only three genera, each with a single species. Two of them are antshrikes: the grey, black-capped Spot-winged Antshrike, *Pygiptila stellaris*, from the Amazon, and the Russet Antshrike, *Thamnistes anabatinus*, of Andean foothills. The third, the Wing-banded Antbird, *Myrmornis torquata*, is sparsely distributed in parts of northern South America. It is an oddly proportioned bird – rotund, very short-tailed, short legged and long-billed – with a complex plumage pattern of chestnut, brown, buff, black and white. It is far less shy of humans than most antbirds.

CRESCENTCHESTS Melanopareiidae

GENERA: 1   **SPECIES:** 4

LENGTH: 14.5–16 cm (5.7–6 in)

WEIGHT: 16–23 g (0.6–0.8 oz)

RANGE AND HABITAT: two species have restricted ranges in Ecuador and Peru, and two inhabit very large areas in eastern central and central North America; all live in dense arid scrub, with one also in dense dry grassland and one in undergrowth in semi-arid woodland

SOCIAL BEHAVIOUR: probably monogamous, with both sexes sharing incubation and care of young; usually seen singly or in pairs

NEST: the few nests that have been recorded were ball-shaped nests of strips of cactus and dry plants with a side entrance, or cups of grass, plant fibres and leaves and sited on the ground among grass or dense shrub cover

EGGS: few records; 2–3, differing between species – white or pale blue with small black, dark reddish brown or grey markings or plain greenish blue

INCUBATION: known only for Collared Crescentchest; 12–16 days

FLEDGING PERIOD: known only for Collared Crescentchest; 12–14 days

FOOD: not known

VOICE: simple, loud songs of repeated 'chuck' or 'chip' notes, and harsh or whistling calls

MIGRATION: probably sedentary

CONSERVATION STATUS: the Marañon Crescentchest, *Melanopareia maranonica*, is Near Threatened

LEFT The Marañon Crescentchest, *Melanopareia maranonica*, is the scarcest member of its small family and human encroachment on its small range could put it at serious risk.

These four handsome little sparrow-sized birds making up this recently created family are all very similar to one another, and placed in a single genus *Melanopareia*. They have a boldly patterned head featuring a black crown and mask separated by a white or cream eyestripe, a tawny buff throat, ending in a black crescent-shaped band across the chest and the rest of the underparts rich chestnut, contrasting with grey upperparts and the long, often jauntily angled tail. The sexes are very similar, apart from males being somewhat more strongly patterned.

The Collared Crescentchest, *M. torquata*, has a wide distribution from eastern Bolivia, across central Brazil to extreme eastern Paraguay, while the Olive-crowned Crescentchest, *M. maximiliani* occurs to the west and south of its relative, in Bolivia, western Paraguay and a small part of northern Argentina. Of the two restricted range species, the Elegant Crescentchest, *M. elegans*, occurs in a small area of western Ecuador and northwest Peru, where it seems to be fairly common and increasing in numbers, perhaps as a result of spreading north into suitable open habitat following deforestation. The same cannot be said, however, of the Marañon Crescentchest, *M. maranonica*, which is confined to a far smaller range in the extreme south of Ecuador and a single river valley in northwest Peru, and is uncommon and probably declining. Threats include logging, cattle-ranching and damage to its habitat from agriculture, especially the spread of oil-palm plantations.

For much of the time, crescentchests remain hidden as they hop or creep about in dense cover, though males are often more visible when they perch at the top of a low shrub to broadcast their loud songs, which then carry a long way. Collared Crescentchests have been known to shelter in burrows dug in the ground by rats and armadillos.

Crescentchests were formerly included in the tapaculo Family Rhinocryptidae (p. 223) but DNA data indicate that they definitely do not belong there. Their near relationships are uncertain, but they have tentatively been placed here closest to the antbirds (Thamnophilidae) and gnateaters (Conopophagidae).

GNATEATERS Conopophagidae

GENERA: 2   **SPECIES:** 10

LENGTH: *Conopophaga*, 10.5–16 cm (4–6 in); *Pittisoma*, 16–19 cm (6–7.5 in)

WEIGHT: *Conopophaga*, 16–43 g (0.6–1.5 oz); *Pittisoma*, 96–110 g (3.4–4 oz)

RANGE AND HABITAT: *Conopophaga*, exclusively South American, with most species in Amazonian rainforests, and others in montane forests in the Andes or in rainforest and woodland in eastern Brazil, Paraguay and northeast Argentina; *Pittisoma*, restricted to extreme north-west South America, with one species just extending into Central America

SOCIAL BEHAVIOUR: little known, apart from a few species of *Conopophaga*; feed solitarily or in pairs, defending territory; probably monogamous, remaining together all year

NEST: little known, documented for some *Conopophaga* species as an untidy cup of rootlets and lichens, camouflaged with twigs and dead leaves, sited among vegetation near ground level

EGGS: little known; clutch of 2, buff, yellowish or pale reddish, recorded for some *Conopophaga*

INCUBATION: about two weeks, known only for the Rufous Gnateater, *C. lineata*

FLEDGING PERIOD: about two weeks in the Rufous Gnateater and Black-cheeked Gnateater, *C. melanops*

FOOD: *Conopophaga* eat arthropods, especially very small beetles, caterpillars, ants, grasshoppers and spiders; little is known of the details of invertebrate prey eaten by *Pittisoma* species

VOICE: harsh calls, with simple songs consisting of whistling, rattling, trilling or chattering notes

MIGRATION: sedentary

CONSERVATION STATUS: one species, the Rufous-crowned Antpitta, *Pittasoma rufopileatum*, is Near Threatened

ABOVE The distinctive white feather tufts of this Rufous Gnateater, *Conopophaga lineata*, are sleeked down and less visible than in display.

The unobtrusive, hard-to-see birds in this very small almost exclusively South American family spend most of their lives just above the floor of tropical forests, generally concealed among dense vegetation. Here they leap about energetically along or between low branches in the undergrowth. Flicking their wings slightly, they fly down to rummage with their bills among the leaf litter for their preferred prey, tiny insects and their larvae and spiders, less than 5 mm (0.2 in) long. They also leap (and occasionally flutter) upwards, or reach up on their long legs, to snatch prey from the foliage above. All but two species are included in the genus *Conopophaga* – a name that means 'gnat-eater', though gnats do not appear to be a feature of their diet.

Small and rotund, with big heads, flattened, slightly hook-tipped bills, short wings, very short tails, long legs and feet, and soft, fluffy plumage, the eight *Conopophaga* species resemble small antpittas (Family Grallariidae, p. 222). Indeed, they were once classified as close relatives of the antpittas and the other ground-dwelling antbirds, which were all subsumed with the antbirds in a single enlarged Family Formicariidae. With conflicting evidence from molecular studies, their precise relationships are still uncertain, but a close relationship with crescentchests (Melanopareiidae, p. 220) seems likely. The *Conopophaga* species are all small, with

the largest, the Black-bellied Gnateater, *C. melanogaster*, only 16 cm (6 in) long, and all the rest measuring only 10.5–14 cm (4–5.5 in). Their plumage is in various combinations and patterns of brown, black, grey, rufous and white, with males brighter than females. All but the Black-cheeked Gnateater, *C. melanops*, have a very distinctive contrasting plume of feathers behind each eye, most prominent and bright silvery white in males, and often greyer in females. These are normally sleeked back or obscured by the overlying crown feathers, but can be erected like little horns during courtship chases or aggressive encounters at territorial boundaries.

The two species in the genus *Pittasoma* were until recently thought to actually belong to the antpitta family, but there is good evidence that they should be included here with the gnateaters. At 16–19 cm (6–7.5 in) long and at a weight of about 100 g (3.5 oz) they are a little longer and more than twice as heavy as the largest *Conopophaga* species, and approaching twice as long and more than twice as heavy as the smallest member of that genus. Both have strikingly marked rufous and black heads, and lack the white plumes of their relatives. Unlike the antpittas, many species of which have pale underparts marked with dark streaks, and unlike the *Conopophaga* species too (which have unmarked underparts) the *Pittasoma* species (apart from one race of the Rufous-crowned Antpitta, *P. rufopileatum*) are strongly barred below. The range of the Rufous-crowned species extends from northwest Ecuador to the central part of the Choco region of Colombia, while the Black-crowned Antpitta, *P. michleri*, replaces it in northern Choco, Panama and Costa Rica. Whereas the *Conopophaga* gnateaters do not join mixed-species flocks of other birds, and have only rarely been recorded at ant swarms, the two *Pittisoma* species are regular attendees, where they tend to dominate both antbirds and woodcreepers.

ANTPITTAS Grallariidae

GENERA: 4   **SPECIES**: 53

LENGTH: 10–24 cm (4–9.5 in)

WEIGHT: 14–266 g (0.5–9.4 oz)

RANGE AND HABITAT: the northern half of South America, from Colombia to northeast Argentina; the range of four of these species extends into central America, one as far north as Costa Rica, two to Honduras and one to southern Mexico; most live in humid forests, with a few in deciduous woodland, bamboo, scrub; the greatest diversity is in the very humid cloud forests of the Andes

SOCIAL BEHAVIOUR: generally solitary, though pairs may forage within earshot of one another; monogamous, defending a territory

NEST: no details available for over half of all species; in the rest, a cup of rootlets, strands of fungi and plant fibres on a small platform of small sticks and leaves and typically sited quite near ground level in a tree, against the trunk or in a fork, though some are among vines, in low bushes, on logs or other sites

EGGS: 1–3, usually 2, colour varying between genera and even between species within a genus; in *Grallaria*, unmarked blue or blue-green, *Hylopezus*, grey, buff or yellowish brown, *Myrmothera*, turquoise to blue-green, *Grallaricula* white, pale green or pale brown; all with different brown markings

INCUBATION: 16–20 days in the few species for which information is available

FLEDGING PERIOD: 13–19 days in the few species for which information is available

FOOD: a wide range of invertebrates, including many insects, as well as earthworms and snails, while some species may also eat small vertebrates such as frogs; occasionally fruit

VOICE: simple, loud, mainly low-pitched ventriloquial songs consisting of single or multiple whistles, hoots, trills or pops; a series of notes may accelerate or decelerate, or rise or fall in pitch or volume

MIGRATION: sedentary

CONSERVATION STATUS: two species, the Tachira Antpitta, *Grallaria chthonia*, and the Urrao Antpitta, *G. fenwickorum*, are Critically Endangered; three species, the Jocotoco Antpitta, *G. ridgelyi*, Cundinamarca Antpitta, *G. kaestneri*, and Ochre-fronted Antpitta, *Grallaricula ochraceifrons*, are Endangered; 10 species, including the Great Antpitta, *Grallaria excelsa*, Giant Antpitta, *G. gigantea*, Moustached Antpitta, *G. alleni*, Masked Antpitta, *Hylopezus auricularis*, and Rusty-tinged Antpitta, *Grallaricula przewalskii*, are Vulnerable; eight species, including the Chestnut Antpitta, *Grallaria blakei*, and Crescent-faced Antpitta, *Grallaricula lineifrons*, are Near Threatened

LEFT The Endangered Jocotoco Antpitta, *Grallaria ridgelyi*, unknown to science until 1997, is known from only five locations in Ecuador.

The antpittas constitute a family of extremely secretive Neotropical birds of the forest floor and dense undergrowth, mostly in Amazonian rainforests and Andean cloud forests. Systematists formerly lumped them together with the ant-thrushes and antbirds in a very large single Family Formicariidae. Subsequently, the antipittas and ant-thrushes were separated as a reduced Family Formicariidae, and known collectively as 'ground antbirds', reflecting the terrestrial habits of both groups in contrast to the less closely related antbirds (now separated in a new family, Thamnophilidae, and called 'typical antbirds'), which spend most of their time in the forest understorey. In addition to these differences in lifestyle, and also in anatomical details, including those of the syrinx ('voice-box'), the 'ground antbirds' show divergence in their DNA. Also, they lack the white interscapular patch (between the 'shoulders') that is a badge of the antbirds, and in contrast to the latter family, the sexes of most species look alike. Currently, the knowledge gained from more recent DNA research indicates that the antpittas and ant-thrushes are not nearly as closely related as had been thought, and so each are given family status. The Family Formicariidae (p. 224) now contain just the ant-thrushes, while the ant-thrushes are in the new Family Grallariidae, with the antbirds remaining in the Thamnophilidae (p. 218).

Antpittas are well adapted for living on the ground, where they move about with powerful, bounding hops, like the unrelated Old World pittas (Family Pittidae, p. 200) from which they take part of their common name (the 'ant' part, a throwback to when they were classified with the antbirds, is not so appropriate, since they rarely feed at army-ant swarms). The antpittas and pittas have similarly odd proportions, too, with big heads, short rotund bodies, extremely short tails, and long, strong legs, and both have a very erect posture. Like pittas, too, many antpittas have big eyes for spotting prey in the gloom of the rainforest floor, and heavy, powerful bills for securing it, but differ from them in their plumage – pittas are so renowned for their brilliant colours that they were sometimes known as 'jewel-birds', whereas antpittas are far more soberly (albeit handsomely) attired, mostly in various combination of brown, chestnut and grey, mostly with paler underparts that are marked with dark streaks or barring in some species.

There are 32 species in the largest genus, *Grallaria*, and three genera of smaller species, *Hylopezus*, *Myrmothera* and *Grallaricula*. Most feed on a wide variety of insects and other invertebrates by rummaging among leaf litter on the forest floor with their strong bills. At 24 cm (9.5 in) long the largest of the three biggest species, the Giant Antpitta, *G. gigantea*, as well as taking large beetle larvae, and slugs, feeds on giant earthworms, slicing them into bite-sized portions with its formidable bill. At the other end of the size scale, the nine very small *Grallaricula* species, most of which measure only 10 cm (4 in) in length, usually use a different feeding method, gleaning small insects and spiders from the lianas or moss-covered tree trunks.

Relatively little is known of the biology of many species, as these birds are secretive and very hard to see in the shaded undergrowth of their forest habitats, so that birders often have to rely on their loud and attractive songs, heard mostly at dawn or dusk, to provide evidence of their presence and identity. Their relatively dull plumage provides good camouflage and they often 'freeze', remaining motionless for long periods. The difficulty of seeing it is celebrated in the common and specific names of one Amazonian species, the Elusive Antpitta, *Grallaria eludens*. One species might have eluded ornithologists completely had it not been discovered – as recently as 1997. This is the Jocotoco Antpitta, *G. ridgleyi*, a very scarce inhabitant of wet, mossy forests with stands of bamboo on the eastern slopes of the Andes in southern Ecuador, at altitudes of about 2,300–2,700 m (7,500–8,900 ft). Subsequently its range was found to extend a short way into northern Peru but it remains rare and seriously threatened (along with various other antpitta species). Its populations are declining slowly but steadily as a result of logging and mining for gold.

TAPACULOS Rhinocryptidae

GENERA: 12   **SPECIES:** 59

LENGTH: 10–23 cm (4–9 in)

WEIGHT: 10.5–185 g (0.4–6.5 oz)

RANGE AND HABITAT: Central America (three species in Panama and Costa Rica) and South America; greatest diversity of species in the northern Andes, but of genera in southern South America; almost all prefer habitats with dense ground cover, mostly in moist montane forest with thick stands of bamboo, ferns or other vegetation; some live above the treeline among grass tussocks or boulders; a few in other habitats, from marshes (the Marsh Tapaculo, *Scytalopus iraiensis*) to arid scrub (the Crested Gallito, *Rhinocrypta lanceolata* and Sandy Gallito, *Teledromas fuscus*)

SOCIAL BEHAVIOUR: often in pairs, in close contact; strongly territorial year-round

NEST: unknown for two-thirds of all species; the rest are very varied, from open cups to globes, with top or side entrance, often of rootlets, moss, grass and twiglets; most are sited at the end of a tunnel they dig in the ground or in a burrow abandoned by or taken over form a rodent, or in a hollow or unused nest hole in a tree

EGGS: usually 2–3; white

INCUBATION: unknown for all except a few species, 15–17 days

FLEDGING PERIOD: unknown except for a few species, 14–15 days

FOOD: mainly insects and spiders, sometimes other invertebrates such as molluscs and centipedes; some also eat berries and seeds

VOICE: loud, simple but distinctive songs, varying from a series of musical notes to harsher trills and churring sounds; in some species, pairs perform duets

MIGRATION: mostly strictly sedentary

CONSERVATION STATUS: one species, Stresemann's Bristlefront, *Merulaxis stresemanni*, is Critically Endangered; seven species, the Ecuadorian Tapaculo, *Scytalopus robbinsi*, Marsh Tapaculo, *S. iraensis*, and Magdalena Tapaculo, *S. rodriguezi*, Magellanic Tapaculo, *S. magellanicus*, Diamantina Tapaculo, *S. diamantinensis*, Boa Nova Tapaculo, *S. gonzogai*, and Bahia Tapaculo, *Eleoscytalopus pyschopompus*, are Endangered; two species, the Perija Tapaculo, *S. perijanus*, and Tacarcuna Tapaculo, *S. panamensis*, are Vulnerable; and five species are Near Threatened

ABOVE The Ocellated Tapaculo, *Acropternis orthonyx*, jumps as it throws leaves backwards with both feet simultaneously to find insect food.

ABOVE Although it spends much of its life on the ground hidden among dense thorny scrub in the Argentine chaco, the Crested Gallito, *Rhinocrypta lanceolata*, sometimes emerges to sing.

ecretive and usually frustratingly difficult to see for more than a eeting view, these small to medium-sized Neotropical birds are ike ovenbirds) unusual in being particularly diverse in the south f the South American continent.

Most have a plump, often neckless body, and generally hold the tail cocked like that of wrens. The common name of the family and most species refers to this habit, whereby the tail covers the bird's rump; it is a colourful Spanish phrase translatable as 'cover your arse'. Tail length varies from very short in little members of the most speciose genus, *Scytalopus*, through medium length as in the two large, thrushlike huet-huets in the genus *Pteroptochos* to long, as in the two bristlefronts in the genus *Merulaxis* named for the short tuft of stiff upright feathers at the base of the bill. All species have a heavy bill and longish legs with big, strong feet that most use for scratching about in soil and leaf litter to expose insects and other food. As well as using one foot to do this like most other birds, they also use both feet simultaneously, in a process called 'kick-scratching'. Other distinctive features are the movable flap or operculum over the nostrils (the family name Rhinocryptidae is from the Greek words for 'hidden nose'), and the loose feathering on flanks and undertail. Their wings are short, and they rarely fly for more than a few metres, depending instead on their relatively long legs with big, strong feet for running, walking or hopping. They usually never roam far from cover, darting about mouselike on the ground among dense cover. Often, the only clues to their presence are their frequent, loud calls and songs.

The plumage is mainly drab, mostly in camouflaging shades of brown, grey or black, but often with areas of brighter chestnut and dark barring, and areas of orange or white in some species. The sexes are similar in most species apart from a few races of *Scytalopus* and the two bristlefronts, *Merulaxis*.

Within the first of the two great suborders of passerines, the suboscines (Tyranni, p. 200), and within that its New World branch (infraorder Tyrannides), the tapaculos are classified within the parvorder Furnariida. This separates the tapaculo family, together with the nine preceding families of antbirds, crescentchests, gnateaters, antpittas, ant-thrushes, leaftossers, woodcreepers and the horneros and relatives, from the parvorder Tyrannida, containing the manakins, cotingas, tyrant-flycatchers and others. As to which families of the Furnariida are most closely related to the tapaculos, there is less certainty, with conflicting results from recent research. They may be closest to the antpittas (Grallariidae, p. 222), with these two together then related in turn to the ant-thrushes (Formicariidae, below) and ovenbirds (p. 227). Alternatively, they may be most closely related to ant-thrushes and ovenbirds, with these three together being related to the antpittas.

The limited DNA evidence available for some species within the family lends support for its division into two subfamilies. The Rhinocryptinae contains seven genera, all but two with just a single species. These monotypic genera include the Crested Gallito, *Rhinocrypta*, and Sandy Gallito, *Teledromas*, their common name, which is Spanish for 'little chicken' referring to their fancied resemblance to little hens, and also the Ocellated Tapaculo, *Acropternis*. The two species of huet-huets get their common name from their distinctive, sharp, loud double (but sometimes treble) calls. The second subfamily, Scytalopodinae, includes the 43 species of *Scytalopus*, most of which look almost identical, and four small genera with just one or two species each, including as well as the two bristlefronts the rare and the little known Spotted Bamboowren, *Psilorhamphus guttatus*.

ANT-THRUSHES Formicariidae

GENERA: 2 **SPECIES**: 12

LENGTH: 17–22.5 cm (7–9 in)

WEIGHT: 40–150 g (1.4–5.3 oz)

RANGE AND HABITAT: Central America, from southern Mexico to Panama, and South America, from Colombia to northeast Argentina; humid tropical forests

SOCIAL BEHAVIOUR: generally solitary; probably all monogamous, with both sexes incubating eggs and caring for young

NEST: a dense platform of sticks, leaves, flowers and other material, sited within a natural tree hole or one excavated and abandoned by another bird

EGGS: known for only a few species; 2, white

INCUBATION: known for only a few species; about 14 days

FLEDGING PERIOD: known for only a few species; about 14 days

FOOD: insects and other invertebrates; some species occasionally eat small snakes and fruit

VOICE: loud whistling, trilling, or other songs; females may sing as well as males

MIGRATION: sedentary

CONSERVATION STATUS: one species, the Rufous-fronted Ant-thrush, *Formicarius rufifrons*, is Near Threatened

ABOVE Like other members of this family, this Blackheaded Ant-thursh, *Formicarius nigricapillus,* is wary and hard to see.

Until recently, these very secretive and relatively little known denizens of dense Neotropical rainforests were lumped together with the antpittas (Family Grallariidae, p. 222) in a larger family, Formicariidae, but as a result of recent DNA studies, they are now known not to be nearly so closely related; instead, their closest relatives appear to be the horneros and relatives in the far larger family, Furnariidae. Compared with the equally highly terrestrial antpittas, which generally adopt very erect posture, ant-thrushes usually have a horizontal carriage. Also, their legs, though relatively long, are not as long and their tails are short but not as stumpy as those of antpittas. Unlike antpittas, which proceed across the forest floor mainly by hopping, ant-thrushes generally walk about slowly and deliberately, often cocking their tail or pumping them up and down in time with each step, quite unlike true thrushes. In fact, they often look like smaller terrestrial members of the completely unrelated rail family, Rallidae. There are six slightly smaller species in the genus *Formicarius*, and six, too, in the other genus, *Chamaeza*.

Ant-thrushes have no relationship at all with the true thrushes (Family Turdidae, p. 391), which are oscine passerines, although the plumage colours and pattern of the ant-thrushes in the genus *Chamaeza* – which are plain brown above and white or warm buff below with dark streaks, apart from one that it strongly barred below – gives them a superficial resemblance to many thrushes. *Formicarius* ant-thrushes are mainly black and dark brown, with patches of rich reddish-brown on the crown, cheeks or undertail and in one species also on the underparts; all but one species have a blue ring around the eye.

Some species may occasionally visit ant swarms with mixed flocks of other birds, keeping to the margins, but usually search for their insect and other invertebrate prey by flicking leaves aside with their stout bills. They are generally extremely hard to see, but can be recognised by their frequent far-carrying songs, simple but often melodic series of whistles, trills and gurgling sounds.

LEAFTOSSERS AND MINERS Scleruridae

GENERA: 2   **SPECIES:** 17

LENGTH: leaftossers, 15–20 cm (6–8 in); miners, 11–18.5 cm (4–7 in)

WEIGHT: leaftossers, 20–45 g (0.7–1.6 oz); miners, 16–54 g (0.6–1.9 oz)

RANGE AND HABITAT: leaftossers in Central and South America, in humid tropical forests; miners in South America, in a wide range of open habitats, from sandy coastal deserts to puna grassland and barren slopes in the Andes

SOCIAL BEHAVIOUR: leaftossers, usually solitary; miners may be seen singly or in pairs, and some may form small flocks after breeding; both groups appear to be monogamous and territorial with the sexes sharing incubation and care of the young

NEST: leaftossers, a shallow cup of twigs, leaf-stems or other plant material at the end of a burrow they dig in soil; miners in a nest chamber with the floor padded with grasses and mammal hair at the end of a burrow in a bank or level ground that they dig themselves, or that have been abandoned by other birds (especially *Upucerthia*, earthcreepers) or mammals (especially tuco-tucos, viscachas and armadillos)

EGGS: leaftossers, usually 2, white; miners 2–3, white

INCUBATION: leaftossers, estimate of at least 21 days; miners, no information

FLEDGING PERIOD: leaftossers, estimate of 14–15 days; miners, no information

FOOD: leaftossers, insects, spiders, earthworms, tiny frogs, seeds; miners, insects, spiders, some seeds

VOICE: leaftossers, simple or more complex songs of clear whistles, in some with chattering, trilling or wheezy notes; miners, simple twittering songs given in a song-flight or from a boulder or other prominent perch

MIGRATION: leaftossers, sedentary; miners, sedentary apart from the Short-billed Miner, *Geositta antarctica*, which migrates northwards after breeding in Tierra del Fuego to as far north as north-central Argentina

CONSERVATION STATUS: one race, *cearensis*, of the Rufous-breasted Leaftosser, *Sclerurus scansor*, sometimes regarded as a separate species, and the Campo Miner, *Geositta poeciloptera*, are Vulnerable; the Grey-throated Leaftosser, *S. albigularis*, is Near Threatened

These two groups of birds are related to the next two families – the woodcreepers, Dendrocolaptidae (p. 226) and the horneros and relatives (Furnariidae, p. 227), and were for long included within the latter family, though were not thought to be closely related to one another. Indeed, the miners were until recently placed at the

ABOVE The Puna Miner, *Geositta punensis*, lives in the Andes, where it depends for nest sites on the burrows of rodents called tuco-tucos.

very beginning of the furnariid family sequence, and the leaftossers at the very end. Recent DNA research has, however, revealed that despite having disparate habitats, lifestyles, and plumage, as well as anatomical and other differences, these two groups are each other's closest relatives, and here they are united within a family of their own, the Scleruridae. The molecular evidence also indicates that the leaftossers and miners are together most closely related to the woodcreepers, and some systematists prefer to include all three of them as subfamilies (Sclerurinae and Dendrocolaptinae) within the Furnariidae.

The six species of leaftossers, occupying a single genus *Sclerurus*, are very shy and elusive and generally encountered only by chance. They have long, oval shaped bodies with a rather hunched back, and hold themselves quite horizontally and close to the ground on short legs as they shuffle about in the leaf litter. All are extremely similar to one another in appearance, mainly dark brown with a reddish-brown rump and breast, a short, broad black tail and a long slender bill, which they use to flick leaves aside (rather than tossing them) to reveal their invertebrate prey. These enigmatic birds are particularly susceptible to deforestation.

There are 11 species of miners, all in the genus *Geositta*. In marked contrast to the leaftossers, they are easier to spot in the open habitats they favour. Although they are well camouflaged and with a habit of crouching motionless to evade detection, they are obvious when they fly. These have a medium to long slim bill and a short notched tail and a distinctively shaped syrinx (voicebox) unlike furnariids. They are dull brownish or greyish above and pale below, in some species with indistinct streaks on the breast. Each species has a unique black-banded tail pattern, revealed when they take wing, and most have dull rufous areas on the wings whose details further aid identification. They are named for their habit of digging nest holes. Miners are strong flyers, with song-flights reminiscent of oscine passerines such as larks and pipits. They hover into the wind to heights of up to about 50 m (160 ft), uttering simple but quite musical twittering songs as they plane down to the ground.

The Campo Miner, *G. poeciloptera*, is endemic to a completely different region of South America from the rest of the genus: it lives in *campo* grassland and the treeless parts of the tropical tall-grass savanna habitat known as *cerrado* in Brazil and adjacent parts of Bolivia and Paraguay. Here, it favours areas that have recently been burned – including those that are still smouldering. It also differs from the other miners in being smaller, with a shorter tail and extensive bright rufous markings on its wings, and was until recently accorded a genus, *Geobates*, of its own. Among the rest, the Slender-billed Miner, *G. tenuirostris*, one of the Andean species, which occurs in puna grassland at up to 4,600 m (15,000 ft), is notable for its particularly long, slender, decurved bill.

WOODCREEPERS Dendrocolaptidae

GENERA: 16   **SPECIES:** 51

LENGTH: 14–36 cm (5.5–14 in)

WEIGHT: 11–160 g (0.4–5.6 oz)

RANGE AND HABITAT: Mexico, Central America and South America; greatest diversity in Amazonia; forests, forest edges and open woodland, mainly in lowlands; one species, the Scimitar-billed Woodcreeper, *Drymornis bridgesii*, occurs in arid scrublands

SOCIAL BEHAVIOUR: solitary or in pairs; mostly monogamous apart from polygamous *Dendrocincla* species

NEST: bed of wood chips or bark flakes or small cup of rootlets, dead leaves, moss and other plant material and sometimes feathers, sited in tree hole or other hollow; sometimes in cavity behind loose bark

EGGS: 1–4, usually 2 or 3, white

INCUBATION: 14–21 days

FLEDGING PERIOD: 17–25 days

FOOD: mostly insects, also some other invertebrates such as spiders, scorpions, millipedes, centipedes and snails; occasionally small reptiles and amphibians

VOICE: varied, with songs heard mainly at dawn and dusk, made up chiefly of whistles, or trills that ascend or descend in pitch; also a wide variety of similar calls heard during the daytime

MIGRATION: almost entirely sedentary apart from altitudinal movements in some upland species

CONSERVATION STATUS: two species, Hoffmann's Woodcreeper, *Dendrocolaptes hoffmansi*, and the Moustached Woodcreeper, *Xiphocolaptes falcirostris*, are Vulnerable; two species the Greater Scythebill, *Drymotoxeres pucheranii* and Zimmer's Woodcreeper, *Dendroplex kienerii*, are Near Threatened

LEFT The Streaked-headed Woodcreeper, *Lepidopcolates souleyetti*, prefers more open habitats than most of its relatives, including savannah.

the long tail with its stiffened feathers as a prop. Unlike those of woodpeckers and other birds that use stiff tails in this way, but like some ovenbirds, such as treerunners, their tips lack vanes and are spiny, wirelike and downcurved, serving as an extra set of claws for maximum purchase. Like treecreepers, woodcreepers usually follow a spiral path as they make their way up a trunk and along branches, and then fly down to the base of the next tree to start again.

Mostly medium-sized birds with a slender body, woodcreepers vary mainly in details of their plumage and in the length of the bill. The plumage is generally brown, with rufous wings and tail. Although a few species are unmarked, most have distinctive patterns of whitish spots, streaks or barring. Some have a short, straight or slightly downcurved, strong bill, suited for gleaning for invertebrates on trunks, branches or foliage; in other species the bill is wider for catching disturbed insects in mid-air. Those with a larger, stronger bill use it to chisel off bark to reach prey beneath or tear apart decaying vegetation on trunks. In others the bill is much longer and used for probing into cavities in trunks or among bromeliads and other vegetation growing on trees. The five species of scythebill have the longest and most strongly downcurved bill of all, for very deep probing. In some, it can be as long as the bird's body. Another species with a long downcurved bill is the Scimitar-billed Woodcreeper, *Drymornis bridgesii*, which unlike all other members of the family regularly feeds on the ground, probing into soil or leaf litter.

Often now classified as a subfamily Dendrocolaptinae within the next large family of horneros and relatives (Furnariidae), but here placed in its traditional Family Dendrocolaptidae, this is a very distinctive group of birds in which all species are very similar in appearance, although they range in size from small to medium-sized.

Apart from a few species that also feed on or near the ground, these birds live in trees and shrubs, moving about with great ease. Like woodpeckers, they do so by using their strong legs and feet, equipped with sharp claws, to grip the bark, and employing

Some woodcreepers, including species of *Dendrocincla*, *Dendrocolaptes* and *Hylexetastes*, feed along with other kinds of birds, including antbirds, in mixed flocks following army-ant swarms. Others wait on a prominent perch and watch for small animals disturbed by mixed feeding flocks in other situations, then fly down to snap up a prey item.

An unusual species is the Wedge-billed Woodcreeper, *Glyphorynchus spirurus*. This is distinctly smaller than the other members of the family and has a different bill shape – short and slightly upturned. It feeds mainly on tiny insects and spiders.

There are two subfamilies. The Sittosominae is by far the smallest, comprising four genera of nine small species with relatively short bills. The genera *Sittasoma*, with just one species, the Olivaceous Woodcreeper, *S. griseicapillus*, and *Dendrocincla*, with six, are among the few plain-coloured species, with no barring or white spotting at all. These four may represent an early evolution of woodcreepers from the next family, Furnariidae, as they share some features with its members; the *Dendrocincla* species in particular, have the least spiny and rigid tail feathers that are adaptations for tree-climbing, and some obtain most of their food from the ground at ant swarms as described above. The Olivaceous Woodcreeper is one of the smallest woodcreepers, only a little larger than the Wedge-billed Woodcreeper.

All the rest of the species, 42 in number, are in the subfamily Dendrocolaptinae. Most of the twelve genera contain only one or a few species, such as *Xiphocolaptes*, with four large species that are the heaviest of all woodcreepers and have the most massive bills, long and laterally compressed. The monotypic genera include the Wedge-billed Woodcreeper, the Long-billed Woodcreeper, *Nasica longirostris*, whose extremely long bill (accounting for a third of its entire length) is only slightly curved, and the biggest of the scythebills, the Greater Scythebill, *Drymotoxeres pucheranii*, whose downcurved bill, though long, is not as relatively long or curved as that of the other four scythebills, in the genus *Campylorhamphus*.

HORNEROS AND RELATIVES Furnariidae

GENERA: 50   **SPECIES:** 231

LENGTH: 10–25 cm (4–10 in)

WEIGHT: 8–109 g (0.3–3.8 oz)

RANGE AND HABITAT: Central and South America; greatest diversity in southern and eastern South America, south of the Tropic of Capricorn; every terrestrial habitat, from constantly wet lowland rainforests or swamps to the driest deserts, and from wild, bleak, high Andean mountains to great cities; two species even live on intertidal rocky beaches (among the very few passerines to do so)

SOCIAL BEHAVIOUR: mainly in pairs or family groups, some forming big flocks outside the breeding season; many are territorial year-round and may roost in a nest outside the breeding season

NEST: extremely varied in type and size; many are large compared with the size of the birds; the main types are hanging purse-shaped structures of sticks; domed nests of sticks or softer plant materials, some with roof or porch; and hard structures of sun-baked mud and straw like native adobe ovens; some species nest in a natural or abandoned bird or mammal tree hole or burrow, making a domed or simple cup nest in a chamber at the end

EGGS: for the few species studied, 1–6, mostly white, some with a pale green, blue or buff tinge

INCUBATION: 14–22 days

FLEDGING PERIOD: known for very few species; 13–29 days

FOOD: most eat insects and other arthropods, also some seeds; a few species eat other invertebrates such as molluscs; others include small frogs or lizards

VOICE: simple, loud songs of mainly unmusical notes, from chattering or screaming notes to creaks and rattles; also whistling sounds

MIGRATION: mostly sedentary; some make altitudinal movements and at least one is nomadic

CONSERVATION STATUS: six species, the Masafuera Rayadito, *Aphrastura masafuerae*, the Royal Cinclodes, *Cinclodes aricomae*, the White-bellied Cinclodes, *C. palliatus*, the Alagoas Foliage-gleaner, *Philydor novaesi*, the Hoary-throated Spinetail, *Synallaxis kollari*, and the Marañon Spinetail, *S. maranonica*, are Critically Endangered; nine species, including the Bolivian Spinetail, *Cranioleuca henricae*, the White-browed Tit-spinetail, *Leptasthenura xenothorax*, Pinto's Spinetail, *Synallaxis infuscata*, and the Perija Thistletail, *Asthenes perijana*, are Endangered; 14 species, including the Pink-legged Gravateiro, *Acrobatornis fonsecai*, the Ash-browed Spinetail, *Cranioleuca curtata*, the Henna-hooded Foliage-gleaner, *Clibanornis erythrocephalus*, and the Russet-mantled Soft-tail, *Thripophaga berpleschi*, are Vulnerable; 24 species are Near Threatened

One of the most species-rich and diverse of all passerine families, the horneros and relatives are unusual in being major constituents of the avifauna of temperate southern South America: in contrast to many of the endemic Neotropical families such as antbirds, ground antbirds, cotingas, manakins, jacamars, toucans and others, they only just extend into the subtropical zone. Almost 90% of species occur in South America, with only 24 in Central America, and only four restricted to that region.

Their hugely varied habitat preferences and lifestyles have led to their being given a large number of wonderfully evocative names, such as foliage-gleaners, treerunners, treehunters, thornbirds, earthcreepers, palmcreepers, streamcreepers, reedhaunters and rushbirds. Their nest structures and sites are also remarkably varied: indeed, no other bird family can rival them in this respect. The nine species of earthcreepers, *Upucerthia*, live among low vegetation in arid scrub and have a longer, more downcurved bill and longer, often cocked tail. The 13 species of cinclodes, *Cinclodes*, are mainly bigger, adapted to life at the edge of water, and include three species that live mainly or entirely on rocky sea coasts. In contrast to these ground dwellers, many ovenbirds have adapted to life in dense vegetation or woodlands. They include 36 species of spinetails, *Synallaxis*, numerous genera of foliage-

ABOVE A Rufous Hornero, *Furnarius rufus*, perches by its immensely strong mud nest in the Mato Grosso, Brazil.

gleaners and the two species of rayaditos, *Aphrastura*. Some are found only in marshland vegetation, reed beds or bamboo thickets, whereas many others live in trees, where they specialise in searching out hidden invertebrate prey behind bark or among curled-up dead leaves.

As would be expected from such a diverse range of lifestyles and feeding habits, there is considerable variation in structure. The bill varies greatly in length and may be thin and pointed for gleaning small insects, robust with an upcurved tip for prying off bark, or downcurved for probing for invertebrates. The tail is particularly variable, as indicated by the common names of groups such as prickletails, wiretails, barbtails and spinetails. Tail shape varies from very short and square or wedge-shaped or slightly forked to extremely long; some, including the treerunners, have stiff feathers with bare, downcurved tips to act as props in tree climbing. The plumage is generally very dull, in camouflaging shades of brown or rufous, often paler and streaked or spotted below, and the sexes are usually more or less similar.

The family's alternative common name of ovenbirds celebrates the most well known of all its species, the Rufous Hornero, *Furnarius rufus*, also known as the Ovenbird. One of six species in the savannah-dwelling hornero genus *Furnarius*, it has adapted to life alongside humans in farmland and cities alike. It builds a big, globular nest from clay, mud, dung and straw that hardens in the sun to produce a structure resembling the old adobe bread-ovens. The scientific name comes from the Latin for 'furnace', whereas the common name 'hornero' is the Spanish word for 'baker'. Rufous Hornero nests, which are 20–30 cm (8–12 in) in diameter, are a common feature of the landscape, built atop tree branches, fence-posts, telephone poles, buildings and many other structures. They weigh as much as 5 kg (11 lb), 100 times that of the bird itself, and their walls, up to 5 cm (2 in) or more thick, make them remarkably strong, able to resist the force of a person standing on top.

In fact, clay nests are unusual among the family as a whole, although the nests of many other genera are renowned for their large size. Some of the most spectacular are those of the Firewood

Gatherer, *Anumbius annumbi*, which builds a huge nest of thorny twigs up to 2 m (7 ft) high in an isolated shrub or tree, and often decorates the entrance hole and tunnel with string, glass and other artefacts; the four species of cachalotes, *Pseudoseisura*, use very long branches, up to 60 cm (2 ft) long, to build their big nests; in two of the species these incorporate snail and crab shells and animal bones and are decorated inside with snakeskin and bark. Some of the *Synallaxis* spinetails adorn their nests with the dried faeces of dogs, cats or other carnivores, or with owl pellets. The odd additions may serve to deter predators.

There are six subfamilies. The first is the Xenopinae, with just three species in a single genus, *Xenops* (used also for their common name), which have odd wedge-shaped bills, flattened from side to side with an upturned lower mandible. The next two subfamilies contain only seven species between them, including one of the most strikingly plumaged and most arboreal members of the family, the large Point-tailed Palmcreeper, *Berlepschia rikeri*, which has bright red-brown back, wings and tail contrasting with boldly black-and-white streaked head and underparts, and resembles a woodcreeper (Dendrocolaptidae, p. 226).

The fourth subfamily, Furnariinae, comprises 34 species in 10 genera. These include the six species of horneros, *Furnarius*, and the 15 species of cinclodes in the genus of the same name, which are sturdy, rather thrushlike birds with a very erect posture that live mainly in the Andes and other high mountains near streams, with a few species along coasts.

There are 46 species in 11 genera in the next subfamily Philydorinae; these include six genera and 35 species of foliage-gleaners. Several species are highly specialised in their habits, searching for their insect prey only among dead leaves for up to 90% of their feeding time.

The final subfamily, Synallaxinae, is by far the largest, containing 136 species in 24 genera. They include many species with highly modified tails. There are nine genera containing birds known as spinetails, the largest being *Synallaxis*, with 36 species. They have long, graduated tails with the outer feathers extending beyond the rest to form two points.

The large genus *Asthenes* contains 27 species, most of which are called canasteros. Their tails, which some hold cocked, are mostly long, and vary in shape: for example, some are bifurcated at the tip, others have broader and more rounded feathers, and some, called thistletails, have extremely long and dishevelled looking tails with frayed tips to the feathers. The four species of Cachalotes, *Pseudoseiura*, are the biggest and heaviest members of the family. Three of them have bright yellow eyes and prominent bushy crests, which together with their general proportions, make them look rather like jays. Their tails are slightly stiffened and end in very short bare spines. The nine species of little tit spinetails, eight of them in the genus *Leptasthenura*, have very long spiky tails ending in two deeply forked spikes, are very active birds that often hang upside down to feed, like their more familiar namesakes the tits (Paridae). The ninth species shares a genus with the owner of the most remarkable appendage of all – Des Murs' Wiretail, *Sylviorthorhynchus desmurii*, whose central tail feathers are twice as long as its body, and so thin that they may appear invisible.

SUBORDER PASSERI

The Passeri, also known as the Oscines, and popularly called songbirds, have a highly developed syrinx ('voice box'), with which they can produce complex, varied songs (although not all do so – for instance the crows). The basic song pattern is inherited as with the Tyranni (Suboscines), but unlike their songs, oscine songs can be modified and developed by learning.

Today, the Tyranni (see p. 200) are only minimally represented in the avifauna of the Old World, and form an important part of the birdlife only in Central and South America. By contrast, the Oscines are found throughout the Old and New Worlds, and form the great majority of passerines, approximately 4,500 of the total number of about 5,700 (almost 80%).

LYREBIRDS Menuridae

GENERA: 1   **SPECIES:** 2

LENGTH: male Superb Lyrebirds, *Menura novaehollandiae*, are about 103 cm (30–40.5 in) of which the tail is 54–71 cm (21–28 in), and females 76–80 cm (30–31 in), with a tail of 25–42 cm (10–16.5 in); Albert's Lyrebirds, *Menura alberti*, are rather smaller and shorter tailed

WEIGHT: 890–930 g (31–33 oz)

RANGE AND HABITAT: East Australia; introduced to Tasmania in the 1930s and 1940s; mainly cool temperate and subtropical rainforest and wet eucalyptus forest (Superb Lyrebird) from sea level to the snowline, and montane subtropical rainforest and wet eucalyptus forest above 300 m (985 ft) (Albert's Lyrebird)

SOCIAL BEHAVIOUR: adults are usually solitary for much of the year, but immature birds often gather in groups; males vigorously defend territories during the breeding season in autumn and winter; the Superb Lyrebird is known to be polygamous and play no part in nesting, incubation or raising the young

NEST: large domed structure of sticks, rootlets, leaves, moss and other vegetation with a side entrance and sometimes an access ramp; usually sited on or near ground, and lined with fine plant material and soft feathers probably plucked by female from her flanks

EGGS: 1 grey or brown with irregular darker markings

INCUBATION: about 50 days

FLEDGING PERIOD: about 39 days in Albert's Lyrebird; 47 days in the Superb Lyrebird

FOOD: invertebrates, including insects, earthworms, spiders and snails; sometimes small frogs and lizards

VOICE: long, loud songs in which they intersperse their own twanging, clicking and other notes with an amazing variety of accurately mimicked sounds – mainly the songs and calls of many other birds and other noises, both natural and occasionally mechanical; both species also have sharp whistling alarm calls

MIGRATION: sedentary

CONSERVATION STATUS: Albert's Lyrebird is Near Threatened

ABOVE A male Superb Lyrebird, *Menura novaehollandiae*, performs his dramatic display in a southeast Tasmanian rainforest.

extremely long incubation period of 7 weeks (80% longer than would be expected for a bird of this size), and the almost equally long fledging time of 6–7 weeks.

Lyrebirds are found only in forests of eastern Australia, and are renowned for the extravagant beauty of the male's tail, which is up to 55 cm (22 in) or more in the larger Superb Lyrebird, *Menura novaehollandiae*, over half the bird's total length. This is displayed to greatest advantage during courtship rituals, performed on a special display mound of earth (Superb Lyrebird) or trampled vegetation (Albert's Lyrebird, *Menura alberti*). The two outer feathers (called lyrates),which are bigger and barred, with club-shaped tips in the Superb species, form a lyre-shape around the cascade of 12 lacy white inner plumes (filamentaries) and two white wirelike central feathers. In his invitation display, the male inverts his tail and thrusts it forward, so that it cascades over his back and head, and vibrates it rapidly. As he does so, he dances, moving quickly from side to side and then jumping repeatedly. An attracted female is then treated to the full display, in which he fans his tail fully, so that he is surrounded by a shimmering white curtain.

Displays are associated with vocal performances too. The males intersperse their own loud repeated phrases with an astonishing range of natural sounds, forming 70–80% of their song in Superb Lyrebirds. These are mainly the calls and songs of a range of other birds as well as other such as creaking tree limbs, the wingbeat noise of a flock of parrots, or the croaking of frogs and mammals. Sometimes they also mimic human voices (including crying babies), and such artificial sounds as sirens, camera shutters, chainsaws and car engines.

Among the world's largest passerines, these chicken-sized songbirds are a basal group of the oscines (together with the scrub-birds, see below); features of their syrinx ('voice box') in particular has even led to proposals that they form a separate suborder, but the consensus is that they are primitive oscines. Earlier, their superficial resemblance in appearance to pheasants led some ornithologists to classify them in the gamebird order Galliformes, until it was realised that they were passerines. Unusual features for passerines are the single-egg clutch, an

SCRUB-BIRDS Atrichornithidae

GENERA: 1   **SPECIES:** 2

LENGTH: 17–23 cm (7–9 in)

WEIGHT: about 30–60 g (1–2 oz)

RANGE AND HABITAT: the Noisy Scrub-bird, *Atrichornis clamosus*, occurs in a small area on the south coast of Western Australia, and birds have also been translocated to several other sites, including an offshore island; it lives in dense scrub and forest understorey shrubs, with some in dense heathland; the Rufous Scrub-bird, *A. rufescens*, hangs on in several fragmented populations in southeast Queensland and northeast New South Wales; its habitat is the dense understorey vegetation of subtropical and temperate rainforest, and also adjacent eucalypt forest with rainforest understorey; both species require plenty of deep leaf-litter for finding food

SOCIAL BEHAVIOUR: probably polygamous (Noisy Scrub-bird) or possibly polygamous (the Rufous Scrub-bird, *A. rufescens*), males and females live apart except for mating; males often defend their territory year-round, and play no part in nest building, incubation or rearing of young

NEST: a domed structure of long sedge and grass leaves with a side entrance, usually sited among dense vegetation 15–80 cm (6–31 in) above the ground

EGGS: Apparently 1 in Noisy Scrub-bird, 2 in Rufous Scrub-bird, pale pinkish or buff with darker markings

INCUBATION: 35–42 days

FLEDGING PERIOD: 21–28 days

FOOD: invertebrates, including insects, spiders and snails; Noisy Scrub-birds include small lizards and frogs in the food they bring to nestlings; Rufous Scrub-birds also eat some seeds

VOICE: the extremely loud song of the male consists of ringing (Noisy Scrub-bird) or 'chipping' (Rufous Scrub-bird) notes; the latter species also occasionally includes mimicry of other birds

MIGRATION: highly sedentary

CONSERVATION STATUS: both species are Endangered

ABOVE The Rufous Scrub-bird, *Atrichornis rufescens*, hangs on in small, isolated populations, threatened by destruction of its habitat.

The extremely disjunct distribution of the two living species in this family on opposite sides of the great Australian landmass suggests that their ancestors once occupied a far greater range when moist forests covered much of the continent during the Tertiary period, about 30 million years ago. Today, they are among Australia's rarest – and most rarely seen – birds. This is especially true of the Noisy Scrub-bird, *Atrichornis clamosus*, with a total population in western Australia likely to number only about 1,000 adults. Unknown to science until 1842, it was regarded as extinct by 1889, when the last individual was seen. Its rediscovery in 1961 was one of the most sensational events of twentieth century ornithology. The Rufous Scrub-bird, *A. rufescens*, was also a surprising find, as it was not known to ornithologists until 1866, far from its relative in a few areas of rainforest along Australia's east coast. Although not as rare as the Noisy Scrub-bird, it is also rarely seen, with a total population probably numbering fewer than 5,000 adults.

Scuttling like small rodents across the ground in their restricted scrubland habitat, these drably plumaged, rare and very localised little birds are among the hardest of all birds to see. They normally remain hidden in dense cover and are well camouflaged with their largely brown, finely barred upperparts. Both species have a sturdy body, strong pointed bill, powerful legs and feet, longish tapered tail and short, rounded wings. They forage for insects and small vertebrates among and under leaf litter, flicking aside the debris with their bill. Being very poor and reluctant flyers, they have been very vulnerable to wildfires.

Both species make up for their inconspicuousness by their loud and varied songs, which include ringing notes and mimicry of other birds. These are among the loudest of all bird sounds, audible up to several miles away, and can even cause discomfort to humans at close range.

These intriguing birds are part of an ancient songbird lineage; their closest relatives are likely to be the lyrebirds (Menuridae, p. 229).

ABOVE The Noisy Scrub-bird, *Atrichornis clamosus*, vies with its close relative and a few other species for the title of most rarely seen of all Australian birds.

BOWERBIRDS Ptilonorhynchidae

GENERA: 8   **SPECIES:** 19

LENGTH: 23–37 cm (9–14.5 in)

WEIGHT: 62–265 g (2–9.3 oz)

RANGE AND HABITAT: New Guinea and adjacent islands, Australia; most live in rainforests and other wet forests or their edges; the five species of grey bowerbird, *Chlamydera*, inhabit more open, drier woodlands, riverine forests and savannahs

SOCIAL BEHAVIOUR: all males except in the two species of catbird, *Ailuroedus*, are polygamous, and males of all of these (except those of the Tooth-billed Bowerbird, *Scenopoeetes dentirostris*) build bowers, elaborate structures for attracting females to mate with them; males of all polygamous species play no part in raising the family; catbirds are monogamous and males share in parental duties; the Satin Bowerbird, *Ptilonorhynchus violaceus*, the Regent Bowerbird, *Sericulus chrysocephalus*, and the grey bowerbirds gather in flocks in winter

Nest: strong cups of twigs, vines, leaves and other plant material, typically sited in a tree-fork or dense cover; the Golden Bowerbird, *Prionodura newtoniana*, hides its nest in a tree crevice

EGGS: 1–3, varying from plain pale pastel colours in dense rainforest species to blotched, streaked or vermiculated with darker colours in more open country species; the Golden Bowerbird lays cream to white eggs

INCUBATION: 17–27 days

FLEDGING PERIOD: 18–22 days

FOOD: mainly berries and other fruit from wide variety of trees and shrubs, but also nectar, leaves, buds, shoots, stems, flowers, insects, spiders, small frogs, lizards and snakes; catbirds take other birds' nestlings to feed to their young

VOICE: often noisy, uttering a wide variety of calls and songs, from harsh chattering, rattling and churring to whistling sounds; also mimicry of other birds, mammals (including human speech) and other natural and artificial noises; catbirds are named for their nasal catlike miaowing songs

MIGRATION: many species are sedentary, but the Satin Bowerbird and other avenue-builders become locally nomadic in winter and some montane species move down to lower altitudes then

CONSERVATION STATUS: two species, Archbold's Bowerbird, *Archboldia papuensis*, and the Fire-maned Bowerbird, *Sericulus bakeri*, are Near Threatened

ABOVE The male Regent Bowerbird, *Sericulus chrysocephalus*, of eastern Australia builds a frail avenue bower that is often destroyed by rival males.

The most remarkable of all avian architects, the bowerbirds are forest and woodland dwellers restricted to Australia and New Guinea. To attract females and entice them to mate with them, the males of all but four species build elaborate structures from sticks, twigs and decorate them with a variety of objects, both natural and artificial, from flowers, fruit, animal bones and snail shells to fragments of glass, plastic objects, spoons and coins. They spend a huge proportion of their lives building and maintaining their bowers, and have to watch vigilantly over them to prevent rival males from stealing their building materials or carefully gathered decorations. The bowers are solely for the purpose of mate attraction and mating, and have nothing to do with nesting.

Most bowerbirds are sturdily built, with a strong, shortish, deep bill (sometimes slightly hooked or notched) and powerful legs. Plumage colours and patterns differ considerably between species. Males of some species are much brighter and more boldly patterned than females, which are generally clad in brown or olive shades, with paler, sometimes barred, scalloped or mottled underparts. A recurring theme in the males is a combination of velvety black and areas of brilliant yellow or gold, the latter colour in several species extending as a mane or cape from the crown to the upper back. Adult males of the best-known species, the Satin Bowerbird, *Ptilonorhynchus violaceus*, of East Australia, have stunning intensely glossy indigo-blue plumage, with violet highlights. Furthermore, they have eyes to match, with vivid purple irides. By contrast, male and female of the three species of catbird, *Ailuroedus*, look alike, being rich green above and paler and spotted or scalloped below.

The catbirds do not build bowers and, unlike all the other bowerbirds, are monogamous. The male Tooth-billed Bowerbird, *Scenopoeetes dentirostris*, a dull-plumaged species, brown above and streaked below, clears a display court encompassing the base of at least one tree on which to display to females, and on the bare forest floor scatters up to 180 fresh leaves, pale side uppermost for maximum contrast, but builds no bower. All other species build bowers of different types and varying degrees of complexity. Those that build the most elaborate bowers have the dullest plumage: this may be because they have transferred the mate-attracting potential of showy plumage, which conveys the fitness of its wearer to the female, to the impressive 'shop-front' display of the bower.

LEFT A male Satin Bowerbird, *Ptilonorhynchus violaceus*, collects a blue bottle top to add to the other blue treasures at his avenue bower.

There are two main types of bower: the avenue bower and the maypole bower. Avenue bowers are built by the four yellow (or gold) and black species *Sericulus*, by the Satin Bowerbird, and the five dull-plumaged species of the grey bowerbird genus *Chlamydera*. The avenues consist of usually two arched walls of sticks or grass stems that enclose a narrow avenue, and features a display platform for the adornments and for the male to display on. Some (perhaps all) of the avenue-building species paint their bower with their bill, using charcoal and vegetable matter masticated with saliva; some even employ a paintbrush, made from a wad of vegetable material, for the purpose.

Maypole bowers include tall and bulky tepee-like towers of sticks, orchid stems and mosses stacked around a tree sapling or on a horizontal perch above a mat of similar materials on which the display materials are presented. The most sophisticated maypole bowers are those of some populations of the dull-plumaged Vogelkop Bowerbird, *Amblyornis inornata*, of New Guinea. These are elaborate hut-like structures that when discovered by nineteenth century Western explorers and naturalists were thought to be the work of local tribespeople.

A number of species are still little known: for instance, the Yellow-fronted Bowerbird, *Amblyornis flavifrons*, with a restricted

ABOVE The hut-like bower with its richly decorated 'garden' of the Vogelkop Bowerbird, *Amblyornis inornata*, is one of the most amazing sights in nature.

range in the remote Foja Mountains in west-central New Guinea, was first scientifically described from skins collected in 1895, but was not seen again for almost a century until it was rediscovered in 1981, and not photographed until 2005.

The bowerbirds were formerly thought to be a member of the great radiation of mainly Australian passerines including the crows, butcherbirds, whistlers and many other families, which make up the Superfamily Corvoidea. They were considered most closely related to a particularly charismatic family in that great group that is, like them, restricted to New Guinea and Australia – the birds-of-paradise (Paradisaeidae, p. 277). More recently, molecular research indicates that bowerbirds are instead more basal members of the oscine suborder, closest to the Australian Treecreepers (Climacteridae, below) and also related to the lyrebirds (Menuridae, p. 229) and scrub-birds (Atrichornithidae, p. 230).

AUSTRALIAN TREECREEPERS Climacteridae

GENERA: 2   **SPECIES:** 7

LENGTH: 14–19 cm (5.5–7.5 in)

WEIGHT: 20–40 g (0.7–1.4 oz)

RANGE AND HABITAT: six species found only in Australia and one, the Papuan Treecreeper, *Cormobates placens*, in New Guinea; forests, woodlands and tall shrublands

SOCIAL BEHAVIOUR: the two *Cormobates* species live in pairs, which strongly defend a territory; *Climacteris* species often live in groups of 3–8 individuals, usually a pair and several male offspring, all cooperating in nest building, feeding the incubating female and young, and territorial defence

NEST: a cup of grasses or bark, often reinforced with animal dung, and lined with feathers, fur or plant down

EGGS: 2–3, white to pink, with brown markings

INCUBATION: 14–24 days

FLEDGING PERIOD: 20–27 days

FOOD: insects (mainly ants and beetles) and other invertebrates, sometimes nectar or seeds; small lizards occasionally recorded for the Rufous Treecreeper, *Climacteris rufus*

VOICE: penetrating high-pitched whistling, piping, rattling, chattering, trilling and insect-like notes

MIGRATION: sedentary

CONSERVATION STATUS: none threatened

Despite the name and their superficially similar appearance and lifestyle, the members of this small family of birds are not related to the treecreepers (Certhiidae) of Eurasia and North America, although they were thought to be until as recently as the 1960s. They are almost certainly among the more ancient of all oscine lineages, and although their affinities are uncertain, they may be, surprisingly, most closely related to bowerbirds.

All species are stout-bodied little birds with a medium-length, slightly downcurved bill and strong legs and feet, with long toes and sharp claws. Unlike those of the certhiid treecreepers in the northern hemisphere or the woodpeckers, their tail feathers are not stiffened to act as a prop when climbing. They feed in a similar way to the certhiids, though, starting near the base of a tree, spiralling up the trunk as they search for insects or other small invertebrates on or beneath the bark, and then flying down to the base of the next tree to start the process over again. Unlike the certhiid treecreepers, three species (the White-browed Treecreeper, *Climacteris affinis*, the Brown Treecreeper, *C. picumnus* and the Rufous Treecreeper, *C. rufus*) regularly forage on the ground, searching for prey among leaf litter and on the bare ground, as well as on logs or at ants' nests.

The plumage is mainly in shades of brown or greyish, with buff, white or black streaks on the underparts and dark barring on the undertail; three species have rufous patches on the head, and two have rufous underparts. The Rufous Treecreeper is rich cinnamon on its head and underparts, while the Black-tailed Treecreeper, *Climacteris melanurus*, is mainly blackish-brown in the nominate race, with dark rufous brown in males of the race *wellsi*.

ABOVE A Brown Treecreeper, *Climacteris picumnus*, scales a tree in a wood near Lexton, Victoria, Australia.

FAIRY-WRENS, EMU-WRENS AND GRASSWRENS Maluridae

GENERA: 6   **SPECIES:** 32

LENGTH: 10–22 cm (4–8.5 in)

WEIGHT: 6–35 g (0.2–1.2 oz)

RANGE AND HABITAT: Australia and New Guinea; all main habitats, from coastal swamps, desert steppes and salt pans to heathland, spinifex tussock grassland and rainforest edge, as well as large suburban gardens and parks in towns and cities

SOCIAL BEHAVIOUR: all fairy-wrens and probably all species in the family breed cooperatively, living in family groups that share in rearing the family and defending the nest site; fairy-wrens are highly polygamous, producing several broods a year; at least some of others breed in territorial pairs

NEST: a domed structure of grass, bark, twigs, moss and other plant materials, lined with feathers, fur or fine plant materials, with a side entrance in *Malurus* fairy-wrens and emu-wrens; half-dome in grasswrens

EGGS: 2–4, whitish, speckled with red-brown

INCUBATION: 12–15 days

FLEDGING PERIOD: 10–12 days

FOOD: mainly insects, also other invertebrates such as spiders and earthworms; some seeds and fruits, especially in grasswrens

VOICE: fairy-wrens and emu-wrens have mechanical-sounding, reeling and trilling songs, louder and lower-pitched in the blue fairy-wrens, weak and higher pitched in emu-wrens; grasswrens have more complex, varied and melodious songs that are a mixture of whistles, buzzing notes, trills and melodious phrases; all have various high-pitched, shrill, chirping and other contact and alarm calls

MIGRATION: most species are sedentary but a few fairy-wrens and the Grey Grasswren, *Amytornis barbatus*, are nomadic in parts of their ranges

CONSERVATION STATUS: one species, the Mallee Emu-wren, *Stipiturus mallee*, is Endangered; two species, the White-throated Grasswren, *Amytornis woodwardi*, and Carpentarian Grasswren, *A. dorotheae* are Vulnerable; two species the Black Grasswren, *A. housei*, and Short-tailed Grasswren, *A. merrotsyi*, are are Near Threatened

These jaunty little birds often hold their long, graduated tail cocked, and have a small, rotund body and often a short, sharp bill, like the unrelated and almost entirely New World true wrens (Family Troglodytidae). They can be subdivided into three distinct groups. The first two, united in the subfamily Malurinae, comprises the fairy-wrens (with four genera and 15 species, found mainly in Australia but with six species in New Guinea) and the emu-wrens (one genus, *Stipiturus*, and three species). The third group, in the subfamily Amytornithinae, are the grasswrens (one genus, *Amytornis*, and 14 species). Both the emu-wrens and the grasswrens are entirely restricted to Australia.

Fairy-wrens live in all major habitats and are the brightest and best-known members of the family, as reflected in the common names of three of them: the Superb Fairy-Wren, *Malurus cyaneus*, the Splendid Fairy-Wren, *Malurus splendens*, and the Lovely Fairy-Wren, *Malurus amabilis*. The Superb Fairy-wren is the most familiar to most Australians, having adapted well to life in suburban parks and gardens since much of its natural habitat of open eucalypt forest has been cleared. An interesting feature of the fairy-wrens is that males occur in two very different plumages – some are very bright, with much blue, violet or black, whereas others are largely dull brownish or grey above and paler or whitish beneath, and resemble the females. Either type of male is capable of breeding, but in the Australian species, the bright plumage is usually only acquired in the breeding season, and females prefer to mate with these more dominant birds, while those remaining in dull plumage generally serve as helpers at the nest. By contrast, males of the three New Guinea species have the same bright plumage year-round.

The secretive emu-wrens live in semi-arid scrublands, from coastal heaths and dune thickets to low mallee woodland and hummocky spinifex grassland. They have an especially long tail with very distinctive filamentous feathers like emu's feathers in miniature, hence their common name. They are tiny birds, even smaller than the fairy-wrens, and are among the smallest of all Australian birds. Mainly rufous, darker and strongly streaked blackish above and with patches of blue on the face, throat and breast in the males. The grasswrens are even more elusive birds and live in a variety of mainly arid grasslands, often with bare rocky areas. They are brown, rufous

and white with black-and-white streaks. Some are almost as small as fairywrens, but others are considerably larger.

The closest relatives of this family appear to be the following four families, which are either endemic to Australia or with many representatives there.

ABOVE A Superb Fairy-wren, *Malurus cyaneus*, broadcasts his loud, trilling song, sometimes compared to the sound of a tinny alarm-clock.

BRISTLEBIRDS Dasyornithidae

GENERA: 1   **SPECIES:** 3

LENGTH: 17–25 cm (7–10 in)

WEIGHT: about 26–77 g (0.9–2.7 oz)

RANGE AND HABITAT: small areas of eastern/south-eastern and south-western Australia; heaths, shrublands and forest, in dense cover

SOCIAL BEHAVIOUR: probably permanently monogamous; usually in pairs or in small groups; territorial during the breeding season

NEST: large, loosely constructed domed structure of twigs, grass, sedges, bark and other vegetable matter, sited low in dense vegetation

EGGS: 2, variable, dull pale brown or sometimes almost white with purplish brown to reddish spots and blotches

INCUBATION: 16–21 days or more

FLEDGING PERIOD: 11–21 days

FOOD: invertebrates, including many beetles, cicadas, ants, flies and other insects, spiders and worms; also many seeds and fruits

VOICE: loud, far-carrying and generally melodious songs, varying greatly between individuals and populations, including sweet whistling notes, ringing trills and squeaking and buzzing notes, uttered by both sexes, sometimes in duets; simple rasping, chattering and whipcrack-like calls

MIGRATION: sedentary

CONSERVATION STATUS: the Eastern Bristlebird, *Dasyornis brachypterus*, and Western Bristlebird, *D. longirostris*, are Endangered

Secretive and hard to see, these thrush-sized Australian endemics have long, graduated tails. Their brown, rufous and grey plumage with subtle scaling streaking or spotting camouflages them well against the dense vegetation among which they spend most of their time. There is no difference in plumage between the sexes. Often the only clue to their presence is when males and females

broadcast their loud, sweet songs in defence of their territory. Pairs regularly duet at the beginning of the breeding season.

Bristlebirds are named for the four or more stiff, forward-curving bristles (modified feathers) between the eyes and the base of the upper mandible of the bill. The function of these bristles is unknown, but as with the variety of other birds, from

ABOVE A rare Eastern Bristlebird, *Dasyornis brachypterus*, feeds its young at a nest hidden among dense grass tussocks.

nightjars to tyrant flycatchers and shrikes, that have such rictal bristles, they may protect the eyes from damage when feeding – for example when sweeping aside leaf litter or poking the bill into the soil in search of insects, as bristlebirds do.

Although bristlebirds have a superficial resemblance to those other highly skulking, brownish Australian endemics, the scrub-birds, they are not closely related. Instead, the three extant species are currently thought to be the relics of an ancient basal group that may be closest to the pardalotes, thornbills and gerygones, Australasian wrens and honeyeaters. Two of the three species, the Western Bristlebird, *Dasyornis longirostris* (the most restricted of the three), and the Eastern Bristlebird, *D. brachypterus*, are threatened by increased burning and drainage of habitat as a result of human settlement. Although the Rufous Bristlebird, *D. broadbenti* is generally not (yet) at risk, its geographically isolated western subspecies *litoralis* is now extinct, probably as a result of fires.

HONEYEATERS Meliphagidae

GENERA: 50   **SPECIES:** 178

LENGTH: 9–50 cm (3.5–20 in)

WEIGHT: 7.4–357 g (0.25–12.6 oz)

RANGE AND HABITAT: by far the most species in New Guinea and Australia, with fewer on islands of the western Pacific, including the Bismarck Archipelago and the Solomon Islands, as far east as Samoa and Tonga; to the south there are two species in New Zealand; and in the west, a few on islands of the Sundas and the Moluccas and one on Bali (the only one in Asia just outside the transitional biogeographic zone of Wallacea); they occur in a very wide range of mainly wooded and shrubby habitats, from rainforests, sclerophyll woodlands, gardens and parks to heaths and other shrublands, arid scrub and mangroves

SOCIAL BEHAVIOUR: most species live singly, in pairs or small family parties, while some often occur in large, loose flocks; some are polygamous, some monogamous, and some have complex cooperative breeding arrangements; many sedentary species maintain nesting territories year-round, others just during the breeding season; some also defend flowering trees and other food resources, but many gather together at good feeding sites

NEST: cup-shaped, sited in a fork in branches or suspended from branches, twigs or leaves

EGGS: 1–5, most often 2 in many species; white, cream, buff or pinkish

with reddish-brown, mauve, purple, or black spots or blotches

INCUBATION: 12–17 days

FLEDGING PERIOD: 10–30 days

FOOD: nectar, also other sweet secretions such as honeydew from various plant-eating bugs and sap directly from plants, also fruit, supplemented by insects and other invertebrates

VOICE: many species are noisy, with a variety of calls and song, more musical in smaller species and often harsher and louder in bigger ones; songs vary from a few whistled notes to more complex twittering ones, a few species are renowned songsters

MIGRATION: most species are at least partially nomadic, following the flowering of favourite food plants, while some make regular migrations

CONSERVATION STATUS: two species, the Crow-Honeyeater, *Gymnomyza aubryana*, and Regent Honeyeater, *Anthochaera phrygia*, are Critically Endangered; one species, the Mao, *Gymnomyza samoensis*, and one race, *melanotis*, of the Yellow-throated Miner, *Manorina flavigula*, which may be a separate species (called the Black-eared Miner) are Endangered; five species, the Painted Honeyeater, *Grantiella picta*, MacGregor's Honeyeater, *Macgregoria pulchra*, Long-bearded Honeyeater, *Melidectes princeps*, Rotuma Myzomela, *Myzomela chermesina*, and Dusky Friarbird, *Philemon fuscicapillus*, are Vulnerable; three species are Near Threatened

Endemic to the southwest Pacific region, this large group of songbirds adapted for nectar-eating has radiated to occupy almost all land habitats and niches with at least some trees or shrubs. They are the largest family of basal oscines, and their closest relatives are the bristlebirds. Although most species live in forests and woodlands of all types, others inhabit savannah, heaths, arid scrublands and mangroves, and some have adapted to gardens, parks and farmland. The latter have been very successful at adapting to artificial habitats: they include well-known Australian species such as the Noisy Miner, *Manorina melanocephala*. Noisy Miners are among the most

abundant of all passerines in Australia, and are hard to ignore as they bustle about in groups in parks and gardens or the roadside verges of cities, living up to their common name with their constant loud, harsh piping, whistling and chuckling calls.

In fact, honeyeaters are in general the most successful family of passerine birds in Australasia, with their centre of diversity in Australia and New Guinea. In Australia they are the most numerous of all passerines, with 71 species in 32 genera, and there are also many in New Guinea, with 60 species in 20 genera. In places and habitats where they are most diverse, as many as 10 different species

ABOVE A male Red-collared Myzomela, *Myzomela rosenbergii*, leans out to sup nectar from a flower in the Western Highlands of Papua New Guinea.

may share a single hectare. By contrast, some of the honeyeaters with restricted ranges have fared far less well; examples include the Crow-Honeyeater, *Gymnomyza aubryana*, of New Caledonia, which is Critically Endangered, and the Endangered Mao (or Black-breasted Honeyeater), *G. samoensis*, restricted to just two small islands of Samoa.

There is a great range of size, from tiny myzomelas, *Myzomela*, similar in size to many sunbirds, to the Yellow Wattlebird, *Anthochaera paradoxa*, similar in size to Eurasian and American magpies, *Pica*. However, most share a fairly slim, streamlined body shape and long pointed wings. Their legs and feet are strong and their toes tipped with sharp claws for moving about among trees or shrubs when feeding. They are very agile and acrobatic, often hanging upside-down or stretching out to reach flowers or other food sources. Unlike the hummingbirds, which can hover for long periods, honeyeaters generally take nectar from flowers while perched (although smaller species may flutter briefly in front of a flower to do this).

Most honeyeaters have a strong, sharp, decurved bill. Its length varies, from short in some, such as the four *Melipotes* species from montane forests of New Guinea, which eat mainly fruit, through medium length in most species to long and more strongly decurved in the many species that feed mainly on nectar. Honeyeaters are adapted to feeding on nectar by having evolved a brushlike tip to the tongue, with which they obtain the sugary fluid. In most species the tongue is long enough to protrude well beyond the bill tip, so they can insert it deeply into long tubular flowers to reach the nectar at the base. They flick it in and out to lap up the nectar at the rate of 10 or more licks per second, and can empty a flower of nectar in less than a second.

Honeyeaters can be very aggressive when competing for food, and some defend territories from other species and members of their own species, chasing rivals away from a group of trees or shrubs, a single one or just part of it.

All honeyeaters probably include at least some nectar in their diet, and this high-energy food forms a major part of their food supply for many species, which are of vital importance as pollinators of Australasian, New Zealand and Pacific island flowers, including those that are pollinated solely by birds. However, nectar is not their sole food. All species supplement their sugar-rich diet with protein and other essential nutrients from insects, flying out from a perch to snap them up in the air as well as taking them from foliage, and they eat spiders too. Many also eat some fruit, and in some species, such as the 15 species of *Meliphaga* honeyeaters of the rainforests of northern Australia and New Guinea this forms a major part of the diet. Honeyeaters also obtain sugary food indirectly from insects: honeydew, excretions of various plant bugs (psyllids, aphids and coccids, or scale-insects), lerp (a substance coating the nymphs of some psyllids, manna. They also feed on sugary sap exuded from plants in response to being eaten by insects, such as manna (from eucalypt leaves) or being eaten by the mammals known as gliders.

As well as the majority of species with this mixed diet, there are a few far more specialist feeders, such as the Strong-billed Honeyeater, *Melithreptus validirostris*, of Tasmania, which uses its short bill to probe beneath or strip off tree bark to obtain insects hiding there, the Painted Honeyeater, *Grantiella picta*, of eastern Australia, which feeds mainly on the fruit and nectar of mistletoes,

ABOVE The Noisy Miner, *Manorina melanocephala*, is well named, for gangs of these very lively, abundant and intensely social birds create a din whenever they feel threatened.

and two other species, the Mangrove Honeyeater, *Gavicalis fasciogularis*, of eastern Australia and the Varied Honeyeater, *G. versicolor*, from New Guinea and northern Queensland, which include crabs and snails in their diet.

Many species have relatively dull green, olive, brown or grey plumage, often streaked or barred, especially beneath, but some are much brighter, with bold yellow, black and white markings. Some, such as the two little spinebills, *Acanthorhynchus*, of Australia are strikingly patterned (in their case in black, white, buff, chestnut and brown, with the males of the western species being distinctly brighter than females, unlike most honeyeaters, in which the sexes have similar plumage). Among the most brightly coloured are the myzomelas, *Myzomela*, the largest genus in the family, with 30 species occupying a vast range from Indonesian island of Sulawesi in the west to New Guinea and Australia (with only a couple of species) and on to the Pacific islands of Samoa and Fiji. Many have large areas of brilliant red (one species is all-red), while three are black. Almost all honeyeaters have patches of coloured bare skin on the gape or face, or as an eye-ring. The colours usually alter with age or at the start of the breeding season, and sometimes also with mood. The bare areas are usually small but are much more extensive in some species, such as some of the 15 species of friarbirds in the genus *Philemon*. All these medium to large, drab brown-and-buff plumaged honeyeaters are similar in appearance, with a bare black head or face, contrasting with the red eyes in the larger species; they have a strong, deep-based decurved bill and several also sport a large triangular casque on the upper mandible. The name 'friarbird' comes from the circular pattern on the crown, likened to a monk's tonsure; an alternative popular name is leatherheads.

ABOVE This Blue-faced Honeyeater, *Entomyzon cyanotis*, is collecting ants to place in its plumage, possibly to make them discharge their formic acid so that they are rendered safer to eat.

Just two genera are endemic to New Zealand. The first is *Prosthemadera*, with a single species, the Tui, *P. novaeseelandiae*. This is a large and striking honeyeater with mainly glossy black iridescent plumage which flashes green, blue, purple and bronze in the sunlight; a lacy collar of filamentous white feathers adorn its neck, and two little tufts of white feathers dangle from its throat. The other genus is *Anthornis*, with a single extant species, the New Zealand Bellbird, *A. melanura*. Another bellbird species, *A. melanocephala*, endemic to the Chatham Islands, was declared extinct following the last record in 1906. Both these widespread and well-known species are much admired for their rich and complex songs, which includes loud, clear ringing notes in the New Zealand Bellbird, often as well as harsh notes, and liquid, melodic sounds in the Tui mixed with wheezes, clicks, coughs and grunts.

The five species of Australian chats, four in the genus *Epthianura* and one in *Ashbyia*, differ in various ways from the rest of the family. Indeed, these Australian endemics were often classified in a family of their own when their relationship with other birds was uncertain, but they share the brush-tipped tongue with the honeyeaters and recent DNA research has shown that they belong in this family. Three of the *Epthianura* species are brightly coloured, especially males, with a mainly yellow, orange or crimson head and body, while the fourth has a striking pied pattern. Mixed flocks are a particularly colourful sight. The Gibberbird, *Ashbyia lovensis*, is yellow below. In contrast to the rest of the family, these are highly terrestrial birds, foraging for insects and seeds on the ground, and siting their nests in low vegetation or on the ground. Also in contrast to most honeyeaters, they live mainly in arid and often desolate country with sparse vegetation, often in salt flats and in some areas in marshes.

Another species now included in the family is *Macgregoria pulchra*, one of the largest members of the family (and the heaviest). This is a striking all-black bird apart from a large bright orange-yellow area of bare skin around each eye and the similarly coloured edges to its primary flight feathers, which form a contrasting panel along the closed wing. Until recently, ornithologists believed it to be this New Guinea species to belong to the bird-of-paradise family (Paradisaeidae, p. 277) but DNA research has shown that it belongs with the honeybirds, so it is now called MacGregor's Honeyeater rather than MacGregor's Bird-of-paradise.

On the other hand, a small group of birds that was previously long thought to belong in the honeyeater family has now been shown not to be at all closely related. These are five species endemic to Hawaii, four known by their Hawaiian names O-o in the genus *Moho*, and another, the Kioea, in the genus *Chaetoptila*. All are, sadly, extinct. The evidence suggests that although they resembled the other honeyeaters in morphology and lifestyle, they were probably more closely related to the waxwings and allies (Bombycillidae, p. 368), and have been placed in a family of their own, the Mohoidae.

The honeyeaters' closest relatives are most likely to be the pardalotes (Pardalotidae, p. 238) and thornbills and relatives (Acanthizidae, p. 239).

PARDALOTES Pardalotidae

GENERA: 1   **SPECIES:** 4

LENGTH: 8.5–12 cm (3.3–4.7 in)

WEIGHT: 7–15 g (0.25–0.5 oz)

RANGE AND HABITAT: Australia; forests and woodlands, mostly dominated by eucalypts

SOCIAL BEHAVIOUR: occur mainly in pairs or small family groups, although in autumn and winter Spotted Pardalotes, *Pardolotus punctatus*, and Striated Pardalotes, *P. striatus*, frequently gather in large (sometimes mixed) flocks, often together with thornbills; largely monogamous; Spotted Pardalotes and Forty-spotted Pardalotes, *P. quadragintus*, defend a nesting territory, but Striated Pardalotes and Red-browed Pardalotes, *P. rubricatus*, often nest colonially

NEST: a cup or dome of grass, bark and other plant materials; Spotted and Red-browed Pardalotes usually nest in burrows they dig in sloping ground, Striated Pardalotes in tree hollows or in ground burrows, and Forty-spotted Pardalotes mainly in tree hollows or in hollow stumps or logs

EGGS: 2–5, white

INCUBATION: 18–24 days

FLEDGING PERIOD: 18–25 days

FOOD: mainly insects and spiders, and particularly lerps, the sugary covering produced by psyllid bugs; also manna, a sugar-rich exudate produced by eucalypt foliage as a response to damage

VOICE: pairs constantly remain in contact with ventriloquial soft whistling calls; songs are loud, simple and melodic

MIGRATION: Spotted and Striated Pardalotes are migrants, moving from moist higher-altitude forests to winter in drier inland plains

CONSERVATION STATUS: one species, the Forty-spotted Pardalote, is Endangered

ABOVE A male Spotted Pardalote, *Pardalotus punctatus*, displays the constellation of shining spots that give the species and family its name.

ABOVE The Striated Pardalote, *Pardalotus striatus*, lacks the spots of its three relatives, although some subspecies have white streaks on the black crown; it also has a red or yellow spot on the wing.

The odd name of these tiny, short-tailed, short-billed, Australian endemics is from the Greek word for 'leopard', from the plumage of the Spotted Pardalote, *Pardolotus punctatus*. They were once known as diamondbirds, from their mainly colourful and boldly marked plumage, with a striking black-and-white head pattern, patches of bright yellow or red and little white spots or white streaks. The male Spotted Pardalote (which is the only sexually dimorphic species) is especially well endowed with a constellation of tiny white spots on the head, upperparts, wings and tail. The female is less boldly patterned and duller, lacking the male's rich golden-yellow breast. The Forty-spotted Pardalote, *P. quadragintus*, is by far the dullest of the four – its forty white spots are small and the only bright feature in the otherwise rather dull greenish, yellowish and greyish plumage. It is also by far the rarest, with a restricted range in Tasmania, with over 90% of the declining population living on just two small offshore islands. It faces ongoing threats from forest clearance and degradation and in the long term, climate change.

Pardalotes feed very actively high in trees, often hanging upside down to glean an insect from beneath a leaf. This, and their very small size, makes them hard to see, but their presence is often revealed by their simple songs, a sequence of repeated rich, staccato, ringing notes that are astonishingly loud for such a tiny bird. They are especially fond of eating lerps, the sugary exudates of psyllid bugs (jumping plant lice) that form protective shelters around the insects, along with the bugs themselves: indeed they are the most specialised of all Australian birds in exploiting this resource, using their strong, short, blunt bill, although they may be driven away by larger and more aggressive colonial honeyeaters. The natural control of psyllids is beneficial to forestry, as large infestations feeding on the leaves and other parts can cause considerable damage to eucalypts, especially if they are already stressed.

THORNBILLS, GERYGONES AND RELATIVES Acanthizidae

GENERA: 13   **SPECIES**: 59

LENGTH: 8–19 cm (3–7.5 in)

WEIGHT: 6– 27 g (0.1–1 oz)

RANGE AND HABITAT: Australia and New Guinea, gerygones also in New Zealand (two species, one widespread on North and South Islands, one only on Chatham Island) and other islands of the south-west Pacific; three species in Asia (two only in Indonesia and one in Southeast Asia); most in rainforests, woodlands and mangroves, but as a whole occupy most terrestrial habitats

SOCIAL BEHAVIOUR: most species occur in pairs or small family groups; a wide range of breeding strategies is found, and although a few species of thornbills, *Acanthiza*, breed as single pairs, many members of the family are cooperative breeders; some adjust their breeding strategies to their habitat, cooperating less in harsher environments

NEST: a large, domed or spherical structure of plant stems and fibres, often lined with feathers, sometimes with a hood over the side entrance; a variety of sites, from tree branches and holes to dense ground cover

EGGS: usually 2–3, mostly white, some with a band of dark spots at the larger end

INCUBATION: 15–21 days

FLEDGING PERIOD: 13–21 days

FOOD: mostly insects, also spiders; some, especially the whitefaces, *Aphelocephala*, also eat seeds and fruit

VOICE: many gerygones in particular utter beautiful songs made up of sweet whistling or warbling notes or silvery trills, often descending in pitch; some others have more buzzing, chattering or rattling songs and calls; various species are expert mimics of other birds

MIGRATION: mostly sedentary, although some thornbills and also the Weebill, *Smicrornis brevirostris*, and whitefaces are locally nomadic after breeding

CONSERVATION STATUS: one species, the Chestnut-breasted Whiteface, *Aphelocephala pectoralis*, is Near Threatened

This large and diverse family includes many of Australia's most familiar small songbirds. As well as names referring to their appearance or behaviour, such as thornbills, *Acanthiza*, gerygones, *Gerygone*, whitefaces, *Aphelocephala*, and Weebill, *Smicrornis brevirostris*, their members have various common names originally bestowed on them by naturalists and settlers because of their supposed similarity to other familiar European songbirds: these include the heathwrens and fieldwrens, *Calamanthus*, the Scrub-tit, *Acanthornis magna*, the mouse warblers, *Crateroscelis*, and the Speckled Warbler, *Chthonicola sagittatus*.

As a group they were often called Australasian warblers (and the gerygones were formerly charmingly known as fairy-warblers or, more prosaically, simply as warblers), but such names are not appropriate as they are related to neither Old World warblers nor New World warblers. Although it sounds as if it might be an Aboriginal word, the name 'gerygone' derives from the Greek words

for 'born of sound', and reflects the sweet songs of these little birds.

Many of the acanthizids are small or tiny birds: at just 8–9.5 cm (3–3.75 in) long, the diminutive Weebill is Australia's smallest bird, at just 6 g (0.2 oz) even lighter than some hummingbirds. Most species are brownish-olive above and buff, cream or pale grey below, and are very difficult to distinguish; some have patches of orange, buff, yellow or red on the rump, and a fair number are altogether brighter, with bright yellow (or in a few cases) orange underparts, and in a few, striking black-and-white head patterns.

Although many species are common and widespread, one oceanic island subspecies, the Lord Howe Island race of the Grey Warbler, *Gerygone igata insularis*, is extinct. Once common, it was wiped out by rats that arrived on the island after a shipwreck in 1918. Several island races of other species are suffering from habitat degradation or introduced mammals. They include another race of the Grey Warbler, on Norfolk Island, *G. i. modesta*. Both

FAR LEFT The Inland Thornbill, *Acanthiza apicalis*, is a widespread bird of scrub, woodland, heath and mangroves across much of Australia.

LEFT The White-throated Gerygone, *Gerygone olivacea*, has a beautiful song of silvery notes on a descending scale.

races are regarded by some authorities as full species, and the race *hypoxantha* of the Large-billed Gerygone, *G. magnirostris*, from two small islands off New Guinea, which is also sometimes accorded species status, when it is classified as Endangered.

There are two subfamilies. The Pachycareinae contain just two species, in two different genera. The Goldenface, *Pachycare flavogriseum*, is a strikingly patterned inhabitant of the mountains of New Guinea whose blue-grey upperparts contrast with bright sulphur yellow underparts. The other species, the Fernwren, *Oreoscopus gutturalis*, by contrast, is brown with a black and white head pattern, and is an Australian endemic, restricted to the rainforests of Queensland. The Acanthizinae contains 57 species in 11 genera. The largest genera are *Gerygone*, comprising 16 species of gerygones, *Acanthiza*, with 14 species of thornbills and *Sericornis* with 10 species of scrubwrens. The closest relatives of the birds in this family appear to be the honeyeaters and pardalotes; the latter have sometimes been amalgamated with the thornbills and allies in the Family Acanthizidae.

LOGRUNNERS Orthonychidae

GENERA: 1   **SPECIES**: 3

LENGTH: 18–29 cm (7–11.5 in)

WEIGHT: 47–215 g (1.6–7.6 oz)

RANGE AND HABITAT: Australia (two species) and New Guinea (one species); rainforest

SOCIAL BEHAVIOUR: live in pairs or small groups of individuals that are not necessarily related to one another; monogamous for at least several years and perhaps for life, and groups defend a territory throughout the year

NEST: a large, dome-shaped structure of sticks, twigs, leaves, moss, ferns and other vegetation, lined with moss, fine rootlets, plant fibres and fungal threads, with a side entrance; sited on or near the ground

EGGS: usually 1 in the Chowchilla, *Orthonyx spaldingii*; 2 in other species; white

INCUBATION: 21–25 days

FLEDGING PERIOD: 18–27 days

FOOD: mostly invertebrates, including insects, spiders, molluscs, leeches and earthworms, and some fruit (the Chowchilla also takes some small frogs or lizards)

VOICE: all very vocal; the Chowchilla is especially noisy, and small groups give loud, ringing songs in unison at twilight, also harsher sounds and mimicry of other birds; other species have loud, penetrating songs made up of a series of whistles, descending in pitch in the Papuan Logrunner, *Orthonyx novaeguineae*; calls are shrill sounds or squawks, clucking or throaty sounds in the Chowchilla

MIGRATION: sedentary

CONSERVATION STATUS: none threatened

ABOVE This female Logrunner, *Orthonyx temmincki*, is searching for food among leaves, logs and other ground debris in Queensland rainforest.

This very small family of rainforest songbirds comprises just three species: two in Australia (the Australian Logrunner, *Orthonyx temminckii*, and the Chowchilla, *O. spaldingii*) and one in New Guinea (the Papuan Logrunner, *O. novaeguineae*). All are local in range, in widely separated regions. The Australian Logrunner is endemic to moist lowland forests along the east coast of Australia, the Chowchilla is restricted to the rainforests of northeastern Queensland, and the Papuan Logrunner lives in subtropical or tropical montane forest of New Guinea.

The plumage of both species of logrunner (which are about the size of a Common Starling, *Sturnus vulgaris*) is a highly cryptic pattern of mottled black, rufous-olive and grey above, with black-and-grey wingbars; the bigger Chowchilla (almost the size of a small feral pigeon) is equally well camouflaged, with very dark brown upperparts and head, and a contrasting pale blue-grey eye-ring. In all three species, males have a white chin and upper breast continuous with the rest of the underparts, whereas the females have an orange chin and upper breast.

In all logrunner species the shafts of the tail feathers extend beyond their vanes as spinelike extensions. These are employed by the birds as a prop when they are energetically and noisily foraging for small animals in leaf litter. All three species also benefit from a modification of their skeleton that allows them to move their legs out sideways (rather than back-to-front as with most passerines) when feeding, to thrust the debris away clear of the body, aided by the bill.

The group name comes from the fact that these birds were often encountered running along logs, where they often place their nest. The common name of the Chowchilla comes from the sound of the loud calls of this species, heard especially at dawn and dusk from small flocks.

AUSTRALASIAN BABBLERS Pomatostomidae

GENERA: 2   **SPECIES**: 5

LENGTH: 17–27 cm (6.5–10.5 in)

WEIGHT: 30–85 g (1–3 oz)

RANGE AND HABITAT: four species in Australia (one shared with New Guinea) and one endemic to New Guinea; Australian species in open woodland, arid or semi-arid scrub and farmland; New Guinea Babbler, *Garritornis isidorei*, in humid forests

SOCIAL BEHAVIOUR: live in family groups and larger flocks of two to 15 or birds, comprising a pair or pairs and extended family members, which share territorial defence; cooperative breeders, helpers from previous broods helping to feed incubating females and young; all species studied are monogamous, usually pairing for life

NEST: a big dome-shaped structure of sticks, on branches of shrubs or trees, often more than one per group as they are used for roosting all year round as well as for nesting

EGGS: 1–6, grey to buff or brown, densely streaked, veined or marbled dark brown, blackish or reddish

INCUBATION: 19–25 (information from two species)

FLEDGING PERIOD: 16–23 (information from two species)

FOOD: insects, spiders, scorpions, small reptiles, eggs and nestlings of small birds, seeds and fruit

VOICE: highly vocal, uttering loud whistling, chuckling, chattering, barking, caterwauling and other sounds; breeding pairs of the Grey-crowned Babbler, *Pomatostomus temporalis*, perform antiphonal duets

MIGRATION: mostly sedentary; Hall's Babbler, *P. halli*, is locally nomadic

CONSERVATION STATUS: none threatened

Genetic data show that this very small family of birds is only very distantly related to that of the Asian and African babblers (families Timaliidae, Pellorneidae and Leiothrichidae). Despite this, its members share with some of them – especially the scimitar babblers, *Pomatorhinus* and *Erythrogenys* – their general appearance, very social habits and noisiness. Indeed, they were included in the formerly much larger 'ragbag' Family Timaliidae. Currently, they are regarded as a very early radiation of the songbird suborder, with their closest relatives possibly being the logrunners (Orthorhynchidae) or perhaps to the Australian treecreepers (Climacteridae). Medium sized birds, roughly the size of thrushes, Australasian babblers have a rather long, downwardly curved bill, a rather long, graduated tail, and a horizontal posture. The Australian species have largely brown plumage with black-and-white head patterns, a blackish bill, a white throat and white tips to the tail feathers. The New Guinea Babbler, *Garritornis isodorei*, is entirely reddish brown with a yellow bill.

Australasian babblers forage for food in noisy groups, moving across the ground or among the lower levels of trees and shrubs in bouncing hops. Although they eat many insects and their larvae,

LEFT The western, northern and central Australian race *rubeculus* of the Grey-crowned Babbler, *Pomatostomus temporalis*, has a rich rufous breast.

they are generally omnivorous, including other small animals as well as seeds and fruit in their diet. Their bulky stick nests, typically sited in a dead or dying tree, are a familiar sight in the Australian outback.

BERRYPECKERS AND LONGBILLS Melanocharitidae

GENERA: 4   **SPECIES**: 10

LENGTH: 7.3–15 cm (2.9–6 in)

WEIGHT: 5–20 g (0.2–0.7 oz)

RANGE AND HABITAT: New Guinea and nearby islands; forests

SOCIAL BEHAVIOUR: mostly occur singly or in pairs; very little known about breeding behaviour

NEST: the few nests found have been cup-shaped, made of fern fronds and stems, dried grass or other vegetation, sometimes bound together with spiders' webs and decorated with lichens or spiders' egg sacs, lined with plant down or other soft material and bound to branches or trailing vines

EGGS: probably 1–2, whitish, cream or pastel pink with darker markings in the few known

INCUBATION: unknown

FLEDGING PERIOD: unknown

FOOD: berrypeckers eat mainly small berries (and in the Spotted Berrypecker, *Rhamphocharis crassirostris*, figs too), also some insects and spiders; longbills feed mainly on insects, spiders and nectar

VOICE: berrypeckers make various buzzing, twittering, rasping and other calls or songs; *Oedistoma* longbills utter various dry, sharp and disyllabic calls or chattering or clicking calls, song not known; *Toxorhamphus* longbills have a sweet song and some harder or buzzing or sneezing calls

MIGRATION: sedentary

CONSERVATION STATUS: none threatened; with relatively few validated records, it is not known if the Obscure Berrypecker, *Melanocharis arfakiana*, is threatened

This is a small family of forest dwellers endemic to the New Guinea region. The six species of berrypeckers were often included in the south Asian/Australasian flowerpecker family (Dicaeidae), but differ in various features, including less specialised tongues. These birds, whose common name reflects their main food, resemble stout-bodied honeyeaters. In most species, males have black upperparts and dull olive-grey underparts, although one, the Fan-tailed Berrypecker, *Melanocharis versteri*, is glossy blue-black above with white flashes on his long tail. Females are even duller, with olive upperparts. Two species differ in that both sexes share the dull olive plumage: these are the rarely seen, well-named Obscure Berrypecker, *M. arfakiana*, and a slightly better known species, the Streaked Berrypecker, *M. striativentris*. The Spotted Berrypecker, *Rhamphocharis crassirostris*, is unusual in that the female is more boldly plumaged than the dull olive male, her dark brown plumage peppered with white spots.

With their long, decurved, sharp-tipped bill, the four species of longbill (not to be confused with the African birds called longbills, which are Old World warblers in the genus *Macrosphenus*, see p. 341) resemble sunbirds or some of the small, short-tailed honeyeaters. Indeed, until quite recently, they were classified in the honeyeater family, before DNA studies showed that they are most closely related to berrypeckers. Unlike the latter, which are almost all mountain dwellers, they are birds of lowland forests. Very active feeders, like berrypeckers, these shy little birds differ in subsisting mainly on nectar and insects, but some take fruit too. The Pygmy Longbill, *Oedistoma pygmaeum*, is New Guinea's smallest bird, at just 7.3 cm (2.9 in) long and weighing only 5 g (0.2 oz), only the size of many small hummingbirds. All species are olive green above with yellowish or whitish underparts in both sexes. The true affinities of this small and relatively little known family are uncertain, but they may turn out to be closest to the satinbirds (Cnemophilidae), also from New Guinea, and the wattlebirds (Family Callaeidae), from New Zealand.

RIGHT The boldly plumaged male Fan-tailed Berrypecker, *Melanocharis versteri*, is the largest member of its genus, and also has the longest tail.

ABOVE The Slaty-headed Longbill, *Toxorhamphus poliopterus*, is usually hard to see, as it lives high in the New Guinea rainforest canopy.

SATINBIRDS Cnemophilidae

GENERA: 2　　**SPECIES:** 3

LENGTH: 17–24 cm (6.5–9.5 in)

WEIGHT: 50–125 g (1.75–4.5 oz)

RANGE AND HABITAT: New Guinea; montane forest and forest edge

SOCIAL BEHAVIOUR: seen alone, in pairs or sometimes in small groups at good food sites in fruiting trees; polygamous, solitary promiscuous male displays to and mates with several females, which build nest, incubate eggs and rear young alone

NEST: a big domed structure, built from orchid stems, mosses and ferns, with a few sticks inserted at the base as a foundation; built in branches or on a mossy tree stump or trunk at moderate height, and well camouflaged against vegetation

EGGS: few details known; probably 1, pale pinkish with fine brown spots

INCUBATION: 25 days recorded from one nest of Loria's Satinbird, *Cnemophilus loriae*

FLEDGING PERIOD: probably more than 30 days

FOOD: almost exclusively or completely fruit eaters, though Loria's Satinbird also eats some earthworms

VOICE: males utter various calls, including harsh rasping, grating or hissing notes, bell-like ringing sounds, explosive muffled barks, and loud clicks; females are less vocal, including softer notes

MIGRATION: sedentary

CONSERVATION STATUS: one species, the Yellow-breasted Satinbird, *Loboparadisea sericea*, is Near Threatened

The three species in this small family, endemic to the mountains of New Guinea, were originally thought to be close relatives of the bowerbirds (Ptilonorynchidae). They were later regarded as members of the bird of paradise family (Paradisaeidae), where they remained as a distinctive subfamily (Cnemophilinae) until recently, when research into their DNA indicated that they should be placed in a family of their own. Recent research suggests that they may be more closely related to the New Zealand wattlebirds (Callaeidae)

LEFT A male Crested Satinbird, *Cnemophilus macgregorii*, visits a fruiting tree in the Western Highlands of Papua New Guinea.

manipulating food items, in contrast to the strong, sturdy crowlike legs and feet of the birds of paradise. Another distinction is their unossified nasal region. The name 'satinbird' has been recently given, referring to the birds' silky plumage.

All three species of satinbird are plump-bodied and short-tailed. The sexes are dimorphic, with relatively boldly plumaged males and drab females. There are two species of *Cnemophilus*. The male Loria's Satinbird, *C. loriae*, is velvety black, with a metallic purple, magenta, blue and greenish gloss, whereas the female is dull olive, browner on the wings and tail. The male Crested Satinbird, *C. macgregorii*, is named for the small erectile crest down the centre of the crown (normally concealed and raised only in display). It has the upper half of its head, and its back, wings and tail brilliant yellow in the nominate race and bright reddish in the other race, *sanguineus*, contrasting in each case with the brownish black underparts, which have a coppery sheen. The female is even duller than the female Loria's Satinbird, plain olive brown above and slightly paler brownish buff below. The male Yellow-breasted Satinbird, *Loboparadisaea sericea*, has a brown head, upperparts, wings and tail, with a coppery sheen in places, and a sulphur-yellow body, whereas the female (unusually, slightly larger than the male) is plain brown above and paler, yellowish buff below with darker greyish streaking.

and the stitchbird (Notiomystidae), or perhaps the rockfowl and relatives (Eupetidae) and Australasian robins (Petroicidae).

As well as the DNA differences, satinbirds differ from birds of paradise in their morphology in several respects. They have a small, fine-tipped, weak bill with an extremely wide gape (they were formerly regarded as the 'wide-gaped birds of paradise' subfamily), suited to their exclusively fruit-based diet – this is very different from the powerful bill of typical birds of paradise, with their omnivorous diet, even when young. Their feet, too, are very different, being slender, weak and not used for holding down or

NEW ZEALAND WATTLEBIRDS Callaeidae

GENERA: 3   **SPECIES**: 4

LENGTH: 25–38 cm (10–15 in)   **WEIGHT**: 70–250 g (2.5–8.8 oz)

RANGE AND HABITAT: originally native forest, now mainly in regenerating forests and plantations after introduction to offshore islands, the kokakos were once found in both islands, now almost certainly only on North Island; the Saddleback is on both islands; the Huia was once widespread in native forest of North Island

SOCIAL BEHAVIOUR: usually singly or in pairs, but may form small family groups after breeding; highly territorial, and often pair for life

NEST: cup-shaped, made of large twigs bound together with lichens, moss and other material, and lined with finer twigs and leaves; that of the kokakos, *Callaeas*, in the fork of a tree, among tangled lianas or other epiphytes, or atop a tree-fern, large but well concealed among vegetation; the Saddleback, *Philesturnus carunculatus*, builds a similar but smaller nest in a hollow tree or tree crevice, or sometimes in a rock crevice in the ground or in a tree among dense epiphytes; the Huia built a saucer-shaped nest of dry grass, leaves and stems on branches or hollows of trees

EGGS: 1–4, usually pale or dark pinkish or purplish grey (sometimes white or deep beige), with dark brown markings

INCUBATION: 16–28 days; unknown for Huia

FLEDGING PERIOD: 25–37 days; unknown unknown for Huia

FOOD: kokakos eat mainly leaves and fruit, with some buds, flowers, nectar and invertebrates; the Saddleback eats mainly invertebrates, also some berries; the Huia ate mainly wood-boring beetle grubs

VOICE: both sexes sing; the kokakos' song is a slow series of loud organ-like notes, the Saddleback has a loud chattering song; all three also have a variety of quieter, softer calls; the Huia had a whistling song

MIGRATION: sedentary

CONSERVATION STATUS: the Huia, *Heterolocha acutirostris*, is Extinct; the South Island Kokako, *Callaeas cinerea*, is Critically Endangered (Perhaps Extinct); two species, the North Island Kokako, *C. wilsoni*, and the Saddleback are Near Threatened

The birds in this tiny family were also known as wattled crows, but they are not really crow-like and are unrelated to the true crows (Family Corvidae). Depending on which taxonomic scheme is followed, there are between two and four species in the two extant genera. In the scheme used in this book, there are two very similar species of kokako in the genus *Callaeas*, the North Island Kokako, *C. wilsoni*, and the South Island Kokako, *C. cinerea* (which are sometimes regarded as subspecies of a single species). They are both about the size of a large pigeon, with a short, deep, decurved bill, a long, broad, decurved tail, and long, sturdy legs. The

plumage of both sexes is mainly blue-grey, with a small black mask around the base of the bill. Both species have a pair of prominent shiny, leathery wattles beneath the bill that touch or overlap across the throat: these are bright blue in the North Island Kokako and orange in the South Island Kokako. The Saddleback, *Philesturnus carunculatus*, has two extremely similar subspecies, the North Island Saddleback, *P. c. rufusater*, and the South Island Saddleback, *P. c. carunculatus*, which are often regarded as full species. These are much smaller birds than the kokakos, about the size of a large thrush. Their plumage is mainly glossy black, contrasting with a

LEFT The Saddleback, *Philesturnus carunculatus*, uses its longish, strong, slightly decurved bill to catch insects by probing in soil or soft wood, tearing off bark, or picking them from foliage.

chestnut 'saddle' and a similarly coloured rump and undertail. The North Island Saddleback is distinguished by a narrow yellowish band edging the forward margin of the saddle.

The song of the kokako is one of the most haunting and beautiful of all the sounds of the New Zealand forests. Both sexes utter its rich, organ-like notes, sometimes in a duet, for just an hour or so after sunrise. Saddlebacks are much noisier, broadcasting their loud, chattering songs throughout the day and all year; regional populations have distinct dialects. Regional dialects are also pronounced in kokakos, which has direct implications for conservation efforts, as it may affect whether or not birds from different populations will mate successfully.

The North Island Kokako is restricted to a few widely separated areas of forest on North Island and some of its offshore islands. Although the South Island Kokako is still classified as Critically Endangered (Perhaps Extinct), the last confirmed sightings were in 2007, and before that in 1967, so it is very likely that it is now extinct. The North Island subspecies of the Saddleback is now restricted to 15 or so predator-free offshore islands and five mainland reserves where predators are excluded by fences or caught in traps. A similar situation applies to the South Island subspecies, which currently survives on 20 or so offshore islands and one mainland sanctuary. All these birds were once common throughout New Zealand's native forests. The cause of the huge declines was originally logging and other large-scale habitat destruction and degradation. There is also a continuing threat from alien mammals, both as predators (especially rats, brush-tailed possums and stoats), and as competitors for food (notably goats and deer, as well as the possums). While the populations of the Northern Kokako and the Saddleback have increased recently as a result of intensive predator control, constant vigilance and action where necessary are essential.

A third species, the Huia, *Heterolocha acutirostris*, endemic to the southern part of North Island, is now extinct; the last confirmed sighting was as long ago as 1907, although there have been some subsequent but unconfirmed reports. The primary reason may have been habitat destruction, in particular the loss of dead trees that were home to the Huia's main prey of wood-boring beetle larvae. It also suffered from the depredations of stoats, cats, rats and other introduced mammals, and the birds had long been hunted by the Maori for their long, glossy black, white-tipped tail feathers, which were prized, along with their dried skins, for ornaments and as barter for other valuable items. Many were hunted by European collectors to supply the lucrative trade in mounted specimens.

The Huia was a striking bird, with black plumage that shone with a green sheen, and bright orange wattles. Males and females were unique among birds in the extreme differences in the shape of their bone-coloured bill. Males used their shorter, only slightly downcurved bill to chisel into bark to reach insects and spiders hiding just beneath, whereas the females employed their much longer, more downcurved bill to probe more deeply for different invertebrate prey.

The closest relatives of this ancient lineage of birds appears to be the Stitchbird (Family Notiomystidae), and these two groups may in turn be related to the satinbirds (Cnemophilidae), berrypeckers (Melanocharitidae), rockfowl and relatives (Eupetidae) and Australasian robins (Petroicidae).

STITCHBIRD (or HIHI) Notiomystidae

GENERA: 1   **SPECIES**: 1

LENGTH: 18 cm (7 in)

WEIGHT: 26–42 g (0.9–1.5 oz)

RANGE AND HABITAT: North Island; dense native forest

SOCIAL BEHAVIOUR: usually in pairs or small groups; breeding system varies among individuals, from the most common arrangement, social monogamy (stay together for at least a season to rear young but may indulge in extra-pair matings) to polyandry (female mating with one or more males), polygny (male mating with one or more females) or polygynandry (both males and females having more than one sexual partner each season)

NEST: a platform of sticks and rootlets supporting a cup of fern rhizomes bound together by spiders' webs, lined with feathers and fern scales, placed in cavity in a tree trunk or branch; built by the female

EGGS: 2–6, usually 4–5, vary from white and unmarked to pale yellowish with dense brown markings

INCUBATION: 13–19 days

FLEDGING PERIOD: 26–32 days

FOOD: nectar, fruit and small insects and spiders, as well as sugary insect and plant exudates including honeydew from nymphs of aphids, psyllid bugs and scale insects, lerps (the crystallised honeydew produced by psyllid bugs as a protective coating) and manna (the secretions of damaged plant material from *Eucalyptus* species and other trees)

VOICE: frequent alarm call is a sharp '*stitch*' sound (probably accounting for both English and Maori names; contact call is a plaintive double '*tseet*'; song is a series of 2–3 loud, high-pitched whistles

MIGRATION: sedentary

CONSERVATION STATUS: Vulnerable

Until very recently, this rare and threatened New Zealand endemic was classified with the honeyeaters. However, despite its apparent resemblance to those birds, the uncertainty about its true relationships has now been resolved by DNA analysis, which indicates that its closest relatives are not honeyeaters but the New Zealand wattlebirds (Family Callaeidae), from which the Stitchbird, *Notiomystis cincta*, split off some 34 million years ago.

Males of this unique songbird have a velvety black hood with a small erectile white nape patch and a golden-yellow shoulder patch, and streaked back and underparts; females are much duller, mainly grey-brown. The longish tail is often held cocked.

The Stitchbird differs in various ways from honeyeaters, including nesting in hollows, having a larger clutch size and a more complex and variable mating system. Most remarkable – and unique among all birds – is the Stitchbird's habit of copulating face-to-face as well as in the usual avian manner, in which the male mounts the female from behind. Face-to-face copulations occur quite often, and are almost always forced upon the female by the male, usually not his mate. The male chases her to the ground and then holds her down with his feet.

The Hihi, to give it its Maori name, is known only from North Island and nearby offshore islands, but by the mid-1880s it had disappeared from the mainland and many of the islands. It had

ABOVE This male Stitchbird (or Hihi), *Notiomystis cincta*, is on predator-free Tiri Matangi Island, off the North Island of New Zealand.

probably been wiped out by a combination of factors, all related to the arrival of European settlers, including the depredations of black rats and other introduced mammals, as well as introduced avian diseases, habitat destruction and large-scale collecting for specimens.

NEW ZEALAND CREEPERS Mohouidae

GENERA: 2   **SPECIES**: 3

LENGTH: 12.5–15 cm (5–6 in)

WEIGHT: 10–32 g (0.35–1.1 oz)

RANGE AND HABITAT: New Zealand, with one species, the Whitehead, *Mohoua albicilla*, on North Island, and two species, the Yellowhead, *M. ochrocephala*, and the New Zealand Brown Creeper, *Finschia novaeseelandiae*, on South Island and Stewart Island; the Whitehead lives in native forest (mainly of southern beech, *Nothofagus*) and manuka, *Leptospermum*, scrub, and also in introduced conifer plantations, the Yellowhead in montane southern beech forests, and the New Zealand Brown Creeper in southern beech forests, introduced pine forests and high-altitude alpine scrub

SOCIAL BEHAVIOUR: monogamous; the Yellowhead and Whitehead breed cooperatively, the latter with up to six helpers assisting with the feeding and care of nestlings

NEST: a deep cup of rootlets, bark, grass, leaves and bark, lined with feathers, wool, moss and bark and covered by spider webs on the outside; the Yellowhead sites its nest in a tree cavity, whereas the other two species build their nests in a forked branch or vine tangle near the ground

EGGS: 2–4, white, pink or pale reddish, with yellowish, brown or purple markings

INCUBATION: 17–21 days

FLEDGING PERIOD: 16–22 days

FOOD: small insects and other arthropods, with some seeds and fruit

VOICE: male Whiteheads and Yellowheads have musical songs of canary-like trills; both male and female New Zealand Brown Creepers sing, male a mixture of whistles, slurs and harsh notes, female a rapid series of brief sounds, ending on a long and high-pitched note; pairs duet

MIGRATION: mainly sedentary, with some local altitudinal or other movements

CONSERVATION STATUS: one species, the Yellowhead, is Endangered

This trio of lively little, large-headed and rotund bodied birds are endemic to New Zealand, with one species, the Yellowhead, restricted to South Island. Here, its small and fragmented mainland population is at risk from predation by introduced rats, mice and stoats, adding to early losses from logging of its forest habitat. Conservationists have had success in increasing numbers by controlling predators and translocating birds to predator-free islands, and also then reintroducing some to the mainland. Although they are declining,

the other two species are still widely distributed – the Whitehead on North Island and the New Zealand Brown Creeper on South Island and Stewart Island – and do not appear to be in immediate danger.

The Yellowhead (also known by its Maori name, Popokotea) has not only the bright yellow head for which it was named but also underparts of the same intense colour; its upperparts and tail are yellowish brown and its eyes, short bill and rather long, strong legs are a contrasting black. Similarly, the Whitehead (or Mohua, in

Maori) has the white on its underparts as well as its head, with its pale brown upperparts and black eye, bill and legs contrasting in the same way as the Yellowhead's. The New Zealand Brown Creeper (or Pipipi in Maori) is much duller, with an ash grey face and neck, reddish brown crown, back and rump and buff underparts.

All three species are very active feeders, typically roaming about in small, noisy groups that move rapidly about among the trees high in the forest canopy, searching for insects on branches and by probing into crevices, and often hanging upside-down to feed.

The Mohouidae were once thought to belong within the whistler Family Pachycephalidae, but recent evidence has disproved such a relationship. They are likely to be an ancient lineage with no obvious close relations to other families.

ABOVE The Maori name of Pipipi for the Brown Creeper, *Finschia novaeseelandiae*, is imitative of this little bird's high-pitched calls.

SITELLAS Neosittidae

GENERA: 1   **SPECIES:** 3

LENGTH: 10–14 cm (4–5.5 in)

WEIGHT: 8–20 g (0.3–0.7 oz)

RANGE AND HABITAT: Australia, New Guinea; the Varied Sitella lives in a wide range of eucalypt woods and forests; the Papuan Sitella in montane rainforest, and the Black Sitella in even higher moss forests

SOCIAL BEHAVIOUR: little is known of the biology of the New Guinea species, especially breeding; Varied Sitellas usually live in family groups or small clans of up to 12 individuals, defending a group territory; members of a clan preen one another and roost huddled together; they are monogamous, breeding as pairs or, most often, as cooperative groups

NEST: in the Varied Sitella, a deep cup of plant fibres and down, superbly camouflaged with fine shreds of bark, sometimes with lichens, mosses, feathers or fur, bound together with spiders' webs, sited mostly in a fork of a branch high in trees

EGGS: 2–3, whitish, boldly blotched or spotted with black, grey, brown, olive or lilac

INCUBATION: 19–20 days

FLEDGING PERIOD: 18–20 days

FOOD: insects and spiders

VOICE: contact calls are simple, monotonously repeated 'chip', squeaking or whistling sounds

MIGRATION: sedentary

CONSERVATION STATUS: none threatened

This tiny family of tree-climbing songbirds is endemic to Australasia. They are superficially similar to the widespread and almost entirely northern hemisphere nuthatches (Family Sittidae). Indeed, until the late 1960s they were usually included in the nuthatch family, and were later linked to the treecreepers (Certhiidae), Australasian treecreepers (Climacteridae) or Australasian babblers (Pomatostomidae). Recent DNA analysis suggests that they represent an ancient linage with uncertain affinities, though one suggestion has been that their closest relative may be the Wattled Ploughbill, *Eulacestoma nigropectus*, of New Guinea.

The Varied Sitella, *Daphoenositta chrysoptera*, is found across much of Australia where there are trees, although not in rainforests. The five races, often formerly regarded as separate species, have distinctive plumage differences, with various permutations of streaked or plainer greyish upperparts, and streaked or unstreaked white underparts, wingbar colour (gold or white) and in most cases a blackish crown in males and blackish hood in females. The six New Guinea races of the Papuan Sitella, *D. papuensis*, show similar variation, while the other, scarcer New Guinea species, the Black Sitella, *D. miranda*, is very different looking, with all-black plumage, apart from a pinkish red area around the forehead and chin, very small amounts of white on the wings and pinkish white on the tail. In contrast to the Varied

Sitella, both these New Guinea endemics are birds of mountain rain and moss forests respectively, with the Black Sitella extending as high as 3,700 m (12,000 ft).

Sitellas spend more time on branches than on tree trunks, and, like nuthatches, can travel with ease downwards as well as upwards. They hold prey by their feet while dealing with it, and may also use their feet to hold strips of bark aside while they pry for insects or spiders hiding beneath them.

LEFT A male Varied Sitella, *Daphoenositta chrysoptera*, brings food to its young, hidden in the well camouflaged nest sited in a tree fork.

CUCKOO-SHRIKES Campephagidae

GENERA: 11   **SPECIES**: 85

LENGTH: 13–38 cm (5–15 in)

WEIGHT: 6–180 g (0.2–6.3 oz)

RANGE AND HABITAT: sub-Saharan Africa, Madagascar, Comoros, Mauritius and Reunion, southern and eastern Asia, Australasia and western Pacific islands; forests, woodlands, savannahs, scrublands and mangroves

SOCIAL BEHAVIOUR: most are monogamous, territorial and usually singly or in pairs, but some are cooperative breeders

NEST: very small relative to the size of the bird, with the egg or eggs only just fitting in, and a sitting adult or nestling(s) spilling over the edges; saucer- or cup-shaped, fragile, of fine twigs, rootlets, grasses, plant down and other plant material, usually bound together and to the branch with spiders' webs and sometimes the birds' own saliva; well hidden on a fork or branch of a tree or shrub

EGGS: 1–5, varying greatly from white, pale green or blue-grey to olive green, yellowish or dark green, with brown spots or blotches

INCUBATION: 14–27 days

FLEDGING PERIOD: 12–30 days

FOOD: mainly insects, such as grasshoppers, mantids, beetles and stick insects, and especially caterpillars in many species; the larger species also eat some small lizards; about 20 species are primarily fruit eaters

VOICE: trilling, churring, chattering and whistling notes, elaborated into longer songs; prolonged insect-like buzzing in cicadabirds

MIGRATION: most are sedentary; some make altitudinal movements and others much longer migrations

CONSERVATION STATUS: one species, the Reunion Cuckoo-shrike, *Lalage newtoni*, is Critically Endangered; two races of the Common Cicadabird, *Edolisoma tenuirostris, nesiotis*, from Yap island, and *insperatum* from Pohnpei island, often regarded as full species, are Endangered; four species, the Western Wattled Cuckoo-shrike, *Lobotos lobatus*, Black-bibbed Cicadabird, *Edolisoma mindanensis*, White-winged Cicadabird, *E. ostentum*, and Mauritius Cuckoo-shrike, *Lalage typica*, are Vulnerable; nine species including the Fiery Minivet, *Pericrocotus igneus*, are Near Threatened

ABOVE This Barred Cuckoo-shrike, *Coracina lineata*, is feeding on wild figs in northern Queensland, Australia.

This largish family of mainly tropical birds has a very wide distribution, occurring in Africa, Madagascar, Asia and Australasia as well as many Pacific islands. Its common name is misleading, as these birds are related to neither the cuckoos (Cuculidae, p. 57) nor the shrikes (Laniidae, p. 270). They were given this name because of morphological similarities to the two other families – the combination of grey upperparts and barred underparts and the yellow eyes of some cuckooshrikes resemble those of some cuckoos and their often strong, slightly hooked bill is rather like that of the shrikes.

There is considerable range in size, from the 12 species of little, sparrow-sized minivets, *Pericrocotus*, to a few jay-sized species, such as the Ground Cuckoo-shrike, *Coracina maxima*, but most species are intermediate in size. Generally, the body is slender. The feet are typically small and quite weak, adapted for perching. Bill shapes vary from the sturdy, strong beak of cuckoo-shrikes, notched and somewhat hooked at the tip, to the shorter, rather more slender bill of the trillers, *Lalage*, and minivets. There are prominent rictal bristles around the base of the bill, which in many species cover the nostrils. The wings are long, with pointed tips, and the tail rather long and either rounded or graduated; uniquely, the Ground Cuckoo Shrike has a deeply forked tail.

The plumage is dense and soft and (as with herons, parrots and a few other groups of birds) incorporates powder down, specially modified feathers that break down in to a talcum-like powder. Many species have erectile feathers on the lower back and rump, which they raise in defensive displays.

There are two subfamilies. The Pericrocotinae contains the single genus of minivets, *Pericrocotus*, with 13 species, all Asian. These are the brightest members of the family, most species having brilliant orange-and-black or red-and-black males and yellow-and-black-and grey females. The other, much larger, family is the Campephaginae, with 72 species in 10 genera. Most species occur in Asia and Australasia, with just 10 in Africa and a single species in Madagascar. The largest genus is *Coracina*, comprising 21 species with plumage in various permutations of black, grey and white, including dark-barred underparts in many, and with the sexes generally looking similar. Another major genus is *Edolisoma*, whose 19 species are known as cicadabirds, from the resemblance of the songs of some species to the sounds made by cicadas. Some have similar plumage to the *Coracina* cuckoo-shrikes, but with females that are duller, paler or barred below, or rich reddish brown; in several species the males are black or dark blue. The males of the 18 species of trillers, *Lalage*, have mainly pied plumage, while females are duller brown and often barred below. A few species in other genera are much brighter. The Golden Cuckoo-shrike, *Campochaera sloetii*, of New Guinea, has a golden yellow body and rump contrasting with a black head, throat and upper breast in males (grey in females). One of the African species, the Blue Cuckoo-shrike, *Cyanograuculus azureus*, lives up to its common and scientific names, with a males resplendent in deep glossy blue plumage, and females azure blue. The two species of wattled cuckoo-shrikes, *Lobotos*, also from Africa, have green upperparts, bright orange or yellow underparts and a glossy black head that sports a contrasting large orange wattle extending from the base of the bill; females are duller with smaller wattles. The males of four other African species, of the genus *Campephaga*, have striking red or yellow shoulder patches as well as small yellow or orange wattles contrasting with their glossy black plumage, very different from the mainly green and yellow females.

Most species are almost entirely arboreal. Some of the trillers are largely insectivorous; some of the larger species, such as the White-bellied Cuckoo-shrike, *Coracina papuensis*, take small lizards. The Ground Cuckoo-shrike, *Coracina maxima*, is unique in foraging wholly on the ground, with much stronger legs than other members of the family although it perches, roosts and nests in trees; pairs or small family groups wander about in sparsely wooded semi-arid areas of inland Australia feeding on insects and other invertebrates, nodding their head back and forth like pigeons as they walk. Minivets, by contrast, move through the treetops in large, noisy groups and often join other birds searching for insects in mixed flocks. Flycatcher-shrikes and some of the trillers sally out to catch flying insects in their short bill with a wide gape.

QUAIL-THRUSHES AND JEWEL-BABBLERS Cinclosomatidae

GENERA: 2   **SPECIES:** 10

LENGTH: 19–30 cm (7.5–12 in)

WEIGHT: 50–120 g (1.8–4.2 oz)

RANGE AND HABITAT: quail-thrushes, *Cinclosoma*, all in Australia apart from one species, the Painted Quail-thrush, *C. ajax*, in New Guinea, and jewel-babblers, *Ptilorrhoa*, only in New Guinea; Australian quail-thrushes in dry woodland and arid plains and scrub, mostly in lowlands, the Painted Quail-thrush and jewel-babblers in rainforest and other humid forests, from lowlands to mountain slopes

SOCIAL BEHAVIOUR: breeding behaviour little known but probably all monogamous and involving helpers at the nest

NEST: cup-shaped and made from twigs, grass, bark and other vegetation, sited on the ground

EGGS: 1–3

INCUBATION: about 14 days

FLEDGING PERIOD: about 14 days

FOOD: insects and other invertebrates, also seeds

VOICE: high-pitched series of whistles, often rapidly repeated

MIGRATION: jewel-babblers probably all sedentary; some quail-thrushes in arid areas may make local movements

CONSERVATION STATUS: none is threatened

ABOVE Among a variety of sounds made by the Spotted Jewel-babbler, *Ptilorrhoa leucosticta*, of New Guinea is a series of clear, bell-like notes.

ABOVE The Cinnamon Quail-thrush, *Cinclosoma cinnamomeum*, lives in stony scrublands and other arid places in parts of central and southern Australia.

This small family of just two genera is restricted to Australia and New Guinea. Five of the six species of quail thrushes, *Cinclosoma*, live only in Australia, with just one, the Painted Quail-thrush, *C. ajax*, in New Guinea, while all four species of jewel-babblers, *Ptilorrhoa*, are endemic to New Guinea, where they live in dense, humid forests. Despite their close relationship, all the Australian *Cinclosoma* species occur in a very different habitat from the jewel-babblers – in woodlands and among scrub in dry, open country. The exception is the Painted Quail-thrush, which is a rainforest dweller like the jewel-babblers.

The size of many of the true thrushes (Turdidae, p. 391), these birds do bear a superficial resemblance to that family, but their proportions are different, with a small head, a long body and long graduated, rounded tail (beneath which the quail-thrushes have especially long undertail coverts). They usually hold themselves more horizontally than thrushes and with their shorter legs appear to hug the ground, where they spend most of their time.

The four species of jewel-babblers are beautiful birds, with mainly rich chestnut or deep blue plumage, or a combination of both, with a black eyestripe and necklace contrasting with a white face, throat or wing-spots. The six species of quail-thrushes lack the blue but are nonetheless strikingly plumaged in more sober browns, black and white, in most species with dark spots, streaks or chevrons on their partly white underparts.

Their closest relatives may be the shrike-tits (Falcunculidae, p. 250) or perhaps the whipbirds and wedgebills (Psophodidae, p. 252) and the painted berrypeckers (Paramythiidae, p. 254).

WHISTLERS Pachycephalidae

GENERA: 5   **SPECIES**: 49

LENGTH: 12.5–28.5 cm (4.5–11 in)

WEIGHT: 13–110 g (0.5–4 oz)

RANGE AND HABITAT: Southeast Asia east through Indonesia and the Philippines to Australasia, New Zealand and central and south Pacific islands; woodland and forest, especially rainforest, some in scrub or mangroves

SOCIAL BEHAVIOUR: they forage alone, in pairs, or as part of mixed-species flocks; of the relatively few species for which details are known, breeding is monogamous and territorial, as separate pairs

NEST: a cup of grass, plant fibres, bark strips and lichens, in a fork of a tree or shrub or among tangled vines

EGGS: 2–4, white, buff, pinkish or olive, with darker markings

INCUBATION: 13–21 days

FLEDGING PERIOD: 10–22 days

FOOD: mainly insects and spiders; some species include other invertebrates such as small snails or crabs, and some also eat fruit and seeds

VOICE: frequent songs consist chiefly of loud whistles; contact and other calls include hissing, piping, twittering or harsh sounds

MIGRATION: most species are sedentary, though a few make altitudinal movements, and the Rufous Whistler, *Pachycephala rufiventris*, makes longer north–south migrations

CONSERVATION STATUS: one species, the Sangir Whistler, *Coracornis sanghirensis*, is Critically Endangered; one species, the Red-lored Whistler, *Pachycephala rufogularis*, is Vulnerable; two species, the Tongan Whistler, *P. jacquinoti*, and the White-bellied Shrike-thrush, *Pseudorectes incertus*, are Near Threatened

ABOVE Renowned for its beautiful song, this Grey Shrike-thrush, *Colluricincla harmonica*, is performing in Tasmania, Australia.

Whistlers are stout-bodied small to medium-sized birds with proportionally large, rounded heads: a less flattering earlier alternative common name (and a transliteration of the scientific name of the main genus and the family) was 'thickheads'. The name used today reflects the powerful, rich, whistling notes of their songs, and the family includes many species renowned in Australia as fine songsters, such as the Rufous Whistler, *Pachycephala rufiventris*. Most species are tree dwellers and most have a strong, stout bill. They feed chiefly on insects, which they catch mainly by gleaning from leaves (especially the undersides), twigs or branches, often after a short flight. Many species join mixed-species feeding flocks.

Most species are drab, but some are brightly coloured, especially with yellow underparts, or boldly marked, including black-and-white patterns. The sexes look similar in some species, but in many the male is more brightly or boldly plumaged. Plumage colours of some species are in combinations of grey, white, orange, chestnut and brown, while others feature olive, yellow, black, grey and white in various patterns.

Of the five genera comprising this family, the largest by far is *Pachycephala*. It contains between 32 and 40 species, depending on different taxonomic assessments: in this book we recognise 39 species. They include the Golden Whistler, *P. pectoralis*, and its close relatives. This species was formerly subdivided into up to as many as 70 or more subspecies, making it among the most geographically diverse of all bird species over a vast range from Indonesia, Australia and New Guinea to many Pacific islands. Their complex taxonomy is still a matter of dispute, with up to 50 or more subspecies still recognised by some researchers, but in the scheme followed here many of these geographical races have been deemed invalid or assigned to other species. As a result, the species contains just seven subspecies, and is called the Australian Golden Whistler (with six species in Australia and one in New Guinea). Males have a black head and collar enclosing a white bib, olive green upperparts, and bright yellow breast and belly, while females of all races except the New Guinea one, *balim*, are much duller, mainly brownish. A very similar species, the Mangrove Warbler, *P. melanura*, is a habitat specialist restricted to coastal areas of northern Australia and southern New Guinea and nearby islands.

As well as the three genera called whistlers, this family contains the shrike-thrushes, almost all in the genus *Colluricincla*. Although the five species are rather thrush-like in shape (but with shorter legs) and have rather heavy, slightly hook-tipped bills reminiscent of those of shrikes, they are not related to either the shrike or the thrush families. One species, the Sooty Shrike-thrush, *C. tenebrosa*, is endemic to New Guinea, one occurs on that island and offshore islands, as well as in northern and eastern Australia, and three are restricted to Australia. Most are drably plumaged in various combinations of greys, buffs and browns, while the Sooty Shrike-thrush is black and brownish-black. In contrast to the whistlers, the sexes are very similar in appearance. Of the Australian species, by far the most common and widespread is the Grey Shrike-thrush, *C. harmonica*, renowned like the Rufous Whistler for producing one of the most beautiful songs of all Australian birds, a series of liquid flutelike notes. As with the whistler, it is a complex song with much regional and individual variation, and both sexes sing. Shrike-thrushes forage in trees and on the ground, and have a mixed diet of invertebrates, including millipedes, worms and snails as well as insects, and plant matter such as seeds, fruits and buds. Some of the larger species also take frogs, lizards, small mammals and nestling birds. The Grey Shrike-thrush is one of the few birds known to use a tool: it has been observed poking a small stick held in its bill into crevices to flush out insects so that it can catch them.

Many shrike-thrushes rear two broods in a single year, while some are capable of producing four or even five in favourable years.

Three other members of this family are among a small group of six birds endemic to New Guinea that share a remarkable adaptation. Until very recently, all these birds were thought to belong to the same genus, *Pitohui*, and all were known as pitohuis. Then, new genetic research revealed that they belonged to three different families. The three species in this family are the single species of whistler in the genus *Melanorectes*, the Black Whistler, *M. nigrescens*, and two species of shrike-thrush in the genus *Pseudorectes*, the Rusty Shrike-thrush, *P. ferrugineus*, and the White-bellied Shrike-thrush, *P. incertus*. The others are the Piping Bellbird (in the Australo-Papuan bellbird Family Oreoicidae, p. 251) and the Variable Pitohui, *Pitohui kirhocephalus* and Hooded Pitohui, *P. dichrous* (in the oriole family, Oriolidae, p. 256). The adaptation they all share (along with just one other bird, the Ifrit, (Family Ifritidae, p. 277) is that they have independently evolved the ability to store highly neurotoxic poisons called batrachotoxins in their feathers and skin (the same type of extremely potent toxins that are used as defence by some of the little poison-dart frogs from Colombia), albeit at a much lower concentration, with the highest levels in pitohuis in the Variable and Hooded species, and none detected at all in the White-bellied species. It is likely that the birds obtain the toxins from *Chloresine* beetles that they eat. Although this came as a recent revelation to biologists, the native New Guineans have long known that the birds should be avoided and are dangerous to eat, hunters calling them 'rubbish birds'. Research suggests it is likely that this is a defence against ectoparasites and bacteria rather than against predators.

The relationships of the Pachycephalidae to other families is not clear, but the removal of various genera to other families has resulted in a scheme that better reflects the close relationships within the family.

SHRIKE-TITS Falcunculidae

GENERA: 1   **SPECIES**: 3

LENGTH: 16–19 cm (6–7 1/2 in)

WEIGHT: 27–33 g (1–1.2 oz)

RANGE AND HABITAT: Australia, New Guinea; in forests and woodlands, mainly with eucalypts

SOCIAL BEHAVIOUR: shrike-tits are monogamous, and territorial when breeding and for much of rest of year; sometimes a pair will benefit from nest helpers

NEST: an inverted cone topped by cup-like cavity, or a deep cup, made from bark strips and dry grass, densely covered with spiders' webs, in a tree fork, typically in the upper canopy

EGGS: 2–3, white with brown, olive and grey markings

INCUBATION: 18–20 days in shrike-tits

FLEDGING PERIOD: 15–17 days (possible up to 21 days)l

FOOD: insects, both adults and larvae, also spiders, and some fruits and seeds

VOICE: songs feature a variety of whistling songs; calls include harsher grating sounds

MIGRATION: shrike-tits are largely sedentary (apart from short local movements)

CONSERVATION STATUS: none threatened

ABOVE A Western Crested Shrike-tit, *Falcunculus leucogaster*, prepares to feed a nestling with an insect it has dismembered with its strong, hooked laterally compressed bill.

This family contains just three species of shrike-tit, in a single genus, *Falcunculus*, restricted to Australia. They are often regarded as merely three sub species of a single species, but there is good evidence for giving each full species status, as here.

As with various other Australian birds, the common name of these small birds is derived from a fancied resemblance to familiar British birds back home. Although a little larger than tits, they do have a bold black-and-white head pattern (in the shrike-tits with a spiky black crest), olive green upperparts and bright yellow underparts, like some tits, and the sexes are similar. They are also active and acrobatic in searching for insect food. As for the resemblance to shrikes, they have a large head and a deep, powerful, hooked bill.

All shrike-tits differ from whistlers, with which they were traditionally united in the same family (Pachycephalidae), in various aspects of breeding. Unlike any species of whistler for which details are known, a pair sometimes use other individuals as helpers at the nest. Another difference from whistlers is that the female builds the nest alone, and it is cone-shaped rather than cup-shaped, and often situated high up, in the forest canopy.

The striking bill shape of these birds is an adaptation to foraging for insects (including many insect larvae) and spiders, especially those hiding under bark. The bird slips its powerful, laterally flattened bill under a piece of bark and twists its head to lever the bark off to reveal prey, which it can then seize. Among the shrike-tits, this feeding technique is particularly important in the Eastern Shrike-tit, *Falcunculus frontatus*, which takes advantage of the high proportion of eucalypt tree species with naturally peeling bark that occur in its range in eastern and south-eastern Australia. The other two shrike-tit species also obtain a good deal of insect food by gleaning from leaves or digging among moss. Males have longer and deeper bills than females.

AUSTRALIAN-PAPUAN BELLBIRDS Oreoicidae

GENERA: 3   **SPECIES**: 3

LENGTH: 16.5–26 cm (6.5–10 in)

WEIGHT: 38–110 g (1.3–3.9 oz)

RANGE AND HABITAT: the Crested Bellbird, *Oreoica gutturalis*, in Australia, in dry woodlands and scrub; the Rufous-naped Bellbird, *Aleadryas rufinucha*, and Piping Bellbird, *Ornorectes cristatus*, in New Guinea, the first in mountain forest and the second in lowland and foothill rainforest

SOCIAL BEHAVIOUR: known for Crested Bellbird and Rufous-naped Bellbird only; both are socially monogamous

NEST: a deep cup of rootlets, leaves, bark, moss or other plant materials, lined with grass and bark strips, and in the Crested Bellbird, with toxic caterpillars; sited in the fork of a tree or in a shrub, or inside a tree-hollow or tree stump; no information for Piping Bellbird

EGGS: 1–4, white with black, grey, brown or olive markings; no information for Piping Bellbird

INCUBATION: 14–17 days; no information for Piping Bellbird

FLEDGING PERIOD: 11–12 days; no information for Piping Bellbird

FOOD: insects, worms and other invertebrates, and some fruit and seeds

VOICE: songs consist of loud, ringing whistles in Crested and Rufous-naped Bellbird; long series of bell-like notes in Piping Bellbird

MIGRATION: all three species are presumed to be sedentary

CONSERVATION STATUS: none threatened

This family unites three species that were formerly dispersed within the whistler family, Pachycephalidae (p. 249) though not thought to be close relatives. Recent molecular studies indicate that they are related closely enough to merit a family of their own, though their affinities with other families is not at all certain. As well as their genetic relationship, all share certain morphological features, including mainly brown and grey plumage, a strong, sturdy bill with a variably hooked tip, a large head on a short neck and medium-length legs and feet.

The Crested Bellbird, *Oreoica gutturalis*, is endemic to Australia, where it is widely distributed throughout most of the interior, as well as extending to southern and western coasts. The size of a Common Starling, *Sturnus vulgaris*, it lives in dry wooded or shrubby habitats, including eucalypt woodland, mallee, acacia scrub and areas of spinifex grassland with scattered trees. The male is boldly marked with a white forehead and throat bordered by a black band that extends downwards through the bright orange eye and broadens into a breastband; as the common name suggests, he also has a short black crest. The female is much duller without the striking head pattern. The name 'bellbird' also refers to its loud, ringing ventriloquial song, which settlers transcribed as the mnemonic 'dick-dick-the-devil'. Crested Bellbirds have a remarkable and possibly unique habit of incorporating into their nests hairy caterpillars that they have paralysed but not killed by pinching them in their bill. They line the rim of the nest with these insect larvae or place them among the eggs. The function of this odd behaviour may be to provide food for the incubating adults to feed to the nestlings or eat themselves, or to repel predators; the caterpillars chosen have hairs that cause severe irritation to human skin at least.

The other two species, endemic to New Guinea, are less well-known; this is especially true of the Piping Bellbird, *Ornorectes cristatus*. It was formerly classified within the whistler family in the New Guinea genus *Pitohui* together with five other species called pitohuis, now moved into three different families; then it was

ABOVE The Rufous-naped Bellbird, *Aleadryas rufinucha*, is found in the mountain forests of Papua New Guinea.

known as the Crested Pitohui. Along with four of the other species, it is unusual in that its skin and feathers are toxic, as a result of the toxin-producing beetles it eats, an adaptation that ornithologists believe helps protect it against ectoparasites. The Piping Bellbird is larger than the Crested Bellbird, with brown upperparts and rufous underparts and a short, spiky crest. Its legs are shorter and stouter than the other members of this family, probably an adaptation to spending more time on the ground.

The Rufous-naped Bellbird, *Aleadryas rufinucha*, is the smallest of the three species, only the size of a House Sparrow, *Passer domesticus*. Before its true affinities were known, it used to be called the Rufous-naped Whistler, and was often placed in the main genus of the whistler family, *Pachycephala*. It is an attractively plumaged bird, with both sexes having a grey head, that contrasts with the russet nape, olive upperparts and white forehead, breast and belly. It forages mainly in the lower storey of the mountain forests it inhabits, creeping along branches or vertically up trunks, but also often visits the ground and occasionally higher up. Its song is a series of high whistling notes often alternating with upslurred ones, and can last for several minutes. Its main call is very different, being an unpleasant rasping hiss.

WHIPBIRDS AND WEDGEBILLS Psophodidae

GENERA: 2   **SPECIES:** 5

LENGTH: 16.5–30 cm (6.5–12 in)

WEIGHT: about 25–75 g (0.9–2.6 oz)

RANGE AND HABITAT: one species, the Papuan Whipbird, *Androphobus viridis*, in New Guinea, in mountain forest; the other four species in Australia, the Eastern Whipbird, *Psophodes olivaceus*, mainly in rainforest, wet eucalypt forest and scrub with dense undergrowth, the three other *Psophodes* species in drier habitats

SOCIAL BEHAVIOUR: known only in detail for Australian whipbirds, which are monogamous, defending territories year-round

NEST: details are unknown for the Papuan Whipbird; the other four species all build a cup-shaped nest of grass, twigs, and other plant material, among dense vegetation

EGGS: details are unknown for the Papuan Whipbird; in other species, 2–3, pale blue or blue-green with black markings

INCUBATION: details are unknown for the Papuan Whipbird; in other species, 14–21 days

FLEDGING PERIOD: details are unknown for the Papuan Whipbird; 10–12 days for other species

FOOD: mainly insects and other invertebrates; diet known in detail only for Eastern Whipbird, which also eats some seeds and fruit

VOICE: the Eastern Whipbird utters a very distinctive song, often in an antiphonal duet, with the female immediately responding with 'chew' notes to the male's whipcrack sound; the Western Whipbird also duets, the male's grating whistle followed by a similar phrase; the two wedgebill species have songs described by their common names (Chiming and Chirruping), with duetting reported only from the Chirruping Wedgebill

MIGRATION: probably all are sedentary

CONSERVATION STATUS: none threatened

ABOVE One of the most iconic sounds of the eastern Australian forests is the explosive whipcrack of male Eastern Whipbirds, *Psophodes olivaceus*, like this one.

This small family of birds from the Australo-Papuan region has been created recently to bring together five species that were previously included either with the jewel-babblers and quail thrushes in the Family Cinclosomatidae (p. 248) or along with an enigmatic species, the Malaysian Rail-babbler, *Eupetes macrocerus*, in the Family Eupetidae (p. 280), which now includes two African bird groups instead. The true relationships of the whipbirds and wedgebills are uncertain, but molecular analysis shows that they are not close to the two other families mentioned above. Their closest relatives may prove to be the vireos (Vireonidae, p. 255) and the painted berrypeckers (Paramythiidae, p. 254).

All five species have strong bills, short wings and a long tail, markedly graduated in all except the Papuan Whipbird (which also lacks the crest on the head of all the others), and strong, sturdy legs and feet suited to their largely terrestrial lifestyle. They forage for invertebrates mainly on the ground, turning over leaf-litter or soil with their strong, sturdy bills.

The three species of whipbirds, *Psophodes*, include two familiar Australian species and one very little-known species in New Guinea. Indeed, the Papuan Whipbird, *Androphobus viridis*, is one of the least known of all birds of that huge island, recorded from only seven sites on New Guinea, mainly in West Papua (administered by Indonesia). There have been few recent sightings, but it is an extremely secretive bird and unlikely to be noticed. Despite the lack of knowledge of its status, conservationists do not, at present anyway, think it is likely to be threatened, especially as the areas where the species is known to occur are on steep mountainsides inaccessible to loggers. At 16.5 cm (6.5 in) long, it is the smallest member of the family. The male is deep olive green, apart from black cheeks separated by a bold white stripe from its black chin, throat and breast. The female lacks the white stripe and the black is replaced by grey.

The Eastern Whipbird, *Psophodes olivaceus*, is by far the least shy and elusive member of the family and hence the best known species. It is widespread in densely vegetated forest understoreys in much of the extreme east of Australia. The male is strikingly patterned, with his black head sporting a prominent, large, triangular black crest, a broad white patch extending from the throat, a black breast and olive green upperparts and tail, the latter with white tips to the feathers. The female is duller, olive brown with only a ghost of the head pattern. It is justly renowned for the remarkable duets between pairs that create a loud and utterly distinctive song. With its ventriloquial quality and the instantaneous response from the female, it sounds as if it were produced by a single bird. The male starts with a few quiet notes, then comes a long whistle, which increases in intensity until it ends abruptly with a very loud sound just like the crack of a whip; this is instantly answered by the female with a quieter 'chew-chew' or 'chew-chew-chew' sound.

The Western Whipbird, *Psophodes nigrogularis*, is far less familiar than the Eastern Whipbird, having a far smaller total range, occurring as four subspecies in widely scattered areas of South Australia and far away in the southwest corner of the continent, and inhabiting dense vegetation, such as thickets of low eucalypt shrubs and tall spinifex grassland. It has a far more uniform plumage than its eastern counterpart, mainly greyish olive, with a much shorter crest, and a greatly reduced black and white pattern restricted to the throat; another difference is that the sexes are alike.

The genus name *Psophodes*, from the Greek word meaning 'noisy' is particularly apt in the case of the two whipbirds. As with its eastern relative, the song of the Western Whipbird is extremely loud, indeed in this species even more so, carrying up to twice as far – as much as 0.8 km (0.5 mile). The male's part in the duetting song is a series of grating whistles, sometimes likened to the sound of a creaking cartwheel; the female answers in seamless timing with a similar series of notes in a simpler pattern. Western Whipbirds have suffered declines as a result of habitat destruction and fires, and though not currently regarded as threatened overall, may be in the future.

The two species of wedgebill are even less familiar, being birds mainly of dense, low vegetation such as acacia and mallee scrub in the arid interior where few people live. This is especially true of the Chiming Wedgebill, *Psophodes occidentalis*, which is shyer and more skulking than the Chirruping Wedgebill, *P. cristatus*, which often perches on the top of a shrub and occurs in small groups as well as singly or in pairs. The two species look almost identical, both sexes being pale brown above and pale grey below with a small crest, but their loud songs differ. Both sexes of the Chiming Wedgebill utter a series of haunting, descending chiming notes (often described as 'did-you-get-drunk'), with no duetting. The Chirruping Wedgebill does duet, its song a monotonous series of sparrow-like chirrups, three notes from the male answered with one from his mate. Both species may begin singing early in the morning and continue until after dark.

PLOUGHBILL Eulacestomatidae

GENERA: 1   **SPECIES:** 1

LENGTH: 12.5–14 cm (5–5.5 in)

WEIGHT: 19–22 g (0.7–0.8 oz)

RANGE AND HABITAT: New Guinea; along the central mountain ranges, mainly at altitudes of 1,900–2,800 m (6,200–9,200 ft) in humid forests with dense undergrowth, especially with climbing bamboo thickets, as well as moss-covered and dead trees

SOCIAL BEHAVIOUR: assumed to be monogamous

NEST: no information

EGGS: no information

INCUBATION: no information

FLEDGING PERIOD: no information

FOOD: insects

VOICE: long, high-pitched whistling song

MIGRATION: sedentary

CONSERVATION STATUS: not threatened

ABOVE The Wattled Ploughbill, *Eulacestoma nigropectus*, hops about on mossy tree branches and bamboo thickets in its search for insect food.

The sole member of this family, the Wattled Ploughbill, *Eulacestoma nigropectus*, is endemic to New Guinea. The male is one of the strangest looking of all passerines, due to having a pair of large fleshy pink wattles sprouting from the base of his bill and extending onto the sides of his throat. These make him look as though he is permanently carrying a brightly coloured butterfly or two flower petals in his bill. He has mainly olive plumage, with golden highlights on the forehead, face and shoulders, black wings and a black patch on his breast. As well as lacking wattles, females are duller and paler below without the black breast patch.

Both common and generic names of this unusual little bird allude to the shape of its bill, which is short, deep and laterally compressed; *Eulacestoma* is from the Greek words for 'ploughshare mouth'. Its wedge shape and slight hook tip is reminiscent of the bills of the shrike-tits (Family Falcunculidae, p. 250); although the two groups have previously sometimes been united in a single enlarged Family Falcunculidae, or close together at the beginning of the whistler family (Pachycephalidae, p. 249) they are not now thought to be closely related. Indeed, it seems to belong to an ancient lineage, with no apparent surviving near-relatives.

Many details of the ploughbill's biology remain to be discovered; there is virtually no information about its breeding habits. It feeds actively, often joining other species in flocks to search for insects among the bamboo and trees, leaning over sideways or hanging upside-down if necessary to reach prey. It will pick insects directly from a branch or twig, but its big wedge of a bill comes into its own when it uses it like a chisel to strip off or chip away bark to reveal the insects hiding beneath. It often visits dead, dry branch tips for this purpose, and also digs into clumps of moss to find prey.

PAINTED BERRYPECKERS Paramythiidae

GENERA: 2　　**SPECIES:** 2

LENGTH: 12–22 cm (4.75–8.5 in)

WEIGHT: 16.5–61 g (0.6–2 oz)

RANGE AND HABITAT: New Guinea; montane forest

SOCIAL BEHAVIOUR: Tit Berrypeckers, *Oreocharis arfaki*, live in pairs or groups of up to 30 individuals; Crested Berrypeckers, *Paramythia montium*, live in pairs or flocks that may contain up to 75 birds; both are monogamous

NEST: cup-shaped in both species; that of the Tit Berrypecker is reportedly made of moss; that of the Crested Berrypecker is large for the bird's size and is mainly of moss or a mosslike liverwort interwoven with woody stems and lichens and lined with fine grass stems, rootlets and other vegetation

EGGS: known only for the Crested Berrypecker: 1, white to pale buff, finely spotted darker

INCUBATION: more than 12 days

FLEDGING PERIOD: unknown

FOOD: almost exclusively berries

VOICE: not well known; the Tit Berrypecker is very vocal, with shrill, wheezy calls; the Crested Berrypecker has short rasping, nasal, squeaking or harsher calls

MIGRATION: neither species makes long migrations, but may be locally nomadic

CONSERVATION STATUS: none threatened

ABOVE The Crested Berrypecker, *Paramythia montium*, raises its crest in excitement or alarm, as here; usually it lies flat on the crown.

ABOVE A male Tit Berrypecker, *Oreocharis arfaki*, reveals his striking head pattern and rich yellow underparts in the humid forest underrstorey of the New Guinea mountains.

This tiny family contains just two arboreal species endemic to mountain forests of New Guinea, separated from other, less closely related species only recently. Relationships with other families are uncertain. Features that unite them are long wirelike plumes on the flanks unique to the family, a similar bill structure, a vestigial tenth primary wing feather and an almost exclusive diet of berries. However, the two species are dissimilar in appearance.

The larger of the two, the Crested Berrypecker, *Paramythia montium*, looks rather like a bulbul (Family Pycnonotidae, p. 351), with a long black crest (although this is normally laid flat along the top of the head). Its plumage is a beautiful combination of blue or blue -grey body and tail, olive-green wings and golden-yellow flanks and undertail, contrasting with the black-and-white head and black bib. The sexes are similar. The Tit Berrypecker, *Oreocharis arfaki*, is just under two-thirds of the length of its close relative, and only about a third of its weight. It does bear a superficial resemblance to the unrelated tits (Family Paridae, p. 335): it is a similar size to many of them, and the male has a similar plumage pattern to that very common Eurasian species, the Great Tit, *Parus major*, accounting for the origin of the common name. The female Tit Berrypecker is much duller, lacking the male's bold black and egg-yellow head pattern and all-yellow underparts.

When the Crested Berrypecker was first described in 1892, it was placed in the starling family (Sturnidae, p. 381) but was soon given a family of its own (Paramythiidae), where it remained for 30 years until being reclassified with the flowerpeckers in the Family Dicaeidae. More recently, its relationship to the Tit Berrypecker was recognised, and both were included in the larger group of New Guinea birds called berrypeckers (Melanocharitidae, p. 241). Recent DNA studies concluded that the two should be separated in the resurrected Paramythiidae.

VIREOS Vireonidae

GENERA: 6   **SPECIES**: 62

LENGTH: 10–20 cm (4–8 in)

WEIGHT: 9–48 g (0.3–1.7 oz)

RANGE AND HABITAT: almost entirely New World, in North America, Caribbean, Central America and South America, with just ten Asian species; most in forests and woodlands; some (especially greenlets) in scrub; a few in mangroves

SOCIAL BEHAVIOUR: mostly in pairs or family groups, and breed in monogamous pairs that defend a territory

NEST: small, usually hanging, cup-shaped, of grass, leaves, twigs, rootlets, bark and lichens in the fork of a tree or tall shrub

EGGS: 2–5, whitish with brown spots

INCUBATION: 11–13 days

FLEDGING PERIOD: 11–13 days

FOOD: mainly insects as well as some spiders and other invertebrates during the breeding season in many species; migratory species before departure and in their winter range eat much fruit, and some tropical species do so all year round; the young are fed mainly on insects

VOICE: very wide variety of calls, including whistling, rasping or harsh nasal sounds; songs mainly simple, repetitive, made up of whistled, slurred or chattering notes, warbling in peppershrikes

MIGRATION: many North American and temperate zone southern South American species are migratory; most subtropical and tropical ones are sedentary

CONSERVATION STATUS: one species, the Choco Vireo, *Vireo masteri*, is Endangered; two species, the Black-capped Vireo, *V. atricapilla*, and the San Andres Vireo, *V. caribaeus*, are Vulnerable; five species are Near Threatened

ABOVE The White-eyed Vireo, *Vireo griseus*, seen here in the Florida Everglades, is widespread in the eastern half of the USA.

Formerly believed to be close relatives of the New World wood-warblers (Family Parulidae) in the great Emberizoid subgroup of the passerines, DNA studies have shown that the vireos are instead members of the Corvidan subgroup, along with the whistlers, orioles, bush-shrikes and various other Old World families. Most vireos look rather like wood-warblers, except for their stronger, generally slightly hook-tipped bill.

Although almost all the members of the family are found only in the Americas, recent molecular evidence has shown that several species formerly included in the Old World family of babblers (Timaliidae, p. 362) are, as here, actually best grouped within the vireo family. This has helped resolve the apparent anomaly of what was previously considered an exclusively New World family being part of the same radiation as Old World families. These new members appear to be basal members of the family, so they are placed first in the sequence. They comprise two genera: *Pteruthius*, with nine species, and Erpornis, with a single species. All of them are Asian, as a group ranging from northeast Pakistan and India across the Himalyan region to China and Southeast Asia. The *Pteruthius* species were known as shrike-babblers when included in the Timaliidae, though they are neither shrikes nor babblers. At present,

they retain this common group name. All have boldly patterned, multicolored plumage in various combinations of black, grey, olive green, chestnut, yellow and white, with marked sexual dimorphism in the five larger species, their females being duller. Three of the four much smaller species, like many vireos and shrike-vireos, have double black-and-white wingbars in males, buff-and-white in females. The single species of Erpornis, *Epornis zantholeuca*, formerly known as the White-bellied Yuhina when it was considered to belong to the babbler genus *Yuhina*, looks more like one of the *Vireo* species with its thinner bill, green head, upperparts and tail and grey underparts, apart from having a crest, a unique feature in the family.

Two genera, those of the peppershrikes and shrike-vireos, are heavy, thickset and big-headed birds that include some of the largest members of the family. They have a heavy bill with a distinct hook, accounting for the shrike part of their name. Their plumage is more colourful with a more complex pattern than that of their smaller relatives the vireos and greenlets. They are found in southern Mexico, Central America and South America; none occur in North America. There are two species of peppershrikes, *Cyclarhis*, with green upperparts, grey or yellow underparts and a chestnut red stripe above each eye. One, the Rufous-browed Peppershrike, *C. gujanensis*, has 22 races occupying a huge range from Mexico to northern Argentina, while the other, the Black-billed Peppershrike, *C. nigrirostris*, is restricted to a small area on the extreme northern slopes of the Andes. The four species of shrike vireos, *Vireolanius*, have less massive but more strongly hooked bills than the peppershrikes. Two species are especially brilliantly coloured, the Green Shrike Vireo, *Vireolanus pulchellus*, of Mexico and Central America, and the Yellow-browed Shrike Vireo, *V. eximius*, of the eastern Darien of Panama and the extreme northwest of South America, which have an intensely emerald green body, with deep sky blue on the crown or nape, and a lemon yellow throat or eyestripe.

The largest genus by far is that of the 'true vireos', *Vireo*, with 31 species. The identical common and generic names are from the Latin word meaning 'I am green', and indeed many of these little birds have olive green upperparts. Some are brown or grey above, and most are yellow or white below. Their plumage pattern camouflages them well among the foliage of trees and shrubs where they spend most of their lives. Many species have pale wingbars and whitish or yellowish eye-rings or 'spectacles'. Others lack wingbars but have eye-stripes, as with a common and widespread North American species, the Red-eyed Vireo, *V. olivaceus*, with its bold, black-margined ones. Most Vireo species live in Mexico, Central America and South America; 13 are North American, though all but one of these are migrants that winter in Mexico, Central America, the Caribbean and northern South America. Although insects and other invertebrates form the bulk of their diet, many of them eat a lot of berries and other fruit in autumn as they prepare to migrate and also in their winter quarters. As with many migratory New World warblers – and Old World warblers too – they do so because the easily digested carbohydrates in this food become converted to fat, which fuels their long journeys. Before they fly, they cram in as much fruit as possible, increasing their body weight by 50% or more to produce a sufficient store of fat. Several of the North American species are seriously declining due to habitat loss and also to brood parasitism by cowbirds, *Molothrus* (see Family Icteridae, p. 321). They include the Black-capped Vireo, *V. atricapilla*, which is classed as Vulnerable, and the Near Threatened Bell's Vireo, *V. bellii*.

The greenlets, *Hylophilus*, are a group of 15 very similar looking Neotropical species that are generally smaller and far more active when foraging than *Vireo* species. Most have plainer green and yellow plumage, lacking wing-bars, and slimmer, more pointed bills that are only slightly hooked at the tip.

Although their songs are neither elaborate nor outstandingly beautiful, some have pleasant warbling songs that they utter constantly throughout the day. The Red-eyed Vireos and Bell's Vireos, *V. bellii*, are the most persistent singers of all North American songbirds. The former species holds the world record, established in 1952, when an individual was heard to sing 22,197 songs on a single May day.

ORIOLES, FIGBIRDS AND RELATIVES Oriolidae

GENERA: 4   **SPECIES:** 35

LENGTH: 17.5–32 cm (7–12.5 in)

WEIGHT: 30–145 g (1–5 oz)

RANGE AND HABITAT: Europe (one species, the Golden Oriole, *Oriolus oriolus*), Africa, Asia, New Guinea, Australia (and two extinct species in New Zealand), with main diversity in Indonesia and New Guinea; woodlands, including mangroves, and forests; some species also in orchards, parks and gardens

SOCIAL BEHAVIOUR: mainly solitary or in pairs and family groups, monogamous, orioles defending nesting territories and figbirds breeding in loose colonies; the Hooded Pitohui, *Pitohui*, may be a cooperative breeder

NEST: oriole nests are typically woven cups of grass, bark strips, moss and lichens, suspended by the rim like a hammock from a forked tree branch; those of figbirds are similarly sited but flimsy and shallow, being constructed mainly from twigs; Hooded Pitohui is also suspended but made of vine tendrils; South Island Piopio built small, neat cup-shaped nests on a tree fork

EGGS: orioles, 1–6, whitish or cream, with darker spots and streaks; figbirds, 2–4, greyish-green to olive with darker markings; Hooded Pitohui, cream or pinkish-grey with darker markings; South Island Piopio, 1–2, white or pinkish-white eggs with dark blotches

INCUBATION: orioles and figbirds, 13–20 days; unknown for others

FLEDGING PERIOD: orioles and figbirds, 13–20 days; unknown for others

FOOD: orioles eat mainly insects for much of the year, but also much fruit in late summer and autumn, and some also eat nectar and pollen; figbirds feed mainly on figs and other fruit; pitohuis, mainly fruit, also insects; piopios, insects, spiders, worms, fruit and seeds

VOICE: most orioles have attractive, flutelike or whistling calls and songs; Indonesian and Australian species include bubbling or rolling sounds; other calls are harsh or like cats' miaows; figbirds have far less melodious songs of repeated phrases of two or three descending notes, and yelping or trilling calls; some orioles and figbirds are good mimics of other bird sounds; pitohuis have songs of rich, upslurred and downslurred whistling notes; piopios had melodious songs

MIGRATION: most orioles, all three figbirds, pitohuis and piopios are sedentary; the Golden Oriole of Eurasia migrates to central and southern Africa and the Black-naped Oriole, *O. chinensis*, of eastern Asia winters westwards as far as western India

CONSERVATION STATUS: two species, the North Island Piopio, *Turnagra capensis*, and South Island Piopio, *T. tanagra*, are Extinct; one species, the Isabela Oriole, *Oriolus isabellae*, is Critically Endangered; one species, the Silver Oriole, *O. mellianus*, is Endangered; one species, the São Tomé Oriole, *O. crassirostris*, is Vulnerable; and two species are Near Threatened

The males of many species of this Old World family of medium-sized songbirds are very colourful (the name 'oriole' may be derived from the Latin word *aureolus* for 'golden', although it perhaps also represents an onomatopoeic approximation of the birds' best known calls). Old World orioles are unrelated to the birds of the same name in the American blackbird or icterid family (Icteridae).

The family is divided into subfamilies. By far the largest is the Oriolinae, containing the 28 species of oriole, *Oriolus*. Orioles have a rather slender body and sturdy, strong, slightly hooked bill. Male European, African and Asian orioles are mostly brilliant golden yellow with black wings and tail; some have a black 'bandit mask' or completely black head. Females and immatures are duller by comparison, mostly greenish yellow with streaked underparts. In some Asian species, the areas of yellow are replaced by equally brilliant crimson, or by maroon or by silvery-white and maroon while two Indonesian species are mainly black. Again, females are duller. Australasian oriole species are much duller, clad mainly in brownish, olive and grey, in some species with dark-streaked pale underparts; in these there is little difference between the sexes.

In five New Guinea and Indonesian oriole species, each mimic the species of friarbird, *Philemon* (in the unrelated honeyeater family (Meliphagidae, p. 235) with which it shares its range and habitat. The resemblance is amazingly close, not only in plumage but also in posture, flight and other movements and, in one

LEFT As well as being one of the most beautiful of all European birds, the male Eurasian Golden Oriole, *Oriolus oriolus*, has a lovely liquid fluting song.

RIGHT The restless, noisy Australasian Figbird, *Sphecotheres vieilloti*, relishes not only figs but also many other fruits, including bananas.

BELOW One of the world's few toxic birds, this is the Hooded Pitohui, *Pitohui dichrous*, from the hill forests of New Guinea.

(possibly two) species, vocalisation. This appears to help the orioles avoid attack from the larger, more aggressive friarbirds. Remarkably, one species, the Brown Oriole, *O. szalayi*, of New Guinea, is itself mimicked by a far smaller honeyeater, the Streak-headed Honeyeater, *Pycnopygius stictocephalus*.

Despite their often brilliant plumage, orioles are generally hard to see, remaining high in the trees, where the bright colours meld into the background of sun-dappled foliage. They are often first detected by their beautiful, far-carrying, flutey calls and songs.

The subfamily Sphecotherinae contains the three species of figbirds, *Sphecotheres*. Their name reflects their fondness for eating figs, although they also eat a wide range of other fruit, including cherries, bananas, and guavas, as well as some seeds and insects (and the *Oriolus* species also include figs in their diet). All three figbird species, two restricted to the Lesser Sunda island group in eastern Indonesia and one in northern and eastern Australia, have a shorter bill than orioles. The males have black heads with distinctive, prominent patches of red bare skin around the eyes, bright olive green upperparts and mainly yellowish or white underparts, while females are much duller, browner above and whitish with extensive dark streaks below, and only small areas of blue-grey skin around the eyes.

Until recently, the last two subfamilies have both been highly enigmatic groups with uncertain affinities. The subfamily Pitohuinae, endemic to New Guinea, contains just two species of pitohuis, *Pitohui*. These were until recently included together with four other *Pitohui* species in the whistler Family Pachycephalidae (p. 249); three of these remain there, and the other one has now been moved to the Australo-Papuan bellbird Family Oreoicidae, (p. 251). Pitohuis are remarkable for having evolved the ability to store very potent batrachotoxins in their feathers and skin as a probably defence against bacteria and ectoparasites, with the highest levels being found in the two species in this family,

the Variable Pitohui, *P. kirhocephalus* and the Hooded Pitohui, *P. dichrous*. Both have a short, slightly hooked bill. The Hooded Pitohui is strikingly plumaged, with a black hood, wings and tail, contrasting with a bright reddish-chestnut body, while the 18 races of the Variable Pitohui live up the species' common name, in having various permutations of black, grey or brown above, with different shades of rufous or orange buff below.

The final species of puzzling origin were the two extinct New Zealand birds called piopios, *Turnagra*, in the subfamily Turnagrinae. Until recently regarded as races of a single species, one species occurred on North Island and the other on South Island and the offshore Stewart Island. Over the years, the piopios have been classified in no fewer than six different families of passerines, including the bowerbirds (Ptilonorhynchidae, p. 231) and whistlers (Pachycephalidae, p. 249), but molecular research now indicates they are members of the oriole family. The size of a very large thrush, these thick-billed, long-legged birds were mainly dark olive-brown above, streaked brown and cream below in the North Island species, and plain grey below in the South Island species. This was renowned as one of New Zealand's finest songsters, while the Maori name 'piopio' comes from the usual call of the little-known North Island species. Both became progressively scarcer in the years following the European settlement of the islands due to the logging of their forest habitat and the depredations of rats and other introduced predators, and the last confirmed sightings were in the early 1900s.

The relationships of the Oriolidae to other passerines is clouded in uncertainty, but their closest relatives may be the whistlers, vireos, whipbirds or painted berrypeckers.

FALSE WHISTLER Rhagologidae

GENERA: 1   **SPECIES:** 1

LENGTH: 15–16.5 cm (6–6.5 in)

WEIGHT: 24–30 g (0.8–1.0 oz)

RANGE AND HABITAT: New Guinea; montane forest on lower and middle slopes of the Central Ranges and the mountains in the Vogelkop (northwest) and Huon (southeast) peninsulas, chiefly at altitudes of 1500–2300 m (4900–7500 ft)

SOCIAL BEHAVIOUR: unknown

NEST: cup woven from rootlets and tendrils, camouflaged on the outside with liverworts and mosses, low down in small branches of tree

EGGS: 1

INCUBATION: no information

FLEDGING PERIOD: no information

FOOD: probably mainly berries and other fruit, with some insects

VOICE: loud series of whistling notes

MIGRATION: presumably sedentary

CONSERVATION STATUS: not threatened

Until recently, this elusive and little-known New Guinea bird was included in the whistler Family Pachycephalidae and was – and often still is – known as the Mottled Whistler. However, recent molecular research has shown that it is only distantly related to the whistlers, and should, as here, be given a family of its own. Recent molecular studies suggest that its closest relatives may be the wood-swallows (Artamidae), ioras (Aegithinidae) or perhaps the boatbills (Macheirirhynchidae). In view of its true relationships, False Whistler is now a more appropriate name than Mottled Whistler. Over the years, some systematists have included this enigmatic species in the major whistler genus *Pachycephala*, while others have recognised its distinctiveness by transferring it to the monotypic genus *Rhagologus*. Here it now resides, with the scientific name of *Rhagologus leucostigma*.

This is a shy bird, not often seen; most encounters are with birds trapped in mist-nets by researchers studying New Guinea montane forest birds. It prefers primary forest, but also lives in secondary forest.

It is sexually dimorphic, the male drab grey, paler below with mottling on the face and the female rather more colourful, being browner above with a rust-coloured cheek patch and heavy dark streaking and scalloping on the pale underparts.

BOATBILLS Machaerirhynchidae

GENERA: 1   **SPECIES:** 2

LENGTH: 11–15 cm (4–6 in)

WEIGHT: 9–12.5 g (0.3–0.4 oz)

RANGE AND HABITAT: 1 species restricted to New Guinea, 1 in New Guinea and northeast Australia; mainly in dense forest

SOCIAL BEHAVIOUR: usually seen in pairs or small groups; sometimes feed in mixed-species flocks

NEST: very fragile basket or saucer of plant fibres, rootlets or vine tendrils bound together with spiders' webs, up to 20 m (65 ft) high in a tree, suspended hammock-style between a narrow horizontal fork among leaves

EGGS: 2–3, white, with reddish or purple spots (known for Yellow-breasted Boatbill only)

INCUBATION: 14 days or more, (Yellow-breasted Boatbill)

FLEDGING PERIOD: unknown

FOOD: insects, caught mainly in a brief flight from a perch, either in mid-air or snatched from foliage, or gleaned from branches or vegetation

VOICE: song of soft whistles, sweet warbling and trills; short, harsh or buzzing calls

MIGRATION: mainly sedentary; Yellow-breasted Boatbill makes local movements to more open woodland after breeding

CONSERVATION STATUS: not threatened

ABOVE The Yellow-breasted Boatbill, *Machaerirhynchus flaviventer*, is more numerous in reserves and other protected areas in extreme north-east Australia than in its far wider range in New Guniea.

The two species in this family of small, lively, boldly plumaged birds earn both their common name and their genus name (from the Greek words meaning 'dagger-bill') from the sturdy, remarkably flattened, black bill, whose upper mandible has a slightly hooked tip. They have a habit of cocking their longish, narrow tail. The Black-breasted Boatbill, *Machaerirhynchus nigripectus*, is endemic to New Guinea, where it is found in montane and submontane forest and forest edge and sometimes visits gardens. The Yellow-breasted Boatbill, *M. flaviventer*, by contrast, is mainly a lowland rainforest species throughout its range. It is widespread in New Guinea, but in Australia is restricted to the far northeast of Queensland. Both species have dark upperparts, dark olive in the

Black-breasted Boatbill and black in the Yellow-breasted Boatbill, with white wing-bars, and yellow underparts, adorned by a black breast patch in the species named for that feature, which is larger in the male.

The boatbills were formerly thought to be unusual members of the monarch flycatcher Family Monarchidae, but recent molecular research indicates that they do not belong there and are best placed in a family of their own since their affinities with other birds are uncertain.

They may prove to be closest to the False Whistler in the immediately preceding Family Rhagologidae, or perhaps to the woodswallows and butcherbirds in the Family Artamidae, or the ioras (Aegithinidae). However, the birds they resemble most closely, in both morphology and behaviour, are the unrelated New World tody-flycatchers, *Todirostrum*, in the sub-oscine Family Pipromorphidae, the flatbills, which have very similar plumage and long, jauntily cocked tail – a remarkable example of convergent evolution.

WOODSWALLOWS, AUSTRALIAN MAGPIES AND RELATIVES Artamidae

GENERA: 6   **SPECIES:** 24

LENGTH: peltops, 18–20 cm (7–8 in); Australian Magpie, *Gymnorhina tibicen*, 37–43 cm (14.5–17 in); butcherbirds and currawongs, 25–57 cm (10–22 in); woodswallows, 12–21 cm (5–8 in)

WEIGHT: peltops, 27–36 g (1–1.3 oz); Australian Magpie, 210–360 g (7.4–12.7 oz); butcherbirds and currawongs, 68–500 g (2.4–18 oz); woodswallows, 13–69 g (0.5–2.4 oz)

RANGE AND HABITAT: peltops in New Guinea, in rainforest, one species in lowlands, other on mountains; Australian Magpie, butcherbirds and currawongs, seven species in Australia, two in New Guinea and adjacent islands and one in both New Guinea and northern Australia, in rainforests, mangroves, eucalypt forest, savannah, with some also in parks and gardens in towns and cities; woodswallows in south and southeast Asia, Australasia, southwest Pacific islands, in open forest and woodland, savannah, grassland and semi-desert scrub

SOCIAL BEHAVIOUR: peltops are territorial but little is known about their breeding and other behaviour; the others are monogamous and territorial, and many are cooperative breeders; woodswallows are highly gregarious at rest or in roosts

NEST: untidy flat cup or bowl of twigs and sticks, lined with grass, rootlets and other plant material, sometimes with artificial materials, in peltops much smaller and neater; generally sited in the fork of a tree

EGGS: peltops, one species, yellowish white with dark brown spots, clutch size unknown; Australian Magpie, butcherbirds and currawongs, 2–4, colour ranges from cream, grey, buff and brown to green and blue, with reddish, brown or purple markings; woodswallows, 2–4, cream with grey or rufous spots

INCUBATION: peltops, unknown; Australian Magpie, butcherbirds and currawongs, 19–23 days; woodswallows, 12–17 days

FLEDGING PERIOD: peltops, unknown; Australian Magpie, butcherbirds and currawongs, 19–33 days; woodswallows, 13–20 days

FOOD: peltops, insects; Australian Magpie, butcherbirds and currawongs, a wide range of animals, from insects, spiders and earthworms to small vertebrates, including lizards and birds, their eggs and chicks, also some seeds and (especially currawongs) fruit, and (butcherbirds) occasionally nectar; woodswallows, insects and occasionally nectar

VOICE: peltops, various twittering and clicking sounds and hoarse, upslurred whistles; Australian Magpie and butcherbirds, beautiful songs include liquid warbling and flute-like notes; currawongs, song and calls include loud, ringing 'curra-wong' phrases and variations, wailing sonds and harsh croaks and screams; woodswallows, loud chirping calls, uttered ceaselessly from perched groups; songs more melodious twittering or jumble of chirps, squawks and trills interspersed with mimicry of other birds

MIGRATION: peltops, Australian Magpie and butcherbirds, sedentary; some Pied Currawongs, *Strepera graculina*, and Black Currawongs, *S. fuliginosa*, make altitudinal migrations; all Australian woodswallows migratory or nomadic, others sedentary

CONSERVATION STATUS: none presently endangered, though one species, the Tagula Butcherbird, *Cracticus louisiadensis*, endemic to the Louisiade Islands, off Papua New Guinea, may become so, being threatened by logging and climate change as well as hunting

The three seemingly diverse groups of birds in this family were previously separated in two families, the highly aerial woodswallows in the Family Artamidae, the mainly much larger, more terrestrial Australian Magpie, butcherbirds and currawongs in the Family Cracticidae, and the two peltops species in the monarch-flycatcher Family Monarchidae. Recent molecular studies have shown that all of them are sufficiently closely related to be included within a single Family Artamidae, with the different groups forming three subfamilies: the woodswallows in the Artaminae, the Australian Magpie, butcherbirds and currawongs in the Cracticinae, and the peltops in the Peltopsinae. Almost two-thirds of all species occur in Australia, including six of the 11 woodswallow species, eight of the 10 butcherbirds and currawongs, and the Australian Magpie (which also occurs in New Guinea); 11 of these, including all three currawongs, are exclusively Australian.

ABOVE Woodswallows, like this Black-faced Woodswallow, *Artamus cinereus*, are the only songbirds whose plumage includes powder down.

ABOVE The fluting song of the Pied Butcherbird, *Cracticus nigrogularis*, often heard at night, is one of the finest of all birds.

ABOVE The Pied Currawong, *Strepera graculina*, is distinguished from the other two currawong species by its white wing patches.

The 11 species of woodswallows, all in the genus *Artamus*, are stocky-bodied, large-headed sparrow-sized to thrush-sized birds that are unrelated to the true swallows (Family Hirundinidae) but rival the latter in their superb aerial skills and also feed on aerial insects. They often hunt high up, with a circling or back-and-forth flight, and make graceful gliding swoops and spirals, and (unusually for songbirds) they can soar high on air currents. They also visit flowering trees and bushes to lap up nectar with their brush-tipped tongue and snap up insects attracted to the flowers. During windy weather, they will feed on the ground, chasing after large beetles, cockroaches, termites, ants and other insects.

They have a much longer, stronger bill than the stub-billed hirundine swallows, slightly downcurved but with a similarly wide gape for trapping fast-flying insects.

Woodswallows were once thought to be members of the shrike (or 'butcherbird') family (Laniidae), when they were called 'swallow-shrikes' (the scientific name comes from the Greek word *artamos*, for 'butcher' or 'murderer') although they are unrelated and do not impale prey. Their wings are long, and broad, tapering to a pointed tip so that they appear almost triangular when the birds are viewed from above or below in flight. The tail is short and slightly forked, and they have short legs and feet. The plumage is in various permutations of black, grey, brown, buff and white, often with just two of these colours in combination. In one species, the White-browed Woodswallow, *Artamus superciliosus*, the male is distinguished from the paler and duller female by the far more intense rich chestnut colour of his underparts, from breast to undertail coverts, and the whiter eyebrow contrasting with his darker grey upperparts. The female Masked Woodswallow, *A. personatus*, too is drabber than the male; in all other species, the sexes look alike.

Although they generally feed alone, these birds are extremely social when resting and roosting, forming flocks of up to 100 or more individuals, sometimes of two or more species. When resting adjacent birds in the large flocks frequently preen one another as they perch on treetop branches or overhead wires. When roosting they huddle tightly together in trees, on branches, in hollows or clinging to the trunk. They breed in pairs or in small groups defending territory fiercely against formidable predatory birds such as butcherbirds, kookaburras and raptors. Although they usually build their nests in a tree or a shrub, they sometimes site them on telephone poles, electricity pylons, fence-posts or other artificial structures.

The second subfamily, Cracticinae, comprises seven species of butcherbird, one in the genus *Melloria* and six in the genus *Cracticus*, a single species, the Australian Magpie in the genus *Gymnorhina* and three species of currawongs in the genus *Strepera*

Like shrikes (Family Laniidae), for which an old English folk name was 'butcherbirds', the unrelated Australasian birds of that name – as well as currawongs – often impale their insect or small vertebrate prey on thorns or spikes such as those of barbed wire or wedge them in a crevice in a tree-trunk, fence post or other site. They then dismember it while it is firmly held, rather than clamping it beneath the feet like most other predatory birds. Currawongs and the Australian Magpie, *Gymnorhina tibicen*, in particular, often cache surplus food to return to later, concealing it by poking it into a grass clump or other suitable hiding place. Butcherbirds and currawongs have a large, powerful, tapering bill that ends in a slight hook and is bluish-white with a black tip in the Australian Magpie and butcherbirds, dark grey in the currawongs. Butcherbirds have the most massive and powerful bills, suited to seizing and dismembering larger prey, while the Australian

Magpie's bill is relatively shorter and stouter with only a slight hook, and is used mainly for digging and probing in the ground or tearing at bark to find insects; the currawongs have longer, slimmer bills without a hook, and a more omnivorous diet, including lots of fruit and seeds, but also invertebrates and small vertebrates – they are particularly partial to snatching small or young from nests, especially to feed to their own nestlings. The butcherbirds and currawongs spend more time in trees, the former typically flying down to the ground to seize prey, while the currawongs find much of the food in trees or shrubs. The Australian Magpie is the most terrestrial forager, adapted for this lifestyle with relatively longer legs and a shorter tail than the others.

Butcherbirds have plumage that is all black, black, grey and white, or black-and-white. Currawongs are either grey-and-white, black-and-white or brown-and-white. Several species have eyes with brightly coloured irides that stand out dramatically against the black plumage of their head: in the Australian Magpie the iris is red, whereas in all three currawongs it is yellow. All of them have short, broad wings. Currawongs have an undulating flight action, with deep wingbeats alternating with swoops, while butcherbirds and the Australian Magpie fly fast, direct and level.

The Australian species are familiar and well known, as they have adapted well to living with humans in suburbs and farmland, and can become very tame when fed. They relish a wide range of food at feeders, including meat, and are also quick to seize waste food at picnic sites, parks and elsewhere. They are some of the most beautiful of all bird sounds to be heard in Australia. Both sexes sing their varied and complex songs throughout the year. Those of the butcherbirds and Australian Magpies are often long-lasting, including duets and antiphonal singing by the butcherbirds and group performances by Australian Magpies, known as 'carolling'.

But although they are justly appreciated for their beautiful songs, they are not for their depredations on nestling songbirds – or their aggression towards other birds, as well as dogs, horses and humans, in the vicinity of their nest. This has led to serious conflict in urban areas as some male Australian Magpies, as well as butcherbirds, are prone to swooping down and pecking people walking or cycling near their nesting sites, sometimes causing serious eye injuries or other damage when a person falls off their bike. They are also disliked by farmers when they devour fruit and cereals, but on the other hand appreciated as efficient predators of pest insects such as locusts.

The final subfamily, Peltopinae, endemic to New Guinea, contains just the two species of peltops in the genus *Peltops*. These are far smaller birds that were until recently classified with the monarch-flycatchers in the Family Monarchidae, but are now known to be an early offshoot of this family. They have mainly black plumage with contrasting patches of white on the head and brilliant red on the rump and undertail. Their bill is short but strong and hook-tipped, as with the rest of the family. They feed in a very different way, though, flying out from a perch and snatching insects in flight, like flycatchers.

ABOVE The boldly pied Australian Magpie, *Gymnorhina tibicen*, is one of the most familiar and widespread of all Australian birds.

BATISES AND WATTLE-EYES Platysteiridae

GENERA: 4   **SPECIES:** 29

LENGTH: 8–16 cm (3–6 in)

WEIGHT: 5–35 g (0.2–1.2 oz)

RANGE AND HABITAT: Sub-Saharan Africa; forests, woodlands, savannahs, acacia thickets, mangroves

SOCIAL BEHAVIOUR: sometimes solitary but usually in pairs or (outside the breeding season) mixed species foraging flocks; monogamous and territorial; helpers at the nest in some species

NEST: small, neat open cup of stems and rootlets, incorporating moss, lichens, fungi and bark, all bound together and to the supporting branch or fork by spiders' webs; in tree or shrub, usually quite exposed, often at considerable height

EGGS: 1–3 whitish, pale bluish or greenish, heavily spotted brown

INCUBATION: 17–19 days

FLEDGING PERIOD: 21–23 days

FOOD: mainly flying insects, often small flies and mosquitoes, but also including larger and tougher insects such as grasshoppers, mantises, butterflies, wasps, bees, ants, cockroaches and beetles; also other invertebrates, such as spiders, scorpions and millipedes

VOICE: very vocal, uttering whistling, piping, trilling, churring, rasping and buzzing calls; songs with similar components included duetting between pairs; also bill-snapping noises and odd whirring, clicking or snapping noises made by wing feathers, called 'fripping'

MIGRATION: most are sedentary, but some make local or altitudinal migrations, mainly related to temperature or drought

CONSERVATION STATUS: one species, the Banded Wattle-eye, *Platysteira laticincta*, is Endangered; one species, the White-fronted Wattle-eye, *Platysteira albifrons*, is Near Threatened

LEFT Only the female Black-throated Wattle-eye, *Platysteira peltata*, has a black throat; the male merely has a narrow black breast band.

The small flycatcher-like birds in this African family were once lumped together with various groups of Old World flycatchers, but today they are generally accorded a family of their own. They are closely related to the vangas (which were completely, and still are mostly, endemic to Madagascar), and have sometimes been included in the same family, Vangidae. In the scheme followed here, the two species of shrike-flycatchers, in the genera *Megabyas* and *Bias* from Africa have been moved from this family to the next family, the Vangidae, as has an enigmatic Madagascan species, *Pseudobias wardi*. As well as this close relationship with the Vangidae, the wattle-eyes and batises may be close to the Bristlehead (Pityriasidae), ioras (Aegithinidae) and bush-shrikes (Malaconotidae).

Most members of the family have a plump body and a relatively big, broad, rounded head, with a broad, slightly hooked bill that is flattened from top to bottom and fringed at its base by stiff bristles. As with flycatchers and other groups that catch flying insects, these probably protect the eyes from being damaged as the bird snaps its bill onto a hard-bodied grasshopper, dragonfly or other insect in mid-air. They may also help the bird sense the movements of the prey when in the bill.

The 18 species of batises are an especially homogeneous group regarding general appearance and behaviour, and all are placed in the genus *Batis*. They are small or tiny: the Pygmy Batis, *Batis perkeo*, is one of the smallest African birds at just 8–9 cm (3–3.5 in) long and weighing only 5–9 g (0.2–0.3 oz). Batises have boldly patterned black, grey, white and often also brown, rufous or orange-fawn plumage. As well as differences between males and females, there is great individual variation, sometimes as much within a species as between species.

There are 10 species of wattle-eyes, split into two genera. All have prominent, fleshy eye-rings. The six *Dyaphorophyia* species are tiny, almost tailless birds; in one species and one subspecies of a second species the underparts are mainly or partly yellow. The plumage of the other members of the genus is in various permutations of black, grey, chestnut and white. Their eye-wattles are pale blue, greenish or pinkish according to species. The White-spotted Wattle-eye *D. tonsa*, has purplish eye-wattles that extend above the eyes like little horns. The four species in the genus *Platysteira* are bigger, with black-and-white or grey-and-white plumage, and red eye-wattles.

VANGAS, HELMET SHRIKES AND RELATIVES Vangidae

GENERA: 21   **SPECIES:** 36

LENGTH: vangas, 13–32 cm (5–12.5 in); helmet-shrikes, 16–26 cm (6–10 in); others, 14–23 cm (5.5–9 in)

WEIGHT: 14–119 g (0.5–4 oz); helmet-shrikes, 20–63 g (0.7–2.2 oz); others, 8.5–46 g (0.3–1.6 oz)

RANGE AND HABITAT: vangas endemic to Madagascar (one species also extending to the Comoro Islands); rainforests, deciduous forests, arid thorn scrub and spiny forests; some also in euphorbia scrublands and plantations; helmet-shrikes, sub-Saharan Africa, in forests, woodlands and savannah; other species in Africa and Asia, in forests, woodlands and scrub

SOCIAL BEHAVIOUR: vangas usually live in groups, often in mixed feeding flocks with other species of vangas and sometimes also other birds; in species studied, monogamous, with cooperative breeding known in the Rufous Vanga, *Schetba rufa*, and several other species; helmet-shrikes are also highly sociable, monogamous, territorial and breed cooperatively; the other species live in monogamous, territorial pairs or small flocks

NEST: almost the entire family build cup- or bowl-shaped nests in the fork of a tree branch, or suspended from a branch tip, made of twigs, roots, moss and other plant material, in some cases bound with spiders' webs; the Sickle-billed Vanga, *Falculea palliata*, is unusual, with its large and untidy stick and twig nest, and the Nuthatch Vanga, *Hypositta corallirostris*, makes a nest mainly of moss inside a tree hollow

EGGS: vangas, 2–4, white to pinkish or bluish-green, with darker markings; helmet-shrikes and shrike-flycatchers, 1–3, pale bluish, greenish or whitish, with brown, reddish, black, grey or purple markings; no information for others

INCUBATION: vangas, 16–19 days; 22–24 days in the Hook-billed Vanga, *Vanga curvirostris*; helmet-shrikes and shrike-flycatchers, 15–19 days; no information for others

FLEDGING PERIOD: vangas, 15–19 days; 20–22 days in the Hook-billed Vanga, and 19–24 days in the Sickle-billed Vanga and White-headed Vanga, *Artamella viridis*; helmet-shrikes and shrike-flycatchers, 15–19 days; no information for others

FOOD: vangas eat mainly insects, such as beetles, cockroaches, crickets and caterpillars, and other invertebrates, including spiders, worms and snails; most also eat small vertebrates, especially small geckos and chameleons; the Hook-billed Vanga includes small frogs, small birds, birds' eggs and young mouse-lemurs in its diet; others eat mainly insects, with a little fruit in some

VOICE: vangas have varied calls and songs, including whistling, hissing, cawing, chattering, rattling and churring notes; helmet-shrikes are highly vocal, with mainly whistling songs and frequent duets between pairs, harsh churring and rasping calls, and mechanical bill-snapping and wing sounds

MIGRATION: sedentary or making only local or altitudinal movements

CONSERVATION STATUS: two species, Van Dam's Vanga, *Xenopirostris damii*, is Endangered; four species, the Red-shouldered Vanga, *Calicalicus rufocarpalis*, the Helmet Vanga, *Euryceros prevostii*, the Red-tailed Newtonia, *Newtonia fanovanae*, and Bernier's Vanga, *Oriolia bernieri*, are Vulnerable; one species is Near Threatened

ABOVE The strikingly plumaged, agile little Blue Vanga, *Cyanolanius madagascarinus*, fills the niche occupied elsewhere by tits (Family Paridae), as these are absent from Madagascar.

This very varied family of tropical and subtropical birds was until recently one of several bird families endemic to the island of Madagascar (with one species, the Blue Vanga, *Cyanolanius madagascarinus*, also found on the nearby Comoro islands). Many species are small to medium-sized shrikelike birds. Although the vangas were once thought to be closely related to the true shrikes in the Family Laniidae, recent DNA studies and other evidence suggest that this is not the case. Their closest relatives are thought to be the helmet shrikes (Prionopidae), and these African endemics are now generally regarded as constituting a subfamily (Prionopinae) within that family, with seven species of helmet-shrikes in a single genus, *Prionops*, and two other African species of shrike-flycatchers in the monotypic genera *Megabyas* and *Bias*. The Prionopinae also includes six Asian species, the two flycatcher-shrikes, *Hemipus*, and the two wood-shrikes, *Tephrodornis*, previously included in the cuckoo-shrike family (Campephagidae) and the two philentomas, *Philentoma*, formerly in the monarch family (Monarchidae). Together with the 15 genera and 21 species of vangas, in the major subfamily Vanginae, these are now referred to collectively as vangids.

Furthermore, several of the species included here as members of the Vanginae were formerly placed in a variety of other, unrelated families. These are: the Madagascar Groundhunter (formerly called Crossley's Babbler), *Mystacornis crossleyi*, from the babbler family, Timaliidae; the three species of newtonias, *Newtonia*, from the Old World warbler Family Sylviidae; and Ward's Vanga (formerly Ward's Flycatcher), *Pseudobias wardi*, from the family of wattle-eyes and batises Platysteiridae.

In a similar way to the far more famous 'Darwin's finches' (also called Galapagos finches) in the subfamily Geospizinae of the Family Emberizidae and the Hawaiian honeycreepers (subfamily Drepanidinae), the vangas are a group that have undergone tremendous adaptive radiation as a result of becoming isolated on an island. The extraordinary range of bill shape and size, in particular, and also of body size, plumage coloration and other characteristics, have enabled the different species to adapt to new habitats and niches in Madagascar. In the more extreme cases, as with the contrast between the thrush-sized Helmet Vanga,

Euryceros prevostii, with its massive arched bill, the Sickle-billed Vanga, *Falculea palliata*, which is of similar size but with an extremely long, slender, strongly decurved bill, and the tiny, short-billed, tree-climbing Nuthatch Vanga, *Hypositta corallirostris*, it is hard to believe that the birds are at all related. Despite these profound differences, they do share other anatomical features, such as the shape of the skull and structure of the bony palate.

The different bill shapes, which also include short and pointed, longer and flycatcher-like, heavier and hook-tipped, and stout and flattened from side to side, fit the birds for a whole range of lifestyles that elsewhere would be occupied by specialists from other families, such as tits, shrikes, nuthatches, treecreepers, woodhoopoes and woodpeckers; none of these occur in Madagascar, which has allowed the vangas to occupy these niches.

The plumage of many species is basically black (often with a green or blue gloss) and white, as in the Hook-billed Vanga, *Vanga curvirostris* (from which the family and various species take their name; *Vanga* is a Malagasy name meaning 'pied bird'). Some species also have grey, fawn or chestnut in various combinations; the Blue Vanga is blue and white, and the Helmet Vanga is black with a broad chestnut 'saddle'. In many, females are slightly duller than males, but the difference is more marked in a few, such as the Red-tailed Vanga, *Calicalicus madagascariensis*, and Red-shouldered Vanga, *C. rufocarpalis*, in which the females lack the males' bold black-and-white head pattern, the Nuthatch Vanga, in which the male is all blue but the female has a brownish-grey head, underparts and wings, and especially in Bernier's Vanga, *Oriola bernieri*, in which the male is glossy blue-black and the female is brown above and ochre below, with dark barring.

The helmet-shrikes take their common name from the stiff feathers on the forehead, which curve forward over the nostrils near the base of the bill and backward onto the crown; in most species they give the head a rather helmet-like shape, whereas in two they form a distinct crest, up to 4.5 cm (1.8 in) long. Two species have an almost entirely white head and body, contrasting with black or black-and-white wings and tail; one species is all black with a

ABOVE The massive bill of the Helmet Vanga, *Euryceros prevostii*, enables it to make short work of lizards as well as large insects.

lemon-yellow helmet; one is a patchwork of black, white and warm buff with contrasting grey head and bright red bill; and the other three species have all-black or black and dark grey plumage and red bill. Almost all have prominent fleshy wattles around the eyes, with the skin brightly coloured red, yellow or orange, similar to those of the wattle-eyes (Platysteiridae), but with a serrated outer edge; this is celebrated in the family and genus's scientific names, from the Greek words *prion*, 'saw', and *ops*, 'eye'.

Helmet shrikes occur throughout the year in groups of six to 12 birds, sometimes more after the breeding season; it is very rare to see just a single bird or even a pair. They do everything together, from feeding and roosting to nesting, territorial defence and driving off predators. Groups are controlled by a strict hierarchy, with the most dominant being the breeding female, followed by the breeding male, non-breeding adult females, non-breeding males, adult offspring, immatures and juveniles. Nests of a particular species are always distant from one another, although two different species may nest fairly near one another. The members of each commune help the breeding pair with nest building, incubation (in some species at least) and feeding the young. Helmet-shrikes hunt in groups for insects and small lizards among the foliage of trees and shrubs and also fly out to seize flying insects, sometimes hovering.

Unlike the helmet-shrikes and the following species, the two shrike-flycatchers, *Megabyas* and *Bias*, are both distinctly sexually dimorphic. Males are boldly pied, with a black head and upperparts extending to the chest in the larger *Bias* species, which has a short crest and white underparts; it has contrasting yellow eyes, while those of *Megabyas* are red. Females are mainly brown above, paler below, strongly streaked and mottled with brown below. The two small species of flycatcher-shrikes, *Hemipus*, have a black cap and white cheeks, pale greyish underparts and black upperparts and wings, in one divided by a large white wing-bar. The two wood-shrikes, *Tephrodornis*, one small and the other almost twice as big, are dark grey or brown above with a black bandit mask through the eyes and faintly streaked whitish and buff below. All catch insects by sallying out from a perch, mainly either picking them off in mid-air or from the underside of leaves; the larger wood-shrike is more sluggish. The two *Philentoma* species are either partly or almost entirely blue-grey; the smaller of the two occurs in

LEFT The Sickle-billed Vanga, *Falculea palliata*, uses its long, slender, decurved bill to extract insect larvae from holes in trees.

ABOVE The White Helmet Shrike, *Prionops plumatus*, has many calls, including growling in aggression, and also snaps its bill audibly.

two different forms (morphs), one with mainly rufous wings and a rufous tail and the other plain blue-grey; the larger and stouter species is also blue-grey, the male being distinguished by a maroon breast-patch. These are relatively slow-moving feeders that forage mainly by searching for insects among the foliage and spend long periods perched motionless.

BRISTLEHEAD Pityriasidae

GENERA: 1   **SPECIES:** 1

LENGTH: 22–26 cm (8.5–10 in)

WEIGHT: 115–150 g (4–5.3 oz)

RANGE AND HABITAT: Borneo; tropical rainforest, mainly in peat-swamp forest

SOCIAL BEHAVIOUR: highly social, almost always seen in flocks; limited anecdotal evidence suggests it may be a cooperative breeder, with other adults helping the breeding pair with nest building and caring for the young

NEST: unknown

EGGS: the 1 egg described was white, sparsely spotted brown and dark grey

INCUBATION: unknown

FLEDGING PERIOD: unknown

FOOD: large insects, such as stick insects, cicadas, katydids, cockroaches and beetles, as well as spiders; sometimes small reptiles and amphibians, as well as fruits

VOICE: very vocal, flocks keeping contact with rather quiet, nasal, mewing calls or loud whistles; other calls include trisyllabic calls interspersed with chattering sounds

MIGRATION: may make seasonal movements, possibly altitudinal

CONSERVATION STATUS: Near Threatened

LEFT The Bornean Bristlehead, *Pityriasis gymnocephala*, is a unique Bornean endemic that is far more often heard than seen.

This strange-looking, elusive and enigmatic bird, endemic to the large island of Borneo, is so distinctive as to be placed in a family of its own. Over the years, the Bristlehead, *Pityriasis gymnocephala*, has been assigned to no fewer than seven different songbird families, including those of starlings (Sturnidae), babblers (Timaliidae) and various different 'shrikes'. It does fill the large-shrike niche in Borneo, where shrikes are absent, but is now considered most closely related to either the ioras (Family Aegithinidae) or bush-shrikes (Malaconotidae). Its secretive habits and tendency to roam widely make it extremely hard to observe, and little is known of its biology. Moreover, it is likely to become threatened as logging and periodic fires destroy much of its forest habitat.

Thrush-sized and stocky-bodied, its very short tail and big head ending in a huge, thick, hooked black bill give this strange bird an ungainly, front-heavy appearance. Its largely black body contrasts dramatically with its brilliant scarlet 'thighs' and similarly bright head. The head has a complex pattern, consisting of a crown of bristlelike outgrowths of yellow to orange bare skin, a pinkish area of bare skin around each of its black eyes, charcoal grey bristly ear coverts and the rest of the head and neck bright red.

IORAS Aegithinidae

GENERA: 1   **SPECIES:** 4

LENGTH: 11.5–15.5 cm (4.5–6 in)

WEIGHT: 10–17 g (0.4–0.6 oz)

RANGE AND HABITAT: south and southeast Asia, from India east as far as Borneo and Bali; evergreen and deciduous forests, woodlands, acacia scrub and mangroves, also wooded gardens and plantations

SOCIAL BEHAVIOUR: often solitary or in pairs, but also forage together and with other small songbirds; ranges from almost permanently social in the Green Iora, *Aegithina viridissima*, to almost entirely solitary in the Common Iora, *A. tiphia*, and Marshall's Iora, *A. nigrolutea*

NEST: small, neat cup of grass and bark strips, bound with spiders' webs in the fork of a tree branch or outer twig

EGGS: 2–4, white, cream, greyish or pinkish, streaked and stippled grey and brown (known for Common Iora, *A. tiphia*, and Marshall's Iora, *A. nigrolutea*, only)

INCUBATION: about 14 days (known for the Common Iora only)

FLEDGING PERIOD: unknown

FOOD: insects, including caterpillars, and spiders

VOICE: loud whistling contact calls from flocks, other calls include harsh rasping and chattering; songs made up of similar sounds

MIGRATION: mainly sedentary

CONSERVATION STATUS: one species, the Green Iora, is Near Threatened

This very small family of small Asian songbirds was previously included as a subfamily with the leafbirds *Chloropsis* and fairy bluebirds *Irena* in the Family Irenidae (and earlier still this was subsumed within the large babbler Family Timaliidae). However, molecular studies suggest ioras are more closely related to the False Whistler (Rhagologidae), the bush-shrikes (Malaconotidae) or the Bristlehead (Pityriasidae), and they clearly deserve a family of their own.

In all species, the plumage is bright olive green or black above, in all but the Great Iora, *Aegithina lafresnayi*, with prominent white wing bars, and bright yellow below. Males are brighter and generally larger than females. They have a thick layer of extra-soft, silky, erectile feathers on the upper flanks, which can be used like a jacket to protect the birds from cold and rain when they are roosting, incubating eggs or brooding nestlings. These are especially well developed in the male, who also uses them in courtship displays, erecting them while perched near a female so that they stand out as he spreads his tail and bows with drooped wings. In another, more dramatic display, performed by Marshall's Iora, *A. nigrolutea*, and perhaps also by the Common

LEFT The Common Iora, *Aegithina tiphia*, is a widespread bird of scrub, open woodland, plantations and gardens.

Iora, *A. tiphia*, and seen only in the Indian subcontinent, the male swoops up in the air, hovers and then parachutes down with not only his flank feathers but also the rest of his body plumage fluffed out, so that he appears like a little green ball.

BUSH-SHRIKES Malaconotidae

GENERA: 9   **SPECIES**: 46

LENGTH: 13–28 cm (5–11 in)

WEIGHT: 15–100 g (0.5–3.5 oz)

RANGE AND HABITAT: sub-Saharan Africa, although some races of Black-crowned Tchagra, *Tchagra senegalus*, live north of the Sahara, as far north as North Africa, and in southern Arabia; woodlands, scrublands (some species also in grassland with shrubs, thorn-scrub or semi-desert) and forests; many also occur in gardens, parks (including in suburbs) and on farmland

SOCIAL BEHAVIOUR: generally highly territorial and monogamous, nesting in solitary pairs; also in small family parties after breeding

NEST: intricately built, neat, compact cup of grass, leaf-stalks, bark, moss and lichen, bound with spiders' webs, and lined with rootlets, grass, bark and lichen, and camouflaged to mimic swellings on tree-branches, rather loosely built cup-shaped structures in trees or bushes of twigs and other plant material, with a lining of fine rootlets or other finer and softer material not woven in but curved to follow the shape of the cup

EGGS: usually 2–5, white, cream, pale grey, pinkish or bluish, with darker markings

INCUBATION: 15–22 days, but unknown for many species

FLEDGING PERIOD: 16–22 days, but unknown for most species

Food: a wide range of invertebrates, including many types of insects, spiders, scorpions, ticks, centipedes, snails, worms, crustaceans; also lizards, snakes, frogs and other small vertebrates, and eggs and nestlings of other birds

VOICE: very vocal, with a great range of sounds, from soft, mellow whistles or fluting notes to rattling, chattering and harsh nasal calls, as well as bill-snapping; songs are complex and melodious, often ventriloquial; pairs or small groups often sing together with perfect timing

MIGRATION: mainly sedentary, although some make local or altitudinal movements

CONSERVATION STATUS: two species, the Uluguru Bush-shrike, *Malaconotus alius*, and the Mount Kupé Bush-shrike, *Chlorophoneus kupeensis* (as well as all but one race of Lühder's Bush-shrike, *Laniarius luehderi*) are Endangered; one species, the Green-breasted Bush-shrike, *Malaconotus gladiator*, is Vulnerable; four species are Near Threatened

Living in densely vegetated habitats, many species of this varied African family are extremely secretive and hard to see for more than brief periods, so details of their biology are little known. They comprise: six species called bush-shrikes, in the genus *Malaconotus*; six species of puffbacks in the genus *Dryoscopus*; a single species in the genus *Bocagia*, the Blackcap Bush-shrike (or Marsh Tchagra), *B. minuta*, four species of tchagras in the genus *Tchagra*; another monotypic genus, *Nilaus*, containing another familiar and common species, the Brubru, *N. afer*; six bush-shrikes, *Chlorophoneus*; 18 species of boubous, gonoleks and bush-shrikes, *Laniarus*; a single species of *Rhodophoneus*, the Rosy-patched Bush-shrike, *R. cruentus*; and three bush-shrikes, *Telephorus*, including the well-known Bokmakierie, *T. zeylonus*.

The smaller species look rather like big warblers in build, but with a considerably stouter, slightly hook-tipped bill. The larger ones, such as the tchagras and especially the *Malaconotus* bush-shrikes are sturdier, with a big head and powerful, heavy, more hooked and notched bill. They have particularly well-developed rictal bristles that protect their face and eyes when catching insects from sharp spines on grasshoppers and other hard insect parts. Unlike true shrikes (Family Laniidae, p. 270), they do not sit and watch for prey but seek it out, usually among dense cover at different levels according to species, mainly in trees or bushes; tchagras catch much of their prey on the ground. Also unlike true shrikes, most bush-shrikes do not impale their prey, although the big *Malaconotus* species may store food in this way.

Some species fluff out their rump feathers in flight during courtship and territorial displays; this accounts for the common name of the puffbacks, in which it is particularly exaggerated.

Being generally so skulking in thick cover, many bush-shrikes are heard far more often then they are seen. They are famous for the astonishing precision of their duets, and some are excellent mimics of other birds.

The family includes some brilliantly plumaged birds. For instance, in the large genus *Laniarius*, the five gonoleks are glossy black above and flame red below – in two species with a golden yellow crown as well. Three of the *Malaconotus* bush-shrikes have bright olive-green upperparts, a grey-and-white head and brilliant yellow, orange or red underparts. Similar patterns, with the addition of black bandit masks or necklaces, are seen in the *Chlorophoneus* and *Telephorus* species, which include species such as the aptly named Many-coloured Bush-shrike, *C. multicolor* (grey, white, black, green, red, orange and yellow) and the Gorgeous Bush-shrike, *T. viridis*. Others are far less flamboyant: examples are the tchagras, with their striped black-and-white head, greyish body and tail and chestnut wings, the black-and-white puffbacks, and the all-black or black-and-white boubous, in the genus *Laniarius*.

ABOVE Generally shy and staying hidden in cover, this Crimson-breasted Gonolek, *Laniarius atrococcineus*, shows off its stunningly bright underparts..

DRONGOS Dicruridae

GENERA: 1   **SPECIES**: 22

LENGTH: 18–56 cm (7–22 in) except for the two racquet-tailed species, in which the exceptionally long outer pair of tail feathers, of variable length, may produce an overall length of up to 70 cm (27.5 in) or more

WEIGHT: 22–124 g (0.75–4.4 oz)

Range and habitat: sub-Saharan Africa, Madagascar and other Indian Ocean islands, southern and southeast Asia, New Guinea and nearby islands, northern and eastern Australia; forests and woodlands, savannah, cultivated land with scattered trees, parks, gardens and urban areas with trees

SOCIAL BEHAVIOUR: generally alone, in pairs or in small family groups; monogamous and mostly highly territorial

NEST: a shallow cup of vines, rootlets, plant fibres and other plant material bound together with spiders' webs, lined with finer material such as horsehair, grasses and lichens, and slung hammock-style between the forks of a tree branch or along its top

EGGS: 1–5, cream to pale pink or deep salmon-pink, with darker markings; known for only seven species

INCUBATION: 13–20 days

FLEDGING PERIOD: known for only 5 species; 15–22 days

FOOD: mainly insects, such as butterflies, moths, dragonflies and beetles; larger species sometimes also catch and eat small birds or lizards, mainly in colder weather when insects are scarce; some species also eat fruits, and Spangled Drongos, *Dicrurus bracteatus*, will take a wide range of food at bird feeders in Australia

VOICE: very noisy, with a huge range of calls, from squeaks, buzzing and rasping sounds to whistling, fluting, chattering, churring and twanging notes; songs consist of a jumble of similar sounds, often mixed with mimicry of other birds' calls or songs

MIGRATION: most tropical species are sedentary, but some species migrate from the Himalayas and northern China to winter in India, Sri Lanka and Southeast Asia, and some Spangled Drongos breeding in Australia winter in New Guinea

CONSERVATION STATUS: two species, the Comoro Drongo, *Dicrurus fuscipennis*, and the Tablas Drongo, *D. menagei*, are Endangered; one species the Mayotte Drongo, *D. waldenii*, is Vulnerable; three species are Near Threatened

ABOVE The Black Drongo, *Dicrurus macrocercus*, is a common South Asian bird of open country, perching on a branch or wire on the lookout for prey.

This smallish family from tropical and subtropical Africa, Asia and Australasia comprises a rather uniform group of birds, all in a single genus, *Dicrurus*. Almost all have glossy black plumage and a long tail, in almost all species deeply forked. The glossy feathers occur in both sexes mainly on the head, neck, mantle, breast, wings and tail and their iridescence varies from greenish to bluish or purple, which along with other morphological features, such as tail length and shape, helps both humans and presumably the birds themselves to distinguish which species (and often which subspecies) they belong to. In some species, the gloss is restricted to the tips of the feathers, as celebrated in the common name of the Spangled Drongo, *Dicrurus bracteatus*, and the neck feathers are elongated and pointed to form spear-shaped hackles. There are also patches of non-iridescent, velvet black plumage, mainly on the forehead, on the chin, and between the bill and the eyes (which have contrasting irides, mainly brilliant red, orange or brown).

The races of one Asian species, the Ashy Drongo, *D. leucophaeus*, range from pale to dark grey, while the nominate race of another, the White-bellied Drongo, *D. caerulescens*, is grey above and on its breast, with a white belly.

Plumage adornments in some species are elongated frontal feathers, ranging from a few hairlike feathers to a crest, that in some species points upwards or forwards and in others curls backwards. The strong black bill is broad-based with a curving upper mandible, and hooked at the tip, for seizing and holding prey. At its base are well-developed rictal bristles, perhaps an adaptation to avoiding injury to the eyes when dealing with hard, sharp and often spikey insects. The legs are short and the feet small, well adapted for spending time perched watching for prey.

The forking of the tail varies between species from a very slight notch in the Square-tailed Drongo, *D. ludwigii*, at one extreme to the deeply divided tails of several species. Most species have markedly forked tails. In some, the forks curve outwards or curl upwards, while the Ribbon-tailed Drongo, *D. megarhynchus*, has a very long, deeply forked tail whose outer feathers resemble a pair of twisted ribbons. Even longer are the tails of Lesser and Greater Racquet-tailed Drongos, *D. remifer* and *D. paradiseus*, with a pair of extremely thin, wirelike outer tail feathers each ending in a long plume that trail out behind them when they fly and have been described as resembling a couple of large insects in hot pursuit of the bird.

Combined with their longish, pointed wings, their specialised tail gives these expert catchers of aerial insects great manoeuvrability as they sally out from a perch such as a bare branch, overhead wire or fence-post to chase a wide range of insects, from small flies to butterflies and large dragonflies or tough-bodied beetles and mantises in flight. Returning to the perch, they may hold the

ABOVE Like all members of this small family, the Black Drongo, *Dicrurus macrocercus*, hunts its prey in flight, snatching insects in mid-air or from foliage.

prey down with their strong feet on short legs while they tear it up and eat it. They often accompany large mammals, both wild and domesticated, to take advantage of the prey they disturb, and some species perch on the backs of these animals.

Drongos are highly territorial and remarkably aggressive when breeding, fiercely defending an area around the nest from rivals of their own species and other drongos, and from potential predators. They will even attack birds as large as cranes, herons or eagles, as well as large mammals and snakes.

The family includes both very local and scarce species and a few that are common and familiar birds, especially three species with a very wide distribution in both natural and urban habitats, from all sorts of woodland and farmland to suburban gardens, city parks, and roadsides. These are the Fork-tailed Drongo, *D. adsimilis*, found in many parts of Africa, the Black Drongo, *D. macrocercus*, abundant around Indian villages, with a range extending from southern Iran to China, and two races of the Spangled Drongo, *D. bracteatus*, in northern and eastern Australia.

The name 'drongo' is reputed to have been derived from an old Malagasy name for the birds. Its more recent use in Australian slang, to refer to a stupid person or a loser, is not directly related to any perceived character of the bird itself, but comes from a 1920s racehorse that was probably named after the Spangled Drongo, *Dicrurus bracteatus*; this unlucky animal failed to win a single race.

FANTAILS Rhipiduridae

GENERA: 3   **SPECIES**: 46

LENGTH: 11.5–21 cm (4.5–8 in)

WEIGHT: 6–25 g (0.2–0.9 oz)

RANGE AND HABITAT: south and southeast Asia, New Guinea, Australia, New Zealand, Pacific islands; greatest diversity in New Guinea; forests and woodlands of many types, mainly in rainforests but some in desert woodland or mangroves; Willie-Wagtail, *Rhipidura leucophrys*, in more open habitats, including parks, gardens, roadsides etc.

SOCIAL BEHAVIOUR: occur alone, in pairs or among big mixed-species feeding flocks; monogamous, pairs defending territories fiercely in the breeding season or year-round

NEST: a cup of grasses, rootlets, leaf fragments, bark strips and other vegetation, often held together with spiders' webs or cemented with mud, on a tree branch, with a 'tail' hanging from the base in many species

EGGS: 2–5, white, cream or pale pink, with darker markings

INCUBATION: 12–14 days

Fledging period: 12–15 days; up to 17 days in the Willie-Wagtail, *Rhipidura leucophrys*

FOOD: insects

VOICE: squeaking contact calls and harsher scolding alarm calls; songs a series of simple, rapid, high-pitched phrases

MIGRATION: most, especially the tropical and island species, are sedentary but some of those breeding in the north and south of the family's range make seasonal or altitudinal migrations

CONSERVATION STATUS: two species, the Malaita Fantail, *R. malaitae*, and the Manus Fantail, *R. semirubra*, are Vulnerable; six species are Near Threatened

All but two species in this family of south Asian, Australasian and Pacific island flycatchers are very similar and accordingly included in one genus, *Rhipidura*. Small to medium-sized, with a compact body and a short, finely hook-tipped bill, they tend to perch horizontally, unlike many other flycatchers. They have a long tail, which they often raise and suddenly spread into a fan shape – giving them their common name – and also swing from side to side. These rapid tail movements, made even more dramatic by the bright white tips to the tail feathers or entirely white outer feathers, may help to startle insect prey hiding among the foliage. Additionally, they may serve as communication between the birds. As well as the tail

movements, most species when foraging often move continuously from side to side or even spin round and round, movements also likely to flush out prey. Fantails have particularly well-developed rictal bristles around the bill protecting their face and eyes from the hard flailing bodies of their insect prey. Some species are mainly combinations of black, grey, white, brown or rufous, while others are more brightly coloured, including yellow and blue. In most species, the plumage is almost the same in both sexes.

The family includes many lesser known species but also some very familiar birds. The latter include three species that are common in Australia. These are the Rufous Fantail, *R. rufifrons*,

ᴀʙᴏᴠᴇ One of Australia's best-known birds, the little Willie-Wagtail, *Rhipidura leucophrys*, is fierce in defence of its territory.

Most species of fantail are restless birds, seeking out insect food by darting along branches or making sallies from a perch to snap up flying prey in mid-air. They make their characteristic tail movements even when in flight, which may involve complex manouevres such as looping the loop, and can take them up to 50 m (160 ft) or more before they land again on a perch. Fantails tend to be highly aggressive when defending territory. Unusually, females are often more territorial than males, attacking intruding birds many times as large as themselves, such as crows, ravens and even birds of prey.

The two species not in the genus *Rhipidura* are the Pygmy Drongo, *Chaetorhynchus papuensis*, from New Guinea, and the Silktail, *Lamprolia victoriae*, from Fiji. The Pygmy Drongo was until recently classified with the drongos (Family Dicruridae). But DNA evidence shows it to be a distinctive member of this family.

The Silktail is a dumpy little bird with strikingly pied plumage: it is mainly glossy blue-black, with iridescent blue and green tips to the feathers of the head, breast and shoulders giving them a spangled appearance, contrasting with a brilliant silky white rump and central tail feathers. This attractive little bird is endemic to Fiji, where it lives in rainforest. It hunts for insect prey in the understorey among the lower branches and also on the ground, where it searches among the leaf litter, producing flashes of white in the shade as it exposes its rump and flicks its tail. It is usually seen in small groups. With an alternative name of Satin Flycatcher, its systematic position had long been uncertain. It was until recently included in the monarch family (Monarchidae), and before that it was included with the Australasian robins (Petroicidae), regarded as a possible member of the bird-of-paradise family (Paradisaeidae) or even thought to deserve a family of its own. The molecular research now indicates not only that it is best included in the fantail family but also that it is most closely related to the Pygmy Drongo.

from the southeast of that continent, the more widespread Grey Fantail, *R. albiscapa*, and the striking and relatively large Willie-Wagtail, *R. leucophrys*, most familiar of all and one of Australia's best-loved birds, which often lives alongside people, when it becomes very tame. Found throughout the country, including northern Tasmania and some smaller islands, it follows people in parks or playing fields, flying up, catching the insects they disturb from the grass. Contrasting with harsh rattling alarm calls is its sweet song, often rendered as 'sweet, pretty creature', which it often delivers for hours on end, and even into the night. Another common and well-known species is the New Zealand Fantail, *R. fuliginosa*, which has two distinctive plumage types (morphs), one with a grey, white and black head pattern and brown and buff body, the other all-black.

ᴀʙᴏᴠᴇ A Rufous Fantail, *Rhipidura rufifrons*, visits its recently hatched nestlings in an Australian rainforest.

ᴀʙᴏᴠᴇ The Friendly Fantail, *Rhipidura albolimbata*, is common in the mountains of New Guinea, living up to its name by being tame; it often approaches humans, probably to catch insects they disturb.

SHRIKES Laniidae

GENERA: 4   **SPECIES**: 34

LENGTH: 14–50 cm (5.5–20 in)

WEIGHT: 14–100 g (0.5–3.5 oz)

RANGE AND HABITAT: Europe, Asia, North America and Africa; greatest diversity in Africa; most live in open or semi-open country, especially habitats such as savannah or steppe with a mosaic of short grass, shrubs or trees that provide hunting sites, perches for watching out for prey, and cover for nesting; some along the edges of forests or woodlands; a few in dense forest

SOCIAL BEHAVIOUR: mainly solitary or in pairs; mainly monogamous and territorial; some are cooperative breeders

NEST: typically large, untidy cups of twigs, bark and rootlets with wide range of lining material, from grasses, mosses and lichens to feathers and animal fur or hair, and often incorporating human-made materials, such as string or cloth, sited in thorny shrubs or trees

EGGS: 1–9, ground colour and pattern of markings often variable within species, cream, buff, pale green or grey with darker markings

INCUBATION: 12–20 days

FLEDGING PERIOD: 13–21 days

FOOD: mainly large insects such as grasshoppers, beetles and bees; also small mammals, birds, reptiles and amphibians

VOICE: harsh, grating or screeching calls; songs of *Lanius* species generally quiet and not often uttered, include melodious warbling often interspersed with mimicry of other birds; other genera have mainly harsher songs

MIGRATION: many are sedentary, but some make long migrations, such as the Eurasian Red-backed and Lesser Grey Shrikes, *Lanius collurio* and *L. minor*, which winter in southern Africa

CONSERVATION STATUS: one species, the Sao Tome (or Newton's) Fiscal Shrike, *L. newtoni*, is Critically Endangered, one species, the Iberian Grey Shrike, *L. meridionalis*, is Vulnerable and two species, the Mountain Shrike, *L. validirostris*, and the Loggerhead Shrike, *L. ludovicianus*, are Near Threatened

ABOVE A male Red-backed Shrike, *Lanius collurio*, perches by its 'larder' during a late spring snow fall in the Great Caucasus, Georgia.

Medium-sized, mainly strikingly plumaged songbirds, the shrikes are unusual among passerines in having evolved a lifestyle similar to that of small birds of prey. They are mainly sit-and-wait predators that scan for prey from bare tree branches, posts or other prominent perches affording them a clear view over relatively open country, then swoop down and seize it on the ground before flying back to a perch to tear it apart and eat it. To deal with a diet consisting mainly of large insects and small vertebrates such as rodents, lizards and songbirds, they have a powerful, deep, strongly hooked bill and strong legs and feet equipped with sharp claws, heightening their resemblance to miniature raptors.

Another key feature of this unusual bird family is their habit of impaling prey on thorns and their more recent artificial equivalent, barbed wire: this they do both to make larger prey easier to dismember, to store surplus food as an insurance against lean periods, or perhaps in some cases to allow toxins to degrade and become relatively harmless.

Many shrikes have plumage in various patterns of grey, brown, black and white; many feature a broad black 'bandit mask' through the eyes or a black head. In some, there are brighter areas of rufous or pale pink plumage. The sexes are alike in most species.

Of the four shrike genera, two that are monotypic and one with just a pair of species are endemic to Africa. The genus *Corvinella* contains only the Yellow-billed Shrike, *C. corvina*, a streaky brown bird with a very long, graduated tail, while the sole species in *Urolestes* is the Magpie Shrike, *U. melanoleucus*, named for its magpie-like pied plumage and even longer tail, up to twice the length of its head and body. *Eurocephalus* comprises the Northern White-crowned Shrike, *E. ruppelli*, and Southern White-crowned Shrike, *E. anguitimens*, with a white head and body, black mask through the eye and grey upperparts and tail.

The fourth and major genus, *Lanius*, is by far the most speciose with 30 species covering a huge overall geographic range. Well known species of Europe and western Asia include the Red-backed Shrike, *L. collurio*, Woodchat Shrike, *L. senator*, and Masked Shrike, *L. nubicus*, of Eurasia, and Lesser Grey Shrike, *L. minor*, all of which winter in Africa, and the Great Grey Shrike, *L. excubitor*, with a vast range from northern Europe, the Canary Islands and North Africa east to as far as north-west China. There are two species in North America, the Northern Shrike, *L. borealis*, and the more southerly Loggerhead Shrike, *L. ludovicianus*.

CROWS AND JAYS Corvidae

GENERA: 22   **SPECIES:** 127

LENGTH: 20–69 cm (8–27 in)

WEIGHT: 40 g–2 Kg (1.4 oz–4.4 lb)

RANGE AND HABITAT: virtually worldwide apart from Antarctica, southern South America and some islands, including New Zealand (a raven species, *Corvus antipodum*, that inhabited New Zealand became extinct after human colonisation); almost all terrestrial habitats, from dense northern coniferous forests and rainforests to grassland, farmland, mountains and deserts; many species in villages and towns

SOCIAL BEHAVIOUR: usually in pairs, family groups or, in many species, larger flocks, which often roost communally, sometimes in mixed-species groups; some establish temporary feeding territories as well as breeding territories, others defend territories year-round; mostly monogamous, often pairing for life; some are cooperative breeders

NEST: typically a bulky cup or platform of sticks, twigs and other plant material with a lining of lichens, feathers, animal hair or other soft material, sited in a tree or shrub, on a rock ledge or in a cave, occasionally among vegetation on the ground, on a telegraph pole, pylon, building or other artificial structure; dome-shaped in a few species – notably magpies, *Pica* – and a mass of sticks and other material in a hole in a tree, cliff or chimney in jackdaws

EGGS: 2–9, typically pale blue or pale green, in some species whitish, cream or buff, often with darker markings

INCUBATION: 12–45 days, usually 16–22 days

FLEDGING PERIOD: 18–45 days

FOOD: most species are omnivorous, taking a very wide range of food, from insects and other invertebrates, small vertebrates, other birds' eggs, carrion, seeds, fruit, and human food from waste or bird feeders

VOICE: each species typically has a very wide repertoire of calls, some of them harsh and loud, but others softer and quieter; the song is not well developed; mimicry of other birds or sounds, including human speech, are highly developed in a few species

MIGRATION: mainly sedentary, although northernmost populations of some northern species, such as the Eurasian Jay, *Garrulus glandarius*, and the North American Blue Jay, *Cyanocitta cristata*, make fairly long migrations, and others such as the nutcrackers, *Nucifraga*, make irruptive movements when their staple food of pine seeds fails to crop

CONSERVATION STATUS: one species, the Hawaiian Crow, *Corvus hawaiiensis*, is Extinct in the Wild; three species, the Banggai Crow, *Corvus unicolor*, the Mariana Crow, *C. kubaryi*, and the Javan Green Magpie, *Cissa thalassina*, are Critically Endangered; two species, the Flores Crow, *C. florensis*, and the Ethiopian Bush-Crow, *Zavattariornis stresemanni*, are Endangered; nine species, including the Florida Scrub Jay, *Aphelocoma coerulescens*, and the Pinyon Jay, *Gymnorhinus cyanocephalus*, are Vulnerable; 12 species are Near Threatened

This large family includes the world's largest passerine, the Common Raven, *Corvus corax*, which is as big as a Common Buzzard, *Buteo buteo*, or a Red-tailed Hawk, *B. jamaicensis*.

Although some cultural associations, as with those among the Norse people in Europe and native North Americans, have celebrated Northern Ravens as messengers from the gods, as folk heroes or magical creatures involved in creation myths, the black corvids have been regarded by many peoples as birds of ill omen, partly due to their association with eating dead bodies on battlefields. Although many people still think of sinister black birds when they consider corvids, and the family does include a good number of black or mainly black species, it also includes some very colourful and beautiful birds. Corvid plumage is often very glossy, with blue, green, purple, bronze or reddish iridescence.

Body shape ranges from stout to slender, and the wings from short and rounded in jays to long and more tapered, as in many crows and ravens. Tail length also varies, but is usually medium length to long (very long in some, such as the magpies). The general-purpose bill is typically sturdy and very strong, enabling the bird to deal with a wide range of food, from killing and dismembering live prey or feeding on carrion to breaking open seeds or nuts or digging in the ground, and is an efficient tool for tearing into food or breaking it up.

The most diverse genus is *Corvus*, with 47 species of crow, rook, jackdaw and raven. These include all-black species, including many species known as crows, such as the abundant Carrion Crow, *C. corone*, and American Crow, *C. brachyrhynchos*, and the Common Raven, as well as various black-and-grey species, such as the Hooded Crow, *C. cornix*, House Crow, *C. splendens*, two species of jackdaw, the Eurasian Jackdaw, *C. monedula*, and Daurian Jackdaw, *C. dauuricus*, some black-and-white ones, like the Pied Crow, *C. albus*, and White-necked Raven, *C. albicollis*, and black-and-brown species, such as

two New Guinea species, the Brown-headed Crow, *C. fuscicapillus*, and the Grey Crow, *C. tristis*. The Rook, *C. frugilegus*, of Eurasia is one of the most closely associated of all birds to human agriculture, intimately tied to lowland arable farmland and grazed grassland, where it probes with its specialised tapering, pointed bill for hidden invertebrates. One adaptation related to this foraging behaviour is that the Rook lacks the nasal bristles found in its relatives such as the Carrion Crow. Another is the featherless, bare, greyish skin of its face (the only other *Corvus* species with bare facial skin is the Grey Crow of New Guinea, in which it is pink).

The two species of chough, *Pyrrhocorax*, also have all-black plumage but their longer, fine, slightly decurved bill for specialised insect feeding by probing into short turf or fossicking among mammal dung, is bright red or yellow and their legs and feet bright red.

Members of a distinctive subgroup of American jays have blue as their predominant plumage colour. In North America these include one of the most familiar birds in woods, parks and gardens, the Blue Jay, *Cyanocitta cristata*, while the Central and South American species constitute a larger group that are coloured in many permutations of blues of various shades, white, grey, black, sometimes with purple, and including a mainly green-and-yellow species and a brown and purplish one. Many of these species sport crests of various shapes, from the short one of the Blue Jay or the longer, spiky one of Steller's Jay, *Cyanocitta stelleri*, to more unusual ones in Neotropical species, such as the rigid recurved topknot of the Curl-crested Jay, *Cyanocorax cristatellus*, the bristly fan-shaped crest of the Tufted Jay, *C. dickey*, or the big busby of the Plush-crested Jay, *C. chrysops*. American jays have a long tail, which is especially long in the two species of magpie-jay, *Calocitta*, of Mexico and Central America, which also have a long crest.

Another genus of three more soberly plumaged mainly grey and brown jays occupy dense coniferous forests across northern North America (the Grey Jay, *Perisoreus canadensis*), Eurasia (the Siberian Jay, *P. infaustus*) and, far more local, in mountains of central China (the Sichuan Jay, *P. internigrans*).

The Old World Jays also include the widespread Eurasian Jay, *Garrulus glandarius*, one of the most beautiful of all corvids, with pinkish brown, black and white plumage and black-barred, intensely bright blue feathers on the wing coverts. Its habit of burying vast numbers of acorns in autumn for later consumption inevitably includes forgetting many, so that this species is directly responsible for the spread of oak forests.

Two species of nutcracker, a white-spotted, chocolate-brown one in the Old World (the Eurasian Nutcracker, *Nucifraga caryocatactes*) and a very pale grey one with black-and-white wings and tail in North America (Clark's Nutcracker, *N. columbiana*), are the most accomplished of all bird hoarders, with an astounding spatial memory that enables them to remember where to find huge numbers of seeds buried in the soil or other sites. Clark's Nutcrackers have been shown to have an efficiency rate of up to 90% when locating their vast stores of 100,000 or more pine seeds, even when they are covered with snow. Food cacheing is in fact common in the family, as

LEFT The Rook, *Corvus frugilegus*, has flourished in the British Isles with the advent of woodland clearance and arable and mixed farming.

BELOW Largest of all crows, and indeed of all passerines, the Common Raven, *Corvus corax*, depends greatly on carrion to sustain it, especially in winter.

BELOW RIGHT The Steller's Jay, *Cyanocitta stelleri*, of western North America observes where other birds or mammals cache food and steals it.

is the habit of carrying food back to digest at leisure or feed to their young in an expandable sublingual pouch, throat or mouth.

There are three species of boldly pied, long-tailed magpie, *Pica*, two in North America, and one in Eurasia and North Africa. The tropical magpies of Asia also have a long tail and include some of the most lovely of all the corvids – the five species of blue magpies, *Urocissa*, with brilliant blue and rufous or blue, black and white plumage, and bright red or yellow bill and eye-rings, and the four green magpies, *Cissa*, with glowing green, chestnut and black colours and red bill and eye-rings. Another long-tailed group, the seven treepies, *Dendrocitta*, also found in southern Asia, are less gaudy but subtly handsome, with their black, grey and rich brown plumage.

Several oddities include: the four small, sandy fawn or grey, black-and-white-winged ground-jays, *Podoces*, of Central Asia, adapted for fast running in desert or semi-desert habitats; the species pair of azure-winged magpies, *Cyanopica*, with a remarkable relict distribution in Iberia and thousands of miles to the east in eastern Asia; the all-black, red-billed and red-eyed, long-tailed Piapiac, *Ptilostomus afer*, of central African savannahs; and the highly localised, starling-like grey-and-black Stresemann's Bush Crow, *Zavattariornis stresemanni*, of acacia savannahs in central Ethiopia. The Crested Jay, *Platylophus galericulatus*, is an enigmatic species whose close relationships remain uncertain. It is instantly recognisable, due to its very long slim crest standing up from the back of its head at an acute angle. Its plumage is blackish, dark brown or rich reddish brown (depending on subspecies), apart from a contrasting white crescent on the sides of its neck and two tiny white marks behind the eye. Although it is clearly part of the corvoid radiation (which also includes drongos, fantails, shrikes, birds-of-paradise and others), recent molecular and morphological research suggests it is not a member of the Corvidae, but might be closer to the shrikes (Laniidae, p. 270). For this reason it has often been called the Shrike-jay or Crested Shrike-jay. Until its precise affinities are discovered, it may be best to move it to a family of its own. Although it is widely distributed in South-east Asia, in the Malay Peninsula, Sumatra, Java and Borneo, it is generally scarce, suffering rapid declines in much of its range due mainly to logging. Ornithologists know relatively little about many aspects of its life.

LEFT The Eurasian Nutcracker, *Nucifraga caryocatactes*, hides huge numbers of pine nuts to see it through the winter.

RIGHT The Common Magpie, *Pica pica*, is one of the most familiar and easily recognised members of the crow family across its huge range in Europe, Asia and North Africa.

Among the least deserving of the popular name of 'songbirds' for the oscine passerines, corvids generally produce harsh and unmelodious sounds, although these make up a complex vocabulary of a great range of different calls (no fewer than 80 are known from the Common Raven). Song is little known in most species. Some corvids, such as the Eurasian Jay and Common Raven, are highly accomplished mimics of the sounds of other birds, other animals and artificial sounds, particularly when in captivity.

Corvids are generally regarded as among the most intelligent of all birds, capable of problem solving and, in several species, notably the New Caledonian Crow, *Corvus moneduloides*, highly sophisticated tool use. Extremely adaptable and often omnivorous, they are quick to take advantage of novel situations, especially in exploiting new foods or new ways of obtaining food. These include dropping molluscs and other hard-shelled food items onto hard surfaces (with the remarkable refinement of using cars to do the job of shelling walnuts, recorded first in Japan and more recently elsewhere, such as California).

Although some corvids, such as the Carrion, Hooded, House and American Crows, *Corvus corone, C. cornix, C. splendens* and *C. brachyrhynchos*, are very common, widespread and successful birds, some species are rare and threatened, and the Hawaiian Crow, *C. hawaiiensis*, is now extinct in the wild.

MONARCHS Monarchidae

GENERA: 16   **SPECIES:** 96

LENGTH: most species 9–21 cm (3.5–8 in) but up to at least 50 cm (20 in) in male Asian Paradise Flycatchers, *Terpsiphone paradisi*, whose very long central tail feathers may project up to 30 cm (12 in) beyond the other tail feathers (which are themselves about as long as the head and body length)

WEIGHT: 5–22 g (0.2–0.8 oz)

RANGE AND HABITAT: sub-Saharan Africa, Madagascar and other Indian Ocean islands, Arabia, south and southeast Asia, New Guinea, Australia and Pacific islands; forests, woodlands, mangroves, savannah, plantations and other cultivated land with trees; some species also in gardens, parks and roadside trees in villages and towns

SOCIAL BEHAVIOUR: seen alone, in pairs or in flocks, in some cases including mixed-species flocks; most are monogamous and territorial, in some species year-round

NEST: in most a small cup of plant fibres, bark strips, mosses and other vegetation, bound together with spiders' webs, on the fork of a tree branch; the exceptions are the frilled flycatchers, *Arses*, with their pendant nests and the mudlarks, *Grallina*, with nest cups made of mud

EGGS: 2–4, white, with reddish-brown blotches or spots

INCUBATION: 12–18 days

FLEDGING PERIOD: 10–18 days

FOOD: mainly flying insects, such as dragonflies, flying ants and grasshoppers, also spiders and other invertebrates; some also eat small fruits and seeds

VOICE: harsh or whistling calls; songs feature high-pitched fluting notes, whistles and trills as well as rasping notes

MIGRATION: tropical species are mainly sedentary; some southern and eastern Australian species move north in winter; the Japanese Paradise Flycatcher, *Terpsiphone atrocaudata*, makes long migrations to winter in Malaysia, Sumatra and the Philippines

CONSERVATION STATUS: three species and one subspecies (often regarded as a full species) are Extinct; one the Ua Pou Monarch, *Pomarina mira*, is Critically Endangered (Possibly Extinct); five species, the Black-chinned Monarch, *Symposiachrus boanensis*, Cerulean Paradise Flycatcher, *Eutrichomyias rowleyi*, Seychelles Paradise Flycatcher, *Terpsiphone corvina*, Tahiti Monarch, *Pomarea nigra*, and Fatu Hiva Monarch, *P. whitneyi*, are Critically Endangered; five species, including the Truk Monarch, *Metabolus rugensis*, the Biak Monarch, *Monarcha brehmii*, White-tipped Monarch, *M. everetti*, are Endangered; seven species, including the Raratonga Monarch, *Pomarea dimidiata*, are Vulnerable; 15 species are Near Threatened

LEFT This male African Paradise Flycatcher, *Terpsiphone viridis*, is of the striking white morph (colour form).

The monarchs, or monarch-flycatchers, are a large family of Old World flycatchers, mostly distributed in wooded habitats right across the tropics and subtropics, from West Africa to islands of the Pacific.

Small to medium-sized arboreal songbirds, they catch insects in flight by flying out from a perch in the typical flycatcher manner, but also glean them from foliage while on a branch or twig or when hovering. They are very active birds, constantly on the move, and quiver their wings and fan their tails as they go. Many species have striking plumage, including bright blue or combinations of chestnut, black, grey and white, while the striking crests and long tails of the paradise flycatchers *Terpsiphone*, with greatly elongated flexible streamers in the males, make them some of the most beautiful of all tropical songbirds.

Monarchs have a short, broad-based, flattened bill (though some species have a hook-tipped and notched bill, which is especially sturdy in the shrike-bills *Clytorhynchus*). The feet are small but strong. Most have a medium-length, square-ended or rather rounded tail, but males of most species of paradise flycatchers, *Terpsiphone*, have a long tail with extremely long central tail streamers; the total length of the tail can be two or even three times the length of the head and body in some males of several species. These include the African Paradise Flycatcher, *T. viridis*, the Japanese Paradise Flycatcher, *T. atrocaudata*, and the Madagascar Paradise Flycatcher, *T. mutata*. The two crested flycatchers, *Trochocercus*, have a long, graduated tail that is about the same length as the body. The forehead is often steeply angled and some have a slight crest; various species, such as the Cerulean Paradise Flycatcher, *Eutrichomias rowleyi*, some races of the Blue-mantled Crested Flycatcher, *Trochocercus cyanomelas*, some of the *Terpsiphone* paradise flycatchers and the three *Hypothymis* monarchs, have much larger and longer crests.

Plumage in many species is grey above with black on the head and rufous underparts; some are almost entirely rufous, grey or black; some are predominantly blue (ranging across different species from pale pastel blue to intense deep blue); a few are black

and yellow; and many others, including most species of the largest genus, *Monarcha*, are black and white, or grey, black and white. Several *Terpsiphone* species have white morphs (colour forms) in which the rufous areas are replaced with white. In some species females are duller; in one, the Chuuk Monarch, *Metabolus rugensis*, the male is almost all white and the female virtually all black. The four species of *Arses* (the name is from a Persian king) have frilled feathering on the neck and fleshy blue eye wattles. Other features that distinguish these frilled flycatchers from the rest of the family are their delicate pendant nests, neat shallow baskets of tendrils and stems usually slung between two vines, and their foraging technique: this involves spiralling up tree trunks like the treecreepers of Eurasia (Family Certhiidae, p. 373) and Australia (Family Climacteridae, p. 232): a good example of convergent evolution, as none of these families is closely related to the others.

The Family Monarchidae also includes two species collectively known as mudlarks. They used to be placed in a family of their own (Grallinidae), but are now regarded as close relatives of the genus *Monarcha*. The far better known one is the Magpie-lark, *Grallina cyanoleuca*, in Australia, extreme southern New Guinea and the Indonesian island of Timor (as well as an introduced population on Lord Howe Island in the Tasman Sea 600 km/372 miles east of the Australian mainland). This is an abundant, widespread and familiar bird across Australia, in town and country alike, where it is often seen on lawns, pastures and other cleared areas, especially near water. Its common name refers to its pied plumage, reminiscent to settlers of the Common Magpie, *Pica pica*, of Europe but it is not a close relative of that member of the crow family or of the larks (Alaudidae, p. 339). Its nearest relative, the Torrent-lark, *Grallina bruijni*, lives only in the foothills and mountains of New Guinea, as its name suggests, near small, fast-flowing streams. The former family name refers to the mud-based nests of both species. They incorporate fibrous plant matter with the mud to create a strong structure when it dries, and line the nest cup with small feathers and fine plant strands.

Both are starling- to thrush-sized birds, 20–30 cm (8–12 in) long, with a small head, relatively long, strong legs for a mainly ground-dwelling life, and with long rounded wings and a longish tail. Plumage of both species is black and white, with least white in the male of the shy, little known and possibly locally scarce Torrent-lark.

ABOVE The Australian Magpie-lark, *Grallina cyanoleuca*, occurs more or less anywhere it can find trees and mud to build its nest.

AUSTRALIAN MUDNESTERS Corcoracidae

GENERA: 2 **SPECIES:** 2

LENGTH: the White-winged Chough, *Corocorax melanorhamphos*, 44–50 cm (17–19.5 in); the Apostlebird, *Struthidea cinerea*, 29–33 cm (11.5–13 in)

WEIGHT: the White-winged Chough 280–425 g (10–15 oz); the Apostlebird 110–155 g (4–5.5 oz)

RANGE AND HABITAT: Australia; woodlands, grassland with scattered trees, orchards, roadside trees and parks

SOCIAL BEHAVIOUR: usually in family or looser groups of up to about 19 members, led by a dominant male and female; all group members help build the nest, incubate, and rear the young, feeding them after they have fledged for up to 28 weeks in the White-winged Chough and about 10 weeks in the Apostlebird; larger assemblies of up to 100 may form at good feeding sites

NEST: a large bowl of grass and bark bound with mud and manure, plastered onto a tree branch

EGGS: 2–5, or up to 9 when two females lay in the same nest, cream, with grey, black or brown blotches

INCUBATION: 18–19 days

FLEDGING PERIOD: 24–30 days for the White-winged Chough; 18–20 days for the Apostlebird

FOOD: seeds and insects

VOICE: the White-winged Chough has a mellow piping whistle, descending in pitch; the Apostlebird's calls are harsher, including a scratchy sound and a nasal two-note call

MIGRATION: sedentary

CONSERVATION STATUS: neither threatened

ABOVE An adult White-winged Chough, *Corcorax melanorhamphos*, feeds one of the youngsters in its communal group.

This exclusively Australian family contains just two very distinctive species that look unalike in size, shape and plumage colour, but share various features such as soft, fluffy plumage, quite short, rounded wings and relatively longish, strong legs and feet for a ground-foraging lifestyle, and mud-nesting. Their close relationship is also supported by the evidence from recent DNA analysis. In the past, they were lumped together in a single family (Grallinidae) with the two species of mudlarks, Grallina, solely on the basis of the unusual mud nests built by all four species, but the two groups are now known to be unrelated. Some authorities prefer to retain the Grallinidae for the mudlarks, but the results of the molecular research strongly indicate that the mudlarks are in fact unusually large members of the monarch flycatcher family (Monarchidae, p. 273), which is where they are placed here.

The White-winged Chough, *Corocorax melanorhamphos*, is sooty black apart from a white panel across the primary wing feathers. It is this black plumage, and the longish, slender decurved bill, that earn it the 'chough' part of its common name; it is not related to the two Eurasian chough species, *Pyrrhocorax*, in the crow Family Corvidae. The eyes have bright red irides. These crow-sized birds have a distinctive display, known as the 'Wing-wave Tail-wag' display, which involves the bird moving its spread wings and fanned tail up and down about once each second, revealing the white wing markings. This is performed in many different contexts, most dramatically as a threat display by dominant males

or all members when two rival groups meet at the edges of their large overlapping feeding territories.

The smaller of the two species, the Apostlebird, *Struthidea cinerea*, has a grey head and body, with the pointed head and neck feathers giving them a shaggy appearance, darker brownish wings and a darker, green-glossed tail. It has a short, deep bill like that of many finches, and very different from that of its relative. Both species forage mainly on the ground for insects in summer and seeds in winter, raking through leaf litter; the White-winged Chough also uses its longer, slender bill to probe into soil or cowpats. Both sometimes catch small mammals such as mice or steal other birds' eggs. In winter they feed mainly on seeds. The Apostlebird can hammer into hard seeds and insects with its strong, stout, short bill and also prises insects from tree bark.

Both White-winged Choughs and Apostlebirds are very sociable birds, living in small groups that huddle together and repeatedly preen one another at resting sites and roosts. As well as feeding, roosting and moving around together in small groups of up to 19 members (averaging six to eight), both species breed cooperatively. The helpers at the nest are usually close relatives, as the offspring remain in the breeding territory for several years after fledging. All share in the tasks of nest building, feeding and caring for the young, defending the territory against rivals and attacking predators. In groups that have persisted for many years, although there may be more than one adult of each sex, generally it is only one dominant pair that breeds each year. If the breeding male or female should die, the survivor together with any immature birds in the group joins a lone mature adult from another group to form a new community. In such groups, where the birds are not so closely related as in the stable groups, more than one male or female mate in various polygamous permutations.

MELAMPITTAS Melampittidae

GENERA: 2 **SPECIES:** 2

LENGTH: Lesser Melampitta, *Melampitta lugubris*, 17–18 cm (7–7.5 in); Greater Melampitta, *Megalampitta gigantea*, 29–32 cm (11.5–12.5 in)

WEIGHT: Lesser Melampitta, about 30 g (1 oz); Greater Melampitta, about 200 g (7 oz)

RANGE AND HABITAT: New Guinea; montane rainforests of the island's mainly central mountains, the Greater Melampitta preferring forests in areas of karst limestone

SOCIAL BEHAVIOUR: unknown

NEST: Lesser Melampitta, a dome-shaped nest of moss, into which is woven tendrils, fern fronds and rootlets, with a side entrance, sited against the trunk of a tree-fern; Greater Melampitta (based on anecdotal information from New Guinea natives), a basket-shaped structure of vines suspended below ground in a karst limestone sinkhole

EGGS: Lesser Melampitta, 1, white with sparse black, grey and purplish markings

INCUBATION: Lesser Melampitta, up to 27 days

FLEDGING PERIOD: Lesser Melampitta, up to 35 days

FOOD: Lesser Melampitta, insects, other invertebrates, including snails and worms, as well as small frogs; also some fruit; no information for Greater Melampitta

VOICE: Lesser Melampitta, song ends in a rapid series of harsh buzzing notes, descending in pitch, calls include loud double clicks (which can be imitated by clicking one's tongue against the roof of the mouth); Greater Melampitta, a loud two-note song repeated monotonously

MIGRATION: both species are probably sedentary

CONSERVATION STATUS: neither species is threatened

This very small family comprises just two relatively little-known species that are endemic to montane forests in the very large island of New Guinea. Both the Lesser Melampitta, *Melampitta lugubris*, and the Greater Melampitta, *Megalampitta gigantea*, have all-black plumage and superficially resemble pittas (Pittidae, p. 200), with a relatively large head and plump body, a stubby tail in the Lesser Melampitta, and erect posture; also like pittas, they have short, rounded wings, long legs and robust feet, suited for a terrestrial lifestyle. They run and hop across the forest floor, searching for insect and other invertebrate prey. Both have all-black plumage: the name 'melampitta' is from the Greek word *melas*, meaning 'black', combined with the genus name *Pitta*. They were originally included within the pitta family when the Lesser Melampitta was first described scientifically in 1871. In 1931 the great evolutionary biologist and ornithologist Ernst Mayr proved by examining the structure of their syrinx (voicebox) that they were unrelated to the pittas (suboscine passerines distinct from the oscine passerines, or songbirds). They languished for a long while in what was a 'ragbag' assortment of birds in the babbler Family Timaliidae (p. 362), after which they were moved to the logrunner Family Orthonychidae (p. 276) and then regarded as relatives of the birds-of-paradise (Paradisaeidae, p. 277) or the jewel-babblers (Cinclosomatidae, p. 248). The recent molecular research suggests

that they are closest to the birds-of-paradise and the Australian mudnesters (Corcoracidae, p. 275), but sufficiently distinct to deserve placement in a family of their own, as here.

The Greater Melampitta is much the larger of the two, almost twice the length of its relative and over six times its weight. It also has a much longer tail and a stouter bill that bears a small hook at the tip. Other differences include the stiffened shafts of its wing and tail feathers; the bare shafts of the tail feathers project a few millimetres beyond the end of the tail.

The Lesser Melampitta has a wide distribution in the forested mountains of the central ranges and also parts of the north, in the Vogelkop peninsula in the west and in the southeast. It has been found generally at altitudes of about 2,000–2,800 m (6,600–9,200 ft) and has even been encountered as high as 3,500 m (11,500 ft).

The Greater Melampitta by contrast, lives at lower altitudes, at about 650–1,400 m (2,100–4,600 ft). It has a far smaller and more fragmented range, and is far more of a habitat specialist. It may be more abundant than realised, since the karst limestone country it inhabits is rarely visited by field biologists and in those areas that have been surveyed it appears to be locally quite common. Also, it runs about like a rodent and often disappears into the sink holes that pepper the karst terrain in which it roosts and is believed to nest, so is accordingly hard to observe. The stiffened wing and tail feathers, which often show signs of wear, may be an adaptation to help the birds climb out as they emerge from their nest or roost deep in a narrow sinkhole.

ABOVE This male Lesser Melampitta, *Melampitta lugubris*, is distinguished from a female by his red eyes; hers are dark brown.

IFRIT Ifritidae

GENERA: 1   **SPECIES**: 1

LENGTH: 16–17 cm (6–6.5 in)

WEIGHT: 34–36 g (1.2–1.3 g)

RANGE AND HABITAT: New Guinea; montane forests

SOCIAL BEHAVIOUR: often seen in small groups

NEST: a deep, thick-walled cup of moss, ferns, rootlets and leaves sited low down in a shrub or small tree

EGGS: 1, white, with a few black and purplish markings

INCUBATION: unknown

FLEDGING PERIOD: unknown

FOOD: mainly insects and other invertebrates, plus some fruit

VOICE: song a series of 5–6 buzzing or squeaking notes, rising then falling; sharp three-note or buzzing calls

MIGRATION: probably sedentary

CONSERVATION STATUS: not threatened

ABOVE The enigmatic Ifrit, *Ifrita kowaldi*, has in the past been classified within many different families, and its precise relationships are still unclear.

The Ifrit, *Ifrita kowaldi*, is a distinctive and little-known New Guinea endemic that inhabits montane forests, especially favouring those with luxuriant growth of mosses. A small, plump-bodied, short-necked and short-tailed bird with a shortish bill, it has olive-brown upperparts and buff underparts, and an iridescent blue crown with a black centre and bordered by a black line. Below this is a pattern of black and white markings in the male and black and buff in the female.

The Ifrit forages by creeping like a nuthatch up moss-covered tree trunks and onto branches, using its tail as a brace as it probes into the moss. It often hangs from the upper surface of a branch to reach prey hiding on the underside, and also occasionally descending lower to search for prey on fallen trunks or branches. It is not at all shy, and small flocks that often form may allow a close approach as they search for food. These may join up with mixed flocks of other species.

The Ifrit is one of a few birds that have been found to have toxic skin; the others are also birds from New Guinea – the pitohuis, now split between several families. Although ornithologists have only relatively recently been aware of this remarkable feature, it was long known to local tribespeople, who are careful to take precautions by removing the skin before eating its flesh; some regarded the Ifrit as more toxic than the Hooded Pitohui, *Pitohui dichrous*. The bird acquires the toxin by eating a particular species of beetle.

BIRDS-OF-PARADISE Paradisaeidae

GENERA: 13   **SPECIES**: 41

LENGTH: 15–44 cm (6–17 in), some species with elongated long central tail feathers (and in some, flank plumes) up to 110 cm (43 in)

WEIGHT: 50–450 g (1.75–15.75 oz)

RANGE AND HABITAT: two species on the Moluccan islands of Indonesia, 36 species in New Guinea and nearby islands, and four species in the extreme north-east of Australia and eastern Australia; mainly in tropical and subtropical rainforest, from near sea level up to almost 3,000 m (9,840 ft) altitude; a few more adaptable species extend to open woodland or mangroves

SOCIAL BEHAVIOUR: most are usually seen singly, although the minority of monogamous species are often in pairs, and in some that gather at fruiting trees, small groups; some polygynous species have communal courtship displays; monogamous species share parental duties but males of polygynous species play no part in nest building, incubation or care of young

NEST: manucodes and the Paradise Crow, *Lycocorax pyrrhopterus*, build a bulky, sparse, shallow cup of vine tendrils, while other species construct a deep, dense, open bowl of orchid stems, leaves, fern fronds and mosses; many nest on tree branches, but some riflebirds, *Ptiloris*, and the Twelve-wired Bird-of-paradise, *Seleucidis melanoleucus*, often nest on the top of a palm, pandanus or among a dense tangle of vines; a single King Bird-of-paradise, *Cicinnurus regius*, nest has been found in a tree hole

EGGS: 1–2, rarely 3, whitish to buff or pinkish, with brown or black markings

INCUBATION: 14–27 days in the relatively few species known

FLEDGING PERIOD: 14–30 or more days

FOOD: mainly fruit, also insects and other invertebrates such as spiders, millipedes and centipedes; some also feed on seeds or nectar; larger species may also eat small frogs and lizards

VOICE: a wide range of sounds, especially during courtship displays, from loud, harsh, rather crow-like notes of many species to the 'machine-gun' rattle of the Brown Sicklebill, *Epimachus meyeri*, or the crackling sound, like radio static, of the King of Saxony Bird-of-paradise, *Pteridophora alberti*, or the weird mechanical-sounding humming, like an electric motor, of the Blue Bird-of-paradise, *Paradisaea rudolphi*; manucodes have a very long, coiled windpipe with which they produce far-carrying, resonant, deep, tremulous sounds

MIGRATION: most are strictly sedentary, some never moving from small territories, but manucodes are non-territorial and wander through forests in search of favourite fruit, especially figs

CONSERVATION STATUS: two species, the Blue Bird-of-paradise and Goldie's Bird-of-paradise, *Paradisaea decora*, are Vulnerable; seven species are Near Threatened

ABOVE A male Raggiana Bird-of-paradise, *Paradisaea raggiana*, calls loudly at a lek in Varirata National Park, in the highlands of Papua New Guinea.

Regarded by some as the most spectacular and beautiful of all birds, the birds-of-paradise acquired their common and scientific names because the first specimens of the extravagantly plumaged adult males to reach the West in the sixteenth century were empty skins from the island of New Guinea, the centre of the family's diversity, where all but two of the 16 genera are found. These 'trade skins' (usually of the Greater Bird-of-Paradise, *Paradisaea apoda*, were prepared by native Papuans for their ceremonial plume trade, and had their legs and feet removed (the specific name of this species is derived from the Greek words meaning 'without feet'). This led naturalists of the day to assert that without feet, the birds would be unable to land and feed, and thus flew about in the air in a heavenly paradise, until they died and fell to earth. The reality of these birds' appearance and biology is just as wonderful as any such myth; no bird family has such a great range of feather structure or more remarkable displays.

The members of this remarkable family range from little birds such as the King Bird-of-paradise, *Cicinnurus regius*, with a sparrow-sized body and long curled central tail feathers, to the crow-sized Curl-crested Manucode, *Manucodia comrii*. All share strong feet adapted for perching, and they have a strong, pointed bill; this is sturdy, slightly hook-tipped, straight to slightly downcurved and short to medium length in most species, though deeper and more arched in some such as the manucodes and slender, very long and strongly downcurved (and lacking any hook) in the aptly named sicklebills, *Epimachus*. The Twelve-wired Bird-of-paradise, *Seleucidis melanoleucus*, has a long and very sturdy, slightly downcurved bill.

While females and immatures of both sexes are mostly drab (in many species brownish with barred underparts), males include some of the most flamboyantly plumaged of all birds. Colours range across the spectrum, and there is an extraordinary variety of elaborate and bizarre adornments, including crests, long head plumes, wattles, beards, greatly elongated tail streamers or flank feathers, and iridescent breast shields. These are all erected or moved in other ways to draw attention to them during courtship displays, which also involve a great variety of exaggerated movements, from leaping up and down or neck stretching to rhythmically swaying the body, hopping from side to side, or dancing round an interested female.

The birds-of-paradise exhibit some of the most striking examples of sexual selection in the natural world. In all but a few species in the family, the males compete for the attention of females, who gather together to carefully assess the males' extravagant plumage adornments and observe their dramatic and elaborate displays before choosing which of them to mate with. Living in rainforests where mammals are few and competition and predation risks relatively low, food is abundant. This means that the female is able to build a nest, incubate her eggs and rear a family with no help from a male after mating. It is to her advantage to spend time choosing a fit and vigorous mate with good genes to pass on to her offspring. In this way, it is females that are the drivers of evolution in respect of male appearance and courtship displays. Often, just one or a few males they deem to be the most attractive are dominant over the others and almost all the females mate only with them, thus reinforcing the evolutionary process that made them attractive.

The exceptions that prove the rule are the Paradise Crow, *Lycocorax pyyrhopterus*, and the four species of manucodes, *Phonygammus* and *Manucodia*. In all these the sexes are alike in their glossy black plumage, are socially monogamous and the male helps the female incubate the eggs and care for the young.

Among the most dramatic-looking species in this generally visually spectacular family are: the Ribbon-tailed Astrapia, *Astrapia mayeri*, whose snow-white central pair of tail feathers extend almost

ABOVE This female Brown Sicklebill, *Epimachus meyeri*, is far less flamboyant than the male, with his black head and upperparts and extremely long central tail feathers glossed with green, blue, purple and magenta.

1 m (3.2 ft) – proportional to the size of the bird, the longest of any species – and contrast with the velvety black, iridescent green, violet, purple and magenta of its body and head; and the King-of-Saxony Bird-of-paradise, *Pteridophora alberti*, which has two amazingly long head plumes (at 50 cm/20 in, over twice the bird's length), along each of which 40–50 plastic-like 'flags' are attached to a bare feather shaft and are waved about dramatically during courtship of females. Also striking, and very beautiful, are the great cascades of filmy yellow, gold, maroon, scarlet or white elongated flank feathers in six of the seven *Paradisaea* species, such as the Raggiana Bird-of-paradise, *P. raggiana*; the seventh, the Blue Bird-of-paradise, *P. rudolphi*, has a glossy jet-black body with turquoise wings and violet-blue and cinnamon flank plumes, which it fans out and shivers in its display as it hangs upside down.

Other astonishing displays include those performed on the ground rather than on branches or other elevated sites. Often, the male diligently removes all the fallen leaves to create a bare earth stage in which his performance will stand out. Remarkable examples are the displays of the Superb Bird-of-paradise, *Lophorina superba*, and the six species of parotia, *Parotia*. The Superb Bird-of-paradise undergoes the most radical transformation of all birds-of-paradise in the culmination of his display, in which he ends up looking nothing like a bird. When he arrives in front of a female, he appears as a black bird with a brilliant iridescent turquoise breast and a tuft of similarly coloured feathers at the front of his crown above the bill. Then, suddenly, he raises and extends his iridescent breast shield and expands the long cape feathers from the back of the neck into a huge black disc to surround his breast shield, and raises his bill to divide the iridescent crown feathers. All this creates an illusion of a broad oval 'smiley face' with a pair of blue-green eyes above a broad blue-green mouth. He displays this apparition to the female by facing her closely as he bounces round and round her as if on springs, without spoiling the illusion by revealing his rear.

Male parotias, *Parotia*, also black with a concealed iridescent breast shield, perform an extraordinary sequence of dance movements, in which they resemble a miniature ballerina. A typical sequence begins with the male lifting himself high on his toes, and expanding his cape of long body plumes that combines with his wings to create a broad circular skirt. He then erects his

ABOVE A Blue Bird-of-paradise, *Paradisaea rudolphi*, reaches the climax of its display, hanging upside-down and sounding like an electric motor.

breast shield to reveal its flashing gold, blue, green, purple or bronze iridescence and jumps rapidly from side to side. Then suddenly he stops and stands stock still for a moment. Next, he balances with feet apart and tail pressed against the ground and twirls his head round and round, making the six very long, wire-like feathers with their pennant tips that extend from his crown bob up and down, before finally leaping into the air to land on the back of one of the watching females and copulate with her. Research has shown that in one species, as many as 58 elements are involved in the display. Young male birds-of-paradise start to practice complex displays such as these before they acquire their adult plumage; it may take them several years before they have perfected them.

ABOVE This male King of Saxony Bird-of-paradise, *Pteridophora alberti*, is in the final stages of his courtship display as he moves his extraordinary, elongated head plumes forward before copulating with a watching female.

ABOVE The very long white central tail feathers of the male Ribbon-tailed Astrapia, *Astrapia mayeri*, are visible at long range, especially when he flies.

ROCKFOWLS AND RELATIVES Eupetidae

GENERA: 3   **SPECIES:** 5

LENGTH: rockfowls, 33–38 cm (13–15 in); rockjumpers, 21–25 cm (8–20 in); Rail-babbler, 28–30 cm (11–12 in)

WEIGHT: rockfowls, 192–250 g (6.8–8.8 oz); rockjumpers, 48–60 g (1.7–2.1 oz); Rail-babbler, 66–72 g (2.3–2.5 oz)

RANGE AND HABITAT: rockfowls, *Picathartes*, west and west-central Africa; mainly in lowland rainforest, with some in second-growth forests and plantations, with cliffs, rocks or caves for nesting and streams with muddy banks for obtaining nest material; after breeding, may visit open country such as clearings, farmland and alongside roads and paths; rockjumpers, *Chaetops*, southern South Africa and Lesotho, in alpine and subalpine grassland and fynbos, with rocky outcrops and gulleys or scree; Rail-babbler, *Eupetes macrocerus*, southern Thailand, Malayan peninsula, Sumatra and Borneo, in mature tropical forests with a relatively open understorey

SOCIAL BEHAVIOUR: rockfowls and rockjumpers, monogamous and territorial, rockfowls breeding as separate pairs or in small colonies, and rockjumpers breeding cooperatively in family groups of up to 12 birds; no information for Rail-babbler

NEST: rockfowls, a large cup of mud incorporating plant fibres, dry leaves and twigs, which hardens to form a strong structure, attached to the walls or roofs of caves or on cliffs; rockjumpers, a deep, untidy cup of grass, twigs, lichen and moss, lined with finer grass, rootlets and sometimes mammal fur, usually sited just above ground in a grass clump or under a shrub or rock; Rail-babbler a shallow, loose cup of plant fibres near the ground

EGGS: 1–3, in the Grey-necked Rockfowl, *Picathartes oreas*, variable, from creamy white to pale grey, pale greenish or fawn, with darker markings, in the White-necked Rockfowl, *P. gymnocephalus*, creamy white with brown markings; rockjumpers, 2–3, white, sometimes with reddish or black speckling; Rail-babbler, 2, plain white

INCUBATION: rockfowls, 23–29 days; rockjumpers, 19–21 days; Rail-babbler, no information

FLEDGING PERIOD: rockfowls, 23–29 days; rockjumpers,18–21; Rail-babbler, no information

FOOD: rockfowls, mainly forest floor invertebrates, including earthworms, slugs and snails, crabs, beetles, termites, ants, grasshoppers and other insects, also small frogs and lizards, which are the main food supplied to nestlings; rockjumpers, mainly insects and other invertebrates, as well as small vertebrates; Rail-babbler, insects, such as beetles and cicadas, and spiders

VOICE: rockfowls generally silent, but known calls include a very loud harsh call of alarm in the White-necked species and a quieter rasping one in the Grey-necked species, as well as churring, melodious whistling and chicken-like clucking sounds; rockjumpers, song a long series of piping notes, calls include short, piercing whistles and harsh churring sounds; Rail-babbler, a ventriloquial song of thin whistling notes increasing and then fading in volume; calls include froglike sounds

MIGRATION: rockfowls basically sedentary, but make local movements outside the breeding season; some rockjumpers make altitudinal migrations; Rail-babbler sedentary

CONSERVATION STATUS: two species, the White-necked Rockfowl and Grey-necked Rockfowl, are Vulnerable; two species, the Cape Rockjumper, *Chaetops frenatus*, and Drakensberg Rockjumper, *C. aurantius*, are Near Threatened

ABOVE The White-necked Rockfowl, *Picathartes gymnocephalus*, is rare and elusive; this photograph is of a captive bird.

Until recently this small family included just two bizarre-looking species endemic to parts of West and west-central Africa and some authorities still restrict it thus, retaining the traditional name Picathartidae. The common name rockfowl refers to their nesting habits, since both species have very specialised requirements. They site their unusual, deep, cup-shaped mud nests on the walls or roofs of caves, on cliffs or in other rocky locations in hilly lowland rainforests, usually on a slope or beneath an overhang. Other names for this enigmatic pair are bald crows (as they were once thought to be related to crows) and, from their scientific name, *picathartes* – a name that combines the Latin word *pica* for magpie, referring to the pied plumage of the White-necked Rockfowl, *Picathartes gymnocephalus*, and the Greek, *cathartes*, for vulture, because of the bare skin on the head of these birds.

Both species of rockfowl are ungainly looking birds, with a proportionally small head and a heavy rather crowlike bill on a big, often hunched body, long broad tail, rounded wings and long legs. The White-necked Rockfowl has almost black upperparts, wings and tail, while the Grey-necked Rockfowl, *P. oreas*, is pale blue-grey above; in both the underparts are white, with a soft yellow to apricot wash on the Grey-necked species. Save for a few short feathers on the crown, the head and nape are unfeathered; in the White-necked species the bare skin is mainly bright yellow with a black area towards the rear of the head, in the Grey-necked it is bright blue on the forecrown, carmine red on the hindcrown and nape, and forms a blackish triangle on each side of the face. Their beautiful combination of colours, silent, graceful bounding progress across the forest floor, as well as their rarity and generally shy and elusive nature make them highly sought-after by birders.

Along with other birds, rockfowl follow army-ant swarms to take advantage of prey flushed out by the column of ants. Both species are potentially at risk due to restricted ranges, habitat destruction, and egg and nestling losses. The latter are due not only to snakes and other predators but also to the habit of the birds themselves destroying the nests of rivals in an attempt to acquire scarce nest sites. The Grey-necked species is most threatened due to its very fragmented range.

This is a group that has puzzled taxonomists for a long time; as well as being allied with the crows, the rockfowls have in the past been placed in several other passerine families, including starlings or even Old World warblers and Old World flycatchers, and most recently with the babblers, before being placed in a family (Picathartidae) of their own. They are currently considered closest to a pair of much smaller birds from the far south of Africa, the rockjumpers, *Chaetops*, and to an enigmatic species found far from Africa, in part of southern Asia, the Rail-babbler, *Eupetes macrocerus*. To reflect this, they are, in the scheme followed here, united with these three other species in the same family.

The first mentioned pair of relatives are the Cape Rockjumper, *C. frenatus*, which lives in rocky and mainly high-altitude areas of the fynbos (flower-rich scrub) of the Western Cape and southwest Eastern Cape regions of the far south of South Africa, and the Drakensberg Rockjumper, *C. aurantius*, which inhabits steep, rocky mountain grasslands in Lesotho and an adjacent area of South Africa. They are the size of a small thrush, with dense, loose plumage with a bold pattern and striking red eyes: males of both species have a white eyestripe and a white stripe extending down from the bill that contrast with the black face, throat and upper breast, streaked grey crown and upperparts; the Cape Rockjumper is bright chestnut below and on the rump, whereas its close relative has those parts paler orange-buff; females are paler and duller. These attractive birds are wary, running fast over the ground and bounding from one rock to the next, often holding the tail slightly cocked, and hard to see as they hide behind a boulder only to reappear some way away. They have often been considered to be subspecies of a single species, but the evidence points to each being given species status, as here. Furthermore, their degree of closeness to the rockfowls is uncertain and they are sometimes given a family, Chaetopidae, of their own. Although both are currently listed as Near Threatened, the conservation status of the Cape Rockjumper may soon be upgraded to Vulnerable, as it faces ongoing declines due to global warming.

The Rail-babbler is an unusual forest floor dweller in the jungles of Malaya, Sumatra and Borneo. Extremely shy and secretive, it is an elegant, small-headed, long-legged bird with a rather long, thin bill and a long graduated tail. It is handsomely plumaged, with a striking rich reddish brown crown contrasting with the white eyestripe and black mask and a mainly olive-brown body. On either side of its neck lie a pair of purplish blue air sacs, which it inflates to produce its long whistling calls. As with the rockjumpers, it is possible that until its detailed relationships are elucidated, this enigmatic species might be better placed in a family, Eupetidae, of its own, leaving the rockfowls to occupy their traditional Family Picathartidae, alone.

AUSTRALASIAN ROBINS Petroicidae

GENERA: 19   **SPECIES**: 49

LENGTH: 10–23 cm (4–9 in)

WEIGHT: 7–48 g (0.25–1.7 oz)

RANGE AND HABITAT: New Guinea, Australia, New Zealand, islands of south-west Pacific; a wide range of mainly wooded habitats, from semi-arid scrubland to tropical rainforest and mangroves, and from lowland savannah to mountain forests, alpine grassland, cliffs and rocky slopes above 2,500 m (8,200 ft)

SOCIAL BEHAVIOUR: typically seen alone or in pairs, although some species form small family groups or larger flocks outside the breeding season; most are monogamous, sometimes for more than one season, and territorial; several are cooperative breeders

NEST: usually a small, saucer-shaped, nest of plant fibres, grasses, bark strips and lichens, bound with spiders' webs, in the fork of a tree or shrub branch; scrub-robins and ground-robins build a bigger, cup-shaped nest on the ground

EGGS: 2–3, pale buff or grey to pale olive or greenish-blue, with brown or grey spots

INCUBATION: 14–20 days

FLEDGING PERIOD: 12–17 days

FOOD: mainly insects; also earthworms, spiders, centipedes, molluscs, berries and seeds

VOICE: brief, high-pitched trills or whistles, undulating piping notes, harsh alarm calls; some have attractive songs

MIGRATION: mostly sedentary

CONSERVATION STATUS: one species, the Chatham Island Robin, *Petroica traversi*, is Endangered; three species are Near Threatened

Although, like the American Robin, *Turdus migratorius* (of the thrush Family Turdidae), the Australasian robins were named by homesick European settlers after the 'true' (European) Robin, *Erithacus rubecula*, of Europe, they are not at all closely related. They were, nonetheless, originally classified with the European Robin and other chats in a subgroup of Old World flycatchers within the very large Family Muscicapidae. Some ornithologists placed them with the whistlers, Pachycephalidae, but the consensus today is that they deserve a family of their own.

Most members of this family are stocky birds with a relatively large, rounded head, large, prominent eyes and a thin, short, straight bill, in some species with a strongly hooked tip. The wings of most species are short and more or less rounded, while the 12-feathered, usually square-ended tail is short in some species but longer in others. These birds typically have an upright posture and often flick their wings and tail. Some species (such as the Eastern Yellow Robin, *Eopsaltria australis*, the Dusky Robin, *Melanodryas vittata*, and a pair of New Zealand endemics, the North Island

LEFT The Pale-yellow Robin, *Tregellasia capito*, is a common inhabitant of rainforests in eastern Australia.

RIGHT This is a male White-winged Robin, *Peneothello sigillatus*, in mountain forest of the western highlands of Papua New Guinea.

Robin, *Petroica longipes*, and the South Island Robin, *P. australis*) are familiar birds, noted for their loud or attractive songs and in some cases for their tameness. Others, by contrast, including most of the New Guinea species, are wary and difficult to see, skulking in dense undergrowth. Most species forage by watching and waiting, then flying down onto their invertebrate prey, but some also catch insects in flight.

There are six subfamilies. The first, Amalocichlinae, contains just one genus, *Amalocichla*, containing two sturdy, strong-legged, brown-plumaged and rather thrush-like species from the mountane forests of New Guinea – the Greater and Lesser Ground Robin, *A. sclateriana*, and *A. incerta*. They forage on the forest floor, running in short bursts and then stopping to snap up their insect prey.

The second subfamily is the Pachycephalopsinae, again with two species in a single genus, *Pachycephalopsis*, endemic to New Guinea montane forests. One of these small birds is very dark grey above and pale grey below, the other with a grey head, olive and brown upperparts and yellow-green underparts.

The third subfamily, Petroicinae, contains two genera. One is monotypic, containing the diminutive Garnet Robin, *Eugerygone rubra*, yet another New Guinea endemic. The other genus is *Petroica*, with 12 species, two in the mountains of New Guinea, four in Australia, one in many islands of the west Pacific, from the Solomns to Fiji and Samoa, and four in New Zealand. They have – at least in males – a reddish breast rather like that of the European Robin, though the red varies from bright pinkish to paler, more diffuse orange-red. The rest of the underparts are usually white or yellow, the head black with a distinctive white spot on the forehead, and the upperparts black. In contrast to the European Robin, and most other Australasian robins too, the sexes look quite different, with the females being mainly brown, darker above. The genus contains all four of New Zealand's robins, including the Endangered Chatham Island Robin, *P. traversi*, found only on the remote Chatham Islands, lying about 800 km (500 miles) east of New Zealand's South Island, and governed by that nation. Also called the Black Robin, from its entirely dull black plumage, the change in fortune of this little, big-headed bird is a renowned conservation success story. As a result mainly of predation by cats and rats introduced by settlers, it declined rapidly and by 1980 the total population was just five birds – the smallest of any bird species for which precise figures were

known – and it seemed doomed to extinction. As a result of using the other, common, robin species on the islands, the tiny Tomtit, *P. macrocephala*, as a foster parent, providing nest boxes, carrying out reforestation and controlling predators, the population now numbers over 250 adults. Continuing threats include predation of adults, eggs and young by introduced Common Starlings, *Sturnus vulgaris*, severe storms and the loss of genetic diversity.

The fourth subfamily is the Microecinae, containing 11 species in five genera. They include three species of *Microeca*. One, the Golden-bellied Robin, *M. hemixantha*, is found only in the Tanimbar Islands, lying to the southwest of New Guinea. The other two are shared between New Guinea and Australia. The first of these is the Lemon-bellied Robin, *M. flavigaster*, with a scattered range in New Guinea and in Australia found only in the far north. The third species, *M. fascinans*, by contrast, despite its drab brown and grey plumage, is one of Australia's best-known and most loved birds, accounting for its affectionate common name of Jacky Winter. This has nothing to do with its seasonal occurrence, as it is generally present throughout the year, but is onomatopoeic, a rough transliteration of its cheery song of repeated four-note phrases; a similarly imitative alternative local name is Peter-Peter.

The subfamily Drymodinae comprises just three species of scrub robins in a single genus, *Drymodes*. One, the Papuan Scrub Robin, *D. beccarii*, is widespread in New Guinea and on the Aru Islands between Australia and New Guinea, while another, the Northern Scrub Robin, *D. superciliaris*, is restricted to the extreme north of the Cape York Peninsula in northwest Australia. These two are boldly patterned in brown, black, white and buff. By contrast, the third species, the Southern Scrub Robin, *D. brunneopygia*, found in scattered locations in southern Australia, is almost uniformly plain brown.

The final subfamily, the Eopsaltrinae, is the most diverse, with 21 species in nine genera. It includes species that are boldly marked in browns, buffs, black and white, all-dark grey, mainly grey with black-and-white markings, or olive, grey or black, lemon yellow and white.

SUGARBIRDS AND RELATIVES Promeropidae

GENERA: 4   **SPECIES**: 5

LENGTH: sugarbirds, 23–44 cm (9–17 in), including elongated tail-feathers of 15–32 cm (6–12.5 in); the three other species, 15–19 cm (6–7.5 in)

WEIGHT: sugarbirds, 23–46 g (0.8–1.6 oz); other three species, 26–42 g (0.9–1.5 oz)

RANGE AND HABITAT: sugarbirds, southern Africa, one, the Cape Sugarbird, *Promerops afer*, in fynbos heathland from lowlands to mountain slopes, the other, Gurney's Sugarbird, *P. gurneyi*, in montane scrub, in both cases heavily dependent on *Protea* flowers for nectar; also visits gardens, parks, botanical gardens and nurseries with *Protea*; the three other species occur in a few small isolated areas of montane forests across Africa

SOCIAL BEHAVIOUR: sugarbirds, often seen in pairs, solitary or loosely colonial breeders; largely monogamous, strongly territorial; little information about the other three species, though probably all are solitary or in pairs, sometimes in small groups, and territorial

NEST: sugarbirds, a deep cup of twigs, heath stems and dry grass, lined with soft *Protea* seed down, sited in a *Protea* bush or a solitary tree; no information for the other three species, except for a nest of the Spot-throat, *Modulatrix stictigula*, which was a neat cup of twigs lined with a felt of leaf skeletons

EGGS: sugarbirds, 2, fawn to dull salmon pink in the Cape Sugarbird, cream to pale brown in Gurney's Sugarbird, in both with dark brown markings; Spot-throat, 2, pinkish with heavy crimson markings; Grey-chested Kakamega, *Kakamega poliothorax*, 2, whitish; unknown for Dapple-chest

INCUBATION: sugarbirds, 16–17; unknown for the three other species

FLEDGING PERIOD: sugarbirds, 17–23 days; unknown for the three other species

FOOD: sugarbirds, in the breeding season, chiefly nectar from a wide variety of different *Protea* species of shrubs, as well as some other tubular-flowered plants, supplemented by small insects and spiders, many of which are fed to nestlings; after breeding, mainly nectar from other flowering shrubs and trees, such as aloes and agaves, and insects; the three other species eat insects and other invertebrates (and, some at least, berries), probing into the soil or flicking away leaf-litter with their bill

VOICE: sugarbirds, song is a medley of harsh, liquid, twanging, twittering or squeaking notes, and calls include harsh, rasping alarm calls; the other three species have loud, melodious whistling songs and warbling, chattering or harsh calls

MIGRATION: sugarbirds, sedentary apart from relatively short nomadic movements after breeding in response to flowering times of food plants; three other species are presumed to be sedentary, apart from some possible altitudinal movements

CONSERVATION STATUS: one species, the Dapple-chest, *Arcanator orostruthus*, is Vulnerable, and one species, Gurney's Sugarbird, *Promerops gurneyi*, is Near Threatened

Specialised feeders on the nectar of southern African shrubs belonging to the genus *Protea*, the sugarbirds probably evolved in parallel with their food source. They depend on it not only for their staple diet in the breeding season but also for nest material, nest sites and roosting places. In return the *Protea* shrubs benefit from the birds being their main pollinators, and also seed distributors, when the seeds in unused or abandoned nests are blown out of the nest bush by the wind and rain, to germinate in the ground.

The sugarbirds' breeding season, in the Southern Hemisphere winter, between April and August is closely synchronised to the flowering period of most species of proteas. Outside the breeding season, they also drink nectar from other plants, such as agaves, aloes, red-hot pokers (*Kniphofia*), eucalypts and ericas.

There are two species of sugarbird in a single genus, *Promerops*. The Cape Sugarbird, *P. cafer*, occurs farthest south, in the western and southern Cape Province of South Africa, while Gurney's Sugarbird, *P. gurneyi*, lives in north and east South Africa and in the eastern highlands of Zimbabwe and adjacent western Mozambique.

Both are long bodied, long-billed and very long-tailed birds, and look like big, long-tailed sunbirds. The male Cape Sugarbird has a particularly long tail, which may account for as much as 86% of the bird's total length. The female has a shorter tail, but it

LEFT The Cape Sugarbird, *Promerops cafer*, has co-evolved with protea flowers, which provide it with its staple diet of nectar. In return, the sugarbirds serve as the plants' main pollinators as pollen is brushed onto their bills and heads and they carry it to the next bloom. Each bird may visit as many as 300 flower-heads every day.

is still about half the bird's total length. Gurney's Sugarbird has a bigger head and stouter body than its relative, and a shorter tail, about half the total length in males, and somewhat less in females. Both species have a long, narrow, slightly decurved, pointed bill. Both species have grey-brown upperparts with darker streaks and an off-white belly and flanks, also streaked darker, and a bright yellow undertail. They differ in details of the head and throat pattern, with the Cape Sugarbird having a dull, mainly grey-brown, crown rather than a deep rufous one, and being less strikingly patterned and more strongly streaked below; Gurney's Sugarbird has a larger, more rufous breast and looks whiter below. Another difference between the two species is in their breeding behaviour: the Cape Sugarbird is a solitary nester, while Gurney's Sugarbird breeds in loose colonies. Although both species spend much time (especially during the middle of the day) hidden within the protea bushes, males are highly visible as they perch on top of the proteas, singing for long periods, interspersed with bouts of preening or feeding.

The long bill of the sugarbirds is well adapted for probing deep into the tubular flowers of proteas, and their long, protrusible tongue, too, is specialised for nectar feeding. In contrast to that of sunbirds, and much more like the tongue of honeyeaters (Family Meliphagidae; see p. 235), the end portion is almost tubular, with a brushlike, frilled tip; the bristles at the tip can be splayed out, to collect nectar from a wider area and channel the nectar by capillary action into a central trough. Sugarbirds also feed on insects, most often gleaning them from the flowers but sometimes catching aerial insects such as flies and wasps in brief flights.

Systematists have always puzzled over where to classify these next three species of scarce and very localised African birds, and they have at various times been rather reluctantly included in the original large babbler family (Timaliidae, p. 362), with the bulbuls (Pycnonotidae, p. 351) or thrushes (Turdidae, p. 391). Recently, molecular research has revealed them to be close relatives of the sugarbirds, and in this book they are regarded as members of the same family, though they are sometimes given a family of their own, called Modulatricidae after the genus name of one of them. They are rather thrush-like or babbler-like birds with short rounded wings and brown or partly brown plumage. All are restricted in range to very small areas of dense montane tropical forest and generally very shy, unobtrusive and elusive, keeping mainly to the darker areas of the forest and often hidden amongst dense cover and when they do show themselves, take off at the first sign of an observer, often with a mixture of hopping and flying. As a result, details of their biology are little-known.

The Spot-throat, *Modulatrix stictigula*, is known from a few areas of forest in the western Usambara Mountains and Iringa highlands of Tanzania and from northern Malawi. It is brown above and orange-buff below, save for the brown-spotted white throat, which is difficult to distinguish in the dim light of the forest floor; the whitish or pale grey eye-ring is more obvious as it contrasts with the dark brown of the head. The genus name is from the Latin word meaning 'a female musician' and this bird has a very loud song of piercing whistles ending in a flourish.

The Dapple-chest, *Arcanator orostruthus*, is also found in a few parts of the Usambara Mountains, and also in the Udzungwa mountains of southeastern Tanzania and mountain ranges in northern Mozambique. It is brown above and pale yellowish cream below with broad olive streaks. Its shy and retiring behaviour is celebrated in the genus name: *Arcanator* is from the Latin word *arcanus*, meaning 'secret' or 'hidden'.

The final member of this interesting but elusive trio is the Grey-chested Kakamega, *Kakamega poliothorax*. It has the most extensive range of the three, occurring in two regions far from each other, at a few sites in West Africa, and parts of East Africa. It has rich reddish-brown upperparts, a whitish throat and grey underparts. Like the Dapple-chest, it is often found alongside streams, and like its relative too it has an attractive song of flute-like notes rising and falling in pitch.

FLOWERPECKERS Dicaeidae

GENERA: 2   **SPECIES**: 45

LENGTH: 7–13 cm (2.75–5 in)

WEIGHT: 4–13 g (0.14–0.45 oz)

RANGE AND HABITAT: south and southeast Asia, New Guinea and southwest Pacific islands, Australia; forests, mangroves, sometimes in scrub, plantations and gardens

SOCIAL BEHAVIOUR: usually solitary or in pairs, apart from small groups assembling to feed at fruiting trees

NEST: purse-shaped or pouch-shaped structures of grass, vegetable down, moss, lichen, spiders' webs and many other materials, usually in a tree or shrub and often suspended from the tip of a branch or twig

EGGS: 1–4, white or very pale grey, pink, green, blue, with brown, red, purple or grey markings

INCUBATION: about 10–12 days for the few species known

FLEDGING PERIOD: about 15 days, for the few species known

FOOD: nectar and pollen, berries, small fruit and fruit pulp, especially of mistletoes; some species also eat small insects

VOICE: loud, high-pitched, sharp calls, including rasping, buzzing or insect-like sounds; songs consist of similar sounds and trilling notes

MIGRATION: most species are sedentary, apart from some that make seasonal altitudinal movements or are nomadic

CONSERVATION STATUS: one species, the Cebu Flowerpecker, *Dicaeum quadricolor*, is Critically Endangered; two species, the Black-belted Flowerpecker, *D. haematostictum*, and the Scarlet-collared Flowerpecker, *D. retrocinctum* are Vulnerable; four species are Near Threatened

ABOVE A male Mistletoe Bird, *Dicaeum hirundinaceum*, lives up to his name as he prepares to swallow whole a mistletoe berry in South Australia.

ABOVE The Orange-bellied Flowerpecker, *Dicaeum trigonostigma*, like this brightly plumaged male, visits gardens to feed on fruiting trees.

True to its common name, this mainly tropical family of diminutive, dumpy birds is closely associated with flowers, from which they feed on nectar and pollen; they also feed extensively on fruit and berries, especially mistletoes, which are an important food, and many species are known to eat insects too. Restricted to the Old World, they are found in greatest variety in Southeast Asia, from Thailand to Indonesia and the Philippines. The family's overall range is considerably greater, extending from India and Burma northwards and eastwards as far as Taiwan and central China, and southwards as far as New Guinea and Australia. Their closest relatives are those in the next family, that of the sunbirds, Nectariniidae.

There are just two genera, *Prionochilus*, with only six species, restricted to the Philippines, Malaysia and Indonesia, and *Dicaeum*, containing the remaining 39. A major difference is that the outermost primary flight feather is well developed in *Prionochilus* species, but vestigial in most of the *Dicaeum* flowerpeckers. Also, *Prionochilus* species have a short, broad, deep, slightly hooked bill. Many of the *Dicaeum* species have a similarly shaped bill, but in others it is narrow, far less deep and in some slightly decurved. In most species, the bill has serrated edges towards its tip. The tongue is long, flattened and slightly concave, with a two-pronged or four-pronged tip, and in some cases is more or less tubular.

All flowerpeckers have a more or less neckless appearance, a compact body and a very short tail. The wings are rather long, with rounded tips. The legs are short and the feet rather slender, suited for clinging to twigs and flower stems or among fruit. One species, the Scarlet-breasted Flowerpecker, *Prionochilus thoracicus*, has also been seen climbing tree trunks like a nuthatch. The plumage varies from quite plain and drab in both sexes of some species to boldly patterned with bright colours in males of others, with females

much duller. The brightly coloured males generally have bluish-grey or bluish-black upperparts, with black upper wings and tail. A few species have a bright red or yellow crown or small patches of those colours on the back or rump. Underpart colours and patterns are more varied, mainly yellow or white, or with patches of red, yellow, dark bluish, black, pinkish or creamy buff. Most females as well as both sexes of drab species have dull olive-green upperparts, with pale yellow, greyish or whitish underparts.

Flowerpeckers are important as pollinators of many flowering trees and shrubs, and also as seed dispersers, when they eat fruit and excrete the seeds. They forage at all levels of the forest, but mainly in the canopy. For almost all species, mistletoes (of one or more of many species) appear to be important foods, at least for part of the year. They can close off the muscular lower part of the stomach, the ventriculus, or gizzard, by a sphincter so that the mistletoe berries, which the birds eat whole, pass directly and rapidly from the glandular upper stomach (the proventriculus) to the duodenum, where they are digested. The seeds pass through the digestive tract unharmed. They emerge as a slimy and sticky mass, with many often held together by gelatinous strings. When they are excreted, the bird wipes its cloacal region against a branch with jerky movements to remove them. Research into this behaviour in the single Australian species, the widespread and common Mistletoe Bird, *Dicaeum hirundinaceum*, (whose range also includes the Aru Islands off New Guinea, some of the southeast Moluccas and the Tanimbar Islands) has shown that the seeds remaining stuck to the branch have a very high average germination rate, of 85% (in one study this ranged from 93–100%). Over half of all species are known to include in their diet many insects, such as beetles, flies, aphids and caterpillars, and some have also been recorded taking spiders.

SUNBIRDS Nectariniidae

GENERA: 16   **SPECIES**: 136

LENGTH: 8–23 cm (3–9 in)

WEIGHT: 4–49 g (0.15–1.7 oz)

RANGE AND HABITAT: Africa and southern and southeast Asia, New Guinea and nearby islands, north-west Australia; a wide range of vegetated habitats

SOCIAL BEHAVIOUR: mostly seen alone or in pairs; almost all are monogamous and territorial, many very aggressively

NEST: sunbird nests are made of leaves, plant fibres, grass and feathers, bound together with spiders' webs, and are purse-shaped with a side entrance, often covered with a porch-like projection, usually suspended from twigs or foliage of a tree or shrub, but sometimes attached; those of spiderhunters are rounded or cup-shaped, attached by the birds to the undersides of large leaves with plant fibres or spiders' webs that they sew through the leaf with the long, sharp bill

EGGS: 2–3, very variable, both in shape, ground-colour and pigmentation: white, pink, blue, some unmarked, others speckled, spotted or streaked

INCUBATION: 13–15 days

FLEDGING PERIOD: 14–18 days

FOOD: mainly nectar, also small insects, and some pulp from fruits and berries

VOICE: high-pitched, fast songs of sharp tinkling or warbling notes, typically rising and falling in pitch; calls mainly sharp, thin and squeaky

MIGRATION: almost all are sedentary or make nomadic movements in response to the availability of flowers, or altitudinal shifts; a few are long-distance migrants

CONSERVATION STATUS: three species, the Amani Sunbird, *Hedydipna pallidigaster*, Loveridge's Sunbird, *Cinnyris loveridgei*, and Elegant Sunbird, *Aethopyga duyvenbodei*, are Endangered; four species, the Banded Green Sunbird, *Anthreptes rubritorques*, the Giant Sunbird, *Dreptes thomensis*, Rockefeller's Sunbird, *Cinnyris rockefelleri*, and the Rufous-winged Sunbird, *C. rufipennis*, are Vulnerable; eight species are Near Threatened

ABOVE The male Hunter's Sunbird, *Chalcomitra hunteri*, of East Africa has a large area of iridescent scarlet feathers on his throat and breast.

With the iridescent colours of most males, their fine, pointed bill, fast, acrobatic flight and nectar-feeding habit, these beautiful, little, mainly tropical birds are often regarded as the Old World ecological equivalents of the New World hummingbirds. These two families are unrelated but have indeed evolved adaptations to a broadly similar lifestyle. Although none are as miniature as some of the hummingbirds, most species are tiny or at least small, ranging in length from 8 to 23 cm (3 to 9 in), apart from a few species; in those with a greater overall length, much of it is taken up by the extra long bill or long tail.

There are two main groups within the family, although it is generally quite a uniform one and these are not deemed to deserve subfamily status. All but 12 of the 127 species, in 15 out of the 16 genera, are called sunbirds, with a wide distribution across Africa and southern Asia, with just two species occurring in New Guinea, one of which also lives in north-west Australia, while the remaining 12 are the spiderhunters, *Arachnothera*, found only in southern Asia. The greatest diversity of sunbirds is in Africa, followed by the area encompassing Malaysia and Indonesia.

Sunbirds have short, rounded wings, and direct, dashing flight. While both sexes of many species have a short or medium-length, square-tipped or somewhat rounded tail, in some species the males have a much longer tail than the females, either markedly graduated or extended into needle-like points, and one species has a forked tail. The legs are short and sturdy, with short, strong toes ending in fine, sharp claws.

Sunbirds have a narrow, sharply pointed bill that in all but one species is very finely serrated near the tip. The bill is typically decurved to a greater or lesser degree. It varies in length from being a little shorter than the head to about three times its length. The longest-billed species are some of the spiderhunters, some of which have a very long, strong and markedly decurved bill. The external nostrils are situated in a groove in the upper mandible, and are each protected by a flap (operculum) to prevent them from being clogged by pollen when the birds are feeding. As with many hummingbirds, the bill of some species is adapted to fit the tubes of certain flowers. The tongue is highly modified, tubular and divided into two or four at the tip. The edges are fringed or frayed, enabling the sunbird to take in nectar by capillary action. Together with two grooves in the palate, the tubular structure of the tongue acts as a suction pump. The combination of capillary action and suction is highly effective at pulling the nectar into the mouth – in contrast to hummingbirds, which lick it up.

Sunbirds feed mainly on nectar from a wide range of flowers with over 450 plant species from about 100 families known to be used by the family as a whole. They include many species of the pea family, Leguminosae, the lily family, Liliaceae, the mallow family Malvaceae, including *Hibiscus*, figs, *Ficus*, plantains and bananas *Musa*, *Fuschia* species and in Africa the Family Protaceae.

In contrast to hummingbirds, sunbirds rarely hover in front of flowers, and lack the former birds' ability to do so with great manoeuvrability for long periods. Instead, they flit from flower to flower, stopping and perching to feed. If flowers are large and the nectar source well hidden, the sunbird may use the bill to tear of the petals or rip into the base of the flower to get at it. As well as nectar, sunbirds eat the fleshy part of berries or fruit. They also feed on insects, such as flies and butterflies and their larvae, especially during the breeding season. These they take in different ways: by gleaning them from flowers or foliage, by hawking for them in the air, or snatching them from spiders' webs. Despite their name, spiderhunters are not the only species to feed on spiders, and in fact like the rest of the sunbirds, usually feed mainly on nectar. In fact, over half of all the total of 127 sunbird species often eat spiders.

Most sunbirds spend much of each day searching for plants that have just bloomed, and making regular circuits of flowering trees and shrubs within their territories. Some are extremely aggressive in defence of these against all comers, including larger species of sunbirds as well as rivals of their own species .

Male sunbirds are adorned in a great variety of brilliant colours, including scarlet, orange, purple, green and yellow. They include iridescent areas, which as with those of hummingbirds look dark and dull until they are illuminated by sunlight, when they suddenly sparkle with scintillating colours. Females are mainly duller olive green or greyish, in some species with small patches of brighter colours. Both sexes of spiderhunters are similar, olive green or brownish above, and yellow or off-white below, often with pale or darker streaks; one species, Whitehead's Spiderhunter, *Arachnothera juliae*, from the mountains of Borneo, is very distinct, with a white-streaked chocolate-brown head and back, blackish wings and tail, a bright yellow rump and boldly dark-streaked white underparts. Males of some species moult into duller, more female-like plumage after breeding. A distinctive feature is that males of about half of all sunbirds (and females of a few species) have pectoral tufts, little bunches of feathers, usually red or yellow, sprouting from the upper flanks at the sides of a coloured breastband, that can be erected during displays.

RIGHT The Beautiful Sunbird, *Cinnyris pulchellus*, is common in thorn scrub and gardens from Senegal east to Eritrea, Ethiopia, Kenya and Tanzania.

BELOW Spiderhunters, like this Streaked Spiderhunter, *Arachnothera magna*, lack the brilliant iridescent colours of many male sunbirds and are restricted to southern Asia.

FAIRY BLUEBIRDS AND LEAFBIRDS Irenidae

GENERA: 2   **SPECIES**: 13

LENGTH: 21–27.5 cm (8–11 in)

WEIGHT: 52–96 g (1.8–3.4 oz)

RANGE AND HABITAT: Parts of southern Asia, in evergreen or semi-evergreen forests, from sea level to about 1,800 m (5,900 ft)

SOCIAL BEHAVIOUR: rarely solitary, seen in pairs or small loose groups; monogamous, breeding as pairs

NEST: very shallow, quite flimsy saucer of twigs, often lined with green bryophytes, small relative to the birds' size, site (known for Asian species) in the fork of a young tree or on palm frond in dense, shaded parts of the forest understorey

EGGS: 2, pale greyish green with darker flecks

INCUBATION: 14 days

FLEDGING PERIOD: 11-18 days

FOOD: mainly fruit, and also some insects; nestlings fed mainly on insects

VOICE: a variety of often loud, liquid whistling sounds make up the calls and probable songs

MIGRATION: sedentary, apart from some local movements

CONSERVATION STATUS: three species, the Greater Green Leafbird, *Chloropsis sonnerati*, the Sumatran Leafbird, *C. media*, and the Philippine Leafbird, *C. flavipennis*, are Vulnerable, and four species are Near Threatened

This small family of beautifully plumaged south Asian birds contains two groups of birds, the delightfully named fairy bluebirds and the leafbirds that have recently been shown by molecular evidence to be closely related. Systematists differ in their assessment of the closeness of the relationship. In the scheme followed in this book, they are regarded as subfamilies within a single family, Irenidae,

whereas in other arrangements they are treated as two separate families, Irenidae and Chloropsidae.

There are just two species in the fairy-bluebird subfamily Ireninae, both in the genus *Irena* (taken from Irene, the name of the Greek goddess of peace). They show some morphological similarities not only to the leafbirds but also to birds belonging to

ABOVE The intense blue areas of the plumage of the male Asian Fairy Bluebird, *Irena puella*, appear as if enamelled, due to special naked barbs at the feather tips.

three other tropical families, the bulbuls (Pycnonotidae, p. 351), the Old World Orioles (Oriolidae, p. 256), and the ioras (Aegithinidae, p. 265). Indeed, they have in the past been considered close relatives of one or other of these families, or even members of them, and before that were thought by some ornithologists to be allied to drongos or rollers.

The Asian Fairy Bluebird, *Irena puella*, is much the more widespread of the two species, occurring in the subtropics and tropics down the far west of the Indian subcontinent as well as in two isolated populations in the north-east and south-east, and across Southeast Asia to extreme southern China, as well as Malaysia, Sumatra, Java, Borneo and the western Philippines. By contrast, the Philippine Fairy Bluebird, *I. cyanogastra*, is restricted to the islands for which it is named and which straddle the tropics.

Both species eat mainly fruit, either plucking them from the tree or shrub while perched or snatching them in flight (both species are powerful fliers). They concentrate mainly on wild figs of various species. Their strong, quite deep and laterally compressed bill with a distinct notch and a slight, fine hook at the tip is well suited for grasping fruit and then squashing it before swallowing it. In addition, many reports refer to the Asian species (but not its Philippine sibling) as feeding on nectar. The powerful bill also serves to deal with insects, such as beetles, and the Asian species has on occasion been observed hawking for the flying sexual stages (alates) of termites. The Asian Fairy Bluebird is highly regarded as a beautiful cagebird by zoos and private aviculturalists, and studies of captive-bred birds have shown that nestlings thrived when fed by their parents solely on insects, such as mealworms and caterpillars provided to them. Much of the time fairy bluebirds are hard to see as they remain high in the canopy, where they can find the greatest concentrations of fig fruits, but the Asian species at least nest quite near the ground, typically at just 2–6 m (6.5–20 ft).

In the early nineteenth century, the leafbirds were regarded as similar to the honeyeaters (Meliphagidae, p. 235) and sunbirds (Nectariniidae, p. 286) with which they share a brush-tipped tongue suited for lapping up nectar; later they were thought to be related to the bulbuls; the first person to link them with the fairy-bluebirds and the ioras was the great ornithologist Edward Blyth who worked for most of his life in India, though he considered them together with those two groups as a subfamily of the bulbul family.

Today, the subfamily Chloropseinae is regarded as containing 11 species of leafbirds, attractive little songbirds named for their predominantly bright green plumage, resembling a fresh new leaf. The name of the single genus, *Chloropsis*, in which they are all included, also relates to this dominant feature, from the Greek meaning 'of green appearance'.

In all but one species, the main differences between the sexes are confined to the head and throat markings and, in some species the wings. Males of most species have a strikingly contrasting black area on the head from the bill to the eye and extending down to the uppermost breast, surrounding a bright blue flash along the jawline, while females of all but two species lack the black. The exceptions are the Bornean Leafbird, *C. kinabaluensis*, and the Golden-fronted Leafbird, *C. aurifrons*, in which the sexes look far more alike, or in the case of the latter species, almost identical. Some species have a blue streak on the 'shoulders' or larger area of blue along the edge of the folded wing, more prominent in the males. The Philippine Leafbird, *C. flavipennis*, is unique in having almost completely green plumage (apart from yellow on the face and along the edge of the folded wings) in both sexes. The most flamboyant species is the Orange-bellied Leafbird, *C. hardwickei*, a widespread species whose range extends eastwards from northern India to southeast China and southwards to Indochina and the Malaysian peninsula. Males not only have by far the biggest black face and breast marking enclosing a large patch of shining violet-blue, but also a brilliant electric blue shoulder patch and black and deep purplish-blue flight feathers and tail, set off with a rich orange or yellow lower breast and belly. Females lack the black and purplish blue, and in two races the oranges or yellow.

All species live mainly in the upper canopy, where they obtain most of their food. Their predominantly green plumage provides excellent camouflage against the background of foliage.

Leafbird songs can be confusing to birdwatchers as they often consist mainly of sounds copied from other bird (and occasionally small mammal) sounds. In some species at least, females as well as males sing.

ABOVE The stunning male Orange-bellied Leafbird, *Chloropsis hardwickei*, appear quite distinct from his mate, unlike other leafbirds.

PRZEVALSKI'S ROSEFINCH Urocynchramidae

GENERA: 1 **SPECIES:** 1

LENGTH: 15.5–16.5 cm (6–6.5 in)

WEIGHT: unknown

RANGE AND HABITAT: endemic to central China, where it lives in alpine scrub at altitudes of 3,000–5,000 m (9,800–16,400 ft)

SOCIAL BEHAVIOUR: probably monogamous; usually seen in pairs or singly during the breeding season and in small flocks in winter

NEST: cup-shaped, made of grass, lined with rootlets, small twigs and yak hair, sited low down in shrubs

EGGS: 2–4, greyish or olive green, densely mottled with brown speckles so that they look all-brown

INCUBATION: unknown

FLEDGING PERIOD: unknown

FOOD: probably seeds and flowers, with some insects

VOICE: the song is simple and brief, consisting of a few sharp chattering notes, and likened by the ornithologist who first described it to that of the Eurasian Reed Bunting, *Schoeniclus schoeniclus*; clear, ringing alarm calls

MIGRATION: sedentary

CONSERVATION STATUS: not threatened

RIGHT A male Przevalski's Rosefinch, *Urocynchramus pylzowi*, reveals his handsome plumage as he perches on top of a bush. This bird spends most of its time hidden in dense cover; the first nest was only found twelve years ago.

A wary, enigmatic and uncommon little songbird from alpine scrub on the slopes of the Quinghai-Tibet Plateau region of central China, Przevalski's Rosefinch, *Urocynchramus pylzowi*, has a conical seed-eating bill like that of finches, sparrows and buntings, but it is relatively slim. Its tail is long and unlike that of finches or buntings is distinctly graduated, with the outer feathers much shorter than the central ones. The very short, rounded wings also have relatively long outer primary feathers, giving it a total of ten primaries compared with the vestigial ones of finches and buntings, which are thus effectively nine-primaried. Males have a bright pink face, a dark-streaked brown crown and upperparts and mainly pink underparts; the tail is pink beneath and with the outer feathers pink above. Females are brown and streaked, with a pale pinkish orange base to the tail. This unusual species was given its common name in honour of the great nineteenth century Russian explorer and naturalist, Nikolai Przhevalsky, who first described it scientifically. He was a Belarusian of Polish origin, and his name in Polish is spelled Przevalski.

At various times this bird has been classified with the rosefinches, *Carpodacus*, in the finch Family Fringillidae or with the buntings in the Family Emberizidae – an alternative common name is the Pink-tailed Bunting. Its true relationships are, however, uncertain, but the latest molecular evidence supports that from morphological features in indicating that it does not belong to either of those two families, and so should be given a family of its own – as was originally proposed by the Polish ornithologist Janusz Domaniewski as long ago as 1918. And perhaps a better common name is the recently proposed 'Przevalski's Pinktail'.

ACCENTORS Prunellidae

GENERA: 1 **SPECIES:** 12

LENGTH: 14.5–18 cm (5.75–7 in)

WEIGHT: 17.5–45 g (0.6–1.6 oz)

RANGE AND HABITAT: Europe, North Africa, Asia; mostly in montane habitats, from forested slopes and alpine grassland to well above the treeline; also some in more open lowland woodland, forest edge, scrub, farmland, parks and gardens

SOCIAL BEHAVIOUR: often seen singly or in pairs; outside the breeding season most species regularly gather in flocks; some breed as monogamous pairs, a few are known to have complex polyandrous, polygynous or polygynandrous breeding arrangements

NEST: cup of grass, moss, roots and similar material, lined with hair and other soft material, sited on the ground, among rocks or other cover, in shrubs or in trees

EGGS: 2–5, blue or blue-green

INCUBATION: 10–15 days

FLEDGING PERIOD: 10–16 days

FOOD: insects, spiders, earthworms and other small invertebrates; small seeds and in some species berries, especially in late autumn and winter

VOICE: thin, high-pitched single or repeated call notes; songs a complex mixture of warbling notes and trills

MIGRATION: most are sedentary or short-range migrants, especially altitudinal; northern populations of some widespread species migrate to temperate regions farther south

CONSERVATION STATUS: none is threatened

This small family of roughly sparrow-sized, Old World songbirds occur almost entirely in montane habitats, apart from one, the Siberian Accentor, *Prunella montanella*, which breeds mainly in the tundra of the far north, and one, the Dunnock, *Prunella modularis*, which is mainly a lowland species in western Europe. They are the only family of birds that is (virtually) restricted to the Palearctic region (the zoogeographic region encompassing Europe, Africa north of the Sahara, and Asia north of the Himalayan foothills). Most species have relatively restricted ranges, some are highly localised and just three are widespread. All 12 accentors are included in the single genus *Prunella*.

Four species occur in Europe as well as Asia. Two of these, the Siberian Accentor and Black-throated Accentor, *P. atrogularis*, are only very marginally European, each with a subspecies having small populations on the European flanks of the Ural Mountains, with the huge majority of birds on the Asian side. The Siberian Accentor breeds across northern Siberia and very locally farther south, and winters in China and Korea, while the Black-throated Accentor is far more restricted, with one race in part of the Urals and another in the mountains of west-central Asia, migrating to southwest Asia.

The two with extensive ranges in Europe are the Alpine Accentor, *P. collaris*, and the Dunnock. The former has a wide but very patchy distribution from Western Europe and North Africa and right across Asia to Japan, and breeds mainly in alpine meadows and a wide range of rocky habitats above the treeline at up to 3,000 m (9,800 ft) in the west of its range, but up to 5,000 m (16,400 ft) in the Himalayas; it has been sighted at almost 8,000 m (26,250 ft) on Mt Everest.

The Dunnock, by contrast, is the most abundant, adaptable and familiar species, found across the whole of Europe and in a small area of southwest Asia. It is a common inhabitant of woodlands, lowland scrub, hedgerows, parks and gardens in western Europe, from remote, wild country to the heart of cities, while in Scandinavia and eastern Europe it occurs in alpine, subarctic and tundra regions, and in southern and central Europe also breeds in mountains at up to 2,000 m (6,600 ft) or so. It was also introduced into New Zealand by settlers in the nineteenth century and, having successfully colonised scrub and woodland habitats, now breeds throughout the islands.

The range of four species, the Robin Accentor, *P. rubeculoides*, Rufous-breasted Accentor, *P. strophiata*, Brown Accentor, *P. fulvescens*, and Maroon-backed Accentor, *P. immaculata*, includes the Himalayas. The Altai Accentor, *P. himalayana*, named for the Central Asian mountain system where part of its population breeds, does not (despite its specific name) breed in the Himalayas, although it does winter there.

These are all short-necked birds, with a compact body. Most species have a medium-length tail, but three species, the Alpine Accentor, its very close relative the Altai Accentor, and the Maroon-backed Accentor, have a shorter tail. The wings are short and rounded in some species, and rather longer and more pointed in others, and also in migratory subspecies of several species.

The plumage is brownish grey or rufous above, streaked darker in most species, and greyish below, often with rufous markings

LEFT The Alpine Accentor, *Prunella collaris*, breeds on mountains up to the snowline, as here in the Caucasus, Georgia, between Europe and Asia.

and brown streaking on the flanks, belly or more extensively. Six species have a bold head pattern, with a black or blackish mask and a broad white or ochre eyebrow, and six have much plainer, mainly grey head plumage. The Maroon-backed Accentor looks the most different, with its mainly dark grey plumage, contrasting with its pale eyes, with a whitish or yellowish iris, the plain rich chestnut back, wings and rump, and cinnamon flanks and undertail. In all species, the sexes are similar but males are slightly brighter, heavier and longer-winged.

Accentors are largely insectivorous during the breeding season though for the rest of the year they live mainly on seeds, which (like finches) they store in a crop and break down with the aid of a muscular gizzard. Although some that occur in woodlands do perch in shrubs and trees, all accentors are ground feeders. They have a distinctive gait, walking or making little hops with a shuffling action. Those living in open, high-mountain habitats forage among rocks, grass, moss and lichens, where their cryptic plumage camouflages them well, while others feed mainly under cover of scrub or other low vegetation. They are all unobtrusive, without being shy; indeed, most species are generally easy to approach quite closely. The one time when they are most obvious is when singing their complex and varied warbling and trilling songs from a rock or the top of a shrub.

In contrast to the others, the Dunnock is a well-known and much-studied species. Its breeding behaviour is remarkably complex. Although some pairs are monogamous, many females are polyandrous, mating with two males, who share the defence of her territory. Some males are polygynous, mating with two females and defending both their territories, and sometimes two or three males mate with two or three females. Each of the polygamous systems tends to favour one or other sex in terms of the number of offspring raised, and has led to the evolution of the extraordinary precopulatory display. This involves the female standing with her wings drooped and quivering as she cocks her tail and vibrates it rapidly from side to side. The male responds by pecking vigorously and repeatedly at her cloaca, until she ejects a drop of sperm from copulations by rival males. This is followed by the male mating with the female. The whole process may be repeated hourly during the entire 10-day mating period. In this way, a dominant (alpha) male greatly improves the chance that it will be his sperm that will fertilise the female's egg cells and thus his genes rather than a rival's that will be passed on to the offspring. The mating system of the Alpine Accentor is even more involved, with two to five males sharing the large range of a similar number of females. A female tries to copulate with all the males to increase their input in caring for her young, while the alpha male attempts to prevent other males from mating with the females, employing a rate of mating even greater than that of the Dunnock. To produce the huge amount of sperm needed, his testes make up an amazing 7.7% of his entire body weight during the breeding season; the equivalent for a man weighing 70 kg (11 stone/154 lb) would be testes weighing 5.4 kg (11.75 lb)!

The Dunnock is a major host of that famous brood parasite, the Common Cuckoo, *Cuculus canorus*, and the relationship features in Chaucer's *The Parlement of Foules* (1382) and Shakespeare's *King Lear* (1606). Its odd name, one of the oldest of all bird names in the English language, is derived from an Old English word meaning 'little brown bird' (*dun* being a word, still in use, for a greyish-brown colour). Despite its fine warbler-like bill, very different from the stout, conical bill of the sparrows, the Dunnock was for a long time known as the Hedge Sparrow, due to its superficially sparrow-like plumage. The name Hedge Accentor was for a while preferred but is now not so often used.

ABOVE A Dunnock, *Prunella modularis*, delivers his cheery warbling song from the top of a hedge in Norfolk, England.

OLIVE WARBLER Peucedramidae

GENERA: 1   **SPECIES:** 1

LENGTH: 13–14 cm (5–5.5 in)

WEIGHT: 10–12 g (0.35–0.4 oz)

RANGE AND HABITAT: extreme south-western USA, Mexico and northern Central America; open montane coniferous and mixed forests

SOCIAL BEHAVIOUR: generally solitary or in pairs, but two or three, or sometimes up to 15, join mixed-species foraging flocks in winter; monogamous and territorial

NEST: a compact, deep cup of rootlets, mosses and lichens, lined with finer rootlets and plant down, sited at the end of a conifer branch, often hidden among a clump of mistletoe or pine needles

EGGS: 3–4, greyish or bluish-white, very heavily marked with dark olive or brown

INCUBATION: unknown

FLEDGING PERIOD: unknown

FOOD: insects and other invertebrates

VOICE: loud song consists of repeated two-note whistling phrases; usual call a short, plaintive whistle

MIGRATION: mostly sedentary, apart from some northern breeders in south-western USA wintering in northern Mexico and some altitudinal migration

CONSERVATION STATUS: not threatened

The sole species in this New World family, the Olive Warbler, *Peucedramus taeniatus*, was for a very long time thought to be an unusual member of the New World warbler Family Parulidae, bearing a marked – though, as it turns out, superficial – resemblance to many parulids, especially those in a major genus, *Dendroica*. The evidence for its being placed in a family of its own comes from recent research. This has involved genetic analysis, and study of various aspects of its anatomy (notably the shape of the basihyal bone of the tongue and the arrangement of jaw, limb and hyoid muscles). Further evidence of its distinctiveness comes from egg colour and behavioural features such as the parents allowing their nestlings to soil the nest with droppings. Other differences, noticeable to the birdwatcher, are its distinctly graduated, strongly notched tail and thinner and more decurved bill compared with a wood warbler, its habit of wing-flicking, and its whistling call notes. Unlike the familiar wood warblers that breed in Canada and the USA, most Olive Warblers do not migrate south in winter (apart from some of the northernmost breeders in the race *arizonae*), and

it may be that its longer, finer bill is one reason that it can find enough insect food in the cold winters of its montane breeding grounds. It uses this as a precision tool for probing deeply into bark crevices and needle clusters of pine trees.

ABOVE At the northern edge of its range, the Olive Warbler, *Peucedramus taeniatus*, breeds in southwest New Mexico and like this one, in southern Arizona.

WEAVERS Ploceidae

GENERA: 15   **SPECIES:** 115

LENGTH: 11–26 cm (4–11 in); some male widowbirds, *Euplectes*, with a long tail in breeding plumage, up to 65 cm (26 in)

WEIGHT: 10–85 g (0.35–3 oz)

Range and habitat: mainly in sub-Saharan Africa, with just a few elsewhere; varied, from tropical rainforest, open woodland, savannah, scrublands and cultivated land to marshes, mountains and desert fringes

SOCIAL BEHAVIOUR: many are very sociable and usually seen in flocks, which may be huge, while others are solitary for most of the year; wide range of breeding arrangements, from solitary monogamous pairs defending territories to polygamous males in colonies, or family groups with cooperative breeding; the Sociable Weaver, *Philetairus socius*, forms very large nest colonies, with more than several hundred pairs at a single nest

NEST: typical weavers build complex, elaborate and often large nests, typically shaped like flasks, retorts, purses or spheres with a narrow side or bottom entrance and suspended from a branch, or low down among grasses, reeds or other vegetation; they may be neat or looser and more untidy structures intricately woven from fine materials, especially very narrow strips torn from grass or reed leaves, palm fibres, vines and other plants and lined with softer materials such as plant down; some build big untidy nests of thorny sticks or stiff grass stems, supported by branches of a shrub or tree; Sociable Weavers build a huge communal domed nest of grass in which each pair occupies a single nest chamber

EGGS: 2–5, with a variety of ground colours, typically blotched or spotted darker, but plain white or pale blue in fodies, *Foudia*, and some *Ploceus* species

INCUBATION: 11–17 days

FLEDGING PERIOD: 11–20 days

FOOD: most open-country species eat both seeds and insects, although some eat only seeds, especially grains, while forest species are mainly insectivorous

VOICE: harsh, unmusical songs, typically made up of a series of chattering or rattling notes, usually rising and falling in pitch, and in some species incorporating trills, squeaks, buzzing, fizzing or other sounds; call notes of similar sounds

MIGRATION: some are nomadic after breeding, and queleas make extensive movements following rain while some Himalayan species make altitudinal movements

CONSERVATION STATUS: seven species, Bates's Weaver, *Ploceus batesi*, Clarke's Weaver, *P. golandi*, the Golden-naped Weaver, *P. aureonucha*, Usambara Weaver, *P. nicolli*, Gola Malimbe, *Malimbus ballmanni*, Ibadan Malimbe *M. ibadanensis* and Mauritius Fody, *Foudia rubra*, are Endangered; five species, including Bannerman's Weaver, *Ploceus bannermani*, Kilombero Weaver, *P. burnieri*, and Finn's Weaver, *P. megarhynchus* are Vulnerable; six species are Near Threatened

This large Old World family is well named, for these are the most accomplished of all birds at nest building. The elaborate and often durable constructions of many species are some of the most impressive of all examples of animal architecture, and their building involves complex, instinctive weaving actions. The male builds the nest and displays from it to attract a mate. Then, when a female has examined it and approved, she lines it.

Almost all genera and species are restricted to sub-Saharan Africa, and there are four species on the island of São Tomé of which two are introduced and one on neighbouring Principe (which together constitute a very small island country off the coast of equatorial west-central Africa). Eight species are endemic to Madagascar and several other Indian Ocean islands. A single species, Rüppell's Weaver, *Ploceus galbula*, lives in the Arabian Peninsula as well as north-east Africa. The remaining five species are Asian, occurring from Pakistan, India and Sri Lanka east to southeast China, Indo-China and Indonesia.

All species have a smallish head and a short neck, with a rather slim body in many species, although others, such as the bishops in the genus *Euplectes*, are plumper. The bill varies from straight and slender and sharply pointed to deeper-based or of the cone shape typical of a seed eater; some species have a bigger, deeper bill. The legs are rather short and strong, with prominent, well-developed, powerful feet. The wings are long and rounded, while the tail is short or very short and square-tipped or rather more rounded, although the males of the widowbirds, *Euplectes*, develop long to extremely long flowing tail feathers for the breeding season.

Most species of weaver are highly gregarious: they nest in large, noisy colonies, and forage and roost in large flocks after breeding. The most extreme development of this flocking behaviour is

LEFT A male Southern Red Bishop, *Euplectes orix*, in South Africa fluffs out his brilliant red feathers and sings a sizzling, hissing song to attract a female.

seen in the three species of quelea, the Cardinal Quelea, *Quelea cardinalis*, the Red-headed Quelea, *Q. erythrops*, and the Red-billed Quelea, *Q. quelea*, especially in the last-named. Whereas feeding and roosting flocks and breeding colonies of the other two may contain thousands of birds, the Red-billed species breeds in truly vast colonies containing millions of nests, up to 6,000 in a single tree. Red-billed Queleas are the most widespread species, breeding across much of sub-Saharan Africa and recorded in every country. Quelea numbers fluctuate largely in response to rainfall on their breeding grounds, but they exist in staggering numbers. A single roost can hold millions of individuals, and some flocks can take as many as five hours to fly past. When a large flock descends to perch on a branch, they may break it with their combined weight.

These little birds, about the size of a small titmouse or chickadee, though heavier, have been dubbed 'locust birds' or 'feathered locusts' because they are serious agricultural pests in areas growing millet and rice. On average, each quelea may eat about 10 g (0.35 oz) a day, so that a flock of two million of the birds could devour 20 tonnes of grain in a single day. Extreme measures have been employed for over 50 years in attempts to control their numbers, to little effect. The onslaught has included the use of flame-throwers and ignition of drums of petroleum by means of explosive charges detonated from a distance, as well as extensive aerial spraying of the birds at their roosts with organophosphate pesticides, especially fenthion (also known as 'quelea-tox').

Despite killing tens of millions every year, the attempts at control have had no significant effect on their total population. Indeed, Red-billed Queleas are probably still the most numerous of all the world's wild birds, with estimates of the total peak post-breeding population at various times varying from 1 billion to as many as 10 billion, but probably most likely to be about 1.5 billion. Furthermore, the spraying has often resulted in deaths of other birds and mammals, including those eating the queleas.

The three species of buffalo-weavers, with several distinctive features, have at times been placed in a subfamily, or even a family, of their own. The largest members of the family, they are widely distributed in Africa, and are split between two genera. The sole member of the genus *Dinemellia*, the White-headed Buffalo Weaver, *D. dinemelli*, has a mainly white body as well as a white head, contrasting with a striking orange-red hind body. The other two, all-blackish plumaged, species in the genus *Bubalornis* are unique in possessing an odd structure called the 'phalloid organ', which has been studied in the Red-billed Buffalo Weaver, *B. niger*. The allusion to a phallus is misleading, as the solid structure has no internal connection with the bird's reproductive system. Moreover, it is found on females as well as males, although it is vestigial in the former. Aviary studies show that the male rubs this organ against the female's cloacal region during mating, and it may be that the greater the stimulation a particular male could achieve the more likely the female is to retain his sperm rather than a rival's. In this remarkable species copulation may last for up to 30 minutes or so, compared to just two seconds for most other birds.

Another, rather larger group of 11 species in five genera was formerly included together with the Old World Sparrows and relatives in the Family Passeridae; they have also sometimes been given subfamily status within the weaver family.

The four species of African sparrow-weavers, *Plocepasser*, are, as their name implies, distinctly sparrow-like in appearance, with striking striped head patterns and white wing bars in most species. The Rufous-tailed Weaver, *Histurgops ruficauda*, is far bigger than other members of the family. It has very distinct plumage, grey above with a scaly pattern of pale feather edges, large dark spots on the white underparts, and a rufous rump and tail. It is restricted to a small area of Tanzania. The two species of social weaver, *Pseudonigrita*, are small, rather finch-like birds with restricted ranges in East Africa. In all these species, and the next one, the sexes look alike.

ABOVE The African Golden Weaver, *Ploceus subaureus*, often builds his nest attached to a single reed stem but sometimes he bridges two stems.

ABOVE A male Red-billed Quelea, *Quelea quelea*, perches by the entrance to his nest of grass strips, one of a huge number in a thorn tree in South Africa.

The single species in the genus *Philetairus* is the Sociable Weaver, *P. socius*. This bird, a common species in parts of south-west Africa, is very aptly named, for it is one of the most intensely colonial nesters of all songbirds. Sociable Weavers, which look rather like boldly plumaged male House Sparrows, live closely packed together in large, noisy colonies that may contain as many as 300 individuals. Remarkably, the whole group lives in a single huge dome built mainly of grass, the largest nest structure built by any bird. It grows in size over the years as the birds add to it, and may eventually reach almost a tonne in weight and 4 m (13 ft) in depth. Each pair has its own nest hole, like a human apartment dweller in a huge housing block. Even though it may be only 10 cm (4 in) from its neighbour, each 'apartment' is separate.

There are two distinctive small species of *Sporopipes*, both with a striking head pattern of black feathers with white tips on the crown

ABOVE A Red-billed Buffalo Weaver, *Bubalornis niger*, bathes in a pool at Selinda Reserve, Botswana.

and a 'moustache' stripe; this accounts for the common names of Scaly-fronted Weaver for *S. squamifrons* and Speckle-fronted Weaver for *S. frontalis*. The sexes are alike in appearance. Adapted to life in arid thornbush scrub, they are tough birds: individuals of the Scaly-fronted Weaver studied after capture in the wild survived for up to 62 days without drinking water; like many other arid-zone granivorous birds, they can produce water metabolically on a diet of dry seeds.

The Grosbeak Weaver (or Thick-billed Weaver), *Amblyospiza albifrons*, the sole member of its genus, is a large, thickset, weaver with a very deep bill, which it uses to crack hard seeds. The male is mainly brown with a striking white forehead and white wing patch, while the female is brown above with thick brown streaks on her white underparts.

By far the most speciose of the nine genera of Ploceinae is *Ploceus*, with 64 species (indeed, it is one of the world's largest bird genera). In some species, the sexes look more or less alike, but in many they differ strikingly, with males having a bright breeding plumage and females being duller. Many breeding males have bright yellow or golden yellow as the predominant colour, with greenish-yellow upperparts and tail, and usually a striking black face marking, often in the form of a broad 'bandit mask', but sometimes with smaller or larger areas of black or entirely black head and upperparts. Others have chestnut or orange, sometimes also with black, on the head or body, and a few are mainly or entirely black or black-and-chestnut. Many look very similar until one gets to know the often small differences, especially in head and back pattern and eye colour. This is even more true of non-breeding males and females, in which most species have similar plumage (often streaked olive and brown above and pale or dull yellow below) with fewer distinguishing features.

There are 10 species of malimbe, *Malimbus*: striking red-and-black forest dwellers that are mainly insectivorous. The different species feed at different levels in the canopy, using different foraging styles that helps avoid competition for resources in species with overlapping ranges. For instance, the Red-vented Malimbe, *M. scutatus*, works the highest strata of the forest, gleaning insects from outermost twigs of the canopy like a tit, the Red-headed Malimbe, *M. rubricollis*, forages lower down but still in the canopy, hammering the bark with its bill like a woodpecker and probing bark and moss clumps, and the Blue-billed Malimbe, *M. nitens*, forages near the forest floor, pulling apart and probing clumps of dry leaves and vine tangles.

The distinctive Red-headed Weaver, *Anaplectes rubriceps*, is the only member of its genus. Breeding males of most subspecies are red on the mantle and breast as well as the head, but those of one race, *jubaensis* from southern Somalia and northern coastal Kenya, are almost entirely red. This weaver is widespread and locally common in woodland, savannah and gardens.

The three quelea species mentioned above are strongly streaked black and buff above, with paler buff or whitish underparts; breeding males differ, with the Red-billed species easily distinguished by the strikingly coloured bill of its name, while the other two species are red-headed (the red extending farther onto the breast in the Cardinal Quelea) with a black bill. The Red-billed Quelea has distinctive heritable colour morphs producing a complex range of plumages; the face mask varies from black, purplish or pink to creamy white and the area surrounding it on the crown and breast pink or straw-coloured.

There are six species of fody, *Foudia*, a genus restricted to various islands of the Indian Ocean, with two found in Madagascar. In three of them, breeding males have a brilliant red head, breast and rump; in the most abundant species, the Red Fody, *F. madagascariensis*, found throughout Madagascar, they have an entirely crimson body; in the Rodrigues Fody, *F. flavicans*, they are bright yellow with a thin black mask surrounded by orange; and in the Seychelles Fody, *F. sechellarum*, they are mainly olive green with a dull yellow crown and throat. The Red Fody has been introduced to many other Indian Ocean islands, where it is not only a serious pest in rice fields but also may cause problems for other, scarcer and threatened fodies as a result of competition or hybridisation.

The genus *Euplectes* is divided into two groups with a very different appearance. Eight species are known as widowbirds. Males

ABOVE A Sociable Weaver, *Philetairus socius*, carries out repairs to his personal nest hole in a giant communal nest of dried grass in South Africa.

ABOVE This Red (or Madagascar) Fody, *Foudia madagascariensis*, belongs to an introduced population on Praslin Island, in the Seychelles.

ABOVE This male Jackson's Golden-backed Weaver, *Ploceus jacksoni*, is busily weaving his intricate grass nest at Baringo Lake, Kenya.

LEFT The Baglafecht Weaver, *Ploceus baglafecht*, is most common in upland woodland, but also occurs in gardens in cities such as Nairobi.

of all these species (though not some shorter-tailed subspecies) grow long or very long tail feathers with which to attract females in the breeding season. Confusingly, they have been called whydahs, a name better reserved for a group of superficially similar, long-tailed birds in the Family Viduidae that are all brood parasites. Widowbirds are birds of open country, breeding in such habitats as wet grassland with tall grass, marshes, wheatfields, overgrown areas of cultivation and rank herbage. The males perform dramatic aerial displays to attract mates, flying up from the ground or a low perch when a female appears and flying round with slow, laboured wingbeats or hovering, the long tail rippling sinuously out behind, singing as they go. Jackson's Widowbird, *E. jacksoni*, has a unique, ground-based display: males assemble at leks and vie for the attention of females by leaping up and down over and over again from their own small circle of flattened grass.

The eight other species of *Euplectes*, are called bishops, and, by contrast, they have extremely short tails. The males are boldly coloured little birds. Four of the nine species have red-and-black plumage, one is entirely black or almost all black (with red restricted to the head or as a narrow collar, according to subspecies), two are black and yellow and two black and orange. Non-breeding males and females are extremely difficult to identify as to species. Bishops live in similar open habitats to their relatives the widowbirds. Like the latter, males may display in the air. They sing in flight and while hovering or gliding to attract females and deter rival males; some perform a dramatic 'bumble flight', when they fluff out their body feathers so that they resemble big black-and-red bumblebees.

ABOVE A male Long-tailed Widowbird, *Euplectes progne*, performs his remarkable display flight to impress a female in Kenya.

WAXBILLS Estrildidae

GENERA: 34   **SPECIES:** 131

LENGTH: 8–15.5 cm (3–6 in)

WEIGHT: 6–30 g (0.2–1 oz)

RANGE AND HABITAT: Africa, Asia, Australasia (though not New Zealand) and various tropical Pacific islands; mainly open country, especially in grassland (including in semi-arid regions), also reed beds, marshes, savannahs, with some in woodlands and forests

SOCIAL BEHAVIOUR: some are solitary or live in pairs, but most are gregarious throughout the year, living in flocks and sometimes assembling in huge flocks when feeding; monogamous and territorial, semi-colonial or solitary breeders

NEST: mostly untidy balls or domes of grasses, leaves, bark strips and feathers, mainly in shrubs or small trees, but in some species high in taller trees, or among tall grass, reeds or other vegetation, or on the ground; a few species nest in tree holes or abandoned nests of other birds

EGGS: 2–8, white

INCUBATION: 10–14 days

FLEDGING PERIOD: 14–21 days

FOOD: chiefly seeds of grasses, including cereals; also insects in the breeding season in most species; some also eat fruit, and a few live mainly on insects all year

VOICE: calls varied, mainly high-pitched and sharp, ranging from chirps, chattering notes and purring sounds to whistles; songs made up of soft warbling, whistling, wheezing, trilling or other sounds

MIGRATION: none truly migratory, but many are nomadic, in search of seed crops

CONSERVATION STATUS: one species, Shelley's Crimsonwing, *Cryptospiza shelleyi*, is Endangered; five species, the Green Avadavat, *Amandava formosa*, the Pink-billed Parrotfinch, *Erythrura kleinschmidti*, the Green-faced Parrotfinch, *E. viridifacies*, the Java Sparrow, *Lonchura oryzivora*, and the Grey-banded Mannikin, *Lonchura vana*, are Vulnerable; seven species are Near Threatened

Sometimes known as estrildid finches, elstrildids or grassfinches, waxbills are found only in the Old World and Australasia, being widespread across the globe in tropical and subtropical regions, mainly in open habitats. Many are kept as cage birds. Others are reared in captivity by biologists and are important as research subjects, especially in the field of behavioural studies, including investigations of song development.

Ornithologists believe that the Estrildidae originated in Africa before spreading eastwards, and 73 species – over half of the family total – are native to Africa today. The other main centre of diversity is in Australasia, where Australia contains 18 species, New Guinea 15 species and a further eight are native to New Britain, the Solomons, Fiji and a few other islands of the south-west Pacific. Finally 22 species are native to southern Asia, just two to Arabia and one to Madagascar. In addition, various species, popular as cage birds, have become established in many places far from the family's natural range as a result of having been introduced and subsequently escaped or deliberately set free. For instance, various Pacific islands are home to one or more introduced waxbill species, with at least 10 species established in the Hawaiian islands alone.

Waxbills are all small or very small, finch-like birds, often with bright, boldly patterned plumage, and a prominent, usually short, broad-based and conical bill that is bright waxy red in many species, hence the name. They have short, rounded wings and a short to medium-length tail that is typically strongly graduated, or pointed in some species. Plumage varies widely across the family, from mainly dull brown or plain grey, sometimes with areas of black, chestnut or orange, to being adorned with patches of striking colours, often two or more combined together. Many species have areas of black-and-white, grey-and-white or brown-and-white barring or bold white spots on a black, brown or red background. The sexes are similar in many species, while in others females are duller, lacking some of the males' patches of bright colour. A few waxbills are more strikingly dichromatic. As well as bright red, the bill colour in some species is silvery grey, shiny black, pink or two-toned. The unfeathered eye-rings of many species are coloured,

ABOVE Native to parts of southern Asia, the Chestnut Munia, *Lonchura malacca*, lives in grassland and wetlands, from marshes to mangroves, and also in gardens.

and their colour and size may differ between the sexes or alter for the breeding season.

Most species forage on the ground in more or less open country and seeds form the major part of their diet, but there are some that live in forests and a few that eat mainly insects. Although the forest dwellers tend to be rather solitary, or live in pairs, most open country waxbills are encountered in flocks throughout the year, while others form flocks after breeding as separate pairs. Pairs, and often also flock members, are usually very close companions, spending much or all of the day together, feeding, drinking, bathing and resting (when they often preen one another), and also roosting huddled closely together at night.

Mated pairs have particularly strong bonds, and are usually almost inseparable, spending almost all their time together. Lively courtship displays include the male bobbing his body up and down, bowing, curtseying, fluffing out his belly feathers, and showing the female a feather, grass blade or seed head held in his bill. In most species males have a song whose function is wholly or primarily sexual, rather than also serving as a signal proclaiming territory, ownership as with most other songbirds. Such 'directed' songs are relatively quiet and the males deliver them at close range to the females; often they are audible only at a range of a metre or so. Males also sing a similar 'solitary' song when they are alone, and a different 'social' song directed at another individual in a non-sexual context.

Waxbill nestlings have striking, complex mouth markings that vary between genera and species in size, shape and colour. Swellings on the gape, at the fleshy corners of the mouth, take the form of little flanges, pads, balls, shiny reflective 'pearls' or other small protruberances (papillae). Inside the mouth, the palate and often the tongue are spotted or barred with black, as well as marked with colours that soon disappear in preserved museum specimens. Various theories have been advanced as to their function, from helping the parents recognise their own young and reducing competition from brood parasite nestlings such as those of indigobirds and whydahs (Family Viduidae, see p. 299) or from other waxbill species that occasionally lay their eggs in another species' nest to helping the parents see the young more clearly. It may well be that the varied patterns simply reflect the evolutionary divergence of the family.

Another feature of the nestlings is their distinctive begging behaviour. Like other nestlings, they direct their open bill upwards when the parent arrives at the nest with food, but in this case they also hold the neck low and twist it to one side.

The family is divided into two subfamilies. The first is the Estrildinae, comprising 70 species. All live in Africa, apart from two of the three species in the genus *Amandava*. The Green Avadavat, *A. formosa*, is restricted to central India, where it is increasingly scarce due to a combination of trapping for the cage bird trade and habitat destruction. The Red Avadavat, *A. amandava*, is both more abundant and more widespread, with a range extending from parts of Pakistan and India to southern China and the Lesser Sundas.

There are 19 other genera in this subfamily. These include the four negro-finches of the genus *Nigrita*. They are highly arboreal forest dwellers with a strong but more slender and elongated bill than that of other waxbills, suited for dealing with insects (which they glean mainly in the trees) rather than the seed-based diet typical of most of the family. They have black-and-grey, chestnut-and-grey or brown-and-white plumage. Another small group of insectivorous forest dwellers are the three species of antpecker, *Parmoptila*, which have an even slimmer bill and mainly brown and rufous plumage, barred in both sexes in one species and just in males in the other. The six twinspots are shared among four genera, *Mandingoa*, *Clytospiza*, *Hypargos* and *Euschistospiza*. Their shared common name refers to the prominent white (or in one species, pale pink) spots arranged in pairs on each feather of the lower breast and flanks, and sometimes also elsewhere, standing out against the black, grey or cinnamon of the rest of each feather.

Another distinctive group is that of the firefinches, *Lagonosticta*. Males of most of the 10 species have largely red plumage, and some species have a red bill, too, whereas females are much duller. A common and widespread species, the Red-billed Firefinch, *L. senegala*, can become very tame, scavenging grain from people grinding it for food and even entering huts or other dwellings. The three species of cordon-bleus in the genus *Uraeginthus* are grey above and bright pale blue below, while males of the two species of grenadier, *Granatina*, have areas of brilliant violet or purple as well as rich chestnut. These are birds of semi-arid savannah with *Acacia* and other thornbush scrub, and also bushy grassland and open woodland in some species.

The largest genus in this subfamily is *Estrilda*, with 13 species. Most are grey, greyish brown with fine dark barring or olive above and yellowish buff below, typically with a narrow red mask and red on the rump and tail in most; three species have a black cap and grey plumage, barred above, with striking red flanks, rump and upper tail coverts. Instead of gleaning fallen seed like many waxbills, many prefer to feed by taking seeds from growing plants. They do this in one of two ways. Either they perch on the swaying stem below or next to the seed head, or jump up from the ground to pull down the seed head with the bill and then prevent it from springing back up by holding it down with one foot, while they extract the seeds.

The second subfamily *Lonchurinae*, includes a group known collectively as the grassfinches, with 14 species in six genera. Almost all are confined to Australia, with one species in New Guinea and

ABOVE A male Red-Billed Firefinch, *Lagonosticta senegala*; this species forages for fallen grass and cereal seeds only on the ground.

ABOVE A male Red-Cheeked Cordon-bleu, *Uraeginthus bengalus*; the French part of its name refers not to culinary excellence but to the 'blue ribbon' of its plumage.

one race of another in Timor and many other islands in the Lesser Sundas. There are four species called firetails from the brilliant scarlet colour of their rump and upper tail coverts. Three, in the genus *Stagonopleura*, are endemic to southern Australia, while the other, the Mountain Firetail, *Oreostruthus fuliginosus*, is restricted to New Guinea. This is another of those few groups of waxbills that regularly nest in trees. A very common Australian species is the Zebra Finch, *Taeniopygia guttata*, which also has a race on the Lesser Sunda islands. Named for the black-and-white striped tail, it has grey upperparts and chest, with a cream lower breast and belly, with orange ear coverts and white-spotted chestnut flanks in the brighter males. Very popular as a cage bird, it flourishes and breeds readily in captivity, and has also been of great importance as a subject for research into song development, sex determination, parental care and other aspects of bird biology.

The 10 colourful species of parrotfinches, *Erythrura*, live in southern Asia, New Guinea, Australia and Pacific islands. Several have longish tails with a pointed tip, longer in the males. A close relative (formerly included in *Erythrura*) is the Endangered Gouldian Finch, *Chloebia gouldiae*, of northern Australia, whose striking multicoloured plumage and variability has made it a very popular cage bird. Both sexes have an almost rainbow combination of colours, with a green back, blue rump, purple chest and yellow belly. The head pattern is variable: there are three distinct colour morphs, which may all be found in the same population. The most common form has a black face, while the other two have red or orange faces and are rarer. Birds of a particular morph prefer to mate with those of the same morph, although this does not always happen, perhaps because of the scarcity of some morphs, and overall up to 30% of pairs are mixed. Many more different colour variants have been produced by aviculturalists using selective breeding.

The genus *Lonchura* is the largest in the whole waxbill family. It contains 28 species known as munias and mannikins, with 13 species in southern Asia (mostly in Southeast Asia), 14 in New Guinea and neighbouring islands, and one species in Australia (another species in the subfamily, the Pictorella Finch, *Heteromunia*

ABOVE LEFT The Zebra Finch, *Taeniopygia guttata*, of Australia and the Lesser Sunda islands is a tiny bird that is superbly adapted to life in arid regions.

ABOVE This pair of Gouldian Finches, *Chloebia gouldiae*, with the male in front, are of the most common, black-headed, form.

RIGHT A recent survey found only 109 Java Sparrows, *Lonchura oryzivora*, in the island of their name.

pectoralis, occurs there; formerly included in *Lonchura*, it has a large, more conical bill, and relatively longer wings and shorter tail). Just five species live in Africa, divided between three genera, and one in Madagascar. Their plumage is mainly various combinations of brown, black and white, with a few species almost entirely brown or black.

Although some species are very common and widespread, other waxbills are threatened. As recently as the early 1970s, the Java Sparrow, *Lonchura oryzivora*, was one of the most common of all birds on the island for which it is named, as well as being found on Bali. Today, following a catastrophic decline, it has been listed as Vulnerable. Much larger than almost all other waxbills, it has striking plumage, pale bluish and purplish grey with a black cap, chin and necklace enclosing the white lower face, and a massive pinkish red bill. It has been popular as a cage bird for centuries and very widely introduced elsewhere in the world, from northern South America, Hawaii and East Africa to many parts of Asia, but in its native range it is now rare, mainly as a result of trapping for the cage-bird trade, exacerbated by being persecuted in the past for its depredations on rice crops and hunting for food.

INDIGOBIRDS AND RELATIVES Viduidae

GENERA: 2   **SPECIES**: 20

LENGTH: Parasitic Weaver, *Anomalospiza imberbis*, 11–12 cm (4–5 in); indigobirds 10–11 cm (4 in); whydahs 10–14 cm (4–5.5 in), males in breeding season 26–43 cm (10–17 in), including elongated tail feathers

WEIGHT: 9–27 g (0.3–0.9 oz)

RANGE AND HABITAT: sub-Saharan Africa; open grassland, savannah, open woodland

SOCIAL BEHAVIOUR: sometimes seen alone, in pairs or in family groups, but often in flocks at all times of year; promiscuous

NEST: all are brood parasites, laying their eggs in the nests of other birds

EGGS: sets of 1–4 eggs are laid at the rate of one per day, and there are a few days between sets; one (sometimes more) is laid in each of several host nests, or several eggs may be laid in one nest (sometimes by more than one female); details of the mean total are known for a few species only and varies from about 21 to 30 eggs in a season, according to species

INCUBATION: 11–12 days, known for some species only

FLEDGING PERIOD: 14–21 days

FOOD: almost entirely seeds, rarely small insects; Parasitic Weaver females (and sometimes females of some *Vidua* species) eat the eggs of their hosts

VOICE: complex, large range of up to 24 different song themes, in two groups, one imitating songs and calls of the host species, and the other of harsh chattering notes; a variety of mainly harsh calls, including chattering, hissing and abrupt notes, also softer sounds

MIGRATION: sedentary

CONSERVATION STATUS: none threatened

This small family of superficially finch-like birds is confined to sub-Saharan Africa. All are brood parasites, laying their eggs in other birds' nests. The hosts then rear the parasite's young, usually along with their own. They are close relatives of the waxbills (see p. 296), and formerly were usually included as a subfamily in the waxbill Family Estrildidae. Apart from the distinct though probably closely related Parasitic Weaver (or Cuckoo Finch), *Anomalospiza imberbis*, all species are included in a single genus, *Vidua*, and are collectively often referred to as 'viduines'. There are two major groups: the 10 short-tailed species called indigobirds, and the nine species with long-tailed males known as whydahs.

All but the Parasitic Weaver lay their eggs in the nests of waxbills, specialising in parasitising just one or a few species. In the case of widespread viduine species, such as the Pin-tailed Whydah, *V. macroura*, host choice shows regional differences. Most of the indigobirds have firefinches, *Lagonosticta*, as their hosts, while paradise whydahs select pytilias, *Pytilia*. The Parasitic Weaver, on the other hand, specialises in parasitising various species of warblers in the genera *Cisticola* and *Prinia*.

Female Parasitic Weavers usually remove and eat the host's eggs before laying one of their own (although they sometimes fail to do so with those of the largest hosts), so that their own offspring is the sole occupant of the nest. All the other species do not behave in this cuckoo-like manner, and one or more of their young share the nest with the host's offspring. Typically, they lay sets of two to four eggs in a nest, sometimes distributed between more than one nest, and on occasion more than one female will lay in the same nest. The eggs of the indigobirds and whydahs are white, like those of the host species. Their nestlings (but not those of the Parasitic Weaver) have mouth markings that mimic with great precision the unique markings of their particular host's young, as well as having a very similar first plumage. They also deceive the hosts by imitating the host nestlings' begging calls. This mimicry helps to avoid the danger of the host not feeding them or even ejecting them from the nest.

All members of the family have a lek-type of mating system, where a number of males gather in the same area to display to females. Males space themselves out in separate display territories, perching on branches of trees and shrubs, fences or overhead wires, and sing

ABOVE The Dusky Indigobird, *Vidua funerea*, specialises in parasitizing the nests of the African Firefinch, *Lagonosticta rubricata*.

for long periods. They respond to the arrival of females with aerial displays, including hovering. The male indigobirds and whydahs learn the song of their particular waxbill hosts when in the nest. Females do not sing, but are able to recognise the imitated songs of the males, and by always choosing males with the same song, perpetuate the link between their species and the particular species of host waxbill.

Indigobirds have sometimes been called indigo-finches, widow-finches, widows or steel-finches; all their common names refer to the distinctive glossy blackish breeding plumage of the males. The gloss varies between species, and may be blue, purple or greenish. All are very similar looking, and indeed the indigobirds were once all classified as a single species. Differences are subtle, involving leg colour as well as the colour of the gloss, and it may only be possible to separate some species in the field by mating behaviour, observing the host waxbill they parasitise or listening to the indigobird's mimicked song of its host. Non-breeding males and females are all virtually identical in appearance, rather sparrow-like birds having a streaky brown head and upperparts, with a paler eye-stripe and underparts. Both sexes have a white bill, except for one red-billed race of the Village Indigobird, *V. chalybeata*.

The breeding plumage of most male whydahs is a combination of black, white, buff or yellow and chestnut; the Pin-tailed Whydah is black-and-white, while the Steel-blue Whydah, *V. hypocherina*, appears entirely blue-black, as suggested by its common name,

LEFT This male Pin-tailed Whydah, *Vidua macroura*, is in his full breeding plumage, with two central pairs of tail feathers greatly elongated.

RIGHT The tail of the breeding male Eastern (or Long-tailed) Paradise Whydah, *Vidua paradisaea*, is particularly flamboyant, with the long tail feathers broadened at the base.

although it actually has a small white patch on its upper flank, usually concealed by its back feathers. Non-breeding males and females are very similar to those of indigobirds and, as with them, the species are very hard to distinguish.

The male Parasitic Weaver has a very different bright yellow breeding plumage, and his non-breeding plumage is duller but with a yellowish face and streaked olive-green upperparts, distinguishing him even then from the streaked brown female, which looks like a particularly short-tailed version of females of the rest of the family.

All species feed almost exclusively on seeds, chiefly the small seeds of annual grasses; they usually feed on the same kinds of seed as their particular estrildid host species. The habit of feeding on seeds still borne on the grass plant while perched on a stem, as seen in many waxbills, is rare in these birds. Instead they feed on fallen seeds on the ground, using a distinctive 'double-scratching' foraging technique. This involves scratching almost simultaneously with both feet in loose soil or plant litter to uncover the seeds, then neatly hopping backwards to pick up each seed in the bill; they then dehusk them by rolling each seed against a ridge on the palate.

OLD WORLD SPARROWS AND RELATIVES Passeridae

GENERA: 8   **SPECIES**: 39

LENGTH: 10.5–21 cm (4–8 in)

WEIGHT: 11–70 g (0.4–2.5 oz)

RANGE AND HABITAT: Europe, Africa, Asia; introduced to many other parts of the world; mainly in a wide range of more or less open habitats, including savannah, scrubland, heath, alpine pastures and rocky areas at high altitudes, farmland and urban areas, but some species in more open woodland

SOCIAL BEHAVIOUR: most are highly social, often in family groups or larger flocks; some breed as solitary pairs, but others are colonial or semi-colonial breeders

NEST: mostly roughly spherical or more shapeless, untidy masses of grasses, plant fibres, moss and other materials, including paper or string in some species, sited in a cavity in a cliff, wall, building or other site, or at the tip of a branch on a tree or shrub

EGGS: 3–7, whitish, cream or pink, with brownish, lilac or greyish markings

INCUBATION: 10–14 days

FLEDGING PERIOD: 13–17 days

FOOD: mainly seeds, including grain in many species; most species also supplement this diet with insects, and feed their young on them; some species, especially the House Sparrow, *Passer domesticus*, have a very wide diet, including bread and other human food waste

VOICE: calls mainly consist of chirping, twittering and harsher churring notes; songs are simple series of sounds like those in the calls, often jumbled together

MIGRATION: mostly sedentary; snowfinches make altitudinal migrations

CONSERVATION STATUS: two species, the Italian Sparrow, *Passer italiae*, and the Abd al Kuri Sparrow, *P. hemileucus*, are Vulnerable

The sparrows and other birds in this family, all of which are native to the Old World, are not closely related to the American sparrows, which, together with the brush finches, towhees, juncos and others, belong to the Family Passerellidae (p. 314). As well as the very widespread Old World sparrows, the Family Passeridae includes rock sparrows (also known as petronias or bush sparrows) and snow finches (some of which are alternatively called ground sparrows), as well as a surprising new member, the Cinnamon Ibon.

There are 23 species of sparrow in the genus *Passer*. All have a rounded head, short neck and compact, stocky body, rather short, broad and blunt-tipped wings and a medium-length tail that is square-ended or slightly notched. The bill is typical of birds that feed mainly on seeds, being stubby and conical, with specialised structures and muscles that, as in finches, work together to manipulate a seed, remove and dispose the husk efficiently and rapidly, and swallow the nutritious kernel. It also has a unique structure for stiffening the tongue, which helps the bird hold the latter against the horny palate when dehusking. The legs and feet are rather short and strong.

Best known by far is the House Sparrow, *P. domesticus*. Throughout recorded history it has been a very well-known bird in Europe, and has since become equally familiar throughout the world as a result of numerous introductions and a rapid spread. This highly adaptable and successful species is likely to be the most widely distributed of all landbirds. Wherever humans have come to inhabit, from remote oceanic islands to the centres of great cities such as New York or Tokyo, these cocky, chirpy little songbirds have become part of everyday life, benefiting from our grain, kitchen scraps and other food and the nest sites afforded by buildings, from rudimentary earth huts to skyscrapers and great industrial buildings.

The Eurasian Tree Sparrow, *P. montanus*, is often referred to as the House Sparrow's 'country cousin' in Western Europe, but in eastern Asia, where House Sparrows are largely absent, it is a common bird in villages, towns and cities as well as in the countryside.

Plumage in the *Passer* sparrows generally differs between the sexes. Males of many species have brown upperparts, strongly streaked with black and chestnut, with a striking, typically chestnut, black and white head pattern, a black bib and usually plain, pale greyish or whitish underparts; two species have pale yellowish underparts. Females of these species are much plainer, streaky brown birds, paler below. Two very similar African species, known collectively as grey-headed sparrows, have a plain grey head and body, and brown wings with a chestnut shoulder patch and single white wing bar. The sexes look almost alike.

Three species are very distinctive: the males of two of these, the golden sparrows, have mainly bright golden yellow plumage; the Sudan Golden Sparrow, *P. luteus*, is distinguished by his chestnut brown mantle, scapulars and back from the Arabian Golden Sparrow, *P. euchlorus*, with his paler yellow upper wing coverts and white-edged black flight feathers. The former species (which, despite its common name, breeds right across Africa in the Sahel semi-desert zone immediately to the south of the Sahara) breeds in very large colonies of up to 65,000 pairs. The Arabian Golden Sparrow breeds in northern Somalia as well as in Southwest Arabia. The male Chestnut Sparrow, *P. eminibey*, of north-east Africa is entirely dark chestnut. Females of these three species are much duller.

Rock sparrows, often collectively called petronias, are divided between three genera. The best-known is the single species in

ABOVE A male House Sparrow, *Passer domesticus*, leaves his nest in the ventilation shaft of a derelict building, Shetland, Scotland, UK.

Petronia, commonly known as *the* Rock Sparrow, *P. petronia*. Distinguished by a very short tail, it has a big bill and streaky plumage, and is widespread and common from the Canary Islands, North Africa, southern Europe (with most of the population in Spain), and eastwards across Asia as far as extreme north-west China. The four *Gymnoris* species, although frequently called petronias, are alternatively called bush-sparrows, and these mainly grey and brown birds, which share with the Rock Sparrow a small, inconspicuous yellow spot (in some species in males only) on the lower throat, are found in savannah, scrublands and cultivated land and gardens. Three live in Africa; one in Asia. The Pale Rock Sparrow, *Carpospiza brachydactyla*, which breeds in the northern Middle East, extreme south-east Turkey and central Asia, and winters in Saudi Arabia and north-east Africa, differs from the other rock sparrows in its more uniform mainly sandy-grey plumage, finchlike song, open cup nest of thorny twigs, and egg colour (white with sparse small black spots and tiny black specks), and may possibly be better placed with the large group of cardueline finches instead.

ABOVE A flock of Eurasian Tree Sparrows, *Passer montanus*, busily feed on seeds on a short winter's day in Norfolk, England UK.

ABOVE The male Sudan Golden Sparrow, *Passer luteus*, is one of a few brightly coloured members of the sparrow family.

ABOVE A White-winged Snowfinch, *Montifringilla nivalis*, survives high in the Great Caucasus mountains of Georgia in April.

The eight species of snowfinch are divided between three genera. These are mainly large, stout, grey, brown, black and white birds with the longest, most pointed wings and most exclusively terrestrial habits in the family. As with the rock sparrows, the sexes are alike or very similar. The three species of *Montifringilla* include the only species with part of its wide though very patchy range in Europe, the White-winged Snowfinch, *M. nivalis*. It lives in alpine meadows above the treeline, on barren rocky terrain, on mountains at altitudes of 2,000–5,300 m (6,500–17,400 ft), from the Pyrenees on the French/Spanish border across the Alps, Corsica and south-eastern Europe to Turkey, the Caucasus and across central Asia to north-west China. In winter, it often frequents ski resorts, where it takes advantage of food scraps and shelter.

The single member of the genus *Onychostruthus*, the White-rumped Snowfinch, *O. taczanowskii*, and the four species of *Pyrgilauda* snowfinches, all Asian, are often called ground-sparrows.

Finally, molecular studies indicate that another, quite different looking bird should be included in the Passeridae. This is the Cinnamon Ibon, *Hypocryptadius cinnamomeus*, from the Philippines, where it has a restricted range in mossy mountain forests above 1,000 m (3,300 ft) on the island of Mindanao. Until recently, it was thought to belong to the white-eye Family Zosteropidae (p. 360), but it differs from the other members of this family in various ways, and its skull and other skeletal features resemble those of the sparrows, supporting the DNA evidence that it should be included here, though it may deserve a subfamily (or even a family) of its own.

WAGTAILS AND PIPITS Motacillidae

GENERA: 7   **SPECIES:** 68

LENGTH: 11.5–24 cm (4.5–9.5 in)

WEIGHT: 11–64 g (0.4–2.3 oz)

RANGE AND HABITAT: worldwide, apart from Antarctica, mostly Old World; mainly open country, especially grassland, also tundra, moorland, heathland, semi-desert, farmland, marsh, some in scrub or lightly wooded country, some near streams and rivers, and a few on sea coasts; a few species in woodlands, often near water

SOCIAL BEHAVIOUR: usually seen singly or in pairs, though migratory species usually in flocks when on the move, and often in winter, when many species also form communal roosts; monogamous and territorial

NEST: typically a deep cup, made mostly of grass lined with hair, wool and finer material, almost always on the ground in pipits and longclaws and most species of wagtail, often in the hoofprint of a grazing mammal among vegetation, or concealed among rocks or by a tussock; some wagtails nest in crevices, holes or ledges in banks, cliffs or walls, beneath bridges or on buildings; a few sometimes and one always (the Forest Wagtail, *Dendronanthus indicus*) nest in trees or shrubs

EGGS: 2–7, typically cream, buff or greenish with brown markings

INCUBATION: 11–16 days

FLEDGING PERIOD: 11–17 days

FOOD: mainly insects, also spiders and other small invertebrates, occasionally small fish or tadpoles; some seeds in autumn and winter

VOICE: calls of wagtails are mostly loud, sharp, metallic, double or single notes, given especially in flight; those of pipits typically consist of a series of single or double, thin, often squeaky and sometimes more forceful sounds; wagtail songs are usually simple and repetitive sequences of high-pitched notes, those of pipits may be simple and monotonous but in some species more complex and melodious, including trills, rattling or buzzing sounds and whistles; the calls and songs of longclaws include piping or whistling sounds

MIGRATION: many species of pipit and wagtail are migratory, especially those breeding in northern latitudes, which make often long journeys to and from more southerly wintering grounds; longclaws are sedentary

CONSERVATION STATUS: three species, Sharpe's Longclaw, *Macronyx sharpei*, the Sokoke Pipit, *Anthus sokokensis*, and the Madanga, *Madanga ruficollis*, are Endangered; five species, the Nilgiri Pipit, *A. nilghiriensis*, Ochre-breasted Pipit, *A. nattereri*, Sprague's Pipit, *A. spragueii*, Yellow-breasted Pipit, *Hemimacronyx chloris*, and the São Tomé Short-tail, *Amaurocichla bocagii*, are Vulnerable; six species including the Meadow Pipit, *A. pratensis* are Near Threatened

This is a family of small, basically terrestrial birds, most of which live in the Old World. The family is divided into three main groups.

The 11 species of wagtail in the genus *Motacilla* are almost entirely restricted to the Old World, with just one race (*tschutschensis*) of the Eastern Yellow Wagtail, *M. tschutschensis*, breeding in Alaska (as well as far northeastern Russia). The ten races of the very widespread Yellow Wagtail, *M. flava*, breed right across Europe, in parts of North Africa and across Asia, from Britain, Portugal and Morocco to Japan and extreme southeastern Russia. Three other species are also very widespread in Europe and Asia: these are the more easterly Citrine Wagtail, *M. citreola*, the Grey Wagtail, *M. cinerea*, and the White Wagtail, *M. alba*; the two latter species also breed in parts of North Africa. Three species, the Cape Wagtail, *M. capensis*, the Mountain Wagtail, *M. clara*, and the African Pied Wagtail, *M. aguimp*, are confined to sub-Saharan Africa, and one, the Madagascan Wagtail, *M. flaviventris*, to the island of its common name. The other three, the White-browed Wagtail, *M. maderaspatensis*, the Mekong Wagtail, *M. samveasnae*, and the Japanese Pied Wagtail, *M. grandis*, are all Asian.

Almost all wagtails are birds of more or less open habitats and are good, fast walkers and runners, on longish, often pale-coloured legs, strong toes and long hind claws. They have a shortish, slender, pointed bill, short neck, slim, tapering body and long tail, and are named for their habit of frequently or continually moving their tail up and down (though generally not wagging them from side to side) as they walk and when they land. Most have a strongly undulating flight action.

Wagtails are strikingly plumaged, with small differences between the sexes in some species. Six species have bold black-and-white or black-grey-and-white patterns (the White, Mountain, African Pied, White-browed, Mekong and Japanese Wagtails), and a black breast band or upper breast. Four are mainly greenish or grey above and bright yellow below (the Yellow, Citrine, Grey and Madagascar species); males of the Grey Wagtail have a black chin and throat patch, and both sexes of the Madagascar Wagtail have a black necklace. The Cape Wagtail is duller, with dark olive-grey upperparts, cream throat, dusky necklace and buff underparts.

All wagtails have white outer tail feathers. The Yellow Wagtail is renowned among birdwatchers and ornithologists alike for having very different looking plumage between the various different subspecies, most noticeable in males; some have a pure yellow head, while others have an olive, ash-grey, blue-grey or blackish crown and ear coverts, with or without a white or yellow eye-stripe. Despite these marked differences, all 11 subspecies are genetically very similar, and regularly interbreed in regions of overlap, producing fertile hybrids. On the other hand, the consistent differences in voice as well as plumage of some of the races on either side of the divide indicate they may be well on the way to evolving into separate species.

The Forest Wagtail, *Dendronanthus indicus*, is atypical in various ways. Living in well-wooded habitats as its common name indicates, it habitually nests in trees, in contrast to its relatives. The nest material too differs – instead of grass as the chief element, pairs construct their compact cup nest mainly from twigs, leaves and moss, bound together with moss and spiders' webs and draped with lichen for camouflage. It behaves like a pipit, but has a plumage pattern of brown, black and white more like a wagtail's, yet is more arboreal than either. A unique feature is that it waves its tail and rear body from side to side, with an exaggerated swaying motion.

The 43 pipits of the genus *Anthus* are rather more compact-bodied and shorter tailed. They have much duller, streaked plumage than wagtails, typically brown above and paler below, reminiscent of many of the unrelated larks (Family Alaudidae, p. 339). Most have white or whitish outer tail feathers. The name 'pipit' is derived from the typical flight call of many species. Overall, pipits have the widest distribution of all members of the family, with 16 species breeding in Eurasia (including six solely Asian species), 16 in Africa (including one whose discontinuous range includes Asia, to as far east as Burma), a single species in the Canaries and Madeira, one in both Australia and New Guinea, one endemic to New Guinea and one to New Zealand. There are 10 species in the New World: two are regular breeders in North America one with a subspecies in Asia, the other endemic to North America, while one Eurasian species has bred in extreme western

ABOVE A male Yellow Wagtail, *Motacilla flava*, brings food for his young in a nest hidden under a cabbage leaf in a field in Lincolnshire England.

ABOVE The White Wagtail, *Motacilla alba*, is widespread right across Eurasia, and is at home in a wide range of habitats from remote uplands to city centres.

ABOVE A Tree Pipit, *Anthus trivialis*, performs his parachuting song flight on a May morning in Breckland, Norfolk, England.

Alaska; seven others breed in South America (with the range of one just extending into Central America, in Panama), and one of these has a race on the sub-Antarctic Falkland Islands. Finally, there is one species endemic to another sub-Antarctic archipelago, that of South Georgia.

The fourth group consists of eight species of African birds called longclaws, all in the genus *Macronyx*. Most are distinctly larger than the other members of the family. They are named for the especially long hind claws. All species have brown upperparts, strongly streaked with black, variable amounts of yellow, orange or red below, and a black band or streaking on the breast. Four yellow-throated and black-necklaced species in particular, the Yellow-throated, Fülleborn's, Abyssinian and Pangani Longclaws, *M. croceus*, *M. fuellebornii*, *M. flavicollis*, *M. aurantiigula*, bear a remarkable resemblance in appearance, habitat and behviour to two species of unrelated New World passerines called meadowlarks, *Sturnella*, in the Family Icteridae (p. 321). This striking example of convergent evolution led to a major error by the originator of the binomial system of classification, the great Swedish biologist Linnaeus, in preparing his *Systema Naturae* of 1758, when he listed meadowlarks as occurring in Africa as well as the Americas, though he did correct his error less than a decade later.

ABOVE The Water Pipit, *Anthus spinoletta*, breeds by mountain streams and damp grassland from central Europe to China, wintering in lowland wetland habitats.

Like the Forest Wagtail, four other species in the family are sufficiently distinct to be placed in genera of their own. The first is the Yellow-breasted Pipit, *Hemimacronyx chloris*, from eastern South Africa and Lesotho. This scarce and Vulnerable species is sometimes included in the major genus *Anthus*, but looks more like one of the longclaws, with its dark-streaked upperparts and yellow underparts. The second is Golden Pipit, *Tmetothylacus tenellus*, an inhabitant of scrubby grasslands in north-east Africa. It, too, has a more similar plumage pattern to the longclaws than to the *Anthus* pipits, at least in the case of the male, with his rich yellow underparts with a black necklace. However, he differs from the longclaws, and indeed from all other members of the family, in having almost entirely bright yellow wings, revealed in flight. This species is also distinguished – not only from other motacillids but from almost all other passerines and from all oscine passerines (songbirds) – by a curious feature of its legs. The lower part of the tibia is unfeathered. No advantage has been found for this modification, and no explanation as to why it should appear in this species of oscine only. The only other passerine known to share this feature is a sub-oscine, the Short-tailed Field Tyrant, *Muscigralla brevicauda*, of South America.

The final two monotypic species are both very recent additions to the family from other, unrelated passerine families, as a result of molecular studies. Both are scarce and threatened birds with restricted ranges on small islands, one in Africa and the other in Asia. The first, *Amaurocichla bocagii*, restricted to the floor and undergrowth of humid mossy forest by streams on the island of São Tomé in the Gulf of Guinea off the coast of Gabon, was originally given the common name Bocage's Longbill. It was classified close to several other African longbills, *Macrosphenus*, in the big Family Sylviidae, comprising all the Old World warblers (the latter has now been split into several families, with the longbills and relatives in the Family Macrosphenidae, p. 341). This little bird, just 11 cm (a little over 4 in) long, appears to have diverged from the rest of the wagtail and pipit family in both structure and plumage. It is oddly proportioned, with a disproportionately long bill, short body, very short, rounded wings and a very short tail. Its plumage is dark brown above and reddish buff below. The molecular analysis suggests it is most closely related to the wagtails. In view of its position, it is now generally known as the São Tomé Short-tail.

A name change is also appropriate for the second recently included species, *Madanga ruficollis*, from the little Indonesian island of Buru. Formerly classified in the white-eye family, Zosteropidae (p. 360), it is still sometimes referred to as the Rufous-throated White-eye, but a better name is Rufous-throated Madanga or, since it is the only member of its genus, simply Madanga. Its overall structure is more like that of the pipits to which the molecular evidence suggests it is most closely related, but its plumage is different, with a grey head and body, olive green upperparts and a rufous throat and upper chest. This may have arisen during its evolution as the result of natural selection for camouflage among trees and epiphytic plants: unlike any pipits, it is arboreal, living in isolated areas of stunted elfin forest, where it forages for insects, often climbing up and down trunks like a nuthatch (Sittidae, p. 374), assisted by its pointed tail feathers and strong toes.

All members of the family feed mainly on insects and invertebrates, which they usually catch in one or other of three ways. The first, and most common, method is by walking or running about and picking up prey in the bill from the ground, vegetation and so on. The second method, characteristic of many wagtails but not of many pipits and longclaws, is by 'flycatching' in the air after the bird launches itself on a brief flight from a rock, fence-post, wall or other perch. Many wagtails use this method, and they (along with some longclaws) also employ a third technique, that may greatly enhance their success rate (up to twice the rate of other methods, or more). This entails accompanying grazing mammals such as cattle or sheep, running along near the latter's head or feet and darting out to seize insects disturbed from the ground or vegetation by the mammal's progress. Wagtails also often use their 'beaters' as a mobile perch from which to flycatch and sometimes pick insects directly off the mammal's head or body and from their dung!

Another time when wagtails and pipits are very obvious is when the males are performing their song-flights. These are especially well developed in pipits, with many species singing continually while ascending, often to as much as 100 m (330 ft) or more, and

ABOVE A Yellow-throated Longclaw, *Macronyx croceus*, pauses before feeding its young at Lake Nakuru National Park, Kenya.

then flying along into the wind before planing down to earth or in some species to a perch. Such flights may last only a few minutes or up to 30 minutes, and in a few, such as the North American Sprague's Pipit, *A. spragueii*, as long as 3 hours. Wagtails have more modest song-flights, and also often deliver their songs while perched or foraging.

FINCHES, EUPHONIAS AND HAWAIIAN HONEYCREEPERS Fringillidae

GENERA: 57   **SPECIES:** 222

LENGTH: 9–25 cm (3.5–10 in)

WEIGHT: 8–99 g (0.3–3.5 oz)

RANGE AND HABITAT: fringilline finches in Europe, Asia, North Africa, the Canaries, Madeira, the Azores; euphonias in Mexico, Central America, and South America (except for southern Chile and Argentina), with one species in Jamaica; carduline finches in Europe, Asia, Africa, North America, Central America, South America; Hawaiian finches endemic to Hawaiian islands; mainly woodlands and forests, but some in scrublands, grasslands, deserts, tundra or high mountains, and some in farmland, parks and gardens

SOCIAL BEHAVIOUR: often in pairs or alone in breeding season, but some breed in loose colonies; often form large single-species or mixed flocks in winter; monogamous and territorial

NEST: typically open cups including grasses, twigs, leaves, rootlets, mosses and lichens, though euphonias build domed nests with a side entrance ; usually in trees or shrubs, but in open-country species may be in rock crevices or on the ground

EGGS: 2–7, dark greenish blue with purple-brown markings in fringilline finches; mainly whitish or pastel colours with brownish markings in others

INCUBATION: 9–18 days

FLEDGING PERIOD: 11–17 days (15–27 days in Hawaiian finches)

FOOD: mainly seeds but also some insects in fringilline finches, which feed young only on insects at first; seeds in cardueline finches, which feed young on seeds and insects, or seeds alone; a wide range in Hawaiian finches, mainly nectar and invertebrates but in some species also fruit, fruit juices, seeds, tree sap, seabird eggs or carrion; euphonias eat mainly fruit

VOICE: very varied, with songs often including both sweet musical sounds and hard, harsh, nasal notes; wide vocabularies of equally varied calls; many have specifically and individually distinct flight calls

MIGRATION: most species, especially those breeding in the north, make irregular nomadic or irruptive movements in response to food availability, though some, such as the Chaffinch, *Fringilla coelebs*, the Brambling, *F. montifringilla*, and the rosefinches, make true migrations; most tropical and subtropical species are largely resident

CONSERVATION STATUS: 17 species, all but one (the Bonin Grosbeak, *Chaunoproctus ferreorostris*) Hawaiian finches, including the Greater Koa Finch, *Rhodacanthis palmeri*, the Lesser Koa Finch, *R. flaviceps*, the Kona Grosbeak, *Chloridops kona*, the Black Mamo, *Drepanis funerea*, and the Hawaiian Mamo, *D. pacifica*, are Extinct; six Hawaiian finches, including the Maui Nukupuu, *Hemignathus affinis*, the Poo-uli, *Melamprosops phaeosoma*, the Oahu Alauahio, *Paroreomyza maculata*, and the Ou, *Psittirostra psittacea*, are Critically Endangered (Possibly Extinct); seven species, all but one (the Saõ Tomé Grosbeak, *Neospiza concolor*) Hawaiian finches, including the Palila, *Loxioides bailleui*, the Akekee, *Loxops caeruleirostris*, the Akikiki, *Oreomystis bairdi*, and the Maui Parrotbill, *Pseudonestor xanthophrys*, are Critically Endangered; eight species, including the Red Siskin, *Spinus cucullatus*, the Yellow-throated Canary, *Crithagra flavigula* and four Hawaiian finches, are Endangered; 11 species are Vulnerable; six species are Near Threatened

Although birds from numerous other families (Passeridae, Ploceidae, Estrildidae, Viduidae, Emberizidae, Thraupidae and Cardinalidae) have (or have had) 'finch' as part of their common names, the Fringillidae are the family of the 'true' finches. Although many of its members (such as serins, siskins, canaries, seedeaters, linnets, redpolls, crossbills and some grosbeaks) do not include the word 'finch' in their common name, many do (for example chaffinches, greenfinches, goldfinches, mountain finches, rosy finches, rosefinches and bullfinches).

The Fringillidae is a family of mainly seed-eating songbirds, mostly sparrow-sized (but with some smaller and a few as large as a Common Starling, *Sturnus vulgaris*). Typically, they have a stocky, compact body, rather long, rather pointed wings, a longish, slightly forked tail, short legs and (except for the Hawiian finches) a short, conical bill of various sizes, adapted for a primarily seed diet, with seed-husking grooves and ridges. This large family is divided into three subfamilies. A combination of features unites all three and distinguishes them from other seed-eating passerines. These include having nine (not 10) primary feathers in each wing and 12 large tail feathers, details of skull morphology, the lack of a crop and the non-involvement of males in nest building, incubation and brooding (though not feeding) of the young.

The true finches are most diverse in the northern hemisphere, although the largest subfamily, Carduelinae, does have representatives in the southern hemisphere, in South America, southern Africa and also in extreme southern Asia (where there is just one species, the Mountain Serin, *Chrysocorythus estherae*, whose range includes southern Sumatra, Java and Sulawesi). No species occur naturally in Australasia, although several have been introduced to Australia and New Zealand, and a few elsewhere. A remarkable radiation of species arose in the North Pacific islands of Hawaii after these were colonised millions of years ago by finch ancestors. Today their descendants, the Hawaiian honeycreepers, though greatly diminished, continue to reflect their evolution of an unparalleled diversity of bill and feeding adaptations. Contrasting with this unique and gravely threatened group of specialists, various other finch species are familiar farmland or garden birds, some occurring in the heart of big conurbations. A good many have for centuries been popular as cage birds, the most famous being the domesticated form of the Atlantic Canary, *Serinus canaria*, with its attractive song. Captive breeding began in the seventeenth century and has produced many colour varieties compared with the rather dull, streaky greenish plumage of the wild birds, as well as forms selected for their shape, plumage characteristics and song. They were also used as an 'early-warning system' to alert coal miners of toxic gases (in British mines until the late 1980s) and extensively in neurological research on both humans and birds.

The Fringillinae is the smallest subfamily, containing just three species of fringilline finch, all in the genus *Fringilla*. Two of them are the well-known and very common and widespread Chaffinch, *F. coelebs*, of woodlands, farmland with trees, parks and gardens in Europe, North Africa and Asia, to as far east as Central Siberia, and its northern counterpart the Brambling, *F. montifringilla*, also a common bird, found across northern and eastern Europe and across northern Asia to north-east Siberia, Kamchatka and Sakhalin. In the far north, it is especially common in open birch and conifer woods near the limit of trees. Chaffinches and especially Bramblings are notable for their often very large winter flocks; Brambling flocks in winter quarters in central and southern Europe far from their breeding range can contain millions of birds. The third fringilline finch, by contrast, is a sedentary species with a very restricted range. This is the Blue Chaffinch, *F. teydea*, which lives only in high-altitude coniferous forests, tree-heath and scrub on Tenerife and Gran Canaria, two of the Canary islands.

The fringilline finches are all similar in shape and size (about 15 cm/6 in long), with a longer tail than most other finches. Males

are colourful (bluish, greenish and pink in the Chaffinch; black, buff, orange and white in the Brambling; and all blue in the Blue Chaffinch) and females much duller. The first two have prominent black-and-white wing markings, the Blue Chaffinch paler blue wing bars. All have a peaked crown and a medium-sized conical bill, and are less specialised in their diet than other finches, eating mainly invertebrates in summer and seeds in winter, and (unlike the others) feeding their nestlings on insects, which the young take directly from the parent's bill. They are thought to be the basal group from which the other two subfamilies evolved.

The second subfamily is the Euphoniinae, comprising 32 species that are endemic to the Neotropics. They are divided into two genera: *Chlorophonia*, containing the five species of chlorophonias, and *Euphonia*, with 27 species of euphonias. Formerly included in the very large tanager family (Thraupidae, p. 329), these rotund-bodied, short-tailed little birds, like many tanagers, have very colourful plumage. Chlorophonias are brilliant green above and on the breast and yellow beneath, with patches of bright blue in most species, while euphonias are dark grey blue above and yellow or orange below, with bright blue on the crown and nape of some species. Despite their bright colours, as with many tropical birds, they can be fairly hard to spot in the darkness of a tropical forest or against sun-dappled foliage. Euphonias and chlorophonias feed mainly on small fruit, such as figs and various berries, either reaching for them when perched or while hovering briefly. They squeeze the fruit to drink the juice, which they can do without tilting their head back. They have a highly specialised digestive tract, adapted for gentle and rapid passage of the seeds mixed with the fruit pulp. This enables them to eat many mistletoe berries, which are avoided by most other Neotropical birds, since their

ABOVE Bramblings, *Fringilla montifringilla*, like this male in Kent, England, winter well to the south of their northern Eurasian breeding grounds.

seeds are highly toxic. They excrete the sticky seeds untouched in long strings, wiping their rear parts against a branch vigorously. As well as ensuring that they can capitalise on a food source for which there is little competition, it also benefits the mistletoes, as it allows the seeds of these epiphytes to germinate and grow into new plants.

The third subfamily Carduelinae contains the great majority of birds in the family, with 187 species in 54 genera. Cardueline finches differ in various ways from their fringilline relatives. Whereas fringillines breed as separate pairs and defend large territories, where they forage solitarily, carduelines generally nest in loose colonies and have only small breeding territories, finding their food outside these, typically in flocks. Songs tend to be longer, quieter and less stereotyped than those of the fringillines. They feed their nestlings mainly on seeds, usually rather infrequently, by regurgitation; some carduelines have special throat pouches for storing seeds. The different groups have a great range of plumage colours and patterns, with males in particular sporting bright red, orange, yellow, green, purple or pink, usually in various combinations, frequently also with black on head, upperparts and tail. Head and throat are often boldly patterned, and bars or patches of yellow, pink or white are often a feature of wings. Females (and especially juveniles) of most species have duller, streaked plumage, and many largely or completely lack bright colours.

Carduelines range in size from 9 cm (3.5 in) in the Andean Siskin, *Spinus spinescens*, which weighs 11 g (0.4 oz) or so, and 10 cm (4 in) and as little as 8 g (0.3 oz) in the Anianiau, *Magumma parva*, to 24 cm (9.5 in) long and a weight of up to 80–99 g (2.8–3.5 oz) in some of the Asian grosbeaks. They have a rounded crown and a great variation in bill size and shape, from the delicate, sharply pointed 'tweezers' of the European Goldfinch, *Carduelis carduelis*, adapted for tweaking out soft seeds from deep within prickly seed heads of thistles, teasels and related plants, through the stouter and sturdier bill of many other species to the massive, powerful bill of the Hawfinch, *Coccothraustes coccothraustes*, capable of cracking immensely hard cherry and olive stones. As well as the Hawaiian finches, with their astonishing range of bill shapes and sizes, the

RIGHT The Grey-crowned Rosy Finch, *Leucosticte tephrocotis*, breeds on coastal cliffs and tundra in Alaska and in the Rockies and Sierra Nevada farther south.

most remarkable are the crossbills, *Loxia*, with the curved tips of the mandibles markedly crossed, so that they overlap when the bill is closed – an adaptation for extracting seeds from tightly closed conifer cones.

The subfamily Carduelinae is divided into five tribes. The first of these is Coccothraustini, comprising the three genera and eight species of grosbeaks and the monotypic genus *Coccothraustes*, containing the Hawfinch, *C. coccothraustes*. This large, plump finch with a massive bill and very short tail has distinctive tawny or orange-brown, chestnut, blue-grey and rich chocolate brown plumage, with a large white wing bar on glossy blue-black wings. The tips of the inner primary flight feathers have strange, notched and recurved extensions visible on the folded wing when the bird is perched or on the ground. These odd structures are unique among finches, and indeed, have no counterpart in any other birds, and probably play a part in courtship displays. The eight large species called grosbeaks share their most distinctive feature, an oversized, deep bill, not only with their close relative the Hawfinch and with two species in two other tribes of the Carduelinae, but also with 17 species of less closely

ABOVE A European Goldfinch, *Carduelis carduelis*, perches on a teasel on a frosty winter morning; teasel and thistle seeds are important in this finch's diet.

ABOVE The formidable bill of the Hawfinch, *Coccothraustes coccothraustes*, powered by massive muscles, is capable of cracking very hard cherry or olive stones.

related birds in the cardinal family (Cardinalidae) and tanager family (Thraupidae). Two of the three genera in this tribe, each containing two species, are Asian – *Eophona* in the Far East, and *Mycerobas*, mainly in central Asia, while the other, *Hesperiphona*, also with two species, is American. The latter includes the Evening Grosbeak, *H. vespertina*, a familiar bird of North American gardens and parks as well as forests and woodlands, with striking mainly yellow-and black-plumage in the male.

The second, very distinctive tribe of the Carduelinae is endemic to the Hawaiian islands. This is the Drepanini, known as the Hawaiian honeycreepers. They are sometimes called Hawaiian finches, and have often been treated as a separate family (Drepanididae) or a subfamily (Drepanidinae) of the Fringillidae. This atypical and diverse group represents the most striking avian example of both adaptive radiation and rapid, human-induced extinction. All Hawaiian honeycreepers are descendants of finches that arrived in Hawaii over 4.5 million years ago, where they diversified into a great variety of species, with especially diverse bill shapes.

At least 51 species are thought to have existed in historic times, many of which became extinct after the Polynesian settlers arrived on the islands from about 750–800 years ago, while many more soon disappeared after European colonisation. The result is that today just 17 species in 13 genera (seven of which are monotypic) are known for certain to remain, while six species in four genera (two of which are monotypic) are regarded as Critically Endangered/Possibly Extinct. Only two are categorised as of Least Concern: these are the Hawaii Amakihi, *Chlorodrepanis virens* (which is found on three islands in different habitats, with a wide diet and relative adaptability to habitat changes) and the Apapane, *Himatione sanguinea*, found on six islands, but with most on the Big Island (Hawaii). All the rest are threatened to various degrees.

These remarkable birds continue to face multiple threats. They have for long suffered from habitat destruction and degradation, caused not only by humans but also by pigs, goats and other ungulates, feral descendants of those originally brought by the settlers to the islands, which do a great deal of damage to the native vegetation on which almost all the honeycreepers depend.

They are also vulnerable to the depredations on adults, eggs and young by introduced mammal predators, especially rats, cats and mongooses. An especially acute problem on these islands in more recent times is the prevalence of avian malaria and avian pox, spread by introduced mosquitoes from introduced birds. Because they evolved free from exposure to avian malaria and pox, the honeycreepers are particularly susceptible to the diseases. As a result, many species are now restricted to higher altitudes, as the mosquitoes are less abundant in the cool conditions there. However, even these last refuges may be threatened as a result of the mosquitoes evolving adaptations to lower temperatures, and the effects of global warming.

The range of bill and feeding adaptations that has resulted from their dramatic radiation is greater in the Hawaiian honeycreepers than in any other comparable group (including the oft-quoted example of the Galapagos finches or 'Darwin's finches'). The many different bill and tongue shapes and associated niches of these honeycreepers include a typical conical finch bill like that of other finches in a number of species, with a mainly conventional seed-eating diet, with each specialising on particular native Hawaiian trees. The Palila, *Loxioides bailleui*, for instance, is adapted for feeding on the toxic immature green seeds of the mamane, *Sophora chrysophylla*, holding the seed pods in its feet and tearing them open with its heavy bill. Although various species will eat fruit opportunistically, only a few species at most appear to be true frugivores. One that does seem to have – or have had – a largely fruit-based diet is the hook-billed Ou, *Psittirostra psittacea*, now Critically Endangered (Possibly Extinct).

Other specialists include the three members of the genus *Pareomyza* (one of which has been declared extinct). These have a short, thin, pointed bill like that of warblers and, like those unrelated birds, feed mainly on insects. Other species live on tree trunks and branches, shuffling up them like the unrelated nuthatches or treecreepers, although none uses the tail as a brace like the treecreepers do. Two species are habitual 'creepers'. The Hawaii Creeper, *Manucerthia mana* (unusual in having no known Hawaiian name), has a slender, conical, slightly decurved bill, with which it pries, probes, pecks and pulls bark aside to reveal insects

ABOVE An Apapane, *Himatione sanguinea*, feeds on nectar from a flower of the ohia-lehua tree (of which it is the main pollinator), on the Big Island of Hawaii.

ABOVE The Critically Endangered Palila, *Loxioides bailleui*, is restricted to dry mamane-naio forests in the north of the Big Island of Hawaii.

ABOVE Though abundant locally and found on all the main Hawaiian islands, the Iiwi, *Vestiaria coccinea*, is declining and classed as Vulnerable.

ABOVE The Akiapolaau, *Hemignathus wilsoni*, with its unique 'double-action' bill, though once widespread, is now Endangered.

and spiders. Like nuthatches, it can climb down tree trunks head first as well as ascending them. The Akikiki, *Oreomystis bairdi* (also known as the Kauai Creeper), is very similar in appearance and has almost identical feeding behaviour; but, remarkably, DNA studies indicate that it is not a close relative. This appears to be an outstanding example of evolutionary convergence.

The most extraordinary bill shape among living forms is seen in the Akiapolaau, *Hemignathus wilsoni*. This small mainly insectivorous bird is equipped with a remarkably versatile 'multi-tool'. The lower mandible of its bill is short, straight and stout, adapted as an all-in-one hammer-and-chisel for making small holes into the soft wood of trees to obtain insects and their larvae hidden within. The sharply decurved upper mandible is twice as long, so that it extends way beyond the lower mandible, and serves as a probe for investigating the holes and also as a rake for gathering insect larvae hidden within, in this case using the lower mandible as a fulcrum. The two mandibles are independently hinged, so that when it has extracted an insect the bird can manipulate it, bringing the tips of the mandibles together like a pair of tweezers despite their differing lengths.

The different species of Hawaiian honeycreeper vary greatly in plumage. Males are brighter than females in most species. Many are olive green above and yellow below, but a few, such as the Iiwi, *Vestiaria coccinea*, and the Apapane, have mainly bright red plumage; the Poo-uli, *Melamprosops phaeosoma*, is brown above with a grey cap, black mask and white and cinnamon underparts; the Akikiki is grey and white; and the Akohekohe, *Palmeria dolei*, is mainly black with silver and orange-red streaks and a small stiff white crest.

Despite such considerable differences, all Hawaiian honeycreepers share various common features that support their inclusion in a single tribe: as well as genetic similarity, these include anatomical features (especially of the skull and tongue) and their unusual musky odour.

The third tribe of the Carduelinae is the Carpodacini. This contains 24 species of almost entirely Asian species known as rosefinches. One, the Common Rosefinch, *Erythrina erythrina*, in a genus of its own, has a huge range, breeding from northern,

central and southeast Europe across Turkey and eastwards as far as northeast China, and wintering southwards to as far as southern India. The other 23 species, all in the genus *Carpodacus*, have more restricted ranges across Asia, with one species, the Sinai Rosefinch, *C. synoicus*, in the Middle East. The males of all these species live up to their name by having the head and body mainly red or pink in various shades, while the females are brown above and pale and streaked below. The Carpodacini also includes two distinctive monotypic species. The Scarlet Finch, *Haematospiza sipahi*, is a stout-bodied bird with a short, deep pale bill. Males are particularly striking, with their bright scarlet plumage, while females are olive green above, paler below and with a bright yellow rump. The final member of the tribe was the Bonin Grosbeak, *Chaunoproctus ferreorostris*, which lived on one or more small islands in the Ogasawara (Bonin) islands, about 1,000 km (600 miles) south of Tokyo. Predominantly terrestrial, and thus vulnerable to ground predators introduced by whalers, this large finch with a massive bill became extinct sometime between 1828 and 1854. Males had a scarlet head and breast, while females were mainly brown. There are only about ten surviving specimens.

The fourth tribe in the Carduelinae is the Pyrrhulini. Its 20 species are divided between ten genera, eight of which are monotypic. The latter include the Pine Grosbeak, *Pinicola enucleator*, a sturdy species up to 25.5 cm (10 in) long, with deep pink males and dull olive yellow females. It is found right around the northern forests, from northern Scandinavia to northeast China and across Canada, in Alaska and western USA.

There are seven species of bullfinch, *Pyrrhula*, mostly largish, big-headed, bull-necked, plump-bodied, finches with a deep, stubby, sharp edged, curved bill, adapted for feeding on softer buds, flowers and berries, stripping the flesh from the latter and also eating the soft seeds within. This contrast with the typical diet of hard seeds found in most members of the Carduelinae. Bullfinches are among those finches that develop a buccal pouch in the base of the mouth for transporting food to their nestlings. All have mainly bluish-black wings with a white or pale wing bar, and white on the rump contrasting with the black tail. Three species have relatively sober plumage in both sexes, but in the other four males have areas of brighter colours. Most beautiful of all is the male Eurasian Bullfinch, *P. pyrrhula*, with his deep pink underparts set off by the glossy black crown and chin and blue-grey back. This is the only bullfinch to occur in Europe, including Britain and Ireland; its huge range extends right across Asia. Its habit of stripping fruit trees of buds at a phenomenal rate has led to persecution by owners of commercial orchards, although the birds usually turn to this source of food only when facing a shortage of ash seeds or other natural food.

The five species of *Leucosticte* include three central and east Asian species called mountain finches, since they are found in high-altitude mountainsides and plateaus. They are rather sparrow-like in appearance, with lightly streaked brown plumage. The other two *Leucosticte* species are the rosy finches, one in eastern Asia and the other in western North America, mainly in the tundra and mountains. Males are somewhat brighter than the mountain finches, dark brown or blackish with pink or reddish brown on the underparts and wings.

The remaining seven species in monotypic genera include three small finches specialised for living in hot deserts or semi-deserts. The best known and most widespread is the Trumpeter Finch, *Bucanetes githagineus*, from the Canary Islands, North Africa, the Middle East and Central Asia. The male's greyish and buff plumage is tinged with pink on the underparts and wings in the breeding season and his deep, stubby little bill is bright waxy red, while the appearance of the female (and also of the male after breeding) is much plainer, almost uniform sandy grey. They blend into the rocks and sand as they shuffle or hop across the ground, though their presence is often indicated by the male's distinctive and unusual song – a prolonged nasal wheeze often followed by a sound like a toy trumpet – which is celebrated in their common name.

ABOVE This male House Finch, *Haemorhous mexicanus*, is from part of its original native range, in this case in San Diego, California.

The fifth and final tribe in the Carduelinae, the Carduelini, is by far the most speciose, with 92 species in 14 genera. The House Finch, *Haemorhous mexicanus*, was formerly classified together with the rosefinches, *Carpodacus*, in the tribe Carpodacini, but recent molecular studies have indicated that it should be moved to the Carduelini. Until about 65 years ago it was restricted to semi-arid habitats in the south-western USA and Mexico. In the 1940s it was introduced as a cage bird to the eastern USA, being advertised in New York as 'the Hollywood Finch,' after which escapes and deliberate releases resulted in the build-up of a feral population. During the 1990s, it suffered a major crash in populations in the eastern states, due to infection with a bacterium, *Mycoplasma gallisepticum*, which caused highly infectious chronic sinusitis. Today, though, it is an abundant resident and familiar visitor to bird feeders throughout much of the continental USA, in country and suburbs alike, and extends in the north into much of extreme southern Canada and in the south into Mexico.

There are five species of greenfinch, *Chloris*. These include the well-known and common European Greenfinch, *C. chloris*, and its Asian counterpart the Grey-capped Greenfinch, *C. sinica*, as well as three other Asian species with more restricted ranges. The linnets comprise two abundant Eurasian species, the well-known Common Linnet, *Linaria cannabina*, and its far less familiar close relative the Twite, *L. flavirostris*, restricted when breeding to moorland and mountain habitats, and two species with very restricted ranges in Somalia and Arabia, respectively. The two redpolls, *Acanthis*, are northern or mountain species that occur right across Eurasia and North America; the two other species in that genus are restricted to the Arabian peninsula and Somalia. The plumage in these two genera is patterned in various combinations of brown and grey with streaking and areas of red in most species, especially in the males.

The eight species remaining in the formerly large genus *Serinus* following reclassification resulting from DNA studies include the widespread, tiny and very small-billed European Serin, *S. serinus*. This is the only member of the genus in Europe, whose range extends into North Africa and Asia Minor. Of the other seven species, one, the Syrian Serin, *S. syriacus*, is endemic to Syria and Lebanon, another, the Red-fronted Serin, *S. pusillus*, is mainly Central Asian and four are African. The seventh has become one of the best known of all the world's birds, due to its huge popularity worldwide as a cagebird: this is the Atlantic Canary, *S. canaria*, whose natural range is on the Atlantic islands of the Canaries, Azores and Madeira.

The rest of the *Serinus* species have all recently been moved to another genus, *Crithagra*, resurrected from previous use in 1827. With a total of 36 species, this is the largest genus in the entire Family Fringillidae. All but one, the Yemen Serin, *C. menachensis*, are endemic to Africa. Some of these have olive green and yellow plumage, while others are much duller, browner or greyer and boldly streaked; the latter are often known as 'seedeaters' but this name is better reserved for the unrelated Central and South American birds in the tanager Family Thraupidae, in the large genus *Sporophila* (p. 329). All the *Crithagra* species are then called canaries, apart from the Yemen Serin, three species called citrils and two called siskins.

There are three species in the genus *Carduelis*, the well-known and common European Goldfinch, *Carduelis carduelis*, the Citril Finch, *C. citronella*, and its close relative the Corsican Finch, *C. corsicana*, until recently regarded as a race of the Citril Finch. The best known by far is the European Goldfinch, which has a vast range extending from Ireland, Britain and across western Europe to as far as northwest China. Like various other finches, has a very long history as a cage bird, admired both for its pretty black, white and red face pattern and delicate, liquid, tinkling song, and important as a Christian religious symbol in medieval times. Its relatively long, slender, fine-pointed, tweezer-like bill is adapted for feeding on very small, soft seeds, especially those of the composite flowers in the Family Asteraceae, such as thistles, teasels, ragworts and groundsels. It often balances on the swaying seed heads, frequently feeding head downwards, or bends the stems of lighter plants down to the ground and holds them down under its feet. The Citril Finch, which is patterned in grey and yellowish-green, is a mountain specialist, breeding in Spain, France and the Alps in forests from 700 m (2,300 ft) to the tree line, while the Corsican Finch is brighter yellow below and occurs at lower altitudes, down to sea-level, in Sardinia as well as Corsica.

The exclusively New World genus *Spinus* comprises 20 species. Three of these are the North American goldfinches, which have similar bills and diet to their European counterpart. The mainly bright yellow American Goldfinch, *S. tristis*, is the most widespread, breeding right across southern Canada and much of the USA; the black-and-yellow Lesser Goldfinch, *S. psaltria*, breeds in western USA, Mexico, Central America and northeast South America, while the Lawrence's Goldfinch, *S. lawrencei*, mainly grey with black-and-yellow markings, is restricted to southwestern USA. The remaining 17 *Spinus* species are called siskins. Like the goldfinches, they have a relatively long, tweezerlike bills, in this case for probing into small cones of conifer trees as well as seed heads of flowers. Also like goldfinches, they are lightweight and agile, capable of hanging upside down from twigs, titlike, when feeding on tree seeds. This group includes common and very widespread species such as the Eurasian Siskin, *S. spinus*, which breeds from Europe across northern and central Asia east to the Russian Far East and Japan, and the Pine Siskin, *S. pinus*, which breeds across Canada and the western USA and south as far as southern Mexico and Guatemala. The remaining 15 species are found variously in Mexico, Central America and South America, with a single species on the Caribbean island of Hispaniola (comprising Haiti and the Dominican Republic). They include wide-ranging and common species and also scarcer ones, notably the Red Siskin, *S. cucullatus*, a rare and Endangered species hanging on in very small, isolated populations in Colombia, Venezuela and Guyana. Apart from the latter, most have green, yellow and black plumage in various patterns.

The five species of crossbills, *Loxia*, are distributed right across the northern hemisphere. Their peculiar looking bills, in which the upper mandible crosses over the lower towards its end, are a superb adaptation to feeding on the seeds of conifers without having to wait for the cone to open or the seeds to fall out. This gives the birds great advantage over other birds that eat conifer seeds but are unable to take them from closed cones. The crossbills insert their bills between the tough protective scales of the cone, then use the upper mandible as a lever to prise the scales apart, so that they can then remove the seeds using the spoon-shaped tip of their tongue. They deal with larger cones *in situ*, but remove smaller ones by snipping them off at the base and flying to a more convenient perch to deal with them, manipulating them with their strong, dextrous feet, in a manner reminiscent of a parrot. A crossbill can deal with several thousand cones in a single day.

One species, the Scottish Crossbill, *L. scotica*, has a very restricted range in the ancient pinewoods of Scotland: it is renowned as Britain's only endemic bird, and is one of very few birds restricted to Europe. The Parrot Crossbill, *L. pytyopsittacus*, named for its especially large bill, breeds from northern Europe to western Siberia, while the Red Crossbill, *L. curvirostra*, has a huge range, encompassing most of Europe, North Africa, a great swathe of Asia and North America, Mexico and parts of Central America. The White-winged Crossbill, *L. leucoptera*, is not so widespread, breeding from northeast Europe to eastern Siberia and in northern North America. Recently separated as a species from the White-winged Crossbill, the Hispaniolan Crossbill, *L. megaplaga*, is endemic to the Caribbean island of Hispaniola. Each species has a bill of a different size, adapted for feeding on a particular range of conifer seeds. It seems, though, that this straightforward arrangement masks complexity, and some researchers adduce evidence (including analysis of vocalisations, as well as morphology, including bill size, and lack of interbreeding) that some, perhaps many, populations conventionally regarded as subspecies may deserve species status. All species have mainly red plumage in mature males and green in females; the White-winged Crossbill, has prominent double white wing bars, earning it the alternative name of Two-barred Crossbill.

ABOVE Mature males of the Red Crossbill, *Loxia curvirostra*, are indeed mainly red on the head and body, but females are olive or greyish green. The curiously crossed bill is superbly adapted to extracting seeds from conifer cones.

LONGSPURS AND ARCTIC BUNTINGS Plectrophenacidae

GENERA: 3   **SPECIES**: 6

LENGTH: 13.5–19 cm (5–7.5 in)

WEIGHT: 21–56 g (0.7–2.0 oz)

RANGE AND HABITAT: all species breed at high latitudes in the northern hemisphere, two species (the Lapland Longspur, *Calcarius lapponicus*, and the Snow Bunting, *Plectrophenax nivalis*), in both Eurasia and North America, and the other four in North America only, one of them with very restricted breeding range on islands of the Bering Sea only; all are birds of open country, four species in Arctic tundra and on shores, (Snow Bunting also locally in barren rocky areas of high mountains farther south), Chestnut-collared Longspur, *C. ornatus*, and McCown's Longspur, *Rhynchophanes mccownii*, both breed in sparse, arid prairie in the Great Plains region of southern Canada and northern USA; all species winter in a wider variety of open habitats, from bare or ploughed fields to sandy beaches

SOCIAL BEHAVIOUR: socially monogamous, apart from Smith's Longspur, *C. pictus*, which has a polygynandrous mating system (each sex mating with multiple partners); seen singly or in pairs in the breeding season, typically in flocks during the non-breeding season

NEST: cup-shaped nest, woven from dry grasses and sedges, sometimes also with moss or lichen, lined with softer material such as fine grasses, feathers or mammal fur; that of longspurs sited on ground, usually concealed by a grass clump or other vegetation, and of Snow Bunting usually in a rock crevice but sometimes in an artificial site such as a nest box or among driftwood

EGGS: 1–8 (typically 3–6); pale whitish, greenish, bluish, buff or greyish, with brownish, reddish or purplish markings

INCUBATION: 10–13 days

FLEDGING PERIOD: 7–14 days

FOOD: mainly insects in breeding season, seeds and small fruit in non-breeding season

VOICE: warbling songs and whistling or staccato rattling calls

MIGRATION: all species migratory; McKay's Bunting winters to east of its breeding range, in western and southwestern coasts of Alaska, the five other species migrating considerable distances farther south

CONSERVATION STATUS: one species, the Chestnut-collared Longspur, *C. ornatus*, is Vulnerable

ABOVE The Snow Bunting, *Plectrophenax nivalis*, often lives up to its name as it lives in open rocky country in the Arctic and on high mountains.

Until recently, this small family of nine-primaried songbirds was included within the formerly much larger Family Emberizidae, along with the Old World buntings and the New World sparrows (now in a separate family, Passerellidae, p. 314) and in some schemes it included even more families, such as the tanagers (Thraupidae, p. 329) and Cardinals, Grosbeaks and relatives, Cardinalidae (p. 327), as subfamilies within a vast Family Emberizidae. The latest genetic research, however, has revealed that the longspurs and two Arctic *Plectrophenax* buntings are only distantly related to the emberizids, and so they have been given a family of their own.

These birds are similar to short-billed finches, but have a longer tail, and are highly terrestrial, feeding mainly from the ground, though also perching above it, such as on rocks or grassy mounds.

The name 'longspur' refers to the long claw on the hind toe, a feature shared with other highly terrestrial birds, including pipit and larks. The genus name also alludes to this feature: *calcar* i Latin for a cock's spur.

In all species, the sexes differ in plumage, especially in the breeding season, when males are much more brightly coloure than females, with bolder markings. These are acquired in sprin not by moult but by wearing away of the dull tips of their feathers (a process also seen in some other songbirds, including various othe buntings, finches and *Passer* sparrows). In winter, both sexes of al but the *Plectrophenax* buntings are brown and streaked, then in th breeding season males acquire their brighter, strongly patterne breeding plumage in various combinations of black, chestnut cream, orange-buff and white. In winter, both sexes of the tw *Plectrophenax* species have tawny brown fringes to the feathers o the head and back and forming a smudgy breast band; by sprin these have worn off to reveal the largely white plumage, especially in the males, in which it contrasts dramatically with a black back, wingtips and much of the tail in the Snow Bunting, *P. nivalis*. The male McKay's Bunting, *P. hyperboreus*, is almost all white, with black only on his wingtips and near the end of his tail.

In contrast to the other members of the family, Smith's Longspur, *Calcarius pictus*, has an unusual mating system, shared with only a few other songbirds such as the Dunnock, *Prunella modularis*, and Alpine Accentor, *P. collaris*, in the unrelated family of accentors, Prunellidae (p. 289). Called polygynandry, this involves the female of a pair mating with two or three males to produce a single clutch of eggs, and simultaneously the male mating with two or more females. The male, who does not defend a territory, copulates with amazing frequency – on average over 350 times in a single week – to displace sperm in the female's cloaca from her matings with rival males. This is one of the highest copulation rates known for any bird. Two or more males may help provide food to the nestlings of the many broods containing chicks of mixed paternity; the amount of such provisioning by a male depends on the number of chicks he has fathered.

During winter, when these birds migrate long distances to temperate wintering grounds, they may form very large flocks, often joining other birds, such as other buntings, finches and larks, at good feeding sites. Sometimes adverse weather on these journeys have resulted in the deaths of large numbers, often due to collisions, notably the estimated one-and-a-half million Lapland Longspurs, *Calcarius lapponicus*, killed in the USA during a snowstorm in 1904 across parts of Iowa and Minnesota. Despite this, and other threats from habitat loss and climate change, only one species currently has threatened status. The Chestnut-collared Longspur, *C. ornatus*, has suffered a rapid and huge decline of almost 89% since 1966, due mainly to conversion of its prairie breeding grounds to agricultural land or urban development.

THRUSH TANAGER Rhodinocichlidae

GENERA: 1 **SPECIES:** 1

LENGTH: 19–20 cm (7.5–8 in)

WEIGHT: 43–52 g (1.5–1.8 oz)

RANGE AND HABITAT: western Mexico, Costa Rica, Panama, northern and central Colombia and northwest Venezuela; second-growth forest, woodlands and plantations with dense undergrowth

SOCIAL BEHAVIOUR: socially monogamous, usually seen singly or in pairs

NEST: cup-shaped, made of plant stems on a foundation of twigs and sometimes lined with black strands of fungus, sited low down in a dense shrub

EGGS: 2–3, pale blue or white with black markings

INCUBATION: no information

FLEDGING PERIOD: no information

FOOD: insects and other invertebrates, fruit and seeds

VOICE: song is a musical series of ringing whistles, uttered by both sexes, both separately and as antiphonal duets

MIGRATION: sedentary

CONSERVATION STATUS: not threatened

ABOVE The intense rosy pink breast of the Thrush Tanager, *Rhodinocichla rosea*, identifies it as a male; both sexes of these rarely seen birds sing their beautiful song in duets.

As its common name suggests, this strikingly coloured Neotropical bird, *Rhodinocichla rosea*, has long been the subject of uncertainty as to its taxonomic position. At various times, it has been included in five different families – the tanagers (Thraupidae), horneros and relatives (Furnariidae), New World wood warblers (Parulidae), wrens (Troglodytidae), and mockingbirds (Mimidae). The most recent molecular research suggests that it is the only survivor of an ancient lineage, and hence it has been accorded a family of its own.

Both sexes are beautiful birds. The male is slate grey or black (varying between subspecies) on the crown, cheeks and upperparts, also as a broad patch on his flanks, and brilliant rose pink or carmine on the rest of his underparts, with a similarly coloured stripe running from the base of his bill and becoming white as it extends back over the eye. The female is similar but with orange where he is pink. The bill is sturdy, very slightly curved and ending in a slight hook; the birds use it to toss leaves or other woodland debris to one side as they search for beetles, bugs or other invertebrate prey. Despite its bright plumage, this is a notoriously difficult bird to see; it is very difficult to get even a glimpse as it tends to remain hidden within thickets and other dense undergrowth. It is usually identified by its very fine, rich song, which is reminiscent of the songs of many thrushes (Turdidae), and also of various Neotropical wrens.

NEW WORLD SPARROWS Passerellidae

GENERA: 30   **SPECIES:** 130

LENGTH: 10.5–24 cm (4–9.5 in)

WEIGHT: 9–60 g (0.3–2.1 oz)

RANGE AND HABITAT: throughout the Americas (apart from the highest latitudes in Canada), south as far as the southernmost tip of South America, with almost all species north of the Canadian border breeding as summer visitors; occupy a very wide range of habitats, from tundra and boreal marshes to rainforest, grassland and desert scrub

SOCIAL BEHAVIOUR: mostly socially monogamous, though some species are polygynous; strictly territorial when breeding, when they are usually seen singly or in pairs, but many are sociable afterwards

NEST: most species build a cup of grass, twigs and other vegetation low down in a tree or shrub, or on the ground, usually well concealed by vegetation, sometimes accessed by a grass tunnel; some, such tropical species, as *Arremon* brush finches, build a domed nest

EGGS: 1–7, white, cream, pale brown, blue or green, usually with darker spots, blotches or scribbles

INCUBATION: 11–15 days

FLEDGING PERIOD: 7–15 days

FOOD: mostly seeds, especially of grasses, and small fruit as well as many insects and other invertebrates, which are fed exclusively to nestlings in most species

VOICE: very variable; songs are loud and musical in some species (which may broadcast them in a song-flight), with sweet, whistled notes and clear trills, but in others mainly harsh or chattering notes; many grassland species in particular sing monotonous insect-like buzzing songs; most calls are brief metallic or more liquid notes

MIGRATION: species breeding in Alaska and Canada migrate south to winter in the USA or Mexico, and some of those living in southern South America migrate north, but tropical species are generally sedentary; some species make altitudinal migrations

CONSERVATION STATUS: one species, the Bermuda Towhee, *Pipilo naufragus*, is Extinct; one species, the Antioquia Brush Finch, *Atlapetes blancae*, is Critically Endangered; eight species, including the Black-spectacled Brush Finch, *A. melanopsis*, the Sierra Madre Sparrow, *Xenospiza baileyi*, the Saltmarsh Sparrow, *Ammospiza caudacuta*, the Guadalupe Junco, *Junco insularis*, and the Zapata Sparrow, *Torreornis inexpectata*, are Endangered; four species, incuding the Yellow-green Finch, *Peliophorus luteoviridis*, and the Yellow-breasted Tanager Finch, *Oreothraupias arremonops*, are Vulnerable; 10 species are Near Threatened

This exclusively New World family of terrestrial songbirds includes some of the most abundant and widespread of all North American songbirds, as well as highly localised, rare and threatened Neotropical species. Although they are not close relatives of the Old World sparrows (Family Passeridae, p. 300) or the true finches (Family Fringillidae, p. 305), almost half the species in this family are called sparrows or finches; others are named towhees and juncos. The family probably originated in South America, then spread to Central and North America. The New World sparrows were until recently included with the Old World Buntings and various Neotropical genera, including the seedeaters, *Sporophila*, sierra finches, *Phrygilus*, yellow finches, *Sicalis*, and the various genera of endemic Galapagos finches, in a considerably enlarged Family Emberizidae. The Old World buntings are now included in a reduced Family Emberizidae (p. 316), while the Neotropical species have been moved to the tanager Family Thraupidae (p. 329). Such transfers have not all been one-way; the nine *Chlorospingus* species of Mexico, Central America and South America have been added to this family from the tanager family. Traditionally known as bush-tanagers, they are now better called tanager finches.

Previous assessments of relationships relied too much on the external morphology of the bill, and ornithologists have found that deep, seed-eating bills have evolved independently in several unrelated groups of songbirds. The internal structure of the bill, the muscles working the jaws and the digestive tract, by contrast, shows major differences between families, adding to the recent evidence from DNA studies.

These are mostly small songbirds, sparrow-sized species measuring about 15 cm (6 in); the smallest is Le Conte's Sparrow, *Ammodramus leconteii*, at 10.5–12.5 cm (4–5 in) long, and the largest are the towhees, *Pipilo*, which are bigger and longer tailed

ABOVE The Song Sparrow, *Melospiza melodia*, is widespread and abundant throughout much of its range across North America.

than sparrows, measuring 17–25 cm (7–10 in) long. Most have a compact, stocky build, but in some, such as the large towhees and the brush finches, *Atlapetes*, the body is more elongated. All members of the family have a short, strong, conical, finchlike bill, suited to cracking seeds as well as dealing with insects. Its size varies, from the stubby bill of *Spizella* species, such as the North American Chipping Sparrow, *S. passerine*, through the medium sized but still short bills of most species to the more massive ones of species such as the towhees and the Lark Bunting, *Calamospiza melanocorys*. In some cases, particular races have a far larger bill than others, as in the Sierra Nevada race *megarhyncha* of the Fox Sparrow.

New World sparrows are predominantly terrestrial, and have shortish, strong legs with large feet and well-developed claws, which many of them use to scratch in soil, leaf litter or other substrates to reveal food. The towhees have a very distinctive 'double-scratching' feeding action, in which they rake the ground with both feet simultaneously. Although eating a lot of seeds, and sometimes small fruit such as berries, most eat many insects, as well as some spiders and other invertebrates. Unlike finches (Fringillidae), many species have a strong preference for the seeds of grasses. The diet of the temperate North American species is far better known than that for tropical members of the family, for which there is generally little detailed information.

The wings of all passerellids have nine visible primary feathers (a small tenth one is usually present but greatly reduced and usually concealed). This feature unites them in a broad grouping (the superfamily Passeroidea) with such families as those of the tanagers (Thraupidae), New World warblers (Parulidae, p. 319) and New World blackbirds (Icteridae, p. 321). The wings of sedentary tropical species such as the brush finches are relatively short and rounded, while those of northerly, temperate breeding species making long migrations are longer and relatively pointed. The tail is of medium length in most species, but is noticeably shorter in some, such as the Savannah Sparrow, *Passerculus sandwichensis*, and *Ammodramus* sparrows of North America, and much longer in some, such as the towhees and the Large-footed Finch, *Pezopetes capitalis*, of the mountains of Costa Rica and Panama.

The plumage of most species is in various combinations of brown, grey, olive, buff and whitish, with most streaked darker, helping to camouflage them by blending into their background; some, such as the towhees, have bolder disruptive patterns, including black, reddish brown and cream markings that may camouflage the birds

ABOVE The Black-throated Sparrow, *Amphispiza bilineata*, is restricted to western USA and Mexico, in arid country with scattered shrubs and cacti.

by breaking up their outline. Some tropical species, have different plumage, such as the nine species of tanager finches, *Chlorospingus*, are olive green above and grey or yellow below. Some of them are more brightly coloured, notably the 28 species of brush finches, *Atlapetes*, most of which have olive backs, bright yellow underparts and heads marked with cinnamon or black or a combination of the two. In almost all species, males and females look alike or very similar. A noticeable exception is the Lark Bunting, in which males in their breeding plumage are entirely jet black apart from a white wing patch and white tips to the tail, while females are pale brown above and whitish below with dark streaks.

Although they are generally strictly territorial when breeding, many members of the family form flocks (usually small and loose) outside the breeding season. These are often of mixed species, such as those of North American sparrows, whose similar appearance tests the identification skills of North American birders. Most species are found year-round in open habitats, such as tundra, grassland, marshes or scrub, but as a whole the family is found in a great range of habitats and climates.

Many species are very common, extremely widespread and well known: examples are the Song Sparrow, *Melospiza melodia*, and the White-crowned Sparrow, *Zonotrichia leucophrys*, in North America, and in South America the Rufous-collared Sparrow, *Z. capensis*, the only tropical member of a primarily North American genus, which has a vast range from southern Mexico to Tierra del Fuego, and is divided into as many as 28 geographical races. Others, by contrast, have extremely small ranges; the major threat to their survival comes from destruction of their habitat by conversion to agriculture or for other development. They include

ABOVE The White-crowned Sparrow, *Zonotrichia leucophrys*, breeds mainly in Canada, wintering mainly in western USA and south to Mexico.

the Endangered Sierra Madre Sparrow, *Xeonspiza baileyi*, known from just two small sites in the mountains of Central Mexico and the Endangered Pale-headed Brush Finch, *Atlapetes pallidiceps*, with a minuscule range in the Andes of southern Ecuador, estimated to be no more than 1 km² (0.4 sq mile). The Critically Endangered Antioquia Brush Finch, *A. blancae*, is known from only three specimens, the last one collected in 1971. Searches have

failed to locate any living birds, and even if it does still exist any population is likely to be minimal.

Two North American species have been of great importance in ornithological research. These are the White-crowned Sparrow, which has been used for many studies of avian physiology and ecology, including timing of migration and breeding, and the Song Sparrow, the species chosen for much research into territoriality.

OLD WORLD BUNTINGS Emberizidae

GENERA: 5   **SPECIES:** 41

LENGTH: 12–19 cm (5–7.5 in)

WEIGHT: 12–67 g (0.4–2.4 oz)

RANGE AND HABITAT: across all of Eurasia apart from far north of Russia (with the most northerly breeding birds summer visitors only) and from southern Asia, also in many parts of Africa and parts of the Arabian peninsula; found in a very wide range of open habitats, from barren rocky areas in high mountains to forest edges and clearings, open woodland, savannah, arid scrubland, grassland, marshes and agricultural habitats

SOCIAL BEHAVIOUR: generally monogamous and territorial, seen singly or in pairs in breeding season, more social after breeding

NEST: open cup of grasses, twigs and other vegetation, often lined with softer material, such as rootlets, fine grasses, or animal hair, sited near or on the ground, hidden by vegetation

EGGS: 2–6, whitish, pale greyish, blueish, greenish or pinkish, with dark markings, including intricate scribbles

INCUBATION: 11–15 days

FLEDGING PERIOD: 8–13 days

FOOD: both invertebrates and seeds, the former especially during the breeding season and for feeding young

VOICE: songs of most species are a simple series of rattling, warbling, twittering or buzzing notes; calls typically brief, high-pitched, sharp or metallic sounding

MIGRATION: the most northerly breeders, from northern Scandinavia and Finland eastwards across much of Russia, all migrate south and west for winter; farther south some are partial migrants, others are sedentary; African species tend to be nomadic, moving in response to rainfall

CONSERVATION STATUS: one species, the Yellow breasted Bunting, *Schoeniclus aureolus*, is Critically Endangered; one species, Jankowski's Bunting, *Emberiza jankowskii*, is Endangered; two species, the Japanese Yellow Bunting, *S. sulphuratus*, and the Rustic Bunting, *S. rusticus*, are Vulnerable, and four species are Near Threatened

This family was formerly a huge and unwieldy assemblage of disparate birds that have recently been reclassified in families of their own, as a result of molecular research.

At one time it used to include a good many large New World families, including the New World sparrows and relatives (Passerellidae, p. 314), the cardinals and grosbeaks (Cardinalidae, p. 327), and Tanagers (Thraupidae, p. 329), the New World wood warblers (Parulidae, p. 319) and the New World Blackbirds (Icteridae, p. 321). Today, the slimmed down Emberizidae consists solely of the Old World buntings. Although they look similar to the Old World sparrows (Passeridae, p. 300), and to the New World sparrows. The small group of six species of longspurs (Plectrophenacidae, p. 312), including the two Arctic buntings, *Plectrophenax*, were until recently lumped in with the Old World buntings, but again the molecular research indicates they are not close relatives.

Nine species, all in the genus *Fringillaria*, are endemic to Africa. Almost 60% of the rest are Asian endemics. They are divided between four genera. The two smallest are *Melophus*, with just a single species, the Crested Bunting, *M. lathami*, from southern Asia and *Granativora*, with two species, the Black-headed Bunting, *G. melanocephala*, found in southeast Europe and from the Caucasus to Iran and the Red-headed Bunting, *G. bruniceps*, in Iran, Afghanistan, central Asia and northwest China. The two largest genera are *Emberiza*, with 15 species, eight of them

restricted to Asia and the other seven also found in Europe, and *Schoeniclus*, with 14 species, seven found only in Asia and the other seven also occurring in Europe.

Most species are about the size of a House Sparrow, *Passer domesticus*, or a little larger. The largest is the Corn Bunting, *Emberiza calandra*, of grassland and cereal cultivation from the Canary Islands, North Africa, and Europe east across Asia to as far as west-central China – or more specifically the male of that species, which averages about 20% larger than the female. In contrast to other members of the family, in which males have brighter plumage than females, in the Corn Bunting both sexes are plain brown streaked birds. And unlike most other emberizids, which are socially monogamous, this species is often polygynous, males mating with up to 18 females in his territory, and maintaining only weak bonds with the females.

The males of the African *Fringillaria* species have varied head patterns of black-and-white stripes, four of them combined with yellow underparts (in one species also with a golden orange breast band), and five with duller, buff or pale grey underparts. The two *Granativora* species have uniformly coloured hoods, reddish brown in the Red-headed Bunting, and black in the Black-headed Bunting, extending onto the upper breast, and in each case combined with a bright yellow collar and underparts. Females are dull brown above and buff below. The Crested Bunting is uniquely plumaged within the family, the male in breeding plumage having a glossy black body and head, the latter adorned by a tall spiky crest, contrasting dramatically with bright reddish brown wings and tail. Females are sandy grey with dark streaks, with a smaller crest and less reddish brown on wings and tail. The Slaty Bunting, *Schoeniclus siemsenni*, too is uniquely plumaged, the male being almost entirely slate grey, apart from a white belly and undertail; in the female the grey is replaced by brown, with a redder tinge to the head and chest. The other 13 *Schoeniclus* species and the 15 *Emberiza* buntings have bold head patterns or colourful underparts, sometimes in combination. A well-known example is the Yellowhammer (also known as the Eurasian Yellow Bunting), *Emberiza citrinella*, a widespread but declining European species, in which the male has a bright lemon-yellow head and underparts, with greyish crown streaks and head stripes and bright chestnut-and-black upperparts and chestnut streaks on the flanks. The males of the three species of reed buntings have a jet-black head contrasting with chestnut-and-black streaked upperparts and white underparts, while various other species of *Emberiza* and *Schoeniclus* have a black-and-white head pattern, especially in the males.

A number of bunting species are suffering serious declines, with eight being of conservation concern; the main threats come from loss of habitat and trapping for food. The most seriously threatened is the Critically Endangered Yellow-breasted Bunting, *Schoeniclus aureola*. It once bred in huge numbers in parts of eastern Europe and in a broad central swathe right across northern Asia, where it was once one of the most abundant breeding birds. Recently it has declined at an alarming rate, with numbers plummeting over a

ABOVE The Rock Bunting, *Emberiza cia*, breeds in uplands from southern Europe to the Himalayas, in areas with rocks and sparse vegetation.

wide range in just over a decade, due to threats faced on its far-off wintering grounds in southern Asia. These are loss of its reedbed roosting sites to agriculture and widespread trapping of huge numbers of the birds for human food, especially in China.

WARBLER TANAGERS Phaenicophilidae

GENERA: 5   **SPECIES:** 9

LENGTH: 14–20 cm (5.5–8 in)

WEIGHT: 9.5–65 g (0.3–2.3 oz)

RANGE AND HABITAT: the three most closely related genera are restricted to the island of Hispaniola, while one of the other two is endemic to Puerto Rico and the other is the most widespread, found across the Greater Antilles; they occur in a wide range of habitats, from arid scrub and shrubby second growth to coffee and other plantations, open woodland and forest of various types

SOCIAL BEHAVIOUR: information about breeding behaviour is sparse, but they are assumed to be socially monogamous

NEST: a cup of twigs, grass, moss, rootlets, leaves or other plant material and sometimes feathers, sited in a tree or shrub

EGGS: 2–3, white, cream, or pale blue, green or grey, with darker markings

INCUBATION: no information

FLEDGING PERIOD: no information

FOOD: fruit, seeds, insects and other invertebrates

VOICE: songs generally simple and unmelodic, and composed of harsh or sibilant sounds, with a whispering song recorded from females; calls similar, also chattering and twittering

MIGRATION: sedentary, apart from local movements in search of food

CONSERVATION STATUS: one species, the White-winged Warbler Tanager, *Xenoligea montana*, is Vulnerable, and one species, the Grey-crowned Palm Tanager, *Phaenicophilus poliocephalus*, is Near Threatened

This small family of birds from the Caribbean region was created to bring together several atypical species from two other families which molecular studies indicated to be close relatives. Seven of the nine species, in the genera *Phaenicophilus* (with two species), *Nesospingus* (a single species) and *Spindalis* (four species) were previously included in the large tanager family (Thraupidae, p. 329). The other two, one in the genus *Xenoligia*, and one in the genus *Microligea*, were formerly considered to be members of the

New World wood warbler family (Parulidae, p. 319). The core group consists of the two *Phaenicophilus* species together with *Xenoligia* and *Microligea*. The two other genera are likely to be their nearest relatives, but often they are thought to each deserve family status of their own until their close relationships are better studied.

The two *Phaenicophilus* species, called palm tanagers, have similar plumage, with a striking black-and-white head pattern, olive green back, wings and tail and grey underparts. Both species

ABOVE The Black-crowned Palm Tanager, *Phaenicophilus palmarum*, has adapted very well to life in human-modified habitats in both Haiti and the Dominican Republic.

are endemic to the island of Hispaniola (divided between two countries, Haiti and the Dominican Republic). The Grey-crowned Palm Tanager, *P. poliocephalus*, has the more restricted distribution,

almost entirely in the southern peninsula of Haiti and on two small offshore islands, while the Black-crowned Palm Tanager, *P. palmarum*, is found over the whole of Hispaniola except where its close relative lives.

The two species moved here from the New World wood warbler family are the smallest members of the family, at only 14.5 cm (5 in) long. Both are endemic to Hispaniola, and have a grey head, olive green upperparts and pale underparts. The Green-tailed Warbler Tanager, *Microligea palustris*, is duller greyish below, while the White-winged Warbler Tanager, *Xenoligea montana*, is white below with a white wing-bar.

The four species of *Spindalis* are sometimes collectively called stripe-headed tanagers; this is apposite as far as the males are concerned, in which the bold black-and-white head pattern is their most striking feature. They are colourful little birds, the rest of their plumage including a beautiful combination of a green back and tail with mainly orange and bright yellow underparts. Females, by contrast, are dull olive-green. Both sexes of the single species of *Nesospingus*, the Puerto Rican Tanager, *N. speculiferus*, have even drabber plumage, dull grey-brown above and off-white with faint grey streaks below.

WREN-THRUSH AND RELATIVES Zeledoniidae

GENERA: 2   **SPECIES:** 3

LENGTH: 12–13 cm (4.75–5 in)

WEIGHT: 6–21 g (0.2–0.7 oz)

RANGE AND HABITAT: the Wren-thrush, *Zeledonia coronata*, endemic to Costa Rica and western Panama; lives in thickets and dense second growth in cloud forest in mountains; the two *Teretistris* species are endemic to Cuba; it is found in various habitats, from arid scrub thickets to forests

SOCIAL BEHAVIOUR: presumed to be monogamous

NEST: the Wren-thrush builds a ball shaped nest of moss, with a hollow egg chamber within and a side entrance, concealed by vegetation on the ground, typically on a mossy bank; the two Cuban warblers build a cup of grasses, leaves, rootlets and other vegetation, well concealed low down in a shrub or among a clump of bromeliads

EGGS: 2 in the Wren-thrush; 2–3 in the two Cuban warblers

INCUBATION: no information for the Wren-thrush or Yellow-headed Warbler, *Teretistris fernandinae*; 8–9 days for the Oriente Warbler, *T. fornsi*

FLEDGING PERIOD: at least 17 days for Wren-thrush; 10–11 days Oriente Warbler; no information for Yellow-headed Warbler

FOOD: mainly insects and other invertebrates; the two Cuban warblers also eat some fruit and small lizards

VOICE: song of Wren-thrush a short series of loud, piercing whistles; songs of *Teretistris* a series of sweet notes alternating with dry, buzzing notes, sometimes mixed with chattering sounds; calls of Wren-thrush long, thin and sibilant, rising in pitch; those of the Cuban warblers include a rasping trill and various harsh or buzzing notes

MIGRATION: sedentary

CONSERVATION STATUS: none is threatened

As its name suggests, the Wrenthrush, *Zeledonia coronata*, of Costa Rica and the western highlands of Panama has at various times been thought to be most closely related to the wrens (Family Troglodytidae, p. 376) or thrushes (Turdidae, p. 391). More recently, it has been tentatively considered to be a member of the New World Wood Warbler family, Parulidae (opposite page), closest to members of the genus *Basileuterus*. However, new research suggests it may not belong here after all. With short wings and a very short tail, it has become adapted to a highly terrestrial lifestyle, and is almost flightless.

This little bird is very hard to observe as it generally remains hidden as it creeps about like a wren in the dense mist shrouded cloud-forest thickets that are its home. Its plumage resembles that

of the unrelated goldcrests and kinglets of the Family Regulidae (p. 366).

In the scheme followed in this book, the very small family Zeledoniidae, created for it after it was moved from the Parulidae, also includes two other species until very recently included within that family. Endemic to Cuba, they are closely related to one another, in the genus *Teretistris*. Some systematists prefer to give these small grey-and-yellow songbirds a family of their own, Teretistridae. As with the Wren-thrush, they spend much time foraging for insects and other small prey low down among dense cover or on the ground beneath, and much remains to be learned about their breeding behaviour and other aspects of their lives.

NEW WORLD WOOD WARBLERS Parulidae

GENERA: 18   **SPECIES**: 108

LENGTH: 11–15 cm (4–6 in)

WEIGHT: mostly 6–17.5 g (0.2–0.6 oz)

RANGE AND HABITAT: North America, Caribbean, Central America, South America; most in forests and woodlands, some in grasslands, scrubland, marshes, reed beds and salt marshes

SOCIAL BEHAVIOUR: most are seen singly or in pairs, although tropical species and migrants from North America wintering there may join mixed-species foraging flocks; males usually establish territories, although some species breed in loose colonies; some North American species may be monogamous for a single season, while others may mate with several females

NEST: most northern species build a neat, open cup of grass, bark strips or other vegetation bound with spiders' webs and lined with feathers, hair, rootlets or other soft material; some northern species, such as the Ovenbird, *Seiurus aurocapilla*, and Northern Parula, *Parula americana*, build domed nests with a side entrance, as do many tropical species; a few nest in tree holes or other cavities

EGGS: 3–8 in northern species; 2–4 in tropical species; usually white speckled with various colours (pure white in a few species)

INCUBATION: 10–14 days in northern species; 13–17 days in tropical species (details known for very few)

FLEDGING PERIOD: 8–14 days for northern species; 12–15 days for tropical species (details known for very few)

FOOD: most are primarily insectivorous, taking a wide range of insects, including many caterpillars, and also eating some other invertebrates; some migratory species supplement this diet with plant material, especially berries or nectar, eaten either in the north after breeding or after arriving in their southern winter quarters, while most tropical species are sedentary, though montane species make altitudinal migrations

VOICE: songs range from sweet, varied phrases to unmusical buzzing, trilling or chipping notes or loud, ringing sounds; males of many species have two song types – a primary song for defending a territory, and an alternate song, used in other situations, including to females; calls are usually brief, harsh or chipping

MIGRATION: most northern species make long migrations to tropical winter quarters

CONSERVATION STATUS: one species, Bachman's Warbler, *Vermivora bachmanii*, is Critically Endangered (Possibly Extinct); one species, Semper's Warbler, *Leucopeza semperi*, is Critically Endangered; six species, the Golden-cheeked Warbler, *Setophaga chrysoparia*, the Whistling Warbler, *Catharopeza bishopi*, the Elfin Woods Warbler, *Setophaga angelae*, the Black-polled Yellowthroat, *Geothlypis speciosa*, the Grey-headed Warbler, *Basileuterus griseiceps*, and the Paria Whitestart, *Myioborus pariae*, are Endangered; six species, including the Cerulean Warbler, *Setophaga cerulea*, the Belding's Yellowthroat, *Geothlypis beldingi*, the Pirre Warbler, *Basileuterus ignotus*, and the Pink-headed Warbler, *Cardellina versicolor*, are Vulnerable; nine species including Kirtland's Warbler, *Setophaga kirtlandii*, and the Golden-winged Warbler, *Vermivora chrysoptera*, are Near Threatened

Also known as wood-warblers or parulids, this major group of New World songbirds is very popular with North American birdwatchers and anyone who appreciates the return of these lively little birds in spring from their mainly tropical American wintering quarters with their colourful breeding plumage and frequent, varied songs. About 50 species – about 45% of the total – are found north of Mexico, and many keen birdwatchers see about 30 species during the peak of spring migration, when the birds return from winter quarters farther south. The distribution, behaviour and ecology of tropical species are far less well known.

By and large, the various genera and species of parulids are similar in their overall shape, body proportions and bill structure, differing mainly in size. Generally, they have a fairly short, slender bill, adapted for gleaning small insects and other invertebrates from foliage. They are very small or small birds, 11–15 cm (4– 6 in) long and normally weighing only 5 to 17.5 g (0.2–0.6 oz). As with other long-distance migrants, the North American breeders may put on a huge amount of weight in the form of fat before departure to see them through the arduous flight: a Connecticut Warbler, *Oporornis agilis*, has been recorded at a weight of 26.8 g (0.95 oz): about double its normal weight.

Contrasting with their homogeneous morphology, the plumage, particularly of those species breeding in North America, is very varied. In a few, such as the Tennessee Warbler, *Leiothlypis peregrina*, with its olive-green upperparts and grey head, or the grey-and-white Plumbeous Warbler, *Setophaga plumbea*, of Dominica, it is relatively subdued. Most northern parulids, though, have bright colours or bold patterns. In many species, there is a marked difference between the males in their bright breeding plumage and the duller females. Many species are grey or blue-grey above and bright yellow below, while some have orange or chestnut markings or are boldly patterned in black-and-white. Stripes are common, too, and one species, the Black-and-white Warbler, *Mniotilta varia*, is almost entirely striped apart from its flight feathers. One species, the Cerulean Warbler, *Setophaga cerulea*, has blue upperparts, deep blue in the male

BOVE This male Chestnut-sided Warbler, *Setophaga pensylvanica*, is just one of 1 strikingly plumaged species that breed in North America.

ABOVE The Hooded Warblers, *Setophaga citrina*, is widespread in mature deciduous woodland in eastern USA, wintering in Central America and the Caribbean.

ABOVE This Tropical Parula, *Setophaga pitiayumi*, is the only member of its genus found in South America; its huge range is from Mexico to northern Argentina.

and duller, turquoise blue in the female. The Ovenbird, *Seiurus aurocapilla*, and two species of waterthrush, *Parkesia*, have plumage resembling that of many thrushes – brown or olive above with pale, dark-streaked and spotted underparts.

Most tropical parulids are olive green above and yellow below, providing good camouflage against a background of sun-dappled foliage in forests. Many have striking head patterns as in some of the *Basileuterus* and *Myioborus* species. A few are brilliantly coloured, such as two Mexican species, the Red Warbler, *Cardellina rubra*, which is almost entirely bright rose-red, and the Pink-headed Warbler, *C. versicolor*, which is deep maroon with a beautiful silvery pink hood. On the whole, there is little sexual dimorphism.

Most parulids are arboreal, although many of the South American species spend much time in dense undergrowth. Some, such as the three North American species of *Seiurus*, the Ovenbird, *S. aurocapilla*, and the two waterthrushes, the Northern Waterthrush, *Parkesia noveboracensis*, and Lousiana Waterthrush, *P. motacilla*, are largely terrestrial. The Ovenbird lives in forests with abundant leaf litter, which it flicks aside to reveal insect and other invertebrate prey, including spiders, snails and earthworms. The waterthrushes inhabit woodlands and thickets alongside water – pools, bogs and slow-moving rivers and other standing water in the case of the Northern Waterthrush and fast-flowing streams and other running water for the Louisiana species. Both feed on aquatic insects, molluscs and crustaceans, and sometimes eat small fish and frogs.

Wood warblers are often the victims of cowbird nest parasites. Some deal with this by removing the cowbirds' eggs, and the Yellow Warbler, *Setophaga petechia*, avoids the problem by building a new nest on top of the old one containing the usurper's eggs.

Just over three-quarters of all species in the family belong to just four genera. The nine species of *Vermivora* are the Critically Endangered Bachman's Warbler, *V. bachmanii*, which is (along with Semper's Warbler, *Leucopeza semperi*, of St Lucia) the rarest of all the New World warblers, or even already extinct. *Setophaga* warblers include many well-known and abundant

North American birds, such as the Yellow-rumped Warbler, *S. coronata*, the Chestnut-sided Warbler, *Setophaga pensylvanica*, and the Yellow Warbler, which has a huge range, from Alaska and the far north of western Canada to as far south as the Galapagos islands and north-west Peru, with over 40 subspecies. All races have yellow-olive upperparts, but the head and underparts vary from all yellow, plain in some and streaked chestnut in others, to races with a chestnut crown or head.

Also well known in the eastern USA is the only one of the two species of parula to breed there, the Northern Parula, *S. americana*. It is extremely active, and often hovers briefly or hangs upside down when gleaning insects from beneath leaves. So titlike is this little bird in its feeding actions that Linnaeus described it as a member of the tit family, Paridae (p. 335), giving it the name *Parus americanus*. When it was realised that it was not a tit, the generic name was modified to *Parulus*, and later to *Parula*, though now this genus has been lost and both parulas are included in the genus *Setophaga*. The other species the Tropical Parula, *S. pitiayumi*, also feed in this way. The single species in the genus *Mniotilta* is the Black-and-white Warbler, *M. varia*, unique among this family in its adoption of a nuthatch-like lifestyle, foraging on tree trunks and branches by probing into bark crevices for insects.

Males of the 12 species of yellowthroat, *Geothlypis*, are strikingly marked with a black mask. Both sexes are olive-green above and mainly yellow below. All but one are Neotropical; the exception is the Common Yellowthroat, *G. trichas*, found right across the USA and southern Canada. Most species live in freshwater marshes and other wetland habitats.

Members of two different genera of wood-warblers are known as redstarts, after the Old World chats, *Phoenicurus*, that were given that name earlier in reference to their rusty-red outer tail feathers ('start' being derived from an Old English word for 'tail'). The American Redstart, *Setophaga ruticilla*, widespread across central and southern Canada and the USA, has brightly coloured feathers on the sides of the tail, although these are orange or yellow and not red. It also has orange wing bars and orange along the sides of the breast, contrasting with its mainly glossy black plumage. The others, 12 species in the genus *Myioborus*, have no red at all in the tail, and are now known instead as whitestarts, which accurately describes the colour of their outer tail feathers (they were originally included with the American Redstart in the genus *Setophaga* but they were found not to be so closely related). The range of just one, the Painted Whitestart, *M. pictus*, includes the extreme south-west of the USA, while the others are mainly South American, with a few in Mexico and Central America. Unlike most members of the family, both redstarts and whitestarts feed mainly by flycatching, the American Redstart being highly specialised in this technique. It flashes the bright patches of colour by opening its wings and fanning its tail, which alarms insects on the foliage so that they fly up, when the bird can dart out to catch them. In addition to *Myioborus*, the most diverse genra in the tropics and subtropics are *Myiothlypis* (with 15 species) and *Basileuterus*, with nine species. Apart from the Painted Whitestart, all these are restricted to Mexico, Central America and South America. Compared with *Myioborus* warblers, all but one of these have olive-green rather than slate-grey upperparts that contrast less with their underparts, which are in many species yellow as in *Myioborus* but in some greyish, buff or whitish.

Ornithologists think that the wood-warblers originated in northern Central America, which still holds the greatest diversity of species. From this ancestral home they radiated north during a number of interglacial periods, and evolved in isolation. They were forced to migrate south each year by the cold northern winters. Moving in the opposite direction, ancestors of the genera *Myioborus*

ABOVE The Northern Waterthrush, *Parkesia noveboracensis*, is rarely found far from water, preferring woodland by slow moving rivers, pools, and swamps.

and *Basileuterus* spread south into South America before the Panama gap closed about three million years ago and linked the sub-continents of North and South America. At this time a period of mountain building may have isolated these southern genera from one another, resulting in a period of rapid speciation.

NEW WORLD BLACKBIRDS Icteridae

GENERA: 31 **SPECIES**: 105

LENGTH: 16–54 cm (6–21 in)

WEIGHT: 16–528 g (0.6–19 oz)

RANGE AND HABITAT: North America, the Caribbean, Central America, South America; grassland, savannah, farmland, gardens, parks, urban habitats, woodland, forests, scrub, marshes

SOCIAL BEHAVIOUR: many are gregarious, some highly so, both in winter feeding flocks and roosts and in breeding colonies; breeding arrangements vary, with some species monogamous and others polygynous, some territorial and others not territorial; the cowbirds, *Molothrus*, are brood parasites

NEST: varied, including pouches or baskets suspended from tree branches woven from grasses and other plant material, domed nests of grass on the ground concealed among cover, often accessed by runways or even covered tunnels, and open, cups of vegetation lined with mud or dung; some orioles and the Baywinged Blackbirds, *Agelaioides*, use the nests of other birds while cowbirds lay their eggs in other birds' nests

EGGS: typically 2–3 for tropical species and 4–7 for northern ones, variable in background colour and amount of markings

INCUBATION: 11–15 days for most species, up to 20 for the biggest oropendolas

FLEDGING PERIOD: the overall range is 9–35 days, but most species fledge in 10–15 days

FOOD: varied, including both insects and other invertebrates (and nestlings of most species fed largely on these) and some small vertebrates, as well as plant matter (northern species eat mainly seeds and grain when in their winter quarters, while tropical species include fruit in their diet

VOICE: most species are loud and noisy; some, such as orioles and meadowlarks, have sweet, melodious songs, while those of others, such as grackles and blackbirds, often include harsh sounds; some caciques and orioles are excellent mimics of other birds; some oropendolas sing two different notes at once

MIGRATION: many northern species migrate south (or in some cases eastwards) in autumn, while most tropical species are sedentary or make only short-distance migrations; Bobolinks are very long-distance migrants

CONSERVATION STATUS: one species, the Slender-billed Grackle, *Quiscalus palustris*, is Extinct; one species, the Bahama Oriole, *Icterus northropi*, is Critically Endangered; seven species, including the Tricoloured Blackbird, *Agelaius tricolor*, the Selva Cacique, *Cacicus koepckeae*, the Jamaican Blackbird, *Nesopsar nigerrimus*, and the Baudo Oropendola, *Psarocolius cassini*, are Endangered; six species, including the Red-bellied Grackle, *Hypopyrrhus pyrohypogaster*, the Rusty Blackbird, *Euphagus carolinus*, and the Pampas Meadowlark, *Leistes defilippii*, are Vulnerable; one species, the St. Lucia Oriole, *Icterus laudabilis*, is Near Threatened

ABOVE A male Red-winged Blackbird, *Agelaius phoeniceus*, fluffs out his plumage and sings his hoarse gurgling song in the Florida Everglades, USA.

The family of New World (or American) blackbirds was named by British settlers to the Americas because some of its black-plumaged members reminded them of the Blackbird, *Turdus merula*, of the Old World, which is a member of the thrush family (Turdidae, p. 391) and unrelated to these birds. In fact, although the predominant plumage colour of the New World blackbirds is indeed black, often with a blue or purple gloss, most are also patterned with small or large areas of red, orange, yellow or brown, and some have no black at all. As well as birds called blackbirds, this family also includes a diverse array of different groups called grackles, American orioles (sometimes called troupials), cowbirds, meadowlarks, oropendolas and caciques. The family as a whole is sometimes known as the American (or New World) orioles (a name again derived from a superficial resemblance to the Old World family of that name, the Oriolidae p. 256), troupials or (perhaps most sensibly) as the icterids, after the scientific name of the family, Icteridae. This also refers to a colour, in this case the yellow of many species of the genus *Icterus*, the American orioles. The name is from a Greek word *ikteros* for a yellow bird, perhaps the Eurasian Golden Oriole, *Oriolus oriolus*, the sighting of which was believed to cure jaundice.

As its name suggests, the family is entirely endemic to the Americas. All the groups mentioned above have representatives in North America and the Caribbean apart from the caciques, represented by various species in Mexico, Central America and South America, and the oropendolas, restricted to tropical South America. Overall, this very successful and adaptable family occupies a huge range, from Alaska to Tierra del Fuego. Representatives are found in many different habitats, from dense tropical forests to open grassland, from Arctic bogs to hot deserts, and from oceanic islands to city centres.

New World blackbirds appear to be related most closely to the wood-warblers (Family Parulidae, p. 319), and more distantly to the New World sparrows (Family Passerellidae, p. 314), and Old World buntings (Family Emberizidae, p.316), the tanagers (Family Thraupidae, p. 329) and cardinal-grosbeaks (Family Cardinalidae, p. 327). All these and a few other small families were once included in a vastly enlarged Emberizidae, but this is now regarded as lumping together groups not sharing a common ancestor. New World blackbirds have strong, often quite long, legs and, in most species, a long tail, which is used for balancing in tree-dwelling species; in others, such as grackles, their long, keel-shaped tail is important in providing lift for slow flight, and in these and other groups, the tail also plays a major part in sexual displays. Species that have become adapted to life on the ground, such as meadowlarks, have a short tail. All members of the family have relatively short, broad wings and fly with rapid wingbeats to lift them quickly into the air.

New World blackbirds have a straight, conical, sharply pointed bill. A major feature of the family is that the bill is operated by a special skull anatomy and associated arrangement of muscles working the bill that enables them to open their bill with force against considerable pressure, rather than passively. This gives them a great advantage over most birds when they thrust the bill into the soil or into an opening of some sort, such as a gap in the bark of a tree trunk or clump of grass, one in a dense flower head, among a bromeliad or other epiphyte, among pine needles, between rocks or among cowpats, or one made by piercing a large fruit or the stem of a sedge. Known as 'gaping' or 'open-bill probing', this technique enables them to expand the gap so that they can detect and extract food items more easily. This feature and feeding behaviour also evolved, independently, in the genus *Sturnus* of Old World starlings (Family Sturnidae, p. 381). In both these and the New World blackbirds, it is thought to be an important factor in their very wide overall range and success.

Some species in the family are among the most abundant of all the world's birds, with the family's total population probably approaching 200 million individuals. At certain times of year, mainly after breeding, they form vast flocks. The most numerous of all is the Red-winged Blackbird, *Agelaius phoeniceus*, which is North America's most abundant songbird. It breeds right across North America from Alaska and much of Canada and through the whole of the USA south through Mexico and Central America to Costa Rica. Young males and non-breeding males form roosts during the breeding season, but when breeding is over, the great bulk of birds living to the north of Mexico move south for short to medium distances and in winter become concentrated in immense roosts containing tens or hundreds of thousands of birds. These usually contain smaller numbers of Common Grackles, *Quiscalus quiscula*, Brown-headed Cowbirds, *Molothrus ater*, and Common Starlings, *Sturnus vulgaris*. They usually forage within about 20 km (12.5 miles) of their roost sites, but may travel up to 80 km (50 miles) to take advantage of good feeding sites. At such times, all these birds, and some other icterids, too, can cause significant damage to agriculture by devouring large amounts of grain from farmland. Flocks of these and other ground-feeding species have a characteristic feeding action in fields of crops or on grassland, in which those at the rear fly over the backs of the others until they are in the front, then feed in one spot while others fly over to replace them at the front until they are once more at the rear, so the whole flock appears to travel across the ground with a rolling action.

ABOVE A male Yellow-headed Blackbird, *Xanthocephalus xanthocephalus*, flies over his territory in a cattail marsh, in California, USA.

LEFT The largest member of the icterid family is the Montezuma Oropendola, *Psarocolius montezuma*, of Mexico and Central America.

ABOVE The Great-tailed Grackle, *Quiscalus mexicanus*, is widespread in southern USA, Mexico, Central America and northeast South America.

When it is perched or on the ground, the male Red-winged Blackbird shows bright red-and-yellow 'epaulettes' at the shoulders, which stand out against the black of the rest of his plumage. In flight these become 'flashes' as the wings beat. Striking coloured markings like this are a feature of many members of the family; for instance, most caciques have red or yellow 'flash' colours on the shoulders or rump, while all oropendolas have bright yellow sides to the uppertail and most have an all-yellow undertail. Eye colour, too, is a distinctive feature in many groups, such as the blue eyes of five of the 11 species of oropendolas, the yellow, blue or white ones of caciques and the yellow ones of many grackles.

In some species, especially the northern migratory and polygynous species, females are very different from the black or boldly patterned males, usually with more cryptic plumage in browns and greys. In others, particularly sedentary and monogamous tropical ones, the sexes look alike, and, unusually compared with most other birds, the females share the bright plumage of the males. Sexual dichromatism may vary even within a species, as with the Baltimore Oriole, *Icterus galbula*, in which some females are much duller than males, while others are indistinguishable from their male counterparts in the field. In most species, the non-breeding plumage is identical to that worn during the breeding season, but in some of the species with all-black or mainly black males, their feathers become tipped with brown during a post-breeding moult, so that the birds look duller; then these tips are worn away by the following spring to produce the striking breeding plumage.

In general, males are distinctly bigger than females. This reaches an extreme in some of the oropendolas; males of the Montezuma Oropendola, *Psarocolius montezuma*, may be more than twice the size of females. Mating systems show a great variation across the whole family. Most orioles are monogamous. The oropendolas, caciques, the larger species of grackles and marsh-nesting blackbirds are polygamous; and in the first three of these groups a dominant male defends the tree in which his harem of females have set up their breeding colony. The males do not play much of a part in family life: only a very few share nest-building duties, and none incubates the eggs or feeds their mates, although most do help to feed the young. They court females with ritualised movements of body, tail and wings, including rapidly vibrating the wings and fluffing out the feathers, while singing. Tilting the bill skywards while sleeking the body plumage, by contrast, is a method of conveying aggression.

There are two subfamilies. The first, Icteriinae, was recently created to accommodate a single species, the Yellow-breasted Chat, *Icteria virens*, that was moved to the Icteridae from the closely related New World wood warbler Family Parulidae, as a result of molecular evidence. This is a widespread breeder in dense thickets and scrub in much of North America, from southern Canada to central Mexico, wintering mainly in Mexico and Central America. It resembles many parulid wood warblers in appearance, with a grey head, white eye-ring, olive green upperparts, a bright yellow throat and chest and white belly, but is considerably larger than them, at up to 19 cm (7.5 in) long, and often weighs more than twice as much. Differences from the parulids include a much stouter bill, its habit of holding down food items with its feet while eating them, and its very different song – a very variable medley of clucks, whistles, rattles, cackles and squealing or mewing sounds – and calls, which include harsh notes and mimicry of other birds.

All the remaining members of the family – over a hundred species in 30 genera – are included in the second subfamily, Icterinae. There are many genera commonly known as 'blackbirds'. The small genus *Agelaius* of marshland-breeding blackbirds includes one other North American species in addition to the Red-winged Blackbird. This is the very similar Tricoloured Blackbird, *A. tricolor*, which unlike its very widespread relative has a restricted range, being confined to the western USA, with most of its very dense breeding colonies in California. There are three other *Agelaius* species all restricted to the Caribbean. Two species of *Chrysomus* are also marshland breeders, both in South America: the striking Yellow-hooded Blackbird, *C. icterocephalus*, and the much duller Chestnut-capped Blackbird, *C. ruficapillus*. The Yellow-headed Blackbird, *Xanthocephalus xanthocephalus*, is another handsome yellow-and-black species, in this case with a large white wing patch, and is widespread in marshes and other wetlands across southwest Canada, western USA and western Mexico. Other blackbirds are found in drier habitats. These include the all-black Austral Blackbird, *Curaeus curaeus*, of southern South America. It is an abundant and successful species that has adapted to a wide range of habitats, including thickets, woodlands, farmland and urban parks; in the far south, in Tierra del Fuego, it forages along rocky beaches. By contrast, the only other member of its genus,

the very similar Forbes's Blackbird, *C. forbesi*, is a very rare and highly restricted species from Brazil, classified as Endangered and vulnerable to extinction. The two *Euphagus* blackbirds, with black males and brown or dark grey females, are both North American; the Rusty Blackbird, *E. carolinus*, is a common but declining bird of Canada and northeast and central USA, where it breeds in wooded swamps, while Brewer's Blackbird, *E. cyanocephalus*, is far more catholic in its choice of habitat. It is found in grassland, farmland and beaches as well as being abundant in urban areas and over the past 100 or so years has undergone a considerable eastward expansion in range from its original range in southwest Canada and the western half of the USA.

The New World blackbirds known as grackles are glossy black birds, readily distinguished by their long, keeled tails. They are divided between four genera. The main genus is *Quiscalus*, with six extant species and one, the Slender-billed Grackle, *Q. palustris*, which was declared extinct after having last been recorded in 1910. It was a casualty of drainage of its marshland breeding habitat in a very small area of central Mexico. By contrast the other six species are generally highly adaptable and successful birds that are expanding their range and occur in a variety of habitats, from marshes, grassland and farmland to mangroves and beaches. Many have colonised urban areas, and are a common sight in large, very noisy flocks on the lawns of city parks. Grackles are bold, and the males often strut about with a very upright gait, uttering their raucous calls almost constantly. They have very wide diets, ranging

ABOVE A female Brown-headed Cowbird, *Molothrus ater*, perches on the back of a bison in the Badlands of North Dakota, USA.

ABOVE The Bobolink, *Dolichonyx oryzivorus*, is the champion migrant of a mainly resident family, breeding in North America and wintering in South America.

from seeds, grains, rice and fruit to insects, lizards, eggs, nestlings and small adult birds and small mammals; the Common Grackle, *Q. quiscula*, often eats crayfish and dives to catch small fish.

The 32 species of *Icterus* orioles are particularly brightly plumaged, with males of northern species and both sexes of most tropical ones having large areas of orange or yellow contrasting with black markings. Some also have patches of white. Orioles feed on insects throughout the year, including species with irritant, toxic hairs that are avoided by most other birds. They also sip nectar from flowers, and some have learned to take sugar solution put out by people to attract hummingbirds. They build intricate, pendant basket nests that in some species may be as deep as 60 cm (2 ft).

Oropendolas, with nine species in the genus *Psarocolius* and two in *Cacicus*, are very striking, large and dramatic-looking birds, with black, dark brown, chestnut or olive-green plumage and a very prominent, long bill whose upper mandible is expanded or swollen at the base to form a conspicuous frontal shield. The bill colour in different species includes ivory, pale yellow, or two-tone bright green or grey with a red tip. Some species have areas of bare pale blue or pink skin around the eye or beneath it. Their size range is 32–53 cm (12.5–21 in) for males and 23–43 cm (9–17 in) for females. These birds feed mainly on fruit, and their big bill with sharp cutting edges is well equipped for cutting away the tough outer skin after they have inserted the pointed end and forced the bill open. While singing, male oropendolas display to females by exaggerated bowing movements, their long tail held up at an angle, and may end the performance by hanging upside down from their perch. Some species can produce two notes simultaneously, one ascending in pitch, the other descending, to produce a complex cascade of sound. The intricately woven hanging nests are shaped like a deep purse, some up to 1 m (3.3 ft) deep, with an entrance near the top. They are made of very narrow strips torn by the female from the large leaves of plants such as bananas, or in some species from strips of bark, orchid roots or coconut fibres, and are suspended from slender twigs or the leaf stalks of trees or even from the leaves themselves, so that it is very difficult for monkeys to reach them to steal the eggs or young. Also, they often choose isolated trees, which also prevents snakes reaching the nests. Colonies typically contain just a few to 10 or so nests, though some are bigger. Many nestlings succumb to fly parasites.

The caciques are similar in appearance to oropendolas, but smaller, with females measuring 19–25 cm (7.5–10 in) long and males 23–30 cm (9–12 in). There are seven species of *Cacicus*, a single one of *Procacicus*, one of *Amblycercus* and also one of *Cassiculus*. Like oropendolas, they feed mainly on fruit, and build hanging nests.

Now placed on its own in a separate genus, the bird formerly known as the Baywinged Cowbird, *Agelaioides badius*, was lumped with the *Molothrus* cowbirds, but unlike them it is not a brood parasite and is not so closely related; the alternative names, Baywing, or, as here, Baywinged Blackbird, is thus more accurate and are often now used instead. These birds are, however, nest parasites, usually appropriating the nests of other birds rather than building their own, and often driving off the rightful owners

with considerable aggression before laying their eggs. The true cowbirds, *Molothrus*, are a small group of five species. The name comes from their habit of following herds of cattle (and originally buffalo) to take advantage of the rich supply of insect food that are flushed out from the grass as the mammals graze. All are brood parasites, the females laying their eggs in the nests of a wide range of other birds, including other members of this family. The best-known and most successful species, with a population estimated at maybe as many as 40 million individuals, is the Brown-headed Cowbird, *M. ater*, of southern Canada, the USA and Mexico. It has been able to expand its range and increase its numbers due to the conversion of forest into agricultural land. It may produce more eggs than any other wild bird: each female can lay at the rate of almost one egg per day at the peak of the breeding season, and may produce as many as 100 eggs over the 2–3 month laying period. As a result, it has been referred to as 'the passerine chicken'! Brown-headed Cowbirds have been recorded laying their eggs in the nests of 226 different host species, and 140 of these are known to have reared the cowbirds' young.

Male cowbirds are glossy black (one species with a brown head) and females brown, and all except one are smallish, 18–22 cm (7–8.5 in) long; the exception is the Giant Cowbird, *M. oryzivorus*, with males twice the size at 35–38 cm (14–15 in), as big as some oropendolas. Appropriately for such a large bird, it specialises in parasitising oropendolas and caciques.

Meadowlarks have strongly streaked brown, buff and black upperparts that provide good camouflage from predators in the open grasslands or farmland where they live. The two northern species, in the genus *Sturnella*, have bright yellow underparts, while the three subtropical and tropical ones in the genus *Leistes* are mainly or partially vivid red below; members of both groups have bold black head stripes, breast bands and flank markings, which help to break up their outline. The species in each genus, especially the northern pair, the Eastern Meadowlark, *Sturnella magna*, and Western Meadowlark, *S. neglecta*, look very similar to one another and are most easily distinguished by their songs. Living in open country without natural perches on which to court females by bowing or hanging upside down, meadowlarks display on the ground, by fluttering jumps or in song-flights. They are, however, often seen perching on fence-posts.

The single species of Bobolink, *Dolichonyx oryzivorus*, is a 17–18 cm (7 in) long, short-tailed bird with a short, almost finchlike bill. In his breeding plumage, the larger male is strikingly patterned in black and white with a big pale buff patch on the back of the head and nape. After breeding, he is far duller, streaked with brown, buff and black, and resembles the female. The Bobolink makes by far the longest migrations of any of the icterids, involving a round trip of 20,000 km (12,400 miles) or more between its North American breeding grounds and its wintering range, mainly in northern Argentina. An old name was 'Ricebird' from the depredations by its large migratory flocks on the rice fields of the southern USA. This habit is also referred to in the specific name – *oryzivorus* means 'rice eater'. Bobolinks are still regarded as agricultural pests in Argentina. In Jamaica, they are nicknamed 'butterbirds' as the plump migrants with their stored fat are trapped for food.

CHAT-TANAGERS Calyptophilidae

GENERA: 1   **SPECIES:** 2

LENGTH: 18–21 cm (7–8 in)

WEIGHT: 26–55 g (0.9–1.9 oz)

RANGE AND HABITAT: found only on the island of Hispaniola; mainly in dense broadleaf evergreen rainforests and pine forests with dense undergrowth in the mountains, especially near water; also in streamside thickets at lower altitudes

SOCIAL BEHAVIOUR: presumed to be socially monogamous; little is known of their breeding behaviour

NEST: only a few have been described; these were large, partly domed structures made from twigs, moss, lichens and vine tendrils, with an inner cup lined with leaf fragments and fine plant stems

EGGS: 2, pale blue with brown spots

INCUBATION: no information

FLEDGING PERIOD: no information

FOOD: mainly insects and other invertebrates, with a few fruits and seeds

VOICE: simple, loud songs of whistling notes, uttered mainly at dawn by both sexes; pairs perform antiphonal duets

MIGRATION: sedentary

CONSERVATION STATUS: one species, the Western Chat Tanager, *Calyptophilus tertius*, is Vulnerable, and the other, the Eastern Chat Tanager, *C. frugivorus*, is Near Threatened

This family of just two species in a single genus is endemic to the island of Hispaniola, divided between two countries, Haiti and the Dominican Republic. They were formerly included within the large tanager family, Thraupidae (p. 329), before recent molecular research indicated that they were sufficiently distinct to deserve a family of their own. As well as the tanagers, their closest relatives appear to be the cardinals (Cardinalidae, p. 327) and aberrant tanagers (Mitrospingidae, p. 326).

Both the Eastern Chat-tanager, *Calyptophilus frugivorus*, and the slightly larger Western Chat-tanager, *C. tertius*, have a relatively long and pointed bill, short wings, quite long and sturdy legs with strong feet, and a long, slightly graduated tail with a rather rounded

tip – features combining to give them a resemblance to one of the unrelated mockingbirds (Mimidae, p. 380). They have sombre plumage, with dark brown upperparts and tail, a white throat and central underparts, with the flanks greyish brown and in all but one of the two races of the Eastern species a rather obscure broken yellow eye-ring.

The generic name is from the Greek meaning 'loving to hide', and they certainly live up to it by remaining hidden in the dense undergrowth of the understorey of the wet forests they inhabit. As a result, there is little information on their breeding habits or other aspects of their biology. Unfortunately, both species are threatened by loss of habitat as the forests are logged or cleared for agriculture.

ABERRANT TANAGERS Mitrospingidae

GENERA: 3   **SPECIES:** 4

LENGTH: 17–19 cm (7–7.5 in)

WEIGHT: 24–46 g (0.8–1.6 oz)

RANGE AND HABITAT: Central America and South America; tropical forest

SOCIAL BEHAVIOUR: little known, but assumed to be socially monogamous; the Dusky-faced Tanager is likely to be a cooperative breeder

NEST: a cup nest built from rootlets, flower stalks and filaments of black fungus, slung between two branches

EGGS: 1–2, white, with brown or reddish brown spots (information for Dusky-faced Tanager, *Mitrospingus cassini*, only)

INCUBATION: no information

FLEDGING PERIOD: no information

FOOD: insects and other invertebrates, fruit

VOICE: songs of the four species are varied, including sharp, high-pitched notes, chattering sounds and loud nasal notes; various calls resemble notes of songs

MIGRATION: sedentary

CONSERVATION STATUS: no species is threatened

This very small family comprises four Neotropical species that were until recently included within the large tanager Family Thraupidae (p. 329), until genetic research indicated they were each other's closest relatives and deserved to be separated from the Thraupidae in a family of their own. Their nearest relatives apart from the thraupine tanagers appear to be the cardinals, grosbeaks and relatives (Cardinalidae, p. 327) and the chat-tanagers (Calyptophilidae, above).

The two *Mitrospingus* species have yellowish olive and grey plumage. The Dusky-faced Tanager, *M. cassinii*, has a wide range, extending from Costa Rica and Panama down the west of Colombia and as far as central Ecuador. It is locally common along the edges of various forested and woodland habitats, where it lives among dense shrub cover, often near streams. This is a shy bird, and usually hard to see as small flocks move about rapidly through the undergrowth. By contrast the Olive-backed Tanager

M. oleagineus, which is dull olive above and olive yellow below, with a grey throat and face, has a restricted range and habitat, being found only in rainforest on the slopes of the remarkable flat-topped mountains known as *tepuis* in a small area of southern Venezuela and immediately adjacent western Guyana and northern Brazil. Unlike its close relative, it is arboreal, foraging for insects by moving slowly along branches, may form much larger groups, and often joins mixed-species flocks.

The single *Orthogonys* species, the Olive-green Tanager, *O. chloricterus*, lives in part of southeast Brazil in the upper and middle storeys of rainforest, mostly in the mountains. It has olive green upperparts and olive yellow underparts, and like the Olive-backed Tanager forms large noisy flocks.

The final species, the sole member of the genus *Lamprospiza*, the Red-billed Pied Tanager, *L. melanoleuca*, is very different in appearance. As its name suggests, it has bold black-and-white plumage and a bright scarlet bill. The head, upperparts and tail are glossy blue-black, extending onto the throat and chest, while the rest of the underparts are white, except for a pair of narrow blue-black bands that almost cross one another at the centre of the breast. This Amazonian species tends to forage high up in the rainforest canopy, and eats more fruit than its relatives.

CARDINALS, GROSBEAKS AND RELATIVES Cardinalidae

GENERA: 11   **SPECIES:** 48

LENGTH: 11–24 cm (4–9.5 in)

WEIGHT: 11.5–85 g (0.4–3 oz)

RANGE AND HABITAT: North America, the Caribbean, Central America, South America; forests and woodlands, grasslands, scrub, farmland, parks and gardens

SOCIAL BEHAVIOUR: mainly solitary or in pairs, but a few form flocks after breeding; the species for which details known (almost all North American) are largely monogamous and territorial

NEST: a big, often loosely built cup of grass and other plant matter, usually in a tree or shrub, in a cactus or among mosses and other epiphytes, but in some species almost on the ground

EGGS: 2–4, white, bluish, blue or greenish

INCUBATION: 11–14 days

FLEDGING PERIOD: 9–15 days

FOOD: seeds, grain, fruits, buds, flowers, insects

VOICE: calls are varied, including hard, metallic sounds and squeaking notes; many have attractive whistling or warbling songs

MIGRATION: many northern species migrate south, while most tropical ones are sedentary

CONSERVATION STATUS: one species, the Black-cheeked Ant Tanager, *Habia atrimaxillaris*, is Endangered; four species, the Sooty Ant Tanager, *H. gutturalis*, the Painted Bunting, *Passerina ciris*, the Rose-bellied Bunting, *P. rositae*, and the Red-and-black Grosbeak, *Caryothraustes erythromelas*, are Near Threatened

ABOVE One of the most familiar and welcomed birds at feeders in the USA is the Northern Cardinal, *Cardinalis cardinalis*.

Restricted to the New World, this family includes some of the most familiar, colourful and best-loved songbirds enjoyed by people feeding birds in backyards and gardens in suburban North America. The family is named for the bright red plumage of males of the Northern Cardinal, *Cardinalis cardinalis*, of North America, the first member of the family to be scientifically described (by Linnaeus), in allusion to the scarlet robes and caps of Catholic cardinals. A total of 15 species occur in the USA, with the ranges of seven of these extending north into southern Canada. The remaining 33 species are largely sedentary birds of Mexico, Central America and South America. The greatest diversity of genera and species occurs in Mexico, Central America and northern South America.

The precise limits of this family have for long been uncertain, and recent genetic research has shown that the saltators, *Saltator*, and Yellow-shouldered Grosbeak, *Parkerthraustes humeralis*, do not belong here; they have now been included in the large tanager family (Thraupidae, p. 329). Such ongoing investigations also suggest equally that some species that have been included within other New World families turn out to belong in this family. These comprise the *Amaurospiza* seedeaters from the New World sparrow family (Passerellidae, p. 314), *Granatellus* chats (formerly tentatively placed in the New World wood warbler family (Parulidae, p. 319), and the ant-tanagers, *Habia*, and the *Piranga* tanagers (moved here from the tanager family).

Cardinals and grosbeaks are finchlike birds with a short, strong, conical bill adapted for crushing seeds. Most have a relatively heavy bill, but in some species (the cardinals, *Cardinalis*, and the ones with 'grosbeak' in their name) the bill is massive and deep. By contrast, the *Passerina* species, confusingly known as buntings (and actually placed by some ornithologists with the Old World buntings and relatives in the Family Emberizidae), have the smallest bill. Cardinalids generally have a compact, stocky body and a relatively large head. The three members of the genus *Cardinalis* have a prominent crest. There is not a great range of size, from species the size of sparrows to those as big as starlings. Males are generally rather larger than females; in the case of the Dickcissel, *Spiza americana*, which is (in contrast to other species) polygynous, males are 30% heavier. The wings are short and rounded in sedentary species, but longer and more pointed in those such as the Dickcissel and Rose-breasted Grosbeak, *Pheucticus ludovicianus*, which make long migrations. Tails range from short to medium length (longest in *Cardinalis*) and usually have a rounded or a slightly notched tip.

The sexes of most species are dichromatic, often strikingly so, with the males sporting bright colours and the females generally cryptically coloured and much drabber. Exceptions are two of the four species of *Caryothraustes*, and three species of *Habia*. Various species are sought after as cage birds for their beautiful plumage. Male colours include red, orange, yellow and blue.

Four of the six species of grosbeaks in the genus *Pheuctictus* are found in Mexico (the Yellow Grosbeak, *P. chrysopeplus*), Costa Rica and Panama (the Black-thighed Grosbeak, *P. tibialis*), or tropical South America (the Golden Grosbeak, *P. chrysogaster*, and Black-backed Grosbeak, *P. aureoventris*) and the males have bold black-and-yellow (or in one race black-and-gold) plumage, and heavily streaked females. The other two are North American, the male of the Rose-breasted Grosbeak being black-and-white and that of the Black-headed Grosbeak, *P. melanocephalus*, having an orange brown body contrasting with a black head, upperparts and tail; females are largely brown and streaked.

In the nine species of *Piranga* tangers, of which five are North American, including the Scarlet Tanager, *P. olivacea*, and Summer Tanager, *P. rubra*, the males have red, orange or orange-and-yellow bodies (contrasting strikingly with black wings and tail in the Scarlet Tanager), while the females are mainly greenish-and-yellow. Five of the eight Neotropical species of ant-tangers, *Habia*, have brighter males, with reddish brown or reddish brown and grey or black plumage (as well as a red crown stripe or crest in two species), while their females are olive green; in the three other species, males resemble the females.

The males of the two sexually dimorphic species of *Caryothraustes* have reddish bodies contrasting with a black hood and, in one, black wings and tail; the females also have the black hood but their bodies are olive green, as they are in both sexes of the other two, black-faced, species in this genus, in one with a grey lower body. The three *Granatellus* chats have males with black, grey, white and rose patterns, while the females are grey above and pale buff below.

Partially or wholly blue plumage features in the males of four genera. In the seven species of *Passerina*, the Indigo Bunting, *P. cyanea*, of North America is almost entirely blue, as is the Blue Grosbeak, *P. caerulea*, found in both the USA and Central America, while other species have the blue partnered with reddish brown, yellow, green or white. The most flamboyant of all is the multi-coloured Painted Bunting, *Passerina ciris*, of the USA, whose males have a blue head, yellow, green, bronze and maroon upperparts

ABOVE This Black-faced Grosbeak, *Caryothraustes palogaster*, will use its huge bill to crush several of these unripe *Hamelia* berries to suck out their juice.

and red underparts. Among Neotropical species, the males of the three little species of seedeaters in the genus *Amaurospiza* are entirely dark blue, while the females are brown. The other all-blue males and brown females are also Neotropical species – the three grosbeaks in the genus *Cyanoloxia* and the single species of *Cyanocompsa*, the Blue Bunting, *C. parellina*.

The predominant colour of the males of two of the three strikingly crested *Cardinalis* species is red; in both the Northern Cardinal, *C. cardinalus*, whose 19 races range from eastern and southern USA to southern Mexico, and the South American Vermilion Cardinal, *C. phoeniceus*, they are all-red apart from a black area around the bill and on the chin. The Northern Cardinal also has a red bill. The male Pyrrhuloxia, *C. sinuatus*, of southern USA and Mexico, is pale grey, with red on his crest and face, extending as a tapering band down his breast, and forming a patch on his wings. Females are brown and buff with red restricted to the crest and wings.

Most members of this family are opportunistic omnivores. Although generally taking more plant matter, including a wide range, from fruits, seeds, buds and flowers to stems, and sometimes nectar, they also eat animals, especially during the breeding season. All species feed their young mainly on insects at first. The animal food taken by adults consists mainly of insects, as well as spiders and other arthropods. Grosbeaks forage mainly in trees and bushes, while many other members of the family feed on the ground or in vegetation.

The Dickcissel makes a long migration from USA to winter in Trinidad and Venezuela, where it is persecuted by farmers. It used to feed there on the seeds of wild grasses in native grasslands but with the spread of agriculture, it nowadays gathers in huge flocks to eat rice and sorghum crops. The species making the longest journey is the Rose-breasted Grosbeak, one of the much-admired birds visiting suburban feeders in North America; breeding as far north as Canada, it winters as far south as Peru. By contrast, the Northern Cardinal is one of the most sedentary of all North American birds. It continues to delight bird-lovers through the depths of winter, continuing to visit feeders when they are dusted with snow, providing a cheering contrast on grey days with its brilliant red plumage.

TANAGERS Thraupidae

GENERA: 98   **SPECIES**: 375

LENGTH: 9–28 cm (3.5–11 in)

WEIGHT: 6–114 g (0.2–4 oz)

RANGE AND HABITAT: apart from the White-collared Seedeater, *Sporophila torqueola*, the family is restricted to Mexico, the Caribbean, Central America and South America (and overwhelmingly in the Neotropics); in varied habitats, chiefly rainforests and other forests, woodlands, plantations, parks and gardens; some in arid scrublands or grasslands and some in relatively barren rocky habitats at high altitudes

SOCIAL BEHAVIOUR: some are largely solitary or live as pairs, others are sociable, both with their own kind and with mixed-species foraging flocks; most are monogamous and some are known to be territorial, although breeding details are not well known for many species

NEST: most species build a cup of grass, plant fibres and other material in a tree, some species nesting near or on the ground among cover; uniquely, the Swallow Tanager, *Tersina viridis*, nests in a hole in a cliff, an earth bank or the wall of a building

EGGS: in most species, 1–4; in most, blue, grey, blue or blue-green, sometimes cream or white, and invariably blotched, spotted or scrawled with darker markings, apart from those of the Swallow Tanager, usually white and unmarked or only lightly marked

INCUBATION: 12–14 days; Swallow Tanager 13–17 days

FLEDGING PERIOD: generally 11–16 days, but up to 20 days in *Thraupis* species, and about 24 days in the Swallow Tanager

FOOD: insects and fruit; some species eat seeds, nectar or flowers

VOICE: songs, uttered mainly at dawn, are often simple and unmelodious repetitions of high-pitched notes, but some species have longer and more complex warbling songs; contact calls tend to be high pitched and thin, alarm calls louder and harsher

MIGRATION: most species are sedentary, but some make nomadic movements to avoid dry seasons or extreme weather at higher altitudes, and some that breed in southern South America migrate north for winter

CONSERVATION STATUS: four species, the Gough Island Finch, *Rowettia goughensis*, the Cherry-throated Tanager, *Nemosia rourei*, the Medium Tree Finch, *Camarhynchus pauper*, and the Mangrove Finch, *C. heliobates*, are Critically Endangered; 14 species, including the Gold-ringed Tanager, *Bangsia aureocincta*, the Venezuelan Flowerpiercer, *Diglossa venezuelensis*, the Great-billed Seed Finch, *Sporophila maximiliani*, the Azure-rumped Tanager, *Tangara cabanisi*, the Black-and-white Tanager, *Conothraupis speculigera*, and the Yellow Cardinal, *Gubernatrix cristata*, are Endangered; 31 species, including the Black-and-gold Tanager, *Bangsia melanochlamys*, the Multicoloured Tanager, *Chlorochrysa nitidissima*, and the Turquoise Dacnis, *Dacnis hartlaubi*, are Vulnerable; 26 species are Near Threatened

Of the closely related groups of New World nine-primaried songbirds, many of the members of this huge family are among the brightest, with every colour in the palette represented in the family as a whole. Such species provide some of the most beautiful and memorable sights that a birder can experience in the Neotropics. Some are completely clothed in one or more stunningly bright colours or are many-hued while others have black plumage that contrasts dramatically with small highlights of vivid colours. An indication of the prevalence of this feature is their common names. Over two-thirds of all of these refer to the colours of the birds, in evocative names such as Cherry-throated Tanager, Flame-crested Tanager, Scarlet-rumped Tanager, Glistening-green Tanager, Seven-coloured Tanager, Viridian Dacnis, Purple Honeycreeper or Deep Blue Flowerpiercer. However, especially after the inclusion in the tanager family of various genera formerly classified in other New World families, there are also a good many species with relatively dull plumage, and in some other species females lack the bright colours of the males.

As with other members of the nine-primaried New World assemblage, the taxonomy of this family is in a great state of flux. As a result of recent DNA research, about 80 species formerly included in the Thraupidae have been found not to be closely related to the rest of its members and hence have been moved to other families. These include the colourful little chlorophonias, *Chlorophonia*, and euphonias, *Euphonia*, whose 32 species are now members of the finch Family Fringillidae (p. 305). The eight species of dull reddish ant-tanagers, *Habia*, and the nine far more colourful *Piranga* species have been moved to the cardinal family (Cardinalidae, p. 327). The latter genus includes four much admired North American birds: the Scarlet Tanager, *P. olivacea*, Summer Tanager, *P. rubra*,

ABOVE The tanager family includes some of the most lovely of all Neotropical birds, like this Blue-gray Tanager, *Thraupis episcopus*, at El Valle, Panama.

Hepatic Tanager, *P. flava*, and Western Tanager, *P. ludoviciana*. Their removal means that the only member of the family now found north of Mexico is one of the seedeaters, the White-collared Seedeater, *Sporophila torqueola*. This has a mere toehold in the USA, breeding in a small area of extreme southern Texas as the northern outpost of its main range in Mexico and Central America.

The nine species of bush tanagers, *Chlorospingus*, have now been found to be relatives of the New World sparrows and have accordingly been transferred to the Family Passerellidae (p. 314). Additionally, various smaller genera have been moved into small families of their own: the single species of thrush tanager (Rhodinocichlidae, p. 313), the warbler tanagers (Phaenicophilidae,

ABOVE The Silver-throated Tanager, *Tangara icterocephala*, is found in wet and humid forests, especially with moss, from Costa Rica to northeast Peru.

p. 317), the chat-tanagers (Calyptophilidae, p. 326), and the aberrant tanagers (Mitrospingidae, p. 326).

Various other species, mainly seedeaters, have been moved in the other direction, into the tanagers from elsewhere. They include the 39 species of seedeaters, *Sporophila*, the six species of *Paroaria* cardinals, and the Galapagos (or Darwin's) finches, *Geospiza*, *Camarynchus*, *Certhidea*, *Pinaroloxias* and *Platyspiza*, moved from the enlarged Emberizidae (before it was split into the New World Passerellidae and Old World buntings Emberizidae, as it appears in this book), and the 14 species of saltators, *Saltator*, until recently included in the Cardinalidae.

This very varied family of songbirds is the largest bird family in the world. Tanagers comprise about 4% of all living bird species and 12% of all birds in the Neotropics, where they constitute the largest of all radiations of songbirds. They exhibit a remarkable range of plumage colours and patterns, and of also of diet and feeding habits, reflected in the great variation of bill shapes and

sizes. Tanagers range in size from tiny birds like some of the smaller species of seedeaters, *Sporophila*, conebills, *Conirostrum*, dacnises, *Dacnis*, honeycreepers, *Cyanerpes*, or flowerpiercers, *Diglossa*, which are only 9–12 cm (3.5–5 in) long, and weigh about 7–11 g (0.25–0.4 oz), to a few much larger species, such as the 14 species of saltators, *Saltator*, ranging from 19–25 cm (7.5–10 in) and weighing up to 100 g (3.5 oz) in the largest species, the White-capped Tanager, *Sericossypha albocristata*, which at 25 cm (10 in) and a weight of 100 g (3.5 oz) or more is as big as a large thrush, or the lighter but longer Magpie Tanager, *Cissopis leverianus*, with a length of 28 cm (11 in), including its long tail. Many of them though, such as those in the very speciose genus *Tangara*, are 12–14 cm (5–5.5 in) long and weigh about 20 g (0.7 oz).

Tails, too, differ widely between different groups, with some such as honeycreepers, dacnises and Darwin's finches having a very short tail and others, like the flowerpiercers and the Magpie Tanager having a longer or much longer tail. Bills differ greatly both in length and shape; although in many species it is powerful, conical and rather finch-like, honeycreepers have a slender, decurved bill, conebills have a rather long, finely pointed one, and the bill of dacnises is short and pointed. In a famous example of evolution in action, bill size and shape within the Darwin's finches have undergone evolutionary changes related to feeding opportunities, which are affected by climatic El Niño and La Niña cycles in the Pacific. These five genera are now often known as Galapagos finches, as apart from the Cocos Island Finch, *Pinaroloxias inornata*, from the Cocos Islands off Costa Rica, they are found only on the Galapagos archipelago. They have become renowned as a superb example of evolution in action: from the arrival, probably about 2–3 million years ago, of an original group of ancestors (either from the South American mainland or from the Caribbean region), they radiated on the different islands of the archipelago into a whole range of species with very different bill sizes and shapes, adapted to a diverse array of lifestyles. These include the Vegetarian Finch, *Platyspiza crassirostris*, the ground-

ABOVE The dapper Black-hooded Sierra Finch, *Phrygilus atriceps*, is one of a group of ground dwelling finches of the high Andes found from the treeline upwards.

ABOVE Like other honeycreepers, the Green Honeycreeper, *Chlorophanes spiza*, feeds on fruit, as well as some nectar, insects and spiders.

ABOVE A Grey-headed Tanager, *Eucometis pencillata*, looks out for insects fleeing from an army ant swarm, at Soberiana National Park, Panama.

finches, all in the single genus *Geospiza*, which specialise in eating seeds of various sizes with a whole array of differently sized bills; the two species of warbler finches, *Certhidea*, which specialise in insect eating with a fine, pointed bill; and five species of tree finch, *Camarynchus*, including the Woodpecker Finch, *C. pallidus*, which is among the few birds known to use tools, as it probes with cactus spines or twigs to extract insect larvae and termites hiding beneath bark or within tree cavities.

Plumage colours, too, are extremely varied; some species, such as the Glistening-green Tanager, *Chlorochrysa phoenicotis*, the Blue-and-black Tanager, *Tangara vassorii*, or males of the Green Honeycreeper, *Chlorophanes spiza*, and the male Purple Honeycreeper, *Cyanerpes caeruleus*, have just one bright colour, with contrasting black markings. The Seven-coloured Tanager, *Tangara fastuosa*, of north-east Brazil is one of a group of species with a kaleidoscope of different colours, in this case including turquoise, blue, violet, purple, yellow, orange and black. Despite their bright colours, as with many tropical birds, such species can often be fairly hard to spot in the darkness of a tropical forest or against sun-dappled foliage. In many tanagers, females look like the brightly coloured males, while in about half the total number of species in the family, they are less colourful, typically dull green, olive, yellowish, brown or grey. In the latter, the males may moult into a duller non-breeding plumage. In some the males too are quite drably coloured, or black-and white, or all-black (as in the males of Galapagos ground finches, *Geospiza*, in which females are brown and heavily streaked) or black-and-white. Some of the flowerpiercers are almost entirely black or blue-grey apart from small patches of rusty red or blue or grey, while others have partly or entirely rufous underparts and some are entirely blue apart from a black face mask in two species.

Although some species are relatively solitary or usually seen in pairs, many are gregarious, forming small flocks when foraging or, often, joining mixed-species groups. Many tanagers feed on both insects and fruit. Some such as the Black-goggled Tanager, *Trichothraupis melanops*, and the Grey-headed Tanager, *Eucometis penicillata*, regularly join a variety of other ant-following birds at army-ant swarms to take advantage of the horde of invertebrates fleeing from the inexorable advance of these formidable ants, though none are obligate ant-followers that only feed in this way. Many tanagers find insect prey by searching the undersides of branches or both surfaces of leaves, while others concentrate their attentions on clusters of mosses or bromeliads, especially those living in cloud forests, where these epiphytic plants are abundant. Various species, formerly included in the Emberizidae, regularly forage on the ground. They include the seedeaters, *Sporophila* and *Catamenia*, the grassquits, *Tiaris*, the sierra finches, *Phrygilus*, and the Galapagos ground finches, *Geospiza*. A few atypical tanagers, such as the Swallow Tanager, *Tersina viridis*, (with long wings but only a shallowly forked tail) and the four species of shrike-tanagers, *Lanio*, which have a strongly hooked shrike-like bill, catch insects in flight.

Overall, the tanagers include more fruit in their diet than most other Neotropical songbirds. Many species eat small fruit that they swallow whole, including the seeds, although they may extract large seeds and drop them. The saltators, which forage in trees mainly at the edges of forests or in scrub, have the odd habit of balancing a fruit they have plucked on a branch of the tree or shrub before taking repeated bites. Fleshy seed coverings called arils are important in the diet of some tanagers, while others eat many of the catkin-like fruits of *Cecropia* trees, which are common in tropical forest clearings. A few species eat flowers or nectar. The flowerpiercers are effectively nectar thieves, obtaining nectar without 'paying for' it. Other nectar feeders such as their relatives the honeycreepers (and the unrelated hummingbirds), probe deeply with their long bills into a tubular flower to obtain the nectar (and in the process help to pollinate the plant as they brush past the stamens and anthers). A flowerpiercer bypasses this route. It has a short but highly specialised bill, with a finely hooked tip to the upper mandible that it uses to hold the corolla of a tubular flower steady while piercing the base of the flower with the sharply pointed lower mandible so that it can extract nectar (and possibly insects too) with its tongue.

LEFT The Large Ground Finch, *Geospiza magnirostris*, one of the famous Galapagos (or Darwin's) finches; recent evidence suggests they may be better placed in the tanager family.

ABOVE The Blue Dacnis, *Dacnis cayana*, occurs in moist or wet forest over a vast range in Central America and the northern half of South America.

ABOVE This striking bird is a male Flame-rumped Tanager, *Ramphocelus flammigerus* of the race *icteronotus*; another race has a red rump.

There is great variation in the size and shape of the bill, from the stubby ones of the seedeaters, *Sporophila*, through the longer and medium-sized ones of many species to the more massive ones of species such as the saltators, *Saltator*, the Caribbean bullfinches, *Melopyrrha*, or many of the Darwin's finches, *Geospiza*, *Platyspiza* and *Camarhynchus*.

The tail is of medium length in most species, but is short in some, such as the honeycreepers, dacnises or the Galapagos ground finches, *Geospiza*, and long in others, including the Long-tailed Reed Finch, *Donacospiza albifrons*, and the grass finches, *Emberizoides*, and especially long in the saltators, and in the Magpie Tanager mentioned above.

Most species live in humid tropical forests or woodland, but some are birds of more open country. The mountain dwellers often live higher up than most other passerines; these hardy little birds include many South American genera in the Andes and other mountains, such as the sierra finches, *Phrygilus*, the yellow finches, *Sicalis*, the diuca finches, *Diuca*, and the Inca finches, *Incaspiza*. Some, especially the latter four genera and others formerly regarded as belonging to other families, have adapted to conditions in extremely arid habitats, such as arid grasslands and dry puna grassland in the Andes. Other tanagers, by contrast, are birds of the perpetually wet, misty Andean cloud forests.

An odd recent inclusion in the family is the little bird called the Bananaquit, *Coereba flaveola*. (The 'quit' ending to the name denotes a small bird in the Caribbean, as in the three species of grassquits, *Tiaris*, and the Orangequit, *Euneornis campestris*, of Jamaica, formerly in the Family Emberizidae but now included in the tanager family). Because of long standing uncertainty about the Bananaquit's true relationships, this widespread and generally common inhabitant of Mexico, Central America, the Caribbean and the northern half of South America it has at various times been included in the wood warbler Family Parulidae, and with the New World sparrows in the Family Passerellidae. Most recently it was placed in a family of its own, the Coerebidae. Its combination of various distinctive features make it unlike any other birds: these include its longish, thin, decurved bill with fleshy red patches at the corners of the gape, a fringed, brushlike tongue and globe-shaped nest.

The Bananaquit has a compact body, with a large head and a very short, almost square tail and short broad wings. It shows a good deal of plumage variation in different parts of its wide range, but basically has grey upperparts and a striking, striped head pattern, with a narrow grey crown, a white supercilium and a grey eye-stripe that broadens out behind the eye to join the nape. The white underparts have a large yellow patch on the belly, and the rump is bright yellow too.

This lively little bird is chiefly a nectar eater, either taking that energy-rich food directly by thrusting the bill into open flowers or 'cheating' like the flowerpiercers mentioned above, by piercing a hole in the base of a flower, although it does not have their particularly specialised bill. Like them, it does not hover in front of

ABOVE Shining Honeycreeper, *Cyanerpes lucidus*, is one of four very similar species in which the males are stunningly blue and velvety black.

a flower like a hummingbird, but perches next to it. The Bananaquit also eats fruit (including snipping off small pieces from bananas), insects and spiders, and often hangs upside down or creeps up branches when feeding. In many places it is unafraid of people, and will steal sweet foods such as jam and sugar from tables. One of its many nicknames in the Caribbean is 'sugar bird' and it can be attracted to bowls or feeders stocked with granular sugar.

The Bananaquit has a high reproductive rate, which in combination with its propensity for the young to disperse, has enabled the species to colonise many Caribbean islands. Birds from the Bahamas occasionally turn up as vagrants in Florida. Most of the remarkable number of 41 subspecies are similar in appearance, although some of the races, especially those on islands, show marked differences in size, bill length and plumage details (for instance, the throat varies from white to black, the extent of yellow on the underparts varies, and all-black morphs occur on St Vincent and Grenada). There is considerable regional variation in their songs.

ABOVE The Bananaquit, *Coereba flaveola*, has adapted to a very wide range of habitats in the Caribbean and northern South America.

HYLIOTAS Hyliotidae

GENERA: 1   **SPECIES**: 4

LENGTH: 10–13 cm (4–5 in)

WEIGHT: 9.5–17 g (0.3–0.6 oz)

RANGE AND HABITAT: sub-Saharan Africa, in the canopy of lowland forests, woodlands, savannah and cultivated land, including coffee or cocoa plantations

SOCIAL BEHAVIOUR: monogamous and territorial; often encountered in pairs or small groups when foraging

NEST: small, neat cup of, rootlets and plant stems camouflaged with mosses and lichens, usually sited in a tree fork

EGGS: 2–4, white or cream, with brown and grey or lilac markings

INCUBATION: no information

FLEDGING PERIOD: no information

FOOD: insects

VOICE: tuneless babbling songs; twittering, whistling and other calls

MIGRATION: sedentary

CONSERVATION STATUS: one species, the Usambara Hyliota, *Hyliota usambara*, is Endangered

Until recently, this very small family of exclusively African birds was usually included in the erstwhile very large family of Old World warblers, Sylviidae, whose 70-odd genera contained over 400 species. Following extensive molecular analysis, this turned out to contain many groups not closely related to one another, and the Sylviidae was accordingly reduced to a far smaller family of mainly Eurasian species (p. 358). Some systematists considered that the hyliotas belonged instead with the endemic African family of batises and wattle-eyes (Platysteiridae, p. 261), or with one or other of two widespread families, the monarchs (Monarchidae, p. 273) and the Old World chats and flycatchers (Muscicapidae, p. 387). The latest DNA research indicates that the hyliotas have no close relatives and should be given their own family, Hyliotidae.

There are four species, all in the genus *Hyliota*: the Yellow-bellied Hyliota, *H. flavigaster*, has the largest range, from Senegal to western Ethiopia and Kenya and from Angola to Mozambique; the Southern Hyliota, *H. australis*, overlaps with it in the southern parts of the Yellow-bellied Hyliota's range. Both these species are birds of open woodlands and savannah. The Violet-backed Hyliota, *H. violacea*, is largely restricted to a few areas of West Africa, and the Usambara Hyliota, *H. usambara*, has a very small range in the Usambara mountains of northeast Tanzania. The last two species are largely forest dwellers, and also found in coffee plantations. They all forage energetically for insects mainly in the canopy layer of forests or at the tops of tall trees in savannah and woodlands, singly or in pairs, and often in mixed-species flocks with other birds. They find most of their food among the smaller branches, hopping or bounding about and often hanging upside-down to snatch prey from the underside of leaves or branches. Sometimes they sally out to snap up insects in flight.

All four species are similar in appearance, with a large head and a flattened bill ending in a very slight hook, a relatively slim body, held horizontally, a short tail and longish legs. They have dark upperparts and pale underparts, and except for the Violet-backed Hyliota they have a prominent, broad white wing bar. The upperparts of the Southern Hyliota are velvety matte black, while in the three other species they are glossy blue-black or in the Violet-backed Hyliota, glossy violet-black. The underparts of males are creamy white and those of females pale tawny orange, brighter on the breast, except in the Usambara Hyliota, in which the male resembles the female.

All species are threatened by deforestation, in the case of the rare Usambara Hyliota in the short term, leading to its classification as Endangered.

FAIRY FLYCATCHER AND RELATIVES Stenostiridae

GENERA: 4   **SPECIES**: 9

LENGTH: 11–18 cm (4–7 in)

WEIGHT: 4–12 g (0.14–3 oz)

RANGE AND HABITAT: Fairy Flycatcher, *Stenostira scita*, in southern Africa, breeding in scrubland and riverine woodland and wintering in acacia savannah, montane scrub, plantations and gardens; crested and blue flycatchers, *Elminia*, right across tropical Africa, mainly in forests, but blue flycatchers also in more open woodland, plantations and gardens; Fairy-fantail, *Chelidorhynx hypoxanthus*, in Himalayan foothills, south-central China and mountains of north and west continental Southeast Asia east to Vietnam, mainly in moist evergreen forests; canary-flycatchers, *Culicicapa*, widespread across southern Asia, from northern Pakistan east to central China and south to Sri Lanka, the Philippines and as far south as southeastern Indonesia, in dry broadleaved forests and woodlands, especially clothing ravines and gorges with streams, also in abandoned plantations and large gardens

SOCIAL BEHAVIOUR: for those species where information is available, socially monogamous (often long-term) apart from the Blue Crested-flycatcher, *E. longicauda*, which is either monogamous or polygamous,

when it breeds communally, with helpers defending the territory and helping to raise the young

NEST: small cup of grass, plant stems, shredded bark or other plant material, bound with spider webs or fine mammal hair and camouflaged with lichen, bark or dried leaves, and lined with plant down, moss, hair, feathers or other soft materials; sited in fork or along a branch of tree or shrub

EGGS: 1–4, white or cream with brown, olive or greyish markings

INCUBATION: 15–18 days, but unknown for some species

FLEDGING PERIOD: 12–14 days, but unknown for some species

FOOD: small insects and other invertebrates

VOICE: songs a medley of whistles, trills and buzzing or chattering sounds, or a series of high-pitched squeaky notes, in some ending in a trill; calls consist of similar sounds

MIGRATION: some sedentary but others make altitudinal migrations

CONSERVATION STATUS: none is threatened

ABOVE The Grey-headed Canary Flycatcher, *Culicicapa ceylonensis*, is a common inhabitant of dry broadleaved forests, especially along wooded gorges and ravines with streams.

The four genera and nine species making up this newly erected family were until very recently each classified in a different family, until genetic research showed them to be close relatives. One of the two Africa genera, *Stenostira*, containing a single species, the Fairy Flycatcher, *S. scita*, was formerly thought to be a close relative of the African warblers called apalises, *Apalis*, and tailorbirds, *Orthotomus*, currently in the Family Cisticolidae (see p. 342); the five species in the other African genus, *Elminia*, were included in the monarch family (Monarchidae, p. 273); one of the two Asian genera, *Chelidorhynx*, containing a single species, the Fairy-fantail, *C. hypoxanthus*, was previously assigned to the genus *Rhipidura* and included in the fantail family (Rhipiduridae, p. 268); and the two canary-flycatchers in the other Asian genus, *Culicicapa*, were regarded as members of the Old World flycatcher family (Muscicapidae, p. 387). Their closest relatives may prove to be the tits and relatives (Paridae, p. 335) and penduline tits (Remizidae, p. 337).

These are lively, active little birds with small bodies, a slender but broad short or medium length bill, and medium length or long, graduated tails. The smallest, the African Fairy-flycatcher, measures less than 12 cm (4.75 in), including its long tail, and may weigh as little as 4 or 5 g (less than 0.2 oz). The African Fairy-flycatcher is mainly blue-grey, with a black 'bandit mask' contrasting with a white eyestripe above and white throat below; its wings are black-and-white, and its tail black with white outer feathers. Three of the *Elminia* species are mainly dark grey and blackish, while the other two are mainly blue; all members of this genus have a short crest. The Fairy-fantail is boldly patterned, dark greyish olive from its crown to its back, with a bright yellow stripe above the eye, a black mask, bright yellow underparts and dark brown wings and tail. The two canary flycatchers are green above and yellow below, in one species with a grey head.

These attractive little birds obtain much of their food – small insects, including flies, moths and bees, by flying out from a perch to catch them in flight, but they also glean insects and spiders from branches and foliage of the forests and woodlands where they live. While foraging, they frequently shake their wings, or droop and fan both their wings and tail.

TITS, TITMICE AND CHICKADEES Paridae

GENERA: 14   **SPECIES**: 62

LENGTH: all but the four monotypic species are 10–16 cm (4–6 in); the Fire-capped Tit, *Cephalopyrus flammiceps*, is 8.5–9.5 com (3–3.75 in); the Yellow-browed Tit, *Sylviparus modestus*, is 9–10 cm (3.5–4 in); the Sultan Tit, *Melanochlora sultanea*, is 20–21 cm (8 in)

WEIGHT: all but the four monotypic species are 7–29 g (0.2–0.9 oz); the Fire-capped Tit is about 7 g (0.2 oz); the Yellow-browed Tit is 5–9 g (0.2–0.3 oz); the Ground Tit is 42–48 g (1.5–1.7 oz); the Sultan Tit is 35–49 g (1.2–1.7 oz)

RANGE AND HABITAT: North America, Europe, North Africa and sub-Saharan Africa, Asia; a wide range of forests, woods and shrubby habitats, scrub, some in urban areas

SOCIAL BEHAVIOUR: most species are monogamous and pair for life; typically territorial; usually in pairs or family groups during the breeding season; afterwards many species form flocks of their own or mixed with other tits and often also nuthatches, woodpeckers, kinglets and woodpeckers

NEST: all species are hole nesters; some species excavate their own holes in soft, decaying wood of tree trunks or branches, while other species select natural holes in trees, among rocks etc., or use the nest holes excavated by other birds such as woodpeckers, or rodents; the nest is typically a mass of fine grass, rootlets, moss, feathers, hair, bark strips or other materials

EGGS: 2–14, typically white with reddish-brown spots, but in a few species and odd individuals of others, pure white

INCUBATION: 12–18 days

FLEDGING PERIOD: typically 16–22 days

FOOD: insects and other invertebrates; also seeds and fruit; many northern species cache food to see them through lean times in winter

VOICE: very vocal, with a rich vocabulary of single or multiple notes; calls mainly high-pitched, ranging from quiet *see-see-see* notes, used mainly for contact, through harsher churring or mixed sounds to explosive calls, often for alarm; the songs are usually more complex and given by males

MIGRATION: mostly sedentary, but some species disperse widely after leaving the nest; some make seasonal altitudinal movements, and many make eruptive movements, especially after large-scale failure of food supplies, such as seeds in autumn

CONSERVATION STATUS: one species, the Izu Tit, *Sittiparus owstoni*, is Endangered; one species, the White-naped Tit, *Parus nuchalis*, is Vulnerable; three species are Near Threatened

This medium-sized family of almost entirely small, lively songbirds of woodland and shrubby habitats contains a number of species that have been intensively studied by ornithologists and are much loved as visitors to bird feeders by many more people. Known simply as tits in the British Isles, they are called chickadees and titmice in North America. In this context, *tit* is an Old English word for something small, while the 'mouse' part of the name is from the Old English name, *mase*, for these birds. Chickadee is straightforwardly onomatopoeic, relating to the distinctive alarm calls of species bearing the name.

Apart from two unusual monotypic genera, all members of the family are very similar in shape: plump-bodied, with a big, short-necked head and stubby pointed bill, which is finer in the more insectivorous species and thicker in those that eat more seeds. These birds have strong legs and feet, with which they can hold down food items such as seeds or insects while hacking into them or breaking them up, and are adept at moving acrobatically in trees and shrubs. They bustle about energetically in search of food, and are skilled at hanging upside down from twigs or bird feeders.

In Europe (especially in the British Isles) and North America, a number of species are amongst the best known, and most admired, of all garden visitors. They include three species with a very wide range across Europe and Asia: the Blue Tit, *Cyanistes caeruleus*, Coal Tit, *Periparus ater*, and the Great Tit, *Parus major*, which is one of the most extensively scientifically studied of all the world's wild birds, and in North America, the Black-capped Chickadee, *Poecile atricapillus*, Carolina Chickadee, *Poecile carolinensis*, and Tufted Titmouse, *Baeolophus bicolor*.

After breeding, many species, especially in temperate regions, form mixed species flocks, often including not only several species of tits but other small insectivorous birds too, such as nuthatches, kinglets, goldcrests or firecrests, and treecreepers.

ABOVE The Blue Tit, *Cyanistes caeruleus*, is one of the most familiar and best-loved of all British garden birds.

Along with corvids and parrots, the tits are thought to be among the most intelligent and adaptable of all birds. Their ability to solve problems using insight learning (that is, by using insight rather than trial and error) has been demonstrated by experiments such as those involving Great Tits working their way through mazes and obtaining nuts by removing matches from matchboxes. A famous example of their adaptability was seen when Great Tits and Blue Tits started accessing the cream at the top of doorstep milk bottles in Britain by pecking through the foil caps (they even learned to distinguish them by colour and avoid homogenised or lower-fat milk). This behaviour was first noted in 1921, and quickly spread throughout populations nationwide over the next couple of decades. Many northern species demonstrate their highly developed spatial memory by their habit of hoarding seeds for winter, hiding them and remembering the location of their caches – in a similar way to some of the corvids, notably the nutcrackers, *Nucifraga*. These include the Old World coal tits, crested tits, and the group known as chickadees in the New World, such as the

Marsh Tit, *Poecile palustris,* Willow Tit, *P. montanus* in Eurasia and the Siberian Tit, *P. cinctus* of Eurasia and Alaska, as well as the four North American species of chickadees, and the five species of North American titmice *Baeolophus.* Another group, including the Great Tit and Blue Tit as well as the 14 *Melaniparus* species occurring in sub-Saharan Africa, are not hoarders.

In contrast to their overall close similarity of structure, plumage patterns are rather varied. In most species, the sexes are very similar in plumage (usually with females being duller), although in the Yellow-bellied Tit, *Pardaliparus venustulus,* the male has a different black-and-white rather than grey-and-white head pattern. Most species feature various combinations of brown (from dull to chestnut), grey, black and white, some include yellow, green, or red, two are mainly bright blue and yellow, and one blue and white. Within a particular group, the plumages of the different species tend to be similar, often extremely so, as in the chickadee group, which are almost all brownish or greyish above, paler below and with a dark brown or black cap and bib. Some species bear a crest on the head: they include the Crested Tit, *Lophophanes cristatus,* and the Grey-crested Tit, *L. dichrous,* in Europe and Asia, several Asian species such as the Rufous-vented Tit, *Periparus rubidiventris,* Rufous-naped Tit, *P. rufonuchalis,* and Black-lored Tit, *P. xanthogenys,* and in North America the Tufted Titmouse, Bridled Titmouse, *Machlolophus wollweberi,* and two other closely related titmice species.

Two monotypic Asian genera differ considerably from the rest in plumage, as well as in size and other characteristics. The Sultan Tit, *Melanochlora sultanea,* is much larger than the rest of the family, and has striking, soft, silky black and yellow plumage, with a long, floppy, spiky-ended yellow or black crest. It is found in the eastern Himalayas, a few areas of southern China, and in Myanmar, Thailand, the Malay Peninsula and northern Indochina.

The Yellow-browed Tit, *Sylviparus modestus,* is, at 9–10 cm (3.5–4 in) long, the second smallest member of a family of generally small birds, is a tiny, drab almost featureless olive-green and yellowish bird. It is found in a long narrow belt across the Himalayas and scattered across China, Myanmar, Thailand and Indochina.

In contrast to these two species, which have long been considered members (albeit aberrant ones) of the Paridae, two Asian birds, are far more recent candidates for admittance to the tit family. The first of these, *Pseudopodoces humilis,* is the most surprising addition. It was previously considered an unusual member of the crow family (Corvidae), with the common name of Hume's Ground-jay, Tibetan Ground Jay or Ground Chough. It does bear a superficial resemblance in shape and its longish, decurved bill to other, larger corvids known as ground-jays, in the genus *Podoces.* However, evidence from its bone structure, voice and preen gland chemistry, backed up by DNA studies, indicate that it is definitely not a corvid and probably should be included in the Paridae, under the common name of Ground Tit. Its soft, dull brown and fawn plumage camouflage it well in its arid steppe or scrub habitat, from the Himalayas to central and south-west China. The nest site is unusual in being a tunnel in an earth bank up to 1.6 m (5.25 ft) long; often this is dug out by the birds themselves but sometimes they will use an existing cavity, including the burrows of some mammals, such as those of the little relatives of rabbits and hares called pikas.

ABOVE A Crested Tit, *Lophophanes cristatus,* the only crested European tit species, perches on the hoof of a dead Roe Deer, in Finland, in winter.

ABOVE In North America crested tit species, like this Tufted Titmouse, *Baeolophus bicolor,* are called titmice while the rest are called chickadees.

Another unusual Asian species that has also recently been added to this family is the Fire-capped Tit, *Cephalopyrus flammiceps.* This tiny bird, which at a mere 8.5–9.5 cm (3.3–3.75 in) and weighing only 7 g or so (0.25 oz) becomes its smallest member, was previously rather dubiously included in the penduline tit family (Remizidae), despite various differences, including its nest site in tree holes, totally unlike that of penduline tits. Before that it was often included in the goldcrest and kinglet family (Regulidae, p. 366). Its common and specific names both refer to the bright flame-red or orange forecrown, chin and throat of the male's breeding plumage, contrasting with its olive green upperparts and bright yellow underparts. Females and non-breeding males lack the fiery markings. It breeds in broadleaved mountain forest in the Himalayas, and in spruce, fir and rhododendron forests in China.

PENDULINE TITS Remizidae

GENERA: 3 **SPECIES**: 10

LENGTH: 7.5–11 cm (3–4.3 in)

WEIGHT: 4.6–12.5 g (0.2–0.5 oz)

RANGE AND HABITAT: Europe, Asia, sub-Saharan Africa; one species (the Verdin, *Auriparus flaviceps*) in southwest North America; mainly open country with scattered trees and bushes or other tall vegetation, including desert scrub and open *Acacia* woodland, marshy areas near rivers and reed beds; one species, the Forest Penduline Tit, *Anthoscopus flavifrons*, in rainforests

SOCIAL BEHAVIOUR: most are strongly gregarious, feeding in flocks of up to 20; the Verdin usually found in pairs; mostly monogamous, but some populations of penduline tits, *Remiz*, are polygamous; some *Anthoscopus* species are cooperative breeders

NEST: almost all build large, elaborate, strong, elastic, feltlike pear-shaped nests of plant fibres and grasses, covered with plant down and animal fur, and with a short, tunnel-like side entrance (or sometimes two); those of the African *Anthoscopus* species are more complex, with an anti-predator device in the shape of a false entrance above the real one, leading to a false chamber; the birds access the actual nest chamber by opening a hidden flap, and closing it once they are safely inside, with spiders' webs to seal it; the Verdin makes a spherical nest up to 20 cm (8 in) across of up to 2,000 spiny twigs (spines facing outwards), woven around a branch, with a soft lining of feathers and a side entrance

EGGS: 2–10, (usually 3–8), white

INCUBATION: 14–17 days

FLEDGING PERIOD: 17–24 days

FOOD: mainly insects and small spiders; also seeds, fruit and nectar in some seasons

VOICE: high-pitched whistling or wheezing contact calls; brief, simple songs of repeated sounds similar to calls

MIGRATION: the tropical species are sedentary; *Remiz* species make long migrations south for winter

CONSERVATION STATUS: none threatened

ABOVE A Eurasian Penduline Tit, *Remiz pendulinus*, perches near the entrance to its felted nest suspended from a branch in Lleida, Spain.

This family is related to the true tits (Paridae), and has sometimes been included as a subfamily (Remizinae) within them. It is less speciose, containing less than a fifth as many species as the Paridae. All are very small songbirds, plump-bodied, with a short, sharply pointed, conical bill that is finer than that of the true tits. Although, like the latter, they are acrobatic feeders and often hang upside down as they probe bark crevices, foliage, flower clusters or other hiding places for their invertebrate or nectar food, this ability is not the origin of the family's common name. Instead, this refers to the siting of the remarkable, long-lasting baglike nest in all species, which except in the Verdin, *Auriparus flaviceps*, is slung by the narrow 'handle' at the top from the end of a branch.

The most sophisticated nest design is that of the endemic African *Anthoscopus* species and is one of the most effective anti-predator devices in nature – the very obvious side entrance fools the predator as it leads only to a false chamber. The tube forming the parents' entrance to the real nest chamber is cunningly concealed as it is closed up to form the roof of the false entrance. When the coast is clear and the birds are ready to enter, they open the concealed entrance flap using one foot, then once in the nest chamber, close it again by means of the Velcro-like action of the spiders' webs they have incorporated into its structure. It takes a pair working together up to a month to construct this type of nest.

This is an almost entirely Old World family, the exception being the Verdin of the deserts of southwestern USA and northern Mexico, one of North America's smallest passerines. The three species in the genus *Remiz* are Eurasian, ranging from Portugal right across the temperate regions of Europe and Asia to as far east as Japan. They have complex patterns of chestnut, grey, brown and cream plumage, with a broad black mask through the eyes or a black hood; males are somewhat brighter. The six *Anthoscopus* species range across much of sub-Saharan Africa, from the southern fringes of the Sahara to South Africa. They are green or grey above with whitish, buff or yellow underparts.

The Verdin is a small dull grey bird with a yellow face, chin and throat, and has sometimes been classified with the true tits. It lays blue-green eggs speckled with reddish brown, which are utterly different from the white eggs laid by the rest of the family. Its nest, though, is more of the general penduline-tit type, a large globe up to 20 cm (8 in) across, but fashioned from spiny twigs woven around a branch and incorporating wool, feathers and other soft materials. The spines are arranged facing outwards, providing a formidable challenge to any would-be predators.

Studies of the Eurasian Penduline Tit, *Remiz pendulinus*, have shown that although most pairs are monogamous, a fair number indulge in polygynous mating arrangements. An unmated male may start building as many as five or six nests in a season to attract females. An interested female may cooperate with him to finish building a part-constructed nest and lay eggs, but sometimes she chases him away once they have mated, then finishes constructing the nest and incubates her eggs alone. The male may then make more nests and attract more females. Since the females are often just as promiscuous as the males, he may be the one who is left to incubate the eggs and rear the resulting brood.

ABOVE The North American Verdin, *Auriparus flaviceps*, builds several nests in dense, arid thorn scrub, including roosting nests maintained all year.

NICATORS Nicatoridae

GENERA: 1   **SPECIES**: 3

LENGTH: 15–23 cm (6–9 in)

WEIGHT: 21–67 g (0.7–2.4 oz

RANGE AND HABITAT: the Western Nicator, *Nicator chloris*, has a more or less continuous distribution from Senegal south to northern Angola and east to eastern Uganda; the Eastern Nicator, *N. gularis*, has a fragmented range in East Africa, from Somalia south to eastern South Africa, and the Yellow-throated Nicator, *N. vireo*, lives in central Africa from Cameroon east to Uganda; mainly in forests with dense understory, but also in more open woodland with dense thickets or other cover, abandoned plantations and suburban gardens

SOCIAL BEHAVIOUR: most likely all three species are socially monogamous and territorial; seen singly or in pairs, and may join with other birds in mixed-species flocks

NEST: a simple, very small and flimsy structure of sticks, with some twigs and plant tendrils and sometimes leaves, rootlets and moss, bound fast to the branch by the network of threads of a fungus, *Marasmius*; usually hidden among undergrowth

EGGS: 1–4, variable, from white, cream, or yellowish green to dark olive green, with purple, brown, grey or other coloured markings

INCUBATION: 17–18 days

FLEDGING PERIOD: 16–18 days

FOOD: mainly insects, also other invertebrates, and small vertebrates such as lizards and frogs

VOICE: loud songs include whistling, chuckling and guttural notes, and sometimes mimicry of other species, from orioles to owls, with those of the two larger species likened to the famous song of the Nightingale, *Luscinia megarhynchos*; calls range from dry, hollow sounds to harsh or nasal notes

MIGRATION: thought to be sedentary

CONSERVATION STATUS: none is threatened

For a long time, the members of this very small family of African endemics were often considered to belong to the bulbuls in the Family Pycnonotidae (p. 351); at times, they were thought to be related to the shrikes (Laniidae, p. 270) or the bush-shrikes and relatives (Malaconotidae, p. 266). Support for the supposed relationship with the bulbuls came from analysis of their feather proteins and early DNA studies, but subsequent DNA research indicated otherwise, and suggested that the nicators should be given a family of their own – a suggestion backed up by the genus having several unique morphological and behavioural features, including their building of makeshift nests, small, sparse, flat platforms of sticks resembling those of pigeons rather than passerines. These can be so flimsy that the eggs fall through them when the nest is rocked by wind. Moreover, the nest itself may fall to the ground just after being built, before the fungus that the birds incorporate into the structure develops a network of threads that binds it securely to the branch. The nicators' closest relatives appear to be the larks (Alaudidae) and the Bearded Reedling (Panuridae, p. 340) but may include a number of other families.

Nicators have a thick, prominently hooked bill, distinctive upward-pointing bristles in front of the eyes, and a long, rounded tail. The Western Nicator, *Nicator chloris*, and Eastern Nicator, *Nicator gularis*, are both about as big as a thrush, whereas the Yellow-throated Nicator, *N. vireo*, is only the size of a sparrow. The three species have very similar plumage, with a yellowish olive head and upperparts and greyish white underparts, distinctive yellow or cream spots on the wings, and a yellowish olive tail with yellow corners; *Nicator vireo* has a yellow throat, and also lacks the prominent yellow eye-ring of its two larger relatives. Although males and females have the same plumage, there is a marked size difference between the sexes, at least for the two larger species: male Eastern Nicators can be 50% heavier than females.

These are shy birds that are usually very hard to see as they spend much of their time in dense cover, mainly at lower levels of the forest, and the best clue to their presence is generally their loud songs, typically combining rich whistled or bubbling notes and dry rattling ones, or their often harsh contact and alarm calls. They may show themselves as they forage for prey, which includes frogs and lizards as well grasshoppers, beetles, caterpillars or other insects. As they search among vine-clad tree trunks, lianas, and tangles of dead leaves, or on the ground among leaf litter, they frequently flick open their wings and fan their tails to startle their prey from hiding places.

LARKS Alaudidae

GENERA: 21   **SPECIES:** 93

LENGTH: 10–23 cm (4–9 in)

WEIGHT: 12–76 g (0.4–2.7 oz)

RANGE AND HABITAT: Europe, much of Asia, Africa, with a single endemic species (the Madagascar Sparrow Lark, *Eremopterix hova*) in Madagascar; one Asian species extending to Australasia (the Horsfield's (or Australasian) Bushlark, *Mirafra javanica*), and one Eurasian species (the Horned Lark [or Shore Lark] *Eremophila alpestris*) also in North America; a single isolated population of Horned Larks in the Andes near Bologna, Colombia, South America; the greatest diversity in Africa (with 80% of species); a wide range of open country, especially grassland, desert and semi-desert and scrub; some species have adapted to agriculture

SOCIAL BEHAVIOUR: singly or in pairs in the breeding season, but many species become gregarious after it, in some cases forming large feeding or migrating flocks; monogamous, territorial, breeding solitarily or in loose colonies

NEST: sited on the ground, in most species a cup consisting mainly of dead grasses, sometimes with a foundation of twigs, lined with softer plant material, feathers or hair, in some a more complex domed structure; some build pathways or encircling ramparts of pebbles, twigs or mammal dung that may protect the eggs or nestlings from high temperatures

EGGS: 1–8, white to pale bluish, superbly camouflaged with dark spots and blotches

INCUBATION: 11–16 days

FLEDGING PERIOD: 8–14 days

FOOD: species with a short, stout bill feed mainly on seeds; those with a longer, thinner and sometimes decurved bill eat mainly insects and other invertebrates; many feed on both types of food

VOICE: calls range from short buzzing notes to sweet, liquid sounds; songs, often delivered in song-flight, are often complex, varied and melodious; some species are skilled mimics of other birds

MIGRATION: many Eurasian species and the Horned Lark in both Eurasia and North America are partial or complete migrants

CONSERVATION STATUS: two species, Archer's Lark, *Heteromirafra archeri*, and the Raso Lark, *Alauda razae*, are Critically Endangered; three species, Ash's Lark, *Mirafra ashi*, and Botha's Lark, *Spizocorys fringillaris*, and Rudd's Lark, *Heteromirafra ruddi*, are Endangered; one species, the Red Lark, *Certhilauda burra*, is Vulnerable; two species are Near Threatened

ABOVE Like some other larks, the Crested Lark, *Galerida cristata*, has a prominent crest, which it raises frequently when alarmed or excited.

Larks are mainly sparrow-sized to starling-sized birds, large-winged and in some species short-tailed. Most have a strong, short to medium-length, straight or slightly decurved bill. In some the bill is thinner, and in a few of these, such as the Greater Hoopoe Lark, *Alaemon alaudipes*, and the Cape Long-billed Lark, *Certhilauda curvirostris*, it is long and distinctly decurved. Such a bill is especially good for digging into soil for seeds or insects. At the other extreme, some species, such as the Thick-billed Lark, *Ramphocoris clotbey*, have a very large, deep bill, similar in size and weight to that of the unrelated Old World hawfinches, *Coccothraustes* (Family Fringillidae), and New World cardinal-grosbeaks (Family Cardinalidae); as with these birds, it is used for cracking very hard seeds.

The legs are strong and rather long and, like some ground-dwelling birds, most larks have long, straight hind claws, which may provide extra stability when standing. Those that run particularly fast, such as the two hoopoe-larks, *Alaemon*, have longer legs and feet with shorter hind-claws.

Most species have camouflaging plumage, typically in various shades of brown, buff, rufous, grey, black and white, often with much streaking, enabling them to blend in impressively to the background of earth, sand, grass or other vegetation, and so escape detection by predators, especially when sitting on the nest. Some have more prominent patterns – for example, the hoopoe larks, whose black-and-white wing markings and pinkish-buff body give them a superficial resemblance to the unrelated (non-passerine) bird for which they are named, and the two species of horned larks, *Eremophila*, which have bold black-and-yellow head and upper breast patterns, and little black 'horns', spikes of elongated feathers that project backwards from the crown and are most prominent in the male's breeding plumage. The male Black Lark, *Melanocorypha yeltoniensis*, of Central Asia is entirely black in his breeding plumage, and the male Black-eared Sparrow-lark, *Eremopterix australis*, of southern Africa is black below and chestnut above. Some species have crests, and these are especially well-developed in the genus *Galerida*, including the widespread Crested Lark, *G. cristata*, of Eurasia and Africa. Larks are among the few passerines known to lose all their feathers (even the flight feathers) during their first true moult from juvenile to adult plumage.

Apart from the Horsfield's (or Australasian) Bushlark, *Mirafra javanica*, all species in this family of ground-dwelling songbirds are birds of the Old World, although one of these, the Horned Lark (known in the UK as the Shore Lark), *Eremophila alpestris*, also occurs widely in North America. Indeed, the latter species is likely to be one of the most widespread of all the world's passerines, with 40-odd subspecies found across Eurasia, North Africa and North America. Similarly, despite major declines, including the huge decline in the UK that has seen the population halve during the 1990s (and continue to decline especially in its preferred farmland habitat), the Eurasian Skylark, *Alauda arvensis*, is one of the most widespread birds in Britain and some other parts of Europe.

ABOVE A Eurasian Skylark, *Alauda arvensis*, begins its long, vertical song flight on a fine spring morning in Norfolk, England.

LEFT The Wood Lark, *Lullula arborea*, sings its beautiful song – regarded as among the finest of all European birds – both in flight and from a perch.

Many species are renowned for the beauty and length of their songs, and have become celebrated in poetry, prose and music. These are often delivered in a song-flight, which is particularly impressive in: the Eurasian Skylark – which towers high, often until lost from view, hovering on fast-fluttering wings and constantly pouring out a stream of song; the Wood Lark, *Lullula arborea* – with a long circling flight and a very beautiful song; and the Greater Hoopoe Lark, with its melancholy piping song in an ascending flight, in which it twists in flight and often somersaults. Some others, particularly the bushlarks, *Mirafra*, have switchback song-flights in which they clap their wings together loudly while singing.

Unfortunately, despite their relatively small size, larks have also traditionally been highly valued for their meat. From medieval times until the 1930s, huge numbers of Skylarks were trapped in Britain and other parts of Europe, and many are still are caught in some southern parts of the continent, but the main threats now facing this widespread and numerous species are from agricultural intensification and destruction or degradation of habitat. This is, true, too, for many far rarer species, including those that have been brought to the brink of extinction in Africa, such as the Critically Endangered Archer's Lark, *Heteromirafra archeri*, now restricted to a single location in southern Ethiopia, as a result of overgrazing and other damage to its grassland habitat. Another Critically Endangered species is the Raso Lark, *Alauda razae*, endemic to a single very small uninhabited island, Raso, in the Cape Verde islands of the Atlantic off West Africa, which is at the mercy of drought, likely to be exacerbated by global warming, and also vulnerable to predation by geckos and, potentially by the introduction of cats, dogs or non-native plants that may result from visits by fishermen and increasing tourism.

BEARDED REEDLING Panuridae

GENERA: 1   **SPECIES:** 1

LENGTH: 14.5–17 cm (6–7 in)

WEIGHT: 11–21 g (0.4–0.7 oz)

RANGE AND HABITAT: scattered across Europe and central Asia and east to as far as the Russian Far East, primarily of specific habitat of dense reedbeds, with some in other vegetated wetland habitats, among rushes and other dense vegetation

SOCIAL BEHAVIOUR: usually monogamous, but some males are polygynous, mating and rearing young with two females simultaneously; generally very gregarious

NEST: a deep cup of dead *Phragmites* reed leaves and leaves of other marsh plants, lined with the fluff from reed flower-heads, feathers and sometimes mammal hair, sited among close vertical stems of reeds or sedges and other marsh plants, which form a roof over it

EGGS: 3–11 recorded, usually 4–8, white or cream, with fine dark brown markings

INCUBATION: 10–14 days

FLEDGING PERIOD: usually 12–13 days, sometimes up to 16 days

FOOD: major seasonal difference in diet; in spring and summer, the birds eat mainly insects and other invertebrates, then in autumn and winter they switch to feeding mainly on reed seeds

VOICE: the song is a brief trill; main call is a distinctive nasal, ringing 'ping ping'

MIGRATION: often more or less sedentary, but make extensive eruptive movements, some of which lead to the establishment of new breeding colonies

CONSERVATION STATUS: not threatened

An unusual species, the Bearded Reedling, *Panurus biarmicus*, has a restricted range across temperate Europe and Asia as an extreme habitat specialist, being chiefly tied to extensive reedbeds and adjoining vegetation, where it nests, roosts and feeds. At various times this attractive little songbird has been given monotypic family status, or alternatively has been regarded first as a member

of the tit family (Paridae), when its English name was the Bearded Tit, then placed in the babbler family as a distinctive member of the parrotbill group, with the common name of Bearded Parrotbill. Recent DNA research, however, suggests that it may have no especially close relatives; as a result, it is given a family of its own; an old vernacular name, 'reedling' which accurately describes its specialised habitat requirements, has been resurrected and the species is now once again called Bearded Reedling.

About half the total length of 14.5–17 cm (6–7 in) is taken up by the long tail. The Bearded Reedling bears a superficial resemblance in shape to the long-tailed tits, but its long tail is broader and strongly graduated and its yellow bill longer and more pointed. With its short, broad wings whirring and its tail trailing behind, it resembles a tiny pheasant in flight. The soft plumage is mainly rich orangey brown, with black, cream and white markings on the wings. Unlike other parrotbills, it is sexually dimorphic. Males have a pale blue-grey head and a distinctive broad black 'moustache' stripe extending from each eye, rather than a 'beard' as alluded to in the species' common name.

Like true tits, and also like other parrotbills, these are very active and acrobatic little birds, with a distinctive habit of moving about in dense reed beds by grasping a pair of adjacent stems, one with each foot. And like other parrotbills, too, they are very gregarious, remaining in flocks of varying sizes for most of the year. Bearded Reedlings are especially vulnerable to hard winters, although the propensity of juvenile birds in particular for making

LEFT The Bearded Reedling, *Panurus biarmicus*, has evolved strong legs and large feet that help it to grasp reed stems and move about with great agility in its reedbed habitat.

eruptive movements after breeding can result in their remaining in a distant reed bed after winter has ended and establishing a new colony. The species is unusual in having a digestive system adapted to dealing with two very different diets; after feeding mainly on insects for much of the year, the birds develop hard plates in their stomachs for digesting tough seeds, a process aided by their habit of swallowing small stones, which are excreted the following spring.

CROMBECS, LONGBILLS AND RELATIVES Macrosphenidae

GENERA: 6   **SPECIES:** 18

LENGTH: 8–23 cm (3–9 in)

WEIGHT: 6–40 g (0.2–1.4 oz)

RANGE AND HABITAT: sub-Saharan Africa, found in a wide range of habitats, the crombecs, *Sylvietta*, mainly in savannah and arid acacia scrub, the Rockrunner, *Achaetops pycnopygius*, in scree and rocky outcrops with scattered trees, especially along streams, Victorin's Warbler, *Cryptillas victorini*, in a variety of damp habitats, from streamside vegetation to mountainsides and coastal heathland; the Moustached Grass Warbler, *Melocichla mentalis*, in wet grassland with scattered shrubs and Cape Grassbird, *Sphenoeacus afer*, in grassland and scrub; longbills in tropical forests

SOCIAL BEHAVIOUR: little information for most species, but all appear to be socially monogamous and territorial

NEST: materials include grass, leaves, twigs and rootlets; in crombecs the nest is a bag-shaped or pear-shaped structure suspended from a branch, with a broad entrance on one side near the top, bound together with spider webs, which also help attach them to the branch; they are often

camouflaged with bark fragments, seeds or other material; the other species build cup-shaped nests, usually hidden on or near the ground among dense vegetation

EGGS: 1–3, white or pale pink with brown, reddish or grey markings

INCUBATION: 14–17 days in the species for which information is available

FLEDGING PERIOD: 14–17 days in the species for which information is available

FOOD: mainly insects and other invertebrates, with some species also occasionally eating seeds or fruit

VOICE: songs vary from simple and repetitive in some species to rich and melodious warbling in others

MIGRATION: sedentary, apart from localised movements relating to rainfall in the Northern Crombec and Moustached Grass Warbler

CONSERVATION STATUS: one subspecies (*chaplini*) of the White-browed Crombec, *S. leucophrys*, which may be a separate species, the Lendu (or Chapin's) Crombec, *Sylvietta chapini*, is Critically Endangered; one species, Pulitzer's Longbill, *Macrosphenus pulitzeri*, is Endangered

LEFT The Red-faced Crombec, *Sylvietta whytii*, is a common and widespread bird in eastern Africa, living in various wooded and bushy habitats from sea-level to about 2,000 m (6,500 ft).

This small endemic African family was recently created to bring together six genera of birds that were previously scattered in the former huge family of some 400 species of Old World warblers, Sylviidae (now reduced to include just the scrub warblers in the single genus *Sylvia*). The molecular evidence that indicates their close relationship also suggests that they are an ancient lineage that branched off early in the evolution of the large group of songbirds containing the various families of warblers and many other families, such as the tits, the swallows and martins, and the bulbuls. As a result, this appears to be a distinctive family with no close relatives.

There are four monotypic genera and two genera that each contain several species. The crombecs, *Sylvietta*, comprise nine species of very small birds, just 8–10 cm (3–4 in) long, with short, slightly decurved and pointed bills, and extremely short tails that barely extend beyond their wingtips when they are perched. They have brown upperparts and buff or cinnamon underparts. They are restless little birds, constantly on the move as they move from tree to tree in search of insect food. The longbills, *Macrosphenus*, are rather larger, and as their common name suggests, have long, straight bills, with a very slight hook at the tip; their tails, while still very short, are longer than the stubby ones of the crombecs. They are mainly olive green or brownish above and paler below, yellow, yellowish, greyish or buff. Both crombecs and longbills forage singly, in pairs or sometimes small groups, and usually remain in the tree canopy or in shrubs. The other species, by contrast, are largely terrestrial. All of them have medium length bills and long, graduated tails.

The two grassland species are the largest and bulkiest members of the family, with the stoutest bills. The more widespread of the two, the Moustached Grass Warbler, *Melocichla mentalis*, has a

particularly sturdy bill and brown plumage, darker above, with a prominent white area above the eye and on the throat, where it contrasts with a thin black streak. The Cape Grassbird (or Cape Grass Warbler), *Sphenoeacus afer*, is largely restricted to southern Africa, and is also brown, with a similar (though more muted) face pattern, but strongly streaked with black above. The Rockrunner, *Achaetops pycnopygius*, which lives in Namibia and southwest Angola, has strikingly patterned plumage, with the head and front half of its body heavily streaked with black, contrasting strongly with its white throat and chest, and the rest of its body rich reddish brown. It scurries about like a mouse across the rocks and damp grass of its mountain habitat, often holding its tail cocked, and has a loud song of clear warbling and bubbling notes. The final member of the family, Victorin's Warbler, *Cryptillas victorini*, is an inhabitant of the wet mountain slopes and fynbos coastal heathland in the Cape region of South Africa. It is dark brown on its crown and upperparts, with a greyish patch around its eye and cinnamon brown below.

CISTICOLAS AND RELATIVES Cisticolidae

GENERA: 27   **SPECIES:** 139

LENGTH: 7–20 cm (2.75–10.5in)

WEIGHT: 5–32 g (0.2–1.1 oz)

RANGE AND HABITAT: Africa, southern Europe (only one species, the Zitting Cisticola, *Cisticola juncidis*, which has a huge range extending from Portugal and sub-Saharan Africa east as far as Japan and Australia), south-central and southern Asia, and Australasia (two species); by far the most species are in sub-Saharan Africa; forests, woodlands, savannah, grassland, scrubland (including semi-arid or arid scrub), marshes

SOCIAL BEHAVIOUR: mostly seen alone or in pairs; sometimes in small family groups, and some may form mixed feeding flocks outside the breeding season; most are monogamous and territorial; a few are sometimes polygynous and a few are cooperative breeders

NEST: a deep cup or oval ball with a side entrance, made of grass, leaves, moss, plant fibres and down that may be bound with spiders' webs; some nest low in vegetation, others higher in trees or shrubs; tailorbirds, all camaropteras and several others in the genera *Cisticola*, *Prinia*, *Artisornis*, *Calamonastes* and *Schistolais* build remarkable nests in a pouch constructed by the bird sewing two or more leaves together (or one folded over) using its bill as a needle and spiders' web, insect cocoon silk or plant fibres (or even cotton, wool or other human-made fibres) as thread

EGGS: 1–7, mainly white, pale blue, pink but deep brick red in some marsh *Cisticola* species, usually with darker markings but very variable in some

INCUBATION: 10–18 days

FLEDGING PERIOD: 12–17 days

FOOD: mainly small insects and other invertebrates, with some taking larger ones

VOICE: Cisticolas have long songs combining more melodious whistling notes with harsh scratchy, trilling, clicking, churring, wailing or other notes; other groups have a variety of whistling or less musical rasping or other sounds; many species make mechanical sounds, including bill clicking and wing-snapping

MIGRATION: almost all are essentially sedentary; some populations of Zitting Cisticola in eastern Asia migrate to winter farther south

CONSERVATION STATUS: one species, the Taita Apalis, *Apalis fuscigularis*, is Critically Endangered; three species, the Sierra Leone Prinia, *Schistolais leontica*, the Yellow-throated Apalis, *A. flavigularis*, and Turner's Eremomela, *Eremomila turneri*, are Endangered; five species, the Karamoja Apalis, *A. karamojae*, the White-winged Apalis, *A. chariessa*, the Grey-crowned Prinia, *Prinea cinereocapilla*, the Aberdare Cisticola, *Cisticola aberdare*, and Winifred's (or Mrs Moreau's) Warbler, *Scepomycter winifredae*, are Vulnerable; and seven species are Near Threatened

LEFT The Zitting Cisticola (formerly known as the Fan-tailed Warbler), *Cisticola juncidis*, is the only member of its family to occur in Europe.

As a result of early developments in molecular analysis, this family of mainly African Old World warblers was removed about 30 years ago from the very large, polyphyletic grouping that constituted the original Family Sylviidae. One little known species, Grauer's Forest Warbler, *Graueria vittata*, from Central Africa, may belong either in this family or with the crombecs and relatives in the Macrosphenidae (p. 341), and until further evidence is available, is perhaps best regarded as of uncertain affinity (*Genera Incertae Sedis*).

Apart from one species, these are small warblers, mostly measuring 9–13 cm (3.5–5 in) and weighing 5–15 g (0.2–0.5 oz), although some of the very long-tailed species approach 20 cm (10.5 in) and a few males approach 25 g (0.9 oz). The exception is the Oriole Warbler, *Hypergerus atriceps*, which is up to 20 cm (10.5 in) long and weighs up to 32 g (1.1 oz). Most have short, rounded wings, but tail size and shape vary, from very short and rounded, as in some of the cisticolas (*Cisticola*) and the camaropteras (*Camaroptera*) to very long in other genera, such as the prinias (*Prinia* and *Schistolais*) and apalises (*Apalis*). Often tail length varies markedly between the sexes, with males of some species having a tail that is about 20–30% longer than those of females, and up to 90% longer in an island race of the Green Longtail, *Urolais epichlorus*. Some, such as the prinias and apalises, have a strongly graduated, wedge-shaped tail.

Plumage colour varies between genera: cisticolas are brownish above and paler below, in some species with brighter golden or rufous on the head, and most are either plain or with heavily dark-streaked upperparts; tailorbirds are olive green above and pale below (in three species with bright yellow), with rich russet brown on the head in most and black in three species; prinias are mostly brown or grey above and white below, though some species are strongly streaked, one is barred, and a few have areas of yellow below; apalises are the most boldly plumaged of the major genera, including colourful species with bright green upperparts and mainly yellow underparts, often with black on head or breast, as well as black and white or grey and white species. The sexes look alike in most species but differ somewhat in various apalises, with females being less brightly or boldly marked.

There are four subfamilies. The first, Neomixinae, contains just three species called jeries in the same genus, *Neomixa*, endemic to the island of Madagascar. The second subfamily is the Eremomelinae, with 47 species divided between 16 genera, all but one in Africa. They include the nine species of eremomelas, *Eremomela*, and the 18 species (or more, when some regarded as subspecies are promoted to full species status) of apalises, *Apalis*. The eremomelas are small, and have relatively short tails that are never strongly graduated or with white tips to the feathers as in many other members of the family. These are very active warblers when foraging in the canopy or at lower levels, often in small family groups and as part of mixed-bird feeding parties. The apalises are also small bodied but with much longer tails, and, like the eremomelas, are often encountered in pairs or small groups in the forest trees. Another well known genus is that of the camaropteras, *Camaroptera*, whose three species are widespread across Africa south of the Sahara apart from most of South Africa. These are generally shy and skulking forest dwellers and often cock their very short tails like wrens (Troglodytidae, p. 376). Both sexes of one species, the Yellow-browed Camaroptera, *C. superciliaris*, have a little patch of bright blue naked skin on each side of their throat, which they inflate and reveals by raising their throat feathers when calling or singing. Another one, the Grey-backed Camaroptera, *C. brachyura*, has an unusual bleating or mewing alarm call, which often reveals its presence when hidden among cover, accounting for an alternative name of Bleating Warbler. Another distinctive group are the three species of wren warblers in the genus *Calamonastes*, which have much longer tails that they often not only cock but

ABOVE The Ashy Prinia, *Prinia socialis*, is one of the most familiar birds of the Indian subcontinent, having adapted well to living near people.

also fan. The only non-African genus, *Microcmacronus*, contains two really tiny species from Asia that was until recently included within the very large former version of the Timaliidae (see p. 362) until genetic research indicated their true affinity. Endemic to the Philippines, they are known as miniature babblers or tit-babblers, and apart from hummingbirds – compete for the title of the world's smallest birds, measuring only 7–8 cm (2.75–3 in) long and weighing as little as 5.5 g (0.2 oz). The Visayan Miniature Babbler, *M. leytensis*, is olive green above with rich yellow underparts, while the Mindanao Miniature Babbler, *M. sordidus*, is duller greyish olive all over, but both are remarkable in having a cascade of bare white feather shafts extending back from the lower back, rump and flanks. These are longer, extending beyond the tail tip, in the Visayan species.

The next subfamily, the Cisticolinae, is a little larger, containing 53 species in eight genera. The principal genus, and the largest in the whole family with 45 species, is that of the cisticolas, *Cisticola*. These little brown warblers, which include some of the most common and familiar songbirds throughout sub-Saharan Africa in open habitats such as grassland, savannah, and marshes, are renowned as one of the most maddeningly difficult of all birds for those not familiar with them to distinguish between species. They are generally more easily distinguished by their distinctive and very varied songs. These account for the rather comical common names of many species, including Trilling, Tinkling, Whistling, Wailing, Rattling, Bubbling, Chattering, Chirping, Churring, Croaking and Zitting Cisticolas. Many of the smallest, shortest tailed cisticolas, such as the aptly named Cloud Cisticola (or Cloud-scraping Cisticola), *C. textrix*, perform spectacular song-flights that involve great endurance and aerobatic ability. They rise and circle high in the sky, so that they are often invisible even through binoculars, and may career about and make dramatic dives, then zoom up again at the last moment before hitting the ground. Some song-flighting cisticolas add to their vocalisations by making sharp cracks with their wing feathers, which are especially loud in the Wing-snapping Cisticola, *C. ayresii*. Mechanical noises, including purring sounds as well as snapping are a feature of other members of the family, too, including some apalises, prinias, camaropteras, and wren warblers.

Another distinctive member of this subfamily, and the giant among the whole family, the Oriole Warbler of West Africa has a long, slightly decurved black bill and a long graduated tail. As well as being so much larger than any of its relatives , it has distinctive plumage: a black head, neck, throat and upper breast, with silvery fringes to the feathers, yellowish olive upperparts and tail and a bright yellow lower breast and belly. It is sometimes known by its local name of Moho – although use of this is best avoided, to prevent confusion with the generic name of the four extinct Hawaiian species of birds (see Mohoidae, p. 372). This striking bird has among the most attractive songs in the Cisticolidae, consisting of a series of rich, fluty notes. The male and female often perform duets, as do pairs of some other species in the family, including cisticolas, apalises and prinias; in some species, a second female may join in as a trio, or nearby pairs may form a quartet or quintet.

The final subfamily, Priniinae, comprises 36 species in two genera, *Prinia*, the 23 species of prinias, and *Orthotomus*, the 13 species of tailorbirds. Thirteen species of prinias are Asian, including one, the Graceful Prinia, *P. gracilis*, is found not only in Asia from the Middle East to Nepal and Bangladesh but also in North Africa, and ten species are African. They vary in size from tiny, like the Graceful Prinia, which can measure as little as 10 cm (4 in), almost half of which is taken up by the long, graduated tail, through very small for most species, at 11–13 cm (4.3–5 in) to the largest members of the genus, six Asian species that are 16–20 cm (6–8 in) long but still small bodied due to the length of the tail.

Prinias are mainly birds of more open country, such as grassland, scrub, open woodland, forest edges and clearings, reedbeds and mangroves. Although they usually spend much of their time hidden among foliage while foraging, they may emerge to perch prominently and utter alarm calls, swivelling and fanning their long tails or cocking them high over their backs. The *Orthotomus* tailorbirds are entirely Asian, and are renowned for their unusual and beautiful nest sites, fashioned by the birds themselves sewing leaves together. To perform this feat, they employ a remarkable technique, in which they use the slender, sharply pointed bill as a needle to perforate the edges of large leaves and then sew them together using individual stitches of cotton-like plant material or the silk from insect cocoons or spiders' webs. Those nesting in town gardens may use actual cotton thread or wool that they have gathered. The builder teases apart the end of the thread to form a tiny ball to prevent it becoming loose. Up to 200 stitches have been counted at some nests. Within this shelter, the birds build their cup-shaped or ball-like nest made of plant fibres, spiders' webs and other material. Leaf tailoring has evolved several times within the family; as well as the tailorbirds, some of the prinias, several cisticolas, camaropteras, the wren warblers and the Red capped Forest Warbler (also known as the African Tailorbird), *Artisornis metopias*, all shelter their nests using the technique, in some cases using just a single leaf, or in others several leaves. This amazing behaviour is unique among all the world's birds to these members of the Cisticolidae.

GRASSBIRDS, GRASSHOPPER WARBLERS AND RELATIVES Locustellidae

GENERA: 13　　**SPECIES:** 57

LENGTH: 12–28 cm (4.75–11 in)

WEIGHT: 9–84 g (0.3–3 oz)

RANGE AND HABITAT: Europe, Africa, Madagascar, Asia, New Guinea and several south Pacific islands, New Zealand; in a wide range of habitats with dense undergrowth, from forests and scrub to grasslands, swamps and marshes

SOCIAL BEHAVIOUR: most species are socially monogamous, some are partly polygynous and songlarks, *Cincloramphus*, are strongly polygynous

NEST: a deep cup made of twigs, grasses, reeds, rootlets, moss or other plant material, lined with hair and other fine material in many species with a domed roof and a side entrance, generally well concealed among dense vegetation near the ground or water

EGGS: 1–7, white, cream, pale pinkish, greenish or grey, with brown, purple or other darker markings

INCUBATION: 10–16 days

FLEDGING PERIOD: 10–17 days

FOOD: a wide range of insects and also other invertebrates, such as spiders, small snails and worms; also occasionally seeds in some species

VOICE: songs include long, very high-pitched insect-like trills, especially in *Locustella* species; in some a series of buzzing, twittering, clicking notes, whistling, warbling or other notes; calls mainly brief and harsh, including rattling, chirping and churring sounds

MIGRATION: species breeding in Europe and in Asia north of the Himalayas migrate south to winter in Africa or southern Asia

CONSERVATION STATUS: two species, Grauer's Swamp Warbler, *Bradypterus graueri*, and the Long-legged Thicketbird, *Megalurulus rufus*, are Endangered; five species, including the Fly River Grassbird, *Poodytes albolimbatus*, Pleske's Grasshopper Warbler, *Locustella pleskei*, and the Knysna Warbler, *Bradypterus sylvaticus*, are Vulnerable; and five species are Near Threatened

These birds were formerly subsumed in two subfamilies of the very large 'ragbag' family Sylviidae, before genetic research indicated that this was polyphyletic and that they should be one of several distinctive groups separated in a family of their own, along with a few species previously considered as members of another originally very large polyphyletic family, the babblers and relatives (Timaliidae). As well as those called grassbirds, others are known as songlarks, grasshopper (or grass) warblers, bushbirds, swamp

warblers and thicketbirds. They are among the most terrestrial of all Old World warblers, which search for their insect food among dense undergrowth or on the ground. Many of its members spend much of their time hidden within dense undergrowth, making them highly frustrating for birders and ornithologists to observe. They are supremely good at manouevring their way through the densest of vegetation, running fast through the tangled cover like mice when disturbed rather than flying away.

ABOVE The Grasshopper Warbler, *Locustella naevia*, remains hidden in dense cover, but it will emerge in the breeding season to broadcast its insect-like reeling song.

These are mainly small or very small birds, with a few larger species. The largest member of the family is the Striated Grassbird, *Megalurus palustris*, of Asia, which is about the size of a thrush. The bill ranges from rather short to medium length, and is generally narrow and pointed, though shorter and thicker in some, such as the two grassbirds in the genus *Schoenicola* one from Africa and one from India, and especially in the Bristled Grassbird, *Chaetornis striata*, of the Indian subcontinent. In most genera, the tail is long and graduated; that of the *Locustella* species appears shorter as they have very long undertail coverts. Several genera have tails in which the feathers are sharply pointed and separate at the end of the tail, and often become frayed at their tips. Their plumage is generally brown, grey-brown or buff; many species have paler underparts, with the upperparts adorned with bold, dark streaks, while others look far more uniform, including several mainly rufous species, such as all four species of thicketbird, *Megalurulus*, from Timor, the Solomon Islands and other Melanesian islands, the Bangwa Forest Warbler, *Bradypterus bangwaensis*, from Cameroon, West Africa, and the Friendly Grasshopper (or Grass) Warbler, *Locustella accentor*, from Borneo.

The single species of *Megalurus*, the Striated Grassbird, *M. palustris*, has a very extensive range across Asia, from northeast Pakistan and northern and central India south to the Philippines and Java, in marshes, reedbeds and other wetlands, especially rice paddies. Its plumage is brown with broad black streaks above and white below. Unlike most of the rest of the family, this relatively large bird with its loud, ringing warbling song, is conspicuous and not shy, often flying clumsily to perch prominently at the top of a reed stem or other vegetation or walking along on the ground.

The genus *Cincloramphus* contains four species, three of which are found in Australia. These are the Tawny Grassbird, *C. timoriensis*, which occurs just in the north and east of that country as part of a wider range that also includes New Guinea. Sulawesi and the Philippines, and two species that are both endemic to Australia, where they are found in most of that country, are the Rufous Songlark, *C. matthewsi*, and the Brown Songlark, *C. cruralis*. Although both called songlarks, they are not related to larks. In all other members of this family, the sexes look alike or are very similar, but the Brown Songlark is a notable exception, being highly sexually dimorphic. The male has a grey head and blackish upperparts with prominent brown fringes to the feathers and black underparts, while the streaky brown and pale grey female looks very different, with her strongly buff-fringed blackish back and white underparts with a buff breastband. Furthermore, he is 24–26 cm (9.5–10 in) long and weighs 70–84 g (2.5–3 oz), while she is 18–20 cm (7–8 in) and, at 25–30 g (0.9–1 oz), can be only a third of his weight. This is the greatest sexual size difference in any passerine.

The Little Grassbird, *M. gramineus*, is widely distributed in Australia and also occurs in the mountains of west-central New Guinea. There are also four species in the genus *Poodytes*. The Fernbird, *Poodytes punctatus*, is endemic to New Zealand. It is locally common on both North and South islands and some offshore islands, but one race, the Chatham Island Fernbird, *P. punctatus rufescens*, is now extinct, having last been recorded in 1900. Its extinction is likely to have been due to habitat loss resulting from overgrazing by introduced goats and rabbits, and predation by introduced cats. These two species have tails ending in sharp points and often fraying. The other two species are the Spinifexbird, *P. carteri*, which as its name suggests, is a specialist inhabitant of spinifex grassland, and the Fly River Grassbird, *P. albolimbatus*, of the Trans-Fly river region of New Guinea.

The 12 species of mainly plain brown *Bradypterus* brush warblers are widely distributed, with about half the species in sub-Saharan Africa and half in southern Asia. They are generally shy birds that skulk in marshland vegetation or dense forest undergrowth, and include many similar looking species, and hence are more easily identified by their loud songs, which vary from ringing notes and trills to a series of low-pitched, far-carrying notes like the sound made by a bouncing ball. One unusual species is the Brown Emu-tail, *B. brunneus*, which is endemic to dense undergrowth in humid rainforests of Madagascar. This tiny warbler has a very long tail with just six bare tail feathers, reduced to dark brown shafts only. Its wings are extremely short, and it rarely flies.

The largest genus is *Locustella*, with 24 species collectively known as grasshopper (or grass) warblers. They have plain or dark-streaked brown, buff and cream plumage, and many look similar to one another. With very reclusive habits in dense cover, they are often best identified by their voice. Many have long, insect-like or reeling songs, including the widespread Grasshopper Warbler (or Common Grasshopper Warbler), *L. naevia*, which breeds from Europe to central Asia, and Pallas's Grasshopper Warbler, *L. certhiola*, with a breeding range extending from southwest Siberia east to the Russian Far East. The largest and stoutest-billed *Locustella* is Gray's Grasshopper Warbler, *L. fasciata*, which breeds from western Siberia south to Korea.

Two differently plumaged species that are somewhat tentatively included in this family are the Malia, *Malia grata*, and the Rabor's Ground Warbler (also sometimes still called the Rusty-headed Babbler, *Robsonius rabori*, as it was originally considered a member of the former 'ragbag' babbler family). The Malia, endemic to the mountains of the Indonesian island of Sulawesi, has a unique appearance with its yellow olive crown, cheeks and upperparts and its bright yellow underparts with a smudgy brownish breast band. Rabor's Ground Warbler is boldly patterned in chestnut brown, black, white and grey and has a sturdy bill.

DONACOBIUS Donacobiidae

GENERA: 1   **SPECIES**: 1

LENGTH: 21.5–22 cm (8.5–8.75 in)

WEIGHT: 30–40 g (1–1.4 oz)

RANGE AND HABITAT: from eastern Panama (where it is scarce) to as far south as extreme northern Argentina, in marshy places among dense shrubs and other vegetation by rivers, especially around oxbow lakes, and next to artificial watercourses

SOCIAL BEHAVIOUR: monogamous and territory, often breeding cooperatively; usually in pairs or family groups

NEST: a big, deep cup of pliable material such as plant fibres and snake skins, usually sited in reeds or other marsh vegetation low over water

EGGS: 2–3, pale purplish, heavily marked with purplish and reddish blotches and spots

INCUBATION: 16–18 days

FLEDGING PERIOD: 17–18 days

FOOD: almost entirely insects and other invertebrates

VOICE: both sexes sing a loud song, often answering one another in a duet, and utter various harsh calls

MIGRATION: sedentary

CONSERVATION STATUS: not threatened

ABOVE The Donacobius, *Donacobius atricapilla*, is easy to identify as pairs or small groups perch conspicuously atop low shrubs or clumps of grass in marshes and other damp habitats.

The Donacobius, *Donacobius atricapilla*, is a strikingly plumaged bird, with a mainly glossy black head, dark chocolate brown upperparts and tail contrasting with the yellowish buff and whitish underparts, often finely barred on the flanks, a rich brown rump, a white wing patch and white tips to the tail feathers; its eyes have a bright yellow iris. It has a wide range, in eastern Panama and much of the northern half of South America, east of the Andes, where it is restricted to dense vegetation in marshy areas: its genus name *Donacobius* is from the Greek translateable as 'marsh dweller'. Its taxonomic position has long been disputed, and it was previously classified until the twentieth century as a thrush (Family Turdidae, p. 391), and then in the mockingbird Family Mimidae (p. 380), being given the common name of Black-capped Mockingthrush. Later, it was regarded as belonging to the wren Family Troglodytidae (p. 376). With its rather long, sturdy bill, long slender body and long graduated tail, it does resemble a mockingbird in form, and its loud whistling and churring song sounds rather like that of a large wren. Surprisingly, however, the latest DNA evidence indicates that its closest relatives are not in the New World, but the grassbirds and relatives of the Old World warbler Family Locustellidae (p. 344) and the Madagascan warblers, in the Family Bernieridae (below).

Donacobius are often very obvious, as pairs or small family groups often perch in full view at the tops of low shrubs or clumps of grass or make brief, weak flights, and further draw attention to themselves by their loud and varied calls, including harsh churring and grating sounds. Both sexes sing, often in an antiphonal duet in which they perch close together, usually facing in opposite directions, bob their heads and wag their partly fanned tails asynchronously, as the male utters a series of loud, liquid 'quoit-quoit-quoit' notes that sound like a car alarm, to which the female responds with a harsh grating note. As they call, they expose a patch of bare orange skin on the side of the neck that is normally concealed. Sometimes a family group will perform together.

MADAGASCAN WARBLERS Bernieridae

GENERA: 8   **SPECIES**: 11

LENGTH: 12–18 cm (4.75–7 in)

WEIGHT: 8–30 g (0.3–1 oz)

RANGE AND HABITAT: Madagascar, in various habitats and at different altitudes, most in dense evergreen rainforests, but one, the Thamnornis Warbler, *Thamnornis chloropetoides*, lives in subdeserts with spiny vegetation, coastal scrub and edges of deciduous forest

SOCIAL BEHAVIOUR: little known, though most appear to be socially monogamous, and some, such as the four species of tetrakas, *Xanthomixis*, are cooperative breeders

NEST: little information on most species, though nests are cup-shaped and built from grass, fresh and dead leaves, moss and plant fibres, in some cases bound with spiders' webs, which may also be used to attach camouflaging material to the outer surface

EGGS: 2–4, pinkish white or reddish, with brown or maroon spots, in the few species for which information is available

INCUBATION: 13–17 days in the few species for which information is available

FLEDGING PERIOD: unknown

FOOD: little information, probably mainly insects and spiders, with the Long-billed Tetraka, *Berniera madagscariensis*, also recorded as feeding on geckos and other small vertebrates

VOICE: songs include sequences of whistling, spluttering, trilling, or rasping sounds; calls varied including brief hard or high-pitched sounds, rattles of alarm

MIGRATION: all presumed to be sedentary

CONSERVATION STATUS: two species, Appert's Tetraka, *Xanthomixis apperti*, and the Dusky Tetraka, *X. tenebrosa*, are Vulnerable, and three species, the Grey-crowned Tetraka, *X. cinereiceps*, the Wedge-tailed Jery, *Hartertula flavoviridis*, and the Madagascar Yellowbrow, *Crossleyia xanthophrys*, are Near Threatened

This new family, formally named as recently as 2010, brings together 11 species of small songbirds shown by molecular studies to be closely related. They had traditionally been assigned on the basis of morphological and ecological similarities to three different large 'wastebin' families, but the genetic research indicated that the similarities were due to convergent evolution rather than reflecting true relationship. The families in which they had lingered so long were the bulbuls (Pycnonotidae, p. 351), the original huge grouping named Sylviidae (now slimmed down hugely to include just the scrub warblers and parrotbills, p. 358) and another very large former family, the babbler family Timaliidae (now greatly reduced to include just the tree babblers).

All but one of the large number of eight genera for such a small family of just 11 species are monotypic, the only genus with more than one species being *Xanthomixis*. This is an example of the dramatic adaptive radiation into species with different ecological niches that are such a feature of the birdlife of Madagascar, resulting from its very long isolation of about 160 million years from the African continent and from the Indian peninsula about 88 million years ago, as well as the large size of the island and relatively little immigration of birds from elsewhere. (Remarkably, half of all the bird species and an amazing 80% of all songbird species breeding on the island are endemic.)

Most of the Madagascan warblers are little known, and some have only relatively recently been discovered and described scientifically: the aptly named Cryptic Warbler, *Cryptosylvicola randrianasoloi*, was unknown to science until 1992. This is a tiny bird, with short wings and quite long, slender legs, and is olive green above and greyish white below with a yellowish throat and upper breast. It is one of four genera with a distinctly graduated tail. It is a bird of hills and mountains, where it favours *Podocarpus* conifer forests with bamboo thickets, moss and lichens, and sometimes ventures above the tree line to forage in heathland.

The four species of tetrakas, *Xanthomixis*, have olive green upperparts and mainly yellow underparts. Two similar species, Appert's Tetraka, *X. apperti*, and the Grey-crowned Tetraka, *X. cinereiceps*, have a blue-grey head and a white throat. In their forest habitats, they often perch on vertical branches of trees, shrubs and creepers, working their way up them rapidly as they forage for insects, which they often catch in short flights or snap up from the undersides of leaves. These birds were originally included in the greenbul genus *Phyllastrephus*, in the bulbul family Pycnonotidae.

The largest member of the family, the White-throated Oxylabes, *Oxylabes madagascariensis*, is a sturdy, short-winged with a fairly long and strong bill and a large head. It is dark brown all over apart from a narrow white stripe through its eye and a white throat. This species was formerly included in the original very large babbler family Timaliidae. Like many other members of this family, it often joins mixed-species flocks as it forages for food in rainforests, on the ground or among low vegetation. It eats a wide range of invertebrates, from beetles and grasshoppers to spiders. Pairs perform duets, one partner uttering a short sequence of whistles and the other joining in part way through with a loud rattling sound.

Another rainforest dweller, the Long-billed Tetraka, *Bernieria madagascariensis*, lives up to its name by having a disproportionately long bill, which is, like most other members of the family, slightly but distinctly hooked at the tip. The sexes differ markedly in size, males measuring as much as 20 cm (8 in) long and weighing up to 39 g (1.4 oz) and females, which have a proportionately shorter bill, as little as 17.5 cm (7 in) and 21 g (0.7 oz). Their plumage is similar, combining green upperparts and yellow underparts.

REED, BRUSH AND SWAMP WARBLERS Acrocephalidae

GENERA: 6   **SPECIES:** 53

LENGTH: 12–20 cm (4.75–8 in)

WEIGHT: 8–34 g (0.3–1.2 oz)

RANGE AND HABITAT: all of Europe, much of Africa, Madagscar and much of Asia, Australia (single species); many in marshes, swamps and reedbeds, but others in drier habitats, including forests and scrub

SOCIAL BEHAVIOUR: most species are socially monogamous, but some are polygynous and at least one, the Seychelles Reed Warbler, *Acrocephalus sechellensis*, is a cooperative breeder

NEST: mostly cup shaped and built from grasses, reeds, dead leaves, moss and other plant matter, often bound with spiders' webs, with a softer lining of feathers, plant down or other material; in many *Acrocephalus* species sited among reeds or other vegetation, often woven around vertical stems, and often over water, or in forest, scrub or other dry habitat species such as all species of *Hippolais* or *Iduna* in a shrub or tree

EGGS: 2–6, cream, pale buff, greyish, greenish or pinkish, with darker markings

INCUBATION: 12–14 days

FLEDGING PERIOD: 12–14 days

FOOD: mainly insects, with some other invertebrates and small aquatic vertebrates, such as small fish and frogs, and sometimes fruit

VOICE: songs vary, and they are often loud; some *Acrocephalus* species have long, rambling songs combining harsh grating, chattering, squeaking and twittering sounds with sweeter notes, while some of the island *Acrocephalus* species utter very melodious warbling songs; the songs of other species include whistled notes and trills, harsh scratchy sounds and twittering; various species mimic other bird sounds

MIGRATION: European and Asian breeding species other than those in southern Asia make long migrations to winter in sub-Saharan Africa and southern Asia

CONSERVATION STATUS: six species, the Aldabra Brush Warbler, *Nesillas aldabrana*, Pagan Reed Warbler, *Acrocephalus yamashinae*, Aguijan Reed Warbler, *A. nijoi*, Mangareva Reed Warbler, *A. astrolabii*, Forster's Reed Warbler, *A. musae*, and Guam Reed Warbler, *A. luscinius*, are Extinct; one species, the Moorea Reed Warbler, *A. longirostris*, is Critically Endangered (Perhaps Extinct); three species, the Saipan Reed Warbler, *A. hiwae*, Rimatara Reed Warbler, *A. rimitarae*, and Hawiian Reed Warbler (or Millerbird), *A. familiaris*, are Critically Endangered; five species, the Pitcairn Reed Warbler, *A. vaughani*, Tahiti Reed Warbler, *A. caffer*, Basra Reed Warbler, *A. griseidis*, Streaked Reed Warbler, *A. sorghophilus*, Kiritimati Warbler, *A. aequinoctialis*, are Endangered; six species, including the Aquatic Warbler, *A. paludicola*, Henderson Island Reed Warbler, *A. taiti*, and Papyrus Yellow Warbler, *Calamonastides gracilirostris*, are Vulnerable; three species are Near Threatened

LEFT The long, repetitive, chattering song of the Eurasian Reed Warbler, *Acrocephalus scirpaceus*, fills the air above reedbeds in spring.

This family was originally included within the huge former family Sylviidae of Old World warblers, but recently, after molecular research confirmed that this unwieldy grouping was polyphyletic, it was one of a number of subgroups that have been given a family of its own. Its closest relatives appear to be the bush warblers and relatives (Locustellidae, p. 344).

Apart from a few species with yellow underparts, these are generally soberly plumaged birds, with brown or olive upperparts and paler buff or whitish underparts; many species have dark stripes on the back. The sexes are similar. They mostly have shortish, rounded wings and their medium length tails (longer in a few species) are often graduated. Most species have a medium length bill, but some of the reed-warblers, such as the Thick-billed Warbler, *Arundinax aedon*, the sole member of its genus, from Russia and Mongolia, the Large-billed Reed Warbler, *Acrocephalus orinus*, breeding in Afghanistan and Tadjikistan, and the Great Reed Warbler, *A. arundinaceus*, of Eurasia and North Africa, have a heavier, stronger bill, while in several island species, like the Guam Reed Warbler, *A. luscinius*, and Tahiti Reed Warbler, *A. caffer*, from Tahiti, the bill is also much longer.

The largest and most widespread genus, *Acrocephalus*, contains 32 species. Collectively, they extend over a vast range, including Europe, Asia, Africa, Australia (just one species, the Australian Reed Warbler, *A. australis*) and various Pacific islands (numerous species). They have a very wide size range, from small species such as the Moustached Warbler, *A. melanopogon*, at about 12 cm (4.75 in) to the very big (for a warbler) Great Reed Warbler, the size of a small thrush at 19–20 cm (7.5–8 in), though far less heavy. Along with the aptly named Clamorous Reed Warbler, *A. stentoreus*, the Great Reed Warbler has a particularly loud song, carrying up to 1 km (0.6 mile) or more. Plumage is of two basic types, plain and streaked: one large group has plain brownish, rufous or grey-brown upperparts and plain cream to buff underparts. Examples are the Eurasian Reed Warbler, *A. scirpaceus*, and very similar Marsh Warbler, *A. palustris*, both of which breed across Europe and much of Asia, with the Reed Warbler having the greatest range, breeding also in Africa. Along with several other *Acrocephalus* species, these are among the major hosts of that famous nest parasite the Common Cuckoo, *Cuculus canorus*, in marshland. The Marsh Warbler is also one of the avian

world's greatest mimics, whose song, which it can broadcast for hours on end with scarcely a break, consists almost entirely of mimicry of song and calls of other species. Across its European breeding range, the species as a whole can imitate perfectly at least 99 species the birds hear in their nesting areas, and as many as 113 African species that they encounter when wintering on that continent; individuals average a total of 76 species, 31 European and 45 African. The birds imitated range are mainly those of other songbirds, including sparrows, swallows and other warblers, but also others such as hornbills, puffbacks, helmet shrikes, magpies and waders.

The second, small group has strikingly black-and-cream striped rufous brown or yellowish brown upperparts; this includes the Moustached Warbler, Aquatic Warbler, *A. paludicola*, and Sedge Warbler, *A. schoenobaenus*. Although some can be found in open woodland and brushland, the *Acrocephalus* warblers live mainly in vegetation associated with wetlands and other damp habitats, such as marshes, reedbeds, rice paddies, damp grassland such as meadows with a lush herb layer, riverside vegetation and mangroves. They have relatively long legs, adapting them for clinging onto the vertical stems of reeds and other marsh or waterside plants. Recently rediscovered is the Large-billed Reed Warbler, *A. orinus*, which is now known to breed in Afghanistan and Tadjikistan. For almost 140 years, this enigmatic bird was known only from a single specimen collected in the Sutlej Valley, Himachal Pradesh, India. Then, in 2006 one was trapped in south-west Thailand, and its identity confirmed by DNA analysis of two of its feathers, backed up by photographs. Remarkably, only six months later, another individual came to light in the skin collection of the Natural History Museum at Tring, in a drawer of Blyth's Reed Warblers, *A. dumetorum*, collected in India in the nineteenth century. Since then, 25 further specimens have been identified as being of this species in museum collections worldwide.

All the other five genera are small, containing between one and six species. The genus *Nesillas* comprises four extant species of brush warblers endemic to several Indian Ocean islands: Madagascar (a single species), Madagascar and the Comoros (one species), and the Comoros (two species). All live in dense tropical evergreen forests, except for the Subdesert Brush Warbler, *N. lantzii*, which as its common name suggests, inhabits dry forest and low coastal scrub, and has a restricted range in southern Madagascar. They are rather large and slender with long, graduated tails, with very similar plumage in all, dark brown above and paler brown below with faint streaks. The largest species, the Aldabra Brush Warbler, *N. aldabrana*, is now extinct. It was unknown to science until 1967, when it was found living on a tiny strip of scrub, about 2 km (1.2 miles) long by 50 m (165 ft) wide, on a single island in the Aldabra atoll, the world's second largest coral atoll. During the mid-1970s, the population hovered at around a maximum of 25 birds, and the last one was seen in 1983. Its demise on such an isolated island was probably due to historic introductions of alien mammals, resulting in goats eating the plants and rats predating the birds' nests.

Distinctly smaller and brighter plumaged, with its olive green upperparts and yellow underparts, is the single species in the genus *Calamonastides*, the Papyrus Yellow Warbler, *C. gracilirostris*. This is a very restricted range and Vulnerable species, known from papyrus and other swamps in just a few small areas in central Africa.

It was until recently lumped together in a now abandoned genus *Chloropetes*, with two other species of African yellow warbler, that have larger but fragmented ranges. These have now been moved to the next genus, *Iduna*, which also contains four much duller species with grey or greyish brown upperparts and whitish underparts from Europe, North Africa and western Asia. Finally, the genus *Hippolais* contains four more Eurasian and North African species, two of which have a similar dull plumage to those in the previous genus (one of which, the Olive-tree Warbler, *H. olivetorum*, is larger and with a longer, stronger bill) and two European breeders, the Melodious Warbler, *H. polyglotta*, and Icterine Warbler, *H. icterina*, that are olive green above and yellow below.

CUPWINGS Pnoepygidae

GENERA: 1   **SPECIES:** 4

LENGTH: 7.5–10 cm (3–4 in)

WEIGHT: 11–23 g (0.4–0.8 oz)

RANGE AND HABITAT: Pygmy Cupwing, *Pnoepyga pusilla*, Himalayan foothills of India and Nepal and east to far eastern China, south through parts of Southeast Asia as far as Java and Bali; Nepal Cupwing, *P. immaculata*, Himalayan foothills of India and Nepal; Scaly-breasted Cupwing, *P. albiventer*, Himalayan foothills east to central China and south to northwest Vietnam; Taiwan Cupwing, *P. formosana*, endemic to Taiwan; breed in wet mountain forests with moss and dense undergrowth, descend lower in winter

SOCIAL BEHAVIOUR: little known, but appear to be monogamous

NEST: spherical nest with a side entrance near the top, made of moss, rootlets, shreds of bark and other materials, with the nest chamber woven around moss or epiphytic plants growing on a rock, tree trunk, on a bank or among rocks or upturned tree roots

EGGS: 2–6, white

INCUBATION: 12–14 days, known for one species only

FLEDGING PERIOD: unknown

FOOD: mainly insects and other invertebrates (including spiders and snails), also seeds (revealed by examining stomach contents of specimens)

VOICE: high pitched warbling or whistling songs; varied calls

MIGRATION: the Taiwan Cupwing, *Pnoepyga formosana*, is essentially sedentary but the others make altitudinal migrations

CONSERVATION STATUS: none is threatened

LEFT The tiny, virtually tailless Pygmy Cupwing, *Pnoepyga pusilla*, has two distinct colour varieties, or 'morphs'. This is a pale morph, with white scaling on its underparts; in dark morph birds the white is replaced by ochre. Heard far more often than seen, these birds have very high-pitched, piercing songs and loud sibilant calls.

even the largest, the Scaly-breasted Cupwing, *P. albiventer*, and the Nepal Cupwing, *P. immaculata*, are just 10 cm (4 in) at most. Their plumage is a subtly beautiful combination of warm brown upperparts (in one species prominently mottled golden buff on the head and back) and with a black-and-white or black-and-gold-scaling pattern below. They appear neckless, with their large heads merging into their miniature plump bodies, and are almost tailless. They have thin, sharp bills, and long, thick legs with disproportionately long, strong toes. In an example of convergent evolution producing a similar appearance among unrelated groups of birds due to adaptation to a similar lifestyle, these features give them a profile rather like a miniature version of the pittas (Pittidae, p. 200), antpittas (Grallariidae, p. 222), or gnateaters (Conopophagidae, p. 221), all unrelated sub-oscine passerines, or more closely related, among the oscines, the little warblers in the genera *Tesia*, *Hemitesia*, and *Urosphena* in the bush warbler family Scotocercidae (p. 354). Like these, the cupwings are well adapted for fast hopping or darting along the ground in forests with dense undergrowth in search of invertebrate prey. They flick their wings as they move, and may venture a little way up a low branch or fallen trunk. Their plumage is a subtly beautiful combination of warm brown upperparts (in one species prominently mottled golden buff on the head and back) and with a black-and-white or black-and-gold-scaling pattern below.

Since they spend much time hidden among the dense undergrowth of the wet forests that are their home, cupwings are often heard rather than seen. Their songs are a series of high-pitched whistling, warbling or piercing notes, varying in spacing between species, and the different species also have a variety of high-pitched, abrupt or more prolonged hard, sibilant, whistling, or wheezing calls.

Cupwings breed in foothill and high mountain forests, as high as 3,000 m (9,800 ft), or in the case of the Scaly-breasted Cupwing, *Pnoepyga albiventer*, up to 3,900 m (12,800 ft) in parts of its Chinese range. In winter they may descend as low as 200–275 m (650–900 ft).

Also known as wren babblers, this very small family of just four species in a single genus, *Pnoepyga*, were until recently, believed to be members of the formerly very large babbler family Timaliidae now used for just 11 genera of scimitar babblers and others that are often called the 'tree babblers'; see p. 362). Since molecular research showed this to be a polyphyletic 'ragbag' grouping, their members have either been placed in other existing families or assigned to newly erected ones, of which this is by far the smallest. The common name of 'cupwings' used here for the family refers to the very short, rounded wings with feathers that curve inwards towards the body, forming a rather cuplike shape when viewed from above. An alternative name is 'wren babblers' but these are not babblers, and there are other genera of birds with this common name, one in the new, restricted family Timaliidae and five in the family of ground babblers and relatives Pellorneidae, p. 363).

These four Himalayan, Chinese and Southeast Asian birds are tiny, the smallest species (and the one with the most extensive range), the Pygmy Cupwing, measuring only 7.5–9 cm (3–3.5 in) long, while

SWALLOWS AND MARTINS Hirundinidae

GENERA: 20   **SPECIES:** 84

LENGTH: 11–25 cm (4.3–10 in) including tail streamers in some species (the longest up to 14 cm/5.5 in, in the Blue Swallow, *Hirundo atrocaerulea*)

WEIGHT: 10–64 g (0.35–2.25 oz)

RANGE AND HABITAT: almost worldwide, except for some remote oceanic islands, the Antarctic and the high Arctic; generally in open habitats of all kinds, often near water (including hunting over rivers or lakes with forested banks); many species have adapted to farmland or urban environments

SOCIAL BEHAVIOUR: some species nest solitarily, others in small, medium or huge colonies; most forage communally; monogamous, defending an area around the nest

NEST: an open cup or enclosed nest with a small entrance made of mud pellets, often reinforced with straw, dried grass, animal hair or other plant matter, attached to vertical faces of cliffs, caves, trees and in some species mainly now onto walls or eaves of houses and other human-made structures; some build a simple cup of vegetation in a nest chamber at the end of a tunnel dug in a sandy or other soft bank or in a tree cavity; one, the Blue Swallow, nests in potholes or Aardvark burrows underground; some add a lining of feathers for insulation

EGGS: 3–6 in most temperate region species, 2–3 in tropical ones, usually plain white but with reddish or purplish speckles and blotches in some, especially open cup nesters

INCUBATION: 10–21 days

FLEDGING PERIOD: 17–30 days

FOOD: almost exclusively aerial insects, including flies (from tiny midges to large horseflies), beetles, aphids and other bugs, dragonflies, damselflies, butterflies and moths, and grasshoppers; the Tree Swallow, *Tachycineta bicolor*, of North America eats many fruits and seeds to enable it to survive the winter relatively far north; also eats small crustaceans

VOICE: calls are mainly short harsh twittering, buzzing or nasal sounds or longer '*tseet*' alarm calls; songs are a simple jumble of similar notes, in some interspersed with sweeter warbling

MIGRATION: many temperate zone species make long migrations (some, such as those of the Barn Swallow, are among the longest of any passerines)

CONSERVATION STATUS: one species, the White-eyed River-martin, *Pseudochelidon sirintarae*, is Critically Endangered; two species, the Bahama Swallow, *Tachycineta cyaneoviridis*, and the Galapagos Martin, *Progne modesta*, are Endangered; five species, including the Golden Swallow, *Tachycineta euchrysea*, Peruvian Martin, *Progne murphyi*, and Blue Swallow, are Vulnerable

ABOVE The Blue-and-white Swallow, *Pygochelidon cyanoleuca*, which has a huge range in tropical America, is among the smallest of all swallows.

The birds in this large family (collectively known as hirundines) include much-loved long-distance migrants across the world that are celebrated as harbingers of spring, such as the Barn Swallow, *Hirundo rustica*, breeding in Eurasia and North America, the Purple Martin, *Progne subis*, breeding in North America and the Welcome Swallow, *H. neoxena*, breeding in Australia and New Zealand.

All are aerobatic feeders on aerial insects, the most developed in this respect of any passerines, and their distinctive appearance reflects adaptations to this specialised lifestyle. They have a slender streamlined body and long, pointed wings that give them both endurance (they spend most of their lives in the air and are the most aerial of all passerines) and great efficiency (with an energy cost of about 50–75% less than that of other passerines of the same size). The shape of the wings, which generates a large amount of lift with minimum drag, enables them to alternate bursts of wingbeats with frequent periods of gliding. They generally hunt by circling round or

flying one way and then back in the opposite direction. Compared with short, broad wings, their wing shape would on its own bring the penalty of reduced manoeuvrability, but a forked tail compensates for this and enables them to make sudden twists and turns to catch fast-flying insects. Many species drink in flight, barely pausing to dip their bill in water as they swoop down at a shallow angle.

Species with a short, square-ended or only shallowly forked tail (often known as martins) are thus better adapted to foraging high in the sky, where their relative lack of manoeuvrability is less important. Those with a deeply forked tail and, often, a pair of elongated outer tail feathers (called 'streamers') are more suited to hunting low down, where the birds need to be as manoeuvrable as possible to catch low-flying insects and to avoid hitting obstacles. They are usually called swallows, although there are exceptions to the allotment of 'martin' and 'swallow' in the common names.

Hirundines have a bill that is very short but has a very wide gape and can be opened and shut very rapidly by strong, fast-acting jaws – like the unrelated (non-passerine) swifts and nightjars. All hunt for aerial insects in a similar way by targeting an insect (and not simply trawling with the bill constantly open as is sometimes thought), and then opening their wide gape and snapping it shut to trap the prey.

The legs of swallows and martins are short and their feet are adapted for perching, in contrast to the superficially similar but even more aerial swifts, which (like their relatives the hummingbirds) have tiny very weak feet used only for clinging onto vertical surfaces. Unlike the swifts, hirundines can walk and even run, with a shuffling gait. The three species of house martin, *Delichon* (the familiar and widespread House Martin, *D. urbicum*, of Eurasia, the Asian House Martin, *D. dasypus*, and the Nepal House Martin, *D. nipalense*) are unique among passerines in having feathered tarsi. Species such as the Sand Martin (called Bank Swallow in North America), *Riparia riparia*, which cling onto sandy vertical banks while excavating their nest holes, and the four species of crag and rock martins of Africa, Europe and Asia, *Ptyonoprogne*, nesting on cliffs, have stronger legs and feet; those of the two species of river martin, *Pseudochelidon* (one of which was not known to science until 1968), are bigger and stronger still. Separated in a subfamily (Ptyonoprogninae) of their own, these two also have a stouter bill and may represent an ancestral group linking the hirundines with the rest of the passerines.

A common plumage pattern is glossy dark blue or green above with white, cream or rufous underparts, which are plain in many species but striped in some. Burrowers in banks or those that nest on cliffs are often brown above and pale beneath, sometimes with a brown chest-band. Some, notably the two river-martins and the five species of saw-wings, *Psalidoprocne*, are glossy dark brown or black, or all-blue, as in the glossy dark blue males of the Purple Martin, *Progne subis*, and most of its Caribbean and Latin American relatives, or the scarce, restricted range Blue Swallow, *Hirundo atrocaerulea*, of eastern Africa. Apart from the general rule that in species with tail streamers, these average longer in males, and the *Progne* martins, in which the females are browner above with pale underparts, there is little difference in appearance between the sexes.

ABOVE Like other hirundines, the Purple Martin, *Progne subis*, catches its insect prey in flight, with many glides on its broad wings.

The saw-wings and also the two species of mainly drab brown plumaged roughwings, *Stelgidopteryx*, from the New World are so named because of their rough outer edge of the male's outer primary wingtip feather, the serrations of which may produce sounds in territorial or courtship display flights.

BULBULS Pycnonotidae

GENERA: 30 **SPECIES:** 152

LENGTH: 13–29 cm (5–11.5 in)

WEIGHT: 12–80 g (0.4–2.8 oz)

RANGE AND HABITAT: North Africa, the Nile valley, sub-Saharan Africa, Madagascar, Indian Ocean islands, southern Asia, from Turkey and the Middle East to Japan, Korea, eastern China, the Philippines and Borneo; forests, woodlands, scrublands

SOCIAL BEHAVIOUR: varies from solitary and secretive in most forest species to gregarious and confiding in open-country ones; all except the lek-forming Yellow-whiskered Greenbul, *Andropadus latirostris*, of Africa are monogamous and territorial; some are cooperative breeders

NEST: a cup of grasses and plant fibres bound with spiders' webs, usually in a tree or shrub, although the White-headed Bulbul, *Cerasophila thompsoni*, of Burma sometimes sites its nest in a hole in a bank

EGGS: 1–5, usually pale, often whitish, cream or pale pink, with dark markings

INCUBATION: 11–14 days

FLEDGING PERIOD: 9–21 days (mostly 12–16 days)

FOOD: mainly fruit and insects; may also include other invertebrates, seeds, buds, pollen and nectar; some include small lizards, birds' eggs, beeswax or carrion

VOICE: very vocal, mostly with whistling, harsh chattering or nasal calls; songs are typically unmelodic variations and repetitions of call notes

MIGRATION: most species are sedentary; some make short altitudinal migrations; some northern breeders such as populations of the Brown-eared Bulbul, *Microscelis amaurotis*, make quite long migrations south for winter

CONSERVATION STATUS: four species, the Straw-headed Bulbul, *Pycnonotus zeylanicus*, Prigogine's Bulbul, *Chlorocichla prigoginei*, the Streak-breasted Bulbul, *Hypsipetes siquijorensis*, and the Moheli Bulbul, *H. moheliensis*, are Endangered; eight species, including the Yellow-bearded Bulbul, *Criniger olivaceus*, the Mauritius Bulbul, *Hypsipetes olivaceus*, the Hook-billed Bulbul, *Setornis criniger*, and the Grand Comoro Bulbul, *H. parvirostris*, are Vulnerable; 18 species are Near Threatened

This is a large, exclusively Old World family that is widespread across wooded country, in Africa and southern Asia, mainly in tropical and subtropical regions. There are roughly the same number of species in Africa and Asia. The common name is thought to be of Arabic, Persian, Hindu or Urdu origin (still being used in all these languages today) and is possibly onomatopoeic. However, for much of the time, when used in the past, it was often in reference to the Common Nightingale, *Luscinia megarhynchos*, (see p. 200) – a bird of huge importance in Muslim culture, in poetry and other literature, music and art. Since this famed songster bred, and sang, only in North Africa and Persia and not in the other Muslim countries, the name became transferred to bulbuls, which though having far less impressive songs, were

common around human dwellings and often kept as cagebirds for their lively antics and simple but cheerful sounding songs, which in various species consist of bubbling or whistling sounds. In South Asia they were also kept for fighting, with gambling as a major part of the contests. One Asian species, the Straw-headed Bulbul, *Pycnonotus zeylanicus*, has a much more attractive and melodious loud and fluty song, and has suffered greatly as a consequence, huge numbers being trapped to be kept in captivity, so that it is one of the bulbuls now classed as Endangered. By contrast, a number of bulbul species, such as the Red-vented Bulbuls, *P. cafer*, in India, White-eared Bulbuls, *P. leucotis*, in the Middle East, and Common Bulbuls, *P. barbatus*, in Africa, are very common and become tame around people, ever ready to snatch food from tables. Indeed, the

ABOVE The Yellow-browed Bulbul, *Acritillas indica*, of the hill forests of western India and Sri Lanka often plucks fruits and seeds from trees in flight.

ABOVE A Common Bulbul, *Pycnonotus barbatus*, quenches its thirst from a dripping tap in the heat of the Masai Mara, Kenya.

Common Bulbul deserves its name as one of the most abundant and best known birds in Africa. Although many species are called bulbuls, and many more are called greenbuls, others are known variously as brownbuls, finchbills or bristlebills.

Most species are starling-sized, but the range is from birds such as the Tiny Greenbul, *Phyllastrephus debilis*, only the size of a small warbler, to the Straw-headed Bulbul, *Pycnonotus zeylanicus*, which is as big as a small pigeon. They are generally slender bodied with short, rounded wings and a long tail. The bills of most species are shortish and rather slender, with a slight hook at the tip; those of the finchbills are much shorter and blunt-tipped. A distinctive feature is the oval external nostrils, with a thin layer of bone or cartilage covering the rear section. All bulbuls have well-developed rictal bristles around the bill base; in the bristlebills, *Bleda*, these may be as long as the bill itself.

Most bulbuls have luxurious, soft, fluffy plumage, especially on the back and rump (the family name Pycnonotidae, from the Greek words meaning 'dense-backed' probably refers to this); some species have a crest, either erect and pointed, as in the widespread Red-whiskered Bulbul, *Pycnonotus jocosus*, or loose and floppy. Most species are relatively dull coloured and pretty featureless, in browns, fawns, greys, greens and yellows, usually paler below. Whole groups of species, especially the greenbuls, are so similar to one another that birdwatchers often find them almost impossible to distinguish in the field. Some have bolder patterns, such as the black-and-grey or black-and-white plumages of members of the genus *Hypsipetes*, with their contrasting red bill and legs, and the black, white and grey Red-whiskered Bulbul, with its jaunty tuft of bright red feathers sticking out behind the eye and red vent. A curious (though not exclusive) feature of the family is that many species have groups of bare, hair-like feathers called filoplumes growing from the nape. These are also found in all sorts of other birds, and differ from rictal (or other) bristles in lacking contrasting muscles, and are finer, either lacking barbs completely or with only a tiny tuft at the tip (bristles have a bristle tuft at the base). In most bulbuls, as with most other bird families, these are short, very fine and not apparent being hidden among the contour feathers that make up the plumage covering the head and body, but in others, such as the Hairy-backed Bulbul, *Tricholestes criniger*, they are longer and sometimes visible to observers. Suggestions for their possible function include that of a display function, and to help detect disturbance via sensory cells at their base to the feather coat in a region not accessible to the bird.

Many species have conspicuously coloured bright red, orange, yellow, blue or white eyes, eye-rings, wattles and other areas of naked skin. Often, a species with relatively dull-coloured eyes has contrastingly bright coloured eye-rings: for example, red eyes surrounded by blue skin. There are differences in the combinations of colours not only between but also sometimes within species, with different subspecies having different colours. Such distinctive patterns probably serve as badges of specific, subspecific or sexual identity or to denote an individual's status or other quality. Otherwise, the sexes are usually alike, although males are usually bigger and heavier sometimes distinctly so, as in some *Phyllastrephus* greenbuls.

OLD WORLD LEAF WARBLERS Phylloscopidae

GENERA: 4   **SPECIES:** 77

LENGTH: 9–14 cm (3.5–5.5 in)

WEIGHT: 4.3–15 g (0.15–0.5 oz)

RANGE AND HABITAT: Europe, Asia, Africa; the Arctic Warbler, *Seicercus borealis*, breeds in Alaska as well as northern Eurasia; in a wide range of wooded habitats, from conifer and broadleaved forests to tropical forests, bamboo thickets, scrub, with some also in gardens

SOCIAL BEHAVIOUR: most species are socially monogamous, but some are polygynous

NEST: in most species, a ball of dried grass with a side entrance, constructed from leaves, moss, small twigs and rootlets, lined with softer material including hair, fur, feathers, plant down; typically low down or on the ground, well hidden among vegetation, or in such places as a mossy bank, a hollow under a fallen tree, or among tree roots

EGGS: 2–8, white, unmarked or with a few or many darker markings

INCUBATION: 11–17 days

FLEDGING PERIOD: 10–22 days

FOOD: chiefly insects, and also spiders, mites, small molluscs, and some seeds and berries, especially in autumn by migrants

VOICE: songs generally quite simple and repetitive series of thin warbling, piping, twittering or buzzing notes; calls range from brief dry sounds to softer ones

MIGRATION: most European and Asian species apart from those breeding in the south make long migrations to southerly wintering grounds

CONSERVATION STATUS: three species, the Hainan Leaf Warbler, *Seicercus hainanus*, Ijima's Leaf Warbler, *S. ijimae*, and Kolombangara Leaf Warbler, *S. amoenus*, are Vulnerable; one species, Tytler's Leaf Warbler, *Phylloscopus tytleri*, is Near Threatened

LEFT The tiny Pallas's Leaf Warbler, *Abrornis proregulus*, which breeds in Siberia, Mongolia and northeast China, has a striking head pattern.

RIGHT The Willow Warbler, *Phylloscopus trochilus*, is the commonest of all summer migrants to the UK and other European countries.

This family was until recently included along with many other warblers within the huge original family Sylviidae, until molecular research showed this to be a polyphyletic assortment with distinct evolutionary origins. Its closest relatives appear to be the bush warblers (Scotocercidae, p. 354) and the long-tailed tits (Aegithalidae, p. 357).

In some classification schemes, all species within this family are included in a single genus, *Phylloscopus*, but here they are apportioned between four genera. The largest by far is *Seicercus*, with 48 species. The other genera are *Rhadina*, containing just three species, *Abrornis*, with 10 species, and *Phylloscopus*, with 16 species.

Leaf warblers are small birds that live mainly in trees and shrubs, where they are generally very active, restlessly moving about as they forage for insects which they catch with short, fine bills. As their family name suggests, they obtain much of their food from leaves, by gleaning while perched or moving along a branch or twig, by hovering in front of the foliage, or by making short sallies from a perch. Most are inconspicuous and hard to see because of their predilection for keeping hidden for much of the time in dense foliage or undergrowth. Plumage colours are generally muted in the three smaller genera, most being greenish above (some greyish or brownish) and dull greyish white below (in some species at least partly yellow), with a pale stripe above the eye. The genus *Phylloscopus* appears to be among the most homogeneous of all Palaearctic passerine genera, with many subgroups of species having such a similar appearance

that they can be difficult to distinguish, even in the hand. It turns out, though, that they contain various 'cryptic' species, which may prove to be distinguished by vocalisations and molecular genetics.

The three *Rhadina* species include one of the larger members of the family, the Wood Warbler, *R. sibilatrix*, which favours woods of beech and sessile oaks with a dense canopy but sparse ground cover. It is brighter than most *Phylloscopus* species, and has two very different songs – one is a series of soft, piping 'pew' notes, and the other begins with rising and accelerating 'tsip' notes culminating in a fast trill that has been likened to the sound of a coin spinning on a marble slab. By contrast, the ten *Abrornis* species, which breed collectively across Siberia to eastern China, make up the tiniest and most intensely active members of the family, at just 9–10 cm (3.5–4 in) long and weighing as little as 4.5 g (0.16 oz). They include the extravagantly striped Pallas's Leaf Warbler, *A. proregulus*, which delights birders in western Europe as a rare autumn migrant, wildly off-course from its normal migration to wintering grounds in northern India.

Almost half of the species in the genus *Seicercus* are much brighter and more boldly patterned. Most have brighter green upperparts and bright yellow underparts, sometimes combined with grey or white. Some of these have prominent double yellow wingbars, and many have a distinctive head pattern, in some species with a black and grey crown stripe, or with a grey upper head and a broad white stripe above the eye, or with a bright chestnut crown or hood with a black stripe or throat patch. Many have prominent yellow or whitish eye-rings.

LEFT The Wood Warbler, *Rhadina sibilatrix*, is one of the most beautiful members of its family, both in plumage and song. Sadly, it has declined over much of its breeding range, especially in the UK where the decline is almost 70% since the mid-1990s.

RIGHT The Common Chiffchaff, *Phylloscopus collybita*, is one of the most abundant of all summer visitors to Europe, singing its name, 'chiff-chaff', from early spring onwards.

Sometimes known as flycatcher-warblers, *Seicercus* species have a broader, blunter bill than *Phylloscopus*, often with much longer rictal bristles around its base, and 10 rather than 12 tail feathers. Most are Asian, with an overall breeding range from the Himalayas to eastern China and south as far as Indonesia.

Of the less colourful *Seicercus* species, the six brownish and pale buff or whitish woodland warblers are the only members of the family Phylloscopidae to breed in sub-Saharan Africa, with the very range of one species also extending to northeast Africa and the Arabian peninsula. At the opposite extreme from tropical heat is the Arctic Warbler, *S. borealis*. This large greyish olive and pale grey warbler breeds in the boreal forests of high northern latitudes, among birches, conifers and dwarf willows, from northern Scandinavia across Finland and Russia to far eastern Siberia, and Alaska (it is the only member of this family to breed in the New World).

Many species are long distance migrants, making impressive journeys for such tiny birds of thousands of kilometres. Geographically these can be subdivided into those breeding in Europe and western Asia, which migrate to winter mainly in Africa, and those breeding in central and eastern Asia, which winter in southern Asia. The Willow Warbler, *P. trochilus*, and Common Chiffchaff, *P. collybita*, of Eurasia are the best-known species and are two of the most abundant of all summer migrants to these continents. The Willow Warbler's longer wings are an adaptation for the greater journeys it makes between Europe and western Siberia to sub-Saharan Africa (even Asian breeders migrate there rather than to southern Asia), compared to the very similar looking but shorter-winged Chiffchaff, *P. collybita*, whose European races winter mainly in southern Europe, North Africa and the Middle East and Asian ones to southwest and central Asia and the northern part of the Indian subcontinent.

BUSH WARBLERS AND RELATIVES Scotocercidae

GENERA: 12   **SPECIES:** 36

LENGTH: 7–18 cm (2.75–7 in)

WEIGHT: 4.5–27 g (0.16–0.95 oz)

RANGE AND HABITAT: western and southern Europe (one species), Africa (seven species), and Asia (the great majority); occupy various habitats with plentiful dense undergrowth, including woodland, reedbeds and marshes, and some in scrub; the Streaked Scrub Warbler, *Scotocerca inquieta*, lives in arid habitats

SOCIAL BEHAVIOUR: presumably socially monogamous, but some, including *Cettia* species, may be partly polygynous

NEST: among dense vegetation, mossy banks or other sites nests ball-shaped in some, cup-shaped nests with a side entrance near the top in others, built from grass, twigs, rootlets, leaves, moss or other material; the ball nest of the Tit Hylia, *Pholidornis rushiae*, is made of soft plant material with an entrance spout facing vertically downwards

EGGS: 1–6, vary from white with very fine red or purplish speckling in Streaked Scrub Warbler to deep chestnut red in Cetti's Warbler, *Cettia cetti*

INCUBATION: 13–17 days

FLEDGING PERIOD: 13–17 days

FOOD: mostly insects, also other invertebrates, especially small snails and spiders, also seeds

VOICE: varies considerably between genera; loud and explosive in *Tesia*, *Cettia* and *Hemitesia* species, and can seem ventriloquial as songs are delivered while bird moves about; some species have trilling, whistling, warbling, twittering and chattering songs; songs of stubtails, *Urosphena*, consist of thin, very high-pitched notes, in some almost inaudible, as is the song of the Broad-billed Warbler, *Tickellia hodgsoni*; *Horornis* bush warblers and the Green Hylia, *Hylia prasina*, have whistling songs; the song of the Tit Hylia, *Pholidornis rushiae*, is a double trill

MIGRATION: sedentary apart from two of the more northerly breeding *Horornis* species, the Manchurian Bush Warbler, *H. canturians*, and one race of the Japanese Bush Warbler, *H. diphone*, which migrate south after breeding

CONSERVATION STATUS: two species, the Tanimbar Bush Warbler, *H. carolinae*, and Bougainville Bush Warbler, *H. haddeni*, are Near Threatened

This smallish family of Old World warblers was formerly included in the huge traditional Family Sylviidae, which has recently been shown to be polyphyletic and so split into several families. Although some of the genera now in this family were considered closely related, others appeared scattered about in various places in the sequence. The common name of 'bush warblers' we use here as the family name (and which appears as part of the names of various species within it) has been hedged about with a degree of confusion, in that it has also been applied to some of the members of the Family Locustellidae (see p. 344), in the genera *Locustella* and *Bradypterus*. The latter, which are endemic to Africa apart from one only on Madagascar, were previously lumped together with the bush warblers now in this family, but the genetic research shows that they are unrelated, their similarities the result of convergent evolution. The closest relatives of the Scotocercidae appear to be the leaf warblers (Phylloscopidae, p. 353) and Long-tailed Tits (Aegithalidae, p. 357).

The individual members of this family are variously known as bush warblers, scrub warblers, flycatcher warblers, tesias and stubtails. In general, these are small birds – the smallest, the Javan Tesia, *Tesia superciliaris*, is one of the smallest of all passerines, at only 7 cm (2.75 in) long – while many are 10–15 cm (4–6 in) long. Some of the bush warblers are rather larger, with some males of one species, the Japanese Bush Warbler, *Horornis diphone*, attaining lengths of up to 18 cm (7 in) and weights of up to 27 g (0.95 g).

The twelve genera differ considerably in appearance, both in their plumage and in their proportions, particularly the length of their tail. Most genera have 10 tail feathers, but some, such as *Erythrocercus*, have 12. Many species cock their tails and flick their wings frequently when alarmed, and may fan their tails and flick their wings to flush out invertebrate prey. In the scheme followed here, there are three subfamilies, which are regarded by some systematists as each deserving separate family status.

The first family, Erythrocercinae, contains the three species of flycatcher warblers, *Erythrocercus*, endemic to Africa. They are known as flycatcher warblers, having been previously regarded as members of the family that includes the monarch flycatchers (see Monarchidae, p. 273). They are colourful little birds, one olive yellow above and bright golden yellow below, a second strikingly patterned with a bright chestnut crown and tail, grey upperparts and buff and white underparts, and the third with a grey crown, white face, olive and yellow body and a chestnut tail. Despite their name, they do not generally catch insects by flying out from a perch, mainly gleaning them from foliage.

The Family Scotocercinae contains just a single very distinctively plumaged species, the Streaked Scrub Warbler, *Scotocercus inquieta*, which has a wide range from North Africa and the Arabian peninsula across central Asia to northwest India, where it is restricted to arid scrub and grassland, including sandy and rocky areas with shrubs and open savannah. This very small but plump bird, has streaky greyish and sandy brown upperparts with a long, graduated, brown, white-tipped tail, which it often cocks.

The major family, with eight genera containing a total of 30 species is the Cettiinae. Most are dull-plumaged in shades of brown, buff, olive and grey, and many have a pale stripe above each eye. In nine species – the tesias, stubtails and one other species – the tail is extremely short, so much so that most of them appear virtually tailless. All but one are from southern Asia. Four of the five species of tesias are in the genus *Tesia* (two widespread, one on Java and one on Flores and Sumbawa), while the other is included with longer-tailed species in the genus *Cettia*: this is the Chestnut-headed Tesia, *C. castaneocoronata*, found from the Himalayan foothills and northern Southeast Asia east to Vietnam. There are three species of stubtails, *Urosphena* (one with a wide breeding range in eastern Asia, from the Russian Far East to Japan and northeast China, and the other two far more local, one in northeast Borneo and the other in Timor and Babar islands). The only non-Asian member of this short-tailed group is Neumann's Warbler, *Hemitesia neumanni*, which has a restricted range in the Rift Mountains of Africa. The other species in *Hemitesia*, which has a much longer tail, is the Pale-footed Bush Warbler, *H. pallidipes*, from southern Asia. The Chestnut-headed Tesia is the most strikingly plumaged of these,

ABOVE Streaked Scrub Warblers, *Scotocerca inquieta*, are often secretive, but will emerge from cover to scold an intruder, cocking their long tails or waving them sideways or up-and-down.

ABOVE The Chestnut-headed Tesia, *Cettia castaneocoronata*, shares features with the four other tesias, despite its removal to a different genus. Almost tailless, it is a ground dweller that can bound deftly through dense vegetation on its long legs.

ABOVE This Manchurian Bush Warbler, *Horornis canturians*, was photographed at its nest in Ussuriland, in the far southeast of Russia.

ABOVE The only member of this mainly Asian family with a population in Europe, Cetti's Warbler, *Cettia cetti*, first colonised England in 1972.

with its olive upperparts contrasting with a rich chestnut head, a white crescent around the eye, and bright yellow. All are active little birds with very skulking habits, generally remaining on or near the ground among dense undergrowth. They have an odd habit of moving along branches sideways on their long, strong legs when alarmed.

As well as the Chestnut-crowned Tesia, the genus *Cettia* contains three other species, the best known of which is Cetti's Warbler, *C. cetti*, with a range including not only northwest Africa and western and central Asia but also, uniquely in the family, western and southern Europe. (It was named for an eighteenth century Italian mathematician and zoologist, whose surname is pronounced 'Chetteya'.) This rufous brown and greyish warbler is renowned among birders as a bird they do not often see, as it is usually hidden deep within its reedbed or other marshland home, but cannot fail to hear, as its song is extraordinarily loud and explosive for such a small bird, a fusillade of staccato liquid notes, and can be heard all year.

The remaining four genera in the Cettiinae are a varied bunch. There are three species of *Abroscopus* warblers, tiny birds with brightly coloured plumage in various combinations including olive green, bright yellow, grey, white, chestnut brown and black. They dwell in evergreen forests from the Himalayan foothills to China and Southeast Asia, where they specialise in eating tiny invertebrates, from diminutive flies and spiders to butterfly eggs. The two species of *Phyllergates*, from southern Asia, have green upperparts and a yellow breast combined with a grey or rufous head and breast, and a long, thin bill. They were originally classified together with other birds (also from Asia apart from one African species) known as tailorbirds from their remarkable habit of concealing their nests within large leaves which they sew together (see p. 344). Recently, since this grouping was found to be polyphyletic, its members have been distributed between several families. Although all the others are known to have this unique nesting habit, it is not confirmed for these two species. There is a single member of the genus *Tickellia*, the Broad-billed Warbler, *Tickellia hodgsoni*, from southern Asia. This is another species with green, bright yellow, grey and chestnut

plumage, and a relatively broad, flattened bill that is furnished with exceptionally long rictal bristles, reaching from its base almost to the tip. The largest genus in the whole family is *Horornis*, comprising 13 species of bush warblers with a collective range from the northeast of the Indian subcontinent to extreme southeast Russia, China, Japan, Korea and Southeast Asia to various Pacific islands. These are generally very similar in appearance, with brown upperparts with a pale stripe above the eye and buff or pale grey underparts. They include the largest members of the family, the Japanese Bush Warbler, *H. diphone*, and the Manchurian Bush Warbler, *H. canturians*.

Finally, two African species are provisionally included, pending further investigation, within this predominantly Asian family. The Green Hylia, *Hylia prasina*, is a rather drably plumaged bird, superficially similar to some of the leaf warblers (Family Phylloscopidae, p. 353), dark olive green above and paler greyish olive below with a contrasting pale yellow stripe above the eye and a blackish one through it. In the past, this enigmatic species has been included as a result of some anatomical similarities within the sunbird family (Nectariniidae), the tit family (Paridae) or even the weaver family (Ploceidae).

Over the long course of debate about its true affinities, the Tit Hylia, *Pholidornis rushiae*, has been shuffled about into no fewer than seven families, ranging from the sunbirds (Nectariniidae), flowerpeckers (Dicaeidae) and weavers (Ploceidae) to the tits (Paridae) and penduline tits (Remizidae). It has been recorded from scattered areas of rainforests and other wooded habitats within a broad belt across the west and Central Africa. However, it doubtless often goes unnoticed, due to its diminutive size – it is the smallest bird in Africa – and habit of often foraging quite high up in trees along the undersides of branches. When it is seen, however, this very short-tailed bird is easy to recognise, with its combination of strongly streaked brown and white head and breast, dark-streaked brown back and wings, and bright yellow hind body, as well as bright orange legs. Some researchers prefer to include these two unusual little birds in a separate family, Hyliidae.

LONG-TAILED TITS Aegithalidae

GENERA: 4   **SPECIES**: 13

LENGTH: 8.5–16 cm (3.3–6.3 in), of which about half is tail

WEIGHT: 4–10 g (0.1–0.35 oz)

RANGE AND HABITAT: Europe, Asia (most in Asia); one species (the Bushtit, *Psaltriparus minimus*) in the New World; woods and forests with rich understorey and shrub layer, often along edges, rivers and clearings, with many species only in mountains; the White-browed Tit-warbler, *Leptopoecile sophiae*, lives at up to 5,000 m/16,400 ft; the Bushtit is most abundant in mixed woodland but also occurs in arid shrublands such as sagebrush

SOCIAL BEHAVIOUR: highly gregarious most of the year, feeding in flocks and roosting together on cold nights, and join mixed-species foraging flocks after breeding; generally solitary nesters, monogamous; often cooperative breeders

NEST: purselike or baglike structure of moss and feathers, superbly camouflaged with lichens, bound together with spiders' webs, with an entrance near the top; sited low in a tree or shrub; an oval ball shape in all except the Bushtit, in which it is gourd-shaped

EGGS: in the few species known, 6–15, white or white with reddish spots

INCUBATION: 12–18 days

FLEDGING PERIOD: in the few species known, 14–18 days

FOOD: mainly insects, spiders, also some seeds and fruit, especially in winter

VOICE: flocks are very vocal, keeping in contact with trilling, churring, nasal and high-pitched calls

MIGRATION: mainly sedentary, though some southward migration of northern breeding species, and some seasonal altitudinal movements of high-mountain species

CONSERVATION STATUS: none threatened

ABOVE A brood of Long-tailed Tit nestlings demand food from the nest where they are warmed by thousands of feathers.

ABOVE A Long-tailed Tit, *Aegithalos caudatus*, searches for food in winter, a hard time for these tiny-bodied birds.

Sometimes known as the bushtits, especially in North America, from the sole New World representative, the Bushtit, *Psaltriparus minimus*, this small family of very small insectivorous songbirds is otherwise widely distributed across Eurasia, with most species in Asia. The Long-tailed Tit, *Aegithalos caudatus*, the most widespread member of the family (ranging from extreme western Europe in a broad band right across Europe and the middle of Asia east as far as Kamchatka and Japan), and the Bushtit (found in extreme southwest Canada, western USA, Mexico and Guatemala) are the best-studied species.

All have a tiny, very compact, plump body, with a long tail that accounts for about half their total length in *Aegithalos* species, and short rounded wings. They appear neckless, and have an extremely short, stubby cone-shaped bill. They spend most of their time in trees or shrubs. Their remarkable spherical gourd-shaped nests are among the most elaborate of all bird nests, with over 2,000 feathers found in single nests of Eurasian Long-tailed Tits.

Plumage in most of the nine species in the largest genus, *Aegithalos*, is a mixture of grey and brown, with black-and-white head or chin markings. The Eurasian Long-tailed Tit has a mainly white body with variable amounts of black or black, grey and pink on the upperparts; the 17 races of Eurasian Long-tailed Tit that have evolved over its huge range also differ in their head patterns, featuring broad black stripes in most but being all-white in the northernmost race *A. c. caudatus*, which breeds from northern and eastern Europe east to Japan. The Black-throated Tit, *Aegithalos concinnus*, the White-throated Tit, *A. niveogularis*, and the Rufous-fronted Tit, *A. iouschistos*, include rich cinnamon on the crown or body.

The Bushtit, the only member of the genus *Psaltriparus*, is even tinier, with a body only about 5 cm (2 in) long, and is one of North America's smallest songbirds. It is more drably plumaged than the *Aegithalos* species, with mainly grey-brown upperparts and dull fawn underparts, although males of several races have a bold black face mask. The Pygmy Tit, *Psaltria exilis*, the sole member of its genus, with a restricted range in the mountains of western and central Java, is similarly coloured to the Bushtit, but smaller still.

The males of the two species of tit-warbler, *Leptopoecile*, of central Asia and China are, by contrast, beautifully coloured, including exquisite combinations of pale grey, rich rufous, magenta, purple, violet, blue and turquoise. The male Crested Tit-warbler, *L. elegans*, also sports a short, silky white-tipped ash-grey crest. Their females are drabber, especially those of the White-browed Tit-warbler, *L. sophiae*. As the last part of their common names suggest, this atypical pair were for a long time included in the huge Old World warbler Family Sylviidae, but recent DNA studies indicate that their true home is with the rest of the long-tailed tits.

The long-tailed tits have often been included together with the tits and chickadees and also the penduline tits as three subfamilies in an enlarged version of the Family Paridae (p. 335). More recently, these

ABOVE The Bushtit, *Psaltriparus minimus*, is the sole New World member of the Family Aegithalidae, with a wide range from Canada to Guatemala.

three groups have been shown to deserve family status, and while the penduline tits are closely related to the tits, the long-tailed tits are only distant relatives. The most recent molecular research indicates that their closest relatives are the bush warblers (Scotocercidae, p. 354) and the leaf warblers (Phylloscopidae, p. 353).

SYLVIID WARBLERS, PARROTBILLS AND RELATIVES Sylviidae

GENERA: 18   **SPECIES:** 62

LENGTH: 9.5–28.5 cm (3.75–11 in)

WEIGHT: 5–110 g (0.17–3.88 oz)

RANGE AND HABITAT: Europe, Africa, Asia; a wide range of habitats, from semi-desert scrub and bamboo thickets to temperate woodland and tropical rainforests

SOCIAL BEHAVIOUR: socially monogamous

NEST: cup-shaped in most species, domed and with a side entrance in a few, such as the Fire-tailed Myzornis, *Myzornis pyrrhoura*, including grass, reeds, leaves, bark fragments and moss, often bound with spiders' webs, lined with feathers, mammal hair or fine plant matter, sited in a shrub, tree, reeds or bamboo

EGGS: 2–8, in *Sylvia* and *Curruca* warblers white, buff, very pale green or blue, with darker markings; babblers, white, pink, pale blue or green unmarked or with darker markings; parrotbills, mostly white or whitish with darker markings

INCUBATION: 10–18 days

FLEDGING PERIOD: 11–19 days

FOOD: mainly insects; some species also eat seeds, fruit, buds and flowers

VOICE: *Sylvia* warblers are fine singers, while *Curruca* species have simpler, less musical songs consisting mainly of scratchy or rattling notes; those of almost all the babblers are simple sequences of thin, high-pitched notes; parrotbill songs are varied, including series of high, staccato notes and wheezing or buzzing sounds; calls of all species are variable, but in many are harsh, consisting of grating, churring or other sounds

MIGRATION: most warbler species breeding in Europe and Asia migrate south after breeding in southern Europe, Africa, the Middle East or southern Asia; the others and all the babbler and parrotbill species are sedentary

CONSERVATION STATUS: five species, the Bush Blackcap, *Sylvia nigricapillus*, Jerdon's Babbler, *Chrysomma altirostre*, the Black-breasted Parrotbill, *Paradoxornis flavirostris*, the Grey-hooded Parrotbill, *Sinosuthora zappyi*, and the Rusty-throated Parrotbill, *S. przewalskii*, are Vulnerable; three species, including the Dartford Warbler, *Sylvia undata*, are Near Threatened

As currently recognised following extensive DNA studies, this family is far smaller than the former incarnation of the Sylviidae, a huge 'ragbag' assemblage of many groups of Old World warblers (and earlier still, including also the babblers, chats and thrushes in an even vaster Family Muscicapidae). The other warblers have been moved to families of their own, starting with the Cistocolidae, and more recently including the Macrosphenidae, Bernieridae, Locustellidae, Acrocephalidae, Phylloscopidae and Scotocercidae. The greatly slimmed down Sylviidae now comprises a mix of genera. These include not only warblers in the genus *Sylvia* and a

recently established genus *Curruca*, but also nine genera originally classified in the formerly large and also polyphyletic babbler Family Timaliidae and eight genera of parrotbills. The latter were originally included briefly in the crow Family Corvidae, then with the babblers and then given a family of their own. Although the members of the genus *Sylvia* and *Curruca* are still referred to as warblers, the genetic evidence shows that they are not closely related to any of the rest of the Old World warblers mentioned above. They are in fact most closely related to the three families of babblers – the reduced Timaliidae, Pellorneidae and Leiotrichidae

LEFT The Black-breasted Parrotbill, *Paradoxornis flavirostris*, of northeast India is a Vulnerable species, suffering loss of its reedbed and grassland habitat.

RIGHT The White-Browed Fulvetta, *Fulvetta vinipectus*, is a denizen of high-altitude scrub and light forest in the Himalayas and farther east.

BELOW A male Dartford Warbler, *Curruca undata*, perches on top of a heathland gorse bush in England, where this species is resident.

(see p. 364, p. 363, p. 364) and to the white-eyes (Zosteropidae, p. 360), and it may be better to give them alternative common names to reflect this. Indeed, the family is nowadays often referred to as the sylviid babblers.

In the scheme followed here, the genus *Sylvia* contains five species, with the other twenty-five species of 'warblers' in the genus *Curruca*, to reflect genetic studies indicating a marked divergence between the two groups. An alternative scheme that is far more widely adopted retains all of these in their traditional position in the genus *Sylvia*. They include widespread, abundant and well-known Eurasian species such as the Blackcap, *S. atricapilla*, and Garden Warbler, *S. borin*, both renowned for their beautiful, rich warbling songs, and the Common Whitethroat, *Curruca communis*, which frequently delivers its scratchy, rattling song while launching itself in a brief upward song-flight before diving back into the cover of a hedge, or alternatively from a prominent perch. The two genera also include rather less familiar species in Europe (most with mainly or exclusively southern distributions), Africa, Arabia and south-west and central Asia.

Plumage is generally brown, grey and buff or whitish, in some species with bolder markings, including black or brown caps or

heads, rich wine-red underparts (the Dartford Warbler, *Curruca undata*) and partly or wholly rusty-orange underparts in several species. Many species have conspicuous red, orange, yellow or white eye-rings or eyes. An example is the Barred Warbler, *C. nisoria*, largest member of the genus with a particularly prominent glaring yellow iris, and also distinctively barred underparts, most strongly marked in the male. Five species of *Curruca* were formerly included in the genus *Parisoma* (three species, still incorporate parisoma as part of their common names). They include a single species in Saudi Arabia and Yemen, with the rest in various parts of Africa, from Ethiopia to South Africa. Another African species, endemic to eastern South Africa, is the Bush Blackcap, which looks rather like an oversized Blackcap, *Sylvia atricapilla*. Formerly included in the babbler family, this is best placed on its own in a third, genus, *Lioptilus*, although often included within *Sylvia*.

The eight other genera that were previously included with the babblers are all monotypic apart from one, *Chrysomma*, with two species, and another, *Fulvetta*, with five species (or in some schemes, as many as eight species). All are Asian, with a collective range from northern India and China to parts of Southeast Asia, apart from two. One is the Juniper Babbler, *Parophasma galinieri*, endemic to the highlands of Ethiopia. A distinctive almost entirely grey bird with a chestnut vent, it is like the Bush Blackcap, larger than most other members of the family. Also known as the Abyssinian Catbird, it has a superficial similarity with members of the unrelated New World Grey Catbird, *Dumatella carolinensis* (see Family Mimidae, p. 380). Its song is a melodious trill, and as its other name suggests, favours juniper woodland with dense vegetation. The other non-African babbler is the Wrentit, *Chamaea fasciata*, which is remarkable for being the only New World member of this family, restricted to the extreme west of the USA in California and Oregon, where it lives in dense brush and shrubby places in many habitats, from montane chaparral to scrubby desert, coastal sage scrub and suburban woodland. With a greyish head, brown upperparts and pinkish buff underparts, it has a tiny rotund body and a long, strongly graduated tail.

The other babbler species vary considerably in appearance and plumage. *Moupina* and *Chrysomma* species are plain reddish brown, the latter paler below, while the Chinese Bush Warbler, *Rhopophilus pekinensis*, has a black streaked head and upperparts and rufous streaks on white underparts. All three have long, graduated tails, in contrast to the other three genera. The little fulvettas in the genus *Fulvetta* are boldly patterned in a mixture of brown, chestnut black and white, and have the shortest tails, while the tiny Golden-breasted Fulvetta, *Lioparus chrysotis*, is a beautiful sight with plumage in a sunset-like combination of grey, white, gold and black. The most colourful member of the family by far is the stunning Fire-tailed Myzornis, *Myzornis pyrrhoura*, which is almost entirely brilliant green with dramatic highlights of fiery red on its breast, wings and tail, and has a very slender, slightly decurved bill.

The exclusively Asian parrotbills have been sometimes placed in a subfamily or even a family of their own. Formerly they were generally shoehorned into just two genera, but recent research has increased this to no fewer than eight genera, three of them monotypic. The 19 species live in dense grasslands, bamboo stands, reed beds and similar habitats, where they are specialist feeders on grass seeds, splitting them with the aid of the big, very deep bill that is so different from the fine insect-eating bills of the rest of the family, and accounts for their collective name. They are acrobatic birds, almost all with a long tail, and their plumage is predominantly rich rufous, with various combinations of bluish grey, fawn, black and white. Eleven species in four genera consist of small birds, mostly 11.5–15 cm (4.5–6 in) in length; the smallest of them, *Neosuthora davidiana*, is a tiny bird, just 9.5–10 cm (3.75–4 in) long and weighing as little as 8 g (0.3 oz), and unlike the rest of the parrotbills has a very short tail, hence its common name, the Short-tailed Parrotbill. There are three genera of medium-sized birds, between about 18 cm and 22 cm long; these include the three species now remaining in the genus *Paradoxornis*. One of these, the Three-toed Parrotbill, *P. paradoxus*, endemic to central China, is the truly paradoxical one, since it is the only passerine to have just three toes, two facing forwards and one backwards rather than the usual three forwards and one backwards of all other members of the order. Dwarfing them all, and the biggest member of the whole family is the aptly named Great Parrotbill, *Conostoma oemodium*, which measures 27.5–28.5 cm (11 in) long and weighs about 88–110 g (3–3.9 oz).

WHITE-EYES, YUHINAS AND RELATIVES Zosteropidae

GENERA: 13   **SPECIES.** 123

LENGTH: 9–18 cm (3.5–7 in)

WEIGHT: 8–31 g (0.3–1.1 oz)

RANGE AND HABITAT: sub-Saharan Africa, the Arabian peninsula, southern and south-eastern Asia, from Afghanistan to Japan, Australasia, New Zealand, many Pacific islands; most species live in forests or woodlands, including mangroves, or along their edges, but some extend into parks and gardens and others are found in scrub, in some cases in arid places

SOCIAL BEHAVIOUR: socially monogamous and territorial; some yuhinas, *Yuhina*, are cooperative breeders; most species are very sociable outside the breeding season, often in large flocks

NEST: in white-eyes, a small, delicate cup, typically of plant stems, bark, lichen and other material, lined with plant down, bound with spiders' webs, and suspended between the tips of a forked branch or twig of a tree or shrub; yuhinas nest in similar sites, building either a flimsy cup or a domed nest

EGGS: 1–4 in most species, usually 2–3, but up to 6 in the two most northerly breeders, the Chestnut-flanked White-eye, *Zosterops erythropleurus*, and the Japanese White-eye, *Z. japonicus*; usually pale blue, occasionally white

INCUBATION: 10–16 days

FLEDGING PERIOD: 10–17 days

FOOD: mainly insects, spiders, small snails, also nectar, pollen and fruit and some seeds

VOICE: thin, nasal, down-slurred 'zeeee-er' calls in *Zosterops* species; other genera have squeaky, rasping, buzzing, chattering or chirping calls; songs are typically a rambling mixture of warbling notes and call notes

MIGRATION: almost all species are sedentary, but some disperse over very wide areas, in the process colonising new islands, while the Chestnut-flanked White-eye and northern populations of the Japanese White-eye make regular migrations south for winter

CONSERVATION STATUS: three species, the Robust White-eye, *Zosterops strenuus*, the Marianne White-eye, *Z. semiflavus*, and the Bridled White-eye, *Z. conspicillatus*, are Extinct; five species, the Mauritius Olive White-eye, *Z. chloronothos*, the Rota Bridled White-eye, *Z. rotensis*, the Sangihe White-eye, *Z. nehrkorni*, the White-chested White-eye, *Z. albogularis*, and the Golden White-eye, *Cleptornis marchei*, are Critically Endangered; six species, the Gizo White-eye, *Z. luteirostris*, Taita White-eye, *Zosterops silvanus*, Saipan White-eye, *Z. saypani*, Teardrop White-eye, *Rukia ruki*, Negros Striped Babbler, *Zosterornis nigrorum*, and Flame-templed Babbler, *Dasycrotapha speciosa*, are Endangered; 10 species, including the Samoan White-eye, *Z. samoensis*, and Mt. Cameroon Speirops, *Z. melanocephalus*, are Vulnerable; 21 species are Near Threatened

These small, compact, mainly forest and woodland songbirds are widespread across much of the more southerly regions of the Old World, from westernmost Africa across southern Asia to Japan, Australasia, New Zealand and on many islands in the Indian and Pacific Oceans. This is one of those families in which new species, especially on remote islands, are still being discovered by ornithologists. The Togian White-eye, *Zosterops somadikartai*, from the Togian islands of northern Sulawesi, Indonesia, and the Vanikoro White-eye, *Z. gibbsi*, from one of the Solomon Islands, were both described as recently as 2008. Many other species are endemic to particular archipelagos or single islands. They are remarkable in forming new species at such a rapid rate, probably faster than any other bird family, a feat that led to their being dubbed the 'Great Speciators'.

Most of the members of this family are known as white-eyes, and the overwhelming number of these, 84 in total (or more in some classification schemes) are in the genus *Zosterops*, accounting for two-thirds of the total number of species in the family. There are also eight other small genera of white-eyes, six of them containing just a single species (the other two comprise two and

ABOVE An Oriental White-eye, *Zosterops palpebrosus*, feeds on fruit at a bird feeder in a Singapore garden.

ten species). Despite their wide range and extensive diversification, most *Zosterops* species look very similar, being largely olive green above and mainly pale grey below. Many have patches or larger areas of yellow or white below or on the forehead or throat, while a few have black on the head, or chestnut flanks, or are uniform olive green or grey, brown or with other colour combinations. As the common name suggests, many species have a very distinctive, prominent ring of tiny white feathers surrounding each eye.

The bill is short, slender and pointed, and the tongue grooved and equipped with a brush tip. As with other birds possessing this modification, it is an adaptation for a diet containing a good deal of nectar. They can suck up large volumes quickly without needing to tilt the head back. They also eat large amounts of insects and fruit.

Some common species, such as the Silvereye, *Zosterops lateralis*, in Australia and New Zealand, Cape White-eye, *Z. pallidus*, in South Africa and the widespread south Asian Oriental White-eye, *Z. palpebrosus*, have caused problems for fruit growers and wine producers as a result of their depredations in orchards and vineyards, in which they damage more fruit than they eat. On the other hand, white-eyes of various species have long been valued for their charm, adaptability and easy maintenance as cage birds. They are also extensively used as subjects for scientific investigation into migration and other topics.

Although many of the other genera of white-eyes include largely green and olive birds rather similar to the *Zosterops* species, some have far more distinctive plumage. A striking example is the single species of *Cleptornis*, the Golden White-eye, *C. marchei*, with a rich golden yellow body, contrasting with its olive green wings and tail, and a bright red bill and legs. Another very different species is the Bicoloured White-eye, *Tephrozosterops stalkeri*, the two colours in question being bright chestnut, on the crown, upperparts and

tail, and bright yellow, beneath the tail; it also has a greyish face and white underparts. Other distinctive species include the Giant White-eye, *Megazosterops palauensis*, from some of the Palau islands in the western Pacific, which is almost uniformly dark olive green and has a stout bill. This is one of several genera that are larger than most white-eyes, including the two species of Rukia, from the Caroline Islands in the southwest Pacific, with a similar mainly dull olive plumage and a long, slender, decurved bill.

As a result of DNA research, the family has recently acquired four genera of birds that were previously included in the original very large and polyphyletic version of the babbler family, Timaliidae. They include the 11 species of yuhinas, *Yuhina*, sprightly little birds distinguished by having a jaunty crest that gives their crown a triangular profile. With plumage in various combinations of brown, grey, black and white, they bear a superficial resemblance to the crested members of the unrelated tit family (Paridae, p. 335), a likeness enhanced by the sight of feeding parties of these active little birds moving fast through the trees of their forest homes. The other three genera are all endemic to the Philippines. The two species of *Dasycrotapha* are the Flame-templed Babbler, *D. speciosa*, with a plain greyish-green body but a strikingly patterned black and gold head, and a much smaller bird, the Pygmy Babbler, *D. plateni*, its two races (sometimes elevated to species rank) with a dark brown or reddish brown head and upperparts, a grey or chestnut breast with fine white streaks and a white belly. Four of the five species of *Zosterornis* have brown upperparts and cream underparts with bold black streaks, while the other is paler brown above, plain buff below and with a chestnut and grey head. Finally, the three species of *Sterrhoptilus* are dark grey and brown above and pale below, and with distinctively coloured crowns, chestnut in one species, golden yellow in the second and black in the third.

The babblers, now split into three families (see p. 362, p. 363, p. 364), are now thought to be the closest relatives of this family. Although the white-eyes have at various times been included in the original large 'ragbag' versions of both the Old World Family Sylviidae and the babbler Family Timaliidae, they have also often been considered to be closely related to the honeyeaters (Meliphagidae, p. 235) and sunbirds (Nectariniidae, p. 286), because of their grooved and brush-tipped tongues, a feature they share with those two nectar-feeding families. The recent molecular studies, however, show conclusively that their true relationships are with the babblers.

A worryingly large and increasing proportion of species – a third of the total in the family – are globally threatened, especially those on islands. Prime among the causes of this sorry state of affairs are habitat destruction and degradation, and predation by introduced animals such as rats and snakes. Introduced diseases (avian malaria and bird pox) and, in some cases, trapping for the cage-bird trade, also take their toll. Already three species have become extinct within the last 70 or so years. These include the ironically named Robust White-eye, *Z. strenuus*, endemic to Lord Howe island, 780 km (480 miles) east of Sydney, Australia. Its downfall was due to the Black Rats introduced to the island, and was extremely rapid: though still common until 1918, none could be found just 10 years later.

SCIMITAR BABBLERS AND RELATIVES Timaliidae

GENERA: 11   **SPECIES:** 46

LENGTH: 9–28 cm (3.5–11 in)

WEIGHT: 6–79 g (0.2–2.8 oz)

RANGE AND HABITAT: northern Pakistan and India east to southeastern China and south throughout mainland Southeast Asia and islands as far south and east as the Philippines, Sumatra, Borneo, Java, Bali and Sulawesi; inhabit a wide range of habitats, from humid rainforests to dry forests, including some at quite high altitudes, as well as dense scrub, abandoned plantations, tall grassland, bamboo thickets and reedbeds

SOCIAL BEHAVIOUR: socially monogamous, some defending territories, though a few may possibly be cooperative breeders; some form small flocks and also join mixed-species feeding groups

NEST: usually domed or spherical, but open cups in some species, made of twigs, leaves, rootlets, moss and other plant material, generally sited on or near the ground concealed among dense vegetation, or in a tree or log hollow

EGGS: 2–5, usually white or cream, in some species with darker markings

INCUBATION: 10–15 days

FLEDGING PERIOD: 10–14 days

FOOD: mainly insects and other invertebrates, with some species also eating seeds, berries, and nectar

VOICE: varied, with songs including mellow hooting or fluting notes, sounds like a bouncing ball, complex warbling and trilling sequences, churring, creaking, croaking or whinnying sounds; calls range from guttural rattling and whiplash-like notes to soft bubbling or gurgling notes

MIGRATION: sedentary

CONSERVATION STATUS: four species, the Nonggang Babbler, *Stachyris nonggangensis*, Snowy-throated Babbler, *S. oglei*, Rusty-throated Wren Babbler, *Spelaeornis badeigularis*, and Tawny-breasted Wren Babbler, *S. longicaudatus*, are Vulnerable; nine species are Near Threatened

Until recent DNA research indicated they should be placed in a family of their own, the birds in this family were buried within a greatly enlarged Timaliidae that also included all the babblers now assigned to two other families, the ground babblers (Pellorneidae, p. 363) and the laughing thrushes and relatives (Leiotrichidae, p. 364). Before that, for a long time all these babblers, together with many others (such as Australasian babblers, sylviid warblers and parrotbills, Old World flycatchers and chats, and thrushes), now removed to various other families, were subsumed in a vast 'ragbag' assemblage, the Muscicapidae; it was referred to by the renowned British nineteenth-century ornithologist as 'a festering mass'! The family name Muscicapidae is now reserved for the Old World flycatchers and chats (p. 387), still one of the largest of all bird families.

The birds in this entirely Asian family span a considerable size range, from the eight species of very small wren babblers in the genus *Spelaeornis* and some of the seven species in the genus *Cyanoderma*, at 9–10 cm (3.5–4 in) long, via those progressively larger, like the two genera of tit babblers, *Mixornis*, at around 11–14 cm (4–5.5 in) and *Macronus*, 13–17 cm, to the bigger scimitar babblers, *Pomatorhinus*, 16–24 cm (6–9.5 in), and *Erythrogenys*, all but one 21–25 cm (8–10 in), with the largest, the aptly named Large Scimitar Babbler, *E. hypoleucos*, at 26–28 cm (10–11 in) long. Most have longish oval bodies and have a rather hunched posture, but the wren babblers are rotund little birds that hold themselves more erect with their tail often angled upwards. The tail of many species is of medium length and graduated, but longer in the scimitar babblers. The bills of the smaller species are quite short and straight, relatively slim in many but stouter in a few others, such as the Chestnut-capped Babbler, *Timalia pileata*. The scimitar babblers take their collective name from their long, decurved bills, which in the *Pomatorhinus* species are bright yellow or in one species (often regarded as two species) red, and in another black; in the latter, the Slender-billed Scimitar Babbler, *P. superciliaris*, is remarkably long, slender and strongly decurved. The bills of the Erythrogenys species are grey or blackish.

This family is also known as the tree babblers, reflecting the fact that most of them are forest dwellers that live mainly off the ground at various levels, depending on species. Exceptions include some of the scimitar babblers that spend much of their time searching for food on or just above the ground, proceeding by ungainly hops and rummaging among the leaf litter or digging into soil to extract insect prey with their long, strong, decurved and laterally compressed bills. As with the other babbler families, those in this family are generally shy birds that remain well hidden among the foliage or other cover, and are far more often heard than seen; again, like their relatives, they are noisy birds and have a wide repertoire of loud and often distinctive songs and calls.

Helping to provide camouflage, the dominant colour in the plumage of most species is a range of browns, from pale buff or orangey brown to deep chestnut or duller olive brown, often with contrasting areas of white or black in the form of white underparts, black-and-white eyestripes or black flank streaks; other patterns include dark streaked underparts in two of the tit babblers, and complex arrangements of black-and-white mottling or barring and white or black spots on rufous underparts in the wren babblers. In most species the tail is plain brown; the Bar-winged Wren Babbler, *Spelaeornis troglodytoides*, has a much longer tail than the other members of its genus, and rather than being plain rufous brown, it is boldly barred black and buff, as are its stubby wings. One species, the Golden Babbler, *Cyanoderma chrysaeum*, is very distinctive, with yellowish olive upperparts, a black-striped crown and bright golden yellow underparts, whereas the six other members of its genus are plain brown with a chestnut cap or a black chin, or a mixture of chestnut, blue-grey and fawn, in one species with black markings. A few species in the genus *Stachyris* are almost entirely blackish or dark brown. Two species of *Macronus* tit babblers have a peculiar plumage feature – a group of elongated, bare whitish or pale buff shafts cascade out from the flanks and lower back and over the base of the tail. Two other far smaller species, the Philippine miniature babblers, *Micromacronus*, share this odd feature to an even greater degree, and were originally included here as close relatives until DNA studies led to their removal to a different family, Sylviidae (see p. 358). Some babblers in this family have blue throat sacs that are noticeable when they inflate them as they sing. The sexes generally look very similar.

GROUND BABBLERS Pellorneidae

GENERA: 16   **SPECIES:** 57

LENGTH: 10–21 cm (4–8 in)

WEIGHT: 8–70 g (0.3–2.5 oz)

RANGE AND HABITAT: equatorial Africa, from Senegal to Tanzania and Zanzibar and in southern Asia, discontinuously in far northern, western and eastern India, east to eastern China and south through Southeast Asia to the Philippines, Sumatra, Java, Borneo and Sulawesi; in forests of various kinds, from low-altitude tropical rainforests to mountain forests, usually with dense undergrowth

SOCIAL BEHAVIOUR: monogamous; a few species are probably cooperative breeders; many species are gregarious and often seen in small groups

NEST: made of twigs, leaves, rootlets and moss, lined with finer materials; structure varies considerably, from small, neat open cups, in some species slung from branches, to semi-domed or domed nests; sited concealed among dense foliage low down in a tree or shrub, or among dense vegetation or other cover on the ground

EGGS: 2–5, white, cream, pale blue or green or grey, pink, with darker markings

INCUBATION: 10–15 days

FLEDGING PERIOD: 10–14 days

FOOD: insects and other invertebrates, including spiders, snails and worms

VOICE: songs are mainly simple series of high-pitched whistling notes; many calls are harsh and rattling or rasping

MIGRATION: sedentary

CONSERVATION STATUS: one species, the White-throated Wren Babbler, *Rimator pasquieri*, is Endangered; five species, including the Bornean Wren Babbler, *Ptilocichla leucogrammica*, Falcated Wren Babbler, *P. falcata*, Naung Mung Wren Babbler, *Jabouilleia naungmanensis*, and Gold-fronted Fulvetta, *Schoeniparus variegaticeps*, are Vulnerable; and 13 species are Near Threatened

ABOVE The Rufous-throated Fulvetta, *Schoeniparus rufogularis*, is a shy, secretive resident of evergreen forests, scrub and bamboo from northeast India to Southeast Thailand.

As a result of many molecular studies, this family was created to embrace various closely related genera that had previously been buried within the huge 'dustbin' assemblage of babblers in the original Family Timaliidae. The name Timaliidae is now reserved for one of the two other families resulting from this division, containing the tree babblers (see p. 362). These are predominantly Asian birds, with just one genus of eight species known as illadopsis or thrush babblers, *Illadopsis*, found in a diagonal belt across Africa extending either side of the Equator.

These are indeed largely ground-dwelling, although they also forage among dense undergrowth in the lower levels of the forests where they live. Most species in this family are shy and secretive, and like other babblers, these are very vocal birds, often heard rather than seen, with loud songs and calls. They are small to medium sized, with soft, fluffy plumage featuring mainly browns, greys, black and white in various patterns. These muted colours, usually darker above than below and often with crown or eye stripes and with strong streaking or mottling in some genera that help to break up their outline, render them very difficult to spot among the foliage and leaf litter in the low light of the forest interior.

Two of the six tiny species of tit-like fulvettas in the genus *Schoeniparus* have plumage that includes brighter colours. The Gold-fronted Fulvetta, *S. variegaticeps*, has a bright yellow forehead, a large black patch under its eye, and bright yellow and black wing panel, while the Yellow-throated Fulvetta, *S. cinereus*, is olive green above with a striking pattern of black and yellow eye-stripes and yellow underparts. The other four fulvetta species have boldly patterned brown, rufous, grey, black and white plumage. The common name of these little birds measuring just that resemble tits (Paridae) is now shared with various diminutive babblers in two other families, both the laughing thrushes and relatives (Leiotrichidae, p. 364) and the sylviid warblers and parrotbills (Sylviidae, p. 358) each having a genus of little birds called fulvettas.

Many of the smaller members of the family look rather like warblers in proportions, while the bigger species mostly recall thrushes or jays. As with the two other babbler families, there is a great diversity of bill sizes, shapes and lengths, associated with the many different niches this remarkably diverse group of birds has occupied. Most species have rather short wings and all have long legs with large feet. Their tails vary, from very short in some of the wren-babblers to medium length in most, with a few having longer tails, such as the two species of *Gampsorhynchus* and the Rufous-rumped Grass Babbler, *Graminicola striatus*, transferred to this family from the family of warblers known as the grassbirds and relatives (Locustellidae, p. 344). Another strikingly long-tailed member of this family that was until recently included in a warbler family (as one of the prinias in the family of cisticolas and relatives, Cisticolidae, p. 342) is the Long-tailed Grass Babbler, *Laticilla cinerascens*. Two species in the genus *Gampsorhynchus*, have a snow-white head and upper breast.

There are six genera with the collective name of wren-babblers. The largest of these, and the largest members of the whole family, are the seven species in the genus *Turdinus*. They have sturdy plump breasted bodies, a medium length tail and a relatively long, stout bill. All have brown upperparts combined in most with white or rufous underparts, often with striking patterns of streaks (or in one case crescents). The three species of *Ptilocichla*, also known as ground babblers, are smaller, with a similar build and bill to the *Turdinus* babblers but very short tails. They too are boldly patterned, brown above with long black-and-white stripes below; one species, the Falcated Wren Babbler, *P. falcata*, has the entire body covered with especially long, loose spiky white feathers on a black background, contrasting with its rich reddish brown crown, wings and tail. The remaining wren babblers are much smaller and plump bodied. Two of the smaller genera of wren-babblers, *Rimator*, and *Jabouilleia*, have

long, strongly decurved bills. The three species of *Rimator* appear almost tailless. They are almost entirely brown with black streaks, apart from a white throat in two of them, while the two species of *Jabouilleia* are longer tailed, with similar but paler brown plumage. Of the three others, two, *Napothera* and *Kenopia*, are also monotypic. Both have a much shorter, relatively stout bill; *Napothera* is brown above with a striking white eyebrow and streaky brown below, and has an extremely short tail, while *Kenopia* is more boldly patterned, with a distinctive white face and underparts and white streaking on its black crown and reddish brown back.

LAUGHING THRUSHES AND RELATED BABBLERS Leiotrichidae

GENERA: 21   **SPECIES**: 125

LENGTH: 12.5–35.5 cm (5–14 in)

WEIGHT: 12–170 g (0.4–6 oz)

RANGE AND HABITAT: Africa and southern Asia, in a wide range of wooded habitats, ranging from dense lowland rainforest and wet montane forests to open woodland and savannah, with some in scrubland, thickets of bamboo or other plants, and a few in semi-arid landscapes

SOCIAL BEHAVIOUR: socially monogamous with some males in the genus *Turdoides* serially polygynous; many *Turdoides* species are cooperative breeders; most are highly gregarious

NEST: mostly cup shaped, made of twigs, roots, dead leaves, bark, grasses and other plant material, often camouflaged with mosses and lichens and incorporating spiders' webs, often lined with softer material such as fine grasses, mammal hair or fur, and moss

EGGS: 2–6, mostly pale to bright blue or blue-green, some white, pinkish or grey; usually with darker markings

INCUBATION: 13–17 days

FLEDGING PERIOD: 9–21 days

FOOD: chiefly insects, also spiders and other invertebrates such as small molluscs, with some species also including fruit, seeds or nectar in their diet

VOICE: varied in these very vocal birds, including whistling, warbling, chuckling and babbling songs, and harsh chattering, grating and churring calls

MIGRATION: this is a highly sedentary family, with just a few species making altitudinal migrations

CONSERVATION STATUS: three species, the Rufous-fronted Laughing-thrush, *Garrulax rufifrons*, Blue-crowned Laughing-thrush, *G. courtoisi*, and Bugun Liocichla, *Liocichla bugunorum*, are Critically Endangered; five species, the Nilgiri Laughing-thrush, *Trochalopteron cachinnans*, Banasura Laughing-thrush, *T. jerdoni*, Collared Laughing-thrush, *T. yersini*, Sumatran Laughing-thrush, *Garrulax bicolor*, and Grey-crowned Crocias, *Laniellus langbianus*, are Endangered; 10 species, including the Snowy-cheeked Laughing-thrush, *Garrulax sukatschewi*, White-throated Mountain Babbler, *Kupeornis gilberti*, Slender-billed Babbler, *Chatarrhaea longirostris*, and Hinde's Babbler, *Turdoides hindei*, are Vulnerable; 15 species are Near Threatened

The birds in this large family, the third and by far the largest of all three new families of babblers, were originally included, together with those in the other two families in the huge original 'dustbin' Family Timaliidae, which molecular analysis showed to contain many genera and species that were not in fact close relatives. There is still uncertainty over the status of several genera, including the large ones of *Turdoides* and *Garrulax*, and evidence suggests that these are polyphyletic and that their limits need to be revised. The Family Timaliidae is now reserved for the scimitar babblers and allies, also known as the tree babblers, p. 362. The name of this family, Leotrichidae, has been spelled in a variety of different ways; the most recent evidence (in press) is that the one used here is the original spelling, and the rules of nomenclature indicate that it is this that should be used rather than the most usual alternative, Leiotrichidae.

This is the one family among the three babbler families with most African representatives (a total of 21 species in three genera in the classification scheme used in this book), although these still represent just 16% of the total number of species and only 14% of the genera in the family, the rest being Asian. The latter range from the Middle East and across central Asia to the Indian subcontinent and further east into China and throughout most of Southeast Asia.

This family includes the greatest number of strikingly plumaged and colourful babblers. Most genera are attired in various combinations of browns, greys, black and white, often in bold patterns, while five genera contain some with areas of brighter colours as well. They have sturdy bodies, short, rounded wings and usually a long tail. The laughing thrushes look rather like the unrelated jays (Family Corvidae), while the seven species of sibias, *Heterophasia* with their long tails, recall the magpies (also in the Corvidae).

Getting on for half of all species are called laughing thrushes, divided between two genera, *Garrulax*, with 40 species and *Trochalopteron*, with 15 species. The name *Garrulax* is from the Latin word *garrulus* meaning talkative or chattering (in English 'garrulous'), and is aptly bestowed, for these are very noisy birds. Various *Garrulax* species, exemplified by the common and widespread White-crested Laughing Thrush, *G. leucolophus*, account for the name of this group of birds. As a flock roams in search of food through a forest, often in the company of a whole range of other birds, such as fantails, drongos and woodpeckers, their subdued, conversational chattering suddenly erupts into peals of very loud cackling laughter, before dying away again with a few quiet calls. One species, the Melodious Laughing Thrush, *Garrulax canorus*, is

ABOVE The Arrow-marked Babbler, *Turdoides jardineii*, is locally common in woodland and savannah with dense cover in Africa south of the Sahara.

ABOVE The Jungle Babbler, *Turdoides striata*, is widely distributed in forests and cultivated land throughout the Indian subcontinent.

particularly renowned as a singer, and as a result has become one of the most popular and highly valued cagebirds in Asia. Relatively common from south and east-central China to northern Laos and Vietnam, it is better known by its Chinese name of Hwamei, meaning 'painted eyebrow', a reference to the very pale blue ring surrounding its eye and extending back in an eyebrow shape. Its loud song is a mixture of warbling and sweet ringing notes, and champion singers are pitted against one another in singing competitions.

Although brown forms a major part of the plumage of most species, laughing thrushes have a wide range of colours and patterns. Many have striking head markings, such as a black, grey or blue grey cap, usually combined with a black 'bandit mask' often extending onto the chest as a bib; some have a large white or rufous ear-patch, or a white throat that may be bordered by a black necklace. Three species have yellow or partly yellow underparts. Several have a chestnut coloured back peppered with black-and-white spots. In the *Trochalopteron* species, wings are often patterned, too, with contrasting panels of yellow, orange or red. Other species have simpler patterns, such as the White-crested Laughing Thrush, with its snow-white hood and breast contrasting with a chestnut brown body and wings and blackish tail; this is unusual among babblers in having a crest, which it raises frequently. One other species is crested: in a genus of its own, *Grammoptila*, this is the Striated Laughing Thrush, *G. striata*. It has white-streaked brown plumage with a large, bushy crest.

The 17 species of *Turdoides* have predominantly brown plumage, often featuring dark or pale streaks, chevrons, scales or mottling, long tails and striking pale white, greyish, yellow or red eyes. Two African species have a white head, and one has a black head, and one has an all-white body contrasting with black wings and tail. These are mainly birds of Africa, with 14 of the 17 species being endemic to that continent. Most dwell in more open habitats than the rest of the family, in open woodland, savannah, tall grassland and marshes with dense cover, and arid scrub. They include some of the most familiar babblers. Of the three Asian species, one, the Jungle Babbler, *T. striata*, is a very common and familiar bird in India. The other two are the Orange-billed Babbler, *T. rufescens*, endemic to Sri Lanka, and the Yellow-billed Babbler, *T. affinis*, found in south India as well as Sri Lanka. Two other very abundant and well known Asian species were recently

moved from their traditional position in *Turdoides* to a new genus, *Argya*. These are the Common Babbler, *A. caudata*, and the Large Grey Babbler, *A. malcolmi*. Like the majority of babblers, these are extremely gregarious birds, spending much of their time in groups of various sizes. When a number of these birds are resting on a branch or other perch during the day, and also at nocturnal roosts, they usually huddle closely together and indulge in bouts of mutual preening.

The two species in the genus *Leiothrix* include the beautiful little Red-billed Leiothrix, *L. lutea*. This is one of the best known of all babblers, as a result of its being highly regarded as a cagebird, both in Asia and abroad, where it is often known by aviculturalists and dealers as the 'Pekin Robin'. Its mainly grey plumage is lit up by its yellow throat, shading into a glowing apricot colour on its breast and a long yellow and orange-red panel on its wing. As its common name indicates, it has a brilliant red bill. It is also unusual for a babbler in having a distinctly forked tail. The cagebird trade has resulted in a decline in numbers in parts of its range, though it remains common across much of its wide range in China. Trapping has had a far more serious effect on other species in this family, especially of laughing thrushes, such as the Critically Endangered Rufous-fronted Laughing Thrush, *Garrulax rufifrons*, endemic to Java. Many other species suffer mainly from habitat destruction.

Other very attractive small birds in this family are the five species of *Liocichla*, which have orange-buff, grey or greenish bodies contrasting with patches of scarlet or yellow. There are three genera of little babblers called minlas, each with a single species and complex plumage patterns. The male Red-tailed Minla, *Minla ignotincta*, has a boldly black-and-white striped head and creamy yellow coloured underparts with faint streaks, the black-and-white wings have a red panel, while the black tail has a white stripe at its base and red outer feathers; the female is duller, lacking the red markings. The Bar-throated Minla, *Chrysominla strigula*, has a grey body, with black-and-white wings featuring a contrasting bright orange panel, yellow underparts and a short, ragged orange crown. The Blue-winged Minla, *Siva cyanouroptera*, has a white-streaked black crown, a brown body, mainly bright blue wings and tail, and grey-streaked whitish underparts. The seven species of fulvettas, *Alcippe*, are much plainer, with mainly brown and grey plumage, and long blackish stripes over the eye in all but two.

The cutia, *Cutia* (often considered as two species) is another strikingly patterned little bird, its plumage a patchwork of chestnut, blue grey, buff, and black with strongly black-barred white underparts. Living in broadleaved evergreen mountain forests with a discontinuous distribution in the Himalayan foothills, China, and parts of Southeast Asia, flocks of these small birds live mainly in the forest canopy, where they creep about on tree branches and trunks like nuthatches, which they resemble somewhat in shape and the shortness of their tails, a contrast with other babblers. This is one of the few babbler species in which the sexes differ in plumage, females being duller, especially in the Vietnamese race (or species) *legalleni*, which lacks the blue-grey crown and wing panel of the male.

GOLDCRESTS AND KINGLETS Regulidae

GENERA: 1   **SPECIES:** 6

LENGTH: 8–11 cm (3–4 in)

WEIGHT: 6–8 g (0.2–0.3 oz)

RANGE AND HABITAT: North America, Europe, North Africa, the Canary Islands, the Azores, Madeira, Asia; coniferous forests, also mixed and deciduous forests, smaller wooded areas (including large gardens), on Atlantic islands (especially the Madeira Firecrest, *Regulus madeirensis*) in laurel forest with tree-heath

SOCIAL BEHAVIOUR: after breeding, they often form loose foraging flocks, and also join mixed-species flocks of other birds such as tits, nuthatches, treecreepers and woodpeckers, and they also roost huddled together in cold weather to reduce heat loss; monogamous and territorial breeders

NEST: tiny, neat, very strong cups of moss and lichen bound together with spiders' webs, lined with feathers and animal hair, with feathers over nest contents to hide and insulate them, suspended from twigs at the end of a high tree branch (among twigs or between horizontal branches of tree-heath in Atlantic island races of the Goldcrest, *R. regulus*, and Madeira Firecrest)

EGGS: 4–12, white to pale buff, sometimes with fine dark spots

INCUBATION: 14–17 days

FLEDGING PERIOD: about 17–22 days

FOOD: small insects and spiders; they take some insects trapped from spiders' webs, when, rarely, the bird can be stuck fast and die of starvation

VOICE: extremely high-pitched calls and song, based on 'si' or 'seee' notes, in song typically with terminal flourish

MIGRATION: all but the island forms make southward migrations for winter

CONSERVATION STATUS: none threatened

ABOVE The prominent flaming orange crown and striking pied head stripes of this Firecrest, *Regulus ignicapillus*, are its most distinctive feature.

This is a tiny family of tiny birds, among the smallest of all the world's birds, and the smallest in Europe. Like hummingbirds and some other passerines, they have a phenomenally high metabolic rate, and must search for food almost constantly, even when singing and nesting, to stay alive. If a Goldcrest, *Regulus regulus*, is unable to feed, it may lose a third of its total weight in just 20 minutes, and captive individuals have starved to death in less than an hour. They feed mainly on insects such as aphids and springtails and on spiders, all of which have relatively soft cuticles ('skins'), and these are often in very short supply during cold winters, when many kinglets perish.

The name 'kinglet' for the two North American species is often also used to describe the whole family (along with the alternatives 'crests' and 'regulids'). Along with the scientific name of the genus and family (from Latin *regulus* meaning 'little king'), it is derived from an old fable found in many different European cultures from Classical Greek times onwards concerning the election of the 'king of the birds'.

Although the eagle apparently flew higher than all the others, at the last moment a tiny bird hidden in its plumage flew up higher still, and was thus awarded the title of king instead of the eagle; this was said to be the smallest of birds, and its identity has variously been ascribed to the Eurasian Wren, *Troglodytes troglodytes*, and to the Goldcrest. There is also a kingly link in the appearance of the Goldcrest and the other species, which all have a gold, yellow or bright red crown. The Goldcrest was often known in the past as the Golden-crested Wren, but recent research suggests that, along with the other members of its family, it is neither related to wrens (Family Trogolodytidae) nor to the Old World warblers (Sylviidae), despite having frequently been included within the latter family. In fact, these little birds seem to represent an ancient lineage with no close relatives.

The two North American species, the Ruby-crowned Kinglet, *R. calendula*, and the Golden-crowned Kinglet, *R. satrapa*, are common and widespread breeders across most of Canada (though not in the north) and in southern Alaska, and also in the USA; there the Golden-crowned Kinglet has the more extensive range, breeding in a large area of the west and in many parts of the east, to as far south as the Appalachian mountains in Tennessee. After breeding, most Golden-crowned Kinglets from Canada migrate to winter in other parts of the USA, with some travelling as far as northeast Mexico, but populations breeding in the USA mostly stay put. There are also two races of Golden-crowned Kinglets that are resident breeders in the mountains of southern Mexico, with the range of one extending to Guatemala. The Ruby-crowned Kinglet breeds mainly in western and west-central USA, elsewhere only in the extreme northeast. It is less hardy than its Golden-crested relative, with a wintering range that extends much farther south, throughout Mexico and into Guatemala. The subspecies *obscurus*, endemic to Mexico's Guadalupe Island, was last recorded in 1953 and is now considered extinct. The Firecrest, *R. ignicapillus*, has a widespread range across Europe and east to Turkey and the Caucasus, as well as in parts of North Africa, but is less common than the Goldcrest, which breeds discontinuously from the far west of Europe and the Atlantic islands off Africa across central Russia and the Himalayas to as far east as Japan. As well as several races of the Goldcrest in the Canaries and Azores, there is a race of the Firecrest (*madeirensis*) often now regarded as a separate species, the Madeira Firecrest. The sixth species is also a very localised island form, the Flamecrest, *R. goodfellowi*, found only in the mountain forests of central Taiwan.

All species have a tiny, plump body, a big head and a short, needle-like bill, and have each nostril covered by a single stiff feather (or several bristles in the Ruby-crowned Kinglet). Plumage is olive green to grey-green (brightest green in the Firecrest and Flamecrest) with paler underparts (ranging from pale buff to brighter, silvery grey in the Firecrest and with bright yellow flanks, undertail and rump in the Flamecrest), with two pale wingbars on each wing. In all but the Ruby-crowned Kinglet (in which males have just a small scarlet crown patch and females none at all) there is a striking head pattern, with a black lateral stripe on either

ABOVE A Ruby-crowned Kinglet, *Regulus calendula*, hunts for tiny insects in the brush near in Stoney Creek, Ontario, Canada.

side of the central stripe, which is mainly bright yellow, orange-red and yellow or brilliant orange, depending on species (with females rather duller than males and juveniles lacking the pattern altogether). In the Flamecrest, Firecrest and Madeira Firecrest the pattern is more complex, with a white stripe above each eye and black through it and below it.

PALMCHAT Dulidae

GENERA: 1   **SPECIES:** 1

LENGTH: 20 cm (8 in)

WEIGHT: 42–52 g (1.5–1.8 oz)

RANGE AND HABITAT: Hispaniola and Gonave islands; various open habitats, from open woodland and woodland edges to scrub, gardens, parks and roadside trees; most abundant in lowland palm woods

SOCIAL BEHAVIOUR: highly gregarious throughout the year; nest and roost communally; each pair in its very big communal nests lives independently

NEST: a massive, domed structure of sticks, almost always sited in the high crown of the Royal Palm; the 10–50 or more nesting chambers, each occupied by a single pair, are roughly lined with strips of palm fronds and dried grass

EGGS: 2–7, very variable, from whitish or cream to beige or pale green, with darker markings

INCUBATION: about 15 days

FLEDGING PERIOD: about 32 days

FOOD: mainly fruits, especially of the Royal Palm, also of other palms and other trees or shrubs, flowers, leaves, insects

VOICE: noisy, especially at or near nests; very varied calls from cawing, gurgling and chattering, to more melodious whistling and cheeping; no real song identified

MIGRATION: sedentary

CONSERVATION STATUS: not threatened

The Palmchat, *Dulus dominicus*, is an odd bird that is usually placed in a family of its own. It is found only on Hispaniola, in both the nations that share this large Caribbean island, Haiti in the west and the Dominican Republic, which occupies a larger central and eastern area. It is the national bird of the Dominican Republic. Despite local fluctuations, it is one of the commonest of all Hispaniola's birds.

This family is one of only two endemic to the Caribbean; the other is that of the unrelated, non-passerine todies (Todidae). Recent genetic analysis supports the long held opinion that the Palmchat is most closely related to the waxwings, silky flycatchers and hypocolius, often previously included together as subfamilies in a larger Family Bombycillidae. The latest research also suggests that the Palmchat and these other birds are also related to another

ABOVE In the Dominican Republic, a Palmchat, *Dulus dominicus*, prepares to feed its two hungry fledglings.

ABOVE Although abundant and widespread, the Palmchat can be hard to see as it spends most of its time foraging high up in trees or palms.

enigmatic bird in a monotypic genus, *Hylocitrea bonensis*, previously placed in the whistler family, Pachycephalidae when it was known as the Olive-flanked Whistler (see Bombycillidae). Surprisingly, this is not a New World species like the Palmchat and most of the other bombicyllids (the whistlers being an exclusively old world family); it is endemic to the Indonesian island of Sulawesi. Finally, the Palmchat may be related to the five recently extinct Hawaiian species in the Family Mohoidae.

Looking rather like a cross between an Australasian figbird and a big, dull-plumaged tanager, the Palmchat is rather ungainly looking, with its short but deep, rather curved bill on a small head, and its long neck. Male and female look alike, plain olive brown on head and upperparts and pale buff below, boldly streaked with dark brown. The eyes are red.

The Palmchat is one of just a very few bird species that build many-chambered communal nests. Bulky affairs of sticks, these are commonly over 1 m (3 ft) in both diameter and height, and occasionally twice that size. Each pair typically accesses its own private nest compartment via an entrance tunnel 5–40 or more centimetres (2–16 or more inches) long, though some nests have a central 'hallway' off which the tunnels to the individual 'rooms' lead. In most cases the commune is occupied by four to 10 pairs, although the largest nests may be home to over 50 pairs. The nests, which may be used for several years, are repaired and added to throughout the year, and are used not only for egg laying and the rearing of families but also for roosting outside the breeding season. The nests are almost always sited in Royal Palms, *Roystonea hispaniola*, and the abundant fruit of this species forms the bird's staple diet (accounting for its common name). It takes some fruit from other palms and trees, and, unlike most birds, also seems to be partial to eating leaves and flowers. Its generic name is from the Greek word meaning 'a slave', apparently in reference to its subservient behaviour when challenged by the Grey Kingbird, *Tyrannus dominicensis*.

WAXWINGS Bombycillidae

GENERA: 1   **SPECIES:** 3

LENGTH: 15–23 cm (6–9 in)

WEIGHT: 32–85 g (1–3 oz)

RANGE AND HABITAT: North America, Central America, northern and eastern Europe, northern and eastern Asia, in coniferous and broadleaved open woodland or forest clearings with bushes and small trees; in winter often seen on more isolated berry-bearing bushes, including by streets in urban centres, and in parks and gardens

SOCIAL BEHAVIOUR: outside the breeding season almost always in flocks, which may be very large in winter; at least seasonally monogamous, and males defend mates against other males but not a breeding territory

NEST: a cup of small twigs, rootlets and grasses or other material, sited in a tree or shrub

EGGS: 2–7, usually 4 or 5, pale bluish grey with grey or blackish markings

INCUBATION: 11–17 days

FLEDGING PERIOD: 14–18 days

FOOD: mainly sugar-rich berries and other fruits, especially in autumn and winter, supplemented by insects, especially in spring and summer

VOICE: high-pitched trills, hissing whistles

MIGRATION: wholly or partly migratory, and in years when the fruit supply is poor in their usual range they make large-scale irruptions to find food

CONSERVATION STATUS: one species, the Japanese Waxwing, *Bombycilla japonica*, is Near Threatened

ABOVE A group of Bohemian Waxwings, *Bombycilla garrulus*, stuff berries into their mouths at top speed during winter in Finland.

This small family includes just the three species of waxwing, intensely gregarious, lively birds with a collective distribution right across the northern and temperate forests of the world, from the whole width of North America and Europe and Asia as far east as Japan. The most familiar species, the Bohemian Waxwing, *B. garrulus*, breeds in both northern Eurasia and North America, while the Cedar Waxwing, *B. cedrorum*, is restricted to North America, breeding not only in the north but also as far south in the USA as northern Calidfornia and Georgia. The Japanese Waxwing, *B. japonica*, despite its name, does not breed in Japan, although it winters throughout the Japanese islands and in eastern China and Korea; its breeding grounds lie in southeast Russia.

Like their close relatives, the silky flycatchers and Hypocolius, waxwings have soft, thick plumage and a crest; also they rely on fruit as a staple diet, and are able to pluck berries and drupes very quickly and swallow them whole. They supplement this with insects in the breeding season. These they catch both in the air and by gleaning from branches or foliage. Waxwings breed later in the year than most birds around them, mostly in summer, since they depend so greatly on fruit, more so than any other birds of temperate climes. Moreover, although they also provide them with some insects for their protein, they feed their young mainly on fruit; they are the only birds outside the tropics to do so.

It is surprising that they have a strong preference for fruits that are rich in sugars but low in other nutrients. These birds eat a wide range of fruits, many of them red ones; in the breeding season they include strawberries and mulberries early in summer, and raspberries, cherries and blueberries from midsummer onwards. In autumn and winter, Waxwings include a much wider range in their diet, but are especially fond of berries from rowan, hawthorn, holly, cotoneaster and pyracantha, as well as rose hips and crabapples. Juniper berries are especially important for Cedar Waxwings in America, where they can make up as much as 80% of their winter diet, while Japanese Waxwings are great consumers of mistletoe berries.

Waxwings have evolved a range of structural and behavioural adaptations for dealing with their high-fruit, high-sugar diet. These include the very wide gape of their bill and the broad gullet enabling them to eat relatively large fruit such as cherries whole and their short, strong legs and feet that give them good balance as they climb rapidly in a tree or shrub and reach up or down from a branch for a fruit or hang upside down to snatch it from above. In winter as the fruit dry they lose much of their water, so the birds must drink water or eat snow frequently to compensate. Because they contain few nutrients apart from the energy-providing sugars, the birds must eat prodigious amounts, at rates of up to three or more fruits every minute. A large winter flock produces a constant shower of droppings. These contain the undigested seeds, each coated in a gelatinous layer so that they resemble a string of pearls. Occasionally, waxwings become drunk when they have eaten fallen fruit that has fermented and produced alcohol, due to its high sugar content.

All three species are similar in appearance, with a short neck and stubby, slightly hook-tipped bill, a very short, square-ended tail, short legs with strong feet, and almost triangular, pointed wings. The head sports a prominent, jaunty, pointed crest and a striking black 'bandit mask' and black chin. They are very handsome birds, with luxuriously soft, dense, silky plumage that is mainly subtly varied shades of foxy brown, greyer brown and grey with paler underparts that are greyish on the Bohemian Waxwing, *Bombycilla garrulus*, and often with a yellow tinge to the belly on the other two species. The undertail is bright red in the Bohemian species and the Japanese Waxwing, *B. japonica*, and white in the smallest species, the exclusively New World Cedar Waxwing, *B. cedrorum*; the band at the end of the tail is yellow in that species and the Bohemian Waxwing, but red in the Japanese Waxwing, which also has a red patch on the wing coverts. The sexes look alike.

The feature that earned these birds their common name is the cluster of little bright red waxy tips that extend a short way from the tips of the adults' boldly marked black, white and yellow secondary flight feathers, looking like club-shaped blobs of sealing-wax. In the Japanese Waxwing they are rare and if present usually reduced to rudiments, and usually there are wax-like red or pink spots on the tips of the feather vanes instead. These odd appendages, which are unique among birds, seem to function as indicators of age.

After they have finished breeding – late in the year compared to most other birds, due to their reliance on fruit – the more northerly populations of waxwings move south, often using different areas from one year to the next. They tend to be highly nomadic, behaviour celebrated in the common name of the Bohemian Waxwing. Flocks roam from place to place, exhausting the supply of fruit in one area and then moving on in search of another. At irregular intervals, a major build-up of numbers in the breeding grounds lead to a shortage of food, and huge numbers leave to winter farther south than usual. They often then visit towns and cities, to take advantage of the bounty provided by berry-bearing trees planted by roadsides or in parks and gardens, as well as providing warmth for roosting. At such times, they delight people who may have never encountered these beautiful and unusual looking birds before, and are very approachable as they concentrate on gorging on berries.

Although the other two species are still common and widespread, the Japanese Waxwing is far more local and generally scarce, and is suspected to be declining in numbers. It faces threats from logging of the Russian forests it depends on for breeding, and maybe also from the pesticides used by fruit-growers, as well as trapping for the cagebird trade.

HYPOCOLIUS AND RELATIVES Hypocoliidae

GENERA: 2   **SPECIES**: 2

LENGTH: Hypocolius, 23 cm (9 in); Olive-flanked Whistler, 14–15 cm

WEIGHT: Hypocolius, 48–57 g (1.7–2 oz); Olive-flanked Whistler, unknown

RANGE AND HABITAT: Hypocolius, eastern Iraq, southern Iran, southern Turkmenistan and western Afghanistan and winters mainly in western and central Saudi Arabia, the Gulf States, southern Iran and southern Pakistan; breeds mainly in open woodland in river valleys fringed by desert or semi-desert, especially in date palm and poplar woods, with thorn trees such as acacias and tamarisk for nesting; more widespread outside breeding season; water supply important; Olive-flanked Whistler, north, central and southeast Sulawesi; montane forest, especially with plentiful moss

SOCIAL BEHAVIOUR: Hypocolius, gregarious year-round, especially outside the breeding season; socially monogamous, nesting in loose colonies of a few to as many as 40 pairs, each pair defending a territory around the nest; Olive-flanked Whistler, breeding details unknown, may join mixed species flocks when foraging

NEST: Hypocolius, a cup of small twigs, rootlets and grasses or other material in a tree or thorny shrub

EGGS: Hypocolius, 3–5, white to pale grey with dark grey or brown markings

INCUBATION: Hypocolius, 14 days

FLEDGING PERIOD: Hypocolius, 13–14 days

FOOD: Hypocolius, mainly fruits, especially those of the Toothbrush Tree, *Salvadora persica*, and often many dates, usually unharvested ones on the ground, as well as mulberries and the fruit of desert shrubs in the non-breeding season, also some insects; Olive-flanked Whistler, berries and some insects and spiders

VOICE: Hypocolius, a melodious, liquid three-note flight call, descending whistle, and loud continuous 'kirrr' calls during courtship displays; Olive-flanked Whistler, song of high-pitched buzzing notes, loud piping calls

MIGRATION: Hypocolius, a short-distance migrant, wintering mainly to the south and east of its breeding range; ; Olive-flanked Whistler, thought to be sedentary

CONSERVATION STATUS: neither is threatened

An enigmatic monotypic species, the Hypocolius (or Grey Hypocolius), *Hypocolius ampelinus*, has sometimes been placed in a subfamily (Hypocoliinae) of the waxwing family (Bombycillidae). It is related to the other members of the bombycillid group, but at present, it is not clear which of the constituent families (waxwings, silky flycatchers or palmchat) are its closest relatives.

A thrush-sized, sleek-bodied bird with a long, narrow tail, the Hypocolius is endemic to various parts of southwest Asia. It looks rather like a bulbul, and also resembles a *Lanius* shrike or one of the *Turdoides* babblers, but has other features similar to those of the waxwings. These include its short, stubby bill, and the short crest it creates when it is agitated by raising the feathers of its ear coverts and nape, as well as the black face mask of the male. Behavioural features in common with the waxwings and silky flycatchers are its habit of breeding in loose colonies and, as with waxwings, its intense gregariousness outside the breeding season, usually feeding or flying about with whirring wingbeats in small groups; its communal roosts may include as many as 500 birds.

Both sexes are mainly greyish, with a pale chin, into a short crest. The female's plumage is browner and she lacks the black mask on the male's face and his bold wing pattern of contrasting black primary feathers with white tips. Although it is often elusive and wary when breeding, it can be very tame and approachable at other times of the year. Because its range includes many countries ravaged by war, further details of this interesting bird's biology and lifestyle remain to be discovered.

Another far less well-known species, the Olive-flanked Whistler, *Hylocitrea bonensis*, is also here tentatively included in this family, pending further analysis that hopefully will provide more certainty as to its close relationships. Its established common name relates to the fact that it was until recently included in the whistler family Pachycephalidae, and earlier in the crow family Corvidae or with the Old World flycatchers and chats (Muscicapidae). It may be better to call it the Hylocitrea and to give it a family of its own, while recognising that it belongs to the bombycillid group and is probably most closely related to the Hypocolius. It is endemic to the Indonesian island of Sulawesi, where it lives in montane forests at altitudes of between 1200 m (3,900 ft) and 3,500 m (11,500 ft). A sparrow-sized bird, it has short legs, a short, thick neck and a short, broad based, slightly hook-tipped bill, and medium length, square-ended tail. Its plumage is drab and rather featureless, dull greyish with olive brown on the head, back and wings and yellowish olive flanks and undertail feathers; females have a grey-streaked cinnamon buff throat. Much remains to be learned about this little bird, including details of its breeding habits, which are unknown.

SILKY FLYCATCHERS Ptiliogonatidae

GENERA: 3   **SPECIES**: 4

LENGTH: 18–24.5 cm (7–9.5 in)

WEIGHT: 22–60 g (0.8–2 oz)

RANGE AND HABITAT: south-western USA, Mexico, Guatemala, Costa Rica, Panama; in montane forests and alpine pastures, deserts and riverside woods

SOCIAL BEHAVIOUR: the Black-and-yellow Silky Flycatcher, *Phainoptila melanoxantha*, is usually seen singly or in solitary pairs, at least in the breeding season, while the other three silky flycatcher species are mainly loosely gregarious

NEST: a bulky cup of small twigs, rootlets and grasses or other material, incorporating or consisting mostly of lichens or mosses in tropical species, bound with spiders' webs or caterpillar silk; usually sited in a fork of a tree or in a shrub

EGGS: usually 2 except for the Phainopepla, *Phainopepla nitens*, which lays 2–3 and very occasionally 4, pale grey or lilac with brown or lilac markings

INCUBATION: 14 days in the Phainopepla; 16–17 days in the Long-tailed Silky Flycatcher, *Ptilogonys caudatus*

FLEDGING PERIOD: 20 days in the Phainopepla; 24–25 days in the Long-tailed Silky Flycatcher

FOOD: mainly sugar-rich berries and other fruits, supplemented by insects; the Phainopepla eats the most fruit

VOICE: the Black-and-yellow Silky Flycatcher has weak, thin 'tsip' call or twittering; other silky flycatchers have a variety of loud calls, including clicking, churring, rattling, buzzing and whistling notes, and imitations of other bird calls, especially by the Phainopepla

MIGRATION: sedentary or make just short-distance movements either altitudinally or in the Phainopepla between different breeding habitats

CONSERVATION STATUS: none is threatened

Like their relatives the waxwings and Hypocolius, the birds in this very small family have thick plumage and except for one species, a crest. They rely on fruit as a staple diet, and are able to pluck berries and drupes very quickly and swallow them whole. They supplement this with insects in the breeding season. They often perch high up on the topmost branch of a bare tree to scan for passing insects, which they chase and catch in mid-air. They are particularly adept at aerial insect catching, turning and diving gracefully in pursuit of their prey. The four species have especially soft, silky plumage that accounts for the family's common name. Unlike the waxwings, they are restricted to the New World, where they occupy a relatively small range.

The Grey Silky Flycatcher, *Ptilogonys cinereus*, of Mexico and Guatemala, and the Long-tailed Silky Flycatcher, *P. caudatus*, of the highlands of Costa Rica and western Panama, are similar in size, although the latter has two elongated central tail feathers. Both have tall, plush, erectile crests. The Phainopepla, *Phainopepla nitens*, of Mexico and southwest USA is a smaller, more slender bird with a spiky-edged crest and bright red eyes. The Black-and-yellow Silky Flycatcher, *Phainoptila melanoxantha*, with a similar range to that of the Long-tailed Silky Flycatcher, is larger, bulkier and thrush-like in appearance if not plumage, without a crest, and differs in other ways from the rest of the family so that its inclusion has been questioned, though recent DNA results suggests that it is a close relative of the others. Differences between the sexes are relatively subtle, except for the Phainopepla, in which males are glossy jet black while females are grey.

The south-western US populations of Phainopepla are unusual in breeding in two completely different habitats at different times

RIGHT The Long-tailed Silky Flycatcher, *Ptilogonys caudatus*, usually perches high in the trees of its highland forest home.

of year: from October to mid-April, each pair defends its own separate territory in deserts, including the Sonora desert of Arizona, where they nest in spring; after this, by June or July, almost all have moved to breed again in riverside oak–sycamore woodlands, this time in loose colonies. Although it is uncertain whether the same individuals are involved, this may represent a strategy whereby the birds can raise two broods each year by alternating between habitats where major food sources reach a peak at different seasons. In the desert, they rely on Desert Mistletoe berries (which grow on the trees used for nesting and are thus easily defended by each pair), as well as insects. In the riparian woodlands, they depend on insects and then the fruits of Redberry, Sumac and Blue Elderberry.

The silky flycatchers are closely related to the waxwings (Bombycillidae). One of the most remarkable discoveries about bird relationships in recent years concerns an apparently very different group, the five species of Hawaiian birds that had always been regarded as belonging to the large honeyeater family (Meliphagidae) of Australasia. Four species, known as 'o'os (pronounced oh-oh's) are in the genus *Moho*, each on a different island of the Hawiian archipelago, and the fifth, the Kioea is in the genus *Chaetophila*. Sadly, all are now extinct, due to the depredations of introduced mammals, avian mosquito-borne diseases and hunting. The last

Kioea was seen in 1859, and the rest by the early twentieth century, apart from the Kauai O'o, *Moho braccatus*, which lingered on until the last sighting of a solitary male in 1985. So similar were these birds in morphology, behaviour and ecology, including their plumage (black and gold in the o'os and striped brown in the Kioea) and brush-tipped tongues adapted for nectar feeding, that not a single ornithologist had ever questioned that they were honeyeaters since the birds were first known to science after James Cook's third expedition visited Hawaii in 1778–9. It was only by the diligent work of researchers investigating the DNA extracted from museum specimens collected in Hawaii between 125 and 168 years ago that the true relationships of these striking birds with their long curved bills and long tails was revealed, with the amazing conclusion that they belong to a group (the bombycillids) of birds that bear no resemblance to them in appearance or lifestyle, including the palmchat, waxwings, Hypocolius and their closest relatives, the silky flycatchers. They are now posthumously accorded a family of their own, the Mohoidae, making them the only entire family of songbirds to have been rendered extinct during the last two centuries. This is one of the most extreme – and deceptive – examples of convergent evolution.

ELACHURAS Elachuridae

GENERA: 1 **SPECIES:** 1

LENGTH: 10 cm (4 in)

WEIGHT: not known

RANGE AND HABITAT: Himalayan foothills of northeast India and eastern Nepal, northeast Bangladesh, north and west Burma, southeast China, Laos and Vietnam; it lives in dense thickets in broadleaf evergreen subtropical and tropical hill and mountain forests, favouring thickets with dense growth of ferns rhododendrons and other plants, moss-covered rocks and rotting tree trunks, often near steep-sided streams or creeks

SOCIAL BEHAVIOUR: unknown

NEST: single nest described was a deep, partly domed cup of leaves, twigs, grass and other plant material, with a soft feather lining, sited on the ground among dense vegetation

EGGS: 3 or 4 in the nest described above

INCUBATION: unknown

FLEDGING PERIOD: unknown

FOOD: insects

VOICE: thin, high-pitched song and trilling call

MIGRATION: sedentary apart from some local downhill movements

CONSERVATION STATUS: not threatened

The tiny bird in this single-species family was formerly known as the Spotted Wren-Babbler, *Elachura formosa*, and included with various other species of wren-babblers in the genus *Spelaeornis* which with several different genera also known as wren-babblers, was contained in the very large original, polytypic babbler family Timaliidae. (This is now situated within a far smaller subset of the babblers, the tree-babbler family, which retains the name Timaliidae.)

The *Spelaeornis* wren-babblers are all very similar to one another, so there was no reason to suppose that this species was the odd one out, and although it was moved later into a different genus, *Elachura*, this was still considered closely related to *Spelaeornis*. But anomalous it has certainly proved to be, since recent molecular research has demonstrated that its true position is very far removed

from the babblers, and it belongs in the bombycillid group that includes the waxwings, silky-flycatchers, Hypocolius and another previously misplaced oddity, the Olive-flanked Whistler. The Elachura appears to represent an ancient basal lineage that diverged from the others at a very early date.

Its name is from the Greek words meaning 'short tail', and this is an accurate description; its wings are very short and rounded, and it has a big head on a very short, thick neck. It has a medium length, slim, sharply pointed bill and long legs with very long feet. The sexes look alike, with mainly brown plumage peppered with a constellation of tiny white spots and its rich russet wings and tail are barred with black. Its voice is unlike that of the other timaliid wren-babblers, with a song of very high-pitched tinkling notes and a call described as a spluttering trill.

TREECREEPERS Certhiidae

GENERA: 1   **SPECIES**: 9

LENGTH: 12–14 cm (5–5.5 in)

WEIGHT: 7.5–12.5 g (0.26–0.44 oz)

RANGE AND HABITAT: Europe, Asia and North America, except for the far north, with a single race (*mauretanica*) of one species, the Short-toed Treecreeper, *Certhia brachydactyla*, in northwest Africa; closely tied to woodlands and forests; rarely far from trees except for migrants while travelling

SOCIAL BEHAVIOUR: usually singly or in pairs, but in small family parties for 2–3 weeks after the young fledge and sometimes in small flocks on migration; at least three treecreeper species roost communally, and in winter all may join mixed-species feeding flocks of tits, nuthatches, kinglets and other small songbirds; Eurasian and American species are known to be usually monogamous and territorial

NEST: a loose, untidy structure of twigs, bark fragments, moss, lichen and other materials lined with feathers, animal hair, plant down, spiders' webs, cocoons and eggs and other softer material, all wedged in a hidden space, typically the tight gap between the trunk of a tree and a flap of loose, peeling bark

EGGS: 3–6 white eggs with reddish brown markings

INCUBATION: 12–20 days (usually 14–16); unknown for some species

FLEDGING PERIOD: 14–21 days for well-known species; otherwise unknown

FOOD: small insects, spiders and pseudoscorpions and their eggs and larvae; some small seeds and other plant matter, mainly in winter

VOICE: rather quiet calls and song, consisting of high-pitched whistles and trills, with more complex songs in some species, including sweet warbling notes

MIGRATION: most species are highly sedentary, but some individuals of northern breeders migrate south for winter, and south Asian species make altitudinal migrations

CONSERVATION STATUS: the Sichuan Treecreeper, *Certhia tianquanensis*, is Near Threatened

ABOVE The intricately marked, bark-like upperparts of this Eurasian Treecreeper, *Certhia familiaris*, provide camouflage as it shuffles up a tree trunk.

All nine species in this family are small brown-and-white arboreal songbirds. They are all intimately tied to wooded habitats, and are rarely encountered far from trees, as reflected in the word 'treecreeper'. All nine species are members of a single genus, *Certhia*. They all look extremely similar to one another, differing mainly in subtle details, notably the degree of streaking of the upperparts and the colour of the underparts.

The 'creeper' part of the names refers to the very distinctive habit of these birds of scurrying, mouselike, hopping with a jerky shuffling action up tree trunks and along larger branches. Usually, they fly to the base of the trunk, then work their way upwards in spirals around the trunk, then fly to the bottom of another nearby tree to repeat the process. Research on feeding habits of the Eurasian Treecreeper, *Certhia familiaris*, has revealed that females tend to forage mostly higher on tree trunks, while males usually remain lower down.

All members of the family have a large head with a rounded crown merging with no obvious neck into the slim body. The bill is very slender, laterally compressed and decurved, and ends in a sharp point. As they spiral up a tree, feeding birds continually thrust the fine bill into cracks and crevices in the bark to probe for insects and spiders. They have short legs and long toes ending in long, very sharp, curved claws, which give them a firm grip. The tail of all species has a distinctive frayed appearance, with long, pointed and stiffened feathers, and serves as a balancing prop as the bird braces it against the trunk. The unrelated Australasian treecreepers (Family Climacteridae, p. 232) also feed by spiralling up trees, placing one foot above the other and bringing the other up after it. The members of this family, by contrast, hold their feet parallel to one another when climbing, moving them simultaneously.

All members of the family have long, thick, soft plumage. The upperparts of treecreepers are brown or brownish-grey, intricately patterned with buff streaks and spots and darker brown and blackish bars and chevrons; the upperwings have prominent buff or whitish zigzag wing bars. The rump and tail are unpatterned and usually brighter or rufous in all but one species, the Bar-tailed Treecreeper, *C. himalayana*, in which it bears fine dark bars. The underparts are pale, bright silvery white in some species, greyish or with rusty tones, especially on the flanks, in others. The sexes look alike.

With their highly cryptic plumage, in which the upperparts blend into their usual background of tree bark, and high-pitched songs and calls, these subtly beautiful birds are unobtrusive and easily overlooked by the casual observer. For this reason, some of the less-well-known species may actually be rather more common than surveys suggest. However, all members of the family are subject to potential declines as a result of deforestation and the fragmentation and degradation of the old-growth woodlands that they prefer.

The best-known species are the Brown Creeper (also known as the American Treecreeper), *Certhia americana*, which is a widespread breeder from Alaska and northwest Canada across

Canada and south through the western and eastern USA to as far as northern Central America (and even more widespread as a winter visitor) and the two common Eurasian ones, the more widespread Eurasian Treecreeper, whose range extends from the British Isles to as far east as Japan, and the Short-toed Treecreeper, *C. brachydactyla*, in western Europe, northwest Africa and south-west Asia. Three forms from the Himalayas and southern China that have traditionally been regarded as subspecies of the Eurasian Treecreeper are now regarded as constituting a full species: Hodgson's Treecreeper, *C. hodgsoni*. There are five other species from central and southern Asia, the Bar-tailed Treecreeper, *C. himalayana*, the Rusty-flanked Treecreeper, *C. nipalensis*, the Sichuan Treecreeper, *C. tianquanensis*, the Sikkim Treecreeper, *C. discolor*, and the Manipur Treecreeper, *C. manipurensis*.

NUTHATCHES, WALLCREEPER AND SPOTTED CREEPERS Sittidae

GENERA: 3   **SPECIES**: 28

LENGTH: 11 cm (4.25 in) to 19.5 cm (almost 8 in)

WEIGHT: 9 g to 47 g (0.33 to 1.6 oz)

RANGE AND HABITAT: nuthatches, *Sitta*, in Eurasia, North Africa and North America; the greatest diversity is found in southern Asia (15 species); the Wallcreeper, *Tichodroma muraria*, lives in the mountains of Eurasia, from Spain to China; one of the two species of spotted creepers, *Salpornis*, is in Africa and the other in India; spotted creepers in open woodland; nuthatches live mostly in forests and woodlands of various types with two species among rocks; the Wallcreeper is a high-mountain specialist

SOCIAL BEHAVIOUR: socially monogamous and strongly territorial; two species, the Pygmy Nuthatch, *Sitta pygmaea*, and Brown-headed Nuthatch, *S. pusilla*, are cooperative breeders; usually seen singly or in pairs, though some species of nuthatch as well as the two spotted creepers (and occasionally the Wallcreeper) form small flocks outside the breeding season

NEST: nuthatches nest in a hole in a tree or rock, often reduced in size by dried mud; the nest chamber is lined with a variety of materials, from bark flakes or seed wings to grass, moss, feathers and hair; the Wallcreeper nests in a crevice in a rock face, or among rocks, often close to a waterfall, sometimes with two entrances; it builds a nest of moss, lichen, pine needles, grass and roots, lined with hair, wool, feathers and rootlets; spotted creepers build a superbly camouflaged neat cup nest of flower and leaf stalks, bark chips and rootlets lined with softer material, siting it in the open, on a tree fork

EGGS: usually 4–8 in nuthatches, white with reddish, brown or lilac spots; 3–5 in the Wallcreeper, white with dark red to blackish spots; spotted creepers lay 1–3 pale greyish, greenish or bluish eggs with darker markings

INCUBATION: 14–18 days in nuthatches; 18.5–20 days in the Wallcreeper; no information for spotted creepers

FLEDGING PERIOD: 12–18 days in nuthatches; 28.5–30 days in the Wallcreeper; no information for spotted creepers

FOOD: insects, other invertebrates such as spiders and snails, seeds and nuts for nuthatches; insects, spiders and other invertebrates for the Wallcreeper and spotted creepers

VOICE: very vocal, with loud whistling, piping and trilling calls; songs simple combinations of similar sounds

MIGRATION: no species is a regular migrant; some nuthatches make irregular invasive movements in winter; the Wallcreeper usually moves downslope in winter, with a few wandering farther away

CONSERVATION STATUS: three species, the Algerian Nuthatch, *S. ledanti*, the Giant Nuthatch, *S. magna*, and the White-browed Nuthatch, *S. victoriae* (and also the race *insularis* of the Brown-headed Nuthatch, *S. pusilla*, often regarded as a separate species, the Bahama Nuthatch), are Endangered; two species, the Beautiful Nuthatch, *S. formosa*, and the Corsican Nuthatch, *S. whiteheadi*, are Vulnerable; two species are Near Threatened

ABOVE A male Wallcreeper, *Tichodroma muraria*, graces a cliff with its exquisite presence in the Great Caucasus, Georgia, in April.

This small family of distinctive birds is currently divided into three subfamilies. The first and by far the largest is that of the nuthatches, Sittinae. These small, compact-bodied, large headed, short-necked and short-tailed birds are almost all forest or woodland dwellers. Most species are sparrow sized, at about 12–15 cm (4.75–6 in) long, but one, the Pygmy Nuthatch, *Sitta pygmaea*, is significantly smaller, at 11 cm (4.25 in) long only the size of a small warbler, and one, the Giant Nuthatch, *S. magna*, is four times its weight, and at 19.5 cm (almost 8 in) nearly twice as long, the size of a small thrush. As well as the distinctive proportions of their head, body and tail, all species share other features: short, broad wings, a square end to the tail, and a longish, strong, pointed bill.

The upperparts of many species are blue-grey or violet-blue, while the underparts may be white, buff, orange or chestnut; some have contrasting white spots on the undertail feathers, and most have a prominent black stripe through the eye, sometimes set off by a pale stripe over the eye or a black cap. Males are usually somewhat brighter.

LEFT The Eurasian Nuthatch, *Sitta europaea*, is a highly sedentary bird of mature deciduous and mixed woodland.

RIGHT The White-breasted Nuthatch, *Sitta carolinensis*, is widespread in North America, from southwest Canada to southern Mexico.

Nuthatches are agile climbers, with strong legs and large, powerful toes equipped with long sharp claws, and spend most of their life on trees (or, in some species, rocks). The scientific name of the single genus (*Sitta*) and family (Sittidae) come from the Greek word *sitte*, used by Aristotle and other Ancient Greek writers for a bird like a woodpecker, but they are not related to woodpeckers. While other tree-climbing birds, such as woodpeckers and treecreepers, move upwards (or sometimes short distances downwards tail first), nuthatches are able to travel down tree trunks head-first with the same ease and speed as they ascend them. Unlike the woodpeckers and treecreepers, which climb with feet more or less parallel, nuthatches do not have stiffened tail feathers that they press against the bark to use as a prop. Instead, they place one leg high to hang from, and the other one low, for support, and hold their short tails away from the trunk as they move.

Some species are widely distributed: examples are the Eurasian Nuthatch, *S. europaea*, found from Portugal and North Africa to far eastern Russia and Japan, and the White-breasted Nuthatch, *S. carolinensis*, which occurs over much of North America. Others are very local, even to the extent of being restricted to small mountain ranges, like the Corsican Nuthatch, *S. whiteheadi*, and Algerian Nuthatch, *S. ledanti*, – the latter was not known to science until 1976.

All but two species are forest dwellers, preferring mature woodland, either broadleaved or coniferous (or mixed) at various altitudes, where they can find natural tree holes for nesting, take over those abandoned by woodpeckers, or excavate their own in rotten wood. As their name suggests, the two rock nuthatches, the Western Rock Nuthatch, *S. neumayer*, and the Eastern Rock Nuthatch, *S. tephronota*, have forsaken the tree-dwelling niche and do their climbing on bare rocks, where they nest in crevices. The Eurasian Nuthatch and relatives plaster around the nest hole with mud to reduce the size of the entrance, leaving just enough space for them to get in and out, so as to discourage predators and rivals for the nest site, while rock nuthatches build a mud tube leading to their mud-fringed nest crevice.

The common family name comes from the habit of the Eurasian Nuthatch of hacking at nuts with its powerful bill to open them; it usually wedges them in a tree crevice. The other species, too, treat hard-coated food, including seeds and insects as well as nuts, in a similar way: unlike tits, they do not use a foot to hold them down. Most nuthatches store large numbers of food items singly in crevices. Three North American species are among the few birds known to use a tool. The Brown-headed Nuthatch, *S. pusilla*, sometimes uses a bark scale to lever up bark to get at insects hiding beneath, while the Pygmy Nuthatch has been seen using a twig to probe the bark. The Red-breasted Nuthatch, *S. canadensis*, uses a bark scale – not for obtaining food but for smearing the entrance to its nest hole with sticky tree resin, to deter predators.

The subfamily Tichodromadinae contains just a single species, the Wallcreeper, *Tichodroma muraria*. This is one of the most beautiful of all mountain birds, charmingly known as the 'rock flower' in Chinese. Its plumage is mainly soft grey (with dull black on throat and breast in the male during the breeding season), adorned with large bright crimson patches on the wings. These are most noticeable when the bird flicks its wings, which it does constantly when foraging, and especially in flight, when large white spots are also visible on the long, broad wings. Its fluttery, jerky flight makes it look like a huge butterfly. Although it may be tolerant of humans, it is often elusive, remaining high on a sheer rock face or disappearing from view behind a rock. This charismatic bird, always one of the most sought after by birdwatchers, breeds at high altitudes in mountains, where it is local and generally uncommon. It descends to lower levels, including valleys, in winter, and it may then turn up in vicinity of buildings, even in towns, as well as on cliffs.

Recently added to this family following DNA analysis as a third subfamily, Salpornithinae, are the two species of spotted creepers, *Salpornis*. They were previously included as a single distinctive species within the treecreeper Family Certhiidae (see p. 373), but they are now known to be more closely related to the nuthatches and the single species with a very disjunct range in both Africa and India has been divided into two species. The African Spotted Creeper, *S. salvadori*, is found from Gambia east to southern Ethiopia, and south to Zimbabwe, while its close relative, the Indian Spotted Creeper, *S. spilonota*, occurs from Rajasthan in the north-west and in central India.

Like the nuthatches, but unlike the treecreepers, the spotted creepers lack the distinctive frayed tail of long, pointed stiffened feathers used as a brace when spiralling up tree trunks; their tails are short and rather rounded, but they are still efficient climbers. Indeed, they are, along with their recently recognised closest relatives the nuthatches, unique in being the only birds that can climb head-first down tree-trunks as well as up them. Both species are very strikingly patterned, having a dark brownish-grey ground colour with large cream or whitish spots almost all over, and a broadly banded pale and dark tail.

WRENS Troglodytidae

GENERA: 19   **SPECIES**: 82

LENGTH: 9–22 cm (3.5–8.5 in)

WEIGHT: 6–57 g (0.2–2 oz)

RANGE AND HABITAT: all but one species are found only in the New World, from southern Canada to the southernmost tip of South America and the Falkland Islands; the exception is the Eurasian Wren, *Troglodytes troglodytes*, found right across Eurasia and in North Africa; forests, woodlands, scrublands, marshes, rocky terrain (including on offshore islands), desert and semi-desert scrub, marshes and reed beds; a few in gardens and other habitats with cover even in large cities

SOCIAL BEHAVIOUR: mostly seen singly, in pairs or family parties; most species, especially tropical ones, are monogamous and territorial, though some (including the Eurasian Wren and the Marsh Wren, *Cistothorus palustris*, of North America) are partially polygamous and some are cooperative breeders; temperate zone species also often keep warm in cold weather by roosting packed tightly together in nests, nest boxes, natural holes or cavities in buildings, with up to 96 Eurasian Wrens together in Europe

NEST: small, domed or roofed, with side entrances, built of grass, leaves, moss and other plant material, lined with feathers and animal hair, and usually sited among vegetation or in cavities of many sorts, from tree holes in woodland species to piles of rocks in desert dwellers; unusually, males of some species build many (up to 20 or so) nests, only one of which will be chosen and completed by the female and used to rear the family

EGGS: usually 2–3 in many tropical species, 3–8 in temperate ones; often white, but can be pale blue, bluish-green or even deep sky blue, and marked or unmarked, often with variation within a single genus, species or even subspecies

INCUBATION: 12–20 days

FLEDGING PERIOD: 14–19 days

FOOD: mainly insects and spiders, also other invertebrates, such as small snails; some larger species also take smallish lizards, snakes and frogs, and some species include seeds and fruit in their diet

VOICE: calls generally loud, ranging from harsh churring to whistling and other sounds; songs are usually complex and very loud for the size of the bird, with whistling and extremely rapid trilling as well as less musical notes; females sing and duet in many tropical species

MIGRATION: most are sedentary, although a few make long migrations

CONSERVATION STATUS: three species, Niceforo's Wren, *Thryothorus nicefori*, the Santa Marta Wren, *Troglodytes monticola*, and the Munchique Wood Wren, *Henicorhina negreti*, are Critically Endangered; three species, Apolinar's Wren, *Cistothorus apolinari*, the Antioquia Wren, *Thryophilus sernai*, and the Zapata Wren, *Ferminia cerverai*, are Endangered; two species, Nava's Wren, *Hylorchilus navai*, and Clarion Wren, *Troglodytes tanneri*, are Vulnerable; five species are Near Threatened

RIGHT The loudness of the song of the Eurasian Wren, *Troglodytes troglodytes* – a brief, explosive rattling trill – is out of all proportion to the bird's diminutive size. It can on occasion carry for almost 1 km (0.5 miles).

This large family is almost entirely restricted to the New World, with only one species, the Eurasian Wren, *Troglodytes troglodytes*, in most of Eurasia and parts of North Africa. With no other wrens in the Old World, this little bird is often known simply as *the* Wren in the British Isles. This was until recently known as the Northern Wren, with a vast range not only including the Old World but also North America. In North America, evidence from DNA and song differences has led to its split into two further species, the Winter Wren, *T. hiemalis*, which is largely a winter visitor only to eastern USA from its mainly Canadian breeding range, and the Pacific Wren, *T. pacificus*, in western Canada and USA. The greatest diversity of wren species is in Central America and northwest South America. The gnatcatchers and gnatwrens (Polioptilidae), treecreepers (Certhiidae) and nuthatches (Sittidae) are their closest relatives.

Most wren species are small and remain for much of the time well hidden in dense cover, although they are often not particularly shy and many species may emerge briefly to sing or examine a human observer. They are usually most noticed by their very loud, often long and complex songs, which in many tropical species (in which females sing far more often than in temperate species) are delivered in duets by pairs. The songs of some of these are especially beautiful, as celebrated in the common names of four Neotropical species – the Flutist Wren, *Microcerculus ustulatus*, the Nightingale Wren, *M. philomela*, the Song Wren, *Cyphorhinus phaeocephalus*, and the Musician Wren, *C. arada*. All feature haunting, melancholy-sounding, pure-toned whistling notes. In the case of the *Cyphorhinus* species, these are interspersed with guttural notes, and pairs often duet.

Wrens are generally very active birds that spend a great deal of time foraging for insect food in cover, usually near or on the ground (although a few species are tree dwellers). The typical wren has a big head and plump, rotund body, and short, broad wings, with a fast whirring flight. The tail is usually short, and is very short in some species, such as those in the genus *Troglodytes*, including the Eurasian, Winter and Pacific Wrens and the House Wren, *T. aedon*, common in the USA. These and other species have a very distinctive habit of holding their tail stiffly upright or even pointing forwards over the back. The bill is slender and with as fine pointed tip, generally quite long and in many species slightly decurved.

Plumage is soft and dense and generally in various shades of brown, ranging from cold grey brown to rich reddish-brown, with smaller patches of grey, fawn, black and white. A few species are mainly black and white and a single, very distinctive species, the White-headed Wren, *Campylorhynchus albobrunneus*, is entirely black (on the upperparts and tail) and white. Many are extensively patterned with dark brown or black bars or spots; unusually for passerines, the tail is often barred. The sexes look alike, and there is often little difference between adults and juvenile birds. In a

LEFT A Carolina Wren, *Thryothorus ludovicianus*, broadcasts its melodious bubbling song in Cape May, New Jersey, USA.

few species, such as the Spotted Wren, *Campylorhynchus gularis*, of Mexico, the juvenile is easily distinguished, and others have more subtle differences between adult and juvenile, recognisable when the birds are examined in the hand by ringers (known in North America as banding). An example is seen in the Eurasian Wren, in which the barring on the wings and tail of juveniles is more or less continuous, reflecting the simultaneous growth of the feathers, whereas on adults the bars are staggered, as feathers are replaced at different times.

The 13 long-tailed species in the genus *Campylorhynchus* include species of arid or semi-arid areas, such as the Cactus Wren, *C. brunneicapillus*, of south-western USA and Mexico, or the Fasciated Wren, *C. fasciatus*, of Peru and Ecuador, but also species (such as the Grey-barred Wren, *C. megalopterus*, of highlands in Mexico or the White-headed Wren, *C. albobrunneus*, of Panama and extreme northwest Colombia) that inhabit humid forest. *Campylorhynchus* species are large (for wrens), and include the biggest member of the family, the Giant Wren, *C. chiapensis*, which has a restricted range in the Pacific lowlands of Chiapas, southern Mexico. Even this 'giant' is only about the size of a small thrush, at 20–22 cm (8–8.5 in) and a weight of up to 57 g (2 oz).

The single species in the genus *Salpinctes*, the Rock Wren, *S. obsoletus*, is a common species in much of western North America and also in Central America, in suitable habitat – which, as its name suggests, consists of hillsides with boulders and stones, quarries and other rocky landscapes. Also a bird of rocky terrain, in this case requiring rock faces, such as those found on inland cliffs or canyons, or ruined buildings, is the Canyon Wren, *Catherpes mexicanus*, another bird of western North America. Another group of wrens, in the genus *Cistothorus*, live among dense vegetation in damp habitats such as marshes, bogs, lakesides and wet fields. They include two North American species, the Sedge Wren, *C. platensis*, and the Marsh Wren, *C. palustris*. Yet another well-known North American species is Bewick's Wren, *Thryomanes bewickii*, which is a very adaptable bird that is equally at home in suburban scrub, farmland and woodland, and in Mexico also lives in arid cactus scrub and city parks. The Zapata Wren, *Ferminia cerverai*, by contrast, is an Endangered species restricted to just one small area of the swamp in western Cuba from which it takes its name.

Also familiar is the Carolina Wren, *Thryothorus ludovicianus*, which has adapted to life in such altered habitats as suburban parks and gardens and abandoned farmland. The large genus *Pheugopedius* includes the delightfully named Happy Wren, *P. felix*, from Mexico. This is one of several wren species that often site their nests in a thorny acacia shrub defended by belligerent *Pseudomyrmicus* ants or next to a hornet nest: in both cases the aggressive reaction of the insects to intruders helps provide protection from predators, such as monkeys. Other unusual wren nests include those of the Rock Wren, which have a foundation of stones. The accumulation of many pebbles or small flat stones can weigh as much as 2.2 kg (4.9 lb), over 120 times the bird's weight, and the largest stones moved by the little bird, at up to 6 g (0.2 oz), can account for about a third of its weight.

GNATCATCHERS AND GNATWRENS Polioptilidae

GENERA: 3   **SPECIES:** 15

LENGTH: 9–13 cm (3.5–5 in)

WEIGHT: 5–14 g (0.2–0.5 oz)

RANGE AND HABITAT: North America, Mexico, Central America, Caribbean islands, much of South America; some in forests and woodlands, others in arid or semi-arid scrublands

SOCIAL BEHAVIOUR: usually in pairs; gnatwrens often join mixed-species foraging flocks in tropical forest understorey; monogamous and territorial

NEST: small, deep cup of grass, leaves and other vegetation, bound with spiders' webs or caterpillar silk, lined with feathers, animal fur and plant down, and often camouflaged on the outside with lichens; often sited in a tree or shrub

EGGS: pale blue or greenish-blue with fine red-brown speckling

INCUBATION: about 14 days

FLEDGING PERIOD: about 14 days

FOOD: almost entirely insects (occasionally includes gnats!) and spiders

VOICE: calls mainly rasping or mewing; songs include soft, prolonged medleys of whistles, nasal notes, chips and trills and much louder, simpler repetitions of sounds like calls, sometimes uttered almost constantly

MIGRATION: most are sedentary, but the Blue-grey Gnatcatcher, *Polioptila caerulea*, makes regular southward migrations for winter

CONSERVATION STATUS: one species, the Creamy-bellied Gnatcatcher, *P. lactea*, is Near Threatened

This small, exclusively New World family consists of species known as gnatcatchers (all 12 species of which are classified within the genus *Polioptila*) and gnatwrens (placed in two genera, *Microbates*, with just

two species, and *Ramphocaenus*, with a single species, the Long-billed Gnatwren, *R. melanurus*). There are just four species in the USA: one (the Blue-grey Gnatcatcher, *Polioptila caerulea*) is common and

LEFT A Blue-grey Gnatcatcher, *Polioptila caerulea*, pauses on a branch of a redbud tree in Long Point, Ontario, Canada.

RIGHT This Long-billed Gnatwren, *Ramphocaenus melanurus*, is at its roost in the Amazon rainforest, Peru.

widespread, the other three (Black-capped, California and Black-tailed Gnatcatchers, *P. nigriceps*, *P. californica*, and *P. melanura*) are Mexican species that just extend into the south-western USA, and have very restricted distributions there. A bird with an extremely small total range and a tiny population was described in 2005 as the Iquitos Gnatcatcher, *P. clementsi*, although it is currently regarded as a subspecies of the Guianan Gnatcatcher, *P. guianensis*. It is known only from a newly established nature reserve in northwest Peru, where it is threatened by deforestation. Another subspecies of the same species, named *attenboroughi* for the great broadcaster Sir David Attenborough, was discovered even more recently, in 2013. It, too, was previously classified as a full species, with the common name of Inambari Gnatcatcher. Some authorities recognise both these as having specific rank.

Previously, the gnatwrens were at first not even considered to belong the major, songbird, subgroup of the passerine order, but were thought to be antbirds. When the Long-billed Gnatwren was found to possess a typical oscine syrinx ('voice box'), they were regarded as New World representatives of the Old World warblers (in the original very large Family Sylviidae). The gnatcatchers, on the other hand, were placed by different workers in various songbird families, including the Old World warblers and the mockingbirds and thrashers (Mimidae); they were even considered by some authorities to be closely allied to the tits (Parulidae), kinglets (Regulidae) or parrotbills (Paradoxornithidae). Genetic research reveals that all these schemes are misleading and that the group deserves a family of its own, closely related to the wrens (Troglodytidae).

Very small songbirds, all but two species in the family have a long, graduated tail that they frequently cock upright or at an angle and flick from side to side. The tail is much shorter in the two *Microbates* gnatwrens, especially the Tawny-faced Gnatwren, *M. cinereiventris*, which has a very short, stubby tail. All have a slender, pointed insect-eating bill, which in most species is of medium length; that of the gnatwrens is far longer, especially in the Long-billed Gnatwren. The gnatwrens are particularly tiny birds, with a body that is among the shortest of all passerines, although their plumper body does help to make them about double the weight of the gnatcatchers.

The *Polioptila* gnatcatchers all have similar plumage: grey above and pale grey or white below (with a brown wash in the female California Gnatcatcher and creamy yellow underparts in the Creamy-bellied Gnatcatcher, *P. lactea*). Males have a black tail with white outer feathers, and in many species also a black hood, crown or eye-patch, which are lacking or reduced in the females. A few others are largely plain grey, with no difference between the sexes. The Collared Gnatwren, *Microbates collaris*, is brown above with a brown crown and striped black-and-white head and pale underparts divided by a black breastband, while the Tawny-faced Gnatwren has rusty orange cheeks, and black breast streaks and is darker grey beneath. Some races of the Long-billed Gnatwren, *Ramphocaenus melanurus*, are all-brown, while others are grey above.

OXPECKERS Buphagidae

GENERA: 1 **SPECIES:** 2

LENGTH: 20 cm (8 in)

WEIGHT: 40–70 g (1.4–2.5 oz)

RANGE AND HABITAT: widespread in parts of sub-Saharan Africa, in open habitats from grassland to savannah, where there are large ungulate mammals; the Yellow-billed Oxpecker, *Buphagus africanus*, is found mainly in West Africa, and the Red-billed Oxpecker, *Buphagus erythrorhynchus*, is a bird of East Africa, from Ethiopia to South Africa

SOCIAL BEHAVIOUR: socially monogamous; pairs breed cooperatively, with one to six extra helpers (mostly siblings but sometimes unrelated adults) feeding young (and sometimes collecting nest material too)

NEST: usually in a tree hole but sometimes in other cavities, such as holes in walls, lining the base with dry grass and hair from host mammals

EGGS: 2–3 (occasionally up to 5 in the Red-billed Oxpecker), very pale blue or pink, heavily speckled with reddish brown, lilac grey, pink or maroon and sometimes also blotched grey or lavender

INCUBATION: about 13 days

FLEDGING PERIOD: 25–30 days

FOOD: exclusively from on or about hosts, mainly ticks, also other ectoparasites including fly larvae and leeches and insects caught in flight, also some blood and dead skin, mucus from the nostrils or eyes of their hosts and ear wax

VOICE: trilling and whistling notes and buzzing flight-calls; sharp hissing alarm calls

MIGRATION: essentially sedentary

CONSERVATION STATUS: neither is threatened

ABOVE Both species of oxpeckers are often seen on the backs and heads of zebras; this is a Yellow-billed Oxpecker, *Buphagus africanus*.

This fascinating species pair of birds have often been included in the starling Family Sturnidae as a distinctive genus or subfamily. Recent molecular research confirms that the two groups are indeed close relatives, but it shows that the oxpeckers are equally close to the mockingbirds and thrashers (Family Mimidae, p. 380). It indicates that they should be placed in a family of their own, which is sister to both the other families.

Both the Yellow-billed Oxpecker, *Buphagus africanus*, and Red-billed Oxpecker, *B. erythrorhynchus*, have very similar plumage, dull olive brown to olive grey on the head, back, wings and tail and on the chest, shading to pale buff on the lower breast; as their common names indicate, the main difference is in the colour of the bill. That of the Red-billed species is entirely bright red, while the Yellow-billed Oxpecker's bill is actually bicoloured, yellow at the base and red at the end. Both species have a red, orange or yellow iris (the colours may be controlled by the birds depending on mood) and the eye is ringed by a fleshy granular wattle of bare skin, bright yellow in the Red-billed species and plain brown in the Yellow-billed Oxpecker.

As suggested by their common name (and the generic name too, for 'buphagus' is Greek for 'beefeater'), oxpeckers do peck the skins of cattle while riding on them, though they are also commonly found on a wide range of wild ungulate mammals, too. The reason they do so, however, is not to eat flesh, but to feed on the often abundant insects that parasitize their hosts. Their favourite prey are ticks (which they can eat at a rate of up to 100 adult ticks or over 13,000 larvae per day), but they also devour avian mites and lice, leeches and fly larvae taken from the host as well as making brief flights to catch aerial insects.

They have a unique lifestyle in that their whole lives are intimately tied up with that of their large mammal hosts. Other birds, including starlings, magpies and jackdaws, perch on the backs of cattle, sheep or wild grazing mammals, and pick off insect parasites, while cattle egrets walk among them and bee-eaters ride on the backs of big Kori Bustards, *Ardeotis kori*, darting out to snap up the insects they disturb, but none spend virtually all of their waking lives apart from when at the nest attached to their hosts. They may fly off at day's end in flocks to roost in trees or reedbeds, but have also been seen to remain sleeping on the backs of their hosts. They also defecate without leaving the host, taking care to hold their tail up and spray their waste well away from its body.

As would be expected for such birds with such a specialised lifestyle, oxpeckers have evolved a suite of anatomical adaptations that help them remain securely on their host and feed efficiently. Their legs and feet are specialised for hopping (and sometimes walking) about on their hosts. They are adept at moving forwards, sideways or backwards, and climb about on the host's body, head and legs with ease. Their legs are short, like those of woodpeckers, nuthatches and other specialist climbers, giving them good balance, and have a muscle arrangement that maximises the grasping power of the feet. Their claws too, resemble those of tree-climbing birds, being very sharp and fine tipped to help them grip the host's thick hide for a safe ride, even when it is moving about when feeding or running. Their tail feathers are stiff and pointed, just like that of woodpeckers, providing a prop for a secure support when moving. The bill is stout, rather bulbous at the centre, and flattened from side to side, and is used for feeding in two different ways. In the first, the oxpecker lays it on one side flat against the host's skin and then opens and closes it in a rapid snipping action like a pair of scissors. The second technique involves simply plucking the insect out using the tip of the bill, aided by powerful jaw muscles. This is used mainly on hosts such as hippos or rhinos with smooth skin, whereas the bird switches to the scissoring technique when visiting long-haired mammals. The greatest concentrations of insects are usually to be found on the host's head and ears or around its eyes, and this is where the birds concentrate their attention, helping the host as they can access these areas it cannot reach by itself.

Usually, instead of flying off to drink and bathe like other songbirds, they wait until the host goes down to a river or a water-hole to drink, then run down the mammal's leg until low enough to reach out and take a few sips of water without leaving it, though they may do so briefly to bathe, but return to the host to dry off. They have also been seen sunbathing on a rhinoceros's back with spread wings and tail.

Some observers have suggested that as well as benefitting their hosts by removing their burden of blood-sucking and disease-carrying or egg-laying parasites, they may instead act partly as oversized ectoparasites themselves by worrying at wounds. Also, some researchers think that they may not make much of a difference to the parasite burden suffered by their hosts. It is true that various large mammals, such as elephants and most species of antelope, reject them by dislodging them with their tail, trunk or horns, or even by rolling on the ground. They have also been seen feeding at carcases, and in captivity thrive on raw minced meat. But although they will take a little blood, for instance from the large wounds found on hippopotamuses after fights between rivals, they do not appear to impede wound healing, and their hosts seem to tolerate or even welcome their attentions. And they also perform a service to their hosts of alerting them to predators such as lions or leopards and human hunters, since the mammals recognize their alarm calls and respond by taking evasive action. And even though oxpeckers do sometimes open new wounds on cattle to feed on their blood, causing local problems for farmers, their relationship with their wild hosts does seem generally truly symbiotic.

Although neither species is currently threatened, there have been serious declines in some parts of their range as a result of the hunting of the game mammals on which they depend and also the use of toxic chemicals used by farmers to control ticks on cattle. Reintroduction programmes coupled with the promotion of less toxic pesticides have helped greatly.

MOCKINGBIRDS & THRASHERS Mimidae

GENERA: 10   **SPECIES:** 34

LENGTH: 19–32 cm (7.5–12.5 in)

WEIGHT: 23–142 g (0.8–5 oz)

RANGE AND HABITAT: the New World, from southern Canada to extreme southern South America; open woodland, scrub and desert or semi-desert

SOCIAL BEHAVIOUR: usually solitary or in pairs; most are territorial and monogamous, with the sexes playing a more or less equal part in defence, nest building, incubation and rearing the young

NEST: a big, bulky cup of twigs, grass and plant fibres, usually on the ground or in a shrub, less often in a tree at up to 15 m (50 ft) high, or in a cactus in desert species

EGGS: 2–6, whitish, pale or darker green or blue, sometimes very bright, often heavily blotched or streaked darker

INCUBATION: usually 12–14 days

FLEDGING PERIOD: usually 12–14 days

FOOD: insects, spiders, worms and other invertebrates, especially in the breeding season, also fruits, berries, seeds, with more eaten in the non-breeding season

VOICE: varied, often loud, calls, including whistling, mewing and harsher notes; songs typically loud and complex, including warbling or scratchy notes, and mimicry of other birds in many species

MIGRATION: mostly sedentary, although the Canadian and northern US populations of several species winter south, to as far as Mexico

CONSERVATION STATUS: two species, the Socorro Mockingbird, *Mimodes graysoni*, and Cozumel Thrasher, *Toxostoma guttatum*, are Critically Endangered; three species, the Floreana Mockingbird, *Nesomimus trifasciatus*, San Cristobal Mockingbird, *Nesomimus melanotis*, and White-breasted Thrasher, *Ramphocinclus brachyurus*, are Endangered; two species, the Española Mockingbird (or Hood Island Mockingbird), *Mimus macdonaldi*, and Bendire's Thrasher, *Toxostoma bendirei*, are Vulnerable; one species the Black Catbird, *Melanoptila glabrirostris*, is Near Threatened

This New World family has its greatest diversity in the south-western USA and Mexico, and also in northern Central America, as well as on some islands off both Atlantic and Pacific coasts of these regions.

Most species are placed in two genera: *Mimus* and *Toxostoma*. The 14 species of *Mimus* mockingbirds include the common and well-known Northern Mockingbird, *Mimus polyglottos*, widespread from the Canadian border through the whole USA and as far south as southern Mexico and the Caribbean. In the Pacific, the Socorro Mockingbird, *M. graysoni*, is endemic to Socorro Island off Mexico's west coast, while the Galapagos mockingbirds – with four species including, in the Galapagos Mockingbird, *N. parvulus*, a complex array of subspecies – are each restricted to one or more islands of that archipelago. The latter were discovered by Charles Darwin in 1835, during his visit to the islands on the *Beagle* voyage, when he became more intrigued by their origin as different species than the finches that later bore his name. The ten species of *Toxostoma* are known as thrashers, from their habit of swiping their bills from side to side across the ground to displace leaf litter, twigs, sand or other material on the ground to disturb and reveal prey. The larger species can even move sizeable sticks and stones aside. The Brown Thrasher, *T. rufum*, is the best known of the North American thrashers and by far the most widespread, found in central and eastern parts of the continent from southern Canada to Texas. The rest are mainly Central American. Placed in a separate monotypic genus is the Sage Thrasher, *Oreoscoptes montanus*, which breeds in the sagebrush plains of extreme southwestern Canada and the western USA, wintering south to central Mexico.

The two species of catbird, each in a separate genus, are so called because of their catlike mewing calls. They are the smallest members of the family, at 19–24 cm (7.5–9 in long) and are shaped rather like small thrushes. The Grey Catbird, *Dumetella carolinensis*, is a well-known bird of southern Canada and the USA that migrates to winter farther south, some as far as Panama and Colombia. The Black Catbird, *Melanoptila glabrirostris*, has a far more restricted range, in the Yucatan peninsula of Mexico and adjacent Guatemala and Belize. There are two species of *Melanotis*: the Blue Mockingbird, *M. caerulescens*, in Mexico and the Blue-and-white Mockingbird, *M. hypoleucus*, of southern Mexico and northern Central America. The two tremblers, *Cinclocerthia*, are restricted to the Caribbean region. Their common name refers to their odd habit of drooping and quivering their wings during most social interactions. This is also seen in another Caribbean species, the monotypic White-breasted Thrasher, *Ramphocinclus brachyurus*. Also in that geographic region are the two Caribbean thrashers, the Pearly-eyed Thrasher, *Margarops fuscatus* – biggest of all mockingbirds at up to 30 cm (12 in) long – and the Scaly-breasted Thrasher, *Allenia fusca*.

Most species are ground dwellers or birds of low, scrubby habitats, although a few are arboreal: notably the tremblers and the catbirds. Many spend much of their time hidden or foraging within scrub or among ground cover, although when singing, they typically choose a prominent, exposed perch.

Almost all these roughly thrush-sized birds have a long, graduated tail, and many have a strong, medium-length or long,

LEFT The Grey Catbird, *Dumetella carolinensis*, mews like a cat as well as mimicking other birds, frogs and mechanical sounds in its long, rambling song.

LEFT A pair of Española (or Hood Island) Mockingbirds, *Mimus macdonaldi*, investigates a tourist's bag on the beach at the island of Española (formerly Hood Island), in the Galapagos archipelago.

RIGHT The Brown Thrasher, *Toxostoma rufum*, is renowned for its long, loud, fluting song that incorporates an amazing variety of different phrases.

decurved bill, and rather long, strong legs for fast running. They prefer to run from danger than fly on their short, rounded wings. The tremblers have a much shorter tail, often held cocked over the back. They also have short legs, suited for hunting insects among foliage, when they often probe with their long decurved bill among tangles of lianas and other epiphytic plants.

Plumage is generally a sober mixture of browns or greys above and whitish to buff below. Many *Mimus* mockingbirds are lightly streaked below, especially on the flanks, while the two *Margarops* thrashers have a scaly pattern of brown crescentic markings on the underparts, and some *Toxostoma* thrashers have boldly streaked or spotted underparts. Some species, such as the Brown Thrasher, of North America and the Brown Trembler, *Cinclocerthia ruficauda*, have brighter, more rufous upperparts. Four species are strikingly different. The Grey Catbird is entirely grey apart from its black forehead, crown and tail and chestnut undertail coverts and the Black Catbird has uniformly glossy blue-black plumage. Brightest are the two *Melanotis* species: the Blue Mockingbird is deep blue with a black mask through the eyes, and the Blue-and-white

Mockingbird differs in having white underparts. Many species have strikingly contrasting bright red, yellow or white eyes. The sexes look alike.

The males of all species have loud, penetrating songs, usually of great complexity and duration. They are made up of a succession of varied phrases, each often being repeated several times, and containing both harsh and mellow notes. Studies have shown that the Brown Thrasher has more than 2,000 different song types. The name of the family, Mimidae, refers to the prowess of many of its members at mimicking the sounds of other birds, and in some cases, a wide range of sounds made by other animals or resulting from human activities. These range from the croaking of frogs and barking of dogs to the howls of a Coyote, *Canis latrans*, and from human whistling to the squeaking of an unoiled gate or wheel. As its specific name suggests, the Northern Mockingbird, *Mimus polyglottos*, has a wide repertoire, while the Grey Catbird (but not the Black Catbird) is also a renowned mimic. Although these two are the best known in this respect, many other members of the family are expert mimics.

STARLINGS Sturnidae

GENERA: 34   **SPECIES**: 114

LENGTH: 15–45 cm (6–18 in)

WEIGHT: 33–290 g (1.1–10 oz)

RANGE AND HABITAT: Europe, Africa, Madagascar, Asia, New Guinea, northeast Australia (one species) and Pacific islands; some species introduced elsewhere (one, the Common Starling, *Sturnus vulgaris*, now worldwide except for the polar regions); forest, woodland, scrubland, savannah, grassland, farmland, gardens, villages and urban habitats

SOCIAL BEHAVIOUR: most are social, often seen in flocks, especially outside the breeding season; monogamous, solitary or semi-colonial breeders

NEST: typically untidy mass of dry grass and other material sited in existing holes in trees, buildings or nest boxes

EGGS: 1–6, pale blue, brighter blue or blue-green, in most species with brownish spots or blotches

INCUBATION: 11–18 days

FLEDGING PERIOD: 15–25 days

FOOD: in many species, fruit or insects form the bulk of the diet, but some are more omnivorous, at least at certain times of year, including pollen, spiders, worms, snails, small crabs and other invertebrates, fish, small amphibians and reptiles, birds' eggs and nestlings, and carrion

VOICE: a wide range of sounds, from harsh, squawks, buzzes and creaks to melodious whistling and warbling; some are mimics

MIGRATION: mostly resident, nomadic or short-distance migrants

CONSERVATION STATUS: four species, the Kosrae Starling, *Aplonis corvina*, Tasman Starling, *A. fusca*, Mysterious Starling, *A. mavornata*, and Réunion Starling, *Fregilupus varius*, are Extinct; three species, the Pohnpei Starling, *Aplonis pelzelni*, Bali Myna (or Bali Starling), *Leucopsar rothschildi*, and Black-winged Myna, *Acridotheres melanopterus*, and also four subspecies often regarded as species, are Critically Endangered; one species, the White-eyed Starling, *Aplonis brunneicapillus*, and one subspecies often regarded as a species, are Endangered; five species are Vulnerable; nine species are Near Threatened

ABOVE A Common Starling, *Sturnus vulgaris*, prepares to feast on fallen apples in an orchard, in Kent, England, UK.

ABOVE This Bali Starling, *Leucopsar rothschildi*, is one of the 1,000 or so individuals in captivity that represent 95% of the total population of the species.

ABOVE Like the Common Starling, the Common Myna, *Acridotheres tristis*, of southern Asia has been widely introduced; this one is in Australia.

This large family of Old World passerines include some well-known species, notably the aptly named Common Starling, *Sturnus vulgaris*, whose very extensive natural range in Eurasia has been extended throughout the world as a result of introductions elsewhere, including North America, the Caribbean, South Africa, Australia and New Zealand. Two other familiar starlings, both from southern Asia, are the Hill Myna, *Gracula religiosa*, and the Common Myna, *Acridotheres tristis*. All three are among the few starling species that are known to be accomplished mimics. The Common Starling incorporates song fragments and calls of many species of birds into its song, which is a rambling medley of whistles, creaky sounds, throaty warbling, gurgling, spluttering squawks and softer clicking, and also includes mimicry of animal sounds and even artificial noises such as the ringing of telephones. Captive individuals may learn to imitate the human voice very accurately, while the Common Myna and particularly the Hill Myna are renowned for this ability among cage birds.

The greatest diversity of starlings is found in Africa, with 47 species in 12 genera, followed by Asia (42 species in 11 genera), then New Guinea and islands of the southwest Pacific Ocean (24 species in three genera). The closest relatives of the starlings are the mockingbirds and thrashers in the previous family, Mimidae.

The family is divided into three subfamilies. By far the largest is the Sturninae, with 73 species in 23 genera. The genus *Sturnus* comprises one extremely widespread species, the Common Starling, and its more localised close relative the Spotless Starling, *Sturnus unicolor*, found in Iberia, extreme southern France, Corsica, Sardinia, Sicily, and North Africa. Close to these two in the subfamily Sturninae is the striking Rose-coloured Starling, *Pastor roseus*, a mainly central Asian species whose range extends into eastern Europe. This pastel-pink and glossy black bird, with a long crest, is a bird of open steppes where there is an abundance of its main summer diet of locusts and grasshoppers, and may breed in huge colonies of up to tens of thousands of pairs. In response to local fluctuations of its staple food, birds may sporadically range much farther west and some of the nomads stay to breed in countries as far west as the Czech Republic, Hungary and Italy, while vagrants may reach Britain and even Iceland.

The many African species in this subfamily include some of the most stunningly plumaged of all that continent's birds. Most are members of the large genus *Lamprotornis*, many of whose 22 species are called glossy starlings. They have shimmering, glossy plumage in various combinations of blue, violet, purple and blue-green, and in a few species contrasting areas of rich rufous, brilliant

ABOVE This Superb Starling, *Lamprotornis superbus*, is just one of many beautiful African starlings with glossy plumage.

ABOVE This male Wattled Starling, *Creatophora cinerea*, sports large fleshy black wattles and bare yellow skin on his head in the breeding season.

yellow (in the Superb Starling, *L. superbus*), or bright green (in the Emerald Starling, *L. iris*). Another very striking African species is the Amethyst Starling, *Cinnyricinclus leucogaster*, in which males have an iridescent purple head, upperparts and chest and white underparts. This is one of relatively few starlings in which the sexes look very different; females lack any gloss, being streaky brown above and white with bold brown streaks below. The Wattled Starling, *Creatophora cinerea*, is unique among African starlings in having areas of bare skin on the head. These are small and inconspicuous in females, immature males and non-breeding males, in which they are restricted to a small area of yellow skin behind the dark eyes. Breeding males, however, have an extensive area of yellow bare skin on the head with a narrow black border, and prominent black wattles on the forehead and throat.

Among the Asian members of the subfamily Sturninae are 10 species in the genus *Acridotheres* known as mynas, the best known of which are the Bank Myna, *A. ginginianus*, and the Common Myna, mentioned above. The other bird in this subfamily often called a myna is the beautiful Bali Myna (or Bali Starling), *Leucopsar rothschildi*. Pure white, apart from the black wing and tail tips and patch of blue skin around each eye, and with a luxurious, erectile crest, it is one of the world's rarest birds, with just a handful of wild birds surviving, and is classified as Critically Endangered.

The next subfamily is the Rhabdornithinae, containing just a single genus, *Rhabdornis*, of two species (or in some recent classification schemes, three or four species, here regarded as subspecies). These are little-known birds which, until recently, were known as Philippine creepers, as they are endemic to the Philippine islands, and were thought to climb tree-trunks like the treecreepers in the family Certhiidae (p. 373). Although they are highly arboreal and superficially similar in appearance to the true treecreepers they do not share the latter birds' morphological adaptations to tree climbing

(elongated toes with long, flat pads, long, powerful, markedly curved claws and stiffened tail feathers) and, unlike them, rarely if ever creep up branches and trunks. Instead, they perch crosswise on branches and move about through the trees like many other small songbirds, by walking or hopping along, and jumping from branch to branch. For this reason, they are now known as rhabdornises, after their generic name. Although previously included with the treecreepers in the Certhiidae, or in the huge jumble of the original babbler family, Timaliidae, or often in a family of their own, recent molecular studies indicate that they belong here in the starling family.

Although just two species, the Stripe-headed Rhabdornis, *R. mystacalis*, and the Stripe-breasted Rhabdornis, *R. inornatus*, are recognised in this book, some authorities split off two of the races (*grandis* and *rabori*) of the Stripe-breasted Rhabdornis as separate species, the Grand Rhabdornis (or Long-billed Rhabdornis), *R. grandis*, and the Visayan Rhabdornis, *R. rabori*. All are very short-necked, with a longish bill that is slender, gently decurved and laterally compressed. They have short, rather pointed wings and a short and square-ended tail. They may fly some distance between trees, with a markedly undulating action, as when going to roost. Some flocks flying in to roost in trees in forest clearings have been seen to contain several hundred birds.

The plumage of both species is similar, with brown head and upperparts, wings and tail, and a broad black mask from the base of the bill through the eye and onto the ear coverts. The Stripe-headed Rhabdornis is heavily streaked with white on the head and upper back. The underparts of both species are whitish with broad streaks of brown on the flanks of the Stripe-breasted Rhabdornis and blackish ones in the Stripe-headed species. The sexes look very similar.

Rhabdornises are omnivores, eating a wide range of insects, seeds and fruits. They often roam the forests in company with other birds such as tits, nuthatches, fantails and bulbuls.

The third subfamily is the Mainatinae, containing 29 species in 10 genera, with a few in mainland southeastern Asia but most in the islands of Indonesia, New Guinea, New Britain and other nearby islands, the Solomons and other islands of the western Pacific. By far the largest genus is *Aplonis*, containing 24 species. Almost all of them are restricted to various islands in the Pacific (including three extinct species). In contrast, one species, the Asian Glossy Starling, *A. panayensis*, is a common bird over a huge range, from extreme northeast India and southern Burma to Malaysia, Indonesia and the Philippines, while another, the Shining Starling, *A. metallica*, is the sole member of the family to occur naturally in Australia, extending to northeast Queensland from its main range in New Guinea and neighbouring islands.

Many of the other members of the Mainatinae are called mynas. As well as the two species of *Gracula* (the widespread Hill Myna and the Sri Lanka Myna, *G. ptilogenys*), which are often enlarged to five species in other classification schemes, there are five other genera of mynas in this subfamily: these include *Basilornis*, with three Indonesian species that sport prominent bushy crests, two in Sulawesi and one on the island of Seram in the Moluccas and a single species of *Goodfellowia*, in the Philippines, the Apo Myna, *G. miranda*, with a smaller, long crest of finer feathers; *Mino*, with three species, two in New Guinea and one in the Bismarck Archipelago and the Solomon Islands, and the monotypic Finch-billed Myna, *Scissirostrum dubium*, of the Sulawesi region. An unusual looking, monotypic Asian starling is the Coleto (or Bald Starling), *Sarcops calvus*, of the Philippines, a grey-and-black plumaged bird with almost its entire face covered with bare pink skin, with a vary narrow line of black bristles along the top of the head.

Although some starling species are slim-bodied, others are stockier. Most have a relatively thin bill, typically with a pointed tip. Several species have evolved a highly effective method of feeding

ABOVE The Coleto (or Bald Starling), *Sarcops calvus*, a distinctive species endemic to the Philippines, has a bald pink head.

on insect larvae such as 'leatherjackets' (the larvae of craneflies) and worms that live beneath the surface of grassland. This feeding method, called open-bill probing, or 'prying' involves the birds forcing the closed bill into the ground and then using specially strengthened protractor muscles in the jaw to open the bill and create a narrow hole so that they can search for and pull out the prey. In the three species in which this method of feeding is most highly developed (the Common Starling, the Asian Pied Starling, *Gracupica contra*, and another Asian species, the White-cheeked Starling, *Spodiopsar cineraceus*) the protractor muscles are very powerful and the skull greatly narrowed, enabling the bird to move its eyes forwards to peer down the bill and spot the prey. Starlings were probably originally fruit eaters, but as they evolved, they have adapted to become omnivorous, including nectar, seeds and insects and other invertebrates in their diet. The bill is thicker, stronger and more curved in some species, especially the *Gracula* hill mynas. These bigger-billed species can overpower small vertebrates such as lizards, frogs and nestling birds. A very few species are regular predators of other birds' eggs. Three species are known to be important egg predators of seabirds on some oceanic islands. They include a species that is native to various Pacific islands – the Micronesian Starling, *Aplonis opaca* – and two introduced species, the Common Myna, established on many islands in the Pacific, Indian and Atlantic oceans, and the Common Starling, known to plunder many eggs at a colony of Roseate Terns, *Sterna dougallii*, on the Azores, in the Atlantic.

The legs and feet of starlings are fairly large and strong. Their length and the birds' gait vary according to lifestyle: the mainly tree-dwelling starlings have shorter legs and usually hop, while more terrestrial species have longer legs and normally walk or run. The wings are short and rounded in many species, but rather longer and more pointed in some of the fast-flying species of open country and those that make longer movements. The tail of many species is short and square-ended, but in some it is longer and pointed or graduated.

Many species have mainly or entirely black plumage, often with an iridescent purple, violet, blue, green or bronzy sheen; others range from dull brown to the brilliant metallic plumage of the glossy starlings described above. Various Asian starlings have a crest of feathers on the head: they include the four species of *Basilornis*, the 10 species of *Acridotheres* mynas, two species of *Aplonis*, the Golden-crested Myna, *Ampeliceps coronatus*, the Bali Myna, the Brahminy Starling, *Sturnia pagodarum*, and the Rose-coloured Starling. An East African species, the Bristle-crowned Starling, *Onychognathus salvadorii*, also sports a small crown of bristly feathers sprouting from its forehead. The adults of many species have eyes with a bright red, yellow or creamy white iris. The size of the coloured area may be at least partly under the bird's voluntary control, and its relative prominence may serve to signal dominance in social encounters.

Females of various species sing as well as males, although not so frequently and often using different notes. Starling song is important not just for attracting mates and defending breeding territory against rivals. Also, many African and Asian species sing for long periods in groups. In African species these are usually birds that assemble to rest during the hottest part of the day, and in Asian species – and the Common Starling – at their night-time roosts. These choral performances may be connected to defending a habitual perch from rivals, or even impart information about feeding opportunities.

The roosts of many species are large, and none are larger than those of the Common Starling, which as well as roosting in reed beds and similar cover in rural areas has also adapted to doing so on buildings and other structures such as piers. Some of the largest rural roosts of this species in Europe have been estimated to contain about two million birds, while a few in Israel may even contain as many as eight million. In tight flocks that constantly change shape, expanding and contracting like a single giant organism, the birds perform spectacular aerial manoeuvres before suddenly diving down into the roost. The beating of all those wings in their highly coordinated movements make a whooshing sound that can be heard a long way away.

Most starlings make their nests in natural tree holes or those excavated by woodpeckers or barbets, often unused ones, but in some cases after usurping their rightful owners. Many species have also become adapted to using artificial sites, in the roofs, eaves or walls of buildings or in other artificial structures. A few species excavate their own nest holes in sand or earth banks, especially along rivers, while some others build cup-shaped or domed nests in the open. Introduced Common Mynas and Common Starlings can be very aggressive at competing with native hole-nesting birds

ABOVE A Stripe-headed Creeper, *Rhabdornis mystacalis*, endemic to the Philippines, adopts a characteristic upright pose when perching.

for breeding sites, and have often been accused of having a serious impact on populations of native species, but there is relatively little robust evidence for major declines due to the aggressive intruders. Along with other species, both invasive and naturally occurring, these species have often acquired pest status for the depredations by large flocks on agricultural crops, especially soft fruits and cereals. On the other hand, other starling species, such as the locust-eating Rosy Starling, have long been valued for their destruction of insects harmful to agriculture.

DIPPERS Cinclidae

GENERA: 1   **SPECIES:** 5

LENGTH: 14–23 cm (5.5–9 in)

Weight: 40–88 g (1.4–3 oz)

RANGE AND HABITAT: Western North America, Central America and western South America, Europe, North Africa, parts of Asia; fast-flowing streams and rivers, mainly in uplands, some in slower waters, generally outside the breeding season

SOCIAL BEHAVIOUR: usually solitary, in pairs at nest; most are monogamous and strongly territorial

NEST: domed nest of moss, sometimes also with roots, grass and plant fibres, typically lined with leaves, sited next to or over running water beneath an overhanging bank, in a hole or among rocks, with the entrance hole facing downwards

EGGS: 2–7, white

INCUBATION: 14–20 days

FLEDGING PERIOD: 20–28 days

FOOD: mainly aquatic invertebrates and their larvae, also some tadpoles, fish eggs and small fish

VOICE: loud, high-pitched metallic calls, musical warbling and trilling song

MIGRATION: almost completely sedentary

CONSERVATION STATUS: one species, the Rufous-throated Dipper, *Cinclus schulzii*, is Vulnerable

ABOVE The White-throated Dipper, *Cinclus cinclus*, varies in plumage across its huge range; this one is of the main UK race with a fairly broad chestnut breast band.

The five species of this small but very widespread family of songbirds all share a similar specialised structure and lifestyle. They are remarkable in being the most adapted of all members of the great passerine order to a semi-aquatic existence. Not only are they intimately tied to living along fast-flowing streams and rivers, mainly in uplands, but, unlike the few other water-feeding passerines such as wagtails (see p. 302), at least three species actually hunt their aquatic prey underwater, using their wingbeats backed up by the running action of the legs, to drive them forwards along the bottom. They also regularly float or paddle on the surface.

Dippers look almost neckless, with a rotund body and very short, often cocked tail, resembling a cross between a plump thrush and a large wren. The bill is short, straight and relatively slim but strong and slightly hook-tipped. The legs are of medium length, strong with sturdy, powerful feet and big, sharp, strongly curved claws for gripping onto wet rocks and moss on boulders and when they want to pause on the riverbed. The narrow nostrils are an adaptation for submerging underwater and can be closed by a membrane to prevent water entering. The eyes are also modified, with great powers of accommodation (the ability of the eye to adjust its optical power so that it can focus a sharp image at different distances). The powerful iris muscles can quickly alter the shape of the lens, enabling the birds to see well both in air and under water. Also, like other birds, dippers are equipped with a protective semi-transparent nictitating membrane. When the bird is submerged, it flicks this across the eye, protecting it from damage; it may also help to remove pieces of grit or other debris carried towards the dipper as it swims or walks against the current. In addition, the eyelids are covered with prominent white feathers, providing a striking visual signal as the bird blinks, as it frequently does, at up to 50 times a minute. This is usually done at the same time as the dipper bobs its body up and down vigorously, as if on springs (this 'dipping' is responsible for the family's common name), and flicks its tail downwards. This is thought to serve variously as a courtship display, a threat display, and to warn a potential predator that the dipper is alerted to its presence. Dipping is a very common sight in all but the two South American species, where it is only rarely seen; instead, these birds flick their wings rapidly to reveal white flashes by exposing the inner webs of the primary feathers.

The plumage is adapted to keeping the birds warm and dry, being dense and with more contour feathers on the body than other passerines of similar size; these feathers are soft and long, and they overlay a thick layer of down feathers; together, these provide excellent insulation from the near-freezing water these tough birds venture into much of the time. The oil gland is especially large and provides copious oil with which the dipper can preen its plumage to render it waterproof. In addition, the heart rate drops considerably as the birds plunge into the water and then more once they are submerged. They can store more oxygen for respiration underwater, as their blood cells have a higher haemoglobin concentration than those of other passerines of similar size. Dippers can remain underwater for at least 23 seconds in the wild (and there is a record of 30 seconds for one in captivity).

Dippers are highly territorial, often all year, and pairs defend a long, linear territory along a stream or river, by regularly patrolling it to check for rivals. They make their presence known by their loud, high-pitched calls, which are well above the frequency of the noise made by the tumbling water, even in torrents and weirs, and their songs too are loud and far-carrying. They occasionally become more sociable during periods of freezing cold weather

ABOVE Dippers, like this American Dipper, *Cinclus mexicanus*, are hardy birds that usually stay put in winter as long as they can find unfrozen water for feeding.

when small numbers gather at unfrozen stretches of water to feed, or sometimes at communal roosts, especially those at artificial sites, notably bridges, with drainage holes, ledges or other sites providing especially good insulation from the cold.

The White-throated Dipper, *Cinclus cinclus*, of Europe, northwest Africa and Asia has a dark brown head and underparts, with a white chin and breast; most races are dark brown to rufous from belly to vent. The Brown Dipper, *C. pallasii*, an Asian species ranging from Afghanistan to the Himalayas, Burma, northern Thailand, Korea, eastern Siberia and China, lives up to its common name by being all brown. Also with a huge range, extending from western Canada and Alaska, and south through the rest of the western USA through Central America to Panama, the American Dipper, *C. mexicanus*, is dark grey, in the nominate Mexican race with a brown head. There are two South American species. The White-capped Dipper, *C. leucocephalus*, of western South America from Colombia south to Peru and Bolivia is dark brown or grey with a whitish crown and nape with fine dark spots and streaks; in one race the chin and throat are pure white, and in another they are white with fine dark streaks; the third race is almost entirely white from chin to belly. By far the scarcest and most localised of all five species is the Rufous-throated Dipper, *C. schulzii*, restricted to northwest Argentina. It is all grey apart from its reddish chin and throat.

The dippers' closest relatives are the Old World flycatchers and chats (Muscicapidae, opposite) and the thrushes (Turdidae p. 391), and perhaps also the starlings (Sturnidae, p. 381 and the mockingbirds and thrashers (Mimidae, p. 380).

CHATS AND OLD WORLD FLYCATCHERS Muscicapidae

GENERA: 57   **SPECIES**: 303

LENGTH: 9–35 cm (3.5–14 in)

WEIGHT: 4–230 g (0.14–8 oz)

RANGE AND HABITAT: Europe, Africa, Asia, North America (migratory populations of a single species, the Northern Wheatear, *Oenanthe oenanthe*, breed in Canada and Alaska); wide range, from forests, woodlands and scrublands to savannah, grasslands, semi-desert and desert edge; mostly chats in the more open areas

SOCIAL BEHAVIOUR: usually solitary or in pairs, but some tropical species join mixed-species feeding flocks; territorial, most monogamous, some polygamous; a few are cooperative breeders

NEST: cup, dome or loose platform of twigs, leaves, grasses, mosses and other plant material, usually sited in the fork of a tree branch, tree hole or nest box

EGGS: 2–6, very variable, whitish, blue, greenish or buff, with brown or blackish markings, or unmarked in hole-nesting species

INCUBATION: 12–15 days

FLEDGING PERIOD: 11–18 days

FOOD: insects and other invertebrates, and some fruit; mainly insects in Old World flycatchers

VOICE: some species, especially chats, are renowned singers with loud, complex songs and extensive mimicry; calls include 'chacking' calls for which the chats were so named, softer whistles and other notes

MIGRATION: most tropical species are sedentary or make only local movements, but those at higher latitudes include some champion migrants, most notably the Northern Wheatear

CONSERVATION STATUS: one species, Rück's Blue Flycatcher, *Cyornis ruecki*, is Critically Endangered; 13 species, including the Black Shama, *Kittacincla cebuensis*, Seychelles Magpie Robin, *Copsychus sechellarum*, Lompobattang Flycatcher, *Ficedula bonthaina*, Rufous-headed Robin, *Larvivora ruficeps*, and White-throated Jungle Flycatcher, *Vauriella albigularis*, are Endangered; 16 species, including the Blackthroat, *Calliope obscura*, Luzon Water Redstart, *Rhyacornis bicolor*, White-tailed Stonechat, *Saxicola leucurus*, Little Slaty Flycatcher, *Ficedula basilanica*, Swynnerton's Robin, *Swynnertonia swynnertoni*, Large-billed Blue Flycatcher, *Cyornis caerulatus*, and Brown-chested Jungle Flycatcher, *C. brunneatus*, are Vulnerable; 29 species are Near Threatened

This very large family was originally far larger, constituting a vast assemblage that included not only many other groups of flycatchers and chats now known to be unrelated, but also expanded versions of the thrush family, Turdidae, the Old Warbler family, Sylviidae, and the babbler family, Timaliidae. Even after these three were separated, they were still unwieldy, and molecular research proved them to be polyphyletic. As a result, there have been many discoveries of new relationships; in particular, various genera were moved between the two closely related families of Muscicapidae and Turdidae, especially from the latter to the former, and the Muscicapidae has been subdivided into four subfamilies rather than the previous two.

This is still the largest of all the passerine families that are endemic to the Old World (or virtually endemic, with just two species, the Northern Wheatear, *Oenanthe oenanthe*, with toeholds in the New World, in far northeast and northwest Canada and Alaska, and the Bluethroat, *Luscinia svecica*, in northern Alaska and Yukon Territory, Canada). It is the second largest of all passerine families, only the tanager Family Thraupidae exceeding it, by a good margin. Indeed it is one of the largest of all the world's bird families.

This huge, diverse assemblage contains two major subfamilies, the Muscicapinae, which contains most of the Old World flycatchers, as well as a mixture of other small genera, and the Saxicolinae, consisting mainly of chats, which were formerly lumped together with the thrushes. Both include representatives in Africa, Europe and Asia, as well as some in western New Guinea and various Pacific islands. They are absent from Australia and New Zealand. The two smaller subfamilies are the Niltavinae, containing the rest of the Old World flycatchers, all found only in Asia, where they occur right across that continent; and the Cossyphinae, known variously as robins, robin-chats and other names alluding to their link with the saxicoline chats. All members of the Cossyphinae are African, apart from the best known member of the entire family,

ABOVE This male Siberian Rubythroat, *Luscinia calliope*, at Beidaihe, China, starts to sing its complex song before leaving for its northern breeding grounds.

the European Robin, *Erithacus rubecula*, which despite its common name has a range that extends into western Asia as far as the Urals and southwest Siberia, and also includes North Africa and Atlantic islands off West Africa.

All members of the family are small to medium-sized, often plump-chested birds, in many species with a relatively big, broad head on a very short neck. The bill is typically short, relatively slim and pointed in most of the chats, but broad-based and slightly hook-tipped in most typical flycatchers, with rictal bristles around the nostrils. Most of the more sedentary species, especially those in forested habitats, have short, rounded wings, while migratory species have longer, more pointed wings. Most species have a short or medium-length tail, but in the shamas, scrub-robins and forktails, it is much longer, graduated in the first two, and deeply forked in the latter. Most chats and many

ABOVE A male Common Redstart, *Phoenicurus phoenicurus*; the 'start' part of its common name is from the old English word, steort, for tail.

ABOVE Northern Wheatears, *Oenanthe oenanthe*, like this male at Westfjords, Iceland, like to use a boulder as a lookout and song-perch.

flycatchers too habitually flick their wings and flirt or cock their tails to communicate with others of their own kind. Most of the chats are ground feeders that run after their insect prey, and have relatively long, strong legs and feet, while many of the typical flycatchers spend a great deal of time perching and have shorter, weaker legs and feet. Almost all the flycatchers are birds of forest, woodland, savannah and shrubby country, and most require trees or bushes both for nest sites (most species are hole nesters in trunks or branches) and for hunting perches, although many may also use a fence-post or other artificial substitute for the latter purpose. From such vantage points they can scan for insect prey, then sally out to snap it up in the air before returning to the perch; alternatively, they may hunt for insects on branches or foliage, either by moving through the tree or shrub on foot or by hovering among its leaves. There is a great deal of variety in plumage, with many species being drab plain brown or grey, while others are all black or boldly pied, and some (apart from a few species, males only) are brightly coloured, including all-blue, blue-and-red, blue-and-orange or green-and-yellow plumage. Despite their showy plumage, the latter are not necessarily conspicuous, as they tend to perch motionless for long periods and are hard to spot among foliage. Some, though, are very obvious as they forage from higher, open perches, including overhead wires, or move about from tree to tree calling noisily. In contrast to the chats, most Old World flycatchers have relatively simple, weak and unremarkable songs.

The subfamily Muscicapinae contains 64 species in 15 genera, and is subdivided into two tribes. The first, Copsychini, comprises 23 species in seven genera. These include the two species of alethes, *Alethe*, endemic to Africa. They are brown above and whitish below and are shy dwellers in dense undergrowth. Although generally solitary, they sometimes join together when foraging for insects, and often follow swarms of army ants to feed on the insects fleeing from those fierce marauders.

In a genus of its own, the Indian Robin, *Saxicoloides fulicata*, is widespread and common in much of the Indian subcontinent and

Sri Lanka. Males are strikingly plumaged, its glossy black plumage contrasting with a brown back in northern races; southern ones are almost entirely all-black; all have a chestnut red patch under the tail and bright white shoulders; females are much duller, brownish grey above and blue gray below. This little bird often cocks its long tail vertically. All but one of the 10 species of scrub robins, *Cercotrichas*, are endemic to Africa, where they live in scrub or open woodland. The exception is the Rufous Scrub Robin, *C. galactotes*, whose huge range includes Iberia, Greece, the Middle East and into southwest Asia as far as west Pakistan as well as Africa. This is plain reddish brown above and buff or whitish below, with a prominent white stripe above the eye. The African species are similarly plumaged, but several have striking patterns of black-and-white stripes on the head, and one is all-black. They all have quite broad, graduated tails with white tips to the feathers.

The collective name of the four species in the genus *Copsychus* – magpie robins – was well chosen, for with their pied plumage and long tail they look like miniature versions of magpies, *Pica*, especially the two with the most similar plumage pattern. Like the Indian Robin and the scrub-robins, they often hold their tails cocked at an angle. One species is found only in Madagascar, one in the Seychelles, one in the Philippines, while the fourth, the Oriental Magpie Robin, *C. saularis*, is widespread in southern Asia, from Pakistan and India to Malaysia and Indonesia. Magpie robins have attractive songs of warbling, whistling, trilling, fluting and chuckling notes, that may incorporate mimicry of other birds.

The tribe Copsychini also includes two Asian genera known as shamas, *Trichixos*, with a single, broad-tailed species, and *Kittacincla*, with four species, mostly with long tails. Their plumage is in various combinations of black, bright rufous and white apart from one all-black and one that is black with a white rump; Like the magpie-robins, they are renowned vocalists, some with richer and more melodious songs. The best known and longest tailed species, the White-rumped Shama, *K. malabarica* is widespread across south Asia in India, Sri Lanka, southwest China and Southeast Asia, and its popularity as a cagebird has led to it being introduced to Hawaii and Taiwan. While some of its many races are threatened with extinction due to the cagebird trade, concern has been expressed about the burgeoning populations of introduced birds on Hawaii and Taiwan, which may be competing with native birds for food and nest sites. The other three *Kittacincla* species are all endemic to various islands of the Philippines.

The second tribe of the Muscicapinae, *Muscicapini*, comprises 41 species in eight genera. One of the few large genera in the family, Muscicapa contains 23 species of flycatchers. A well-known European species is the Spotted Flycatcher, *Muscicapa striata*. Like other members of its genus, the Spotted Flycatcher is one of the drably plumaged species, mousey grey-brown above and whitish below, with a streaked crown and breast. Once very common and widespread, it has declined dramatically in the British Isles and many other parts of Europe in recent years. The other 22 *Muscicapa* species are mainly found in Africa, with 13 species there and one other found also in southwest Arabia, and there are also eight species in Asia. The four species of *Bradornis* are all African, and are dull plumaged little birds, mostly brown above and buff or grey below. The seven species of *Melaenornis*, also all endemic to Africa, have mainly brown, grey or black plumage.

The subfamily Niltavinae contains 47 species in six genera, found across southern Asia. In two genera, *Cyornis*, with 25 species, and *Niltava*, with six species, the males sport mainly blue plumage of various shades. In the *Cyornis* species these range from entirely cobalt blue in the Pale Blue Flycatcher, *C. unicolor*, to azure blue and an intense deep blue in others, which have partly or almost wholly reddish orange underparts. Most of the six species of *Niltava*, too, including the aptly named Vivid Niltava, *N. vivida*, and the Beautiful (or Rufous-bellied) Niltava, *N. sundara*, have brilliant blue upperparts and rich rufous underparts. One, the Large Niltava, *N. grandis*, is a rather sluggish and stocky bird, the biggest Asian flycatcher (and one of the largest of all Old World flycatchers) at up to 22 cm (8.5 in). It is mainly dark blue, tinged purple below, and with black-and-indigo flight feathers and a black-and-violet-blue tail. Yet another beautiful little mainly blue bird in this subfamily is the male Blue-and-white Flycatcher, *Cyanoptila cyanomelana*. In all these, the females are dull brownish birds with whitish, buff or greyish underparts.

The subfamily Cossyphinae comprises 36 species in 10 genera. All but one are endemic to Africa, including the 14 species of robin-chat, *Cossypha*, the ten species of akalats, *Sheppardia* and several monotypic genera, mostly with 'robin' as the second part of their common name. Most of them are brown above with orange red on the underparts or breast. The bird from which the names of these and so many other red-breasted birds the world over has been derived, as a result of homesick explorers or settlers, is the European Robin, *Erithacus rubecula*. Usually known simply as the Robin, this is an abundant, widespread and much loved garden bird in the British Isles, where it is found from wild countryside to city centres. It has a very attractive sweet warbling song, more wistful in winter. Celebrated in folklore

and on Christmas cards, it readily takes to nest boxes and bird feeders, often becoming very tame – in contrast to the situation in much of the rest of its range, in continental Europe, North Africa and western Asia, where it is much shyer and in some places still targeted by hunters.

The subfamily Saxicolinae comprises 26 genera and 156 species. It is a member of this subfamily that is most renowned as a vocalist, celebrated in poetry and music from early times: the Nightingale, *Luscinia megarhynchos*. It is justly regarded as one of the world's finest songsters, helped by the male's habit of delivering his powerful, rich and varied song at night, when there are few other sounds to compete with it. (This is reflected in its common name, whose early, Anglo-Saxon, form *nihtingale*, meant 'night songstress', as the female was presumed to sing.) After arriving on the European breeding grounds in spring from winter quarters in Africa, a male sings by day at first, to proclaim his territorial boundary and deter rivals. Later, he delivers a more complex version at night to attract a mate, pouring out a long sequence of loud, rich, rising and falling, fluting, piping, bubbling, churring and rattling notes, separated by brief but dramatic silences, for long periods. Some other chats, too, have rich and dramatic songs, including some of the African species mentioned above.

The Nightingale and its close relative the Thrush Nightingale, *L. luscinia*, found farther east, are plain, warm brown birds with a chestnut-red tail. This feature is shared by another group of chats, the redstarts, *Phoenicurus*, but the males are very much more strikingly plumaged than those of the nightingales, in which the sexes look alike. These are some of the loveliest of all Old World songbirds, with ash-grey or blue-grey upperparts contrasting with intensely orange-red underparts, and in most a striking black-and-white head pattern. Some redstarts, such as the widespread Common Redstart, *P. phoenicurus*, of northwest Africa, Europe and central Asia, are woodland birds, but others live in more open rocky country, often on mountains, and several breed near rivers and streams, as do two closely related Asian genera, the White-capped Water Redstart, *Chaimarrornis leucocephalus*, and the two water redstarts, *Rhyacornis*, males of the latter being entirely dark slaty blue apart from a chestnut rear body and tail. Females of all these species are much duller, mainly brown plumaged birds, but with the rufous tail. All these redstarts have a distinctive habit of frequently quivering (and in some species, dipping and raising) their tail.

Another genus of chats is that of the stonechats, bushchats and whinchats, *Saxicola*, 10 small, large-headed birds of open scrubby country that like to perch on the top of a bush and have a very fast, whirring flight. The wheatears, *Oenanthe*, are a larger genus of 22 species found in open country, including deserts, tundra, rocky areas in mountains and meadows of Eurasia, Africa and India. These are bigger and slimmer than the *Saxicola* chats, and the males of most species have bold plumage patterns consisting of various combinations of buff, black, grey and white, with a black face mask. The very widespread Northern Wheatear, *Oenanthe oenanthe*, is one of the world's champion migrants, with northerly populations flying each way between northern Europe, Siberia and Alaska to their wintering areas in sub-Saharan Africa. It has a grey crown, nape and mantle. A distinctive feature of all wheatears is the bold tail pattern, with an inverted 'T' on the white tail; most species have a white rump (the name wheatear being derived not from an ear of wheat but from 'white-arse').

The forktails, *Enicurus*, are very distinctive birds, with their slender body, black-and-white plumage and mostly long, deeply forked tails. They are strongly attached to fast-flowing streams and rivers in the Himalayas and other mountains of Asia, where they catch aquatic insects, mainly along the banks but also gleaning them from the rocks in the water or the water itself, especially in the vicinity of waterfalls or the most turbulent stretches.

The 13 species of rock thrush, *Monticola*, are among the largest members of the Family Muscicapidae, the size of a Eurasian Starling, *Sturnus vulgaris*. Most species have a longer bill than other chats, and a shorter tail than true thrushes (Turdidae). Rock thrushes are fond of perching in a prominent position on a boulder, clifftop or building. Generally shy and wary, they are apt to dash off when spotted, with a strong, fast flight, and disappear behind a boulder or over a ridge. The males are handsome birds, blue or grey-blue on the head, upper breast and mantle, and reddish-orange below in most species. Females are brownish or greyish, paler below, with barring or scaly markings. They are mostly birds of semi-arid, rocky country in hills and mountains. Six species are endemic to Africa, two to Madagascar and three to Asia. The other two are widespread: the Common Rock Thrush, *M. saxatilis*, breeds from northwest Africa and southern and central Europe to southwest and central Asia across southwest Siberia and as far east as northern China, with all populations migrating to winter almost entirely in Africa; the Blue Rock Thrush, *M. solitarius*, with all-blue males, has an even wider range, breeding much farther east and south, including in Japan and the Thai-Malay peninsula, and wintering in North Africa and southern Asia.

The seven species of whistling thrushes, *Myophonus*, of southern Asia are mainly velvety bluish-black. In the gloom of the forest understorey they inhabit, they look black, but a shaft of sunlight reveals patches of dazzling metallic blue on the forehead, shoulder and tail, while some species are spangled all over their body with royal blue. They are mainly tied to rocky mountain streams and rivers, and are usually very wary and hard to see. Unlike the rest of this family, whistling thrushes have a heavy, deep bill with which they can tackle small reptiles and amphibians as well as such invertebrate prey as water beetles, snails and crabs. Their common name celebrates their rich, mournful songs, consisting of loud, often uncannily human-sounding whistles. They include the largest members of this family, notably the most widespread species, the Blue Whistling Thrush, *M. caeruleus*, which is 29-35 cm (11.5-14 in) long and weighs 136-230 g (5-8 oz). Most species occur on islands. The three subspecies of the Sunda Whistling Thrush, *M. glaucinus*, are often regarded as full species, one on Sumatra, another on Borneo, and the third on Java and Bali. The species with the most restricted range, the Sri Lanka Whistling Thush, *M. blighi*, is Endangered.

The large genus *Ficedula*, with 54 species, contains most of the Old World flycatchers. A well-known European species is the Pied Flycatcher, *Ficedula hypoleuca*, which also breed eastwards as far as western Siberia. The male is a dapper little black-and-white bird (the female – and the male after breeding – having the same pattern but with the black mainly replaced by brown). Other members of the very large genus *Ficedula* (containing 54 species) are mainly Asian; apart from Pied Flycatcher populations in northwest Africa, none breed on that continent, though the Pied Flycatcher, along with two very similar European species, migrate to winter in sub-Saharan Africa.

Many flycatcher species breeding in northern Asia migrate to southern Asia for winter, and so do the European populations of one of them, the Red-breasted Flycatcher, *F. parva*, which looks superficially like a miniature European Robin. This is one of the few European breeding birds that migrate exclusively to southern Asia rather than Africa. Like many members of the Family Muscicapidae, this little bird, just 11.5 cm (4.5 in) long, is a long-distance migrant. Some birds travel between the forests of southern Sweden or Kamchatka, at either end of the species' huge Eurasian breeding range, and wintering areas as far south as central India or Thailand respectively, a round trip of up to 16,000 km (10,000 miles). Most of the brightest and most beautiful species in this genus are Asian. They include the Narcissus Flycatcher, *Ficedula narcissina*, with brilliant yellow-and-black plumage and bold white wing patches.

ABOVE The beautiful Narcissus Flycatcher, *Ficedula narcissina*, breeds in the far east of Russia and in Japan, and migrates to winter in southern China and southeast Asia.

THRUSHES Turdidae

GENERA: 20   **SPECIES:** 159

LENGTH: 15–33 cm (6–13 in)

WEIGHT: 25–170 g (0.9–6 oz)

RANGE AND HABITAT: worldwide, apart from Antarctica, and New Zealand (apart from the introduced Eurasian Blackbird, *Turdus merula*, and Song Thrush, *T. philomelos*); very varied, most in forests and woodlands, but many species also in other, open habitats, from mountains, moorlands, desert edges and grassland to farmland and gardens and parks in cities

SOCIAL BEHAVIOUR: mostly solitary or in pairs, but northerly breeding species in particular migrate in flocks or form large foraging and roosting flocks in winter, and some tropical species also roost communally; most are monogamous and territorial

NEST: usually an open cup of twigs, plants stems, moss and feathers, lined with mud by some species, sited in forks or on branches of trees or shrubs; whistling thrushes often nest on streamside rock ledges or behind waterfalls, while a few species such as solitaires nest on or near the ground, hidden by exposed tree roots, boulders and so on, or on steep banks or cliff ledges among cover, and a few nest in tree holes; some readily use nest boxes

EGGS: 3–6, whitish, buff, blue or green, either unmarked or with darker markings

INCUBATION: 12–15 days

FLEDGING PERIOD: 12–15 days

FOOD: mainly insects and other invertebrates, especially earthworms, snails and slugs; also berries and other fruit in autumn and winter

VOICE: calls include harsh, loud, rattling, chattering, clucking or chinking sounds, and quieter, high-pitched warning calls; songs often melodic, a sequence of rich, fluting whistles, warbling, trilling or harsher notes that are either repeated singly or uttered as short phrases; some species are skilled mimics of the songs and calls of other birds and in some species of other sounds, including telephone ringing or other human-made sounds

MIGRATION: most species are sedentary but some species and populations breeding in higher northern latitudes migrate south for winter

CONSERVATION STATUS: four species, the Bonin Thrush, *Zoothera terrestris*, Kamao, *Myadestes myadestinus*, Amaui, *M. woahensis*, and Grand Cayman Thrush, *Turdus ravidus*, are Extinct; one species, the Olomao, *Myadestes lanaiensis*, is Critically Endangered (Possibly Extinct); three species, the Puaiohi, *M. palmeri*, Taita Thrush, *Turdus helleri*, and Principe Thrush, *T. xanthorhynchus*, are Critically Endangered; two species, the La Selle Thrush, *T. swalesi*, and Spotted Thrush, *Geokichla guttata*, and one race, *leucogenys*, of the Rufous-brown Solitaire, *Cichlopsis leucogenys* (often regarded as a full species), are Endangered; nine species, including Bicknell's Thrush, *Catharus bicknelli*, Javan Cochoa, *Cochoa azurea*, Ashy Thrush, *Turdus feae*, and Somali Thrush, *T. ludoviciae*, are Vulnerable; 24 species are Near Threatened

Many species of this large, cosmopolitan family of songbirds are renowned for the beauty of their songs, among the very finest of any birds'. Some are shy and skulking denizens of vast northern coniferous forests or tropical rainforest, but others are among our most familiar garden birds, in both rural and urban surroundings. These generally very adaptable birds have moved from their original homes in wooded habitats to a wide range of other, more open, landscapes, from dry semi-desert and scrubland to savannah, grassland and farmland, and from mangroves to remote moorland and high mountains.

The thrushes were until a few years ago lumped together with the chats in a large family called Muscicapidae. Recently, molecular evidence has indicated that the chats are more closely related to the Old World flycatchers. As a result, the latter two groups have been combined in a reduced Family Muscicapidae (see p. 387), separate from the thrush Family Turdidae. The thrushes appear to have evolved in the Old World, probably in Asia, which contains the largest number of species. Their closest relatives are the Old World flycatchers and chats, mentioned above, and the dippers (Family Cinclidae, p. 385).

Thrushes have a rounded head and relatively long, tapering body with a rounded, rather plump breast. They have a strong, sharp, straight, short bill that is fairly slender except in a few species, and at its base sprout a few rictal bristles. The eyes are quite large, and many species forage in dark forests or in twilight. They are almost entirely ground feeders, finding food by digging in the soil, rummaging in and sweeping aside dead leaves or conifer needles and twigs, and are generally omnivorous, eating a wide range of insects, worms, molluscs and other invertebrates as well as fruit. The legs are of medium length, strong and 'booted' (that is, not divided into separate scales on the leading edge). Thrushes can move fast on the ground

ABOVE A Rufous-throated Solitaire, *Myadestes genibarbis*, in the Dominican Republic broadcasts its hauntingly lovely song.

in big, bounding hops, and some only hop, but others walk or run too. The wings are of medium length, generally rather rounded, but more pointed in migratory species, and the tail, too, is usually of medium length. Thrushes are strong flyers, with a direct flight path in many species, but a rather or markedly undulating one in others. The medium length tail aids balance when hopping or running fast, and manoeuvrability in flight.

The plumage of most thrushes is predominantly brown, grey and white or cream, but with patches of bright colour in many and in some mainly or entirely black, grey or even bright blue, green or purple. Females are usually similar but duller. A characteristic thrushes share with the chats and Old World flycatchers is that the juveniles have spotted plumage.

ABOVE A male Eastern Bluebird, *Sialia sialis*, delights the eye as it perches amid springtime blossoms in New York State, USA.

There are two subfamilies, the Myadestinae, with 19 species, and the far larger Turdinae, containing the remaining 140 species. The Myadestinae are a small assemblage of five genera in the New World and Africa that differ from the typical thrush appearance and lifestyle. Despite their huge geographical spread, there is strong evidence from DNA analyses that they are closely related to one another and to the rest of the family, but distinct enough to deserve a subfamily of their own, Myadestinae. The largest genus, *Myadestes*, comprises 11 extant species, mostly in the New World, which have earned the common name of solitaires from the tendency of these shy birds to keep to themselves. They have mainly sombre brown and grey plumage, with a broad, short bill and a long tail. Three species live only in Hawaii, one Critically Endangered (Perhaps Extinct), another Critically Endangered, and the third Vulnerable. There are also two other recently extinct species; all are listed in the accompanying fact box. A single Myadestes species, Townsend's Solitaire, *M. townsendi*, lives in Canada and the continental USA; the others are spread across Mexico, the Caribbean, Central America and one species in the northern half of South America. One Caribbean species, the Rufous-throated Solitaire, *M. genibarbis*, has what is generally regarded as one of the most beautiful of all bird songs, made up of melancholy whistles in a minor key.

The genus *Neocossyphus* contains two species of ant-thrushes, endemic to Africa, and the third, another African duo, the two species of flycatcher-thrush, *Stizorhina*. All four species look similar, brown above with a contrasting orange wing panel and grey head, and rich rufous-orange below. The group is almost exclusively arboreal and the juveniles lack the spotting found in the young of other thrushes.

By far the best known members of this group are in the genus *Sialia*, which comprises three lovely and much-loved North American birds, the bluebirds. Males of two species, the Eastern Bluebird, *S. sialis*, and its western counterpart the Western Bluebird, *S. mexicana*, are mainly blue above with chestnut-orange on the underparts. The blue of Western Bluebird males is deeper and richer, especially some males of one of the Mexican races, which lack the rufous breast and flank patch of typical individuals of this race, and are almost entirely intensely blue. Males of the Mountain Bluebird, *S. currucoides*, are stunning, too, being bright cobalt blue above and azure blue below.

Also with stunningly blue plumage is the final member of this subfamily, formerly included in the Old World flycatcher and chat family, which is given a genus of its own: the Grandala, *Grandala coelicolor*. Living in the Himalayas, it is a high-altitude specialist, surviving way above the treeline at heights of 3,900-5,500 m (12,800-18,000 ft). The male has astonishingly bright blue plumage, and is one of the relatively few entirely bright blue birds in the world. The female is dull streaky brownish grey, with a faint blue tinge to her rump.

The 15 genera of the major subfamily Turdinae includes two small New World genera that share the common name of solitaires with the *Myadestes* species in the first subfamily, described above. These are *Entomodestes*, with two species in the Andes, one black and the other black and brown, and both with a striking large white face patch, and *Cichlopsis*, with a very widespread brown-plumaged South American species that is sometimes considered as four species.

Larger species include the 33 species often called ground thrushes. They were formerly all placed in the genus *Zoothera*, but are now divided between that genus, with members only in Asia, and another one, *Geokichla*, including both Asian and African species. These include some of the largest birds in the family. They generally have stronger and longer bills than most other thrushes, stouter legs and shorter tails, a striking, usually black-and-white,

ABOVE A stunning male Grandala, *Grandala coelicolor*, surveys the January scene near the snowline at Sela Pass, Arunachal Pradesh, India.

RIGHT One of the best loved sounds of European woods and gardens is the loud, challenging repetitive song of the Song Thrush, *Turdus philomelos*.

BELOW A migrant from its Siberian breeding range, this Dusky Thrush, *Turdus naumanni*, is wintering in the city of Kushiro, Hokkaido, Japan.

underwing pattern, and are specialised for ground foraging in dense forest. Almost all are restricted to Africa and Asia, except for one species, White's Thrush, *Zoothera aurea*. Its breeding range, from southern Siberia to Japan, extends marginally to the eastern edge of European Russia. This is one of about a dozen Asian species that are brown above and white or golden-buff below, and distinctively marked over the whole head and body with black crescentic markings, giving them a scaly appearance (some are called scaly thrushes for this reason). Two other scaly thrushes are the only members of the family native to Australia, the Bassian Thrush, *Z. lunulata*, endemic to that continent, and the Russet-tailed Thrush, *Z. heinei*, found also in New Guinea, the Solomons and some other nearby islands.

Two others, the Long-billed Thrush, *Z. monticola*, and the Dark-sided Thrush, *Z. marginata*, have evolved a longer, deeper, more powerful bill with a strongly curved upper mandible. This is an adaptation for gouging deeply into soil or rotting ground vegetation for invertebrates such as earthworms; many thrushes obtain part of their food by ground probing, but these two have become specialists. Both have a scattered range from the Himalayas to Burma and Indochina. The other species in this genus are either orange-chestnut on head and body with brown or grey back, wings and tail, or brown above and white with large black spots below. Many *Zoothera* thrushes have striking songs composed of rich, fluty whistling notes, in some cases mixed with trills and other sounds, including mimicry of other birds.

The single species in the genus *Ixoreus* is the Varied Thrush, *I. naevius*. Widespread across the west of North America, from Alaska south to north-western California, its common name refers to its complex plumage pattern, a bold mixture of black, slate grey and orange.

The 12 species of *Catharus* are mainly brown above and greyish or whitish below, either plain or with spots restricted mainly to the breast. They include four North American species noted for the beauty of their songs, consisting of a trio of ethereal, fluted whistles rising or falling in pitch: the Hermit Thrush, *C. guttatus*, Swainson's Thrush, *C. ustulatus*, and the Veery, *C. fuscescens*. The genus also contains seven far less well-known species, the nightingale-thrushes, found in Mexico, Central America and northern South America. They do superficially resemble nightingales (see Muscicapidae, p. 387) and, in some species, have dramatic and complex songs too.

Another well-known North American thrush with a superb and variable song is placed in a different genus: this is the Wood Thrush, *Hylocichla mustelina*, which has reddish-brown upperparts and boldly black-spotted white underparts.

By far the largest and most widespread of all genera of thrushes is *Turdus*, with 80 species in most parts of Europe, Africa and Asia, many islands in the Pacific Ocean, and Mexico, Central America and South America. These are mainly large species, including the biggest members of the whole family, such as the Mistle Thrush, *T. viscivorus* and Fieldfare, *T. pilaris* of Eurasia, and, largest of all at up to 33 cm (13 in) long, the Great Thrush, *T. fuscater*, which lives on the eastern slopes of the Andes, from Colombia to Peru. Plumage varies considerably, from various permutations of grey, brown and orange to all black, black with white markings or all brown; a few are brown above and pale below with bold spots. This very large genus includes many common, widespread and familiar species with strikingly beautiful songs, including in Eurasia, the Eurasian Blackbird, *T. merula*, and Song Thrush, *T. philomelos*, and in North America the American Robin, *T. migratorius*. Others include the Clay-coloured Thrush, *T. grayi*, one of the commonest songbirds in Central America, and the Island Thrush, *T. poliocephalus*. The latter species has colonised many islands in its huge range across the Indian and Pacific Oceans, resulting in its diversification into almost 50 extant subspecies (as well as three extinct ones), with a corresponding diversity of plumage, from all black with a golden yellow bill and eye-ring just like a male Eurasian Blackbird (but with yellow feet in all races) to black with a white or orange front, all brown or brown and orange.

There are four species of cochoa, *Cochoa*, in Asia, all scarce or rare birds of mountain forests, often along ravines or near small streams. Males in particular are brilliantly plumaged, mainly purple, blue or green according to species, though they are usually hard to see, unlike most other thrushes, they spend long periods perching unobtrusively high up in the forest, in the middle storey and beneath the canopy, and are rarely seen on the ground. Cochoas feed mainly on fruits and berries, swallowing large ones relative to their size in their broad-gaped bill, reminiscent of that of a cotinga (see p. 206), and take relatively few insects and molluscs.

GLOSSARY

Words in *italics* refer to other entries in the glossary

adaptive radiation the relatively rapid evolutionary process of *speciation* within a single *lineage* that results in many new genera or species adapted to different *niches*

advertising call a bird sound that announces the presence of a bird to rivals or prospective mates; often used in place of 'song' for non-passerines

air sacs part of a bird's respiratory system within the body cavity and extending into some of the bones that bring air into the body and supply it to the lungs

air speed the speed of a bird relative to the air mass through which it is flying (see also *ground speed*)

Afrotropical region the zoogeographic region embracing sub-Saharan Africa, southern Arabia and Madagascar

altitudinal migration regular movements between higher and lower altitudes

altricial describing young that hatch naked, blind and helpless and remain in the nest until they *fledge* (also called nidicolous)

alula a group of small, stiff feathers projecting from the bird's first finger at the bend of the wing, used for minimising turbulence in slow flight

antiphonal duetting of a pair (usually a mated pair) of birds in which each utters its part of a song alternately, rather than simultaneously

arboreal living mainly or entirely in trees

arena communal display ground

arthropod member of a major group of jointed-limbed *invertebrates* with a chitinous exoskeleton (external skeleton); examples are insects, crustaceans and spiders

arachnids spiders, scorpions and relatives

arm the inner section of the wing, between the *shoulder* and the *carpal joint*.

aspect ratio the figure obtained by dividing the length of a wing by its mean width, which gives a measure of a bird's flight style and ability

Australasian region zoogeographical region embracing Australia, New Guinea and other islands south and east of the *Indomalayan region*, New Zealand and its smaller islands

Australo-Papuan of a species, genus or family found in Australia and New Guinea

avifauna all the birds of a particular geographical area

band/banding term used in North America for ring/ringing

bare parts exposed areas of skin, such as patches on the face, around the eye or as wattles or other outgrowths, and also the horny covering of the bill and the legs and feet

basal group a genus, family or other group at the base of a *lineage*, from which more recent groups evolved

belly the area of the *underparts* between the breast and the undertail *coverts*

bib a patch of plumage of contrasting colour on the chin, or one extending to the throat or upper breast

bill the term preferred by ornithologists for the beak

bird of prey term usually used for any of the birds in the order Falconiformes, such as eagles, hawks and falcons, all *diurnal* birds of prey; sometimes extended to owls, then referred to as nocturnal birds of prey; synonymous with raptors

breast the area of the underparts between the throat and the belly, sometimes called the chest

breastband a band of contrasting colour encircling the breast

brood all the young hatched from the same *clutch* of eggs

brood parasite a bird that lays its eggs in the nests of other species (interspecific brood parasite) or individuals of its own species (intraspecific brood parasite) so that they bring up its young

brood patch an area on the lower breast and/or belly from which feathers are shed before incubation, and from which swollen blood vessels transfer heat to the eggs for incubation

cache a store of food made by a bird for later use

caecum (plural: caeca) a blind-ending appendage leading off the lower intestine

calls vocalisations of birds that are typically simpler and shorter than songs; usually associated with particular situations, and conveying a specific message, e.g. contact calls, alarm calls, food begging calls, calls to invite copulation

canopy the uppermost layer of a forest

carpal joint (or carpals) the bird's 'wrist' at the bend of the wing

caruncle a naked, fleshy, often brightly coloured skin growth on the head or neck of some birds

cere the naked, leathery or waxy band of skin covering the base of the upper *mandible* of the bill of some birds, and surrounding the external nostrils

cheek the lower side of the face

chest see *breast*

chin the small area immediately beneath the base of the lower *mandible* of the bill

churring a relatively deep trilling sound (see also *reeling, trilling*)

circumpolar distributed right around the polar regions

cloaca (plural cloacae) a common chamber at the end of the gut into which waste products (faeces from the large intestine, uric acid from the kidneys) and eggs or sperm from the gonads are released and then voided via the *vent*

cloud forest subtropical or tropical mountain forest that is shrouded in fog or clouds

clutch a complete set of eggs laid by a single female during a single incubation period

clutch size the number of eggs in a particular clutch

co-evolution interaction between two or more species in which one evolves an adaptation affecting the other(s), which then responds with a different adaptation, and so on; examples include interactions between plants and their pollinators, predators and prey, and brood parasites and hosts

collar a band of contrastingly coloured plumage around the neck

common name (or vernacular name) the popular name in a local language given to a bird species or group, as opposed to its *scientific name*

convergent evolution the independent evolution of similar forms, behaviours or other characteristics by two or more unrelated birds or groups of birds, resulting from their adaptation to similar environmental factors

cooperative breeding the situation in which individuals (called helpers) other than the breeding pair assist the latter in territory defence, nest building or rearing of young; they are usually non-breeders and often siblings from the previous brood

corvid a member of the crow family, Corvidae

court an area of ground often cleared of dead leaves and so on and defended by a male at a communal display ground, or *lek*; also a similarly cleared area in front of a male bowerbird's bower

courtship feeding the feeding of a female bird by her mate, usually during the periods shortly before and during egg-laying

coverts smaller feathers that partly cover the flight feathers of the wings and tails like overlapping tiles on a roof; they (function)

crepuscular active mainly at dusk or dawn

crest a tuft of elongated feathers on the *crown* of a bird that may be permanently erect or erected and lowered at will

cryptic plumage colour and pattern that helps the bird camouflage itself against its background

crop a pouch leading from a bird's oesophagus, used to store food before it is passed to the stomach or while the bird carries it to feed to its young

crown the top of the head between the *eyebrows*, and between the forehead and the *nape*

decurved (of a bird's bill) curved downward

dichromatic term used for a species in which the plumage varies noticeably between the sexes

dimorphic term used for a species in which there are two distinct forms, including the genetically determined different plumage colours of birds, such as some birds of prey or herons, or (sexually dimorphic) when the sexes differ in size (of the body or of the bill or other parts), plumage or other physical characteristics

display ritualised movements or postures, often enhanced by distinctive sounds, used in situations like courtship, territorial defence or threat

distraction display technique used by some ground-nesting birds in which the parent acts as if it has a broken wing or is incapacitated in some other way in an attempt to draw the attention of a predator away from eggs or young

diurnal active during daylight

diurnal birds of prey members of the Order Falconiformes; also called *raptors*

DNA analysis/research/studies investigation based on examining DNA, used to tease out the relationships between different bird *taxa* and their evolutionary history

double-brooded producing two *clutches* or *broods* in a single breeding season

dynamic soaring energy-saving technique used by albatrosses and some relatives, utilising the gradient of different wind speeds above the sea

ecosystem a community of organisms, together with the non-living components of their environment

ear tufts bunches of elongated feathers on the head that can be erected

during display, in alarm and so on; have nothing to do with hearing

eclipse plumage a drab, *cryptic*, female-like plumage that is acquired in a post-breeding *moult* by some groups of birds, notably ducks, in which it helps protect them from predation during the flightless period when they moult all their wing feathers in one brief period

emarginated term used to describe a feather, especially the *flight feathers* called *primaries*, in which one of the *vanes* narrows abruptly, producing a notch near the tip

endemic restricted to a particular area; an endemic is a species, family or other group so restricted

epiphyte a plant that grows on another plant but is not parasitic on it; epiphytic plants include many orchids and bromeliads in rainforests

eruption refers to the departure phase of an *irruptive* species

eyelash the structure found in a few bird families similar to that of mammalian eyes but made up of modified feathers (bristles) rather than hairs

eyebrow a stripe of contrasting colour above the eye; more technically known as the supercilium

eye-ring a circle of often contrastingly coloured small feathers or bare skin surrounding the eye; also more technically known as orbital ring (especially of skin)

eyeshine the brilliant reflection of coloured light from the tapetum, a layer at the back of the eyes of nightjars and relatives (Order Caprimulgiformes); the red eyeshine from other birds (and mammals) is less bright

eyestripe a narrow stripe of contrastingly coloured feathers running through both sides of the eye

eyrie the nest of an eagle or other large bird of prey

face the front of a bird's head, including the *lores*, the area around the eyes and the *cheeks*

facial disc (or facial ruff) the disc-shaped front of an owl or harrier, with an outer ruff of stiffened feathers, that aids hearing by funnelling sound into the ears

family level of classification above *genus* and below *order*, containing closely related *genera*

feral term used for individuals of a domesticated species that has established a viable breeding population in the wild

flanks the sides of the body, between the belly and the axillary ('armpit') feathers; partly obscured when the wings are closed

fledge strictly speaking, used to grow feathers, but usually used to denote the point at which a young bird first flies, having acquired a more or less complete set of feathers

fledging period the time between hatching and fledging

fledgling for young reared in the nest, sometimes used for the time when the bird leaves it or (as in this book) for all birds (except of course flightless ones) when it is first capable of flight

flight feathers collective term for the *primaries* and *secondaries* of the wings, and often also those of the tail

foraging the obtaining of food

fossil record the record of the occurrence through time and evolutionary history of birds or a particular group of birds (or other organisms) as inferred from fossils

freeze to become motionless in an attempt to avoid detection, as when faced by a predator

frontal shield an area of often brightly coloured bare horny or fleshy skin on the forehead, above the upper *mandible* of the bill

game bird although sometimes used to describe any bird that is hunted, in this book it is used for birds, such as grouse and pheasants, in the Order Galliformes

gape the open mouth, brightly coloured in some birds

gape flanges the area of skin in the angle between the two *mandibles* of the bill, brightly coloured in many nestlings

generic name the name of a genus, which appears as the first part of the scientific name of a species

genetic analysis/research term sometimes used to describe studies involving *DNA analysis*

genus (plural genera) the level of classification above species and below family

gizzard the muscular forepart of the stomach

gleaning plucking an insect or other *invertebrate* prey from foliage, branches, or other surfaces; the bird may walk or hop, hover, or combine it with *sallying*

gliding unpowered level or descending flight (see also *soaring*)

gonydeal angle the angle formed by the keel-like projection (gonys) on the ventral surface of the lower mandible of the bill, especially noticeable in gulls and some other birds

graduated a term describing the tail shape of some birds in which the feathers become abruptly longer from the outside in, giving a stepped appearance

ground colour of eggs bearing markings, the underlying colour

ground speed the flight speed of a bird relative to the ground (or water) over which it is flying (see also *air speed*)

guano the hardened accumulation of droppings, especially at seabird breeding colonies

gular pouch a throat pouch

hand the outer part of the wing, extending from the *carpal joint* (wrist)

hawking the aerial pursuit of prey, especially insects; sometimes used to describe a bird that flies out from a perch to do so (see also *sallying*)

Holarctic of a bird having a distribution that includes part of both the *Nearctic* and the *Palaearctic* zoogeographic regions

hyoid apparatus/bones/horns or hyoids refers to the structures supporting the tongue and the muscles that control it

incubation period the interval between the laying of the last egg of a *clutch* and the hatching of the last egg

Indomalayan region the zoogeographic region embracing subtropical and tropical areas of southern Asia

invertebrate an animal without a backbone, including insects, crustaceans, worms, molluscs, and many others

iris (plural irides, or irises) the coloured part surrounding the pupil of the eye; it is this that is referred to when a bird's eye is described as being yellow, red etc.

irruptive species a bird that leaves its normal range at irregular intervals, usually prompted by shortage of its

usual food; large numbers arriving in areas where it does not normally occur are called invasions

keratin the protein forming the feathers, bill, claws and other horny structures

kleptoparasite a bird that specialises in feeding by stealing food from another of a different species

knee sometimes used to describe the joint between the *tibia* and the *tarsus* which is actually its ankle joint; the true knee is at the top of the tibia, usually hidden by body feathers

krill shrimplike marine crustaceans of the Order Euphausiacea

lamella (plural lamellae) projections from the inner edge of the bills of birds such as some ducks and flamingos that filter small food particles from the water

lek the place where a group of males meet to compete with courtship displays for the attention of females

lineage a group (population, species, genus or higher taxonomic level) of birds having common descent

loafing resting, as opposed to *roosting*, when birds sleep

lores the area between the base of the upper *mandible* and the eye

lump to combine *taxa* into larger taxonomic units, for instance to regard two species as a single species (see also *split*)

Malagasy occurring in Madagascar

mallee semi-arid shrub habitat in Australia dominated by many-stemmed eucalypts

mandibles the two parts of the bill, consisting of the upper mandible (also called maxilla) and the lower mandible

mantle the upper part of the back; sometimes used to describe the mantle, back and *scapulars* when these areas are uniformly and distinctly coloured

maturity used to describe a bird that is sexually mature and capable of reproduction

maxilla see *mandibles*

mechanical sounds all the non-vocal sounds produced by birds, such as bill rattling and wing snapping

metabolism all the biochemical processes that take place within the cells of the body, such as those that maintain body temperature and make muscles work

mimicry imitation of the form, plumage or behaviour of another species, such as mimicking songs or calls, imitating a more dangerous species or the eggs of another bird in *brood parasites*

mobbing the habit of one or (usually) more birds, often of several species, and often with loud calls, harassing a species perceived as a threat

molecular analysis/research using data from DNA or RNA studies to determine relationships between different bird *taxa*

monogamy mating system in which one male pairs with one female, at least for the duration of a single breeding season (see also *sexual monogamy* and *social monogamy*)

monophyletic term describing a group of birds that contain all the living descendants of their most recent common ancestor (see also *paraphyletic* and *polyphyletic*)

monotypic term describing a *taxon* with no further subdivisions; e.g. a monotypic family contains only a single genus, a monotypic genus only a single species and a monotypic

species no subspecies (it cannot have a single subspecies)

montane pertaining to mountains

morphs term used for two or more distinct forms within a single species that differ in plumage colour or pattern, body size, or bill size or shape; sometimes called a phase

morphology the form and structure of a bird, especially externally

moult the process of renewing feathers

moustache loose term used to embrace various contrastingly coloured stripes running from the base of the bill down the sides of the head at an angle

multi-brooded term used for a bird laying more than one *clutch* of eggs a year

nape the area between the crown and the hind neck

nares (singular naris) the external nostrils

Nearctic the zoogeographic region comprising North America south to the northern border of tropical forest in Mexico sometimes, as in this book, excluding Greenland

necklace a band of contrasting colour around the neck or across the upper breast of a bird

Neotropical, Neotropics the zoogeographic region comprising tropical Mexico, Central America, the Caribbean and South America

New World the whole of the Americas; see also *Old World*

niche the ecological niche of a species that reflects the many ways in which it interacts with its environment, from diet and feeding methods to its relation to competitors and predators

nomadic term used to describe species that are frequently on the move, and do not usually return to the same area each breeding season, instead settling to breed in areas where food is plentiful

non-passerine birds those belonging to any *order* other than the great order of *passerines*

non-vocal sounds (see *mechanical sounds*)

Oceanic the zoogeographic region embracing islands of the west central and central Pacific Ocean

oil glands glands at the base of the tail in most birds that produce preen oil, which they apply to their plumage to condition it

Old World the area comprising the continents of Europe, Africa and Asia, but excluding Australia

operculum a flap partly covering and protecting the external nostrils (*nares*)

order a higher taxonomic category consisting of one or more families (see also *family*)

oscines the major *suborder* of *passerines*, also called *songbirds*

osteology the study of bones and skeletal anatomy, used in classification

Palaearctic the zoogeographic region comprising Europe and Asia north of the Himalayas

panel an area of plumage of contrasting colour, usually either on the wings or tail

pantropical distributed throughout the tropics

papilla (plural papillae) a tiny spine or bump; also used for the cone-shaped structure from which a feather develops

paraphyletic term used to describe a group of birds with a single evolutionary origin but not including

all descendants of their last common ancestor (see also *monophyletic* and *polyphyletic*)

passerine a member of the great Order Passeriformes, often called perching birds

pelagic species those occurring in the open ocean, far from land, which they normally visit only to breed

pellet a compact mass of indigestible food remains, such as bones, fur, feathers or the hard parts of insects, that is regurgitated through the mouth

phytoplankton plant *plankton*

plankton microscopic organisms that move passively with water currents in freshwaters or the sea

plunge diver a bird that dives from the air into the water to pursue prey beneath the surface

polyandry mating system in which one female mates with two or more males in the same breeding season

polygamy mating system in which males or females mate with more than one partner in the same breeding season; comprises *polyandry* and *polygyny*

polygynandry mating system in which both males and females mate with more than one partner in the same breeding season

polygyny mating system in which one male mates with two or more females in the same breeding season

polymorphic term used for species in which there are two or more distinct forms, or *morphs*, differing in colour, size or such features as bill size

polyphyletic term used for a group of birds that have different evolutionary origins

powder down modified down feathers that disintegrate to form a fine powder used in *preening*

preening the act of keeping feathers in good condition using the bill (and sometimes claws) to clean and smooth them, often using preen oil from the preen gland

primaries the outer flight feathers of the wings, attached to the *hand*

race or geographical race, see *subspecies*

racquets (tail racquets) the vaned tip of a central tail feather that is bare and wirelike for the rest of its length

radiation see *adaptive radiation*

raptor see *bird of prey*

ratite any of the orders of big flightless birds (Ostrich, rheas, cassowaries, emus, kiwis and two extinct orders) that lack a keel on the breast bone

reeling term used to describe a monotonous, high-pitched trilling song

regurgitation the ejection of food for nestlings or of a *pellet* via the mouth

relict term used for an isolated population of a formerly widespread bird or group of birds

resident remaining in the same area year-round; non-migratory; see also *sedentary*

rictal bristle bare, stiff, hairlike feathers surrounding the base of the bill in many insect-eating birds

ringing (called *banding* in North America) fitting a metal (or plastic) ring (North American: band) bearing a unique number or colour around the leg of a bird to identify it for research, especially the study of migration

riparian inhabiting or associated with a riverbank

roost to sleep; also used for the place where birds sleep, often communally

rump the area between the lower back and the upper tail *coverts*

sallying flying out from a perch to catch an insect in mid-air, then returning to the same or another perch; sally-gleaning involves the bird flying out and then gleaning an insect from a leaf or other surface

scapulars a group of elongated feathers growing from the *shoulder*

scavenger a bird eating dead creatures or other organic matter, including food discarded by humans

sclerophyll a plant with tough leaves, adapted to arid areas

scientific name the formal, internationally agreed, name of a taxon, used particularly in reference to the two-part (binomial) species name (or binomen) or for *subspecies* the three-part name; often incorrectly known as the Latin name (Latinised is preferable, since many of the names include Latinised forms of words from Ancient Greek and other languages)

scrape a shallow hollow made in the ground by a bird to serve as a nest

seabird strictly speaking, a bird that finds most or all of its food in the sea, but sometimes extended to those that only do so at some seasons, such as various ducks and phalaropes

secondaries the inner flight feathers of the wings, attached to the 'arm' (see also *tertials*)

sedentary often used interchangeably with *resident*, but may imply that the bird is especially tied to a single restricted area all year

sexual role reversal used of species where the female is typically more brightly plumaged and is the dominant sex, defending a territory, taking the lead in courtship, competing for males and leaving the male to incubate the eggs and rear the young, while they mate with another male

sexual monogamy the situation, relatively rare in birds, in which pairs remain sexually faithful to one another, at least for one season; see also *social monogamy*

shaft of a feather, the stiff central rod from which the flat *vanes* extend on either side

shoulder informal term for the area at the front of the closed wing where it joins the body

sister group the most closely related group to a particular group of birds at each taxonomic level (sister species, sister family etc.)

slotting the separation of narrow *primaries* at the wingtips when the bird spreads these feathers in flight; particularly a feature of large soaring birds

soaring unpowered flight in which the bird gains height by using the rising air of *thermals* (see also *gliding*)

social monogamy mating system in which male and female remain together as a pair at least for a season and raise a family but may not remain faithful sexually

songbirds see *oscines*; they have an especially complex *syrinx*, enabling them to produce more complex *songs*

songs typically complex vocalisations of birds that are connected with defending a territory and attracting a mate; sometimes regarded as exclusive to *songbirds* but often used for the similar vocalisations made by other birds (see also *advertising call*)

spatulate term describing a bill shaped like a spatula or a spoon

species the primary taxonomic unit, below a *genus*, often defined as a group of freely interbreeding natural populations that are reproductively isolated from other such groups

specific name the second part of the scientific name of a species

speciation the process by which new species evolve through natural selection

speciose term used to describe a family, genus or other taxonomic category that contains many species; also called species-rich

spectacles a combination of contrastingly coloured eye rings and a stripe from bill-base to eye that make it look as though a bird is wearing spectacles

split to subdivide *taxa*, typically a single species into two or more subspecies or species (compare *lump*)

streamers see *tail streamers*

subcanopy middle storey layers of a forest below the topmost level, the canopy

subfamily taxonomic level between family and genus

subfossil remains of a bird that has been only partly preserved and has not been mineralised due to lack of time or unsuitable conditions

suborder taxonomic level below order

subspecies a population of a species that is morphologically distinct from other populations of the same species but still capable of interbreeding with them; also called a *race*, or geographical race; the subspecific name is the third part of a *scientific name*

surface diver a bird that dives underwater from the surface of the water

syrinx the bird's 'voicebox'

tail streamers very elongated and narrow tail feathers

tarsus (plural tarsi) colloquially regarded as the lower part of a bird's leg; more properly called the tarsometatarsus, and in fact the foot and ankle bones combined

taxon (plural taxa) any group of organisms irrespective of their particular taxonomic rank, used when referring to different ranks together or when doubt exists as to whether a species or subspecies is being discussed

taxonomy strictly speaking, the classification of organisms into separate *taxa*, based on their similarities and differences; often used to include what is more formally called systematics, the study of the evolutionary relationships between taxa

taxonomists scientist specialising in the naming and classification of organisms

tertiaries found only in long-winged birds such as albatrosses, they are attached to the upper arm bone (the humerus); these are sometimes referred to as 'true tertials'.

tertials the innermost *secondaries*, that form a cover for the wing when it is folded, and are often distinguished by a different colour or pattern

thermal a column of warm air rising from a surface heated by the sun, used by many *soaring* birds

throat the area between the chin and the breast

tibia colloquially, the upper part of the bird's leg, sometimes called its thigh; more properly called the tibiotarsus, and actually the lower part of its leg; often largely hidden by feathers

trill a vocal sound resulting from the rapid repetition of similar notes

tubenose a bird belonging to the order Procellariiformes, including albatrosses, shearwaters, petrels and fulmars, storm perels and diving petrels, that have tubular external nostrils

underparts the entire undersurface of the body, including the *chin*, *throat*, *breast*, *belly*, *flanks* and under tail *coverts*.

upending submerging the head, neck and front of the body into water to feed

upperparts the upper surface of the body, including the *mantle*, back, *scapulars*, *rump* and upper tail *coverts*; may also include the forehead, *crown*, *nape*, and hind neck

vanes the flat sides of a feather on either side of the *shaft*

vent the external opening of the *cloaca*; sometimes used in relation to the area of plumage surrounding it

vernacular name (see *common name*)

wattle a flap of often brightly coloured skin dangling from the head or neck of a bird

wing bar a bar or stripe of contrasting colour on the upper wing *coverts*

wing loading the ratio of body mass to the total area of both wings, related to flight capabilities

wrist colloquial term for the *carpal* joint

zooplankton animal *plankton*

APPENDIX

DEFINITION OF BIRDLIFE/IUCN RED LIST THREAT CATEGORIES

It is a sad fact that today more than 1,470 species of bird are at risk of extinction. This number represents 13.4%, just over one in eight, of the total number of almost 10,000 species that inhabit the planet today. Of these, 222 are Critically Endangered and face an extremely high risk of extinction in the immediate future.

To understand the threats affecting each species, and to help work out the most effective strategies for reversing declines, it is vital to categorise the degree of threat, based on such parameters as the total population, the size of the species' range, and the rate of decline. The International Union for Conservation of Nature (IUCN), the world's largest and oldest global environmental network, maintains the Red List of Threatened Species of plants and animals. The official authority for the status of the world's birds for inclusion in the Red List is BirdLife International, the worldwide partnership of over 120 non-governmental conservation organisations with a special focus on birds and their habitats. Throughout this book, we use these categories when referring to

threatened birds, listing them under the final heading 'Conservation Status' in the fact boxes accompanying the text for each bird family. The total number of species in each threat category at the time of writing is given. This may occasionally differ from the official BirdLife/ IUCN Red List where the classification used by BirdLife International disagrees with that we have followed in this book. Similarly, we do not include some species listed as Extinct by BirdLife International because of such differences. In addition, different authorities disagree as to where to draw the line between species for which there is evidence from at least fragments of skin and feathers and the many species described only as subfossils (in which the fossilisation process is not complete and the remains are of not yet mineralised skeletons) or fossils (in which the skeleton is mineralised and preserved in rock, or preserved in amber or tar).

Sometimes we give the common and scientific names of all the species in a particular threat category, but where many species in a family are threatened, especially for the lower categories of threat, we give representative examples only, because of space constraints.

Note: As well as the threat categories, we include one of the non-threatened categories, Near Threatened, but not the other two (Least Concern and Data Deficient). You can find the complete list of species in all categories on the BirdLife website (see Further Information, p. 397), in the Data Zone section.

Each of the different categories has a precise definition, as follows, taken from the BirdLife International website:

EXTINCT

This category is used for a species for which there is no reasonable doubt that the last individual has died, after exhaustive surveys of its known or expected habitat at appropriate times (diurnal, seasonal or annual) throughout its historic range have failed to record an individual. Surveys should be conducted over a time frame appropriate to the species' life history.

EXTINCT IN THE WILD

This category is used for a species known only to survive in captivity or as a naturalized population (or populations) well outside the past range. A species is presumed Extinct in the Wild when exhaustive surveys in known and/or expected habitat at appropriate times (diurnal, seasonal, annual) throughout its historic range have failed to record an individual. Surveys should be over a time frame appropriate to the species' life history.

CRITICALLY ENDANGERED

This category is used for a species when the best available evidence indicates that it meets any of the criteria A to E for Critically Endangered (see the 'Assessing risk' section, below) and it is therefore considered to be facing an extremely high risk of extinction in the wild.

POSSIBLY EXTINCT

BirdLife applies a 'Possibly Extinct' tag to certain Critically Endangered species. The definition for this, and guidelines for its application, have been developed by examining information on species that have not been recorded for a long time or with dwindling populations that may have finally disappeared.

Species classified as Critically Endangered (Possibly Extinct) are defined by BirdLife as 'species that are likely to be extinct, but for which there is a small chance that they may still be extant, hence they should not be listed as Extinct until local or unconfirmed reports have been discounted, and adequate surveys have failed to find any individuals.' For each species, the following information is considered: (1) evidence pertaining to the timing of the last confirmed records; (2) any subsequent unconfirmed records or local reports; (3) knowledge about the strength of threatening processes currently and historically operating; (4) the adequacy of fieldwork relative to the (presumed) ease of detection of the species; and (5) the extent and quality of remaining suitable habitat (where 'suitable' incorporates the absence of introduced predators, pathogens, etc.). Species are tagged as Possibly Extinct if, on balance, the evidence that they may be extinct outweighs any evidence that they may still be extant (although the latter remains a slim possibility, so they are not yet classified as Extinct).

ENDANGERED

This category is used for a species when the best available evidence indicates that it meets any of the criteria A to E for Endangered (see the 'Assessing risk' section, below),

and it is therefore considered to be facing a very high risk of extinction in the wild.

VULNERABLE

This category is used for a species when the best available evidence indicates that it meets any of the criteria A to E for Vulnerable (see the 'Assessing risk' section, below), and it is therefore considered to be facing a high risk of extinction in the wild.

NEAR THREATENED

This category is used for a species when it has been evaluated against the criteria but does not qualify for Critically Endangered, Endangered or Vulnerable now, but is close to qualifying for, or is likely to qualify for, a threatened category in the near future.

LEAST CONCERN

This category is used for a species when it has been evaluated against the criteria and does not qualify for Critically Endangered, Endangered, Vulnerable or Near Threatened. Widespread and abundant species are included in this category.

DATA DEFICIENT

This category is used for a species when there is inadequate information to make a direct, or indirect, assessment of its risk of extinction based on its distribution and/or population status. A species in this category may be well studied, and its biology well known, but appropriate data on abundance and/or distribution are lacking. Data Deficient is therefore not a category of threat. Listing of species in this category indicates

that more information is required and acknowledges the possibility that future research will show that threatened classification is appropriate. It is important to make positive use of whatever data are available. In many cases great care is exercised in choosing between Data Deficient and a threatened status. If the range of a species is suspected to be relatively circumscribed, and a considerable period of time has elapsed since the last record of the species, threatened status may well be justified.

Note: When used in its strict official sense, the term 'threatened' applies collectively to the three categories of Critically Endangered, Endangered and Vulnerable.

Assessing risk

The three 'threatened' categories are defined by decreasing probabilities of extinction of the species in question over increasing timescales, and by five criteria which differ for each level. To qualify for listing within any of the three categories, the species needs to meet any one of these criteria. The criteria are as follows:

A   A high rate of decline
B   A small range area and decline
C   A small population size and decline
D   Very small population size
E   Unfavourable quantitative analysis (this refers to the measure to the probability of extinction in the wild, e.g. for a species to qualify for Critically Endangered status, the probability of its extinction in the wild must be less than 50% in 10 years, or three generations).

FURTHER INFORMATION

REFERENCE SOURCES

This is a selection of books and online resources; space restrictions preclude the inclusion of all titles or of the many hundreds of journal articles that were also consulted in the preparation of this book.

The world bird list followed (with a few exceptions) in the preparation of this book:
Dickinson, E. C., & Remsen, J. V, Jr, Eds., (2013), *The Howard and Moore Complete Checklist of the Birds of the World*: 4th edn., Vol.1, Non-Passerines.
Dickinson, E.C., & Christidis, L., Eds., (2014), *The Howard and Moore Complete Checklist of the Birds of the World*: 4th edn., Vol.2, Passerines.
Another source used for checking various taxonomic details is the IOC World Bird List, produced by the International Ornithologists' Union, and available online at: www.worldbirdnames.org

A source that has been constantly referred to during the preparation of this book is the magisterial and monumental *Handbook of Birds of the World (HBW)*, whose 17 huge volumes were produced and published over a period of 22 years, from 1992 to 2013, by the specialist Spanish publishers, Lynx Edicions and edited by Josep del Hoyo, Andrew Elliott, Jordi Sargatal and David Christie. This is the first work ever to illustrate and deal in detail with all the living species of birds. The publisher's website at www.lynxeds.com offers two outstanding resources: first, *HBW Alive* – for a modest annual suscription, it is possible to view the whole work, including both still and moving images and sounds, all continually updated. The second, the *Internet Bird Collection*, is a free collection of constantly updated photos, videos and sounds. In addition, Lynx Edicions have published, in association with BirdLife International, the two-volume *Illustrated Checklist of the Birds of the World*: Vol 1, Non-passerines (2014) and Vol 2, Passerines (2017), and with the Cornell Lab of Ornithology, the single-volume *Bird Families of the World* (2015).

Other major multi-volume works covering all the species of each region in detail are:
The Birds of the Western Palaearctic (BWP), published

1977–1996 in nine volumes by Oxford University Press, Oxford; a 2-volume Concise Edition was published in 1998.
The Birds of Africa, published 1982–2004 in eight volumes, initially by Academic Press, now by Christopher Helm, the last one dealing with the birds of Madagascar.
The Birds of North America, originally published as a collectible series of loose leaf species accounts, covering all North American species; this vital resource is now available for a very small annual subscription on a website of the Cornell Lab of Ornithology (see below under organisations).
The Handbook of Australian, New Zealand and Antarctic Birds (HANZAB), published 1990–2006 by Oxford University Press in 7 volumes (of which Vols. 1 and 7 are each in two parts).

In addition, there are numerous other individual titles, their number growing constantly, on the particular families or larger groups of birds, and on the birds of various countries and regions. They include the excellent series of guides published by Bloomsbury Publishing, under their imprints Christopher Helm and Poyser, by HarperCollins (including titles dealing with birds in their superb *New Naturalist* series), and by Princeton University Press. An important series of books dealing in detail with individual bird families is the Bird Families series published 1995–2006 by Oxford University Press, Oxford.

CDs AND DVDs

The following list is just a small sample of those available; WildSounds (see below under websites) have a very large selection.
Attenborough, David (1998, 2012), *The Life of Birds* (DVD), BBC, London.
Birds of the Western Palearctic Interactive (BWPi) (2014), A full searchable, updated DVD of the 9-volume print version together with the updated 2-volume Concise Edition, including videos, photos and illustrations of every species, with species comparison facilities, as well as calls, songs, BirdGuides, London.
Roche, J. *Bird Songs and Calls of Britain and Europe*, WildSounds, Salthouse, Norfolk.
Sample, G. (2010), *Collins Bird Songs and Calls*, HarperCollins, London.
Constantine, M. (2006), *The Sound Approach to Birding: A guide to understanding bird sound*, The Sound Approach, Poole, Dorset.

Walton, R.K. & Lawson, R.W. (2000 and 2002), *Birding by Ear and More Birding by Ear: Eastern and Central North America: A guide to bird song identification*, Houghton Mifflin, New York.
Walton, R.K. & Lawson, R.W. (1999), *Birding by Ear: Western North America: A guide to bird song identification*, Houghton Mifflin, New York.

ORGANISATIONS & WEBSITES

This list includes just a few of the many organisations devoted to the study and conservation of the world's birds, together with their websites.

African Bird Club (ABC)
www.africanbirdclub.org
Publishes a checklist of birds of the whole of Africa, Madagascar and some Indian Ocean and Atlantic Ocean islands as well as lists for individual countries.

American Ornithologists Union (AOU)
www.aou.org
Publishes a checklist of all bird species of North and Middle America and also that of South America; both are accessible via its website. Its quarterly journal, *The Auk*, has been published since 1884.

BirdLife Australia
www.birdlife.org.au
Publishes a quarterly journal, *Emu-Austral Ornithology* and a quarterly magazine, *Australian Birdlife*, as well as an online database of Australian bird distribution.

BirdLife International
www.birdlife.org
Often referred to simply as BirdLife, this is the world's biggest nature conservation partnership, involving 13 million members and still growing. It works tirelessly across the globe to save species and conserve their habitats with 120 partner organisations, one in each country. BirdLife has published definitive books and reports on the status and conservation of birds and their habitats, and a huge amount of detailed information on its website, including in its Data Zone the complete listing of the conservation status of every one of the world's bird species. Publishes *World Birdwatch* quarterly.

British Ornithologists Union (BOU)
www.bou.org.uk
One of the world's oldest and most important ornitholological societies. Its quarterly journal, *Ibis*,

has been published since 1859 and is a major research source, with papers on all aspects of our scientific understanding of the world's birdlife.

British Trust for Ornithology (BTO)
www.bto.org
An independent charitable research institute combining professional and citizen science aimed at using evidence of change in wildlife populations, particularly birds, to inform the public, opinion-formers and environmental policy- and decision-makers. Publishes the quarterly journal *Bird Study*, the quarterly magazine *BTO News* and a range of books and reports.

Cornell Lab of Ornithology
www.birds.cornell.edu
The pre-eminent academically based North American institution for the study and conservation of birds, and a leader in the development of citizen science programmes in conjunction with the National Audubon Society, involving the public in data collection and other activities. Its extensive online resources include two in-depth multi-media regional accounts of New World bird species:

Birds of North America online
https://birdsna.org/Species-Account/bna/home

Neotropical Birds
www.neotropical.birds.cornell.edu

National Audubon Society
www.audubon.org
This is the major non-profit organisation working for bird conservation throughout the USA, with almost 500 local chapters, and in the rest of the Americas. Publishes a quarterly magazine *Audubon*.

Neotropical Bird Club (NBC)
www.neotropicalbirdclub.org
Promotes the study, identification and conservation of birds of Central America, the Caribbean, and South America; publishes *Neotropical Birding* bi-annually and *Cotinga* annually.

Oriental Bird Club (OBC)
www.orientalbirdclub.org
Promotes the study, identification and conservation of wild birds of the Oriental region.

Royal Society for the Protection of Birds (RPSB)
www.rspb.org.uk
With over a million members, this is the UK's largest nature charity, carrying out vital research and managing some 200 nature reserves. Publishes the magazine *Nature's Home* quarterly.

Natural History Museum at Tring, Bird Group www. nhm.ac.uk/tring
Home to the world-class research and collections of the Natural History Museum's Bird Group, based in a beautiful Victorian museum in Tring, near London. Free entry with a changing programme of exhibitions and events.

Wildfowl & Wetlands Trust (WWT)
www.wwt.org.uk
Charity founded by Sir Peter Scott to conserve wetlands and their birds and other biodiversity, with nine regional centres in the UK

Zoological Society of London (ZSL)
www.zsl.org
Has major collections of birds and carries out varied research on birds and their conservation worldwide; the library has a very large collection of ornithological books and journals.

OTHER WEBSITES
Avibase
avibase.bsc-eoc.org
An extensive database information system about all the world's birds, including links to other bird websites worldwide.

Birdfair
www.birdfair.org.uk
Full details of the annual gathering at Rutland Water Nature Reserve, Leicestershire, UK, which is the world's largest wildlife event.

Fatbirder
www.fatbirder.com
Regularly updated resources and links to thousands of other birding websites worldwide.

Surfbirds
www.surfbirds.com
Worldwide coverage with a huge number of blogs, trip reports, discussions and resources.

Xeno-Canto
www.xeno-canto.org
A vast collaborative online collection of bird sounds from all over the world.

Online international booksellers for a huge selection of books and other media on birds:

NHBS
www.nhbs.com

Subbuteo
www.wildlifebooks.com

WildSounds
www.wildsounds.com

BIRD FAMILIES AND NAMES INDEX

INDEXER'S NOTE: Bird common names are indexed according to their groups, with an additional index entry for those names that do not conform to their group names.

Page numbers in *italic* refer to illustration captions. Alternative common names referred to in the text are given in brackets; NA indicates a North American common name.

Abrornis proregulus 353, *353*
Abroscopus 356
Acanthis 310
Acanthisitta chloris 199, *199*
Acanthisittidae 199
Acanthiza 239, 240
　A. apicalis 239
Acanthizidae 239–40
Acanthorhynchus 237
Acanthornis magna 239
accentors 289–91
　Alpine 290, *290*, 313
　Altai 290
　Black-throated 290
　Brown 290
　Maroon-backed 290
　Robin Accentor 290
　Rufous-breasted 290
　Siberian 290
　see also Dunnock
Accipiter 60, 140, 185
　A. cooperii 140
　A. gentilis 136, 140, 147
　A. gundlachi 140
　A. imitator 140

A. nisus 136, 140
A. striatus 140
A. superciliosus 136
Accipitridae 136–40
Aceros nipalensis 153, 156
Achaetops pycnopygius 341, 342
Acridotheres 384
　A. ginginianus 383
　A. melanopterus 381
　A. tristis 382, *382*, 383, 384, 385
Acritillas indica 352
Acrobatornis fonsecai 227
Acrocephalidae 347–9
Acrocephalus aequinoctialis 347
　A. arundinaceus 348
　A. astrolabii 347
　A. australis 348
　A. caffer 347, 348
　A. dumetorum 348
　A. familiaris 347
　A. griseldis 347
　A. hiwae 347
　A. longirostris 347
　A. luscinius 347, 348
　A. melanopogon 348
　A. musae 347
　A. nijoi 347
　A. orinus 348
　A. paludicola 347, 348
　A. palustris 348
　A. rimatarae 347
　A. schoenobaenus 348
　A. scirpaceus 348, *348*
　A. sechellensis 347
　A. sorghophilus 347
　A. stentoreus 348
　A. taiti 347
　A. vaughani 347

A. yamashinae 347
Acropternis orthonyx 223, 224
Acryllium vulturinum 22, 23, *23*
Actenoides bougainvillei 180
　A. hombroni 180
Actitis macularius 118
Actophilornis albinucha 115
adjutants
　Greater 88, 89, 90, 132
　Lesser 88, 90
Aechmophorus clarkii 30, 31
　A. occidentalis 30, 31
Aegithalidae 357–8
Aegithalos caudatus 357, *357*
　A. c. caudatus 357
　A. concinnus 357
　A. iouschistos 357
　A. niveogularis 357
Aegithina lafresnayi 265
　A. nigrolutea 265
　A. tiphia 265, *265*
　A. viridissima 265
Aegithinidae 265
Aegolius acadicus 146
　A. funereus 147
　A. harrisii 147
Aegotheles albertisi 47
　A. bennettii 47
　A. cristatus 47
　A. insignis 47
　A. savesi 47
Aegothelidae 47
Aegypius monachus 132, 136, 138
Aepypodius bruijnii 19
　A. lathami 20
Aerodramus 49
　A. bartschi 48
　A. elaphrus 48
　A. fuciphagus 50
　A. maximus 50
Aeronautes saxatilis 50, 51
Aethia 123
　A. cristatella 125, *125*
　A. pusilla 124
Aethopyga duyvenbodei 286

African Firefinch 299
Agamia agami 94, 95
Agapornis 188
　A. nigrigennis 194
　A. roseicollis 197
Agelaioides 321
　A. badius 325
Agelaius phoeniceus 322, *322*, 323, 324
　A. tricolor 321, 324
Agelastes meleagrides 22
　A. niger 22
Aglaeactis aliciae 52
Aglaiocercus 52, 54
　A. berlepschi 52
Agriornis 217
　A. lividus 215
Ailuroedus 231
Aix galericulata 16, 18
　A. sponsa 16, 18
Ajaja ajaja 98
Akekee 305
Akiapolaau 309, *309*
Akikiki (Kauai Creeper) 305, 308–9
Akohekohe 309
Alaemon 339
　A. audipes 339, 340
Alagoas Tyrannulet 213
Alauda arvensis 339, 340, *340*
　A. razae 339, 340
Alaudidae 339–40
albatrosses 79–82
　Amsterdam 79
　Black-browed 79, 80, *81*, 84
　Black-footed 80, 81
　Buller's 80
　Grey-headed 79, 80, *80*
　Laysan 80
　Light-mantled 80, 81, *81*
　Royal 79, 80, 82
　Short-tailed 79, 80
　Shy 80
　Sooty 80, 81
　Wandering 79, 80, 81, 82, *82*

Waved (Galapagos) 79, 80, 81, 82, *82*
Alca torda 123, 124, *124*, 125
Alcedinidae 180–3
Alcedo atthis 181, *181*, 182
Alcidae 123–5
Alcippe vinipectus 359
Aleadryas rufinucha 251, *251*
Alectoris rufa 26
Alectroenas nitidissima 31
Alectrurus risora 215, 217
　A. tricolor 215
Alethe 388
Alisterus scapularis 195
Alle alle 123, 124, 125
Allenia fusca 380
Alopochen aegyptiaca 15
　A. kervazoi 15
Amalocichla incerta 282
　A. sclateriana 282
Amandava amandava 297
　A. formosa 296, 297
Amaui 391
Amaurocichla bocagii 302, 304
Amaurornis flavirostra 62
Amaurospiza 327, 328
Amazilia 53
　A. edward 53
　A. luciae 52
Amazona 189
　A. festiva 193
　A. finschi 192
　A. guildingii 192
　A. imperialis 192
　A. oratrix 192
　A. pretrei 192
　A. versicolor 192
　A. vittata 192
amazons
　Festive *193*
　Imperial 192
　Lilac-crowned 192
　Puerto Rican 192
　Red-spectacled 192
　St Lucia 192
　St Vincent 192

Yellow-headed 192
Amblycercus 325
Amblyornis flavifrons 232
A. inornata 232, *232*
Amblyospiza albifrons 294
American Goldfinch 311
American Redstart 320
American Robin 281, 393
Ammodramus 315
A. leconteii 314
Ammospiza caudacuta 314
Ampeliceps coronatus 384
Amphispiza bilineata *315*
Amytornis 234
A. barbatus 233
A. dorotheae 233
A. housei 233
A. merrotsyi 233
A. woodwardi 233
Anairetes 216
A. alpinus 215
Anaplectes rubriceps 294
A. r. jubaensis 294
Anarhynchus frontalis 111
Anas 16, 18
A. acuta 16
A. bernieri 15
A. chlorotis 15
A. crecca 16
A. laysanensis 15
A. platyrhynchos 16, 19
A. wyvilliana 15
Anastomus lamelligerus 89
A. oscitans 89
Anatidae 15–19
Andean Cock-of-the-Rock *208*
Andean Siskin 307
Andigena 170
Androdon aequatorialis 54
Andropadus latirostris 351
Androphobus viridis 252
Anhima cornuta 14, *14*
Anhimidae 13–14
Anhinga 104, *104*
Anhinga anhinga 104, *104*
A. melanogaster 104
A. novaehollandiae 104
A. rufa 104
Anhingidae 104
Anianiau 307
Annumbius annumbi 189
Anodorhynchus glaucus 192
A. leari 192
Anomalospiza imberbis 299, 300
Anorrhinus 156
Anous 127, 130
Anser anser 15, 19, *19*
A. caerulescens 18
A. cygnoides 15, 19
A. erythropus 15
Anseranas semipalmata *14*, 14–15
Anseranatidae 14–15
ant-tanagers
Black-cheeked 327
Sooty 327
ant-thrushes 224–5
Black-headed *224*
Rufous-fronted 224
antbirds 218–20
Alagoas Antwren 218
Bananal Antbird 218
Bare-crowned Antbird 220
Barred Antshrike 219
Bicoloured Antbird *219*
Black-hooded Antwren 218
Dot-winged Antwren 219
Fringe-backed Fire-eye 218
Giant Antshrike 219
Marsh Antwren 218
Moustached Antwren 219
Ocellated Antbird *218*, 220
Orange-bellied Antwren 218
Pectoral Antwren 218
Plumbeous Antvireo 218
Pygmy Antwren 219
Recurve-billed Bushbird 218
Rio Branco Antbird 218
Rufous-throated Antbird 219
Russet Antshrike 220
Scalloped Antbird 218
Spiny-faced Antshrike 218
Spot-winged Antshrike 220
Spotted Antbird *218*
White-bearded Antshrike 218
White-plumed Antbird 219
Wing-banded Antbird 220
Yellow-rumped Antwren 218
Anthocephala floriceps 52
Anthochaera paradoxa 236
A. phrygia 235
Anthornis melanocephala 237
A. melanura 237
Anthoscopus flavifrons 337
Anthracoceros 156
A. marchei 153
A. montani 153
Anthracocorax 53
A. nigricollis 55
A. prevostii *55*
Anthreptes rubritorques 286
Anthus 303
A. campestris 302
A. nattereri 302
A. nilghiriensis 302
A. sokokensis 302
A. spinoletta *304*
A. spragueii 302, 305
A. trivialis *304*
Antigone antigone 67, 68
A. canadensis 67, 68, *68*
A. rubicunda 67
Antilophia bokermanni 205
A. galatea 205
Antioquia Bristle Tyrant 213
Antioquia Brush Finch 314, 316
antpittas 222–3
Chestnut 222
Crescent-faced 222
Cundinamarca 222
Elusive 223
Giant 222
Great 222
Jocotoco 222, *222*, 223
Masked 222
Moustached 222
Ochre-fronted 222
Rusty-tinged 222
Tachira 222
Urrao 222
Antrostomus arizonae 45
A. carolinensis 45
A. noctitherus 44
A. vociferus 45
Anumbius annumbi 228
Apalharpactes mackloti 152
A. reinwardtii 150, 152
Apalis 334, 343
A. chariessa 343
A. flavigularis 342
A. fuscigularis 342
A. karamojae 343
apalises
Karamoja 343
Taita 342
White-winged 343
Yellow-throated 342
Apaloderma narina 152
Apapane 308, *308*, 309
Aphelocephala pectoralis 239
Aphelocoma coerulescens 271
Aphrastura 228
A. masafuerae 227
Aphrodroma brevirostris 85
Aplonis brunneicapillus 381
A. corvina 381
A. fusca 381
A. mavornata 381
A. metallica 384
A. opaca 384
A. panayensis 384
A. pelzelni 381
Apodidae 48–51
Apostlebird 275
Appert's Tetraka 346, 347
Aptenodytes forsteri 74, 75, *75*, 76
A. patagonicus 74, 76, *76*
Apterygidae 10–11
Apteryx australis 10
A. a. lawryi 10
A. haastii 10
A. mantelli 10, *10*
A. owenii 10
A. rowi 10
Apus acuticauda 48
A. affinis 50
A. apus 48, 49, 50, 51
A. barbatus 50
Aquila audax 137, 139
A. chrysaetos 137, 139
A. verreauxii 139
Ara ambiguus 192
A. ararauna 193
A. glaucogularis 192
A. hyacinthinus 188, 189, 192, 193
A. macao 193
A. militaris 192
A. rubrogenys 192
A. tricolor 192, 193
araçaris
Collared *169*
Curl-crested *170*, 171
Arachnothera 286
A. juliae 287
A. magna *287*
Aramidae 66
Aramides cajanea *62*
Aramus guarauna 66, *66*
Aratinga jandaya 194
A. solstitialis 192, 194, *194*
Arborophila 26
Arcanator orostruthus 283, 284
Archaeopteryx 56
Archboldia papuensis 231
Archilochus alexandri 53
A. colubris 53, 55
Arctic buntings 312–13
Arctitis hypoleucos 118, *119*
Ardea alba 95, 96
A. cinerea 94, 96, *96*
A. goliath 95
A. herodias 95, 96
A. humbloti 94
A. insignis 94
A. purpurea *95*
Ardeidae 94–7
Ardenna 85
A. creatopus 84
A. gravis 86
A. grisea 85, *87*
Ardeola 95
A. idae 94, 96
A. ralloides 96
Ardeotis kori 174, 379
A. nigriceps 69
Arenaria interpres 117
A. melanocephala 117
Argentavis magnificens 132
Argusianus 26
Argya caudata 365
A. malcolmi 365
Arses 273, 274
Artamella viridis 262
Artamidae 259–61
Artamus cinereus *259*
A. personatus 260
A. superciliosus 260
Artisornis 342
A. metopias 344
Arundinax aedon 348
Ashbyia lovensis 237
Ashy-faced Owl 142
Asian Houbara 69
Asio capensis 143, 144, 147
A. flammeus 143, 144, 146, 147
A. otus 143, 147
asities 202–3
Common Sunbird Asity 202, *202*
Schlegel's Asity 202, 203
Velvet Asity 202, 203
Yellow-bellied Sunbird Asity 202, 203
Aspatha gularis 179, 180
Asthenes 228
A. perijana 227
Astrapia mayeri *279*
Atelornis crossleyi 176, 177
A. pittoides 177, *177*
Athene brama 147
A. cunicularia 143, *143*, 144, 145, 146, 147
A. noctua 144, 145, 147
Atlantic Canary 306, 310
Atlapetes 315
A. blancae 314, 316
A. melanopsis 314
A. palliceps 316
Atrichornis clamosus 230, *230*
A. rufescens 230, *230*
Atrichornithidae 230
Attagis gayi 114
Attila torridus 215
auks and auklets 123–5
Cassin's Auklet 124
Crested Auklet 125, *125*
Great Auk 123, 124, 125
Least Auklet 124, 125
Little Auk (NA Dovekie) 123, 124, 125
Razorbill 123, 124, *124*, 125
Rhinoceros Auklet 123, 125
see also guillemots; murrelets *and* puffins
Aulacorhynchus 170, 171
A. huallagae 168
A. prasinus *169*, 170
Auriparus flaviceps 337–8, *338*
Australasian babblers
Grey-crowned 241
Hall's 241
New Guinea 241
Australasian Figbird *257*
Australasian robins 281–2
Chatham Island (Black) 281, 282
Dusky 281
Eastern Yellow 281
Garnet 282
Golden-bellied 282
Greater Ground 282
Lemon-bellied 282
Lesser Ground 282
North Island 281–2
Northern Scrub 282
Pale-yellow *282*
Papuan Scrub 282
South Island 282
Southern Scrub 282
White-winged *282*
see also Jacky Winter *and* Tomtit
Australasian wrens *see* emu-wrens; fairy-wrens *and* grasswrens
Australian Magpie 259, 260–1, *261*
Australian mudnesters
Apostlebird 275
White-winged Chough 275, *275*
Australian-Papuan bellbirds 251
Crested 251
Rufous-naped 251, *251*
Piping 250, 251
Australian treecreepers 232–3
Black-tailed 233
Brown 233, *233*
Papuan 232
Rufous 232, 233
White-browed 233
Aviceda 138
avocets 109–10
American 109, 110
Andean 110
Pied 109, 110, *110*
Red-necked 109, 110
Aythya americana 16
A. baeri 15
A. collaris 16
A. ferina 16, *17*
A. fuligula 16
A. innotata 15
A. marila 16
A. valisineria 16

babblers
Arrow-marked Babbler *365*
Bar-throated Minla 365
Blue-winged Minla 365
Bugun Liocichla 364
Common Babbler 365
Flame-templed Babbler 360, 361
Grey-crowned Crocias 364
Hinde's Babbler 364
Jungle Babbler 365, *365*
Large Grey Babbler 365
Negros Striped Babbler 360
Orange-billed Babbler 365
Pygmy Babbler 361
Red-tailed Minla 365
Slender-billed Babbler 364
White-throated Mountain-babbler 364
Yellow-billed Babbler 365
see also Australasian babblers
babblers, *Micromacronus*
Mindanao Miniature 343
Visayan Miniature 343
Baeolophus 336
B. bicolor 335, 336, *336*
Bahia Tyrannulet 213
Baillonius bailloni 171
Balaeniceps rex 88, *93*, 93–4
Balaenicipitidae 93–4
bald crows *see* rockfowls
Balearica pavonina 67
B. regulorum 67
Bananaquit 332–3, *333*
Bangsia aureocincta 329
B. melanochlamys 329
Bangwa Forest Warbler 345
Bar-throated Minla 365
Bar-winged Wren Babbler 362
barbets 171–2
Black-girdled 168
Brown 172
Coppersmith 172
Five-coloured 168
Golden-fronted *172*
Great 172
Prong-billed 172
Red-fronted *171*
Red and Yellow *171*
Scarlet-banded 168
White-mantled 168
Yellow-billed 172
Zambian 168
see also Toucan-barbet
barn owls 141–2
Ashy-faced Owl 142
Australian (Pearly Owl) 142
Barn Owl 93, 141, 142, *142*
Bismarck Masked (Golden) Owl 141
Greater Sooty Owl 142, *142*
Lesser Sooty Owl 142
Manus Masked Owl 141
Minahassa Masked Owl 141
Bartramia longicauda 117
Baryphthengus martii 179
B. ruficapillus 179
Basileuterus 318, 320, 321
B. griseiceps 319
B. ignotus 319
Basilornis 384
Batara cinerea 219
Bateleur 138
Batis perkeo 262
batises 261–2
Pygmy 262
Batrachostomus auritus 42
B. poliolophus 42
bay owls
Congo 141, 142
Oriental 142
Bearded Reedling 340–1, *341*
Bearded Wood-partridge 23

becards
Rose-throated 211
Slaty 210
bee-eaters 173–5
Black-headed 174
Blue-bearded 173, 174
Blue-cheeked 174
Blue-moustached 173
Blue-throated *174*
European *173*, 174
Green 174
Little 175
Northern Carmine 174
Olive 174
Purple-bearded 173
Rainbow 174
Red-bearded 173, 174
Rosy 175
Southern Carmine 174, *175*
Swallow-tailed 174
White-throated 174
Belding's Yellowthroat 319
bellbirds
Bare-throated 207
Bearded 207
Three-wattled 206, 207, *207*
White 207
see also Australian-Papuan
bellbirds *and* New Zealand
Bellbird
Berenicornis comatus 156
Berlepschia rikeri 228
Bermuda Towhee 314
Berniera madagascariensis 346,
347
Bernieridae 346–7
berrypeckers
Fan-tailed 242, *242*
Obscure 241, 242
Spotted 241, 242
Streaked 242
Bias 262, 263, 264
Biatas nigropectus 218
birds-of-paradise 277–9
Blue 277, 278, *278*
Goldie's 277
Greater 278
King 277, 278
King of Saxony 277, 279, *279*
Raggiana *278*, 279
Superb 279
Twelve-wired 277, 278
see also Brown Sicklebill;
Curl-crested Manucode;
Paradise Crow *and* Ribbon-
tailed Astrapia
Bismarck Masked (Golden)
Owl 141
bitterns
Australasian 94
Eurasian *95*
Forest 95
Least 95
New Zealand 94
Biziura lobata 17
Black-billed Magpie 259
Black-breasted Puffleg 52
Black-capped Pygmy Tyrant
214
Black Crake 62
Black-crowned Antpitta 221
Black-crowned Palm Tanager
318, *318*
Black-crowned Tchagra 266
Black-eared Miner 235
Black-hooded Sierra Finch 330
Black Inca 52
Black Mamo 305
Black Phoebe 217
Black-polled Yellowthroat 319
Black Shama 387
Black-spectacled Brush Finch
314
Black-throated Mango 55
Black-and-white Monjita 215
Black-and-white Tody
Tyrant 214
Blackbird, Eurasian 322, 391, 393

blackbirds, New World 321–5
Austral 324
Brewer's 324
Chestnut-capped 324
Forbes's 324
Jamaican 321
Red-winged 322, *322*, 323,
324
Rusty 321, 324
Tricoloured 321, 324
Yellow-headed *323*, 324
Yellow-hooded 324
see also Bobolink; cowbirds;
grackles; meadowlarks;
orioles; oropendolas; Selva
Cacique *and* Yellow-breasted
Chat
Blackcap 359
Blackthroat 387
Bleda 352
bleeding hearts
Mindanao 31
Mindoro 31
Negros 31
Sulu 31
Blossomcrown 52
Blue Bunting 328
Blue Chaffinch 306
Blue Crested-flycatcher 334
Blue-winged Goose 15
Blue-winged Minla 365
bluebirds
Eastern 392, *392*
Mountain 392
Western 392
Bluethroat 387
boatbills
Black-breasted 258, 259
Yellow-breasted 258, *258*,
259
Bobolink *324*, 325
Bocagia minuta 266
Bokmakierie 266
Bolbopsittacus 188
B. lunulatus 197
Bolborhynchus orbygnesius 193
Bombycilla cedrorum 369
B. garrulus 369, *369*
B. japonica 368, 369, 370
Bombycillidae 368–70
Bonasa umbellus 26
Bonin Grosbeak 305, 309
boobies 100–2
Abbott's 100, 102
Blue-footed *101*, 102
Brown 101, 102
Masked 101, 102
Nazca 101, 102
Peruvian 100, 102
Red-footed 100, 101, 102
boobooks
Christmas Island 143
Least 143
Northern 146
Papuan 146
Bornean Wren Babbler 363
Bostrychia bocagei 97
B. olivacea 98
Botaurus 95
B. poiciloptilus 94
B. stellaris 95
bowerbirds 231–2
Archbold's 231
Fire-maned 231
Golden 231
Regent 231, *231*
Satin 231, 232, *232*
Tooth-billed 231
Vogelkop 232, *232*
Yellow-fronted 232
Brace's Emerald 52
Brachygalba 161
Brachypteracias leptosomus 176,
177
Brachypteraciidae 176–7
Brachyramphus 123
B. brevirostris 123, 125
B. marmoratus 123, 125

B. perdix 123, 125
Bradornis 389
Bradypterus 355
B. bangwaensis 345
B. brunneus 345
B. graueri 344
B. sylvaticus 344
Brambling 305, 306, *306*
Branta canadensis 15, 19 *B.
ruficollis* 15
B. sandvicensis 15
bristlebirds 234–5
Eastern 234, 235, *235*
Rufous 235
Western 234, 235
Bristlehead 264–5, *265*
broadbills 201–2, 203–4
African 203
Banded 202
Black-and-red 201, *201*
Black-and-yellow 201, 202
Dusky 201
Grauer's 201, 202
Green 203, 204, *204*
Grey-headed 203
Hose's 203, 204
Long-tailed 201
Rufous-sided 203
Silver-breasted 202
Wattled 201, 202
Whitehead's 204
Brolga 67
Brown Emutail 345
Brown Sicklebill 277, *278*
Brown Songlark 345
Brown Trembler 381
Brubru 266
Bruijn's Brush-turkey 19
Brush Turkey 20
Bubalornis niger 293, *294*
Bubo blakistoni 143, *144*, 147
B. bubo 143, 147
B. lacteus 93
B. philippensis 143
B. scandiacus 143, 144, 146,
147
B. shelleyi 143
B. virginianus 146, 147, 189
Bucanetes githagineus 310
Bucco 162
B. noanamae 161
Bucconidae 161–2
Bucephala albeola 16
B. clangula 16, 18
B. islandica 16, 17
Buceros bicornis 154, 156
B. rhinoceros 155
Bucerotidae 153–7
Bucorvus abyssinicus 154, 155
B. leadbeateri 154, 155, *155*
Budgerigar 188, 194, 197
Buff-throated Purpletuft 210
Bufflehead 16
Bugun Liocichla 364
bulbuls 351–2
Brown-eared 351
Common 351–2, *352*
Grand Comoro 351
Hairy-backed 352
Hook-billed 351
Mauritius 351
Moheli 351
Red-vented 351
Red-whiskered 352
Straw-headed 351, 352
Streak-breasted 351
White-eared 351
White-headed 351
Yellow-bearded 351
Yellow-browed 352
see also greenbuls
Bulweria 85
buntings, Arctic
McKay's 312, 313
Snow 312, *312*, 313
buntings, Old World
Black-headed 316

Corn 316
Crested 316
Jankowski's 316
Japanese Yellow 316
Long-legged 199
Red-headed 316
Reed 289
Rock *317*
Rustic 316
Slaty 317
Yellow-breasted 316, 317
see also Yellowhammer
Buphagidae 378–9
Buphagus africanus 378, 379,
379
B. erythrorhynchus 378, 379
Burhinidae 105–6
Burhinus 106
B. bistriatus 105
B. capensis 105
B. grallarius 105
B. oedicnemus 105, *105*
B. senegalensis 105
B. superciliaris 105
B. vermiculatus 105
Bush Blackcap 358, 359
bush-shrikes
Black-crowned Tchagra 266
Blackcap Bush-shrike
(Marsh Tchagra) 266
Bokmakierie 266
Brubru 266
Crimson-breasted Gonolek
266
Gorgeous Bush-shrike 266
Green-breasted Bush-shrike
266
Lühder's Bush-shrike 266
Many-coloured Bush-shrike
266
Mount Kupé Bush-shrike
266
Rosy-patched Bush-shrike
266
Uluguru Bush-shrike 266
Bushtit 357, 358, *358*
Bushwren 199
bustards 69–71
African Black-bellied 71
Asian Houbara 69
Great 69, 70, *70*, 132
Great Indian 69
Houbara 70
Kori 174, 379
Little 70, 71
Ludwig's 69
Red-crested 71
see also floricans
butcherbirds 260, 261
Pied *260*
Tagula 259
Buteo buteo 140, 271
B. jamaicensis 140, *140*, 271
B. lagopus 140
B. platypterus 140
B. ridgwayi 136
B. swainsoni 140
Buteogallus aequinoctialis 140
B. coronatus 136
Butorides striata 95, 96, 97
B. s. sundevalli 96
B. virescens 95, 97
buttonquails
Black-breasted 120
Black-rumped 120
Buff-breasted 120
Common 120
Painted 120
Sumba 120
Yellow-legged 120, *120*
buzzards
Common 140, 271
Rough-legged (NA Rough-
legged Hawk) 140
Bycanistes 156
B. cylindricus 153

Cacatua alba 191, 192

C. galerita 192, *192*
C. goffiniana 191
C. haematuropygia 191, 192
C. leadbeateri 189, 191, 192
C. moluccensis 189, 191
C. ophthalmica 191
C. sanguinea 192
C. sulphurea 191, 192
Cacatuidae 191–2
cachalotes 228
Cacicus 325
C. koepckeae 321
Cacomantis variolosus 59
Cairina moschata 16, 19
Calamanthus 239
Calamonastes 342, 343
Calamonastides gracilirostris
347, 348
Calamospiza melanocorys 314
Calcarius lapponicus 312, 313
C. ornatus 312, 313
C. pictus 312, 313
Calicalicus madagascariensis
263
C. rufocarpalis 262, 263
Calidris 117
C. canutus 119
C. ferruginea 119
C. mauri 117
C. pusilla 117
C. pygmea 116, 119
C. tenuirostris 116
Callaeas cinereus 243, 244
C. wilsoni 243, 244
Callaeidae 243–4
Calliope obscura 387
Callipepla gambelii 24
Callocephalon fimbriatum 189,
191, 192
Calocitta 271
Caloenas nicobarica 33, 34
Calonectris 85
Calorhamphus fuliginosus 169,
172
Calypte anna 53
Calyptomena hosii 203, 204
C. viridis 203, 204, *204*
C. whiteheadi 204
Calyptomenidae 203–4
Calyptophilidae 326
Calyptophilus frugivorus 326
C. tertius 326
Calyptorhynchus 191
C. banksii 192
C. funerea 192
C. lathami 191, 192
Calyptura cristata 211
Camarhynchus 330, 332
C. heliobates 329
C. pallidus 331
C. pauper 329
Camaroptera 343
C. brachyura 343
C. superciliaris 343
camaropteras
Grey-backed 343
Yellow-browed 343
Campephaga 248
Campephagidae 247–8
Campephilus 168
C. imperialis 164, 165, 166
C. principalis 164, 165, 166
Campethera 166
Campochaera sloetii 247
Camptorhynchus labradorius
15, 16
Campylopterus 53
C. phainopeplus 52
Campylorhamphus 227
Campylorhynchus albobrunneus
376, 377
C. brunneicapillus 377
C. chiapensis 377
C. fasciatus 377
C. gularis 377
C. megalopterus 377
Canachites canadensis 26
Canirallus oculeus 63

Canvasback 16
Cape Grassbird 341, 342
capercaillies
    Black-billed 26
    Western 26
Capito 169, 172
    C. dayi 168
    C. hypoleucus 168
    C. quinticolor 168
    C. wallacei 168
Caprimulgidae 44–6
Caprimulgus concretus 44
    C. europaeus 45, *45*, 46
    C. longipennis 45
    C. macrurus 45
    C. prigoginei 44
    C. solala 44
    C. vexillarius 45
Capuchinbird 207
Caracara cheriway 185
    C. lutosa 184, 185
    C. plancus 185
caracaras
    Black 184, 187
    Chimango *186*, 187
    Crested 185
    Guadalupe 184, 185
    Mountain 185
    Red-throated 184, 185
    Southern 185
    Striated 184, 185, 187
Cardellina rubra 320
    C. versicolor 319, 320
Cardinalidae 327–8
Cardinalis cardinalis 327, *327*, 328
    C. phoeniceus 328
    C. sinuatus 328
cardinals
    Northern 327, *327*, 328
    Vermilion 328
Carduelis carduelis 307, *307*, 311
    C. citrinella 311
    C. corsicana 311
Cariama cristata 183, 184
Cariamidae 183–4
Caribbean Emerald 52
Carocopsis barklyi 194, 195
Carpococcyx radiceus 60
    C. renauldi 58, 60
    C. viridis 57
Carpodacus 289
    C. synoicus 309
Carpodectes 207
    C. antoniae 206
Carpornis 207
Carpospiza brachydactyla 301
Caryothraustes 328
    C. erythromelas 327
    C. palogaster *328*
Cassiculus 325
cassowaries 11–12
    Dwarf 12
    Northern (Single-wattled) 12
    Southern (Two-wattled) *11*, 12
Casuariidae 11–13
Casuarius 11
    C. bennetti 12
    C. casuarius *11*, 12
    C. unappendiculatus 12
Catamenia 331
catbirds
    Black 380, 381
    Grey 359, 380, *380*, 381
Cathartes aura 131, 132, *132*, 133, *133*
    C. burrovianus 132
    C. melambrotus 132
Cathartidae 131–4
Catharus bicknelli 391
    C. fuscescens 393
    C. guttatus 393
    C. ustulatus 393
Cathatropeza bishopi 319
Catherpes mexicanus 377
Celeus flavus 166

C. obrieni 164
Centrocercus 26
    C. urophasianus 26
Centropus 57, 58
    C. chlororhynchos 57
    C. menbeki 59
    C. phasianinus 58, 60
    C. steerii 57
Cephalopterus glabricollis 206, 207
    C. ornatus 207
    C. penduliger 206, 207, *207*
Cephalopyrus flammiceps 335, 336
Cepphus 123, 124, 125
Cerasophila thompsoni 351
Ceratogymna 156
    C. elata 153
Ceratopipra mentalis 206
Cercomacra carbonaria 218
Cercotrichas 388
    C. galactotes 388
Cercromacra ferdinandi 218
Cereopsis novaehollandiae 15, 18
Cerorhinca monocerata 123, 125
Certhia americana 373
    C. brachydactyla 374
    C. b. mauretanica 374
    C. discolor 374
    C. familiaris 373, *373*, 374
    C. himalayana 373, 374
    C. hodgsoni 374
    C. manipurensis 374
    C. nipalensis 374
    C. tianquanensis 373, 374
Certhidea 330, 331
Certhiidae 373–4
Certhilauda burra 339
    C. curvirostris 339
Ceryle rudis 182
Cettia castaneocoronata 355, 355
    C. cetti 354, 356, *356*
Ceyx 181
    C. fallax 180
    C. melanurus 180
    C. webster 180
chacalacas
    Grey-headed *21*
    Rufous-headed 21
Chaetops aurantius 280, 281
    C. frenatus 280, 281
Chaetoptila 237, 372
Chaetorhynchus papuensis 269
Chaetornis striata 345
Chaetura pelagica 48, 50
    C. vauxi 50
Chaffinch 305, 306
Chaimarrornis leucocephalus 389
Chalcites lucidus 59, 60
    C. minutillus 59
Chalcomitra hunteri 286
Chamaea fasciata 359
Chamaeza 225
Charadriidae 11–13
Charadrius bicinctus 112
    C. hiaticula 111, *112*
    C. nivosus 111
    C. obscurus obscurus 111
    C. sanctaehelenae 111
    C. semipalmatus 111
    C. thoracicus 111
    C. vociferus 111
Charmosyna amabilis 194
    C. diadema 194
    C. toxopei 194
Chat-tanagers
    Eastern 326
    Western 326
Chatarrhaea longirostris 364
Chatham Island Fernbird 345
chats 387–90
    Black Shama 387
    Blackthroat 387
    Bluethroat 387

Common Nightingale 338, 351, 389
    Siberian Rubythroat *387*
    Thrush Nightingale 389
    White-rumped Sharma 388
    see also Northern Wheatear; redstarts; robins; rock thrushes *and* White-tailed Stonechat
Chauna chavaria 13, 14
    C. torquata *13*, 14
Chaunoproctus ferreorostris 305, 309
Chelictinia riocourii 137
Chelidoptera tenebrosa 161, 162
Chelidorhynx hypoxanthus 334
Chenonetta jubata 16
Chestnut-breasted Whiteface 239
Chestnut-capped Piha 206
Chestnut-headed Tesia 355, 355
Chestnut Munia *296*
chickadees
    Black-capped 335
    Carolina 335
Chiffchaff, Common 354, *354*
Chinese Bush Warbler 359
Chionidae 106–7
Chionis albus 106, *107*
    C. minor 106
Chiroxiphia 205
    C. linearis 206
Chlamydera 231, 232
Chlamydotis macqueenii 69
    C. undulata 70
Chlidonias 129
    C. albostriatus 127, 130
    C. hybrida 130
    C. leucopterus 130
    C. niger 130
Chloebia gouldiae 298, *298*
Chloephaga 15
Chloridops kona 305
Chloris chloris 310
    C. sinica 310
Chloroceryle aenea 181
    C. amazona 182
    C. americana 181, *182*
    C. inda 182
Chlorochrysa nitidissima 329
    C. phoenicotis 331
Chlorocichla prigoginei 351
Chlorodrepanis virens 308
Chloropsis 349
Chlorophanes spiza 330, 331
Chlorophoneus kupeensis 266
    C. multicolor 266
Chlorophonia 306, 329
Chloropicos 167
Chloropipo flavicapilla 205
Chloropsis 265
    C. aurifrons 265
    C. flavipennis 287, 288
    C. hardwickei 288, *288*
    C. kinabaluensis 288
    C. media 287
    C. sonnerati 287
Chlorospingus 314, 315, 329
Chlorostilbon 53
    C. bracei 52
    C. elegans 52
Chondrohierax uncinatus 138
Chordeiles acutipennis 46
    C. minor 46
    C. nacunda 46
choughs 271
Chowchilla 240
Chroicocephalus bulleri 127
    C. philadelphia 127
    C. ridibundus 128, *128*
Chrysococcyx cupreus 59
    C. maculatus 59
    C. xanthorhynchus 60
Chrysocolaptes lucidus 166
Chrysocorythus estherae 306
Chrysomitris strigula 365
Chrysomma 359

C. altirostre 358
Chrysomus icterocephalus 324
    C. ruficapillus 324
Chthonicola sagittatus 239
Chuck-will's-widow 45
Chunga burmeisteri 184
cicadabirds
    Black-bibbed 247
    Common 247
    White-winged 247
Cichlopis 392
    C. leucogenys 391
Cicinnurus regius 277, 278
Ciconia abdimii 88
    C. boyciana 88
    C. ciconia 88, 89, 90, *90*
    C. episcopus 88, 89
    C. maguari 88, 89
    C. nigra 88, 89
    C. stormi 88
Ciconiidae 88–90
Cinclidae 385–6
Cinclocerthia 380
    C. ruficauda 381
cinclodes
    Royal 227
    White-bellied 227
Cinclodes aricomae 227
    C. palliatus 227
Cincloramphus 344
    C. cruralis 345
    C. mathewsi 345
    C. timoriensis 345
Cinclosoma ajax 248
    C. cinnamomeum 248
Cinclosomatidae 248
Cinclus cinclus 385, 386
    C. leucocephalus 386
    C. mexicanus 386, *386*
    C. pallasii 386
    C. schulzii 385, 386
Cinnamon-breasted Tody Tyrant 213
Cinnamon Ibon 301, 302
Cinnamon Tyrant 211
Cinnyricinclus leucogaster 383
Cinnyris loveridgei 286
    C. pulchellus *287*
    C. rockefelleri 286
    C. rufipennis 286
Circaetus 138
Circus 136
    C. cyaneus 139
    C. maillardi 136
Cissa 272
    C. thalassina 271
Cissopis leverianus 330, 332
Cisticola 299
    C. aberdare 342
    C. ayresii 343
    C. juncidis 342, *342*
    C. textrix 343
cisticolas 342–4
    Aberdare 342
    Cloud 343
    Wing-snapping 343
    Zitting Cisticola 342, *342*
Cisticolidae 342–4
Cistothorus apolinari 376
    C. palustris 376, 377
    C. platensis 377
Cladorhynchus leucocephalus 109, 110
Clamator 59
    C. glandarius 59
    C. jacobinus 59
Clangula hyemalis 16, 18, 19
Cleptornis marchei 361
Clibanornis erythrocephalus 227
Climacteridae 232–3
Climacteris affinis 233
    C. melanurus 233
    C. m. wellsi 233
    C. picumnus 233, *233*
    C. rufus 232, 233
Clytoctantes alixii 218
Clytorhynchus 274

Clytospiza 297
Cnemophilidae 242–3
Cnemophilus loriae 242, 243
    C. macgregorii 243, *243*
    C. m. macgregorii 243
    C. m. sanguineus 243
Cnipodectes 214
    C. superrufus 213
Coccothraustes 339
    C. coccothraustes 307, *307*
Coccyua minuta 59
    C. pumila 59
Coccyzus americanus 59
    C. erythropthalmus 59
    C. rufigularis 57
Cochlearius cochlearius 95
Cochoa 393
    C. azurea 391
Cockatiel 189, 191, 192
cockatoos 191–2
    Blue-eyed 191
    Gang-gang 189, 191, 192
    Glossy Black 191, 192
    Long-billed Black 191, 192
    Major Mitchell's 189, 191, 192
    Palm 189, 191
    Philippine 191, 192
    Red-tailed Black 192
    Salmon-crested 189, 191
    Short-billed Black 191, 192
    Sulphur-crested 192, *192*
    White 191, 192
    Yellow-crested 191, 192
    Yellow-tailed Black 192
Cocos Island Finch 330
Coeligena 53
    C. prunellei 52
Coenocorypha aucklandica 118
Coereba flaveola 332–3, *333*
Colaptes auratus 166
    C. chrysoides 166
    C. fernandinae 164
    C. rupicola 166
Colibri 53
Coliidae 148–9
Colius 148
    C. castanotus 149
    C. colius 149
    C. leucocephalus 149
    C. striatus 148, 149
Collocalia esculenta 49, *50*
    C. troglodytes 49
Colluricincla harmonica 249, *249*
    C. tenebrosa 249
Colourful Puffleg 52, 55
Columba 34
    C. argentina 31
    C. livia 32
    C. palumbus 33
    C. torrington 31
    C. versicolor 31
Columbidae 31–4
Columbina 32, 34
condors
    Andean 131, 132, 133
    California 131, 132, 133, *133*
Conirostrum 330
Conopias albovittatus 216
Conopophaga lineata 221, *221*
    C. melanogaster 221
    C. melanops 221
Conopophagidae 221
Conostoma oemodium 360
Conothraupis speculigera 329
Contopus 215
    C. sordidulus 217
    C. virens 217
Conuropsis carolinensis 192, 194
coots
    Common 63
    Horned 63
Copsychus saularis 388
    C. sechellarum 387
Coracias abyssinicus 175

C. benghalensis 176
C. caudatus 175, *176*
C. cyanogaster 175
C. garrulus 175
C. naevius 175
C. spatulatus 175, 176
C. temminckii 176
Coraciidae 175–6
Coracina lineata 247
C. maxima 247, 248
C. papuensis 248
Coracopsis nigra 195
C. vasa 195
Coracornis sanghirensis 249
Coragyps atratus 131, 132, *132*,
133
Corcoracidae 275
corellas
Little 192
Tanimbar 191
Cormobates placens 232
cormorants 102–3
Bank 102
Cape 102
Double-crested 102
Flightless 102, 103
Great 102, 103
Guanay 102
Little Pied *103*
Neotropic 102
Pygmy 102, 103, *103*
Red-legged 103
Socotra 102
Spectacled 102
see also shags
Corocorax melanorhamphos
275, *275*
Corvidae 271–3
Corvinella corvina 270
Corvus alba 271
C. albicollis 271
C. antipodum 271
C. brachyrhynchos 271, 273
C. corax 147, 191, 198, 207,
271, *272*
C. cornix 271, 273
C. corone 271, 273
C. dauuricus 271
C. florensis 271
C. frugilegus 184, 271, *272*
C. fuscicapillus 271
C. hawaiiensis 271, 273
C. kubaryi 271
C. monedula 271
C. moneduloides 273
C. splendens 271, 273
C. tristis 271
C. unicolor 271
Corydon sumatranus 201
Corythaeola cristata 71, 72
Corythaixoides concolor 72
C. leucogaster 72, *72*
C. personatus 72
Corythopis 214
Corythornis 181
Coscoroba coscoroba 15, 18
Cossypha 389
Cotinga amabilis 207
C. cayana 208
C. maculata 206
C. ridgwayi 206
cotingas 206–8
Andean Cock-of-the-Rock
208
Banded Cotinga 206
Capuchinbird 207
Chestnut-capped Piha 206
Fiery-throated Fruiteater 207
Lovely Cotinga 207
Orange-breasted Fruiteater
208
Peruvian Plantcutter 206
Purple-throated Fruitcrow 207
Red-ruffed Fruitcrow 207
Spangled Cotinga *208*
Swallow-tailed Cotinga 207
Turquoise Cotinga 206
Yellow-billed Cotinga 206

see also bellbirds *and*
umbrellabirds
Cotingidae 206–8
Coturnix chinensis 26
C. coturnix 24
Coua delalandiae 57, 58
coucals
Black-headed 57
Greater Black 59
Green-billed 57
Pheasant 58, 60
coursers 122
Cream-coloured 122, *122*
Indian 122
Jerdon's 122
cowbirds
Baywinged 325
Brown-headed 322, *324*, 325
Giant 325
Crab Plover 121, *121*
Cracidae 21–2
Cracticus louisiadensis 259
C. nigrogularis 260
cranes 67–9
Black Crowned 67
Black-necked 67
Blue 67, 68
Common 67, 69, *69*
Crowned 67
Demoiselle 67, *67*, 68
Hooded 67
Red-crowned (Japanese;
Manchurian) 67, *68*
Sandhill 67, 68, *68*
Sarus 67, 68
Siberian 67, 68, 69
Wattled 67
White-naped 67
Whooping 67, 68, 69
see also Brolga
Cranioleuca curtata 227
C. henricae 227
Crateroscelis 239
Crax alberti 21
C. globulosa 21
C. rubra 22
Creagrus furcatus 128, 129
Creatophora cinerea 383, *383*
creepers, New Zealand 245–6
crescentchests
Collared 220
Elegant 220
Marañon 220, *221*
Olive-crowned 220
Crested Gallito 223, *223*
Crested Tit-warbler 358
Crimson-breasted Gonolek 266
Crimson Rosella 196, 197
Crinifer 71, 72
Criniger olivaceus 351
Crithagra flavigula 305
C. menachensis 310
crombecs 341–2
Lendu (Chapin's) 341
Northern 341
Red-faced *341*
White-browed 341
Crossleyia xanthophrys 346
Crotophaga 57
C. major 60
crows 271–3
American 271, 273
Banggai 271
Brown-headed 271
Carrion 271, 273
Ethiopian Bush-Crow 271
Flores 271
Grey 271
Hawaiian 271, 273
Hooded 271, 273
House 271, 273
Mariana 271
New Caledonian 273
Pied 271
Stresemann's Bush Crow 272
see also choughs; jackdaws;
magpies; Piapiac; ravens *and*
Rook

Cryptillas victorini 341, 342
Cryptospiza shelleyi 296
Cryptosylvicola randrianasoloi
347
Crypturellus kerriae 9
Cuckoo-roller *149*, 149–50, 173
cuckoo-shrikes 247–8
Barred *247*
Blue 247
Golden 247
Ground 247, 248
Mauritius 247
Reunion 247
Western Wattled 247
White-bellied 248
see also cicadabirds *and*
Fiery Minivet
cuckoos 57–60
Banded Ground 57
Bay-breasted 57
Black 60
Black-bellied *58*
Black-billed 59
Bornean Ground 60
Brush 59
Channel-billed 57, 59, 60
Common 57, *58*, 59, 60,
291, 348
Coral-billed Ground 58, 60
Drongo 60
Dwarf 59
Great Spotted 59
Guira 57, 58
Jacobin 59
Little 59
Little Bronze 59
Pavonine 58
Pheasant 58
Rufous-vented Ground 57
Shining Bronze 59, 60
Squirrel 59
Striped 58
Sumatran Ground 57
Violet 60
Yellow-billed 59
see also coucals; Greater
Ani; Red-faced Malkoha;
roadrunners *and* Snail-
eating Coua
Cuculidae 57–60
Cuculus 59, 60, 138
C. canorus 57, *58*, 59, 60,
291, 348
C. clamosus 60
Culicicapa 334
C. ceylonensis 334
Culicivora caudacuta 215
cupwings
Nepal 349
Pygmy 349, *349*
Scaly-breasted 349
Taiwan 349
Curaeus curaeus 324
C. forbesi 324
curassows 21
Alagoas 21
Blue-billed 21
Great *22*
Helmeted 21
Horned 21
Wattled 21
Curl-crested Manucode 278
curlews
Bristle-thighed 116
Eskimo 116, 119
Eurasian 117, *117*
Far Eastern 116, 117
Little 117
Slender-billed 116, 119
currawongs
Black 259
Pied 259, *260*
Curruca communis 359
C. nisoria 359
C. undata 358, 359, *359*
Cursorius coromandelicus 122
C. cursor 122, *122*
Cutia 366

Cutia legalleni 366
Cyanerpes 330
C. caeruleus 331
C. lucidus 332
Cyanistes caeruleus 335, *335*
Cyanochen cyanoptera 15
Cyanocitta cristata 271
C. stelleri 271, *272*
Cyanocompsa perellina 328
Cyanocorax chrysops 271
C. cristatellus 271
C. dickey 271
Cyanoderma chrysaeum 362
Cyanograuculus azureus 247
Cyanolanius madagascarinus
263, *263*
Cyanolimnas cerverai 61
Cyanoliseus patagonicus 189,
194
Cyanoloxia 328
Cyanopica 272
Cyanopsitta spixii 192, 194
Cyanoptila cyanomelana 389
Cyanoramphus 196
C. ulietanus 194
C. unicolor 196
C. zealandicus 194
Cyclarhis gujanensis 255
C. nigrirostris 255
Cyclopsitta 188, 197
Cygnus 17
C. atratus 15
C. buccinator 15
C. columbianus 15
C. cygnus 15
C. melanocoryphus 15, 17
C. olor 15, 17, 18, *18*, 132
Cymbirhynchus macrorhynchus
201, *201*
Cyornis brunneatus 387
C. caeruleus 387
C. ruecki 387
C. unicolor 389
Cyphorhinus arada 376
C. phaeocephalus 376
Cypseloides niger 49, 51
C. senex 49, *49*
Cypsiurus 50
C. parvus 50
Cyrtonyx ocellatus 23

Dacelo gaudichaud 181
D. leachii 181
D. novaeguineae 180, 181,
182
D. rex 182
D. tyro 181
Dacnis 330
D. cayana 332
D. hartlaubi 329
dacnises
Blue *332*
Turquoise 329
Viridian 329
Daphoenositta chrysoptera 246,
246
D. miranda 246
D. papuensis 246
Dapple-chest 283, 284
Daption capense 84, *86*
Daptrius ater 184, 187
darters
African 104
Australasian 104
Oriental 104
see also Anhinga
Dasycrotapha plateni 361
D. speciosa 360, 361
Dasyornis brachypterus 234,
235, 235
D. broadbenti 235
D. b. litoralis 235
D. longirostris 234, 235
Dasyornithidae 234–5
Delichon dasypus 350
D. nipalense 350
D. urbicum 350
Dendragapus obscurus 26

Dendrocincla 226, 227
Dendrocitta 272
Dendrocolaptes 227
D. hoffmansi 226
Dendrocolaptidae 226–7
Dendrocopos kizuki 165
D. maculatus 165
D. major 165, 167, *167*
D. minor 167
D. noguchii 164
Dendrocygna 15, 189
Dendroica 291
Dendronanthus indicus 302,
303
Dendropicos 167
Dendroplex kienerii 226
Dendrortyx barbatus 23
Dendroscansor decurvirostris
199
Deroptyus accipitrinus 194
Des Murs' Wiretail 228
Dicaeidae 284–5
Dicaeum haematostictum 284
D. hirundinaceum 285, *285*
D. quadricolor 284
D. retrocinctum 284
D. trigonostigma 285
Dickcissel 328
Dicruridae 267–8
Dicrurus adsimilis 268
D. bracteatus 267, 268
D. caerulescens 267
D. fuscipennis 267
D. leucophaeus 267
D. ludwigii 267
D. macrocercus 267, 268, *268*
D. megarhynchus 267
D. menagei 267
D. paradiseus 267
D. remifer 267
D. waldenii 267
Didunculus strigirostris* 31, 32,
33, 34
Diglossa 54, 330
D. venezuelensis 329
dikkops
Spotted 105
Water 105
Dinemellia dinemelli 293
Dinopium 166, 168
Diomedea 79, 80, 132
D. epomophora 80, 82
D. e. sanfordi 79
D. exulans 79, 80, 81, 82, *82*
D. e. amsterdamensis 79
D. e. antipodensis 79
D. e. dabbenena 79
Diomedeidae 79–82
Diopsittaca nobilis 193
dippers
American 386, *386*
Brown 386
Rufous-throated 385, 386
White-capped 386
White-throated *385*, 386
Diuca 332
divers 73–4
Black- throated (NA Black-
throated Loon) 73
Great Northern (NA
Common Loon) 73, *73*
Pacific (NA Pacific Loon) 73
Red-throated (NA Red-
throated Loon) 73, *74*
White-billed (NA Yellow-
billed Loon) 73
diving-petrels
Common 87, *87*
Magellanic 86
Peruvian 87
South Georgia 87
Dixiphia pipra 206
Dodo 31, 34
Dolichonyx oryzivorus 324, 325
Dollarbird 175, 176
Donacobiidae 346
Donacobius 346, *346*
Donacobius atricapilla 346, *346*

Donacospiza albifrons 332
Doryfera 53
dotterels
Eurasian 111, 112
Hooded 111
Shore (Shore Plover) 111
Tawny-throated 111
doves 32
Atoll Fruit 32
Grenada 31
Mourning 34
Red-moustached Fruit 31
Rock (Rock Pigeon) 32
Socorro 31
Zebra 32
see also bleeding hearts
Drepanis funerea 305
D. pacifica 305
Dreptes thomensis 286
Dromadidae 121
Dromaius 11
D. baudinianus 13
D. minor 13
D. novaehollandiae 12, *12*
D. n. diemenensis 13
Dromas ardeola 121, *121*
Dromococcyx pavoninus 58
D. phasianellus 58
drongos 267–8
Ashy 267
Black *267*, 268, *268*
Fork-tailed 268
Grand Comoro 267
Greater Raquet-tailed 267
Lesser Raquet-tailed 267
Mayotte 267
Pygmy 269
Ribbon-tailed 267
Spangled 267, 268
Square-tailed 267
Tablas 267
White-bellied 267
Drymodes beccarii 282
D. brunneopygia 282
D. superciliaris 282
Drymornis bridgesii 226
Drymotoxeres pucherannii 226, 227
Dryocopus 166, 168
D. galeatus 164
D. hodgei 164, 166
D. martius 166, *166*
D. pileatus 166
Dryoscopus 266
Dryotriorchis 138
ducks
Black-headed 17
Blue 15, 16, 18
Comb 16, 17
Freckled 16
Harlequin 16, 18
Hawaiian 15
Labrador 15, 16
Lake 17
Laysan 15
Long-tailed 16, 18, 19
Mandarin 16, 18
Maned 16
Masked 17
Muscovy 16, 19
Musk 17
Pink-eared 16, 17, 18
Pink-headed 15
Ring-necked 16
Ruddy 17
Torrent 16, 18
Tufted 16
White-headed 15, 17
Wood 16, 18
see also Blue-winged Goose;
Canvasback; Egyptian
Goose; goldeneyes; Greater
Scaup; Mallard; mergansers;
Northern Pintail; Orinoco
Goose; pochards; Redhead;
shelducks; shovelers; Smew;
Steller's Eider; teal *and*
wigeon

Ducula 34
D. cineracea 31
Dulidae 367–8
Dulus dominicus 367–8, *368*
Dumetella carolinensis 359, 380, *380*, 381
Dunnock 290, *291*, 313
Dusky Friarbird 235
Dusky Tetraka 346
Dyaphorophyia tonsa 262
Dysithamnus 219
D. plumbeus 218

eagles
Bald *137*, 140
Bateleur 138
Black 139
Black-chested Buzzard Eagle 140
Booted 139
Crested 138, 139
Crowned 139, *139*
Crowned Solitary 136
Golden 137, 139
Haast's 139
Harpy 136, 138, 139
Little 139
Long-crested 139
Madagascar Fish-eagle 136
Martial 139
Papuan 138, 139
Philippine 136, 138
Steller's Sea 136, 140
Verreaux's 139
Wedge-tailed 137, 139
earthcreepers 225, 227
Eastern Kingbird 217
Eastern Phoebe 217
Eastern Wood Pewee 217
Eclectus roratus 189, 195
Ectopistes migratorius 31, 34
Edolisoma mindanensis 247
E. ostentum 247
E. tenuirostris insperatum 247
E. t. nesiotis 247
egrets
Cattle 95, 96, 97
Chinese 94
Great 95, 96
Little 96
Pacific Reef 96
Reddish 96
Slaty 94
Snowy 96
Western Reef 96
Egretta 95, 97
E. ardesiaca 96
E. caerulea 96
E. eulophotes 94
E. garzetta 96
E. gularis 96
E. rufescens 96
E. sacra 96
E. thula 96
E. vinaceigula 94
Egyptian Goose 15
Egyptian Plover 107, 122
Elachura formosa 372
Elachuridae 372
Elaenia 215, 216
Elanoides 136
E. forficatus 138
Elanus axillaris 137
E. caeruleus 137
E. leucurus 137
E. scriptus 137
Electron carinatum 179
E. platyrhynchum 179, *180*
Elegant Mourner 210, 211
Eleoscytalopus pyschopompus 223
Eleothreptus anomalus 46
E. candicans 44
Elminia longicauda 334
Emberiza 317
E. alcoveri 199
E. calandra 316

E. cia 317
E. citrinella 317
E. jankowskii 316
Emberizidae 316
Emberizoides 332
Empidonax 215, 217
emu-wrens 234
Mallee 233
emus 11, 12–13
Kangaroo Island 13
King Island 13
Enicurus 389
Ensifera ensifera 53, 54
Entomodestes 392
Entomyzon cyanotis 237
Eolophus roseicapillus 191, 192
Eophona 308
Eopsaltria australis 281
Eos cyanogenia 194
Ephippiorhynchus 88
E. asiaticus 89
E. senegalensis 89, 90
Epimachus 277
E. meyeri 277, *278*
Epthianura 237
Eremomela 343
E. turneri 342
Eremophila alpestris 339
Eremopterix australis 339
E. hova 339
Eriocnemis godini 52
E. isabellae 52
E. mirabilis 52, 55
E. nigrivestis 52
Erithacus rubecula 281, 387, 389
Erpornis 255
Erpornis zantholeuca 255
Erythrina erythrina 309
Erythrocercus 355
Erythrogenys 241
E. hypoleucos 362
Erythropitta 200
Erythrotriorchis 140
Erythrura 298
E. kleinschmidti 296
E. viridifacies 296
Esacus 106
E. magnirostris 105
E. recurvirostris 105
Estrilda 297
Estrildidae 296–8
Euaegotheles crinifrons 47
Eubucco 169, 172
Euchrepornis 219
E. sharpei 218
Eucometis pencillata 331, *331*
Eudocimus ruber 98
Eudromias morinellus 111, 112
Eudynamys scolopaceus 59
Eudyptes chrysocome 75
E. chrysolophus 74
E. moseleyi 74
E. pachyrhynchus 74
E. sclateri 74
Eudyptula minor 75
Eugenes fulgens 52
Eugerygone rubra 282
Eulacestoma nigropectus 246, 253, *253*
Eulacestomatidae 253
Eulipoa wallacei 19, 20
Eumomota superciliosa 179, 180
Euneornis campestris 332
Eunymphicus cornutus 196
E. uvaeensis 196
Eupetes macrocerus 252, 280, 281
Eupetidae 280–1
Euphagus carolinus 321, 324
E. cyanocephalus 324
Euphonia 306, 329
Euplectes 292, 294, 295
E. jacksoni 295
E. orix 292
E. progne 295
Eupodotis 69
Euptilotis neoxenus 152

Eurasian Bullfinch 310
Eurasian Siskin 311
Eurocephalus anguitimens 270
E. ruppelli 270
European Goldfinch 307, *307*, 311
European Greenfinch 310
European Serin 310
Eurostopodus diabolicus 44
E. exul 44
Euryceros prevostii 262, 263, *263*
Eurylaimidae 201–2
Eurylaimus javanicus 202
E. ochromalus 201, 202
Eurypyga helias 37, *37*
Eurypygidae 37
Eurystomus azureus 175, 176
E. glaucurus 175, 176
E. gularis 176
E. orientalis 175, 176
Euschistospiza 297
Eutoxeres 53, 54
Eutrichomyias rowleyi 273, 274
Evening Grosbeak 308

fairy bluebirds 287–8
Asian 288, *288*
Philippine 288
Fairy-fantail 334
Fairy Flycatcher 334
fairy-wrens 233
Lovely 234
Splendid 234
Superb 233, *234*
Falcated Wren Babbler 364
Falcipennis falcipennis 26
Falco amurensis 184, 186, 188
F. araea 184, 186
F. biarmicus 186
F. cherrug 184, 185, 186
F. columbarius 186, 187
F. concolor 184, 186, 188
F. cuvieri 186
F. deiroleucus 187
F. eleonorae 184, 186, *186*, 187, 188
F. fasclinucha 184, 187
F. femoralis 186
F. hypoleucos 184
F. jugger 186
F. longipennis 186
F. mexicanus 187
F. naumanni 186
F. novaeseelandiae 184
F. pelegrinoides 187
F. peregrinus 147, 184, 185, 187, *187*, 188
F. punctatus 184, 186
F. rufigularius 186
F. rusticolus 147, 185, 187
F. severus 186
F. sparverius 185, 186, 187, *187*, 188
F. subbuteo 186
F. tinnunculus 184, 185
F. vespertinus 184, 186, 187
F. zoniventris 186
falconets
Black-thighed 185
Spot-winged 185
White-fronted 184
Falconidae 184–8
falcons
African Pygmy 185
Amur 184, 186, 188
Aplomado 186
Barbary 186
Bat 186
Eleonora's 184, 186, *186*, 187, 188
Grey 184
Gyr 147, 185, 187
Laggar 186
Lanner 186
Laughing 184, 185, 187
New Zealand 184
Orange-breasted 187

Peregrine 147, 184, 185, 187, *187*, 188
Prairie 187
Red-footed 184, 186, 187
Saker 184, 185, 186
Sooty 184, 186, 188
Taita 184, 187
White-rumped Pygmy 185
see also falconets; forest-
falcons; hobbies, kestrels *and*
Merlin
Falculea palliata 262, 263, *264*
Falcunculidae 250–1
Falcunculus 250
F. frontatus 251
F. leucogaster *250*
False Whistler 258
fantails
Friendly *269*
Grey 269
Malaita 268
Manus 268
New Zealand 269
Rufous 268, *269*
see also Willie-Wagtail
Ferminia cerverai 376, *377*
Fernbird 345
Fernwren 240
Ficedula basilanica 387
F. bonthaina 387
F. hypoleuca 390
F. narcissina 390, *390*
F. parva 390
Fieldfare 393
Fiery Minivet 247
finches
American Goldfinch 311
Andean Siskin 307
Atlantic Canary 306, 310
Blue Chaffinch 306
Bonin Grosbeak 305, 309
Brambling 305, 306, *306*
Chaffinch 305, 306
Citril Finch 311
Common Linnet 310
Common Rosefinch 309
Corsican Finch 311
Eurasian Bullfinch 310
Eurasian Siskin 311
European Goldfinch 307, *307*, 311
European Greenfinch 310
European Serin 310
Evening Grosbeak 308
Grey-capped Greenfinch 310
Grey-crowned Rosy Finch *307*
Hawfinch 307, *307*
Hispaniolan Crossbill 311
House Finch 305, *310*
Lawrence's Goldfinch 311
Lesser Goldfinch 311
Mountain Serin 306
Parrot Crossbill 311
Pine Grosbeak 309
Pine Siskin 311
Red Crossbill 311, *311*
Red-fronted Serin 310
Red Siskin 305, 311
Saõ Tomé Grosbeak 305
Scarlet Finch 309
Scottish Crossbill 311
Sinai Rosefinch 309
Syrian Serin 310
Trumpeter Finch 310
Twite 310
White-winged (Two-barred)
Crossbill 311
Yellow-throated Canary 305
Yemen Serin 310
finfoots
African 64, *64*
Masked 64
see also Sungrebe
Finschia novaeseelandiae 245, 246, *246*
Fire-tailed Myzornis 358, 360
Firecrest *366*, 367

Firewood Gatherer 189, 228
Flame-templed Babbler 360,
361
Flamecrest 367
flamingos 27–8
American 27
Andean 27, 28
Chilean 27, 28
Eurasian 27, 29
Greater 27, 28, 29
James's (Puna) 27, 28
Lesser 27, 28, 28
flatbills 213–14
Alagoas Tyrannulet 213
Antioquia Bristle Tyrant 213
Bahia Tyrannulet 213
Black-capped Pygmy Tyrant
214
Black-and-white Tody
Tyrant 214
Cinnamon-breasted Tody
Tyrant 213
Common Tody Flycatcher
214
Fork-tailed Tody Tyrant 213
Johnson's Tody Tyrant 213
Kaempfer's Tody Tyrant 213
Minas Gerais Tyrannulet 213
Restinga Tyrannulet 213
Rufous-headed Pygmy
Tyrant 214
Rufous Twistwing 213
Short-tailed Pygmy Tyrant
198, 214
Yellow-olive Flycatcher 214
flickers
Andean 166
Fernandina's 164
Gilded 166
Northern 166
floricans
Bengal 69
Lesser 69, 70, 71
Florisuga 53
flowerpeckers 284–5
Black-belted 284
Cebu 284
Orange-bellied 285
Scarlet-breasted 285
Scarlet-collared 284
see also Mistletoe Bird
flowerpiercers 330, 331
Deep Blue 329
Venezuelan 329
flufftails
Slender-billed 63
White-winged 63
Fluvicola 217
F. pica 216
flycatchers, Old World 387–90
Blue-and-white 389
Brown-chested Jungle 387
Large-billed Blue 387
Little Slaty 387
Lompobattang 387
Narcissus 390, 390
Pale Blue 389
Pied 390
Red-breasted 390
Rück's Blue 387
Spotted 389
White-throated Jungle 387
see also niltavas
fodies
Mauritius 292
Red (Madagascar) 294, 295
Rodrigues 294
Seychelles 294
foliage-gleaners
Alagoas 227
Henna-hooded 227
forest-falcons
Barred 187
Collared 187
Plumbeous 184
Fork-tailed Tody Tyrant 213
Formicariidae 224–5
Formicarius 225

F. nigricapillus 224
F. rufifrons 224
Formicivora 219
F. erythronotos 218
F. paludicola 218
Forpus 193
F. xanthops 192
Foudia flavicans 294
F. madagascariensis 294, 295
F. rubra 292
F. sechellarum 294
francolins
Djibouti 24
Nahan's 24, 26
Francolinus nahani 24, 26
F. ochropectus 24
Fratercula arctica 123, 125, 128
F. cirrhata 123, 125
F. corniculata 123
Fregata andrewsi 99, 99, 100
F. aquila 99, 100
F. ariel 99, 100
F. magnificens 99, 100
F. minor 99, 100
Fregatidae 99–100
Fregetta maoriana 77
Fregilupus varius 381
frigatebirds 99–100
Ascension 99, 100
Christmas Island 99, 99, 100
Great 99, 100
Lesser 99, 100
Magnificent 99, 100
Fringe-backed Fire-eye 218
Fringilla coelebs 305, 306
F. montifringilla 305, 306,
306
F. teydea 306
Fringillaria 316
Fringillidae 305–11
frogmouths 42–3
Large 42
Marbled 42
Papuan 42
Short-tailed 42
Solomon Islands
(Cinnamon) 42
Tawny 42, 43
Fulica 63
F. atra 63
F. cornuta 63
fulmars
Northern 84
Southern 84
Fulmarus glacialis 84
F. glacialoides 84
Fulveta 359, 360
F. vinipectus 359
fulvettas
Golden-breasted 360
White-browed 359
Furnariidae 227–8
Furnarius rufus 228, 228

Galah 191, 192
Galapagos (Darwin's) finches
263,
308, 330–1, 332, 380
Galbalcyrhynchus 161
Galbula 161
G. albirostris 160
G. dea 161
G. pastazae 160
G. ruficauda 160
Galbulidae 160–1
Galerida cristata 339, 339
Gallicolumba 32, 34
G. crinigera 31
G. keayi 31
G. menagei 31
G. platenae 31
Gallinago 118
G. gallinago 118
G. macrodactyla 116
G. media 118
Gallinula 62
Gallirallus australis 61
G. lafresnayanus 61

G. owstoni 61
Gallus gallus 26
G. sonneratii 26, 27
Gampsonyx swainsonii 136, 137
Gampsorhynchus 363
gannets 100–2
Australasian 100, 101
Cape 100
Northern 101
Garritornis isidorei 241
Garrulax bicolor 364
G. canorus 364
G. courtoisi 364
G. leucolophus 364
G. ruufifrons 364, 365
G. sukatschewi 364
Garrulus glandarius 272, 273
Gavia adamsii 73
G. arctica 73
G. immer 73, 73
G. pacifica 73
G. stellata 73, 74
Gaviidae 73–4
Gavicalis fasciogularis 237
G. versicolor 237
geese
African Pygmy 17
Canada 15, 19
Cape Barren 15, 18
Greylag 15, 19, 19
Hawaiian 15
Lesser White-fronted 15
Red-breasted 15
Snow 15
Swan Goose 15, 19
Geobates tenuirostris 226
Geobiastes squamiger 176, 177
Geochelidon nilotica 129
Geococcyx 57, 58
G. californianus 58, 60
G. velox 58
Geocolaptes olivaceus 165
Geokichla 392
G. guttata 391
Geopelia striata 32
Geophaps plumifera 32, 33
G. scripta 32
Geositta antarctica 225
G. poeciloptera 225, 226
G. punensis 225
Geospiza 330, 331, 332
G. magnirostris 331
Geothlypis beldingi 319
G. speciosa 319
G. trichas 320
Geotrygon 34
Geranoaetus melanoleucus 140
Geranospiza caerulescens 140
Geronticus calvus 97, 98
G. eremita 97, 98
Gerygone igata insularis 239
G. i. modesta 239
G. magnirostris 240
G. olivacea 239
gerygones 239
Grey Warbler 239
Large-billed Gerygone 240
White-throated Gerygone
239
Giant Kingbird 216
Gibberbird 237
Glareola cinerea 123
G. maldivarum 122
G. nordmanni 122, 123
G. ocularis 122
G. pratincola 123, 123
Glareolidae 122–3
Glaucidium 147
G. brasilianum 146
G. capense 144
G. cuculoides 144
G. gnoma 144, 146
G. minutissimum 143
G. mooreorum 143
G. passerinum 144, 146
G. siju 146
Glaucis dohrnii 52
Glyphorynchus spirurus 227

gnatcatchers
Black-capped 378
Black-tailed 378
Blue-grey 377, 378
California 378
Creamy-bellied 377, 378
Guianan 378
Inambari 378
Iquitos 378
gnateaters
Black-bellied Gnateater 221
Black-cheeked Gnateater 221
Black-crowned Antpitta 221
Rufous-crowned Antpitta
221
Rufous Gnateater 221, 221
gnatwrens
Collared 378
Long-billed 377, 378, 378
Tawny-faced 378
go-away birds
Bare-faced 72
Grey 72
White-bellied 72, 72
godwits
Bar-tailed 119
Black-tailed 117
Marbled 117
goldcrests
Firecrest 366, 367
Flamecrest 367
Goldcrest 366
Madeira Firecrest 366, 367
goldeneyes 18
Barrow's 16, 17
Common 16, 18
see also Bufflehead
Goldenface 240
Goodfellowia miranda 384
Goosander (NA Common
Merganser) 16
Gorgeted Puffleg 52
Gorgeted Wood-quail 23
Gorsachius 95
G. goisagi 94
G. magnificus 94
Gough Island Finch 329
Gouldian Finch 298, 298
Goura 32, 34
G. victoria 31
grackles
Common 322, 325
Great-tailed 323
Red-bellied 321
Slender-billed 321, 324
Gracula ptilogenys 384
G. religiosa 382, 384
Gracupica contra 384
Grallaria alleni 222
G. blakei 222
G. chthonia 222
G. eludens 223
G. excelsa 222
G. fenwickorum 222
G. gigantea 222
G. kaestneri 222
G. przewalskii 222
G. ridgelyi 222, 222, 223
Grallaricula lineifrons 222
Grallariidae 222–3
Grallina 273
G. bruijni 274
G. cyanoleuca 274, 274
Gralluricula ochraceifrons 222
Graminicola striatus 363
Grammoptila striata 365
Granatellus 327, 328
Granatina 297
Granativora bruniceps 316
G. melanocephala 316
Grandala 392, 392
Grandala coelicolor 392, 392
Grantiella picta 235, 236
grass owls 142
African 142
Eastern 142
see also Madagascan Red
Owl

grassbirds
Bristled 345
Fly River 344, 345
Little 345
Striated 345
Tawny 345
grasshopper warblers 345, 345
Friendly 345
Gray's 345
Pallas's 345
Pleske's 344
grasswrens 234
Black 233
Carpentarian 233
Grey 233
Short-tailed 233
White-throated 233
Graueria vittata 342
Grauer's Forest Warbler 342
Grauer's Swamp Warbler 344
Great-billed Seed Finch 329
Great Kiskadee 216, 217
Greater Ani 60
Greater Koa Finch 305
Greater Scaup 16
Greater Scythebill 226, 227
Greater Sooty Owl 142, 142
Greater Yellowlegs 118
grebes 29–31
Alaotra 29, 31
Atitlan 29, 30, 31
Clark's 30, 31
Colombian 29, 31
Great Crested 30, 30, 31
Hooded 29, 31
Junin Flightless 29, 30, 31
Least 30
Little 30
Madagascar 29
New Zealand 29
Pied-billed 30, 30
Red-necked 30
Titicaca (Short-winged) 29,
30, 31
Western 30, 31
Green Avadavat 296, 297
Green-backed Firecrown 55
Green-breasted Mango 55
Green-faced Parrotfinch 296
Green Hylia 354, 356
Green Longtail 343
greenbuls
Prigogine's 351
Tiny 352
Yellow-whiskered 351
Grey-banded Mannikin 296
Grey-capped Greenfinch 310
Grey-chested Kakamega 283,
284
Grey-crowned Crocias 364
Grey-crowned Palm Tanager
317, 318
Grey-crowned Rosy Finch 307
Grey-crowned Tetraka 346, 347
Grey-headed Canary
Flycatcher 334
Grey Kingbird 368
Grey Warbler 239
grosbeaks
Black-backed 328
Black-faced 328
Black-headed 328
Black-thighed 328
Blue 328
Golden 328
Red-and-black 327
Rose-breasted 328
Yellow 328
ground antbirds see antpittas
ground babblers
Bornean Wren Babbler 363
Falcated Wren Babbler 364
Gold-fronted Fulvetta 363
Long-tailed Grass Babbler
363
Naung Mung Wren Babbler
363
Rufous-rumped Grass

Babbler 363
Rufous-throated Fulvetta *363*
White-throated Wren
Babbler 363
Yellow-throated Fulvetta 363
ground-parrots
Eastern 196
Western 196
ground rollers 176–7
Long-tailed 176, 177, *177*
Pitta-like 177, *177*
Rufous-headed 176, 177
Scaly 176, 177
Short-legged 176, 177
grouse 25–6
Blue 26
Eurasian Black 26
Red 25
Ruffed 26
Sage 26
Siberian Grouse 26
Spruce Grouse 26
Willow 25
see also capercaillies; prairie-chickens *and* ptarmigans
Gruidae 67–9
Grus americana 67, 68, 69
G. carunculatus 67
G. grus 67, 69, 69
G. japonensis 67, 68
G. monacha 67
G. nigricollis 67
G. paradiseus 67, 68
G. vipio 67
G. virgo 67, 67, 68
Guadalupe Junco 314
Guaiabero 197
guans
Black-fronted Piping 21
Crested *22*
Highland 21
Horned 21
Trinidad Piping 21
White-winged 21
Gubernatrix cristata 329
Gubernetes yetapa 217
guillemots
Brünnich's (NA Thick-billed
Murre) 124, 125
Common (NA Common
Murre) *124*
guineafowl 22–3
Black 22
Crested 22, 23
Helmeted 22, 23, *23*
Plumed 22, 23
Vulturine 22, 23, *23*
White-breasted 22
Guira guira 57, 58
gulls 127–9
Black-billed 127
Black-headed 128, *128*
Bonaparte's 127
Franklin's 129
Grey 127, 129
Herring 128, *128*
Ivory 128, 129
Laughing 128, 129
Lava 127
Ross's 128
Sabine's 127, 128
Swallow-tailed 128, 129
see also kittiwakes
Guttera plumifera 22, 23
G. pucherani 22, 23
Gygis 127
G. alba 127, 130
Gymnocichla nudiceps 220
Gymnogyps californianus 131, 132, 133, *133*
Gymnomyza aubryana 235, 236
G. samoensis 235, 236
Gymnopithys bicolor 219
Gymnopythis rufigula 220
Gymnorhina tibicen 259, 260–1, *261*
Gymnorhinus cyanocephalus 271

Gymnoris 301
Gypaetus barbatus 136, 137, 138
Gypohierax angolensis 136, 138
Gyps africanus 136
G. bengalensis 136, 138, 139
G. coprotheres 136
G. himalayensis 136
G. indicus 139
G. rueppellii 136
G. tenuirostris 136, 139

Habia 328, 329
H. atrimaxillaris 327
H. gutturalis 327
Habroptila wallacii 61, 62
Haematoderus 207
Haematopodidae 108–9
Haematopus ater 108
H. bachmani 108
H. chathamensis 108
H. finschi 108
H. fuliginosus 108
H. leucopodus 108
H. longirostris 108
H. meadewaldoi 108
H. moquini 108
H. ostralegus 108, *109*
H. palliatus 108
H. unicolor 108
H. u. chathamensis 108
Haematospiza sipahi 309
Haemorhous mexicanus 310, 310
Halcyon chelicuti 182
H. coromanda 181, 183
H. leucocephala 182
H. smyrnensis 181
Haliaeetus 137
H. leucocephalus 137, 140
H. pelagicus 136, 140
H. vociferoides 136
Haliastur indus 140
H. spenurus 140
Halobaena caerulea 85
Hamerkop 88, 92–3, *93*
Hapalopsittaca fuertesi 192
Hapaloptila castanea 162
Haplophaedia 53
Harpactes kasumba 150
Harpagornis moorei 139
Harpia harpyja 136, 138, 139
Harpyopsis novaeguineae 138, 139
harriers
Hen 139
Réunion 136
Hartertula flavoriviridis 347
Hawaii Amakihi 308
Hawaiian honeycreepers 263, 306, 308
Akekee 305
Akiapolaau 309, *309*
Akikiki (Kauai Creeper) 305, 308–9
Akohekohe 309
Anianiau 307
Apapane 308, *308*, 309
Black Mamo 305
Greater Koa Finch 305
Hawaii Amakihi 308
Hawaii Creeper 308
Hawaiian Mamo 305
Iiwi 309, *309*
Kona Grosbeak 305
Lesser Koa Finch 305
Maui Nukupuu 305
Maui Parrotbill 305
Oahu Alauahio 305
Ou 305, 308
Palila 305, 308, *308*
Poo-uli 305, 309
Hawaiian Mamo 305
Hawfinch 307, *307*
hawks
Bat 136, 139
Broad-winged 140
Cooper's 140

Crane 140
Gundlach's 140
Harris's (Bay-winged) 136, 140
Red-tailed 140, *140*, 271
Ridgway's 140
Rufous Crab-Hawk 140
Sharp-shinned 140
Swainson's 140
Tiny 136
White 140
see also buzzards; Northern Goshawk *and* sparrowhawks
Hedydipna pallidigaster 286
Heliangelus 53
H. regalis 52
Helicolestes hamatus 140
Heliodoxa 54
Heliopais personatus 64
Heliornis fulica 64
Heliornithidae 64
Heliothryx 54
helmet shrikes 262, 263–4
White *264*
Hemicircus 165
Hemignathus affinis 305
H. wilsoni 309, *309*
Hemimacronyx chloris 302, 304
Hemiphaga novaeseelandiae 34
Hemiprocne comata 51
H. coronata 51
H. longipennis 51
H. mystacea 51, *51*
Hemipus 263, 264
Hemitesia 349, 354
H. neumanni 355
H. pallidipes 355
Hemitriccus 214
H. cinnamomeipectus 213
H. furcatus 213
H. kaempferi 213
Henicorhina negreti 376
herons 94–7
Agami 94, 95
Black 96
Boat-billed 95
Capped 95
Goliath 95
Great Blue 95, 96
Green 95, 97
Grey 94, 96, *96*
Humblot's 94
Japanese Night 94
Little Blue 96
Madagascan Pond 94, 96
Purple 95
Squacco 96
Striated 95, 96, 97
Whistling 95
White-bellied 94
White-eared Night 94
Zigzag 95
see also bitterns *and* egrets
Herpetotheres cachinnans 184, 185, 187
Herpsilochmus pectoralis 218
Hesperiphona vespertina 308
Heteroglaux blewitti 143, 146
Heteroglocha acutirostris 243, 244
Heteromirafra archeri 339, 340
H. ruddi 339
Heteromunia pectoralis 298
Heteronetta atricapilla 17
Heterophasia 364
Heteroscelus brevipes 119
H. incanus 119
Hieraaetus morphnoides 139
H. pennatus 139
Himantopus himantopus 109, 110, *110*
H. novaezelandiae 109, 110
Himatione sanguinea 308, *308*, 309
Hippolais 347, 349
H. icterina 349
H. olivetorum 349
H. polyglotta 349

Hirundapus 49
H. caudacutus 48
H. celebensis 50
H. giganteus 50
Hirundinea ferruginea 216
Hirundinidae 350–1
Hirundo atrocaerulea 350, 351
H. neoxena 350
H. rustica 350
H. indicus 350
Hispaniolan Crossbill 311
Histrionicus histrionicus 16, 18
Histurgops ruficauda 293
Hoatzin 56, 56–7, 64
hobbies
African 186
Australian 186
Eurasian 186
Oriental 186
Honduran Emerald 52
honey buzzards 136, 138
honeycreepers
Green *330*, 331
Purple 329, 331
Shining *332*
see also Hawaiian honeycreepers
honeyeaters 235–7
Black-eared Miner 235
Blue-faced *237*
Crow-Honeyeater 235, 236
Dusky Friarbird 235
Gibberbird 237
Long-bearded Honeyeater 235
MacGregor's Honeyeater 235, 237
Mangrove Honeyeater 237
Mao (Black-breasted Honeyeater) 235, 236
New Zealand Bellbird 237
Noisy Miner 235, *236*
Painted Honeyeater 235, 236
Red-collared Myzomela *236*
Regent Honeyeater 235
Rotuma Myzomela 235
Streak-headed Honeyeater 257
Strong-billed Honeyeater 236
Tui 237
Varied Honeyeater 237
Yellow-throated Miner 235
Yellow Wattlebird 236
honeyguides 162–4
Dwarf 162
Greater 162, 163, *163*, 164
Green-backed 162
Lesser 162, *163*, 164
Lyre-tailed 163
Malaysian 162
Scaly-throated 163
Yellow-footed 162
Yellow-rumped 162, 163
Hook-billed Hermit 52
Hoopoe 157–8, *158*
hornbills 12, 153–7
African Grey 153
Brown-cheeked 153
Eastern Yellow-billed *153*
Great 154, 156
Helmeted 153, 156
Indian Grey 154
Knobbed 153
Long-tailed 155, 156
Narcondam 153
Northern ground 154, 155
Palawan 153
Papuan 153
Plain-pouched 153
Red-billed *154*
Red-billed Dwarf 155
Rhinoceros *155*
Rufous-headed 153
Rufous-necked 153, 156
Southern ground 154, 155, *155*
Sulu 153
Sulwesi 153

Sumba 153
Tarictic *156*
White-crowned 156
Yellow-casqued 153
horneros 227
Rufous (Ovenbird) 228, *228*
Horornis canturians 354, 356, *356*
H. carolinae 354
H. diphone 354, 355, 356
H. haddeni 354
Houbaropsis bengalensis 69
Huia 243, 244
hummingbirds 52–5
Allen's Hummingbird 53
Anna's Hummingbird 53
Bee Hummingbird 52, 53, 55
Black-breasted Puffleg 52
Black-chinned Hummingbird 53
Black Inca 52
Black-throated Mango 55
Blossomcrown 52
Brace's Emerald 52
Calliope Hummingbird 55
Caribbean Emerald 52
Colourful Puffleg 52, 55
Giant Hummingbird 53, 54
Glow-throated Hummingbird 52
Gorgeted Puffleg 52
Green-backed Firecrown 55
Green-breasted Mango *55*
Honduran Emerald 52
Hook-billed Hermit 52
Juan Fernandez Firecrown 52
Long-tailed Hermit *55*
Magnificent Hummingbird *52*
Marvellous Spatuletail 52, 53, 54
Mexican Woodnymph 52
Peruvian Sheartail 54
Purple-backed Sunbeam 52
Purple-backed Thornbill 54
Reddish Hermit 52
Royal Sunangel 52
Ruby-throated Hummingbird 53, 55
Rufous-crested Coquette 55
Rufous Hummingbird 53, 55
Santa Marta Sabrewing 52
Sapphire-bellied Hummingbird 52
Short-crested Coquette 52
Snowy-bellied Hummingbird 53
Sword-billed Hummingbird 53, 54
Toothbilled Hummingbird 54
Turquoise-throated Puffleg 52
Venezuelan Sylph 52
Hydrobates furcatus 83
H. homochroa 83
H. hornbyi 83
H. leucorhous 83
H. macrodactylus 83
H. matsudairae 83
H. monorhis 83
H. monteiroi 83
H. pelagicus 77, 78, 83
H. tristrami 83
Hydrobatidae 83
Hydrochous gigas 48, 49
Hydromis 200
Hydrophasianus chirurgus 115, 116
Hydroprogne caspia 129
Hydropsalis climacocerca 45
H. torquata 45
Hyemnops perspicillatus 217
Hylexetastes 227
Hylia prasina 354, 356
Hyliota australis 333
H. flavigaster 333

H. usambara 333
H. violacea 333
hyliotas
　Southern 333
　Usambara 333
　Violet-backed 333
　Yellow-bellied 333
Hyliotidae 333
Hylocichla mustelina 393
Hylocitrea bonensis 368, 370–1
Hylomanes momotula 178, 179
Hylopezus auricularis 222
Hylophilus 256
Hylophylax naevioides 218
Hylorchilus navai 376
Hymenolaimus malacorhynchos 15, 16, 18
Hypargos 297
Hypergerus atriceps 343, 344
Hypnelus 162
Hypocoliidae 370–1
Hypocolius (Grey Hypocolius) 370
Hypocolius ampelinus 370
Hypocryptadius cinnamomeus 301, 302
Hypopyrrhus pyrohypogaster 321
Hypositta corallirostris 262, 263
Hypotaenidia okinawae 61
Hypothymis 274
Hypsipetes 352
　H. olivaceus 351
　H. parvirostris 351
　H. siquijorensis 351
　H. moheliensis 351

Ibidorhyncha struthersii 108, 109, *109*
Ibisbill 108, 109, *109*
ibises 97–8
　Australian 98
　Black-faced *97*, 98
　Crested 97, 98
　Giant 97
　Green 98
　Madagascan Crested 98
　Madagascar Sacred 97
　Northern Bald 97, 98
　Olive 98
　Puna 98
　Reunion 97
　Sacred 98
　São Tomé 97
　Scarlet 98
　Southern Bald 97, 98
　White-shouldered 97
Ibycter americanus 184, 185
Ichthyophaga 140
Icteria virens 323
Icteridae 321–5
Icterus 322, 325
　I. galbula 323
　I. laudabilis 321
　I. northropi 321
Ictinaetus malayensis 139
Ictinia 136
　I. mississippiensis 140
　I. plumbea 140
Iduna 347, 349
Ifrit 250, 277, *277*
Ifrita kowaldi 250, 277, *277*
Ifritidae 277
Iiwi 309, *309*
Illadopsis 363
Incaspiza 332
Indian Peafowl 26, 27
Indicator archipelagicus 162
　I. indicator 162, 163, *163*, 164
　I. minor 162, *163*, 164
　I. pumilio 162
　I. variegatus 163
　I. xanthonotus 162, 163
Indicatoridae 162–4
Indigo Bunting 328
indigobirds
　Dusky *299*
　Village 299

Iodopleura 211
　I. pipra 210
ioras
　Common 265, *265*
　Great 265
　Green 265
　Marshall's 265
Ipophilus 167
Irediparra gallinacea 116
Irena 265, 287
　I. cyanogastra 288
　I. puella 288, *288*
Irenidae 287–8
Ispidina lecontei 180, 181
Ixobrychus minutus 95
　I. novaezelandiae 94
Ixoreus naevius 393

Jabiru 88, 89, 90
Jabiru mycteria 88, 89, 90
Jabouilleia 364
　J. naungmanensis 363
Jacamaralcyon tridactyla 160, 161
jacamars 160–1
　Coppery-chested 160
　Great 160, 161
　Paradise 161
　Rufous-tailed *160*
　Three-toed 160, 161
　Yellow-billed 160
Jacamerops aureus 160, 161
Jacana jacana 116
　J. spinosa 116, *116*
jacanas 115–16
　Comb-crested 116
　Lesser 115, 116
　Madagascar 115
　Northern 116, *116*
　Pheasant-tailed 115, 116
　Wattled 116
Jacanidae 115–16
jackdaws
　Daurian 271
　Eurasian 271
Jacky Winter 282
Java Sparrow 296, 298, *298*
Javan Cochoa 391
Javan Tesia 355
jays 271–2, *273*
　Blue 271
　Crested 272
　Curl-crested 271
　Eurasian 272, 273
　Florida Scrub 271
　Grey 272
　Pinyon Jay 271
　Plush-crested 271
　Siberian 272
　Sichuan 272
　Steller's 271, *272*
　Tufted 271
Jerdon's Babbler 358
Johnson's Tody Tyrant 213
Juan Fernandez Firecrown 52
Jubula 147
Junco insularis 314
junglefowl
　Grey 26, 27
　Red 26
Juniper Babbler (Abyssinian Catbird) 359
Jynx ruficollis 164
　J. torquilla 164

Kaempfer's Tody Tyrant 213
Kagu 38, *38*
Kakamega poliothorax 283, 284
Kakapo 188, 189, 190, *190*, 196
kakas
　New Zealand 188, 190
　Norfolk Island 190
Kamao 391
Kca 188, 190
Kenopia 364
Kokako 243, 244
Kona Grosbeak 305
kookaburras
　Blue-winged 181

Banded 186
Common (European) 184, 185
Lesser 184
Mauritius 184, 186
Seychelles 184, 186
Ketupa 147
Killdeer 111
kingfishers 180–3
　African Dwarf 180, 181
　Amazon 182
　American Pygmy 181
　Beach 182
　Belted 182
　Bismarck 180
　Blue-capped 180
　Brown-winged 180
　Buff-breasted Paradise 181
　Collared 181
　Common 181, *181*, 182
　Crested 182
　Giant 182, 183
　Green 181, *182*
　Green-and-rufous 182
　Grey-headed *182*
　Hook-billed 182
　Kafiau Paradise 180
　Marquesan 180
　Moustached 180
　Numfor Paradise 180
　Philippine Dwarf 180
　Pied 182
　Red-backed 182
　Ringed 182
　Ruddy 181, 183
　Rufous-lored 180
　Shovel-billed 182
　Sombre 180
　Stork-billed 183
　Striped 182
　Sulawesi Dwarf 180
　Tuamotu 180
　White-throated 181
　see also kookaburras
Kinglet Calyptura 211
kinglets
　Golden-crowned 366, 367
　Ruby-crowned 366, 367, *367*
Kioea 237, 372
kites
　Black 140
　Black-shouldered 137
　Black-winged 137
　Brahminy 140
　Hook-billed 138
　Letter-winged 137
　Mississippi 140
　Pearl 136, 137
　Plumbaceous 140
　Red 136, 140
　Scissor-tailed 137
　Slender-billed 140
　Snail 136, 137, 140
　Swallow-tailed 138
　Whistling 140
　White-tailed 137
Kittacincla 388, 389
　K. cebuensis 387
　K. malabarica 388
kittiwakes
　Black-legged 127
　Red-legged 127, 128
kiwis 10–11
　Great Spotted 10
　Little Spotted 10
　Northern Brown 10, *10*
　Okarito Brown 10
　Southern Brown 10
Knipolegus 217
knot
　Great 116
　Red 119
Knysna Warbler 344
Koel, Common 59
Kokako 243, 244

Laughing 180, 181, *182*
Rufous-bellied 181
Spangled 181
Kupeornis gilberti 364

Lagonosticta 297, 299
　L. rubricata 299
　L. senegala 297, *297*
Lagopus lagopus 25
　L. l. scoticus 25
　L. leucura 25
　L. mutus 25
Lalage newtoni 247
　L. typica 247
Lammergeier (Bearded Vulture) 136, 137, 138
Lamprolia victoriae 269
Lamprospiza melanoleuca 327
Lamprotornis 382
　L. iris 383
　L. superbus 383, *383*
Lanceolated Monklet 162
Laniarius atrococcineus 266
　L. luehderi 266
Laniellus langbianus 364
Laniidae 270
Laniisoma elegans 210, 211
Lanio 331
Laniocera 210
Lanius borealis 270
　L. collurio 270, *270*
　L. excubitor 270
　L. ludovicianus 270
　L. meridionalis 270
　L. minor 270
　L. newtoni 270
　L. nubicus 270
　L. senator 270
　L. validirostris 270
lapwings
　Javan Wattled 111
　Masked *111*, 112
　Northern 111, 112
　Red-wattled 112
　Sociable 111, 112
　Southern 112
Large-footed Finch 315
Large Ground Finch *331*
Laridae 127–30
Lark Bunting 314
larks 339–40
　Archer's Lark 339, 340
　Ash's Lark 339
　Black-eared Sparrow-lark 339
　Black Lark 339
　Botha's Lark 339
　Cape Long-billed Lark 339
　Crested Lark 339, *339*
　Eurasian Skylark 339, 340, *340*
　Greater Hoopoe Lark 339, 340
　Horsfield's (Australasian) Bushlark 339
　Madagascar Sparrow Lark 339
　Raso Lark 339, 340
　Red Lark 339
　Rudd's Lark 339
　Shore (NA Horned) Lark 339
　Thick-billed Lark 339
　Wood Lark 340, *340*
Larosterna inca 130
Larus 127
　L. argentatus 128, *128*
Larvivora ruficeps 387
Laterallus spilonota 61
Lathamus discolor 189, 194
Laticilla cinerascens 363
laughing-thrushes
　Banasura 364
　Blue-crowned 364
　Collared 364
　Melodious 364
　Nilgiri 364
　Rufous-fronted 364, 365
　Snowy-cheeked 364
　Striated 365

Sumatran 364
White-crested 364
Lawrence's Goldfinch 311
leafbirds 287, 288
　Bornean 288
　Golden-fronted 288
　Greater Green 287
　Orange-bellied 288, *288*
　Philippine 287, 288
　Sumatran 287
leaftossers
　Grey-throated 225
　Rufous-breasted 225
Legatus leucophaius 215
Leiothlypis peregrina 319
Leiothrix lutea 365
Leiotrichidae 364–6
Leipoa ocellata 19, 20, *20*
Leistes 325
　L. defilippii 321
Lepidocolaptes souleyetti 226
Lepidopyga lilliae 52
Lepidothrix iris 205
　L. isidorei 205
　L. vilasboasi 205
Leptasthenura 228
　L. xenothorax 227
Leptopilos 90
Leptopoecile elegans 358
　L. sophiae 357, *358*
Leptoptilos crumenifer 29, 88, 89, 89, 90, 132
　L. dubius 88, 89, 90, 132
　L. javanicus 88, 90
Leptosoma discolor 173
Leptosomidae 149–50
Leptosomus discolor *149*, 149–50
Leptotila wellsi 31
Lesbia 54
Lesser Goldfinch 311
Lesser Koa Finch 305
Lesser Sooty Owl 142
Lesser Yellowlegs 118
Leucogeranus leucogeranus 67, 68, 69
Leucopeza semperi 319, 320
Leucophaeus atricilla 128, 129
　L. fuliginosus 127
　L. modestus 127, 129
　L. pipixcan 129
Leucopsar rothschildi 381, *382*, 383, 384
Leucosarcia melanoleuca 33
Leucosticte 310
　L. tephrocotis *307*
Limnodromus 118
Limosa fedoa 117
　L. lapponica 119
　L. limosa 117
Limpkin 66, 66
Linaria cannabina 310
　L. flavirostris 310
Linnet, Common 310
Liocichla 365
　L. bugunorum 364
Lioparus chrysotis 360
Lioptilus 359
Lipaugus 207
　L. weberi 206
Lissotis melanogaster 71
Loboparadisaea sericea 242, 243
Lobotos lobatus 247
Locustella 345, 355
　L. accentor 345
　L. certhiola 345
　L. fasciata 345
　L. naevia 345, *345*
　L. pleskei 344
Locustellidae 344–5
Loddigesia mirabilis 52, 53, 54
logrunners
　Australian 240, *240*
　Papuan 240
　see also Chowchilla
Lonchura 298
　L. malacca 296
　L. oryzivora 296, 298, *298*
　L. vana 296

Long-billed Tetraka 346, 347
Long-legged Thicketbird 344
Long-tailed Hermit 55
Long-tailed Reed Finch 332
long-tailed tits 357–8
  Black-throated Tit 357
  Bushtit 357, 358, *358*
  Crested Tit-warbler 358
  Long-tailed Tit 357, *357*
  Pygmy Tit 358
  Rufous-fronted Tit 357
  White-browed Tit-warbler
    357, 358
  White-throated Tit 357
longbills, *Macrosphenus* 341,
    342
  Pulitzer's 341
longbills, *Oedistoma* and
  Toxorhamphus 241, 242
  Pygmy 242
  Slaty-headed *242*
longclaws
  Abyssinian 304
  Fülleborn's 304
  Pangani 304
  Sharpe's 302
  Yellow-throated 304, *305*
longspurs
  Chestnut Collared 312, 313
  Lapland 312, 313
  McCown's 312
  Smith's 312, 313
loons *see* divers
Lophaetus occipitalis 139
Lophodytes cucullatus 16
Lopholaimus antarcticus 33
Lophophanes cristatus 336, *336*
Lophornis 53, 54
  L. brachylophus 52
  L. delattrei 55
Lophostrix cristata 147
Lophotibis cristata 98
Lophotis ruficrista 71
Lophotriccus 214
Lophura bulweri 26
Loriculus 188, 197
  L. flosculus 194
lories
  Black-winged 194
  Chattering 194
lorikeets
  Blue-fronted 194
  New Caledonian 194
  Rainbow 196, *196*, 197
  Red-throated 194
  Ultramarine 194
Lorius garrulus 194
Lousiana Waterthrush 320
lovebirds
  Black-cheeked 194
  Rosy-faced 194
Loxia curvirostra 311, *311*
  L. leucoptera 311
  L. megaplaga 311
  L. pytyopsittacus 311
  L. scotica 311
Loxioides bailleui 305, 308,
    308
Loxops caeruleirostris 305
Lullula arborea 340, *340*
Luscinia calliope 387
  L. luscinia 389
  L. megarhynchos 338, 351,
    389
  L. svecica 387
Lybius 172
  L. chaplini 168
Lycocorax pyrrhopterus 277,
    278
Lymnocryptes minimus 118
Lyncornis macrotis 46
  L. temminckii 46
lyrebirds
  Albert's 229
  Superb 229, *229*
Lyrurus tetrix 26

macaws
  Blue-throated 192
  Blue-and-yellow 193
  Cuban 192, 193
  Glaucous 192
  Great Green 192
  Hyacinth 188, 189, 192, 193
  Lear's 192
  Military 192
  Red-fronted 192
  Red-shouldered 193
  Scarlet 193
  Spix's 192, 194
Macgregoria pulchra 235, 237
Machaerirhynchidae 258–9
Machaerirhynchus flaviventer
  258, *258*, 259
  M. nigripectus 258, 259
Macheiramphus alcinus 136, 139
Machlolophus wollweberi 336
Macrocephalon maleo 19, 20
Macrodipteryx 44
Macronectes 84
  M. giganteus 85
Macronus 362
Macronyx aurantiigula 304
  M. croceus 304, *305*
  M. flavicollis 304
  M. fuellebornii 304
  M. sharpei 302
Macropygia 32, 34
Macropsalis forcipata 45
Macrosphenidae 341–2
Macrosphenus 304, 342
  M. pulitzeri 341
Madagascan Red Owl 141, 142
Madagascan warblers
  Appert's Tetraka 346, 347
  Cryptic Warbler 347
  Dusky Tetraka 346
  Grey-crowned Tetraka 346,
    347
  Long-billed Tetraka 346, 347
  Madagascar Yellowbrow 346
  Thamnornis Warbler 346
  Wedge-tailed Jery 347
  White-throated Oxylabes 347
Madagascar Groundhunter 263
Madagascar Yellowbrow 346
Madanga 302, 304
Madanga ruficollis 302, 304
Madeira Firecrest 366, 367
Magpie, Common *273*, 274
Magpie Goose *14*, 14–15
Magpie-lark 274, *274*
magpies
  Black-billed 59
  Common *273*, 274
  Javan Green 271
Magumma parva 307
Malaconotidae 266
Malaconotus alius 266
Malacoptila 161, 162
  M. semicincta 161
  M. striata 161
  M. s. striata 161
Malacorhynchus membranaceus
  16, 17, 18
Malanocotus gladiator 266
Malaysian Rail-babbler 252
Maleo 19, 20
Malia 345
Malia grata 345
malimbes
  Blue-billed 294
  Gola 292
  Ibadan 292
  Red-headed 294
  Red-vented 294
Malimbus ballmanni 292
  M. ibadanensis 292
  M. nitens 294
  M. rubricollis 294
  M. scutatus 294
Mallard 16, 18, 19
Malleefowl 19, 20, *20*
Malurus 233

M. amabilis 234
M. cyaneus 234, *234*
M. splendens 234
Manacus manacus 205
  M. m. candei 205
manakins 205–6
  Araripe 205
  Bearded 205, *205*
  Blue-rumped 205
  Golden-crowned 205
  Helmeted 205
  Long-tailed 206
  Opal-crowned 205
  Red-capped *206*
  White-crowned *206*
  Wire-tailed 205, *206*
  Yellow-headed 205
  see also Wied's Tyrant-
    manakin
Mandingoa 297
Mangrove Finch 329
Mangrove Warbler 249
Manorina flavigula melanotis
  235
  M. melanocephala 235, *236*
Manucerthia mana 308
Manucodia comrii 278
Manus Masked Owl 141
Many-coloured Rush Tyrant
  212, 213, *213*
Mao 235, 236
Marabou 29, 88, 89, *89*, 90, 132
Mareca americana 16
  M. penelope 16, *17*
  M. sibilatrix 16
Margarops 381
  M. fuscatus 380
martins
  Asian House 350
  Galapagos 350
  House 350
  Nepal House 350
  Peruvian 350
  Purple 350, 351, *351*
  Sand (NA Bank Swallow) 350
  White-eyed River-martin 350
Marvellous Spatuletail 52,
  53, 54
Mascarinus mascarin 194
Masked Tityra *210*
Maui Nukupuu 305
Maui Parrotbill 305
meadowlarks
  Eastern 325
  Pampas 321
  Western 325
Mearnsia picina 48
Medium Tree Finch 329
Megabyas 262, 263, 264
Megaceryle alcyon 182
  M. lugubris 182
  M. maxima 182, 183
  M. torquata 182
Megadyptes antipodes 74
Megalurulus 345
  M. rufus 344
Megalurus gramineus 345
  M. palustris 345
megapodes 19–21
  Bruijn's Brush-turkey 19
  Brush Turkey 20
  Maleo 19, 20
  Malleefowl 19, 20, *20*
  Micronesian Megapode 19
  Moluccan Megapode 19, 20
  Orange-footed Scrubfowl
    20, *20*
  Tanimbar Megapode 19
  Tongan Megapode 19
Megapodiidae 19–21
Megapodius 20
  M. laperouse 19
  M. pritchardii 19
  M. reinwardt 20, *20*
  M. tenimberensis 19
Megarynchus pitangua 216
Megascops asio 145, 147
  M. kennicottii 145, 147

M. marshalli 143
Megatriorchis 140
Megazosterops palauensis 361
Melaenornis 389
  M. lugubris 276, *276*
melampittas
  Greater 276
  Lesser 276, *276*
Melampittidae 276
Melamprosops phaeosoma 305,
  309
Melanerpes carolinus 167
  M. cruentatus 167
  M. erythrocephalus 165, 167
  M. formicivorus 167
  M. lewis 167
  M. uropygialis 167
Melaniparus 336
Melanitta 16
Melanocharis arfakiana 241, 242
  M. striativentris 242
  M. versteri 242, *242*
Melanocharitidae 241–2
Melanochlora sultanea 335, 336
Melanocorypha yeltoniensis 339
Melanodryas vittata 281
Melanopareia elegans 220
  M. maranonica 220, *221*
  M. maximiliani 220
  M. torquata 220
Melanopareiidae 220
Melanoptila glabrirostris 380,
  381
Melanorectes nigrescens 250
Melanotis caerulescens 380, 381
  M. hypoleucus 380, 381
Meleagris gallopavo 25, *25*
  M. ocellata 25
Melichneutes robustus 163
Melidectes princeps 235
Melidora macrorrhina 182
Melignomon 163
  M. elsentrauti 162
Meliphaga 236
Meliphagidae 235–7
Melithreptus validirostris 236
Mellisuga helenae 52, 53, 55
Melloria 260
Melocichla mentalis 341, 342
Melophus lathami 305
Melopsittacus undulatus 188,
  194, 197
Melopyrrha 332
Melospiza melodia 314, 315
Melozone alberti 229
Menura 229
  M. novaehollandiae 229, *229*
Menuridae 229
Merganetta armata 16, 18
mergansers
  Auckland Islands 15, 16
  Brazilian 15, 16
  Hooded 16
  Red-breasted 16, *16*
  Scaly-sided 15, 16
Mergellus albellus 16
Mergus australis 15, 16
  M. merganser 16
  M. octosetaceus 15, 16
  M. serrator 16, *16*
  M. squamatus 15, 16
Merlin 186, 187
Meropidae 173–5
Meropogon forsteni 173
Merops albicollis 174
  M. apiaster 173, 174
  M. breweri 174
  M. hirundineus 174
  M. malimbicus 175
  M. mentalis 173
  M. nubicoides 174, *175*
  M. nubicus 174
  M. orientalis 174
  M. ornatus 174
  M. persicus 174
  M. pusillus 175
  M. superciliosus 174

M. viridis 174
Merulaxis 224
  M. stresemanni 223
Mesembrinibis cayennensis 98
mesites
  Brown 36
  Sub-desert 36, *36*
  White-breasted 36, *36*
Mesitornis unicolor 36
  M. variegatus 36, *36*
Mesitornithidae 36
Mesopicos 167
Metabolus rugensis 273, 274
Metallura 53
Mexican Woodnymph 52
Micrastur 185
  M. plumbeus 184
  M. ruficollis 187
  M. semitorquatus 187
Micrathene whitneyi 143, 144,
  146
Micrimacronus 362
Microbates 377
  M. cinereiventris 378
  M. collaris 378
*Microcarbo melanoleucos
  brevirostris* 103
  M. pygmeus 102, 103, *103*
Microcerculus philomela 376
  M. ustulatus 376
Microeca fascinans 282
  M. flavigaster 282
  M. hemixantha 282
Microhierax fringillarius 185
  M. latifrons 184
Microligea 317
  M. palustris 318
Micromacronus leytensis 343
  M. sordidus 343
Micromonacha lanceolata 162
Microparra capensis 115, 116
Micropsitta 195
  M. pusio 189
Microrhopias quixensis 219
Microscelis amaurotis 351
Milvago chimango 186, 187
Milvus migrans 140
  M. milvus 136, 140
Mimidae 380–1
Mimodes graysoni 380
Mimus polyglottos 380, 381
Minahassa Masked Owl 141
Minas Gerais Tyrannulet 213
miners
  Campo 225, 226
  Puna *225*
  Short-billed 225
  Slender-billed 226
Minla ignotincta 365
Mirafra 340
  M. ashi 339
  M. javanica 339
Mistletoe Bird 285, *285*
Mitrospingidae 326–7
Mitrospingus cassini 326
  M. oleagineus 326–7
Mitu mitu 21
Mixornis 362
Mniotilta varia 319, 320
mockingbirds
  Blue 380, 381
  Blue-and-white 380, 381
  Española (Hood Island)
    380, *381*
  Floreana 380
  Galapagos 380
  Northern 380, 381
  San Cristobal 380
  Socorro 380
Modulatrix stictigula 283, 284
Moho 237, 372
  M. braccatus 372
Mohoidae 237, 245–6
Mohoua albicilla 245
  M. ochrocephala 245
Molothrus ater 322, *324*, 325
  M. oryzivorus 325
Momotidae 179–80

Momotus aequatorialis 179
  M. mexicanus 179
  M. momota 179, *179*
Monarcha 274
  M. boanensis 273
  M. brehmii 273
  M. everetti 273
Monarchidae 273–4
monarchs 273–4
  African Paradise Flycatcher 274, *274*
  Asian Paradise Flycatcher 273
  Biak Monarch 273
  Black-chinned Monarch 273
  Blue-mantled Crested Flycatcher 274
  Cerulean Paradise Flycatcher 273, *274*
  Chuuk Monarch 274
  Fatu Hiva Monarch 273
  Japanese Paradise Flycatcher 273, *274*
  Madagascar Paradise Flycatcher 274
  Magpie-lark 274, *274*
  Raratonga Monarch 273
  Seychelles Paradise Flycatcher 273
  Tahiti Monarch 273
  Torrent-lark 274
  Truk Monarch 273
  Ua Pou Monarch 273
  White-tipped Monarch 273
Monasa 161, *162*
  M. benschi 36, *36*
Monticola saxatilis 390
  M. solitarius 390
Montifringilla nivalis 302, *302*
moorhens
  Makira 61
  Samoan 61
Morphnus guianensis 138, 139
Morus bassanus 101
  M. capensis 100
  M. serrator 100, *101*
Motacilla aguimp 303
  M. alba 303, *303*
  M. capensis 303
  M. cinerea 303
  M. citreola 303
  M. clara 303
  M. flava 303, *303*
  M. flaviventris 303
  M. grandis 303
  M. maderaspatensis 303
  M. samveasnae 303
  M. tschutschensis 303
  M. t. tschutschensis 303
Motacillidae 302–5
motmots 179–80
  Amazonian 179, *179*
  Blue-crowned 179
  Blue-throated 179, 180
  Broad-billed 179, *180*
  Highland 179
  Keel-billed 179
  Rufous 179
  Rufous-capped 179
  Russet-crowned 179
  Tody 178, 179
  Turquoise-browed 179, *180*
Mount Cameroon Speirops 360
Mountain Firetail 298
Mountain Serin 306
Moupina 359
mousebirds 148–9
  Blue-naped *148*, 149
  Red-backed 149
  Red-faced 149
  Speckled *148*, 149
  White-backed 149
  White-headed 149
Moustached Grass Warbler 341, 342
mudlarks 274
mudnesters *see* Australian mudnesters
Mulleripicus pulverulentus 164,

165, 166
murrelets
  Ancient 123
  Craveri's 123
  Guadelupe 123
  Japanese 123
  Kittlitz's 123, 125
  Long-billed 123, 125
  Marbled 123, 125
  Scripp's 123
Musciaxicola 217
Muscicapa striata 389
Muscicapidae 387–90
Muscigralla brevicauda 216, 304
Musophaga rossae 72
  M. violacea 72
Musophagidae 71–2
Myadestes genibarbis 391, 392
  M. lanaiensis 391
  M. myadestinus 391
  M. palmeri 391
  M. townsendi 392
  M. woahensis 391
Mycerobas 308
Mycteria 88
  M. americana 89, *89*, 90
  M. cinerea 88, 89, 90
  M. ibis 89
  M. leucocephala 90
Myiarchus cinerascens 217
  M. crinitis 217
  M. semirufus 215
Myiobius 208, 210
  M. barbatus 209
Myioborus 320, 321
  M. pariae 319
  M. pictus 321
Myiodynastes luteiventris 217
  M. maculatus 215
Myiopagis 216
Myiopsitta monachus 184, 189, 192, 193
Myiornis atricapillus 214
  M. ecaudatus 198, 214
Myiotheretes pernix 215
Myiozetetes similis 216
mynas
  Apo 384
  Bali (Bali Starling) 381, *382*, 383, 384
  Bank 383
  Black-winged 381
  Common 382, *382*, 383, 384, 385
  Finch-billed 384
  Golden-crested 384
  Hill 382, 384
  Sri Lanka 384
Myophonus blighi 390
  M. caeruleus 390
  M. glaucinus 390
Myrmoderus ruficauda 218
Myrmornis torquata 220
Myrmothera 222
Myrmotherula brachyura 219
  M. ignota 219
  M. snowi 218
Mystacornis crossleyi 263
Myzomela 236, 237
  M. chermesina 235
  M. rosenbergii 236
Myzornis pyrrhoura 358, 360

Nannopsittaca panychlora 193
Napothera 364
Nasica longirostris 227
Naung Mung Wren Babbler 363
Necrosyrtes monachus 136, 138
Nectariniidae 286–7
needletails
  Brown-backed 50
  Purple 50
  White-throated 48
Negros Striped Babbler 360
Nemosia rourei 329
Neochen jubata 15
Neocossyphus 392
Neodrepanis coruscans 202, *202*

N. hypoxantha 202, 203
Neomixa 343
Neomorphus 58, 60
  N. geoffroyi 57
  N. radiolosus 57
Neopelma aurifrons 205
Neophema chrysogaster 189, 194
Neophron percnopterus 136, 138
Neopipo cinnamomea 211
Neosittidae 246
Neospiza concolor 305
Neosuthora davidiana 360
Neotis ludwigii 69
Nesasio solomonensis 143, 147
Nesillas aldabrana 347, 348
  N. lantzii 348
Nesoctites micromegas 165
Nesoenas mayeri 31, 34
Nesofregetta fuliginosa 77
Nesomimus macdonaldi 380, *381*
  N. melanotis 380
  N. parvulus 380
  N. trifasciatus 380
Nesopsar nigerrimus 321
Nesospingus 317
  N. speculiferus 318
Nestor meridionalis 188, 190
  N. notabilis 188, 190
  N. productus 190
Netta 16
  N. peposaca 17
Nettapus 16
  N. auritus 17
New Zealand Bellbird 237
New Zealand Brown Creeper 245, 246, *246*
New Zealand wattlebirds
  Huia 243, 244
  North Island Kokako 243, 244
  Saddleback 243, *244*
  South Island Kokako 243, 244
New Zealand wrens
  Alpine (New Zealand) Rockwren 199
  Bushwren 199
  Long-billed Wren 199
  Lyall's (Stephens Island) Rockwren 199
  Rifleman 199, *199*
  Stout-legged Wren 199
Newtonia 263
  N. fanovanae 262
Nicator chloris 338
  N. gularis 338
  N. vireo 338
Nicatoridae 338
nicators
  Eastern 338
  Western 338
  Yellow-throated 338
nighthawks
  Common 46
  Lesser 46
  Nacunda 46
Nightingale, Common 338, 351, 389
nightjars 44–6
  Bonaparte's 44
  Brown 44
  European 45, *45*, 46
  Great Eared 46
  Heinrich's 44
  Itombwe 44
  Ladder-tailed 45
  Large-tailed 46
  Long-trained 45
  Lyre-tailed 45
  Malaysian Eared 46
  Nechisar 44
  Pennant-winged 45
  Puerto Rican 44
  Scissor-tailed 45
  Sickle-winged 46
  Silver 44
  Standard-winged 45
  Swallow-tailed *44*, 45

White-winged 44
  see also Chuck-will's-widow; nighthawks; pauraques; Poorwill, Common *and* whip-poor-wills
Nigrita 297
Nilaus afer 266
Niltava grandis 389
  N. sundara 389
  N. vivida 389
niltavas
  Beautiful (Rufous-bellied) 389
  Large 389
  Vivid 389
Ninox japonica 146
  N. natalis 143
  N. sumbaensis 143
Nipponia nippon 97, 98
Nisaetus 139
noddies
  Blue 130
  Grey 130
Noisy Miner 235, *236*
Nomonyx dominicus 17
Nonnula 162
Northern Bobwhite 23, 24
Northern Goshawk *136*, 140, 147
Northern Parula 319, 320
Northern Pintail 16
Northern Rockhopper 74
Northern Waterthrush 320, *321*
Northern Wheatear 387, *388*, 389
Notharchus 162
Nothocercus nigrocapillus 9
Nothura maculosa 10
Notiomystidae 244–5
Notiomystis cincta 244–5, *245*
Nucifraga 335
  N. caryocatactes 272, *273*
  N. columbiana 272
Numenius arquata 117, *117*
  N. borealis 116, 119
  N. madagascariensis 116, 117
  N. minutus 117
  N. tahitiensis 116
  N. tenuirostris 116, 119
Numida meleagris 22, 23, *23*
  N. m. sabyi 22
Numididae 22–3
nutcrackers
  Clark's 272
  Eurasian 272, *273*
nuthatches
  Algerian 374, 375
  Bahama 374, 375
  Beautiful 374
  Brown-headed 374, 375
  Corsican 374, 375
  Eastern Rock 375
  Eurasian 374, *375*
  Giant 374
  Pygmy 374
  Red-breasted 375
  Western Rock 375
  White-breasted 374, *375*
  White-browed 374
Nyctanassa 95
Nyctibiidae 43–4
Nyctibius bracteatus 43
  N. grandis 43
  N. griseus 43
  N. maculosus 43
Nycticorax 95, 96
Nycticryphes semicollaris 114, 115
Nyctidromus albicollis 45, 46
Nyctiphrynus 46
Nyctyornis 175
  N. amictus 173, 174
  N. athertoni 173, 174
Nymphicus hollandicus 189, 191, 192
Nystalus 162

Oahu Alauahio 305

Oceanites oceanicus 78, *78*
Oceanitidae 77–8
Ochraceous Attila 215
Ocyceros 156
  O. birostris 154
Ocyphaps lophotes 33
Odontophoridae 23–4
Odontophorus atrifrons 23
  O. dialeucos 23
  O. melanonotus 23
  O. strophium 23
Oedistoma 241
  O. pygmaeum 242
Oenanthe oenanthe 387, *388*, 389
Oilbird 40, 41, *41*, 49
Olive-flanked Whistler 368, 370–1
Olive Warbler 291, *291*
Olomao 391
Oncostoma 214
Onychognathus salvadorii 384
Onychoprion fuscatus 127, 129
Onychorhynchidae 209–10
Onychorhynchus 208
  O. coronatus 209, *209*, 210
  O. c. occidentalis 209
  O. c. swainsoni 209
Onychostruthus taczanowskii 302
o'os
  Kauai O'o 372
  O'o 237, 372
openbills
  African 89
  Asian 89
Ophrysia superciliosa 24
Opisthocomidae 56–7
Opisthocomus hoazin 56, 56–7, 64
Oporornis agilis 319
Orange-breasted Fruiteater *208*
Orange-footed Scrubfowl 20, *20*
Orangequit 332
Oreocharis arfaki 254, *254*
Oreoica gutturalis 251
Oreoicidae 251
Oreomystis bairdi 305, 308–9
Oreophasis derbianus 21
Oreopholus ruficollis 111
Oreoscoptes montanus 380
Oreoscopus gutturalis 240
Oreostruthus fuliginosus 298
Oreothraupias arremonops 314
Oriente Warbler 318
Orinoco Goose 15
Oriola bernieri 262, 263
Oriole Warbler 343, 344
orioles
  Black-naped 256
  Brown 257
  Golden 256, *257*, 322
  Isabela 256
  São Tomé 256
  Silver 256
orioles [New World blackbirds]
  Bahama 321
  Baltimore 323
  St. Lucia 321
Oriolidae 256–7
Oriolus chinensis 256
  O. crassirostris 256
  O. isabellae 256
  O. mellianus 256
  O. oriolus 256, *257*, 322
  O. szalayi 257
Ornithion brunneicapillus 215
Ornorectes cristatus 250, 251
oropendolas
  Baudo 321
  Montezuma 323, *323*
Ortalis cinereiceps 21
  O. erythroptera 21
Orthogonys chloricterus 327
Orthonychidae 240
Orthonyx novaeguineae 240
  O. spaldingii 240
  O. temminckii 240, *240*

Orthotomus 334, 344
Osprey 131, 135, *135*
ostriches 6–8
  Common 6, *7*, 8, 138
  Somali 6, 8
Otididae 69–71
Otidiphaps nobilis 34
Otis tarda 69, 70, *70*, 132
Otus alfredi 143
  O. insularis 143
  O. scops 143, 144, 147
Ovenbird [hornero] 228, *228*
Ovenbird [New World warbler] 319, 320
owlet-nightjars
  Australian 47
  Barred *47*
  Feline 47
  Moluccan 47
  Mountain 47
  New Caledonian 47
owlets
  African Barred 144
  Asian Barred 144
  Asian Spotted 147
  Forest 143, 146
  Long-whiskered 143, 146
owls, typical 143–7
  African Wood 147
  Barred 147
  Blakiston's Eagle 143, *144*, 147
  Brown Wood 147
  Buff-fronted 147
  Burrowing 143, *143*, 144, 145, 146, 147
  Cloud Forest Screech 143
  Crested 147
  Cuban Pygmy 146
  Eastern Screech 145, 147
  Elf 143, 144, 146
  Eurasian Eagle 143, 147
  Eurasian Pygmy 144, 146
  Eurasian Scops 143, 144, 147
  Fearful 143, 147
  Ferruginous Pygmy 146
  Flammulated 147
  Flores Scops 147
  Great Grey 141, 145, *145*, 147
  Great Horned 146, 147, 189
  Hawk 144, *144*, 146
  Hume's 144, 147
  Jamaican 147
  Laughing (Whekau) 143, 146
  Least Pygmy 143
  Little 144, 145, 147
  Long-eared 143, 147
  Maned 147
  Marsh 143, 144, 147
  Northern Pygmy 144, 146
  Northern Saw-whet *146*
  Pernàmbuco Pygmy 143
  Philippine Eagle 143
  Seychelles Scops 143
  Shelley's Eagle 143
  Short-eared 143, 144, 146, 147
  Snowy 143, 144, 146, 147
  Spectacled 143, 147
  Spotted 143, 147
  Striped 143
  Tawny 145, 147
  Tengmalm's (NA Boreal) 147
  Ural 146
  Verreaux's Eagle 93
  Western Screech 145, 147
  see also Boobooks *and* owlets
oxpeckers
  Red-billed 378, 379
  Yellow-billed 378, 379, *379*
Oxylabes madagascariensis 347
Oxyruncidae 208–9
Oxyruncus cristatus 208–9
Oxyura 18
  O. jamaicensis 17
  O. leucocephala 15, 17
  O. vittata 17

oystercatchers 108–9
  African Black 108
  American 108
  American Black 108
  Australian Pied 108
  Blackish 108
  Canary Islands 108
  Chatham 108
  Eurasian 108, *109*
  Magellanic 108
  Sooty 108
  South Island Pied 108
  Variable 108

Pachycare flavogriseum 240
Pachycephala 258
  P. jacquinoti 249
  P. melanura 249
  P. pectoralis 249
  P. p. balim 249
  P. rufiventris 249
  P. rufogularis 249
Pachycephalidae 249–10
Pachycephalopsis 282
Pachyplichas yaldwyni 199
Pachyptila crassirostris 85
  P. desolata 86
Pachyramphus 212
  P. aglaiae 211
  P. spodiurus 210
Pagodroma nivea 84
Pagophila eburnea 128, 129
painted berrypeckers
  Tit 254, *254*
  Crested 254, *254*
Painted Bunting 327, 328
painted-snipes 114–15
  Australian 114
  Greater 114, *115*
  South American 114, 115
Painted Whitestart 321
Pale-headed Brush Finch 316
Palila 305, 308, *308*
Palmchat 367–8, *368*
Palmeria dolei 309
Pandion haliaetus 131, 135, *135*
Pandionidae 135
Panuridae 340–1
Panurus biarmicus 340–1, *341*
Panyptila 50
Papasula abbotti 100, 102
Parabuteo unicinctus 136, 140
  P. u. harrisi 140
Paradisaea apoda 278
  P. decora 277
  P. raggiana 278, 279
  P. rudolphi 277, 278, *278*
Paradisaeidae 277–9
Paradise Crow 277, 278
Paradoxornis flavirostris 358, *359*
  P. paradoxus 360
parakeets
  Andean 193
  Antipodes 196
  Black-fronted 194
  Burrowing 189, 194
  Carolina 192, 194
  Echo 194
  Jandaya 194
  Long-horned 196
  Monk 184, 189, 192, 193
  Ralatea 194
  Rodrigues 194
  Rose-ringed 195, *197*
  Seychelles 194, 196
  Short-horned 196
  Sun 192, 194, *194*
Paramythia montium 254, *254*
Paramythiidae 254
Parasitic Weaver (Cuckoo Finch) 299, 300
Pardaliparus venustulus 336
pardalotes
  Forty-spotted 238
  Red-browed 238
  Spotted 238, *238*
  Striated 238, *238*

Pardalotidae 238
Pardolotus punctatus 238, *238*
  P. quadragintus 238
  P. rubricatus 238
  P. striatus 238, *238*
Pareomyza 308
Pareudiastes pacificus 61
  P. silvestris 61
Paria Whitestart 319
Paridae 335–6
Parisoma 339
Parkerthraustes humeralis 327
Parkesia motacilla 320
  P. noveboracensis 320, *321*
Parmoptila 297
Paroaria 330
Parophasma galinieri 359
Paroreomyza maculata 305
Parotia 279
Parrot Crossbill 311
parrotbills
  Black-breasted 358, *359*
  Great 360
  Grey-hooded 358
  Rusty-throated 358
  Short-tailed 360
  Three-toed 360
parrotlets
  Red-fronted 192
  Tepui 193
  Yellow-faced 192
parrots
  Australian King Parrot 195
  Budgerigar 188, 194, 197
  Buff-faced Pygmy Parrot 189
  Cockatiel 189, 191, 192
  Eclectus Parrot 189, 195
  Galah 191, 192
  Greater Vasa Parrot 195
  Grey Parrot 192, 193
  Guaiabero 197
  Indigo-winged Parrot 192
  Kakapo 188, 189, 190, *190*, 196
  Kea 188, 190
  Lesser Vasa Parrot 195
  Mascarene Parrot 194
  Mulga Parrot 195
  Night Parrot 194, 196
  Orange-bellied Parrot 189, 194
  Paradise Parrot 194, 196
  Pesquet's Parrot 193, 194, 195
  Red-fan Parrot 194
  Seychelles Black Parrot 194, 195
  Swift Parrot 189, 194
  Vulturine Parrot 192, 193, 195
  Wallace's Hanging Parrot 194
  see also amazons; cockatoos; corellas; Crimson Rosella; ground-parrots; kakas; lories; lorikeets; lovebirds; macaws; parakeets; parrotlets *and* raquet-tails
partridges
  Grey 26, *26*
  Red-legged 26
  Stone Partridge 24, 26
Parula americana 319, 320
Parulidae 319–21
Parus major 335
  P. nuchalis 335
Passer domesticus 251, 293, 300, 301, *301*, 316
  P. eminbey 301
  P. euchlorus 301
  P. hemileucus 300
  P. italiae 301
  P. luteus 301, *302*
  P. montanus 301, *301*
Passerculus sandwichensis 315
Passerella iliaca megarhyncha 314
Passerellidae 314–16
Passeridae 300–2
Passerina 327

P. caerulea 328
  P. ciris 327, 328
  P. cyanea 328
  P. rositae 327
Pastor roseus 382, 384, 385
Patagioenas 34
Patagona gigas 53, 54
pauraques
  Common 45, 46, *46*
  Jamaican 44, 46
Pauxi 22
  P. pauxi 21
  P. unicornis 21
Pavo cristatus 26, 27
Pedionomidae 113
Pedionomus torquatus 113, *113*
Pelagodroma marina 77
Pelecanidae 91–2
Pelecanoides garnotii 87
  P. georgicus 87
  P. magellani 86
  P. urinatrix 87, *87*
Pelecanus conspicillatus 91, *91*, *91*
  P. crispus 91, *91*
  P. erythrorhynchos 91, 92, *92*
  P. occidentalis 91, 92, *92*
  P. onocrotalus 91
  P. philippensis 91, 92
  P. rufescens 92
  P. thagus 91, 92, 102
pelicans 91–2
  American White 91, 92, *92*
  Australian 91, 92
  Brown 91, 92, *92*
  Dalmatian 91, *91*
  Great White 91
  Peruvian 91, 92, 102
  Pink-backed 92
  Spot-billed 91, 92
Peliohaporus luteoviridis 314
Pellomeidae 363
Peltops 261
penduline tits 337–8
  Eurasian Penduline Tit *337*, 338
  Forest Penduline Tit 337
  Verdin 337–8, *338*
Penelope albipennis 21
  P. purpurascens 22
Penelopides 156
  P. exarhatus 153
  P. manillae 156
Penelopina nigra 21
Peneothello sigillatus 282
penguins 74–6
  Adélie 76
  African 74
  Chinstrap 76
  Emperor 74, 75, *75*, 76
  Erect-crested 74
  Fiordland 74
  Galapagos 74, 75
  Gentoo 76
  King 74, 76, *76*
  Little 75
  Macaroni 74
  Magellanic 74
  Northern Rockhopper 74
  Rockhopper *75*
  Yellow-eyed 74
peppershrikes
  Black-billed 255
  Rufous-browed 255
Perdix perdix 26
Pericrocotus igneus 247
Perija Thistletail 227
Periparus ater 335
  P. rubidiventris 336
  P. rufonuchalis 336
  P. xanthogenys 336
Perisoreus canadensis 272
  P. infaustus 272
  P. internigrans 272
Perissocephalus tricolor 207

Pernis 136, 138
Peruvian Plantcutter 206
Peruvian Sheartail 54
petrels
  Antarctic 84
  Beck's 84, 85
  Bermuda 84
  Black-capped 84
  Blue 85
  Cape 84, *86*
  Chatham 84
  Cook's 84
  Fiji 84, 85
  Galapagos 84
  Hawaiian 84
  Juan Fernandez 84
  Kerguelen 85
  Madeira 84
  Magenta 84
  Mascarene 84, 85
  Phoenix 84
  Snow 84
  Southern Giant *85*
  White-chinned *87*
  see also fulmars *and* prions
Petroica australis 282
  P. longipes 282
  P. macrocephala 282
  P. traversi 281, 282
Petroicidae 281–2
Petronia petronia 301
Peucedramidae 291
Peucedramus taeniatus 291, *291*
Pezopetes capitalis 315
Pezophaps solitaria 31
Pezoporus flaviventris 196
  P. occidentalis 194, 196
  P. wallicus 196
Phaenicophaeus 59
  P. pyrrocephalus 57
Phaenicophilidae 317–18
Phaenicophilus palmarum 318, *318*
  P. poliocephalus 317, 318
Phaenostictus mcleannani 218, 220
Phaethon aethereus 39, *39*, 40
  P. lepturus 39, 40, *40*
  P. l. fulvus 39
  P. rubricauda 39, 40
Phaethontidae 39–40
Phaethornis ruber 52
  P. superciliosus 55
Phainopepla 371
Phainopepla nitens 371
Phainoptila melanoxantha 371
Phalacrocoracidae 102–3
Phalacrocorax atriceps 103
  P. auritus 102
  P. bougainvillii 102
  P. brasilianus 102
  P. capensis 102
  P. carbo 102, 103
  P. carunculatus 102
  P. featherstoni 102
  P. gaimardi 103
  P. harrisi 102, 103
  P. neglectus 102
  P. nigrogularis 102
  P. onslowi 102
  P. perspicillatus 102
  P. punctatus 103
Phalaenoptilus nuttallii 46
phalaropes
  Grey (NA Red Phalarope) 119
  Red-necked 119, *119*
  Wilson's 119
Phalaropus fulicarius 119
  P. lobatus 119, *119*
  P. tricolor 119
Phalcoboenus australis 184, 185, 187
  P. megalopterus 185
Pharomachrus auriceps 152
  P. mocinno 150, 152, *152*
Phasianidae 24–7
Phasianus colchicus 26, 27, *136*

pheasants
  Bulwer's 26
  Common 26, 27, *136*
  see also Indian Peafowl
Phegornis mitchellii 111
Pheucticus aureoventris 328
  P. chrysogaster 328
  P. chrysopeplus 328
  P. ludovicianus 328
  P. melanocephalus 328
  P. tibialis 328
Pheugopedius felix 377
Phibalura flavirostris 207
  P. f. boliviana 208
  P. f. phibalura 208
Philemon 237, 256
  P. fuscicapillus 235
Philentoma 263, 264
Philepitta castanea 202, 203
  P. schlegeli 202, 203
Philepittidae 202–3
Philesturnus carunculatus
  243–4, *244*
  P. c. carunculatus 243
  P. c. rufusater 243, 244
Philetairus socius 292, 293, *294*
Philippine Spinetail 48
Philomachus pugnax 117
Philomyias urichi 215
Philydor novaesi 227
Phodilus badius 142
Phoebastria albatrus 79, 80
  P. immutabilis 80
  P. irrorata 80, 81, 82, *82*
  P. nigripes 80, 81
Phoebetria fusca 79, 80, 81
  P. palpebrata 80, 81, *81*
Phoenicircus 207
Phoeniconaias minor 27, 28, *28*
Phoenicoparrus andinus 27, 28
  P. jamesi 27, 28
Phoenicopteridae 27–9
Phoenicopterus chilensis 27, 28
  P. ruber 27, 28, *29*
  P. r. roseus 27, *29*
  P. r. ruber 27
Phoeniculidae 158–9
Phoeniculus bollei 159
  P. castaneiceps 158, *159*
  P. damarensis 158, *159*
  P. purpureus 159, *159*
  P. somaliensis 159
Phoenicurus 320, 389
  P. phoenicurus 388, 389
Pholidornis rushiae 354, 356
Phonygammus 278
Phrygilus 314, 330, 332
  P. atriceps *330*
Phyllastrephus 347
  P. debilis 352
Phyllergates 356
Phylloscartes beckeri 213
  P. ceciliae 213
  P. kronei 213
  P. roquettei 213
Phylloscopidae 353–4
Phylloscopus collybita 354, *354*
  P. trochilus 353, 354
  P. tytleri 353
Phytotoma raimondii 206
Piapiac 272
Piaya cayana 59
  P. melanogaster *58*
Pica 236, 272
  P. pica 273, 274, 388
Picathartes gymnocephalus 280,
  280
  P. oreas 280, 281
Picidae 164–8
Picoides 168
  P. dorsalis 167
  P. pubescens 167
  P. ramsayi 164
  P. tridactylus 167
  P. villosus 167
Pictorella Finch 298
piculets
  African 165

Antillean 165
  Bar-breasted 165
  Olivaceous 165
  Rufous *165*
  Speckle-chested 164
  Speckled 162, 163
  Varzea 164
  White-bellied 164
Picumnus aurifrons 165
  P. innominatus 162, 163
  P. olivaceus 165
  P. spilogaster 164
  P. steindachneri 164
  P. varzeae 164
Picus canus 166
  P. viridis 166, *166*
pigeons 31–4, 36
  Bonin 31
  Crested 33
  Feral 32
  Mauritius Blue 31
  New Zealand *34*
  Nicobar 32, 34
  Passenger 31, 34
  Pheasant 34
  Pink 31, 34
  Silvery 31
  Spinifex 32, 33
  Squatter *32*
  Sri Lanka 31
  Timor Green 31
  Timor Imperial 31
  Tooth-billed 31, 32, 33, 34
  Topknot 33
  Victoria Crowned 31
  Wonga *33*
  Wood *33*
Pilherodius pileatus 95
Pinaroloxias inornata 330
Pine Grosbeak 309
Pine Siskin 311
Pinguinus impennis 123, 124,
  125
Pinicola enucleator 309
Pink-billed Parrotfinch 296
Pink-legged Gravateiro 227
piopios 257
  North Island 256
  South Island 256
Pipile jacutinga 21
  P. pipile 21
Pipilo naufragus 314
pipits 303–5
  Golden 217, 304
  Meadow 302
  Nilgiri 302
  Ochre-breasted 302
  Sokoke 302
  Sprague's 302, 305
  Tree *304*
  Water *304*
  Yellow-breasted 302, 304
Pipra filicauda 205, *206*
Pipreola chlorolepidota 207
  P. jucunda 208
Pipridae 205–6
piprites
  Black-capped 212, *212*
  Grey-headed 212
  Wing-barred 212
Piprites chloris 212
  P. griseiceps 212
  P. pileata 212, *212*
Pipritidae 212
Pipromorphidae 213–14
Piranga 327
  P. flava 329
  P. ludoviciana 329
  P. olivacea 328, 329
  P. rubra 328, 329
Pitangus sulphuratus 216, 217
Pithecophaga jefferyi 136, 138
Pithys albifrons 219
Pitohui 250, 251, 256, 257
  P. dichrous 250, 256, 257,
  257, 277
  P. kirhocephalus 250, 257
pitohuis

Hooded 250 , 256, 257, *257*,
  277
  Variable 250, 257
Pitta anerythra 200
  P. angolensis 200
  P. baudii 200
  P. brachyura 200
  P. caerulea 200
  P. gurneyi 200
  P. kochi 200
  P. megarhyncha 200
  P. moluccensis 200, 201
  P. nympha 200
  P. steerii 200
  P. superba 200
  P. venusta 200
  P. versicolor 200, *200*
pittas 200–1
  African 200
  Azure-breasted 200
  Black-faced 200
  Blue-headed 200
  Blue-winged 200, 201
  Fairy 200
  Giant 200
  Graceful 200
  Gurney's 200
  Indian 200
  Mangrove 200
  Noisy 200, *200*
  Superb 200
  Whiskered 200
Pittasoma michleri 221
  P. rufopileatum 221
Pittidae 200
Pityriasidae 264–5
Pityriasis gymnocephala 264–5,
  265
Plains-wanderer 113, *113*
Platalea leucorodia 98
  P. minor 97
Platycercus elegans 196, 197
Platylophus galericulatus 272
Platyrinchidae 211–12
Platyrinchus leucoryphus 211
  P. myastaceus 211, *211*
Platyspiza 330, 332
  P. crassirostris 330
Platysteira 262
  P. albifrons 261
  P. laticincta 261
  P. peltata 262
Platysteiridae 261–2
Plecopterus gambensis 16
Plectrophenacidae 312–13
Plectrophenax 316
  P. hyperboreus 312, 313
  P. nivalis 312, *312*, 313
Plegadis ridgwayi 98
Ploceidae 292–5
Plocepasser 293
Ploceus 294
  P. aureonucha 292
  P. baglafecht 295
  P. bannermani 292
  P. batesi 292
  P. burnieri 292
  P. galbula 292
  P. golandi 292
  P. jacksoni 295
  P. megarhynchus 292
  P. nicolli 292
  P. subaureus 293
Ploughbill 246, 253, *253*
plovers 111–13
  American Golden 111
  Common Ringed 111, *112*
  Diademed 111
  Double-banded 112
  Eurasian Golden 111, *112*
  Grey (NA Black-bellied
  Plover) 111
  Madagascan 111
  Magellanic 106, 107
  Pacific Golden 111, 113
  Red-breasted 111
  Semipalmated 111
  Snowy 111

St Helena 111
  see also Crab plover;
  dotterels; Egyptian Plover;
  Killdeer; lapwings *and*
  Wrybill
Pluvialis apricaria 111, *112*
  P. dominica 111
  P. fulva 111, 113
  P. squatarola 111
Pluvianellus socialis 106, 107
Pluvianidae 107
Pluvianus aegyptius 107, 122
Pnoepyga albiventer 349
  P. formosana 349
  P. immaculata 349
  P. pusilla 349, *349*
Pnoepygidae 349
pochards 18
  Baer's Pochard 15
  Common 16, *17*
  Madagascar 15
  Rosy-billed 17
Podargidae 42–3
Podargus ocellatus 42
  P. papuensis 42
  P. strigoides 42, *43*
Podica senegalensis 64, *64*
Podiceps andinus 29, 31
  P. cristatus 30, *30*, 31
  P. gallardoi 29, 31
  P. grisegena 30
  P. taczanowskii 29, 30, 31
Podicipedidae 29–31
Podilymbus gigas 29, 30, 31
  P. podiceps 30, *30*
Podoces 272, 336
Poecile atricapillus 335
  P. carolinensis 335
  P. cinctus 336
  P. montanus 336
  P. palustris 336
Poecilotriccus capitalis 214
  P. lululae 213
Pogoniulus 171
Pogonotriccus lanyoni 213
Point-tailed Palmcreeper 228
Polemaetus bellicosus 139
Polihierax insignis 185
  P. semitorquatus 185
Poliocephalus rufopectus 29
Polioptila caerulea 377, *378*
  P. californica 378
  P. clementsi 378
  P. guanensis 378
  P. g. attenboroughi 378
  P. lactea 377, 378
  P. melanura 378
  P. nigriceps 378
Polioptilidae 377–8
Polyboroides 138, 140
Polysticta stelleri 15, 16
Pomarea dimidiata 273
  P. nigra 273
  P. whitneyi 273
Pomarina mira 273
Pomatorhinus 241
  P. superciliaris 362
Pomatostomidae 241
Pomatostomus halli 241
  P. temporalis 241
  P. t. rubeculus 241
Poo-uli 305, 309
Poodytes albolimbatus 344, 345
  P. carteri 345
  P. punctatus 345
  P. p. rufescens 345
Poorwill, Common 46
Porphyrio albus 63
  P. hochstetteri 61, 62, *62*
  P. porphyrio 62, 63
potoos 41, 43–4
  Andean 43
  Common *43*
  Great 43
  Rufous 43
prairie-chickens 26
  Greater *25*
pratincoles 122, 123

Australian 123
  Black-winged 122, 123
  Collared 123, *123*
  Grey 123
  Madagascar 122
  Oriental 122
Prinia 299, 343
  P. cinereocapilla 342
  P. gracilis 344
  P. socialis 343
prinias
  Ashy *343*
  Graceful 344
  Grey-crowned 342
  Sierra Leone 342
Prioniturus 189, 195
  P. luconensis 194
  P. verticalis 194
Prionochilus thoracicus 285
Prionodura newtoniana 231
Prionops 263
  P. plumatus *264*
prions
  Antarctic *86*
  Fulmar Prion 85
Priotelus roseigaster 150, 152
  P. temnurus 152
Probosciger aterrimus 189, 191
Procaccius 325
Procellaria 85
  P. aequinoctialis *87*
Procellariidae 84–7
Procelsterna 127
  P. albivitta 130
  P. cerulea 130
Procnias albus 207
  P. averano 207
  P. nudicollis 207
  P. tricarunculatus 206, 207,
  207
Prodotiscus 163
  P. zambesiae 162
Progne modesta 350
  P. murphyi 350
  P. subis 350, 351, *351*
Promeropidae 283–4
Promerops cafer 283, 283–4
  P. gurneyi 283–4
Prosobonia cancellata 116
  P. ellisi 116
  P. leucoptera 116
  P. parvirostris 116, 117
Prosthemadera novaeseelandiae
  237
Prunella atrogularis 290
  P. collaris 290, *290*, 313
  P. fulvescens 290
  P. himalayana 290
  P. immaculata 290
  P. modularis 290, *291*, 313
  P. montanella 290
  P. rubeculoides 290
  P. strophiata 290
Prunellidae 289–91
Przevalski's Rosefinch 289, *289*
Psalidorprocne 351
Psaltria exilis 358
Psaltriparus minimus 357, 358,
  358
Psarisomus dalhousiae 201
Psarocolius 325
  P. cassini 321
  P. montezuma 323, *323*
Psephotellus pulcherrimus
  194, 196
  P. varius 196
Pseudastur albicollis 140
Pseudibis davisoni 97
  P. gigantea 97
Pseudobias wardi 262, 263
Pseudobulweria aterrima 84, 85
  P. becki 84, 85
  P. macgillivrayi 84, 85
Pseudocalyptomena graueri
  201, 202
Pseudochelidon 351
  P. sirintarae 350
Pseudocolopteryx 216

Pseudonestor xanthophrys 305
Pseudonigrita 293
Pseudopodoces humilis 336
Pseudorectes ferrugineus 250
  P. incertus 249, 250
Pseudoscops clamator 143
  P. grammicus 147
Pseudoseisura 228
Pseudotriccus ruficeps 214
Psilopogon 169
  P. franklinii 172
  P. haemacephalus 172
  P. virens 172
Psilorhamphus guttatus 224
Psiloscops flammeolus 147
Psiphodes occidentalis 253
Psittacidae 192–4
Psittacula eques 194
  P. exsul 194, 196
  P. krameri 195, *197*
  P. wardi 194, 196
Psittaculidae 194–7
Psittaculirostris 188, 197
Psittacus erithacus 192, 193
  P. e. timneh 193
Psittirostra psittacea 305, 308
Psittrichas fulgidus 193, 194, 195
Psophia crepitans 65, *65*
  P. leucoptera 65
  P. l. ochroptera 65
  P. viridis dextralis 65
  P. v. obscura 65
  P. v. viridis 65
Psophiidae 65
Psophodes cristatus 252, 253
  P. nigrogularis 252
  P. olivaceus 252, *252*
Psophodidae 252–3
ptarmigans
  Rock 25
  White-tailed 25
Pteridophora alberti 277, 279, *279*
Pterocles alchata 35
  P. indicus 35
Pteroclidae 35
Pterocnemia pennata 8, *8*
  P. p. tarapacensis 8
Pterodroma 85
  P. alba 84
  P. axillaris 84
  P. cahow 84
  P. cookii 84
  P. externa 84
  P. hasitata caribbaea 84
  P. madeira 84
  P. magentae 84
  P. phaeopygia 84
  P. sandwichensis 84
Pteroglossus 168, 171
  P. beauharnaesii *170*, 171
  P. torquatus 169
Pteroptochos 223
Pteruthius 255
Ptilinopus 33, 34
  P. coralensis 32
  P. mercierii 31
Ptiliogonatidae 371–2
Ptilocichla falcata 364
  P. leucogrammica 363
Ptilogonys caudatus 371, *371*
  P. cinereus 371
Ptilolaemus 156
Ptilonorhynchidae 231–2
Ptilonorhynchus violaceus 231, 232, *232*
Ptilopachus petrosus 24, 26
Ptiloris 277
Ptilorrhoa leucosticta 248
Ptilostomus afer 272
Ptychoramphus aleuticus 124
Ptyonoprogne 351
Puaiohi 391
puffbacks 266
puffbirds 161–2
  Crescent-chested 161
  Semi-collared *161*
  Sooty-capped 161

Swallow-winged 161, 162
  see also Lanceolated Monklet *and* White-faced Nunbird
puffins
  Atlantic 123, 125, *128*
  Horned 123
  Tufted 123, 125
Puffinus auricularis 84
  P. bryani 84
  P. huttoni 84
  P. mauretanicus 84
  P. puffinus 85
Pulsatrix perspicillata 143, 147
Purple-backed Sunbeam 52
Purple-backed Thornbill 54
Purple-throated Fruitcrow 207
Pycnonotidae 351–2
Pycnonotus barbatus 351–2, *352*
  P. cafer 351
  P. jocosus 352
  P. leucotis 351
  P. zeylanicus 351, 352
Pycnopygius stictocephalus 257
Pygiptila stellaris 220
Pygochelidon cyanoleuca 350
Pygoscelis adeliae 76
  P. antarctica 76
  P. papua 76
Pyrgilauda 302
Pyriglena 220
  P. atra 218
Pyrilia vulturina 192, 193, 195
Pyrocephalus rubinus 216, *216*, 217
Pyroderus scutatus 207
Pyrrhocorax 271, 275
Pyrrhula 309
  P. pyrrhula 310
Pyrrhuloxia 328
Pyrrhura 194
Pytilia 299

quail-thrushes
  Cinnamon *248*
  Painted 248
quails, New World 23–4
  Bearded Wood-partridge 23
  Black-fronted Wood-quail 23
  Dark-backed Wood-quail 23
  Gambel's Quail *24*
  Gorgeted Wood-quail 23
  Northern Bobwhite 23, 24
  Ocellated Quail 23
  Tacarcuna Wood-quail 23
quails, Old World
  Common Quail 24
  Himalayan Quail 24
  King Quail 26
Quelea cardinalis 292, 294
  Q. erythrops 292
  Q. quelea 292, *293*, 294
queleas
  Cardinal 292
  Red-billed 292, *293*, 294
  Red-headed 292
Querula purpurata 207
quetzals
  Eared 152
  Golden-headed 152
  Resplendent 150, 152, *152*
Quiscalus mexicanus 323
  Q. palustris 321, 324
  Q. quiscula 322, 325

Rabor's Ground Warbler 345
Rail Babbler 280, 281
rails 61–3
  Bogota 61
  Galapagos 61
  Grey-necked Wood *62*
  Grey-throated 63
  Guam 61
  Invisible 61, 62
  New Caledonian 61
  Okinawa 61
  Western Water 61
  Zapata 61
  see also Black Crake; coots;

moorhens; swamphens *and* Weka
Rallidae 61–3
Rallus aquaticus 61
  R. semiplumbeus 61
Ramphastidae 168–72
Ramphastos 169, 170
  R. sulfuratus 170, *170*
  R. toco 170
  R. vitellinus 168
Ramphocaenus melanurus 377, 378, *378*
Ramphocelus flammigerus icteronotus 332
Ramphocinclus brachyurus 380
Ramphocoris clotbey 339
Ramphomicron microrhynchum 54
Raphus cucullatus 31, 34
raquet-tails 195
  Blue-winged 194
  Green 194
ravens
  Common (Northern) 147, 191, 198, 207, 271, *272*
  New Zealand 271
  White-necked 271
rayaditos
  Masafuera 227
Razorbill 123, 124, *124*, 125
Recurve-billed Bushbird 218
Recurvirostra americana 109, 110
  R. andina 110
  R. avosetta 109, 110, *110*
  R. novaehollandiae 109, 110
Recurvirostridae 109–10
Red Avadavat 297
Red-billed Firefinch 297, *297*
Red-billed Leiothrix 365
Red-capped Forest Warbler (African Tailorbird) 344
Red-cheeked Cordon-bleu 297
Red-collared Myzomela *236*
Red Crossbill 311, *311*
Red-faced Malkoha 57
Red-fronted Serin 310
Red-ruffed Fruitcrow 207
Red Siskin 305, 311
Red-tailed Minla 365
Red-tailed Newtonia 262
Reddish Hermit 52
Redhead 16
redstarts
  Common *388*, 389
  Luzon Water 387
  White-capped Water 389
Regulidae 366–7
Regulus calendula 366, 367, 367
  R. c. obscurus 367
  R. goodfellowi 367
  R. ignicapillus 366, 367
  R. i. madeirensis 367
  R. madeirensis 366, 367
  R. regulus 366
  R. satrapa 366, 367
Remiz pendulinus *337*, 338
Remizidae 337–8
Restinga Tyrannulet 213
Rhabdornis grandis 383
  R. inornatus 383
  R. mystacalis 383, *385*
  R. rabori 383
rhabdornises
  Grand (Long-billed) 383
  Stripe-breasted 383
  Stripe-headed 383, *385*
  Visayan 383
Rhadina sibilatrix 353, *354*
Rhagologidae 258
Rhagologus leucostigma 258
Rhamphocharis crassirostris 241, 242
Rhea americana 8
rheas 8–9
  Greater 8
  Lesser 8, *8*

Puna 8
Rheidae 8–9
Rheinardia 26
Rhinocrypta 224
  R. lanceolata 223, *223*
Rhinocryptidae 223–4
Rhinoplax vigil 153, 156
Rhinopomastus 158, 159
  R. aterrimus 159
  R. cyanomelas 159
  R. minor 159
Rhinoptilus bitorquatus 122
Rhipidura 334
  R. albiscapa 269
  R. albolimbata 269
  R. fuliginosa 269
  R. leucophrys 268, 269, *269*
  R. malaitae 268
  R. rufifrons 268, *269*
  R. semirubra 268
Rhipiduridae 268–9
Rhodinocichla rosea 313, *313*
Rhodinocichlidae 313
Rhodocanthis flaviceps 305
  R. palmeri 305
Rhodonessa caryophyllacea 15
Rhodophoneus cruentus 266
Rhodostethia rosea 128
Rhopophilus pekinensis 359
Rhyacornis 389
  R. bicolor 387
Rhynchocyclus 214
Rhynchophanes mccownii 312
Rhynochetidae 38
Rhynochetos jubatus 38, *38*
Rhyticeros 156
  R. cassidix 153
  R. everetti 153
  R. narcondami 153
  R. plicatus 153
  R. subruficollis 153
  R. waldeni 153
Ribbon-tailed Astrapia *279*
Rifleman 199, *199*
Rigidipenna inexpectata 42
Rimator 364
  R. pasquieri 363
Riparia riparia 350
Rissa brevirostris 127, *128*
  R. tridactyla 128
roadrunners
  Greater 58, *60*
  Lesser 58
robins
  European 281, 387, 389
  Indian 388
  Oriental Magpie Robin 388
  Rufous Scrub 388
  Seychelles Magpie Robin 387
  Swynnerton's 387
  see also Australasian robins
Robsonius rabori 345
rock sparrows 301
  Pale 301
rock thrushes
  Blue 390
  Common 390
rockfowls 280–1
  Grey-necked 280, 281
  White-necked 280, *280*
rockjumpers
  Cape 280, 281
  Drakensberg 280, 281
Rockrunner 341, 342
rockwrens 199
Rodrigues Solitaire 31
Rollandia microptera 29, 30, 31
rollers 175–6
  Abyssinian 175
  Blue-bellied 175
  Blue-throated 176
  Broad-billed 175, 176
  European 175
  Indian 176
  Lilac-breasted 175, *176*
  Purple 175, 176
  Purple-winged (Sulawesi) 176
  Racquet-tailed 175, 176

Rufous-crowned 175
  see also Dollarbird
Rook 184, 271, *272*
Rose-bellied Bunting 327
Rosefinch, Common 309
Rostratula australis 114
  R. benghalensis 114, *115*
Rostratulidae 114–15
Rostrhamus sociabilis 136, 137, 140
Rotuma Myzomela 235
Rowettia goughensis 329
royal flycatchers 209, *209*, *210*
  Atlantic 209
  Pacific 209
Royal Sunangel 52
Ruddy-tailed Flycatcher 209
Ruff 117
Rufous-crested Coquette *55*
Rufous-crowned Antpitta 221
Rufous-headed Pygmy Tyrant 214
Rufous Songlark 345
Rufous Twistwing 213
Rukia ruki 360
Rupicola 206, 207
  R. peruvianus *208*
Russet-mantled Soft-tail 227
Rusty-throated Wren Babbler 362
Ruwenzororornis johnstoni 72
Rynchops albicollis 127, 130
  R. flavirostris 130
  R. niger 127, 130, *130*
  R. n. cinerascens 130
  R. n. intercedens 130
  R. n. niger 130

Saddleback 243-4, *244*
Sagittariidae 134
Sagittarius serpentarius 131, 134, 183
Salpinctes obsoletus 377
Salpornis 374
  S. salvadori 375
  S. spilonota 375
Saltator 327, 330, 331, 332
sandgrouse 35, 36
  Painted *35*
  Pin-tailed 35
sandpipers
  Christmas Island 116
  Common 118, *119*
  Curlew 119
  Moorea 116
  Semipalmated 117
  Spoon-billed 116, 119
  Spotted 118
  Tahiti 116
  Tuamotu 116, 117
  Upland 117
  Western *117*
  see also Ruff
Sandy Gallito 223, 224
Santa Marta Sabrewing 52
Saõ Tomé Grosbeak 305
Saõ Tomé Short-tail 302, 304
Sapayo 204
Sapayoa aenigma 204
Sapayoaidae 204
Sarcogyps calvus 136
Sarcophanops steerii 201, 202
Sarcops calvus 384, *384*
Sarcoramphus papa 132, 133, *133*
Sarkidiornis melanotos 16, 17
Sarothrura ayresi 63
  S. watersi 63
Sarothruridae 63
Sasia 165
  S. abnormis *165*
satinbirds 242–3
  Crested 243, *243*
  Loria's 242, 243
  Yellow-breasted 242, 243
Saurothera 60
Saxicola 389
  S. leucurus 387

Saxicoloides fulicata 388
Sayornis nigricans 217
  S. phoebe 217
  S. saya 217
Say's Phoebe 217
Sceloglaux albifacies 143, 146
Scenopoeetes dentirostris 231
Scepomycter winifredae 342
Schetba rufa 262
Schiffornis 210
Schistolais 343
  S. leontica 342
Schoeniclus aureola 316, 317
  S. rusticus 316
  S. schoeniclus 289
  S. siemsenni 317
  S. sulphuratus 316
Schoenicola 345
Schoeniparus cinereus 363
  S. rufogularis 363
  S. variegaticeps 363
Schoutedenapus schoutedeni 48
scimitar babblers
  Bar-winged Wren Babbler
    362
  Chestnut-capped Babbler 362
  Golden Babbler 362
  Large Scimitar Babbler 362
  Nonggang Babbler 362
  Rusty-throated Wren Babbler
    362
  Slender-billed Scimitar
    Babbler 362
  Snowy-throated Babbler 362
  Tawny-breasted Wren
    Babbler 362
scimitarbills
  Abyssinian 159
  Common *159*
Scissirostrum dubium 384
Scleruridae 225–6
Sclerurus albigularis 225
  S. scansor cearensis 225
Scolopacidae 116–19
Scolopax 118
  S. minor 118
  S. mira 116
  S. rochussenii 116
  S. rusticola 118
Scopidae 92–3
Scopus umbretta 88, 92–3, *93*
Scotocerca inquieta 354, 355,
  355
Scotocercidae 354–6
Scotopelia 147
Scottish Crossbill 311
screamers 13–14
  Horned 14, *14*
  Northern 13, 14
  Southern *13*, 14
scrub-birds
  Noisy 230, *230*
  Rufous 230, *230*
Scrub-tit 239
Scytalopus 224
  S. diamantinensis 223
  S. gonzogai 223
  S. iraiensis 223
  S. magellanicus 223
  S. panamensis 223
  S. perijanus 223
  S. robbinsi 223
  S. rodriguezi 223
Scythrops novaehollandiae 57,
  59, 60
Secretary Bird 131, 134, 183
seedsnipes 114
  Grey-breasted *114*
  Least 114
  Rufous-bellied 114
Seicercus amoenus 353
  S. borealis 353, 354
  S. hainanus 353
  S. ijimae 353
Seiurus aurocapilla 319, 320
Selasphorus ardens 52
  S. rufus 53, 55
  S. sasin 53

Selenidera 171
Seleucidis melanoleucus 277, 278
Selva Cacique 321
Semnornis 169
  S. frantzii 172
  S. ramphastinus 172, *172*
Sephanoides fernandensis 52
  S. sephaniodes 55
Sericossypha albocristata 330
Sericulus bakeri 231
  S. chrysocephalus 231, *231*
seriemas 183–4
  Black-legged 184
  Red-legged *183*, 184
Serilophus lunatus 202
Serinus canaria 306, 310
  S. pusillus 310
  S. serinus 310
  S. syriacus 310
Setophaga angelae 319
  S. cerulea 319
  S. chrysoparia 319
  S. citrina 319
  S. coronata 320
  S. kirtlandii 319
  S. pensylvanica 319, 320
  S. petechia 320
  S. pitiayumi 320, *320*
  S. plumbea 319
  S. ruticilla 320
Setornis criniger 351
shags
  Chatham 102
  Imperial *103*
  Pitt 102
  Rough-faced 102
  Spotted 103
shanks
  Common Redshank 118
  Greater Yellowlegs 118
  Lesser Yellowlegs 118
  Nordmann's Greenshank 116
  Spotted Redshank 119
Sharpbill 208–9
shearwaters
  Balearic 84
  Bryan's 84
  Great 86
  Hutton's 84
  Manx 85
  Pink-footed 84
  Sooty 85, *87*
  Townsend's 84
sheathbills 106–7
  Black-faced (Lesser) 106
  Snowy (American or Pale-
    faced) 106, *107*
sheldgeese 15
shelducks 18
  Common 17
  Crested 15
  Reunion 15
Shelley's Crimsonwing 296
Sheppardia 389
Shoebill (Whale-headed Stork)
  88, *93*, 93–4
Short-crested Coquette 52
Short-tailed Pygmy Tyrant
  198, 214
shovelers 18
shrike-thrushes
  Grey 249, *249*
  Rusty 250
  Sooty 249
  White-bellied 249, 250
shrike-tits 250–1
  Eastern 251
  Western Crested *250*
shrikes 270
  Great Grey 270
  Iberian Grey 270
  Lesser Grey 270
  Loggerhead 270
  Magpie 270
  Masked 270
  Mountain 270
  Northern 270
  Red-backed 270, *270*

Sao Tome (Newton's) Fiscal
  270
  Southern White-crowned 270
  White-crowned 270
  Woodchat 270
  Yellow-billed 270
Sialia currucoides 392
  S. mexicana 392
  S. sialis 392, *392*
Siberian Rubythroat *387*
Sibirionetta formosa 16
Sicalis 314, 332
Silktail (Satin Flycatcher) 269
silky flycatchers
  Black-and-yellow 371
  Grey 371
  Long-tailed 371, *371*
  see also Phainopepla
Silvereye 361
Sinai Rosefinch 309
Sinosuthora przewalskii 358
  S. zappyi 358
Siphonorhis americana 44, 46
sitellas
  Black 246
  Papuan 246
  Varied 246, *246*
Sitta canadensis 375
  S. carolinensis 375, 375
  S. europaea 375, *375*
  S. formosa 374
  S. ledanti 374, 375
  S. magna 374
  S. neumayer 375
  S. pusilla 374, 375
  S. pygmaea 374
  S. tephronota 375
  S. victoriae 374
  S. v. insularis 374
Sittaparus owstoni 335
Sittasoma griseicapillus 227
Sittidae 374–5
Siva cyanouroptera 365
skimmers 127, 130
  African 130
  Black 127, 130, *130*
  Indian 127, 130
skuas 126–7
  Arctic (NA Parasitic Jaeger)
    126, *126*
  Brown (or Southern) 126,
    126, 127
  Chilean 126, 127
  Great 126, 127
  Long-tailed (NA Long-tailed
    Jaeger) 126
  Pomarine (NA Pomarine
    Jaeger) 126
  South Polar 126
Smew 16
Smicrornis brevirostris 239
  S. capensis 203
  S. rufolateralis 203
  S. sharpei 203
Snail-eating Coua 57, 58
snipes 116
  Common *118*
  Great 118
  Jack 118
  Madagascar 116
  New Zealand 118
snowcocks 26
  Himalayan 26
snowfinches
  White-rumped 302
  White-winged 302, *302*
Solitaire, Rodrigues 31
solitaires [thrushes]
  Rufous-brown 391
  Rufous-throated *391*, 392
  Townsend's 392
Somateria 16
South Island Takahe 61, 62, *62*
Southern Red Bishop 292
spadebills
  Russet-winged 211
  White-throated 211, *211*

Spangled Cotinga *208*
sparrowhawks
  Eurasian 136, 140
  Imitator 140
sparrows, New World 314–16
  Antioquia Brush Finch 314,
    316
  Bermuda Towhee 314
  Black-spectacled Brush Finch
    314
  Black-throated Sparrow *315*
  Chipping Sparrow 314
  Fox Sparrow 314
  Guadalupe Junco 314
  Large-footed Finch 315
  Lark Bunting 314
  Le Conte's Sparrow 314
  Pale-headed Brush Finch 316
  Rufous-collared Sparrow 315
  Saltmarsh Sparrow 314
  Savannah Sparrow 315
  Sierra Madre Sparrow 314,
    316
  Song Sparrow *314*, 315
  White-crowned Sparrow 315,
    315, 316
  Yellow-breasted Tanager
    Finch 314
  Yellow-green Finch 314
  Zapata Sparrow 314
sparrows, Old World 300–1
  Abd al Kuri 300
  Arabian Golden 301
  Chestnut 301
  Eurasian Tree 301, *301*
  House 251, 293, 300, 301,
    301, 316
  Italian 300
  Sudan Golden 301, *302*
Spatula discors 16
  S. hottentota 16, 17
Speckled Warbler 239
Spelaeornis 362
  S. badeigularis 362
  S. longicaudatus 362
  S. troglodytoides 362
Sphecotheres 257
  S. vieilloti 257
Spheniscidae 74–6
Spheniscus demersus 74
  S. magellanicus 74
  S. mendiculus 74, 75
Sphenoeacus afer 341, 342
Sphyrapicus 167
spiderhunters
  Streaked *287*
  Whitehead's *287*
Spilornis 138
Spindalis 317, 318
spinetails 227, 228
  Ash-browed 227
  Bolivian 227
  Hoary-throated 227
  Marañon 227
  Pinto's 227
Spinifexbird 345
Spinus cucullatus 305, 311
  S. lawrencei 311
  S. pinus 311
  S. psaltria 311
  S. spinescens 307
  S. spinus 311
  S. tristis 311
Spiza americana 328
Spizaetus 139
Spizella passerine 314
Spiziapteryx circumcinctus 185
Spizocorys fringillaris 339
Spodiopsar cineraceus 384
spoonbills 97, 98
  Black-faced 97
  Eurasian *98*
  Roseate 98
Sporophila 310, 314, 330, 331,
  332
  S. maximiliani 329
  S. torqueola 329
Sporopipes 293

  S. frontalis 294
  S. squamifrons 294
Spot-throat 283, 284
Spotted Bamboowren 224
spotted creepers 374
  African 375
  Indian 375
Spotted Jewel-babbler *248*
Spotted Nothura 10
Spotted Wren-babbler 372
Spur-winged Goose 16
Stachyris 362
  S. nonggangensis 362
  S. oglei 362
Stagonopleura 298
starlings 381–5
  Amethyst 383
  Asian Glossy 384
  Asian Pied 384
  Brahminy 384
  Bristle-crowned 384
  Coleto (Bald Starling) 384,
    384
  Common 240, 282, 306, 322,
    381, 382, *382*, 384, 385, 390
  Emerald 383
  Kosrae 381
  Micronesian 384
  Mysterious 381
  Pohnpei 381
  Réunion 381
  Rose-coloured (Rosy) 382,
    384, 385
  Shining 384
  Spotless 382
  Superb 383, *383*
  Tasman 381
  Wattled 383, *383*
  White-cheeked 384
  White-eyed 381
  see also mynas *and*
    rhabdornises
Steatornis caripensis 40, 41,
  41, 49
Steatornithidae 41
Stelgidopteryx 351
Steller's Eider 15, 16
Stellula calliope 55
Stenostira scita 334
Stenostiridae 334
Stephanoaetus coronatus 139,
  139
Stercorariidae 126–7
Stercorarius antarcticus 126,
  126, 127
  S. chilensis 126, 127
  S. longicaudus 126
  S. maccormicki 126, 127
  S. parasiticus 126, *126*
  S. pomarinus 126
  S. skua 126, 127
Sterna acuticauda 127
  S. dougallii 286
  S. paradisaea 129, *129*
Sternula albifrons 129
  S. antillarum 129
  S. lorata 127
  S. nereis 127
Sterrhoptilus 361
Stictonetta naevosa 16
Stigmatura 216
Stiltia isabella 123
stilts 109–10
  Banded 109, 110
  Black 109, 110
  Black-winged 109, 110, *110*
Stipiturus mallee 233
Stitchbird (Hihi) 244–5, *245*
Stizorhina 392
stone-curlews
  Beach 105
  Bush 105
  Eurasian 105, *105*
  Great 105
storks 88–90
  Abdim's 88
  Black 88, 89
  Black-necked 89

European White 88, 89, 90, *90*
Maguari 88, 89
Milky 88, 89, 90
Oriental White 88
Painted 90
Saddle-billed 89, 90
Storm's 88
Wood 88, 89, 90
Woolly-necked 88, 89
Yellow-billed 90
see also adjutants; Jabiru; Marabou *and* openbills
storm-petrels, northern 83
Ashy 83
European 77, 78, *83*
Fork-tailed 83
Guadalupe 83
Hornby's 83
Leach's 83
Matsudaira's 83
Monteiro's 83
Swinhoe's 83
Tristram's 83
storm-petrels, southern 77–8
New Zealand 77
Polynesian 77
White-faced 77
Wilson's 78, *78*
Strepera fuliginosa 259
S. graculina 259, *260*
Streptopelia 34
Streptoprocne phelpsi 50
S. rutila 50
S. semicollaris 51
S. zonaris 51
Stresemann's Bristlefront 223
Strigidae 143–7
Strigopidae 190–1
Strigops habroptilus 188, 189, 190, *190*, 196
Strix aluco 145, 147
S. butleri 144, 147
S. leptogrammica 147
S. nebulosa 141, 145, *145*, 147
S. occidentalis 143, 147
S. uralensis 146
S. varia 147
S. woodfordi 147
Struthidea cinerea 275
Struthio camelus 6, *7*, 8, 138
S. c. molybdophanes 6, 8
S. c. syriacus 6, 8
Struthionidae 6–8
Sturnella 304
S. magna 325
S. neglecta 325
Sturnia pagodarum 384
Sturnidae 381–5
Sturnus unicolor 382
S. vulgaris 240, 282, 306, 322, 381, 382, *382*, 384, 385, 390
sugarbirds
Cape *283*, 283–4
Gurney's 283–4
Sula dactylatra 101, 102
S. granti 101, 102
S. leucogaster 101, 102
S. nebouxii 101, 102
S. sula 100, 101, 102
S. variegata 100, 102
Sulidae 100–2
Sulphur-rumped Flycatcher 209
sunbirds 286–7
Amani 286
Banded Green 286
Beautiful *287*
Elegant 286
Giant 286
Hunter's *286*
Loveridge's 286
Rockefeller's 286
Rufous-winged 286
see also spiderhunters
Sunbittern 37, *37*
Sungrebe 64
Surnia ulula 144, *144*, 146
Surniculus lugubris 60

Swallow-tailed Cotinga 207
swallows
Bahama 350
Barn 350
Blue 350, 351
Blue-and-white *350*
Golden 350
Tree 350
Welcome 350
swamphens
Lord Howe (White) Swamphen 63
Purple Swamphen 62, 63
South Island Takahe 61, 62, *62*
swans
Black 15
Black-necked 15, 17
Coscoroba 15, 18
Mute 15, 17, 18, *18*, 132
Trumpeter 15
Tundra 15
Whooper 15
swiftlets
Black-nest 50
Edible-nest 50
Glossy 49, *50*
Mariana 48
Pygmy 49
Seychelles 48
swifts 48–51
African 50
African Palm 50
Alpine 49, 50
Black 49, 51
Chestnut-collared 50
Chimney 48, 51
Common 48, 49, 50, 51
Dark-rumped 48
Fork-tailed Palm 50
Great Dusky 49, *49*
Little 50
Mottled 50
Schouteden's 48
Tepui 50
Vaux's 51
Waterfall 48, 49
White-collared 51
White-naped 51
White-throated 50, 51
see also needletails; Philippine Spinetail; swiftlets *and* treeswifts
Swynnertonia swynnertoni 387
Sylvia 341
S. atricapilla 359
S. borin 359
S. nigricapillus 358, 359
Sylvietta 341–2
S. chapini 341
S. leucophrys chapini 341
S. whytii *341*
Sylviidae 358–60
Sylviorthorhynchus desmursii 228
Sylviparus modestus 335, 336
Synallaxis 228
S. infuscata 227
S. kollari 227
S. maranonica 227
Synthliboramphus 124
S. antiquus 123
S. craveri 123
S. hypoleucus 123
S. scrippsi 123
S. wumizusume 123
Sypheotides indicus 69, 70, 71
Syrian Serin 310
Syrigma sibilatrix 95
Syrrhaptes 35

Tachornis squamata 50
Tachurididae 213
Tachuris rubigastra 212, 213, *213*
Tachybaptus dominicus 30
T. pelzelnii 29
T. ruficollis 30
T. rufolavatus 29, 31

Tachycineta bicolor 350
T. cyaneoviridis 350
T. euchrysea 350
Tachyeres 16, 17
Tachymarptis aequatorialis 50
T. melba 49, 50
Tadorna cristata 15
T. tadorna 17, 18
Taenopygia guttata 298, *298*
Talegalla 20
tanagers 329–33
Azure-rumped Tanager 329
Bananaquit 332–3, *333*
Black-goggled Tanager 331
Black-and-gold Tanager 329
Black-hooded Sierra Finch *330*
Black-and-white Tanager 329
Blue-and-black Tanager 331
Blue-gray Tanager *329*
Cherry-throated Tanager 329
Cocos Island Finch 330
Flame-crested Tanager 329
Flame-rumped Tanager *332*
Glistening-green Tanager 329, 331
Gold-ringed Tanager 329
Gough Island Finch 329
Great-billed Seed Finch 329
Grey-headed Tanager 331, *331*
Hepatic Tanager 329
Large Ground Finch *331*
Long-tailed Reed Finch 332
Magpie Tanager 330, 332
Mangrove Finch 329
Medium Tree Finch 329
Multicoloured Tanager 329
Orangequit 332
Scarlet-rumped Tanager 329
Scarlet Tanager 328, 329
Seven-coloured Tanager 329, 331
Silver-throated Tanager *330*
Summer Tanager 328, 329
Vegetarian Finch 330
Western Tanager 329
White-capped Tanager 330
White-collared Seedeater 329
Woodpecker Finch 331
Yellow Cardinal 329
Yellow-shouldered Grosbeak 327
see also dacnises; flowerpiercers; Galapagos (Darwin's) finches *and* honeycreepers
Tanagers, Aberrant
Dusky-faced Tanager 326
Olive-backed Tanager 326–7
Olive-green Tanager 327
Red-billed Pied Tanager 327
Tangara 330
T. cabanisi 329
T. fastuosa 331
T. icterocephala *330*
T. vassorii 331
Tanysiptera carolinae 180
T. ellioti 180
T. sylvia 181
Taoniscus nanus 9
tapaculos 223–4
Bahia Tapaculo 223
Boa Nova Tapaculo 223
Crested Gallito 223, *223*, 224
Diamantina Tapaculo 223
Ecuadorian Tapaculo 223
Magdalena Tapaculo 223
Magellanic Tapaculo 223
Marsh Tapaculo 223
Ocellated Tapaculo *223*, 224
Perija Tapaculo 223
Sandy Gallito 223, 224
Spotted Bamboowren 224
Stresemann's Bristlefront 223
Tacarcuna Tapaculo 223
Tapera 58
T. naevia 58

tattlers
Grey-tailed 119
Wandering 119
Tauraco bannermani 71
T. fischeri 71
T. ruspolii 71
Tawny-breasted Wren Babbler 362
Tchagra senegalus 266
teal 18
Baikal 16
Blue-winged 16
Brown 15
Green-winged 16
Hottentot 16, 17
Madagascar 15
Teledromas fuscus 223, 224
Telephorus viridis 266
T. zeylonus 266
Tephrodornis 263, 264
Tephrozosterops stalkeri 361
Terathopius ecaudatus 138
Terenotriccus 208
T. erythrurus 209
Terenura sicki 218
Teretistris fernandinae 318
T. fornsi 318
terns 127, 129–30
Arctic *129*, *129*
Black 130
Black-bellied 127
Black-fronted 127, 130
Caspian 129
Chinese Crested 127
Elegant 129
Fairy 127
Gull-billed 129
Inca 130
Least 129
Little 129
Peruvian 127
Roseate 384
Royal 129
Sandwich 129
Sooty 127, 129
Whiskered 130
White 127, 130
White-winged Black 130
see also noddies
Terpsiphone atrocaudata 273, 274
T. corvina 273
T. mutata 274
T. paradisi 273
T. viridis 274, *274*
Tesia 349, *354*
T. superciliaris 355
Tetrao parvirostris 26
T. urogallus 26
Tetraogallus himalayensis 26
Tetrastes 26
Tetrax tetrax 70, *70*, 71
Thalanuria ridgwayi 52
Thalassarche bulleri 80
T. cauta 80
T. chlororhynchos 79, 80
T. chrysostoma 79, 80, *80*
T. melanophris 79, 80, *81*, 84
Thalasseus bernsteini 127
T. elegans 129
T. maxima 129
T. sandvicensis 129
Thalassoica antarctica 84
Thalassornis 15
Thalurania 53, 54
Thamnistes anabatinus 220
Thamnomanes 219
Thamnophilidae 218–20
Thamnophilus doliatus 219
Thamnornis chloropetoides 346
Thaumastura cora 54
Theristicus melanopis 97, 98

Thinocoridae 114
Thinocorus orbignyianus *114*
T. rumicivorus 114
Thinornis cucullatus 111
T. novaeseelandiae 111
thornbills 239
Inland *239*
thrashers
Bendire's 380
Brown 380, 381, *381*
Cozumel 380
Pearly-eyed 380
Sage 380
Scaly-breasted 380
White-breasted 380
see also Brown Trembler
Thraupidae 329–33
Thraupis episcopus 329
Threnetes 53
Threskiornis aethiopicus 98
T. bernieri 97
T. moluccus 98
T. solitarius 97
Threskiornithidae 97–8
Thripophaga berlepschi 227
Thrush Nightingale 389
Thrush Tanager 313, *313*
thrushes
Ashy 391
Bassian 393
Bicknell's 391
Bonin 391
Clay-coloured 393
Dark-sided 393
Dusky *393*
Grand Cayman 391
Hermit 393
Island 393
La Selle 391
Long-billed 393
Mistle 393
Principe 391
Russet-tailed 393
Somali 391
Song 201, 391, 393, *393*
Spotted 391
Swainson's 393
Taita 391
Varied 393
White's 393
Wood 393
see also Amaui; American Robin; Blackbird, Eurasian; bluebirds; Fieldfare; Grandala; Javan Cochoa; Kamao; Olomao; Puaiohi; solitaires [thrushes] *and* Veery
Thryomanes bewickii 377
Thryophilus sernai 376
Thryothorus ludovicianus 377, *377*
T. nicefori 376
Tiaris 331, 332
Tichodroma muraria 374, *375*, 375
Tickellia hodgsoni 354, 355
Tigriornis 95
Tigrisoma 95
Timalia pileata 262
Timaliidae 362
Tinamidae 9–10
tinamous 9–10
Choco 9
Dwarf 9
Elegant-crested
Great 9, *9*
Grey 9
Hooded 9
Solitary 9
see also Spotted Nothura
Tinamus major 9, *9*
T. solitarius 9
T. tao 9
Tit Hylia 354, 356
tit spinetails 228
White-browed 227
titmice

Bridled 336
Tufted 335, 336, *336*
tits (NA chickadees, titmice)
335–6
Black-lored 336
Blue 335, *335*
Coal 335
Crested 336, *336*
Fire-capped 335, 336
Great 335
Grey-crested 336
Ground 336
Izu 335
Marsh 336
Rufous-naped 336
Rufous-vented 336
Siberian 336
Sultan 335, 336
White-naped 335
Willow 336
Yellow-bellied 336
Yellow-browed 335, 336
see also chickadees; long-
tailed tits *and* titmice
Tityra semifasciata 210
tityras 210–11
Tityridae 210–11
Tmetothylacus tenellus 217, 304
Tockus 154, 156
T. camurus 155
T. erythrorhynchus 154
T. flavirostris 153
T. nasutus 153
Todidae 178
todies
Broad-billed 178, *178*
Cuban 178
Jamaican 178
Narrow-billed 178
Puerto Rican 178
Todiramphus chloris 181
T. funebris 180
T. gambieri 180
T. godeffroyi 180
T. pyrrhopygius 182
T. saurophagus 182
T. winchelli 180
Todirostrum 214, 259
T. cinereum 214
Todus angustirostris 178
T. mexicanus 178
T. multicolor 178
T. subulatus 178, *178*
T. todus 178
Tody Flycatcher, Common *214*
Tolmomyias 214
T. sulphurescens *214*
Tomtit 282
Topaz 53, 54
Torgos tracheliotos 138
Torrent-lark 274
Torreornis inexpectata 314
Toucan-barbet 172, *172*
toucanets
Emerald *169*, 170
Saffron 171
Yellow-browed 168
toucans 168, 169–71
Channel-billed 168
Keel-billed 170, *170*
Toco 168
see also araçaris *and*
toucanets
Touit 193
T. costaricensis 192
Toxorhamphus 241
T. poliopterus 242
Toxostoma bendirei 380
T. guttatum 380
T. rufum 380, 381, *381*
Trachylaemus purpuratus 172
Trachyphonini 169
Trachyphonus 172
T. erythrocephalus 171
Tragopan 26
Traversia lyalli 199
treecreepers 373–4
Bar-tailed 373, 374

Brown Creeper (American
Treecreeper) 373
Eurasian 373, *373*, 374
Hodgson's 374
Manipur 374
Rusty-flanked 374
Short-toed 374
Sichuan 373, 374
Sikkim 374
see also Australian
treecreepers
treeswifts
Crested 51
Grey-rumped 51 Moustached
51, *51*
Whiskered 51
Tregellasia capito 282
Treron 34
T. psittaceus 31
Trichixos 388
Trichoglossus haematodus 196,
196, 197
Tricholaema diademata 171
Tricholestes criniger 352
Trichothraupis melanops 331
Trigonoceps occipitalis 136
Tringa erythropus 119
T. flavipes 118
T. guttifer 116
T. melanoleuca 118
T. totanus 118
Trochalopteron 365
T. cachinnans 364
T. jerdoni 364
T. yersini 364
Trochilidae 52–5
Trochilus 54
Trochocercus cyanomelas 274
Troglodytes aedon 376
T. hiemalis 195, 376
T. monticola 376
T. pacificus 376
T. tanneri 376
T. troglodytes 195, 366, 376,
376
Troglodytidae 376–7
Trogon bairdii 150
T. collaris 152
T. elegans 152
T. massena *151*
T. violaceus 150, *151*
Trogonidae 150–2
trogons 150–2
Baird's 150
Collared 152
Cuban 152
Elegant 152
Hispaniolan 150, 152
Javan 150, 152
Narina's 152
Red-naped 150
Slaty-tailed Trogon *151*
Sumatran 152
Violaceous Trogon 150,
151
see also quetzals
Tropical Parula 320, *320*
tropicbirds 39–40
Red-billed 39, *39*, 40
Red-tailed 39, 40
White-tailed 39, 40, *40*
Tropicranus albocristatus 155,
156
trumpeters 65
Black-winged 65
Green-winged 65
Grey-winged 65, *65*
Ochre-winged 65
Olive-winged 65
Pale-winged 65
Tui 237
turacos 71–2
Bannerman's 71
Fischer's 71
Great Blue 71, 72
Ross's 72
Ruspoli's 71
Ruwenzori 72

Violet 72
see also go-away birds
Turdidae 391–3
Turdinus 364
Turdoides affinis 365
T. hindei 364
T. jardineii 365
T. rufescens 365
T. striata 365, *365*
Turdus feae 391
T. grayi 393
T. helleri 391
T. ludoviciae 391
T. merula 322, 391, 393
T. migratorius 281, 393
T. naumanni 393
T. philomelos 201, 391, 393,
393
T. pilaris 393
T. poliocephalus 393
T. ravidus 391
T. swalesi 391
T. viscivorus 393
T. xanthorhynchus 391
turkeys
Ocellated 25
Wild 25, *25*
Turnagra 257
T. capensis 256
T. tanagra 256
Turner's Eremomela 342
Turnicidae 120
Turnix everetti 120
T. melanogaster 120
T. nanus hottentotus 120
T. olivii 120
T. sylvaticus 120
T. tanki 120
T. t. blanfordii 120
T. varius novaecaledoniae 120
turnstones
Black 117
Ruddy 117
Turquoise-throated Puffleg 52
Twite 310
Tympanuchus 26
T. cupido 25
Tyrannidae 215–17
Tyrannus cubensis 215, 216
T. dominicensis 368
T. forficatus 215, *215*, 217
T. savana 217
T. tyrannus 217
T. verticalis 217
tyrant-flycatchers 215–17
Ash-breasted Tit Tyrant 215
Ash-throated Flycatcher 217
Black Phoebe 217
Black-and-white Monjita 215
Boat-billed Flycatcher 216
Brown-capped Tyrannulet
215
Cliff Flycatcher 216
Cock-tailed Tyrant 215
Cuban Tyrannulet 215
Eastern Kingbird 217
Eastern Phoebe 217
Eastern Wood Pewee 217
Fork-tailed Flycatcher 217
Giant Kingbird 216
Great Crested Flycatcher 217
Great Kiskadee 216, 217
Great Shrike-Tyrant 215
Grey Kingbird 368
Ochraceous Attila 215
Pied Water-Tyrant 216
Piratic Flycatcher 215
Red-billed Tyrannulet 215
Rufous Flycatcher 215
Santa Marta Bush Tyrant 215
Say's Phoebe 217
Scissor-tailed Flycatcher 215,
215, 217
Sharp-tailed Tyrant 215
Short-tailed Field Tyrant
216, 304
Social Flycatcher 216
Spectacled Tyrant 217

Strange-tailed Tyrant 215,
217
Streaked Flycatcher *215*
Streamer-tailed Tyrant 217
Sulphur-bellied Flycatcher
217
Urich's Tyrannulet 215
Vermilion Flycatcher 216,
216, 217
Western Kingbird 217
Western Wood Pewee 217
White-ringed Flycatcher *216*
Tyto alba 93, 141, 142, *142*
T. aurantia 141
T. capensis 142
T. delicatula 142
T. glaucops 142
T. inexspectata 141
T. longimembris 142
T. manusi 141
T. multipunctatus 142
T. prigoginei 141, 142
T. soumagnei 141, 142
T. tenebricosa 142, *142*
Tytonidae 141–2

umbrellabirds
Amazonian 207
Bare-necked 206, 207
Long-wattled 206, 207, *207*
Upucerthia 225, 227
Upupa epops 157–8, *158*
Upupidae 157–8
Uraeginthus 297
U. bengalus 297
Uratelornis chimaera 176, 177,
177
Uria aalge *124*
U. lomvia 124, 125
Urocissa 272
Urocolius 148
U. indicus 149
U. macrourus *148*, 149
Urocynchramidae 289
Urocynchramus pylzowi 289,
289
Uroglaux albifacies 146
Urolais epichlorus 343
Urolestes melanoleucus 270
Uromyias 216
Uropsalis 44
U. lyra 45
U. segmentata 44, 45
Urosphena 349, 354, 355
Urotriorchis 140

Vanellus chilensis 112
V. gregarius 111, 112
V. indicus 112
V. macropterus 111
V. miles *111*, 112
V. vanellus 111, 112
Vanga curvirostris 262, 263
vangas 262–3
Bernier's 262, 263
Blue 262, *263*
Helmet 262, 263, *263*
Hook-billed 262, 263
Nuthatch 262, 263
Red-shouldered 262, 263
Red-tailed 263
Rufous 262
Sickle-billed 262, 263, *264*
Van Dam's 262
Ward's 263
White-headed 262
see also Madagascar
Groundhunter *and* Red-
tailed Newtonia
Vangidae 262–4
Vauriella albigularis 387
Veery 393
Vegetarian Finch 330
Veles binotatus 46
Venezuelan Sylph 52
Veniliornis 167
Verdin 337–8, *338*
Vermivora bachmanii 319, 320

V. chrysoptera 319
Verniliornis callonotus 165
Verrauxia africana 165
Vestiaria coccinea 309, *309*
Victorin's Warbler 341, 342
Vidua chalybeata 299
V. funerea 299
V. hypocherina 299
V. macroura 299, *300*
V. paradisaea 300
Viduidae 299–300
Vini ultramarina 194
Vireo atricapilla 255, 256
V. bellii 256
V. caribaeus 255
V. griseus 255
V. masteri 255
V. olivaceus 256
Vireolanius eximius 255
V. pulchellus 255
Vireonidae 255–6
vireos 255–6
Bell's 256
Black-capped 255, 256
Choco 255
Green Shrike 255
Red-eyed 256
San Andres 255
White-eyed *255*
Yellow-browed Shrike 255
see also Erpornis *and*
peppershrikes
Vultur gryphus 131, 132, 133
vultures, New World 131–4
Black 131, 132, *132*, 133
Cinereous 132
Greater Yellow-headed 132
King 132, 133, *133*
Lesser Yellow-headed 132
Turkey 131, 132, *132*, 133,
133
see also condors
vultures, Old World
Bearded (Lammergeier) 136,
137, 138
Cape 136
Cinereous 136, 138
Egyptian 136, 138
Himalayan 136
Hooded 136, 138
Lappet-faced 138
Long-billed 139
Palm-nut 136, 138
Red-headed 136
Rüppell's 136
Slender-billed 136, 139
White-backed 136
White-headed 136
White-rumped 136, 138, 139

wagtails 302–3
African Pied 303
Cape 303
Citrine 303
Eastern Yellow 303
Forest 302, 303
Grey 303
Japanese Pied 303
Madagascan 303
Mekong 303
Mountain 303
White 303, *303*
White-browed 303
Yellow 303, *303*
Wallcreeper 374, *374*, 375
warbler tanagers
Black-crowned Palm Tanager
318, *318*
Green-tailed Warbler Tanager
318
Grey-crowned Palm Tanager
317, 318
Puerto Rican Tanager 318
White-winged Warbler
Tanager 317, 318
warblers (bush) 354–6
Bougainville Bush Warbler
354

Broad-billed Warbler 354, 356
Cetti's Warbler 354, 356, *356*
Chestnut-headed Tesia 355, *355*
Green Hylia 354, 356
Japanese Bush Warbler 354, 355, 356
Javan Tesia 355
Manchurian Bush Warbler 354, 356, *356*
Neumann's Warbler 355
Pale-footed Bush Warbler 355
Streaked Scrub Warbler 354, 355, *355*
Tanibar Bush Warbler 354
Tit Hylia 354, 356
warblers (leaf), Old World 353–4
Arctic Warbler 353, 354
Common Chiffchaff 354, *354*
Hainan Leaf Warbler 353
Ijima's Leaf Warbler 353
Kolombangara Leaf Warbler 353
Pallas's Warbler 353, *353*
Tytler's Leaf Warbler 353
Willow Warbler *353*, 354
Wood Warbler 353, *354*
warblers (reed, brush and swamp) 347–9
Aguijan Reed Warbler 347
Aldabra Brush Warbler 347, 348
Aquatic Warbler 347, 348
Australian Reed Warbler 348
Basra Reed Warbler 347
Blyth's Reed Warbler 348
Clamorous Reed Warbler 348
Eurasian Reed Warbler 348, *348*
Forster's Reed Warbler 347
Great Reed Warbler 348
Guam Reed Warbler 347, 348
Hawaiian (Millerbird) Reed Warbler 347
Henderson Island Reed Warbler 347
Icterine Warbler 349
Kiritimati Warbler 347
Large-billed Reed Warbler 348
Mangareva Reed Warbler 347
Marsh Warbler 348
Melodious Warbler 349
Moorea Reed Warbler 347
Moustached Warbler 348
Olive-tree Warbler 349
Pagan Reed Warbler 347
Papyrus Yellow Warbler 347, 348
Pitcairn Reed Warbler 347
Rimatara Reed Warbler 347
Saipan Reed Warbler 347
Sedge Warbler 348
Seychelles Reed Warbler 347
Streaked Reed Warbler 347
Subdesert Brush Warbler 348
Tahiti Reed Warbler 347, 348
Thick-billed Warbler 348
warblers (wood) *see* wood warblers, New World
warblers, Sylviid
Barred Warbler 359
Blackcap 359
Common Whitethroat 359
Dartford Warbler 358, 359, *359*
Garden Warbler 359
wattle-eyes
Banded 261
Black-throated *262*
White-fronted 261
White-spotted 262
wattlebirds *see* New Zealand wattlebirds *and* Yellow Wattlebird
Wattled Ploughbill 253, *253*

waxbills 296–8
African Firefinch *299*
Chestnut Munia 296
Gouldian Finch 298, *298*
Green Avadavat 296, 297
Green-faced Parrotfinch 296
Grey-banded Mannikin 296
Java Sparrow 296, 298, *298*
Mountain Firetail 298
Pictorella Finch 298
Pink-billed Parrotfinch 296
Red Avadavat 297
Red-billed Firefinch 297, *297*
Red-cheeked Cordon-bleu *297*
Shelley's Crimsonwing 296
Zebra Finch 298, *298*
waxwings
Bohemian 369, *369*
Cedar 369
Japanese 368, 369, 370
weavers 292–5
African Golden *293*
Baglafecht *295*
Bannerman's 292
Bates's 292
Clarke's 292
Finn's 292
Golden-naped 292
Grosbeak (Thick-billed) 294
Jackson's Golden-backed *295*
Kilombero 292
Red-billed Buffalo 293, *294*
Red-headed 294
Rufous-tailed 293
Rüppell's 292
Scaly-fronted 294
Sociable 292, 293, *294*
Speckle-fronted 294
Usambara 292
White-headed Buffalo 293
see also fodies; malimbes; queleas; Southern Red Bishop *and* widowbirds
Wedge-tailed Jery 347
wedgebills
Chiming 253
Chirruping 252, 253
Weebill 239
Weka 61
Western Kingbird 217
Western Wattled Cuckoo-shrike 247
Western Wood Pewee 217
whip-poor-wills
Eastern 45
Mexican 45
whipbirds
Eastern 252, *252*
Papuan 252
Western 252
whistlers 249–50
Black 250
Golden 249
Red-lored 249
Rufous 249
Sangir 249
Tongan 249
see also shrike-thrushes
whistling thrushes
Blue 390
Sri Lanka 390
Sunda 390
White-browed Tit-warbler 357, 358
White-collared Seedeater 329
white-eyes
Bicoloured 361
Bridled 360
Cape 361
Chestnut-flanked 360
Giant 361
Gizo 360
Golden 361
Japanese 360
Marianne 360
Mauritius Olive 360
Oriental 361, *361*

Robust 360, 361
Rota Bridled 360
Saipan 360
Samoan 360
Sangihe 360
Taiti 360
Teardrop 360
Togian 360
Vanikoro 360
White-chested 360
see also Mount Cameroon Speirops *and* Silvereye
White-faced Nunbird 162
White-naped Xenopsaris 211
White-tailed Stonechat 387
White-throated Oxylabes 347
White-throated Wren Babbler 363
White-winged Chough 275, *275*
White-winged Crossbill 311
Whitehead 245
Whitethroat, Common 359
whydahs
Eastern (Long-tailed)
Paradise 300
Pin-tailed 299, *300*
Steel-blue 299
widowbirds
Jackson's 295
Long-tailed *295*
Wied's Tyrant-manakin 205
wigeon
American 16
Chiloe 16
Eurasian 16, *17*
Willie-Wagtail 268, 269, *269*
Winifrede's (Mrs Moreau's) Warbler 342
wood-hoopoes 158–9
Black 159
Black-billed 159
Forest 158, 159
Green 159, *159*
Violet 158, 159
White-headed 159
see also scimitarbills
wood warblers, New World
American Redstart 320
Bachman's Warbler 319, 320
Belding's Yellowthroat 319
Black-polled Yellowthroat 319
Black-and-white Warbler 319, 320
Cerulean Warbler 319
Chestnut-sided Warbler 319, 320
Common Yellowthroat 320
Connecticut Warbler 319
Elfin Woods Warbler 319
Golden-cheeked Warbler 319
Golden-winged Warbler 319
Grey-headed Warbler 319
Hooded Warbler *320*
Kirtland's Warbler 319
Lousiana Waterthrush 320
Northern Parula 319, 320
Northern Waterthrush 320, 321
Ovenbird 319, 320
Painted Whitestart 321
Paria Whitestart 319
Pink-headed Warbler 319, 320
Pirre Warbler 319
Plumbeous Warbler 319
Red Warbler 320
Semper's Warbler 319, 320
Tennessee Warbler 319
Tropical Parula 320, *320*
Whistling Warbler 319
Yellow-rumped Warbler 320
Yellow Warbler 320
woodcocks 118
American 118
Anami 116
Eurasian 118
Moluccan 116

woodcreepers 226–7
Hoffmann's 226
Long-billed 227
Moustached 226
Olivaceous 227
Scimitar-billed 226
Streaked-headed *226*
Wedge-billed 227
Zimmer's 226
see also Greater Scythebill
Woodpecker Finch 331
woodpeckers 164–8
Acorn 167
American Three-toed 167
Andaman 164, 166
Black 166, *166*
Cream-coloured 166
Downy 167
Eurasian Three-toed 167
Gila 167
Great Slaty 164, 165, 166
Great Spotted 165, 167, *167*
Greater Flame-backed 166
Green 166, *166*
Grey-headed 166
Ground 165
Hairy 167
Helmeted 166
Imperial 164, 165, 166
Ivory-billed 164, 165, 166
Japanese Pygmy 165
Kaempfer's 164
Lesser Spotted 167
Lewis's 167
Okinawan164
Philippine Pygmy 165
Pileated 166
Red-bellied 167
Red-headed 165, 167
Scarlet-backed 165
Sulawesi Pygmy 164
Yellow-tufted *167*
see also flickers; piculets *and* wrynecks
woodswallows
Black-faced *259*
Masked 260
White-browed 260
wrens
Antioquia 376
Apolinar's 376
Bewick's 377
Cactus 377
Canyon 377
Carolina 377, *377*
Clarion 376
Eurasian 195, 366, 376, *376*
Fasciated 377
Flutist 376
Giant 377
Grey-barred 377
Happy 377
House 376
Marsh 376, 377
Munchique Wood 376
Musician 376
Nava's 376
Nicéforo's 376
Nightingale 376
Pacific 376
Rock 377
Santa Marta 376
Sedge 377
Song 376
Spotted 377
White-headed 376, 377
Winter 195, 376
Zapata 376, 377
see also emu-wrens; fairy-wrens; grasswrens *and* New Zealand wrens
Wrenthrush 318
Wrentit 359
Wrybill 111
wrynecks
Northern 164
Rufous-breasted 164

Xanthocephalus xanthocephalus 323, 324
Xanthomixis apperti 346, 347
X. cinereiceps 346, 347
X. tenebrosa 346
Xema sabini 127, 128
Xenicus gilviventris 199
X. longipes 199
Xenoglaux loweryi 143, 146
Xenoligea montana 317, 318
Xenopirostris damii 262
Xenops 228
Xenopsaris albinucha 211
Xenornis setifrons 218
Xenospiza baileyi 314, 316
Xiphocolaptes 227
X. falcirostris 226
Xipholena 207
Xolmis 217
X. dominicanus 215

Yellow-breasted Chat 323
Yellow-breasted Tanager Finch 314
Yellow Cardinal 329
Yellow-green Finch 314
Yellow-headed Warbler 318
Yellow-olive Flycatcher *214*
Yellow-throated Canary 305
Yellow-throated Miner 235
Yellow Wattlebird 236
Yellowhammer (Eurasian Yellow Bunting) 317
Yellowhead 245
Yellowthroat, Common 320
Yemen Serin 310
Yuhina 255, 361
Yuhinas 255, 360, 361

Zanda baudinii 191, 192
Z. latirostris 191, 192
Zavattariornis stresemanni 271, 272
Zebra Finch 298, *298*
Zebrilus undulatus 95
Zeledonia coronata 318
Zeledoniidae 318
Zenaida graysoni 31
Z. macroura 34
Zimmerius cinereicapilla 215
Zonerodius heliosylus 95
Zonotrichia capensis 315
Z. leucophrys 315, *315*, 316
Zoothera 392
Z. aurea 393
Z. heinei 393
Z. lunulata 393
Z. marginata 393
Z. monticola 393
Z. terrestris 391
Zosteropidae 360–1
Zosterops albogularis 360
Z. chloronothos 360
Z. conspicillatus 360
Z. erythropleurus 360
Z. gibbsi 360
Z. japonicus 360
Z. lateralis 361
Z. luteirostris 360
Z. melanocephalus 360
Z. nehrkorni 360
Z. pallidus 361
Z. palpebrosus 361, *361*
Z. rotensis 360
Z. samoensis 360
Z. saypani 360
Z. semiflavus 360
Z. silvanus 360
Z. somadikartai 360
Z. strenuus 360, 361
Zosterornis 361
Z. nigrorum 360

PICTURE CREDITS

p.4, 5, 17 (bottom, right), 34, 91(top), 236(bottom), 237 ©Jonathan Elphick; p.7, 8, 10, 11, 12, 13, 14(top), 16, 17(top and bottom,left), 18, 19, 20(top), 21, 22, 23, 24, 25, 26, 28, 29, 30, 32, 33, 35, 37, 41, 42, 43, 44, 45, 46, 47, 50, 51, 52, 53, 55, 56, 58, 59, 60, 62, 63, 65, 66, 67, 68, 69, 70, 72(top), 73, 74, 75, 77, 79, 80, 81, 82(top), 83, 85, 86, 87(top,left and bottom), 89, 90, 91(bottom), 92, 93, 95, 96, 97, 98, 101(top), 103, 104, 105, 107, 109(left), 110, 111, 112, 114, 116, 117, 118, 119, 124, 125, 126(bottom), 128, 129, 132, 133(bottom), 135, 136, 137, 140, 142(bottom), 143, 144, 145, 148, 151, 152, 153, 154, 155, 156, 158, 159(top), 160, 161, 169, 170, 171, 173, 174, 176, 179, 180, 181, 182, 186, 187, 192, 193, 196, 197(bottom), 199, 200, 205, 206, 208(top,left and bottom), 215(right), 216(bottom), 218, 219 223(top), 231, 232(left), 234, 236(top), 240, 243, 245, 247, 251, 255, 257(top,right), 260, 261, 267, 268, 269(top), 270, 272, 273, 278, 279(top and bottom, right), 282, 286, 287(top), 288(top), 290, 291(top), 295(middle), 296, 301, 302(right), 303, 304, 306, 307, 310, 311, 312, 314, 315, 317, 319, 320(left), 322, 327, 328, 329, 330(top and bottom,right), 331(top), 332, 333, 335, 336(top), 339, 340, 342, 343, 348, 351, 352(left), 353, 357(right), 359(bottom), 361, 365, 369, 373, 374, 375, 376, 377, 382, 383(left), 385(bottom), 387, 393 ©David Tipling; p.14, (bottom), 350 ©Mike Lane/NHPA/Photoshot;; p.20 (bottom), 266 ©Dave Watts/naturepl.com; p.36(top), 82(bottom), 133(top), 183, 208(top,right), 264(top), 331(bottom) ©Pete Oxford/naturepl. com; p.36 (bottom), 177, 263(bottom), 300(left) ©Nick Garbutt/naturepl. com; p.38, 298(bottom) ©Joe Blossom/NHPA/Photoshot; p.39 ©M. Watson/ardea.com; p.40 ©Martin Harvey/NHPA/Photoshot; p.49 ©Tom Stephenson; p.64 ©Anup Shah/naturepl. com; p.72 ©Mike Wilkes/naturepl. com; p.78, 123 ©Markus Varesvuo/naturepl.com; p.87 (top,right) ©Alan Greensmith/ardea.com; p.99©Taketomo Shiratori/NHPA/Photoshot; p.100 ©Carolyn Jenkins/PictureNature/NHPA/Photoshot; p.101(bottom) ©Christopher Swann/Science Photo Library; p.109(right), 368(right) ©Neil Bowman/FLPA; p.113 ©Mélanie and Kyle Elliott; p.114 ©Francois Gohier/ardea.com; p.120 ©Hans Reinhard/Photoshot; p.121, 265(bottom) ©Hanne & Jens Eriksen/naturepl.com; p.122 ©Bruno D'Amicis/naturepl.com; p.120(top) ©Jose Luis Gomeaz de Francisco/naturepl.com; p.130 ©Rolf Nussbaumer/naturepl.com; p.139 ©Michel Gunther/Biosphoto/ardea.com; p.142(top), 298(top, left) ©ANT Photo Library/ NHPA/Photoshot; p.146 ©Ron Austing/FLPA; p.149 ©Loic Poidevin/naturepl.com; p.159(bottom) ©Greg & Yvonne Dean/WorldWildlifeImages. com; p.163,300(right) ©Nigel J. Dennis/NHPA/Photoshot; p.165 Bendiks Westerink/Minden Pictures/FLPA; p.172(right), 207(right), 216(top), 320(right) ©Murray Cooper/MindenPictures/FLPA; p172(left) ©Xi Zhinong/naturepl.com; p.175 ©Thomas Dressler/ardea.com; p.178, 368(left), 391 ©Eladio Fernandez/NHPA/Photoshot; p.190 ©Tui De Roy/naturepl.com; p.194 ©Lynn M

Stone/naturepl.com; p.197 (top) © Karl Terblanche / ardea.com; p.201 ©Kenneth W. Fink /ardea.com; p.202 ©Alan Greensmith/ardea.com; p.204 ©John Mason/ardea.com; p.207(left) ©Michael_Patricia Fogden/Minden Pictures/FLPA; p.209, 220 ©Doug Wechsler/naturepl.com; p.210(top), 378(right) ©Mark Bowler/naturepl.com; p.210(bottom) ©Visuals Unlimited/naturepl.com; p.211 Leonardo Mercon/Shutterstock; p.212, 228, 346 ©Luiz Claudio Marigo/naturepl.com; p.213 ©Jean-Paul Chatagn/Biosphoto/FLPA; p.214(left) ©Gualberto Becerra/Shutterstock; p.214(right) ©Salparadis/Shutterstock; p.215(left) ©Rolf Nussbaumer/naturepl.com; p.221, 224 ©John S. Dunning/ardea.com; p.222, 378(left), 381(right) ©Glenn Bartley/NHPA/Photoshot; p.223(bottom) ©Melanie and Kyle Elliott; p.225, 330(bottom,left) ©James Lowen/FLPA; p.226, 232(right) ©Konrad Wothe/naturepl.com; p.229, 249 © Dave Watts/NHPA/Photoshot; p.230(top), 235, 248(right), 269(bottom, left) ©Ellis McNamara/ardea.com; p.230(bottom) ©Jiri Lochman/naturepl.com; p.233, 239, 241, 244, 259 ©Don Hadden/ardea.com; p.238(top) ©Graeme Chapman/ardea.com; p.238(bottom) ©Tom and Pam Gardner/FLPA; p.242(top) ©Sarah Blair; p.242(bottom) Gerry Ellis/Minden Pictures/FLPA; p.246(top), 356(right) ©Martin Pelanek/Shutterstock; p.246(bottom) ©A.N.T. Photo Library/NHPA/Photoshot; p.248(left) ©Bruce Beehler/NHPA/Photoshot; p.250 ©Michael Morcombe/NHPA/Photoshot; p.252 ©Jason Benz Bennee/Shutterstock; p.253, 276 Markus Lilje; p.254(top) ©Otto Plantema/Minden Pictures/FLPA; p.254(bottom) ©Nik Borrow; p.257(left) ©Kerstin Hinze/naturepl.com; p.257(bottom, right) ©Daniel Heuclin/NHPA/Photoshot; p.258 ©Ralph & Daphne Keller/NHPA/Photoshot; p.262 ©Pat Morris/ardea.com; p.263 (top) ©Dubi Shapiro; p.264(bottom) ©R.M. Bloomfield/ardea.com; p.265(top) ©Cede Prudente/NHPA/Photoshot; p.269(bottom, right) ©David Tipling/naturepl.com; p.274(top), 295(top,right), 297(right) ©Tony Crocetta/NHPA/Photoshot; p.274(bottom), 275 ©Ken Griffiths/NHPA/Photoshot; p.277 ©Tim Laman/naturepl.com; p.279(bottom, left) ©Brian J. Coates/Photoshot; p.280 ©Kevin Schafer/naturepl.com; p.283 ©Martin Harvey/NHPA/Photoshot; p.285(left), 298(top, left) ©Gerhard Koertner/NHPA/Photoshot; p.285(right), 287(bottom), 288(bottom) ©Morten Strange/NHPA/Photoshot; p.288(bottom) ©Dong Lei/naturepl.com; p.291(bottom) ©Jim Zipp/Photo Researchers/NHPA/Photoshot; p.292 ©Nigel J. Dennis/NHPA/Photoshot; p.293 ©Neil Aldridge/NHPA/Photoshot; p.294(top) ©Daryl Balfour/NHPA/Photoshot; p.294(bottom) ©Ann & Steve Toon/NHPA/Photoshot; p.295(top, left), 308(left), 309(left) ©Bill Coster/NHPA/Photoshot; p.295(bottom), 305 ©James Warwick/ NHPA/Photoshot; p.297(left) ©Roger Tidman/NHPA/Photoshot; p.299 ©Warwick Tarboton; p.302(left) ©Brian Bevan/ardea.com; p.308(right) ©Peter La Tourette/birdphotography.com; p.309(right) ©Jack Jeffrey Photography; p.313 ©Murray Cooper/Minden Pictures/naturepl.com; p.318

©Dax Roman; p.321, 323(top,left) ©Marie Read/NHPA/Photoshot; p.323(top, right), 371 ©Joe McDonald/NHPA/Photoshot; p.323(bottom), 338 ©Larry Ditto/NHPA/Photoshot; p.324(left) ©Daphne Kinzler/FLPA; p.324(right) ©Tim Fitzharris/Minden Pictures/FLPA; p.334 ©Felis Images/naturepl.com; p.336(bottom), 392(top) ©Marie Read/Woodfall Wild Images/Photoshot; p.337 ©Jordi Bas Casas/NHPA/Photoshot; p.341(top) ©Mriya Wildlife/Shutterstock; p.341(bottom) ©Mike Read/naturepl.com; p.345 ©SanderMeertins Photography/Shutterstock; p.349 ©Yusuf Madi/Shutterstock; p.352(right) ©John Holmes/FLPA; p.354(left) Andy Rouse/2020Vision/naturepl; p.354(right) ©Menno Schaefer/Shutterstock; p.355(left) ©Dimitry Fch/Shutterstock; p.355(right) ©Wang LiQiang/Shutterstock; p.356(left) ©Yuri Shibnev/naturepl; p.357(right) ©Ernie Janes/Photoshot; p.358 ©AllCanadaPhotos/Photoshot; p.359(top) ©Dhritiman Mukherjee/NHPA/Photoshot; p.363 ©non15/Shutterstock; p.366, 367 ©Raymond James Barlow/PictureNature/ NHPA/Photoshot; p.379 ©Sharon Heald/naturepl.com; p.380

©Lang Elliott/Woodfall/Photoshot; p.381(left) ©Bob Gibbons/Photoshot; p.383(right) ©Richard Du Toit/Mindem Pictures/FLPA; p.384, 385(top) Romy Ocon/NHPA/Photoshot; p.386 ©D. Robert Franz/Bruce Coleman/Photoshot; p.388(left), 392(bottom) ©Melvin Grey/NHPA/Photoshot; p.388 (top,right) ©Imagebroker/FLPA; p.390 ©Alfo/naturepl; .

t, top; m, middle; b, bottom; l, left; r, right

NHM London ©The Trustees of the Natural History Museum, London 2014. All Rights Reserved.

Picture Library www.piclib.nhm.ac.uk

Every effort has been made to contact and accurately credit all copyright holders. If we have been unsuccessful, we apologise and welcome corrections for future editions.

NOTE: Imperial measurements are given in decimals as the measurements are very specific.

ACKNOWLEDGEMENTS

In Publishing at the Natural History Museum, London, I thank Colin Ziegler, Head of Publishing, Lynn Millhouse, Production Manager, and Lewis Morgan, Sales and Marketing Executive, for their help and commitment. Picture Researcher Anna Smith coped magnificently with frequent requests for hard-to-find images, last-minute substitutions and much else. Above all, creating this book would have been so much more difficult without Editorial Manager, Trudy Brannan, with whom I have worked on a variety of Natural History Museum books for the past 20 years. She saw the whole project through the ups and downs of its incubation and fledging period with her characteristic skill, determination, patience and attention to detail, together with her constantly unflappable and reassuring Editor Gemma Simmons; their positive attitude kept me going through difficult times. Others who made vital contributions were the copy-editor Amanda Harman, designer Zoe Mercer and indexer Angie Hipkin.

I owe a very special gratitude to David Tipling, with whom I have been involved in several projects over the years, for his stunningly beautiful photographs that grace so many of the pages. My thanks also go to my redoubtable agent Pat White and her assistant Miriam Tobin.

I thank the many people too numerous to mention by name, who helped by answering queries and correcting errors, or acting as hosts or knowledgeable guides during my travels. As with all my endeavours, I am hugely grateful to dear friends Mark Cocker and Jeremy Mynott for their advice and for their constant encouragement and support when, as often, I felt I was flagging.

For nurturing my passion for birds through childhood and adolescence, I am forever indebted to my parents Walter and Mimi, my brothers Michael and Richard, my inspirational biology teacher Tony Angell, the ornithologist and ecologist Peter Hope Jones, and the entire Walton family.

Above all, I acknowledge an eternal debt of gratitude to my wife Melanie, who until her untimely death two and a half years ago provided constant support and encouragement in all my endeavours and was my beloved companion for 35 years at home and on our many adventures travelling the world.

Likewise, I thank my children Becky, Alys and Tom, and my grandsons Callum and Jacob, for my not always having spent as much time with them as I'd have liked and for my habit while on walks of saying "you go on, I just want to check out this bird …"

JONATHAN ELPHICK